Lecture Notes in Artificial Intelligence 4139

Edited by J. G. Carbonell and J. Siekmann

Subseries of Lecture Notes in Computer Science

Tapio Salakoski Filip Ginter
Sampo Pyysalo Tapio Pahikkala (Eds.)

Advances in Natural Language Processing

5th International Conference on NLP, FinTAL 2006
Turku, Finland, August 23-25, 2006
Proceedings

Springer

Series Editors

Jaime G. Carbonell, Carnegie Mellon University, Pittsburgh, PA, USA
Jörg Siekmann, University of Saarland, Saarbrücken, Germany

Volume Editors

Tapio Salakoski
Filip Ginter
Sampo Pyysalo
Tapio Pahikkala

University of Turku
Department of Information Technology
20014 Turku, Finland
E-mail: {Tapio.Salakoski, Filip.Ginter, Sampo.Pyysalo, Tapio.Pahikkala}@it.utu.fi

Library of Congress Control Number: 2006930503

CR Subject Classification (1998): I.2.7, F.4.2-3, I.2, H.3, I.7

LNCS Sublibrary: SL 7 – Artificial Intelligence

ISSN 0302-9743
ISBN-10 3-540-37334-9 Springer Berlin Heidelberg New York
ISBN-13 978-3-540-37334-6 Springer Berlin Heidelberg New York

Springer is a part of Springer Science+Business Media

springer.com

Printed in Germany

Typesetting: Camera-ready by author, data conversion by Scientific Publishing Services, Chennai, India
Printed on acid-free paper SPIN: 11816508 06/3142 5 4 3 2 1 0

Preface

The research papers in this volume comprise the proceedings of FinTAL 2006, a Natural Language Processing conference continuing the TAL series of events: FracTAL 1997 at Université de Franche-Comté in Besançon, France; VexTAL 1999 at Università Ca' Foscari di Venezia in Venice, Italy; PorTAL 2002 at Universidade do Algarve in Faro, Portugal; and EsTAL 2004 at Universitat d'Alacant in Alicante, Spain. The main goals of the TAL conferences have been to bring together the international NLP community, to strengthen local NLP research, and to provide a forum for discussion of new NLP research and applications.

FinTAL 2006, organized by Turku Centre for Computer Science (TUCS) in Turku, Finland, also contributed to the goals mentioned above, further increasing the high international standing of the TAL conference series. We called for submissions both from academia and industry on any topic that is of interest to the NLP community, particularly encouraging research emphasizing multidisciplinary aspects of NLP and the interplay between linguistics, computer science and application domains such as biomedicine, communication systems, public services, and educational technology.

As a response, we received as many as 150 submissions from 38 countries in Europe, Asia, Africa, and the Americas. The manuscripts were reviewed by three members of FinTAL Program Committee, composed of researchers in the field, or external reviewers designated by the PC members. The PC members as well as the external reviewers are gratefully acknowledged in the following pages for their valuable contribution.

We would like to express here our gratitude to Turku Centre for Computer Science (TUCS), University of Turku, and Åbo Akademi University, as well as to our sponsors the city of Turku, Nokia, Lingsoft, PARC, and Sanako. We also thank our keynote speakers, the highly esteemed scholars Fred Karlsson, Lauri Karttunen, and Igor Mel'čuk. Last but obviously not least, we would like to thank all the individuals involved in organizing the event; without you it would not have been possible at all.

The careful evaluation of the submissions finally led to the selection of 72 papers to be presented at the conference and published in this volume. It is our firm belief that the accepted papers provide a significant contribution to the advance of science and technology. We hope that you will enjoy reading the articles and find them inspiring for your work, whether in basic NLP research or in the development of human language technology applications.

Turku, Finland, June 2006 Tapio Salakoski

Organization

FinTAL 2006 was organized by Turku Centre for Computer Science (TUCS) in conjunction with the University of Turku and Åbo Akademi University.

TUCS UNIVERSITY OF TURKU ÅBO AKADEMI

Program Committee

Tapio Salakoski	University of Turku, Finland (Chair)
Olli Aaltonen	University of Turku, Finland
Walid El Abed	Nestlé Corp., Switzerland
Jorge Baptista	University of Faro, Portugal
Florence Beaujard	Airbus Corp., France
Krzysztof Bogacki	University of Warsaw, Poland
Caroline Brun	Xerox Corp., France
Sylviane Cardey	University of Franche-Comte, France
Nigel Collier	National Institute of Informatics, Japan
Walter Daelemans	University of Antwerp, Belgium
Rodolfo Delmonte	University of Venice, Italy
Pasi Fränti	University of Joensuu, Finland
Peter Greenfield	University of Franche-Comté, France
Jari Kangas	Nokia Research Center, Finland
Kimmo Koskenniemi	University of Helsinki, Finland
Kyoko Kuroda	Shimane College, Japan
Hsiang-I Lin	National Taiwan University (NTU), Taiwan
Nuno Mamede	University of Lisbon, Portugal
Patricio Martínez-Barco	University of Alicante, Spain
Einar Meister	Tallinn University of Technology, Estonia
Rada Mihalcea	University of North Texas, USA
Leonel Ruiz Miyares	University of Santiago de Cuba, Cuba
Adeline Nazarenko	University Paris-Nord, France
Elisabete Ranchhod	University of Lisbon, Portugal
Karl-Michael Schneider	Textkernel BV, Amsterdam, The Netherlands
Rolf Schwitter	Macquarie University, Australia
John Tait	University of Sunderland, UK
José Luis Vicedo	University of Alicante, Spain
Simo Vihjanen	Lingsoft Ltd., Finland
Roman Yangarber	University of Helsinki, Finland

Local Organizers

Filip Ginter
Sampo Pyysalo
Hanna Suominen
Tapio Pahikkala
Tomi 'bgt' Mäntylä
Irmeli Laine
Christel Donner

Reviewers

Adeline Nazarenko
Agnes Sandor
Amanda Bouffier
Annu Paganus
Anssi Yli-Jyrä
Antoine Doucet
Antoine Rozenknop
Armando Suárez-Cueto
Borja Navarro
Caroline Brun
Caroline Hagege
Christopher Stokoe
Cristina Mota
David Martins de Matos
David Tomás
Davy Weissenbacher
Diamantino Caseiro
Duygu Can
Einar Meister
Elisabete Ranchhod
Evgeni Tsivtsivadze
Evgenia Chernenko
Felipe Sánchez-Martínez
Filip Ginter
Florence Beaujard
Graham Wilcock
Guillaume Bouchard
Guillaume Jacquet
Hanna Suominen
Hervé Déjean
Hsiang-I Lin
Hugo Meinedo
Ismo Kärkkäinen
Jari Kangas
Jean-Sébastien Tisserand
Joana L. Paulo
Joao Cabral
John Tait
Jorge Baptista
Jorma Boberg
José Luis Vicedo
Jouni Järvinen
Juhani Saastamoinen
Jussi Hakokari
Jussi Piitulainen
Jyri Paakkulainen
Karl-Michael Schneider
Kimmo Koskenniemi
Krister Lindén
Krzysztof Bogacki
Kyoko Kuroda
Leonel Ruiz Miyares
Luisa Coheur
Manuel Célio Conceição
Marc Dymetman
Marketta Hiissa
Maud Ehrmann
Michael Oakes
Navid Atar Sharghi
Nigel Collier
Nuno Mamede
Olli Aaltonen
Paloma Moreda
Pasi Fränti
Patricio Martínez-Barco
Paula Carvalho
Peter Greenfield
Rada Mihalcea
Rafael Carrasco
Rafael Muñoz
Ricardo Ribeiro
Rodolfo Delmonte
Rolf Schwitter
Roman Yangarber
Sampo Pyysalo
Shao Fen Liang
Simo Vihjanen
Siobhan Devlin
Sylviane Cardey
Séverine Vienney
Tanja Kavander
Tapio Pahikkala
Tapio Salakoski
Thierry Poibeau
Timo Honkela
Timo Knuutila
Tomi 'bgt' Mäntylä
Tony Mullen
Tuomo Saarni
Ville Hautamäki
Walid El Abed
Walter Daelemans
Xiaohong Wu

Conference Sponsors

turku

NOKIA
Connecting People

Lingsoft®
LANGUAGE SOLUTIONS

parc®
Palo Alto Research Center

sanako

Table of Contents

Keynote Addresses

Research Papers

Recursion in Natural Languages

Fred Karlsson

Department of General Linguistics
P.O. Box 9, FI-00014 University of Helsinki, Finland
fgk@ling.helsinki.fi

Abstract. The received view is that there are no grammatical constraints on clausal embedding complexity in sentences in languages of the 'Standard Average European' (SAE) type like English, Finnish, and Russian. The foremost proponent of this thesis is Noam Chomsky. This hypothesis of unbounded clausal embedding complexity is closely related to the hypothesis of unbounded syntactic recursion.

Psycholinguistic experimentation in the 1960's established that there are clear performance-related preferences especially regarding center-embedding. The acceptability of repeated center-embeddings (nesting) below depth 1 steeply decreases with each successive level of embedding.

Not much corpus-based work has been done to find out what the empirical 'facts' of clausal embedding complexity are. I have conducted extensive corpus studies of English, Finnish, German, Latin, and Swedish, with the aim of determining the most complex clausal embedding patterns actually used. The basic constraint on nested center-embedding in written language turns out to be two (with a marginal cline to three), in spoken language one. There are further specific restrictions on which types of clauses may be nested. The practical limit of final embedding (right-branching) is five. Repeated initial embedding (left-branching) of clauses below depth two is not possible.

These written language constraints were reached already in Sumerian, Akkadian, and Latin along with the advent of written language and have remained the same ever since.

The constraints on center-embedding imply that SAE syntax is finite-state, type 3 in the Chomsky hierarchy. Clause-level recursion is thus not unbounded. The special case of right-branching relative clauses is rather an instance of depth-preserving iteration.

T. Salakoski et al. (Eds.): FinTAL 2006, LNAI 4139, p. 1, 2006.

The Explanatory Combinatorial Dictionary as the Key Tool in Machine Translation

Igor Mel'čuk

Department of linguistics and translation
University of Montreal
C.P. 6128, Succ. Centre-Ville
Montreal (Quebec) H3C 3J7
Canada
Igor.Melcuk@umontreal.ca

Abstract. Lexical and syntactic mismatches between languages are the main challenge for every translation (especially formidable for Machine Translation; see Mel'čuk & Wanner 2001, 2006). An example of mismatches in English-to-Russian translation:

a. *The demonstrators were brutally beaten and tear-gassed by the police.*
b. Rus. *Demonstranty podverglis´ zverskomu izbieniju so storony policii; protiv nix byl primenën slezotočivyj gaz* lit. 'Demonstrators underwent bestial beating from_side of_police; against them was applied tear-gas'.

The only way to resolve inter-linguistic mismatches is paraphrasing—intra- or interlinguistic. To explain better what I mean I will refer to mismatches found in the example. Thus, in Russian:

— The verb with the meaning '[to] tear-gas' does not exist, so you have to use the semantically equivalent expression '[to] apply tear-gas'.
— The passive of the verb '[to] beat'—with the Actor 'police'—does not readily combine with the noun 'police' as the syntactic Agent (it is not official enough!), so you have to use the semantically equivalent expression '[to] undergo a beating' (with the Subject 'demonstrators').
— The expression '[to] apply tear-gas' does not have a passive and therefore cannot be directly conjoined with '[to] undergo a beating' (the two clauses have different Subjects), so you have to use loose coordination of two complete clauses.

Such paraphrases are described by Deep-Syntactic Paraphrasing System of the Meaning-Text Theory: a few dozens universal paraphrasing rules (Mel'čuk 1992; Milićević 2006).

Paraphrasing at the semantic and/or deep-syntactic level can be ensured only by an extremely rich dictionary. Thus, the transformation '[to] tear-gas' ⇒ '[to] apply tear-gas' is triggered by the information in the lexical entry of the Russian nominal expression SLEZOTOČIVYJ GAZ 'tear-gas' (where the semi-auxiliary verb PRIMENJAT´ '[to] apply' is found).

Such a dictionary, semantically-based and lexical co-occurrence centered, is the *Explanatory Combinatorial Dictionary* (Mel'čuk & Žolkovskyj 1984, Mel'čuk *et al.* 1984-1999, Mel'čuk *et al.* 1995). Three major zones of its lexical entry for headword L present:

T. Salakoski et al. (Eds.): FinTAL 2006, LNAI 4139, pp. 2 – 3, 2006.

— L's meaning, in the form of a formalized analytical lexicographic definition equivalent to a semantic network of the Meaning-Text Theory;
— L's Government Pattern, which contains complete information about L's actants and their surface realization;
— L's restricted lexical cooccurrence, in the form of Lexical Functions, which supply complete information about L's collocations (for instance: Real_1(*slezotočivyj gaz* 'tear-gas') = *primenjat´* [~ *protiv* 'against' N_Y]; [AntiBon + Magn](*izbivat´* '[to] beat') = *zverski* lit. 'bestially'; Fact_2(*policija* 'police') = *izbivat´* '[to] beat', not **bit´* '[to] beat', which is semantically quite plausible).

A Finite-State Approximation of Optimality Theory: The Case of Finnish Prosody

Lauri Karttunen

Palo Alto Research Center, 3333 Coyote Hill Rd, Palo Alto CA 94304, USA
karttunen@parc.com
http://www2.parc.com/istl/members/karttune/

Abstract. This paper gives a finite-state formulation of two closely related descriptions of Finnish prosody proposed by Paul Kiparsky and Nine Elenbaas in the framework of OPTIMALITY THEORY. In native Finnish words, the primary stress falls on the first syllable. Secondary stress generally falls on every second syllable. However, secondary stress skips a light syllable that is followed by a heavy syllable. Kiparsky and Elenbaas attempt to show that the ternary pattern arises from the interaction of universal metrical constraints.

This paper formalizes the Kiparsky and Elenbaas analyses using the PARC/XRCE regular expression calculus. It shows how output forms with syllabification, stress and metrical feet are constructed from unmarked input forms. The optimality constraints proposed by Kiparsky and Elenbaas are reformulated in finite-state terms using lenient composition. The formalization shows that both analyses fail for many types of words.

1 Introduction

This article is a companion piece to Karttunen [1] that refutes the account proposed by Paul Kiparsky [2] and Nine Elenbaas [3,4] in the framework of OPTIMALITY THEORY [5,6,7] for ternary rhythm in Finnish. The purpose of this follow-up article is to fill in the missing technical details and provide a complete account of the finite-state implementation that was used to derive the result.

In general, Finnish prosody is trochaic with the main stress on the first syllable and a secondary stress on every other following syllable. Finnish also has a ternary stress pattern that surfaces in words where the stress would fall on a light syllable that is followed by a heavy syllable. A light syllable ends with a short vowel (*ta*); a heavy syllable ends with a coda consonant (*jat*, *an*) or a long vowel (*kuu*, *aa*) or a diphthong (*voi*, *ei*). Example (1a) shows the usual trochaic pattern; (1b) starts off with a ternary foot.[1]

(1) a. (rá.kas).(tà.ja).(tàr.ta) 'mistress' (Sg. Par.)
    b. (rá.kas).ta.(jàt.ta).(rè.na) 'mistress' (Sg. Ess.)

[1] Kiparsky and Elenbaas treat the third syllable of a dactyl as extrametrical, that is, (rá.kas).ta. instead of (rá.kas.ta). This decision of not recognizing a ternary foot as a primitive is of no consequence as far as the topic of this paper is concerned.

T. Salakoski et al. (Eds.): FinTAL 2006, LNAI 4139, pp. 4–15, 2006.

The acute accent indicates primary stress and the grave accents mark secondary stress. Periods mark syllable boundaries and feet are enclosed in parentheses.

The fundamental idea in the Kiparsky and Elenbaas studies is that the ternary rhythm in examples such as (1b) arises naturally from the interaction of constraints that in other types of words produce a binary stress pattern. The fundamental assumption in the OT framework is that all types of prosodic structures are always available in principle. It is the constraints and the ranking between them that determines which of the competing candidates emerges as the winner. In some circumstances the constraints select the binary rhythm, in other circumstances the trochaic pattern wins. Unfortunately the constraints they propose pick out the wrong pattern in many cases. This fact has not been noticed by the proponents of the OT analyses. It is practically impossible to detect such errors without a computational implementation.

2 OT Constraints for Finnish Prosody

Under Kiparsky's analysis (p. 111), the prosody of Finnish is characterized by the system in (2). The constraints are listed in the order of their priority.

(2) a. *CLASH: No stresses on adjacent syllables.
   b. LEFT-HANDEDNESS: The stressed syllable is initial in the foot.
   c. MAIN STRESS: The primary stress in Finnish is on the first syllable.
   d. FOOTBIN: Feet are minimally bimoraic and maximally disyllabic.
   e. *LAPSE: Every unstressed syllable must be adjacent to a stressed syllable or to the word edge.
   f. NON-FINAL: The final syllable is not stressed.
   g. STRESS-TO-WEIGHT: Stressed syllables are heavy.
   h. LICENSE-σ: Syllables are parsed into feet.
   i. ALL-FT-LEFT: The left edge of every foot coincides with the left edge of some prosodic word.

Elenbaas [3] and Elenbaas and Kager [4] give essentially the same analysis except that they replace Kiparsky's STRESS-TO-WEIGHT constraint with the more specific one in (3).

(3) *(L̀H): If the second syllable of a foot is heavy, the stressed syllable should not be light.

3 Finite-State Approximation of OT

As we will see shortly, classical OT constraints such as those in (2) and (3) are REGULAR (= RATIONAL) in power. They can be implemented by finite-state networks. Nevertheless, it has been known for a long time (Frank and Satta [8], Karttunen [9], Eisner [10]) that OT as a whole is not a finite-state system. Although the official OT rhetoric suggests otherwise, OT is fundamentally more complex than finite-state models of phonology such as classical Chomsky-Halle phonology [11] and Koskenniemi's two-level model [12]. The reason is that OT takes into account not just the ranking of the constraints but the number of constraint violations. For example, (4a) and (4b) win over (4c) because (4c) contains two violations of *LAPSE whereas (4a) and (4b) have no violations.[2]

(4) a. (ér.go).(nò.mi).a 'ergonomics' (Nom. Sg.)
 b. (ér.go).no.(mì.a)
 c. (ér.go).no.mi.a

Furthermore, for GRADIENT constraints such as ALL-FT-LEFT, it is not just the number of instances of non-compliance that counts but the SEVERITY of the offense. Candidates (4a) and (4b) both contain one foot that is not at the left edge of the word. But they are not equally optimal. In (4a) the foot not conforming to ALL-FT-LEFT, (nò.mi), is two syllables away from the left edge whereas in (4b) the noncompliant (mì.a) is three syllables away from the beginning. Consequently, (4b) with three violations of ALL-FT-LEFT loses to (4a) that only has two violations of that constraint.

If the number of constraint violations is bounded, the classical OT theory of [5] can be approximated by a finite-state cascade where the input is first composed with a transducer, GEN, that maps the input to a set of output candidates (possibly infinite) and the resulting input/output transducer is then "leniently" composed with constraint automata starting with the most highly ranked constraint. We will use this technique, first described in [9], to implement the two OT descriptions of Finnish prosody. The key operation, LENIENT COMPOSITION, is a combination of ordinary composition and PRIORITY UNION [13].

Priority Union. The priority union operator `.P.` is defined in terms of other regular expression operators in the PARC/XRCE calculus.[3] The definition of priority union is given in (5).

(5) `Q .P. R` $=_{def}$ `Q | [~[Q.u] .o. R]`

The `.u` operator in (5) extracts the "upper" language from a regular relation; ~ is negation. Thus the expression `~[Q.u]` denotes the set of strings that do not occur on the upper side of the `Q` relation. The symbol `.o.` is the composition operator and `|` stands for union. The effect of the composition `[~[Q.u] .o. R]` is to restrict `R` to mappings of strings that are not mapped into anything in `Q`. Only this subrelation of `R` is unioned with `Q`. In other words, `[Q .P. R]` gives precedence to the mappings in `Q` over the mappings in `R`.

Lenient Composition. The basic idea of lenient composition can be explained as follows. Assume that `R` is a relation, a mapping that assigns to each input form some number of outputs, and that `C` is a constraint that prohibits some of the output forms. The lenient composition of `R` and `C`, denoted as `[R .O. C]`, is the relation that eliminates all the output candidates of a given input that do

[2] It is important to keep in mind that the actual scores, 0 vs. 2, are not relevant. What matters is that (4a) and (4b) have **fewer** violations than (4c).

[3] The PARC/XRCE regular expression formalism is presented in Chapter 2 of [14].

not conform to C, provided that the input has at least one output that meets the constraint. If none of the output candidates of a given input meet the constraint, lenient composition spares all of them. Consequently, every input will have at least one output, no matter how many violations it incurs.[4]

We define the desired operation, denoted `.O.`, as a combination of ordinary composition and priority union in (6).

(6) `R .O. C` $=_{def}$ `[R .o. C] .P. R`

The left side of the priority union in (6), `[R .o. C]` restricts `R` to mappings that satisfy the constraint `C`. That is, any pair whose lower side string is not in `C` will be eliminated. If some string in the upper language of `R` has no counterpart on the lower side that meets the constraint, then it is not present in `[R .o. C].u` but, for that very reason, it will be "rescued" by the priority union. In other words, if an underlying form has some output that can meet the given constraint, lenient composition enforces the constraint. If an underlying form has no output candidates that meet the constraint, then the underlying form and all its outputs are retained. The definition of lenient composition entails that the upper language of `R` is preserved in `[R .O. C]`.

In order to be able to give preference to output forms that incur the fewest violations of a constraint `C`, we first mark the violations and then select the best candidates using lenient composition. We set a limit n, an upper bound for the number of violations that the system will consider, and employ a set of auxiliary constraints, V_{n-1}, V_{n-2}, ..., V_0, where V_i accepts the output candidates that violate the constraint at most i times. The most stringent enforcer, V_0, allows no violations. Given a relation `R`, a mapping from the inputs to the current set of output candidates, we mark all the violations of `C` and then prune the resulting `R'` with lenient composition: `R' .O.` V_{n-1} `.O.` V_{n-2} `... .O.` V_0. If an input form has output candidates that are accepted by V_i, where $n > i \geq 0$, all the ones that are rejected by V_i are eliminated; otherwise the set of output candidates is not reduced. The details of this strategy are explained in Section 4.2.

4 Finite-State OT Prosody

In this section, we will show how the two OT descriptions of Finnish prosody in Section 2 can be implemented in a finite-state system. The regular expression formalism in this section and the **xfst** application used for computation are described in the book *Finite State Morphology* [14].

The first objective is to provide a definition of the GEN function for Finnish prosody. The function must accomplish three tasks: (1) parse the input into syllables, (2) assign optional stress, and (3) combine syllables optionally into metrical feet. In keeping with the hallmark OT thesis of "freedom of analysis", we need a prolific GEN. Every conceivable output candidate, however bizarre, should be made available for evaluation by the constraints.

---

[4] Frank and Satta [8, pp. 8–9] call this operation "conditional intersection."

The second objective is to express Kiparsky's nine constraints in (2) in finite-state terms and bundle them together in the order of their ranking. Combined with GEN, the system should map any input into its optimal metrical realization in Finnish.

4.1 The GEN Function

To simplify our definitions of complex regular expressions, it is useful to start with some elementary notions and define higher-level concepts with the help of the finite-state calculus.

Basic Definitions. Each of the definitions in (7) is a formula in the PARC/XRCE extended regular expression language and compiles into a finite-state network. The vertical bar, |, is the union operator. Consequently, the first statement in (7) defines `HighV` as the language consisting of the strings *u*, *y* and *i*. The text following `#` is a comment.

(7)
```
define HighV [u | y | i];                              # High vowel
define MidV [e | o | ö];                                # Mid vowel
define LowV [a | ä] ;                                   # Low vowel
define USV [HighV | MidV | LowV];               # Unstressed Vowel
define C [b | c | d | f | g | h | j | k | l | m |
          n | p | q | r | s | t | v | w | x | z]; # Consonant

define MSV [á | é | í | ó| ú | ý | ä́ | ö́];          # Main stress
define SSV [à | è | ì | ò | ù | ỳ | ä̀ | ö̀];# Secondary stress
define SV [MSV | SSV];                              # Stressed vowel
define V [USV | SV] ;                                        # Vowel
define P [V | C];                                          # Phoneme
```

We also need some auxiliary symbols to mark syllable and foot boundaries. The auxiliary alphabet is defined in (8). The period, `.`, marks internal syllable boundaries. The parentheses, `( )`, enclose a metrical foot. We use a special symbol, `.#.`, to refer to the beginning or the end of a string. The suffix operator, `+`, creates a "one-or-more" iterative language from whatever it is attached to.

(8)
```
define B [["(" | ")" | "." ]+ | .#.];                    # Boundary
define E .#. | ".";                                          # Edge
```

Two basic types of syllables are defined in (9). The onset of a syllable may contain zero or more consonants, `C*`. The nucleus of a light syllable, `LS`, consists of a single short vowel. For example, *a*, *ta* and *stra* are light syllables.

(9)
```
define LS [C* V];                                # Light Syllable
define HS [LS P+];                               # Heavy Syllable
define S [HS | LS];                                     # Syllable
```

In addition to knowing whether a syllable is light or heavy, we also need to know about the stress. The ampersand, `&`, in (10) stands for intersection and the dollar sign, $, is the "contains" operator. A stressed syllable, SS, is thus the intersection of all syllables with anything that contains a stressed vowel. With ~ standing for negation, an unstressed syllable, US, is the intersection of all syllables with anything that does not contain a stressed vowel. Finally, MSS is a syllable with a vowel that has the main stress.

(10)
```
define SS [S & $SV];                          # Stressed Syllable
define US [S & ~$SV];                       # Unstressed Syllable
define MSS [S & $MSV] ;               # Syllable with Main Stress
```

With the help of the basic concepts in (7)-(10) we can proceed to the first real task, the definition of Finnish syllabification.

Syllabification. Assigning the correct syllable structure is a non-trivial task in Finnish because the nucleus of a syllable may consist of a short vowel, a long vowel, or a diphthong. A diphthong is a combination of two unlike vowels that together form the nucleus of a syllable. Adjacent vowels that cannot constitute a long vowel or a diphthong must be separated by a syllable boundary. In general, Finnish diphthongs end in a high vowel. However, in the first syllable there are three exceptional high-mid diphthongs: *ie*, *uo*, and *yö* that historically come from long *ee*, *oo*, and *öö*, respectively. All other adjacent vowels must be separated by a syllable boundary. For example, the first *ie* in the input *sienien* 'mushroom' (Pl. Gen.) constitutes a diphthong but the second *ie* does not because it is not in the first syllable. The correct syllabification is *sie.ni.en.*[5]

We will define Syllabification as a transducer that takes any input and inserts periods to mark syllable boundaries. Because of the issue with diphthongs, it is convenient to build the final syllabification transducer from two components. The first one, MarkNonDiphth, in (11) inserts syllable boundaries (periods) between vowels that cannot form the nucleus of a syllable.

(11)
```
define MarkNonDiphth [ [. .] -> "." ||
                              [HighV | MidV] _ LowV, # i.a, e.a
                              LowV _ MidV,           # a.e
                              i _ [MidV - e],        # i.o, i.ö
                              u _ [MidV - o],        # u.e
                              y _ [MidV - ö],        # y.e
                              $V i _ e ];            # sieni.en
```

The arrow, -> is the "replace" operator. The first line of (11) specifies that an epsilon (empty string), [. .][6], is replaced by a period in certain contexts, defined on the six lines following ||. The underscore, _, marks the site of the of the replacement between left and right contexts. For example, the last context line

[5] Instead of providing the syllabification directly as part of GEN, it would of course be possible to generate a set of possible syllabification candidates from which the winners would emerge through an interaction with OT constraints such as HAVEONSET, FILLNUCLEUS, NOCODA, etc.

[6] For an explanation of the [. .] notation, see [14, pp. 67–68].

in (11) inserts a syllable boundary between i and e when there is some preceding vowel. Thus it breaks the second, but not the first, *ie*-cluster in in words such as *sienien* 'mushroom' (Pl. Gen.). The minus symbol, `-`, in the preceding three lines denotes subtraction, e.g. `[MidV - e]` is any mid vowel other than *e*.

The second component of syllabification is defined in (12). Here `@->` is the left-to-right, longest-match replace operator. The effect of the rule is to insert a syllable boundary after a maximal match for the `C* V+ C*` pattern provided that it is followed by a consonant and a vowel. Here ... mark the match for the pattern and "." is the insertion after the match. Applying `MaximizeSyll` to an input string such as *strukturalismi* yields *struk.tu.ra.lis.mi.*

(12) `define MaximizeSyll [ C* V+ C* @-> ... "." || _ C V ];`

Having defined the two components separately, we can now define the general syllabification rule by composing them together into a single transducer, as shown in (13) where `.o.` is the ordinary composition operator.

(13) `define Syllabify [MarkNonDiphth .o. MaximizeSyll];`

For example, when `Syllabify` is applied to the input *sienien*, the outcome is *sie.ni.en* where the second syllable boundary comes from `MarkNonDiphth` and the first one from `MaximizeSyll`.

The general syllabification rule in (13) has exceptions. In particular, some loan words such as *ate.isti* 'atheist' must be partially syllabified in the lexicon. Compound boundaries must be indicated to prevent bad syllabifications such as **i.soi.sä* for *i.so#i.sä* 'grand father'.

Stress. Because the proper distribution of primary and secondary stress is determined by the optimality constraints, all that the GEN function needs to do is to allow any vowel to have a main stress, a secondary stress or be unstressed. This is accomplished by the definition in (14) where `(->)` is the "optional replace" operator. The effect of the rule is to optionally replace each of the six vowels by the two stressed versions of the same vowel. For example, `OptStress` maps the input *maa* into *maa*, *máa* and *màa*.

```
(14) define OptStress [ a (->) á|à, e (->) é|è, i (->) í|ì,
                        o (->) ó|ò, u (->) ú|ù, y (->) ý|ỳ,
                        ä (->) ä́|ä̀, ö (->) ö́|ö̀  ||  E C* _ ];
```

Because of the context restriction, `E C* _`, in (14), the stress is always assigned to the first component of a long vowel or a diphthong. As defined in (8), `E` stands here for a syllable boundary or the beginning of a word.

Metrical Structure. In keeping with the OT philosophy, the grouping of syllables into metrical feet should also be done optionally and in every possible way to create a rich candidate set for the evaluation by optimality constraints. The definion of `OptScan` in (15) yields a foot-building transducer that optionally wraps parentheses around one, two or three adjacent syllables. The expression to the left of the optional replace operator, `[S ("." S ("." S)) & $SS]`, defines a pattern that matches one or two or three syllables with their syllable boundary marks. The intersection with `$SS` guarantees that at least one of them is a stressed syllable. The right side of the rule wraps any instance of such a pattern within parentheses thus creating a metrical foot. The context restriction, `E _ E`, has the effect that feet consist of whole syllables with no part left behind.

```
(15) define OptScan [[S ("." S ("." S)) & $SS] (->) "(" ... ")"
                     || E _ E];
```

Assembling the GEN Function. Having defined separately the three components of GEN, syllabification, stress assignment and footing, we can now build the GEN function by composing the three transducers with the definition in (16).

```
(16) define GEN(X) [ X .o. Syllabify .o. OptStress .o. OptScan ];
```

where `X` can be a single input form or a symbol representing a set of input forms or an entire language. The result of compiling a regular expression of the form `GEN(X)` is a transducer that maps each input form in `X` into all of its possible output forms.

Because stress assignment and footing are optional, The `GEN()` function produces a large number of alternative prosodic structures for even short inputs. For example, for the input *kala* 'fish' (Sg. Nom.), `GEN({kala})` produces the 33 output forms shown in (17).

(17) kà.là, kà.lá, kà.la, kà.(lá), kà.(là), ká.là, ká.lá, ká.la, ká.(lá), ká.(là), ka.là, ka.lá, ka.la, ka.(lá), ka.(là), (ká).là, (ká).lá, (ká).la, (ká).(lá), (ká).(là), **(ká.la)**, (ká.lá), (ká.là), (kà).là, (kà).lá, (kà).la, (kà).(lá), (kà).(là), (kà.la), (kà.lá), (kà.là), (ka.lá), (ka.là)

As the analyses by Elenbaas and Kiparsky predict, the correct output is (ká.la).

4.2 The Constraints

There are two types of violable OT constraints. For CATEGORICAL constraints, the penalty is the same no matter where the violation occurs. For GRADIENT constraints, the site of violation matters. For example, ALL-FEET-LEFT assigns to non-initial feet a penalty that increases with the distance from the beginning of the word.

Our general strategy is as follows. We first define an evaluation template for the two constraint types and then define the constraints themselves with the help of the templates. We use asterisks as violation marks and use lenient composition to select the output candidates with the fewest violation marks. Categorical constraints mark each violation with an asterisk. Gradient constraints mark violations with sequences of asterisks starting from one and increasing with the distance from the word edge.

The initial set of output candidates is obtained by composing the input with GEN. As the constraints are evaluated in the order of their ranking, the number of output forms is successively reduced. At the end of the evaluation, each input form typically should have just one correct output form.

An evaluation template for categorical constraints, shown in (18), needs four arguments: the current output mapping, a regular expression pattern describing what counts as a violation, a left context, and a right context.[7]

(18)
```
define Cat(Candidates, Violation, Left, Right) [
  Candidates .o. Violation -> ... "*" || Left _ Right
  .O. Viol3 .O. Viol2 .O. Viol1 .O. Viol0
  .o. Pardon ];
```

The first part of the definition composes the candidate set with a rule transducer that inserts an asterisk whenever it sees a violation that occurs in the specified context. The second part of the definition is a sequence of lenient compositions. The first one eliminates all candidates with more than three violations, provided that some candidates have only three or fewer violations. Finally, we try to eliminate all candidates with even one violation. This will succeed only if there are some output strings with no asterisks. The auxiliary terms `Viol3`, `Viol2`, `Viol1`, `Viol0` limit the number of asterisks. For example, `Viol1`, is defined as `~[$"*"]^2`. It prohibits having two or more violation marks. The third part, `Pardon`, is defined as `"*" -> 0`. It removes any remaining violation marks from the output strings. Because we are counting violations only up to three, we cannot distinguish strings that have four violations from strings with more than four violations. It turns out that three is an empirically sufficient limit for our categorical prosody constraints.

The evaluation template for gradient constraints counts up to 14 violations and each violation incurs more and more asterisks as we count instances of the left context. The definition is given in (19).

(19)
```
define GradLeft(Candidates, Violation, Left, Right) [
  Candidates
  .o. Violation -> "*" ... ||.#. Left _ Right
  .o. Violation -> "*"^2 ... ||.#. Left^2 _ Right
  .o. Violation -> "*"^3 ... ||.#. Left^3 _ Right
  .o. Violation -> "*"^4 ... ||.#. Left^4 _ Right
  .o. Violation -> "*"^5 ... ||.#. Left^5 _ Right
  .o. Violation -> "*"^6 ... ||.#. Left^6 _ Right
  .o. Violation -> "*"^7 ... ||.#. Left^7 _ Right
  .o. Violation -> "*"^8 ... ||.#. Left^8 _ Right
  .o. Violation -> "*"^9 ... ||.#. Left^9 _ Right
  .o. Violation -> "*"^10 ... ||.#. Left^10 _ Right
  .o. Violation -> "*"^11 ... ||.#. Left^11 _ Right
  .o. Violation -> "*"^12... || .#. Left^12 _ Right
  .o. Violation -> "*"^13 ... ||.#. Left^13 _ Right
```

[7] Some constraints can be specified without referring to a particular left or right context. The expression `?*` stands for any unspecified context.

```
.o. Violation -> "*"^14 ... ||.#. Left^14 _ Right
.O. Viol14 .O. Viol13 .O. Viol12 .O.Viol11 .O. Viol10
.O. Viol9 .O. Viol8 .O. Viol7 .O. Viol6 .O. Viol5
.O. Viol4 .O. Viol3 .O. Viol2 .O. Viol1 .O.  Viol0
.o. Pardon ];
```

Using the two templates in (18) and (19), we can now give very simple definitions for Kiparsky's nine constraints in (2).

(20) a. *CLASH: No stress on adjacent syllables.
`define Clash(X) Cat(X, SS, SS B, ?*);`

b. LEFT-HANDEDNESS: The stressed syllable is initial in the foot.
`define AlignLeft(X) Cat(X, SS, ".", ?*);`

c. MAIN STRESS: The primary stress in Finnish is on the first syllable.
```
define MainStress(X)
  Cat(X, ~[B MSS ~$MSS], .#., .#.);
```

d. FOOT-BIN: Feet are minimally bimoraic and maximally bisyllabic.
```
define FootBin(X)
  Cat(X, ["(" LS ")" | "(" S ["." S]^>1], ?*, ?*);
```

e. LAPSE: Every unstressed syllable must be adjacent to a stressed syllable or to the word edge.
`define Lapse(X) Cat(X, US, [B US B], [B US B]);`

f. NON-FINAL: The final syllable is not stressed.
`define NonFinal(X) Cat(X, SS, ?*, ~$S .#.);`

g. STRESS-TO-WEIGHT: Stressed syllables are heavy.
`define StressToWeight(X) Cat(X, [SS & LS], ?*, B);`

h. LICENSE-σ: Syllables are parsed into feet.
`define Parse(X) Cat(X, S, E, E);`

i. ALL-FT-LEFT: The left edge of every foot coincides with the left edge of some prosodic word.
```
define AllFeetFirst(X)
  GradLeft(X, "(", [~$"." "." ~$"."], ?*);
```

To take just one example, let us consider the `StressToWeight` function. The violation part of the definition, `[SS & LS]`, picks out syllables such as *tí* and *tì* that are light and contain a stressed vowel. The left context is irrelevant, represented as `?*`. The right context matters. It must be some kind of boundary; otherwise perfectly well-formed outputs such as (má.te).ma.(tìik.ka) would get two violation marks: (má*.te).ma.(tì*ik.ka). That is because *tì* by itself is a stressed light syllable but *tìik* is not. The violation mark on the initial syllable *má* is correct but has no consequence because the higher-ranked `MainStress` constraint has removed all competing output candidates for *matematiikka* 'mathematics' (Sg. Nom.) that started with a secondary stress, *mà*, or without any stress, *ma*.

4.3 Combining GEN with the Constraints

Having defined both the GEN function and Kiparsky's nine prosody constraints, we can now put it all together creating a single function, `FinnishProsody`, that should map any Finnish input into its correct prosodic form. The definition is given in (21).

(21) `define FinnishProsody(Input) [ AllFeetFirst( Parse( StressToWeight(NonFinal(Lapse( FootBin( MainStress( AlignLeft( Clash( GEN( Input )))))))))) ];`

A regular expression of the form `FinnishProsody(X)` is computed "inside-out." First the GEN function defined in (16) maps each of the input forms in `X` into all of its possible output forms. Then the constraints defined in Section 4.2 are applied in the order of their ranking to eliminate violators, making sure that at least one output form remains for all the inputs. For example, the compilation of the regular expression in (22)

(22) `FinnishProsody({rakastajatarta} | {rakastajattarena});`

produces a transducer with the mappings in (23) and (24).

```
(23)   r a     k a s       t a   j a       t a r   t a
     ( r á . k a s ) . ( t à . j a ) . ( t à r . t a )

(24)   r a     k a s     t a     j a t   t a       r e   n a
     ( r á . k a s ) . t a . ( j à t . t a ) . ( r è . n a )
```

This is the right result we already saw in (1). Unfortunately there are many input patters that yield an incorrect result. Some examples are given in (25). We use `L` for light, `H` for heavy syllable and `X` when the distinction between `L` and `H` does not matter. For a discussion of what goes wrong, see [1].

```
(25)     XXLLLX: *(ká.las).te.(lè.mi).nen
         XXHHLX: *(há.pa).roi.(tùt.ta).vaa
        XXLHHLX: *(pú.hu).(tè.tuim).(mìs.ta).kin
      XXHHLHHLX: *(jā́r.jes).tel.(mā̀l.li).syy.(dèl.lä).ni
```

Replacing Kiparsky's `StressToWeight` by Elenbaas' more specific *(L̀H) constraint helps in some cases and hurts in others. The last of the four patterns in (25) comes out correct but a new type of error appears, as shown in (26).

```
(26)     XXHLLX: *(kú.ti).tet.(tù.ja).kin
      XXHHLHHLX: (jā́r.jes).(tèl.mäl).li.(sȳ̀y.del).(lā̀.ni)
```

5 Conclusion

The basic assumption in the Kiparsky and Elenbaas & Kager studies is that the alternation between binary and ternary patterns in Finnish arises in a natural way from the interaction of universal constraints. It would be a satisfying result but, unfortunately, it is not true for the constraints that have been proposed so far. The traditional tableau method commonly used by phonologists cannot handle the vast number of competing output candidates that the theory postulates. Computational techniques such as those developed in this article are indispensable in finding and verifying an OT solution to Finnish prosody. And even with the best computational tools, debugging OT constraints is a hard problem.

References

1. Karttunen, L.: The insufficiency of paper-and-pencil linguistics: the case of Finnish prosody. In Butt, M., Dalrymple, M., King, T.H., eds.: Intelligent Linguistic Architectures: Variations on Themes by Ronald M. Kaplan. CSLI Publications, Stanford, California (2006) 287–300
2. Kiparsky, P.: Finnish noun inflection. In Nelson, D., Manninen, S., eds.: Generative Approaches to Finnic and Saami Linguistics: Case, Features and Constraints. CSLI Publications, Stanford, California (2003) 109–161
3. Elenbaas, N.: A Unified Account of Binary and Ternary Stress. Graduate School of Linguistics, Utrecht, Netherlands (1999)
4. Elenbaas, N., Kager, R.: Ternary rhythm and the lapse constraint. Phonology **16** (1999) 273–329
5. Prince, A., Smolensky, P.: Optimality Theory: Constraint Interaction in Generative Grammar. Cognitive Science Center, Rutgers, New Jersey (1993) ROA Version, 8/2002
6. Kager, R.: Optimality Theory. Cambridge University Press, Cambridge, England (1999)
7. McCarthy, J.J.: The Foundations of Optimality Theory. Cambridge University Press, Cambridge, England (2002)
8. Frank, R., Satta, G.: Optimality theory and the generative complexity of constraint violability. Computational Linguistics **24**(2) (1998) 307–316
9. Karttunen, L.: The proper treatment of optimality in computational phonology. In: FSMNLP'98., Ankara, Turkey, Bilkent University (1998) cmp-lg/9804002.
10. Eisner, J.: Directional constraint evaluation in Optimality Theory. In: Proceedings of the 18th International Conference on Computational Linguistics (COLING 2000), Saarbrücken, Germany (2000) 257–263
11. Kaplan, R.M., Kay, M.: Regular models of phonological rule systems. Computational Linguistics **20**(3) (1994) 331–378
12. Koskenniemi, K.: Two-level morphology. Publication 11, University of Helsinki, Department of General Linguistics, Helsinki (1983)
13. Kaplan, R.M., Newman, P.S.: Lexical resource reconciliation in the Xerox Linguistic Environment. In: ACL/EACL'98 Workshop on Computational Environments for Grammar Development and Linguistic Engineering, Madrid, Spain (1997) 54–61
14. Beesley, K.R., Karttunen, L.: Finite State Morphology. CSLI Publications, Stanford, CA (2003)

A Bilingual Corpus of Novels Aligned at Paragraph Level*

Alexander Gelbukh, Grigori Sidorov, and José Ángel Vera-Félix

Natural Language and Text Processing Laboratory,
Center for Research in Computer Science,
National Polytechnic Institute,
Av. Juan Dios Batiz, s/n, Zacatenco, 07738, Mexico City,
Mexico
sidorov@cic.ipn.mx
www.Gelbukh.com

Abstract. The paper presents a bilingual English-Spanish parallel corpus aligned at the paragraph level. The corpus consists of twelve large novels found in Internet and converted into text format with manual correction of formatting problems and errors. We used a dictionary-based algorithm for automatic alignment of the corpus. Evaluation of the results of alignment is given. There are very few available resources as far as parallel fiction texts are concerned, while they are non-trivial case of alignment of a considerable size. Usually, approaches for automatic alignment that are based on linguistic data are applied for texts in the restricted areas, like laws, manuals, etc. It is not obvious that these methods are applicable for fiction texts because these texts have much more cases of non-literal translation than the texts in the restricted areas. We show that the results of alignment for fiction texts using dictionary based method are good, namely, produce state of art precision value.

1 Introduction

There are many sources of linguistic data. Nowadays, Internet is one of the most important sources of texts of various kinds that are used for investigations in the field of computational linguistics. Also, advances of corpus linguistics give more and more possibilities of accessing of various types of corpora – raw texts as well as texts marked with certain additional linguistic information: phonetic, morphological, syntactic, information about word senses, semantic roles, etc. One of the important types of the linguistic information is the "relative" information that is not specific to the text itself, but is related to some other text or pragmatic situation, in contrast with the "absolute" information specific to the text itself.

One of the clear examples of the relative information is the case of parallel texts, i.e., the texts that are translations of each other, or, maybe, translations of some other text. Sometimes it is interesting to compare two different translation of the same text. The relative information is represented by the relation between different structural

* The work was done under partial support of Mexican Government (CONACyT, SNI) and National Polytechnic Institute, Mexico (CGPI, COFAA, PIFI).

T. Salakoski et al. (Eds.): FinTAL 2006, LNAI 4139, pp. 16 – 23, 2006.

parts (units) of these texts. The procedure of establishing these relations is called alignment, and the resulting parallel corpus is called aligned. Obviously, there are various levels of alignment: text, i.e., we just know that the texts are parallel (it may be useful in case of very short texts, like news messages or paper abstracts, for example); paragraphs; sentences; words and phraseological units.

It is important to emphasize that each unit in a parallel text can have one, several or zero correspondences in the other text, for example, one sentence can be translated with various, some words can be omitted, etc. Thus, the alignment of parallel texts is not a trivial task. This situation is especially frequent in fiction texts that we discuss in the present paper.

One of the most accessible sources of parallel texts is Internet. Unfortunately, the texts presented in Internet are very "dirty", i.e., they may have pictures, special formatting, special HTML symbols, etc. Often, the texts are in the PDF format and during their conversion into the plain text format the information about the ends of paragraphs is lost. Thus, rather extended preprocessing, sometimes inevitably manual, is necessary.

The importance of the aligned parallel corpora is related with the fact that there are structural differences between languages. These differences can be exploited for automatic extraction of various linguistic phenomena. The other obvious application of these corpora is machine translation [1], especially, machine translation based on examples. Another application is automatic extraction of data for machine learning methods. Also, these resources are useful in bilingual lexicography [7], [11]. Another natural application is language teaching. The famous example of the application of parallel texts is deciphering of Egyptian hieroglyphs based on the parallel texts of Rosetta stone.

Generally speaking, there are two very large classes of methods in computational linguistics. One class is based on statistical data, while the other one applies additional linguistic knowledge. Note that the basis of this distinction is related with the kind of data being processed independently of the methods of processing. This is typical situation, for example, the same happens in word sense disambiguation [6].

As far as alignment methods are concerned, the classic statistical methods exploit the expected correlation of length of text units (paragraphs or sentences) in different languages [4], [8] and try to establish the correspondence between the units of the expected size. The size can be measured in number of words or characters.

On the other hand, the linguistic methods, one of which was used for obtaining the results presented in this paper, use linguistic data (usually, dictionaries) for establishing the correspondence between structural units. Application of dictionary data for text alignment was used, for example, in [2], [9], [10], [11]. Among more recent works, let us also mention the paper [3]. The experiments described in this paper were conducted using texts of laws. This is typical for parallel texts because there are many translations of specialized texts, like technical manuals, parliament debates (European or Canadian), law texts, etc. Still, fiction texts are different from these types of technical texts because translation of fiction is much less literal than translation of specialized documents.

The motivation of our paper is presentation of a bilingual parallel corpus of novels and evaluation of how a dictionary-based method performs for fiction texts.

2 Corpus Description

We present the English-Spanish parallel corpus of fiction texts aligned at the paragraph level. The first step is preparation of a corpus, i.e., compilation and preprocessing of the parallel texts. In our case, we chose novels because it is one of the most non-trivial cases of translation of the data of considerable size, for example, advertising is even more complicated, but the corresponding texts are very short. The titles that we included in our corpus are presented in Table 1, as well as the number of paragraphs of each text.

Table 1. Texts included in the corpus with correspoding number of paragraphs

Author	English title	Par.	Spanish title	Par.
Carroll, Lewis	*Alice's adventures in wonderland*	905	*Alicia en el país de las maravillas*	1,148
Carroll, Lewis	*Through the looking-glass*	1,190	*Alicia a través del espejo*	1,230
Conan Doyle, Arthur	*The adventures of Sherlock Holmes*	2,260	*Las aventuras de Sherlock Holmes*	2,550
James, Henry	*The turn of the screw*	820	*Otra vuelta de tuerca*	1,141
Kipling, Rudyard	*The jungle book*	1,219	*El libro de la selva*	1,428
Shelley, Mary	*Frankenstein*	787	*Frankenstein*	835
Stoker, Bram	*Dracula*	2,276	*Drácula*	2,430
Ubídia, Abdón	*Advances in genetics*[2]	116	*De la genética y sus logros*	109
Verne, Jules	*Five weeks in a balloon*	2,068	*Cinco semanas en globo*	2,860
Verne, Jules	*From the earth to the moon*	894	*De la tierra a la luna*	1,235
Verne, Jules	*Michael Strogoff*	2464	*Miguel Strogoff*	3,059
Verne, Jules	*Twenty thousand leagues under the sea*[3]	3,702	*Veinte mil leguas de viaje submarino*	3,515

[2] This is a fiction text, not a scientific text.
[3] There are two English translations of this novel available.

The texts had originally the PDF format. They were converted into plain text and preprocessed manually. Special formatting elements were eliminated and the paragraph structure was restored. The total size of corpus is more than 11.5 MB. The corpus size might seem too small, but let us remind that it is a parallel corpus, where the data is not so easy to obtain. The corpus is freely available on request for research purposes.

Table 2. Some corpus parameters

Corpus parameter	English part	Spanish part
Number of words	848,040	844,156
Tokens (wordforms)	25,877	43,176
Paragraphs	18,701	21,540
Most frequent words	52,597 (*the*) 25,159 (*and*) 25,147 (*of*) 22,041 (*to*) 18,225 (*I*) 17,280 (*a*) 13,473 (*in*)...	43,451 (*de*) 28,714 (*que*) 26,768 (*la*) 24,498 (*y*) 21,871 (*el*) 20,043 (*a*) 18,182 (*en*)...

The difference between numbers of tokens is explained by the presence of morphological variants in Spanish as compared with English.

3 Method Used for Corpus Alignment

Let us remind that the correspondence of paragraphs in source and target texts is not necessarily one-to-one. One of such examples is presented in Table 3.

Table 3. Example of alignment of paragraphs with pattern "2-1"

... Antes de que yo dijese una palabra, María se apresuró a decirme, azorada: *-Es mi madre.*	*Before I could say a word, Maria, disturbed, said hastily, "It's my mother."*
(Lit.: *...Before I could say a word, Maria hurried to say hastily:* "*It is my mother.*")	

This often happens in English-Spanish text pairs, when the direct speech constitutes a separate paragraph in Spanish, while it is part of the previous paragraph in English.

According to the used method, the texts are compared using bilingual dictionaries. Dictionaries have their entries as normalized words. So, it is necessary to implement morphological normalization of tokens (wordforms) converting them into types (lemmas). We performed normalization of Spanish texts using our morphological analyzer AGME [12]. The number of entries of the morphological dictionary is about 26,000 that is equivalent to more than 1,000,000 wordforms.

We have similar morphological analyzer [5] for English language. It is based on WordNet dictionary. The English morphological dictionary contains about 60,000 entries.

Another necessary feature in text alignment is filtering of the auxiliary words. These words should be ignored because their presence is arbitrary and can carry false information about paragraph matching.

Our alignment was based on Spanish-English dictionary that contains about 30,000 entries.

For the moment, we developed a heuristic algorithm that performs the alignment. The algorithm takes into account possible patterns of three paragraphs in each text, starting from the beginning of the texts, and tries to find the best match calculating the similarity for possible patterns of three paragraphs: 1 to 1, 1 to 2, 1 to 3, 2 to 1, 3 to 1. The best possible correspondence is taken. Then the algorithm proceeds to the next three available paragraphs. This algorithm implies the usage of the local optimization as in [3]. It cannot use the global optimization like in [9]. In future, we plan to try the global optimization strategies as well, for example, it is possible to apply genetic algorithm as we already did for word sense disambiguation [6] or, say, dynamic programming [4].

We also implemented the anchor point technique. It implies that we search the small paragraphs, where we are very sure of the alignment (=anchor points). It happens when the paragraphs contain dates or numbers or proper names or some metadata, like chapters. Further, the main algorithm works only between anchor points. It allows avoiding the completely wrong alignment that could be produced due to only one error influencing the rest of alignment.

For calculation of the similarity measure used in the algorithm, we used Dice coefficient with the only modification that we penalize paragraphs with too different sizes. Dice coefficient for two sets – in our case, the set of words and the set of their possible translations– is equal to the intersection (multiplied by two) of these sets, normalized by dividing to the total size of both sets. The penalization is made by multiplication to the number that is the difference of the expected correlation of lengths of sets and the actual correlation.

4 Example of Non-literal Translation

Let us consider an example of non-literal translation of paragraphs. This case is presented in Table 4. The example is taken from the text 8 of the corpus.

The English paragraph has only 85 words, while the Spanish one has 157 words (nearly double size). Note that alignment of these paragraphs is difficult for statistical methods because of the difference in sizes. Obviously, the final correct or incorrect alignment depends on the structure of the context paragraphs.

Table 4. Example of non-literal translation of a paragraph

<table>
<tr><td colspan="2">(Original) Le hice ver que no había dado importancia al asunto. Pero (y hablo de esa vez), a duras penas pude controlar la emoción que me vapuleó de arriba a abajo. "Qué puedes temer del tiempo, si tiempo es lo que más tienes", le dije desde mi interior, pensando en que su turbación se debía al súbito sufrimiento que le ocasionaba el solo pensar que, de todas maneras, en aquella foto, en aquel rostro desdibujado, estaba escrito ya el arribo inevitable, el futuro corrupto y degradado que mis ojos inquisidores (y mis teorías acerca de las herencias físicas) podían prefigurar para ella; algo como una vergüenza impuesta por un pecado aún no cometido, algo como una culpa asumida sin razón; en el fondo, la réplica infantil de una conciencia demasiado tierna. "Qué puedes temer del tiempo, chiquilla", le repetí desde mí mismo, mientras me alejaba de ella para darle lugar a recomponerse, a retomar su serenidad de siempre.</td></tr>
<tr><td>(Translation) I shrugged and smiled and nodded. But I could barely control the emotion that shook me from head to toe. I figured that she must have been upset by the thought that in that blurry face in the photo was written the inevitable, corrupted, degraded future of her own old age. "What do you have to fear from time, little girl, if you have so much of it?" I wondered, as I withdrew to give her space to compose herself and regain her customary serenity.</td><td>(Literal translation) I made her see that I did not give importance to the situation. But (and I speak about this time) I could barely control the emotion that whipped me from head to toe. “Why should you be afraid of time, if you have a lot of time?” I told her in my inside, thinking that her abashment is due to the abrupt anguish that was caused by the mere idea that, anyway, at the photograph, in that blurry face, there was written something inevitable, the corrupted and degraded future, which my inquisitional eyes (and my theories about physical inheritance) could foresee for her. Something like a shame of a sin not committed yet or a fault assumed without any reason, deep down, the infantile copy of a too immature conscience. “Why are you afraid of time, little girl” I repeated inside, while I was withdrawing to allow her to compose herself and regain her customary serenity.</td></tr>
</table>

If we calculate the words that these paragraphs have in common according to their translations in dictionaries, then we will get the value that usually would not appear in relatively big paragraphs, namely, 20 words, i.e., 23% for English and 12% for Spanish. Still, this value keeps being rather solid for their alignment using the dictionary-based method.

5 Alignment Evaluation

We made the experiment for 50 patterns of paragraphs of the text *Dracula*. The results presented in Table 5 were obtained.

Note that we deal with translations of the fiction texts that are not literate; still the precision of the method in this experiment is 94%. The result is the state of art value that shows that the dictionary-based method can be applied to the alignment of fiction texts.

Table 5. Alignment results for 50 patterns of paragraphs

Patterns found	Correct	Incorrect
1 – 1	27	0
1 – 2	8	2
1 – 3	6	0
2 – 1	7	0
3 – 1	2	1

The errors of the alignment methods based on dictionaries happened for paragraphs that have small sizes, because they do not have enough significant words for using them in alignment. Note that from the point of view of statistical methods, the small-size paragraphs are also unreliable.

For a dictionary-based method, a possible solution can be the following: if there are very few o none significant words, some kinds of auxiliary words that have reasonable translations (say, prepositions) can be used in comparison, i.e., treated like significant words.

We expect that adding more dictionary information (synonyms, hyponyms), syntactic information will allow improvements in resolving this problem.

6 Conclusions and Future Work

The paper describes the English-Spanish parallel corpus of novels of a considerable size. Also, we present the evaluation of the performance of the dictionary-based method of alignment at the paragraphs level applied to this corpus. Note that the corpus contains fiction texts that usually do not have very literal translation. The experiment conducted on a small sample and verified manually shows that the dictionary based method has high precision (94%) for this type of non-literal translations. So, we expect that this kind of methods is applicable for fiction texts.

The corpus is freely available for research purposes.

In future, we plan to implement better algorithm of alignment instead of the described heuristic-based algorithm. For example, we plan to use genetic algorithm with global optimization and dynamic programming.

Another direction of improvement of the method is usage of other types of the dictionaries with synonymic and homonymic relations, like WordNet. Also, the method can beneficiate from weighting of the distance between a word and its possible translation, especially in case of the large paragraphs, because some words can occur in a paragraph as a translation of the other word, and not the one that we are searching.

References

[1] Brown, P. F., Lai, J. C. & Mercer, R. L. 1991. Aligning Sentences in Parallel Corpora. In: *Proceedings of the 29th Annual Meeting of the Association for Computational Linguistics,* Berkeley, California, pp 169 – 176.

[2] Chen, S. 1993. Aligning sentences in bilingual corpora using lexical information. In: *Proceeding of ACL-93*, pp. 9-16.

[3] Kit, Chunyu, Jonathan J. Webster, King Kui Sin, Haihua Pan, Heng Li. 2004. Clause alignment for Hong Kong legal texts: A lexical-based approach. *International Journal of Corpus Linguistics* 9:1. pp. 29–51.

[4] Gale, W. A. & Church, K. W. 1991. A program for Aligning Sentences in Bilingual Corpora. In: *Proceedings of the 29th Annual Meeting of the Association for Computational Linguistics*, Berkeley, California.

[5] Gelbukh, Alexander, and Grigori Sidorov. 2003. *Approach to construction of automatic morphological analysis systems for inflective languages with little effort.* Lecture Notes in Computer Science, N 2588, Springer-Verlag, pp. 215–220.

[6] Gelbukh, Alexander, Grigori Sidorov, SangYong Han. 2005. On Some Optimization Heuristics for Lesk-Like WSD Algorithms. *Lecture Notes in Computer Science, N 3513*, Springer-Verlag, pp. 402–405.

[7] McEnery, A. M. & Oakes, M. P. 1996. Sentence and word alignment in the CRATER project. In: J. Thomas & M. Short (eds), *Using Corpora for Language Research*, London, pp. 211 – 231.

[8] Mikhailov, M. 2001. Two Approaches to Automated Text Aligning of Parallel Fiction Texts. *Across Languages and Cultures, 2:1*, pp. 87 – 96.

[9] Kay, Martin and Martin Roscheisen. 1993. Text-translation alignment. *Computational Linguistics*, 19(1):121-142.

[10] Langlais, Ph., M. Simard, J. Veronis. 1998. Methods and practical issues in evaluation alignment techniques. In: *Proceeding of Coling-ACL-98.*

[11] Meyers, Adam, Michiko Kosaka, and Ralph Grishman. 1998. A Multilingual Procedure for Dictionary-Based Sentence Alignment. In: *Proceedings of AMTA'98: Machine Translation and the Information Soup*, pages 187-198.

[12] Velásquez, F., Gelbukh, A. & Sidorov, G. 2002. AGME: un sistema de análisis y generación de la morfología del español. In: *Proc. Of Workshop Multilingual information access & natural language processing of IBERAMIA 2002 (8th Iberoamerican conference on Artificial Intelligence)*, Sevilla, España, November, 12, pp 1-6.

A Computational Implementation of Internally Headed Relative Clause Constructions

Jong-Bok Kim[1], Peter Sells[2], and Jaehyung Yang[3]

[1] School of English, Kyung Hee University, Seoul, Korea 130-701
jongbok@khu.ac.kr
[2] Dept. of Linguistics, Stanford University, USA
sells@stanford.edu
[3] School of Computer Engineering, Kangnam University, Kyunggi, 446-702, Korea
jhyang@kangnam.ac.kr

Abstract. The so-called Internally Headed Relative Clause (IHRC) construction found in the head-final languages Korean and Japanese has received little attention from computational perspectives even though it is frequently found in both text and speech. This is partly because there have been no grammars precise enough to allow deep processing of the construction's syntactic and semantic properties. This paper shows that the typed feature structure grammar HPSG (together with the semantic representations of Minimal Recursion Semantics) offers a computationally feasible and useful way of deep-parsing the construction in question.

1 Introduction

In terms of truth conditions, there is no clear difference between a (Korean) IHRC (internally head relative clause) like (1)a and and EHRC (externally headed relative clause) like (1)b.[1]

(1) a. Tom-un [sakwa-ka cayngpan-wi-ey iss-nun kes]-ul mekessta
Tom-TOP apple-NOM tray-TOP-LOC exist-PNE KES-ACC ate
'Tom ate an apple, which was on the tray.'

b. Tom-un [__ cayngpan-wi-ey iss-nun sakwa]-ul mekessta.
Tom-TOP tray-TOP-LOC exist-PNE apple-ACC ate
'Tom ate an apple that was on the tray.'

Both describe an event in which an apple is on the tray, and Tom's eating it.[2]

Yet, there exist several intriguing differences between the two constructions. One crucial difference between the IHRC and EHRC comes from the fact that

[1] We thank anonymous reviewers for their helpful comments and suggestions. This work was supported by the Korea Research Foundation Grant funded by the Korean Government (KRF-2005-042-A00056).

[2] The following is the abbreviations used for glosses and feature attributes in this paper: ACC (ACCUSATIVE), COMP (COMPLEMENTIZER), LOC (LOCATIVE), NOM (NOMINATIVE), PNE (PRENOMINAL), TOP (TOPIC), etc.

T. Salakoski et al. (Eds.): FinTAL 2006, LNAI 4139, pp. 24–31, 2006.

the semantic object of *mekessta* 'ate' in the IHRC example (1)a is the NP *sakwa* 'apple' buried inside the embedded clause. It is thus the subject of the embedded clause that serves as the semantic argument of the main predicate ([1], [2]).

In the analysis of such IHRCs, the central questions thus involve (a) the key syntactic properties, (b) the association of the internal head of the IHRC clause with the matrix predicate so that the head can function as its semantic argument, and (c) the differences between the IHRC and EHRC. This paper provides a constraint-based analysis within the framework of HPSG (Head-driven Phrase Structure Grammar) and implements it in the existing HPSG grammar for Korean using the LKB (Linguistic Building Knowledge) system to check the computational feasibility of the proposed analysis.[3]

2 Implementing an Analysis

2.1 Syntactic Aspects of the IHRC

One main morphological property of the IHRC construction is shown in (2)b: the embedded clausal predicate should be in the adnominal present form of *(n)un*, followed by the so-called bound noun *kes*. This clearly contrasts with the EHRC example (2)a, in which the predicate can have any of the three different markers of tense information:[4]

(2) a. Tom-i $\_\_{i}$ ilk-nun/un/ul chayk$_i$
Tom-NOM read-PRES.PNE/PST.PNE/FUT.PNE book
'the book that Tom reads/read/will read'
b. Tom-un [sakwa-ka caygnpan-wi-ey **iss-nun/*ul** kes]-ul mekessta
Tom-TOP apple-NOM tray-TOP-LOC exist-PNE KES-ACC ate
'Tom ate an apple, which was (lit. 'is') on the tray.'

In traditional Korean grammar, *kes* in the IHRC is called a 'dependent noun', in that it always requires either a modifying determiner or clause, even in a non-IHRC usage:

(3) a.*(i/ku/ce) kes '*(this/that) thing'
b.*(nay-ka mek-un) kes 'the thing (*that I ate)'

This close syntactic relation between the clause and the noun *kes* can also be found in the fact that unlike canonical nouns, it must combine with a preceding adnominal clause:

(4) Na-nun *(kangto-ka unhayng-eyse nao-nun) kes-ul capassta
I-TOP robber-NOM bank-from come-out-PNE KES-ACC caught
'I arrested the robber who was coming out of the bank.'

[3] The LKB, freely available with open source (`http://lingo.stanford.edu`), is a grammar and lexicon development environment for use with constraint-based linguistic formalisms such as HPSG. cf. [3].

[4] These three prenominal markers in the EHRC extend their meanings to denote aspects when combined with (preceding) tense suffixes.

These examples show that the pronoun *kes* selects an adnominal clause as its complement, and that the IHRC requires a specific inflected form of its predicate.

Then, what is the relationship between the whole IHRC clause including *kes* and the matrix verb? To relate the matrix verb with this construction with an 'internal semantic head', it was assumed in transformational grammar that it was necessary to introduce an empty category such as *pro* to the right of the adnominal clause, on the assumption that the IHRC is an adjunct clause (Jhang 1991). However, there is ample evidence showing that the clause is a direct syntactic nominal complement of the matrix predicate. One strong argument against an adjunct treatment centers on the passivization of the IHRC clause. As shown in (5), an object IHRC clause can be promoted to the subject of the sentence.

(5) [Tom-i talli-nun kes]-i Mary-eyeuyhayse caphiessta
Tom-NOM run-PNE KES-NOM Mary-by be.caught
'Tom, who was running, was caught by Mary.'

Another fact concerning the status of the IHRC comes from stacking: whereas more than one EHRC clause can be stacked, only one IHRC clause is possible:

(6) a.*kyongchal-i [**kangto-ka unhayng-eyse nao-nun**]
police-NOM [robber-NOM bank-from come.out-PNE]
[ton-ul hwumchi-n] **kes**-ul chephohayssta
money-ACC steal-PNE KES-ACC arrested
'(int.) The police arrested a thief coming out of the bank, stealing money.'

b. kyongchal-i [__ **unhayng-eyse nao-nun**]
police-NOM [bank-from come.out-PNE]
[ton-ul hwumchi-n] **kangto**-lul chephohayssta
money-ACC steal-PNE robber-ACC arrested
'(int.) The police arrested a thief coming out of the bank, stealing money.'

This contrast implies that the adnominal clause which is the IHRC has the canonical properties of a complement clause.

Based on these observations, we assume the structure (7) for the internal and external structure of the IHRC in (1)a:

(7)

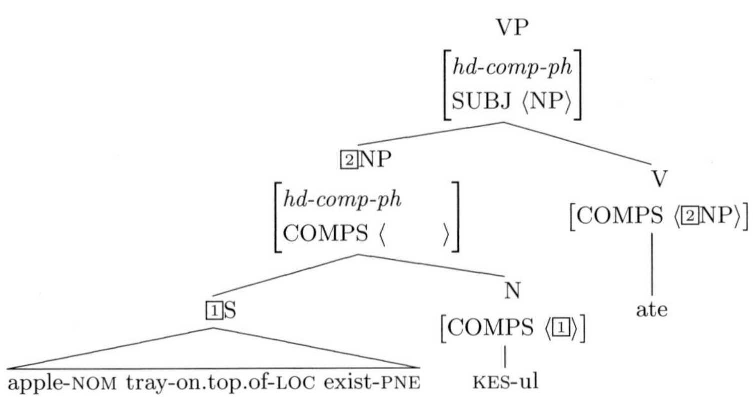

As represented in the tree, *kes* combines with its complement clause, forming a *hd-comp-ph* (*head-complement-ph*). This resulting NP also functions as the complement of the matrix verb *ate*.

2.2 Semantic Aspects of the IHRC and Related Constructions

One thing to note is that IHRCs are syntactically very similar to DPCs (direct perception constructions). IHRCs and DPCs both function as the syntactic argument of a matrix predicate. However, in the IHRC (8)a, the internal argument *John* within the embedded clause functions as the semantic argument of 'caught'. Meanwhile, in (8)b it is the whole embedded clausal complement that functions as its semantic argument:

(8) a. Mary-nun [John-i talli-nun kes]-ul **capassta**.
Mary-TOP John-NOM run-PNE KES-ACC caught
'Mary caught John who was running.'

b. Mary-nun [John-i talli-nun kes]-ul **poassta**.
Mary-TOP John-NOM run-PNE KES-ACC saw
'Mary saw John running.'

The only difference between (8)a and (8)b is the matrix predicate, which correlates with the meaning difference. When the matrix predicate is an action verb such as *capta* 'catch', *chepohata* 'arrest', or *mekta* 'eat' as in (8)a, we obtain an entity reading for the clausal complement. But as in (8)b we will have only an event reading when the matrix predicate is a type of perception verb such as *po-ta* 'see', *al-ta* 'know', and *kiekhata* 'remember'.

The key point in our analysis is thus that the interpretation of *kes* is dependent upon the type of matrix predicate. Hence the lexical entries in our grammar involve not only syntax but also semantics. For example, the verb *cap-ta* 'catch' in (9) lexically requires its object to refer to a *ref-ind* (referential-index) whereas the verb *po-ta* 'see' in (10) selects an object complement whose index is *indiv-ind* (individual index) whose subtypes include *ref-ind* and *event-ind*, indicating that its object can be either a referential individual or an event.[5]

---

[5] The meaning representations adopted here involve Minimal Recursion Semantics (MRS), developed by [4]. This is a framework of computational semantics designed to enable semantic composition using only the unification of type feature structures. The value of the attribute SEM(ANTICS) we used here represents simplified MRS, though it originally includes HOOK, RELS, and HCONS. The feature HOOK represents externally visible attributes of the atomic predications in RELS (RELATIONS). The value of LTOP is the local top handle, the handle of the relations with the widest scope within the constituent. The value of XARG is linked to the external argument of the predicate. See [4] and [5] for the exact function(s) of each attribute. We suppress irrelevant features.

(9)

a. $\begin{bmatrix} \langle\text{cap-ta 'catch'}\rangle \\ \text{SYN}\,|\,\text{VAL}\begin{bmatrix}\text{SUBJ }\langle\text{NP}_i\rangle \\ \text{COMPS }\langle\text{NP}_j\rangle\end{bmatrix} \\ \text{SEM}\,|\,\text{RELS}\left\langle\begin{bmatrix}\text{PRED } \textit{catch\_v\_rel} \\ \text{ARG0 } \textit{e1} \\ \text{ARG1 }{}_i[\textit{ref-ind}] \\ \text{ARG2 }{}_j[\textit{ref-ind}]\end{bmatrix}\right\rangle \end{bmatrix}$

b. $\begin{bmatrix} \langle\text{po-ta 'see'}\rangle \\ \text{SYN}\,|\,\text{VAL}\begin{bmatrix}\text{SUBJ }\langle\text{NP}_i\rangle \\ \text{COMPS }\langle\text{NP}_j\rangle\end{bmatrix} \\ \text{SEM}\,|\,\text{RELS}\left\langle\begin{bmatrix}\text{PRED } \textit{see\_v\_rel} \\ \text{ARG0 } \textit{e1} \\ \text{ARG1 }{}_i[\textit{ref-ind}] \\ \text{ARG2 }{}_j[\textit{ind-ind}]\end{bmatrix}\right\rangle \end{bmatrix}$

These lexical entries will then project an identical syntactic structure for (8)a and (8)b, represented together here in (10):

(10)

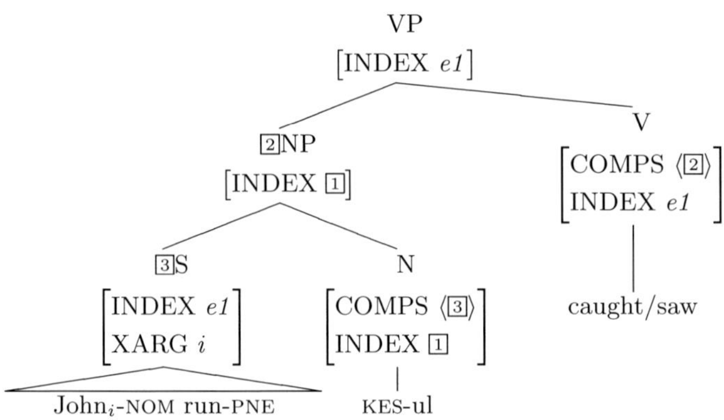

As represented in the structure, in both constructions *kes* selects an adnominal S as its complement and forms a *hd-comp-ph* with it. The resulting NP serves the complement of the main verb *caught* or *saw*. However, semantically, due to the lexical entries in (9), the object of *caught* is linked to the external argument (XARG) *robber* whereas that of *saw* in (9)b is linked to the event denoted by the S.[6] The type of predicate thus determines whether the INDEX value of *kes* will be identified with that of the S or that of its XARG, as presented in the lexical entries:

(11)

a. $\begin{bmatrix} \langle\text{kes}\rangle \\ \text{SYN}\begin{bmatrix}\text{HEAD}\,|\,\text{POS } \textit{noun} \\ \text{VAL}\,|\,\text{COMPS }\langle\text{S[INDEX } \textit{e1}]\rangle\end{bmatrix} \\ \text{SEM}\,|\,\text{HOOK}\,|\,\text{INDEX } \textit{e1} \end{bmatrix}$

b. $\begin{bmatrix} \langle\text{kes}\rangle \\ \text{SYN}\begin{bmatrix}\text{HEAD}\,|\,\text{POS } \textit{noun} \\ \text{VAL}\,|\,\text{COMPS }\langle\text{S}\begin{bmatrix}\text{XARG } i\end{bmatrix}\rangle\end{bmatrix} \\ \text{SEM}\,|\,\text{HOOK}\,|\,\text{INDEX } i \end{bmatrix}$

---

[6] The feature XARG refers to the external argument in control constructions like *John tries to run*. The XARG of *run* is thus identified the matrix subject *John*. See [5] for details.

This grammar in which lexical information interacts with the other syntactic components ensures that the perception verb *saw* combines with an NP projected from (11)a whereas the action verb *caught* with an NP projected from (11)b. Otherwise, the resulting structure will not satisfy the selectional restrictions of the predicates.

Incorporating this into our Korean grammar,[7] we implemented this analysis in the LKB and obtained the following two parsed trees and MRSs for the two examples:

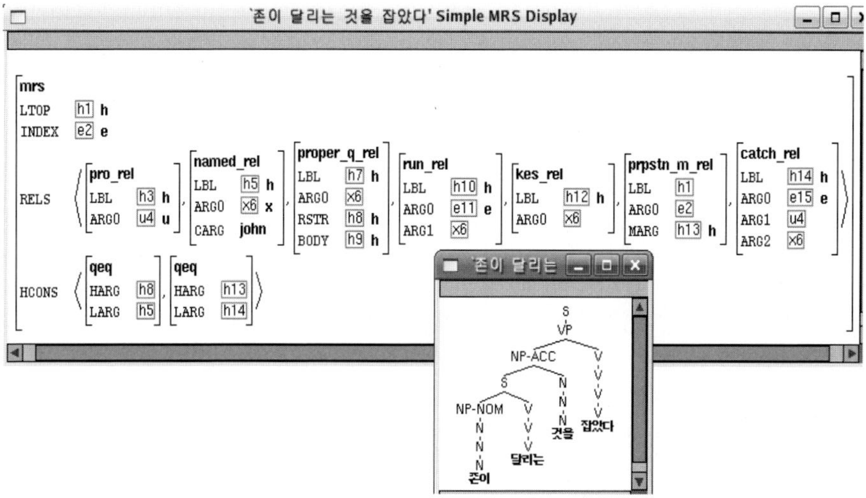

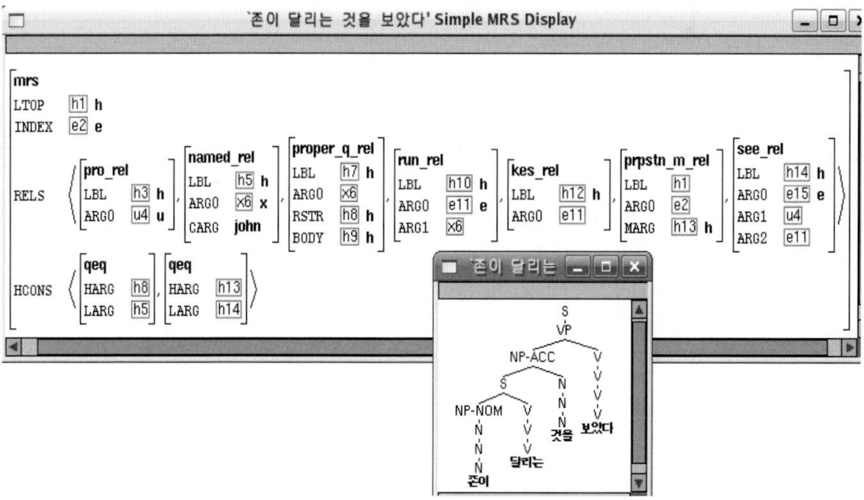

[7] The current Korean Resource Grammar has 394 type definitions, 36 grammar rules, 77 inflectional rules, 1100 lexical entries, and 2100 test-suite sentences, and aims to expand its coverage on real-life data.

Leaving aside the irrelevant parts, we can see that the two have the identical syntactic structures but different semantics. In the former, the ARG0 value of *kes* is identified with the *named_rel* (for 'John') but in the latter it is identified with *run_rel*.

The analysis thus provides a clean account of the complementary distribution of the IHRC and the DPC. That is, according to our analysis, we obtain an entity reading when the index value of *kes* is identified with that of the external argument. Meanwhile, we have an event reading when the index value is structure-shared with that of the adnominal S. This analysis thus correctly predicts that there exist no cases where the two readings are available simultaneously.

One of the welcome predictions that this analysis brings is that the canonical antecedent of the pronoun *kes* is the external argument:

(12) [haksayng-i aktang-ul cha-nun kes-ul] capassta
student-NOM rascal-ACC kick-PNE KES-ACC caught
'(I) caught a student, who was then kicking a rascal.'

Even though one can catch either a student or a rascal, the semantic object of the verb 'catch' is not the object but the external argument *haksayng* (attested by our implementation but not included here because of limits on space).

3 Discussion and Conclusion

The analysis we have presented so far, part of the typed-feature structure grammar HPSG for Korean aiming at working with real-world data, has been implemented into LKB (Linguistic Knowledge Building System) to test its performance and feasibility.

We first inspected the Sejong Treebank Corpus (33,953 sentences) and identified 4,610 sentences with [S[FORM *nun*] + *kes*]. Of these, we inspected the 518 ACC marked examples, but found only 3 IHRC examples. Another 154 examples used *kes* in a cleft construction, and 361 as direct perception examples. Among these, we selected canonical types of the IHRC constructions to check if the grammar can parse them both in terms of syntax and semantics. As we have shown in section 2.2, the grammar is quite successful in picking up the appropriate semantic head from the IHRC. Of course, issues remain of extending the coverage of our grammar to parse more real-life data and further identifying other constructional types of *kes*, such as cleft usages.

Any grammar, aiming for real world application, needs to provide a correct syntax from which we can build semantic representations in compositional ways. In addition, these semantic representations must be rich enough to capture compositional as well as constructional meanings. In this respect, the analysis we have sketched here seems to be promising in the sense that it provides appropriate semantic representations for the IHRC and DPC in a compositional way, suitable for applications requiring deep natural language understanding.

References

1. Kim, Y.B.: Relevance in internally headed relative clauses in korean. Lingua **112** (2002) 541–559
2. Chung, C., Kim, J.B.: Differences between externally and internally headed relative clause constructions. In: Proceedings of HPSG 2002, CSLI Publications (2003) 3–25
3. Copestake, A.: Implementing Typed Feature Structure Grammars. CSLI Publications, Stanford (2002)
4. Copestake, A., Flickenger, D., Sag, I., Pollard, C.: Minimal recursion semantics: An introduction. Manuscript (2003)
5. Bender, E.M., Flickinger, D.P., Oepen, S.: The grammar matrix: An open-source starter-kit for the rapid development of cross-linguistically consistent broad-coverage precision grammars. In Carroll, J., Oostdijk, N., Sutcliffe, R., eds.: Proceedings of the Workshop on Grammar Engineering and Evaluation at the 19th International Conference on Computational Linguistics, Taipei, Taiwan (2002) 8–14

A Corpus-Based Empirical Account of Adverbial Clauses Across Speech and Writing in Contemporary British English

Alex Chengyu Fang

Department of Chinese, Translation and Linguistics
City University of Hong Kong
Tat Chee Avenue, Kowloon, Hong Kong
acfang@cityu.edu.hk

Abstract. Adverbial subordinators are an important index of different types of discourse and have been used, for example, in automatic text classification. This article reports an investigation of the use of adverbial clauses based on a corpus of contemporary British English. It demonstrates on the basis of empirical evidence that it is simply a misconceived notion that adverbial clauses are typically associated with informal, unplanned types of discourse and hence spoken English. The investigation initially examined samples from both spoken and written English, followed by a contrastive analysis of spontaneous and prepared speech, to be finally confirmed by evidence from a further experiment based on timed and untimed university essays. The three sets of experiments consistently produced empirical evidence which irrefutably suggests that, contrary to claims by previous studies, the proportion of adverbial clauses are consistently much lower in speech than in writing and that adverbial clauses are a significant characteristic of planned, elaborated discourse.

1 Introduction

It is commonly accepted that adverbial clauses are registerially important, especially between speech and writing as two major modes of discourse. A recent consensus is that there are more adverbial clauses in speech than in writing. In his research on linguistic variations across speech and writing, Biber reports that "*that*-clauses, *WH*-clauses and adverbial subordinators co-occur frequently with interpersonal and reduced-content features such as first and second person pronouns, questions, contractions, hedges, and emphatics. These types of subordination occur frequently in spoken genres, both interactional (conversation) and informational (speeches), but they occur relatively infrequently in informational written genres" ([1], p230). More recently, this observation has been extended and introduced in the automatic analysis of biochemical text. In [2], Biber and Jones introduce a research approach that "combines corpus-linguistic and discourse-analytic perspectives to analyse the discourse patterns

T. Salakoski et al. (Eds.): FinTAL 2006, LNAI 4139, pp. 32 – 43, 2006.

in a large corpus of biology research articles. The primary goals of the study are to identify vocabulary-based Discourse Units (DUs) using computational techniques, to describe the basic types of DUs in biology research articles as distinguished by their primary linguistic characteristics (using Multi-Dimentional analysis), to interpret those Discourse Unit Types in functional terms, and to then illustrate how the internal organization of a text can be described as a sequence of DUs, shifting among various Discourse Unit Types (p151).

Biber's claim is by no means unique. Thompson in [3] presents a similar claim, showing that the presence of subordination has to do with the formal/informal division and that, in terms of clause preference, speech appears to make use of more adverbial clauses and writing more non-finite clauses. More famously, in [4] and [5], Halliday observes that speech and writing are both complex systems but in different ways: speech is more complex in terms of sentence structures while writing in terms of high lexical density. In his opinion, the structural complex found in speech is characterised by a relatively higher degree of hypotaxis which involves subordination of various kinds such as adverbial clauses.

However, results of these past empirically based studies are far from conclusive. For one reason, they seem to have based their claims on either small samples or data that is not adequately defined or validated. In [1], for instance, it is not clear at all how many tokens of the spoken genre were used in the study. Instead, the basic figures were all normalised to a text length of 1,000 words. But even so, one easily questions the reliability of the data and indeed the validity of the analysis. For the mean frequencies of face-to-face conversations used in [1], as another example, the average number of infinitives per thousand tokens is as many as 13.8, far too high when compared with results of more recent studies such as [6], where infinitives account for fewer than 9 occurrences per thousand tokens in direct conversations. Indeed, [1] is based on frequencies collected from automatically analysed texts for its spoken and written samples. It is also worth pointing out that [1] makes use of the London-Lund corpus of English, which was produced over half a century ago.

This article reports an experiment that was aimed at a full review of the distribution of adverbial clauses across speech and writing. The experiment was performed on the basis of the understanding that conclusive results can only be obtained from first of all samples of authentic contemporary data and secondly from carefully designed analysis of the material that is manually validated and hence reliable. The next section will describe the data used in the experiment in terms of corpus composition and annotation.

2 Methodology

The methodology adopted in the current study was to investigate the distribution of different types of adverbial clauses across speech and writing based on a representative corpus of contemporary English. The scope of investigation would cover not only finite adverbial clauses but the non-finite ones, including infinitival, present participial and past participial constructions. The aim was to conclusively establish the differences in the use of adverbial clauses, in frequential terms, across speech and writing. A second step would be to ascertain the variation of these clauses within the spoken and the written genres respectively.

Table 1. The composition of ICE-GB

Spoken			
Dialogue	Private		
	S1A1	direct conversations	90
	S1A2	distanced conversations	10
	Public		
	S1B1	class lessons	20
	S1B2	broadcast discussions	20
	S1B3	broadcast interviews	10
	S1B4	parliamentary debates	10
	S1B5	legal cross-examinations	10
	S1B6	business transactions	10
Monologue	Unscripted		
	S2A1	spontaneous commentaries	20
	S2A2	unscripted speeches	30
	S2A3	Demonstrations	10
	S2A4	legal presentations	10
	Mixed		
	S2B1	broadcast news	20
	Scripted		
	S2B2	broadcast talks	20
	S2B3	non-broadcast talks	10

Written			
Non-Printed	Student Writing		
	W1A1	untimed essays	10
	W1A2	timed essays	10
	Correspondence		
	W1B1	social letters	15
	W1B2	business letters	15
Printed	Informational		
	W2A1	Learned: humanities	10
	W2A2	Learned: social sciences	10
	W2A3	Learned: natural sciences	10
	W2A4	Learned: technology	10
	W2B1	Popular: humanities	10
	W2B2	Popular: social sciences	10
	W2B3	Popular: natural sciences	10
	W2B4	Popular: technology	10
	W2C1	Press news reports	20
	Instructional		
	W2D1	Administrative writing	10
	W2D2	Skills and hobbies	10
	Persuasive		
	W2E1	Press editorials	10
	Creative		
	W2F1	Fiction	20

The International Corpus of English (ICE) corpus was used in the current study as source of empirical evidence. The ICE project was launched by Professor Sidney Greenbaum at the Survey of English Usage, University College London. This project, participated by twenty national and regional teams, aims at the grammatical description of English in countries and regions where it is used either as a first or an official language ([6], p3). The British component of the corpus (ICE-GB) consists of 300 texts of transcribed speech and 200 texts of written samples, of 2,000 word tokens each, generally dated from the period 1990-1994. The component texts were selected according to registerial specifications. The spoken section, which contains 60% of the total corpus in terms of words, is divided between dialogues and monologues. The dialogues range from private direct and distanced conversations to public situations such as broadcast discussions and parliamentary debates. The written samples are divided into two initial categories: non-printed and printed. The former is a collection of university essays and letters of correspondence. The latter has four major divisions: informational, instructional, persuasive, and creative. Table 1 presents an overview of the design of the corpus, with indications of text IDs, categories, and number of samples assigned to the category.

As can be seen from the corpus composition, ICE-GB provides an ideal setting for an empirical investigation of the variation in the use of adverbial clauses across speech and writing. First of all, the corpus is divided into spoken and written sections and thus allows for some general indications of distribution. Secondly, each major mode within the corpus contains genres that display a continuum between the spontaneous and the prepared, the informal and the formal, the timed and untimed, etc, thus allowing for the validation of hypothesis whether the use of adverbial clauses can be discussed along these lines, alongside the spoken-written division.

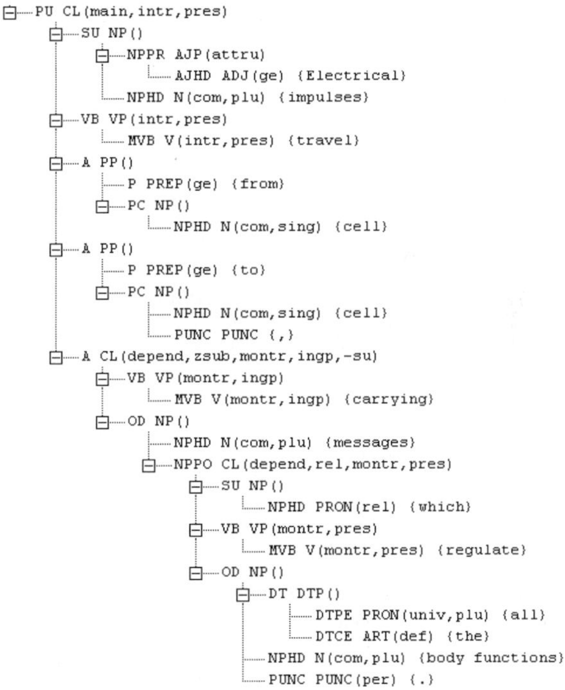

Fig. 1. The ICE parse tree for (1)

ICE-GB has been grammatically tagged, syntactically parsed and manually checked. The parsing scheme indicates a full analysis of the phrase structures and assigns syntactic functions to these constituents. Consider (1).

(1) *Electrical pulses travel from cell to cell, carrying messages which regulate all the body functions. <W2B-023-004>*

This example in ICE-GB, taken from the fourth sentence in Text 23 of Genre W2B, receives the syntactic tree structure in Figure 1.

Each node in an ICE-GB tree comprises two labels: function and category. For example, `SU NP()` is interpreted as 'syntactic subject realised by the category NP or noun phrase'. Similarly, `NPPR AJP(attru)` indicates an attributive adjective phrase performing the function of an NP premodifer. The leaf nodes, i.e., the lexical items, are enclosed within curly brackets. As can be seen from Figure 1, Example (1) is analysed as a main clause consisting of a subject and a verb, with three adverbials: two realised by the prepositional phrases *from cell to cell* and one realised by a non-finite present participial clause *carrying messages which regulate all the body functions*. Features associated with the adverbial clause indicate that it does not have an overt subordinator (*zsub*), that its main verb is present participial (*ingp*), and that this clause does not have an overt subject (*-su*). The detailed annotation thus indicates explicitly the category names such as the clause and the phrase type as well as their syntactic functions such as subject and adverbial. ICE-GB therefore allows for unambiguous retrieval of different types of adverbial clauses.

3 The Experiments

The experiments examined the frequency distribution of finite adverbial clauses as well as the non-finite ones (infinitival, present participial, and past participial) in ICE-GB. There are three procedures. First, the experiment aimed to establish the overall distribution of adverbial clauses across the spoken and the written sections. Secondly, samples of spontaneous and prepared speech were examined to ascertain whether preparedness could be seen as a continuum of changes for the use of adverbial clauses. Finally, samples of timed and untimed university essays were used to validate the hypothesis that adverbial clauses also demonstrate a predictable variation as a function of degrees of preparedness in written English.

3.1 Uses of Adverbial Clauses Across Speech and Writing

As a first step, the complete corpus was used to obtain empirical indications of the different uses of adverbial clauses across speech and writing. Frequencies of occurrence were respectively collected from the spoken and the written sections of ICE-GB. The statistics include the total number of sentences and clauses in these two sections. Statistics were also collected for the total number of sentences involving the use of adverbial clauses and the exact number of adverbial clauses in these two sections. Two proportions were calculated: the total number of sentences with at least one adverbial clause over the total number of sentences, and the total number of adverbial clauses over the total number of sentences. The former indicates the proportion of sentences in ICE-GB that make use of adverbial clauses. The latter shows the proportion of adverbial clauses in the corpus since there often are multiple adverbial clauses in one sentence or utterance and it is useful to have such an indication. These two proportions thus indicate how often adverbial clauses are used and how complex the sentence structure is (assuming that structural complexity can be measured in terms of clause subordination). Table 2 summarises the results.

Table 2. Adverbial clauses across speech and writing

	Spoken (59,470)		Written (24,084)		Total (83,554)	
	#	%	#	%	#	%
Sentence	7124	11.98	6474	26.88	13598	13.27
Clause	7809	13.13	7052	29.28	14861	17.79

Initial results were simply contrary to what previous studies have suggested: the uses of adverbial clauses are more frequent in writing than in speech. As Table 2 clearly indicates, a much higher proportion of sentences in writing make use of adverbial clauses. To be exact, adverbial clauses are more than twice likely to occur in writing than in speech. In writing, 25.42% of the sentences make use of adverbial clauses in contrast to only 12.49% of the sentences with an adverbial clause in speech. The same difference can be observed in terms of the number of adverbial clauses: there are over 30 adverbial clauses per one hundred sentences in writing compared with fewer than 15 adverbial clauses per one hundred sentences in speech.[1]

3.2 Types of Adverbial Clauses Across Speech and Writing

The distribution of different types of adverbial clauses was investigated in order to verify that the observed difference was not the result of a skewed use of any one particular type. The second experiment examined the distribution of finite adverbial clauses with an overt subordinator and the non-finite ones, which include infinitival, present participial and past participial adverbial clauses. They are illustrated respectively by examples (2)-(5) with the relevant sections underlined.

(2) *And I think the question is bigger than that because it's from both sides.* <#S1A-001-054>

(3) *Having said that, I can really only say how it was for me when I came to work.* <#S1A-001-056>

(4) *And you condemn the series having seen a bit of one of them.* <#S1A-006-105>

[1] It makes more sense in terms of sentences rather than words. As a general guide, there are 600,000 words in the spoken section of the corpus and 400,000 words in the written section. In terms of words, therefore, there are 1.46 adverbial clauses per hundred words in speech, compared with 1.86 in writing.

(5) *The actual work surface was a very thick piece of wood, dumped on top, all held in place by words.* <#S1A-009-200>

The results are summarized in Table 3. As can be clearly seen, this second experiment also indicate that written samples of the ICE corpus make much more extensive use of the adverbial clause, be it finite, infinitival, or participial. The finite ones occur twice as many times in writing than in speech. For the other three types of adverbial clauses, the proportion for the written genre is even higher than for the spoken genre. Consider the infinitival clauses, for example. In writing, they are nearly three times more likely to be used than in spoken discourse (5.43% vs 1.98%), largely echoing previous observations that writing is characterised by a higher content of infinitives compared with spoken English (see, for example, [6] and [8]). This proportion is even greater with the other two types of non-finite adverbial clauses.

Table 3. Types of adverbial clauses across speech and writing

		Spoken (59,470)		Written (24,084)		Total (83,554)	
		#	%	#	%	#	%
A_{sub}	Sentence	5172	8.69	3954	16.42	9126	10.92
	Clause	5787	9.73	4430	18.39	10217	12.23
A_{infin}	Sentence	1122	1.89	1254	5.21	2376	2.84
	Clause	1177	1.98	1308	5.43	2485	2.97
A_{ing}	Sentence	691	1.16	1023	4.25	1714	2.05
	Clause	704	1.18	1066	4.43	1770	2.12
A_{edp}	Sentence	139	0.23	243	1.01	382	0.46
	Clause	141	0.24	248	1.03	389	0.47
Total	Sentence	7124	11.98	6474	26.88	13598	16.27
	Clause	7809	13.13	7052	29.28	14861	17.79

We may incidentally note that past participial clauses are the least frequent type of adverbial clauses, with only 141 found in speech and 248 in writing in the whole corpus.

3.3 Types of Adverbial Clauses Across Spontaneous and Prepared Speech

Empirical indications thus irrefutably suggest that, contrary to previous claims, adverbial clauses are a marked characteristic of the written genre, in line with non-finite clauses that also characterise writing. However, to conclude that this difference in terms of use is due to different levels of elaboration, we need further empirical evidence. We need to prove that such variations can be observed not only across speech and writing, but also within the spoken and the written sections as a function of varying degrees of elaboration.

To this end, a sub-corpus of 180,000 words was created with S1A texts in ICE-GB, representing spontaneous private conversations. A second sub-corpus was also created, this time with the first 40 texts in S2B, representing talks prepared and scripted for public broadcast. These two genres thus may be seen as forming a continuum between what was unprepared and what was carefully prepared, therefore a measure of different degrees of elaboration.

The results are summarised in Table 4, where we can read that, as an example, the subcorpus of spontaneous conversations contains a total number of 1,574 sentences that make use of finite adverbial clauses, accounting for 5.34% of the total number of sentences in the sub-corpus. On the other end of the continuum, as another example, we duly observe a higher proportion of finite adverbial clauses, that is, 12.81% in terms of sentences and 13.53% in terms of clauses. It is important to note that this general trend can be observed for all of the different types of adverbial clauses.

Table 4. Types of adverbial clauses across samples of spontaneous and scripted speech

		Spontaneous (29,490)		Scripted (5,793)		Total (35,283)	
		#	%	#	%	#	%
A_{sub}	Sentence	1574	5.34	742	12.81	2316	6.56
	Clause	1757	5.96	784	13.53	2541	7.20
A_{infin}	Sentence	271	0.92	253	4.37	524	1.49
	Clause	279	0.95	260	4.49	539	1.53
A_{ing}	Sentence	190	0.64	161	2.78	351	0.99
	Clause	193	0.65	163	2.81	356	1.01
A_{edp}	Sentence	21	0.07	35	0.60	56	0.16
	Clause	21	0.07	36	0.62	57	0.16
Total	Sentence	2056	6.97	1191	20.56	3247	9.20
	Clause	2250	7.63	1243	21.46	3493	9.89

It is thus reasonable to suggest that within speech the proportion of adverbial clauses increases as a function of degrees of elaboration, formality, and preparedness.

3.4 Types of Adverbial Clauses Across Timed and Untimed Essays

Having established that in speech the proportion of adverbial clauses is largely a function of elaboration or formality or preparedness, we want to do the same for the written samples. We want to argue, on empirical basis, that adverbial clauses not only mark a spoken-written division, that they also mark a continuum between what is spontaneous and what is scripted in speech, and that they also mark a degree of preparedness in writing.

Conveniently, the ICE-GB corpus contains a category coded W1A, which includes 20 texts evenly divided into two sets. Both sets were unpublished essays written by university students. The only difference is that the first set was written within a pre-designated period of time while the second set comprises samples written without the time constraint. If the higher use of adverbial clauses were indeed the result of a higher degree of elaboration or preparedness, then we would observe more uses in the untimed set than in the timed set. This consideration led to a third experiment, whose results are summarised in Table 4.

Table 5. Types of adverbial clauses across samples of timed and untimed essays

		Timed (1,057)		Untimed (1,046)		Total (2,103)	
		#	%	#	%	#	%
A_{sub}	Sentence	156	14.76	203	19.41	359	17.07
	Clause	171	16.18	235	22.47	406	19.31
A_{infin}	Sentence	62	5.87	61	5.83	123	5.85
	Clause	65	6.15	64	6.12	129	6.13
A_{ing}	Sentence	59	5.58	51	4.88	110	5.23
	Clause	59	5.58	55	5.26	114	5.42
A_{edp}	Sentence	10	0.94	16	1.53	26	1.23
	Clause	10	0.94	16	1.53	26	1.23
Total	Sentence	287	27.15	331	31.64	618	29.29
	Clause	305	28.86	370	35.37	675	32.09

Again, we duly observed a consistent increase in the proportion of adverbial clauses from one end of the continuum, timed essays, to the other end of the continuum, untimed essays. For instance, we observe that there are 16.18 finite adverbial clauses per 100 sentences for the timed essays. The untimed essays make more uses of finite adverbial clauses, 22.47 per 100 sentences. The same trend can be observed for all of the different types of adverbial clauses, except the infinitival ones. 62 sentences were observed to contain a total of 65 adverbial clauses in timed essays. In the untimed essays, 61 sentences were found to use a total of 64 infinitival adverbial clauses. While the differences are only marginal and can be dismissed as occasional, this group of texts will be examined in a future study for a possible relation between text types and uses of infinitival clauses.

For the purpose of the current study, it can be observed that in the untimed essays as a whole 31.64% of the sentences made use of adverbial clauses, almost 4.5% higher than 27.15% for the timed group. The results thus support the suggestion that within writing the proportion of adverbial clauses indicates different degrees of preparedness in terms of time.

3.5 Discussions

We have thus observed that, in the first place, adverbial clauses mark a division between spoken and written English in the sense that the spoken samples have a lower proportion of adverbial clauses than the written samples. This is true not only for finite adverbial clauses but non-finite ones, including infinitival, present participial and past participial constructions. Secondly, the experiments also produced empirical evidence that the frequency distribution of adverbial clauses follows a predictable and regular growth curve from spontaneous conversations to scripted public speeches. The same trend can be observed from within the written sample themselves, where the proportion of adverbial clauses in general increase from timed essays to untimed essays. As Figure 2 clearly demonstrates[2], the proportion of adverbial clauses per 100 sentences in ICE-GB consistently increases along a continuum between spontaneous conversations and untimed university essays. What is remarkably surprising is the fact that the occurrence of adverbial clauses in spontaneous conversations accounts for only about 7.5% of the utterances. What is equally surprising is that the occurrence of adverbial clauses in untimed university essays accounts for over 35% of the sentences, over 4.6 times as much as that in speech. The sharp contrast between speech and writing shown in Figure 2 argues strongly against the claims of past studies.

The graph also shows the average proportions of adverbial clauses in the two modes are nicely situated between the two sections within the same continuum. First of all, the average proportion of adverbial clauses in speech is shown in the figure to be between spontaneous conversations and scripted public speeches, suggesting a consistent increase in speech along the 'preparedness' register. In the written section of the continuum, the average proportion of adverbial clauses in writing rests between timed and untimed essays, again suggesting a consistent increase, continuing the trend from the spoken section, along the 'preparedness' register.

This is clear and irrefutable evidence that, contrary to results of previous studies, there are more adverbial clauses in writing than in speech, at least as far as contemporary British English is concerned and there is no obvious reason why other varieties of English should be seen otherwise. In the light of the evidence that the experiments came up with, observations such as the following is plainly not in line with what can be empirically observed in contemporary data: "Adverbial clauses appear to be an important device for indicating information relations in a text. Overall, Thompson (1984 [3]) and Biber (1988 [9]) find more adverbial clauses in speech than in writing." ([1], p235).

While it is evident from Figure 2 that speech and writing demonstrate a vast difference in terms of the use of adverbial clauses, it is clear at the same time that adverbial clauses are not as much a factor of speech vs writing division as a degree of preparedness in discourse. To be exact, it is acceptable to suggest on the basis of empirical evidence that degrees of information elaboration dictate the proportion of

---

[2] The *X* axis in Figure 2 has legends indicating the proportion of adverbial clauses in the following groups of samples in ICE-GB:

- *Spon*: spontaneous conversations
- *Speech*: complete spoken samples
- *Scripted*: scripted broadcast news and talks
- *Timed*: timed university essays
- *Writing*: complete written samples
- *Untimed*: untimed university essays

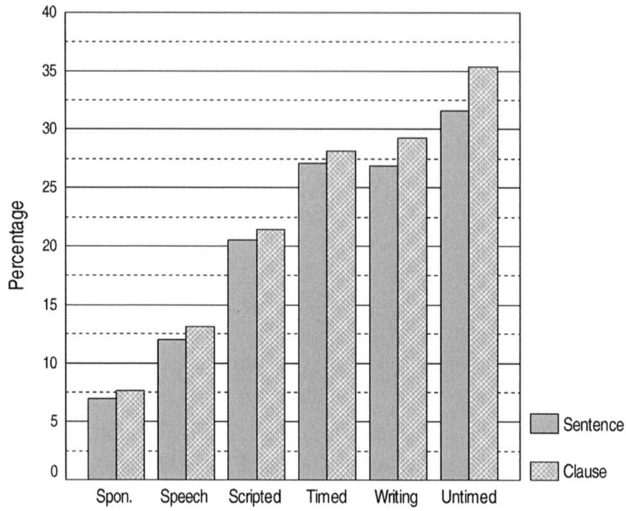

Fig. 2. The increase of adverbial clauses as a function of degrees of preparedness

adverbial clauses: the more elaborate the sample (defined in terms of preparedness), the more adverbial clauses, thus again contrary to a previous claim that '[t]he subordination features grouped on Factor 6 apparently mark informational elaboration that is produced under strict real-time constraints, resulting in a fragmented presentation of information accomplished by tacking on additional dependent clauses, rather than an integrated presentation that packs information into fewer constructions containing more high-content words and phrases" ([1]).

4 Conclusion

To conclude, this article reported an experiment to investigate the distribution of adverbial clauses across speech and writing. The experiment used ICE-GB, a corpus of contemporary British English that contains both transcribed speech and written samples. The detailed syntactic annotation of the corpus and manual validation of the analysis ensured that adverbial clauses could be accurately retrieved. These two features of the experiment are a clear advancement on past studies that made use of either old-fashioned data produced over half a century ago or unreliable analysis automatically performed by the computer without manual checking. The results irrefutably demonstrate that, contrary to claims by past studies, the proportion of adverbial clauses is much lower in speech than in writing. It is also shown that adverbial clauses do not simply mark a division between the spoken and written genres. Empirical evidence strongly suggests that the proportion of adverbial clauses is also a function of varying degrees of preparedness, which can be independently demonstrated from within the spoken and written genres. It is thus reasonable to postulate that the spoken-written division is perhaps better perceived as a continuum of preparedness, from spontaneous private conversations at one extreme to untimed carefully prepared writing at the other, along which the proportion of adverbial clauses consistently change in a predictable fashion.

Acknowlegement

The author would like to thank Professor M.A.K. Halliday for comments on an earlier draft of the article.

References

1. Biber, D. 1988. *Variation across Speech and Writing*. Cambridge: Cambridge University Press.
2. Biber, D. and J. Jones. 2005. Merging corpus linguistic and discourse analytic research goals: Discourse units in biology research articles. In *Corpus Linguistics and Linguistic Theory 1-2 (2005)*. pp 151-182.
3. Thompson, S. 1984. Subordination in Formal and Informal Discourse. In D. Schffrin (ed), *Meaning, Form, and Use in Context: Linguistic Applications*. Washington DC: Georgetown University Press. pp 85-94.
4. Halliday, M.A.K. 1979. Differences between Spoken and Written Language: Some Implications for Literacy Teaching. In G. Page, J. Elkins, B. O'Connor (eds), *Communication through Reading: Proceedings of the Fourth Australilan Reading Conference, Brisbane, 25-27 August 1978, Vol. 2, Diverse Needs: Creative Approaches*. Australian Reading Association. Pp 37-52.
5. Halliday, M.A.K. 1985. *Spoken and Written Language*. Victoria: Keakin University Press.
6. Fang, A.C. 1995. The Distribution of Infinitives of Contemporary British English: A Study Based on the British ICE Corpus. In *Oxford Literary and Linguistic Computing, 10:4*. pp 247-257.
7. Greenbaum, S. (ed) 1996. *Comparing English World Wide: The International Corpus of English*. Oxford: Oxford University Press.
8. Mair, C. 1990. *Infinitival Complement Clauses in English*. Cambridge: Cambridge University Press.
9. Biber, D. 1988. Adverbial stance types in English. In *Discourse Processes 11*. pp 1-34.

A Korean Syntactic Parser Customized for Korean-English Patent MT System

Chang-Hyun Kim and Munpyo Hong

ETRI, NLP Team
161 Gajeong-dong, Yuseong-gu
305-350 Daejeon, Korea
{chkim, munpyo}@etri.re.kr

Abstract. Patent MT is emerging as a killer application domain for MT, as there is a strong need for fast and cheap translations for patent documents. Most of the Korean-English MT engines hitherto have suffered from the poor syntactic analysis performance and the lack of linguistic resources. We customized a Korean syntactic parser based on the linguistic characteristics of the patent documents, especially focusing on minimizing the noise in acquiring the co-occurrence data for Korean syntactic parsing. We will show that the improvement of the quality of co-occurrence data and other customization processes can lead to the improvement of the parsing accuracy and thus the improvement of the translation quality.

1 Introduction

Recently, the natural language processing of intellectual property documents is gaining more and more attentions from the NLP society. Especially, the multilinguality of patent documents has become a hot research topic in the IR community. The importance of the creation and the dissemination of multilingual patent documents also seems to be gaining much attention from MT community because of its importance and the economic impact ([2]).

In the era of globalization, it is urgent to enforce the distribution of patent information to foreign countries for the protection of technologies of one's own country. As a result, the opening of all information on how to do examination in the patent and trademark office of each country (such as Japan, U.S.A, EU, etc.) through Internet was proposed. As the recent decision of WIPO (World Intellectual Property Organization)[1] shows, the demands for the distribution of Korean patent information in English have been rapidly increased due to the interests in Korean technologies from foreign countries. Considering the time and cost for the distribution of the content in English, an MT system for the patent translation is highly needed for this purpose.[2]

Although there is a strong need for Korean to English MT, Korean to English MT systems have been rarely used in serious applications due to their low trans lation accuracy. Some reasons can be found for the comparably poor translation

[1] When examining IT-related patents filed in European countries, the Korean patents in the area must be consulted as a prior art study.

[2] In Korea, about 100,000 patents are filed in annually.

T. Salakoski et al. (Eds.): FinTAL 2006, LNAI 4139, pp. 44 – 55, 2006.

performance for Korean-English MT. The biggest reason lies in the difficulty of Korean syntactic analysis. Though intensive research has been made on Korean syntactic analysis, there still remain many issues to be tackled. In addition to that, in our opinion, one of the biggest reasons is that few noteworthy customizations, if any, have been made for general domain Korean-English MT engines yet. In [3],[4], we presented our customization effort for a patent-domain Korean-English MT system. The focus of the papers was rather put on the lexical resource construction process. In this paper we will present our customization effort for Korean syntactic parser for patent using co-occurrence data.

Accurate co-occurrence patterns assume a crucial role in predicate-argument structure analysis. In previous works employing co-occurrence patterns, regardless they are lexical- or semantic co-occurrence, the co-occurrence data led in many cases to wrong parsing result due to the noise in the co-occurrence data. We improve the accuracy of co-occurrence patterns by detecting noisy patterns and then re-computing their frequency in proportion to the degree of reliability.

We also analyze the characteristics of patent domain documents and reflect them in the parsing. Having pursued the mentioned methods, we could improve the parsing performance by 4 %.

The present research was conducted in the context of the project ETRI has carried out since 2004 under the auspices of the MIC. The aim of the project is to develop a Korean-English patent MT system. The result of the research has been successfully embedded in the information system of KIPO (Korean Intellectual Property Office). The MT service is provided under the name of K-PION (Korean Patent Information Online Network) for foreign patent examiners.[3]

In section 2 we briefly introduce some characteristics of Korean patent documents. In section 3 we will discuss about the syntactic analysis issued in Korean. We will show the method for reducing the noise in acquiring the co-occurrence data. Section 4 will show the evaluation result of the propose method. Finally, in section 5 we will conclude the discussion and present the future research direction.

2 Linguistic Characteristics of Korean Patents from the Viewpoint of Parsing

It is generally recognized that the patent domain features overwhelmingly long and complex sentences and peculiar style. As we have shown in [4], a sentence in a patent document is composed of 18.45 Eojeols[4] on the average, compared with 12.3 Eojeols in general Korean newspaper articles.

Extremely long sentences are often found in the detailed description part of a patent. A patent applicant may try to describe his or her invention in full in the detailed description section. A long sentence usually consists of several simple sentences connected with a verbal connective ending.

[3] K-PION (URL: http://kposd.kipo.go.kr:8088/up/kpion/) is currently opened to registered foreign patent examiners only. The issue of the opening of the service to the public is still under discussion.

[4] An Eojeol is a spacing unit. It corresponds to a bunsetsu in Japanese.

In long sentences we found not only many verbs with connective endings but also many long NPs. The long NPs are generally an NP connected with the conjunctions like "wa (and)", "mit (and)", "geurigo (and)", "hokeun(or)", and "ttoneun (or)". These long NPs are often found in the abstracts and the claims of patents ([1]).

In addition to the long and complex sentences, the distribution of some part-of-speech is quite different from the general domain texts. Firstly, the frequency of topic markers is relatively low.[5] A topic marker distinguishes a topic noun. The NP with a topic marker is underspecified w.r.t. its case. So, a frequent use of a topic marker may cause a misunderstanding of the content or at least make it more difficult to understand the content ([6]). From this reason topic markers are seldom used. Secondly, adverbs are also not frequently used and its vocabulary is limited. Thirdly, unknown predicates are often encountered. Even if we set the correct lexical goals and construct the term dictionary, we cannot cover all the possible predicates in patent documents. The unknown predicates belong to an open class like technical terms.

As is the case in the US- or Japanese patents, the Korean patent documents have its peculiar styles that are widely accepted in the patent offices. In particular, patent claims are formulated according to a set of precise syntactic, lexical and stylistic guidelines ([5]).

3 Korean Syntactic Analysis

3.1 Predicate-Argument Structure Analysis

The most important information in predicate-argument structure analysis is collocation patterns which are constructed automatically from large corpora using Korean morphological analyzer and syntactic analyzer. For example, from (1), two lexical co-occurrence patterns are acquired.

(1)	아이-가	사과-를	먹_는_다
	kid-subj	apple-obj	eat_present_declarative

아이-가-먹_v	1.0	: kid-subj-eat
사과-를-먹_v	1.0	: apple-obj-eat

But, lexical co-occurrence patterns(LC Patterns) inevitably cause data sparseness problem and we cope with it by using semantic co-occurrence patterns(SC Patterns). SC patterns are generated from LC patterns by applying semantic codes of each noun to LC patterns.

아이-가-먹_v =>	$사람-가-먹_v	1.0	:: SemCode(아이)={$사람:person}
사과-를-먹_v =>	$과일-를-먹_v	0.5	:: SemCode(사과)={$과일:fruit,$말:word}
	$말-를-먹_v	0.5	

[5] 'nun' is a representative topic marker in Korean. It corresponds to the Japanese topic marker 'wa'.

As in the case of '사과-를-먹_v', the frequency of each SC pattern is generally computed by dividing the frequency of LC pattern by the number of semantic codes of a noun ([8]). However, the computation of the frequency of SC patterns in this manner deteriorates the reliability of SC patterns. For example, as for the meaning of '사과-를-먹_v (to eat an apple)', '$과일-를-먹_v (to eat $**FRUIT**)' is far more preferable than '$말-를-먹_v (to eat $**WORD**)'. But this kind of preference is not considered during the construction process at all, resulting in the overestimation of '$말-를-먹_v'.

3.2 Refining SC Patterns

SC patterns are used not only for parsing but word sense disambiguation and other processes. So, the distortion of the frequencies of SC patterns can lead to the wrong results in the translation overall. In this section, we are going to refine the SC pattern construction process, by which the preference of each LC pattern can be reflected. The refining process of the SC patterns consists of the following two steps:

- Locate LC patterns that participate only in LC pattern construction without joining in the construction of SC pattern construction
- Readjust SC pattern frequencies for the remaining LC patterns according to the reliability of each SC pattern

3.2.1 Detection of Lexical Only Co-occurrence Patterns

The reason some LC patterns need to be excluded in the construction of SC patterns is that they can distort the reliability of SC patterns seriously. In case of '사과-를-먹_v', we know that the correct SC pattern is '$과일-를-먹_v (to eat $**FRUIT**)' and not '$말-를-먹_v (to eat $**WORD**)'. And empirically we can also know that the frequency of '$과일-를-먹_v' is larger than the frequency of '$말-를-먹_v'. Then let's loot at the result of SC pattern construction.

$FREQ_{sc}$ ($과일 - 를 - 먹_v) = 269.3

$FREQ_{SC}$ ($말 - 를 - 먹_v) = 383.5

The result is against our expectation. To find out what caused this, let's look at the inside of SC patterns in more detail.

말씀-를-먹_v	**5**	SemCode(말씀) = { $말:word } : hear the word
사과-를-먹_v	41	SemCode(사과) = { $과일:fruit, $말 } : eat an apple
성원-를-먹_v	2	SemCode(성원) = { $말, $사람:person } : hear words of cheer
식사-를-먹_v	4	SemCode(식사) = { $말, $음식:food } : have a dinner
욕-를-먹_v	**353**	SemCode(욕) = { $말 } : get insulted
함성-를-먹_v	**2**	SemCode(함성) = { $말 } : hear a shout

Boldfaced LC patterns have no semantic ambiguities while lightfaced LC patterns do. Here, the frequency of $말-를-먹_v, FREQ($말-를-먹_v) is 383.5 and 욕-를-먹_v contributes 92% to the total frequency. In fact, 욕-를-먹_v is almost idiomatically used and therefore is more desirable to participate only in LC pattern construction without participating in SC pattern construction. In that case, the SC pattern frequencies can be adjusted empirically more reasonably as follows :

$$FREQ_{sc}(\$과일-를-먹\_v) = 269.3$$

$$FREQ_{SC}(\$말-를-먹\_v) = 30.5$$

Based on the adjusted frequencies, 사과-를-먹_v can be determined to be $과일-를-먹_v. Henceforth, we will call the dictionary having LC only patterns as LC_ONLY dictionary. To detect LC_ONLY patterns, firstly, it is necessary to divide SC dictionary into 2 dictionaries.

- DISAMBI_SEM_1 : an SC pattern dictionary constructed from LC patterns with no semantic ambiguities
- AMBI_SEM_1 : an SC pattern dictionary constructed from LC patterns with semantic ambiguities

DISAMBI_SEM_1 and AMBI_SEM_1 have the format SEM_1(sPat) = (frequency, LC pattern list with each frequency) as the example in the below shows :

DISAMBI_SEM_1($말-를-먹_v)=(360,[[말씀-를-먹_v,5],[욕-를-먹_v,353],[함성-를-먹_v,2]])

Each SEM_1 has its corresponding LEX_1, that is, AMBI_LEX_1 and DISAMBI_LEX_1 of the format LEX_1(lPat) = (frequency, SC pattern list with the corresponding frequency) as the example below :

AMBI_LEX_1(사과-를-먹_v)=(41,[[$과일-를-먹_v, 20.5],[$말-를-먹_v,20.5]])

LC_ONLY construction from DISAMBI_LEX_1
Here, every LC patterns in DISAMBI_LEX_1 is considered to decide whether it belongs to LC_ONLY or not. The algorithm is as follows :

```
for every lPat in DISAMBI_LEX_1 do :
          for every sPat of lPat  do :[6]
                    sRatio = FREQDS1(sPat) [7] /  FREQ(sPat)
                    lRatio = FREQDS1(sPat|lPat)[8] / FREQDS1(sPat)
I                   if sRatio >= sThreshold && lRatio >= lThreshold  :
                              lPat belongs to LC_ONLY
```

According to our dictionary, about 80 % of nouns are unambiguous and DISAMBI_SEM_1 can be considered reliable in itself with respect to its statistics. sRatio measures the ratio of sPat in DISAMBI_SEM_1 with respect to the total sPat. High sRatio implies that DISAMB_SEM_1(sPat) is highly reliable and has the meaning in itself even if AMBI_SEM_1(sPat) is not referred. Only after the reliability of

[6] Here, the number of sPat for each lPat is only 1.
[7] $FREQ_{DS1}$(sPat) means the frequency of sPat in DISAMBI_SEM_1 and sPat an SC pattern.
[8] $FREQ_{DS1}$(sPat|lPat) means the frequency of sPat in LC pattern lPat.

DISAMB_ISEM_1(sPat) is approved, then can any LC_ONLY candidate has its meaning. Let's look at the above example again.

$$\text{sRatio} = \frac{\text{DISAMBI\_SEM\_1(\$말\_를\_먹\_v)}}{\text{DISAMBI\_SEM\_1(\$말\_를\_먹\_v)} + \text{AMBI\_SEM\_1(\$말\_를\_먹\_v)}}$$

$$= \frac{360}{360 + 23.5} = 0.9387$$

$$\text{lRatio} = \frac{\text{DISAMBI\_SEM\_1(\$말\_를\_먹\_v | 욕\_를\_먹\_v)}}{\text{DISAMBI\_SEM\_1(\$말\_를\_먹\_v)}} = \frac{353}{360} = 0.98$$

The sRatio of \$말_를_먹_v is very high. As a matter of course, the reliability of \$말_를_먹_v is also very high and therefore lRatio has its meaning now. In the example, lRatio is also very high and 욕_를_먹_v is determined to be an LC_ONLY pattern.

LC_ONLY construction from AMBI_LEX_1

LC_ONLY patterns exist not only in DISAMBI_LEX_1 but also in AMBI_LEX_1, where the difference is only whether an LC pattern has semantic ambiguities or not. But since the reliability of an SC pattern cannot be computed in this case, we have to find another method.

In this step also, every LC patterns in AMBI_LEX_1 is considered. Although the reliability of an SC pattern cannot be calculated, we still need DISAMBI_SEM_1 to decide whether each SC pattern of an LC pattern in AMBI_LEX_1 is meaningful or not. For example, if a semantic pattern sPat in AMBI_SEM_1 doesn't exist in DISAMBI_SEM_1, then it can be considered to be meaningless. The algorithm is as follows :

```
for every lPat in AMBI_LEX_1 do :
        LC_ONLY_flag = true
        for every sPat in lPat do :
                if sPat exists in DISAMBI_SEM_1 :
                        LC_ONLY_flag = false
                        break

        If LC_ONLY_flag == true :
                sRatioLowest = 2.
                for every sPat in lPat do:
                        sRatio = FREQ_AS1(sPat|lPat) / FREQ_AS1(sPat)
                        if sRatioLow > sRatio : sRatioLow = sRatio
                if sRatioLowest <= 1. && sRatio >= sThreshold :
                        lPat belongs to LC_ONLY
```

If any SC pattern doesn't exist in DISAMBI_SEM_1, then the SC pattern can be considered to be very unlikely. Likewise, every SC pattern of any LC pattern in AMBI_SEM_1 doesn't exist in DISAMBI_SEM_1, then, the real SC pattern(s) of the LC pattern is(are) very unique with respect to other SC patterns resulting in noisy SC pattern(s). So, such LC patterns are better not to participate in SC pattern construction and belong to LC_ONLY dictionary. But, there is still a possibility that any specific SC pattern of an LC pattern has the meaning and thus should remain as an SC pattern, but, doesn't exist in DISAMBI_SEM_1 by some reasons such as all LC patterns with any specific SC pattern happen to be semantically ambiguous resulting in no entry in DISAMBI_SEM_1. We verify such possibility by sRatio. After confirming that no SC pattern of an LC pattern doesn't exist in DISAMBI_SEM_1, we weigh the importance of each SC pattern of an LC pattern. If the number of LC patterns with an SC pattern is one, that LC pattern belongs to LC_ONLY. If the number is more than one, the ratio of each SC pattern of an LC pattern is computed with respect to the SC pattern in total. If the lowest ratio among the ratios of all SC patterns of an LC pattern is over the threshold, that LC pattern belongs to LC_ONLY. Ratio over the threshold means the SC pattern from other LC patterns is not meaningful compared to the SC pattern from the LC pattern in LC_ONLY. Let's look at an example for 눈-를-흘기_v (eye-obj-give a sharp sidelong glance).

눈-를-흘기_v 126 SemCode(눈) = { $기상, $식물기관, $신체부분}
DISAMBI_SEM_1($기상-를-흘기_v) =0 sRatio = 42 / 42 = 1
DISAMBI_SEM_1($식물기관-를-흘기_v)=0 sRatio = 42 / 42 = 1
DISAMBI_SEM_1($신체부분-를-흘기_v)=0 sRatio = 42 / 42 = 1

According to the above computation, 눈-를-흘기_v is decided to be an LC_ONLY pattern since every SC pattern doesn't appear in DISAMBI_SEM_1 and the lowest sRatio is 1, which is surely above the sThreshold. The true SC pattern of 눈-를-흘기_v is $신체부분-를-흘기_v, but, to our knowledge no other LC patterns do not exist that have $신체부분-를-흘기_v as its SC pattern.

3.2.2 Frequency Readjustment of Ambiguous SC Patterns Based on Reliability

DISAMBI_SEM_2 and AMBI_SEM_2 are constructed from DISAMBI_SEM_1 and AMBI_SEM_1 by reflecting LC_ONLY dictionary. DISAMBI_SEM_2 is fixed and no longer changed, but, AMBI_SEM_2 still needs to be readjusted according to the reliability of each SC pattern. We first define the degree of reliability as follows :

$$SURE(sPat) = FREQ_{DS2}(sPat) / (FREQ_{DS2}(sPat) + FREQ_{AS2}(sPat))$$

SURE(sPat) tells how reliable sPat is. SURE() is based on the fact that most of nouns in the dictionary are unambiguous and DISAMBI_SEM_2 can be considered reliable in itself with respect to its statistics. First, the reliability of every SC pattern in AMBI_SEM_2 is computed, and then, for every LC pattern in AMBI_LEX_2, the frequencies of each SC pattern is recomputed according to their reliability. The algorithm is as follows :

```
for every sPat in AMBI_SEM_2 do :
        SURE(sPat)=FREQDS2(sPat) / ( FREQDS2(sPat)+FREQAS2(sPat) )

for every lPat in AMBI_LEX_2 do :
    SURE_SUM=0.
    for every sPat in lPat do :
        SURE_SUM = SURE_SUM + SURE(sPat)
```

For every sPat in lPat do :
FREQ$_{DS3}$(sPat|lPat)=FREQ$_{AL2}$(lPat)*SURE(sPat)/SURE_SUM

In this way, we can adjust the SC pattern frequencies of ambiguous LC patterns. For example :

AMBI_LEX_2(사과-를-먹_v)=(41,[[$말-를-먹_v,20.5],[$과일-를-먹_v,20.5]])

SURE($말_를_먹_v)

$$= \frac{\text{DISAMBI\_SEM\_2(\$말\_를\_먹\_v)}}{\text{DISAMBI\_SEM\_2(\$말\_를\_먹\_v)} + \text{AMBI\_SEM\_2(\$말\_를\_먹\_v)}}$$

$$= \frac{7}{7 + 23.5} = 0.23$$

SURE($과일_를_먹_v)

$$= \frac{\text{DISAMBI\_SEM\_2(\$과일\_를\_먹\_v)}}{\text{DISAMBI\_SEM\_2(\$과일\_를\_먹\_v)} + \text{AMBI\_SEM\_2(\$과일\_를\_먹\_v)}}$$

$$= \frac{210}{210 + 59} = 0.78$$

The readjusted result is as follows :

AMBI_SEM_3($말-를-먹_v |사과-를-먹_v) = 41 * 0.23 / (0.23 + 0.78) = 9.337
AMBI_SEM_3($과일-를-먹_v|사과-를-먹_v) = 41 * 0.78 / (0.23 + 0.78) = 31.663

We can see that 사과-를-먹_v shows a preference to $과일-를-먹_v than $말-를-먹_v. The result is also stored in AMBI_LEX_3.

AMBI_LEX_3(사과-를-먹_v)=(41, [[$말-를-먹_v,9.337], [$과일-를-먹_v,31.663]])

The final SC pattern dictionary SEM_4 is constructed by merging AMBI_SEM_3 and DISAMBI_SEM_2.

3.3 Patent Domain Consideration

Among characteristics of the patent documents, some findings can be used to improve the performance of parsing as follows.

Firstly, unknown predicates are often encountered. Even if we set the correct lexical goals and construct the term dictionary, we cannot cover all the possible predicates in patent documents. The unknown predicates belong to an open class like technical terms. For unknown technical predicates there is no information about their valency. But, deeper investigation of many unknown predicates revealed that the locality can be a good clue to the solution. The application of the locality clue to the syntactic analysis is also satisfying.

Secondly, noun phrases show very complex structures. When testing the performance of a syntactic analyzer for general purpose, it showed the worst performance in dealing with the noun phrases. The complexity of noun phrases in patent domain is mainly attributed to the coordination and technical terms. From this reason, compared with the general domain, the window size for coordination detection needed to be extended. For the technical terms, we use lexical and/or structural information. Especially, suffix and prefix information is quite useful and effective. Nonetheless, it's still a very difficult task and has its limits. We believe that certain kind of ontology or any form of semantic information is urgent for each technical domain to cope with NP analysis properly.

Thirdly, for long sentences, we use some syntactic clues to partition a long sentence into several "proper sized" sentences so that each of which can be parsed easily. The clues for partitioning a long sentence are exemplified below:

Clue 1: verbal ending morphemes followed by "," such as:
- "verb stem + 지만 (but) + comma"
- "verb stem + 고 (and) + comma"
- "verb stem + ㄹ때 (when) + comma"

Clue 2: conjunctions and specific lexical tokens in NPs such as:
NP1와(and); NP2와(and); ... NPn을 포함하여(including) 이루어진다(be composed of) ➔ It is composed of the following: NP1, NP2, ..., NPn

Fourthly, the Korean patent documents have its peculiar styles that are widely accepted in the patent offices as is the case in the US- or Japanese patents. In particular, patent claims are formulated according to a set of precise syntactic, lexical and stylistic guidelines (Sheremetyeva, 2003). This fact enables to employ sentence patterns for the translation without complex syntactic parsing after morphological analysis. To detect stereotyped sentence styles in patent documents, we performed the linguistic study of 1,000 sample Korean patent documents and extracted sentence patterns based on certain syntactic, lexical and stylistic features. In each section of a patent document, there are different types of sentence patterns as follows:

Abstract: the introduction about the invention is described in a specific form like:
- 본 발명은 ~에 관한 것이다: the present invention relates to ~
- 본 발명은 ~를 개시한다: the present invention discloses ~

Detailed description of the invention: the idiomatic adverb phrases are frequently repeated:
- 종래 기술에 따르면...: according to prior art ...
- 도n에 도시되어 있는 바와 같이...: as shown in Fig. N ...

Brief descriptions of the drawing: it is mainly composed of noun phrases that explain the drawings:
- 도 n은 ...를 설명하기 위한 도면: Fig. n is a view for explaining ...

The effect of the invention: the sentences are mainly for explaining the effects of the invention:
- 본 발명은 ...는 효과가 있다: the present invention has the effect that ...

Claims : it is mainly composed of noun phrases that describe the patent claims:

- 제 n항에 있어서, ...를 더 포함하는 것을 특징으로 하는...: ... of claim n, further comprising ...

4 Evaluation

The goal of the evaluation was to see:

i) How accurately the collocation patterns were generated
ii) How much do the semantic collocation patterns improve the parser
iii) How much does the patent-domain customization improves the parser

The accuracy of collocation pattern was tested for both LEX_ONLY dictionary and the final semantic collocation dictionary SEM_4. The number of extracted LEX_ONLY patterns were 8,061 and we selected 100 patterns randomly for evaluation. The result was as follows:

Correct		Wrong	
Good	No Harm	SemCode Error	Data Sparseness
81	12	5	2

On the table, 'Good' means the extracted patterns are good for LEX_ONLY patterns. 'No Harm' means the semantic pattern of the extracted pattern is correct, but due to the bias of the corpus and thus over-counting of that pattern, it is better to consider that pattern as LEX_ONLY patterns. 'SemCode Error' means the case where the semantic error caused the error. 'Data Sparseness' means the case where the semantic pattern of the extracted patterns is correct but due to the data sparseness, the patterns happen to be considered as LEX_ONLY pattern.

The final semantic collocation dictionary SEM_4 was evaluated for each lexical collocation pattern with respect to ERR(Error Reduction Rate). For example, in case of '사과-를-먹_v' with frequency 50, ERR is 60% as follows :

LC pat	SC pat	Freq. Before	Freq. After	ERR
사과-를-먹v	$과일-를-먹v	25	40	60%
	$말-를-먹v	25	10	
accuracy		50%	80%	

We selected 50 ambiguous LC patterns and the average ERR was 74%. None of the tested LC patterns were deteriorated and the more ambiguous the LC patterns were, the better the result was.

Improved SC patterns can improve the parsing and the translation, but, the application ratio or hit ratio of SC patterns may not be that high. So, to evaluate the effect of SC patterns more closely, we selected 100 sentences that are affected by the new SC patterns. The parsing results are represented by dependency trees in our system and the accuracy of the affected dependency relations were 91%.

To evaluate the performance of the parser after the frequency adjustment and customization, we selected 200 test sentences randomly from patent corpus. The test set was organized in such a way that it reflects a real patent document. Among 200 sentences, about 120 sentences were selected from the "detailed description" section of patents, 40 were extracted from the "claim" section, the rest from the "description of the drawing" and the "effects of the invention" section. The average length of a sentence was 23.7 words. The length was normalized in order to reflect the length of the real patent sentences. The parsing accuracy with respect to dependency relation was 93.4 %, 3.8% higher than the original, general domain parser(89.6%), which is quite good results showing the importance of customization.

Among the sections in patent documents, the parsing accuracy of the description of the drawings part was best, while the accuracy of the detailed description part scored worst. The reason for the best accuracy of the description of the drawing section is that the ratio of the application of sentence patterns was relatively high. The detailed description part contained, as expected, many long sentences.

5 Conclusion

In this paper we showed an effective method to reduce the noise of lexical- and semantic co-occurrence data and customization process for patent documents.

Firstly, by detecting the lexical-only co-occurrence data, we could reduce the noise caused by over-contributed LC patterns. Secondly, by computing the reliability of each semantic pattern, we could minimize the effect of wrong semantic patterns.

Customization was done for patent domain and contributed to the improvement of parsing accuracy. But, the application ratio was different from section to section of patent documents.

We found that our proposed method to reduce the noise of co-occurrence data contributes to parsing accuracy and thus translation quality. In fact, our method can be applied to general domain also, although we applied our method to patent domain for the first time. We also found that customization for specific domain can contribute to the parsing accuracy.

Acknowledgement

This work was funded by the Ministry of Information and Communication of Korean government.

References

1. Shinmori, A., Okumura, M., Marukawa, Y., Iwayama, M.: *Patent Claim Processing for Readability.* In "Proceedings of ACL 2003 Workshop on Patent Corpus Processing Workshop" (2003)
2. Kobayashi, A.: *Machine Translation and Japio's role in disseminating Japanese information.* http://www.european-patent-office.org/epidos/conf/jpinfo/2004/_pdf/pres/japio_kobayashi_machine_translation_and_japio_role.pdf (2004)
3. Kim, Y., Hong, M., Kim, C., Park, S.: *Word Sense Disambiguation Using Lexical and Semantic Information within Local Syntactic Relations.* In "Proceedings of the 30th Annual Conference of the IEEE Industrial Electronics Society" (2004)

4. Hong, M., Kim, Y., Kim, C., Yang, S., Seo, Y., Ryu, C., Park, S.: Customizing a Korean-English MT System for Patent Translation, in Proceedings of the tenth MT Summit (2005)
5. Sheremetyeva, S. : *Natural Language Analysis of Patent Claims.* In "Proceedings of ACL 2003 Workshop on Patent Corpus Processing Workshop" (2003)
6. Lee, H., Kang, I., Lee,J.: D*etermination of Unknown Syntactic Relation in Korean using Concept patterns and Statistical Information*, Conference on Korean Information Processing, pp.261-266 (1998)

A Scalable and Distributed NLP Architecture for Web Document Annotation

Julien Deriviere, Thierry Hamon, and Adeline Nazarenko

LIPN – UMR CNRS 7030
99 av. J.B. Clément, F-93430 Villetaneuse, France
Tél.: 33 1 49 40 28 32, Fax: 33 1 48 26 07 12
firstname.lastname@lipn.univ-paris13.fr,
www-lipn.univ-paris13.fr/~lastname

Abstract. In the context of the ALVIS project, which aims at integrating linguistic information in topic-specific search engines, we develop a NLP architecture to linguistically annotate large collections of web documents. This context leads us to face the scalability aspect of Natural Language Processing. The platform can be viewed as a framework using existing NLP tools. We focus on the efficiency of the platform by distributing linguistic processing on several machines. We carry out an an experiment on 55,329 web documents focusing on biology. These 79 million-word collections of web documents have been processed in 3 days on 16 computers.

1 Introduction

As existing search engines provide poor foundation for linguistic and semantic web operations, the ALVIS[1] project aims at proposing a peer-to-peer network of topic-specific search engines. Given the specificity of the information in specialized documents, we argue that their indexation requires linguistic analysis. Thus, each peer should also integrate a Natural Language Processing (NLP) architecture with domain-specific annotations. For instance, processing life science literature implies adding a biological named entity recognizer, a gene interaction identifier, etc. This paper focuses on the design and the development of a text processing architecture exploiting specialized NLP tools to produce linguistically annotated documents.

This platform is designed to be generic for processing large collections of specialized documents. Input documents have been crawled on the web by a topic-specific harvester [1], normalized in XML files and sent to the NLP platform. Even if those documents focus on a specific domain, they are heterogeneous regarding the language, the size, and the content. Given this non-traditional constraint in NLP, texts must be analysed quickly and robustly. We designed the NLP platform as a distributed and modular framework integrating existing NLP tools. Each tool is wrapped in the platform. Most of them can be tuned by

[1] European Project STREP IST-1-002068-STP, http://www.alvis.info/alvis/

T. Salakoski et al. (Eds.): FinTAL 2006, LNAI 4139, pp. 56–67, 2006.

adding domain specific lexical resources. Moreover, each document is analysed by a instance of the platform.

We describe the NLP platform in section 2. Then, its performances are analysed in section 3, based on an experiment on 55,329 web documents focusing on biology. In section 4, we discuss the contribution of our approach given the existing architectures designed for document annotation. We then conclude in section 5.

2 A Modular and Tunable Platform

We develop a platform exploiting existing NLP tools rather than developing new ones[2], which allows us to quickly annotate a large amount of documents. For instance, the platform allows us to test the various combinations of annotations to identify which ones have a significant impact on the extraction rule learning. In that respect, the platform can be viewed as a modular software architecture tunable according to the targeted domain.

2.1 Specific Constraints

The reuse of NLP tools imposes specific constraints regarding software engineering and processing domain specific documents relies on the tuning of the NLP tools for the corresponding sublanguage.

From the software engineering point of view, constraints concern above all the heterogeneity of the input/output formats of the integrated NLP tools. Each NLP tool has its specific input and output format. Linking together several tools requires defining an interchange format. Testing various combinations of annotations, including processing time of various linguistic analyses (named entity recognition or term tagging) incites us to propose a distributed architecture.

Proposing a platform to annotate topic-specific texts implies also NLP constraints like the availability of lexical and ontological resources, or the tuning of NLP tools to improve Part-of-Speech tagging or parsing. Specialized linguistic processing can be required according to specific domains. For instance, we argued in [2] that the identification of gene interaction requires gene name tagging, and term recognition.

2.2 General Architecture

The NLP platform is organized according the traditional client/server schema, but it can also be run in stand-alone mode. The client requests a document from the server. Then, the document is linguistically annoted and sent back to the server. The server aims at selecting documents requested by the clients and recording the annotated documents. Input documents and output documents are stored in a spool. We designed a protocol to insure that no document is lost.

In the following sections, we focus on the description of the NLP client layout.

---

[2] We only develop unexisting or unavailable NLP systems regarding our requirements: GPL or free licence for research.

2.3 Overview of the Linguistic Analysis

The different processing steps are traditionally separated in modules [3]. Each module carries out a specific processing: named entity recognition, word segmentation, POS tagging and parsing. It wraps an NLP tool to ensure the conformity of the input/output format with the DTD. Annotations are recorded in an stand-off XML format to deal with the heterogeneousness of NLP tools input/output (the DTD is fully described in [4]).

The modularity of the architecture simplifies the substitution of a tool with another. This implies module switching without any impact on the whole architecture.

Tuning to a specific field is insured by the resources used by each module. For instance, a targeted species or gene list can be added to the biology-specific named entity recognizer to process biological texts. It only depends on the availability of such a resource.

Figure 1 gives an overview of the architecture of the NLP clients. The various modules composing the NLP line are represented as boxes. The description of these modules are given in section 2.4. The arrows represent the data processing flow. The dotted arrows represent alternative types of outputs that the platform may produce.

We assume that input web documents (sent by the server) are already downloaded, cleaned, encoded into the UTF-8 character set, and formatted in XML [4]. Documents are first tokenized to define offsets for further linguistic units to annotate and to ensure the homogeneity of the various annotations. Then, documents are processed through several modules: named entity recognition, word and sentence segmentation, lemmatization, part-of-speech tagging, term tagging, and parsing.

Although this architecture is quite traditional, a few points should be highlighted:

- Tokenisation is a first step to compute a first non-linguistic basic segmentation, and is used for further reference. Those are the basic textual units in the text processing line. Tokenization serves no other purpose but to provide a starting point for segmentation. This level of annotation follows the recommendations of the TC37SC4/TEI workgroup, even if we refer to the character offset rather than pointer mark-up (TEI element ptr) in the textual signal to mark the token boundaries.
  To simplify further processing, we distinguish different types of tokens: alphabetical tokens, numerical tokens,separating tokens and symbolic tokens.
- Named Entity tagging takes place very early in the NLP line because unrecognized named entities hinder most NLP steps in many sublanguages;

2.4 NLP Module Description

For each document, the NLP modules are called sequentially. The output of each module is stored in memory until the end of the processing. The XML output

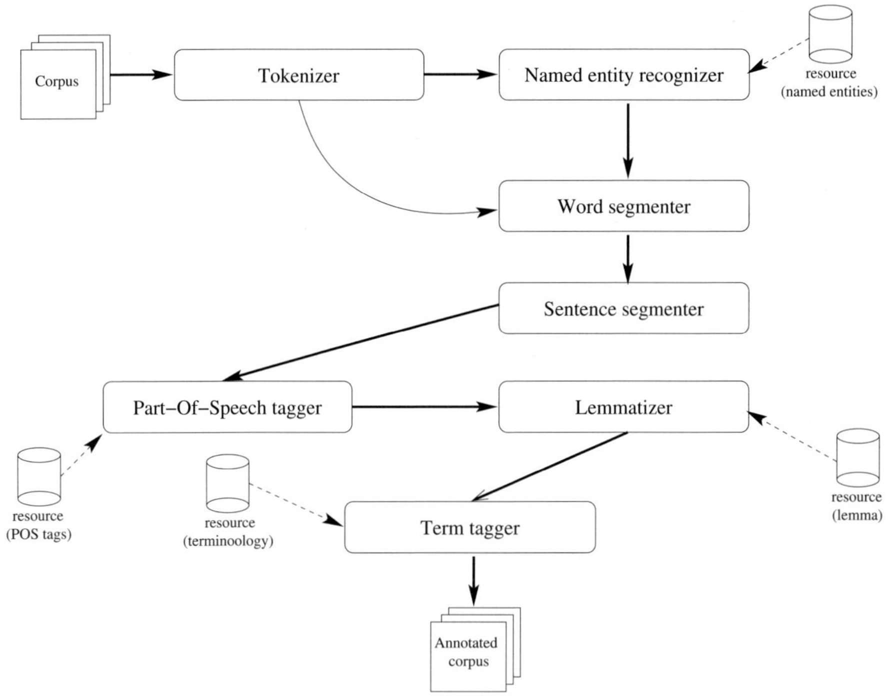

Fig. 1. Architecture of the text processing line

is recorded every time a document is processed. Figure 3 presents sample of the annotation of a Medline abstract (id PMID10788508) used as input (figure 2).

This section describes the general specifications of the various modules of the NLP line that produces various types of linguistic annotations. The tools wrapped in the modules are examples of NLP tools integration, and they can be substituted with others.

Named Entity Tagging. The Named entity tagging module aims at annotating semantic units with syntactic and semantic types. Each text sequence corresponding to a named entity will be tagged with a unique tag corresponding to its semantic value (for example a "gene" type for gene names, "species" type for species names, etc.). All these text sequences are also assumed to be equivalent to nouns: the tagger dynamically produces linguistic units equivalent to words or noun phrases. We integrated our Named entity tagger, TagEn [5], which is based on a set of linguistic resources and grammars.

Word and Sentence Segmentation. This module identifies sentence and word boundaries. We use simple regular expressions, based on the algorithm proposed in [6]. Part of the segmentation has been implicitly performed by the Named Entity tagging to resolve some ambiguities, such as the identification of the sequence "B. subtilis", by providing information on "B." as a short form of "Bacillus". Word and sentence segmentation steps are thus made simpler.

Morpho-Syntactic Tagging. This module aims at associating a part of speech (POS) tag to each word.It assumes that word and sentence segmentations have been performed. We are using the probabilistic Part-Of-Speech tagger TreeTagger [7]. We also integrated the GeniaTagger[8] in the platform. However, for the sake of processing time, we will not be using it in the following experiments, even though it proposes a better POS tagging.

Lemmatisation. The module associates a lemma, i.e. a canonical form to each word. If the word cannot be lemmatized (for instance a number or a foreign word where none of the rules apply), the information is omitted. It assumes that word segmentation and morpho-syntactic information are provided. While it is a distinct module, we are currently using the TreeTagger's output which provides lemma as well as POS tags. An external resource could be required depending on the lemmatizer and the domain tuning requirements. This resource would provide an association between the inflectional forms of a word and its lemma.

Terminology Tagging. This module aims at recognizing terms in the documents differing from named entities, like *gene expression*, *spore coat cell.* Term lists can be provided as terminological resources such as the Gene Ontology [9], the MeSH [10] or more widely UMLS [11]. They can also be acquired through corpus analysis. Providing a given terminology tunes the term tagging to the corresponding domain. Previous annotation levels, such as lemmatisation and word segmentation but also named entities, are required.

2.5 Implementation

We implemented the platform in Perl, a language which suits our character string processing needs. The availability of packages such as *UTF8* or *XMLParser* makes Perl a very interesting developing language, even if it may not be as fast as compiled languages such as *C++*.

The NLP client reads documents requested by the server, and processes them one after the other. The processing line is the following:

1. A XML document is loaded into memory.
2. NLP modules are called.
3. The XML annotated document is sent back to the server.

```
<documentCollection> <documentRecord
id="A79ACA58DEB7E6114747710B9A85059F">
  <acquisition>
      <acquisitionData>
        <modifiedDate>2004-11-21 15:59:14</modifiedDate>
        <urls>
          <url>http://www.ncbi.nlm.nih.gov/entrez/query.fcgi?cmd=
               Retrieve&amp;db=pubmed&amp;dopt=MEDLINE&amp;list_uids
               =10788508</url>
        </urls>
      </acquisitionData>
      <canonicalDocument>
        <section>
          <section title="Combined action of two transcription factors
               regulates genes encoding spore coat proteins of Bacillus
               subtilis.">
        <section>Combined action of two transcription factors regulates
            genes encoding spore coat proteins of Bacillus subtilis.
        </section>
            ...
      </section>
    </section>
      </canonicalDocument>
  </acquisition>
```


Fig. 2. Sample of the input of the platform

3 Performance Analysis

We carry out an experiment on a collection of 55,329 web documents focusing biology. Figure 4 gives the distribution of the document size in input (both axes are on a logarithmic scale). Most documents have a XML size between 1KB and 100KB. The size of the biggest document is about 5.7 MB.

We used 16 machines to annotate them. Most of these machines are standard Personal Computers with 1GB of RAM and a 3.1 or 2.9 GHz processor. Others are four elements of a cluster with a similar configurations and a computer with 8GB of RAM and two 2.8GHz Xeon (dual-core) processors. Their operating system is either Debian Linux or Mandrake Linux. The server and three NLP clients processes were running on the 8GB/biprocessor. Only one NLP client was running on each standard Personal Computer with a low priority.

We consider these performances as an indication of the platform processing time. A real benchmark requires several tests to evaluate the performance. Timers are run between each function call in order to measure how long each step is taking user-time-wise. We use the functions provided in the `Time::Hires` package. All the time results are recorded in the annotated XML documents, except for the XML rendering step.

The annotation of the documents was completed in three days, which represents 25 days and 20h39'23" of sequential processing. Each client processes an average of 2790 documents. Figure 1 shows the total number of entities found in the document collection. The platform processed 79 million words and 3.6 million sentences. It also identified 7.2 million named entities and 17 million terms. Each document contains an average of 1494 words, 68 sentences, 136

```
<linguisticAnalysis>
  <token_level>
  <token>
    <content>Combined</content>
    <from>0</from>
    <id>token1</id>
    <to>7</to>
    <type>alpha</type>
  </token>
  ...
  </token_level>
  <sentence_level>
  <sentence>
    <form>Combined action of two
         transcription factors
        regulates genes encoding
         spore coat proteins of
        Bacillus subtilis .</
        form>
    <id>sentence1</id>
    <refid_end_token>token30</
        refid_end_token>
    <refid_start_token>token1</
        refid_start_token>
  </sentence>
  ...
  </sentence_level>
  <word_level>
  <word>
    <form>Combined</form>
    <id>word1</id>
    <list_refid_token>
      <refid_token>
        <refid_token>token1</
            refid_token>
      </refid_token>
    </list_refid_token>
  </word>
  ...
  </word_level>
  <lemma_level>
  <lemma>
    <canonical_form>combined</
        canonical_form>
    <id>lemma1</id>
    <refid_word>word1</
        refid_word>
  </lemma>
  ...
  </lemma_level>
  <semantic_unit_level>
  <semantic_unit>
    <named_entity>
      <form>Bacillus subtilis</
          form>
      <id>named_entity0</id>
      <list_refid_token>
        <refid_token>
          <refid_token>token27</
              refid_token>
        </refid_token>
        <refid_token>
          <refid_token>token28</
              refid_token>
        </refid_token>
        <refid_token>
          <refid_token>token29</
              refid_token>
        </refid_token>
      </list_refid_token>
      <named_entity_type>species</
          named_entity_type>
    </named_entity>
  </semantic_unit>
  ...
  </semantic_unit_level>
  <morphosyntactic_features_level>
  <morphosyntactic_features>
    <id>morphosyntactic_features1<
        /id>
    <refid_word>word1</refid_word>
    <syntactic_category>JJ</
        syntactic_category>
  </morphosyntactic_features>
  <morphosyntactic_features>
    <id>morphosyntactic_features10
        </id>
    <refid_word>word10</refid_word
        >
    <syntactic_category>NN</
        syntactic_category>
  </morphosyntactic_features>
  ...
  </morphosyntactic_features_level
      >
 </linguisticAnalysis>
</documentRecord>
</documentCollection>
```

Fig. 3. Sample of the output of the platform

named entities and 326 terms. 176 of the documents contained no words at all, they therefore underwent the tokenization step only. One of our NLP clients processed a 350,444-word document.

Figure 2 shows the average processing time for each document. Less than one minute is required to process each document. The most time-consuming steps are the term tagging (78% of the overall processing time) and the named entity recognition (12% of the overall processing time). In the current version of the

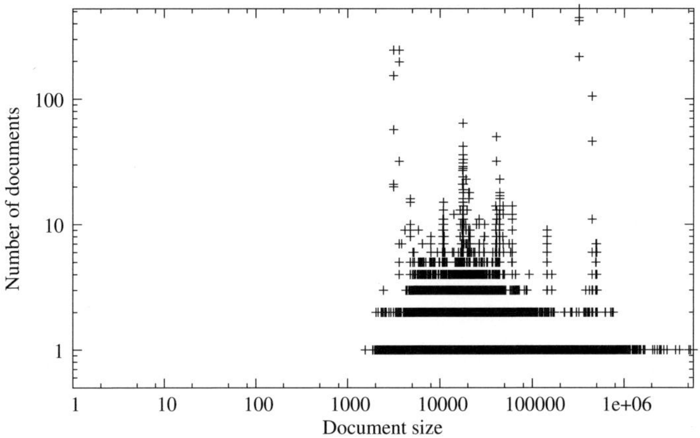

Fig. 4. Range of input document size

platform, these tools are invoked for each document, then unloaded from memory until the next document record is loaded. The high processing time is probably due to the time needed for the tools to load their resources.

A possible workaround which remains yet to be implemented would be to load these tools in memory and keep them there until the entire processing is done. For some tools, this would however imply taking into account a possible buffering of the tool output. For other tools like TagEN, it is probably not even possible. Such an enhancement remains to be explored.

Only 27 documents out of the total amount (0.04%) were not annotated. This is mainly due to an unidentified bug in a NLP tool we use, which froze some of our client machines. We found a workaround for this bug after the experiments were complete. This problem increased processing times; we approximate the overall processing time to an average of 2 days and 7 hours, since the slowest client machine completed its task in 2 days and 7 hours. Moreover, standard personal computers were being used by other connected users. In that respect, the CPU load varied and computers have been rebooted. We have also noticed that certain external NLP tools can encouter difficulties with the UTF8 character set when used on different machines with various environments.

Table 1. Average and total of linguistic units

	Average number of units by document	Total number of units in the document collection
Tokens	5,290.72	276,532,529
Named entities	136.61	7,202,367
Words	1,494.23	79,165,931
Sentences	67.96	3,639,945
Part-of-speech tags and lemma	992.79	53,594,958
Terms	326.29	17,193,097

Table 2. Average of document time processing in second

	Average document time processing	Percentage Percentage
XML loading	0.67	1.2
tokenization	0.56	1
named entity recognition	6.68	12
word segmentation	1.39	2.5
sentence segmentation	0.38	0.7
part-of-speech tagging and lemmatization	2.2	4
term tagging	43.63	78.6
Total	55.52	100

4 Background

Several text engineering architectures have been proposed to manage text processing for the last decade [12]. GATE (General Architecture for Text Engineering) [3] has been essentially designed for information extraction tasks. It aims at reusing NLP tools in built-in components. The interchange annotation format (CPSL – Common Pattern Specific Language) is based on the TIPSTER annotation format [13].

Based on an external linguistic annotation platform, namely GATE, the KIM platform [14] can be considered as a "meta-platform". It is an ontology population, semantic indexing and information retrieval architecture. KIM has been integrated in massive semantic annotation projects such as the SWAN clusters[3] and SEKT[4]. The authors deem scalability is a critical parameter for two reasons: (1) KIM has to be able to process large amounts of data, in order to build and train statistical models for Information Extraction; (2) it has to be suitable for use as an online public service.

UIMA[15], a new implementation architecture of TEXTRACT [16], is similar to GATE. It mainly differs from GATE in the data representation model. UIMA is a framework for the development of analysis engines. It offers components for the analysis of unstructured information streams such as HTML web pages. These components are supposed to range from lightweight to highly scalable implementations.The UIMA annotation format is called CAS (Common Analysis Structure). It is mainly based on the TIPSTER format [13]. Annotations in the CAS are stand-off for the sake of flexibility. Documents can be processed either at a single document level or at a collection level. Collections are handled in UIMA by the Collection Processing Engine, which has some interesting features such as filtering, performance monitoring and parallelization.

The Textpresso system [17] has been specifically developed to mine biological documents, abstracts as well as articles. Focusing on *Caenorhabditis elegans*, the system processes 16,000 abstracts and 3,000 full text articles. It is designed as

[3] `http://deri.ie/projects/swan`

[4] `http://sekt.semanticweb.org`

a curation system extracting gene-gene interaction that is also used as a search engine. NLP modules are integrated: a tokenizer, a sentence segmenter, a Part-Of-Speech (POS) tagger, and an ontology tagger based on information provided by Gene Ontology[18].

While Textpresso is specifically designed for biomedical texts, our platform is closer to GATE, since it also aims at proposing a generic platform to process large document collections. Our first test shows that GATE is not suited to process large collections of documents. GATE has been designed as a powerful environment for the conception and development of NLP applications in information extraction. Scalability is not central in its design, and information extraction deals with small sets of documents.

Our approach is quite similar to those of [19], although the implementation and communication are different. They propose a distributed architecture in order to address scalability and modularity issues. Contrary to our platform, each NLP component is embedded in a server performing the requested processing. We rather plan to implemente each client integrating NLP components as a real pipeline using FIFOs.

Regarding the above approach, very little information is generally given to evaluate the behavior of the systems on a collection of documents whereas from our point of view, this aspect is crucial for such a system. We intend that our platform insures interoperability between components as well as efficiency and concurrent annotations.

5 Conclusion

We present a platform to enrich domain-specific web documents with linguistic annotations. In our approach, we intend to take into account the interoperability of the NLP components, as well as scalability and robustness due to the amount of documents to annotate. In that respect, the platform is designed as a framework using existing NLP tools which can be substituted with others if necessary. Several NLP modules have been integrated: Named entity tagging, word and sentence segmentation, POS tagging, lemmatization and term tagging. The platform produces an stand-off XML annotated corpus. We address the scalability problems by distributing linguistic processing on several computers, according to a client/server architecture. Each NLP client requests a document from the document server, annotates it and sends it back to the server. Robustness is insured at the client level (large document annotation is problematic, but it does not freeze the entire platform), as well as at the component level (a problem on a annotation step only affects the given annotation level).

We carry out an experiment on a large collection of 55,329 web documents in three days, on 16 computers. Only 0.04% of the documents were not annotated, due to a bug in a integrated NLP component, or a user reboot of some computers. A workaround was found for this bug after the experiments were completed. Such problems left aside, the NLP annotations would have been completed in 2 days and 7 hours.

Further developments will be the integration of syntactic parsing in the platform although it remains the main critical point as far as processing time is concerned. We are convinced that a good recognition of the terms can significantly reduce the parsing time. We are currently investigating various complementary methods to reduce the paring time. Our first results show that a proper handling of unknown words and the reduction of sentence complexity are promising leads [20].

We are also further investigating the distribution layout by using processing capacity balancing: we note that the server does not take into account the capacity of clients to process a document in a acceptable time. Documents requested by a client will be selected by taking into account processing time of the already annotated documents by the same client.

References

1. Ardö, A.: Focused crawling in the alvis semantic search engine. In: Poster in ESWC2005 – 2nd Annual European Semantic Web Conference, Heraklion, Crete (2005)
2. Alphonse, E., Aubin, S., Bessieres, P., Bisson, G., Hamon, T., Laguarrigue, S., Manine, A.P., Nazarenko, A., Nedellec, C., Vetah, M.O.A., Poibeau, T., Weissenbacher, D.: Event-based information extraction for the biomedical domain: the caderige project. In: Workshop BioNLP (Biology and Natural language Processing), Conférence Computational Linguisitics (Coling 2004), Geneva (2004)
3. Bontcheva, K., Tablan, V., Maynard, D., Cunningham, H.: Evolving gate to meet new challenges in language engineering. Natural Language Engineering **10**(3-4) (2004) 349–374
4. Nazarenko, A., Alphonse, E., Derivière, J., Hamon, T., Vauvert, G., Weissenbacher, D.: The alvis format for linguistically annotated documents. In: Summitted to LREC 2006. (2006)
5. Berroyer, J.F.: Tagen, un analyseur d"entités nommées : conception, développement et évaluation. Mémoire de d.e.a. d'intelligence artificielle, Université Paris-Nord (2004)
6. Grefenstette, G.: Exploration in Automatic Thesaurus Discovery. Kluwer Academic Publishers, Boston, USA (1994)
7. Schmid, H.: Probabilistic part-of-speech tagging using decision trees. In Jones, D., Somers, H., eds.: New Methods in Language Processing Studies in Computational Linguistics. (1997)
8. Tsuruoka, Y., Tateishi, Y., Kim, J.D., Ohta, T., McNaught, J., Ananiadou, S., Tsujii, J.: Developing a robust part-of-speech tagger for biomedical text. In: Proceedings of Advances in Informatics - 10th Panhellenic Conference on Informatics. LNCS 3746 (2005) 382–392
9. Consortium, T.G.O.: Gene ontology: tool for the unification of biology. Nature genetics **25** (2000) 25–29
10. MeSH: Medical subject headings. Library of Medicine, Bethesda, Maryland, WWW page `http://www.nlm.nih.gov/mesh/meshhome.html`, (1998)
11. National Library of Medicine, ed.: UMLS Knowledge Source. 13th edn. (2003)
12. Cunningham, H., Bontcheva, K., Tablan, V., Wilks, Y.: Software infrastructure for language resources: a taxonomy of previous work and a requirements analysis. In: Proceedings of the 2nd International Conference on Language Resources and Evaluation (LREC-2), Athens (2000)

13. Grishman, R.: Tipster architecture design document version 2.3. Technical report, DARPA (1997)
14. Popov, B., Kiryakov, A., Ognyanoff, D., Manov, D., Kirilov, A.: Kim – a semantic platform for information extraction and retrieval. Natural Language Engineering **10**(3-4) (2004) 375–392
15. Ferrucci, D., Lally, A.: Uima: an architecture approach to unstructured information processing in a corporate research environment. Natural Language Engineering **10**(3-4) (2004) 327–348
16. Neff, M.S., Byrd, R.J., Boguraev, B.K.: The talent system: Textract architecture and data model. Natural Language Engineering **10**(3-4) (2004) 307–326
17. Müller, H.M., Kenny, E.E., Sternberg, P.W.: Textpresso: an ontology-based information retrieval and extraction system for biological literature. PLoS Biology **2**(11) (2004) 1984–1998
18. Consortium, T.G.O.: Creating the Gene Ontology Resource: Design and Implementation. Genome Res. **11**(8) (2001) 1425–1433
19. Zajac, R., Casper, M., Sharples, N.: An open distributed architecture for reuse and integration of heterogeneous nlp components. In: Proceedings of the fifth Conference on Applied Natural Language Processing (ANLP'97). (1997)
20. Aubin, S., Nazarenko, A., Nédellec, C.: Adapting a general parser to a sublanguage. In: The international conference RANLP 2005, Borovets, Bulgaria (2005)

A Straightforward Method for Automatic Identification of Marginalized Languages

Ana Lilia Reyes-Herrera, Luis Villaseñor-Pineda, and Manuel Montes-y-Gómez

Language Technologies Group, Computer Science Department,
National Institute of Astrophysics, Optics and Electronics (INAOE), Mexico
{ana_reyes, villasen, mmontesg}@inaoep.mx

Abstract. Spoken language identification consists in recognizing a language based on a sample of speech from an unknown speaker. The traditional approach for this task mainly considers the phonothactic information of languages. However, for marginalized languages –languages with few speakers or oral languages without a fixed writing standard–, this information is practically not at hand and consequently the usual approach is not applicable. In this paper, we present a method that only considers the acoustic features of the speech signal and does not use any kind of linguistic information. The experimental results on a pairwise discrimination task among nine languages demonstrated that our proposal is comparable to other similar methods. Nevertheless, its great advantage is the straightforward characterization of the acoustic signal.

1 Introduction

Automatic language identification consists in recognizing a language based on a sample of speech from an unknown speaker. There are two main approaches for this task. The first approach is based on the use of the phonothactic information of languages. It differentiates languages by the proportion and combination of phonemes in the elocutions. In particular, it considers the segmentation of the speech signal into phonemes and the use of a language model –which capture all possible combinations of phonemes from a particular language– to determine the language at issue [1, 2]. On the other hand, the second approach does not take into consideration the phonothactic information. It identifies languages exclusively using acoustic features from the speech signal such as the prosody [3], the rhythm [4] and some others perceptual features [5].

At present, the best classification results have been achieved by the first approach [1]. However, its application requires carrying out a study on the target languages in order to determine all valid phoneme combinations as well as their probabilities of occurrence. This study can be only completed for well-systematized languages, i.e., it can be done for languages having a fixed writing standard and an ample set of digital documents available. Unfortunately, this is not case for most marginalized languages, and especially, it is not the case for most of the 62 indigenous languages of Mexico.

In this paper, we propose a straightforward method for language identification. This method just considers the acoustic features of the speech signal and does not apply any linguistic information of the languages. In particular, it characterize the

T. Salakoski et al. (Eds.): FinTAL 2006, LNAI 4139, pp. 68–75, 2006.

speech signals by set of general –language independent– features that capture the variations in the Mel frequency cepstral coefficients and take advantage of the secondary frequencies.

The proposed method will encourage the construction of systems for automatic identification of indigenous languages, which will facilitate the medical and judicial assistance of more than five million of monolingual indigenous speakers.[1]

The rest of the paper is organized as follows. Section 2 describes some previous works on language identification using acoustic features. Section 3 describes a straightforward characterization of the speech signal, which is specially suited for the language identification task. Section 4 shows the experimental results on a pairwise discrimination task among nine languages. Finally, section 4 depicts our conclusions and future work.

2 Related Work

Just a few works has tackled the problem of spoken language identification without using the phonothactic information of languages. These works are founded on the hypothesis that each language has its own rhythm (indeed, linguistics clusters languages in three major rhythmical groups: sylabe-timed, stress-timed, mora-timed). One of the first works in trying to classify languages under this assumption was that of Cummings et al. [3]. In this work, the authors proposed exploiting the variations in the fundamental frequency to perceive the rhythm of the speech. Table 1 shows their experimental results on a pairwise discrimination task among five languages. For the experiments, they implemented a neural net and used the OGI_TS corpus [6]. In particular, they considered 50 different speakers per language for training and 20 for test, and used speech samples of 50 seconds.

Table 1. Accuracy percentages reported by Cummins et al. [3]

	German	Spanish	Japanase	Mandarin
English	52	62	57	58
German	-	51	58	65
Spanish	-	-	66	47
Japanese	-	-	-	60

In other relevant work, Rouas [4] proposed a method for language identification based on the rhythm. It recaptured the linguistic theory of Ramus [7], and tried to characterize the speech rhythm in function of its vocalic and consonantal intervals. According to Ramus, the duration of these intervals determines the rhythm of the languages. Therefore, to obtain the parameters of the rhythm, Rouas segmented the speech signal in intervals formed by vowels and in intervals formed by consonants. In practice, he used the fundamental frequency F0 of each segment to obtain the intonation parameters. He considered four parameters: the stocking, the standard

[1] Initially, the idea is assisting a call operator to identify the used language, and therefore to contact an adequate interpreter who provide the required assistance.

deviation, the F0 skewness and the F0 kurtosis. In order to probe his method Rouas used nine languages of the OGI_TS corpus, and generated a classifier –based on the Gaussian Mixtures Models– for each pair of languages. For the experiments, he considered samples of 45 seconds. Table 2 shows their experimental results.

Table 2. Accuracy percentages reported by Rouas [4]

	German	Spanish	Mandarin	Vietnamese	Japanese	Korean	Tamil	Farsi
English	59.5	67.7	75.0	67.7	67.6	79.4	77.4	76.3
German	-	59.4	62.2	65.7	65.8	71.4	69.7	71.8
Spanish	-	-	80.6	62.1	62.5	75.9	65.4	66.7
Mandarin	-	-	-	50.0	50.6	73.5	74.2	76.3
Vietnamese	-	-	-	-	68.6	56.2	71.4	66.7
Japanese	-	-	-	-	-	65.7	59.4	66.7
Korean	-	-	-	-	-	-	62.1	75.0
Tamil	-	-	-	-	-	-		69.7

Finally, Samouelian [5] proposed an alternative method for the signal characterization. First, he breaks the signal into fixed segments and obtains 12 Mel frequency cepstral coefficients for each segment. Then, he computes the deltas of these coefficients. That is, he calculates the change of each coefficient between to contiguous segments. This way, each signal is represented by a set of deltas. In order to probe the representation, he generated a decision tree (based on the C4.5 algorithm) from a training corpus of 50 speakers of three different languages extracted from the OGI_TS corpus. He obtained 53% of accuracy when using samples of 45 seconds, and 48.6% when using 10 seconds samples.

It is important to mention that the results reported by Samouelain correspond to a multi-class classifier (3-languages: English, German and Japanese), while the other two works report results on a pairwise (binary) classification task.

The signal characterization proposed in this paper extends Samouelain's ideas. On the one hand, it uses 16 Mel frequency cepstral coefficients instead of just 12. This increment in the number of coefficients allows a better description of the secondary frequencies. On the other hand, it not only considers the changes between contiguous segments, it also includes the deltas among non-contiguous signal segments. The following section details the proposed acoustic characterization.

3 Acoustic Characterization

In this paper, we propose a straightforward characterization of the acoustic signal. This characterization allows differentiating languages by their rhythm, but avoids the demanding representation of the vocalic and consonantal intervals. It is based on two simple ideas.

On the one hand, we represent the acoustic signal by fixed-size segments and characterize each segment using the Mel Frequency Cepstral Coefficients (MFCC). We take this representation from speech recognition. In this task, it is common to use only 12 MFCC since it has been empirically demonstrated that the use of more coefficients does not improve the accuracy [8]. However, for language identification, we suggest to employ additional coefficients in order to obtain more detail on the secondary frequencies. This suggestion is supported in the works by Cummings et al. [3] and Samouelain [5], which indirectly demonstrated that using the fundamental frequency is not sufficient for this task.

On the other hand, we consider that the Mel frequency cepstral coefficients cannot directly capture the rhythm of the speech. Therefore, we propose expressing their information by a set of more general –and time independent– features. In particular, we characterize the signals by their coefficient's variations. That is, we calculate the change of the coefficient's values between two signal segments. Different to Samouelain's proposal, we not only compute the differences between adjacent segments, but also the changes between non-contiguous fragments (two or three positions away from each other). This idea allows our characterization to represent the rhythm, since it presumably captures the changes at the syllabic level.

In order to enrich the acoustic characterization we also compute the averages of the coefficient's variations as well as their maximum and minimum values. In total, we use 192 features to represent each signal sample.

Table 3. The proposed set of features

Description	Calculation	#Features
Average value of the coefficients	$\tilde{c}_i = \frac{1}{N}\sum_{k=1}^{N} c_{ik}$	16
Maximum value of the coefficients	$\hat{c}_i = \max_{k=1}^{N}(c_{ik})$	16
Minimum value of the coefficients	$\breve{c}_i = \min_{k=1}^{N}(c_{ik})$	16
Average value of the coefficient's changes	$\tilde{\Delta}_1 c_i = \frac{1}{N-1}\sum_{k=2}^{N} c_{ik} - c_{i(k-1)}$ $\tilde{\Delta}_2 c_i = \frac{1}{N-2}\sum_{k=3}^{N} c_{ik} - c_{i(k-2)}$ $\tilde{\Delta}_3 c_i = \frac{1}{N-3}\sum_{k=4}^{N} c_{ik} - c_{i(k-3)}$	48
Maximum value of the coefficient's changes	$\hat{\Delta}_1 c_i = \max_{k=2}^{N}(c_{ik} - c_{i(k-1)})$ $\hat{\Delta}_2 c_i = \max_{k=3}^{N}(c_{ik} - c_{i(k-2)})$ $\hat{\Delta}_3 c_i = \max_{k=4}^{N}(c_{ik} - c_{i(k-3)})$	48
Minimum value of the coefficient's changes	$\breve{\Delta}_1 c_i = \min_{k=2}^{N}(c_{ik} - c_{i(k-1)})$ $\breve{\Delta}_2 c_i = \min_{k=3}^{N}(c_{ik} - c_{i(k-2)})$ $\breve{\Delta}_3 c_i = \min_{k=4}^{N}(c_{ik} - c_{i(k-3)})$	48

Table 3 describes the used features. It focuses on the description of the features related with each one of the 16 Mel frequency cepstral coefficients. In this table, C_{ik} denotes the coefficient i of the segment k, N indicates the number of considered segments, and Δ_1, Δ_2, and Δ_3 represent the coefficient's changes between fragments separated by one, two and three positions respectively.

4 Experimental Results

The motivation of our work was the identification of marginalized languages, especially, the identification of Mexican indigenous languages. However, in order to evaluate and compare our proposal with other methods we decided to carry out the experiments using the standard OGI_TS corpus [6]. Particularly, we considered nine languages from this corpus: English, German, Spanish, Japanese, Chinese Mandarin, Korean, Tamil, Vietnamese and Farsi. We excluded the French, since it was recently eliminated from the corpus.

The OGI Multilanguage Telephone Speech Corpus consists of recordings of telephone calls (8 KHz), where people spontaneously answer questions such as: describe the way to your work?, describe your house?, how is the weather in your country?, etc. For the experiments, we considered 50 different speakers for each language, and selected samples of 10 and 45 seconds per speaker. We used four different classifiers (KNN, Support Vector Machines, Naïve Bayes and C4.5) in order to be able to validate the proposed signal characterization. In addition, we used the information gain for dimensionality reduction, and the 10-fold cross-validation as evaluation scheme.

Table 4 shows the results corresponding to the samples of 45 seconds. These results were achieved using Naïve Bayes, which was indeed the best classifier in the whole experiments. From this table, it is clear that our results constantly outperformed those reported by Rouas et al. [4] (indicated in parenthesis), even though the proposed characterization method is much simpler than that of them. As explained in section 2, they used the rhythm units of the signal (e.g., the relation-ship between the vocalic and consonantal intervals) as main features, and the Gausssian Mixture Models (GMM) as classification technique.

Table 4. Accuracy percentages using samples of 45 seconds

	German	Spanish	Mandarin	Vietnamese	Japanese	Korean	Tamil	Farsi
English	**77** (59.5)	**88** (67.7)	73 (**75.0**)	**73** (67.7)	**82** (67.6)	79 (**79.4**)	**88** (77.4)	**83** (76.3)
German	-	**50** (59.4)	**75** (62.2)	**58** (65.7)	**62** (65.8)	65 (**71.4**)	**75** (69.7)	64 (**71.8**)
Spanish	-	-	78 (**80.6**)	**77** (62.1)	**72** (62.5)	72 (**75.9**)	**67** (65.4)	63 (**66.7**)
Mandarin	-	-	-	**72** (50.0)	**78** (50.6)	64 (**73.5**)	**79** (74.2)	**75** (76.3)
Vietnamese	-	-	-	-	**72** (68.6)	**71** (56.2)	68(**71.4**)	**79** (66.7)
Japanese	-	-	-	-	-	**65** (65.7)	**70**(59.4)	**76** (66.7)
Korean	-	-	-	-	-	-	**77**(62.1)	63 (75.0)
Tamil	-	-	-	-	-	-	-	**75** (69.7)

We performed the experiments using four different classifiers. In this case, our purpose was to demonstrate the pertinence of the proposed signal characterization. Mainly, we tried to prove that we could obtain similar results using different classification techniques. Figure 1 shows the average accuracy of each classifier per each language. The figure indicates that Naïve Bayes and SVM reached the best results. On the contrary, KNN and C4.5 achieved –in the majority of cases– the lowest results. However, it is noticeable that the four classifiers are relatively consistent. Therefore, we can assert about the pertinence of the characterization. That is, we confirmed that the reached results are a consequence of the characterization and not only a result of the selected classification algorithm.

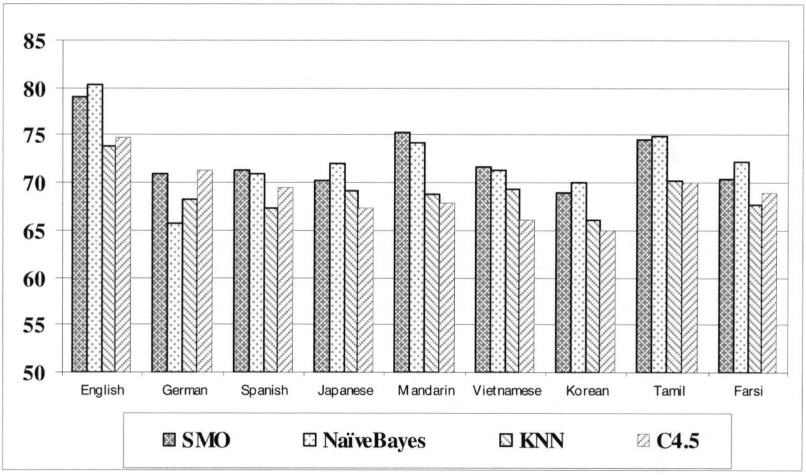

Fig. 1. Average accuracy per language using different classifiers

Table 5. Accuracy percentages using samples of 10 seconds

	German	Spanish	Mandarin	Vietnamese	Japanese	Korean	Tamil	Farsi
English	86	87	75	85	87	77	89	84
German	-	75	83	81	68	71	69	77
Spanish	-	-	79	73	69	69	52	61
Mandarin	-	-	-	83	70	61	80	74
Vietnamese	-	-	-	-	68	68	59	64
Japanese	-	-	-	-	-	69	68	61
Korean	-	-	-	-	-	-	65	74
Tamil	-	-	-	-	-	-	-	74

We performed a third experiment using samples of 10 seconds. The objective was to determine the convenience of the proposed characterization when using small samples, which are –indeed– commonly used for language identification. Table 5 shows the results obtained by the Naïve Bayes classifier. Comparing these results with those of table 4 we can observed some variations.

In order to emphasize these variations, table 6 presents the average accuracy per language. In most cases, the variations were lesser than ± 2%. However, for English and German there is a noticeable difference favoring samples of 10 seconds, while for Tamil the best results were obtained using samples of 45 seconds.

Table 6. Comparison of accuracies using samples of 45 and 10 seconds

	English	German	Spanish	Mandarin	Vietnamese	Japanese	Korean	Tamil	Farsi
45 seconds	80	66	71	72	74	71	70	75	72
10 seconds	84	76	71	70	76	73	69	70	72

Finally, we applied the proposed method for the identification of two indigenous languages of Mexico, namely, the Náhualt and the Zoque [9]. This experiment considered 20 different speakers per language, samples of 10 seconds per speaker, the naïve Bayes classifier, and a 10-cross-fold validation schema. The achieved results were very satisfactory and encouraging (see table 7). However, we believe it is necessary to perform more experiments, with bigger corpora, in order to confirm the pertinence of our method for the treatment of Mexican indigenous languages.

Table 7. Classification between Náhualt and the Zoque

	Náhuatl	Zoque	Accuracy
Náhuatl	16	4	87.5%
Zoque	1	19	

5 Conclusions

In this paper, we presented a straightforward method for spoken language identification task. This method considers an acoustic characterization specially suited for the identification of marginalized languages, where there are not sufficient elements to apply the phonothactic approach.

We evaluated the proposed signal characterization in a pairwise discrimination task among nine languages. The achieved results were comparable to others from similar methods. However, our signal characterization is much simpler. It represents the signal through the changes in the Mel frequency cepstral coefficients and takes advantage of the secondary frequencies.

We also evaluated our signal characterization using four different classification techniques. This evaluation demonstrated the pertinence of the proposed characterization.

Although current results are encouraging, it is still necessary to do more experiments in order to determine with greater precision the scope of the characterization as well as to understand the accuracy variations caused by the sample sizes.

Acknowledgements

This work was done under partial support of CONACYT (scholarship 184660, and project Grants 43990 and U39957-Y) and SNI-Mexico.

References

1. D. Casseiro, and I. Troncoso (1998). *Language Identification Using Minimum Linguistic Information.* 10th Portuguese on Pattern Recognition RECPAD'98. Lisbon, Portugal, 1998.
2. O. Andersen, and P. Dalsgaard (1997). *Language Identification based on Cross-Language Acoustic models and Optimized Information Combination.* EUROSPEECH-97. Rhodes, Greece, 1997.
3. F. Cummins, F. Gers, and J. Schmidhuber (1999). *Language Identification from Prosody without explicit Features.* EUROSPEECH'99. Budapest, Hungary, 1999.
4. J.-L. Rouas, J. Farinas, F. Pellegrino and R. André-Obrecht (2003). *Modeling prosody for language identification on read and spontaneous speech.* IEEE ICASSP-2003, Hong Kong, 2003.
5. A. Samouelian (1996). Automatic *Language Identification using Inductive Inference.* 4th International Conference on Spoken Language Processing ICSLP-96. Philadelphia, USA, 1996.
6. Y. K. Muthusamy, R. Cole, B. Oshika (1992). *The OGI multi-language telephone speech corpus.* International Conference on Spoken Language Processing. Alberta, Canada, 1992.
7. F. Ramus, M. Nespor, J. Mehler. (1999). Correlates of linguistic rhythm in the speech signal. *Cognition* 73(3), pp. 265-293. Elsevier, 1999.
8. X. Huang, A. Acero, H-W. Hon (2001). *Spoken Language Processing. A Guide to Theory, Algorithm ans System Development.* Prentice Hall, 2001.
9. H. Johnson and J. Amith (2005). http://www.ailla.org: *Archive of the Indigenous Languages of Latin America.* Access=public. Texas University. USA.

A Text Mining Approach for Definition Question Answering

Claudia Denicia-Carral, Manuel Montes-y-Gómez,
Luis Villaseñor-Pineda, and René García Hernández

Language Technologies Group, Computer Science Department,
National Institute of Astrophysics, Optics and Electronics (INAOE), Mexico
{cdenicia, mmontesg, villasen, renearnulfo}@inaoep.mx

Abstract. This paper describes a method for definition question answering based on the use of surface text patterns. The method is specially suited to answer questions about person's positions and acronym's descriptions. It considers two main steps. First, it applies a sequence-mining algorithm to discover a set of definition-related text patterns from the Web. Then, using these patterns, it extracts a collection of concept-description pairs from a target document database, and applies the sequence-mining algorithm to determine the most adequate answer to a given question. Experimental results on the Spanish CLEF 2005 data set indicate that this method can be a practical solution for answering this kind of definition questions, reaching a precision as high as 84%.

1 Introduction

Nowadays, thanks to the Internet explosion, there is an enormous volume of available data. This data may satisfy almost every information need, but without the appropriate search facilities, it is practically useless. This situation motivated the emergence of new approaches for information retrieval such as question answering.

A question answering (QA) system is an information retrieval application whose aim is to provide inexperienced users with a flexible access to information, allowing them writing a query in natural language and obtaining not a set of documents that contain the answer, but the concise answer itself [11]. At present, most QA systems focus on treating short-answer questions such as factoid, definition and temporal. This paper focuses on answering definition questions as delimited in the CLEF[1]. These questions, in contrast to those of TREC[2], exclusively ask for the position of a person, e.g., Who is George Bush?, and for the description of an acronym, e.g., What is UNICEF?.

There are several approaches to extract answers from free text for this kind of questions. Most of them take advantage of some stylistic conventions frequently used by writers to introduce new concepts. These conventions include some typographic elements that can be expressed by a set of lexical patterns. In the initial attempts, these patterns were manually created [5, 9]. However, because they are difficult to

[1] Cross-Language Evaluation Forum (www.clef-campaign.org).
[2] Text REtrieval Conference (trec.nist.gov/).

T. Salakoski et al. (Eds.): FinTAL 2006, LNAI 4139, pp. 76 – 86, 2006.

extract and domain dependent, current approaches tend to construct them automatically [2, 8].

In this paper, we explore a text mining approach for answering this kind of definition questions. In particular, we use a sequence-mining algorithm [1] to discover definition patterns from the Web as well as to identify the best candidate answer to a given question from a set of matched concept-description pairs. The double use of the sequence-mining algorithm gives our method its power. It allows the discovery of surface definition patterns for any kind of text or domain, and enables taking advantage on the redundancy of the target document collection to determine with finer precision the answers to the questions.

In order to evaluate this method, we consider the definition questions from the Spanish CLEF 2005 evaluation exercise. Our results demonstrate that our approximation can be effectively used to answer definition questions from free-text documents.

The rest of the paper is organized as follows. Section 2 discuses some related work. Section 3 presents the general scheme of the method. Section 4 describes their main components. Section 5 introduces the task of sequence mining and explains our approach to answer ranking. Section 6 shows the experimental results, and finally, section 7 presents our conclusions and future work.

2 Related Work

There are several approaches for answering definition questions. Most of them use lexical patterns to extract the answer to a given question from a target document collection. Depending on the complexity of the requested definition, it is the complexity of the useful patterns. For the simplest case, i.e., the introduction of a new referent in the discourse, the stylistic conventions used by authors are clear and stable. In consequence, the practical lexical patterns are simple and precise. Under this assumption, the questions like "What is X?" and "Who is Y?" are resolved.

The existing approaches for answering definition questions diverge in the way they determine the definition patterns and in the way they use them. There are some works that applies patterns that were manually constructed [5, 9, 3], and other works that automatically construct the patterns from a set of usage examples [2, 8]. Our method considers the automatic construction of the patterns. It consists of two main steps:

In the first step, the method applies a mining algorithm in order to discover a set of definition-related text patterns from the Web. These lexical patterns allow associating persons with their positions, and acronyms with their descriptions. This step is similar to other previous approaches (especially to [8]). Nevertheless, our method differs from them in that it considers all discovered patterns, i.e., it does not evaluate and select the mined patterns. Therefore, the main difference in this first step is that while others focus on selecting a small number of very precise patterns, we concentrate on discovering the major number of mutually exclusive patterns.

In the second step, the method applies the patterns over a target document collection in order to answer the specified questions. The way we use the patterns to answer definition questions is quite novel. Previous works [8, 5, 9] apply the patterns over a set of "relevant" passages, and trust that the best (high-precision) patterns will allow identifying the answer. In contrast, our method applies all discovered patterns to the entire target document collection and constructs a “general catalog”. Then, when a question arrives, it mines the definition catalog in order to determine the best answer for the given question. In this way, the answer extraction does not depend on a passage retrieval system and takes advantage on the redundancy of the entire collection.

3 Method at a Glance

Figure 1 shows the general scheme of our method. It consists of two main modules; one focuses on the discovery of definition patterns and the other one on the answer extraction.

The module for pattern discovery uses a small set of concept-description pairs to collect from the Web an extended set of definition instances. Then, it applies a text mining method on the collected instances to discover a set of definition surface patterns.

The module for answer extraction applies the discovered patterns over a target document collection in order to create a definition catalog consisting of a set of potential concept-description pairs. Later, given a question, it extracts from the catalog the set of associated descriptions to the requested concept. Finally, it mines the selected descriptions to find the more adequate answer to the given question.

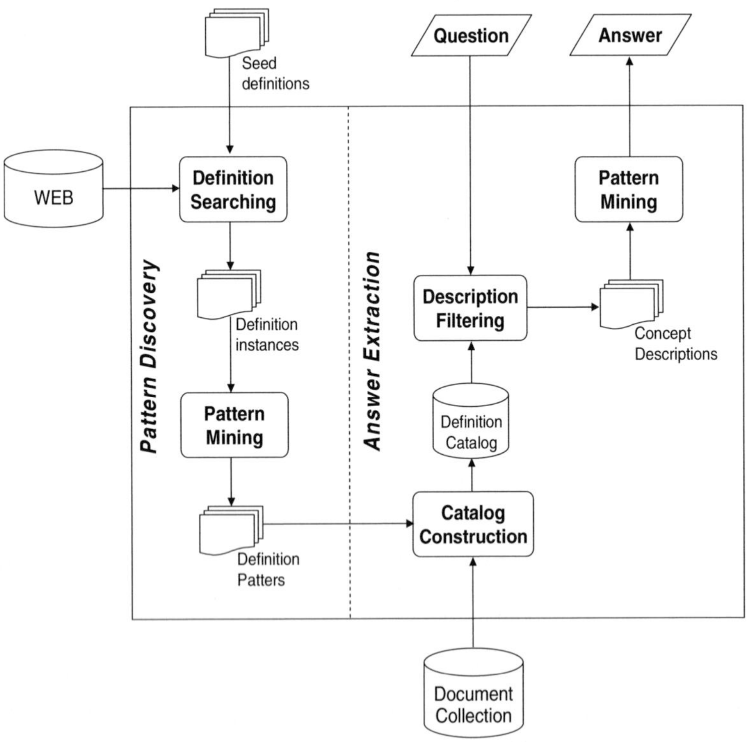

Fig. 1. General diagram of the method

It is important to notice that the process of pattern discovery is done offline, while the answer extraction, except for the construction of the definition catalog, is done online. It is also important to mention that different to traditional QA approaches, the proposed method does not consider any module for document or passage retrieval. The following section describes in detail these two modules.

4 Answering Definition Questions

4.1 Pattern Discovery

As we mentioned, there are certain stylistic conventions frequently used by authors to introduce new concepts in a text. Several QA approaches exploit these conventions by means of a set of lexical patterns. Unfortunately, there are so many ways in which concepts are described in natural language that it is difficult to come up with a complete set of linguistics patterns to solve the problem. In addition, these patterns depend on the text domain, writing style and language.

In order to solve these difficulties we use a very general method for pattern discovery [8]. The method captures the definition conventions through their repetition. It considers two main subtasks:

Definition searching. This task is triggered by a small set of empirically defined concept-description pairs. The pairs are used to retrieve a number of usage examples from the Web[3]. Each usage example represents a definition instance. To be relevant, a definition instance must contain the concept and its description in one single phrase.

Pattern mining. It is divided in three main steps: data preparation, data mining and pattern filtering.

The purpose of the data preparation phase is to normalize the input data. In this case, it transforms all definition instances into the same format, using special tags for the concepts and their descriptions.

In the data mining phase, a sequence mining algorithm (refer to section 5.1) is used to obtain all maximal frequent sequences –of words and punctuation marks– from the set of definition instances. The sequences express lexicographic patterns highly related to concept definitions.

Finally, the pattern-filtering phase allows choosing the more discriminative patterns. It selects the patterns satisfying the following general regular expressions:

<left-frontier-string> DESCRIPTION <center-string> CONCEPT < right-frontier-string>

<left-frontier-string> CONCEPT <center-string>DESCRIPTION < right-frontier-string>

Figure 2 illustrates the information treatment through the pattern discovery process. The idea is to obtain several surface definition patterns starting up with a small set of concept-description example pairs. First, using a small set of concept-description seeds, for instance, "*Wolfgang Clement – German Federal Minister of Economics and Labor*" and "*Vicente Fox – President of Mexico*", we obtained a set of definition instances. One example of these instances is "*…meeting between the Cuban leader and the president of Mexico, Vicente Fox.*". Then, the instances were normalized, and finally a sequence-mining algorithm was used to obtain lexicographic

[3] At present, we are using Google for searching the Web.

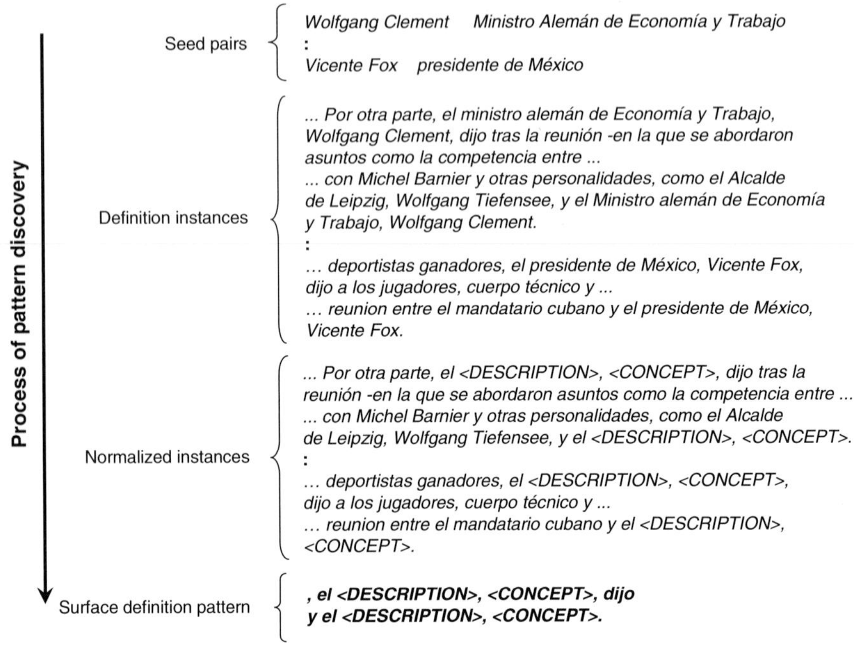

Fig. 2. Data flow in the pattern discovery process

patterns highly related to concept definitions. The figure shows two obtained patterns: "*, the <DESCRIPTION>, <CONCEPT>, says*" and "*and the <DESCRIPTION>, <CONCEPT>.*". It is important to notice that the patterns not only include words as frontier elements but also punctuation marks.

4.2 Answer Extraction

This second module handles the extraction of the answer for a given definition question. It is also based on a text mining approach. Its purpose is to find the more adequate description for a requested concept from an automatically constructed definition catalog.

Because the definition patterns guide the construction of the definition catalog, it contains a huge diversity of information, including incomplete and incorrect descriptions for many concepts. However, it is expected that the correct information will be more abundant than the incorrect one. This expectation supports the idea of using a text mining technique to distinguish between the adequate and the improbable answers to a given question.

This module considers the following steps:

Catalog construction. In this phase, the definition patterns discovered in the previous stage (i.e., in the pattern discovery module) are applied over the target document collection. The result is a set of matched segments that presumably contain a concept and its description. The definition catalog is created gathering all matched segments.

Description filtering. Given a specific question, this procedure extracts from the definition catalog all descriptions corresponding to the requested concept. As we mentioned, these "presumable" descriptions may include incomplete and incorrect information. However, it is expected that many of them will contain, maybe as a substring, the required answer.

Answer mining. This process aims to detect a single answer to the given question from the set of extracted descriptions. It is divided in three main phases: data preparation, data mining and answer ranking.

The data preparation phase focuses on homogenizing the descriptions related to the requested concept. The main action is to convert these descriptions to a lower case format.

In the data mining phase, a sequence mining algorithm (refer to section 5.1) is used to obtain all maximal frequent word sequences from the set of descriptions. Each sequence indicates a candidate answer to the given question.

Then, in the answer raking phase, each candidate answer is evaluated according to the frequency of occurrence of its subsequences. The idea is that a candidate answer assembled from frequent subsequences has more probability of being the correct answer than one formed by rare ones. Therefore, the sequence with the greatest ranking score is selected as the correct answer. The section 5.2 introduces the ranking score.

Figure 3 shows the process of answer extraction for the question "*Who is Diego Armando Maradona?*". First, we obtained all descriptions associated with the requested concept. It is clear that there are erroneous or incomplete descriptions (e.g. "*Argentina soccer team*"). However, most of them contain a partially satisfactory explanation of the concept. Actually, we detected correct descriptions such as "*captain of the Argentine soccer team*" and "*Argentine star*". Then, a mining process allowed detecting a set of maximal frequent sequences. Each sequence was considered a candidate answer. In this case, we detected three sequences: "*argentine*", "*captain of the Argentine soccer team*" and "*supposed overuse of Ephedrine by the star of the Argentine team*". Finally, the candidate answers were ranked based on the frequency of occurrence of its subsequences in the whole description set. In this way, we took advantage of the incomplete descriptions of the concept. The selected answer was "*captain of the Argentine national football soccer team*", since it was conformed from frequent subsequences such as "*captain of the*", "*soccer team*" and "*Argentine*".

It is important to clarify that a question may have several correct answers. In accordance with the CLEF, an answer is correct if there is a passage that supports it. Therefore, for the question at hand there are other correct answers such as "*ex capitán de la selección argentina de futbol*" and "*astro argentino*".

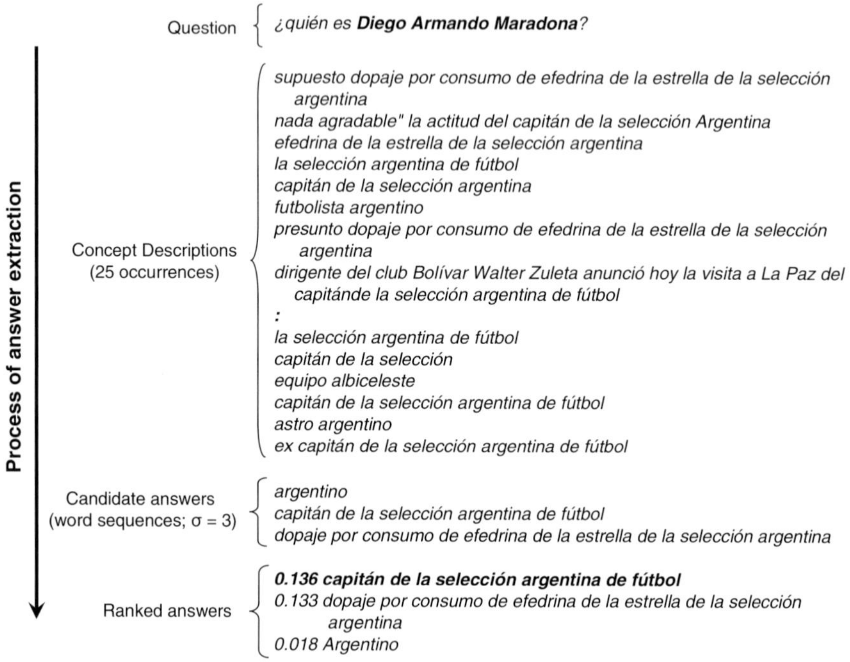

Fig. 3. Data flow in the answer extraction process

5 Text Mining Techniques

5.1 Mining Maximal Frequent Word Sequences

Assume that D is a set of texts (a text may represent a complete document or even just a single sentence), and each text consists of a sequence of words. Then, we have the following definitions [1].

Definition 1. A sequence $p = a_1 \ldots a_k$ is a *subsequence* of a sequence q if all the items a_i, $1 \leq i \leq k$, occur in q and they occur in the same order as in p. If a sequence p is a subsequence of a sequence q, we also say that p occurs in q.

Definition 2. A sequence p is *frequent* in D if p is a subsequence of at least σ texts of D, where σ is a given frequency threshold.

Definition 3. A sequence p is a *maximal frequent sequence* in D if there does not exist any sequence p' in D such that p is a subsequence of p' and p' is frequent in D.

Once introduced the maximal frequent word sequences, the problem of mining maximal frequent word sequences can formally state as follows: Given a text collection D and an arbitrary integer value σ such that $1 \leq \sigma \leq |D|$, enumerate all maximal frequent word sequences in D.

The implementation of a method for sequence mining is not a trivial task because of its computational complexity. The algorithm used in our experiments is described in [4].

5.2 Ranking Score

This measure aims to establish the better answer for a given definition question. Given a set of candidate answers (the maximal frequent sequences obtained from the set of concept descriptions), this measure selects the final unique answer taking into consideration the frequency of occurrence of its subsequences.

The ranking score R for a word sequence indicates its compensated frequency. It is calculated as follows:

$$R_{p(n)} = \frac{1}{n} \sum_{i=1}^{n} \sum_{j=1}^{n-i+1} \frac{f_{p_j(i)}}{\sum_{\forall q \in S_i} f_{q(i)}} \quad (1)$$

In this formula, we have introduced the following notation for the sake of simplicity. S_i indicates the set of sequences of size i, $q(i)$ represents the sequence q of size i, $p_j(i)$ is the j-th subsequence of size i included in the sequence $p(n)$, $f_{q(i)}$ specifies the frequency of occurrence of the sequence q in the set of concept descriptions, and finally $R_{p(n)}$ indicates the compensated frequency of the sequence p.

The idea behind this ranking score is that a candidate answer assembled from frequent subsequences has more probability of being the correct answer than one formed by rare substrings. Evidently, the frequency of occurrence of the stopwords is not considered into the calculation of the ranking score.

6 Experimental Results

In order to evaluate the proposed method, we considered the task of definition question answering. In particular, we contemplated questions asking about the position of a person as well as questions demanding the description of an acronym.

Table 1 shows some numbers on the process of pattern discovery. It is important to notice that using only 20 definition seed pairs we discovered 78 definition patterns related to positions and 122 related to acronyms. Some of these patterns are shown in table 2.

The quality of the discovered patterns is very diverse. Some are too specific and precise but not so applicable. Some others are too general, but guarantee a high coverage. The combined application of all of them represents a good compromise between precision and coverage, and produces the data redundancy required by the process of answer extraction.

Table 1. Statistics on the process of pattern discovery

Question Type	Seed Definitions	Collected Snippets	Maximal Frequent Sequences	Surface Definition Patterns
Positions	10	6523	875	78
Acronym	10	10526	1504	122

Table 2. Examples of definition patterns

Position related patterns	Acronym related patterns
El <DESCRIPTION>, <CONCEPT>, ha	*del <DESCRIPTION> (<CONCEPT>).*
del <DESCRIPTION>, <CONCEPT>.	*que la <DESCRIPTION> (<CONCEPT>)*
El ex <DESCRIPTION>, <CONCEPT>,	*de la <DESCRIPTION> (<CONCEPT>) en*
por el <DESCRIPTION>, <CONCEPT>.	*del <DESCRIPTION> (<CONCEPT>) y*
El <DESCRIPTION>, <CONCEPT>, se	*en el <DESCRIPTION> (<CONCEPT>)*

The evaluation of the answer extraction process was based on the Spanish CLEF05 data set. This set includes a collection of 454,045 documents, and a set of 50 definition questions related to person's positions and acronym's descriptions.

Table 3 shows some data on the process of answer extraction. It shows that initially we extracted quite a lot of "presumable" related descriptions per question. The purpose is to catch an answer for all questions, and to capture most of their occurrences. Then, using a text-mining technique, we detected just a few high-precision candidate answers (sequences) per question. It is important to point out that the number of candidate answers is smaller for the questions about acronyms than for those about person's positions. We consider this situation happened because positions are regularly expressed in several ways, while acronyms tend to have only one meaning.

Table 3. Statistics on the process of answer extraction

Question Type	Average Descriptions per Question	Average Candidate Answers per Question
Positions	633	5.04
Acronym	1352.96	1.67

Table 4 presents the overall precision results for the question answering evaluation exercise. The second column indicates the precision when the answers were extracted using only the sequence mining algorithm, i.e., when answers were defined as the most frequent sequences in the set of descriptions related to the requested concept. On the other hand, the last column shows the precision rates achieved when the answers were selected using the proposed ranking score.

Table 4. Overall results on definition question answering

	Answer Selection	
Question Type	Most Frequent Sequence	Highest Ranking Score
Positions	64%	80%
Acronym	80%	88%
Total	**72%**	**84%**

The results demonstrated that our method could be a practical solution to answer this kind of definition questions, reaching a precision as high as 84%. We consider that these results are very significant, since the average precision rate for definition questions on the CLEF 2005 edition was 48%, being 80% the best result and 0% de worst [10]. Indeed, the best result at CLEF 2005 for definition questions was achieved by other method proposed by our Lab. The main difference between these methods is that while the old one uses manually constructed patterns, the new approach applies automatically discovered patterns.

It is important to mention that our method could not determine the correct answer for all questions. This situation was mainly caused by the lack of information for the requested concepts in the definition catalog. In particular, the definition catalog does not contain any information related to six questions. For instance, we could not find any description for the organization "*Medicos sin Fronteras*" ("*Doctors Without Borders*"). This was because the discovered definition patterns only allow extracting descriptions related to acronyms but not locating descriptions related to complete organization names. In order to reduce this problem it is necessary to have more definition patterns that consider several different ways of describing a concept.

Finally, it is also important to mention that a major weakness of the proposed method is that it greatly depends on the redundancy of the target collection, and especially, on the redundancy of the searched answer. Therefore, if there is just one single occurrence of the searched answer in the whole collection, then our method will not have sufficient evidence to resolve the given question.

7 Conclusions and Future Work

In this paper, we presented a method for answering definition questions. This method considers two main tasks: the discovery of definition patterns from the Web, and the extraction of the most adequate answer for a given question. The use of a text mining technique in both tasks gives our method its power. It allows the discovery of surface definition patterns for any kind of text or domain, and enables taking advantage on the redundancy of the target document collection to determine with finer precision the answer to a question.

The method was evaluated on the definition questions from the Spanish CLEF 2005 data set. These questions ask about person's positions and acronym's descriptions. The obtained results are highly significant since they are superior to those reported in the CLEF 2005 working notes [10].

In addition, the results demonstrated that it is possible to answer this kind of definition questions without using any kind of linguistic resource or knowledge. Even more, they also evidenced that a non-standard QA approach, which does not contemplate an IR phase, can be a good scheme for answering dcfinitions questions.

As future work, we plan to:

- Consider more types of definition questions. In particular we are interested in using this approach to answer questions about general things, for instance questions like "what is an aspirin?". In order to do that it will be necessary to extend the proposed approach to consider patterns beyond the lexical level.

- Apply the method on different languages. Since our method does not use any sophisticated tool for language analysis, we believe that it could be easily adapted to other languages. This way, we plan to work with other languages considered by the CLEF, such as Italian, French and Portuguese.
- Use the method to discover different kind of patterns. For instance, patterns related to different semantic relations (e.g. synonymy, hyperonymy, etc.).

Acknowledgements

This work was done under partial support of CONACYT (Project Grants 43990 and U39957-Y) and SNI-Mexico. We also thanks to the CLEF for the resources provided.

References

1. Ahonen-Myka H. (2002). Discovery of Frequent Word Sequences in Text Source. Proceedings of the ESF Exploratory Workshop on Pattern Detection and Discovery. London, UK, 2002.
2. Cui H., Kan M., and Chua T. (2004). Unsupervised Learning of Soft Patterns for Generating Definitions from Online News. Proceedings International WWW Conference. New York, USA, 2004.
3. Fleischman M., Hovy E. and Echihabi A. (2003). Offline Strategies for Online Question Answering: Answering Question Before they are Asked. Proceedings of the ACL-2003, Sapporo, Japan, 2003.
4. García-Hernández, R., Martínez-Trinidad F., and Carrasco-Ochoa A. (2006). A New Algorithm for Fast Discovery of Maximal Sequential Patterns in a Document Collection. International Conference on Computational Linguistics and text Processing, CICLing-2006. Mexico City, Mexico, 2006.
5. Hildebrandt W., Katz B., and Lin J. (2004). Answering Definition Questions Using Multiple Knowledge Sources. Proceedings of Human Language Technology Conference. Boston, USA, 2004.
6. Montes-y-Gómez M., Villaseñor-Pineda L., Pérez-Coutiño M., Gómez-Soriano J. M., Sanchis-Arnal E. and Rosso, P. (2003). INAOE-UPV Joint Participation in CLEF 2005: Experiments in Monolingual Question Answering. Working Notes of CLEF 2005. Vienna, Austria, 2005.
7. Pantel P., Ravichandran D. and Hovy E. (2004). Towards Terascale Knowledge Acquisition. Proceedings of the COLING 2004 Conference. Geneva, Switzerland, 2004.
8. Ravichandran D., and Hovy E. (2002). Learning Surface Text Patterns for a Question Answering System. Proceedings of the ACL-2002 Conference. Philadelphia, USA, 2002.
9. Soubbotin M. M., and Soubbotin S. M. (2001). Patterns of Potential Answer Expressions as Clues to the Right Answer. Proceedings of the TREC-10 Conference. Gaithersburg, 2001.
10. Vallin A., Giampiccolo D., Aunimo L., Ayache C., Osenova P., Peñas A., de Rijke M., Sacaleanu B., Santos D., and Sutcliffe R. (2005). Overview of the CLEF 2005 Multilingual Question Answering Track. Working Notes of the CLEF 2005. Vienna, Austria, 2005.
11. Vicedo J. L., Rodríguez H., Peñas A., and Massot M. (2003). Los sistemas de Búsqueda de Respuestas desde una perspectiva actual. Revista de la Sociedad Española para el Procesamiento del Lenguaje Natural. Num.31, 2003.

Accommodating Multiword Expressions in an Arabic LFG Grammar

Mohammed A. Attia

School of Informatics, The University of Manchester, UK
mohammed.attia@postgrad.manchester.ac.uk

Abstract. Multiword expressions (MWEs) vary in syntactic category, structure, the degree of semantic opaqueness, the ability of one or more constituents to undergo inflection and processes such as passivization, and the possibility of having intervening elements. Therefore, there is no straight-forward way of dealing with them. This paper shows how MWEs can be dealt with at different levels of analysis starting with tokenization, and going through the stages of morphological analysis and syntactic parsing.

1 Introduction

There was a tendency to ignore MWEs in linguistic analysis due to their complexity and idiosyncrasy. However, it is now recognized that MWEs have a high frequency in day-to-day interactions (Venkatapathy, 2004), that they account for 41% of the entries in WordNet 1.7 (Fellbaum, 1998, Sag et al., 2001), that phrasal verbs account for "about one third of the English verb vocabulary" (Li et al., 2003), and that technical domains rely heavily on them. This makes it imperative to handle MWEs if we want to make large-scale, linguistically-motivated, and precise processing of the language.

MWEs constitute serious pitfalls for machine translation systems and human translators as well (Volk, 1998). When they are translated compositionally, they give textbook examples of highly intolerable, blind and literal translation. It is also underestimation to the problem to assume that it should be handled during higher phases of processing such as transfer. In fact MWEs require deep analysis that starts as early as the tokenization, and goes through morphological analysis and into the syntactic rules. The focus of this paper is to explain how MWEs can be accommodated in each step in the preprocessing and the processing stages. The advantages of handling MWEs in the pre-processing stage are avoidance of needless analysis of idiosyncratic structures, reduction of parsing ambiguity, and reduction of parse time (Brun, 1998). This is why there are growing calls to construct MWE dictionaries (Guenthner and Blanco, 2004), lexicons (Calzolari et al., 2002), and phrasets (Bentivogli and Pianta, 2003).

This paper shows how several devices can be applied to handle MWEs properly at several stages of processing. All the solutions are applied to Arabic, yet, most of the solutions are general and are applicable to other languages as well. The software used for writing grammar rules is XLE (Xerox Linguistic Environment) (Butt et al., 1999,

T. Salakoski et al. (Eds.): FinTAL 2006, LNAI 4139, pp. 87 – 98, 2006.

Dipper, 2003). It is a platform created by Palo Alto Research Center (PARC) for developing large-scale grammars using LFG (Lexical Functional Grammar) notations. Morphological transducers, tokenizers and MWE transducers are all developed using Finite State Technology (Beesley and Karttunen, 2003).

2 Definition

MWEs encompass a wide range of linguistically related phenomena that share the criterion of being composed of two words or more, whether adjacent or separate. MWEs have been defined as "idiosyncratic interpretations that cross word boundaries (or spaces)" (Sag et al., 2001). In an MWE, the structure and the semantics of the expression are dependant on the phrase as a whole, and not on its individual components (Venkatapathy, 2004). MWEs cover expressions that are traditionally classified as idioms (e.g. *down the drain*), prepositional verbs (e.g. *rely on*), verbs with particles (e.g. *give up*), compound nouns (e.g. *book cover*) and collocations (e.g. *do a favour*).

Although there is no clear-cut definition with which we can decide what expressions can be considered MWEs, there is a set of criteria (adapted from (Baldwin, 2004, Calzolari et al., 2002, Guenthner and Blanco, 2004)) when one or more of which applies the expression can safely be considered as an MWE.

1. Lexogrammatical fixedness. The expression has come to a rigid or frozen state. This fixedness can be identified through a number of tests. Components of the expression must be immune to the following operations:
   - Substitutability. The word *many* in (1.a) can be substituted with its synonym *several*, while in (1.b) it cannot.
     (1.a) *many books -> several books* (1.b) *many thanks -> * several thanks*
   - Deletion. The adjective in (2.a) can be deleted, while in (2.b) it cannot.
     (2.a) *black sheep -> the sheep* (2.b) *black hole -> * the hole*
   - Category transformation. The adjective in (3.a) can be changed to noun, while in (3.b) it cannot.
     (3.a) *black sheep -> the blackness of the sheep*
     (3.b) *black hole -> * the blackness of the hole*
   - Permutation. A noun-noun compound can usually be expressed by a noun-preposition-noun as in (4.a), but not in MWEs as in (4.b) and (4.c).
     (4.a) *the hospital staff -> the staff of the hospital*
     (4.b) *life guard -> * the guard of life* (4.c) *kiss of life -> * life kiss*
2. Semantic non-compositionality. The meaning of the expression is not derived from the component parts, such as *kick the bucket* which means *die*.
3. Syntactic irregularity. The expression exhibits a structure that is inexplicable by regular grammatical rules, such as *long time, no see* and *by and large*.
4. Single-word paraphrasability. The expression can be paraphrased by a single word, such as *give up* which means *abandon*.
5. Translatability into a single word or into a non-compositional expression. Expressions can be considered as "terms when the corresponding … translation is a unit, or when their translation differs from a word to word translation" (Brun, 1998). In various projects a corpus of translated texts is used to judge or detect

MWEs (Butt et al., 1999, Nerima et al., 2003, Smadja et al., 1996). Sometimes a unilingual analysis may be confused about whether an expression is a regular combination of words or an MWE. Translation usually helps to show expressions in perspective.

(5) *looking glass* = مرآة *[mir'aah]* (Arabic)

3 Classification of Multiword Expressions

In order for an expression to be classified as an MWE, it must show a degree of semantic non-compositionality and/or a degree of morpho-syntactic inflexibility. MWEs are classified with regard to their semantic compositionality into lexicalized and institu-tionalized expressions. Moreover, they are classified with regard to their flexibility into fixed, semi-fixed and syntactically flexible expressions (adapted from (Sag et al., 2001)).

3.1 Compositional vs. Non-compositional MWEs

Semantic compositionality, sometimes termed *decomposability*, is "a means of describing how the overall sense of a given idiom is related to its parts" (Sag et al., 2001). An illustrative example of non-compositionality is the expression *kick the bucket*, where the meaning "die" has no relation to any word in the expression. An example of compositional expressions is the compound noun *book cover*, where the meaning is directly related to the component parts. Unfortunately, the assignment of a plus/minus feature of compositionality to an expression is sometimes very elusive. Most of the time "one cannot really make a binary distinction between compositional and non-compositional MWEs" (Venkatapathy, 2004). They occupy a continuum in a large scale. At one end of the scale there are those expressions that are highly opaque and non-compositional, where the meaning is not traceable to any of the component parts, such as *kick the bucket*. In the middle of the scale there are those where one or more words are used in an idiosyncratic sense, or use "semantics unavailable outside the MWE" (Baldwin et al., 2003), such as *spill the beans*, which means "to disclose a secret". At the other end of the scale there are those which are highly compositional, such as *book cover*, *traffic light*, *health crisis* and *party meeting*.

Non-compositional expressions, or, more accurately, expressions that show any degree of non-compositionality, are termed *lexicalized* and are automatically eligible to be considered as MWEs. However, in order for compositional expressions to be included in an MWE lexicon, they need to be conventionalized or *institutionalized*. This means that these expressions have come to such a frequent use that they block the use of other synonyms and near synonyms (Nerima et al., 2003). When words co-occur in a statistically meaningful way like this they are called *collocations*. This way, expressions such as *book cover* and *traffic light* can be safely added to an MWE lexicon, while *health crisis* and *party meeting* cannot.

3.2 Flexible vs. Inflexible MWEs

With regard to syntactic and morphological flexibility, MWEs are classified into three types: fixed, semi-fixed and syntactically flexible expressions (Baldwin, 2004, Oflazer et al., 2004, Sag et al., 2001).

3.2.1 Fixed Expressions

These expressions are lexically, syntactically and morphologically rigid. An expression of this type is considered as a word with spaces (a single word that happens to contain spaces), such as *San Francisco* and *in a nutshell.* Some expressions are frozen at the level of the sentence, sometimes termed "frozen texts" (Guenthner and Blanco, 2004). These include proverbs such as *Buy cheap, buy twice*, and pragmatically fixed expressions such as *Good morning*.

3.2.2 Semi-fixed Expressions

These expressions can undergo morphological and lexical variations, but still the components of the expression are adjacent. They cannot be reordered or separated by external elements. The variations that can affect semi-fixed expressions are of two types:

1. Morphological variations that express person, number, tense, gender, etc., such as *traffic light/lights* and *kick/kicks/kicked the bucket.*
2. Lexical variations. This is the case when a position in the expression is filled by a choice from the set of reflexive pronouns (e.g. *prostrate himself/herself*), or when one word can be replaced by another (e.g. *to sweep something under the carpet/rug*).

3.2.3 Syntactically Flexible Expressions

These are the expressions that can either undergo reordering, such as passivization (e.g. *the cat was let out of the bag*), or allow external elements to intervene between the components (e.g. *slow the car down*). Here the adjacency of the MWE is disrupted.

4 Handling MWEs

This section shows how an MWE transducer is built to complement the morphological transducer, and how the MWE transducer interacts with other processing and preprocessing components. It also shows how the grammar is responsible for detecting and interpreting syntactically flexible expressions.

4.1 Building the MWE Transducer

A specialized two-sided transducer is build for MWEs using a finite state regular expression (Beesley and Karttunen, 2003) to provide correct analysis on the lexical side (upper side) and correct generation on the surface side (lower side). This transducer covers two types of MWEs: fixed and semi-fixed expressions, leaving syntactically-flexible expressions to be handled by the grammar. This entails that the

MWE transducer will not handle verbs at all (in the case of Arabic), and will not handle compound nouns that allow external elements to intervene. In order for the transducer to account for the morphological flexibility of some components, it consults the core morphological transducer (Attia, 2005) to obtain all available forms of certain words. This is how the MWE is enabled to search through the core morphological transducer. First the morphological transducer is loaded and put in a defined variable:

(6) load ArabicTransducer.fst
define AllWords

For the word وزير (wazir [minister]), for instance, the transducer has the following upper and lower structures.

(7) +noun [وزير]+masc+sg
وزير

In order to capture all different forms of the word (number and gender variations) we compose the rule in (11) above the finite state network (or transducer).

(8) $[?* "[" {وزير} "]" ?*] .o. AllWords

The sign "$", in finite state notations, means only paths that contain the specified string, and "?*" is a regular expression that means any string of any length. This gives us all surface forms that contain the wanted stem.

Arabic Multiword Nouns

Fixed compound nouns are entered in the lexicon as a list of words with spaces. Example (9) shows how the compound noun حفظ الأمن (hifz al-amn [peace keeping]) is coded in a finite state regular expression.

(9) ["+noun" "+masc" "+def"]:{حفظ} sp {الأمن}

The string "sp" here indicates a separator or space between the two words, so that each word can be identified in case there is need to access it. Compound proper names, including names of persons, places and organizations, are treated in the same way.

Semi-fixed compound nouns that undergo limited morphological/lexical variations are also entered in the lexicon with the variations explicitly stated. Example (10) shows the expression نزع سلاح (naz' silah [lit. removing a weapon: disarming]) which can have a definite variant.

(10) ["+noun" "+masc"]:{نزع} sp ("+def":{ال}) {سلاح}

Example (11) illustrates lexical variation. The expression مدعى عليه (mudda'a 'alaih [lit. the charged against him: defendant]) can choose from a fixed set of third person pronouns to indicate the number and gender of the noun.

(11)["+noun"]:0 ("+def":{ال}) {مدعى} sp {علي} ["+sg" "+masc":ه
|"+sg" "+fem":{ها}| "+dual":{هما} | "+pl" "+masc":{هم} | "+pl" "+fem":{هن}]

As for Semi-fixed compound nouns that undergo full morphological variations, a morphological transducer is consulted to obtain all possible variations.

First we need to explain how Arabic compound nouns are formed and what morphological variations they may have. They are generally formed according to the re-write rule in (12).

(12) NP[_Compound] -> [N N* A*] & ~N

This means that a compound noun can be formed by a noun optionally followed by one or more nouns, optionally followed by one or more adjectives. The condition "&~N" is to disallow the possibility of a compound noun being composed of a single noun. In an N_N construction, the first noun is inflected for number and gender, while the second is inflected for definiteness. When the compound noun is indefinite there is no article attached anywhere, but when it is definite, the definite article ال (al [the]) is attached only to the last noun in the structure. The compound وزير الخارجية (wazir al-kharijiyah [foreign minister]) is formatted as in (13).

(13) $[?* "[" {وزير} "]" ?*] .o. AllWords sp ("+def":{ال}) {خارجية}

In an N_A structure the noun and adjective are both inflected for number and gender and can take the definite article. The regular expression in (14) shows the format of the expression سيارة مفخخة (saiyarah mufakhakhah [lit. trapping car: car bomb]).

(14) $[?* "[" {سيارة} "]" ?*] .o. AllWords sp $[?* "[" {مفخخ} "]" ?*] .o. AllWords

This regular expression, however, is prone to overgenerate allowing for a masculine adjective to modify a feminine noun in contradiction to agreement rules. This is why paths need to be filtered by a set of combinatorial rules (or local grammars). The rules in (15) discard from the network paths that contain conflicting features:

(15) ~$["+dual" <> ["+sg" | "+pl"] /?*] .o. ~$["+fem" <> "+masc" /?*]

The notation "~$" means "does not contain," "<>" means "order is not important" and "/?*" means "ignore noise from any intervening strings".

After the words are combined correctly, they need to be analyzed correctly. First we do not need features to be repeated in the upper language. In example (16.a), the noun سيارة (saiyarah [car]) is analayzed as +fem+sg, and the adjective مفخخة (mufakhakhah [trapping]) has the same features +fem+sg. Second we do not want features to be contradictory. The first word is analyzed as +noun, while the second is analyzed as +adj. This is shown by the representation in (16.b).

(16.a) سيارة مفخخة

saiyarah mufakhakhah
car.noun.fem.sg trapping.adj.fem.sg (bomb car)

(16.b) +noun+fem+sgسيارة +adj+fem+sg مفخخة
سيارة مفخخة

We need to remove all features from non-head components, and the rules in (17) serve this purpose.

(17) "+sg" -> [] || sp ?* _ .o. "+fem" -> [] || sp ?* _
.o. "+adj" -> [] || sp ?* _ .o. "+noun" -> [] || sp ?* _

When these rules are applied to the upper language in the transducer, they remove all specified features from non-initial words, leaving features unique and consistent.

(18) +noun+fem+sgسيارة مفخخة
سيارة مفخخة

Special attention, however, should be given to cases where some features are drawn from non-initial nouns like definiteness in (13) above and the features of number and gender in (11).

Adjectives, Adverbs and Others

Adjectives are treated to a great extent like semi-fixed expressions, as they can undergo morphological variations, such as the examples in (19).

(19.a) قصير النظر qasir al-nazar short.masc.sg sighted	(19.b) قصيرات النظر qasirat al-nazar short.fem.pl sighted

Some adverbs have regular forms and can be easily classified and detected. They are usually composed of a preposition, noun and a modifying adjective. The preposition and the noun are relatively fixed while the adjective changes to convey the meaning, as shown by (20).

(20) بطريقة عشوائية (bi-tariqah 'ashwa'iyah [randomly / lit.: in a random way])

Some MWEs, however, are less easily classified. They include expressions that function as linking words, as in (21), and highly repetitive complete phrases as in (22).

(21) وعلى هذا (wa-'ala haza [whereupon])

(22) ومما يذكر أن (wa mimma yuzkar anna [It is to be mentioned that])

One String MWEs

Some MWEs in Arabic are composed of words with clitics. They look like single words but if they are to be treated by the morphological analyzer alone, they will be analyzed compositionally and lose their actual meaning and syntactic function, such as the example in (23).

(23) بالتالي (bit-tali [consequently / lit.: with the second])

4.2 Interaction with the Tokenizer

The function of a tokenizer is to split a running text into tokens, so that they can be fed into a morphological transducer for processing. The tokenizer is responsible for demarcating words, clitics, abbreviated forms, acronyms, and punctuation marks. The output of the tokenizer is a text with a mark after each token; the "@" sign in XLE case. Besides, the tokenizer is responsible for treating MWEs in a special way. They should be treated as single tokens with the inner space(s) preserved.

One way to allow the tokenizer to handle MWEs is to embed them in the Tokenizer (Beesley and Karttunen, 2003). Yet a better approach, described by (Karttunen et al., 1996), is to develop one or several multiword transducers or "staplers" that are composed with the tokenizer. I will explain here how this is implemented in my solution. Let's first look at the composition regular expression:

```
(24) 1  singleTokens.i
     2  .o. ?* 0:"[[[" (MweTokens.l) 0:"]]]" ?*
     3  .o. "@" -> " " || "[[[" [Alphabet* | "@"*] _
     4  .o. "[[[" -> [] .o. "]]]" -> []].i;
```

The tokenizer is defined in the variable *singleTokens* and the MWE transducer is defined in *MweTokens*. In the MWE transducer all spaces in the lower language are replaced by "@" so that the lower language can be matched by the output of the tokenizer. In line 1 the tokenizer is inverted (the upper language is shifted down) by the operator ".i" so that composition goes in the right direction. From the MWE transducer we take only the lower language by the operator ".l" in line 2. Here all MWEs are searched and if they match any string they will be enclosed with three brackets on either side. Line 3 replaces all "@" signs with spaces in MWEs only. The two compositions in line 4 remove the intermediary brackets.

Let's now show how this works with an example:

(25) ولوزير خارجيتها
wa-li-wazir kharijiyati-ha
and-to-minister foreign-its (and to its foreign minister)

The tokenizer first gives the output in (26), among other possibilities:

(26) و@ل@وزير@خارجية@ها@ (approx. and@to@foreign@minister@its@)

Then after the MWEs are composed with the tokenizer, we obtain the result in (27) with the MWE identified as a single token:

(27) و@ل@وزير خارجية@ها (approx. and@to@foreign minister@its@)

4.3 Integration with the Morphological Transducer

The MWE transducer can either complement or substitute the core morphological transducer. If we want to allow the compositional analysis of the expression to be available to the parser we need make the MWE transducer complement the morphological transducer. On the other hand if we are sure enough that MWEs cannot have significant compositional varieties, we need to prioritize the MWE transducer over the main transducer, so that when an expression is found in the MWE transducer no further search is done.

4.4 Interaction with the Grammar

As for fixed and semi-fixed MWEs that are identified both by the tokenizer and the morphological analyzer, they are represented in Lexical Functional Grammar (LFG) as a single word, as shown in (28).

(28.a) جنود حفظ الأمن (junud hifz al-amn [peace keeping soldiers])

(28.b) C-Structure

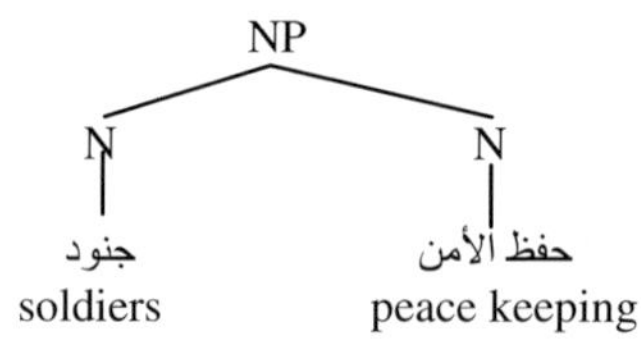

Fig. 1. C-structure of an MWE NP

(28.c) F-Structure
SUBJ PRED 'جنود[soldiers]'
MOD [PRED 'حفظ الأمن[peace keeping]'
DEF +, GEND masc, NUM sg, PERS 3]
DEF +, GEND masc, NUM pl, PERS 3

Fig. 2. F-structure of an MWE NP

When MWEs are syntactically flexible, by either allowing reordering such as passivization or allowing intervening elements such as phrasal verbs, they are handled by the syntactic parser. As passivization in Arabic is not made by configurational restructuring of the sentence, but rather by morphological inflection of verbs, we can say that Arabic shows only one instance of syntactic flexibility in MWEs, that is allowing intervening elements.

Syntactically flexible MWEs are handled through lexical rules where one word selects another word or preposition, and that word's semantic value is determined by this selected element. It will be shown here how this is accommodated in LFG by two examples: adjective noun constructions, and prepositional verbs.

When a noun is modified by an adjective, it usually allows for genitive nouns or pronouns to come in between, even if the expression is highly non-compositional, as shown in (29).

(29.a) دراجة نارية
darrajah nariyah
bike fiery (motorbike)

(29.b) رأيت دراجة الولد الصغير النارية
ra'itu darrajah al-walad al-saghir al-nariyah
saw I bike the-boy the-young the-fiery
(I saw the young boy's motorbike)

(29.c) C-Structure of the object NP in sentence (29.b)

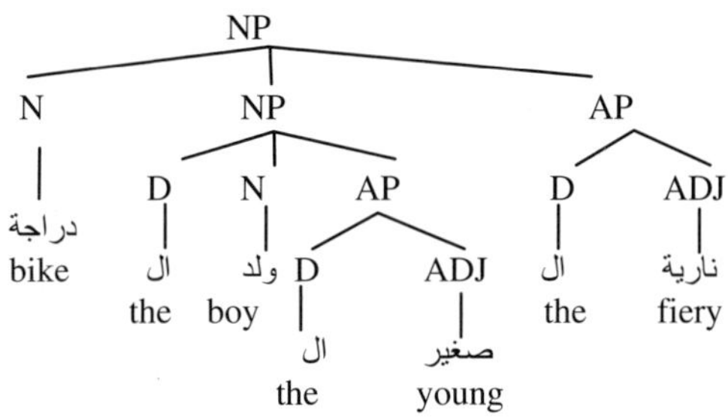

Fig. 3. C-structure of an MWE NP

(29.d) F-Structure of the object NP in sentence (29.b)

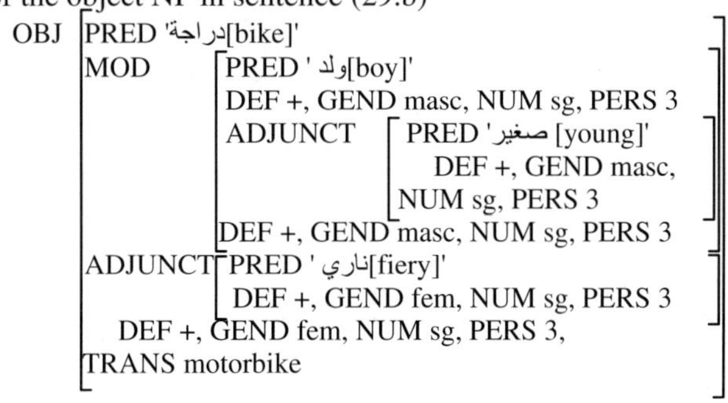

Fig. 4. F-structure of an MWE NP

This is done by allowing the lexical entry of the noun to select its modifier, as shown by the lexical rule in (30).

(30) دراجة[bike] N {(^PRED='دراجة[bike]' (^ ADJUNCT PRED)=c 'ناري[fiery]'
(^ TRANS)=motorbike
| (^PRED='دراجة[bike]' (^ ADJUNCT PRED)~= 'ناري[fiery]'
(^ TRANS)=bike}.

This means that the translation, or the semantic value, of the noun changes according to the value of the adjunct, or the adjectival modifier. The operator "=c" in the rule means "equal", and "~=" means "not equal".

Similarly, prepositional verbs in Arabic allow for subjects to intervene between verbs and objects as shown by the example in (31). This is why they need to be handled in the syntax.

(31.a) اعتمد الولد على البنت
i'tamada al-waladu 'ala al-bint
relied the-boy on the-girl
(The boy relied on the girl)

(31.b) C-Structure

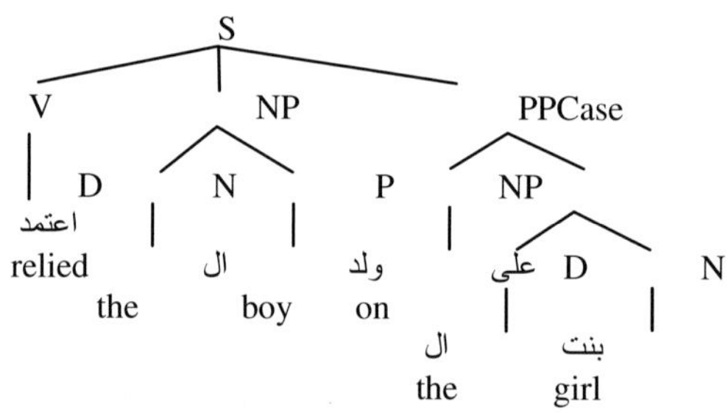

Fig. 5. C-structure of an MWE NP

(31.c) F-Structure

PRED 'اعتمد[rely]<(^ SUBJ)(^ OBJ)'
SUBJ [PRED 'ولد[boy]'
SPEC [DET [DET-TYPE def]]
DEF +, GEND masc, NUM sg, PERS 3]
OBJ [PRED 'بنت[girl]'
SPEC [DET [DET-TYPE def]]
DEF +, GEND fem, NUM sg, PERS 3,
PFORM على[on]]

Fig. 6. F-structure of an MWE NP

In the c-structure the prepositional verbs looks like a verb followed by a PP. In the f-structure, however, the PP functions as the object of the verb. The semantic value, or PRED, of the preposition is removed. The preposition functions only as a case assigner and a feature marker to the main object, but it does not subcategorize for an object itself as shown in (32).

(32) على[on] P (^ PFORM)=على[on] (^ PCASE)=gen.

The lexical entry of the verb, as shown in (33), states that the verb subcategorizes for an object with a certain value for the PFORM feature. This means that the object must be preceded by a specified preposition.

(33) اعتمد[rely] V (^ PRED)='اعتمد[rely]<(^ SUBJ)
(^ OBJ)>' (^ OBJ PFORM)=c على[on].

5 Conclusion

The important lesson of this analysis of MWEs is that they must be integrated in the processing and preprocessing stages if we want to obtain any viable linguistic analysis. When MWEs are properly dealt with, they reduce parse ambiguities and give a noticeable degree of certitude to the analysis and machine translation output. This paper explains different types of MWEs and shows what type can be analyzed at what stage.

References

Attia, Mohammed. 2005. Developing Robust Arabic Morphological Transducer Using Finite State Technology. Paper presented at *The 8th Annual CLUK Research Colloquium*, Manchester, UK.

Baldwin, Timothy, Bannard, Colin, Tanaka, Takaaki, and Widdows, Dominic. 2003. An Empirical Model of Multiword Expression Decomposability. Paper presented at *the ACL-2003 Workshop on Multiword Expressions: Analysis, Acquisition and Treatment*, Sapporo, Japan.

Baldwin, Timothy. 2004. Multiword Expressions, an Advanced Course. Paper presented at *The Australasian Language Technology Summer School (ALTSS 2004)*, Sydney, Australia.

Beesley, K. R., and Karttunen, L. 2003. *Finite State Morphology*. Stanford, Calif.: CSLI Publications.

Bentivogli, L., and Pianta, E. 2003. Beyond Lexical Units: Enriching WordNets with Phrasets. Paper presented at *EACL-03*, Budapest, Hungary.

Brun, Caroline. 1998. Terminology finite-state preprocessing for computational LFG. Paper presented at *The 36th conference on Association for Computational Linguistics*, Montreal, Quebec, Canada.

Butt, Miriam, King, Tracy Holloway, Nino, Maria-Eugenia, and Segond, Frederique. 1999. *A Grammar Writer's Cookbook*. Stanford, CA: CSLI.

Calzolari, N., Lenci, A., and Quochi, V. 2002. Towards Multiword and Multilingual Lexicons: between Theory and Practice. Paper presented at *LP2002*, Urayasu, Japan.

Dipper, Stefanie. 2003. Implementing and Documenting Large-Scale Grammars -- German LFG, Institut f¨ur maschinelle Sprachverarbeitung, Institut f¨ur maschinelle Sprachverarbeitung der Stuttgart University: Ph.D.

Fellbaum, Christine ed. 1998. *WordNet: An Electronic Lexical Database*. Cambridge, MA: MIT Press.

Guenthner, Frantz, and Blanco, Xavier. 2004. Multi-Lexemic Expressions: an overview. In *Lexique, Syntaxe et Lexique-Grammaire*, eds. Christian Leclère, Éric Laporte, Mireille Piot and Max Silberztein. Philadelphia PA, USA: John Benjamins.

Karttunen, Lauri, Chanod, Jean-Pierre, Grefenstette, G., and Schiller, A. 1996. Regular expressions for language engineering. *Natural Language Engineering* 2:305-328.

Li, W., Zhang, X., Niu, C., Jiang, Y., and Srihari, R. K. 2003. An Expert Lexicon Approach to Identifying English Phrasal Verbs. Paper presented at *The Association for Computational Linguistics (ACL- 2003)*, Sapporo, Japan.

Nerima, Luka, Seretan, Violeta, and Wehrli, Eric. 2003. Creating a Multilingual Collocations Dictionary from Large Text Corpora. Paper presented at *10th Conference of the European Chapter of the Association for Computational Linguistics (EACL03)*, Budapest, Hungary.

Oflazer, Kemal, Uglu, Özlem Çetino, and Say, Bilge. 2004. Integrating Morphology with Multi-word Expression Processing in Turkish. Paper presented at *Second ACL Workshop on Multiword Expressions: Integrating Processing*, Spain.

Sag, Ivan A., Baldwin, Timothy, Bond, Francis, Copestake, Ann, and Flickinger, Dan. 2001. Multi-word Expressions: A Pain in the Neck for NLP. Paper presented at *LinGO Working Papers*, Stanford University, CA.

Smadja, Frank, McKeown, Kathleen R., and Hatzivassiloglou, Vasileios. 1996. Translating collocations for bilingual lexicons: a statistical approach. *Computational Linguistics* 22:1-38.

Venkatapathy, Sriram. 2004. Overview of my work on Multi-word expressions and Semantic Role Labeling.

Volk, Martin. 1998. The Automatic Translation of Idioms. Machine Translation vs. Translation Memory Systems. In *Machine Translation: Theory, Applications, and Evaluation. An assessment of the state of the art*, ed. Nico Weber. St. Augustin: gardez-Verlag.

Analysis of EU Languages Through Text Compression

Kimmo Kettunen[1], Markus Sadeniemi[2], Tiina Lindh-Knuutila[2], and Timo Honkela[2]

[1] University of Tampere, Department of Information Studies, Kanslerinrinne 1, FIN-33014, University of Tampere, Finland
Kimmo.kettunen@uta.fi
[2] Helsinki University of Technology, Laboratory of Computer and Information Science
P.O. Box 5400 FI-02015 HUT Finland
Markus.Sadeniemi@iki.fi, tiina.lindh-knuutila@tkk.fi, timo.honkela@tkk.fi

Abstract. In this article, we are studying the differences between the European languages using statistical and unsupervised methods. The analysis is conducted in different levels of language, lexical, morphological and syntactic. Our premise is that the difficulty of the translation could be perceived as differences or similarities in different levels of language. The results are compared to linguistic groupings. The analyses of this paper are based on the concept of Kolmogorov complexity, which is used to compare the language structure in syntactic and morphological levels. The way the languages convey information in these levels is taken as a measure of similarity or dissimilarity between languages and the results are compared to classical linguistic classification. The results will serve as a tool in developing machine translation system(s), e.g., in the following way: if source language conveys more information in the morphological level and the target language more in the syntactic level, it is clear that the (machine) translator must be able to transfer the information from one level to another.

1 Introduction

The European Union has 21 official languages (including Irish from 1st of January 2007), which have approximately 407 million speakers. In this article we analyze parallel corpora in these 21 languages using statistical, unsupervised learning methods to study the similarities and differences of the languages in different levels. We compare these results with traditional linguistic categorizations like division into language groups, morphological complexity and syntactic complexity. The aim of the study is to evaluate the possibility of using statistical methods in different tasks related to statistical machine translation. For instance, for some language pairs the issues related to morphological analysis may be particularly relevant. For some other language pairs, one may have to pay particular attention to the word order. These kinds of questions can be taken into account when the statistical models to be used are chosen.

Much of the material produced by the Union has to be translated to all languages, and the practical problems of translation are huge. The problem gets only worse as new member states bring new languages to the Union. With the current 21 languages

T. Salakoski et al. (Eds.): FinTAL 2006, LNAI 4139, pp. 99 – 109, 2006.

there are 410 language pairs to translate. It is evident that even automatic low-quality translation would be of great help.

EU documents are often difficult for a human to read and understand. For automatic processing and translation the situation might not be so problematic. Language used in documents is typically well structured, uses many words with exactly one translation and still embraces only a small part of human life.

This article provides basic information that could be used in the development of "next generation"' learning machine translation (MT) systems. The basic idea is that one should be able to cover, for instance, 420 pairs of EU languages in not too distant future[1]. This objective cannot be achieved unless the process of developing the MT systems is substantially automated. We do not consider MT itself in this paper, but rather analyze the complexity of EU languages. The analysis aims to support choosing the design principles and learning paradigms for the MT system. The basic insight behind the analysis is the following: two languages that have similar level of complexity when corresponding linguistic characteristics are considered as relatively easier to translate to each other than two languages that differ a lot. Moreover, the nature of the differences can also provide useful information for the MT system design. In the end, the kind of analysis reported in this article might serve as a preliminary phase in the creation of the MT systems, e.g., considering their parameterization.

1.1 Linguistic Comparison of Languages

It is estimated that the number of languages in the world is in several thousands, over 6000 being a usual figure to be mentioned [1, 2]. Of those, 21 are official EU languages: Czech (cs), Danish (da), Dutch (nl), English (en), Estonian (et), Finnish (fi), French (fr), German (de), Greek (el), Hungarian (hu), Irish (ga) (from 1st of January 2007), Italian (it), Latvian (lv), Lithuanian (lt), Maltese (mt), Polish (po), Portuguese (pt), Slovak (sk), Slovene (sl), Spanish (es) and Swedish (sv). Most of these belong to the Indo-European language family. One can divide the Indo-European EU languages into Germanic languages (Danish, Dutch, English, German and Swedish), Romance languages (French, Italian, Portuguese and Spanish), Slavic languages (Czech, Polish, Slovak and Slovene), Hellenic languages (Greek), Celtic languages (Irish) and Baltic languages (Latvian and Lithuanian) [1, 2]. In the present EU, only Estonian, Finnish, Hungarian and Maltese do not belong to Indo-European language family. The three first are Finno-Ugric languages, and Maltese is a Semitic language, Arabic written in Latin alphabet.

A working hypothesis is that the automated translation between two languages that belong to the same group, for example Romance languages, is easier than between those that belong to different groups, let alone different language families. In this article, we conduct statistical analyses to assess whether the differences and similarities of the languages could have significance considering the difficulty of translation. A basic assumption is that if two languages share features or have similarity in a particular level of complexity the translation between these languages is relatively easier.

---

[1] More information on this objective and related research at Helsinki University of Technology can be found at http://www.cis.hut.fi/research/compcogsys/

2 Data and Methods

2.1 Data and Preprocessing

As language material we used parallel texts of EU Constitution in the 21 official languages of the European Union. The texts are smallish but representative, and each text consists of ca. 113 000 – 177 000 word forms and ca. 9100 – 15 000 sentences depending on the language. The character coding of the texts is UTF-8. The total number of files is 987, which means 47 files in each of the 21 languages. The total number of word form tokens in the corpus is 3 099 290. The original files are automatically XML-tagged to include, e.g., sentence, paragraph and word boundary information[2] [3].

The texts of each of the 21 languages were pre-processed by cleaning them from extra tags etc. and making all words lowercased. Then two modifications were made to the cleaned texts, one on the morpheme/word level and another on word order level. In the first modification each word was replaced by a random number in the range 10,000 – 30,000. So each occurrence of the word "competence" was replaced by the same number in the English text but had no relation to the number representing "competences". In another modification the words in each sentence were shuffled to a random order [cf. 4]. The ending punctuation was kept at its place.

After pre-processing we had three versions of the text in each language: original law texts cleaned from XML tags and slightly normalized, one word per line, and files where word forms were randomized and files with shuffled word order.

2.2 Compression Method

Use of (file) compression as a measure for complexity is based on the concept of *Kolmogorov complexity*. Informally, for any sequence of symbols, the Kolmogorov complexity of the sequence is the length of the shortest algorithm that will exactly generate the sequence (and then stop). In other words, the more predictable the sequence, the shorter the algorithm needed is and thus the Kolmogorov complexity of the sequence is also lower [5, 6, 7].

Kolmogorov complexity is uncomputable, but file compression programs can be used to estimate the Kolmogorov complexity of a given file. A decompression program and a compressed file can be used to (re)generate the original string. A more complex string (in the sense of Kolmogorov complexity) will be less compressible [5].

Estimations of complexity using compression has been used for different purposes in many areas. Juola [4] introduces comparison of complexity between languages on morphological level for linguistic purposes. "By selectively altering the expression of morphological information, one can measure the amount of morphological complexity contributes to a corpus by measuring the change in perceived informativeness." Juola's method is simple: after randomization of the morphological level, the size of the original compressed file is divided with the size of the altered compressed file. The resulting ratio is taken as a measure of the morphological complexity of the language in question. With the same procedure of systematic random distortion other levels of language can also be analyzed [8].

---

[2] Materials are available from http://logos.uio.no/opus/index.html

3 Results

3.1 Compression: The Juola Style

For comparison of the complexity of the languages three files were compressed using *bzip2* program[3]. The sizes of modified compressed texts were then compared to the original compressed one to get a measure on the change of information, when morphological and word order information in the texts were destroyed. In Table 1 we have figures of the compressed language files.

Table 1. Compression results of the files. A = original (cleaned) compressed file, B = words replaced by random numbers, file compressed, C = words of sentences shuffled to random order and file compressed, D = language.

A	B	C	D
158606	145956	206540	cs
156115	138097	215904	da
169236	145144	224822	de
181890	158274	249777	el
149490	141982	217175	en
161700	152196	239311	es
151050	137791	193037	et
161067	138409	203658	fi
160846	151428	243122	fr
168550	159304	245621	ga
168831	147829	228542	hu
160627	152720	234036	it
157123	145381	206011	lt
151512	140713	202518	lv
165988	149947	230652	mt
169179	151200	237162	nl
168857	148408	221580	pl
157958	147963	230835	pt
166421	149307	216623	sk
153428	145154	215130	sl
156210	138832	209294	sv

From these figures we made three different relational analyses in the style of [4]. In Figure 1 we have the morphological complexity of the languages shown as relation between columns A and B of Table 1 (A/B), sorted in ascending order.

[3] Available online at http://www.bzip.org

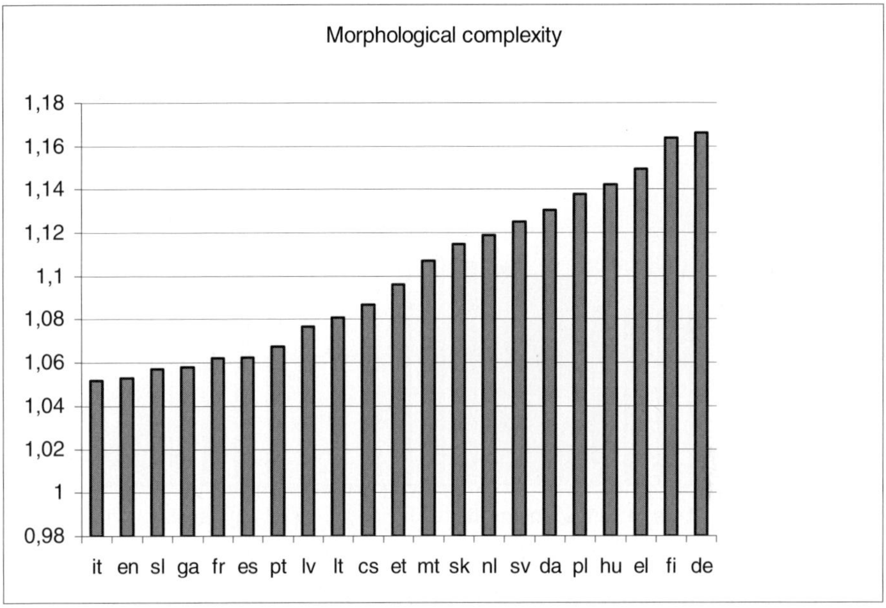

Fig. 1. Morphological complexity of the languages analyzed with compression

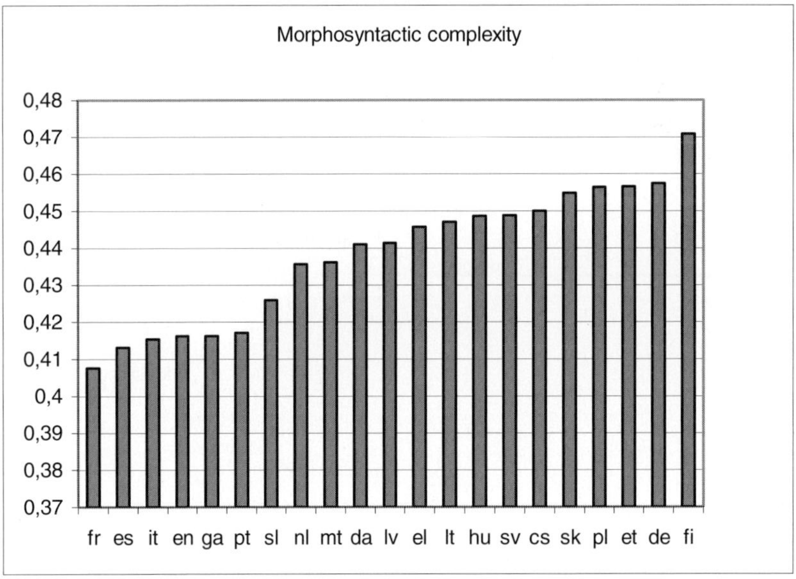

Fig. 2. Morphosyntactic complexity of the languages analyzed with compression

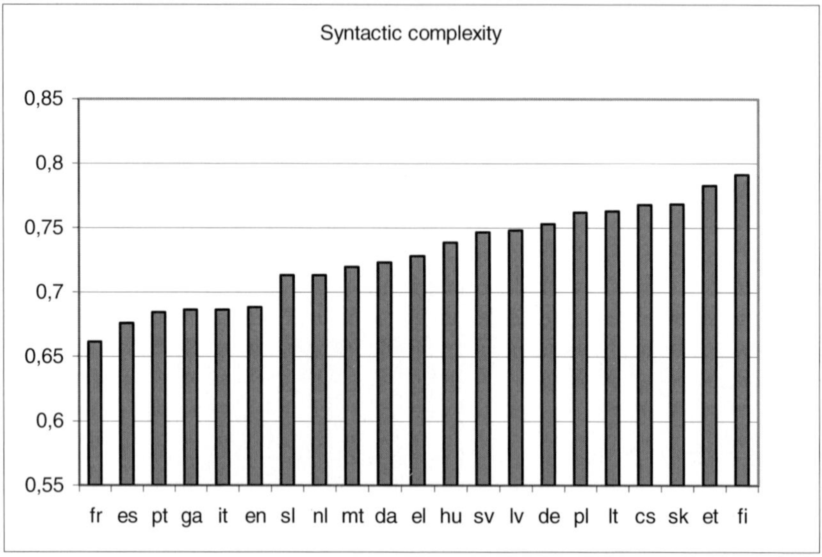

Fig. 3. Syntactic complexity of the languages analyzed with compression

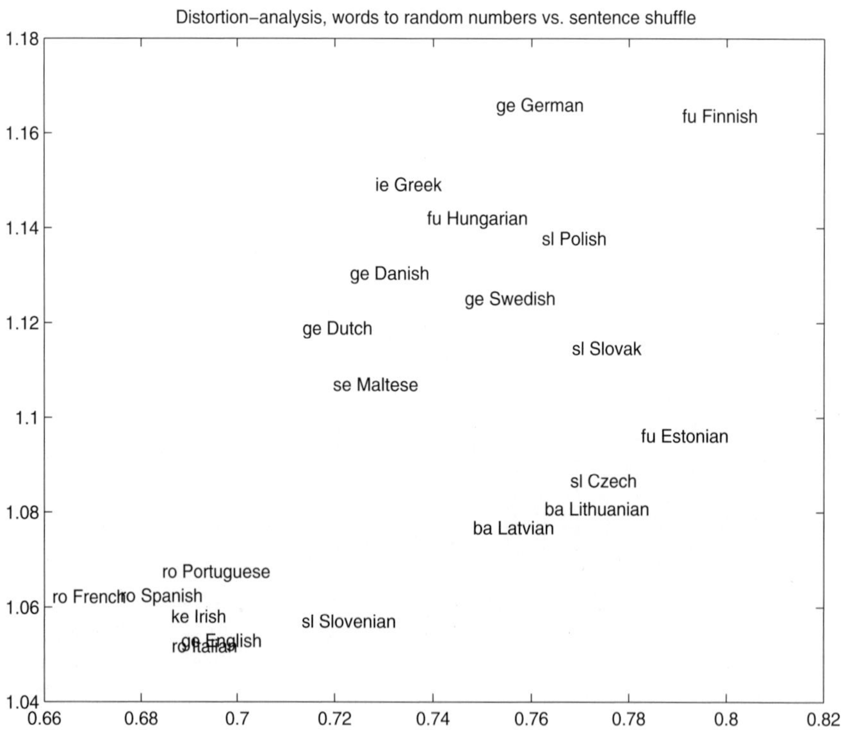

Fig. 4. Morphological and syntactic complexity of the languages in a two-dimensional graph

A few comments of Figure 1 are necessary. Mostly the results are as expected: morphologically simple languages, Italian, English, Irish, French, Portuguese and Spanish are getting low scores and morphologically more complex languages, Finnish, Hungarian and Polish, are in the other end of the scale. But some of the results are not very expected: Slovene, Slovak, Latvian, Czech and Estonian should be higher on the complexity scale. Dutch, Swedish, Danish and German seem to get quite high values, German being even on the top of the scale. It is possible, that compound words cause this effect. Also the type of texts, legalese, could have a boosting effect on the complexity of German and other Germanic languages.

In Figure 2 we show the morphosyntactic complexity of the languages by adding columns B and C together and dividing figure from column A of Table 1 with the result, A/(B + C).

In Figure 3 the syntactic complexity of the languages is shown as a relation of columns A and C from Table 1 (A/C)..

In Figure 4 data of figures 1 and 3 are joined as a two-dimensional graph.

Figure 4 shows the languages plotted on a two-dimensional graph using the variables of morphological and syntactic complexity (A/B and A/C). As we can see, Romance languages are grouped neatly into southwest corner of the picture and seeing English near them is no surprise. Finnish and German are located near the top of the figure. Baltic and other Slavic languages are generally more on the southeast side than Germanic languages, although the separation is not very clear.

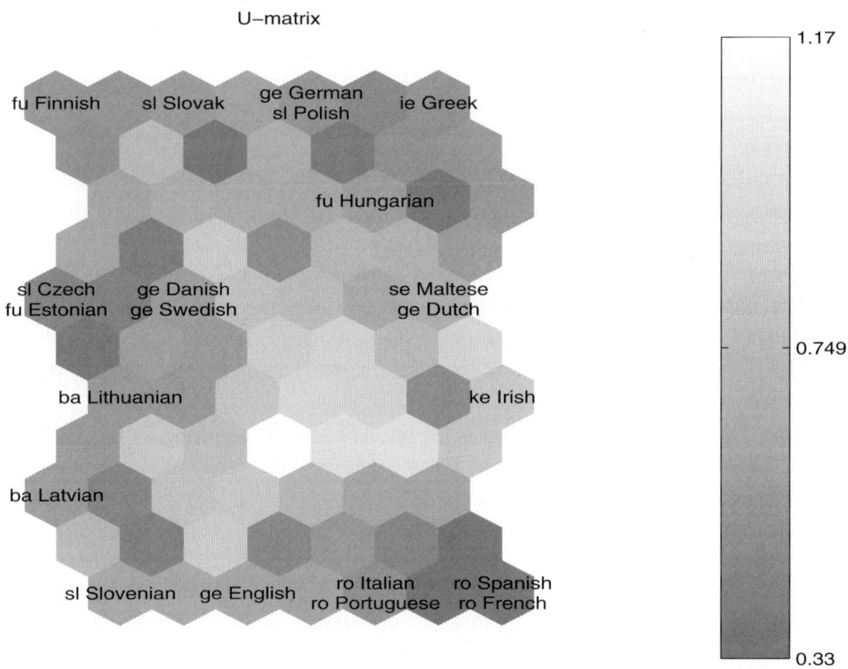

Fig. 5. Languages in a SOM-map: morphology vs. word order information

Overall the results are as expected: Finnish and Estonian have quite free word order, Finnish and German have compound words and a complex morphological structure of words whereas Romance languages and English are on the other end of the scale. It must be remembered, of course, that when talking about word order, we do not only mean clause level SVO-like grammatical structures but also constituent level things, like nominal heads and their different modifiers.

Figure 5 shows languages on a self-organizing map (SOM-map). Input variables in this picture are the three compressed file sizes as such. A SOM map is a highly nonlinear projection from the original feature space to a two-dimensional map. This is done in a way that observations - here languages - that are close in original space remain close on the map. Longer distances don't remain proportional, however. The map in figure 5 shows Romance languages well clustered again and English near them. Danish and Swedish are close as they should, but Estonian should rather be near to Finnish than to Czech.

3.2 Interpretation of Morphosyntactic and Syntactic Complexities

The morphosyntactic complexity of the languages in Figure 2 is partly as expected, partly not. Most of the languages at the complex end of the scale are as expected, Finnish, German, Estonian, Polish, Slovak, Czech and Hungarian being in the top. Only Swedish seems to be higher in the scale than expected and Latvian and Slovene lower than expected.

To get a meaningful interpretation for the order of languages in the word order complexity counting, linguistic literature was consulted for independent figures.

Bakker [9, pp. 387–] introduces flexibility of language's word order, which is based on 10 factors, such as order of verb and object in the language, order of adjective and its head noun, order of genitive and its head noun etc. Altogether Bakker has seven constituent level variables and three clause level variables in his flexibility counting, and thus constituent level variables are more important for the result. The flexibility of the language in Bakker's counting can be given with a numeric value from 0 - 1: if the flexibility figure is close to zero, the language is more inflexible in its word order, if the figure is closer to 1, the language is more flexible in its word order. In the information theoretic framework of the compression approach flexibility and inflexibility can be interpreted naturally as higher and lower degrees of complexity, i.e. predictability.

In Table 2 figures based on Bakker's [9, pp. 417 – 419] counting of the flexibility values for the individual languages are given together with values given by compression analysis.

If we compare the figures given by Bakker in column 2 to figures given by compression based calculation in column 4, we can see, that the overall order of the languages based on these independent calculations converge well. The lower end of the scale is quite analogous in both analyses consisting of same five languages with only minor differences in the order. There are also some bigger differences in the orders given by the two analyses. The syntactic complexity of Lithuanian seems to be estimated higher by compression than by Bakker's flexibility value (16 vs. 8).

Table 2. Bakker's flexibility values for languages with compression relation complexity of the word order. Czech and Hungarian have been omitted from the table, as Bakker is missing data for them. The compession figures for these languages are 0,74 (Hungarian) and 0,77 (Czech).

Order of the languages based on Bakker's flexibility calculation	Bakker's flexibility value	Syntactic complexity order of the languages based on compressional relation calculations from Figure 3.	Complexity figure based on compression
1. fr	0,10	1. fr	0,66
2. ga	0,20	2. es	0,68
3. es	0,30	3. pt	0,68
4. pt	0,30	4. ga	0,69
5. it	0,30	5. it	0,69
6. da	0,30	6. en	0,69
7. mt	0,30	7. sl	0,71
8. lt	0,30	8. nl	0,71
9. en	0,40	9. mt	0,72
10. nl	0,40	10. da	0,72
11. de	0,40	11. el	0,73
12. sv	0,40	12. sv	0,75
13. et	0,40	13. lv	0,75
14. sl	0,50	14. de	0,75
15. lv	0,50	15. pl	0,76
16. sk	0,50	16. lt	0,76
17. el	0,60	17. sk	0,77
18. pl	0,60	18. et	0,78
19. fi	0,60	19. fi	0,79

Slovene has also a higher flexibility value than its complexity value (14 vs. 7). Greek is also higher in Bakker's counting than in complexity analysis (17 vs. 11). In our compression calculations Finnish and Estonian are estimated almost equally complex, but in Bakker's analysis Estonian is less complex than Finnish (18 vs. 13).

3.3 Compression: Cilibrasi and Vitányi Style

Another method for comparing the similarity of languages using compression is described by Cilibrasi and Vitànyi [10]. Again the size of a compressed text file is used to measure its Kolmogorov complexity as described in Li et al. [6].

A compression program (also bzip2 here) learns the characteristics of a language as it processes the text. If the language of the text changes in the middle of processing the compression program has to adapt to a new situation. If the languages are different, it has to unlearn the efficient coding of the first language and learn the characteristics of the new language. On the other hand, if the languages are similar enough, it can use the old coding with perhaps small modifications.

So the similarity of languages can be measured by how well the compression manages this transition. In mathematical terms we can mark the size of compressed text file in language x by *C(x)* and in y by *C(y)* and by *C(xy)* the size of the compressed file for concatenated text *xy*. The distance measure used here is

$$(C(xy) - C(x)) / C(y) \tag{1}$$

which measures the change in compressing language y when using x as model. The expression acknowledges the possibility that the relation can be asymmetric: perhaps x is better explained by y than vice versa.

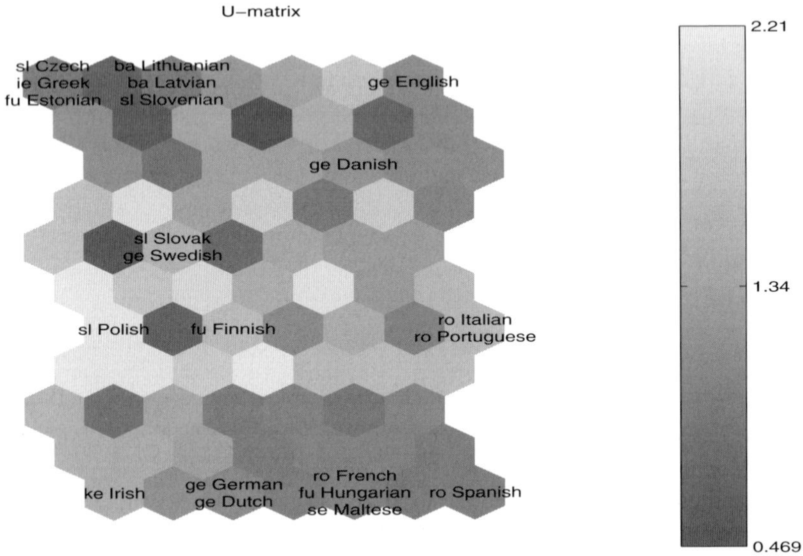

Fig. 6. A SOM-map analysis of languages showing language pair distances

Figure 6 shows languages as they appear on a SOM-map. The results are in many ways problematic. Romance languages are on the lower right corner and English on the upper right, but Hungarian and Maltese being near French is not too logical. In the upper left there is Czech, Slovenian, Latvian and Lithuanian, but Estonian and Greek should not be in the same group.

4 Discussion and Conclusion

In this paper we have used a file compression program as an analysis tool for complexity of the 21 official EU languages on lexical, morphological and syntactic levels. Our analyses have shown that the approach is capable of showing relations between languages on these levels. The level of analysis is, however, relatively coarse, but results given are mainly in accordance with linguistic descriptions of the languages; this is most clearly shown with the syntactic complexity analysis, when compression results are related to Bakker's flexibility values for the languages in Table 2.

What, then, could be the use of this type of general level information theoretic analysis? One suggested way to use the analyses would be in development work of a statistical machine translation system. The basic idea is that the translation process can be divided into interrelated tasks following, e.g., the classical machine translation triangle model. In this case, however, we foresee that all those tasks can be conducted using statistical methods. For instance, a detailed morphological analysis can be made using unsupervised learning method [11] when needed. For some languages, a detailed morphological analysis is not needed. Similarly, for some language pairs one may need to pay special attention to the word order whereas for some other language pairs it may be assumed that the word order in them is rather similar. This assessment influences the complexity of the statistical model needed.

References

1. Gordon, R. G., Jr. (ed.): Ethnologue: Languages of the World, Fifteenth edition. Dallas, Tex.: SIL International (2005). Online version: http://www.ethnologue.com/
2. Haarman, H.: Kleines Lexikon der Sprachen. Von Albanisch bis Zulu. Verlag C.H. Beck, München, 2.,überarbeitete Auflage (2002)
3. Tiedemann, J., Nygaard, L: The OPUS Corpus - Parallel & Free. In Proceedings of the Fourth International Conference on Language Resources and Evaluation (LREC'04). Lisbon, Portugal, May 26-28. 2004 http://www.let.rug.nl/~tiedeman/blog/paper/opus_lrec04.pdf. Accessed 30 January 2006.
4. Juola, P.:. Measuring Linguistic Complexity: the Morphological Tier. Journal of Quantitative Linguistics 5 (1998) 206–213
5. Li, M, Vitanyi, P. An Introduction to Kolmogorov Complexity and its Applicatrions. Springer Verlag, New York Berlin Heidelberg (1994)
6. Li, M., Chen, X., Li, X., Ma, B, Vitányi, P.M.B.:The Similarity Metric. IEEE Transactions on Information Theory. 50 .(2004). 3250 - 3264
7. Bennet, C.H., Gács, P., Li, M., Vitányi, P.M.B., Zurek, W.H.:Information Distance. IEEE Transactions on Information Theory. 44 (1998) 1407 - 1423
8. Juola, P.: Compression-Based Analysis of Language Complexity. Approaches to Complexity in Language, abstracts. (2005) http://www.ling.helsinki.fi/sky/tapahtumat/complexity/Abstracts.pdf. Accessed January 15th 2006
9. Bakker, D.: Flexibility and Consistency in Word Order Patterns in the Languages of Europe. In Siewierska, A. (ed.): Constituent Order in the Languages of Europe. Empirical Approaches to Language Typology. Mouton de Gruyter, Berlin New York (1998). 381 – 419
10. Cilibrasi, R., Vitányi, P. M. B.: Clustering by Compression. IEEE Transactions on Information Theory, 51 (2005), 1523–1545
11. Creutz, M., Lagus, K.: Unsupervised Morpheme Segmentation and Morphology Induction from Text Corpora Using Morfessor 1.0. Espoo: Publications in Computer and Information Science, Helsinki University of Technology, Report A81 (2005)

Applying Latent Dirichlet Allocation to Automatic Essay Grading

Tuomo Kakkonen, Niko Myller, and Erkki Sutinen

University of Joensuu, P.O. Box 111, FI-80101 Joensuu, Finland
firstname.lastname@cs.joensuu.fi

Abstract. We report experiments on automatic essay grading using Latent Dirichlet Allocation (LDA). LDA is a "bag-of-words" type of language modeling and dimension reduction method, reported to outperform other related methods, Latent Semantic Analysis (LSA) and Probabilistic Latent Semantic Analysis (PLSA) in Information Retrieval (IR) domain. We introduce LDA in detail and compare its strengths and weaknesses to LSA and PLSA. We also compare empirically the performance of LDA to LSA and PLSA. The experiments were run with three essay sets consisting in total of 283 essays from different domains. On contrary to the findings in IR, LDA achieved slightly worse results compared to LSA and PLSA in the experiments. We state the reasons for LSA and PLSA outperforming LDA and indicate further research directions.

1 Introduction

Computer-assisted assessment refers to the use of computers for assessing students' learning outcomes. Assessing free-text responses, like essays, is a demanding task even for a human. To reduce the costs and to increase the objectivity of grading, methods to automate the assessment process have been developed. The methods applied for automatic grading can be divided into three groups: surface features-based methods apply statistics of *e.g.* total number of words and commas in an essay for grading. The earliest systems, such as *PEG* [1] relied heavily on such features. More recent systems, such as *E-rater* [2], take into consideration the structure and organization of arguments in the texts to be evaluated. Our focus in this paper is on content-based assessment methods.

Several methods have been applied for automatic content-based grading of essays. For instance, *Latent Semantic Analysis* (LSA) [3] and *Probabilistic Latent Semantic Analysis* (PLSA) [4] have been shown to be suitable for document similarity comparisons in automated essay grading [5,6]. In addition to *Automatic Essay Assessor* (AEA), systems such as *Intelligent Essay Assessor* [5] and *Apex* [7] apply LSA to automatic essay grading. In this paper, we examine the applicability of *Latent Dirichlet Allocation* (LDA) [8] for document similarity comparison in AEA. To our knowledge AEA is the only automatic essay grading system applying LDA.

T. Salakoski et al. (Eds.): FinTAL 2006, LNAI 4139, pp. 110–120, 2006.

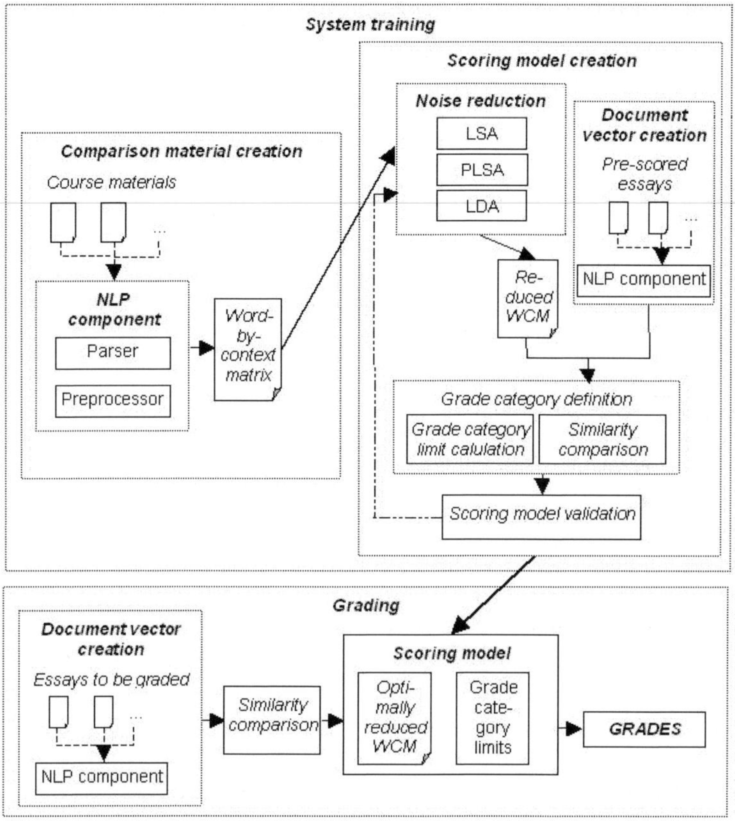

Fig. 1. The architecture of AEA

LDA stems from the same idea as LSA and PLSA. These methods provide the means to compare the semantic similarity between two texts. All the three methods start from the word-by-context matrix, where the content of a context (*e.g.* a document) is represented on a column where the cells stand for the number of occurrences of a specific word in that context. LSA uses *Singular Value Decomposition* (SVD), a form of factor analysis, for reducing the dimensionality of the word-by-context matrix [3]. The aim of the dimensionality reduction step is to trim down noise or unimportant details in the data and to allow the underlying semantic structure to become evident. PLSA and LDA take a statistical approach to the problem. They both build a probabilistic language model from the given documents. The model can be used to infer the probability that a document would appear when another document is given as a query. This probability can be used as a measure of the similarity between the two documents.

The paper is organized as follows. We start in Section 2 by introducing the automatic grading system, AEA. In Section 3, LDA is described and compared to LSA and PLSA in theoretical level. Next, in Section 4, we introduce the tests sets, the configurations of the experiments and summarize the results. Section 5 concludes the findings and introduces some future directions for the research.

2 Automatic Essay Assessor

Automatic Essay Assessor (AEA) is a system, which automatically grades essays written in the agglutinative Finnish language [9]. However, because of its modular design, it is not limited to only one language. AEA determines the grade of an essay based on its similarity to the course content (textbook passages, lecture notes *etc.*) relevant to the essay assignment. We call these assignment-specific texts *corpus*. The similarity is computed using a word-by-context matrix, which essentially contains the occurrence information of each word in the corpus. The corpus is represented as matrix columns, or document vectors, each of which represents a certain sentence, paragraph, or passage of the corpus. Originally, we applied LSA for creating the model of the course content, but later PLSA [6], and in this paper LDA, has been used for the purpose.

The system consists of three main components (see Figure 1: a natural language parser, a method for comparing the similarity between texts, and a method for determining the grades). The system can apply LSA, PLSA or LDA in order to measure the content similarity between the essays and the course materials [9,6]. As Finnish is a morphologically complex language, and words are formed by adding suffixes into the base forms, base forms have to be used instead of inflectional forms, especially if a relatively small corpus is utilized. A syntactic parser and morphological analyzer *Constraint Grammar Parser for Finnish* (FINCG), is applied for lemmatization [10].

The assessment procedure consists of two phases. First, the reference material is created from the essay-prompt representative corpus. The word-by-context matrix is then processed either by LSA, PLSA or LDA. Next, AEA uses human-graded essays for determining threshold similarity values for each grade category by comparing essays to the reference materials. A query vector representing the content of the essay is created and compared to each document of the LSA, PLSA or LDA representation created in the previous phase, giving a similarity score for the essay. The threshold values for grade categories are defined based on the set of human-graded essays distributed equally over all the grade categories.

In the grading phase, the document vectors from each of the essays to be graded are created and compared to the reference material with the same method as in the previous phase. The similarity value of the essay is matched to the grade categories according to their limits to determine the correct grade. An interested reader is referred to [6,11] for a more detailed description of the system and the grading process.

3 Latent Dirichlet Allocation

In addition to LSA and PLSA, LDA [8] has been integrated into AEA. In this section, we explain the generative model of LDA and give the formulas used to estimate the model. In AEA, the LDA model is formed iteratively by using *Expectation Maximization* (EM) -based algorithm introduced by Blei et al. [8].

LDA assumes the following generative process for each document d_i in a corpus D of N documents which contain M distinct words w_m and K distinct latent variables or topics $\mathbf{z} = \{z_1, \ldots, z_K\}$:

1. Choose the length of the document $L \sim Poisson(x)$.
2. Choose a parameter vector for the topic distribution $\theta \sim Dirichlet(\alpha)$, the parameter α is a K-vector with components $\alpha_k > 0$ and θ is a K-vector so that $\theta_k > 0$ and $\sum_{k=1}^{K} \theta_k = 1$ and $P(\theta|\alpha)$ is the probability density function of the Dirichlet distribution.
3. For each of the L words w_l (this also means that $d_i = \{w_1, \ldots, w_L\}$, where there can be $w_i = w_j$ when $i \neq j$ which is not true for distinct words in the corpus marked with w_m):
   (a) Choose a topic $z_l \sim Multinomial(\theta)$.
   (b) Choose a word w_l from $P(w_l|z_l, \beta)$, a multinomial probability conditioned on the topic z_l, where β is a $K \times M$ matrix so that $\beta_{kj} = P(w_m|z_k)$ for all $1 \leq m \leq M$ and $1 \leq k \leq K$.

To do the inference in the language model, the posterior distribution of the hidden variables, when given the document, should be computed for $\forall d_i \in D$ as shown in Equation (1).

$$P(\theta, \mathbf{z}, d_i|\alpha, \beta) = \frac{P(\theta, \mathbf{z}, d_i|\alpha, \beta)}{P(d_i|\alpha, \beta)} \tag{1}$$

However, this equation is intractable and therefore needs to be approximated. Blei et al. [8] introduce an EM-based variational algorithm to approximate the inference and maximize the log likelihood of the model based on the α and β parameters. We describe the algorithm here briefly. An interested reader is directed to Blei et al. [8], and Minka and Lafferty [12] for further details.

In the E-step, the density function in Equation (1) needs to be approximated with a tractable model. This is done with a simplified model shown in Equation (2), where the Dirichlet parameter γ and the multinomial parameters $(\phi_1, \ldots, \phi_N)$ are free variational parameters and need to be estimated for each document.

$$P(\theta, \mathbf{z}|\gamma, \phi) = P(\theta|\gamma) \prod_{n=1}^{L} P(z_l|\phi_l), \tag{2}$$

where each $z_l \in z_1 \ldots z_K$.

This can be translated into a minimization problem to minimize the Kullback-Leibner Divergence between these two probability distributions by finding the minimal values for parameters γ and ϕ. In this way, we are able to search for the optimal γ and ϕ for each document d_i and obtain the update Equations (3) and (4) for these parameters,

$$\phi_{lk}(d_i) \propto \beta_{kw_l} \exp\Big[E_P\big[\log\left(\theta_k|\gamma(d_i)\right)\big]\big)\Big] \tag{3}$$

$$\gamma_k(d_i) = \alpha_k + \sum_{l=1}^{L} \phi_{lk}(d_i), \tag{4}$$

where $E_P[\log(\theta_k|\gamma(d_i))] = \Psi(\gamma_k(d_i)) - \Psi\left(\sum_{j=1}^{K} \gamma_j(d_i)\right)$. The γ parameter vector describes the topic distribution for each document and thus can be used similarly to $P(z_k|d_i)$ in the PLSA model. These two equations are computed repeatedly for all l, k and d_i until the lower bound achieved from Jensen's inequality converges.

In the M-step, we need to estimate the α and β parameters after the new ϕ and γ have been calculated. Blei et al. [8] propose using the Newton-Raphson optimization technique to find the stationary point of the α function by iterating Equation (5). Furthermore, the conditional multinomial parameters α and β are updated as in Equations (5) and (6).

$$\alpha_{new} = \alpha_{old} - H(\alpha_{old})^{-1} g(\alpha_{old}) \tag{5}$$

$$\beta_{km} \propto \sum_{i=1}^{N} \sum_{l=1}^{L_{d_i}} \phi_{lk}(d_i) eq(w_l, w_m), \tag{6}$$

where $H(\alpha)$ and $g(\alpha)$ are the Hessian matrix and gradient respectively at point α and $eq(w_l, w_m)$ is 1 if a word w_l from the document d_i is the same word as mth distinct word w_m in the corpus otherwise 0. After each cycle in the EM algorithm the convergence of the model building is measured with the log-likelihood of the model.

New documents can be added to the model with a similar procedure by doing the inference for each document. However, Blei et al. [8] propose methods for smoothing the distributions in order to avoid zero probabilities when new documents containing unseen words are added.

The γ vector of a document contains the information how the document belongs to the different latent classes or topics. Furthermore, ϕ contains the same information for each word in the document. When the similarities between the documents are compared, the cosine of the angle between the documents' γ vectors can be applied. Two other distance measures that can be used with LDA are the *entropic cosine similarity*, Eq. (7), and *the logarithm of the a posteriori probability for the comparison material passage*, Eq. (8), formulated by Girolami and Kabán [13].

$$d(d_i, q) = \sum_{w_j \in q} n(q, w_j) \log \sum_{k=1}^{K} P(w_j|z_k) P(z_k|d_i) \tag{7}$$

$$d(d_i, q) = \sum_{w_j \in d_i} n(d_i, w_j) \log \sum_{k=1}^{K} P(w_j|z_k) P(z_k|q) \tag{8}$$

3.1 Theoretical Comparison

When compared from a theoretical perspective, PLSA and LDA differ significantly from LSA. LSA is based on SVD, a method from linear algebra. The technique tries to approximate the word-by-context matrix by minimizing the Frobenius norm. From a linguistic point of view, LSA is flawed because the matrix can contain negative values after the dimension reduction, meaning that a document contains negative amount of words. However, this might have a positive effect on performance of LSA in some conditions because it separates the documents into larger are in K-dimensional space. In contrast, PLSA and LDA define generative models of the language and its usage and try to learn the model from the training data. The appropriateness of these generative models can be debated, nevertheless, the assumptions behind these models are closer to the use of the language compared to the assumptions behind LSA. Moreover, PLSA and LDA define generative models and probability distributions for documents and words and thus cannot contain negative values.

The awkwardness of the dimensionality selection in LSA is a well-reported problem [14,3]. As a consequence, the model build by LSA is not interpretable. LDA and PLSA are interpretable with their generative models, latent classes or topics, and graphical models and representations in K-dimensional space [4,8]. Furthermore, it was shown by Hofmann [4] that the accuracy of PLSA can increase when the number of latent variables is increased. However, this increases the time and space complexities and it has not been shown that this continues when the number of topics is higher than the number of documents or words. Another technique for increasing the accuracy of the PLSA and LDA models is to combine (linearly) similarity scores obtained from models using different predefined number of latent variables [4]. Therefore, the selection of optimal dimensionality is not as crucial as in LSA. However, this might not be the case with small data sets [6].

Girolami and Kabán [13] have shown that actually the two frameworks, PLSA and LSA, are related and that PLSA is a maximum a posteriori estimate of LDA model. Thus, these models are just using different techniques to approximate the same intractable theoretical model. The algorithm used in PLSA is probabilistic and can converge to a local maximum. However, according to Hofmann [4] this is not a serious problem in PLSA and the differences between separate runs are small, although the problem might materialize with certain data sets. Similar issue also exists in the variational method used to approximate LDA model, but can be overcome if another method is used to approximate the model, for example Expectation-Maximization [12]. It has been claimed that PLSA is overfitting the model into the training data. Moreover, the generative model of PLSA and the assumptions behind it are accused of being flawed, because the probability to obtain an unseen document needs to be approximated [8]. Both these claims have been later shown to be incorrect by Brants [15]. The algorithm used for building LDA models does not overfit and produces language models with lower perplexity than PLSA [8,12]. The generative model of LDA is consistent and there is no need to approximate the probability to obtain a document. Furthermore, the model learning algorithm of LDA converges faster than that of PLSA. Thus, although the running time of LDA is considerably worse than the running time of LSA , it still is faster than PLSA.

On contrary to LSA and PLSA, it is possible to build an LDA model with several layers forming a tree hierarchy. For instance, a two-layered hierarchy of a document could be created by first dividing it into paragraphs or sentences, forming the first layer, and then into words to compose the second layer of the representation. This would allow one to model the topics within a paragraph or a sentence and in the word level separately and thus utilize the results from a parser more effectively. For example, in the sentence level the subject, predicate and object relations or part-of-speech tagging could be used.

4 Experiment

In the context of automated essay grading, the idea of using the methods from information retrieval and language modeling (*i.e.* LSA, PLSA and LDA) is to compare the documents' similarities, in the case of AEA especially, the similarities between the essays and the corresponding course materials. In this study, we compare the performance of the three methods. Furthermore, to validate the suitability of the grading method applied by AEA, where the grading process is based on both course materials and human-graded essays (illustrated in the Figure 1), we compared it to the *k-nearest neighbor* (k-NN) method that has been commonly used in automatic essay grading systems (cf. [16]).

The grading accuracy of LSA, PLSA and LDA using both grading methods were tested with the essay sets described in Table 1. With LSA, all the possible dimensions (*i.e.*, from two to the number of passages in the comparison materials) were searched in order to find the dimension resulting in the highest accuracy of grading. The accuracy was measured as the Spearman correlation between the grades given by the system and the human assessor. There is no upper limit for the number of latent variables or topics in PLSA and LDA models as there is for the dimensions in LSA. Thus, in order to be fair in the comparison, we used the same range as for LSA to search for the dimension yielding the best accuracy. When building up the PLSA models with TEM, twenty essays from the training sets were used to test the performance of the model for the stopping condition.

We utilized the cosine of the angle between vectors and the logarithm of the a posteriori probability and the entropic cosine as the similarity measures in LSA, PLSA and LDA respectively as these either were only ones applicable to the model or yielded the best results.

A similar procedure was used for k-NN-based grading methods with LSA (*KNN-LSA*), PLSA (*KNN-PLSA*) and LDA (*KNN-LDA)*. The models were built with the human-graded essays. Each essay to be graded was compared to every essay in the model and the grade was defined as the weighted average of the grades of the k nearest neighbor essays. The weighting was based on the similarity score between the essay to be graded and the essay in the model. The experiments were run with the number of nearest neighbors (k) between 1 and 10. Figure 2 illustrates the idea K-NN-based grading.

Table 2 shows the results of the experiment. The results clearly indicate that k-NN-based method is outperformed by the method using both course materials

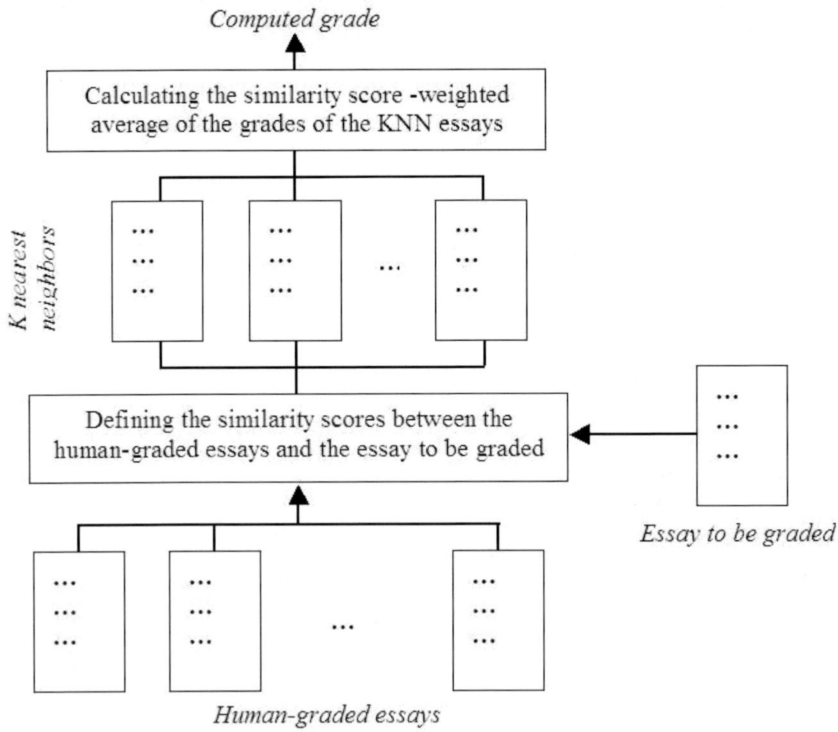

Fig. 2. The KNN-based grading method

and human-graded essays. This shows that the approach taken in AEA is better than the plain k-NN method user previously [16]. For all the methods and test sets the accuracy of the system increased when the course materials used for creating the scoring model were divided into sentences instead of paragraphs. However, in most of the cases the differences were small. On the other hand, dividing the texts into sentences results into larger word-by-context matrices and makes the computations more time-consuming.

The Spearman rank correlations in this experiment (between 0.64 ... 0.95 for two of the sets and 0.42 ... 0.57 for the third when reference materials were divided into sentences) are comparable to the results achieved by the other automated assessment systems based on LSA and to those observed between grades given by two human assessors. For example Landauer et al. [17], Lemaire and Dessus [7] and Folz et al. [18] have reported inter-rater correlations ranging from 0.64 to 0.84 and correlations 0.59 ... 0.89 between the LSA-based system and human graders.

A comparison between LSA, PLSA and LDA indicates that, LSA performs better than the other two methods, although the differences are relatively small, especially between LSA and PLSA. Moreover, PLSA slightly outperforms LDA in the accuracy. On contrary to the findings of Hofmann [4] and Blei el al. [8] in

Table 1. The essay sets used in the experiments. The column labeled "domain" indicates the subject of the essays and the column "level" indicates if the essays were collected from an undergraduate or a graduate course or from a vocational school class. The next two columns show the number of essays used for creating the scoring model and the number of essays graded by the system. The column "grade scale" indicates the scale of the grades given by the system and the grader, who is also stated in the next column. The last three columns indicate the total number of text passages (sentences or paragraphs) and words in the course material corpus related to the essay question, and if the passages were divided into paragraphs or sentences.

Set No.	Domain	Level	Train. essays	Test essays	Grade scale	Grader	Division type	No. pass.	No. words
1	Education	Under-grad.	70	73	0–6	Professor	Paragraphs	26	2397
2	Education	Under-grad.	70	73	0–6	Professor	Sentences	147	2397
3	Communi-cations	Voca-tional	42	45	0–4	Course teacher	Paragraphs	45	1583
4	Communi-cations	Voca-tional	42	45	0–4	Course teacher	Sentences	139	1583
5	Software Engineering	Gradu-ate	26	27	0–10	Assistant	Paragraphs	27	965
6	Software Engineering	Gradu-ate	26	27	0–10	Assistant	Sentences	105	965

IR tasks, PLSA and LDA did not perform better than LSA in our experiments. We attribute the difference at least partially to the size of the collections used to train the model. In the studies in IR domain, the document collections with 1,000-3,000 documents were used, whereas our test sets contained only around 150 documents. However, this is a realistic number of essays for a grading system. Thus, a method applied in AEA should be able to perform well on relatively small document collections. Another possible cause of worse performance

Table 2. The results of the comparison between the language model building methods measured by the Spearman correlation between grades assigned by human and computer. *) Same as previous because no course materials were used.

Set No.	LSA	KNN -LSA	PLSA	KNN-PLSA	LDA	KNN -LDA
1	0.78	0.53	0.75	0.28	0.61	0.44
2	0.80	*	0.78	*	0.64	*
3	0.54	0.45	0.51	0.34	0.25	0.44
4	0.57	*	0.55	*	0.42	*
5	0.88	0.81	0.88	0.88	0.82	0.88
6	0.90	*	0.95	*	0.83	*

of the LDA models is the method used to approximate the LDA model. Minka and Lafferty [12] showed that variational methods may learn inaccurate models. They proposed the Expectation-Propagation method to learn more accurate LDA models. This will be tested in the future experiments.

The performance on the test sets 3 and 4 is seriously flawed compared to the other test sets. We attribute these differences to the inaccurate selection of the course materials used to build the model and to the fact that the question used in the essay prompt was more open-ended than in the two other test sets. Many student were using different real-life examples as the basis of their answers. Thus, comparison with course content or other student's essays did not yield good results.

5 Conclusion and Future Work

We have presented an automatic essay grading system applying LDA for measuring the similarities between the essays and the course content and reported an experiment with test sets consisting of essays written in Finnish. Comparison with related methods, LSA and PLSA was also performed. The results indicate that at least for relatively small test sets with around 100-150 essays, LDA performs worse than LSA and PLSA models. Although LDA achieved worse results, LDA has some theoretical advantages (*e.g.* dimensionality selection, being not so prone to model overfitting, the consistency of the generative model) compared to the two other methods. Thus, we see it worthwhile to continue the research on applying also LDA for automatic essay grading. We plan to test the Expectation-Propagation method proposed by Minka and Lafferty [12] in order to learn more accurate LDA models.

References

1. Page, E.B.: The Imminence of Grading Essays by Computer. Phi Delta Kappan **47** (1966) 238–243
2. Burstein, J.: The E-Rater Scoring Engine: Automated Essay Scoring with Natural Language Processing. In Shermis, M.D., Burstein, J., eds.: Automated Essay Scoring: a Cross-Disciplinary Perspective. Lawrence Erlbaum Associates, Hillsdale, New Jersey, USA (2003) 113–122
3. Landauer, T.K., Foltz, P.W., Laham, D.: Introduction to Latent Semantic Analysis. Discourse Processes **25** (1998) 259–284
4. Hofmann, T.: Unsupervised Learning by Probabilistic Latent Semantic Analysis. Machine Learning Journal **42** (2000) 177–196
5. Landauer, T.K., D. Laham, P.F.: Automatic Essay Assessment. Assessment in Education **10** (2003) 295–308
6. Kakkonen, T., Myller, N., Sutinen, E., Timonen, J.: Automatic Essay Grading with Probabilistic Latent Semantic Analysis. In: Proceedings of the ACL 2005 Second Workshop on Building Educational Applications Using Natural Language Processing, Ann Arbor, Michigan, USA (2005) 29–36
7. Lemaire, B., Dessus, P.: A System to Assess the Semantic Content of Student Essays. Journal of Educational Computing Research **24** (2001) 305–320

8. Blei, D.M., Ng, A.Y., Jordan, M.I.: Latent Dirichlet Allocation. Journal of Machine Learning Research **3** (2003) 993–1022
9. Kakkonen, T., Sutinen, E.: Automatic Assessment of the Content of Essays Based on Course Materials. In: Proceedings of International Conference on Information Technology: Research and Education, London, UK (2004) 126–130
10. Lingsoft: Lingsoft Ltd. WWW-page (2005) http://www.lingsoft.fi (Accessed 1.3.2006).
11. Kakkonen, T., Sutinen, E., Timonen, J.: Applying Validation Methods for Noise Reduction in LSA-based Essay Grading. WSEAS Transactions on Information Science and Applications **2** (2005) 1334–1342
12. Minka, T., Lafferty, J.: Expectation-propagation for the generative aspect model. In: Proceedings of the Eighteenth Conference on Uncertainty in Artificial Intelligence. (2002) 352–359
13. Girolami, M., Kabán, A.: On an Equivalence between PLSI and LDA. In: Proceedings of the 26th Annual International ACM SIGIR Conference on Research and Development in Information Retrieval, NY, ACM Press (2003) 433–434
14. Globerson, A., Tishby, N.: Sufficient Dimensionality Reduction. Journal of Machine Learning Research **3** (2003) 1307–1331
15. Brants, T.: Test Data Likelihood for PLSA Models. Information Retrieval **8** (2005) 181–196
16. Larkey, L.: Automatic Essay Grading Using Text Categorization Techniques. In: Proceedings of 21st Annual International Conference on Research and Development in Information Retrieval. (1998) 90–95
17. Landauer, T., Rehder, B., Schreiner, M.E.: How Well Can Passage Meaning Be Derived without Using Word Order? A Comparison of Latent Semantic Analysis and Humans. In: Proceedings of the 19th Annual Meeting of the Cognitive Science Society. (1997)
18. Foltz, P.W., Gilliam, S., Kendall, S.: Supporting Content-based Feedback in Online Writing Evaluation with LSA. Interactive Learning Environments **8** (2001) 111–129

Automatic Acquisition of Semantic Relationships from Morphological Relatedness

Delphine Bernhard

TIMC-IMAG
Institut de l'Ingénierie et de l'Information de Santé
Faculté de Médecine
38706 La Tronche cedex, France
Delphine.Bernhard@imag.fr

Abstract. Semantic relationships like specialisation can be acquired either by word-external methods relying on the context or word-internal methods based on lexical structure. Word segments are thus a relevant cue for the automatic acquisition of semantic relationships. We have developed an unsupervised method for morphological segmentation devised for this objective. Semantic relationships are deduced from specific morphological structures based on the segments discovered. Evaluation of the validity of the semantic relationships inferred is performed against WordNet and the NCI Thesaurus.

1 Introduction

Structured resources like terminologies or thesauri are usually organised in a hierarchical way through the specialisation relationship. Manual identification of such relationships is a time-consuming process. Many methods thus aim at automatically acquiring semantically related words. These can be subdivided in two main approaches. One is to use the context in which terms occur. Contexts may for instance be described through specific lexico-syntactic patterns like "*X such as Y, ... (and|or) Z*" where Y is X's hyponym, i.e. Y is a kind of X [1]. The other approach relies on the inner structure of words and multi-word expressions. Much work has been devoted to the induction of semantic relationships from the lexical structure of multi-word terms, but corresponding methods for morphologically complex single word terms need resources or tools able to segment words into sub-units. We have therefore devised a system for the unsupervised segmentation of words into labelled segments (stems, prefixes, suffixes and linking elements). These labelled units are then used to discover semantic relationships like subsumption between morphologically complex single word terms. We have tested the method using a corpus of English texts on breast cancer and evaluated the results against two structured resources, namely the NCI Thesaurus and WordNet.

T. Salakoski et al. (Eds.): FinTAL 2006, LNAI 4139, pp. 121–132, 2006.

2 Lexically-Induced Semantic Relationships

In this section we describe methods for the acquisition of semantic relationships from the inner structure of words and multi-word expressions.

2.1 Induction of Semantic Relationships from the Lexical Structure of Multi-word Terms

Multi-word terms are phrases which represent domain-specific concepts like *"radiation therapy"* in oncology. They are composed of several graphical words i.e. character strings separated by spaces. Research on the induction of semantic relationships from the lexical structure of multi-word terms focuses mainly on hypernymy, though other kinds of semantic relationships are addressed as well. Semantic relations are induced from several types of lexical variation patterns, the most important being **lexical inclusion**.

Lexical inclusion is defined as follows by [2]: a term T_1 is lexically included in another term T_2 iff all the normalised content words in T_1 occur in T_2. Lexical inclusion is a hint that T_1 is T_2's hypernym. This is the case for example with the term *"fatty acid"* which is lexically included in the term *"omega-3 fatty acid"*: *"fatty acid"* is the hypernym of *"omega-3 fatty acid"*, i.e. *"omega-3 fatty acid"* is a kind of *"fatty acid"*.

Lexical inclusion can be described even more precisely through different patterns depending on the place where terms T_1 and T_2 differ. We use the same terminology here as [3]:

- **Left expansion:** $T_2 = W + T_1$. W can be an adjective [4,5] as in *"ventricular aneurysm"* - *"aneurysm"* or a noun [5] as in *"compression fracture"* - *"fracture"*.
- **Insertion.** In this case, a new element W is inserted in the middle of T_1 in order to form T_2 as in *"adult brain glioblastoma"* - *"adult glioblastoma"*
- **Right expansion:** $T_2 = T_1 + W$. Example: *"cholesterol"* - *"cholesterol granuloma"*.

All these patterns do not equally well account for hierarchical relationships. According to [5], left expansion and insertion generally induce a hierarchical relationship between terms while right expansion corresponds to a weaker semantic link comparable to *See also* thesaurus links. Results obtained by these methods nevertheless show that they might usefully complement context-based methods. For instance [4] demonstrate that less than half of the hyponymy relationships suggested by adjectival left expansions are present in the hierarchical structure of their gold-standard thesaurus (UMLS: Unified Medical Language System).

Besides lexical inclusion, [3] also defines **substitution** as the replacement of a component word in T_1 by another word in T_2 where T_1 and T_2 have the same length. Modifier substitutions are a hint that both terms belong the same class, i.e. are co-hyponyms. Moreover, morphosyntactic modifications of one of the constituents of a multi-word term can induce semantic relationships other than hypernymy or co-hyponymy like antonymy (*"organic chemical"* - *"inorganic chemical"*) or temporal precedence [6].

2.2 Induction of Semantic Relationships from the Morphological Structure of Single-Word Terms

Work on morphosemantics has been undertaken especially for scientific and technical single-word terms. Since morphemes are the minimal meaning-bearing units they are useful to detect semantic relationships. But segmenting words into subunits is a difficult task. Morphosemantic information is therefore either manually encoded or automatically acquired from semantically related words found in thesauri or dictionaries.

Systems for the acquisition of lexical semantic information may be given as input lists of affixes or combining forms with their corresponding semantic values. For instance, [7] manually analyses a limited number of general language derivational affixes to provide corresponding lexical semantic features like telicity or activity. Other systems, like the rule-based morphosemantic parser described in [8] account for the complex morphological structure of medical language, based on manually-built lists of combining forms associated with semantic information. Of course, such kind of tools, though providing robust analyses, suffer from the drawbacks inherent to lexicon and rule-based approaches in that they require human validation and maintenance of the rules and lexicon.

In order to overcome these limitations, other systems aim at automatically acquiring morphosemantic information, but still necessitate some manually-built resources like thesauri and dictionaries [9,10] or some amount of manual validation [11]. The incremental method presented in [11] focuses on the semi-automatic acquisition of couples of antonyms, starting from a manually-built list of words opposed by their prefixes. New couples of antonyms which have been automatically identified have to be validated by an expert. Couples of semantically-related words can also be extracted from terminologies like SNOMED [9] or specialised dictionaries [10]. Morphological rules are then acquired either by comparing the orthography of both words [9] or by identifying analogies in quadruplets of words [10]. These rules may be used afterwards to discover morphologically related words and suggest a semantic link between these words.

Manual validation or the use of external resources limit the chance that incorrect morphological relationships be induced but on the other hand this requires that such resources or manpower be available. We have therefore built a system to discover morphological structure from a raw list of words.

3 Unsupervised Morphological Segmentation

In order to segment words into morphological sub-units we have used the method described in [12]. Like other systems [13,14] it is not dependent on a given language, nor on a given domain and performs complex morphological segmentation in that it is able to segment compound word forms. It has already been used to segment words in English, Finnish, French and Turkish and compares well to the Morfessor systems described in [13] since it has been shown to achieve an F-measure of about 65% on a morpheme segmentation task for these three languages [15]. It uses a plain word-list as input and can be decomposed in the following stages:

1. Acquisition of prefixes and suffixes using drops in the transitional probability between substrings.
2. Extraction of stems by subtracting prefixes and suffixes from words.
3. Segmentation of words based on the alignment of words containing the same stem.
4. Selection of the best segmentation among all possible segmentations for a word.

As a result of morphological segmentation, words are split in sub-units, belonging to either of the 4 following segment types: stems, prefixes, suffixes, and linking elements. For instance, the word *eyeglasses* is segmented as follows: eye + glass + *es*, where eye and glass are stems and *es* is a suffix.

4 Using Morphological Segments to Retrieve Semantic Relationships

Morphological families can be easily built by grouping words sharing an identical stem. This readily clusters words in morphological and hence semantic groups. There are however different degrees of semantic relatedness within morphological families: inflectional variants are closely related while derivational variants have more distant meanings. We have therefore identified specific morphological constructs which correspond to particular semantic relationships.

Thanks to the morphological tags provided by the segmentation relevant roles like head and modifier are easily identified within the word. In English (as well as in French and German), the head of a compound word form is located at the end of the word. We therefore consider the head to be the rightmost stem. Elements occurring to the left of this stem (prefixes and other stems) are modifiers. Linking elements and suffixes are not considered as relevant semantic elements in our typology, though of course they also contribute to the meaning of the word, especially derivational suffixes.

Several types of lexical relations are induced by morphological segmentation. We focus on two types of morphological patterns for terms sharing the same head: inclusion and substitution. These should make it possible to respectively detect hypernymy and co-hyponymy. We re-use terminology introduced in Section 2.1 to describe lexical inclusion and substitution for multi-word expressions.

1. **Inclusion** corresponds to two different constructs:
   (a) **Left expansion:** term T_2 is a left expansion variant of term T_1 if:
      – they share the same final sequence of morphological elements, necessarily including at least one stem
      – T_2 differs from T_1 by its initial sequence of morphological elements, necessarily including one and only one prefix or stem

For instance, *lymphedema* is a left expansion variant of *edema* while *outpatient* is a left expansion variant of *patient.*

(b) **Insertion:** term T_2 is a modifier insertion variant of term T_1 if T_2 is formed by inserting by either a stem or a prefix in the middle of T_1, before the rightmost stem. For instance, *hepatosplenomegaly* is an insertion variant of *hepatomegaly.*

2. **Substitution** occurs in the following morphological construct: terms T_1 and T_2 are substitution variants if they share the same final sequence of morphological elements but differ by the initial sequence of morphological elements including one and only one prefix or stem. For instance, *magnetotherapy* and *curietherapy* are substitution variants.

5 Results

In order to evaluate the method, we have used a list of about 86,000 word forms extracted from a corpus on breast cancer. The corpus contains 4,549 texts and has been automatically built from the Internet, using the method described in [16]. After performing morphological segmentation, we have extracted word couples using the inclusion and substitution patterns previously described. We have checked semantic relationships against two different resources: a domain specific thesaurus (NCI Thesaurus) and a general language resource (WordNet).

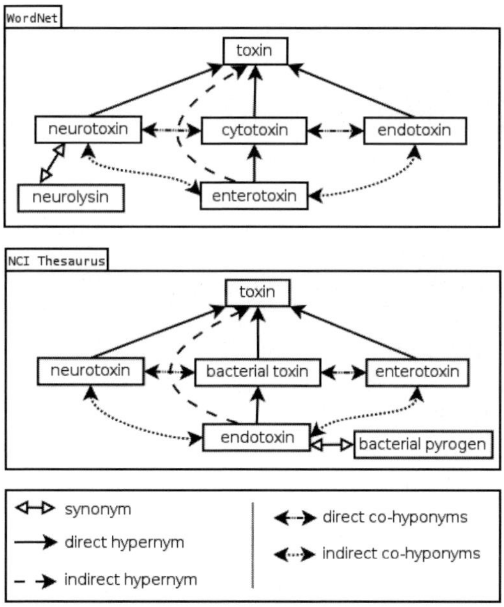

Fig. 1. Example semantic links in the NCI Thesaurus and in WordNet

5.1 Evaluation Using the NCI Thesaurus

The NCI Thesaurus is an open content vocabulary published by the National Cancer Institute and available under Open Source License [17]. For this study we have used the flat file Version 06.01c (January 2006). Included in this format are all the terms associated with NCI Thesaurus concepts (names and synonyms) and subsumption relations. The thesaurus contains about 117,000 terms and 48,000 concepts. Approximately 85% of all concepts are represented by multi-word terms and will thus not be considered in this study which focuses on morphologically complex single-word terms.

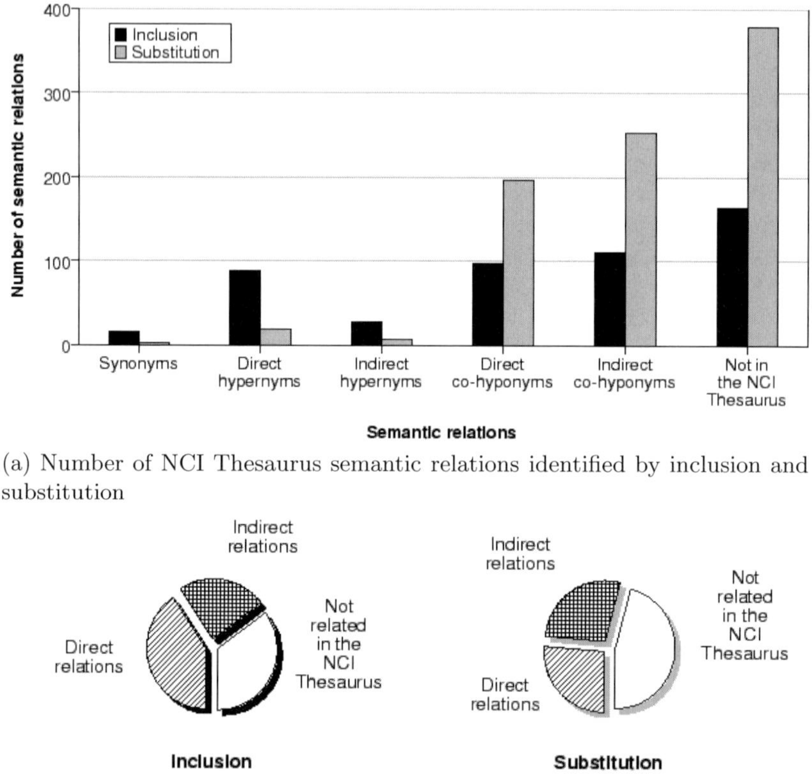

(a) Number of NCI Thesaurus semantic relations identified by inclusion and substitution

(b) Proportions of direct and indirect relations comparatively to relations not found in the NCI Thesaurus

Fig. 2. Results of the evaluation using the NCI Thesaurus

For each pair of words (T_1, T_2) linked either by inclusion or substitution and representing the concepts (C_1, C_2) we checked which semantic relationships are found between these terms and their corresponding concepts in the

NCI Thesaurus (see also Figure 1). Results obtained for the following semantic relationships are detailed in Figure 2:

- **Synonymy:** T_1 and T_2 are synonyms if they represent the same concept.
- **Direct hypernymy:** C_1 is C_2's direct hypernym if C_1 is the direct superconcept of C_2 in the concept hierarchy.
- **Indirect hypernymy:** C_1 is C_2's indirect hypernym if C_1 is one of C_2's ancestors.
- **Direct co-hyponymy:** C_1 and C_2 are direct co-hyponyms if they share the same direct hypernym.
- **Indirect co-hyponymy:** C_1 and C_2 are indirect co-hyponyms if they share an identical ancestor, with a maximum ancestor distance in the hierarchy of 3 (i.e the shared ancestor is at most a great grandparent).

5.2 Evaluation Using WordNet

WordNet is a lexical database for English [18]. In WordNet words are grouped in sets of synonyms (synsets) representing concepts. Noun synsets are hierarchically related by the specialisation, or IS-A, relationship. Part-whole or meronymic relationships between nouns and antonymy are represented as well. For this study we have only used the noun subset of WordNet 2.0. It contains 114,648 unique noun strings, 79,689 synsets and 141,690 word-sense pairs.

Relationships considered for evaluation are the same as those listed before for the NCI Thesaurus, plus **antonymy** (semantic opposition) and **meronymy** (part-of relationship). Synonyms are words which belong to the same synset. Note that in WordNet, semantic relations are defined between synsets (except of course synonymy). We have therefore considered all the different senses attached to each word in WordNet to retrieve semantic relationships. Results are displayed in Figure 3.

6 Discussion

In this section, we discuss the results obtained and give some examples of correct and incorrect semantic relationships.

6.1 Hyper-/Hyponymy

We hypothesised in Section 4 that hyponymic relationships should correspond to the inclusion pattern while co-hyponymy should be reflected by substitution. Indeed, a very small proportion of specialisation relationships are predicted by the substitution pattern and the inclusion pattern performs better for this task. This observation holds for WordNet as well as for the NCI Thesaurus.

6.2 Co-hyponymy

Again, as we hypothesised, couples of co-hyponymic terms predicted by the substitution pattern outnumber those predicted by the inclusion pattern. But the inclusion pattern nevertheless predicts more direct and indirect co-hyponymic

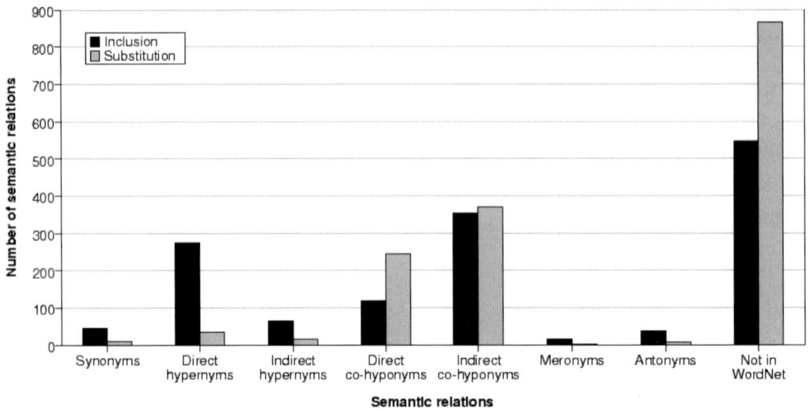

(a) Number of WordNet semantic relations identified by inclusion and substitution

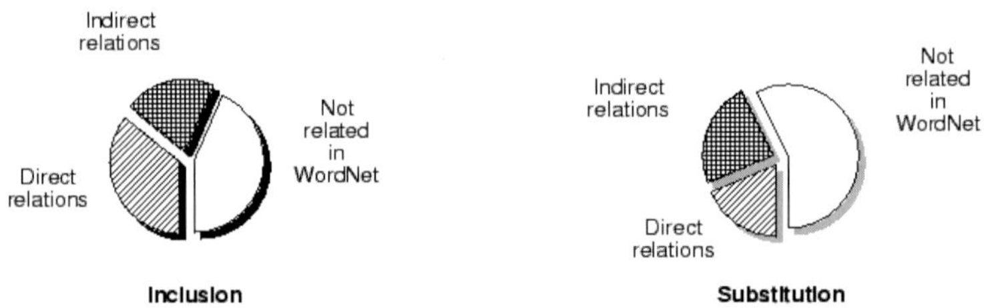

(b) Proportions of direct and indirect relations comparatively to relations not found in WordNet

Fig. 3. Results of the evaluation using WordNet

relationships than specialisation relationships. Indeed, inclusion does not always correspond to specialisation. For instance, consider the following couple of words: (*"hypothalamus"*, *"thalamus"*); the term *"thalamus"* is included in the longer term *"hypothalamus"*. But the *"hypothalamus"* is not a kind of *"thalamus"*; rather, the *"hypothalamus"* is found below the *"thalamus"*. In WordNet, *"thalamus"* and *"hypothalamus"* are therefore co-hyponyms of *"neural structure"* and co-meronyms of *"diencephalon"*. And in the NCI Thesaurus they are co-hyponyms of *"Brain_Part"*.

6.3 Other Semantic Relationships

Synonyms, antonyms and meronyms rarely correspond to the inclusion and substitution patterns. They however display recurrent morphological constructs which could be used for their identification:

Synonyms. Synonyms are often compounds, as for instance (*"paper"*, *"newspaper"*) or (*"tan"*, *"suntan"*). In such cases the initial stem, as *"sun"* in *"suntan"* is optional when used in specific contexts. Orthographical variants like (*"edema"*, *"oedema"*) also belong to that category.

Antonyms. Couples of antonyms are usually opposed by their prefixes like *dis-/ε-* (*"disagreement"*, *"agreement"*), *un-/ε-* (*"unconsciousness"*, *"consciousness"*), *non-/ε-* (*"nonparticipation"*, *"participation"*) , *in-/ε-* (*"inactivity"*, *"activity"*), *hyper-/hypo-* (*"hyperpigmentation"*, *"hypopigmentation"*) or *in-/out-* (*"inflow"*, *"outflow"*). This observation is consistent with the semi-supervised method for the extraction of antonyms described in [11].

Meronyms. Many meronyms are formed by adding one of the following prefixes to their holonym: *mid-* (*"midnight"*, *"night"*), *sub-* (*"subfamily"*, *"family"*), *half-* (*"half-hour"*, *"hour"*) or *quarter* (*"quarter-century"*, *"century"*).

6.4 Missing Relationships

About half of the couples identified by the insertion and substitution patterns are not found in the NCI Thesaurus and WordNet (see Figures 2(b) and 3(b)). The inclusion pattern seems more reliable in that respect since it proportionately retrieves more relationships found either in the NCI Thesaurus or in WordNet than the substitution pattern. Three different explanations can be given:

Inaccurate Morphological Segmentations. The procedure for morphological segmentation is unsupervised and it is therefore only natural that some results should be inaccurate. See for examples the following segmentations (stems are underlined):

- lobule = lobul + e
  globule = g + lobul + e
- kill = kill
  skill = s + kill
- copy = cop + y
  sigmoidoscopy = sigmoid + o + s + cop + y

These terms are considered as inclusion variants while they are neither morphologically nor semantically related.

Ambiguous Segments. Just as words, word segments may have more than one meaning. See for example the following list of words: *"gram"*, *"microgram"*, *"milligram"*, *"arteriogram"*, *"mammogram"*, *"sonogram"*. All of these words share the word-final segment *-gram.* But in these examples *"gram"* has two different meanings: it can either refer to a metric unit as in *"microgram"* and *"milligram"* or to a kind of picture as in *"arteriogram"* and *"mammogram"*. As a consequence, spurious word couples such as (*"arteriogram"*, *"milligram"*) are identified but valid semantic links as (*"sonogram"*, *"arteriogram"*) are retrieved as well.

General Semantic Link. Some of the stems retrieved by the segmentation method correspond to word-forming elements which carry reduced semantic information. Take for example the segment *-logy* found in words as diverse as: *"technology"*, *"pathology"* or *"pharmacology"*. Some of the words sharing the final segment *-logy* are closely related. This is the case for instance with *"nephrology"*, *"hematology"* and *"rheumatology"* which are all co-hyponyms of the superconcept *"Internal_Medicine"* in the NCI Thesaurus. In other cases however the semantic contribution of *-logy* is so tenuous that terms cannot be considered as semantically related, as for instance in the following three words: *"psychology"*, *"opthalmology"* and *"technology"*.

6.5 Overlap and Differences Between Links Found in WordNet and the NCI Thesaurus

The method has been tested on a specialised corpus. In order to be able to assess the usability of this method for general corpora, we have compared the results of the evaluations using WordNet and the NCI Thesaurus (see Figure 4). We

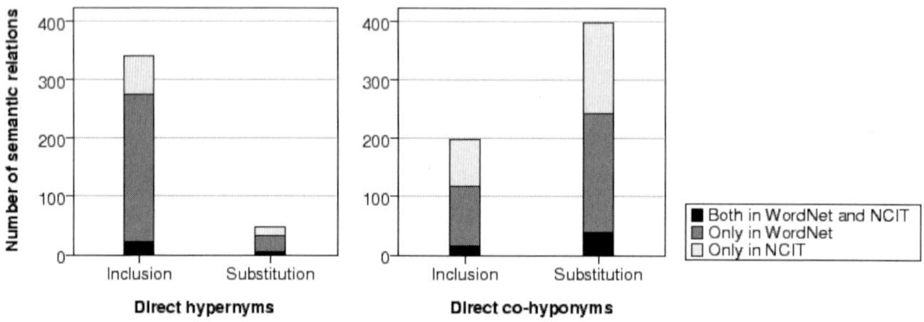

Fig. 4. Number of semantic relations found in WordNet and/or the NCI Thesaurus

notice that the overlap between relations found in WordNet and those found in the NCI Thesaurus is rather small and most of the relations are found in only one of the resources. Theses differences are due to two main causes:

- The NCI Thesaurus contains domain-specific terms while WordNet describes general language. It is thus not surprising that some terms should be found only in one of the resources and that many relations found only in WordNet link general language terms like *"tub"* – *"bathtub"* or *"bedroom"* – *"living-room"*.
- Hierarchical structures differ in both resources. For instance *"edema"* is *"lymphedema"*'s hypernym in WordNet, while they are not related by a specialisation link in the NCI Thesaurus. Figure 1 gives another such example for the terms *"toxin"* and *"endotoxin"*.

7 Conclusions and Future Research

We have presented a method to detect semantic relationships between words relying on morphological segmentation. We have defined two morphological constructs, inclusion and substitution in order to acquire specialisation and cohyponymic relationships. Evaluation performed using WordNet and the NCI

Thesaurus shows an interesting overlap between semantic relationships induced by morphological structure and semantic relationships present in the resources. We have however noticed that even though the inclusion pattern performs well, it also extracts many co-hyponymic links. The semantic relation induced is therefore ambiguous. Also, results could be undoubtedly bettered by improving the recall of the morphological segmentation algorithm and thus augmenting the number of semantic relationships identified.

In this study, we have only considered two morphological patterns. In the future, we plan to investigate if other morphological patterns might be of interest to retrieve semantic relationships. Of course, as has already been shown by [7], morphological cues cannot come as a replacement to other surface cues like distributional information since they are not available for all words. Results obtained should therefore also be compared with contextual approaches based on lexico-syntactic patterns like [1] or co-occurrence vectors like LSA [19] or HAL [20] to see which are the benefits of each and how they could complement one another.

References

1. Hearst, M.A.: Automatic Acquisition of Hyponyms from Large Text Corpora. In: Proceedings of the Fourteenth International Conference on Computational Linguistics, Nantes, France, July 1992. (1992) 539–545
2. Grabar, N., Zweigenbaum, P.: Lexically-based terminology structuring: a feasibility study. In: Proceedings of the LREC Workshop on Using Semantics for Information Retrieval and Filtering, Las Palmas, Canaries (2002) 73–77
3. Ibekwe-SanJuan, F.: Terminological variation, a means of identifying research topics from texts. In: Proceedings of the Joint International Conference on Computational Linguistics (COLING-ACL'98), Montréal, Québec (1998) 564–570
4. Bodenreider, O., Burgun, A., Rindflesch, T.C.: Lexically-suggested hyponymic relations among medical terms and their representation in the UMLS. In: Actes de la Quatrième rencontre Terminologie et Intelligence Artificielle (TIA'01), Nancy, France (2001) 11–21
5. Ibekwe-SanJuan, F.: Inclusion lexicale et proximité sémantique entre termes. In: Actes des Sixièmes rencontres Terminologie et Intelligence Artificielle (TIA'05), Rouen, France (2005) 45–57
6. Daille, B.: Conceptual structuring through term variations. In Bond, F., Korhonen, A., MacCarthy, D., Villacicencio, A., eds.: Proceedings of the ACL 2003 Workshop on Multiword Expressions: Analysis, Acquisition and Treatment. (2003) 9–16
7. Light, M.: Morphological cues for lexical semantics. In: Proceedings of the 34th annual meeting of the Association for Computational Linguistics, Association for Computational Linguistics (1996) 25–31
8. Namer, F., Zweigenbaum, P.: Acquiring meaning for French medical terminology: contribution of morphosemantics. In: Proceedings of Medinfo. 2004. Volume 11., San Francisco CA (2004) 535–539
9. Zweigenbaum, P., Grabar, N.: Liens morphologiques et structuration de terminologie. In: Actes de IC 2000 : Ingénierie des Connaissances. (2000) 325–334
10. Claveau, V., L'Homme, M.C.: Structuring Terminology by Analogy-Based Machine Learning. In: Proceedings of the 7th International Conference on Terminology and Knowledge Engineering, TKE'05. (2005)

11. Schwab, D., Lafourcade, M., Prince, V.: Extraction semi-supervisée de couples d'antonymes grâce à leur morphologie. In: Actes de TALN 2005. (2005) 73–82
12. Bernhard, D.: Unsupervised Morphological Segmentation Based on Segment Predictability and Word Segments Alignment. In: Proceedings of the Pascal Challenges Workshop on the Unsupervised Segmentation of Words into Morphemes, Venice, Italy (2006) 19–23
13. Creutz, M., Lagus, K.: Inducing the Morphological Lexicon of a Natural Language from Unannotated Text. In: Proceedings of the International and Interdisciplinary Conference on Adaptive Knowledge Representation and Reasoning (AKRR'05), Espoo, Finland (2005)
14. Bordag, S.: Unsupervised Knowledge-Free Morpheme Boundary Detection. In: Proceedings of RANLP (Recent Advances in Natural Language Processing) 2005, Borovets, Bulgaria (2005)
15. Kurimo, M., Creutz, M., Varjokallio, M., Arisoy, E., Saraclar, M.: Unsupervised segmentation of words into morphemes – Challenge 2005: An Introduction and Evaluation Report. In: Proceedings of the Pascal Challenges Workshop on the Unsupervised Segmentation of Words into Morphemes, Venice, Italy (2006) 1–11
16. Baroni, M., Bernardini, S.: BootCaT: Bootstrapping Corpora and Terms from the Web. In Lino, M.T., Xavier, M.F., Ferreira, F., Costa, R., Silva, R., eds.: Proceedings of the Fourth International Conference on Language Resources and Evaluation (LREC), Lisbon, Portugal (2004) 1313–1316
17. National Cancer Institute, Office of Communications and Center for Bioinformatics: NCI Thesaurus. ftp://ftp1.nci.nih.gov/pub/cacore/EVS (2006) [Online; accessed 23 March 2006].
18. Miller, G.A.: WordNet: a lexical database for English. Communications of the ACM **38**(11) (1995) 39–41
19. Deerwester, S., Dumais, S.T., Furnas, G.W., Landauer, T.K., Harshman, R.: Indexing by Latent Semantic Analysis. Journal of the American Society for Information Science **41**(6) (1990) 391–407
20. Lund, K., Burgess, C.: Producing high-dimensional semantic spaces from lexical co-occurrence. Behavior Research Methods, Instruments & Computers **28**(2) (1996) 203–208

Automatic Feature Extraction for Question Classification Based on Dissimilarity of Probability Distributions *

David Tomás[1], José L. Vicedo[1], Empar Bisbal[2], and Lidia Moreno[2]

[1] Departamento de Lenguajes y Sistemas Informáticos
Universidad de Alicante, Spain
{dtomas, vicedo}@dlsi.ua.es

[2] Departamento de Sistemas Informáticos y Computación
Universidad Politécnica de Valencia, Spain
{ebisbal, lmoreno}@dsic.upv.es

Abstract. Question classification is one of the first tasks carried out in a Question Answering system. In this paper we present a multilingual question classification system based on machine learning techniques. We use Support Vector Machines to classify the questions. All the features needed to train and test this method are automatically extracted through statistical information in an unsupervised way, comparing *Poisson distributions* of single words in two plain corpora of questions and documents. Thus, we need nothing but plain text to train the system, obtaining a flexible approach easy to adapt to new languages and domains. We have tested it on a bilingual corpus of questions in English and Spanish.

1 Introduction

Question classification is one of the tasks carried out in a Question Answering system. It tries to assign a class or category to the searched answer. The answer extraction process depends on this classification, as different strategies may be used depending on the question type detected. Consequently, the overall performance of the system depends directly on question classification.

In this paper we present a machine learning approach to question classification. We use Support Vector Machines (SVM) for the learning task. All the features needed to train the system are automatically obtained by means of statistical information, comparing how probability distributions of words differ in a plain corpus of questions and a plain corpus of documents. As a result, no complex linguistic knowledge or tools are needed to build the system, resulting in a flexible approach easily adaptable to different languages and domains. The system has been tested on a bilingual corpus of English and Spanish questions.

Next section outlines current research on question classification. Section 3 describes the machine learning framework, the statistical foundations followed

* This work has been developed in the framework of the project CICYT R2D2 (TIC2003-07158-C04).

T. Salakoski et al. (Eds.): FinTAL 2006, LNAI 4139, pp. 133–140, 2006.

in this approach, the resources employed and the feature extraction process. Section 4 shows the experiments carried out and the results obtained. Finally, conclusions and future work are discussed in section 5.

2 Question Classification

The question classification process maps a question to a predefined set of answer types. Most question classification systems are based on heuristic rules and hand made patterns [1] . This kind of systems presents two main problems. First, the great amount of human effort needed to define the patterns as there are many different ways to query the system. Secondly, the lack of flexibility and domain dependency, as changing the domain of application or adding new classes would involve the revision and redefinition of the whole set of heuristics and patterns.

By applying machine learning techniques we want to bypass such limitations, obtaining a system that can automatically learn from experience. Systems that follow this approach normally learn from features obtained through complex linguistic information, like chunking, semantic analysis or named entity recognition [2]. This kind of linguistic knowledge binds the systems to particular tools and resources, creating dependencies that also make them hard to move to new languages and domains.

In our approach, the learning features are exclusively extracted from statistical information obtained from plain corpora of questions and documents. Neither tools nor complex linguistic resources (not even a stopword list) are required to train the system, but just plain text. Moreover, no special heuristics have been used when changing from one language to another. The final goal is to obtain a question classification system that can be automatically adapted to new languages and domains employing nothing but plain text.

Next section describes the machine learning framework and the statistical feature extraction method.

3 Machine Learning Approach

Machine learning is concerned with the task of constructing computer applications that automatically improve with experience. This field of research allows obtaining more flexible applications than those based on linguistic knowledge. While linguistic methods are usually more precise, those based on machine learning sacrifice precision in order to obtain more coverage and robustness. Besides that, the cost of development of such systems is lower than those based on linguistic techniques as knowledge is automatically acquired.

Many different machine learning methods have been applied in classification. In our previous work [3] we tested several techniques from different families of algorithms for question classification. Looking at the results obtained, we have decided to use SVM [4] as the best method for this task of classification.

3.1 Statistical Feature Extraction

All the learning features used in our system are somehow obtained from statistical information acquired from unigrams (single words) in plain text corpora. For instance, we compute the divergence of *Poisson distributions* of unigrams extracted from a corpus of documents and a corpus of questions, in order to decide whether a word in the question may be a relevant feature on our SVM-based question classification system. These words must be carefully selected as questions are very short portions of text.

In the following paragraphs, we first present the statistical basis applied in our approach. Next, we show the resources necessary to obtain the statistical information and finally, we describe the feature vector for the learning task.

3.2 Statistical Foundations

Statistics allow learning from observation and experience. By applying statistical methods to language processing we try to capture regularities in linguistic expressions.

To estimate the parameters of the statistical model we use linguistic corpus. We have a universe of outcomes formed by the words of the corpus, and we have assigned a probability to them, which is exactly the frequency of appearance in the corpus. Probabilities are always members of a distribution, which is a set of non-negative numbers that add up to 1.0. The standard probabilistic model for the distribution of a certain type of event over units of a fixed size is the *Poisson distribution*, defined as follows:

$$p(k;\lambda_i) = e^{-\lambda_i}\frac{\lambda_i^k}{k!}. \qquad (1)$$

In the most common model of the *Poisson distribution* [5], λ_i is the average number of occurrences of word w_i per document, that is $\lambda_i = cf_i/N$, where cf_i is the collection frequency of the word w_i and N is the total number of documents in the collection. The *Poisson distribution* can be used to estimate the probability of a document having exactly k occurrences of w_i.

In our approach $p(k \geq 1, \lambda_i)$ and $p(k = 0; \lambda_i)$ are calculated for every w_i, that is, the probability that a word that follows the *Poisson distribution* appears or not in a text. These values are computed in two different corpora: a corpus of documents and a corpus of questions. With this information we can predict the chance that a word appears in a document or a question.

Another statistical concept we want to introduce is the relative entropy, also known as the *Kullback-Leibler (KL) divergence*. It is a measure of how different are two probability distributions p and q:

$$D(p\|q) = \sum_{x \in X} p(x) log\frac{p(x)}{q(x)}. \qquad (2)$$

We use this value to compare how the distribution of a word differs from a corpus of documents to a corpus of questions.

Finally, another two closely related concepts are employed: the *mean* and the *variance*. The *mean* (or *arithmetic mean*) of a list of numbers is the sum of all the members in the list divided by the number of items in the list. The *variance* measures how much the individual members deviate from the *mean*.

The *mean* of the position where a word appears in a question is calculated. The *variance* is employed to determine weather a word tends to appear always in the same position inside the questions. If the position is the same in all cases, the *variance* is zero.

3.3 Resources

We have collected statistical information for individual words (unigram model) from two different corpora: a corpus of documents and a corpus of questions. This will allow us to compare how word behavior differs in documents and questions. The texts were previously filtered in order to lower case the words and eliminate undesired characters: dots, slashes, hyphenations...

We need two different sets of resources in order to test the system on English and Spanish. The corpora of documents in English consists of newswire texts from the CLEF[1] conferences: the *L.A. Times 94* (113,005 documents) and the *Glasgow Herald 95* (56,472 documents). The corpora of documents for Spanish was also obtained from CLEF, and consists of news from agency *EFE* in years 1994 (215,738 documents) and 1995 (238,307 documents).

As we said before, we also need a corpus of questions to extract statistical information. We first collected all the questions from TREC[2] 1999 to TREC 2003 Question Answering track, obtaining a set of 2393 factoid English samples. To complete the resources for Spanish we just translated them into this language [6].

One of the assumptions when applying *Poisson distributions* is that documents are all the same size. As we want to compare distributions of words between documents and questions, the questions were randomly gathered from TREC in sets about the same size. This size is obtained measuring the average number of words per document in the corpus of documents. Finally, a set of documents exclusively formed by questions was obtained.

Once compiled the corpora, the number of times every word appeared in each corpus was counted, obtaining the collection frequency cf_i of a word w_i in the corpus of documents and in the corpus of questions. With this information, a database with the following statistics for each word was created: (1) the word itself; (2) the probabilities $p_d(k \geq 1, \lambda_i)$ and $p_d(k = 0, \lambda_i)$ in the corpus of documents, i.e., the probabilities that a word w_i following the *Poisson distribution* appears or not in a corpus of documents; (3) the probabilities $p_q(k \geq 1, \lambda_i)$ and $p_q(k = 0, \lambda_i)$ in the corpus of questions, i.e., the probabilities that a word w_i following the *Poisson distribution* appears or not in a set of questions randomly gathered to equal the average size of a document in the corpus of documents; (4) the *KL divergence* of the probability distributions mentioned above; (5) the

[1] Cross Language Evaluation Forum, http://www.clef-campaign.org

[2] Text REtrieval Conference, http://trec.nist.gov

mean of the position of the word in the questions; (6) the *sample deviation* of the position of the word in the questions, which is just the square root of the *variance* described in section 3.2.

Only words appearing in both corpora were taken into account. Of course, we have different statistical databases for every language studied.

3.4 Feature Vector

We use the statistical information collected to obtain two different kinds of features that are employed in the experiments in section 4: (1) the relevant words in the question; (2) the label indicating whether each word in the question is a stopword, a keyword or a definition term[3].

Relevant Words. The statistical information allows us to decide which words in the questions are useful features for the question classification task. Stopwords or rarely appearing words are not useful in order to determine the class of the question we are dealing with. Otherwise, *wh-words* (*what*, *when*, *where*...) are very helpful for this task. Our theoretical assumption here is that a word in the question is a good feature if it behaves as a stopword in the corpus of questions but not in the corpus of documents, that is, if it appears commonly in questions but not so often in documents, being the two probabilities of appearance substantially different.

To obtain these useful words from a question, all the words appearing are taken separately and the statistical information stored in the database is retrieved. If the word is not included in the database or appears only once (*hapax legomenon*), we automatically reject it as a feature: rarely appearing words are not useful for the classification task.

We set two different thresholds to determine whether a word is candidate to be part of the feature vector or not. The first one, th_1, is inspired in the probability $p(k \geq 1, \lambda_i)$ of a word following the *Poisson distribution.* This value indicates the probability of appearance of a word at least once in a document. If this number is high, it indicates that the word tends to appear in every document behaving as a stopword in the corpus.

This threshold is automatically set through the formula of *Poisson distribution* in equation (1). We assume that a stopword is a word that appears at least once in every document, being cf, the frequency of the word in the corpus, equal to the number of documents N. Thus, $\lambda = 1$ and the probability of this kind of words appearing at least once in a document following equation (1) is:

$$th_1 = p(k \geq 1, \lambda) = p(k \geq 1, 1) = 1 - p(k = 0, 1) = 1 - e^{-1} = 0.632121.$$

This value is the same for both English and Spanish classifiers.

[3] Definition terms are those that do not help retrieval systems to locate the correct answer but are useful to determine the kind of information requested, like *wh-words*.

The second threshold ,th_2, is inspired in the *KL divergence* and measures how different must be the probability distributions of a word in the corpora of documents and questions to consider that its role notably changes from one to another. This time the threshold was empirically acquired for the two languages studied, obtaining the best classification results with $th_2 = 0.2$ for English and $th_2 = 2.1$ for Spanish.

This way, we consider a word as candidate for the feature vector only if it does not behave as a stopword in the corpus of documents ($p_d(k \geq 1, \lambda_i) < th_1$), but it does in the corpus of questions ($p_q(k \geq 1, \lambda_i) > th_1$) and the *KL divergence* between these two probability distributions is big enough ($D(p_d \| p_q) > th_2$).

Once eliminated the words not fitting these constraints, the next step is to choose the words with the best *KL divergence*, those which behavior differs more from documents to questions. We empirically set the number of candidate words to four. These words are shorted by its *mean* and *sample deviation*, choosing the one that tends to appear first in the questions and in the same position. We use this word as the first feature of our vector. After that, we choose the three following words in the question. To sum up, we collect four words from the question: after some experiments, this was the optimal number of words to characterize the class of a question.

Stopwords, Keywords and Definition Terms. The thresholds set above are useful to label every word in a question as stopword, keyword or definition term. We label a word as stopword if it behaves as a stopword in the corpus of documents ($p_d(k \geq 1, \lambda_i) > th_1$), and the *KL divergence* is lower than the threshold established ($D(p_d \| p_q) < th_2$). We label a word as keyword if the probability of appearance in the corpus of documents and questions is under the first threshold ($p_d(k \geq 1, \lambda_i) < th_1$ and $p_q(k \geq 1, \lambda_i) < th_1$), that is, it does not behave as a stopword in none of the corpora. Otherwise, we consider the word as a definition term.

This information is included in a set of experiments described in the next section, characterizing words not only for the sequence of characters but for the role they play in the question.

4 Experiments and Results

Every classification task needs a training corpus and a test corpus. The goal is to obtain a model that can predict de class of the samples in the test corpus. In order to test the capabilities of our approach, we trained and tested the system with the DISEQuA [7] corpus. It is an XML corpus of 450 fatoid questions in four different languages (Dutch, Italian, Spanish and English), labelled with seven different question types: PERSON, LOCATION, MEASURE, DATE, ORGANIZATION, OBJECT (concrete things) and OTHER. More information is present for every question, but for the aim of classification only questions and their types where taken into account.

We used the implementation of SVM provided by WEKA [8]. The optimization algorithm used to train the support vector classifiers is an implementation of Platt's sequential minimal optimization algorithm. The kernel function used for mapping the input space was a polynomial of exponent one, the default values of the algorithm. These values are the same we used in our previous work [3]. In the experiments we used 10-fold cross validation.

To compare our results we created a baseline experiment for the task of question classification, where the features were just the eight first words appearing in the question, taken into account nothing else. This number of words results from calculating the average number of terms in the questions in both languages.

We performed the same experiments for both languages. Table 1 shows the results obtained. The first experiment is the baseline. In the second one, the label statistically obtained for each word was added to the baseline, indicating if it is a stopword, a keyword or a definition term. The third experiment uses as features the four words extracted from the question with our statistical approach. Finally, in the fourth experiment we use the features of the baseline plus the features gathered with our statistical approach in the previous two experiments.

Table 1. Question classification performance for English and Spanish. *Experiment 1*: baseline. *Experiment 2*: baseline + label. *Experiment 3*: four useful terms. *Experiment 4*: baseline + label + four useful terms.

Language	**Experiment 1**	**Experiment 2**	**Experiment 3**	**Experiment 4**
English	83,92%	84,38%	81,47%	**85,04%**
Spanish	**80,71%**	79,59%	80,04%	80,22%

The results obtained for the experiments reflects that the baseline approach (*Experiment 1*) achieves pretty good results for both languages, taken into account that it just extracts the words of the questions as features. It makes sense in this particular case because the questions in the test set presents a very simple utterance, with the *wh-words* and the focus words most of the time present at the beginning of the question. In a real environment, where more variable questions are present, the baseline approach would be affected. Our system would face this challenge with more guarantees as it looks into the question for the best words, it does not matter in what position they appear.

In the second experiment, we added the information of the label detected for each word to the baseline, improving the performance for English (84,38%) but losing a bit for Spanish (79,59%). The idea in this case was to classify the words as pertaining to three different types: stopwords, keywords and definition terms. This way we want to equal the terms by the role they play in the question.

The results obtained with the vector of four useful words extracted in the third experiment (81,47% and 80,04%) are very close to the experiments of the baseline for both languages (83,92% and 80,71%). The results are quite good taking into account that only four features are present in the learning process.

Combining all the features extracted statistically with the baseline in the fourth experiment improves the performance for English (85,04%), while in Spanish slightly improves the results in relation to the four words approach (80,22%).

5 Conclusions and Future Work

In this paper we have proposed a method for automatically extract features for question classification. The main idea was to build a system that can learn from features fully obtained from plain text in a completely unsupervised way, avoiding the use of complex linguistic resources, labelled data or tools. This way we want to obtain a flexible system, easily adaptable to new languages and domains with a minimal cost.

The main problem found is that statistical information must be wide enough to cover the range of possible formulations of a question. As we even avoided using a stemmer, words like "do" and "did" are considered completely different (adding the role of the word in the experiments seems to solve the problem in some cases). Thus, enrich the corpus would help to solve this kind of problems. As a first approach, the results seem promising enough to continue with this research line.

The system may also be improved collecting statistical information not only for unigrams but for larger n-grams, capturing information for larger syntactic patterns and treating the words as pertaining to a more complex structure.

On the other hand, we explained in section 3.1 that statistical information can also be used to categorize the words as stopwords, keywords and definition terms. As a future work, we want to test our approach detecting relevant words for the information retrieval task, completing a full question analysis for Question Answering based on statistical information.

References

1. Hermjakob, U.: Parsing and question classification for question answering. Proceedings of the ACL 2001 Workshop on Open-Domain Question Answering (2001)
2. Li, X., Roth, D.: Learning question classifiers. In Proceedings of COLING (2002)
3. Bisbal, E., Tomás, D., Vicedo, José L., Moreno, L.: A multilingual SVM-Based Question Classification System. In Proceedings of MICAI (2005)
4. Vapnik, V.: The Nature of Statistical Learning Theory. ISBN 0-387-94559-8. Springer, N.Y.
5. Manning, C., Schütze, H.: Foundations of Statistical natural Language Processing. MIT Press. Cambridge, MA: May 1999
6. Tomás, D., Bisbal, E., Vicedo, J.L., Moreno, L. and Suárez, A.: Una aproximación multilingüe a la clasificación de preguntas basada en aprendizaje automático. Procesamiento del Lenguaje Natural, n° 35, pp.391-400, SEPLN (2005)
7. Magnini, B., Romagnoli, S., Vallin, A., Herrera, J., Peñas, A., Peinado, V., Verdejo, F., de Rijke, M.: Creating the DISEQuA Corpus: A Test Set for Multilingual Question Answering
8. Witten, Ian H., Frank, E.: Data Mining: Practical machine learning tools and techniques. 2nd Edition, Morgan Kaufmann, San Francisco (2005)

Cat3LB and Cast3LB: From Constituents to Dependencies

Montserrat Civit, Ma. Antònia Martí, and Núria Bufí

CLiC Centre de Llenguatge i Computació
Universitat de Barcelona
{civit, nuria}@thera-clic.com, amarti@ub.edu

Abstract. In this paper we present the conversion of two treebanks (Cat3LB for Catalan, and Cast3LB for Spanish) from its original constituent format into dependencies. The process has been done automatically but by manually writing the head and the function table. The process has also been used to improve the quality of the first annotation and to modifiy the annotation for further extensions of the treebanks. Treebanks in both formats are freely available for research purposes.

1 Introduction

In this paper we aim at presenting the conversion of two constituent treebanks into dependency ones[1]. On the one hand, it is commonly accepted that constituent annotation is richer than that of dependencies since it contains different descriptive levels having a wide range of variability in the internal structure of constituents. Furthermore, in this kind of annotation, the head of each constituent can be easily inferred from the information contained in the constituents. On the other hand, dependencies provide an immediate description, without intermediate descriptive levels, because each tree node corresponds to a word. Therefore, it is easier to go from a constituent structure to a dependency one: heads can be easily obtained and intermediate levels can be avoided so as to obtain a complete standard dependency representation. Whereas, when going from a dependency structure to a constituent one, the result is a quite flat constituent structure laking intermediate description levels. According to [10] and [11], dependency trees allow for more meaningful error measures and comparisons; and further works have confirmed this idea (see [1]).

Our starting point have been two constituent treebanks, one for Catalan and another for Spanish, which have been converted into the dependency format. This way, two corpora in two different formats are made available to the community, with the hope on enlarging the research on NLP for the two concerned languages.

[1] The work described here has been partially funded by the CESS-ECE project (HUM2004-21127).

T. Salakoski et al. (Eds.): FinTAL 2006, LNAI 4139, pp. 141–152, 2006.

In section 2 we present the treebanks from which the conversion has been done; in sections 3 and 4 we discuss about the head table and the function table used for the conversion; in section 5 we deal with constituent tags. In section 6 we discuss about the conversion process and its influence for the improvement of the annotation in the original treebank. Last section, section 7, is devoted to conclusions and further work.

2 Starting Point: 3LB Treebanks

The Spanish treebank, Cast3LB ([3]) and the Catalan one, Cat3LB, ([4])[2] consist of 100,000 words each (aproximately 4,000 sentences for Cast3LB and 2,800 for Cat3LB). For both treebanks a theory-neutral and surface-oriented annotation scheme has been adopted, which follows the linguistic tradition for Romance Languages. There are three levels of annotation: morphology (pos-tag plus lemma), constituency (tree structure with non-terminal and terminal nodes); and functions, although these are only given to sentence structure nodes. No nodes have been added to the trees, except those for elliptical subjects (Spanish and Catalan being *pro-drop* languages). Figure 1 shows the analysis of the Spanish sentence (*Quiero con esto decir que Medardo_Fraile ha escrito un relato extraño y divertido*[3]) in the constituency format.

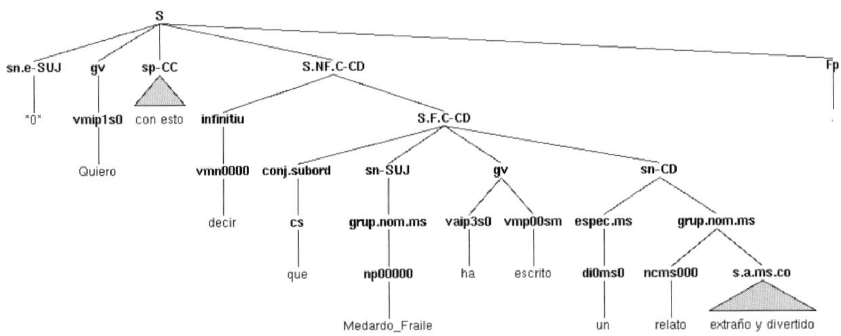

Fig. 1. Constituent format treebank

One of the main problems to be dealt with during the annotation process is discontinuity. In the case of Cat3LB and Cast3LB indexes have been used as suffixes for constituents and function tags when constituents are discontinuous. There are two cases of discontinuity made explicit in Cast3LB and Cat3LB: one related to constituents and the other related to functions. The first one

[2] See [5] and [6] for the Cast3LB annotation guidelines in Spanish, and [12] and [7] for the Catalan ones, in Catalan.

[3] Word-by-word translation: *Want with this to_say that Medardo_Fraile has written a story strange and funny*; Translation: *With this, I mean that Medardo_Fraile wrote a strange, funny story.*

mainly involves noun phrases, for which a noun complement is not immediately dominated by the noun phrase node, mainly because there is another element in between. This usually happens with relative clauses, where the relative pronoun does not immedialety follow the noun. An example of such construction can be found in figure 2. It corresponds to the Catalan sentence *ja_que cada català aporta cada any 220.000 pessetes a Madrid que mai no tornen*[4]. In this sentence, the relative clause *que mai no tornen* is separated from the relative antecedent (*pessetes*) by a verbal complement (*a Madrid*).

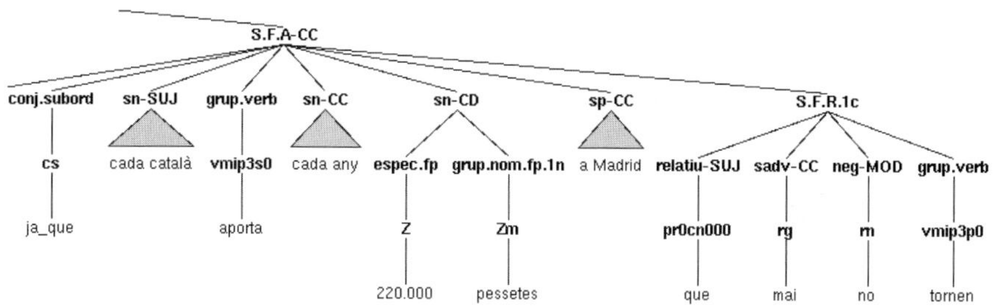

Fig. 2. Constituent discontinuity

The second case concerns clauses and functions: a complement of the clause is outside the clause (*raising structures*). The following text, in Catalan, shows an example of that: *dels pagesos que hi vulguin anar*[5]. This is a prepositional phrase (*sp*) containing a relative clause (*S.F.R*) in which the complement (*hi*) of the infinitive form (*anar*) appears before the main verb form (*vulguin*).

```
(sp
  (prep
    (spcmp dels del))
  (sn
    (grup.nom.mp
      (ncmp000 pagesos pages)
      (S.F.R
        (relatiu-SUJ
          (pr0cn000 que que))
        (sn-CREG.NFc
          (grup.nom
            (pp3cn000 hi hi)))
```

[4] Word-by-word translation: *because each Catalan contributes each year 220,000 pesetas to Madrid which never come back*; translation: *because each Catalan contributes 220,000 pesetas per year to Madrid which never come back.*

[5] Word-by-word translation: *of the farmers who there want go*; translation: *of farmers who want to go there.*

```
(grup.verb
  (vmsp3p0 vulguin voler))
(S.NF.C-CD.NFn
  (infinitiu
    (vmn0000 anar anar)))))))
```

Figures about discontinuity appear in table 1. When dealing with constituent discontinuity, the head gets the suffix **.1n** and the modifier the suffix **.1c**. In the case of discontinuity related to syntactic functions, the complement gets the suffix **.Fc / .NFc**, depending on whether it is related to a finite (F) or a non-finite clause (NF), and the head clause gets the suffix **.Fn or .NFn**, also depending on its type. As it can be appreciated, there is a huge difference between Catalan and Spanish, the former showing much more cases than the latter [6].

Table 1. Discontinuity in Catalan and Spanish

Catalan							
Constituents				**Functions**			
1st case	#	**2nd case**	#	**non-finite S**	#	**finite S**	#
1n	204	**2n**	8	**NFn**	16	**Fn**	16
1c	181	**2c**	11	**NFc**	16	**Fc**	16
Spanish							
Constituents				**Functions**			
1st case	#	**2nd case**	#	**non-finite S**	#	**finite S**	#
1n	36	**2n**	2	**NFn**	37	**Fn**	5
1c	33	**2c**	2	**NFc**	37	**Fc**	5

Once the conversion process has been achieved, the resulting treebank consists of a tuple as follows:

position word pos lemma function head cons

where:

- **position** stands for the word position in the sentence starting at 0
- **word** stands for the word form
- **lemma** stands for the lemma
- **pos** stands for the part-of-speech tag
- **function** stands for the syntactic function of the word

[6] These figures only include discontinuity explicitely marked in the treebanks. There is another case of discontinuiry related to coordination: two coordinated verbs share one or more complements. In our conversion, the complement will only be related to the head of the coordinated structure, in a Negra-style annotation [2].

- **head** stands for the head-position
- **cons** stands for the constituent tag the word has in the treebank

The resulting analysis of the above-mentioned Spanish sentence with the dependency format is presented in table 2.

Table 2. Dependency format

position	word	lemma	pos	function	head	cons
0	Quiero	querer	vmip1s0	ROOT	-	S
1	con	con	sps00	CC	0	sp
2	esto	este	pd0ns000	CPREP	1	sn
3	decir	decir	vmn0000	CD	0	S.NF.C
4	que	que	cs	SUBORD	8	conj.subord
5	Medardo_Fraile	Medardo_Fraile	np00000	SUJ	8	sn
6	ha	haber	vaip3s0	AUX	7	vaip3s0
7	escrito	escribir	vmp00sm	CD	3	S.F.C
8	un	uno	di0ms0	DETER	9	espec.ms
9	relato	relato	ncms000	CD	7	sn
10	extraño	extraño	aq0ms0	CN	9	s.a.ms.co
11	y	y	cc	CO	10	coord
12	divertido	divertido	aq0msp	CONJUNCT	10	S.NF.P
13	.	.	Fp	PUNC-END	0	PUNC(punto)

3 Head Table

As there is no explicit information about head-modifier relationship in the treebank, it was necessary to create a so-called *head table* which indicates which of the daugther nodes of a constituent is its head. So, the goal of the head table is to associate each non-terminal tag with either another non-terminal tag or a pos-tag, its resulting head. Therefore, the subsequent dependencies are simple pairs of elements with no edge labels. Basic assuptions for the head table are that:

1. each non-terminal node in the trees has a head;
2. heads are linguistically-based.

The format of the head table is as follows:

$$\text{tag1} = (\text{operator})\ \text{tag2}$$

where *tag1* is the mother and *tag2* the daughter. There are three operators in the head table: *rigthmost*, *leftmost* and *only_one*. The first two select a given *tag2* according to its place: the rightmost (or the leftmost) element of a given sequence; while *only_one* works for the cases in which there is only one element of a given type[7].

[7] The are also some conventions in the head table: < stands for the beginning of a pos-tag; <> for the whole pos-tag. In other rules, **{** stands for the beginning of a constituent tag, while full constituent tags are directly written.

3.1 Head Selection

The head selection is *linguistically motivated*, that is, the most linguistically natural-sounding head was chosen. In addition to that, there is another crucial element in this table: the order in which daughters are selected as heads. Let's consider the following Catalan verbal forms for the verb *cantar* (*to sing*):

form	**translation**	**grammar rule**
1 *cantes*	(you) sing	verb
2 *ha cantat*	has sung	aux. + participle
3 *vol cantar*	wants to sing	verb + infinitive
4 *ha de cantar*	has to sing	aux. + preposition + infinitive
5 *ha d'haver cantat*	has to have sung	aux. + preposition + past infinitive
6 *està cantant*	is singing	verb + gerund

and the following head rules:

```
grup.verb = rightmost infinitiu
grup.verb = rightmost gerundi
grup.verb = rightmost <vmp
grup.verb = rightmost <vsp
grup.verb = only_one <v
grup.verb = rightmost <vap
grup.verb = rightmost <vmi
```

The first element selected as the head of the verbal node is the infinitive (*infinitiu*). This means that for cases 3, 4 and 5 a head has already been selected. According to the second rule, the next selected head is the gerund (*gerundi*), which means that example 6 is given a head. The third rule selects as head the verbal form whose pos-tag starts by *vmp*, which corresponds to participles; and the example 2 is given the head. For the previous examples, rule number 4 (grup.verb = rightmost $<$vsp) does not apply. Next rule will be *grup.verb* = *only_one* $<$*v* which states that if there is only one verbal form, it is the head, so example 1 is finally given its head.

Another example to be considered for the head selection is the case of determiners. Some rules extracted from the treebank are[8]:

```
espec.fp = di0fp0 da0fp0  (totes les (persones))
espec.fp = dd0fp0 dn0fp0  (aquestes tres (persones))
```

When establishing the heads for determiners, they where selected according to their *determinativeness*: definite articles first ($<$*da*), then possessives ($<$*dp*), then demonstratives ($<$*dd*), and so on.

```
espec.fs = <da
espec.fs = <dp
espec.fs = <dd
```

[8] The translation of the exemples is: *all the people*, *these three people*.

```
espec-fs = <dn
espec.fs = leftmost <di
espec.fs = <dt
espec.fs = <rg>
```

There are also regular expressions in the head table, so as to simplify as much as possible the annotation. Next rule in the head table states that the head for a relative coordinated clause (S.F.R.co) is the leftmost relative clause, no matter whether this is a coordinated one or not ({S.F.R(|.co)$}).

```
S.F.R.co = leftmost {S.F.R(|.co)$
```

3.2 Coordination

The main open question concerning dependency representation is related to coordination. The fundamental difference between coordination and subordination is that while for the latter there is a dependent element and a head, for the former, the two (or more) concerned elements are equivalent. This equivalent relationship cannot be represented by means of a dependency tree, since the basic relation here is the head-modifier one. Different solutions can be found for that, but generally speaking, the head is either the coordinating conjuntion, like in the Prague Dependeny Treebank's analytical level ([8]), or one of the coordinated elements, which is the solution adopted here.

Some examples of rules for coordinated nodes are [9]:

```
grup.nom.co = grup.nom.ms coord grup.nom.fp
grup.nom.co = coord grup.nom.mp coord grup.nom.co
```

Coordination is not only an open question by itself, but also for related phenomena. For instance, for how to deal with complements depending on two (or more) coordinated elements. In the Tiger project ([2]) there are *secondary edges*, and in the Danish Dependency Treebank there are *secondary governors* to represent this phenomenon ([9]). In our case, we have decided, for the moment, to relate those complements only to the head of the coordinated element. This can be illustrated with the case of the nominal group. It is stated that the head for a coordinated nominal group is the leftmost nominal group (no matter its type), thus any complement of the coordinated structure will be related to this element.

```
grup.nom.co = {grup.nom
```

This can be observed in this example[10] where there is a coordinated nominal group (*grup.nom.co*) and an adjoined prepositional phrase (*sp.j*). According to

[9] *grup.nom.***co** stands for a coordinated nominal group; *coord*, for coordinating conjunctions; *grup.nom.***ms** for a **masculine singular** nominal group; *grup.nom.***fp** for a **feminine plural** one; and *grup.nom.***mp** for a **masculine plural** nominal group.

[10] Word-by-word translation: *others bodies and departments of the Generalitat*; translation: *other agencies and departments of the Catalan government.*

the previous head rule, the preposition phrase will have a dependency relationship only with the first nominal group in the coordinated structure, since it is its head.

```
(sn.x
  (espec.mp
    (di0cp0 altres altre))
  (grup.nom.co
    (grup.nom.co
      (grup.nom.mp
        (ncmp000 cossos cos))
      (coord
        (cc i i))
      (grup.nom.mp
        (ncmp000 departaments departament)))
    (sp.j
      (prep
        (sps00 de de))
      (sn
        (espec.fs
          (da0fs0 la el))
        (grup.nom.fs
          (np00000 Generalitat Generalitat))))))
```

3.3 Kinds of Rules

The are two sorts of rules in the head table, ones being specific for the data in the treebank and other ones being general rules that will apply for further non-encountered cases. Examples of general rules are those concernig the verbal node: when dealing with the verb node head, rules state that the rightmost verbform must be selected as the head, even though in the data there is only one verb form of a given type (this will allow, in the future, to recognize heads in sequences that do not appear in the current treebank but that are perfectly possible). For instance, the head table statement:

```
grup.verb = righmost infinitiu
```

is a generalised rule, since in the data there is only one infinitive form (*infinitiu*); but nothing prevents, in the language, for a second (even third) infinitive to appear[11].

4 Function table

Functions only appear in the treebank when nodes are daughters of sentence structures. For the rest of the cases a table of additional conversion (*function*

[11] It should be pointed out that verb node is the sole one to have its head at the rightmost position (any other nodes having the head on the left).

table) is looked at to provide with the relationship expressed in the head table: the edge labels[12].

The format of the function table is as follows:

$$\text{tag1} < \text{tag2} = \text{function\_tag}$$

where *tag1* is the daughter, *tag2* the mother and *function_tag* the function of the daughter with respect to the mother, the edge label.

Some examples of that table are:

```
espec.fs < sn = DETER
sn.co < grup.nom.fp = APOS
sn < sp = CPREP
s.a.ms < sn = CN
sadv < sa = CADJ
```

The first one establishes the edge label *DETER* (*determiner*) for any *espec.fs* (feminine singular specifier) depending on a *sn* (noun phrase). The second sets the edge label *APOS* (apposition) for any *sn.co* (coordinated noun phrase) depending on a *grup.nom.fp* (feminine plural nominal group). *CPREP* (complement of a preposition) is the edge label for any *sn* (noun phrase) depending on a *sp* (prepositional phrase). *CN* (complement of a noun) is the label for any *s.a.ms* (masculine singular adjectival phrase) depending on a *sn*. Finally, *CADJ* is the edge lable for any *sadv* (adverbial phrase) depending on a *sa* (adjectival phrase).

Function tags used for the conversion appear in table 3, together with a gloss of their meaning.

5 Constituent Tags

Last column in the output format corresponds to the constituent tag. The information comes from the treebanks, since almost every terminal-node has its corresponding constituent tag. This information may not be necessary for the dependency format, but as the information is available in the original treebanks, it may also be useful here. Special constituent tags were established for punctuation marks. When there were not such tags in the treebank, we used the pos-tag, instead.

6 Improving Original Annotation

The conversion process was first done for Spanish. During the task, some problems appeared, and were corrected, all of them related to a lack of information in the constituent trees. Main sources of errors were:

1. a functional tag was not given to the *correct* node (for instance, a function tag was given to the *grup.nom.fs* node but should have been attached to the *sn* node)

[12] Verbs being the head of its sentence are given the function **root**.

Table 3. Function tagset

Function	Gloss	Function	Gloss
Coming from the treebank			
ATR	Attribute	CAG	Agent complement
CC	Adjunct	CD	Direct object
CD.Q	Quantitative direct object	CI	Indirect object
CPRED	Predicative complement	CPRED.CD	CD predicative complement
CPRED.SUJ	SUJ predicative complement	CREG	Prepositional complement
ET	Textual element	IMPERS	Impersonal mark
MOD	Verb modifier	PASS	Passive mark
SUJ	Subject	VOC	Vocative
Coming from the function table			
PUNC	Punctuation mark	DETER	Head determiner
CPREP	Complement of a preposition	APOS	Apposition
CN	Complement of a noun	CO	Coordinating element
ESPEC	Non-head determiner	SUBORD	Subordinating element
CONJUNCT	Coordinated element	CADV	Complement of an adverb
CADJ	Complement of an adjective	INSERT	Inserted element
AUX	Auxiliary verb	INTJ	Interjection
MORF	Verbal morpheme	NEG	Negative element
CNEG	Complement of a negation	ADJUNCT	Adjoined element
AO	Sentence adjunct	ROOT	Sentence head

2. missing/extra nodes
3. incorrect function tags
4. incorrect bracketing
5. input irregularities (i.e. no lemma for a given word)

The head-modifier relationship for discontinuous constituents (*1n, 1c* tag suffixes) and functions (*NFn, NFc, Fn, Fc* tag suffixes) was not explicitely marked, and this information had to be added before converting constituent trees into dependencies.

On the other hand, there was one difference between the annotation of adjoined[13] nodes in Spanish and Catalan. In Catalan this relationship was made explicit by adding the suffix **.j** to the adjoined node, but it was not in Spanish, and that meant that cases were to be looked at one by one in order to establish the correct relationship. The lack of markup (for discontinuous constituents and adjunction) was reconsidered for the project of enlarging the annotated data.

[13] Adjunction is marked in the XBar tradition by repeating the node which receives the adjunction (*sn.co = sn.co S.F.R*).

3LB treebanks will be part of CESS-ECE[14] treebanks, and their guidelines now include this new markup.

7 Conclusions and Further Work

We have presented the conversion process of Cat3LB and Cast3LB from constituents to dependencies. Generally speaking, treebanks are mostly annotated following the constituency format, and that is because this annotation allows for the inclusion of declarative information about the syntactic structure at several levels of description and so far it has been the commonest parsers' output. However, when the goal is to compare different parsers and parsing systems, constituents make the comparability a difficult task. The conversion into dependencies is not an arduous task and it can be achieved with a high degree of accuracy, while the opposite is not true.

The systematic conversion of Cat3LB and Cast3LB corpora into dependency structure has also been a way of improving the quality of the original treebank, since the conversion process discussed here has been of great usefulness for the checking of the quality of the annotation.

The conversion process was done automatically, but the head table and the function table were manually written, in order to ensure consistency and coverage.

As for further work, we plan to extend the amount of annotated data in the constituency format up to 500,000 words, that will also be converted into the dependency format.Those corpora, as well as the two presented here will be freely available for research purposes.

References

1. Beil, F., Prescher, D., Schmid, H., Shulte im Walde, S.: Evaluation of the Gramotron parser for German. Beyond Parseval, a LREC02 Workshop (2002)
2. Brants, S., Dipper, S., Hansen, S., Lezius, W., Smith, G.: The TIGER Treebank. Proccedings of the Workshop on Treebanks and Linguistic Theories.(2002)
3. Civit, M., Martí, M.A.: Building Cast3LB: a Spanish Treebank. Research on Language & Computation **2** (4) (2005)
4. Civit, M., Bufí, N, Valverde. M.P CAT3LB: a Treebank for Catalan with Word Sense Annotation. 3rd Workshop on Treebanks and Linguistic Theories, (TLT04) Tuebingen, Germany (2004)
5. Civit, M.: Guía para la anotación sintáctica de Cast3LB: un corpus del español con anotación sintáctica, semántica y pragmática. (2003) Available at http://clic.fil.ub.es/
6. Civit, M.: Guía para la anotación de las funciones sintácticas de Cast3LB: un corpus del español con anotación sintáctica, semántica y pragmática. (2003) Available at http://clic.fil.ub.es/

[14] CESS-ECE is a project funded by the Spanish government whose aim is to enlarge the amount of annotated data up to 500,000 words for each language involved in the project: Catalan, Spanish and Basque.

7. Civit, M., Bufí, N., Valverde, M.P.: Guia per a la anotació de les funcions sintàctiques de Cat3LB: un corpus del català amb anotació sintàctica, semàntica i pragmàtica. (2004) Available at http://clic.fil.ub.es/
8. Hajic, J.: Building a syntactically annotated corpus: the Prague Dependency Treebank. Issues in Valency and Meaning. Studies in honour of Jarmila Panevova (1999)
9. Kromann, M.: The Danish Dependency Treebank and the underlying linguistic theory. Proceedings of the Second Workshop on Treebanks and Linguistic Theories (2003)
10. Lin, D.: A dependency-based method for evaluating broad-coverage parsers. Proceedings of IJCAI-95 (1995) 1420–1425
11. Lin, D.: A dependency-based method for evaluating broad-coverage parsers. Natural Language Engineering **4** (2) (1998) 1420–1425
12. Valverde, M.P., Civit, M., Bufí, N.: Guia per a la anotació sintàctica de Cat3LB: un corpus del català amb anotació sintàctica, semàntica i pragmàtica. (2004) Available at http://clic.fil.ub.es/

Classification of News Web Documents Based on Structural Features

Shisanu Tongchim, Virach Sornlertlamvanich, and Hitoshi Isahara

Thai Computational Linguistics Laboratory
National Institute of Information and Communications Technology
112 Paholyothin Road, Klong 1, Klong Luang, Pathumthani 12120, Thailand
shisanu@tcllab.org, virach@tcllab.org, isahara@nict.go.jp

Abstract. The motivation of this work comes from the need of a Thai web corpus for testing our information retrieval algorithm. Two collections of news web documents are gathered from two different Thai newspaper web sites. Our goal is to find a simple yet effective method to extract news articles from these web collections. We explore the use of machine learning methods to distinguish article pages from non-article pages, e.g. table of contents, advertisements. Then, the selected web articles are compared in a fine-grained manner in order to find informative structures. Both steps of information extraction utilize the structural features of web documents rather than the extracted keywords or terms. Thus, the inherent errors of word segmentation, one of the major problems in Thai text processing, do not affect to this method.

1 Introduction

The web has been proved to be a valuable source of information for computational linguistics studies. With the growing number of web documents and online information, *web mining* plays an important role in extracting useful information from the World Wide Web. According to a taxonomy proposed by Cooley *et al.* [1], the term 'web mining' has been used in two distinct ways, namely *web content mining* and *web usage mining*. The first one refers to information discovery on the World Wide Web, whereas the second one describes the research in analyzing the user access patterns from web servers. Our study can be classified to the web content mining category. This study is motivated by the need of a Thai web corpus for testing our information retrieval algorithm. We use Thai newspaper web sites as sources of information. In general, a newspaper web site consists of thousands of web pages. The desired pages are the article pages. Thus, the first goal is to identify which pages are the article pages. The non-article pages, e.g. table of contents, advertisements, opinion or query submission forms, should be screened out. In the second step, the selected pages are analyzed to eliminate non-informative parts of pages, e.g. the navigation bar.

The rest of this paper is organized as follows: Section 2 discusses related work. Section 3 provides the description of a technique for identifying the article pages. Section 4 presents a technique for analyzing web pages in a fine-grained manner

T. Salakoski et al. (Eds.): FinTAL 2006, LNAI 4139, pp. 153–160, 2006.

in order to eliminate non-informative structures in web documents. Section 5 presents the experimental results and discussion. Finally, Section 6 concludes our work and discusses future research.

2 Related Work

Similarity measurement between web documents is the central idea for web classification. Similarity measurement and Classification can be done on features drawn from web documents. In general, the research in this area can be classified into three groups according to the type of features. The first group utilizes extracted terms and textual information of web documents. The second group is based solely on the structural information of documents. The last group uses a combination of textual information and structural information.

A number of techniques have been proposed based on extracted terms and textual information [2,3,4]. A set of words extracted from web documents are used as features for classification algorithms. In general, the plain text is obtained by removing all HTML tags. Then, the stop words are usually removed from the extracted word list. After this phase, some studies also transfer each word into its stem by using some stemming algorithms. The extracted terms are used to represent web documents and their classes. Typically, only some extracted words are selected as features or attributes for classification algorithms since the extracted word list is usually large and it is impractical for classification algorithms. For the languages which have no explicit word boundary, some word segmentation algorithms are applied to web documents. An example of using a word segmentation algorithm with Chinese web documents before constructing a word list was presented by He *et al.* [5]. In general, the errors from word segmentation are unavoidable. This case also applies to Thai language which perfect word segmentation is hardly achieved. Thus, we intend not to use textual information as features for classification.

Some researchers utilize structural features of web documents for classification [6,7,8]. Joshi *et al.* [6] converted a tree representation of web documents to a simpler representation and measured structural similarity. Cruz *et al.* [7] measured similarity between web pages based on the frequencies of HTML tags. Wong and Fu [8] generalized some knowledge from a hierarchical structure of web documents and used this knowledge to classify web pages.

The last category is to use a combination of textual information and structural information. An example is the article by Tombros and Ali [9]. They experimented the use of three different types of features, namely the textual content from different parts of documents, HTML tag frequencies, and the query terms found in pages.

3 Web Page Classification

We choose the frequencies of HTML tags as structural features for web classification. We adopt the frequencies of tags in percentage from the article by

Cruz *et al.* [7]. Let $T = \{t_1, t_2, ..., t_n\}$ be the collection of n frequent used HTML tags found in a document collection $\mathcal{C}$. Let $m_j(t_i)$ be the number of occurrences of the tag t_i in the document j. The frequency $f_j(t_i)$ (in %) of the tag t_i in the document j can be calculated as follows:

$$f_j(t_i) = \frac{m_j(t_i)}{\sum_{k=1}^{n} m_j(t_k)} \times 100 \tag{1}$$

We define a feature vector $F = \{f_j(t_1), f_j(t_2), ..., f_j(t_n)\}$ as a representation of the document j.

The use of structural information like the tag frequencies for the classification is motivated by the following reasons.

- The construction of feature vectors is simple, fast and straightforward. Thus, it is suitable for a web site with thousands of web pages like a newspaper web site.
- The use of structural information avoids the inherent errors of word segmentation. Unlike the use of textual information, the proposed method does not use the keyword extraction. Thus, word segmentation is unnecessary.
- In general, a newspaper web site contains several categories, e.g. Sport, Politics, Entertainment. The preferred pages are the article pages, no matter what categories they belong to. The structural information should be a better representation than the textual information.

4 Selection of Informative Structures

After selecting article pages from the collected collections, the next task is to eliminate non-informative structures existing in the selected article pages. In general, a web page may contain many information blocks. Some blocks contain information which does not relate to the main content, for example, navigation bars, copyright notices, advertisements, etc. Such information blocks can be regarded as the noisy blocks [10]. If the noisy information blocks have not been eliminated from the collection of web pages, they may affect the evaluation of information retrieval algorithms later. Yi *et al.* [10] pointed out that the elimination of noisy information improves the performance of two data mining tasks.

In this section, we perform a fine-grained analysis on the article pages to estimate the importance of a particular information block. Our intuition is that the noisy blocks tend to appear in many other pages in the same web site, while the main contents are quite unique. To identify which information blocks are likely to be noisy information, the comparisons among pages are performed. The frequency of a particular information block will indicate whether that information block is informative or not.

An HTML document can be modeled as a tree. Figure 1 shows an example of HTML document. By using the relations among tags, a hierarchical structure of this HTML document can be constructed as a tree presented in Figure 2.

```
<html>
<head>
<title>Contact-TCL</title>
</head>
<body>
<table width="800" border="0" cellspacing="0" cellpadding="0">
  <tr>
    <td colspan="2"><h1>Contact Address</h1></td>
  </tr>
  <tr>
    <td width="128"><h2>Address</h2></td>
    <td width="672">Room 224, NECTEC Building,
                    Thailand Science Park 112 Paholyothin Road,
                    Klong 1, Klong Luang, Pathumthani, 12120,
                     Thailand </td>
  </tr>
  <tr>
    <td><h2>Telephone</h2></td>
    <td>(+66)-2564-7990 </td>
  </tr>
  <tr>
    <td><h2>Fax</h2></td>
    <td>(+66)-2564-7992 </td>
  </tr>
  <tr>
    <td><h2>E-mail</h2></td>
    <td><a href="mailto:info.tcllab.org">info@tcllab.org</a></td>
  </tr>
</table>
</body>
</html>
```

Fig. 1. An example of HTML code

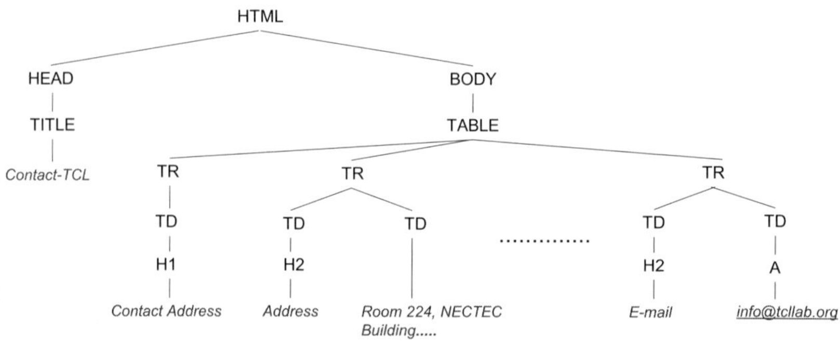

Fig. 2. An example of HTML tag tree

Although the tree representation completely contains the structural information, it is not simple to manipulate. The comparisons among trees represented HTML documents are computational intensive.

To make the tree representation easier to manipulate, the tree structure is converted into a simpler representation. We use the set of paths from the root node to the leaf nodes or the terminal nodes to represent a document. Let m be the number of leaf nodes in the document i, and $L_i = \{l_1, l_2, ..., l_m\}$ be the collection of leaf nodes of the document i. Thus, the number of paths from the root node to the leaf nodes is equal to m. Let $P_i = \{p_1, p_2, ..., p_m\}$ be the collection of paths of the document i. A path p_j contains the root node, the leaf node (l_j) and all the intermediate nodes between the root node and the the leaf node (l_j). From the figure 2, the first path p_1 can be defined as $\{HTML, HEAD, TITLE, Contact - TCL\}$. Let n be the number of documents. By comparing all path collections $P_i, 1 \leq i \leq n$, we can create the collection of distinct paths, $P_{dist} = \{p'_1, p'_2, ..., p'_N\}$. Let $m(p'_j)$ be the number of occurrences of the path p'_j in all path collections $P_i, 1 \leq i \leq n$. We use the ratio of the number of occurrences of a particular path to the number of documents, $m(p'_j)/n$, to identify whether this path is informative or not. If $m(p'_j)/n$ is less than a predefined threshold value, this path is informative. In this study, the threshold is 0.1.

The transformation of the tree structure to parent-child relations is close to the *bag of tree paths model* presented by Joshi *et al.* [6]. However, they used the path information to compute the similarity of documents rather than identifying informative structures. Another difference is that they discarded the textual information. Thus, every text node is ignored. In contrast, we use both textual information and structural information. We consider paths that have text nodes as the leaf nodes.

5 Experimental Results

In this section, we report the results of the proposed method on two collections of news documents. The first collection of 4497 documents is gathered from the Manager web site[1]. The number of article pages in the Manager collection is 1263. The second collection of 623 documents is harvested from the BangkokBiz web site[2]. In the BangkokBiz collection, 416 pages are article documents.

The first experiment is to explore the use of tag frequencies for page classification. By analyzing web pages in both collections, there are 51 commonly used tags. We create feature vectors of these 51 tags as in the section 3. Three machine learning algorithms are compared, namely Support Vector Machine (SVM), C4.5 and Naive Bayes. The experiment is done on the Weka workbench [11]. The parameters of all learning algorithms are set to their default values. For SVM, the linear kernel is used with the complexity parameter of 1.0. For C4.5, the confidence factor is set to 2.5. The labeled collections of pages are split into two parts, namely 5% are considered as training data and 95% are testing data. Therefore, 225 pages from the Manager collection are used as training data, while 31 pages from the BangkokBiz collection are used as training data.

Tables 1 and 2 show the classification results. Table 1 presents the performance of correctly identifying web pages as article pages, whereas table 2 shows the performance of correctly identifying web pages that are not article pages. On two collections, SVM performs better than the other two algorithms. However, the difference among the algorithms is marginal. Overall, the performance of algorithms on the Manager collection is slightly better than that of the BangkokBiz

[1] http://www.manager.co.th
[2] http://www.bangkokbiznews.com

Table 1. Classification results of different algorithms for article pages

Method	Manager			BangkokBiz		
	Pr	*Re*	F_1	*Pr*	*Re*	F_1
SVM	0.976	0.997	0.986	0.968	0.99	0.979
C4.5	0.946	0.967	0.957	0.951	0.913	0.931
Naive Bayes	0.892	0.973	0.931	0.985	0.988	0.986

Table 2. Classification results of different algorithms for non-article pages

Method	Manager			BangkokBiz		
	Pr	*Re*	F_1	*Pr*	*Re*	F_1
SVM	0.999	0.991	0.995	0.978	0.932	0.954
C4.5	0.987	0.978	0.983	0.931	0.901	0.864
Naive Bayes	0.989	0.954	0.971	0.974	0.969	0.971

collection. The results suggest that the use of tag frequencies is feasible and sufficient for our classification problem. Even using a small number of training examples (like 31 pages for the BangkokBiz collection), only a small number of pages are wrongly classified. Moreover, we have illustrated the feasibility of this technique for the classification task by using default parameter values. The algorithms achieve high precision without the need of parameter tuning.

After selecting which pages are article pages, the article pages are compared by using the proposed idea presented in the section 4. We randomly select two sets of 100 article pages from both collections. The first set is obtained from the Manager collection, whereas the second set is acquired from the BangkokBiz collection. The algorithm is implemented in Java. We use HTMLParser[3] to parse the HTML documents. Each document is converted to a tree. Then, the tree representation is transformed to a set of paths. There are 2642 and 2409 distinct paths for the first set and the second set respectively. It is interesting to note that the same path may occur in two or more times even in a single document. Therefore, the number of occurrences of a particular path may be greater than the number of documents. In the set of 100 Manager articles, the most frequent used path is found 2784 times. In contrast, the most frequent used path in the set from the BangkokBiz is found 97 times. Another observation is that the vast majority of paths are unique. They appear only one time in the whole collection. There are 2234 paths that are unique for the first set and 2100 paths for the second set. According to our intuition, these paths are likely to be informative structures.

In both news collections, most article pages have small discussion boards at the end of articles. The discussion boards allow readers to submit their opinions about

[3] http://htmlparser.sourceforge.net/

news articles. The textual information in these discussion boards is problematic for our analysis. Although the textual information of opinion boards loosely relates to the articles, they are not parts of the main contents. They can be considered as noisy information. It is not trivial to detect these parts by using the proposed method since they are quite unique. We will leave this problem to the future work. In this study, these parts are not considered in our experiment.

The 2642 extracted paths of the first set and the 2409 paths of the second set are classified by using the threshold value of 0.1. Then, they are manually checked by hand. Note that the numbers of non-informative blocks are 8.59% and 8.26% for the first set and the second set respectively. The results are shown in Table 3. From the results, the recalls for classifying non-informative structures are 0.423 and 0.839 for the first set and the second set respectively. The recalls for identifying informative structures for both sets are all 1.0. This means that a number of false positives occur, but no false negative. All structures classified as non-informative structures are correct. However, some non-informative structures are still ambiguous. The number of occurrences is not significant enough for the algorithm to detect them as non-informative structures.

Table 3. Classification results for informative and non-informative structures

	Manager			BangkokBiz		
	Pr	*Re*	F_1	*Pr*	*Re*	F_1
Informative Structure	0.948	1.000	0.973	0.986	1.000	0.993
Non-informative Structure	1.000	0.423	0.594	1.000	0.839	0.913

6 Conclusions and Future Work

We have proposed a method to extract some useful textual information from the newspaper web sites. The goal is to construct a Thai web corpus from news articles. The proposed method works in two steps. The first step is to select the article pages from the collections of web documents. To avoid the problem of word segmentation, our proposed method uses only the structural information, namely the tag frequencies. SVM performs better than the other two classifiers. However, the difference among the algorithms is not significant. The second step is to eliminate noisy information in the selected web articles. The results show that the majority of structures are correctly classified. However, there is still a problem with discussion boards. We leave this problem to the future work.

There are several possible extensions to this study. We are currently using the Thai web corpus from this study to examine our information retrieval algorithm. The results will be compared with the use of news web pages without any preprocessing. The second one is to explore a method to detect and eliminate the noisy information of discussion boards. The third one is to use other information for detecting noisy information.

References

1. Cooley, R., Mobasher, B., Srivastava, J.: Web mining: Information and pattern discovery on the world wide web. In: ICTAI. (1997) 558–567
2. Sun, A., Lim, E.P., Ng, W.K.: Web classification using support vector machine. In Chiang, R.H.L., Lim, E.P., eds.: WIDM, ACM (2002) 96–99
3. Holden, N., Freitas, A.A.: Web page classification with an ant colony algorithm. In Yao, X., Burke, E.K., Lozano, J.A., Smith, J., Guervós, J.J.M., Bullinaria, J.A., Rowe, J.E., Tiño, P., Kabán, A., Schwefel, H.P., eds.: PPSN. Volume 3242 of Lecture Notes in Computer Science., Springer (2004) 1092–1102
4. An, A., Huang, Y., Huang, X., Cercone, N.: Feature selection with rough sets for web page classification. In Peters, J.F., Skowron, A., Dubois, D., Grzymala-Busse, J.W., Inuiguchi, M., Polkowski, L., eds.: T. Rough Sets. Volume 3135 of Lecture Notes in Computer Science., Springer (2004) 1–13
5. He, J., Tan, A.H., Tan, C.L.: Machine learning methods for chinese web page categorization. In: ACL'2000 2nd Workshop on Chinese Language Processing, Hongkong, China (2000) 93–100
6. Joshi, S., Agrawal, N., Krishnapuram, R., Negi, S.: A bag of paths model for measuring structural similarity in web documents. [12] 577–582
7. Cruz, I.F., Borisov, S., Marks, M.A., Webb, T.R.: Measuring structural similarity among web documents: Preliminary results. In Hersch, R.D., André, J., Brown, H., eds.: EP. Volume 1375 of Lecture Notes in Computer Science., Springer (1998) 513–524
8. Wong, W.C., Fu, A.W.C.: Finding structure and characteristics of web documents for classification. In: ACM SIGMOD Workshop on Research Issues in Data Mining and Knowledge Discovery. (2000) 96–105
9. Tombros, A., Ali, Z.: Factors affecting web page similarity. In Losada, D.E., Fernández-Luna, J.M., eds.: ECIR. Volume 3408 of Lecture Notes in Computer Science., Springer (2005) 487–501
10. Yi, L., Liu, B., Li, X.: Eliminating noisy information in web pages for data mining. [12] 296–305
11. Witten, I., Frank, E.: Data Mining: Practical machine learning tools and techniques. 2nd edn. Morgan Kaufmann, San Francisco (2005)
12. Getoor, L., Senator, T.E., Domingos, P., Faloutsos, C., eds.: Proceedings of the Ninth ACM SIGKDD International Conference on Knowledge Discovery and Data Mining, Washington, DC, USA, August 24 - 27, 2003. In Getoor, L., Senator, T.E., Domingos, P., Faloutsos, C., eds.: KDD, ACM (2003)

Cognition and Physio-acoustic Correlates — Audio and Audio-visual Effects of a Short English Emotional Statement: On JL2, FL2 and EL1

Toshiko Isei-Jaakkola[1,2]

[1] Graduate School of Information Science and Technology, University of Tokyo, Hongo 7-3-1, Bunkyo-ku, Tokyo, Japan
tijaakkola@gavo.t.u-tokyo.ac.jp
[2] Department of Speech Sciences, University of Helsinki, PL9, Helsinki, Finland
toshiko.jaakkola@helsinki.fi

Abstract. This paper concerns the correlation between cognition test results from audio and audio-visual effects on nine English emotional words and the physio-acoustic distances. Two parameters were selected; F0 and intensity. The two types of distance were calculated: the average and pattern-distance for each emotion. 2 Japanese, 2 Finnish, and 1 English group participated in the cognition tests. Regarding cognition, the correct answer ratios were higher in audio-visual than audio for all three languages. The difference between audio and audio-visual was much smaller in Japanese than in the other languages. Finnish showed different correct answer patterns than the others. The correlation between cognition and distances confirmed that the pattern distance was more correlated with cognition than with average distance in both audio and audio-visual. Also, it seems that intensity was more correlated with cognition than F0.

1 Introduction

In speech communication, emotions play an important role. Emotions are also inevitably related to the culture of the target language to be studied. However, the research materials aimed at finding the correlate between the human cognition of emotions and the acoustic parameters and articulatory settings when producing emotions have often been limited to rather short utterances such as isolated words or words emphasised in a sentence, particularly in speech synthesis and recognition. In addition, the number of subjects has been rather small and thus a lack of sufficient data on cognition. Emotions have been studied not only pycho-acoutically but also physio-acoustically, socio-linguistically, and physio-phonetically. A great number of experiments have been conducted in order to discover the acoustic parameters of emotions (e.g., [5]). [1], [2], [3] and [4] have investigated the emotional cognition of Japanese learners of English (JL2) and English speakers (EL1), using English emotions in either dialogues [1] or in a short statement [2] or in a word [3]. In these tests, only audio = sound (A) or both A and audio-visual (AV) were used. It was found that the order of the correct answer ratios was: dialogues > short statements > word in A, and word > short statements in AV. [4] investigated the correlation between the cognition

T. Salakoski et al. (Eds.): FinTAL 2006, LNAI 4139, pp. 161 – 173, 2006.

test results by JL2 and EL1 and the physio-acoustic distances (area-distance, average distance, and pattern-distance) in A and AV, using a short English emotional sentence. The results confirmed that there was no strong correlation between them, intensity seeming to be more correlated to the cognition test results than F0 for A for both JL2 and EL1. In this paper, I shall add the Finnish learners of English (FL2) to JL2 and EL1 for comparison with the cognition tests. These three languages have never been compared simultaneously in terms of emotional studies, particularly of this type of study, to my knowledge.

In this study, I shall investigate the following:

(1) Whether there are differences between JL2's, FL2's and EL1's cognition of English emotions uttered in a short statement on A and AV
(2) Whether there is a correlation between their correctly selected answers and the physio-acoustic distances
(3) Is the cognitive confusion in judging the correct emotion related to physio-acoustic distances between emotions?

In (2) and (3) I will use two acoustic parameters: pitch and intensity movements (contours or patterns). For physio-acoustic distances, average distance (D) and pattern-distance (PD) will be used for pitch (F0) and intensity.

2 Cognition Test

2.1 Methods

Nine emotion words were used for the cognition test: 'happiness', '(cold) anger', 'suspicion', 'surprise', 'sadness', 'fear', 'hatred', 'disappointment', and 'contempt'. The sentence used for recording purposes was "This is a pen". This was done to prevent as far as possible the linguistic information from affecting the results, so that the subjects could concentrate on only non- and para-linguistic English emotions. The sentence was not written on the answer sheet. It was simultaneously recorded on both a DAT tape (A) and a video tape (AV), and each emotion was uttered twice in sequence by one British female informant (51 years of age, a university lecturer), and based on her own reproduction of her emotions in the recording studio. There were five groups: JL2, FL2 and EL1. The two JL2 groups, participating in Tests A and AV, consisted of male and female university students between 18 and 22 years of age in English classes, majoring in various fields, and numbering 149 (A) and 110 (AV) respectively for the tests. Two FL2 groups participated in these two Tests: 40 (A) and 31 (AV). They were attending English classes at the polytechnic university, and consisted of males and females. Their ages varied between 19 and 43 years (mostly in their 20s), and majoring in various subjects. There was no great difference among JL2 and FL2 in English proficiency. There were 34 in the EL1 group, consisting of both males and females aged between 18 and 64, who participated in both tests. They were from the U.S.A., the U.K., Australia, Canada and New Zealand, and their profiles varied. All of them listened or observed twice. The testing method was forced-choice (chance level 11.1%).

2.2 Results

Overall Results. Figure 1 illustrates the overall correct answer ratios for EL1, JL2 and FL2. The correct answer ratios were higher in AV than V for all three languages. The correct answer ratio of EL1 for AV was 59% and that of FL2 58%, whereas that of A was 31% for EL1 and 20% for FL2. On the other hand, for JL2, the difference (9%) between A (38%) and AV (47%) was the smallest of all three language speakers. The difference between A and AV was the largest of all for FL2 (38%). The range between A and AV was very large in FL2 and EL1 (28%).

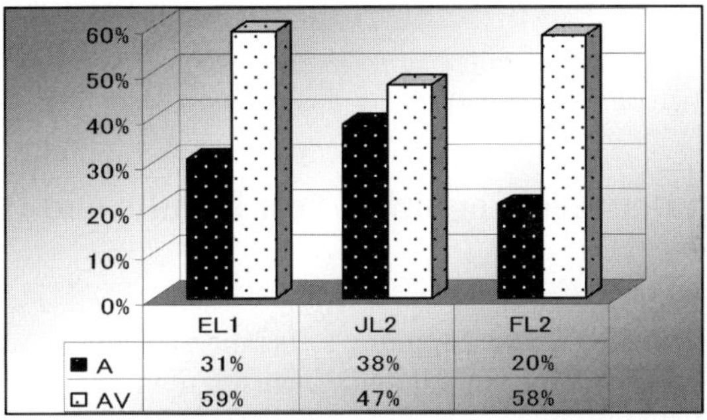

Fig. 1. Overall results of experiment in A and AV effects

Correct Answer Ratios of Each Emotion. Figure 2 illustrates the correct answer ratios according to each emotion word by A (left) and AV (right). The bars show the correct answer ratios of EL1 and the lines of JL2 (with circular spots) and FL2 (with triangular spots) respectively. As for A, the highest emotion word was 'anger' for EL1 (76%) and JL2 (57%), but 'anger' and 'hatred' were the highest of all for FL2 (54%). 'Suspicion' was the lowest of all for all three language speakers (3% for EL1, 5% for JL2 and 2% for FL2). These low correct answer ratios were below the chance level. Regarding AV, the highest emotion word was 'happiness' for EL1 and JL2, although 'hatred' was the highest for FL2. 'Contempt' was the lowest for EL1 (36%) and JL2 (21%), yet 'disappointment' was the lowest (26%) for FL2. Observing the correct answer patterns from the highest to the lowest, EL1 and JL2 appear relatively similar, although FL2 shows a very different pattern from the other two language speakers. Comparing the relationships between the correct answer ratios of each emotion, for JL2 basic emotions such as 'anger', 'sadness', 'surprise', 'happiness', 'fear', and 'hatred', had higher correct answer ratios than paralinguistic emotions such as 'disappointment', 'contempt', and 'suspicion' in both tests, A and AV. Only in A, it was true of FL2. However, for EL1, this did not hold; 'contempt' had a higher correct ratio than some basic emotions in A, and 'disappointment', 'contempt', and 'suspicion' did not have a particularly lower correct answer ratio than did the basic emotions in AV. As for FL2, particular attention must be paid to their relatively high correct answer ratios for negative emotions such as 'hatred' and 'anger' in both A and AV, compared to EL1 and JL2.

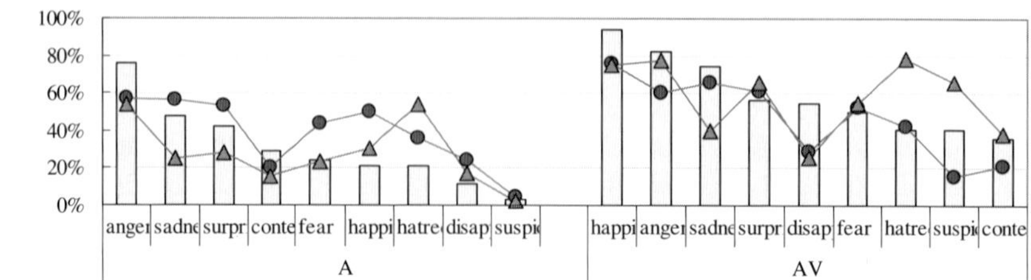

	anger	sadne	surpr	conte	fear	happi	hatre	disap	suspi	happi	anger	sadne	surpr	disap	fear	hatre	suspi	conte
EL1	76%	48%	42%	29%	24%	21%	21%	12%	3%	94%	82%	74%	56%	55%	50%	41%	41%	36%
JL2	57%	56%	53%	20%	44%	50%	36%	24%	5%	76%	60%	66%	61%	29%	52%	42%	16%	21%
FL2	54%	25%	28%	15%	23%	31%	54%	17%	2%	75%	77%	40%	66%	26%	55%	78%	66%	38%

Fig. 2. A (left) and AV (right) effects of experiment according to each emotion

3 Correlation Between Cognition Test Results and Physio-acoustic Distances

The sentence duration used for the cognition tests ranged from 1.082 s. to 2.583 s. In [4] I described the patterns of each F0 and intensity contour for each emotion by normalising the time difference. I predicted that the cognitive confusion among emotions may have been caused by the similarity of the patterns of these contours, e.g., happiness' and 'surprise', and 'contempt' and 'suspicion'. In [4] I used the following equations to calculate two kinds of physio-acoustic distances: (1) D (equation (1)) and (2) PD (equation (2)) between the emotions for F0 (Hz) and intensity (dB), respectively. Below these, distance values will be compared with the cognition test results.

$$D = \frac{\sum_{t=0}^{T} \left| F_i(t) - F_j(t) \right|}{T} . \tag{1}$$

$$D_p = \frac{\sum_{t=0}^{T-1} \left| (F_i(t+1) - F_j(t+1)) - (F_i(t) - F_j(t)) \right|}{T-1} . \tag{2}$$

3.1 Overall Correlation Coefficients Between Correct Cognition and Distances

I examined whether there was a correlation between the overall correct answer ratios for A and AV by JL2, FL2 and EL1 in the cognition tests, and the overall average values of distances for F0 and intensity, respectively. The results are listed in table 1. Coefficiency between them was not high. Yet, it was apparently higher in intensity than in F0 for A for all language speakers, but this was not the case for AV, particularly in FL2. Also, it was highest of all for EL1 in both F0 and intensity in A in both distance types, and also in AV in the case of intensity. But, F0 in AV varied depending on the language and the kinds of distance.

Table 1. Correlation coefficients between the overall correct answer ratios in the cognition tests and distances

		F0		Intensity	
		D	PD	D	PD
A	JL2	-0.06	0.07	0.26	0.24
	EL1	0.13	-0.14	0.59	0.55
	FL2	0.02	0.02	0.35	0.41
AV	JL2	-0.22	0.08	0.06	0.08
	EL1	-0.11	0.20	0.21	0.26
	FL2	-0.16	-0.22	0.04	0.16

3.2 Ratios of High Correlation in the Standard Scores

I calculated the correlation between the standard scores of all emotions and the standard scores of each distance, according to each emotion, each language (JL2, FL2, or EL1), each effect (V or AV), each distance (D or PD) and each parameter (F0 or intensity). The results are listed in appendix 1. Based on appendix 1, I calculated the ratios (%) of the number of higher correlation ratios (over 70%) for all nine emotions including the correct answer emotion (see 'All' in fig. 3) and all eight error emotions, excluding the correct answer emotion (thus, wrong answers, see 'Errors' in fig.3). It shows how many emotions were correlated to the distance. Therefore, the higher the ratio the more the emotions are correlated to distance.

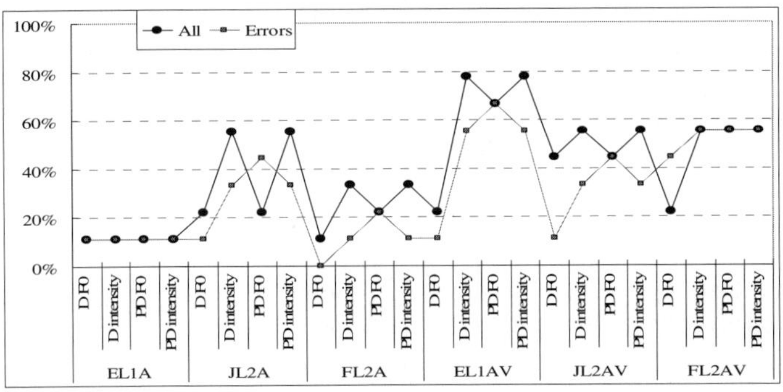

Fig. 3. Ratios of high correlation according to A or AV, languages, distances, F0 and intensity

In terms of the relationships between the emotions and distances, AV showed higher ratios ($\bar{X}$ 53%) than A ($\bar{X}$ 25%) in general, particularly for EL1. This might probably be because the correct answer ratios were higher in AV. In A, JL2 showed the highest ratio ($\bar{X}$ 44%) of all (EL1, FL2: 36%). PD had higher ratios ($\bar{X}$ 43%) than D ($\bar{X}$ 35%). Intensity had higher ratios ($\bar{X}$ 48%) than F0 ($\bar{X}$ 30%). In terms of the relationships between the error emotions and distances, the overall ratio was lower than 'All', probably because the correct answer ratio was not included. AV showed higher ratios ($\bar{X}$ 44%) than A ($\bar{X}$ 18%) in general, particularly for EL1. This was also probably because the answer ratios were higher in AV. In A, JL2 showed the highest ratio of all. PD had higher ratios ($\bar{X}$ 37%) than D ($\bar{X}$ 24%). Intensity had higher ratios ($\bar{X}$ 33%) than F0 ($\bar{X}$ 28%). In comparing 'All' and 'Errors', JL2 showed similar patterns in both A and AV, but EL1 presented a very different pattern between A and AV. FL2 was relatively closer to EL1. Intensity was slightly higher than F0.

3.3 Kurtosis

As far as the kurtosis is concerned there is a gradient in the curve in this case compared to a normal distribution pattern. Based on appendix 1, I calculated the overall correlation between the answer ratios of all emotions, including the correct answer ratio and four kinds of distance (distance F0, distance intensity, pattern distance F0, pattern distance intensity). The results have been converted into figure 4. The mean kurtosis showed that PD had higher values ($\bar{X}$ 0.41) than D ($\bar{X}$ 19.5), that intensity had higher values ($\bar{X}$ 0.30 for A, 0.44 for AV) than F0 ($\bar{X}$ 0.09 for A, 0.38 for AV) in both A and AV, that A had higher values ($\bar{X}$ 0.33) than AV ($\bar{X}$ 0.28), and that EL1 had the highest values ($\bar{X}$ 0.435), FL2 ($\bar{X}$ 0.30), JL2 ($\bar{X}$ 0.18).

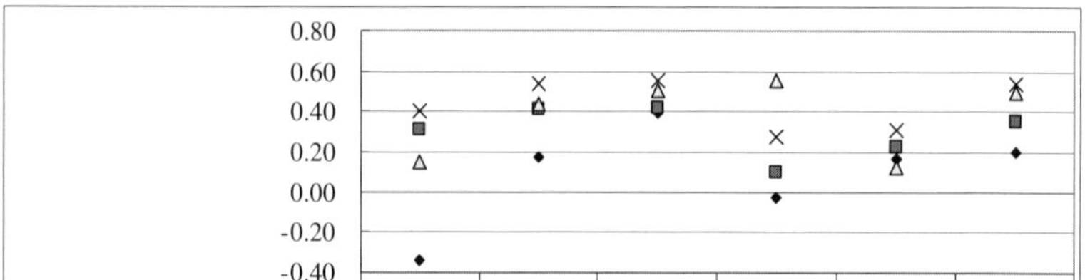

	JL2A	FL2A	EL1A	JL2AV	FL2AV	EL1AV
◆ Distance F0 kutosis	-0.34	0.17	0.40	-0.03	0.16	0.20
■ Distance intensity kutosis	0.31	0.41	0.42	0.10	0.22	0.35
△ Pattern-distance F0 kutosis	0.15	0.44	0.50	0.56	0.12	0.50
× Pattern-distance intensity kutosis	0.40	0.54	0.56	0.28	0.31	0.54

Fig. 4. Overall kurtosis correlation between the answer ratios for each emotion, and distances for each emotion according to the language, A or AV, and F0 or intensity

3.4 Confusion Among the Emotions and Distances

Standard Score. I calculated the standard scores for all nine emotions including one correct answer emotion and the remaining eight error emotions of the answer ratios respectively, and the standard scores of four kinds of distance (D, PD x F0, intensity) according to nine kinds of emotion. The results were converted into the figures in appendix 2, in which the dots (response per cent) connected by a blue line illustrate the distributions of the answers (right and wrong), for each targeted emotion (e.g., 'happiness'), for each distance and for F0 and intensity, respectively. In appendix 2, the upper three figures per each emotion show A by EL1, JL2 and FL2, and the lower three figures AV by the same. In the figures, the legend has been omitted. Distance F0 is shown with circular dots, distance intensity with lozenge dots, pattern-distance F0 with triangular dots, and pattern-distance intensity with square dots.

Level of Confusion. These figures show how the subjects speaking all three language judged English emotional sentences. In the figures, their judgements according to the language were plotted negatively, a style converse to a net graph. The correct answer was calculated as zero, and the closer the other emotions to zero were the greater the subjects' confusion with the correct answer became. For example, in fig. EL1A 'surprise', the correct answer was 'surprise', but there was a confusion with 'anger' and thus the response per centages of these two emotions were closer to the centre in the figure. Also, there were patterns in their answers, highlighting either only one correct answer (e.g., 'anger') or diffusing into two (e.g., 'surprise'), three (e.g., 'hatred'), and more (e.g., 'suspicion' in A and AV, 'fear' in A). This suggests the level of the subjects' confusion.

Distance and Response Percent. The figures in appendix 2 show that the closer the four distances to response per cent are, the more they are correlated. For example, in fig. EL1A 'surprise', 'anger' is far from the distances, but not from the other eight emotions. This means that the rest of the emotions, including the correct answer 'surprise', were almost in correlation with the four distances.

3.5 Variation and Kurtosis

I compared the variation and kurtosis of each emotion with the way in which the subjects made judgements. The variation is illustrated in figure 5 and the kurtosis in figure 6, according to each emotion, language, and A or AV. The variation tended to be smaller for 'suspicion', 'fear', 'disappointment' and 'surprise' and even among all three languages. In general, the kurtosis concentrated on 'anger (high Ku)', 'suspicion (low)', 'sadness (high except FL2AV)'. Otherwise, both the variation and kurtosis varied depending on the languages.

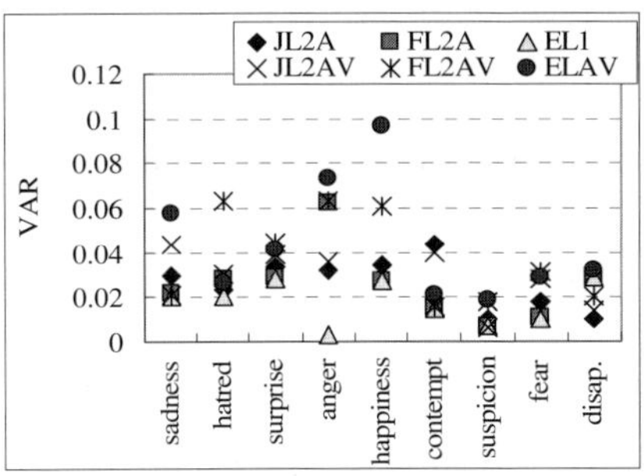

Fig. 5. Variation of each emotion, language, and A or AV

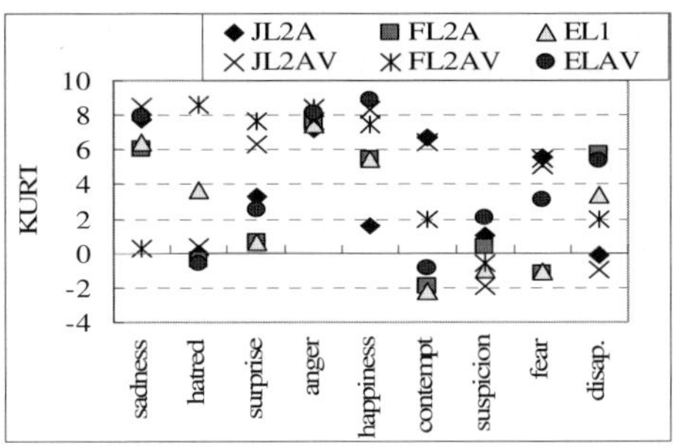

Fig. 6. Kurtosis of each emotion, language, and A or AV

4 Conclusions

The cognition test results confirmed, (1) that the difference in overall correct answer ratios between the A and AV tests was higher in AV, (2) that it was the smallest in JL2, which might imply that JL2 depended more on the sound while watching the video for the judgment of English emotion, compared to EL1 and FL2, (3) that the patterns of correct ratios according to each emotion were somewhat similar in JL2 and EL1, whereas FL2 showed higher correct ratios in the para-linguistic emotions, unlike JL2 and EL1, and (4) that the distribution of the answers according to each emotion were either similar to or different from the others, depending on the language. These differences between A and AV may have been caused by a different (cultural) attitude towards the test methods upon which they were dependent, A or AV, and possibly by the difference in acoustic parameters used in their own languages. Thus, it might be predicted that the cognition of English emotion could be universal or culturally constrained depending on emotions and depending on the test methods. This may accord with previous studies.

The correlation between these cognition tests and the physio-acoustic distances confirmed, (1) that when the overall mean values were directly compared, F0 and intensity did not show a high correlation, yet seem to be higher in intensity for A for all language speakers, although this was not the case for AV, particularly in FL2 ; further, the fact that intensity was higher than F0 was also confirmed by the kurtosis when all the emotions were compared, yet there was one case in which F0 was higher than intensity only when the errors were compared, and (2) that PD was higher than D in both A and AV, which implies that all three language speakers judge emotions by their own patterns for emotions.

In future studies a greater variety of English emotional sentences and more informants will be necessary if the present results are to be confirmed, and also speakers of languages other than Japanese and Finnish could be used in the tests. For physio-acoustic parameters, duration should be compared as well as F0 and intensity in investigating the correlation between cognition and physio-acoustic features.

Acknowledgements

I would like to thank Dr Rika Takegata, psychologist, of Helsinki University for the statistical study and Mr Qinghua Sun, of the Tokyo University for providing the distance values.

References

1. Isei-Jaakkola, T., Neff, P.: Japanese L2 Learner's Emotional Cognition of English Intonation. Proceedings of 7th Annual Congress of EPSJ (2002)
2. Isei-Jaakkola, T., Soga, S., Barat, R.: Audio and Audio-visual Effects on English Emotions by Japanese L2. A Handbook for the EPSJ Kanto Branch 6th Meeting. (2004) 63–68

3. Isei-Jaakkola, T.; Sun, Q.; Hirose, K.: Audio and Audio-visual Effects of English Emotional Word on Japanese L2's Cognition and the Acoustic Correlate. Proceedings of SPECOM 2005, (2005) 455–458
4. Isei-Jaakkola, T., Sun, Q., Hirose K.: Audio and Audio-visual Effects of a Short English Emotional Sentence on Japanese L2's and English L1's Cognition, and Physio-acoustic Correlate. Proceedings of Int. Conf. of Speech Prosody Dresden (2006)
5. Scherer, K. R.: Cross-cultural Investigation of Emotion Inferences from Voice and Speech: Implications of Speech and Technology. Proceedings of ICSLP Beijing, 2, (2000) 379–382

Appendix 1. Correlation Between the Answer Ratios for Each Emotion and the Distances

		sad.	hatred	surp.	anger	happi.	cont.	susp.	fear	disap.
EL1	D F0	0.70	0.41	0.13	0.07	-0.39	0.31	-0.49	0.35	-0.08
A	D dB	0.77	0.46	0.35	0.03	0.17	0.43	-0.19	0.42	0.30
	PD F0	0.78	0.23	0.56	-0.33	-0.25	0.01	-0.51	0.67	0.34
	PD dB	0.86	0.48	0.32	-0.04	0.04	0.40	-0.20	0.44	0.17
JL2	D F0	0.67	0.70	0.59	0.77	0.47	0.39	-0.50	0.61	0.23
A	D dB	0.91	0.39	0.86	0.92	0.90	0.09	-0.32	0.87	0.56
	PD F0	0.81	0.60	0.68	0.84	0.68	0.41	-0.45	0.63	0.60
	PD dB	0.87	0.44	0.86	0.90	0.85	0.11	-0.14	0.86	0.39
FL2	D F0	0.70	0.31	0.44	0.62	-0.07	0.58	0.11	0.18	-0.40
A	D dB	0.91	0.25	0.76	0.92	0.53	0.47	0.16	0.49	0.04
	PD F0	0.77	0.36	0.48	0.90	0.11	0.62	-0.31	0.05	-0.07
	PD dB	0.89	0.29	0.77	0.92	0.47	0.47	0.13	0.49	0.27
EL1	D F0	0.73	0.66	0.52	0.65	0.79	0.60	0.65	0.57	0.52
V	D dB	0.93	0.64	0.84	0.94	0.88	0.52	0.87	0.78	0.86
	PD F0	0.83	0.71	0.61	0.90	0.95	0.73	0.63	0.65	0.82
	PD dB	0.88	0.66	0.86	0.93	0.88	0.52	0.91	0.77	0.89
JL2	D F0	0.73	0.73	0.60	0.72	0.75	0.45	0.16	0.53	0.28
AV	D dB	0.92	0.44	0.87	0.92	0.91	0.15	0.16	0.84	0.65
	PD F0	0.86	0.63	0.73	0.89	0.92	0.45	0.17	0.58	0.66
	PD dB	0.87	0.49	0.88	0.91	0.90	0.18	0.20	0.83	0.53
FL2	D F0	0.40	0.79	0.64	0.71	0.74	0.25	0.36	0.71	0.37
AV	D dB	0.63	0.85	0.88	0.95	0.92	0.60	0.33	0.88	0.68
	PD F0	0.64	0.86	0.77	0.89	0.90	0.73	0.38	0.80	0.41
	PD dB	0.60	0.85	0.91	0.94	0.91	0.52	0.40	0.89	0.56

Appendix 2. Figures of Distribution of Correct Answers for Each Emotion

(1) 'Happiness'

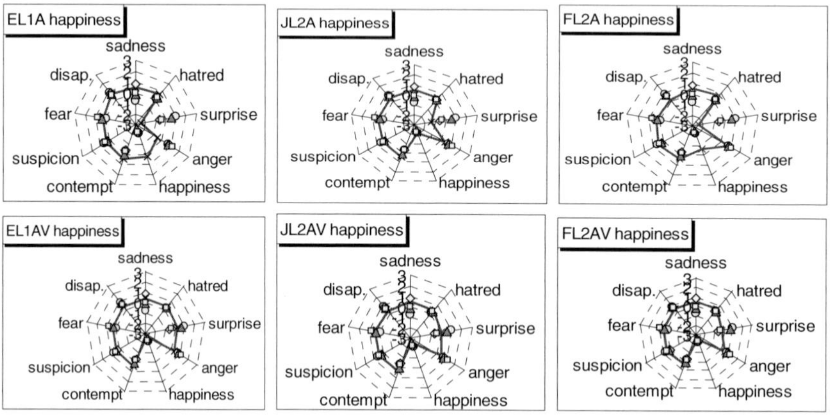

(2) 'Surprise'

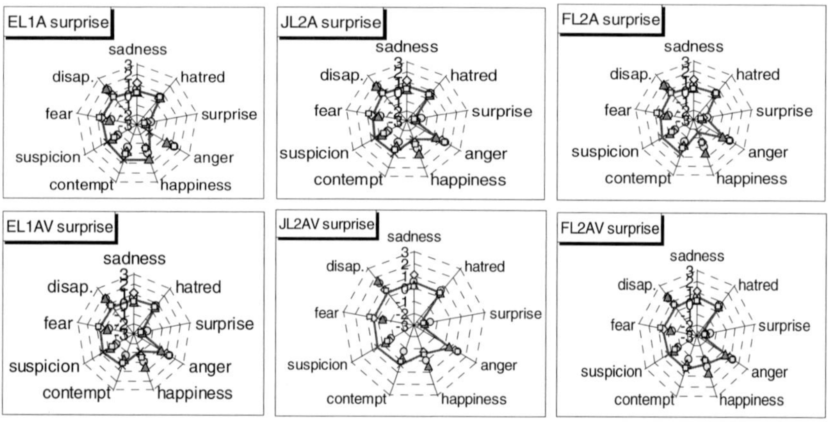

(3) 'Suspicion'

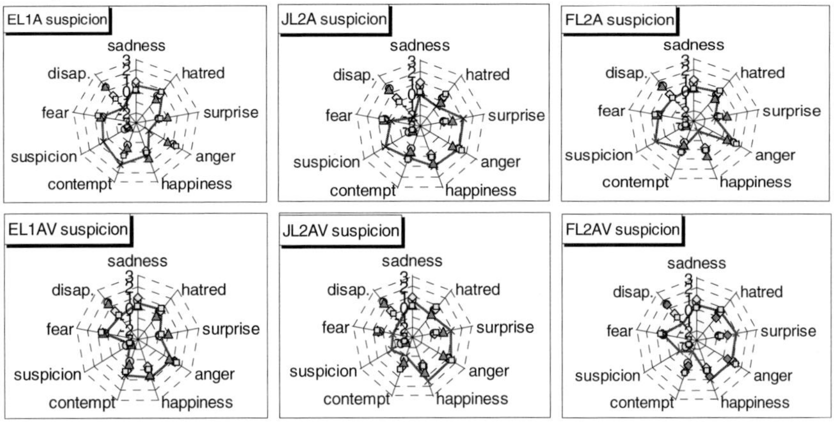

(4) 'Fear'

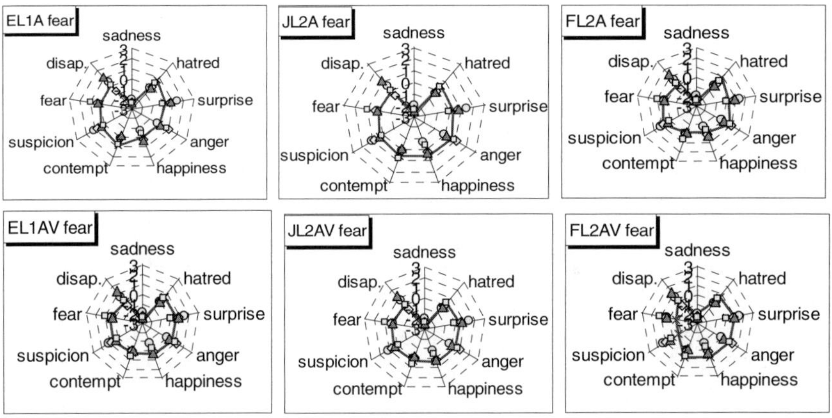

(5) 'Anger'

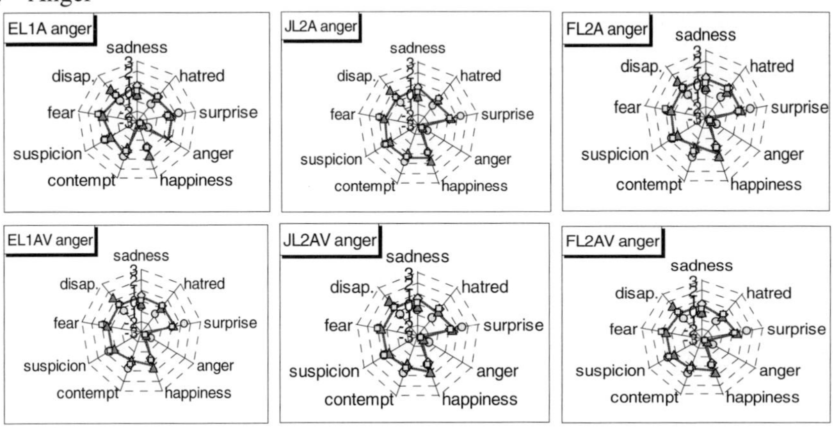

(6) 'Hatred'

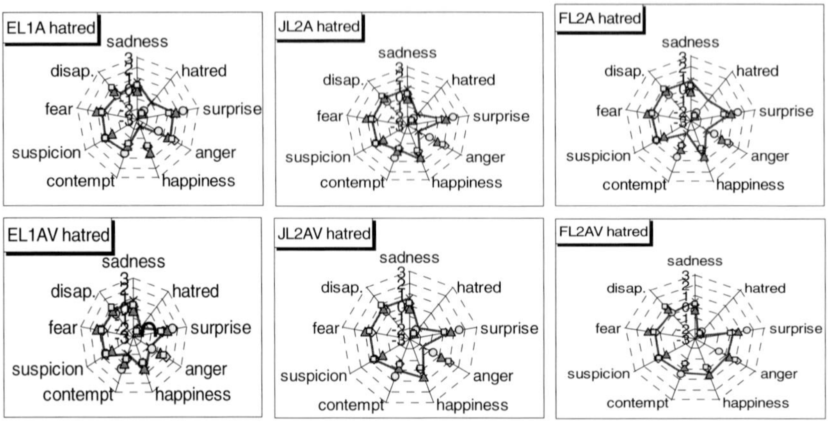

(7) 'Contempt'

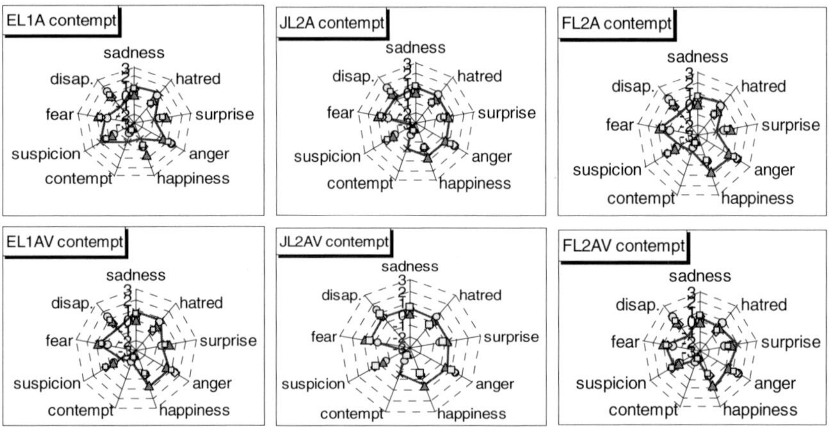

(8) 'Disappointment'

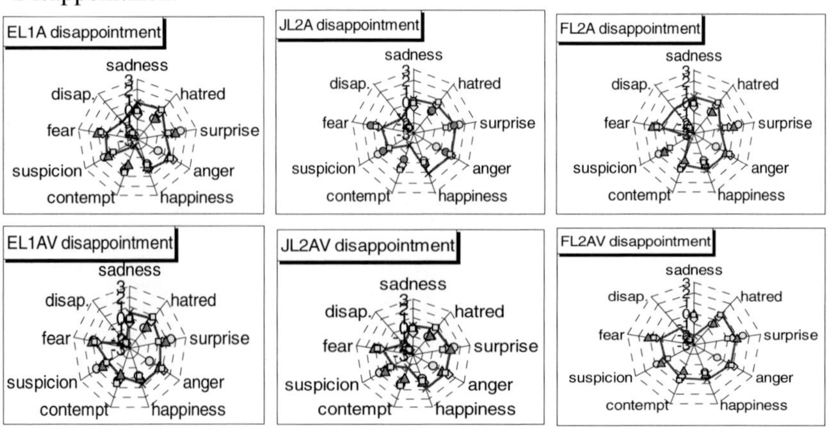

(9) 'Sadness'

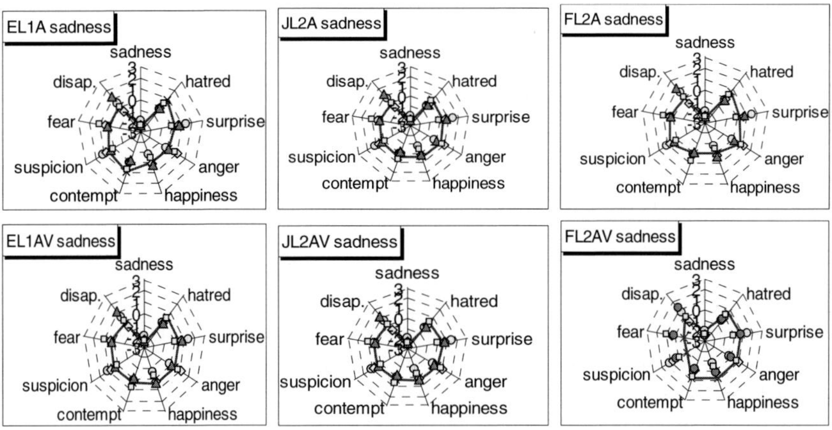
EL1A sadness
JL2A sadness
FL2A sadness
EL1AV sadness
JL2AV sadness
FL2AV sadness
sadness
hatred
surprise
anger
happiness
contempt
suspicion
fear
disap.

Compiling Generalized Two-Level Rules and Grammars

Anssi Yli-Jyrä and Kimmo Koskenniemi

[1] Language Bank Service, CSC Scientific Computing Ltd., Finland
[2] Department of General Linguistics, University of Helsinki, Finland
{aylijyra, koskenni}@ling.helsinki.fi

Abstract. New methods to compile morphophonological two-level rules into finite-state machines are presented. Compilation of the original and new two-level rules and grammars is formulated using an operation called the *generalized restriction* that constructs a one-tape finite-state automaton over an input alphabet of symbol pairs.

The generalized restriction is first used to compile the original two-level formalism where the rules were restricted to single symbol pairs as their centers (i.e. the left-hand sides of the rules). The solution handles also strings of symbol pairs (or regular expressions over the pair alphabet) as centers of two-level rules. Then, the treatment of context conditions is generalized with unions and relative complements etc. Moreover, an extended rule type, the *presence requirement*, combines the generalized context conditions with center conditions at both sides of the rules. The left-hand side specifies where the rule applies and the right-hand side specifies which of the applications are successful.

The original two-level grammars were represented as a separate finite-state machine for each rule and the whole grammar as their intersection. The new methods are used first to redefine this setup, and then to implement a uniform conflict resolution scheme for all rules. The resolution scheme prefers successful and the longest embedded applications of rules, but it treats partially overlapping or explicitly independent applications of rules conjunctively. The composite rules of the original formalism have a marginal status in the new formalism because only identity pairs are allowed in locations where no rule is applicable.

1 Introduction

The aim of this paper is to present a mechanism which we call *generalized restriction* [1] and to use the mechanism to redefine certain earlier versions of finite-state two-level rules and grammars, to present extensions to the existing two-level rule formalism [2,3,4,5] and grammars, and to show how the rules are compiled into finite-state machines and how individual rules are combined into two-level grammars. The paper proceeds in stages along two paths according to (a) the generality of individual rules and (b) the way how rules interact and how they are combined into full grammars.

T. Salakoski et al. (Eds.): FinTAL 2006, LNAI 4139, pp. 174–185, 2006.

Generality of the Rules. We proceed in four steps according to the generality of individual rules:

Rules with Two One-Sided Contexts. The original two-level rules [2] had a written representation for rules, X OP V_Y where X is called the *center* of the rule and V is the left context and Y is the right context. The center X was restricted to single pairs of symbols. Both contexts were regular expressions of pairs. Combining contexts was possible only implicitly and only by intersection, i.e. no explicit operations were allowed for contexts as a whole.

Multi-Character Centers. The center of two-level rules can be generalized to consist of arbitrary regular expressions of pairs in addition to single pairs. This makes it easier to represent certain linguistic phenomena such as metathesis and to handle cases where several symbols are modified as a whole (e.g. if an alphabet represents phonemes by multiple characters).

Rules with Two-Sided Contexts. It is shown that the context part can be reduced into a single regular expression of marked strings, and thus generalize the single rules so that they can have boolean expressions of contexts, including unions, intersections and relative complements. This is a conceptual simplification.

General Rule Operator. It is shown that all original rule types can be collapsed with the *presence requirement* operator (==>). Each of the two arguments of the operator specifies a set of configurations that involve both the centers and their full contexts.

Interplay Between Rules. Two-level rules are not fully independent of each other. The article identifies and discusses four distinct levels of integration:

Intersection. The original two-level grammars treated each rule as a separate and independent finite-state machine. Their intersection, corresponding to the direct product of rule automata, acted as the two-level grammar. The only interaction among the rules was that each rule could introduce further symbol pairs to the common input alphabet. This interaction was quite limited as the symbol pairs were collected in a preprocessing phase.

Right-Arrow Conflicts. Context restriction rules (with the => operator) were sometimes written by grouping phenomena together rather than rules with identical centers. Certain shorthand conventions enabled the linguist to express similar restriction for several centers in a single rule. The combination of these two practices led to problems because the grammar writer usually wished to say that each rule was a permission for those pairs to occur — and not that every constraint had to hold for each occurrence, one constraint for each occurrence would have been more intuitive. As a result, the original intersection did not accomplish what the grammar writer probably wished. Karttunen [4] developed a method of borrowing additional context parts from conflicting rules in order to let the modified rules act as if they were true permissions. The second step of our rule integration shows how to re-implement the resolution of right-arrow conflicts.

Conflicts of Coincident Applications. The generalized restriction gives even further possibilities to widen the principle of rules as permissions rather than just as constraints. Interesting new possibilities arise in handling even other types of conflicts than the right-arrow conflict. Other rule types may also have conflicts, especially the coercion rules among themselves or coercion rules with right-arrow rules. The third step of generalization discusses these possibilities and their compilation methods.

Conflicts of Embedded Applications. New kind of conflicts arise with embedded applications of rules. The fourth step gives precedence to the successful applications of the widest centers over the failures of the contained centers. At the same time, we introduce a possibility to keep independent linguistic phenomena in separation by limiting the conflict resolution to subsets of rules.

2 Basic Definitions

2.1 Operators

Let L_1 and L_2 be arbitrary languages (sets of strings) over an alphabet A. Each letter $a \in A$ denote also the language $\{a\}$ when used as an argument of operations that expect language arguments. The empty string is denoted by ϵ.

Concatenation L_1L_2, exponentiation (L_1^n, where $n \in \mathbf{N}$), (concatenation) closure (L_1^*), positive closure (L_1^+), union ($L_1 \cup L_2$), intersection ($L_1 \cap L_2$), and relative complement ($L_1 - L_2$) are defined in the usual way. The unary operators tie before the binary ones, and binary operators tie in this precedence. Parentheses or square brackets are used for grouping.

A mapping $d_D : (A \cup D)^* \to A^*$, where $D \cap A = \emptyset$, is called a *D-deletion* if $d_D(a_1a_2 \ldots a_n) = a'_1a'_2 \ldots a'_n$ where $a'_i = a_i$ if $a_i \in A$ and $a'_i = \epsilon$ otherwise for all $a_1a_2 \ldots a_n \in (A \cup D)^*$ where every $a_i \in A \cup D$.

2.2 Symbol Pair Strings

Let A and B be alphabets. Set of symbol pairs $A \times B$ is called a *symbol pair alphabet.* Each element $[a, b]$ of alphabet $A \times B$ is denoted by a colon-separated pair of characters $a{:}b$.

Sequences $w \in A \times B$ are called *symbol pair strings*. Each symbol pair string w can be denoted as a sequence of symbol pairs $a_1{:}b_1a_2{:}b_2 \ldots a_n{:}b_n$ or as a colon-separated pair of strings $u{:}v = (a_1a_2 \ldots a_n){:}(b_1b_2 \ldots b_n)$. In such a pair, u is called the *lexical string* and v is called the *surface string.*

2.3 Two-Level Grammars

A two-level grammar is a structure $G = (\Sigma_1, \Sigma_2, 0, \Pi, R, L)$ where

- Σ_1, Σ_2 are the *lexical alphabet* and the *surface alphabet*, respectively,
- $0 \in \Sigma_1, \Sigma_2$ is called a *zero symbol* that is used instead of the empty string ϵ in symbol pair strings. It is often the symbol to be eliminated by deletions.

- $\Pi \subseteq \Sigma_1 \times \Sigma_2$ is a set of *feasible pairs*,
- $R = \{R_1, R_2, \ldots R_q\}$ is a set of two-level rules (two-level rules are defined in Section 3.2),
- L is a mapping from sets of two-level rules to languages Π^* (this mapping is defined in Section 4).

Each two-level grammar defines the following mappings.

- Let $z : (\Sigma_1 \cup \{0\})^* \cup (\Sigma_2 \cup \{0\})^* \rightarrow \Sigma_1^* \cup \Sigma_2^*$ is a 0-deletion.
- Let $\pi_1 : \Pi^* \rightarrow \Sigma_1$ be the mapping for selecting the lexical string of a pair, defined as $\pi_1(w_1{:}w_2) = z(w_1)$ for all $w_1{:}w_2 \in \Pi^*$.
- Let $\pi_2 : \Pi^* \rightarrow \Sigma_2^*$ be mapping for selecting the surface string of a pair, defined as $\pi_2(w_1{:}w_2) = z(w_2)$ for all $w_1{:}w_2 \in \Pi^*$.

Let $[{:}L] = \pi_1^{-1}(\pi_1(L))$ for all $L \subseteq \Pi^*$ and $[L{:}] = \pi_2^{-1}(\pi_2(L))$ for all $L \subseteq \Pi^*$.

Each two-level grammar G defines a regular relation $E(G) \subseteq (\Sigma_1 - \{0\})^* \times (\Sigma_2 - \{0\})^*$ as follows:

$$G = \{z(w_1){:}z(w_2) \mid w_1{:}w_2 \in L(R)\}. \tag{1}$$

In the application area of finite-state morphology [6], a two-level grammar G is typically used to specify productive or otherwise common morphophonemic alternations between lexical word forms and surface word forms. In practical applications such as morphological analysis of surface forms, sufficient accuracy of analysis is achieved best by restricting the relation E with a set of known lexical strings, e.g. by composing the relation $E(G)$ represented by a two-level grammar G with a relation represented by a lexical transducer [7].

2.4 Generalized Restriction

Let Π and M be disjoint alphabets, the latter of which is called the *marker alphabet*. For each $g \in \mathbb{N}$, the operation of *generalized restriction* [1] involves (in addition to the universal language Π^*) two languages:

- set $W \subseteq \Pi^*(M\Pi^*)^g$, called a *generalized precondition*
- set $W' \subseteq \Pi^*(M\Pi^*)^g$, called a *generalized postcondition.*

The operation maps these arguments to the subsets of Π^*, as follows

$$\text{generalized-restriction}(\Pi, M, W, W') = \Pi^* - d_M(W - W'), \tag{2}$$

where $d_M : (\Pi \cup M)^* \rightarrow \Pi^*$ is an M-deletion. The operation has the syntactic form

$$W \overset{gM}{\Rightarrow} W'. \tag{3}$$

3 The Two-Level Rules

3.1 Context Conditions

Let Π be a set of feasible pairs. *Context conditions* are subsets of the *universal context condition* $U = \Pi^*\mathbf{.}\Pi^*\mathbf{.}\Pi^*$ where $\mathbf{.} \notin \Pi$ is a marker symbol rather than the concatenation operator. Define *configurations* as structures (w, v, x, y) where $w \in \Pi^*$ and $w = vxy$. A configuration (w, v, x, y) is said to *satisfy* a context condition $C_i \subseteq U$ if and only if $v\mathbf{.}x\mathbf{.}y \in C_i$.

We will use conventional context conditions [8] as shorthand notations for their more explicit counterparts. For example, conventional context conditions $\_\_b{:}b$, $a{:}a\_\_b{:}b$, $\#a{:}a\_\_b{:}b$ and $\_\_$ correspond to our context conditions $\Pi^*\mathbf{.}\Pi^*\mathbf{.}b{:}b\Pi^*$, $\Pi^* a{:}a\mathbf{.}\Pi^*\mathbf{.}b{:}b\Pi^*$, $a{:}a\mathbf{.}\Pi^*\mathbf{.}b{:}b\Pi^*$ and U.

3.2 Original Two-Level Rules as Implications

Two-level rules R are of the general form

$$X \ \text{OP} \ C \tag{4}$$

where $X \subseteq \Pi^*$ and $C \subseteq U$ are regular sets called the *center* and the context condition, resp., and OP is one of the following operators: *context restriction* (=>), *center prohibition* (/<=), *surface coercion* (<=) or *lexical coercion* [5] (<-).

Every two-level rule R_i specifies a logical condition $\text{CTX}_i(w, v, x, y)$ that must be true for all string configurations (w, v, x, y) of an accepted string $w \in \Pi^*$. The condition $\text{CTX}_i(w, v, x, y)$ is of the general form

$$\begin{aligned} &\text{precondition}(v, x, y) \Longrightarrow \text{postcondition}(v, x, y). \qquad (5) \\ &\text{i.e. } \neg\text{precondition}(v, x, y) \vee \text{postcondition}(v, x, y). \end{aligned}$$

A two-level rule of the form (4) is *traditional* [2] if $X \subseteq \Pi$ and $C = V\mathbf{.}\Pi^*\mathbf{.}Y$, for some $V, Y \subseteq \Pi^*$. Such a rule was written in the form X OP $V\_\_Y$, and it corresponds to implications (5) that are defined for different OPs as

$$\begin{aligned} x \in X &\Longrightarrow v \in V \ \wedge \ y \in Y && (\texttt{=>}) \\ v \in V \ \wedge x \in X \ \wedge \ y \in Y &\Longrightarrow \text{false} && (\texttt{/<=}) \\ v \in V \ \wedge \ x \in [X{:}] \ \wedge \ y \in Y &\Longrightarrow x \in X && (\texttt{<=}) \\ v \in V \ \wedge \ x \in [{:}X] \ \wedge \ y \in Y &\Longrightarrow x \in X. && (\texttt{<-}) \end{aligned}$$

The rule with => operator requires that every occurrence of X must be surrounded by the appropriate context. The rule with /<= operator forbids any occurrences of X in the given context. The rule with operator <= requires that any lexical side of X in the given context must be realized as in X in the given context. The rule with operator <- requires that any surface side of X must correspond to something according to X in the given context.

3.3 Original Two-Level Rules as Generalized Restrictions

Each condition $v \in L_1 \wedge x \in L_2 \wedge y \in L_3$ where $L_1, L_2, L_3 \subseteq \Pi^*$ can also be expressed as $v.x.y \subseteq L_1.L_2.L_3$. Thus the implication (5) for traditional rules is equivalent to implication $v.x.y \subseteq W_i \Longrightarrow v.x.y \in W_i'$ where $W_i, W_i' \subseteq \Pi^*.\Pi^*.\Pi^*$. The complement of (5) reduces to the property $v.x.y \subseteq W_i - W_i'$. The property (5) holds for all configurations (w, v, x, y) if w belongs to the set

$$W_i \overset{2M}{\Rightarrow} W_i' \text{ where } M = \{.\}. \tag{6}$$

The first compilation method for two-level rules is due to Kaplan and Kay [3,8]. According to [1], the early solution was applicable only when $X \subseteq \Pi$. For the formula (6), this restriction is unessential, as X can be any subset of Π^*.

In addition to the multi-character centers, the current method treats epenthesis rules such as $0{:}b$ <= $c{:}c$__$d{:}d$ in an elegant way, with a precondition that checks whether the property $x \in [X{:}]$ holds for configurations (w, v, x, y). The property holds not only when $x = 0{:}b$ but also for $x = \epsilon{:}\epsilon$ and $x = 0{:}b\,0{:}b$. The same effect was achieved earlier [8] by treating the epenthesis rules as special cases.

3.4 Generalized Contexts of Two-Level Rules

Two-level rules (4) whose context conditions are not of the form $V \,.\, \Pi^* \,.\, Y$, where $V, Y \subseteq \Pi^*$, need a more general compilation formula that does not use V and Y. For example, multiple context conditions $\{V_1\_\_Y_1, \ldots, V_k\_\_Y_k\}$ may be given as a single context condition $C = \cup_{i=1}^{k} V_i \,.\, \Pi^* \,.\, Y_i$. To define the semantics in the general case, we will now relate X and C directly to W_i and W_i'.

Let $T_X = \Pi^* \,.\, X \,.\, \Pi^*$ for all $X \subseteq \Pi^*$. The language represented by each simple two-level rule R_i is obtained as $L(R_i) = W_i \overset{2M}{\Rightarrow} W_i'$ where

$$W_i = \begin{cases} T_X & \text{if OP is =>} \\ C \cap T_X & \text{if OP is /<=} \\ C \cap T_{[X:]} & \text{if OP is <=} \\ C \cap T_{[:X]} & \text{if OP is <-} \end{cases} \qquad W_i' = \begin{cases} C & \text{if OP is =>} \\ \emptyset & \text{if OP is /<=} \\ T_X & \text{if OP is <=} \\ T_X & \text{if OP is <-} \end{cases} \tag{7}$$

3.5 The Presence Requirement Rule

We can now generalize over the prohibition and coercion rules by defining the operator of *center presence requirement* (<==) and the corresponding languages W_i and W_i' as $W_i = C$ and $W_i' = T_X$. With this operation, it is possible to express some traditional two-level rules more uniformly:

X /<= V__Y	equals to	$\emptyset$ <== $V \,.\, X \,.\, Y$,
X <= V__Y	equals to	X <== $V \,.\, [X{:}] \,.\, Y$,
X <- V__Y	equals to	X <== $V \,.\, [{:}X] \,.\, Y$.

Finally, we can generalize the format of two-level rules to allow context conditions on both sides. The *presence requirement* rule C ==> C', where $C, C' \subseteq U$, would define W_i and W_i' as $W_i = C$ and $W_i' = C'$. The presence requirement rule can be used to express all traditional rules in a uniform manner. E.g., X<==C and X=>C correspond to C==>T_X and T_X==>C, respectively.

4 A Coarse Interpretation of Two-Level Grammars

A coarse view of two-level rules is that they are just constraints that either accept or reject strings over alphabet Π. When there is a set of two-level rules $R = \{R_1, R_2, \ldots R_q\}$, their combination $L(R)$ is obtained by set intersection

$$\cap_i L(R_i) \tag{8}$$

When the rules R of a two-level grammar $G = (\Sigma_1, \Sigma_2, 0, \Pi, R, L)$ are applied, as constraints, to a string $w \in \Pi^*$, all the rules see the same representation. Therefore, they do not interact with each other like the rules of classical generative phonology (generative phonology includes interaction by feeding, counter-feeding, bleeding and counter-bleeding). A coarsely interpreted two-level formalism might be formally quite capable for the task of morphophonemic grammars.

Morphophonemic two-level rules are usually expected to associate exactly one surface string $v \in \Sigma_2^*$ for any reasonable lexical representation $u \in \Sigma_1^*$. This requires good cooperation among the two-level rules. Some grammars generate, of course, *multiple* surface representations, but they are less common in practical descriptions. It is possible but, again, less common that a lexical representation corresponds to *no* surface representation at all. The coarse interpretation of two-level rules threatens this expectation because two-level constraints often interact with each other so that the grammar is tighter than aimed by the linguist.

5 Adding More Structure to the Interpretation of Rules

In addition to the constraint interpretation of two-level rules, we can view two-level rules as phonological rules that *apply* to different locations in each string pair $w \in \Pi^*$. We say that a configuration (w, v, x, y) is an *application* of a two-level rule R_i if it satisfies the precondition of R_i. This corresponds to the condition $v{\scriptstyle\blacksquare}x{\scriptstyle\blacksquare}y \in W_i$.

When the application also satisfies the postcondition of R_i, it is called *successful*, but otherwise the application is *failing*. The application (w, v, x, y) of rule R_i is a successful application if and only if $v{\scriptstyle\blacksquare}x{\scriptstyle\blacksquare}y \in S_i$, $S_i = W_i \cap W_i'$, and it is a failing application if and only if $v{\scriptstyle\blacksquare}x{\scriptstyle\blacksquare}y \in F_i$, $F_i = W_i - W_i'$. Observe (i) that every application of a single rule is either successful or failing, but not both, and (ii) that there may be also configurations to which R_i is not applicable.

Two-level rules apply in all places where they can apply. Rules often apply in several different places in a symbol pair string. In such cases, all the failing or successful applications (w, v, x, y) share the string w. When the rules are interpreted as constraints, the additional applications of the rule seem meaningless: On one hand, successful applications do not make change to the string. On the other hand, a single failing application suffices to reject the string.

5.1 The Contrast Between Prohibitions and Permissions

Multiple applications of a two-level rule can be given a meaningful interpretation by interpreting each application *contrastively* with respect to the center $x \in \Pi$ in each configuration (w, v, x, y). In this configuration, the rule *either* permits (allows) or prohibits (disallows) the center x. The contrast was captured by Bear [9,10] in his alternative two-level rule formalism that contained two kinds of rules: "X disallowed in C" and "X allowed in C". Bear's rules express a similar kind of distinction as our distinction between successful applications and failing applications.[1]

If two-level rules are viewed as constraints, the basic interpretation does not make use of successful applications. We see that the logical semantics given to the two-level rules when viewed as constraints discards their ability to say that some centers are permitted rather than prohibited. Such detailed interpretation is simply lost when we consider two-level rules as constraints only: Every configuration (w, v, x, y) where $w \in L(R_i)$, satisfies the condition $v \,.\, x \,.\, y \notin F_i \quad \vee \quad v.x.y \in S_i$. The language $L(R_i)$ is indeed equivalent to

$$L(R_i) = \quad F_i \overset{2M}{\Rightarrow} S_i \quad = \quad F_i \overset{2M}{\Rightarrow} \emptyset. \tag{9}$$

In practice, it may be difficult or clumsy for the linguist to express his or her intuitions in a compact and elegant way without writing contradictory rules because the strict logical conjunction of rules forces the author to write only fully true rules. A more practical approach is to detect well-understood types of rule interaction and resolve them using simple principles. An important and well understood family of rule interactions contains left arrow conflicts and right arrow conflicts [5]. We say that a pair of two-level rules R_i and R_j are *in conflict* if a successful application of one rule is a failing application of another rule, i.e. exactly when it holds that

$$S_i \cap F_j \neq \emptyset \quad \vee \quad S_j \cap F_i \neq \emptyset. \tag{10}$$

5.2 Resolving Right-Arrow Conflicts

So called *right-arrow conflicts* consist of a pair of context restriction rules with non-disjoint centers and unequal context conditions. They are difficult to avoid if the rules are organized according to phenomena rather than the similarity of centers. For example, rules *a*:*ä*=>*c*:*c*__ and *a*:*ä*=>*s*:*s*__ are in right-arrow conflict.

The compiler of Karttunen *et al.* [3,4] resolves right-arrow conflicts by collapsing conflicting right-arrow rules to one rule with multiple contexts. While our approach could handle the result – a union of multiple contexts, there is no need to collapse rules before their compilation. Instead, we can compile the rules as such and get the effect of conflict resolution for free. This effect is achieved by modifying languages F_i and F_j as $F_i' = F_i - F_j$ and $F_j' = F_j - F_i$ so that

[1] Note that this opposition is not the same thing as the positive and the negative reading of operators as presented in [5].

$$S_i \cap F'_j = \emptyset \quad \vee \quad S_j \cap F'_i = \emptyset. \tag{11}$$

for all rule pairs (i, j). In fact, the corresponding changes can be made over all right-arrow rules with common rule applications by defining the modified rule language

$$L(R_i) = \quad (F_i - \cup_j S_j) \overset{2M}{\Rightarrow} \emptyset \quad = \quad F_i \overset{2M}{\Rightarrow} \cup_j S_j. \tag{12}$$

where j ranges over all indexes of => rules R_j in the rule set R.

When the right-arrow conflicts are resolved, the redefined language $L(R)$ is given by the formula

$$L(R) = [(\cup_i F_i) \overset{2M}{\Rightarrow} \cup_i S_i] \cap [\cap_j L(R_j)] \tag{13}$$

where i ranges over the indexes of => rules R_i and j ranges over the indexes of the other rules. Observe that the set S_i is now crucial for the implementation of the right-arrow conflict resolution.

5.3 Resolving More General Conflicts of Coincident Applications

The approach of right-arrow conflict resolution can be generalized to other types of rule conflicts so that the sets representing successful applications is taken into account also in these conflicts. To achieve this effect, we simply compute the language of the whole grammar with the formula (13), but this time i ranges over the indexes of all rules and j does not get any values.

With this interpretation, the conflicts are resolved by licensing such configurations that either do not constitute any rule applications or that are successful applications of some rule. For example, the combination of rules *a*:*a*<=*c*:*c*__ and *a*:*ä*<=*c*:*c*__ is rendered as equivalent to rule {*a*:*a*, *a*:*ä*}<=*c*:*c*__.

The generalization would remove all the conflicts that are characterized by the condition (10). As a result, a new kind of rule conflicts are resolved automatically: *left-right arrow conflict*. This occurs between rules *a*:*a*=>*c*:*c*__ and *a*:*ä*<=*c*:*c*__. The latter rule becomes now effectively equivalent to rule {*a*:*a*, *a*:*ä*} <= *c*:*c*__. Furthermore, in the conflicting pair of rules *a*:*a*=>*c*:*c*__ and *a*:*a*<=*d*:*d*__, the first rule is changed effectively to *a*:*a*=>{*c*:*c*, *d*:*d*}__.

6 Conflicts of Embedded Applications of Rules

6.1 Giving Precedence to the Widest Successful Applications

In the original two-level formalism, the center is a subset of Π. However, our definitions allow centers that can be any regular subsets of Π^*. This generalization introduces a new type of conflict: an *embedded-center conflict*. A typical example of an embedded-center conflict is given by the rules

$$a{:}i\ b{:}j\ c{:}k \ \text{OP}\ l{:}l\_\_r{:}r \tag{14}$$

$$a{:}i \ \text{OP}\ m{:}m\_\_. \tag{15}$$

where OP $\in$ {<=, =>}. The centers of these rules are different, so they are not in a normal rule pair conflict. Nevertheless, the latter rule requires that center $a{:}i$ must be preceded by $m{:}m$, which is not possible if the $a{:}a$ occurs after $l{:}l$ as assumed by the first rule. As the result, a successful application of the first rule implies a failing application of the second rule.

The conflict cannot be solved solely on the basis of the previously presented formulas. There is, however, a notational trick (see e.g. in [11]) that implements rules of type (14) as traditional two-level rules

$$a{:}i \text{ OP } l{:}l\_\_[b{:}]\,[c{:}]\,r{:}r \tag{16}$$
$$b{:}j \text{ OP } l{:}l\,[a{:}]\_\_[c{:}]\,r{:}r \tag{17}$$
$$c{:}k \text{ OP } l{:}l\,[a{:}]\,[b{:}]\_\_r{:}r. \tag{18}$$

In the original two-level formalism where the centers were restricted to subsets of Π, the combination of latter kind of rules were used as an expanded alternative for the rule (14) that was not directly expressible. Thus, given the rule (14), it should be perfectly possible to include all the four rules into the grammar, without implying any further restrictions.

If the inclusion of the expanded rules is done, the effect is surprising: rules (15) and (16) are now in conflict, but the right-arrow conflict resolution makes these rules compatible, which will also enable that successful applications of (14) are no more blocked by failing applications of (15).

In practice, the resolution strategy can be implemented with a simple modification to the compilation formulas. This modification would deduce e.g. successful applications of rules (16) - (18) from the successful application of rule (14). The deduction can be realized redefining $L(R)$ as

$$L(R) = (\cup_i F_i) \overset{2M}{\Rightarrow} \mu(\cup_i S_i) \tag{19}$$

where $\mu(L) = \{vx_1{\scriptstyle\blacksquare}x_2{\scriptstyle\blacksquare}x_3y \mid v{\scriptstyle\blacksquare}x_1x_2x_3{\scriptstyle\blacksquare}y \in L\}$.

Rules like 0:b<=$c{:}c$__ used to be a tricky special case in a previous compilation approach [4,8]. When compiled with the formula (19), the rule considers configuration $c{:}c \,{\scriptstyle\blacksquare}\, \epsilon \,{\scriptstyle\blacksquare}\, 0{:}b$ a successful application as required.

6.2 The Default Correspondences

One of the differences of independent two-level rules compared to e.g. replace rules [6] is that they allow character changes that are not described in the rules. For example, rule $a{:}i$ $b{:}j$=>$l{:}l$__$r{:}r$ allows all strings $w \in \Pi^*$ that do not contain the substring $a{:}i$ $b{:}j$. To avoid undesirable character changes, traditional two-level formalisms try to keep Π as small as possible. While Π can be minimized in practical implementations without loss of generality, we assume here that $\Pi = \Sigma_1 \times \Sigma_2$.

It seems to be natural that a grammar $G = (\Sigma_1, \Sigma_2, 0, \Sigma_1 \times \Sigma_2, R, L)$ where $R = \emptyset$ defines the identity mapping $\{w{:}w | w \in (\Sigma_1 \cap \Sigma_2)^*\}$. This interpretation can be implemented by including, by default, occurrences of other symbol pairs than identity pairs to the set of failing configurations. This redefines $L(R)$ as:

$$L(R) = (\cup_i F_i \cup T_N) \overset{2M}{\Rightarrow} \mu(\cup_i S_i) \tag{20}$$

where $N = \Pi - \{a{:}a | a \in \Sigma_1\}$. The semantics of the resulting two-level grammar resembles now that of the replace operator [6]. The current system allows, however, overlapping applications of rules.

An important consequence of the use of successful applications is that there is less need for so-called *composite rules* of the form X<=>C, where the operator <=> is interpreted as a shorthand notation for the combination of rules X=>C and X<=C. The reason is that the left-arrow rules X<=C would have the same successful application as what one would get by including also the corresponding right-arrow rules. However, a composite rule might be useful if we need to restrict occurrences of identity pair strings.

6.3 Simultaneous Phenomena

It seems that the new interpretation of rules given by the formula (20) is sometimes even too permitting. For example in Finnish, selection between stems and endings is largely independent from the rules for consonant gradation. To avoid conflict resolution between rules of distinct phenomena, we could partition the set of rules into independent blocks. The conflicts are resolved within each such block in separation from other blocks. The language of the whole set of rules is then the intersection of the languages of these blocks.

7 Summary

The interpretation given here to two-level grammars removes some differences between the operators. The traditional rules can be expressed with the presence requirement rules. The left-hand side of such rules specify the set of applications of the rules and the right-hand side classifies these applications either as failing or successful. We believe that this uniformity makes the formalism easier to understand.

In contrast to the traditional two-level formalisms and optimality-theoretic phonology, the constraint system presented here does not emphasize failing applications of rules. Moreover, the overall preference of successful applications reduces the annoying rule conflicts of the traditional formalisms substantially.

The current paper does not address all aspects of a practical two-level formalism. In addition to lexical features, the paper does not discuss the subsumption of context conditions or violable rules. It seems possible to use generalized restriction e.g. for disjunctive ordering as well as to add weights to longest applications.

A peculiarity of the system is that it allows overlapping centers in the applications of rules: a failing application cannot be saved by a partially overlapping successful application. Apart from this, the semantics of the grammar resembles the replace operator [6], by using identity pairs of characters in locations where the rules are not applied.

An important aspect of the compilation method is its efficiency and state complexity considerations. Undoubtedly, the proposed formalism allows overly complex rules that are simply impractical. However, on the basis of our initial experiments, the proposed method scales well with usual rules and it can be used to compile practical two-level descriptions and to construct lexical transducers.

References

1. Yli-Jyrä, A.M., Koskenniemi, K.: Compiling contextual restrictions on strings into finite-state automata. In Cleophas, L., Watson, B.W., eds.: The Eindhoven FASTAR Days, Proceedings. Number 04/40 in Computer Science Reports, Eindhoven, The Netherlands, Technische Universiteit Eindhoven (2004) `http://www.ling.helsinki.fi/~aylijyra/dissertation/7.pdf`.
2. Koskenniemi, K.: Two-level morphology: a general computational model for word-form recognition and production. Number 11 in Publications. Department of General Linguistics, University of Helsinki, Helsinki (1983)
3. Karttunen, L., Koskenniemi, K., Kaplan, R.M.: A compiler for two-level phonological rules. Report CSLI-87-108, Center for Study of Language and Information, Stanford University, CA (1987)
4. Karttunen, L., Beesley, K.R.: Two-level rule compiler. Technical Report ISTL-92-2, Xerox Palo Alto Research Center, 3333 Coyote Hill Road, Palo Alto, California (1992) `www.xrce.xerox.com/competencies/content-analysis/fssoft/docs/twolc-92/t wolc92.html`.
5. Karttunen, L., Beesley, K.R.: Two-level rule compiler. An additional documentation file on the CD-ROM supplement of Beesley and Karttunen (2003), March 5 (2003)
6. Beesley, K.R., Karttunen, L.: Finite State Morphology. CSLI Studies in Computational Linguistics. CSLI Publications, Stanford, CA, USA (2003)
7. Karttunen, L.: Constructing lexical transducers. In: 15th COLING 1994, Proceedings of the Conference. Volume 1., Kyoto, Japan (1994) 406–411 `http://acl.ldc.upenn.edu/C/C94/C94-1066.pdf`.
8. Kaplan, R.M., Kay, M.: Regular models of phonological rule systems. Computational Linguistics **20**(3) (1994) 331–378 `http://acl.ldc.upenn.edu/J/J94/J94-3001.pdf`.
9. Bear, J.: A morphological recognizer with syntactic and phonological rules. In: 11th COLING 1986, Proceedings of the Conference, Bonn, Germany (1986) 272–276 `http://acl.ldc.upenn.edu/C/C86/C86-1065.pdf`.
10. Bear, J.: Backwards phonology. In: 13th COLING 1990, Proceedings of the Conference. Volume 3. (1990) 13–20 `http://acl.ldc.upenn.edu/C/C90/C90-3003.pdf`.
11. Kempe, A., Karttunen, L.: Parallel replacement in finite state calculus. In: 16th COLING 1996, Proceedings of the Conference. Volume 2., Copenhagen, Denmark (1996) 622–627 `http://arxiv.org/abs/cmp-lg/9607007`.

Computer Analysis of the Turkmen Language Morphology

A. Cüneyd Tantuğ[1], Eşref Adalı[1], and Kemal Oflazer[2]

[1] İstanbul Teknik Üniversitesi Elektrik-Elektronik Fakültesi
Bilgisayar Mühendisliği Bölümü
34469, Maslak, İstanbul, Türkiye
{cuneyd, adali}@cs.itu.edu.tr
[2] Sabancı Üniversitesi Doğa Bilimleri Fakültesi
Bilgisayar Mühendisliği Bölümü
34956, Orhanlı, Tuzla, Türkiye
oflazer@sabanciuniv.edu

Abstract. This paper describes the implementation of a two-level morphological analyzer for the Turkmen Language. Like all Turkic languages, the Turkmen Language is an agglutinative language that has productive inflectional and derivational suffixes. In this work, we implemented a finite-state two-level morphological analyzer for Turkmen Language by using Xerox Finite State Tools.

1 Introduction

This paper describes the implementation of a two-level morphological analyzer for the Turkmen Language. The Turkmen Language is classified as one of the Turkic languages which are all in the Ural-Altaic language family. Like all Turkic languages, the Turkmen Language is an agglutinative language that has productive inflectional and derivational suffixes which are affixed to a word like "beads on a string" [1]. Hence, the morphological analyzing component is an important first-step component of any natural language processing task for agglutinative languages which have complicated morphological structures. There are lots of work in the literature which have focused on two-level analysis of various languages like Japanese, English and Finnish [2,3,4] but the most valuable work for our developments is the two-level description of Turkish morphology [5]. Since both Turkish and Turkmen are close Turkic languages, some of the morphological structures and word roots are common. Even though both languages are similar, there exist great divergences like different tenses, different subject-verb agreements and etc. Another morphological work for a Turkic language is for Crimean Tatar [6].

In this work, we implemented a finite-state two-level morphological analyzer for Turkmen Language by using Xerox Finite State Tools [7]. Next section gives some information about the Turkmen Language; the following chapter describes a brief overview of two-level morphology. In the fourth section, the two-level rules are explained in detail while the finite state machines for morphotactics are explained in the fifth section. The last section concludes the results of the work.

T. Salakoski et al. (Eds.): FinTAL 2006, LNAI 4139, pp. 186 – 193, 2006.

2 The Turkmen Language

The Turkmen Language is a Turkic language which belongs to Ural-Altaic language family. It is used by nearly 7 million people especially in Turkmenistan, Afghanistan, Iran, and Iraq [8]. Although there are great similarities between Turkish and Turkmen language, these languages are classified as different languages because Turkmen is not intelligible to Turkish speaking people or vice versa. After using Arabic and Cyrillic alphabets, the current Turkmen orthography is composed of 30 Latin letters: ***a b j ç d e ä f g h y i ž k l m n ñ o ö p r s ş t u ü w ý z***. There are 9 vowels (***a e ä y i o ö u ü***) and 21 consonants (***b j ç d f g h ž k l m n ñ p r s ş t w ý z***).

3 Two-Level Morphology

Two-level morphology is a widely used technique in morphological analysis [9]. As the name emphasizes, there are two levels called lexical and surface levels. In the surface level, a word is represented in its original orthographic form. In the lexical level, a word is represented by denoting all of the functional components of the word. The phonological modifications can be implemented by writing rules these four rule types [1]:

`1. a:b => LC _ RC`	A is realized as b only in the context LC (left context) and RC (Right Context), but not necessarily.
`2. a:b <= LC _ RC`	A is **always** realized as b in the context LC and RC.
`3. a:b <=> LC _ RC`	A is **always** realized as b in the context LC and RC and nowhere else.
`4. a:b /<= LC _ RC`	A is **never** realized as b in the context LC and RC.

The rules based on these rule types are used to generate a finite state acceptor which executes all rules in parallel and accepts or rejects a lexical-surface pair. The proper sequencing of morphemes (morphotactics) is done by finite state machines that are built by using roots words lexicons and suffixes.

4 Two-Level Rules

We have defined an alphabet for the two-level description of the language. This alphabet includes the standard Turkmen letters and some additional symbols which are used in the intermediate level and have no usage in orthography. We have represent the non-ASCII Turkmen letters by their uppercase counterparts (***ü⇨U, ö⇨O, ç⇨C, ñ⇨N, ş⇨S, ý⇨Y, ž⇨Z, ä⇨E***). The definitions are listed as the following:

Consonants:	CONS = b C d f g h j Z k l m n N p r s S t w Y z
Vowels :	VOWEL = a E e y i o O u U;
Back Vowels:	BACKV = a y u o
Front Vowels :	FRONTV = e E i O U

Back-Rounded Vowels : BKROV = o u
Back-Unrounded Vowels : BKUNROV = a y
Front-Rounded Vowels : FRROV = O U
Back-Unrounded Vowels : FRUNROV = e i E
First letters of some suffixes which may disappear in some cases: X = s n
Vowels subject to ellipsis under some conditions : VS = y i O o U u

In order to handle phonetic variations, we represent a number of two-level rules taken from various Turkmen language references [10,11,12]. Some important rules are given below:

```
1.  A:a  =>  [:BACKV] [:CONS]* (%':%') (%+:0) [CONS: | :CONS | :0]* _
2.  A:e  =>  [:FRONTV] [:CONS]* (%':%') (%+:0) [CONS: | :CONS | :0]* _
3.  V:a  =>  [:BACKV] [CONS]* (%+:0) [CONS: | :CONS | :0]* _
4.  V:E  =>  [:FRONTV] [CONS]* (%+:0) [CONS: | :CONS | :0]* _
5.  I:y  =>  [:BACKV] [CONS]* (%':%') (%+:0) [CONS: | :CONS | :0]* _
6.  I:i  =>  [:FRONTV] [CONS]* (%':%') (%+:0) [CONS: | :CONS | :0]* _
7.  H:i  =>  [:FRUNROV] [CONS]* (%':%') (%+:0) [CONS: | :CONS | :0]* _
8.  H:y  =>  [:BKUNROV] [CONS]* (%':%') (%+:0) [CONS: | :CONS | :0]* _
9.  H:u  =>  [:BKROV] [CONS]* (%':%') (%+:0) [CONS: | :CONS | :0]* _
10. H:U  =>  [:FRROV] [CONS]* (%':%') (%+:0) [CONS: | :CONS | :0]* _
```

These rules are for the harmony rules of the vowels. The surface realization of ***A***, ***V*** or ***I*** is determined by the backness property of the preceding vowel while an ***H*** is determined by the backness and roundness properties of the preceding vowel.

```
11. H:0  <=>  [:VOWEL] %+:0 _
```

A vowel in ***H*** set is deleted if it is the first letter of a suffix which is affixed to a word (or the previous suffix) which has a vowel as the last letter.

```
12. T:a <=> [:BACKV] [CONS: | :CONS | :0]+ [%+:0] _
13. T:e <=> [:FRONTV] [CONS: | :CONS | :0]+ [%+:0] _
14. Cx:Cy <=> _%+:0 [T:] where Cx in (i e A y) Cy in (E E E a) matched
```

Dative is a non-standard nominal case in Turkmen language. These rules are used to handle these special cases. For example, the words ending with vowels ***i, e*** and ***ä***, these vowels are changed into ***E***.

Lexical :	`Berdi+T`	`(A City Name)+Dative`
Surface:	`BerdE00`	`Berdä`

The vowel ***y*** placed as the last letter of a word is changed into ***a*** in dative case.

Lexical :	`Mary+T`	`(A City Name)+Dative`
Surface:	`Mar00a`	`Mara`

There is no orthographic difference between the nominal case and the dative case for the words ending with the letters ***a*** and ***o***. The diffence is stressed by the duration of the last phoneme in the speech.

Lexical :	`ata+T`	`Noun(father)+Dative`
Surface:	`ata00`	`ata`

```
15. e:E <=>  _ %+:0 [H:] [m: | N: | p:] (I: z:);    _ %+:0 [H:] b e r;
```

This rule changes the letter ***e*** to ***E*** for some cases.

```
Lexical :   iSle+HpdI      to work+Past
Surface:    iSlE00pdi      işläpdi
```

```
16. Cx:Cy <=>  [:CONS] %+:0 _ (CONS VOWEL); where Cx in (s n S Y) Cy in
                                                   (0 0 s 0) matched;
```

This rule deletes the letters ***s, n, S*** and ***Y*** if they are in the beginning of a suffix which is affixed to a morpheme that has a consonant as its last letter.

```
17. A:E => %+:0 m _ [k:] %+:0 [T:]; %+:0 d _ %+:0 k [I:]
```

In two special conditions, the ***A*** is resolved as ***E***. One of these conditions is the cases where a verbal root has ***+mAk*** infinitive root and dative case suffixes. Also in a noun which has ***+dA*** locative case and ***+kI*** relative suffixes, the ***A*** of the locative case morpheme is resolved into an ***E***.

```
Lexical :   ber+mAk+T      to give+Infinitive+Dative
Surface:    ber0mEg0e      bermäge

Lexical :   galam+dA+kI    pencil+Loc+Relative
Surface:    galam0dE0ki    galamdäki
```

```
18. Cx:Cy => _ %+:0 (X:0) [ :VOWEL ]; where Cx in (p t C k)
                                            Cy in (b d j g) matched;
```

This rule realizes the voiced obstruents ***p***, ***t***, ***C***, and ***k*** when they are followed by a suffix beginning with a vowel.

```
Lexical :   kitap+T        book+Dative
Surface:    kitab0a        kitaba
```

```
19. VS:0 <=> %$:0 _  [ CONS %+:0 (X:0) [A: | H: | I: | T:] ];
20. H:0 <=> %$:0 _  [ CONS %+:0 (X:0) [A: | H: | I: | T:] ];
```

In certain words, a vowel ellipsis can occur with some kinds of suffixes. The vowel subject to ellipsis is represented by a preceding ***$*** sign in the lexicon.

5 Morphotactics

The study and modeling of legal word formation is called morphotactic [13]. Morphotactic rules imply the legal ordering of the morphemes. In our implementation, morphotactics are done by finite-state-machines. These machines are depicted in Figure 1 and Figure 2. In these figures, the boxes show the states, the arrows shows the next states that can be reached when a suffix matching one of the labels is found. The circles are the final states which indicate legal word formations. The class of the final word is given in the parentheses beside the final states. The 0 transitions indicate that the transition can be done by the null input. The XFST environment has a module

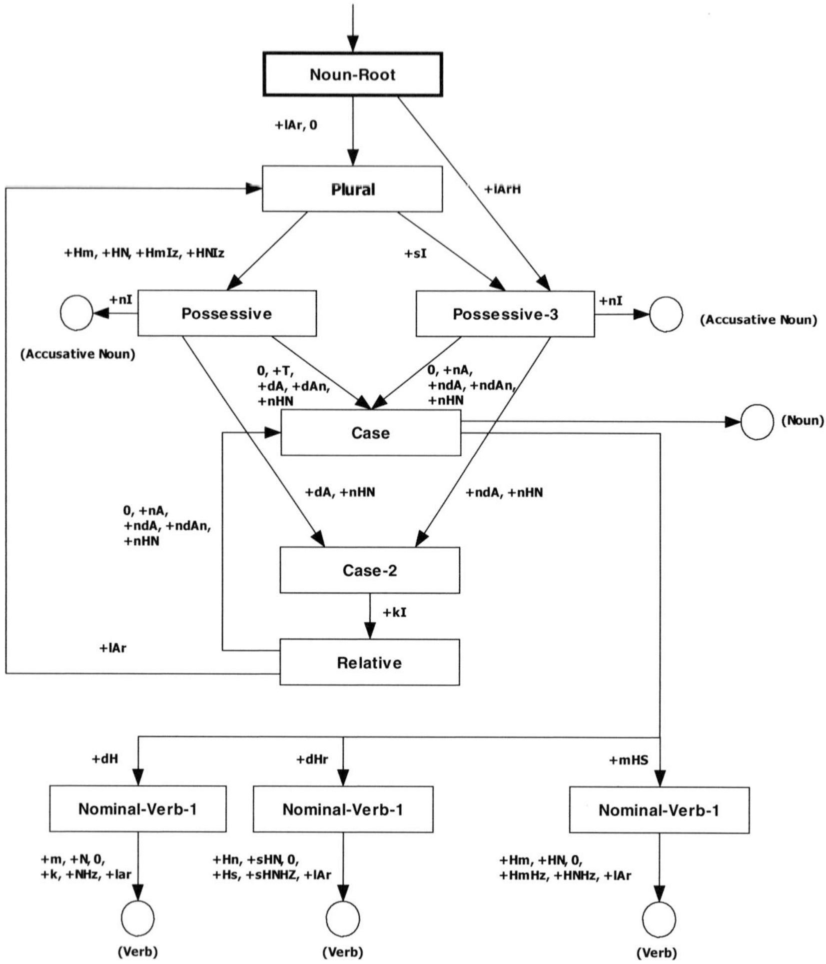

Fig. 1. Finite State Machine for Nominal Morphotactics

called LEXC to build the finite-state-machines as morphotactic rules. A small section of the LEXC lexicons are given below:

```
LEXICON VERBS          LEXICON VERB-POST        LEXICON VERB-ROOT
diY   VERB-POST;       +Verb : 0 VERB-ROOT;     0      : 0     VERB-PASSIVE;
dEl   VERB-POST;                                +Recip : +nHS  VERB-RECIP;
bil   VERB-POST;                                +Recip : +S    VERB-RECIP;
al    VERB-POST;
geple VERB-POST;
```

Each sub-lexicon consists of entries which denote output and input pairs and the name of the next lexicon (state). The system moves to the next state by consuming the input and producing the corresponding output.

Some morphological analysis examples are:

```
galam   0lar      0ym    00yñ   (surface level - galamlarymyñ)
galam   +lAr      +Hm    +nHN   (intermediate level)
pencil  +A3pl     +P1sg  +Gen   (lexical Level - of my pencils)

geple   +mA   +yVr    +Hs   (surface level - geplemeyäris)
geple   0me   0yär    0is   (intermediate level)
talk    +Neg  +Prog1  +A1pl (lexical level - we are not talking)
```

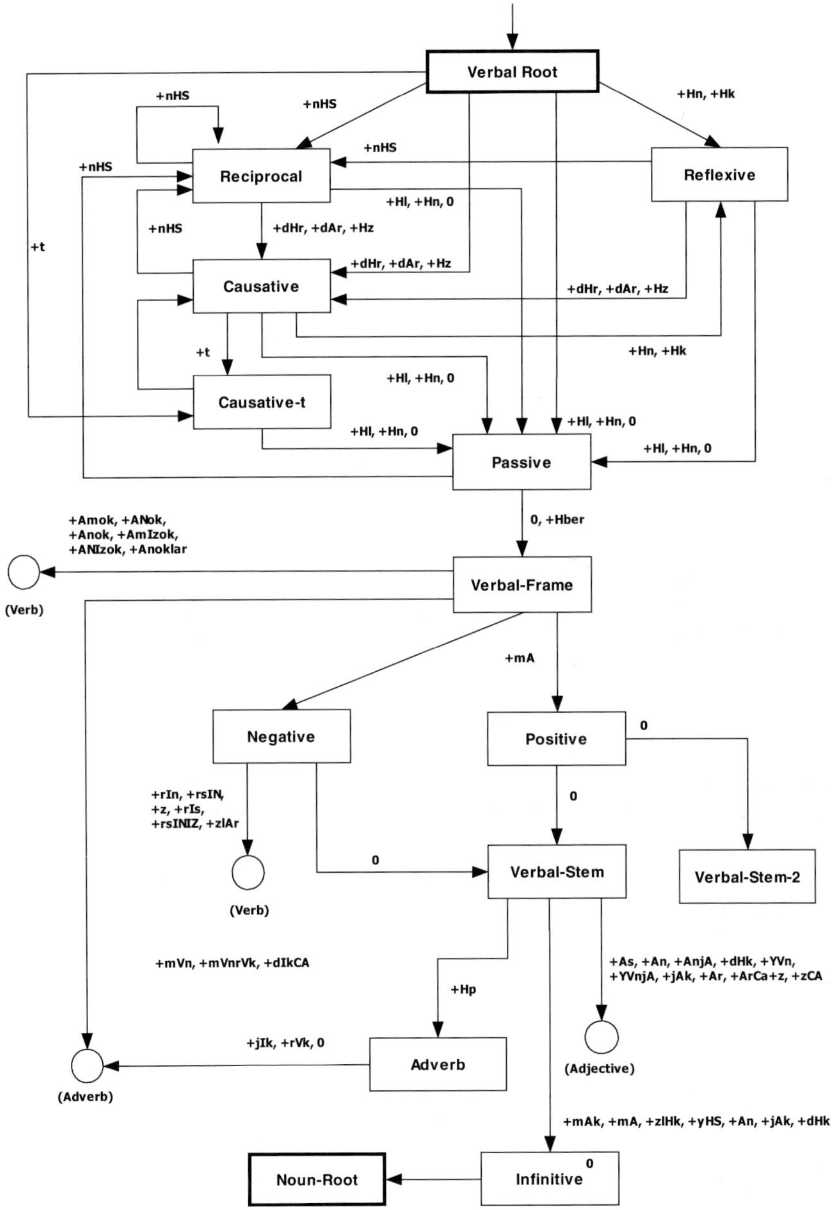

Fig. 2. Finite State Machine for Verbal Morphotactics

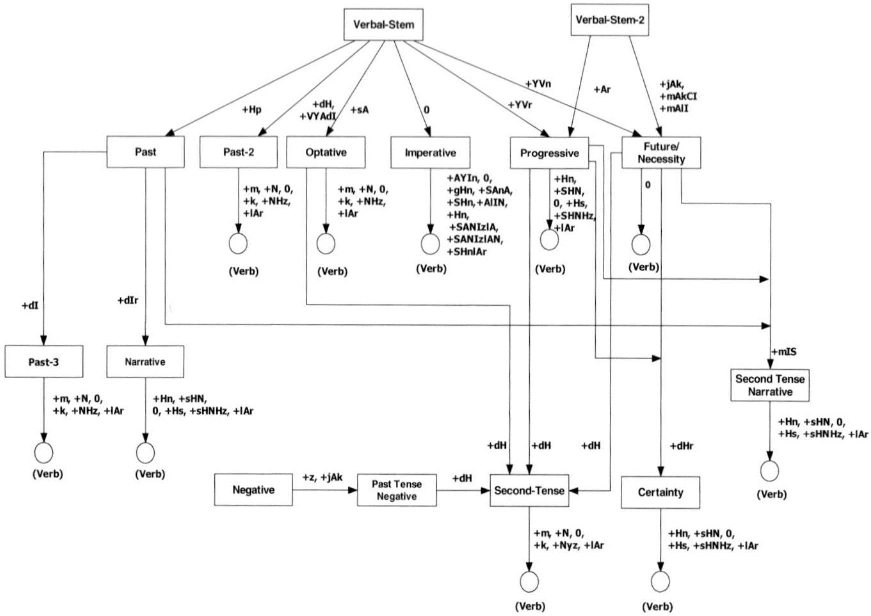

Fig. 2. (*continued*)

6 Conclusion

As a consequence, this work introduces a computer analysis of the Turkmen Language morphology. The well-known two-level morphological analysis method is implemented by finite-state machines. The resulting morphological analyzer is the first step for all kind of NLP tasks because, like Turkish, the Turkmen language has a very complicated inflectional and derivational structure and no other NLP related system can be designed without having the morphological analysis of the words in hand. Even though current version of the implementation does not have large word root lexicons (~1200), it can be easily used for all other NLP related purposes. Since the main goal of implementing a machine translation system between Turkmen and Turkish, we are still improving the performance of the analyzer and enlarging its lexicon size by adding new word roots.

References

1. Sproat, R. : Morphology and Computation, MIT Press (1992)
2. Alam, Y. S. : A Two-Level Morphological Analysis of Japanese. Texas Linguistics Forum, 22:229-252 (1983)
3. Karttunen, L., Wittenburg, K. : A Two-Level Morphological Analysis of English. Texas Linguistics Forum, 22:217-228 (1983)
4. Koskenniemi, K. : An Application of the Two-Level Model to Finnish. In Fred Karlsson, editor, Computational Morphosyntax, a report on research 1981-1984. University of Helsinki Department of General Linguistics (1985)

5. Oflazer, K. : Two-Level Description of Turkish Morphology. Literary and Linguistic Computing, Vol. 9, No:2 (1994)
6. Altintas, K. Cicekli, İ.: A Morphological Analyser for Crimean Tatar. Proceedings of the 10th Turkish Symposium on Artificial Intelligence and Neural Networks (TAINN2001), North Cyprus, pp: 180-189 (2001)
7. Karttunen, L., Gaal, T., Kempe, A. : Xerox Finite-State Tool. Technical Report, Xerox Research Centre, Europe (1997)
8. www.sil.org, www.ethnologue.com
9. Koskenniemi, K. : Two-Level Morphology : A General Computational Model for Word Form Recognition and Production. Publication No:11 , Department of General Linguistics, University of Helsinki
10. Clark, L. : The Turkmen Reference Harrassowitx Verlag, Wiesbaden (1998)
11. Sarı, B., Güder N. : Türkmencenin Grameri (II Morfologiya), Türk Dünyası Gençlerinin Mahtumkulu Yayın Birliği . (1998)
12. Söyegowyñ, M. : Türkmen Diliniñ Grammatikasy – Morfologiya, TDK (2000)
13. Kenneth, B.R., Karttunen, L. : Finite State Morphology, CSLI Publications (2003)

Coordination Structures in a Typed Feature Structure Grammar: Formalization and Implementation

Jong-Bok Kim[1] and Jaehyung Yang[2]

[1] School of English, Kyung Hee University, Seoul, 130-701, Korea
jongbok@khu.ac.kr
[2] School of Computer Engineering, Kangnam University, Kyunggi, 446-702, Korea
jhyang@kangnam.ac.kr

Abstract. Every language employs its own coordination strategies, according to the type of coordinating marking, the pattern of marking, the position of the marker, and the phrase types coordinated. The SOV language Korean is intriguing in the sense that it displays almost all the possibilities of these dimensions. This paper shows how a typed feature structure grammar, HPSG, together with the notions of 'type hierarchy' and 'constructions', can provide a robust basis for parsing the coordination constructions found in the language. We show that this system induces robust syntactic structures as well as enriched semantic representations for real-time applications such as machine translation, which require deep processing of the phenomena concerned.

1 Basic Data: Two Main Types of Coordination

Korean employs two kinds of coordination marking: morphological and lexical marking.[1] In the morphological marking system, the language distinguishes nominal and verbal coordination. As seen in the corpus example (1a), nominal coordination uses suffixal markers (usually called particles in the traditional literature) like *-(k)wa, -hako, -(i)lang* 'and' for conjunctive and *-(i)na* 'or' for disjunctive coordination. Meanwhile, as in (1b), verbal coordination uses the suffixal marker *-ko* 'and' for conjunctive and *-kena* 'or' for disjunctive coordination:[2]

[1] Our thanks go to three anonymous reviewers for the helpful comments and suggestions. This work was supported by the Korea Research Foundation Grant funded by the Korean Government (KRF-2005-042-A00056).

[2] The abbreviations for the glosses and attributes used in this paper are ACC (ACCUSATIVE), ARG (ARGUMENT), CARG (CONSTANT ARGUMENT), C-ARG (CONJUNCT ARGUMENT), C-CONT (CONSTRUCTIONAL CONTENT), DAT (DATIVE), DECL (DECLARATIVE), HON (HONORIFIC), LBL (LABEL), L-INDEX (LEFT INDEX), LTOP (LOCAL TOP), NOM (NOMINATIVE), PNE (PRENOMINAL ENDING), PL (PLURAL), PST (PAST), R-INDEX (RIGHT INDEX), RELS (RELATIONS), TOP (TOPIC), etc.

T. Salakoski et al. (Eds.): FinTAL 2006, LNAI 4139, pp. 194–205, 2006.

(1) a. [khempwuthe-wa/hako/ilang intheneys-ul] paywu-ess-ta
computer-and internet learn-PST-DECL
'(Hc) learned computer and internet.'
b. pelley-ey [mwulli-ko/kena sso-yess-ta]
insect-DAT bite-and/or stung
'(He) was bitten and/or stung by an insect.'

In addition to these morphological markers, the language has words like *kuliko* 'and', *ttonun* 'or' as lexical coordinators. Unlike the morphological coordinators, these coordinators can be used for both nominal and verbal coordination:

(2) a. hay-wa tal kuliko sem-i hamkkey ha-nun kos
sun-and moon and island-NOM together do-PNE place
'the place where sun, moon, and island exist together'
b. mak-kena ttonun phihal swuissta
block-or or avoid can
'(You) can block or avoid it.'

In terms of the patterns of coordination marking, natural languages employ four main types of coordination constructions from asyndeton (with no marking in each conjunct) to omnisyndeton (with one marking for each conjunct) (cf. [1]):

(3) a. Asyndeton: A B C
b. Monosyndeton: A B conj C
c. Polysyndeton: A conj B conj C
d. Omnisyndeton: A conj B conj C conj

Our corpus search reveals that Korean displays all these types in spoken and written texts. We inspected the Sejong Treebank Corpus to check the possible patterns of Korean coordination. The corpus consists of 378,689 words (33,953 sentences). We identified total 6,345 instances of nominal coordination within which we identified all these four types. In particular, the following present the 5,378 instances of top 8 frequent patterns with maximum three conjunts we found in the corpus.[3]

(4)

Patterns	Frequency	Patterns	Frequency
A(-)and B (mono)	3,201	A B(-)and, C (mono)	167
A(-)or B (mono)	860	A(-)and B(-)and C (poly)	70
A, B (asyndeton)	508	A-and B, C (mono)	27
A, B, C (asyndeton)	534	A-and B-and (omni)	11

As shown here, the language uses monosyndeton strategies most often. The corpus also reveals more asyndeton instances than polysyndeton or omnisyndeton.

There has been much debate regarding the syntactic structures of coordination. Among the central questions are whether it allows *n*-ary structures; and

[3] The coordinators with a hyphen are the morphological ones whereas those with no hyphen are the lexical ones.

which of the conjuncts serves as the head of the coordination phrase (cf. [2], [1]). Engineering considerations in our project have indicated that Korean requires both binary and ternary structures (cf. [2]). The descriptive facts also indicate that the final conjunct functions at least as the syntactic head of the coordination phrase. This paper provides an account of how these two basic assumptions, together with appropriate constructional constraints, can bring us an efficient and robust grammar for parsing the intriguing syntactic as well as semantic aspects of Korean coordination.

2 Implementing an Analysis

Needless to say, theoretical and engineering considerations lead us to prefer fewer rules in dealing with all these different types. Empirical data and our implementation results indicate that the most economic way of implementing the analysis in a typed feature structure grammar is to introduce the notion of constructional constraints within a multiple inheritance type hierarchy system.

2.1 Lexical Information

In monosyndeton strategies, as noted, the language can use either morphological marking or a lexical coordinator:

(5) a. A-and/or B salam-kwa/-ina cimsung ('human and/or animal')
    b. A and/or B yokmang kuliko/ttonun pwulan ('desire and/or anxiety')

The attachment of a morphological marker like *-kwa* or *-ina* onto a nominal differentiates it from a canonical nominal and introduces the head feature COORD. The need to treat this as a head feature comes from complex examples in which the marking information needs to pass up to the mother NP:

(6) [[$_{NP}$[nelp-un cip-kwa] [$_{NP}$[alumtaw-un cengwon-ul]] calanghayssta
    wide-PNE house-and pretty-PNE garden-ACC boasted
    'It boasted a wide house and beautiful garden.'

The lexicon thus adds the head feature COORD to a nominal or verbal expression when it hosts a morphological coordination marker:

(7) a. $\begin{bmatrix} \textit{nominal-conj} \\ \left\langle \text{`khempwute-wa'} \right\rangle \quad \text{`computer-and'} \\ \text{SYN} \mid \text{HEAD} \begin{bmatrix} \text{POS } \textit{noun} \\ \text{COORD } \textit{and} \end{bmatrix} \end{bmatrix}$ b. $\begin{bmatrix} \textit{verbal-conj} \\ \left\langle \text{mwulli-kena} \right\rangle \quad \text{`bite-or'} \\ \text{SYN} \begin{bmatrix} \text{HEAD} \begin{bmatrix} \text{POS } \textit{verb} \\ \text{COORD } \textit{or} \end{bmatrix} \end{bmatrix} \end{bmatrix}$

The lexical coordinators are no different. Just like the morphological markers, our grammar takes these words to provide the COORD value, as exemplified in (8):

(8)

a. $\begin{bmatrix} \textit{conj-w} \\ \text{ORTH} \left\langle \text{kuliko} \right\rangle \text{ `and'} \\ \text{SYN} \begin{bmatrix} \text{HEAD} \begin{bmatrix} \text{POS } \textit{conj} \\ \text{COORD } \textit{and} \end{bmatrix} \end{bmatrix} \end{bmatrix}$ b. $\begin{bmatrix} \textit{conj-w} \\ \text{ORTH} \left\langle \text{ttonun} \right\rangle \text{ `or'} \\ \text{SYN} \begin{bmatrix} \text{HEAD} \begin{bmatrix} \text{POS } \textit{conj} \\ \text{COORD } \textit{or} \end{bmatrix} \end{bmatrix} \end{bmatrix}$

2.2 Syntactic Aspects

Different from other languages, Korean coordination appears to assign the syntactic headedness to the last conjunct. For example, the (nominative) CASE or HON value of a nominal coordination and the MOOD value of verbal coordination are projected from the final conjunct.

(9) a. [[haksayng-kwa] [sensayng-nim-i]] o-si-ess-ta
student-and teacher-HON-NOM come-HON-PST-DECL
'Students and teachers came.'
b. [[namca-nun o-ass-ko] [yeca-un ttena-ss-ta]]
men-TOP come-PST-and women leave-PST-DECL
'Men came, and women left.'

However, the coordinated phrases need to be like categories. In particular, the conjuncts need to have the same POS (part of speech) and VAL (valence) values:

(10) a. * $_{NP}$[haksayng-kwa] $_{AdvP}$[ppalli] o-ass-ta
student-and fast come-PST-DECL
b. *[$_{S/NP}$[haksayng-un __ ilk-ess-ko] $_{S}$[sensayng-nim-un
student-TOP read-PST-and teacher-HON-HON
hayngpokha-n] chayk]
happy book
'*the book that students read and teachers were happy'

As shown in (10a), we cannot coordinate an NP with an AdvP. And as shown in (10b), an S with a gap cannot be coordinated with a fully saturated S since they have different VAL values.[4]

Our grammar contributes the following general constraints to the coordination construction defined as *coord-ph*, in terms of a grammar rule:

(11) Coordination Rule:

$$\text{XP}\left[\textit{coord-ph}\right] \rightarrow \text{XP}\begin{bmatrix} \text{POS } \boxed{4} \\ \text{VAL } \boxed{5} \end{bmatrix}, \left(\left[\text{POS } \textit{conj}\right]\right), \textbf{(H)}\text{XP}\begin{bmatrix} \text{COORD } \textit{none} \\ \text{POS } \boxed{4} \\ \text{VAL } \boxed{5} \end{bmatrix}$$

The rule in (11), which all instances of coordination need to observe, basically says that two identical XPs can be conjoined when they share POS and VAL values, while the last conjunct serves as the syntactic head. The first conjunct

[4] Valence values here include subject, complements, and slashed elements.

has no constraint on the value of COORD[5], yet the last conjunct bears the head feature [COORD *none*] value. This will block a coordination-marked phrase from appearing in a final conjunct.[6]

Depending on the appearance of the second conjunction word, the phrase will be realized either as a binary structure *bin-coord-ph* or as a ternary structure *tern-coord-ph*. When the middle element (lexical coordinator) of the phrase is absent, we license a *bin-coord-ph* with patterns like (12). Meanwhile, when the conjunction word occurs, we will have a *tern-coord-ph* with patterns like (13):

(12) a. A, B
  b. A-and B
  c. A-or B

(13) a. A and/or B
  b. A-and and B
  c. A-or or B

When *bin-coord-ph* and *tern-coord-ph* are combined, we will have various patterns of coordination, some of which are as follows:

(14) a. A, [B and C]
  b. A, [B-and and C]
  c. [A-and [B and C]]
  d. A, [B, C]
  e. [A-and [B-and and C]]
  f. [A-and B] and [C-and D]

Notice that the language also uses omnisyndeton strategies in which all conjuncts are marked with a coordination marker. Omnisyndeton is possible only with the morphological coordinators *-hako* and *-(i)lang*:

(15) a. kongchayk-hako/ilang yenphil-hako/ilang ciwukay-hako/ilang sassta.
  notebook-and pencil-and eraser-and bought
  '(I) bought notebooks, pencils, and erasers.'
  b.*kongchayk-kwa yenphil-kwa ciwukay-wa sassta.
  notebook-and pencil-and eraser-and bought

The final conjunct with marking *hako* or *ilang* thus functions just like a canonical NP with no coordination marking. To deal with this, we assume that the nominals with such a marking have an underspecified COORD value:

(16) $\begin{bmatrix} \textit{nominal-ilang-hako} \\ \text{SYN} \mid \text{HEAD} \begin{bmatrix} \text{POS } \textit{noun} \\ \text{COORD } \textit{and-none} \end{bmatrix} \end{bmatrix}$

This lexical information means that words like *ciwukay-hako* 'eraser-and' or *ciwukay-lang* can be either [COORD *none*] or [COORD *and*].

[5] The subtypes of *coord-ph* can place constraints on the COORD value.
[6] The value of [COORD *coord*] is defined as follows:

(i) a. *coord: and-none, or-none*
  b. *and-none: and, none*
  c. *or-none: or, none*

2.3 Semantic Aspects and Constructional Constraints

In deep-processing the coordination structures, complications arise in how to get the appropriate semantics ([3]). We can simply assume that the morphological or lexical coordinator (marked with COORD feature) determines the conjunctive or disjunctive meaning of a coordination phrase. One issue arises from doubly-marked phrases. As noted before, in coordinating two NPs, we can have both the morphological marking -*wa* as well as the lexical conjunction word *kuliko*:

(17) hyencay-(wa) kuliko/ttonun milay-lul saynkakhay poca.
present-and and future-ACC think let
'Let's think about the present and future!'

If each of these morphological and lexical markers induce its own independent semantic relation, we would have too many coordination relations: one at least is redundant. Another issue lies in asyndeton strategies in which no marking appears:

(18) haksayng, hakpwumo, kyosa-tul-i chamsekhayessta
student parent teacher-PL-NOM attended
'Students, parents, and teachers attended.'

In such an example, even though we have only a conjunctive reading, the question arises as to what triggers this meaning.

These observations, together with our trial and error progress from implementations, led us to make the supposition that the coordination relation is invoked as a constructional meaning, represented in (19):

(19)

$$\text{XP}\begin{bmatrix} \textit{coord-ph} \\ \text{SEM}\,|\,\text{HOOK}\,|\,\text{INDEX } \boxed{3} \\ \text{C-CONT}\,|\,\text{RELS}\left\langle \begin{bmatrix} \textit{coord-rel} \\ \text{C-ARG } \boxed{3} \\ \text{L-IND } \boxed{1} \\ \text{R-IND } \boxed{2} \end{bmatrix} \right\rangle \end{bmatrix} \rightarrow \text{XP}\begin{bmatrix}\text{INDEX } \boxed{1}\end{bmatrix},\ (\begin{bmatrix}\text{POS } \textit{conj}\end{bmatrix}),\ \textbf{(H)}\text{XP}\begin{bmatrix}\text{INDEX } \boxed{2}\end{bmatrix}$$

The semantic (SEM) information of the phrase, represented in the format of MRS (Minimal Recursion Semantics), includes an INDEX value. In addition, we can see here that the *coord-ph* introduces a constructional relation *coord-rel* in the C-CONT (constructional content). This relation has three arguments: C-ARG (conjunct argument), L-INDEX (left conjunct's index) and R-INDEX (right conjunct's index value). The value of C-ARG is the conjoined index *conj-index* which serves as a pointer to the separate conjoined entity and thus is identified with the INDEX value of the whole phrase.[7]

The question that follows is then how we can distinguish conjunctive from disjunctive coordination. In answering this, the grammar classifies *coord-ph* into two dimensions as represented in the following multiple inheritance hierarchy:

(20)

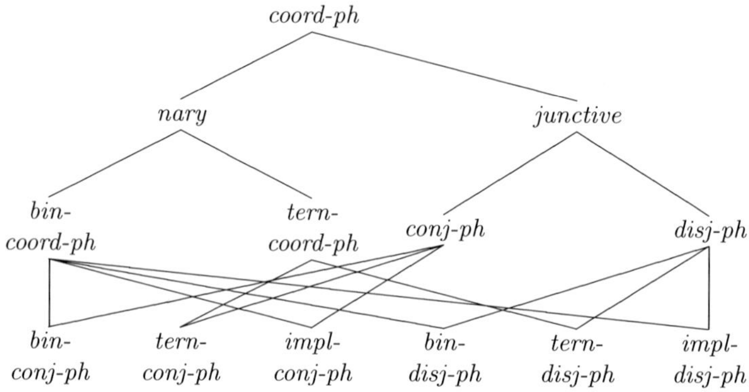

Each type has its own syntactic as well as semantic constraints, capturing the generalizations among types. Any constraints on a supertype will be inherited to its subtypes. The types *bin-coord-ph* and *tern-coord-ph* will determine the syntactic structure of the conjunct daughters as we have seen before. Meanwhile, the phrases *conj-ph* and *disj-ph* introduce a conjunctive or disjunctive relation in the C-CONT:

(21) a. $XP\begin{bmatrix} \textit{conj-ph} \\ \text{C-CONT} \mid \text{RELS}\langle[\textit{and\_coord\_rel}]\rangle \end{bmatrix} \rightarrow XP,...$

b. $XP\begin{bmatrix} \textit{disj-ph} \\ \text{C-CONT} \mid \text{RELS}\langle[\textit{or\_coord\_rel}]\rangle \end{bmatrix} \rightarrow XP,...$

Meanwhile, their subtypes specify which conjunct daughter contributes this coordination meaning together with the constraints on the COORD value:

(22) a. $XP\begin{bmatrix}\textit{bin-conj-ph}\end{bmatrix} \rightarrow XP\begin{bmatrix}\text{COORD } \textit{and-none}\end{bmatrix}, XP$

b. $XP\begin{bmatrix}\textit{tern-conj-ph}\end{bmatrix} \rightarrow XP\begin{bmatrix}\text{COORD } \textit{and-none}\end{bmatrix}, \begin{bmatrix}\text{COORD } \textit{and}\end{bmatrix}, XP$

c. $XP\begin{bmatrix}\textit{bin-disj-ph}\end{bmatrix} \rightarrow XP\begin{bmatrix}\text{COORD } \textit{or}\end{bmatrix}, XP$

d. $XP\begin{bmatrix}\textit{tern-disj-ph}\end{bmatrix} \rightarrow XP\begin{bmatrix}\text{COORD } \textit{or-none}\end{bmatrix}, \begin{bmatrix}\text{COORD } \textit{or}\end{bmatrix}, XP$

[7] Minimal Recursion Semantics, developed by [4], is a framework of computational semantics designed to enable semantic composition using only the unification of type feature structures. See [4] and [5] The value of the attribute SEM(ANTICS) in our system represents a simplified MRS.

In *bin-conj-ph* and *bin-disj-ph*, the first conjunct determines the coordination meaning whereas in *tern-conj-ph* and *tern-disj-ph*, the second element (conjunction word) regulates the meaning.

There are two additional things to be noted here. First, note that the value of COORD in the first conjunct of *tern-conj-ph* and *tern-disj-ph* is *and-none* and *or-none*, implying its value can be either *and/or* or *none*. This constraint on the COORD value allows the grammar to license the symmetric patterns in (23) but not the asymmetric patterns in (24), when we have both the morphological and lexical coordinators:[8]

(23) a. A-(and) and B
     b. A-(or) or B

(24) a.*A-(or) and B
     b.*A-(and) or B

Second, notice the COORD value of the first conjunct in *bin-conj-ph* and *bin-disj-ph*. It is *and-none* in the former whereas it is *or* in the latter. This ensures that the asyndeton strategies will induce only a conjunctive reading:

(25) [kunsim, kekceng-i] epsi cal cinaywassta
     concern anxiety without well spent
     '(I) have been well without worry and anxiety.'

In *bin-conj-ph*, the first conjunct's COORD value is *and-none*. When its value is *none*, the grammar can license examples like (25). Even though the first conjunct has no marking, the combination of *kunsim, kekceng* here will form a *bin-conj-ph* with a *and_coord_rel*. There is no rule that induces a disjunctive reading for such a case, as proved from the parsing results too. Our grammar is thus restrictive in the sense that when there is no coordination marking at all as in (25), we have a conjunctive reading only.

However, a complication arises here from examples in which the interpretation of the top coordination phrase with no coordinator depends on the type of the lower coordination phrase. Consider the following:

(26) a. [si, [kulim-(kwa) (kuliko) iyaki-ka]] iss-nun kos
        poem picture and story exist-PNE place
        'the place where poems, pictures, and stories exist.'
     b. [si, [kulim-(ina) (ttonun) iyaki-ka]] iss-nun kos
        poem picture or story exist-PNE place
        'the place where poems, pictures, or stories exist.'

The example (26a) induces only a conjunctive reading, whereas (26b) only a disjunctive reading.[9] In order to capture these constraints, we have two additional types of coordination as the subtypes as noted in the hierarchy (20):

[8] Our Google web search reveals less than 100 instances of such asymmetric coordination patterns. If such examples are really acceptable, we simply need to remove the constraints on the value of the attribute COORD in the first conjunct.

[9] A flat structure analysis may solve such an issue, but as noted by [1], it will require a great deal of grammar rules in the implementation.

(27) a. $$\text{XP}\begin{bmatrix} \textit{imp-conj-ph} \\ \text{C-CONT} \mid \text{RELS}\langle[\textit{and\_coord\_rel}]\rangle \end{bmatrix} \rightarrow \text{XP}\big[\text{COORD } \textit{none}\big], \text{XP}\big[\text{C-CONT} \mid \text{RELS}\langle[\textit{and\_coord\_rel}]\rangle\big]$$

b. $$\text{XP}\begin{bmatrix} \textit{imp-disj-ph} \\ \text{C-CONT} \mid \text{RELS}\langle[\textit{or\_coord\_rel}]\rangle \end{bmatrix} \rightarrow \text{XP}\big[\text{COORD } \textit{none}\big], \text{XP}\big[\text{C-CONT} \mid \text{RELS}\langle[\textit{or\_coord\_rel}]\rangle\big]$$

These rules will allow us to induce appropriate semantics for the different asyndenton strategies such as "A, [B and C]" (only conjunctive reading) and "A, [B or C]" (only disjunctive reading).

3 Results of the Implementation

The analysis we have presented so far has been incorporated in the typed-feature structure grammar HPSG for Korean (Korean Resource Grammar) aiming at working with real-world data (cf. [6] and [7]). To test its performance and feasibility, it has been implemented into the LKB (Linguistic Knowledge Building).[10] The test results give the proper syntactic as well as semantic structures for all the coordination patterns from simple binary or ternary to complex patterns we find in the language.

For example, (28) is the syntactic and MRS structure for the example *si-wa kulim-kwa kuliko iyaki* 'poem-and, picture-and and story' where the morphological marker -*wa* and the lexical coordinator *kuliko* occur together. In terms of the syntactic structures, the grammar generates only one structure for the NP as given in the output here: *kulim-kwa kuliko iyaki* forms a *tern-conj-ph* and then this resulting phrase will form a *bin-conj-ph* with *si-wa*.[11] We can notice here that the MRS the grammar generates provides enriched information of the phrase. The value of LTOP is the local top handle, the handle of the relation with the widest scope within the constituent. The attribute RELS is basically a bag of elementary predications (EP) each of whose value is a *relation*.[12] Each of the types *relation* has at least three features LBL, PRED (represented here as a type), and ARG0. The INDEX value here is identified with the ARG0 (C-ARG) value of the first *and_rel* within the RELS list here. The L-INDEX value of this relation is identified with the *udef_q_rel* for the noun *poem* that serves as the first conjunct.[13] The R-INDEX value is iden-

[10] The current Korean Resource Grammar has 394 type definitions, 36 grammar rules, 77 inflectional rules, 1100 lexical entries, and 2100 test-suite sentences, and aims to expand its coverage on real-life data.

[11] The system does not combine *si-wa* with *kulim-kwa* first since the latter is marked with [COORD *and*], which would violate the constraint on *coord-ph*.

[12] The attribute HCONS is to represent quantificational information. See [5].

[13] Korean common nouns do not require a determiner to project an NP. Even though a determiner is not available, we need to express an underspecified quantification on the noun in order to make the semantics compatible with the semantic output of other languages, and to make scope restrictions work. Such a move is essential in deep processing aimed at multilingual applications.

tified not with any conjunct but with the ARG0 of the other *and_rel* representing the semantics of *kulim-kwa kuliko iyaki* 'picture and story'.

(28)
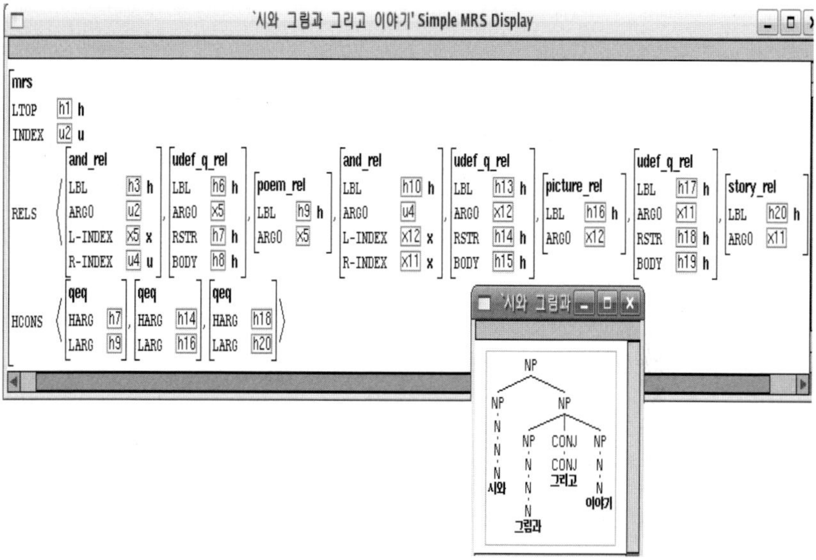

Now let's look at a combination of asyndeton and monosyndeton, *si, kulim kuliko iyaki* 'poem, picture and story':

(29)
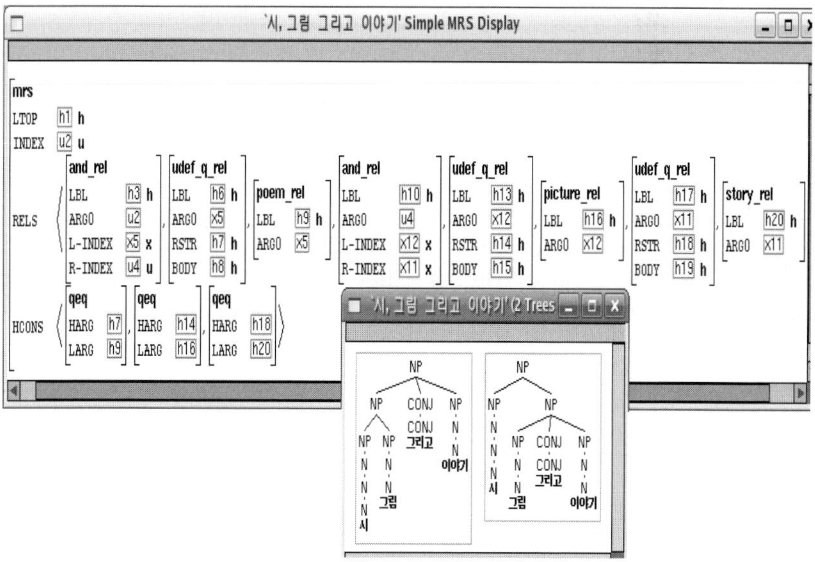

As noted in the parse trees, we have two syntactic structures. In the first tree *si* 'poem' combines with *kulim* 'picture' as an *impl-conj-ph* and the result forms a *tern-conj-ph* together with the conjunction word *kuliko* and *iyaki* 'story'. In the second tree *kulim*, *kuliko* and *iyagi* forms a *tern-conj-ph* first and then forms an *impl-conj-ph* with *si*. The MRS here represents the meaning of the second tree. One thing to note here is that even though there is neither morphological marking nor lexical marking, the constraint on *impl-conj-ph* induces only a conjunctive reading (adding a *and_rel*).

Our system also allows the appropriate syntactic as well as semantic representations for the omnisyndeton coordination. Consider the parsing results of the example *kongchayk-ilang, yenphil-ilang, ciwukay-lang* 'notebook-and, pencil-and, eraser-and':

(30)

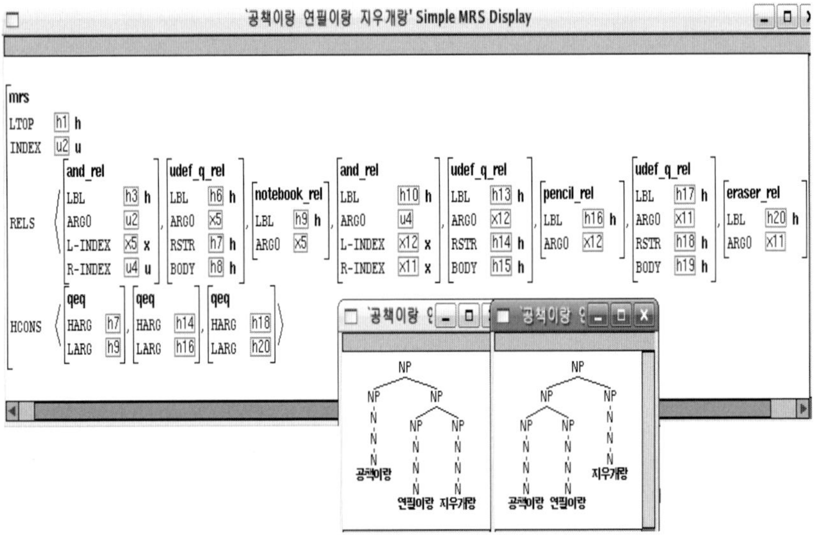

Once again, we have two possible structures depending on the order of combining the conjuncts (each combination forms a *bin-conj-ph* here). Even though the final conjunct is marked with *-ilang*, our lexical specification in (16) allows it to have [COORD *none*]. Also note that our constructional approach invokes no redundant *coord_rel*, proving the efficiency of the grammar.

4 Conclusion

As noted earlier, coordination phrases have a high frequency in real-life texts. In the present analysis, the grammatical constraints are encoded in the multiple inheritance hierarchy where the subtypes of coordination phrases are arranged. This allows us to capture both syntactic and semantic generalizations across all of the different coordination constructions in a systematic way.

Any grammar, aiming for real-world applications, needs to provide a correct syntax from which we can build semantic representations in compositional ways. In addition, these semantic representations must be rich enough to capture compositional as well as constructional meanings. In this respect, the analysis we have sketched here seems to be promising as it provides enriched semantic representations for various types of coordination that should be suitable for applications requiring deep natural language processing.

References

1. Drellishak, S., Bender, E.M.: A coordination module for a crosslinguistic grammar resource. In Müller, S., ed.: The Proceedings of the 12th International Conference on Head-Driven Phrase Structure Grammar, Department of Informatics, University of Lisbon, Stanford, CSLI Publications (2005) 108–128
2. Abeillé, A.: A lexicon- and construction-based approach to coordinations. In Müller, S., ed.: Proceedings of the HPSG-2003 Conference, Michigan State University, East Lansing, Stanford, CSLI Publications (2003) 5–25
3. Bender, E.M., Siegel, M.: Implementing the syntax of Japanese numeral classifiers. In: Proceedings of IJCNLP-04. (2004)
4. Copestake, A., Flickenger, D., Sag, I., Pollard, C.: Minimal recursion semantics: An introduction. Manuscript (2003)
5. Bender, E.M., Flickinger, D.P., Oepen, S.: The grammar matrix: An open-source starter-kit for the rapid development of cross-linguistically consistent broad-coverage precision grammars. In Carroll, J., Oostdijk, N., Sutcliffe, R., eds.: Proceedings of the Workshop on Grammar Engineering and Evaluation at the 19th International Conference on Computational Linguistics, Taipei, Taiwan (2002) 8–14
6. Kim, J.B., Yang, J.: Projections from morphology to syntax in the korean resource grammar: implementing typed feature structures. In: Lecture Notes in Computer Science. Volume 2945. Springer-Verlag (2004) 13–24
7. Kim, J.B.: Korean Phrase Structure Grammar. Hankwuk Publishing, Seoul (2004) In Korean.

Cue-Based Interpretation of Customer's Requests: Analysis of Estonian Dialogue Corpus

Tiit Hennoste[1,2], Olga Gerassimenko[2], Riina Kasterpalu[2], Mare Koit[2], Andriela Rääbis[2], Krista Strandson[2], and Maret Valdisoo[2]

[1] University of Helsinki, P.O. Box 9,
00014 Helsinki, Finland
tiit.hennoste@helsinki.fi
http://www.helsinki.fi/university/
[2] University of Tartu, J. Liivi 2,
50409 Tartu, Estonia
{tiit.hennoste, olga.gerassimenko, riina.kasterpalu, mare.koit, andriela.raabis, krista.strandson, maret}@ut.ee
http://www.cl.ut.ee

Abstract. Estonian spoken human-human information dialogues (calls) have been analyzed with the aim of finding lexical and syntactic cues which can be used for automatic recognition of dialogue acts. We considered a customer's requests where the goal of the speaker is to get some information or trigger an action by the hearer who is an official person. The corpus analysis demonstrates that a limited number of verbs in a limited number of forms are used to form requests, and there is a difference between general requests which only introduce a topic and exact requests where the speaker has to get certain information or trigger an action by the hearer.

1 Introduction

The main problem in case of a dialogue act interpretation is to determine when given an utterance, which dialogue act it realizes. In some cases, it is possible to determine the act by using its lexical or syntactic form, e.g. some questions in English begin with *wh*-words, commands have imperative syntax, etc. There are two main classes of computational models of the interpretation of dialogue acts [6]. The first class is called cue-based or probabilistic. The idea is that the listener uses different cues (lexical, collocational, syntactic, prosodic, or conversational-structure cues) of the utterance to help decide how to build an interpretation. It is motivated by intuitions of a micro grammar [5]. The cue-based models consider interpretation as a classification task, and solve it by training statistical classifiers on labelled examples of dialogue acts. The second class of models implements the inferential approach. A sentence like *Can you tell me the director's phone number?* has the literal meaning of a question: *Do you have the ability to tell me the director's phone number?* The request act *Tell me the director's phone number* is inferred by the hearer after processing the literal question. The

T. Salakoski et al. (Eds.): FinTAL 2006, LNAI 4139, pp. 206–213, 2006.

inferential models are based on belief logics and use logical inferences to reason about the speaker's intentions.

In this paper, we will concentrate on a cue-based model and more specifically, on lexical and syntactic cues. Our aim is to find out lexical and syntactic cues of requests in Estonian spoken dialogues (institutional calls). We limit us with customers' requests here having in mind a further goal to implement a dialogue system which plays the role of an information operator and will be able to recognize a customer's requests and grant them. Some of the lexical cues have been used in an automatic dialogue act classification system which implements artificial neural networks [2].

Our analysis is based on the Estonian Dialogue Corpus which includes more than 800 spoken human-human dialogues, among them 715 institutional calls (`http://www.cs.ut.ee/~koit/Dialoog/EDiC`). Dialogue acts are annotated in EDiC using a typology which departs from conversation analysis. This is a DAMSL-like dialogue act set with some differences [3]. There are about 120 dialogue acts in our typology.

A software tool is being worked out to simplify the corpus analysis [8]. One can choose a sub-corpus and search it for specific words or dialogue acts, according to any combination of constraints from both the transcribed dialogue text and dialogue acts' annotations. Statistical reports can be generated for an entire dialogue corpus or any subset. EDiC is accessible in Internet using the workbench but password-protected (`http://math.ut.ee/~treumuth/`). For this paper, 144 calls (almost 20,000 tokens) were selected from EDiC.

Four situational groups are represented in the dialogues:

- directory inquiries (phone numbers, addresses, etc.)
- calls to travel agencies
- calls to outpatients' offices
- ordering a taxi.

There are 129 customer's requests in our analysed sub-corpus (Table 1).

Our aim is to find lexical and syntactic cues in Estonian dialogues that can be used by the computer in order to recognize a customer's requests. The cues found in other languages can not be transferred in a direct way.

2 What Is a Request?

We make a difference between directives and questions in our typology of dialogue acts [4]. The main difference is formal. Questions have special explicit formal features in Estonian (interrogatives, intonation, specific word order, etc.).

Other information-requests (and directive-actions in sense of DAMSL) are considered as directives in our typology. For example, *Can you give me X?* is an open yes/no question but *Give me X* is a directive (a request).

As mentioned above, there are linguistic features of questions in Estonian which can be used as cues for their automatic recognition. No such features exist for directives.

Table 1. Overview of the used corpus

Type of dialogue	Number of dialogues	tokens	customer's requests
Directory inquiries	60	4,384	55
Travel agency	36	12,104	33
Outpatients' office	26	2,422	22
Taxi	22	1,028	19
Total	144	19,938	129

There are three types of directives in our typology: request, offer and proposal. A request expresses the speaker's need or intent to get some information or trigger an action by the hearer. Requests can be divided into two groups on the basis of the expected reaction:

- a customer needs certain information, e.g. to get a phone number
- a customer expects an action by the operator, e.g to book a reception time with a doctor, to send a taxi.

At the same time, performing an action always is accompanied with giving information: the operator informs the caller if (s)he is able to perform the action, or has performed it [1] (*jaa, takso tuleb teile / yes, a taxi will come*).

In our corpus, a customer's requests are information requests in directory inquiries and calls to travel agencies (e.g *sooviks 'Norrasse sõita / I'd like to travel to Norway*).

The requests expect an action in case of calls to outpatients' offices or ordering a taxi (*hh sooviks 'lasteortopeedile aega 'kinni panna / I'd like to book a time with a children orthopaedist*). If a customer needs a piece of information then (s)he always forms a question, not a request (*kas teil üliõpilastele mingit 'hinnasoodustust ka on. / do you have any discounts for students?*).

3 Lexical and Syntactic Cues of Requests

Utterances that represent requests can be divided into two groups: with and without verbs. Table 2 summarises the results of our analysis.

3.1 Verb Forms Used in Requests

As we can see, a limited number of verbs occur in a customer's requests. The most frequent are *soovima 'to wish/'I'd like'* and *paluma 'to ask'* – 59 cases (46% of requests). In addition, *tahtma 'to want'* and *ütlema 'to tell'* are used in 23 cases (18%). These four verbs make up 64% of all occurrences. Four more verbs

[1] Transcription of conversation analysis is used in examples.

Table 2. Number of customer's requests with different verb forms and without verb

With verb	Mode			Total
	Indicative	Conditional	Imperative	
soovima 'to wish'	2	33		35
tahtma 'to want'	3	12		15
paluma 'to ask'	12	12		24
ütlema 'to tell'			8	8
võtma 'to take'		6		6
vaja olema 'to be needed'		5		5
huvitama 'to interest'	1	3		4
huvitatud olema 'to be interested'	2			2
panema 'to put (book)'	1	1	2	4
andma 'to give'			2	2
küsima 'to ask'	1	1		2
oskama 'to can'	2			2
saama 'to be able'	1			1
olema pakkuda 'to be offered'	1			1
vaatama 'to look'			1	1
vabandama 'to excuse'			1	1
Without verb				16
Total	26	73	14	
				129

are used 4–6 times (19 occurrences in total, or 15%). The remaining verbs are used 1–2 times.

Moreover, the verbs appear only in certain modes and persons. The verbs can be divided into two groups. In the first group, the imperative is used to express a request (*ütle 'tell', pane 'put', here: 'book', anna 'give', vaata 'look'*). 14 requests (11%) are formed by these verbs in the imperative. The same verbs can be used in the conditional in order to express a wish, an intention only in yes/no questions (*kas te (ei) vaataks/annaks/paneks/ütleks 'would you (not) look/give/put/tell'*). Still, questions are excluded from the current analysis.

In the second group of verbs, the first person conditional or indicative is used (*ma soovin/tahan/palun/võtan 'I wish/want/ask/take'*). 99 requests are formed this way. 75 requests from 99 (75%) include a verb in the conditional. The conditional has a certain morphological feature (-*ks*-) in Estonian which can be used as a cue for its automatic recognition [1] (*sooviks/tahaks/paluks/võtaks*). The remaining 22 requests contain a verb in the indicative.

The conditional in general is related to a request, adding politeness to it. Nevertheless, some requests include a verb in the indicative. A problem arises, when (under which conditions) a verb in the indicative can be used to form a request. The indicative is a universal form of declarative acts. In all the analysed cases, it is a (theoretically) parallel variant alongside the conditional, except in the case of the verb *huvitatud olema 'to be interested in'* (2 cases in our corpus; cf. [7]). The indicative is frequently used only in the case of the verb *paluma 'to ask, please'*. This word is used also as a polite formula in Estonian, therefore its meaning includes politeness and it functions as a mitigater of an utterance. Other usages of the indicative represent specific cases.

The verb semantics determines whether a verb can occur in a request. Formulas are used in certain situations:

- *palun/paluks 'I ask/would ask', öelge 'tell', sooviks 'I'd wish, I'd like to'* in directory inquiries
- *palun 'I ask', sooviks 'I'd wish, I'd like to'* ordering a taxi
- *sooviks 'I'd wish, I'd like to'* in calls to an outpatients' office.

Certain verb forms are used at the beginning of an utterance or after the pronoun *I*, in order to start a new theme.

When calling an outpatients' office or ordering a taxi, a customer wants to trigger an action of the operator. The most frequent verbs are *paluma 'to ask, here: please'* and *soovima 'to wish, I'd like to'* in such requests (27 cases out of 34, or 79%).

When calling a travel agency or asking a directory inquiry, customers use more different verbs. The most frequent is *soovima 'to wish'* (13 cases out of 29, or 45% in travel agency dialogues, and 9 cases out of 49, or 18% in directory inquiries). The central verbs are *paluma 'to ask'* (15 cases, or 31%) and *ütlema 'to tell'* (8 cases, or 16%) in directory inquiries.

3.2 Requests Without Verb

Sixteen requests are formed as phrases without a verb. These requests can be divided into three groups. The first group (8 requests) is formed by nominal phrases (*'teisipäeva 'pärastlõuna pärast 'kolme / Tuesday afternoon after 3 o'clock*). The second group (6) contains dialogue particles *jah/jaa/mhmh 'yes, hem'*, and the third group (2) – phrases *see oleks hea / it would be good, no nii, nii /well, so.*

The same phrases can be divided into two groups on the basis of their role in conversation. The first group is formed by 13 requests which are reactions to the operator's previous turn – the operator has offered something, and a customer's agreement is a request at the same time (C – customer, O – operator):

```
O:  .h aga: aga ma saan teile anda ‘Hermann reiside
telefoninumbri.=     OFFER
    but I can give you the phone number of Hermann Travel
C: =jaa?    AGREEMENT + REQUEST
    yes
```

Three requests with a nominal phrase are formulated as exact requests in directory inquiries and ordering a taxi:

```
O: ‘Maria=Takso tere. / Maria taxi, good morning
C:  ‘Lossi: ‘kolmteist. / Lossi thirteen     REQUEST
```

3.3 Features of a Typical Request

A typical customer's request has the following features

- the communication takes place between strangers
- a request is presented by a customer at the beginning of the conversation
- the customer has made up the request before calling therefore the request is the actual reason of the call.

These requests can be divided into two groups:

(1) exact requests where the speaker has to get some concrete information or trigger an action (phone number, taxi, etc.)

(2) general requests which only introduce a topic (e.g. *sooviks 'Norrasse sõita / I'd like to travel to Norway*). An information-sharing sub-dialogue follows, and the exact request will be formulated later.

The requests of the type (1) are used in directory inquiries, calls to outpatients' offices and in ordering a taxi. Travel dialogues, on the other hand, often begin with a general request of the type (2) after which an information-sharing sub-dialogue starts where participants ask and answer questions.

Our study has shown that exact requests are expressed by using verb forms *sooviks 'I'd like to', paluks 'I'd like to ask', palun 'please', öelge 'tell'* in the second person imperative plural. General requests are expressed using the forms *sooviks teada 'I'd like to know'; sooviks küsida 'I'd like to ask'; mind huvitab 'it interests me'/huvitaks 'it would interest me'/ma olen huvitatud 'I'm interested in'.*

Typical requests are formed by using almost exclusively the conditional or imperative. Single usages of the indicative can be found: *palun 'please'* which meaning includes politeness, and *mind huvitab 'it interests me'/ma olen huvitatud 'I'm interested in'* which emphasizes the speaker's interest.

3.4 Experiment

An experiment was carried out to verify the following hypothesis: if the computer finds the verb forms *sooviksin, sooviks '[I]'d wish, I'd like to', tahaksin, tahaks '[I]'d want, I'd like to', paluksin, paluks '[I]'d ask, I'd like to', võtaks '[I]'d take', oleks vaja 'it would be needed', huvitaks '[I]'d be interested in', paneks '[I]'d book', küsiks(in) '[I]'d like to ask'* (in the conditional) in an utterance then this utterance is probably a request. It can be mentioned that 81% of requests in our analysed corpus include these verbs in the conditional.

For the experiment, a test corpus was built (total number of dialogues is 505, total number of tokens – 57,585). The corpus workbench [8] was used to analyse the test corpus. The results are promising – 78% of utterances that include a verb of our list in the conditional (140) are a customer's requests (Table 3). As the total number of a customer's requests is 466 in the test corpus, additional cues should be implemented to recognize them.

Table 3. Test with verbs in the conditional

Verb form	Number of occurrences			
	Initial corpus	In requests	Test corpus	In requests
sooviksin 'I'd like to'	11	7	27	25
sooviks 'I'd like to'	18	17	29	27
tahaks 'I'd want'	11	7	6	2
paluksin 'I'd ask'	2	2	18	8
paluks 'I'd ask'	11	11	31	29
võtaks 'I'd take'	9	6	24	24
oleks vaja 'it would be needed'	5	5	8	2
(h)uvitaks 'I'd be interested in'	6	3	13	7
paneks 'I'd book'	1	1	9	7
küsiksin 'I'd like to ask'	1	1	1	0
tahaks teada 'I'd like to know'	5	4	2	1
tahaks küsida 'I'd like to ask'	1	1	2	1
sooviks teada 'I'd like to know'	1	1	3	0
sooviksin teada 'I'd like to know'	8	7	1	1
sooviksin küsida 'I'd like to ask'	1	1	6	6
Total	91	74 81%	180	140 78%

4 Discussion and Conclusion

As the above analysis demonstrates, only certain modes and persons of certain verbs can be used to form requests. The verb forms used in a customer's requests can be divided into two groups. In the first group, the imperative is used to form a request (*ütle 'tell', pane 'put', anna 'give', vaata 'look'*).

In the second group, the first person of the conditional or indicative is used (*ma soovin/tahan/palun/võtan/küsin 'I wish/want/ask/take/ask'*). The conditional generally is related to a request, inserting additional politeness. The conditional has an explicit morphological feature *-ks-* in Estonian which can be used as a cue for its automatic recognition [1].

Some indicative forms can be used in requests but not in institutional dialogues because they express a strong and impolite command (*sa ütled 'you must say'*).

A typical request has the following features: the communication takes place between strangers, a request is represented by a customer at the beginning of the conversation, the customer has made up the request before calling therefore the request is the actual reason of the call.

Typical requests can be divided into two groups: 1) exact requests for information or an action, 2) general requests used for introducing a topic.

Typical exact requests are expressed with the verb forms *sooviks 'I'd like to wish', paluks 'I'd like to ask', palun 'please', öelge 'tell' in the second person imperative plural.*

Typical general requests are expressed by using the forms *sooviks teada 'I'd like to know', sooviks küsida 'I'd like to ask', mind huvitab 'it interests me'/huvitaks 'it would interest me'/ma olen huvitatud 'I am interested in'.*

Exact requests that arise during a dialogue can be represented by using the forms *võtaks 'I'd take', paneks 'I'd book'/pane 'book' in the imperative /paneme 'we book', andke 'give' in the imperative, vaadake 'look' in the imperative.*

As we have seen, typical requests are formed by using almost always the conditional or imperative. Rare examples of the indicative are represented with the verb forms *palun 'here: please'* which meaning includes politeness, and *mind huvitab 'it interest me'/ma olen huvitatud 'I'm interested in'* which emphasizes the speaker's interest.

Our next goal is to test these cues using decision trees, and to find out more cues for interpreting the a customer's requests.

Acknowledgement

This work is supported by Estonian Science Foundation (grant No 5685).

References

1. Erelt, M. (ed.): Estonian Language. Linguistica Uralica Supplementary Series vol 1. Estonian Academy Publishers, Tallinn (2003)
2. Fishel, M.: Dialogue act recognition in Estonian using artificial neural networks. Proc. of the 2nd Baltic Conference on Human Language Technologies, Tallinn (2005) 231–236.
3. Hennoste, T., Koit, M., Rääbis, A., Valdisoo, M.: Developing a Dialogue Act Coding Scheme: An Experience of Annotating the Estonian Dialogue Corpus. LREC 2004 Satellite Workshop Compiling and Processing Spoken Language Corpora. Ed. Nelleke Oostdijk, Gjert Kristoffersen, Geoffrey Sampson. Lisboa, Portugal (2004) 40–47.
4. Hennoste, T., Koit, M., Rääbis, A., Strandson, K., Valdisoo, M., Vutt, E.: Developing a Typology of Dialogue Acts: Some Boundary Problems. Proceedings of the 4th SIGdial Workshop on Discourse and Dialogue. Sapporo July 5-6 (2003) 226–235
5. Goodwin C.: Transparent vision. Interaction and grammar, ed. by Elinor Ochs, Emanuel A. Schegloff, and Sandra A. Thompson. Cambridge: Cambridge University Press (1996)
6. Jurafsky, D. and Martin, J.H.: An introduction to natural language processing, computational linguistics, and speech recognition. Prentice Hall (2000)
7. Quirk, R., Greenbaum, S., Leech, G., and Svartvik, J.: A Grammar of Contemporary English. Longman (1972)
8. Treumuth, M.: A software tool for the Estonian Dialogue Corpus. Proc. of the Second Baltic Conference on Human Language Technologies. Tallinn (2005) 341–346.

Czech-English Phrase-Based Machine Translation

Ondřej Bojar[1], Evgeny Matusov[2], and Hermann Ney[2]

[1] Institute of Formal and Applied Linguistics*
ÚFAL MFF UK, Malostranské náměstí 25, CZ-11800 Praha, Czech Republic
bojar@ufal.mff.cuni.cz
[2] Lehrstuhl für Informatik 6, Computer Science Department
RWTH Aachen University, D-52056 Aachen, Germany
{matusov, ney}@cs.rwth-aachen.de

Abstract. We describe experiments with Czech-to-English phrase-based machine translation. Several techniques for improving translation quality (in terms of well-established measure BLEU) are evaluated. In total, we are able to achieve BLEU of 0.36 to 0.41 on the examined corpus of Wall Street Journal texts, outperforming all other systems evaluated on this language pair.

1 Introduction

We aim at Czech-to-English machine translation (MT). For the time being, top performing systems of machine translation are statistical and phrase-based.[1]

Czech is a thoroughly studied Slavonic language with extensive language data resources available (most notably the Prague Dependency Treebank, PDT[2], [1]). Czech is an inflective language with rich morphology and relatively free word order allowing non-projective constructions. These properties usually cast some doubt on the applicability of "uninformed" statistical methods that do not attempt at analyzing sentence structure.

Traditionally, most of the research on Czech is performed within the framework of the Functional Generative Description (FGD, [2]), a dependency-based formalism defining the deep syntactic (syntactico-semantic) level of language description. Effort has been invested in the development of linguistically adequate annotated data (PDT and lexicons) and tools (taggers, parsers to surface and deep syntactic levels, see the PDT for references). MT is attempted at the deep syntactic level [3].

In this paper, we describe our experiments with a phrase-based statistical MT system (PBT) developed at RWTH Aachen University [4]. We observe that at least for our particular corpus, translation direction and metrics used, linguistically uninformed methods currently clearly outperform other approaches.

* The work was performed while the first author was a visiting scientist at RWTH Aachen University.

[1] http://www.nist.gov/speech/tests/summaries/2005/mt05.htm

[2] http://ufal.mff.cuni.cz/pdt2.0/

T. Salakoski et al. (Eds.): FinTAL 2006, LNAI 4139, pp. 214–224, 2006.

1.1 Statistical Phrase-Based Machine Translation (Summary)

In statistical MT, the goal is to translate a source (foreign) language sentence $f_1^J = f_1 \ldots f_j \ldots f_J$ into a target language (English) sentence $e_1^I = e_1 \ldots e_j \ldots e_I$. Among all possible target language sentences, we choose the sentence with the highest probability:

$$\hat{e}_1^{\hat{I}} = \underset{I, e_1^I}{\operatorname{argmax}} \{Pr(e_1^I | f_1^J)\} \tag{1}$$

In a log-linear model, the conditional probability of e_1^I being the translation of f_1^J is modelled as a combination of independent feature functions $h_1(\cdot,\cdot) \ldots h_M(\cdot,\cdot)$ describing the relation of the source and target sentences:

$$Pr(e_1^I | f_1^J) = \frac{\exp(\sum_{m=1}^M \lambda_m h_m(e_1^I, f_1^J))}{\sum_{e'^{I'}_1} \exp(\sum_{m=1}^M \lambda_m h_m(e'^{I'}_1, f_1^J))} \tag{2}$$

The model scaling factors λ_1^M are trained either to the maximum entropy principle or optimized with respect to the final translation quality measure.

Among feature functions used, the most important are the phrase-based translation model and the target language model. The phrase-based model captures the basic idea of phrase-based translation: to segment source sentence into phrases, then translate each phrase and finally compose the target sentence from phrase translations. Theoretically, the segmentation s_1^K of the source sentence into K phrases is introduced as a hidden variable to the overall model (thus making the feature functions dependent also on the segmentations, i.e. $h(f_1^J, e_1^I, s_1^K)$) and summing over all possible segmentations. In practice, a maximum approximation to this sum is used:

$$h_{\text{Phr}}(f_1^J, e_1^I) = \max_{s_1^K} \log \prod_{k=1}^{K} p(\tilde{f}_k | \tilde{e}_k) \tag{3}$$

The conditional probability of phrase $\tilde{f}_k$ given phrase $\tilde{e}_k$ is estimated from relative frequencies: $p(\tilde{f}_k|\tilde{e}_k) = N(\tilde{f},\tilde{e})/N(\tilde{e})$ where $N(\tilde{f},\tilde{e})$ denotes the number of co-occurrences of a phrase pair $(\tilde{f},\tilde{e})$ that are consistent with the word alignment. The marginal count $N(\tilde{e})$ is the number of occurrences of the target phrase $\tilde{e}$ in the training corpus.

The phrase-based model is included in the log-linear combination in source-to-target and target-to-source directions: $p(\tilde{f}|\tilde{e})$ and $p(\tilde{e}|\tilde{f})$. In addition, statistical single word based lexica are used in both directions. They are included to smooth the relative frequencies used as estimates of the phrase probabilities.

The target language model is typically the standard n-gram language model:

$$h_{\text{LM}}(f_1^J, e_1^I) = \log \prod_{i=1}^{I} p(e_i | e_{i-n+1}^{i-1}) \tag{4}$$

Finally, two length penalties (counting words and phrases, respectively) are included as additional features.

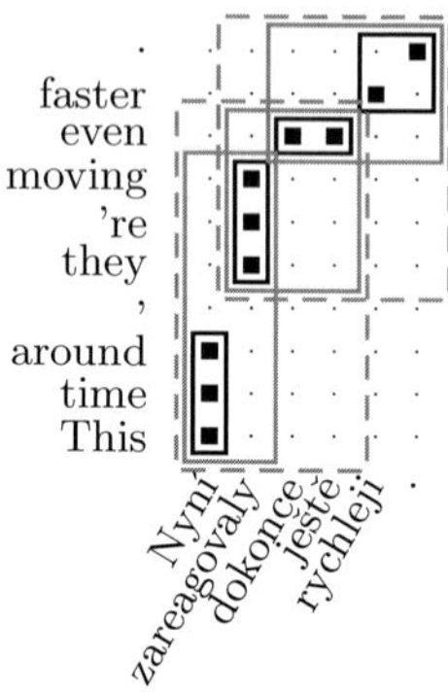

This	=	nyní
time	=	nyní
around	=	nyní
they	=	zareagovaly
...	=	...
This time around	=	Nyní
they 're moving	=	zareagovaly
even	=	dokonce ještě
...	=	...
This time around, they 're moving	=	Nyní zareagovaly
even faster	=	dokonce ještě rychleji
...	=	...

Fig. 1. Sample word alignment and sample phrases consistent with it (not all consistent phrases have been marked)

1.2 Data Description

The Prague Czech-English Dependency Corpus v. 1.0 (PCEDT [5]) consists of half of the Wall Street Journal part of Penn Treebank [6] translated sentence by sentence to Czech. Basic statistics about the training part of the PCEDT are given in Table 1. The PCEDT contains also separate development and evaluation parts (Devtest and Etest), each containing about 250 sentences with 4 independent re-translations back to English. Due to the original English source and nature of translation (sentence by sentence), the Czech sentences might be actually restricted in grammar and might not exhibit all complex word order phenomena as an independent Czech text would do. For a completely fair comparison, when the PCEDT is used to evaluate MT from English to Czech, we would need the reference translations for this direction, too.

Table 1 documents the morphological richness of Czech: the vocabulary size of Czech word forms is nearly twice as large as the vocabulary of English. If the text

Table 1. Characteristics of the Prague Czech-English Dependency Treebank 1.0

		Czech	English
	Sentences	21,141	
	Running Words	475,719	494,349
	Running Words without Punct.	404,523	439,304
Baseline (word forms)	Vocabulary	57,085	30,770
Produkce malých vozů se více než ztrojnásobila .	Singletons	31,458	14,637
Lemmas	Vocabulary	28,007	25,000
produkce malý vůz se hodně než-2 ztrojnásobit .	Singletons	13,009	11,873
Lemmas + Singletons backed off with POS	Vocabulary	15,041	13,150
produkce malý vůz se hodně než-2 UNK-verb .	Singletons	12	2
Stemming	Vocabulary	17,393	13,525
Prod malý vozů se více než ztro .	Singletons	6,347	4,846

is automatically lemmatized (this type of annotation is ready in the PCEDT), the disproportion almost disappears. In order to reduce the vocabulary size by another half, we replace all tokens appearing only once with their part of speech. A simple stemming technique (use first 4 characters of each word) gives us a the vocabulary size somewhere between lemmatization and lemmatization with singletons.

2 Techniques Improving Translation Quality

We evaluate the translation quality with the standard implementation of BLEU [7], as available for NIST evaluation[3] and with the default setting (4-grams, case insensitive). An independent implementation of the BLEU metric was used to estimate confidence intervals for all the scores. Statistically significant improvements over the respective baseline are marked with a star in all the following tables.

We use the designated development and evaluation sections of the PCEDT. Results on the development section are reported with the default weights for all model parameters, results on the test set are reported after some tuning of model parameters (optimization) using the development data.

2.1 Preprocessing Czech and Choosing Type of Word Alignment

We use the GIZA++ toolkit [8] to learn word alignments. The toolkit is capable of guessing 1-n alignments (many target words are assigned to one source word). Typically, it is used twice to obtain alignments in both directions and there are two common ways to join them to a symmetric alignment: either the two directions are combined using intersection or using union.[4] See Figure 1 for a sample union alignment.

Table 2. Translation quality and alignment error rate depending on alignment symmetrization and data preprocessing

	BLEU (ETest)		Alignment Error Rate	
	Intersection	Union	Intersection	Union
Baseline (word forms)	0.282	0.298	27.4	25.5
Stemming	-	0.306	-	-
Lemmas	0.298	**0.320***	15.0	17.2
Lemmas + singletons	0.308*	0.319*	**14.6**	17.4

In addition to the choice of a symmetrization method, we can also employ various techniques of preprocessing tokens in the training corpus. The basic options are illustrated in Table 1: either the tokens are kept as word forms, lemmatized or

[3] `http://www.nist.gov/speech/tests/mt/resources/scoring.htm`, we used the version 11b.

[4] For other symmetrization techniques see [9].

simply stemmed. It should be noted that the preprocessing is used for estimating word alignments only. Phrases consistent with the alignment are extracted using original word forms. The translation process thus remains unchanged, i.e. we translate from source word forms to target word forms directly, only the phrase table is estimated more reliably thanks to the better alignment.

Table 2 summarizes the improvements of translation quality depending on the type of symmetrization used (intersection or union) and on the preprocessing of parallel text for alignment. We report also the alignment error rates (AER) evaluated against manually annotated alignments. See [10] for more details on the AER measurements and manual annotation. The data are directly comparable because we share the set of sentences used for the evaluation.

Similarly to [10], we observe that the reduction of vocabulary size by lemmatization significantly improves not only AER but also translation quality. (Nearly the same level of BLEU is achieved using simple stemming.). The type of symmetrization on the other hand comes out differently: based on the AER, one would choose intersection, but it leads to significantly worse translation compared to the union.

2.2 Handling Numbers

Given the type of texts in the PCEDT (economical texts), special treatment of numbers seems to pay off, see Table 3. The baseline is to treat numbers as normal tokens. To reduce the data sparseness and allow the PBT to extract phrases that correctly reorder numbers and surrounding words (mostly the dollar sign, in our case), we replace all numbers with a special symbol _NUM. Surprisingly, this leads to a lower performance in terms of BLEU. The best behaviour is achieved by a post-processing step to correct the typographic convention about the decimal point. As displayed in Table 3, this correction brings us some improvement, most notable on the test set (2.7% relative).

Table 3. Example of special treatment of numbers and the improvement of BLEU

	Sample input	Input to PBT	Output
Baseline	na 57,375 dolarech	na 57,375 dolarech	at 57,375 $
Numbers	na 57,375 dolarech	na _NUM dolarech	at $ 57,375
Numbers + Correction	na 57,375 dolarech	na _NUM dolarech	**at $ 57.375**

	Devtest	Etest
Baseline	0.346	0.320
Numbers	0.341	0.309
Numbers + Correction	**0.347**	**0.329***

2.3 Dependency-Based Corpus Expansion

Dependency syntax analysis is closely related to the notion of "sentence reduction" [11]. In short, words corresponding to leaves in the dependency structure of the sentence can be (up to a few exceptions) removed without disrupting the grammatical correctness of the sentence. Phrase-based systems in general can learn phrase translation equivalents consisting of adjacent words only. There is a hope that a combination of these two approaches can improve translation quality, and indeed, some recent models are based on this assumption (see [12]).

We use the automatically generated dependency structure available for both Czech and English in the PCEDT to artificially expand the available training data by removing some words in the sentences. The training data for the PBT then consist of the original sentences plus a set of new sentences created by various reductions. Our method cannot be utilized off-line (before the source text to be translated is available) because there are too many possible reductions.

Given the source text, we collect all bigrams to be translated. We then scan the training data for *non-contiguous* occurrences of these bigrams (contiguous occurrences are already covered by the plain phrase extraction algorithm). For each non-contiguous occurrence we mark the two source words and then recursively add all translation equivalents (linked via word alignment) and all neighbours in both the source and the target dependency structures to satisfy some core grammatical requirements. This mainly means that at least the dependency path between all the words has to be added and some words (such as prepositions) require to add their daughters. All marked words are then printed out as a new pair of training sentences, provided that the two seed words have remained next to each other and no word has been inserted between them. (There is no point in producing a sentence pair if the words of the original bigram to be translated are not adjacent in it.)

Figure 2 illustrates the whole process of creating a new parallel phrase for the seed bigram *prověrka neukázala*. The aligned English words *check*, *n't* and *indicate* are marked first, then *seem* is added to make the English subgraph of marked words connected and finally *a*, *did* and *to* are added for grammatical reasons. In total, the new phrase *prověrka neukázala* = *a check did n't seem to indicate* is produced.

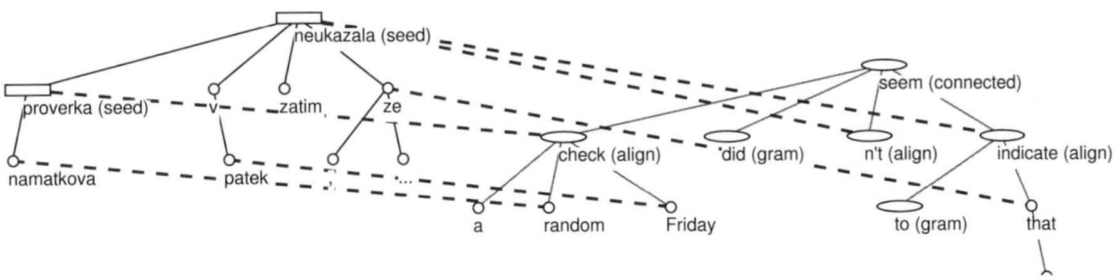

A opravdu , namátková prověrka v pátek zatím neukázala , že by stávka měla dopad na ostatní letecké operace .

Indeed , a random check Friday did n't seem to indicate that the strike was having much of an effect on other airline operations .

Fig. 2. Excerpts from dependency trees of word-aligned sentences illustrating dependency-based corpus expansion

Table 4 summarizes the BLEU scores on the development and evaluation set for various training corpus sizes. We have to conclude that the contribution of dependency-based corpus expansion is not statistically significant. We believe that the main reason for the failure might be inherently implied by the distributional properties of language expressions: if two words tend to depend on each other, they also tend to occur adjacently (and are thus captured by plain phrases). In other words, the situation where our algorithm can apply is rather exceptional. Indeed, only about a thousand distinct translation pairs were generated from the 20k corpus. Moreover, random errors from various sources (errors in the training sentences as such, errors in automatic parsing or limitations of the core grammatical requirements applied in our algorithm) lead to wrong translation pairs that are then inevitably suppressed by the language model.

2.4 Additional Data Sources

As documented in Table 4, doubling the parallel corpus size increases BLEU by about 0.02 to 0.04. A similar observation was reported also by [13] for Arabic-to-English.

Table 5 reports scores achieved using additional training data. Adding out-of-domain parallel texts (a collection of electronically available books) proves to bring another improvement of about 0.02 (less significant on the evaluation set). For alignment training with this additional parallel data, we did not use full lemmatization but only a simple stemming mechanism (keeping first 4 characters of words).

In a separate experiment, we employed a bigger target language model based on a monolingual corpus of the Wall Street Journal (see [3]) instead of a LM derived from the parallel texts only. As we see, adding an in-domain LM can actually serve better than adding parallel texts.

The best results we are able to achieve combine the two additional data sources: for the extraction of translation phrases, we use all parallel texts available, but only the in-domain LM is used.

Table 4. Dependency-based corpus expansion does not improve translation quality

	Devtest			Etest		
Training sentences	5k	10k	20k	5k	10k	20k
Baseline	0.275	0.316	**0.346**	0.254	0.284	0.320
Expanded Corpus	0.274	0.319	0.345	0.250	0.280	**0.323**

Table 5. Impact of additional data sources

	Devtest	Etest
Baseline: 20k sentences	0.346	0.320
20k + 85k out-of-domain sentences	0.366*	0.324
20k sentences, bigger in-domain LM	0.379*	0.337*
20k + 85k out-of-domain sentences, bigger in-domain LM	0.409*	0.370*

2.5 Finding and Fixing Clear Problems

Figure 3 illustrates our method for finding most apparent translation "errors". We compare the set of bigrams of the hypothesis and the four reference translations on the development data. The BLEU metric penalizes our hypothesis if it contains an n-gram not present in any of the hypothesis (*superfluous n-gram*). On the contrary, the hypothesis is suspicious if it does not contain n-grams that all or most reference translations do (*missing n-gram*).

We see that the training data and the reference translations follow different typographic conventions, for instance the system tends to produce "' ' ." but the reference translations expect ". "". Unfortunately, BLEU is sensitive to these differences (see also [14] for suggestions on improving correlation between BLEU and human judgements). Table 6 documents that four simple string-replacement rules inspired by the top missing and superfluous bigrams improve BLEU scores by 1.5% to 5% relative both for small and full training corpus size. The biggest improvement is observed on the development set and the positive effect is slightly reduced on the evaluation set if model parameters are optimized properly.

Top missing bigrams:	
19 , "	12 " said
12 of the	10 Free Europe
10 Radio Free	7 . "
6 L.J. Hooker	6 United States
6 in the	6 the United
6 the strike	5 " We

Top superfluous bigrams:	
26 , ' '	18 ' ' .
14 " said	12 , which
11 Svobodn Evropa	8 , when
8 the state	7 , who
7 J. Hooker	7 L. J.
7 company GM	7 firm Hooker

Fig. 3. Summary of most frequent causes of loss in BLEU score

3 Summary and Related Work

Table 7 compares our best results with the results given in [3] for DBMT (Dependency-Based Machine Translation system by [3]) and ReWrite (word-based statistical MT by [15]). To the best of our knowledge, there are no other reports on the evaluation of Czech-to-English MT quality. The scores are directly comparable, because we use the same training data, language model and development and evaluation sets. Throughout this paper, BLEU scores are based

Table 6. Four patterns fixing typographic conventions significantly improve BLEU

' ' . → . "		L. J. Hooker → L.J. Hooker
' ' → "		the U.S. → the United States
→		

	Devtest		Etest	
	Baseline	Fixed	Baseline	Fixed
5k sentences	0.275	0.291*	0.254	0.256
20k sentences	0.346	0.363*	0.320	0.325
20k sentences + bigger LM	0.379	0.397*	0.337	0.342

Source
Konsorcium soukromých investorů fungující jako LJH Funding Co. sdělilo, že dalo nabídku za 409 milionů dolarů v hotovosti na většinu holdingů v oblasti realit a nákupních center firmy L. J. Hooker Corp. Tato 409 milionová nabídka zahrnuje také odhadovaných 300 milionů dolarů v zaručených závazcích na tyto nemovitosti, jak uvádí nabízející strana. Skupinu vede Jay Shidler, výkonný ředitel Shidler Investment Corp. na Honolulu, a A. Boyd Simpson, výkonný ředitel Simpson Organization Inc. v Atlantě. Firma pana Shidlera se specializuje na investice do obchodních realit a chlubí se majetkem v hodnotě 1 miliardy dolarů; pan Simpson je developer a bývalý vedoucí pracovník ve firmě L. J. Hooker. "Aktiva jsou dobrá, ale vyžadují více peněz a řízení" než může L. J. Hooker v současné situaci nabídnout, řekl pan Simpson v jednom rozhovoru. " Filozofie firmy Hooker byla postavit a prodat. My chceme postavit a ponechat si. L. J. Hooker se sídlem v Atlantě funguje s ochranou proti svým věřitelům podle kapitoly 11 amerického zákona o bankrotu.
Output of the system
The private investors working as LJH Funding Co. said it could offer for $409 million in cash for most holding in the area real-estate and shopping-center firm L.J. Hooker Corp. The 409 million offer includes also an estimated $300 million of secured obligations on those real estate, according union-bidder party. Leading Jay Shidler, executive director Shidler Investment Corp. to Honolulu, and A. Boyd Simpson, executive director of Simpson Organization Inc. in Atlanta. The firm Mr. Shidlera specializes in investment in commercial real-estate and boasts property $1 billion ; Mr. Simpson is the developer and former executive at the company L.J. Hooker. " Assets are good, but require more money and manage " than can L.J. Hooker in the current situation offer, said Mr. Simpson in an interview ". Philosophy Hooker's was to build and sell. We want to build and maintain. L.J. Hooker, based in Atlanta works with protection against their creditors under Chapter 11 of the United States bankruptcy law.
One of the four reference translations
A group of private investors operating under the name LJH Funding Co. has announced that they have submitted a bid of $409 million in cash for the majority of L.J. Hooker Corp. holdings in the field of real-estate and shopping centers. This offer of $409 million also includes a estimated $300 million in secured bonds of this real estate, claimed the bidder. The leaders of the group are Jay Shidler, executive director of Shidler Investment Corp. in Honolulu, and A.Boyd Simpson, executive director of Simpson Organization Inc. in Atlanta. Shidler's company specializes in investments in commercial real estate, and boasts assets of $1 billion; Simpson is a developer and former chief executive of L.J. Hooker. "The assets are sound but they require more money and management" than L.J. Hooker can offer at present, said Simpson in an interview. Hooker's philosophy has been to build and sell. We want to build and keep. L.J. Hooker, based in Atlanta, is protected against its creditors pursuant to chapter 11 of the American bankruptcy act.

Fig. 4. Sample translations using more parallel texts and the bigger in-domain language model

on four re-translations of the Czech text, in [3], the original English text is used as the fifth reference and the average over 4-reference scores (always leaving one reference out) is reported. For the purposes of comparison in Table 7, we evaluated our methods using the same averaging technique, too.

Table 7. Best results of PBT compared to other approaches

	Average over 5 refs.		4 refs. only	
	Devtest	Etest	Devtest	Etest
DBMT with parser I, no LM	0.1857	0.1634	-	-
DBMT with parser II, no LM	0.1916	0.1705	-	-
GIZA++ & ReWrite, bigger LM	0.2222	0.2017	-	-
PBT, no additional LM	0.387±0.015	0.348±0.013	0.363	0.325
PBT, bigger LM	0.413±0.012	0.364±0.013	0.397	0.342
PBT, more parallel texts, bigger LM	0.423±0.011	0.381±0.008	0.410	0.368

The results reported for PBT are based on union alignments of lemmatized training texts and the final hypotheses are typographically corrected as described in section 2.5. The language model used for our experiments is trained either on the English side of parallel texts only ("no additional LM") or on a large monolingual corpus of Wall Street Journal, same as used in [3] ("bigger LM"). The translation of a few sentences of the Devtest are given in Figure 4.

4 Conclusion

We described several experiments with Czech-to-English phrase-based machine translation. Employing a technique of handling morphological richness of Czech is crucial, be it simple stemming or full lemmatization. The type of alignment used for phrase extraction has to be chosen carefully, too. Moreover, the alignment has to be selected on the basis of an end-to-end translation quality metric, because comparing alignments against human-annotated data leads to a sub-optimal selection.

We also experimented with rule-based handling of numbers and with a novel technique for artificial expansion of training corpus using dependency structures of the sentences.

We confirm that adding more training data improves translation quality, but it is documented that the best results are achieved if we use out-of-domain data to extract phrases only and keep the target language model in-domain. We also suggest a simple technique to find the most apparent causes of a loss in the BLEU score.

In conclusion, phrase-based statistical MT from Czech to English performs well, despite the expectations arising from linguistic knowledge about the properties of Czech. The system we experimented with is currently the best performing MT evaluated on this language pair.

Acknowledgement

The work on this experiment was partially supported by the grants GAAV ČR 1ET201120505, GAUK 351/2005 and Collegium Informaticum GAČR 201/05/H014.

References

1. Hajič, J.: Complex Corpus Annotation: The Prague Dependency Treebank. In Šimková, M., ed.: Insight into Slovak and Czech Corpus Linguistics, Bratislava, Slovakia, Veda, vydavateľstvo SAV (2005) 54–73
2. Sgall, P., Hajičová, E., Panevová, J.: The Meaning of the Sentence and Its Semantic and Pragmatic Aspects. Academia/Reidel Publishing Company, Prague, Czech Republic/Dordrecht, Netherlands (1986)
3. Čmejrek, M., Cuřín, J., Havelka, J.: Czech-English Dependency-based Machine Translation. In: EACL 2003 Proceedings of the Conference, Association for Computational Linguistics (2003) 83–90
4. Zens, R., Bender, O., Hasan, S., Khadivi, S., Matusov, E., Xu, J., Zhang, Y., Ney, H.: The RWTH Phrase-based Statistical Machine Translation System. In: Proceedings of the International Workshop on Spoken Language Translation (IWSLT), Pittsburgh, PA (2005) 155–162
5. Čmejrek, M., Cuřín, J., Havelka, J., Hajič, J., Kuboň, V.: Prague Czech-English Dependecy Treebank: Syntactically Annotated Resources for Machine Translation. In: Proceedings of LREC 2004, Lisbon (2004)
6. Linguistic Data Consortium: Penn Treebank 3, LDC99T42 (1999)
7. Papineni, K., Roukos, S., Ward, T., Zhu, W.J.: BLEU: a Method for Automatic Evaluation of Machine Translation. In: ACL 2002, Proceedings of the 40th Annual Meeting of the Association for Computational Linguistics, Philadelphia, Pennsylvania (2002) 311–318
8. Och, F.J., Ney, H.: A systematic comparison of various statistical alignment models. Computational Linguistics **29**(1) (2003) 19–51
9. Matusov, E., Zens, R., Ney, H.: Symmetric Word Alignments for Statistical Machine Translation. In: Proceedings of COLING 2004, Geneva, Switzerland (2004) 219–225
10. Bojar, O., Prokopová, M.: Czech-English Word Alignment. In: Proceedings of the Fifth International Conference on Language Resources and Evaluation (LREC 2006), ELRA (2006) (in print).
11. Lopatková, M., Plátek, M., Kuboň, V.: Modeling syntax of Free Word-Order Languages: Dependency Analysis By Reduction. In Matoušek, V., Mautner, P., Pavelka, T., eds.: Text, Speech and Dialogue: 8th International Conference, TSD 2005, Karlovy Vary, Czech Republic, September 12-15, 2005. Proceedings. Volume LNAI 3658., Springer Verlag (2005) 140–147
12. Chiang, D.: A hierarchical phrase-based model for statistical machine translation. In: Proceedings of the 43rd Annual Meeting of the Association for Computational Linguistics (ACL'05), Ann Arbor, Michigan, Association for Computational Linguistics (2005) 263–270
13. Och, F.J.: Statistical Machine Translation: Foundations and Recent Advances. Tutorial at MT Summit 2005 (2005)
14. Leusch, G., Ueffing, N., Vilar, D., Ney, H.: Preprocessing and Normalization for Automatic Evaluation of Machine Translation. In: Proceedings of the ACL Workshop on Intrinsic and Extrinsic Evaluation Measures for Machine Translation and/or Summarization, Ann Arbor, Michigan, Association for Computational Linguistics (2005) 17–24
15. Germann, U.: Greedy decoding for statistical machine translation in almost linear time. In: HLT-NAACL. (2003)

Deep vs. Shallow Semantic Analysis Applied to Textual Entailment Recognition

Óscar Ferrández, Rafael Muñoz Terol, Rafael Muñoz, Patricio Martínez-Barco, and Manuel Palomar

Natural Language Processing and Information Systems Group
Department of Software and Computing Systems
University of Alicante
Alicante, Spain
{ofe, rafamt, rafael, patricio, mpalomar}@dlsi.ua.es

Abstract. This paper covers two different methods of recognising entailment between the text/hypothesis pair by processing logic forms. These two methods are based on knowledge sources. The logic forms of both the text and the hypothesis are inferred by analysing the syntactic dependency relationships between their words. Both approaches use the WordNet lexical database as knowledge source and obtain a semantic similarity score by means of WordNet relations. The difference between them is the treatment of these relations. Whereas one method carries out a deeper analysis considering many WordNet relations, the other one is shallower and manages only a reduced number of relations. These two approaches have been evaluated using the PASCAL Second RTE Challenge data and evaluation methodology.

1 Introduction

Textual entailment has been recently defined as a common solution for modelling language variability [1] in different NLP tasks. A strict textual entailment is defined as a relation holding between two natural language expressions, a text (T) and an entailment hypothesis (H), that is entailed by T. The following examples show a true entailment and a false entailment between two segments of text, respectively.

T: This is a Hindu temple dedicated to the Lord Shiva, one of 3 major Gods of Hinduism.
H: Lord Shiva is one of the major Gods of Hinduism.

T: The Eiffel Tower was built in the period 1887-1889, to celebrate the 100th anniversary of the French Revolution.
H: The Eiffel Tower was built during the French Revolution.

The pair of sentences (T-H) can carry different facts, but the hypothesis can be inferred from the text. Both the text and the hypothesis have to be meaningful and

T. Salakoski et al. (Eds.): FinTAL 2006, LNAI 4139, pp. 225–236, 2006.

coherent expressions. Depending on the linguistic complexity of the sentences, a shallower or deeper linguistic analysis will be required in order to verify the entailment relation. According to Pazienza et al. [2], from an operational point of view, we can distinguish three types of entailment: (i) *semantic subsumption*, when the text describes the fact more specifically than the hypothesis through semantic operations. For example in H: "the cat eats the mouse and T: "the cat devours the mouse, T is more specific semantically than H; (ii) *syntactic subsumption*, when the situation described in the text is more specific through syntactic operations (e.g. in the pair H: "the cat eats the mouse and T: "the cat eats the mouse in the garden); and (iii) *direct implication*, when the fact expressed in the hypothesis is inferred by the fact in the text. For example in H: "The cat killed the mouse and T: "the cat devours the mouse, H is implied by T. The latter type of entailment relation requires deeper syntactic and semantic analysis than the other ones, whereas for the first and second type, a semantic resources and a detailed syntactic analysis could be profitable in order to detect entailment.

Many NLP applications need to recognize when the meaning of one text can be expressed by, or inferred from, another text. The textual entailment phenomenon captures broadly the reasoning about this language variability. An automatic method, that can determine how two sentences relate to each other in terms of semantic relations or textual entailment, would be very useful for robust NLP applications. For example, in a Question Answering (QA) system the same answer could be expressed in different syntactic and semantic ways, and a textual entailment module could help a QA system in identifying the forecast answers that entail the expected answer. Similarly, in other natural language applications such as Information Extraction a textual entailment tool could help by discovering different variants expressing the same concept. In multi-document summarization, for instance, it could be used to identify redundant information among the most informative sentences and, therefore, eliminate duplicates. In general, a textual entailment tool would be profitable for a better performance of many NLP applications.

The PASCAL RTE (Recognising Textual Entailment) Challenge [3] introduces a common task and evaluation framework for textual entailment, covering a broad range of semantic-oriented inferences needed for practical applications. This task is, therefore, suitable for evaluating and comparing semantic-oriented models in a generic manner. Participants in the evaluation exercise are provided with pairs of small text snippets (one or more sentences in English), which the organizers term Text-Hypothesis (T-H) pairs. Participating systems have to decide for each T-H pair whether T indeed entails H or not, and their results are then compared to the manual annotation.

In this paper we present a system based on knowledge for solving the strict textual entailment. The strict entailment can involve both semantic and syntactic transformations from T to H, but the meaning of H is implied by T. Therefore, strict entailment encompasses all three types of entailment distinguished above (semantic subsumption, syntactic subsumption and direct implication). Our system attempts to recognise textual entailment by determining if the text and the hypothesis are related by deriving logic forms from the text and the hypothesis, and by finding semantic relations between their predicates using WordNet.

The organization of the paper is as follows. The next section presents a brief background of textual entailment. The architecture and the main components of our system are provided in Section 3, evaluation and performance analysis are presented in Section 4, and the conclusions and future work are drawn in Section 5.

2 Background

In this brief state-of-the-art of approaches taken in order to recognize textual entailment, we want to emphasize two different approaches developed by the researchers. Mainly, we distinguish between approaches based on knowledge techniques, which normally use linguistic resources, and other approaches using machine learning and statistical methods to induce specific entailment relations.

Although the latter approaches obtain good results solving the textual entailment phenomenon, the main trend is to provide the systems with knowledge resources. This is due to the fact that recognising textual entailment requires a deep semantic understanding of the texts, and the use of semantic resources such as WordNet seems appropriate for the detection of semantic relations between two different texts.

As we have mentioned in the previous section, the recognition of the textual entailment phenomenon is a novel task within the NLP field and the research community has a strong interest in this task. A clear example of this interest is the organization of several Workshops such as the PASCAL Challenge Workshops[1] and the ACL Workshop on Empirical Modeling of Semantic Equivalence and Entailment[2].

2.1 Based on Machine Learning and Statistical Methods

In Glickman and Dagan previous work [4], a general probabilistic setting that formalises the notion of textual entailment is proposed. They further describe a model based on document cooccurrence probabilities.

In the textual entailment system presented by Bos and Markert [5], a decision tree was trained using features obtained by shallow and deep NLP methods such as word overlap, CCG-parser to generate fine-grained semantic representation, first-order logic, Vampire (a theorem prover for first-order logic) and Paradox (a finite model builder). They also use some background knowledge: generic axioms for the semantics of possessives, active-passive and locations; lexical knowledge (first-order axioms based on WordNet hyperonyms); and geographical knowledge into first-order axioms.

[1] http://www.pascal-network.org/Challenges/RTE/ and http://www.pascal-network.org/Challenges/RTE2

[2] http://acl.ldc.upenn.edu/W/W05/

Another interesting research work was carried out by Zanzotto et al. [6]. In this work, the authors focus on entailment between verbs, due to the fact that verbs generally govern the meaning of sentences. They investigate the prototypical textual forms that describe entailment relations calling them *textual entailment patterns*. These patterns enable the detection of entailment assertions that are analysed in order to be considered true entailment expression. This last analysis is obtained by both investigating large textual collections and by applying statistical measures relevant for the task.

2.2 Based on Knowledge Techniques

In this case, these approaches are characterized by applying lexical resources. Some of the knowledge-based methods employed are the representation of the texts into logic forms, the creation of dependency trees from the texts and the analysis of the semantic similarity measures between the texts.

Akhmatova [7] describes a system based on syntax-driven semantic analysis and uses the notion of atomic proposition as its main element for entailment recognition. Atomic proposition is a minimal declarative statement (or small idea). If for every atomic proposition in the hypothesis sentence there is one in the text sentence from that it could be entailed, then the sentence entailment holds, otherwise the entailment does not hold.

In Fowler et al. [8], each text pair is transformed into logic form representation with semantic relations. Generating automatically NLP axioms serving as linguistic rewriting rules and lexical chain axioms that connect concepts in both texts as well as a light set of simple hand-coded world knowledge axioms are included.

Herrera et al. [9] present an approach that converts both the text and the hypothesis into dependency trees. These trees are compared by a simple matching algorithm focused on searching in all the branches starting from any leaf of the hypothesis tree and showing a matching with any branch of the tree assigned to the text. One branch node of the hypothesis tree matches with one from the text tree, if there is a lexical entailment between them. They define this lexical entailment considering WordNet relations such as synonymy, hyperonymy and entailment, WordNet multiwords and comparing the negation with the WordNet antonymy relation.

Another work on dependency trees is reported by Kouylekov and Magnini [10]. The authors of this work use the tree edit distance algorithm applied to the dependency trees of the text and the hypothesis. The entailment holds if there exists a sequence of transformations applied to text such that we can obtain hypothesis with an overall cost below a certain threshold. The transformations (i.e. deletion, insertion and substitution) are determined by a set of predefined entailment rules, which also determine a cost for each editing operation.

3 System Architecture

Our system carries out the detection of strict entailment between two texts by means of two main components: the first one derives the logic forms and the other one computes the semantic similarity between logic forms. The former embodies various advanced natural language processing techniques that derive from the text and the hypothesis the associated logic forms. The latter component provides us with a score illustrating the semantic similarity between the logic form predicates associated with the text and the hypothesis. Depending on the value of this score, we will decide if the two logic forms (text and hypothesis) are related or not. If the logic forms are related, then the entailment between the text and the hypothesis is true. Otherwise, there is no entailment relation holding between the text and the hypothesis.

An overview of our system is depicted in Figure 1. In the following sections we will describe in detail these main components.

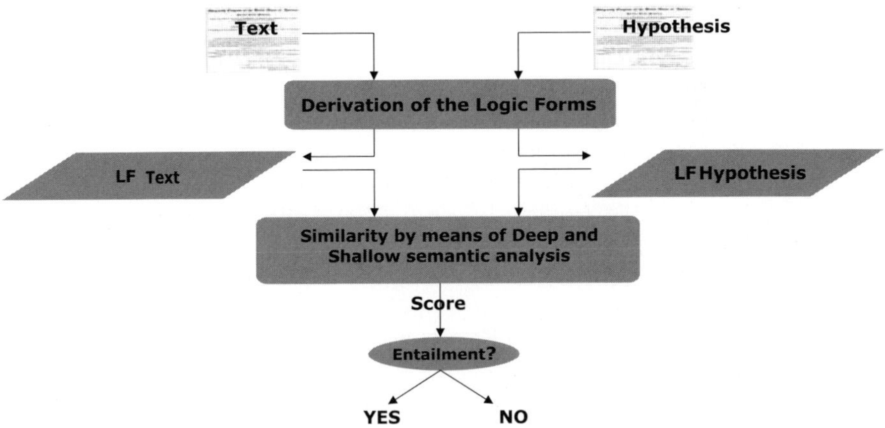

Fig. 1. System architecture

3.1 Derivation of the Logic Forms

Our system makes use of the logic forms of the sentences with the aim of simplifying the sentence treatment process. A logic form can be defined as a set of predicates related among them that have been inferred from a sentence. The logic form of a sentence shows its logic representation by the way of related predicates. The format of a logic form is similar to the format of the lexical resource called Logic Form Transformation of eXtended WordNet (LFT) [11]. The logic form of a sentence is derived through applying NLP rules to the dependency relationship of the words in the sentence. Thus, the first step necessary to infer the logic form of a sentence is to obtain the dependency relationships between the words of the sentence. The NLP resource used to obtain the dependency relationships between the words of the sentence is MINIPAR [12], a broad-coverage parser. Once the dependency relationships have been acquired, the next step to automatically infer the logic form of the sentence is the analysis of these dependency relationships between the words of the sentence. Then, the logic form derivation is a compositional process that starts in the leaves of the dependency tree, continues through the ramifications of the dependency tree and ends in the root of the derivation tree.

We summarize this complex process of inferring the logic form of a sentence through the following example in the sentence "The beach is beautiful". The first step is to find the dependency relationships between the words in the sentence. Figure 2 shows the dependency tree. The second step consists of applying the simple NLP rules to the leaves of this dependency relationship and obtaining the predicates of the logic form derived in these leaves. The next step is based on applying the complex NLP rules to the ramifications and the root of the dependency tree deriving the logic form.

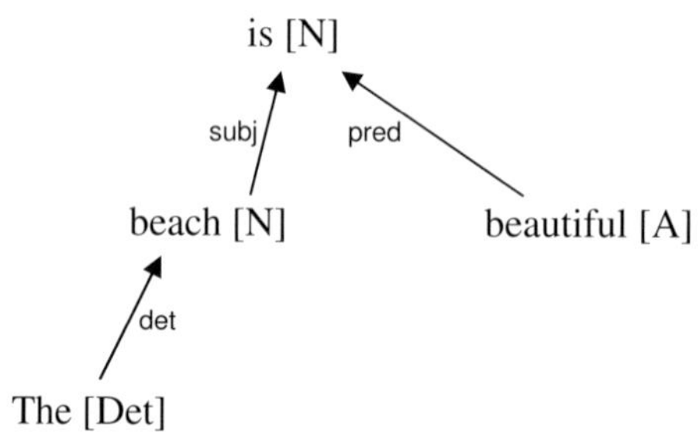

Fig. 2. Dependency tree of the sentence

Once all these rules have been applied to the dependency tree of the sentence "The beach is beautiful", the logic form is inferred as "beach:NN(x2) be:VB(e1, x2, x3) Atributo:IN(e1, x1) beautiful:JJ(x1)". Note that the verb "to be" is intransitive. This fact produces in the logic form that on the one hand the argument of its predicate that represents the object (x3) is dummy and, on the other hand, the predicate "Atributo" links the dependency relationship between the verb and the adjective. This logic representation (logic form) concludes that the noun-assert "beach" is the subject of the verb-assert to "be" and the adjective-assert "beautiful" is an attribute of the verb-assert to "be".

3.2 Semantic Similarity Between Logic Forms

In order to obtain the semantic similarity score between two logic form predicates, we have carried out a method focused on initially analysing the semantic relations between the logic form predicates corresponding to the verbs of the text and the hypothesis, respectively. Then, if there is any relation between the two verbs, the method will analyse the semantic relations between the logic form predicates of the words depending on the two verbs. These analysis provide semantic weights which are summed and normalized, obtaining the final normalized-relation score.

The aforementioned method is implemented as shown in the pseudo-code below.

```
semanticWeight = 0
Tvb = obtainVerbs(T)
Hvb = obtainVerbs(H)
for i = 0 ... size(Tvb) do
  for j = 0 ... size(Hvb) do
    if semanticSimilarity(Tvb(i),Hvb(j)) ≠ 0 then
      semanticWeight += semanticSimilarity(Tvb(i),Hvb(j))
      Telem = obtainElem(Tvb(i))
      Helem = obtainElem(Hvb(j))
      semanticWeight += semanticSimilarity(Telem,Helem)
    end if
  end for
end for
if semanticWeight > threshold then
  return TRUE
else
  return FALSE
end if
```

In order to obtain the semantic similarity between the predicates of the logic forms (*semanticSimilarity(x,y)*), two approaches have been implemented. Both of them are based on WordNet hierarchy, and use the WordNet relations.

One of these two approaches is characterized by applying a deep semantic analysis between the two logic form predicates, whereas the other one realises a shallower analysis. The reason for implementing two different approaches is to find out what kinds of WordNet relations are more adequate for recognising entailment. In this case, the approach that carries out a shallower semantic analysis only includes the WordNet relations which we have considered relevant for the entailment, whereas our other approach incorporates more WordNet relations. In concrete, the relevant relations for the entailment are hyponymy, synonymy and entailment, because of these relations allude to a specific entailment between the text and the hypothesis. A detailed description of the two approaches is shown in the following subsections.

A Word Sense Disambiguation module was not employed in deriving the WordNet relations between any two predicates. Only the first 50% of the WordNet senses were taken into account. We consider only the most frequent senses of a word, because if we had taken into account all the senses, the system would have added more noise making it harder to solve the task.

The threshold, above which one can consider that the text entails the hypothesis, has been obtained empirically using the provided development data. The Figure 3 in the section 4 presents this process in detail.

A Deep Semantic Analysis Using WordNet Relationships. In the WordNet lexical database [13], a synset is a set of concepts that express the same meaning. A concept is defined as the use of one word in one determined context (sense). Thus, this task deals determining if two different concepts are related through the composition of different WordNet relationships: hypernymy, hyponymy, entailment, synonymy, meronymy and holonymy. The length of the path that relates the two different concepts must be lower or equal than 4 synsets. These relations are not representing the same knowledge. This fact produces that we assign an empirical weight between 0 and 1 to each one of these WordNet relations: 0.8 for the hypernymy relationship, 0.7 for the hyponymy and entailment relationships, 0.9 for the synonymy relationship, and 0.5 for the meronymy and holonymy relationships. Then, the weight of the path between two different concepts is calculated as the product of the weights associated to the relations connecting the intermediate synsets. This technique is different from the Spread-Weights algorithm [14], even though derived from it.

Even though these WordNet relationships have used for the textual entailment phenomenon, they can also be used in other NLP task as Question Answering [15]. However, we consider that the application of these WordNet relationships is interesting in order to check their impact on the textual entailment task. Moreover, this way, we are able to investigate which WordNet relations are more adequate for textual entailment.

A Shallow Semantic Analysis Using WordNet Relationships. In this case, we determine if two concepts are related through the composition of the WordNet relationships that we consider as specific entailment relations. Hyponymy, entailment and synonymy are the WordNet relationships that we handle in this approach. We consider that these relations are more adequate for the entailment phenomenon, and we want to check whether using only these three relations the recognition of textual entailment is better than using the relations mentioned in the previous section.

In the same way that the previous approach, the length of the path that relates the two different concepts must be lower or equal than 4 synsets and the weights assigned to each one of the WordNet relations are the same (0.7 for the hyponymy and entailment, and 0.9 for the synonymy relationship). As the aforementioned approach, the weight is also calculated as the product of the weights associated to the relations connecting the intermediate synsets.

4 Evaluation

For evaluating our system we consider appropriate to use the corpus provided by the PASCAL Second Recognising Textual Entailment Challenge. The organizers of this challenge provide participants with development and test corpora, both of them with 800 sentence pairs (text and hypothesis) manually annotated for logical entailment. It consists of four subsets, which correspond to typical success and failure settings in different applications such as Information Extraction (IE),

Information Retrieval (IR), Question Answering (QA) and Multi-document summarization (SUM). Within each application setting the annotators selected both positive entailment examples (annotated YES) as well as negative examples (annotated NO), where entailment does not hold (50%-50% split). The organizers have also established two measures for evaluating the systems. The judgments returned by the systems will be compared to those manually assigned by the human annotators. The percentage of matching judgments will provide the *accuracy* of the run, i.e. the fraction of correct responses. As a second measure, an *Average Precision* measure will be computed. This measure evaluates the ability of systems to rank all the pairs in the test set according to their entailment confidence, in decreasing order from the most certain entailment to the least certain. *Average precision* is a common evaluation measure for system rankings. More formally, it can be written as follows:

$$Average\_Precision = \frac{1}{R}(\sum_{i=1}^{n} E(i)\frac{\#\_correct\_up\_to\_pair\_i}{i}) \qquad (1)$$

where n is the number of the pairs in the test set, R is the total number of positive pairs in the test set, E(i) is 1 if the i-th pair is positive and 0 otherwise, and i ranges over the pairs, ordered by their ranking.

We evaluated two different runs. Both runs were based on deriving the logic forms from the text and the hypothesis. However, the *WNdeep* run computes the comparison between logic forms by means of our module that deals with six WordNet relations (see section 3.2), whereas the *WNshallow* run uses our approach based only on the three WordNet relations (see section 3.2), that we have considered more relevant for the textual entailment task.

The results obtained by the PASCAL RTE2 evaluation script for the development and test data are shown in Table 1.

Table 1. *Results obtained by the PASCAL RTE2 evaluation script*

			overall	IE	IR	QA	SUM
development	WNdeep	Accuracy	0.5273	0.5510	0.5345	0.4677	0.5686
	WNshallow	Accuracy	0.5375	0.5026	0.5357	0.5641	0.5474
test	WNdeep	Accuracy	0.5475	0.4750	0.5850	0.6150	0.5150
		Average Precision	0.5743	0.5853	0.6113	0.5768	0.5589
	WNshallow	Accuracy	0.5513	0.5150	0.5350	0.5950	0.5600
		Average Precision	0.6027	0.5689	0.5891	0.6385	0.6105

In order to adjust the threshold that determines if the text entails the hypothesis, we have carried out several experiments using the development data. The Figure 3 shows an empirical increasing of the thresholds in order to obtain the best performance one for each run. The best threshold for *WNdeep* run had a value of *0.24*, whereas for the *WNshallow* run was *0.25*. Although the adjustment of the thresholds is similar for the two runs, the treatment of different WordNet relations causes a slight difference between them.

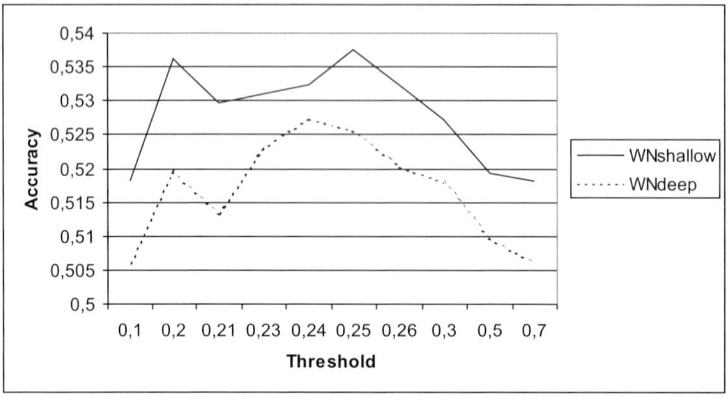

Fig. 3. Adjusting the thresholds on the development data

The run using a weak treatment of the WordNet relations (*WNshallow*) achieves better results than the approach that uses more WordNet relations, both when tested on development, as well as test data (see Table 1).

This improvement of accuracy and average precision is due to the fact that our previous hypothesis about considering only the relevant WordNet relations for the textual entailment task, was correct. Whereas our other approach (*WNdeep*) attempts to establish an objective semantic comparison between the logic forms rather than an entailment relation.

Nevertheless, our system, in both runs (*WNdeep* and *WNshallow*) fails in many cases because it encounters good semantic matching between the logic forms of the text and the hypothesis, even if the two have got different meanings. In the case of the following example:

T: Jose Reyes scored the winner for Arsenal as they ended a three-game league losing streak with a victory over battling Charlton.
H: Jose Reyes scored the winner against Arsenal.

our system produces a true textual entailment due to a huge similarity score.

The reason for this is that the text's and the hypothesis' verbs and their dependent predicates are the same or very similar semantically. However, in the hypothesis "*against* causes a different meaning with respect to the text. Hitherto, our system is not able to recognise these cases. Therefore, a more detailed syntactic processing is needed in order to recognise the words that affect the meaning of the sentence.

5 Conclusions and Future Work

The main contribution of this research is the development of a system for solving the strict textual entailment, this kind of entailment takes into account all the operations (syntactic and semantic) in order to detect when the hypothesis is inferred by the text. Another contribution, is the evaluation of the impact of several types of WordNet relations in improving the detection of the entailment phenomenon.

Our system derives the logic forms for the text/hypothesis pair and computes the semantic comparison between them. This comparison is carried out using two different approaches. On the one hand, our first approach *WNdeep* is managed by a deeper study of the WordNet relations between the predicates of the text and the hypothesis. And on the other hand, we have also implemented another approach (*WNshallow*), that only computes the WordNet relations which we have considered relevant for recognising textual entailment.

The *WNshallow* run produces an improvement of accuracy and average precision. We expected this improvement because the WordNet relations, that this run uses, are adequate for the textual entailment task. Hyponymy, entailment and synonymy relations between the text and the hypothesis point out a clear evidence of the entailment, whereas taking into account other relations for recognizing textual entailment such as meronymy or holonymy is not appropriate. However, these relations can be useful for other applications as Question Answering [15].

As future work, we are interested in two matters. Firstly, we want to improve our method by investigating in more detail the syntactic trees of the text and the hypothesis. Therefore, the errors derived from words that change the meaning of the sentence can be lessened. Finally, we are also interested in testing how other natural language processing tools can help to detect textual entailment. For example, using a Named Entity Recognizer could help in detecting entailment between two segments of text.

Acknowledgements

This research has been partially funded by the Spanish Government under project CICyT number TIC2003-07158-C04-01.

References

1. Dagan, I., Glickman, O.: Probabilistic Textual Entailment: Generic Applied Modeling of Language Variability. In: PASCAL Workshop on Learning Methods for Text Understanding and Mining, Grenoble, France (2004) 26–29
2. Pazienza, M.T., Pennacchiotti, M., Zanzotto, F.M.: Textual Entailment as Syntactic Graph Distance: a rule based and a SVM based approach. In: Proceedings of the PASCAL Challenges Workshop on Recognising Textual Entailment, Southampton, UK (2005) 25–28
3. Dagan, I., Glickman, O., Magnini, B.: The PASCAL Recognising Textual Entailment Challenge. In: Proceedings of the PASCAL Challenges Workshop on Recognising Textual Entailment, Southampton, UK (2005) 1–8

4. Glickman, O., Dagan, I.: A Probabilistic Setting and Lexical Cooccurrence Model for Textual Entailment. In: Proceedings of the ACL Workshop on Empirical Modeling of Semantic Equivalence and Entailmen, Ann Arbor, Michigan, Association for Computational Linguistics (2005) 43–48
5. Bos, J., Markert, K.: Combining Shallow and Deep NLP Methods for Recognizing Textual Entailment. In: Proceedings of the PASCAL Challenges Workshop on Recognising Textual Entailment, Southampton, UK (2005) 65–68
6. Zanzotto, F.M., Pazienza, M.T., Pennacchiotti, M.: Discovering Entailment Relations Using "Textual Entailment Patterns". In: Proceedings of the ACL Workshop on Empirical Modeling of Semantic Equivalence and Entailment, Ann Arbor, Michigan, Association for Computational Linguistics (2005) 37–42
7. Akhmatova, E.: Textual Entailment Resolution via Atomic Propositions. In: Proceedings of the PASCAL Challenges Workshop on Recognising Textual Entailment, Southampton, UK (2005) 61–64
8. Fowler, A., Hauser, B., Hodges, D., Niles, I., Novischi, A., Stephan, J.: Applying COGEX to Recognize Textual Entailment. In: Proceedings of the PASCAL Challenges Workshop on Recognising Textual Entailment, Southampton, UK (2005) 69–72
9. Herrera, J., Peñas, A., Verdejo, F.: Textual Entailment Recognition Based on Dependency Analysis and WordNet. In: Proceedings of the PASCAL Challenges Workshop on Recognising Textual Entailment, Southampton, UK (2005) 21–24
10. Kouylekov, M., Magnini, B.: Recognizing Textual Entailment with Tree Edit Distance Algorithms. In: Proceedings of the PASCAL Challenges Workshop on Recognising Textual Entailment, Southampton, UK (2005) 17–20
11. Harabagiu, S., Miller, G., Moldovan, D.: WordNet 2 - A Morphologically and Semantically Enhanced Resource. In: Proceedings of ACL-SIGLEX99: Standardizing Lexical Resources, Maryland (1999) 1–8
12. Lin, D.: Dependency-based evaluation of minipar. In: Workshop on the Evaluation of Parsing Systems, Southampton, UK (2005) 17–20
13. Miller, G.: WordNet: An on-line lexical database. In: International Journal of Lexicography 3, 4. (1990) 235–312
14. Moldovan, D., Novischi, A.: Lexical Chains for Question Answering. In: Proceedings of the 19th international conference on Computational linguistics - Volume 1, Taipei, Taiwan (2002) 1–7
15. Terol, R.M., Martínez-Barco, P., Palomar, M.: Applying Logic Forms to Biomedical Q-A. In: Proceedings of the International Symposium on Innovations in Intelligent Systems and Applications, Istambul, Turkey (2005)

Dictionary-Free Morphological Classifier of Russian Nouns*

Igor A. Bolshakov[1] and Elena I. Bolshakova[2]

[1] Center for Computing Research (CIC)
National Polytechnic Institute (IPN), Mexico City, Mexico
igor@cic.ipn.mx
[2] Moscow State Lomonosov University
Faculty of Computational Mathematics and Cybernetics, Moscow, Russia
bolsh@cs.msu.su

Abstract. A dictionary-free morphological classifier of nouns for a highly inflective language is developed. The classifier is a front-end utility for acquiring a very large DB of Russian collocations and WordNet-like semantic links. For its main functions, the classifier uses the final letters of standard noun forms and extensive morphological and lexical data. The percentage of nouns correctly classified in a standalone manner is now 99.65%. A completely error-free performance is impossible for context-free methods in principle, primarily because of homonymy: the nouns of various senses may decline in different ways. Therefore the classifier's results are additionally tested against more than 200,000 collocations stored in the DB and, when it is necessary, are automatically corrected.

1 Introduction

Any modern NLP system for a European language requires morphological tools. For highly inflectional languages such as Russian, a full-fledge morphological dictionary is essential. For each entry word, this dictionary should contain classifying features including part of speech, inflection class, and gender (for nouns), among others.

A morpho-dictionary for a new NLP system can be built before the target system or in parallel with it. The first option is good for controllable languages whereby the vocabulary, i.e. the list of relevant lexemes, is known in advance, so that just a few tunings of the dictionary are expected. If the developer cannot evaluate in advance the content of the vocabulary and its size, and some new words that may be absent in common dictionaries are likely to occur, only the second option seems promising.

We chose the parallel development option for the morpho-dictionary in the CrossLexica system—a very large DB of Russian collocations and WordNet-like semantic links [2]. On scanning texts of newspapers, journals, leaflets, and books in

---

* Work done under partial support of Mexican Government (CONACyT, SNI, SIP-IPN) and Russian Foundation of Fundamental Research (RFFI, the grant 06-01-00571). Many thanks to Steve Legrand for good advice and proofreading.

T. Salakoski et al. (Eds.): FinTAL 2006, LNAI 4139, pp. 237–244, 2006.

paper form and especially when browsing the Web, we found a lot of new words—mainly contracted, special or argotic—that cannot be found in standard dictionaries.

Hence we thought of a front-end utility for CrossLexica that would supply in an automatic and context-free manner each word in acquired collocations with a morphological description that would be sufficient both analytically and synthetically. This should then allow CrossLexica to recognize in runtime any already known lexeme in any inflected form and to output its collocations with all the components properly inflected. We do have a morpho-dictionary in CrossLexica, which is a result of the automated front-end processing, and it was not brought from outside. So our approach can be called dictionary-free. We were building a classifier with tangled programming logic and data—both morphological and lexical—and we were prepared to spend a considerable time for it. This paper describes the classifying utility which has taken more than 12 years to bring to perfection.

As for computational morphology, there exist several approaches [3, 4, 5]. For Russian nouns, we took the simplest approach: a wordform is a concatenation of a constant stem string and an optional end string (maybe empty) implied by number and grammatical case. Classification of a noun involves determining its declension class, which in turn determines all endings possible for that noun.

Automatic classification is greatly facilitated by the knowledge of final letters of the standard (dictionary) noun form. The first promoter of this idea in Russian computational linguistics was G.G. Belonogov [1]. However, for classification of tens of thousand of nouns the knowledge of only final letters is insufficient, and rather extensive morphological and lexical data are needed. These are used in our classifier together with the final letters.

The quality of our context-free classifier already seems pretty good, but some rare errors in declension classes are inevitable, mainly because of homonymy of nouns (various senses can decline differently). Therefore, the results are additionally tested by means of another utility, which compares noun endings in the collocations stored in the DB with those implied by the assigned declension class. For the majority of the cases, the assigned class proves to be correct. The rare contradictions that may be found are amended at this stage automatically, with the correction of the previously assigned class and without any message alerting the developer. Such a feature may be called self-learning.

All Russian nouns and their parts are given below with Latin letters, but we hope no knowledge of Russian is needed for making sense of the paper.

2 On Morphology of Russian Nouns

The morphological features of Russian nouns are typical of Slavic languages. The nouns have three genders: masculine, feminine or neuter. They decline according to two numbers and six grammatical cases—nominative, genitive, dative, accusative, instrumental, and prepositional—in each number, having all in all up to ten different case endings.

Since Russian declension does not use prefixes, the simplest morphological model is allowable:

$$wordform = stem + ending \quad (1)$$

where *stem* is the same for the whole morpho-paradigm; *ending* depends on the case and declension class and may be empty; + indicates concatenation. However, there exist many complicated features that increase the number of the declension classes greatly.

First, Russian noun can contain the so-called fugitive vowels *e* or *o* in the penultimate position of the stem and a consonant in the ultimate position. The fugitive vowel disappears when the ending has an initial vowel. This is a kind of morphonological phenomena well-known in general linguistics. To retain the model (1), we shift the border between the stem and the ending two letters back. In this manner we generate new declension classes—for each combination of the fugitive vowel and the ultimate consonant of the original stem. For example, the noun *kivok*+∅ 'nod' (∅ is an empty string) has the same set {∅, *a*, *u*, ∅, *om*, *e*} of endings in singular as *dok* 'dock', but unlike *dok* the penultimate *o* in the stem *kivok* disappears in the cases where the ending initiates with a vowel: *kivk+a, kivk+u, kivk+om, kivk+e.* Shifting the border two letters to the left, we have the paradigm {*kiv+ok, kiv+ka, kiv+ku, kiv+ok, kiv+kom, kiv+ke*} with the shortened stem *kiv* and a new set of endings: {*ok, ka, ku, ok, kom, ke*}. In several classes, because of peculiarities of Russian orthography, the letter *j* or the palatalization sign ' appears at the position of the fugitive *e*, but the method of the standardization of the stem remains the same.

Second, Russian nouns have animate or inanimate denotations, and their endings in accusative are different for masculine singular and plural nouns. We consider 'animate' declension classes separately.

Third, Russian nouns include rather vast sets of substantivized adjectives that have declension patterns corresponding to the original adjectives. Meanwhile each gender of substantivized adjectives forms its own declension class.

An additional factor multiplying declension classes is purely ours. Since many nouns in singular and plural have different sets of supplementing words with which they form collocations, as well as different sets of synonyms, the two numbers of the same noun are considered as different entries. This increases the vocabulary of nouns approximately by 33% and correspondingly increases the total number of declension classes.

Each noun with a fixed number has a morpho-paradigm of six cases, but we should also take into account those few tens of masculine singular nouns (some of them rather frequent) that have two more cases: partitive and locative. These cases are equal respectively to genitive and prepositional in meaning but have the same endings as dative. The choices 'genitive or partitive' and 'prepositional or locative' are usually a matter of style. To consider all nouns in a standard way, we presume eight cases for all 'one-number' nouns, with the last two endings usually empty.

The fragment of the resulting table of endings is given below. Each line begins with the declension class number and ends with an example.

`{11}('a','ov','am','ov','ami','ax','','')`	{*doktora* 'doctors'}
`{12}('a','','am','a','ami','ax' ,'','')`	{*vremena* 'times'}
`{13}('na','on','nam','na','nami','nax ,'','')`	{*volokna* 'fibers'}
`{14}('na','en','nam','na','nami','nax','','')`	{*pjatna* 'stains'}
`{15}('la','ol','lam','la','lami','lax','','')`	{*stekla* 'glasses'}
`{16}('o','a','u','o','om','e','','')`	{*oblako* 'clowd'}

```
{17}('e','ja','ju','e','em','i','','')        {penie 'singing'}
{18}('e','ja','ju','e','em','e','','')        {pole 'camp'}
```

Initially, the number of classes manually derived from standard grammars was 180. During accumulation and testing of the CrossLexica primary DB lasting several years, we introduced 24 classes more, though as many as 22 starting classes are still not represented in the DB. Hence, today the number of classes equals 204.

3 Subsystems of CrossLexica Primary Database

The most relevant item for the classification is the NV subsystem of the CrossLexica primary DB. It consists of a sequence of entries. Each entry is headed by a noun and contains from 1 to 248 lines with collocations of the complement type 'ruling verb—dependent title noun', where the complement noun case is implied by the verb. When necessary, a preposition stands between the verb (in infinitive) and the noun and then the preposition alone implies the case: $ruling\_verb_{\mathrm{INF}}$ [*preposition*] $noun_{CASE}$. In the primary DB, each $noun_{CASE}$ has the shape *~ending,* where ~ stands for the title noun stem. If the ending is as in the standard form, it may be omitted.

Additionally, the majority of entries include collocations with the title noun as the subject of a sentence and a verb in the 3rd person form as its predicate: *noun* $verb_{PERS}$. Russian subjects and predicates agree in gender and number, and this gives additional means for the classification testing, since nearly each class determines number and gender of the classified noun.

The following is an example of an NV subsystem entry:

```
pribežišče              'habitation'
  ~ iščetsja            '~ is searched'
  ~ najdeno             '~ is found'
  ~ predostavleno       '~ is given'
  byt' ~em              'to be ~'
  iskat' ~              'to search ~'
  najti ~               'to found ~'
  okazat'sja ~em        'to turn to be ~'
  predostavit' ~        'to give ~'
  stat' ~em             'to become ~'
```

The total number of entries in NV is 14,066, with the total number of collocations 319,118 (at the average 22.69 per entry). Among them 210,341 contain complement collocations (14.95 per entry), while the rest contain predicate collocations.

There are several other large subsystems in the primary DB playing a minor role in the classification.

The NN subsystem contains entries with a title noun and collocations consisting of other nouns ruling the title one, directly or through a preposition (Cf. the left side of Table 1). Since a set of cases in such an entry differs from the entry with the same title in NV, this sometimes can reveal errors unseen in the NV subsystem. The total number of collocations in NN is 133,038 (13.60 per noun). However, the number of nouns in NN that are absent in NV does not exceed a hundred.

The AN subsystem contains entries with nouns and their possible adjectival modifiers (Cf. the right side of Table 1). Since Russian adjectives always agree with their ruling nouns in gender, number, and case, they sometimes help in detecting wrong classes. The nouns in AN that are absent in NV number about two thousands.

Table 1. Examples of entries in NN and AN subsystems

`kabina`	'cabin'	`alljuzii`	'allusions'
`vysota ~y`	'height of ~'	`mnogočislennye`	'multiple'
`dvertsy ~y`	'doors of ~'	`otdalennye`	'remote'
`dym v2 ~e`	'fume in ~'	`očevidnye`	'evident'
`zadymlenie v2 ~e`	'fumigation in ~'	`prijatnye`	'nice'
`razmery ~y`	'size of ~'	`smutnye`	'nebulous'

A large Synonymous Dictionary of CrossLexica contains 6,270 noun synsets (36% of the total size) with 5.73 synonyms per synset. Together with NV, NN, and AN subsystems, SD helps to manually test classification results *a posteriori* (the classifier outputs a humanly readable protocol for each of the subsystems). The number of nouns in SD that are absent in NV, NN, and AN is about four thousands.

There are about two hundreds animate names for different nationalities in the CrossLexica subsystem of semantic derivatives.

Therefore, the total number of different nouns to be classified in CrossLexica is now about 20,000. These are the nouns most used in Russian.

4 Classification Steps and Final Results

The classifier analyzes final letters of the standard (dictionary) wordform for a given noun. Let us denote these letters SFL(*i*), where SFL(1) is the ultimate letter, SFL(2) is the penultimate one, etc. SFL(1) alone is rarely sufficient for classification. More often than not the utility takes SFL(2), then SFL(3), etc., into account.

However indiscriminative final letters are frequent. E.g., the nouns *metel'* 'snow storm' and *motel'* 'motel' differ only in SFL(5), but they are of a different gender and their endings are the same only in nominative and accusative. If SFLs are ambiguous, the classifier takes into account prefixes (like *v*, *za*, *na* or *s*), prefixoides (like *avia*, *agro* or *anti*), short roots (like *bros*, *val*, *vod* or *grev*), suffixes (like *ist*, *ism* or *ščik*), suffixoides (like *ved*, *fob* or *fil*) or whole words divided into groups with the same SFLs and declension class.

Our main goal was to somehow minimize the total amount of lexical and morphological information used by the classifier, i.e. to diminish both the data and the programming logic directly addressing the data. Minimization of the runtime was a side issue, but we preferred to make first the comparisons with strings more commonly used in texts. To minimize the data, we took into account that in Russian:

- Animate nouns are less numerous than inanimate (up to four times, depending on the compared classes);
- Feminine plural nouns that could be implicated by their SFLs with masculine plural nouns are rarer.

Hence the tables with animate masculine singular and feminine plural nouns prevail among the classifier data. The lists of animate masculine singular classes store more than 1200 entries, and the lists of inanimate feminine plural classes store more than 500 entries. All the other lists are considerably shorter, even if numerous. For example, the lists of as many as 19 classes comprise only one noun (*put', lev, zajac, rot, led, lob...*).

With all these considerations, we have divided nouns to two large types: validated and correctable. The division is not strictly implied by the declension classes, but animate masculine singular and feminine plural nouns are mainly qualified as validated.

The nouns of the validated type are classified with certainty, since available information about them is sufficient in the classifier, and we usually omitted homonymous nouns among them. The comparison of endings for nouns in the CrossLexica DB with those required by the validated classes must have tested the typist who had entered collocations rather than the classes themselves. Sometimes the errors revealed necessitated the introduction of a new class. The **validated** nouns comprise about 59% in the NV subsystem (cf. Table 2).

The nouns of the correctable type are classified transitorily, since available context-free information is considered insufficient. Therefore, their consecutive testing against the collocations in the CrossLexica DB is crucial.

If there is no contradiction between transitory classification and the DB content, the nouns are considered **accepted**. They comprise about 41% of all nouns in NV. Together with the validated type they comprise 99.65% of the nouns that are classified at the outset.

Table 2. Noun types considered in classification

Noun Type	Amount	Percentage	Examples
Validated	8282	58.88	*most* 'bridge'; *akter* 'actor'
Accepted	5731	40.77	*potexa* 'fun'; *kupanija* 'baths'
Animated	37	0.26	$agent_2$ 'spy'; rak_2 'lobster'
Feminized	1	0.01	$pary_2$ 'pairs'
Masculinized	10	0.07	$banki_1$ 'banks'; $belki_2$ 'proteins'
Accentuated	1	0.01	*štyk-nož* 'sword bayonet'
Hard-corrected	4	0.03	$vina_2$ 'vines'; $glava_2$ 'chief'
Total	14066	100.00	

If, for a given noun, some contradictions between the available endings and those required by the transitory class are found in the database, attempts are made to amend the situation. This can be applied for any newly acquired noun, but proves to be absolutely vital when the noun has several senses pertaining to diverse classes.

When accusative ending(s) of a noun contradicts with that required by the transitory assigned class, a corresponding animate class is searched in a special table, and it is taken as the finally assigned class. For example, for both $agent_1$ 'substance' and $agent_2$ 'human', transitory class 1 is assigned, but since for $agent_2$ the collocation *nadejat'sja na agenta̲* 'to rely on the agent' is in the DB with the ending *a* contradicting the class 1, the corresponding animate class 2 is taken. Such changes to **animated** nouns proved to be necessary in 0.26% of the total vocabulary (cf. Table 2).

When contradictions are in the genitive endings, the tests are of two types. If the gender of the noun is transitorily plural masculine, an attempt is made to '**feminize**' it. E.g., both $pary_1$ 'vapor' and $pary_2$ 'pairs' have transitory class 86, but the collocation *izbegat' par* 'avoid the pairs' with an empty ending suggests changing $pary_2$ to class 90. If the gender of the noun is transitorily plural feminine, an attempt is made to '**masculinize**' it. E.g., both $belki_1$ 'squirrels' and $belki_2$ 'proteins' are assigned first with class 42, but then the collocation *sintezirovat' na osnove belkov* 'to synthesize based on proteins' suggests changing $belki_2$ to class 37.

When contradictions are in the instrumental endings, the change of the transitory classes to those giving accentuated endings is attempted. There exists also a small group of nouns for which number should be changed (**hard-corrected** in Table 2). E.g., both $vina_1$ 'blame' and $vina_2$ 'vines' are of transitory class 6, but nearly all the endings of $vina_2$ contradict this hypothesis, so it is re-assigned with class 12.

The total percentage of automatically corrected nouns in the NV subsystem is now very low (0.35%), and so far we have no classification errors after tests by means of this subsystem. However, the long history of replenishing the CrossLexica DB appeals to caution in our evaluations of the future. For example, in any moment a new animate noun with unknown morphs can appear in DB collocations without the accusative expressed in an explicit way, i.e. with the preposition *v* 'into', *na* 'onto', *za* 'behind' or *pod* 'under'. In such a case the newcomer is given an inanimate class until the next replenishing of DB or a manual revision of the classifier source.

The classifier program is a module in Turbo Pascal consisting of 3158 text lines. The size of the corresponding part of the *exe* module is ca. 42.8 KB. If we consider that a morphological dictionary for 20,000 nouns might occupy more than 160 KB, the dictionary-free representation of noun morphology is nearly four times more compact.

5 Conclusions

A noun classifying utility for a very large DB of Russian collocations and WordNet-like semantic links was developed. It determines correctly the declension class of each noun included into the primary DB and does not need any morphological dictionary from outside. All necessary morphological and lexical information, e.g. about animateness or gender of nouns that determine declension, is built into the utility.

The classes of about 59% of all nouns are guaranteed to be correct, while nearly all the rest 41% are also correct, but first considered transitory, since in rare cases the classifier can fail in its task. The main reason is that various senses of the same noun can belong to different classes (human *agent* and *agent* as substance decline differently), meanwhile no context-free classifier distinguishes senses. Other errors can be implied by unknown animate nouns in collocations to be acquired in the future.

For this reason the results of the classification are tested by another utility that compares the endings implied by the classification and those occurred for the same noun among the collocations in the DB. The final tests verify the non-guaranteed nouns and show that only 0.35% of the total noun set have some contradictions in case endings. The preliminary assigned classes with the revealed faults are then automatically corrected, without any alert messages.

In total, the classifier developed was tested against more than 20,000 nouns in the collocation DB that was employed. These nouns are the most used in Russian. The classifier is about four times more compact than any third-party morphological dictionary for the same set of nouns. It is slowly evolves with the database it serves to and thereby is permanently tuned to unknown words, usually automatically but from time to time manually. It can classify any type of Russian nouns that is already known to it.

The proposed 'built-in' method of morphological classification is equally applicable to other languages with declinable nouns, e.g. to other Slavic or Ugro-Finnic languages.

References

1. Belonogov, G.G., *et al.* Algorithm of multi-step morphological analysis of Russian words (in Russian). *Nauchno-Tekhnicheskaya Informatsiya* (NTI), Ser. 2, 1983, No. 1, p. 6-10.
2. Bolshakov, I.A. Getting One's First Million…Collocations. *Lecture Notes in Computer Science*, No. 2945, Springer, 2004, p. 229-242.
3. Gelbukh, A.F. An effectively implementable model of morphology of an inflective language (in Russian). *Nauchno-Tekhnicheskaya Informatsiya* (NTI), Ser. 2, 1992, No. 1, p. 24-31; http://www.gelbukh.com/CV/Publications/1992/NTI-Morph-model.htm.
4. Gelbukh, A., G. Sidorov. Approach to construction of automatic morphological analysis systems for inflective languages with little effort. *Lecture Notes in Computer Science,* No. 2588, Springer, 2003, p. 215–220.
5. Mitkov, R. (Ed.). *The Oxford Handbook of Computational Linguistics*. Oxford University Press, 2003.

Discourse Segmentation of German Written Texts

Harald Lüngen, Csilla Puskás,
Maja Bärenfänger, Mirco Hilbert, and Henning Lobin

Justus-Liebig-Universität Gießen
FB 05 - Applied and Computational Linguistics, Otto-Behaghel-Str. 10 D
{luengen,puskas}@uni-giessen.de

Abstract. Discourse segmentation is the division of a text into minimal discourse segments, which form the leaves in the trees that are used to represent discourse structures. A definition of elementary discourse segments in German is provided by adapting widely used segmentation principles for English minimal units, while considering punctuation, morphology, sytax, and aspects of the logical document structure of a complex text type, namely scientific articles. The algorithm and implementation of a discourse segmenter based on these principles is presented, as well an evaluation of test runs.

1 Introduction

In one subproject of the DFG research group *Text-technological modelling of information*, a discourse parser for a complex text type, i.e. scientific articles, is being developed. Discourse parsing according to Rhetorical Structure Theory (RST, [1]) deals with automatically assigning a text a hierarchical (tree) structure marking *discourse segments* (text spans) and functional-argumentative relations such as BACKGROUND, CONCESSION, and CONTRAST between them. Most discourse relations are binary, and one of the arguments has the status of being a *nucleus* (the more salient piece of information according to the author's intentions) while the other one is the *satellite* (containing supporting information that can potentially be omitted). Discourse segments can be complex or elementary, the latter being the minimal propositional units at the leaves of a discourse tree. The segmentation of an input document into elementary discourse segments is the first step in the discourse parsing process, cf. [2]. In our parsing architecture, this step is performed by a preprocessing component, a discourse segmenter. This paper introduces the discourse segmenter, i.e. is about how the minimal units of discourse should be defined for the relevant language (German), and how they are automatically recognised in text documents.

2 Requirements

What is an elementary discourse segment? In many systems based on RST, the definition is that of an *elementary discourse unit* (EDU) which seems to have

T. Salakoski et al. (Eds.): FinTAL 2006, LNAI 4139, pp. 245–256, 2006.

been introduced by Marcu, e.g. "*[e]dus* are defined functionally as clauses or clause-like units that are unequivocally the NUCLEUS or SATELLITE of a rhetorical relation that holds between two adjacent spans of text" [3]. This definition includes types of main and subordinate clauses, but also certain phrase types. The phrase *in spite of the bad weather conditions*, for example, is an EDU because the preposition *in spite of* introduces a CONCESSION relation between two propositions just like the subordinating conjunction *although.*

This definition of EDUs has been operationalised in terms of a set of criteria relating to English punctuation and grammar and has been applied to the segmentation and manual RST annotation of a large corpus of newspaper articles by Carlson and Marcu [4]. EDUs have subsequently also been used in the discourse parsers proposed in [5], [6], and [7].

We work with a different application scenario, text type, and language than previous approaches to automated discourse segmentation such as [2], [5], and [8]. For the development of our discourse parser and segmenter we use a corpus of 47 German scientific articles in the discipline of linguistics from the journal *Linguistik Online*[1]. The discourse parser is to be used in a hypertext system that supports students in the explorative and selective reading of scientific articles, based on highlighting text structure and on providing automatically generated link lists to different structural elements that contain rhetorically salient parts of the text. Articles chosen by the students themselves shall be automatically analysed by the discourse parser and annotated with an RST structure. Thus, the definition of a minimal unit of discourse is guided by the question whether it will be part of a discourse relation where the nucleus is semantically independent enough so that the satellite can be realised as a separate hypertext unit.

Although we take the methodology to define EDUs as introduced in [4] as a model, we have chosen not to adopt the term *EDU* itself since in several respects we deviate from the definition of English EDUs. Our criteria for segmenting a German text into elementary discourse *segments* (EDSs) refer to the following levels of information: a) logical document structure, b) punctuation, and c) morphology and syntax, including lexical discourse markers.

2.1 EDSs Induced by Logical Document Structure

The logical structure of the documents in our corpus, i.e. their hierarchical division in sections, titles, paragraphs etc. is annotated according to the so-called DOC annotation scheme which was developed in co-operation with a partner project. It comprises about 60 elements from the DocBook DTD [9] plus 14 additional elements for scientific articles such as `<caption>` as well as XHTML elements, integrated in one XML schema using namespace technology. Our segmenter expects a text plus its DOC annotation as input.[2]

The textual content of certain DOC elements shall directly correspond to an EDS (Table 1 shows some). Some of them, e.g. `<blockquote>`, `<blockemphasis>`,

---

[1] http://www.linguistik-online.de/

[2] In later stages of the project, a tool to convert other document formats to DOC will be developed.

Table 1. Elementary discourse segments according to the DOC annotation layer

DOC Element	Semantics
`<title>`	The title of the whole article, or of sections
`<programlisting>`	Code
`<bibliomixed>`	An entry in the bibliography
`<glossterm>`	A term in a definition list
`<ackno>`	Acknowledgments
`<blockquote>`	A quotation that is set apart from the running text
`<blockemphasis>`	Text that is set apart from the running text
`<footnote>`	Text in a footnote
`<log:mediaobject>`	(Empty elements containing) figures, i.e. images or diagrams
`<log:caption>`	The caption of a table, or a figure
`<log:tgroup>`	The body of a table

and `<footnote>`, may contain text that could potentially be further segmented by the punctuational and grammatical criteria. In view of the explorative reading scenario sketched above, however, we want them to always correspond to EDSs. We think that this specification makes sense for other languages and application scenarios, too.

2.2 EDSs Induced by Grammar and Punctuation

In the following, the main types of EDSs according to grammatical and punctuational criteria are formulated independently of the representation of grammatical analysis produced by the syntactic parser that we employ in the segmenter.

1. *Main clauses:* all simplex main clauses form an EDS. Main clauses are separated from other segments by punctuation, and/or coordinating conjunctions. Example: *[Die schwedische Kolonisation dauerte über sog. 600 Jahre,] [und zur selben Zeit sind Handwerker und Kaufleute aus dem ganzen Ostseeraum nach Finnland gezogen.]*[3]
2. *Modal subclauses:* modal subordinate clauses (marked by a modal subordinating conjunction), including modal infinitival constructions (marked by *ohne zu* or *um zu*). Example: *[Es ist auch üblich, dass man zu Hause sowohl Finnisch als auch Schwedisch redet,] [da Ehen oft über die Sprachgrenze hinweg geschlossen werden.]*
3. *Coordinated clauses:* Only in coordinations of the categories S, $\overline{\text{S}}$, and VP are the coordinated parts EDSs. Thus the subject or a subject plus a grammatical auxiliary may be elliptified in an EDS; this is parallel to the definitions for English in [4]. Example: *[Das Land gehörte 600 Jahre lang zu dem schwedischen Reich] [und wurde im Jahre 1809 ein autonomes Grossherzogtum unter dem russischen Zaren.]* We additionally include cases where units consisting of Subject + Complement are coordinated, i.e. in these cases a verb may

[3] Unless otherwise stated, the examples given are taken from [10].

be elliptified in a resulting EDS. Example: *[Ein Drittel von ihnen wohnt in Ostrobothnia (...) an der Westküste des Landes,] [die anderen in Südfinnland und auf den Åland-Inseln.]*

4. *Embedded segments:* embedded segments are segments marked by punctuation (brackets, dashes, or commas) which disrupt other EDSs, and which themselves are EDSs. Exception: Brackets that contain only figures (e.g. *(1999)*) are not segmented. Example: *[Problematisch ist jedoch, dass in Finnland mehrere samische Sprachen [(Nordsamisch, Skoltsamisch und Enaresamisch)] gesprochen werden.]* Note: Embedded segments are not internally segmented.
5. *Quotations* that are delimited by quotation marks and are introduced by reporting verbs. Note: Quotations shall *not* be internally segmented. Example: *["Ein Kind hatte im Spielzeugladen eine Wunschliste hinterlegt. Ich war froh, dass noch ein Aufziehauto für 3,50 Euro zu vergeben war",] [berichtet Rolfs.]*[4] Exception: Quotations that are built into running text without attributional constructions are not separated at all, i.e. in these cases the quotation marks are simply ignored, and segment boundaries are assigned as usual.
6. *Clausal complements of reporting verbs* such as (*meinen, sagen, feststellen*) in connection with a citation or quotation (inducing the rhetorical relation of ATTRIBUTION, cf. [4]). Example: *[Allardt (2000:8) meint], [dass die Einstellung während der letzten Jahrzehnten sich positiv entwickelt hat.]*
7. *Clausal complements and relative clauses preceded by adverbials:* Clausal complements of verbs or nouns, or relative clauses that are preceded by a *discourse marking adverbial* such as *nämlich, namentlich, besonders, insbesondere, d.h., vozugsweise.* Example: *[Das Ergebnis stimmt mit einer ziemlich allgemein verbreiteten Auffassung überein,] [nämlich dass das Sprachprogramm der finnischen Schulen allzu schmal ist.]*
8. *Prepositional phrases of attribution*, i.e. one of the prepositions *nach, laut, gemäß* + a named entity, or a pronoun referring to a named entity, in connection with a citation or quotation. Example: *[Nach Allardt] (...)][hängt dieses damit zusammen, dass die Finnischsprachigen daran gewöhnt sind, mit den Finnlandschweden Finnisch zu sprechen.]*
9. *Appositives.* Appositives are NPs that can be used postnominally as supplements to NPs, with which they mostly agree in number and case. Appositions sometimes start with a discourse-marking adverbial, too.[5] Example: *[Dazu hat das Land seit 1995 drei offizielle Minderheitssprachen,] [Samisch, Romani und Gebärdensprache.]*
   Appositives frequently occur as embedded segments.
10. *PPs that are separated by a comma.* These are similar to the "discourse-salient phrases" in [4], only we do not inventorise a list of strong discourse cues but define every adverbial PP that is separated from the rest of the clause by a comma to be an EDS. Since PPs are not usually separated by

[4] This example is taken from the newspaper article [11].

[5] Cf. *grammis - das grammatische Informationssystem des Instituts für deutsche Sprache*, `http://hypermedia.ids-mannheim.de/index.html`.

commas, the use of a comma in such cases can be considered a strong discourse cue employed by the author. Example: *[Gleichzeitig entstand aber eine Gegenbewegung,] [für das Bewahren der schwedischen Sprache in Finnland.]*

With EDSs defined in the above fashion, note that the following clause types are *not* EDSs:

- Clausal subjects and clausal complements of verbs and nouns, (with the exception of the attributional complements described under 6. and 7.)..
- Restricting relative clauses. Following [1], we do not regard restricting relative clauses as EDSs because unlike other satellites, they contribute to the semantic interpretation of their head noun, and in that way can never be omitted. This treatment is in contrast to [4].
- Conditional clauses: *wenn..., dann..., je..., desto* etc. Unlike in other so-called mononuclear constructions, the nucleus in constructions related by the CONDITION relation seems not comprehensible without the satellite, thus we regard them as together forming one EDS. This treatment is also in contrast to [4].
- Proportional clauses, i.e. clauses combined by comparative connectives such as *mehr... als, weniger... als, so (ADJ)... wie.* Unlike in [4], such a construction is not split into separate EDSs, because neither of its parts seems more salient than the other in terms of nuclearity.

A consequence of denying certain clause types the status of EDS (most notably complemental clauses and restricting relative clauses) is that potential EDSs that are subordinate to such non-segmentable clauses cannot be EDSs, either. Consider a sentence from [10], the clause structure of which is indicated by labelled bracketing:

> ${}_{S}$*[Es ist aber symptomatisch,* ${}_{\bar{S}}$*[dass alle Streitigkeiten sofort vergessen wurden,* ${}_{\bar{S}}$*[als eine gemeinsame Gefahr von AuSSen drohte,* ${}_{NP}$*[d.h. Russifizierung in der Periode 1890-1917 und zwei Kriege in den Jahren 1939-1945]]]].*

According to criterion 2 above, an EDS boundary could potentially be introduced between *wurden,* and *als*, because it is the beginning of a modal subclause. At the same time, no boundary is to be inserted at the previous subordination, i.e. between *symptomatisch,* and *dass*, because an ordinary sentential subject is starting. This means that the correct segment to attach the second subclause to will not be available in the discourse structure, and attaching it to the remaining matrix clause + first subclause EDS would yield a descriptively inadequate structure as in Fig. 1.[6] Thus, we introduce a general exception pertaining to all segmentable clause types as listed above:[7]

- Any potential EDS shall *not* be segmented if it is coordinate or subordinate to a clause that is *not* segmented according to the criteria above, either.

[6] For drawing RST trees we employ the tool sketched in [12].

[7] Note that from the segmentation criteria suggested in [4], the same problem arises, albeit in fewer cases.

Listing 1.1. XML format SEG for segmented text

```
<cds type="para" docIdref="i1119">
  <sds id="s87">
    <eds id="e149">Die Frage der beiden Nationalsprachen ist für die finnische Bevölkerung
       so gut wie eine Selbstverständlichkeit,
    </eds>
    <eds id="e150"> aber vor 150 Jahren war die Sprachfrage ein heikles Thema.
    </eds>
  </sds>
  <sds id="s88">
    <eds id="e151">Es hing mit dem Nationalitätsgedanken zusammen,
    </eds>
    <eds id="e152"> obwohl Finnland damals zu Russland gehörte.
   </eds>
 </sds> [...]
</cds>
```

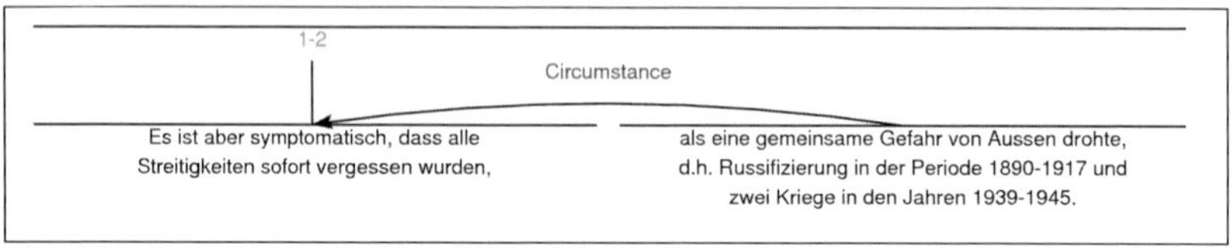

Fig. 1. Example of a potential segment boundary in a subordinate clause leading to a descriptively inadequate discourse structure

2.3 XML Format for Segmented Text

We store a discourse-segmented text in an XML annotation layer called SEG, where EDSs are contained in an element called <`eds`>. But not only EDSs are marked, additionally there are <`sds`> elements for SDSs (*sentential discourse segments*), i.e. text segments that correspond to sentences, as well as <`cds`> elements for CDSs (*complex discourse segments*), i.e. text segments that correspond to elements on the DOC layer. After having been identified by the segmenter, their purpose is to serve as input to and to guide the parsing cycles in the discourse parser, cf. [13]. Listing 1.1 shows an example of text annotated according to the SEG format.[8]

3 Algorithm

Segmentation is performed in three major phases corresponding to the identification of CDS, SDS, and EDS boundaries, cf. Figure 2. The result annotation layer SEG is constructed in a top-down fashion in the three phases. The basic idea for EDS recognition is to first determine all *potential* EDS boundaries by looking at punctuation and coordination, and then to successively remove those that can be established as non-EDS-marking by looking at their syntactic features.

[8] An extract from [10].

The segmentation component is implemented in Perl, using the LibXML and LibXSLT libraries to process the XML input document. Each phase is realised in one perl module. During the segmentation process, the syntactic parser *Machinese Syntax* from Connexor Oy, is repeatedly called. It provides output in XML ("CNX" in Fig. 2), containing morphological and syntactic tags for each token, as well as dependency relations between words based on Functional Dependency Grammar [14].

Phase 1: CDS recognition. The elements of the DOC annotation layer are all straightforwardly transformed into `<cds>` elements, still distinguished by a `@type` attribute specified e.g. for the value `para`, `sect`, `table`, or `title`. The specification `@type="eds"` marks those `<cds>` that at the same time correspond to EDSs according to Table 1.

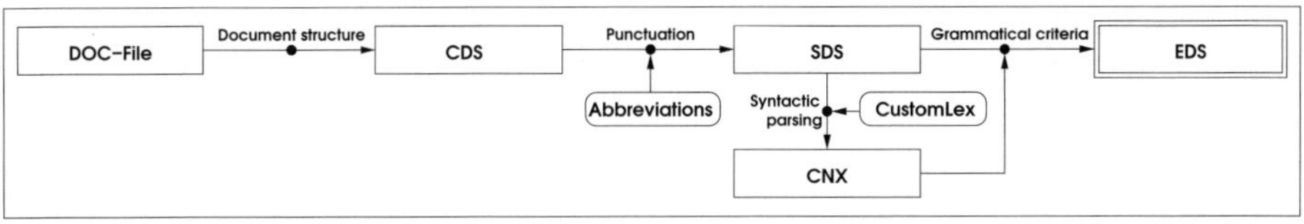

Fig. 2. Three phases of segment identification

Phase 2: SDS recognition and syntactic parsing. In the second phase, the textual content of those `<cds>` elements with `@type="para"` is further segmented. By using punctuation and a list of stop words (abbreviations), the sentence boundaries are determined and `<sds>` tags are added to the SEG annotation layer. Sentence boundaries inside quotations and parentheses as described in criteria 4 and 5 in Sect. 2.2 as well in certain DOC elements (Sect. 2.1) are ignored. Then for each SDS obtained, the syntactic parser *Machinese Syntax* is called. The reason for not doing this in a preprocessing step over the whole document is that the parser has its own internal rules to detect sentence and paragraph boundaries which may contradict the boundaries determined here via the DOC annotation layer.

Phase 3: EDS recognition. In phase 3, elementary discourse segments (EDS) are determined according to the grammatical criteria presented in Sect. 2.2. To this end, the segmenter accesses morphosyntactic information from the syntactic parser, i.e. POS-tags and information about the finiteness of verbs.

To identify EDS boundaries within an SDS, firstly, all *potential EDS boundaries* are marked and numbered. Potential boundaries are commas (except commas in numbers such as in *27,8%*), the lexical discourse markers *und* and *oder* as well as parentheses. Subsequently, boundary markers within parentheses as well as within quotation marks are deleted according to criteria 4 and 5.

At the beginning of the grammatical analysis, the POS tags of a sentence are used to build up phrasal information (NP and PP) and to store it in a string variable called $ic associated with the current SDS.[9] During the analysis, the potential boundary markers are one after the other tested for being a non-boundary, that is, whether they mark enumerations, relative clauses, clausal subjects and complements, proportional clauses, and infinitival complements. Only if all tests are negative, a boundary will be preserved.

An enumeration is a coordination of PPs, NPs, or APs. The recognition of such coordinations is achieved by looking at the variable $ic as explained above. From $ic = "P ART N und ř1ř ART N", simple phrases ($ic = "P NP und ř1ř NP"), then complex phrases ($ic = "PP und ř1ř NP") before and after the conjunction are generated and each time compared with each other. If the POS or phrasal categories match, the potential boundary is identified as enumerative and the actual boundary flag for the respective marker is set to 0.

Clausal subjects and complements start with the subordinating conjunctions *dass*, *ob*, or a wh-pronoun, or are infinitival constructions starting with *zu*. Their identification is combined with a check for attributional constructions which form the matrix clauses of clausal complements but are still EDSs according to criterion 5.

The results of the tests (value 0 or 1 for *boundary* or *non-boundary*) are stored in a complex data structure associated with the current SDS. After the results of all tests for one SDS are available, these are evaluated and actual non-boundary markers are removed in a function called `ignore()`. The order in which the results are evaluated is crucial for the determination of EDSs. The whole process of evaluation (the function `remove-marker()`) of the test results is shown in Figure 3. First, those markers that are associated with the conjunctions *und* and *oder* are removed if the conjunctors were only enumerative. Then, those markers that are associated with a comma are evaluated in order (see Figure 3). If the current comma marker is associated with a sentential subject or complement, or a proportional clause, or an infinitival complement, `ignore()` is called, removing the marker itself and all other markers up to the following comma marker. If the current comma marker is associated with an enumeration, only the current marker is removed. If it is associated with a relative clause, then not only all markers up to the next comma marker ($next) are removed, but also the marker after that one. If $next marked an enumeration or a relative clause, $next is re-calculated, and `ignore()` is called again. This procedure represents a default solution for the general exception sketched in 2.2, i.e. currently all clauses following a main clause and a sub-clause EDS are treated as being sub-subordinated. After this evaluation of tests for potential EDS boundaries, each EDS established so far is checked for further internal boundaries brought about by EDSs below the clause level, i.e. phrases. Currently only attributional PPs are checked for (e.g. *nach Allardt*).

---

[9] Alternatively, phrasal information could be derived from the dependency structure information in the parser output. But since the POS information seems more reliable and is easier to use, for the time being we use only POS information.

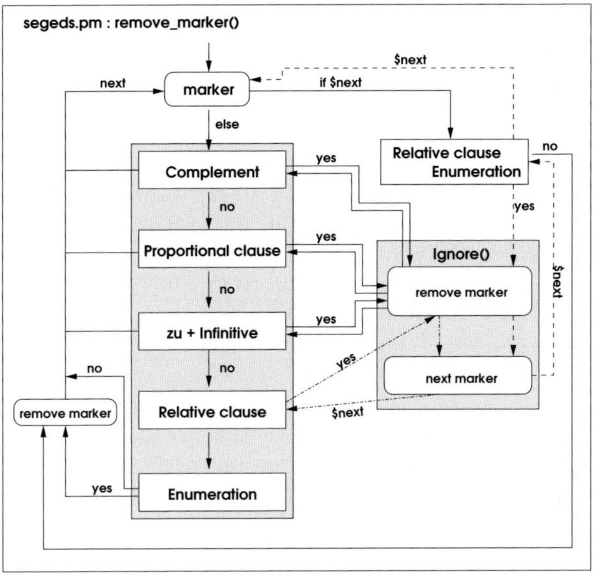

Fig. 3. The function `remove-marker()`

4 Results and Discussion

We performed test runs of the segmenter on six different texts. Four of them were scientific articles from our corpus (A-003, A-010, A-040, and A-023). To evaluate the performance on other text types as well we additionally segmented a web-published article on hypertext (L) and one newspaper article (Z). Manual segmentations of all six texts were provided by experts and served as "master" annotations containing the correct segmentations, against which precision and recall were then calculated. Table 2 gives statistics of the test texts as well as three groups of results of test runs.

The first group shows the performance of a baseline segmenter on all six texts. It executes CDS and SDS segmentation as described above and on top of that simply converts each comma into an EDS boundary. The second group shows the results of the segmenter applying the complete segmentation procedure as described in Sect. 3 to the texts. The final group shows the performance of pure sentence segmentation based on the CDS and SDS segmentation as described above, evaluated against the manually produced sentence segmentations of the six texts.

For all six texts, the performance of the fully informed EDS segmenter was significantly better than the baseline version. The SDS segmenter performed well in general, however text L additionally contained XHTML elements on the DOC layer, which the segmenter simply ignores, but which were considered boundary markers in the master segmentation (e.g. `<xhtml:br>`). This was the cause of many segmentation errors in text L.

Table 2. Results

	Texts	A-003	A-010	A-040	A-023	L	Z
Statistics	# wordforms	12323	2239	6560	5450	3138	1448
	# master eds	758	154	497	338	292	136
	# master sds	470	103	300	231	148	90
Baseline-EDS	% Precision	0.34	0.41	0.39	0.25	0.45	0.43
	% Recall	0.59	0.66	0.62	0.48	0.62	0.59
Segmenter-EDS	% Precision	0.80	0.82	0.78	0.60	0.74	0.76
	% Recall	0.80	0.88	0.77	0.67	0.66	0.80
Segmenter-SDS	% Precision	0.89	0.98	0.92	0.84	0.85	0.98
	% Recall	0.93	0.99	0.92	0.90	0.74	0.99

Text A-003 is the longest text and the one that we inspected most closely when implementing and debugging the segmenter. The texts A-010 and Z were not previously inspected in that way but recall is equally good or even better for them.

The EDS segmenter still has some shortcomings regarding the implementation of some of the segmentation criteria, which were considered not too significant for text A-003. In some texts, however, they produce a higher fraction of errors. Sometimes, for example, the EDS segmenter does not recognise attributional constructions, firstly because not all possible verbs of attribution are inventorised yet, and secondly because even for humans it is sometimes difficult to distinguish attributional constructions from non-attributional ones according to criterion 6. Likewise, the segmenter sometimes does not recognise appositives (criterion 9) well because they can be confused with NP enumerations. In the sentence *Dazu hat das Land seit 1995 drei offizielle Minderheitssprachen, Samisch, Romani und Gebärdensprache*, for example, the first comma is a segment boundary separating the trailing appositive from the main clause. The second comma, however, marks only an enumeration of NPs. The problem is that NP-enumerations are identified by checking for consecutive NPs that agree in their case value, which also holds for appositives, i.e. such constructions are functionally ambiguous.

A second type of segmentation errors is caused by faulty analyses of the syntactic parser which tend to occur with very long and complex sentences. Some such errors could be avoided by tuning our segmenter accordingly. Relative pronouns, for example, are sometimes POS-tagged as determiners, so our implementation checks whether forms such as *der, die, den* are rather relative pronouns, by additionally looking at the POS tags in the context.

The principle of not segmenting certain sub-subordinated or sub-coordinated clauses as described in Sect. 2.2 has proven difficult to implement, because with multiple subordinations it is not uncommon that the output from the syntactic parser is already faulty. At the moment we have implemented a default strategy that regards every subclause following a subclause that was preceded by a main clause as sub-subordinated. Though this seems to cover the majority of cases, it is also the cause of several unidentified boundaries that affect recall figures.

A third type of error turned out to be an author's omission of commas or using too many commas. Several segmentation errors in text A-040 proved to be due to such mispunctuations. A solution could be to rely more systematically on lexical discourse markers as boundary signals as in [2], however for most texts we do not expect this to improve recall figures significantly.

5 Summary and Outlook

We presented an automatic discourse segmenter for German written text to be used in the framework of RST-based discourse parsing in a text-technological environment. We defined the notion of an elementary discourse segment (EDS) by adapting the widely used segmentation principles for English EDUs presented in [4] to German while also considering aspects of the document structure of a complex text type, namely scientific articles. Thus the criteria in defining our EDSs are based on logical document structure, syntax, and punctuation.

Unlike the discourse segmenters presented in [3] and [5], we employ a knowledge-based procedure that does not require a large amount of training data (which is not available for German). And unlike the segmenters presented in [3] and [6], we do not presuppose that an input text comes together with its correct syntactic analysis; instead we have integrated a syntactic parser that is used online in the segmentation process.

Our segmenter first performs a segmentation of CDS induced by elements of the logical document structure, then a segmentation of SDS based on logical document structure and punctuation. Subsequently, the syntactic parser is called for each SDS. EDS segmentation is then performed by marking the potential segment boundaries of an SDS and successively checking whether they are not actual segment boundaries, using the syntactic analyses. By first setting potential boundary markers and then eliminating the actual non-boundaries, we have considerably reduced the amount of analysis (i.e. the number of tests required in Phase 3) in comparison with the opposite strategy of directly establishing the actual EDS boundaries. A strength of our approach lies also in the separation of the syntax checks from the evaluation of their results in phase 3. It enables us to modify or extend segmentation criteria easily if desired.

The performance of our system (EDS and SDS segmentation) on three of the six texts used in the evaluation was slightly worse than that of the knowledge-based segmenter for English reported in [6] (79% overall recall), and our recall figures also remain lower than those reported for the statistical approach to discourse segmentation in [5] (85,4% recall of sentence-internal EDU boundaries). However, on account of our evaluation we reported several types of segmentation errors that can be remedied by further use of the syntactic analysis and that we will tackle in the near future to further improve the performance.

References

1. Mann, W.C., Thompson, S.A.: Rhetorical Structure Theory: Toward a functional theory of text organisation. Text **8**(3) (1988) 243–281
2. Marcu, D.: The Theory and Practice of Discourse Parsing and Summarization. MIT Press, Cambridge, MA (2000)

3. Marcu, D.: A decision-based approach to rhetorical parsing. In: Proceedings of the 37th annual meeting of the ACL, Maryland, Association for Computational Linguistics (1999) 365–372
4. Carlson, L., Marcu, D.: Discourse tagging reference manual. Technical report, Information Science Institute, Marina del Rey, CA (2001) ISI-TR-545.
5. Soricut, R., Marcu, D.: Sentence level discourse parsing using syntactic and lexical information. In: Proceedings of the Human Laanguage Technology and North American Association for Computational Linguistics Conference (HLT/NAACL), Edmonton, Canada (2003)
6. Le Thanh, H., Abeysinghe, G., Huyck, C.: Automated discourse segmentation by syntactic information and cue phrases. In: Proceedings of the IASTED International Conference on Artificial Intelligence and Applications (AIA 2004), Innsbruck, Austria (2004)
7. Sporleder, C., Lapata, M.: Discourse chunking and its application to sentence compression. In: Proceedings of the Human Language Technology Conference and the Conference on Empirical Methods in Natural Language Processing (HLT/EMNLP-05), Vancouver, Canada (2005)
8. Le Thanh, H., Abeysinghe, G., Huyck, C.: Generating discourse structures for written texts. In: Proceedings of COLING'04, Geneva, Switzerland (2004)
9. Walsh, N., Muellner, L.: DocBook: The Definitive Guide. O'Reilly (1999)
10. Saari, M.: Schwedisch als die zweite Nationalsprache Finnlands: Soziolinguistische Aspekte. Linguistik Online **7** (2000) `http://www.linguistik-online.de`.
11. Krohn, P.: Arm, ärmer, kind. Die Zeit **15** (2005) 27
12. O'Donnell, M.: RSTTool 2.4 – A markup tool for Rhetorical Structure Theory. In: Proceedings of the International Natural Language Generation Conference (INLG'2000), Mitzpe Ramon, Israel (2000) 253 – 256
13. Lobin, H., Bärenfänger, M., Hilbert, M., Lüngen, H., Puskàs, C.: Text parsing of a complex genre. In: Proceedings of the Conference on Electronic Publishing (ELPUB), Bansko, Bulgaria (2006) to appear
14. Tapanainen, P., Järvinen, T.: A non-projective dependency parser. In: Proceedings of the 5th Conference on Applied Natural Language Processing, Washington D.C., Association for Computational Linguistics (1997) 64–71

Document Clustering Based on Maximal Frequent Sequences

Edith Hernández-Reyes, Rene A. García-Hernández, J.A. Carrasco-Ochoa, and J.Fco. Martínez-Trinidad

National Institute for Astrophysics, Optics and Electronics
Luis Enrique Erro No.1 Sta. Ma. Tonantzintla, Puebla, México C.P. 72840
{ereyes, renearnulfo, ariel, fmartine}@inaoep.mx

Abstract. Document clustering has the goal of discovering groups with similar documents. The success of the document clustering algorithms depends on the model used for representing these documents. Documents are commonly represented with the vector space model based on words or n-grams. However, these representations have some disadvantages such as high dimensionality and loss of the word sequential order. In this work, we propose a new document representation in which the maximal frequent sequences of words are used as features of the vector space model. The proposed model efficiency is evaluated by clustering different document collections and compared against the vector space model based on words and n-grams, through internal and external measures.

1 Introduction

Document clustering is an important technique widely used in text mining and information retrieval systems [1]. Document clustering was proposed to increase the precision and recall of information retrieval systems. Recently, it has been used for browsing documents and generating hierarchies [2].

Document clustering consists in dividing a set of documents into groups. In a language-independent framework, the most common document representation is the vector space model based on words proposed by Salton in 1975 [3]. Here, every document is represented as a vector of features, where the features correspond to the different words of the document collection. Many works use the vector space model based on words as document representation [4] [5] [6]. However, a disadvantage of the vector space model based on words is the high dimensionality because a document collection might contain a huge amount of words. For example, the well-known Reuters-21578[7] document collection is not considered as a big collection but it contains around 38 thousand different words from 1.4 million words used in the whole collection. In consequence, there are some researches trying to reduce the dimensionality of the vector space model based on words. Another drawback of this representation is that it does not preserve the original order of the words. For example, documents like *"This text is concerned about find gold mining"* and *"Text mining is concerned about find gold text"* are treated as identical in this model, because both are represented with the same words without considering combinations of terms that appear in the document like *"text mining"* and *"gold mining"* which could help to distinguish them.

T. Salakoski et al. (Eds.): FinTAL 2006, LNAI 4139, pp. 257 – 267, 2006.

In a vector space framework, other common representation is based on using n consecutive words obtained from the document *i.e.* the well known n-gram model. In this case, each n-gram appearing in the document collection corresponds to one feature of the vector. However, the high dimensionality also is a disadvantage of the vector space model based on n-grams because the number of word combinations can be enormous. In the n-gram model, the 2-grams are commonly used like in [8] [9], using 1-gram corresponds to the model proposed by Salton.

In a vector space framework, an alternative text representation for document clustering is the employment of consecutive word sequences that are repeated frequently in a document. In this sense, a word sequence will be frequent if it appears at least β times. A maximal frequent sequence (MFS) is a sequence such that it is not contained (subsequence) in other frequent sequence. So, the MFS's are a compact representation of the frequent sequences.

Ahonen[10] developed the first algorithm to find sequential patterns in a document collection. Recently, the MFS's have been used by Doucet [11] in the document retrieval task, his algorithm finds the MFS's from a document collection too. Unlike Ahonen and Doucet algorithms, in [12] an algorithm to find efficiently the maximal consecutive frequent sequences of words but from a single document was proposed.

In this work we propose a document representation for document clustering using the vector space model based on the MFS's obtained from each document in the collection. In this case, the sequential order of the words is preserved which could help to distinguish among documents with almost the same words but in different order. With this proposed document representation we have a smaller size of the vector based on MFS's than using words or n-grams. In order to test the proposed document representation, some document clustering experiments were done with two document collections: the English document collection Reuters-21578 and the Spanish document collection Disasters; this last one contains news of natural disasters divided into four categories (forest, hurricane, inundation and drought). The quality obtained in the document clustering experiments, with the proposed representation, was compared against the one obtained with the other two representations, through internal and external clustering quality measures.

This paper is organized as follows. Section 2 describes the maximal frequent sequences. Section 3 presents the new document representation. Section 4 gives the methodology used in this work and the experimental results. Finally, in section 5 we present our conclusions and some directions for future work.

2 Maximal Frequent Sequences

The text of a document is expressed by words in a sequential order. Therefore, it could be useful to determine the consecutive word sequences that appear frequently in a document. Also, it is possible to determine which of the frequent sequences are not contained in any other frequent sequence *i.e.* which of them are maximal. In this proposal, the main focus is the set of MFS's because they are a compact representation of the frequent sequences.

The maximal frequent sequences are formally defined as follows [12]:

Definition 1. A sequence $P=p_1p_2...p_n$ is a subsequence of a sequence $S=s_1s_2...s_m$, denoted $P\subseteq S$, if there exists an integer $l\leq i$ such that $p_1=s_i, p_2=s_{i+1}, p_3=s_{i+2},...,p_n=s_{i+n-1}$

Definition 2. Let $X\subseteq S$ and $Y\subseteq S$ then X and Y are *mutually excluded* if X and Y do not share items *i.e.*, if ($x_n=s_i$ and $y_1=s_j$) or ($y_n=s_i$ and $x_1=s_j$) then $i<j$.

Definition 3. Given a text T expressed as a sequence and a user-specified threshold β. A sequence S is *frequent* in T, if it is contained at least β times in T in a mutually excluded way.

Definition 4. A frequent sequence is *maximal* if it is not a subsequence of any other frequent sequence.

Table 1 presents an example of MFS's for two documents with β=2

Table 1. MFS's for two documents

d_1= *bank said had provided money market further billion assistance bank afternoon session brings billion bank total help compares revised shortage forecast money market.* **MFS's** = bank, money market, billion
d_2= *bank billion provided money market late assistance system brings bank total help compares money market latest forecast shortage system today.* **MFS's** = bank, money market, system

The MFS's presents some important characteristics. First, they keep the sequential order of words; it means the MFS's do not lose the sequential order of the text. Second, the length of the MFS's is not previously determined; it is determined by the document content. And third, the MFS's can be obtained independently of the language of the documents.

In this work, the algorithm proposed in [12] was used to obtain the MFS's of a document.

3 Vector Space Model Based on MFS's

Common document representations such as vector of words or n-grams have some disadvantages like high dimensionality and loss of important information from the sequential order of the original text. In order to reduce these drawbacks we propose a new document representation using MFS's. This representation, based on the vector space model, consists in obtaining the MFS's from each document and using them to build the vector (figure 1). Every MFS founded is associated to one element of the vector. Therefore, each document of the collection is represented by an M dimensional vector; M is the number of different MFS's founded in all the documents of the collection. The document collection is represented by an NxM matrix where N is the number of documents.

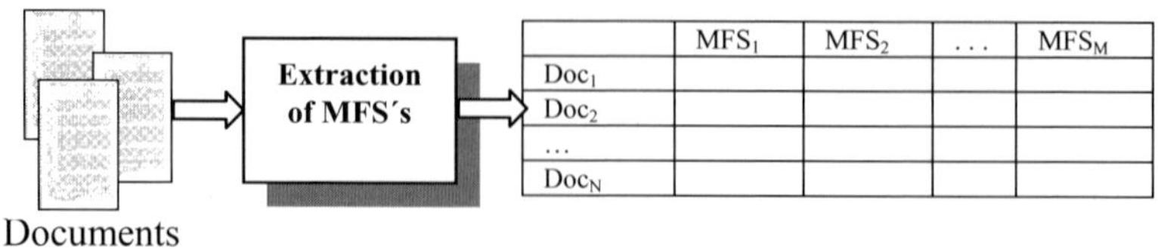

Fig. 1. Proposed representation

Following the idea of the vector space model, the Boolean and TF-IDF weighting are used to assign a weight to each MFS in the vector, both term weightings are widely used for the vector based on words. In Boolean weighting, each MFS receives 1 as weight if it occurs in the document and 0 otherwise. In TF-IDF weighting, the weight of each MFS in the vector for a document *T* is the product of its frequency in *T* and the *log* of its inverse frequency in the collection. Also we propose to use the length of the MFS's as term weighting in order to allow the comparison taking advantage of the size of the MFS's since if two documents are similar in large sequences they must be more similar than if they are similar in short sequences.

Considering the example presented in table 1, we built the vector based on MFS's using the three different term weighting (figure 2).

Boolean term weighting

	bank	money market	billion	system
d_1	1	1	1	0
d_2	1	1	1	1

TF-IDF term weighting

	bank	money market	billion	system
d_1	0	0	0,602	0
d_2	0	0	0,301	0,602

Length term Weighting

	bank	money market	billion	system
d_1	1	2	1	0
d_2	1	2	1	1

Fig. 2. Term weighting

Note that in our example both documents talk about the same topic and we need only 4 MFS's to represent them. In case of the vector based on words, the vector would have 22 elements to represent the documents without considering stop words.

4 Experimentation

In order to test the proposed representation we used the Reuters-21578 and Natural Disasters collection which are written in English and Spanish, respectively. Table 2 and 3 present a description of the data used for the experiments done with Reuters-21578 and Natural Disasters collections. For each experiment, the name of the used classes, number of documents and the number of required clusters are shown. Also, the number of words, n-grams and MFS's with and without stop words (SW) from each experiment, are provided.

Table 2. Data used for the experiments with the Reuters-21578 collection

	Exp. 1	Exp. 2	Exp. 3	Exp. 4
Classes	Acq, earn	Money, acq, earn	Acq, earn, crude	Gold,acq,trade,reserve,earn
Documents	100		120	253
Required clusters	2	3	3	5
Words with SW	2456	3195	3952	5768
2-grams with SW	7697	9128	9541	17534
MFS's with SW	1023	1635	1864	2746
Words without SW	1546	2354	2541	4294
2-grams without SW	3357	7652	7768	12927
MFS's without SW	484	726	821	1693

Table 3. Data used for the experiment with the Natural Disasters collection

	Exp. 1	Exp. 2	Exp. 3	Exp. 4	Exp. 5	Exp. 6
Classes	Forest, hurricane	Forest, inundation	Drought, Inundation	Forest, earth-quake, inundation	Forest, drought, inundation	Forest, drought, hurricane
Documents	80	80	80	120	120	120
Required clusters	2	2	2	3	3	3
Words with SW	4767	4737	4896	6118	6226	5637
2-grams with SW	12685	12613	12726	18462	18742	16686
MFS's with SW	1513	1391	1745	2014	4593	1797
Words without SW	4611	4583	4825	5963	6059	4593
2-grams without SW	12608	12329	12846	16574	17126	15549
MFS's without SW	944	914	953	1286	2652	1133

4.1 Methodology

In all the experiments, the methodology showed in the figure 2 was used. We pre-processed the documents removing punctuation, number and special characters. As we can see in table 2 and table 3, some experiments were done removing stop-words too. Then, the vectors based on words, n-grams and MFS's were obtained. We only use 2-grams since it is the most common n-gram model. For extracting the MFS's, we have used the algorithm described in [12] taking β equal to 2 since it is the lowest threshold which produced longer MFS's. Boolean and TF-IDF weighting were used for the three representations. In addition, for the case of MFS's, the number of words of each MFS was used to weight the features of the vector in order to allow the comparison taking advantage of the size of the MFS's because being similar in big sequences is more important than in small sequences.

Documents were clustered with the k-means algorithm using the cosine similarity measure which is calculated with the next expression:

$$\cos(d_1, d_2) = \frac{d_1 \bullet d_2}{\|d_1\| \|d_2\|}$$

Finally, the clustering was evaluated with internal and external quality measures. Internal measures evaluate the internal cohesion and external separation of the

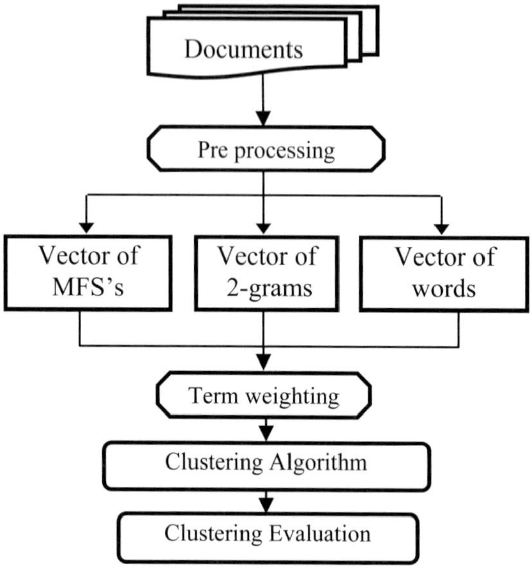

Fig. 3. Methodology of the experiments

resulting groups without using previous knowledge about the original classes of the collection. In this work, the global similarity [5] and the global silhouette (GS) were used as internal measures.

It is appropriate underline that in real clustering problems the original classes are unknown. On the other hand, the external measures are employed to evaluate the quality clustering by comparing the obtained groups against the previously defined classes, which have been determined by a human criterion. In this paper, total entropy and general F-measure [5] were used.

For the global silhouette, global similarity and general F-measure higher values represent better quality of the clusters. In the case of the total entropy, smaller values represent better quality.

The internal and external measures used in this work are described in table 4.

4.2 Results

The results of the experiments for Spanish and English are shown on tables 5-7 and 8-10, respectively. In these tables, the first column specifies the used document representation while the second column shows the term weighting used for each representation; the next columns provide the results of each experiment. For each experiment, the best results are highlighted.

For the experiments whit the Natural Disasters collection, table 5 shows the clustering quality, obtained by the three document representation, evaluated with the internal measures. We can observe that the vector of MFS's obtained clusters with higher internal cohesion and external separation than the groups obtained with the vector based on words or based on 2-grams. This shows that the vector model based on MFS's is a good option for representing documents. Also, we can observe that the highest clustering quality was obtained by the vector representation using MFS's with Boolean weights, and the smallest quality was obtained by the vector representation using words with TF-IDF term weighting.

Table 4. Internal and external measures for clustering quality

INTERNAL MEASURES

Silhouette value of the *i*th document $$s(i) = \frac{MIN(AVGD\_BETWEEN(i,k) - AVGD\_WITHIN(i))}{MAX(AVGD\_WITHIN(i), AVGD\_BETWEEN(i,k))}$$

AVGD_BETWEEN(i,k):average distance from the *i*-th document to all documents in other clusters.
AVGD_WHITHIN(i): average distance from the *i*-th0 document to the others documents in its own cluster.

Cluster Silhoutte $S_j = \sum_{i=1}^{|C_j|} s(i)$ $|C_j|$ = number of documents in cluster C_j

$$GlobalSilhoutte = \frac{1}{K}\sum_{j=1}^{K} S_j$$ K = number of clusters

$$GloabalSimilarity = \frac{\sum_{i=1}^{K} similarity(C_i)}{K}$$

where:
K = number of clusters
C_i = cluster i

$$\text{Similarity}(C_i) = \frac{1}{|C_i|^2}\sum_{\substack{d\in C_i\\ d'\in C_i}} \cos(d, d')$$

EXTERNAL MEASURES

$$GeneralFmeasure = \sum_{i=1}^{K}\left[\frac{|class_i|}{N}\max_{j=1..k}\{Fmeasure(i,j)\}\right]$$

where:
K = number of classes = number of clusters
$|class_i|$ = number of documents in the class i
N = total number of documents

$$\text{Fmeasure}(i,j) = \frac{2P_{ij}R_{ij}}{P_{ij} + R_{ij}}$$

P_{ij} = precision of class i with cluster j
R_{ij} = recall of class i with cluster j

$$TotalEntropy = \sum_{j=1}^{K}\frac{n_j * Entropy_j}{N}$$

where:
K = number of clusters
n_j = number of documents in cluster *i*
N = total number of documents

$$\text{Entropy}_j = -\sum_i p_{ij}\log_2(p_{ij})$$

p_{ij}= probability that a documents from the cluster *j* belongs to class *i*.

Table 5. Clustering quality evaluated with the internal measures

GLOBAL SILHOUETTE							
DOCUMENT REPRESENTATION	WEIGHT	FOREST HURRICANE	FOREST INUNDATION	DROUGHT INUNDATION	FOREST EARTHQUAKE HURRICANE	HURRICANE FOREST INUNDATION	HURRICANE-DROUGHT FOREST
Words	Boolean	0,064406	0,046008	0,042131	0,065106	0,0421860	0,050846
Words	TF-IDF	0,029597	0,018681	0,021302	0,035131	0,0248780	0,048958
2-grams	Boolean	0,076723	0,053462	0,041564	0,068349	0,0418521	0,062495
2-grams	TF-IDF	0,041634	0,029954	0,030108	0,045321	0,0232876	0,046352
MFS's	Boolean	0,129020	0,099217	0,091041	0,124080	0,0782930	0,095101
MFS's	TF-IDF	0,048859	0,034592	0,039286	0,061559	0,0406520	0,049190
MFS's	Length	0,114760	0,088918	0,078969	0,118960	0,0703230	0,084429
GLOBAL SIMILARITY							
DOCUMENT REPRESENTATION	WEIGHT	FOREST HURRICANE	FOREST INUNDATION	DROUGHT INUNDATION	FOREST EARTHQUAKE HURRICANE	HURRICANE FOREST INUNDATION	HURRICANE-DROUGHT FOREST
Words	Boolean	0,037580	0,033401	0,033183	0,016749	0,015970	0,015813
Words	TF-IDF	0,017727	0,015613	0,016410	0,008600	0,007766	0,026858
2-grams	Boolean	0,037580	0,041362	0,041695	0,019643	0,013849	0,023657
2-grams	TF-IDF	0,025612	0,025126	0,012143	0,007163	0,008121	0,036411
MFS's	Boolean	0,063395	0,058079	0,058435	0,027263	0,025613	0,025706
MFS's	TF-IDF	0,024060	0,022078	0,023356	0,012227	0,010648	0,011509
MFS's	Length	0,052862	0,049424	0,047743	0,023666	0,021656	0,021335

Table 6 presents the clustering quality evaluated with the external measures. Although the vector of MFS's was not the best in all the experiments it was the best in most of the cases. As we mentioned before, these external measures are based on evaluating the clusters according to a previously defined classification. However we do not always have this classification in real problems of document clustering.

Table 6. Clustering quality evaluated with the external measures

GENERAL F-MEASURE							
DOCUMENT REPRESENTATION	WEIGHT	FOREST HURRICANE	FOREST INUNDATION	DROUGHT INUNDATION	FOREST EARTHQUAKE HURRICANE	HURRICANE FOREST INUNDATION	HURRICANE-DROUGHT FOREST
Words	Boolean	0,98750	1	0,96245	0,94929	0,94122	0,94996
Words	TF-IDF	1	1	0,94987	0,94929	0,94972	0,94996
2-grams	Boolean	0,98962	1	0,95362	0,94156	0,93123	0,95012
2-grams	TF-IDF	1	1	0,93651	0,95025	0,94136	0,96215
MFS's	Boolean	0,98750	1	0,97500	0,96663	0,92404	0,97499
MFS's	TF-IDF	0,98750	1	0,94987	0,84277	0,94122	0,96666
MFS's	Length	0,93725	1	0,97500	0,95886	0,92404	0,95860
TOTAL ENTROPY							
DOCUMENT REPRESENTATION	WEIGHT	FOREST HURRICANE	FOREST INUNDATION	DROUGHT INUNDATION	FOREST EARTHQUAKE HURRICANE	HURRICANE FOREST INUNDATION	HURRICANE-DROUGHT FOREST
Words	Boolean	0	0	0,14500	0,056521	0,21414	0,19213
Words	TF-IDF	0	0	0,19622	0,056521	0,21414	0,15260
2-grams	Boolean	0	0	0,14121	0,055132	0,22345	0,20103
2-grams	TF-IDF	0	0	0,19254	0,575644	0,23141	0.17236
MFS's	Boolean	0,084781	0	0,14500	0,113340	0,23781	0,15258
MFS's	TF-IDF	0,084781	0	0,19622	0,168650	0,18872	0,15258
MFS's	Length	0	0	0,14500	0,168650	0,21414	0,15258

It is important to mention that in all the experiments carried out the number of terms, obtained with the vector of MFS's, was smaller than the one obtained with the vector of words or n-grams. In table 7 we present the number of terms for each representation and the reduction percentage obtained by the vector of MFS's. The column 5 shows the reduction percentage obtained by using MFS's instead of words and column 6 presents the reduction percentage obtained by using MFS's instead of 2-grams. You can see that reduction is in both cases greater than 60% in all the experiments.

Table 7. Reduction percentage of terms

EXPERIMENTS DISASTERS	NUMBER OF WORDS	NUMBER OF 2-GRAMS	NUMBER OF MFS's	REDUCTION WORDS VS MFS's	REDUCTION 2-GRAMS VS MFS's
1	4611	12608	944	79,52%	92,52%
2	4583	12329	914	80,05%	92,58%
3	4825	12846	953	80,24%	92,58%
4	5963	16574	1286	78,43%	92,24%
5	6059	17126	2652	56,23%	84,51%
6	4593	15544	1133	75,33%	92,71%

Tables 8-9 present the results of the clustering quality, obtained with the documents in English. Thus, Table 8 shows the clustering quality evaluated with internal measures. Again, we can observe that using the vector of MFS's the formed groups have high internal cohesion and external separation. The highest clustering quality was obtained by the vector representation using MFS's with Boolean weights, and the smallest quality was obtained by the vector representation using words with TF-IDF term weighting.

Table 8. Clustering quality evaluated with the internal measures

GLOBAL SILHOUETTE					
DOCUMENT REPRESENTATION	WEIGHT	ACQ, EARN	MONEY,ACQ, EARN	ACQ,ERAN CRUDE	GOLD, ACQ, TRADE, RESERVE, EARN
Words	Boolean	0,121110	0,103910	0,103140	0,13152
Words	TF-IDF	0,072247	0,060720	0,077011	0,09483
2-grams	Boolean	0,123654	0,135121	0,101261	0,12756
2-grams	TF-IDF	0,081652	0,070266	0,065244	0,08273
MFS's	Boolean	0,181210	0,144870	0,153840	0,18023
MFS's	TF-IDF	0,103850	0,076099	0,102890	0,12938
MFS's	Length	0,146760	0,096807	0,126850	0,15021
GLOBAL SIMILARITY					
DOCUMENT REPRESENTATION	WEIGHT	ACQ, EARN	MONEY,ACQ, EARN	ACQ,ERAN CRUDE	GOLD, ACQ, TRADE, RESERVE, EARN
Words	Boolean	0,048405	0,045655	0,019496	0,02511
Words	TF-IDF	0,022866	0,022851	0,010897	0,01360
2-grams	Boolean	0,058621	0,042365	0,019562	0,02347
2-grams	TF-IDF	0,030200	0,012365	0,011236	0,02046
MFS's	Boolean	0,062359	0,059618	0,025336	0,03372
MFS's	TF-IDF	0,030447	0,027392	0,013815	0,02173
MFS's	Length	0,047538	0,043986	0,019786	0,28910

Table 9 presents the result of the clustering quality evaluated with the external measures. The vectors based on words and based on MFS's, both obtained very similar results, and in some cases they were tied.

Table 9. Clustering quality evaluated with the external measures

GENERAL F-MEASURE					
DOCUMENT REPRESENTATION	WEIGHT	ACQ, EARN	MONEY,ACQ, EARN	ACQ,ERAN, CRUDE	GOLD, ACQ, TRADE, RESERVE, EARN
Words	Boolean	0,88865	1	0,90756	0,91238
Words	TF-IDF	0,88865	1	0,90756	0,91238
2-grams	Boolean	0,88865	1	0,90712	0,91221
2-grams	TF-IDF	0,87635	1	0,90765	0,91071
MFS's	Boolean	0,88865	1	0,90076	0,91238
MFS's	TF-IDF	0,87825	1	0,90076	0,91031
MFS's	Length	0,87825	0,98735	0,90076	0,91045
TOTAL ENTROPY					
DOCUMENT REPRESENTATION	WEIGHT	ACQ, EARN	MONEY,ACQ, EARN	ACQ,ERAN, CRUDE	GOLD, ACQ, TRADE, RESERVE, EARN
Words	Boolean	0,41528	0	0,39332	0,42294
Words	TF-IDF	0,41528	0	0,39332	0,42294
2-grams	Boolean	0,41528	0	0,41236	0,43432
2-grams	TF-IDF	0,42345	0	0,40564	0,43251
MFS's	Boolean	0,41528	0	0,40991	0,42294
MFS's	TF-IDF	0,43948	0	0,40991	0,42458
MFS's	Length	0,43948	0,084449	0,40991	0,42981

Also, as in the experiment with documents in Spanish, in the experiments with documents in English the number of obtained MFS's is less than the number of words or n-grams, and it did not affect the clustering quality. The reduction is shown in table 10 where the column 5 shows the reduction percentage obtained by using MFS's instead of words and column 6 presents the reduction percentage obtained by using MFS's instead of 2-grams. The reduction is in both cases greater than 60% in all the experiments. Moreover, when the MFS's are used instead of 2-grams, which preserve part of the word sequential order, the reduction is around 88% in all the experiments. The reduction is possible because the MFS's are a compact representation of the frequent sequences in a document. This reduction of the vector size is an advantage of the representation based on MFS's over the vector based on words or n-grams.

Table 10. Reduction percentage of terms

EXPERIMENTS REUTERS	NUMBER OF WORDS	NUMBER OF 2-GRAMS	NUMBER OF MFS's	REDUCTION WORDS VS MFS's	REDUCTION 2-GRAMS VS MFS's
1	1546	3357	484	68,69%	85,58%
2	2354	7652	726	69,15%	90,51%
3	2541	7768	821	67,69%	89,43%
4	4294	12927	1693	60.58%	86.90%

5 Conclusions

In this paper, we have introduced the vector space model based on MFS's as a document representation. The experiments established that using the maximal frequent sequences as features in the vector space model is a good option for document clustering. In addition, the amount of MFS's, obtained from documents, is smaller than the amount of words or n-grams, therefore our proposal based on MFS's allows a compact document representation. The experimental results showed that the vector based on MFS's always obtained clusters with best internal cohesion and external separation. When the proposed representation was evaluated with external measures, it obtained better quality in most of the experiments.

It is appropriate to underline that the objective of this work was to analyze the MFS's performance as document representation for document clustering. However the MFS's have some useful characteristics that could improve even more the document clustering, therefore as future work we will propose a new document representation using MFS's but without following the vector space model. Also we will define a new way to evaluate the similarity among documents when they are represented by MFS's without the vector space model.

References

1. Zhong Su, Li Zhang, Yue Pan. Document Clustering Based on Vector Quatization and Growing-Cell Structure. Springer-Verlag Berlin Heidelberg, pp 326-336, 2003.
2. Yoelle S., Fagin, Ronald, Ben-Shaul, Israel Z. y Pelleg, Dan. Ephemeral Document Clustering for Web Applications. IBM Research. Report RJ 10186, 2000
3. G. Salton, A. Wang, C.S. Yang. A Vector Space Model for Information Retrieval. Journal of the American Society for information Science, pp 613-620, 1975.
4. L. Jing, Michael k.,Jun Ku, Joshua Z. H. Subspace Clustering of Text Documents with Feature Weighting k-means Algorithm, 9th Pacific-Asia Conference on Knowledge Discovery and Data Mining (PAKDD-05), Springer-Verlag 2005, pp. 802-812.
5. M. Steinbach, G. Karypis, V. Kumar. A Comparison of Document Clustering Techniques. Proc. Text mining workshop, KDD, 2000.
6. Patrick Pantel, Dekang Lin. Efficiently Clustering Documents with Committees. Pacific Rim International Conferences on Artificial Intelligence (PRICAI 2002), Springer-verlag 2002, pp.424-433.
7. [http://www.ics.uci.edu/~kdd/databases/reuters21578/reuters21578.html]
8. Christopher D. Manning, Hinrich Schütze. Foundations of Statical Natural Language Processing. Massachussets Institute of Technology. 2001.
9. Xiao Luo, Nur Zincir-Heywood. Analyzing the Temporal Sequences for Text Categorization. Springer-Verlag Berlin Heildeberg, pp 498-505, 2004.
10. Helena Ahonen-Myka. Finding All Maximal Frequent Sequences in Text. Proc. of the ICML99 Workshop on Machine Learning in Text Data Analysis, pages 11--17, 1999
11. Antoine Doucet. Advanced Document Description, a Sequential Approach. Thesis PhD. University of Helsinki Finland. 2005
12. René A. García-Hernández, José Fco. Martínez-Trinidad and Jesús Ariel Carrasco-Ochoa, A Fast Algorithm to Find All the Maximal Frequent Sequences in a Text, 9th Iberoamerican Congress on Pattern Recognition (CIARP'2004), Lecture Notes in Computer Science vol. 3287 Springer-Verlag 2004.pp. 478-486.

Enriching Thesauri with Hierarchical Relationships by Pattern Matching in Dictionaries*

Lourdes Araujo and José R. Pérez-Agüera

Departamento de Sistemas Informáticos y Programación.
Universidad Complutense de Madrid. Madrid 28040. Spain
lurdes@sip.ucm.es, jose.aguera@fdi.ucm.es

Abstract. This paper proposes a pattern matching method applied to dictionaries to identify hierarchical relationships between terms. In this work we focus on this type of relationship because we use it in the automatic generation of thesauri, which are used to improve information retrieval tasks. However the method can also be applied to identify other semantic relationships. We distinguish two kinds of patterns: structural patterns, composed of a sequence of part-of-speech tags, and key patterns, typical of dictionary entries, composed of some key terms, along with some part-of-speech tags. This kind of patterns are automatically extracted for the dictionary entries by means of stochastic techniques. The thesaurus, that has been partially constructed previously, is then extended with the new relationships obtained by applying the patterns to a dictionary. We have based the system evaluation on the results obtained with and without the thesaurus in an information retrieval task proposed by the Cross-Language Evaluation Forum (CLEF). The results of these experiments have revealed a clear improvement on the performance.

Keywords: automatic thesaurus extraction, information retrieval, query expansion, pattern matching, dictionary.

1 Introduction

Information retrieval (IR) techniques aim at providing fast and effective access to a large amount of information. During the last decades IR has extended its application area from textual documents in static collections to Internet and the Web. Nowadays, IR methods include document indexing, document classification and categorization, etc., most of which try to improve the response to a search query in internet, probably the task most commonly performed everywhere and everytime.

The performance of an IR system is usually proportional to the size of the query [14]. Long queries typically provide enough information for the system to respond with appropriate documents, while short queries usually yield a low

* Supported by Ingeniería del Software e Inteligencia Artificial group, ref. 910494 and project TIC2003-09481-C04.

T. Salakoski et al. (Eds.): FinTAL 2006, LNAI 4139, pp. 268–279, 2006.

performance. In these cases query expansion can improve the retrieval performance. A common technique to expand the query adding related terms is to use thesauri. A thesaurus is a structured list of terms, usually related to a particular domain of knowledge. Thesauri are used to standardize terminology and provide alternative and preferred terms for any application. In particular, they are very useful in keyword searching on the web if they are applied to expand the list of keywords in such a way that the searched concept is given the form it really has in the web pages relevant to a searcher's area of interest.

In spite of the great interest thesaurus have reached nowadays for web applications, most of them are manually generated, what is very expensive and limits its availability to some particular topics. Furthermore, a thesaurus usually requires to be periodically updated to include new terminology, in particular in modern terms, such as those related to computer science. These reasons make the automatic generation of thesauri an interesting area of research which is attracting a lot of interest. Research on automatic thesaurus generation for information retrieval began with Sparck Jones's works on automatic term classification [10], G. Salton's work on automatic thesaurus construction and query expansion [16], and Van Rijsbergen's work on term co-occurrence [17]. Voorhees [18] applied a different approach, based on linguistic information obtained from WordNet, to perform query expansion, with very limited results. In the nineties Qui and Frei [14]. worked on a term-vs-term similarity matrix based on how the terms of the collection are indexed. Recently, Zazo, Berrocal, Figuerola and Rodríguez [2] have developed a work using similarity thesauri for Spanish documents. Jing and Croft [9] have proposed an approach to automatically construct collection-dependent association thesauri using large full-text documents collections. Those approaches obtain promising results when applied to improve information retrieval processes.

The goal of this work is to enrich the structure of a thesaurus with hierarchical relationships or taxonomy extracted from a dictionary. This is done by automatically extracting from a dictionary patterns which indicate this kind of relationship. Many entries to a typical explanatory dictionary usually adopt predefined forms. For example, let us consider some typical entries from the English online dictionary *dictionary.com*:

entry	definition
chemical	Of or relating to chemistry.
physical	Of or relating to material things...
numerical	Of or relating to a number or...

It is easy to observe patterns such as *Of or relating to NOUN* and *Of or relating to ARTICLE NOUN*. These patterns can be automatically extracted from the dictionary.

On the other hand, even dictionary entries which do not contain key expressions usually present a restricted structure which allow extracting semantic information with only a naive analysis. This property has been exploited in different manners in research in natural language processing. Alshawi [1] applies a hierarchy of phrasal patterns to analyze dictionary word sense definitions applied to a particular dictionary: the *Longman Dictionary of Contemporary English*, which uses a restricted vocabulary in its definitions. Chodorow and Byrd [4] propose some semi-automatic procedures for extracting and organizing information implicit in dictionary definitions. The system Mindnet [15], based on the use of a broad-coverage NL-parser, has been applied to dictionary definitions. Jannink [8] uses a kind of PageRank algorithm for extraction of hierarchical relationships between words in a dictionary. Markowitz et al. [12] use dictionary patterns to find the features of a lexicon entries, such as verb categories, selection restrictions, etc. Other works search for patterns to identify semantic relationships in other resources such as large text corpora [7] and free text [11].

To search the hierarchical relationships in dictionary entries which do not contain key expressions we propose to use a collection of simple part-of-speech patterns or structural patterns. In this case the potential relationships are checked by applying vector space similarity measures on a text collection concerning the intended thesaurus domain.

The thesaurus to be enriched has been previously generated applying statistical techniques for the selection of terms and the detection of term relationships. The particular domain of knowledge to which the new thesaurus is devoted, is characterized by a set of terms extracted from a document collection about the intended topic. This is done by applying indexing techniques. Then we use the information previously collected in other thesauri about these terms to construct the initial structure of the new one. Finally, the new thesaurus is enriched by searching for new relationship among its terms. The three basic relationships between the terms of a thesaurus are equivalence (they are synonyms, one is the translation of the other, its archaic form, etc.), hierarchical and associative relationships. Equivalence is directly extracted form a dictionary, while the hierarchical relationship amounts to extracting by the pattern matching. The associative relationship between terms which are not connected by a hierarchy[1] is first detected using co-occurrence measures and, its type is characterized later.

The system has been evaluated by comparing the results obtained in an information retrieval task, for which the expected results are perfectly defined, when a set of query terms are directly consulted, and when they are previously expanded with the generated thesaurus. For the evaluation, we have used one of the document collections provided by the Cross-Language Evaluation Forum (CLEF)[2], which have been specifically developed for testing and evaluating information retrieval systems.

The rest of the paper proceeds as follows: section 2 describes the different techniques used to generate the initial structure of the thesaurus; section 3 is devoted to describe the mechanism to extract the dictionary patterns which indicate hierarchical relationships; section 4 presents and discusses the experiments and results, and section 5 presents the main conclusions of this work.

---

[1] For example because they are narrower terms of different broad terms, but they still present some kind of relationship.

[2] http://www.clef-campaign.org/

2 First Steps in the Thesaurus Generation

In this work we combine different techniques to obtain a new thesaurus for a particular domain of knowledge.

2.1 Term Selection: The Core Set

The first step in the construction of the new thesaurus is the selection of the *core set* of terms which characterize the intended domain, according to the provided text collection. The text collection is previously preprocessed in order to determine the index terms. We perform a POS tagging of the documents to identify nouns, the words which can be included in the thesaurus. We eliminate typical stop words (articles, prepositions, conjunctions, etc). But we also eliminate other terms, that we call *specific stopwords* which are not typical stopwords, but which are too frequent in the collection to be good discriminators for thesaurus construction. Examples of specific stopwords are months, name of the days, etc. Words resulting from the previous step are applied a stemming process. The last step is the selection of the most representative terms of the text to be used as index. This phase is carried out by applying the standard indexing technique TF-IDF, i.e. the construction of an index for each document which characterizes it and allows a quicker access than the whole set of words of the document. We have used the classic inversion technique in information retrieval, constructing an inverted index whose terms have associated a list of pointers to the occurrences of the term in the text collection.

2.2 Generation of the Intersection Thesaurus

The next step of the process is the generation of the *intersection thesaurus* from a set of source thesauri, if there is any. In other case the procedure would go to the next phase. The source thesauri that we have used are the following ones:

- EUROVOC, which contains concepts on the activity of the European Union.
- SPINES, a controlled and structured vocabulary for information processing in the field of science and technology for development.
- ISOC, thesaurus aimed at the treatment of information on economy.

It is not possible to find conflict between the hierarchies provided by different sources thesauri for a same term of the core set, because the norm z39.19 allows the existence of polyhierarchical relationships [13][3]. For this reason, whenever we found two broader terms for the same term in the thesauri source, we used both in the intersection thesaurus generating its respective entries.

Terms which appear in both, the core set and any source thesauri, are the term list of the intersection thesaurus. Furthermore, the relationships among the terms included in the new thesaurus are provided by the source thesauri. Figure 1 shows an example of generation of the intersection thesaurus. When the term *terremoto* (earthquake), which belongs to the core set, is searched in

[3] Page 18.

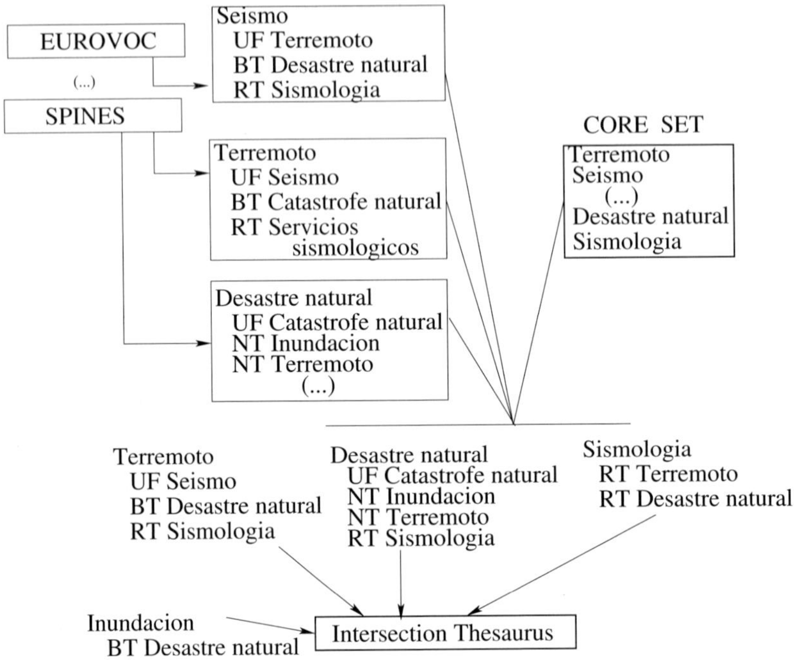

Fig. 1. Example of generation of the intersection thesaurus. UF stands for *used for*, NT for *narrower term*, BT for *broader term* and RT for *related term*.

the source thesauri two entries are found, one in SPINES and the other one in EUROVOC.

In EUROVOC *terremoto* (earthquake) belongs to an entry whose preferred term is *seísmo* (seism) and which also contains *desastre natural* (natural disaster) (BT), and *sismología* (seismology) (RT). In SPINES *terremoto* is the preferred term of an entry which also contains the synonym *seísmo*, the broader term *catástrofe natural* (natural catastrophe) and the related term *servicios sismológicos* (seismological service). In SPINES, *terremoto* also appears in other entry whose preferred term is *desastre natural*, and which also contains the synonym *catástrofe natural*, and the narrower terms *inundación* (flood) and *terremoto*. Accordingly, the intersection thesaurus presents entries whose preferred terms are *terremoto*, *desastre natural*, *sismología* and *inundación*, the terms of the core set. *Seísmo*, which also belongs to the core set, is not given an entry because it is equivalent to *terremoto*, which appears before in the core set. Each entry is composed of the terms connected with the preferred one, or with its equivalent terms, in any of the source thesauri. Thus, the *terremoto* entry is composed of *seísmo*, connected to *terremoto* in both thesauri, *desastre natural*, connected to *seísmo* (which is equivalent to *terremoto* in EUROVOC), etc.

2.3 Generation of the New Thesaurus

Finally, the structure of the new thesaurus is extended with new relationships among its terms. If the couple of terms to be related appears in some of the source thesauri, this indicates the kind of its relationships. If they do not appear in the source thesauri, its possible relationship has to be investigated. Each type of relationship is studied in a different manner. Equivalence is extracted from Eurowordnet [5]. Hierarchical relationships are extracted by the pattern matching techniques described in the next section. To detect associative relationships we determine the pairs of terms for which the semantic similarity is significant enough using the classic measure of cosine (the similarity is above a threshold value of 0.3 in our case).

3 Pattern Matching for Relationships Identification

Let us now consider the technique used to detect hierarchical relationships. It relies on the assumption that in a dictionary the entries for a term which is an instance of a more general concept contain a reference to the term for this general concept. Furthermore, we assume that the references to more general terms usually adopt some predefined patterns. We consider two kinds of patterns: *structural patterns*, which are defined as a sequence of part-of speech tags, and *keyphrase patterns*, which are composed of a keyphrase along with some part-of-speech tags. Each of these types is used in a different manner. Structural patterns are used to check the relationships between the expression which is the entry to the dictionary and the noun phrase expressions which appear in the definition, wherever they appear. Obviously, in general both expressions may not be related at all. Accordingly the relationship of these pairs of terms is checked in the training texts which define the domain.

We have considered the following set of structural patterns for the detection of hierarchical relationships:

noun
noun adjective
noun noun
noun preposition noun
noun preposition article noun

On the other hand, keyphrase patterns automatically identify the expression of the definition which is related with to dictionary entry and the type of this relationship. For example, let us consider the following entries from the RAE (Real Academia Española) Spanish online dictionary:

entry	definition
campesino	Perteneciente o relativo al campo.
ciudadano	Perteneciente o relativo a la ciudad.
marino	Perteneciente o relativo al mar.

It is easy to observe the pattern *perteneciente o relativo a*, which means *belonging or related to*. We have designed a method to automatically detect such keyphrases patterns in an online dictionary. Our method is as follows:

- The first step is the selection of the key terms which form the expression. A sequence of adjacent terms is considered a key expression if it is frequent enough, i.e. if the number of occurrences in the dictionary is above a threshold. Because the key expressions have very different lengths, we compute the frequency of sequences of different length (from 2 to 10). The threshold decreases with the length of the sequence, since short sequences may be frequent even if they are not a key expression.
- The previous step produces lists of key expressions of different length. In general, some key expressions will appear as part of other expressions from other lists. In these cases we must select one of them, as complete and as general as possible. If several expressions from the $ngram_i$ are part of one expression from $ngram_{i+1}$, then we select this expression because it is more complete. For example,

ngram-4:	cada una de las
	una de las partes
ngram-5:	cada una de las partes

  Our method selects the expression *cada una de las partes* from the *ngram-5* which is the most complete one.

  On the other hand, if an expression from the list $ngram_i$ is part of several expressions from the list $ngram_{i+1}$, we consider that the expression of list $ngram_i$ is more general, and thus it is the one selected. For example, we have extracted the following data from the RAE (Real Academia Española) Spanish dictionary.:

ngram-4:	perteneciente o relativo a
ngram-5:	perteneciente o relativo a este
	perteneciente o relativo a esta
	perteneciente o relativo a el
	perteneciente o relativo a la
	perteneciente o relativo a las
	perteneciente o relativo a los
	perteneciente o relativo a un
	perteneciente o relativo a una

  Our method selects the expression *perteneciente o relativo a* from the *ngram-4* because it is more general, since it corresponds to several expression in the ngram-5 list.
- Once we have selected the key terms, patterns must be completed with the part-of-speech tags which give rise to frequent patterns. For example, the key phrases from the examples above give rise to the following patterns:

key expression	pattern
cada una de las partes de	cada una de las partes de ART N
perteneciente o relativo a	perteneciente o relativo a ART N
	perteneciente o relativo a DADJ N

where ART stands for article, N for noun and DADJ for demonstrative adjective. For a word sequence which matches one of these patterns the noun assigned to N is known to be a more general term than the word which is the entry for the dictionary.

Because patterns are dictionary dependent, they must be extracted for each dictionary we want to use. However, the described method is automatic and can be applied to any electronic dictionary and in any language. We have developed our experiments in Spanish, using the RAE (Real Academia Española) dictionary. We have performed a part-of-speech (POS) tagging of the dictionary entries in order to detect the selected structures. We have used SVMTool [6] for tagging, a software which implements a POS-Tagger with Support Vector Machine and achieves an accuracy of 96,7% for Spanish texts and 97,8% for English texts. Figure 2 shows an example of taxonomy generated using only structural patterns (a) and with both kinds of patterns (b) extracted from the RAE dictionary.

4 Experiments and Results

The prototype developed for our experiments has been implemented using the programming language Java. This prototype has been run on a computer Intel Pentium IV Hyper-Threading 3.40 GHz, with 2GB of RAM memory.

In order to provide a quantitative measure for the quality of the generated thesaurus, we have decided to evaluate its usefulness when it is applied to an information retrieval task. Specifically, we used the thesaurus to perform a term-to-term query expansion, i.e. for identifying terms related with the query terms in order to improve the retrieval capability.

For query expansion we use the method proposed by Qiu y Frei [14], which selects expansion terms according to their similarity with all query terms. Given a query q composed of terms $(t_1, t_2, ..., t_n)$ which are assigned weights $(w_1, w_2, ..., w_n)$, the similarity with a term $t\prime$ is defined as follow:

$$sim_{qt\prime}(q, t\prime) = \sum_{t_i \epsilon q} w_i * sim(t_i, t\prime) \tag{1}$$

where $sim(t_i, t\prime)$ is the similarity[4] computed when the thesaurus is generated. The weight of each expansion term $t\prime$ with respect to the query q is defined as:

$$w_{qexp}(q, t\prime) = \frac{sim_{qt\prime}(q, t\prime)}{\sum_{t_i \epsilon q} w_i} \tag{2}$$

[4] It is the measured similarity for terms extracted from texts, and the similarity value of the corresponding dictionary entry for terms taken from the dictionary.

RAE Taxonomy
transporte de personas
vehículo_automóvil
coche

(a)

RAE Taxonomy
transporte de personas
vehículo_automóvil
coche
vagón de ferrocarril
coche_cama
coche_celular
coche_de_camino
coche_de_colleras
coche_de_estribos
autobus
coche_de_línea
coche_de_niño
coche_de_plaza-coche_de_punto
coche_de_rúa
coche_escoba
coche_fúnebre
...

(b)

Fig. 2. Example of taxonomy generated with structural patterns (a) and with both kind of patterns (b)

This weight can be interpreted as the weighted mean of similarities between the candidate term and all terms in the query. We use this weight as a boost factor in the TF-IDF expression of our search engine[5].

With the aim at being as fair as possible, in the selection of tests we have taken a set of tests used in the CLEF (Cross-Language Evaluation Forum) for the Spanish language. The collection and tests used come from EFE94. This document collection came from the international news agency EFE, from all the news received during 1994.

For the evaluation of the system we have used the classic measures of precision and recall [3]. Recall is the fraction of the relevant documents which have been retrieved and precision is the fraction of the retrieved documents which are relevant. Specifically we use R-precision, which is the precision after retrieving R documents, where R is the total number of relevant documents for the query.

As a battery of test we have used a total of 40 extracted queries of the batteries provided by CLEF in 2001 and 2002. The reason why we have made a selection in the batteries of tests is our need of using a set of queries that can be expanded by thesauri source and whose domain is focused on politics and economy. Accordingly, we discard some queries on other topics, such as those related to sports.

Table 1 shows the results obtained using different thesauri to expand a set of queries from the EFE94 collection provided by CLEF[6]. The first row corresponds

[5] We use lucene (http://lucene.apache.org/java/docs/) for the implementation of the our search engine which use Vector Space Model like retrieval paradigm.

[6] http://clef.isti.cnr.it/

Table 1. Precision and recall results for a set of queries from EFE94 provided by CLEF

Query	R-prec	R-prec improvement	Recall	Recall Improvement
Original	0.4891	–	0.61	–
Spines	0.4196	- 14.20%	0.6213	+ 1.81%
Eurovoc	0.4113	- 15.90%	0.6442	+ 5.3%
ISOC-Economy	0.4122	- 15.72%	0.6231	+ 2.1%
Intersection Thesaurus	0.3813	- 22.04%	0.6771	+ 9.9%
RAE-taxonomy-key (only key patterns)	0.4978	+ 1.74%	0.6483	+ 5.9%
RAE-taxonomy (both pattern types)	0.5116	+ 4.39%	0.6663	+ 8,44%
Final Thesaurus	0.5614	+ 12,87%	0.7312	+ 16.57%

to the query without expansion. The next three rows present the results expanding the query with Spines, Eurovoc and ISOC-Economy thesauri, respectively. The fifth row corresponds to an expansion with our intersection thesaurus, composed of terms from the text collection and from source thesauri. The 6th row corresponds to expanding the query with the taxonomy obtained by only applying key patterns. The 7th row presents the results expanding with the taxonomy obtained using both types of patterns. Finally, the last row gives the results expanded with our final thesaurus, which also includes equivalent and associative relationships. We can observe that recall improves in every case since the set of search terms is enlarged with thesaurus terms. Precision also improves in the last three rows because the percentage of relevant documents retrieved with the query expansion is larger than that for the original query, i.e. ambiguity has been reduced. However precision gets worse for the source thesauri and their intersection. This means that they provide too general terms for the query expansion. Results show that both, key and structural patterns, reduce ambiguity and thus improve precision.

5 Conclusions and Future Works

This paper describes a method to use dictionary patterns in the construction of thesauri. Dictionary patterns of different lengths are automatically extracted from the dictionary entries. We also propose a method to automatically generate the thesaurus and enrich it with the hierarchical relationships detected with the extracted patterns. This paper shows how to use handmade thesauri for the automatic generation of new thesauri. There exists a large amount of handmade thesauri and they are very useful as knowledge bases for the automatic generation of thesauri[7]. Furthermore, we have defined a methodology to combine linguistic methods and statistical methods for the automatic generation of thesauri. Results have shown the usefulness of the generated thesauri,

[7] Web Thesaurus Compendium: http://www.ipsi.fraunhofer.de/~lutes/thesoecd.html

improving both, recall and precision measures in an information retrieval task. Key patterns have been proved useful to include new terms in the thesaurus taxonomy without increasing the ambiguity because they correspond to very specific relationships. Structural patterns are also useful, but to avoid increasing ambiguity the terms selected by them are only included in the taxonomy if they belong to the text collection which defines the domain. We have used a Spanish dictionary in our experiments, but the method is valid for any language, though the dictionary patterns extracted will depend on the particular language and on the dictionary used.

For the future we expect to improve results by using more dictionaries in the process. We will also try to improve the performance of the information retrieval tasks by weighting the relationships used in the query expansion. We also plan to extend the method to detect patterns for more specific relationships, such as *be part of*, etc.

References

1. Hiyan Alshawi. Processing dictionary definitions with phrasal pattern hierarchies. *Comput. Linguist.*, 13(3-4):195–202, 1987.
2. Angel F. Zazo and Carlos G. Figuerola and Jose L. Alonso Berrocal and Emilio Rodríguez. Reformulation of queries using similarity thesauri. *Information Processing and Management*, 41(5):1163–1173, 2005.
3. Ricardo A. Baeza-Yates and Berthier A. Ribeiro-Neto. *Modern Information Retrieval.* ACM Press / Addison-Wesley, 1999.
4. Martin S. Chodorow, Roy J. Byrd, and George E. Heidorn. Extracting semantic hierarchies from a large on-line dictionary. In *Proceedings of the 23rd annual meeting on Association for Computational Linguistics*, pages 299–304, Morristown, NJ, USA, 1985. Association for Computational Linguistics.
5. P. Vossen (Ed.). *EuroWordNet A Multilingual Database with Lexical Semantic Networks.* Kluwer Academic publishers., 1998.
6. Jesús Giménez and Lluís Márquez. Svmtool: A general pos tagger generator based on support vector machines. In *Proceedings of the 4th LREC*, 2004.
7. Marti A. Hearst. Automatic acquisition of hyponyms from large text corpora. In *Proceedings of the 14th conference on Computational linguistics*, pages 539–545, Morristown, NJ, USA, 1992. Association for Computational Linguistics.
8. J. Jannink and G. Wiederhold. Thesaurus entry extraction from an on-line dictionary. In *Fusion '99*, pages 110–138, 1999.
9. Y. Jing and W. Bruce Croft. An association thesaurus for information retrieval. In *Proceedings of RIAO-94, 4th International Conference "Recherche d'Information Assistee par Ordinateur"*, pages 146–160, New York, US, 1994.
10. K. Sparck Jones and R.M. Needham. Automatic Term Classification and Retrieval. *Information Processing and Management*, 4(1):91–100, 1968.
11. Juan Lloréns and Hernán Astudillo. Automatic generation of hierarchical taxonomies from free text using linguistic algorithms. In *OOIS Workshops*, pages 74–83, 2002.
12. Judith Markowitz, Thomas Ahlswede, and Martha Evens. Semantically significant patterns in dictionary definitions. In *Proceedings of the 24th annual meeting on Association for Computational Linguistics*, pages 112–119, Morristown, NJ, USA, 1986. Association for Computational Linguistics.

13. National Information Standards Organization (U.S.). *Guidelines for the Construction, Format, and Management of Monolingual Thesauri*, volume ANSI/NISO 239.19-1993 of *National information standards series*. NISO PRESS, 1994.
14. Yonggang Qiu and Hans-Peter Frei. Concept-based query expansion. In *Proceedings of SIGIR-93, 16th ACM International Conference on Research and Development in Information Retrieval*, pages 160–169, Pittsburgh, US, 1993.
15. Stephen D. Richardson, William B. Dolan, and Lucy Vanderwende. Mindnet: acquiring and structuring semantic information from text. In *Proceedings of the 17th international conference on Computational linguistics*, pages 1098–1102. Association for Computational Linguistics, 1998.
16. G. Salton, C. Buckley, and C. T. Yu. An evaluation of term dependence models in information retrieval. In *SIGIR '82: Proceedings of the 5th annual ACM conference on Research and development in information retrieval*, pages 151–173, New York, NY, USA, 1982. Springer-Verlag New York, Inc.
17. C.J van. Rijsbergen, D.J. Harper, and M.F. Porter. The selection of good search terms. *Information Processing and Management*, 17(2):77–91, 1981.
18. Ellen M. Voorhees. Using wordnet to disambiguate word senses for text retrieval. In *SIGIR '93: Proceedings of the 16th annual international ACM SIGIR conference on Research and development in information retrieval*, pages 171–180, New York, NY, USA, 1993. ACM Press.

Evaluation of Alignment Methods for HTML Parallel Text

Enrique Sánchez-Villamil, Susana Santos-Antón,
Sergio Ortiz-Rojas, and Mikel L. Forcada

Transducens group, Departament de Llenguatges i Sistemes Informàtics
Universitat d'Alacant, E-03071 Alacant, Spain
{esvillamil, ssantos, sortiz, mlf}@dlsi.ua.es

Abstract. The Internet constitutes a potential huge store of parallel text that may be collected to be exploited by many applications such as multilingual information retrieval, machine translation, etc. These applications usually require at least sentence-aligned bilingual text. This paper presents new aligners designed for improving the performance of classical sentence-level aligners while aligning structured text such as HTML. The new aligners are compared with other well-known geometric aligners.

1 Introduction

Many machine translation applications are based on machine learning on parallel corpora. The amount of parallel text required to obtain accurate translations using these applications is quite high (up to hundreds of megabytes) although it seems possible to generate such large corpora using the Internet. The utility of the corpora increases dramatically when they are aligned at sentence or word levels.

A number of sentence-alignment approaches have been developed during the last years. The first effective approach at aligning large corpora was based on modeling the relationship between the lengths of sentences that are mutual translations (Brown et al., 1991; Gale and Church, 1991, 1993). Chen (1993) used a different approach, based on lexical information to improve accuracy, but it was slower than sentence-length-based algorithms. Some years later, Melamed (1996) developed a method based on word correspondences and supported by external linguistical knowledge.

All these aligners are designed to work with text segmented in sentences. In our case, collections of hundreds of megabytes of downloaded webpages, which are not segmented, have to be aligned at sentence-level. These pages are turned into XML[1] using the `tidy` program,[2] which may be used to turn HTML into XHTML.[3]

[1] `http://www.w3.org/TR/2004/REC-xml-20040204/`

[2] `http://www.w3.org/People/Raggett/tidy/`

[3] XHTML is a stricter and cleaner XML-version of HTML.

T. Salakoski et al. (Eds.): FinTAL 2006, LNAI 4139, pp. 280–290, 2006.

The aligners proposed in this paper are being used to generate a large collection of aligned text corpora. The corpora will be segmented, and segments will be aligned to build translation units. The resulting translation units may be used to train translation applications.

In particular, this paper presents a type of aligners that combine sentence-splitting and alignment generation, and take advantage of the structured nature of web documents to improve the accuracy of sentence-aligned text in the absence of linguistic knowledge. The aligners are compared to classical approaches in the experiments.

2 Notation

In this paper, we define the *alignment* as a sequence of edit operations, that is, a sequence of insertions, deletions and substitutions of segments.[4] Let $L = (l_1, l_2, ..., l_{|L|})$ and $R = (r_1, r_2, ..., r_{|R|})$ be two parallel texts split in segments and $S = (s_1, s_2, ..., s_{|S|})$, a sequence of edit distance operations, where s_i can be an insertion (m_i), a deletion (m_d) or a substitution (m_s) of a segment. It is straightforward to obtain the aligned segment pairs (l_i, r_i) using the edit distance sequence. We define A as the function returning the edit-distance alignment of two texts, so that $A(L, R) \longrightarrow S$.

Additionally, we define the alignment distance D that is considered as a measure of the similarity of the texts that have been aligned. The distance D is defined as the addition of the differences in length of all aligned segments:

$$D(S) = \sum_{i=1}^{|S|} \text{abs}(|l_i| - |r_i|) \tag{1}$$

where bars $|\cdot|$ are used to represent the length of a text segment. The m_i and m_d operations where either l_i or r_i would be the empty string are also taken into account.

3 Classical Geometric Aligners

Geometric aligners are based only in geometric properties of the documents, such as sentence lengths, word lengths, paragraph lengths, etc. They are fully independent of the language because they do not use linguistic information.

Classical geometric aligners were designed to align plain text segmented in sentences. However, they can be adapted to marked-up corpora, such as XHTML, in several ways. The simplest approach would be the removal of all tags in both sides, so that a pair of plain texts would be obtained and would then be split; such aligner is called *Remover*. A more elaborate algorithm would require the substitution of some tags by sentence boundaries[5] (and the removal of the rest

[4] This definition induces a monotone alignment.

[5] The tags replaced are `hr`, `br`, `p`, `li`, `ul`, `ol`, `tr`, `td`, `th`, `div`.

of tags) and the aligner that implements this algorithm is called *Replacer*. Both aligners will be used as a baseline to evaluate the sentence-alignment algorithms presented in this paper.

4 Geometric Aligners Based on Structure

The sentence-alignment algorithms that are presented in this paper combine sentence splitting with the alignment process. The algorithms work with structured text such as XHTML, but can be generalized easily to be applied to other XML-based formats.

These algorithms are based on a classification of tags that guide the initial splitting of the text. After that, a sequence of tags and text segments is extracted to perform the alignment, which will never allow the alignment of tags to text segments.

4.1 Classification of XHTML Tags

In order to maximize the alignment accuracy, XHTML tags have been classified in several different categories. Originally, tags were divided in *block* and *inline* tags as in the XHTML DTD, but these partition was refined and the following four categories were defined:

- Structural tags: Tags that compose the structure of the webpage and its graphical representation: `blockquote, body, caption, col, colgroup, dd, dir, div, dl, dt, h1, h2, h3, h4, h5, h6, head, hr, html, li, menu, noframes, noscript, ol, optgroup, option, p, q, select, table, tbody, td, tfoot, th, thead, tr, ul.`
- Format tags: Tags that specify the format of some elements of the webpage: `abbr, acronym, b, big, center, cite, code, dfn, em, font, i, pre, s, small, span, strike, strong, style, sub, sup, tt, u.`
- Content tags: Tags that contain relevant elements (for alignment purposes), which are neither structural nor format tags: `a, area, fieldset, form, iframe, img, input, isindex, label, legend, map, object, param, textarea, title.`
- Irrelevant tags: Tags that are ignored[6] during the alignment process: `address, applet, base, basefont, bdo, br, button, del, ins, kbd, link, meta, samp, script, var.`

Most block tags are structural tags, and most inline tags are format tags. Content tags represent basically inline tags that do not contain format. Tags that are not useful in the alignment process are classified as irrelevant tags.

Such a classification allows to set specific substitution costs regarding to the categories of the tags; for instance, the costs of substitutions involving structural tags will be higher than those of substitutions involving format tags.

[6] In fact, irrelevant tags are simply removed before aligning.

Table 1. Triggers applied to the context of dots to score sentence borders

#	Characters before	Characters after	Points
1	-	a number	−0.5
2	-	a blank space	+0.5
3	-	a non-capital letter	−0.2
4	-	another dot	−0.5
5	-	a blank space and a capital letter	+0.5
6	-	a blank space and a non-capital letter	−0.2
7	a capital letter	-	−0.5
8	a word of 3 characters or less	-	−0.5
9	a blank space	-	+0.2
10	a ' or " character	a ' or " character	−0.5
11	another dot	-	+0.4

4.2 Sentence-Splitting Heuristics

Text segments have to be split into sentences so that they can be aligned. The splitting algorithm considers many of the tags as sentence boundaries, which often generates small segments that do not even contain a single sentence. After that, sentence splitting algorithms are applied to ensure that the alignment is performed at sentence-level, so that no segment contains more than one sentence.

The algorithms in this paper use heuristics to find sentence boundaries. Initially, all breaking points[7] inside a text segment are located. After that, question marks and exclamation marks are considered sentence boundaries and dots are analysed to detect if they constitute sentence boundaries.

The analysis of dots is based on a list of triggers, which is shown in table 1, that assign scores to breaking points, so that breaking points with a score higher than a threshold, which was defined as -0.2, will be considered sentence borders. The scores associated with the triggers and the threshold have been experimentally adjusted. The threshold was defined to be negative so that if no trigger is executed the breaking point is considered as a sentence border.

4.3 Text Alignment

The alignment process is performed at the same time for tags and text segments, that is, the edit distance algorithm is applied to generate the best alignment between tags and text segments.

The edit distance costs were specified according to our alignment constraints and some decisions about the alignment of parallel texts:

- A tag cannot be aligned to a text segment or vice versa.
- A structural tag should not be aligned to a format, content or irrelevant tag, and the cost of the alignment with a different structural tag should be high.

[7] Breaking points are dots (.), question marks (?) and exclamation marks (!).

Table 2. Edit distance costs between different items in the text. See text for a definition of Δ.

	Insertion	**Struct. tags**	**Format tags**	**Content tags**	**Text segm.**
Deletion	-	1	0.75	1.25	$0.01\ \lvert r\rvert$
Struct. tags	1	1.5	1.75	H	H
Format tags	0.75	1.75	0.4	H	H
Content tags	1.25	H	H	H	H
Text segm.	$0.01\ \lvert l\rvert$	H	H	H	Δ

- A format tag should not be aligned to a tag of different type, and the cost of the alignment with a different format tag should be low.
- A content tag should only be aligned with the same tag.
- To favor tag alignment, text chunks should only be aligned between them and costs of their aligment should be lower than those that involve tags.

These costs are defined in table 2, where H is a value high enough to be never used in the edit distance process. The value of the symbol Δ will be defined specifically for each aligner.

The *2-in-1 aligner* splits both texts in tags and text sentences and then aligns them. This aligner defines $\Delta = 0.015\ (\text{abs}(|l| - |r|))$, that is, the difference between the text sentences lengths multiplied by a factor. The factor 0.015 has been established to be between the cost of inserting/deleting text characters and the sum of both costs, that was defined experimentally as 0.01 in the table 2.

The *2-steps aligner* splits the text in tags and text segments, which can contain more than one sentence. The first step consists in aligning tags and text segments among them. After that, the second step consists in aligning the sentences contained in the text segments obtained in the first step.

Two variants of this last aligner have been tested: the first one defines $\Delta = 0.015\ (\text{abs}(|l| - |r|))$, that is called *2-steps-L aligner*, where L means length, given that this first variant is based in length differences. The second one defines $\Delta = 0.01\ D(A(l, r))$, that is the alignment distance between the text segments multiplied by a factor, and it is called *2-steps-AD aligner*.[8] The 2-step-L factor is the same used in the 2-in-1 aligner, but the 2-steps-AD factor is the cost of inserting/deleting text characters, so that the substitution cost would remain lower than the sum of the insertion cost plus the deletion costs if the substitution were possible.

5 Experiments

The experiments performed to assess the quality of the aligners are based on several sentence-aligned corpora. These corpora were downloaded from three different websites. Then, all corpora were aligned and manually corrected using

[8] AD stands for *alignment distance*.

a program with a graphical user interface[9] oriented to checking and manipulating alignments.

5.1 Corpora

Three different corpora have been used to evaluate the quality of the alignments. Each of them represents a step forward in alignment difficulty. A measure of the difficulty in the alignment of parallel text could be the number of sentences that are aligned to blank in a manual alignment. The higher the number of blank alignments established, the less parallel the aligned texts are.

The first corpus has been downloaded from the Internet with a collector of parallel corpora called Bitextor (Sánchez-Villamil et al., 2006)[10]. This corpus contains 3.3 megabytes of Spanish–Catalan parallel text that was downloaded from `www.elperiodico.com`, an online daily newspaper.

The second one is a small fragment of the Quixote (196 kilobytes) that was downloaded from the Miguel de Cervantes Digital Library,[11] and it constitutes an Spanish–English corpus.

And the third one is a little collection of parallel text files in Spanish, Portuguese, Italian, Catalan and Galician that compose the help texts of the popular chatting program mIRC.[12] It contains a total of 96 kilobytes distributed in the five languages. All ten possible language pairs were aligned.

The corpus downloaded using Bitextor has 2.14% of sentences aligned to blank, which makes it the easiest one. The Quixote corpus has 19.08% which makes it harder to be aligned, and the 26.42% of the mIRC corpus makes it the hardest one.

5.2 Metrics

The metrics that have been selected to evaluate the quality of the alignment generated by the different aligners are the same as in (Black et al., 1991), that is, the precision, the recall and the F-measure. All of them require a reference alignment to calculate the number of correct alignments and the total of reference alignments. These metrics are based on sentences and are defined as follows:

$$\text{precision} = \frac{\#\ \text{correct alignments}}{\#\ \text{proposed alignments}} \tag{2}$$

$$\text{recall} = \frac{\#\ \text{correct alignments}}{\#\ \text{reference alignments}} \tag{3}$$

$$F = 2 \cdot \frac{\text{recall} \times \text{precision}}{\text{recall} + \text{precision}} \tag{4}$$

[9] Very similar to that of the `bitext2tmx` bitext aligner, `http://www.sourceforge.net/projects/bitext2tmx/`.

[10] `http://www.sourceforge.net/projects/bitextor/`

[11] `http://www.cervantesvirtual.com/`

[12] `http://www.mirc.co.uk/translations/index.html`

However, in our case, the direct comparison of the results of the aligners would not make sense because there is a significant length diference of the resulting alignments generated by different aligners. Therefore, concatenation of alignments was allowed in the comparison. This means that a pair of aligned segments is correct if: (a) the same pair is found in the reference alignment or (b) the same pair can be built by concatenating pairs of the reference alignment.

Furthermore, an additional metric has been applied to perform the evaluation. This metric is based on considering the number of sentence boundaries, instead of sentences, that were aligned properly. In (Melamed, 1996), Melamed used a method of evaluating bitext mapping algorithms which consists in comparing their output to a hand-constructed reference set of points, which, in our case, are the sentence boundaries. This metric allows to handle successfully the differences in length in the alignments proposed, although does not completely guarantee the correction of the alignments proposed.

5.3 Results

The experiments have been performed using five different aligners. The first two, are the basic geometric aligners *Remover* and *Replacer* that were explained in section 3, which are used as a baseline. The last three are the aligners proposed in this paper, i.e., the 2-steps-AD aligner, the 2-steps-L aligner and the 2-in-1 aligner.

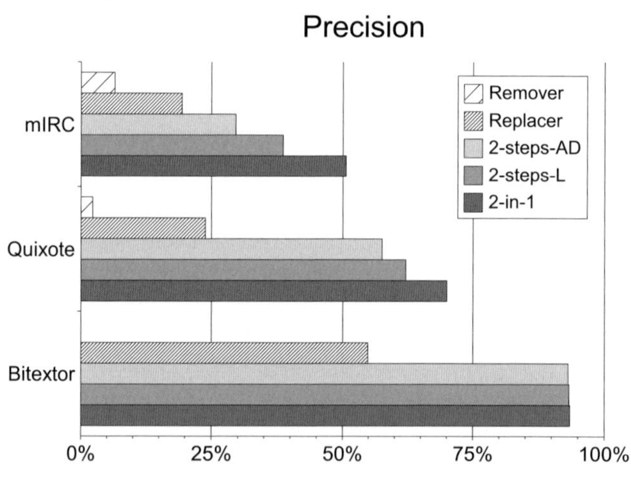

Fig. 1. Precision achieved by the aligners

The results that we obtained with the metrics based on sentences are shown in figures 1, 2 and 3. As can be seen, the precision and recall of the resulting alignments is quite different for each corpus. As expected, the best results were obtained in the Bitextor corpus, and the mIRC corpus had the worst results. The results of the proposed aligners were clearly better than those of the basic geometric aligners.

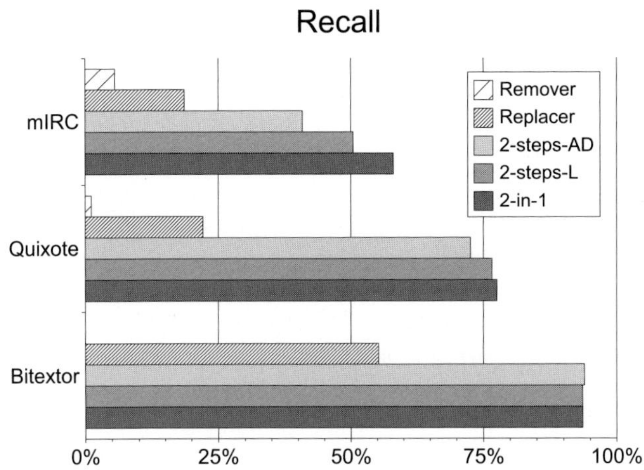

Fig. 2. Recall achieved by the aligners

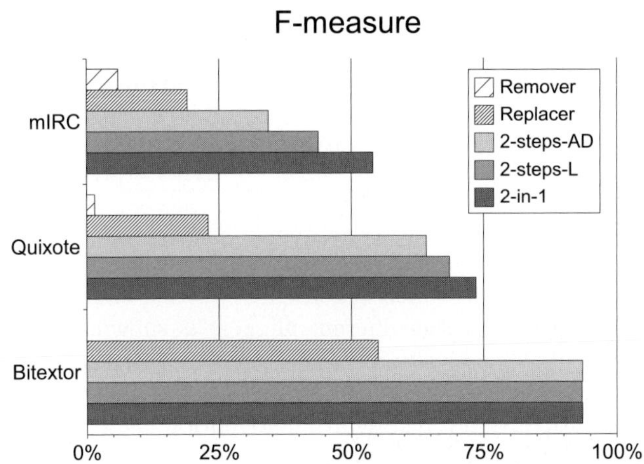

Fig. 3. F-measure achieved by the aligners

Similar results were obtained using the metric based on sentence boundaries, as it is shown in figure 4 (only the F-measure is given). The results were slightly better because the sentence-based metric requires the coincidence of two consecutive sentence boundaries,[13] while the sentence-boundaries metric only requires the coincidence of one of them.

The results obtained by the 2-in-1 aligner were the best in the three corpora, with more than 93% of F-measure in the Bitextor corpus, more than 73% in the Quixote corpus and more than 58% in the mIRC corpus.

[13] Two consecutive sentence boundaries delimit a sentence.

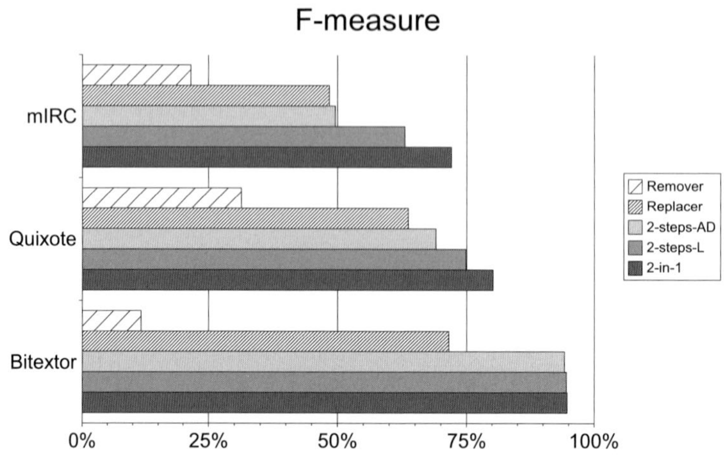

Fig. 4. F-measure achieved by the aligners using the sentence-boundary metric

Table 3. Average segment length (standard deviation) for each corpus and each aligner in characters

	Remover	Replacer	2-steps-AD	2-steps-L	2-in-1
mIRC	38(65)	33(52)	29(46)	29(46)	29(47)
Quixote	75(166)	40(95)	37(85)	37(85)	37(86)
Bitextor	95(285)	22(31)	21(29)	21(29)	21(29)

Additionally, it is worth examining the average in segment length of the different aligners, given that they apply different sentence splitting criteria. In table 3 the comparison of the results of the different aligners is shown. As expected, the proposed aligners build shorter sentences than basic geometric aligners. The standard deviation is much higher than the average because the sentence length distribution in common texts is not a standard distribution, as it is explained in (Sigurd et al., 2003).

Nevertheless, as a counterpart, the tag aligners are slower than basic geometric aligners. Table 4 contains the results of the time comparison of the alignment of the Bitextor corpus. The processing times of basic geometric aligners were aproximately one half of the processing times of the tag aligners. The tag aligners align a higher number of items than basic aligners; this is because basic aligners do not consider the tags as items, which explains the significant difference in processing time.

Finally, some related experiments (changing the classification of tags) have been studied and are shown in figure 5. When format tags are considered as irrelevant tags, the results are slightly worse (7–18% worse for the mIRC corpus, 6–16% worse for the Quixote corpus and 4–5% for the Bitextor corpus). When content tags are considered as irrelevant tags, the results are quite different in each of the corpus: 17–22% worse for the mIRC corpus, similar results for the Quixote corpus and 2–4% better for the Bitextor corpus.

Table 4. Time spent by the aligners while processing the Bitextor corpus

	Remover	Replacer	2-steps-AD	2-steps-L	2-in-1
Time	155 s	153 s	318 s	294 s	323 s

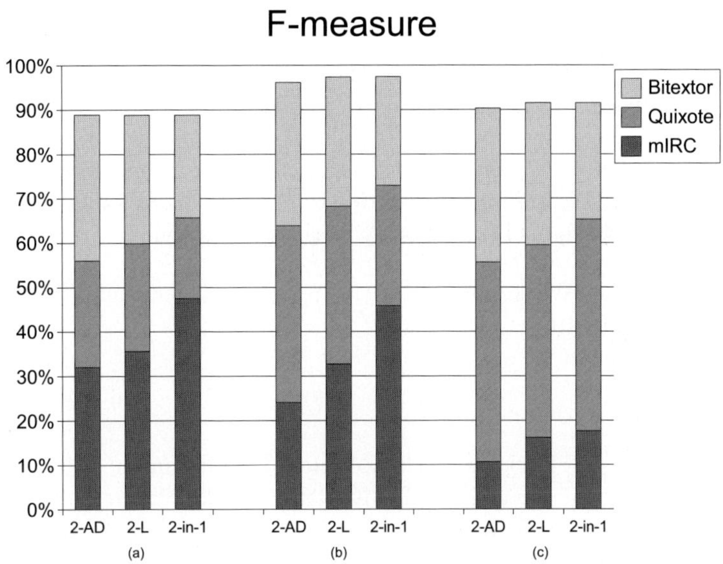

Fig. 5. *F*-measure achieved by the aligners in related experiments: (a) Ignoring format tags. (b) Ignoring content tags. (c) Ignoring format and content tags.

6 Conclusions

The alignment algorithms presented in this paper achieve a better level of quality, compared to classical algorithms, as has been shown in the experiments. This strongly suggests that using the tag structure of the webpages is very useful when aligning bitexts.

The quality of the bitexts used to perform the experiments was not optimal, that is, the bitexts were not accurate translations. In many cases, the tag structure of pairs of real parallel text was slightly different. In spite of this, the results have been clearly better than simply filtering the tags before the alignment.

Additionally, the aligned text segments generated by the proposed aligners have a smaller length than those obtained by basic geometric aligners. This may improve the reusability of the resulting translation units in many translation applications.

The comparison of the aligners revealed that the 2-in-1 aligner obtains the best results in all corpora. This suggests that it is not necessary to apply two steps in the aligners given that the results did not improve, but made the algorithm more complex.

The aligners proposed in this paper can be downloaded freely[14] because they have been released under the GNU General Public License.[15]

7 Future Work

We are developing translation applications that will be trained with the translation units generated by the aligners. They will translate sentences by choosing the best combination of translation units that compose them.

However, it is not clear which one is the best combination of translation units that compose a sentence-pair, although using the most frequent ones appears to give better results. We are researching different ways of combining the harvested translation units to improve the quality of the translation.

Acknowledgements. Work funded by the Spanish Government through grant TIC2003-08681-C02-01.

Bibliography

Black, E., Abney, S., Flickenger, D., Gdaniec, C., Grishman, R., Harrison, P., Hin-dle, D., Ingria, R., Jelinek, F., Klavans, J., Liberman, M., Marcus, M., Roukos, S., Santorini, B., and Strzalkowski, T. (1991). A procedure for quantitatively comparing syntactic coverage of english grammars. In *DARPA Speech and Natural Language Workshop.*

Brown, P. F., Lai, J. C., and Mercer, R. L. (1991). Aligning sentences in parallel corpora. In *Proceedings of the 29th Meeting of the Association for Computational Linguistics*, pages 169–176, Berkeley. University of California.

Chen, S. F. (1993). Aligning sentences in bilingual corpora using lexical information. In *Proceedings of the 31st annual meeting on Association for Computational Linguistics*, pages 9–16, Morristown, NJ, USA. Association for Computational Linguistics.

Gale, W. A. and Church, K. W. (1991). A program for aligning sentences in bilingual corpora. In *Meeting of the Association for Computational Linguistics*, pages 177–184.

Gale, W. A. and Church, K. W. (1993). A program for aligning sentences in bilingual corpora. *Computational Linguistics*, 19:75–102.

Melamed, I. D. (1996). A geometric approach to mapping bitext correspondence. In Brill, E. and Church, K., editors, *Proceedings of the Conference on Empirical Methods in Natural Language Processing*, pages 1–12. Association for Computational Linguistics, Somerset, New Jersey.

Sánchez-Villamil, E., Tomás, J., and Forcada, M. L. (2006). Building parallel text collections for closely related languages. Unpublished.

Sigurd, B., Eeg-Olofsson, M., and van Weijer, J. (2003). Word length, sentence length and frequency - Zipf revisited. *Studia Linguistica*, 58(1):37–52.

[14] `http://sourceforge.net/projects/tag-aligner`

[15] `http://www.gnu.org/licenses/gpl.html`

Experiments in Passage Selection and Answer Identification for Question Answering

Horacio Saggion and Robert Gaizauskas

Department of Computer Science
University of Sheffield
211 Portobello Street
Sheffield - S1 4DP
England - United Kingdom
{saggion, robertg}@dcs.shef.ac.uk

Abstract. Question Answering (QA) aims at providing users with short text units that answer specific, well-formed natural language questions. A two stage architecture is widely adopted for this task consisting of a document retrieval step followed by an answer extraction step. In such an approach two main problems need to be addressed to reduce the search space: better selecting answer bearing passages in the document retrieval step and better pinpointing answers in the answer extraction step. We investigate the effect of word-based and linguistic-based features for the identification of answer-bearing sentences and answer candidates in a QA system and show that both play a significant role.

1 Introduction

Finding textual answers to open domain questions in huge text collections is a challenging problem [Hirschman and Gaizauskas, 2001]. Unlike Information Retrieval (IR) which aims at providing documents satisfying users information needs expressed in the form of a query, Question Answering (QA) aims at providing users with, usually short, text units that answer specific, well-formed natural language questions.

The Text REtrieval Conferences (TREC) [Voorhees, 2002] have clearly defined question types, data, and evaluation methods to assess the performance of QA systems.

In the work reported here we have focused solely on factoid questions which require single facts as answers. The evaluation metric defined by TREC for factoid questions is answer-accuracy: the percent of correct answers found by the system. We have developed a QA system which is composed of an information retrieval (IR) engine followed by an answer extraction (AE) component. This approach is widely adopted by TREC participants. However it has the disadvantage of bounding the performance of the QA system by that of the IR engine. Recent studies in QA [Gaizauskas et al., 2004] have shown that one has to descend deep in the ranked list of documents in order to find passages containing

T. Salakoski et al. (Eds.): FinTAL 2006, LNAI 4139, pp. 291–302, 2006.

the answer[1]. For example, using NIST Z-PRISE system one has to descend to rank 1000 in order to have 87% coverage[2] over the TREC 2003 factoid questions. At the same time, as the AE component is given lower rank documents to consider more answer hypotheses appear, thus decreasing answer-accuracy. One way of obtaining answer bearing passages at higher ranks is by applying re-ranking methods to the IR output to maximise coverage at lower ranks. Another alternative, which we investigate in this work, is to train classifiers for passage identification so that passages unlikely to contain the answer can be identified and discarded as early as possible (or the classifier's outcome probability used for re-ranking purposes).

Based on previous reported success with the use of boolean search for QA [Harabagiu et al., 2000], we have developed an in-house boolean search engine that performs word indexing at the sentence level (see Section 3) that we used in the experiments described here. For the AE component (detailed in Section 4), we have adopted a NLP-based approach where questions and candidate passages are transformed into semantic representations by a process of robust, partial parsing. Each entity in a candidate passage is scored according to (i) its semantic proximity to the expected answer type (EAT), (ii) the number of linguistic-based relations involving an entity from the question that appear in the candidate passage, and (iii) the similarity between the question and the passage where the candidate comes from. The entity with the highest score is proposed as the answer to the question. For example, question 2219 from TREC/QA *"How tall is Al Pacino?"* asks for a measurement EAT. A suitable candidate passage from AQUAINT to answer this question is document NYT19990811.0068 where the following sentence is found:

> *"Other celebs in their stocking feet: Danny DeVito, 5 feet; Spike Lee, 5 feet 5 inches; Al Pacino, 5 feet 6 inches; and Martin Sheen, 5 feet 7 inches."*

Note that there are many candidate answers in this passage. However, because *"Al Pacino"* (a question entity) and *"5 feet 6 inches"* are in a relation of apposition in the passage, the latter should be considered a more likely answer than other competing candidates: this is the approach taken by our extraction component.

In spite of its linguistic appeal, the value of the linguistic-based features used by our extraction component had yet, prior to the work reported here, to be quantitatively assessed. In this work we try to remedy this situation by addressing two related issues: (i) the identification of answer bearing passages returned by the IR engine as a way of reducing noise; and (ii) the identification of answers in answer bearing passages to boost answer-accuracy.

---

[1] We use the term "high ranked" documents to refer to documents that are judged more relevant to a query than documents that are "low ranked", though the numeric rank associated with a high ranked document (e.g. 1) is lower than the rank associated with a low ranked document (e.g. 1000).

[2] *Coverage at rank k* is the proportion of questions for which a correct answer can be found within the top k retrieved documents [Roberts and Gaizauskas, 2004].

We see both tasks as classification problems and adopt a supervised machine learning (ML) research methodology, making use of the WEKA software [Witten and Eibe, 2000]. In order to carry out experimentation we have created a data-set of answer-bearing sentences, non-answer bearing sentences, and answers for a subset of TREC 2003 factoid questions. In the experiments reported below, we study the effect of word-based and linguistic-based features derived from question/passage analysis on the process of identifying answer bearing passages and answers.

More generally, and from an AI perspective, our work tries to assess the question of to what extent linguistic analysis helps in the QA enterprise.

In the rest of the paper we introduce in detail our IR and AE components. Then, we describe the data set, experiments and results on passage and answer identification. Finally, we close with conclusions and suggestions for further research.

2 Related Work

Question Answering has been part of the artificial intelligence agenda for a long time [Woods, 1973]. However, fuelled by the Internet, the huge volume of on-line texts, and the establishment of the TREC/QA track [Voorhees, 2002], Question Answering is nowadays receiving unprecedented attention from research laboratories and commercial companies. In a traditional document retrieval/answer extraction architecture two main problems need to be addressed: document filtering and answer pinpointing. In order to obtain good answer bearing passages as early as possible, a two-pass strategy can be used which will first extract a large number of candidate passages and then re-rank them by using learned ranking functions [Usunier et al., 2004]. Such an approach has been shown to increase coverage with respect to the unranked IR output. One technique that has been applied to combat the noise produced by the IR system is filtering of answer candidates by type checking the expected answer type. Because named entity recognisers of coarse-grained types of named entities (e.g., dates, places, people, organisations) tend to be quite accurate, checking the type of the candidate answer has a positive impact for certain types of question [Schlobach et al., 2004]. However, and in spite of recent advances in the development of fine-grained question type hierarchies [Hovy et al., 2001], open domain question answering may need additional techniques for answer filtering.

3 Boolean Information Retrieval

In the experiments described in this paper we have made use of an in-house boolean retrieval system which performs word indexing at the sentence level (see [Gaizauskas et al., 2003] for a description of the boolean search engine). A basic boolean query language was implemented which supports queries of arbitrarily deeply nested conjunctions and disjunctions of search terms (words); negation is not supported at this point as there has not appeared to be a need for it. For boolean retrieval engines the task of formulating queries to retrieve documents relevant to answering some question is non-trivial. A query formed as a conjunction of the words in the question (omitting stoplist words, perhaps) will commonly be too restrictive, returning few or no documents, whereas a query that is a disjunction of the same words will commonly retrieve too many. The best approach for formulating boolean retrieval queries is an open research topic. However, we have recently carried out extensive experimentation and identified a strategy for question analysis and sentence retrieval [Saggion et al., 2004]. This strategy is an iterative process which starts with an initial query and then modifies it until the required number of sentences have been returned or no further refinements to the query are possible.

The strategy for document retrieval achieved 62.15% coverage at rank 200 (on TREC/QA 2003 factoid data) which compares unfavourably to the 80.4% coverage at the same rank for Z-PRISE. However, while at rank 200 our retrieval system will return on average 137 sentences per question, Z-PRISE will return around 4600, broadening considerably the search space for the AE component.

4 Answer Extraction

Answer extraction receives as input a set of candidate passages and returns one answer per question (or the constant NIL if an answer cannot be found). Depending on the IR retrieval component, passages can be full-documents, paragraphs, or as with the IR approach previously described, sentences matching the query.

AE is a pipeline of freely available components which include named entity recognition, POS-tagging, parsing, and discourse interpretation. The system first carries out partial, robust syntactic and semantic analysis of the passages returned by the search engine and of the question, transducing them both into a predicate-argument or quasi-logical form (QLF) representation (see Figure 1). Note the analysis may well be only partially correct - e.g. the EAT in the representation shown in Figure 1 is not the logical object of the verb *to travel.*

In this representation the predicates are, for the most part, either the unary predicates formed from the morphological roots of nominal (e.g. `submarine`) or verbal (e.g. `travel`) forms in the text or binary predicates from a closed set of grammatical relations (e.g. `lobj` for the verb logical object, `lsubj` for the verb logical subject) or of prepositions (e.g. `in`, `after`) or the special binary predicate `name` to identify the name of a named entity. Identifiers (e_n) are created for each entity in the representation.

In this step, the EAT is determined (e.g., `measure`) and depending on the question, a special attribute (`qattr`) is created which indicates the attribute-value to be output from the answer entity. For example in the case of a measurement, the value to extract is an attribute `count` that should be attached to the answer.

Given these sentence level "semantic" representations of candidate answer-bearing passages and of the question, a discourse interpretation step then creates

1937: *How fast can a nuclear submarine travel? QLF:* travel(e2), submarine(e1), lsubj(e2,e1), lobj(e2,e3), adj(e1,nuclear), qvar(e3), qattr(e3,count), measure(e3)

Fig. 1. Parser output for question 1937. `qvar` represents the sought answer.

a discourse model of each retrieved passage by running a coreference algorithm against the semantic representation of successive sentences in the passage, in order to unify them with the discourse model built for the passage so far. This results in multiple references to the same entity across the passage being merged into a single unified instance. Next, coreference is computed again between the QLF of the question and the discourse model of the passage, in order to unify common references.

In this model, possible answer entities are identified and scored as follows. First each sentence in each passage is given a score based on counting matches of entity types (unary predicates) between the sentence QLF and the question QLF. Next each entity from a passage not so matched with an entity in the question (and hence remaining a possible answer) gets a preliminary score according to (1) its semantic proximity to the EAT using WordNet and (2) whether or not it stands in a relation R to some other entity in the sentence in which it occurs which is itself matched with an entity in the question which stands in relation R to the sought entity (e.g. an entity in a candidate answer passage which is the subject of a verb that matches a verb in the question whose subject is the sought entity will have its score boosted). An overall score is computed for each entity as a function of its preliminary score and the score of the sentence in which it occurs. The final answer to the question is the entity with the highest score.

5 Experiments

One of the main goals of this work is to better understand the contribution of various features in use in our system for the passage selection and answer identification tasks.

5.1 Q&A Data

The data used in the experiments reported here is that used in the TREC 2003 QA track. The text collection used is the AQUAINT corpus consisting of approximately one million documents drawn from three newswire sources for the period 1998-2000 (about 3.2 gigabytes of text). The TREC 2003 question set consists of a subset of 150 factoid questions from the collection. In order to support automated evaluation, NIST produces regular expression patterns for each question which match strings containing the answer. In addition to the regular patterns, NIST also provides the document ids where correct answers can be found. In order to identify answer bearing sentences (ABS) from AQUAINT we relied on the documents judged as correct by NIST analysts: each sentence in an answer bearing document is considered an ABS if it matches a question pattern and an additional manual check to verify that the sentence does answer the question.

For example, consider question 2293 *"How many times a day do observant muslims pray?"*. It has as possible correct answers the strings provided by NIST *"five"* and *"at least five"*. The following two sentences were extracted from answer bearing documents identified by NIST:

(S1) *But at work, it takes about* **five** *minutes counting the time it takes to get to a prayer area and wash their hands if necessary.*

(S2) *As devout Muslims, they consider it their duty to pray* **at least five** *times a day, one of those times while they are at work.*

both (S1) and (S2) contain an instance of an answer string. However only (S2) is an ABS because it allows one to infer an answer to the question.

In order to identify non answer bearing sentences (NABS), we relied on our boolean search engine. For each question we pulled out from AQUAINT at most 100 sentences following the strategy previously described. Sentences which are not ABS were considered NABS. This strategy has been designed so that the instances used for the experiment simulate a natural QA setting where most of the sentences returned by the IR engine will be NABS. The distribution of sentences in the data set is rather skewed with only 25% of the cases being ABS. Each question and sentence was analysed by the AE parser and transformed into a logical representation. Logical forms and linguistic information such as words, word lemmas, and POS categories are available for feature computation. The full process of linguistic analysis is automatic and as a consequence imperfect.

5.2 Features for Passage Identification

In the experiments reported here, we study the effect of word-based and linguistic features as potential sources of information for ABS identification.

During experimentation we fixed the following word-based features (words and lemmas are normalised to lowercase and stop words are removed): (W1) number of common lemmas between question and sentence, and (W2) number of common words between question and sentence. In addition to these two, four more features represent the size of the respective sets of question/sentence lemmas/words. This set of features which we denote WBF is too simple to differentiate cases which are extremely different. Consider for example question 2384 from TREC/QA: *"What is the population of Canberra?"* and two candidate sentences

(S3) "Canberra with a population of 306,400"

and

(S4) "The prospect of an exodus of refugees from a population of 210 million causes alarm from Canberra to Bangkok".

Both sentences match all nonstop question words and lemmas, thus they are identical with respect to W1 and W2. Note, however, that (S3) contains a relation between *"Canberra"* and *"population"* which is not present in sentence (S4). A relation between *"Canberra"* and *"population"* also occurs in the question, thus making (S3) more likely to contain an answer. It is intuitive to think that the presence in a sentence of entities together with relations which also appear in the question should be used to estimate ABS likelihood.

2392: *When was the Red Cross founded? QLF:* qvar(e1), qattr(e1,name), date(e1), found(e2) lsubj(e2,e3), name(e3,'Red Cross'), in(e2,e1)
F1: $date(X)$
F2: $date(X)$
F3: $found(X)$
F4: $name(X,' RedCross')$
F5: $found(X) \wedge date(Y)$
F6: VOID
F7: $found(X) \wedge name(Y,' RedCross')$
F8: VOID

Fig. 2. Sets for feature computation

Therefore, for each question we compute four linguistic-based sets: (F1) the expected answer type set of those predicates in the QLF possibly representing the answer; (F2) the predicates in the QLF derived from nouns (objects); (F3) the predicates in the QLF derived from verbs (events); and (F4) the instances of the binary predicate `name` (the named entities). These sets are used as the basis for computation of sets of pairs of predicates (linguistically motivated bigrams) indicating that a relation exists between: (F5) an object and an event; (F6) two objects; (F7) a name and an event; and finally (F8) a name and an object. These F1-F8 sets are used to compute eight features for each sentence representing the number of elements in each set matching the sentence QLF. For sets of bigrams, it is checked whether or not a relation exists between the two components of the bigram in the QLF. In Figure 2 we show how sets F1-F8 are computed for question 2392. An ABS for question 2392 such as:

1863 - International Committee of the Red Cross is founded in Geneva.

having QLF:

```
date(e1), name(e1,1863), name(e3,'Geneva'), organization(e11),
name(e11,'International Comitee'), of(e11,e12), name(e12,'Red Cross'),
found(e10), in(e10,e13), lobj(e10,e11)
```

will have features instantiated as follows F1=1, F2=1, F3=1, F4=1, F5=0 (because `date` and `found` are not related in the sentence), F6=VOID, F7=0 (because e12 is not related to the event `found`), and F8=VOID. Additionally, the size of the respective sets is computed for each question and used as a feature. We refer to this complete feature set as LBF.

We have made use of different classifiers from the WEKA toolkit in order to identify whether the data described with word-based features (WBF) or linguistic-based features (LBF) helps the learner in this binary classification task. We use the *ZeroR* classifier as a baseline against which we compare the more informed methods. Its strategy is to classify all sentences according to the most frequent category: NABS in our case.

5.3 Results

We have experimented with several algorithms and obtained statistical improvement over the baseline. Table 1 shows the performance (in terms of *%correct*) of J48, a particular WEKA implementation of the C4.5 decision tree algorithm which was one of the most accurate classifiers. It outperforms the baseline (at a 99% confidence level) using either of the two feature sets[3]. Interestingly, there is no statistical difference in classification accuracy between J48 using either WBF ($J48_{WBF}$) or LBF ($J48_{LBF}$). In order to verify if the two sets of features could be used together in order to improve classification accuracy we have specified a pos-hoc classifier (Comb) which uses the outcome and posterior probability of the J48 classifiers. Given a sentence representation S, Comb computes $J48_{WBF}(S)$ and $J48_{LBF}(S)$ and their respective outcome probabilities $P_{WBF}(S)$ and $P_{LBF}(S)$. Comb classifies S as $J48_{WBF}(S)$ if $P_{WBF}(S) \geq P_{LBF}(S)$ otherwise it classifies S as $J48_{LBF}(S)$. This algorithm outperforms significantly (confidence level %99) both WBF and LBF (See Table 1).

Table 1. Experimental results for answer bearing sentence identification. Column ABS indicates the number of ABS instances correctly classified. Column NABS indicates the number of NABS correctly classified. Column ALL indicates the number of instances correctly classified.

Classifier	ABS	NABS	ALL
Baseline	0 (0%)	3507 (100%)	3507 (74%)
$J48_{WBF}$	708 (57%)	3477 (99%)	4185 (88%)
$J48_{LBF}$	824 (66%)	3349 (96%)	4173 (88%)
Comb	861 (69%)	3432 (98%)	4293 (90%)

6 Features for Answer Identification

For the experiments described here, we need to identify for each entity in an answer-bearing sentence whether or not it is an answer. We carry out this task in two steps, firstly identifying the offsets of the answer string provided by NIST,

[3] Apart from differences in *%correct*, statistically significant differences are observed in *precision*, *recall*, and *F-measure*.

and then extracting from the QLF the entity id (e_k) that is realised within those offsets.

We use a set of six features derived from the linguistic intuitions used in the AE component. In order to compute them we first create for each question the following sets of lambda expressions: (L1) the expected answer types set of those predicated in the QLF representing the answer; (L2) the set of expected attributes from the answer (e.g. `qattr`); (L3) the predicate the sought entity is the logical subject of; (L4) the predicate the sought entity is the logical object of; (L5) the set of predicates the sought entity is related to by a relation different from subject or object; (L6) the set of predicates occurring in the question (excluding the EAT). Figure 3 shows the required sets for feature computation for an example question. Given a sentence and an answer candidate, each lambda expression (L1-L6) is instantiated with the candidate hypothesis and matched against the sentence logical form. The corresponding feature will be true if the instantiated expression matches the QLF, otherwise it will be false. Consider again the following answer bearing sentence for question 2392:

1863 - International Committee of the Red Cross is founded in Geneva.

and its partial QLF:

```
...found(e10), in(e10,e13), name(e3,'Geneva'),
date(e1), name(e1,1863)...
```

Figure 4 shows how the features are instantiated for entities $e1$ (an answer) and $e13$ (a non-answer). For example in order to test (L5) with entity $e1$ the goal $found(Y) \wedge in(Y, e1)$ (e.g., $e1$ is attached to the event `found` by relation `in`) will be matched against the sentence QLF. The class of the entity will be 'answer' or 'non-answer' according to the procedure described above.

For this task again, the distribution of answer/non-answers is very skewed with only 6% of positive instances. This again leaves very little space for classification improvement. We have experimented with different classifiers from the WEKA toolkit and have compared them with *ZeroR* classifier which classifies each entity as a non-answer.

6.1 Results

The best performing algorithms were again decision trees (J48). The classification performance of this algorithm is shown in Table 2. Two *J48* instances are presented, one uses the full set of features ($J48_{ALL}$) while the other uses only features L1 and L2 ($J48_{L1;L2}$). Both configurations outperform significantly the baseline at a 99% confidence level. Algorithm $J48_{ALL}$ has a modest absolute improvement in classification accuracy over $J48_{L1;L2}$ which is statistically significant at 99% confidence level.

2392: *When was the Red Cross founded? QLF:* qvar(e1), qattr(e1,name), date(e1), found(e2) lsubj(e2,e3), name(e3,'Red Cross'), in(e2,e1)
L1: $\lambda X.date(X)$
L2: $\lambda X.name(X, Y)$
L3: VOID
L4: VOID
L5: $\lambda X.found(Y) \wedge in(Y, X)$
L6: $\lambda X.found(X) \vee \lambda X.name(X,' RedCross')$

Fig. 3. Features for answer identification (question 2392)

Features	L1	L2	L3	L4	L5	L6
e1	true	true	VOID	VOID	false	false
e13	false	false	VOID	VOID	true	true

Fig. 4. Features computed for entities $e1$ and $e13$ from an ABS from document APW19981023.1385

6.2 Discussion

In our experiments with sentence classification both word-based features and linguistic-based features combine to outperform either of the feature sets individually. It should be noted that in further experiments with the learning environment, we have come to the conclusion that the EAT is not the only feature responsible for classification accuracy.

Our experiments on answer classification provide interesting insights into the role of the linguistic features used in our QA system. Our results seem to indicate that features from question analysis help in the answer classification task and that the EAT is not the only factor in answer identification. This result however should be interpreted with caution: the results of answer classification indicate that from the 150 questions in the set:

- 2 questions (1%) would be incorrectly answered because no true answer is identified as such, instead two false positives are output;
- 14 questions (9%) could be correctly and unambiguously answered using the classifier because only true positives and true negatives are output;
- 16 questions (11%) would need an additional disambiguation step (probably taking into account answer redundancy) because the classifier outputs both true positives and false positives; and finally
- 118 questions (79%) would remain unanswered because all instances were classified as non-answers (true negatives and false negatives)

These results, however considerable, are rather modest. This can be attributed to the following facts. On the one hand, the data used in our experiments, because automatically produced is far from correct, making sophisticated-relational features rather sparse. On the other hand, the features studied here are derived from the 'superficial' forms obtained through question analysis, thus ignoring the mismatch problem between relations in the question and similar relations in

Table 2. Accuracy results for answer identification

Classifier	ANSWER	NON-ANSWER	ALL
Baseline	0 (0%)	6351 (100%)	6351 (93%)
$J48_{ALL}$	111 (24.77%)	6296 (99.16%)	6390 (94.26%)
$J48_{L1;L2}$	91 (20.31%)	6300 (99.22%)	6390 (94.02%)

the answer-bearing sentence. The latter could be addressed by incorporating a sophisticated process of paraphrase identification [Lin and Pantel, 2001].

7 Conclusion and Future Work

A number of valuable results have emerged from this work. First, our experiments on answer-bearing sentence classification show that a number of easy-to-compute word-based features combined with linguistically-motivated ones help in the classification task. However, the success of the classification should be tested in a working environment and the contribution of each individual feature better assessed. Because of the unbalanced characteristic of the data set, it seems better to use the sentence classifiers for sentence ranking, postponing decisions until answer extraction takes place.

Second, in experiments on answer identification, linguistic-features used by our system seem to make a contribution in answer pinpointing. This result should be carefully examined, however. Our experiments depend strongly on a process that accurately identifies answer-bearing sentences and so leaves little space for ambiguity. In order to assess the impact of the parsing process in the accuracy of classification, we intend to either assess the accuracy or our parser or replicate these experiments using an evaluated system. We believe that answer classification could be used here again to rank entities according to their answer likelihood.

In future work, the resources produced in this work will be assessed using TREC/QA evaluation metrics by incorporating the classifiers into our QA system and measuring end-to-end performance.

The approaches we have studied here rely on natural intuitions about how answers to questions should behave in what the linguistic structure of questions and answer bearing passages is concern. However with the ever increasing availability of QA data, an inductive approach could help identify new features which are not directly associated with our linguistic intuitions. This approach is part of our research agenda.

References

[Gaizauskas et al., 2003] Gaizauskas, R., Greenwood, M., Hepple, M., Roberts, I., Saggion, H., and Sargaison, M. (2003). The University of Sheffield's TREC 2003 Q&A Experiments. In *Proceedings of the 12th Text REtrieval Conference.*

[Gaizauskas et al., 2004] Gaizauskas, R., Hepple, M., and Greenwood, M., editors (2004). *IR4QA: Information Retrieval for Question Answering*, SIGIR Workshops.

[Harabagiu et al., 2000] Harabagiu, S., Moldovan, D., Paşca, M., Mihalcea, R., Surdeanu, M., Bunescu, R., Gîrju, R., Rus, V., and Morărescu, P. (2000). FALCON: Boosting Knowledge for Answer Engines. In *Proceedings of the 9th Text REtrieval Conference*.

[Hirschman and Gaizauskas, 2001] Hirschman, L. and Gaizauskas, R. (2001). Natural Language Question Answering: The View From Here. *Natural Language Engineering*, 7(4).

[Hovy et al., 2001] Hovy, E., Geber, L., Hermjakob, U., Lin, C.-Y., and Ravichandran, D. (2001). Question Answering in Webclopedia. In *Proceedings of the 9th Text REtrieval Conference)*.

[Lin and Pantel, 2001] Lin, D. and Pantel, P. (2001). Discovery of Inference Rules for Question Answering. *Natural Language Engineering*, 7(4).

[Roberts and Gaizauskas, 2004] Roberts, I. and Gaizauskas, R. (2004). Evaluating passage retrieval approaches for question answering. In *Advances in Information Retrieval: Proceedings of the 26th European Conference on Information Retrieval (ECIR04)*, number 2997 in LNCS, pages 72–84, Sunderland. Springer.

[Saggion et al., 2004] Saggion, H., Gaizauskas, R., Hepple, M., Roberts, I., and Greenwood, M. A. (2004). Exploring the Performance of Boolean Retrieval Strategies for Open Domain Question Answering. In *Proceedings of the SIGIR Workshop on Information Retrieval for Question Answering (IR4QA)*, Sheffield, UK.

[Schlobach et al., 2004] Schlobach, S., Olsthoorn, M., and de Rijke, M. (2004). Type Checking in Open-Domain Question Answering. In *Proceedings of EACI*, pages 398–402.

[Usunier et al., 2004] Usunier, N., Amini, M., and Gallinari, P. (2004). Boosting Weak Ranking Functions to Enhance Pssage Retrieval for Question Answering. In *Proceedings of the SIGIR Workshop on Information Retrieval for Question Answering*, pages 53–58.

[Voorhees, 2002] Voorhees, E. M. (2002). Overview of the TREC 2002 Question Answering Track. In *Proceedings of the 11th Text REtrieval Conference*.

[Witten and Eibe, 2000] Witten, I. and Eibe, F. (2000). *Data Mining: Practical machine learning tools with Java implementations*. Morgan Kaufmann, San Francisco.

[Woods, 1973] Woods, W. (1973). Progress in Natural Language Understanding - An Application to Lunar Geology. In *AFIPS Conference Proceedings*, volume 42, pages 441–450.

Extracting Idiomatic Hungarian Verb Frames

Bálint Sass

Research Institute for Linguistics, Hungarian Academy of Sciences
joker@nytud.hu

Abstract. We describe a machine learning method for collecting idiomatic fixed stem verb frames. Firstly we collect frequent frame candidates from the output of a partial parser, secondly we apply a certain idiomaticity metric to the list to get the most idiomatic frames. Running our implemented system we get a list of ten thousand frames of more than 900 verbs which will be translated to English and used as a resource in a Hungarian-to-English machine translation system.

1 Introduction

In a project we are currently creating a Hungarian-to-English machine translation system. In such a system it is important to be aware of idiomatic expressions [1], because their translation is irregular. They can not be treated at grammar level, they should get into the lexicon.

By the term *verb frame* we mean a verb with something like its valency, more specifically, how many and what kind of NPs can or must appear together with that verb. *Position* within a frame is defined by either word order, or a given preposition/casemark/postposition. Different frames of the same verb often represent different lexical *senses* [2], therefore if we have all idiomatic verb frames listed, we will be able to use the correct sense in translations.

Though there are recent efforts to extract frames and their translation in one step [1], we follow a more traditional way: frames will be translated manually to English to provide a high-quality lexical resource. We already have a manually built table with Hungarian verb frames. Such tables are usually tend to be incomplete [3,4], so our present task is to collect missing frames. However, our aim is to collect as many frames as possible, we obviously need the most important/frequent ones only.

Hungarian is a free-word-order language, and verbs indicate explicit case markings for their complements. There are many papers dealing with English frames [2,3], but only few dealing with a free-word-order language (eg. Czech) [5]. We build our system mainly on methods described in this paper, and we also go one step further. Concerning the Hungarian language there is a related paper [6], which investigates Hungarian multiword expressions, namely simple verb + noun + casemark patterns.

For translation purposes it is important to have the so-called *fixed stem* frames, where only one (or at most a couple of) defined stem can appear at a given position of the frame. For example in English frames to take stock of sg

T. Salakoski et al. (Eds.): FinTAL 2006, LNAI 4139, pp. 303–309, 2006.

and to take sg into consideration, the fixed stem is stock in 'object' position and consideration in 'into' position respectively. Not just the frequency what matters, we need to collect such stems, where the meaning is not compositional or more importantly the translation is special. In other words: *idiomatic* fixed stem frames are wanted. We mention, that it is not a big problem if we have some frames at the end, which is compositional, but fully fixed: they can be handled at grammar or at lexicon level with same effort.

Many previous researches (esp. dealing with English) are using a predefined restricted set of verb frames [3]. Searching for new fixed stem frames, we do not have a predefined frame set, such as in [5].

In the next two chapters we describe the two-step method we use to extract idiomatic verb frames. When we mention Hungarian frames we will do it in the form of Hungarian frame[English translation strictly word by word]/English frame. If the latter two is nearly the same, then the word by word translation is omitted.

2 Collecting Verb Frames

Hungarian is a highly inflectional language[1]. There are no prepositions, but about twenty cases, and some dozen postpositions in it. Being a free-word-order language the casemark on the head of an NP shows the relation of that NP to the rest of the sentence, eg. whether it is a subject or an object etc. Apart from being separate words postpositions can be handled as cases (as suggested in [6]). We express possessive relations also with suffixes, so it is important to have a detailed representation of morphological information of every wordform.

The corpus[2] is a special 10 million word subcorpus of the Hungarian National Corpus (HNC) [9]. Our focus is to detect frames with NP complements. We want to examine one-frame units. Not having a clause-determiner tool we take sentences of 3 to 10 words length with no punctuation in them. These sentences contain one frame per sentence with a good chance. We deleted duplications from this corpus, every sentence appears now once.

The HNC is morphologically tagged and disambiguated, so we begin with the syntactic parsing step. Our partial parser implements a *cascaded regular grammar* [10] engine, with some extensions:

- *Word position* can be given, it is useful, when dealing with named entities, where being the first word in a sentence matters;
- *negation* can be used;
- every structure gets all the properties of its head automatically;
- annotation categories are *tiered*, we can use sub-categories;
- it is possible to *delete* annotations, it means we can use a temporary annotation to hide something from the scope of a grammar;
- not just real regular grammar: all possibilities of *extended regular expressions* can be used.

[1] You can have a quick overview of grammar of Hungarian in [7].

[2] The corpus and parser we use are described in detail in [8] (in Hungarian).

Our parser does not distinguish between complements and adjuncts. We use a simple grammar for NP-detection, after that we identify verb stems. If we find an infinitive, then we derive the verb stem from it, because the infinitive always bears the verb frame. In Hungarian, verbal affixes appears as separate words when they are not the direct left neighbour of the verb. If we find such an affix, we attach it to the beginning of the verb stem. We also cut off frequent deverbal verb suffixes (now only the most frequent *-hAt* suffix), because they do not affect verb frame usage.

Next step is to generate the verb frame candidates. Initial idea is similar to [5]. In a sentence every NP is ...

- either taken into account as bare case of the head;
- or as stem + case of the head[3];
- or omitted (it is the so-called *optionalization*).

Frame candidates with *every* variation of the above are normalized, using an alphabetical ordering inside the frame, and collected as a long list [4]. Both true fixed stem frames and free stem frames (frames with no fixed stem in any position) will be frequent in this list. But frames with adjuncts in them will be rare, because adjuncts can appear in many ways eg. as different cases. Thank to optionalization we get the same true frame from different sentences, where different adjuncts appear besides the same frame, and get rid of adjuncts automatically. So if we select frequent ones from candidates list – applying a frequency threshold – we get true verb frames. Using this method we automatically catch both fixed and free positions of a frame. If a verb usually cooccurs with an NP with the same casemark, but the head of the NP varies, it becomes a free stem position of this frame: only the case is defined and presumably any NP-head bearing this casemark can fill it. But if the head is usually the same stem, then it becomes a fixed stem position: only this head with this casemark can fill it.

To make it clearer consider the sentence on Fig. 1. This is an example of

(Hungarian)	A polgármesteri hivatal**t**	bér**be** adták	a filmesek**nek**.
	A polgármesteri hivatal**ACC**	bér**ILL** ad-ták	a filmesek**DAT**.
	The town hall**ACC**	**into** payment give-PLUR3	film-makers**DAT**.
(English)	The town hall	was let to	film-makers.

Fig. 1. An example sentence

the frame ad bérILL ACC DAT[to give sg into payment for sy]/to let sg to sy. In Hungarian it is a fixed stem frame: besides the verb ad the stem bér must occur in a particular case (marked with ILL, translated to English with preposition

[3] Actually, apart from stem and case, also the possessive suffix is recorded, because there are many frames, where it plays an important role.

[4] Though there are true frames with nominative case (like derül fény SUB[to clear light on]/to be discovered) we omitted NPs with nominative case because the noise is too much is this case.

'into'), there is also a free object position (with accusative case ACC) and a free receiver position (with dative case DAT) in this frame. Frame candidates of this sentence can be seen on Fig. 2. After the above process only the frame ad bérILL

```
ad      bérILL filmesDAT hivatalACC
ad      bérILL filmesDAT ACC
ad      bérILL filmesDAT
ad      filmesDAT hivatalACC ILL
ad      filmesDAT ACC ILL
ad      filmesDAT ILL
...
ad      bérILL
ad      hivatalACC ILL
ad      ACC ILL
ad      ILL
ad      hivatalACC
ad      ACC
```

Fig. 2. Frame candidates of sentence on Fig. 1. Only the beginning and the end of the list.

ACC DAT (and its subsets) remains, it means that in position of bérILL can occur only that stem with that case, but words from a broad class can occur in the object and receiver positions.

Given a high-frequency true frame, all frames with a subset of its complements are also become highly frequent. There is no method worked out yet to eliminate them in general, it remains future work. (In our practical case that is not a serious problem, because translators will see this bogus frames right by the good one in an alphabetical list, and they can simply leave them out.)

3 Considering Idiomaticity

As we mentioned, in a machine translation system we need *idiomatic* fixed stem frames, frames whose translation is not regular/trivial. Using the above method, there are many cases when we get a fixed stem frame just because the stem is frequent enough in a particular case, without having a special, idiomatic role. To address the task of filtering out those frames we apply an *idiomaticity metric* based on [11] in a second step.

There is a graduality in idiomaticity of frames from completely transparent to very idiomatic [4]:

1. árusít ACC/to sell sg
2. mentesít alól[5][to exempt sy from under sg]/to exempt sy from sg
3. hoz nyilvánosságSUB ACC[to bring sg onto publicity]/to make sg public

[5] *Alól* is a postposition treated as case.

In short, a given frame is more idiomatic if its *generalized frame* (frame without the verb) is used with only few verbs, most idiomatic frames are used with only one verb. That is the property what our metric measures.

The original paper deals with verb–object relation [11]. It is emphasized that this relation is asymmetric, it can be considered, that a distinct sense of a verb is selected according to the object. The suggested metric – namely *distributed frequency (DF)* – works this way: if an object occurs with only a few verbs, then the DF of this object will be high. More precisely, if a given object ($\mathbf{o}$) appears with n different verbs ($V_{1..n}$) more frequently than a threshold (C) and the frequency of ($V_k, \mathbf{o}$) collocates is F_k, then the formula for calculating DF for this object looks as follows:

$$DF(\mathbf{o}) = \sum_{k=1}^{n} \frac{F_k^a}{n^b}$$

In our case we must apply this technique not to two words (a verb and an object) but to a verb and a generalized frame. We simply get the generalized frame as a string, and apply the method. For example in case of ad bérILL ACC DAT the string representation of the generalized frame will be bérILL ACC DAT. For above constants we use: $C = 5$, $a = 1$, $b = 1.2$.

In the paper in question nothing is said about how to assign a DF-value to different verb–frame pairs, they – because of the same generalized frame – seem to have the same DF-value. Somewhat similarly to definition of salience [6], to prefer such pairs where the verb is more frequent, we multiply the DF-value with the relative frequency of verb within the generalized frame, so we define our eventual idiomaticity metric (so-called *DF-score*) as follows:

$$DF\text{-}score(V_k, \mathbf{o}) = DF(\mathbf{o}) \cdot \frac{F_k}{\sum_{i=1}^{n} F_i}$$

If this score is above a certain threshold, the frame get into the list of idiomatic frames. Since the graduality in idiomaticity [4], we can not say that some frames are idiomatic and some frames are not, we can only say that the frames at the top of the list are more idiomatic than the others at the bottom. We set the threshold to have such a list, which is manageable in size to be manually translated.

4 Results

Our final list contains 10100 verb frames for 911 verbs. There are 8859 different frame types in it. Obviously, the cause of the latter number being such big, is that every different fixed stem frame is counted separately.

Frames that appear with one verb alone like tesz kijelentésACC/to make statement, pótol hiányACC/to fill gap get into the list. The generalized frame példaACC appears with many (namely 24) verbs, so these not very idiomatic frames are omitted: mond példaACC/to say example, vesz példaACC/to take example, említ példaACC/to mention example, mutat példaACC/to show example. Conversely, the generalized frame példaACC DAT appears only with one verb: mutat példaACC DAT[to show example for sy]/to set example for sy. As a result of idiomaticity-filtering mutat példaACC appearing 49 times is filtered out, and the idiomatic mutat példaACC DAT appearing only 13 times gets into the final verb frame list. It seems that the idiomaticity-filtering is also useful for throwing off bogus subset-frames, mentioned on page 306.

Firstly, to perform some pilot-measurements on precision and recall of the idiomaticity-filtering step, we manually annotated the frames, "which must be translated some special way" in some parts of the raw list generated by the collecting step. With this definition of goodness we get result seeming rather bad (precision ranges from 12 to 75% and recall ranges from 46 to 81%). It should be noted that from our point of view recall is obviously more important, because manual translators can leave out incorrect frames easily. One possible cause of these results can be, that we do not consider frequency of the frames, when we make the manually annotated list.

Secondly, to have an overview about the adequacy of the whole process we should compare our results to an existing verb frame source, as authoritative as possible. There is no available electronic verb frame dictionaries for Hungarian, so we contrast manually a small sample of 17 frames from our final list with the Hungarian Concise Dictionary. There are 15 frames in the written dictionary, from which we found 5, so at first sight the recall to the dictionary is bad (5/15=33%). Conversely, it turns out that from the 17 frames found, 14 are true frames, so our method presents 9 new frames not appearing in the dictionary. That is the well-known problem of evaluation against dictionaries: we can not find some rare items, because they do not appear in our corpus, and we find additional true items, because of some information gaps in the dictionary [4].

5 Future work

The parser itself needs improvement to be able to parse complex sentences, moreover a better grammar implementing a full-featured Hungarian NP-grammar should be used.

The binomial filtering method described in [12] can be tested for getting rid of frames which only occurs by error.

There is a need of a general solution for throwing off frequent bogus subsets of frequent frames. A good basis can be the method described in [5].

If we want to measure idiomaticity of free stem frames too, perhaps an other, more sensitive idiomacity metric should be worked out.

6 Conclusion

We described a machine learning method for extracting idiomatic fixed stem verb frames from a POS-tagged corpus. We used two level filtering, first on the grounds of frequency and then on the grounds of idiomaticity. We got a list of 10000 frames, which seems to be good enough to be the source of manual translation to English. The bilingual verb frame lexicon will make up an important resource in our Hungarian-to-English machine translation system being prepared. We will use this list also in creating Hungarian EuroWordNet synsets. We also underpined the long-standing statement, that existing non-corpus-based dictionaries can provide incomplete information about verb frames [3,4].

We are grateful to Csaba Oravecz, László Tihanyi, Csaba Merényi, Kata Gábor and the three anonymous reviewers for comments on an earlier draft of this paper.

References

1. Bojar, O., Hajič, J.: Extracting translations verb frames. In: Proceedings of the Modern Approaches in Translation Technologies Workshop, Borovets, Bulgaria (2005) 2–6
2. Briscoe, T., Carroll, J.: Automatic extraction of subcategorization from corpora. In: Proceedings of the 5th Conference on Applied Natural Language Processing (ANLP-97), Washington, DC (1997)
3. Manning, C.D.: Automatic acquisition of a large subcategorization dictionary from corpora. In: Proceedings of the 31st Meeting of the Association for Computational Linguistics, Columbus, Ohio (1993) 235–242
4. McCarthy, D., Keller, B., Carroll, J.: Detecting a continuum of compositionality in phrasal verbs. In: Proceedings of the ACL-SIGLEX Workshop on Multiword Expressions: Analysis, Acquisition and Treatment, Sapporo, Japan (2003) 73–80
5. Zeman, D., Sarkar, A.: Learning verb subcategorization from corpora: Counting frame subsets. In: Proceedings of the 2nd International Conference on Language Resources and Evaluation (LREC2000), Athens, Greece (2000)
6. Kis, B., Villada, B., Bouma, G., Ugray, G., Bíró, T., Pohl, G., Nerbonne, J.: A new approach to the corpus-based statistical investigation of hungarian multi-word lexemes. In: Proceedings of the 4rd International Conference on Language Resources and Evaluation (LREC2004). Volume V., Lisbon, Portugal (2004) 1677–1681
7. Megyesi, B.: The hungarian language. (1998)
8. Sass, B.: Vonzatkeretek a Magyar Nemzeti Szövegtárban [Verb frames in the Hungarian National Corpus]. In: Proceedings of the 3rd Magyar Számítógépes Nyelvészeti Konferencia [Hungarian Conference on Computational Linguistics] (MSZNY2005), Szeged, Hungary (2005) 257–264
9. Váradi, T.: The Hungarian National Corpus. In: Proceedings of the 3rd International Conference on Language Resources and Evaluation (LREC2002), Las Palmas, Spain (2002) 385–389
10. Abney, S.: Partial parsing via finite-state cascades. In: Proceedings of the 8th European Summer School in Logic, Language and Information (ESSLLI96) Robust Parsing Workshop, Prague, Czech Republic (1996) 8–15
11. Tapanainen, P., Piitulainen, J., Järvinen, T.: Idiomatic object usage and support verbs. In: Proceedings of the 17th COLING – 36th ACL, Montreal, Canada (1998) 1289–1293
12. Brent, M.: From grammar to lexicon: Unsupervised learning of lexical syntax. Computational Linguistics **19** (1993) 243–262

Extracting Term Collocations for Directing Users to Informative Web Pages

Eiko Yamamoto and Hitoshi Isahara

National Institute of Information and Communications Technology
3-5 Hikaridai, Seika-cho, Soraku-gun, Kyoto, Japan
{eiko, isahara}@nict.go.jp

Abstract. Due to the rapid increase in the number of existing web pages, accessing the pertinent information we seek has become more difficult, especially when one cannot hit upon the proper keywords for the search engine. When we encounter such a situation, we often try to add more keywords to the previous query. However, adding the appropriate words so as to extract only useful documents is rather difficult. In order to solve this problem, we developed a method of extracting term collocations that could help limit the extracted pages to those that are more informative. In order to verify the usefulness of our approach, we extracted collocations from web documents within the medical domain as an example, and we input those collocations into a search engine and retrieved information from the Internet. The results verified that the collocations extracted by this methodology directed users to more informative web pages.

1 Introduction

Nowadays, due to the rapid increase in the number of existing web pages and the development of high-performance search engines on the Internet, we can easily uncover a vast number of web pages that are somehow related to our interests. At the same time, however, accessing pertinent information that closely matches our objective has become more difficult, especially when we cannot hit upon the proper keywords for the search engines. When we encounter a huge number of web pages extracted by a search engine, we try to add more keywords to the previous query in order to limit the number of pages extracted. However, adding the appropriate keywords in order to extract only useful documents is rather difficult. At least two possible factors contribute to this type of difficulty: first, the user does not know what kinds of things related to the area of interest are described on the web and what expressions can be keywords for accessing such informative pages; and second, when the user is faced with too many pages possibly related to the area of interest, s/he does not know how to limit the pages to those most suitable to the area of interest. In order to solve these problems, acquisition of helpful knowledge for directing users to more informative web pages has been tried.

We have noticed that compound terms and noun phrases such as titles of newspapers and academic papers are useful for retrieving information. In general, a

T. Salakoski et al. (Eds.): FinTAL 2006, LNAI 4139, pp. 310 – 321, 2006.

compound term is a kind of collocation because a collocation is an expression consisting of two or more words that correspond to some conventional way of saying things [3]. There are several methods of acquiring new words and new compound nouns from a large amount of text. In Japanese, there are some of the methods having the high performance in previous research [4]. Against this kind of extraction of words and compound words, we focused on collocations of terms which have a semantic or causal relationship. This kind of collocation can be interpreted as one of knowledge in web documents and can be helpful for directing users to pertinent information. We have focused on extracting such collocations of terms in order to restrict the extracted pages to more informative pages.

We developed a statistical method of extracting such useful information for retrieving web documents. In order to extract useful collocations using inclusive relations between words based on a modifier-modifyee relationship, we applied a method of automatically constructing semantic hierarchies from corpora [2, 5]. This method is based on the Complementary Similarity Measure, which was developed to recognize degraded machine-printed text [1]. Then, we interpreted each of the extracted semantic hierarchies as a collocation of terms with a semantic relationship in the specific domain related to the web documents we treat.

In our experiment, we extracted helpful collocations from web documents within the medical domain as an example. We used three types of experimental data obtained from the web documents. We verified the capability of the Complementary Similarity Measure to select informative word pairs, compared with the typical method of using co-occurrence frequency, which is the simplest method for finding collocations in documents [3]. Then, in order to verify the usefulness of our approach, we input the extracted collocations into a search engine and retrieved information from the Internet. The results verified that this methodology is effective at directing users to suitable web pages.

2 Acquisition of Term Collocation

We applied a method of automatically constructing semantic hierarchies from corpora in order to acquire collocations useful for directing users to suitable web pages. The method utilizes the Complementary Similarity Measure (CSM) to determine the hierarchical structure of words in a corpus.

2.1 Complementary Similarity Measure

CSM was developed as a means of recognizing degraded machine-printed text and was designed to accommodate heavy noise or graphical designs [1]. It has been applied to estimate one-to-many relations between words based on the inclusive relations between the appearance patterns of two words [6]. CSM has also been used to extract hierarchies of abstract nouns that co-occur with adjectives in Japanese [2, 5]. Previous research has determined a hierarchical relationship based on the inclusive relations between the appearance patterns for two words. An appearance pattern is expressed as an n-dimensional binary feature vector. Let $F = (f_1, f_2, ..., f_i, ..., f_n)$ and T

$= (t_1, t_2, ..., t_i, ..., t_n)$, where f_i and t_i are 0 or 1, be the feature vectors of the appearance patterns for two words. The CSM of F to T is defined as follows:

$$a=\sum_{i=1}^{n} f_i \cdot t_i,\ b=\sum_{i=1}^{n} f_i \cdot (1-t_i),\ c=\sum_{i=1}^{n} (1-f_i) \cdot t_i,\ d=\sum_{i=1}^{n} (1-f_i) \cdot (1-t_i),$$

$$CSM(F,\ T)=\frac{ad-bc}{\sqrt{(a+c)(b+d)}},$$

where n = a + b + c + d. CSM is an asymmetric measure because its denominator is asymmetric, that is, *CSM(F, T)* usually differs from *CSM(T, F)*. If *CSM(F, T)* is higher than *CSM(T, F)*, we would be able to determine that the word with appearance pattern *F* is a hypernym of the word with appearance pattern *T*.

2.2 CSM-Based Hierarchy Extraction

We used the CSM-based method to extract term collocations from documents [5]. This method uses CSM to compute the similarity between word appearance patterns, determines the hierarchical relation between two words according to their CSM values, and connects words based on their relationship. Here, let's express the relation between words X and Y as a tuple (X, Y), where X is a hypernym of Y and Y is a hyponym of X. Suppose we have (A, B), (B, C), (Z, B), (C, D), (C, E), and (C, F) in the order of their CSM values. Let (B, C) be an initial hierarchy B->C. We build a hierarchy as follows:

1. First, we find the tuple with the highest CSM value among the tuples where the word at the tail of the current hierarchy is a hypernym and connect the hyponym of the tuple to the tail of the current hierarchy.

   In this example, word "D" is connected to B->C because (C, D) has the highest CSM value of the three tuples (C, D), (C, E), and (C, F), so the current hierarchy is B->C->D.

2. This process is repeated as long as there are tuples with a CSM value above a certain threshold (TH).
3. Next, we find the tuple with the highest CSM value among the tuples where the word at the head of the current hierarchy is a hyponym, and connect the hypernym of the tuple to the head of the current hierarchy.

   Similarly, word "A" is connected to the head of B->C->D because (A, B) has a higher CSM value than (Z, B), so the current hierarchy is A->B->C->D.

4. This process is repeated as long as there are tuples with a CSM value above TH.

In this example, we obtained the hierarchy A->B->C->D. In this way, we build hierarchies from tuples with CSM values above a certain threshold. If a short hierarchy is included in a longer hierarchy and the order of the words remains the same, the shorter one is dropped from the list of hierarchies.

We surmised that extracted hierarchies can be utilized as collocations useful for conducting web searches, which we will verify in the following sections.

3 Experimental Data

In compiling our experimental data, we tried to extract medical term collocations from sentences collected from web pages within the medical domain. For medical terms, we used those that are Japanese translations of descriptors in the 2005 MeSH thesaurus.[1] The number of words used as medical terms in this experiment was 2,557.

The Japanese language has case-marking particles that provide semantic relations between two elements in a dependency relation. We focused on these particles and, using these particles as grounds for extraction, extracted data for our experiment. First, we parsed sentences with the KNP[2] and collected from the parsing results dependency relations matching one of the following five patterns of case-marking particles. With A and B as nouns including compound words, C as a verb, and <*X*> as a case-marking particle, the five patterns are as follows:

- A <*no* (of)> B
- A <*wo* (object)> C
- A <*ga* (subject)> C
- A <*ni* (dative)> C
- A <*ha* (topic)> C

We used five case-marking particles in the above patterns: <*no*>, <*wo*>, <*ga*>, <*ni*>, and <*ha*>. Suppose we have the following sentence:

> *Taro <ha> Mitsuko <kara> Jiro <ga> Hanako <ni> daiya <no> yubiwa <wo> ageta <to> kiita.*

This means "Taro heard from Mitsuko that Jiro gave Hanako a diamond ring." From this sentence, we can extract five dependency relations between words as follows:

- *daiya* (diamond) <*no*> *yubiwa* (ring)
- *yubiwa* <*wo*> *ageta* (gave)
- *Jiro* <*ga*> *ageta*
- *Hanako* <*ni*> *ageta*
- *Taro* <*ha*> *kiita* (heard)

From this set of dependency relations, we compiled the following types of experimental data:

- **NN-data** based on co-occurrence between nouns
  We gathered nouns followed by any of the five case-marking particles and nouns preceded by <*no*> for each sentence in our document collection. For the above sentence, we can gather *Taro*, *Jiro*, *Hanako*, *daiya*, and *yubiwa*.

---

[1] The U.S. National Library of Medicine created, maintains, and provides the Medical Subject Headings (MeSH®) thesaurus.

[2] A Japanese parser developed at Kyoto University.

- **NV-data** based on a dependency relation between noun and verb
  We gathered nouns followed by each of the case-marking particles <*wo*>, <*ga*>, <*ni*>, and <*ha*> for each verb. We named them **Wo-data**, **Ga-data**, **Ni-data**, and **Ha-data**, respectively. For the verb *ageta* in the above sentence, *yubiwa* is added as one element of the data for the verb *ageta* in Wo-data, *Jiro* is added as one element of the data for the verb *ageta* in Ga-data, and so on.
- **SO-data** based on a collocation between subject and object
  We gathered pairs of subjects followed by the case-marking particle <*ga*> and objects followed by the case-marking particle <*wo*> for each verb. Then we made lists of object nouns for each subject noun. For the above example, we can gather the object *yubiwa* for the subject *Jiro* because we identified the dependency relations *Jiro* <*ga*> *yubiwa* <*wo*> *ageta*.

4 Experiment

In applying the CSM-based method, we represented experimental data with binary vectors. For NN-data, a vector corresponds to the appearance pattern of a noun where the number of the dimension of the vector represents the number of sentences. The element for a noun in a vector is 1 if the noun appears in the sentence and 0 if it does not. We can obtain hierarchies for the nouns with this vector expression. Similarly, for NV-data, a vector corresponds to the appearance pattern of a noun where the number of the dimension of the vector is the number of verbs. For SO-data, a vector corresponds to the appearance pattern of a subject noun where the number of the dimension is the number of object nouns. Therefore, if we calculate the CSM value between Vector A and Vector B, each of the parameters a, b, c, and d used for CSM in section 2.1 corresponds to the number of each of the following cases:

- Both Vector A and Vector B have 1 in the dimension.
- Vector A has 1, though Vector B has 0.
- Vector B has 1, though Vector A has 0.
- Both Vector A and Vector B have 0 in the dimension.

For example, if the number of the dimension is 10, Vector A is 1110010111, and Vector B is 1000110110, a is 4, b is 3, c is 1, and d is 2.

To avoid an upsurge in the number of hierarchies extracted, we carefully set the threshold (TH) and chose tuples to build term hierarchies that exceeded the TH. From all hierarchies thus constructed, we utilized hierarchies consisting of three or more terms as collocations.

5 Comparison with the Baseline Method

The simplest method for finding collocations in documents is merely counting. If two words co-occur frequently, that is evidence that they have a special meaning [3]. We verified the capability of our CSM-based method to select informative word pairs, compared to this typical method of counting using co-occurrence frequency. We compiled a list of word pairs that co-occurred at least twice in the NN-data and sorted it by co-occurrence frequency. We also made a list of tuples obtained from the NN-data and sorted it by the CSM values of the tuples. The top 10 tuples are shown in Table 1. Comparing these two lists, we found more informative tuples near the top of the CSM-based list.

Table 1. List of the top 10 tuples extracted from NN-data with the CSM-based method

Tuples	
administration	treatment
daughter	nursery school
attention	referral
iron	transferrin
woods	orangutan
daughter	son
role	cytokine
stroke	epilepsy
secretion	glucocorticoid
nature	rights

For example, both methods gave the highest score to the tuple ("administration," "treatment") in the first row of Table 1. This indicates that if the frequency of the tuple is high, the CSM value of the tuple is also high. Because general terms have a tendency to appear more frequently than technical terms in corpora, we can see many tuples of general terms near the top of the baseline list.

On the other hand, the tuple ("iron," "transferrin") in the fourth row has a high CSM value, though it does not appear near the top of the list sorted by frequency (because the frequency is low). We used the two words in this tuple as keywords for retrieving information on the web and were able to find a page in a medical dictionary that includes the sentence "Iron is taken into the body with the molecule called Transferrin." This shows that we can obtain meaningful information about "iron" in the medical field by using this word pair as keywords for conducting an online search. This suggests that the CSM-based method can extract informative word pairs that can be useful for information retrieval.

Another feature of the CSM-based method is that it can extract not only word pairs but also the hierarchical structures of words. The CSM can calculate the inclusive relations between two words and the results can be merged. That is, once we obtain two tuples (A, B) and (B, C), even though they are tuples extracted from different sentences, we can obtain the hierarchical structure A->B->C. On the other hand, the co-occurrence frequency extracts only the co-occurrence relations and the two tuples cannot be merged easily. Because this feature of CSM is not limited within a given sentence, the CSM-based method is not only relevant for information within a sentence, but also for information from a wider context.

6 Comparison with MeSH Thesaurus

Next, we compared the extracted collocations with the MeSH trees in the 2005 MeSH thesaurus. The MeSH headings are organized into 15 categories. The MeSH trees are hierarchical arrangements of headings with their associated tree numbers, which include information about the category. We show segments of a MeSH tree in Fig. 1. Notice that some headings are classified into more than one category.

In Fig. 1 we can see a hierarchical structure of terms by their tree numbers. For example, the term "thumb" has tree number "A01.378.800.667.430.705." The term "finger" is a hypernym of "thumb" because the tree number of "finger" is "A01.378.800.667.430." Similarly, because "A01.378.800.667" is the tree number of "hand" and "A01.378.800" is the tree number of "upper limb," we can search the hierarchical structures from "thumb" to its hypernyms, i.e., "finger," "hand" and "upper limb." Finally, as we reach the term "body region (A01)" and then "Anatomy (A)," we can see that "thumb" is a hyponym of "Anatomy (A)."

A01	body region
:	
A01.378	limb
A01.378.610	lower limb
A01.378.610.250	foot
A01.378.610.250.149	ankle
A01.378.610.250.510	heel
:	
A01.378.800	upper limb
A01.378.800.075	arm
A01.378.800.420	elbow
A01.378.800.585	forearm
A01.378.800.667	hand
A01.378.800.667.430	finger
A01.378.800.667.430.705	thumb
A01.378.800.667.715	wrist
A01.378.800.750	shoulder
A01.456	head
A01.456.505	face
A01.456.505.580	forehead
:	

Fig. 1. Segments of the MeSH trees

If the CSM-based method extracts hierarchies that agree with the MeSH thesaurus, terms in collocations we extracted are classified into one of the categories in the MeSH trees. However, there are terms which are classified into several categories in the MeSH thesaurus. We examined the distribution of terms in the MeSH categories for each type of experimental data except SO-data (Table 2). By way of exception, for example, we obtained a collocation "tree - forest - Orangutan" from NN-data. "Tree" is classified into two categories "Organisms (B)" and "Technology and Food and Beverages (J)," "forest" is classified into "J," and "Orangutan" is classified into "B."

In such case, we consider that there is a relation between "forest" and "Orangutan" via "tree," and treat this collocation as being distributed in one category.

Table 2. Distribution of terms in CSM-based collocations in MeSH categories[3]

Data		Number of collocations	Distribution in category (percentage)			Percentage of collocations distributed in 3 or fewer categories
			1 category	2 categories	3 categories	
NN		594	42 (7)	148 (25)	120 (20)	52
NV	Wo	199	40 (20)	55 (28)	47 (24)	71
	Ga	62	14 (23)	24 (39)	8 (13)	74
	Ni	37	7 (19)	13 (35)	3 (08)	62
	Ha	85	7 (08)	28 (33)	11 (13)	54

In Table 2, we found that for NN-data and NV-data the percentage of CSM-based collocations whose terms were distributed in two MeSH categories was higher than that of CSM-based collocations whose terms were distributed in three categories, and the total percentage of the CSM-based collocations whose terms were distributed in three or fewer categories was between 52% and 74%. Of the CSM-based collocations, Ga-data provided the highest agreement ratio. The reason for this seems to be that the subject case represented by the case-marking particle <*ga*> restricts nouns more straightforwardly than the others.

7 Verification

Finally, we retrieved web pages using the extracted collocations. First, we will show how collocations whose terms are distributed in a plural number of pages are useful for Web retrieval. Then, we will show some examples of actual collocations and their results of retrieval. In the experiment, we extracted Japanese terms from Web pages and retrieved Web pages in Japanese. The English words and sentences shown below are only for the sake of explanation and have been translated from Japanese using MeSH and glossaries of medical terms.

First, we examined whether collocations whose terms distributed in two categories could help limit the extracted pages to more informative pages. There are collocations composed by three or more terms distributed in two categories, and one of these terms is classified into a category and the rest are classified into another category. Using 60 such collocations extracted from our experimental data, we actually retrieved web

[3] SO-data is the data gathered pairs of subjects and objects that depend on the same verb. For example, when we have "*ningen* (person) <*ga*> *hon* (book) <*wo*> *yomu* (read)," which means "a person reads a book," and "*nezumi* (mouse) <*ga*> *hon* (book) <*wo*> *kajiru* (gnaw)," which means "a mouse gnaws a book," we estimate the relation between *ningen* and *nezumi* with CSM. Therefore, we can surmise that the information we obtain from this data will not agree with a general thesaurus because we do not limit the verbs that subjects and objects depend on. In actuality, our hierarchies obtained from SO-data had very little agreement with the MeSH trees.

pages using all terms in the collocation, with all terms except one in different category, and with all terms except one in the same category as the rest. The results are shown in Fig. 2, where the horizontal axis is the number of web pages Google retrieved with all terms in a collocation, and the vertical axis is the number of web pages retrieved using all but one term in a collocation. A circle shows the results of retrieval with all terms except one in different categories, and a cross shows the results of retrieval with all terms except one in the same category. The diagonal line in the graph shows that adding one term to the search terms does not affect the number of pages extracted. As you can see, most circles fall just above the line and most crosses fall further above the line. This graph indicates that when searching Google, adding an additional search term in a different category makes a bigger difference than adding an additional term in the same category. This means that such terms are crucial in retrieving informative pages.

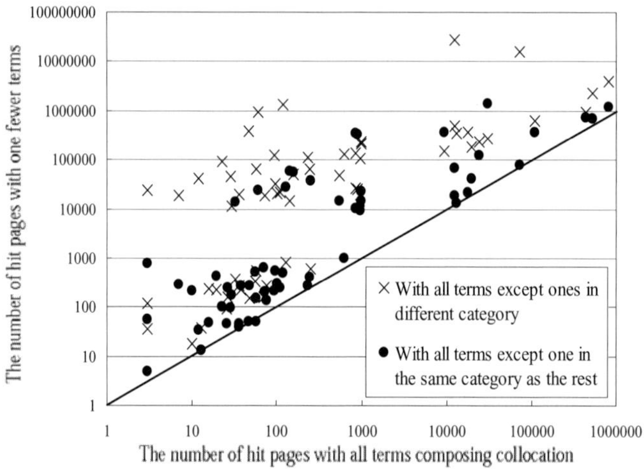

Fig. 2. Distribution of terms classified into different categories when we retrieved web pages

We actually retrieved web pages using some of the extracted collocations from our experimental data. We will explain here some of the interesting results. Figs. 3, 4, and 5 show examples of collocations obtained from NN-data, NV-data, and SO-data, respectively.

For example, using the search words "ovary - spleen - palpation," the first collocation shown in Fig. 3, where "palpation" is classified into a different category in the MeSH thesaurus, Google retrieved web pages that include the information "Diseases of the ovary and spleen can be diagnosed by palpation." We can interpret this as a causal relation. This indicates that this collocation precisely defines the user's intention and can retrieve informative pages. Similarly, we used "data - causation - depression - reduction - platelet count - bone marrow examination," the second collocation in Fig. 3, as search terms. In this case, the terms are classified into three or more categories, indicating that these terms exist in some sort of relationship according to the CSM-based method, yet are not in a hierarchy. The relation would be something semantic, and these terms can be used as keywords for retrieval. This collocation retrieved web pages that include the sentence "Bone marrow examination is necessary because bone marrow illnesses can cause depression and reduced platelet count." We can also interpret this as a causal relation like the collocation "ovary - spleen - palpation."

As another example, we considered "neonate - patent ductus arteriosus - necrotizing enterocolitis," the third collocation shown in Fig. 3. Using only "necrotizing enterocolitis" as a search term, Google retrieves 894 pages that include the information "Necrotizing enterocolitis is a disease which newborns suffer from." Even when "neonate" is added as a search term, Google still retrieves 612 pages related to information about "prophylaxis of necrotizing enterocolitis and cure for this disease." On the other hand, if we input only "patent ductus arteriosus," we obtained 22,600 pages which include the information that "Patent ductus arteriosus is a disease of newborns." However, when all terms in the collocation are used as search terms, that is, "neonate," "patent ductus arteriosus," and "necrotizing enterocolitis," Google retrieves just 252 pages and the top five pages among them are related to "Newborns' patent ductus arteriosus and Mefenamic acid," though these five pages are ranked under pages related to "the prophylaxis and the cure" that are listed at the top of the 612 pages extracted without "patent ductus arteriosus." These five pages include the important information "When Mefenamic acid is used to treat patent dutus arteriosus, necrotizing enterocolitis may react badly to this medicine."

ovary - spleen - palpation
data - causation - depression - reduction - platelet count
  - bone marrow examination
neonate - patent ductus arteriosus - necrotizing enterocolitis
secretion - gastric acid - gastric mucosa - duodenal ulcer
skin - atopic dermatitis - herpes viruses - antiviral drugs
skin - abdomen - cervix - cavitas oris - chest
fatigue - uterine muscle - pregnancy toxemia
water - oxygen - hydrogen - hydrogen ion
person - nicotiana - smoke - oxygen deficiencies

Fig. 3. Examples of collocations obtained from NN-data

ice cream - chocolate - wine (Ni)
bleeding - pyrexia - hematuria - consciousness disorder - vertigo
  - high blood pressure (Ga)
variation - cross reactions - outbreaks - secretion (Wo)
cough - fetus - bronchiolitis obliterans organizing pneumonia (Ha)
cardiovascular disease - coronary artery disease - bronchitis
  - thrombophlebitides - flatulence - hyperuricemia - lower back pain
  - ulnar nerve palsies - brain hemorrhage - obstructive jaundice (Wo)
extrasystole - bronchospasm - acute renal failure - colitides - diabetic coma
  - pancreatitides (Ga)
hand - mouth - ear - finger (Ni)

Fig. 4. Examples of collocations obtained from NV-data

As for the collocations obtained from NV-data, we were able to extract "ice cream - chocolate - wine," shown as the first collocation of Fig. 4. It is obviously a viable collocation from the viewpoint of NLP because all items are edible. However, "ice cream" and "wine" are categorized as foods and "chocolate" is categorized as a plant in the MeSH thesaurus. Similarly, with "bleeding - pyrexia - hematuria - consciousness disorder - vertigo - high blood pressure," the second collocation of Fig. 4, we obtained web pages that include the information that the terms of the collocation can be adverse reactions to a certain medicine. Thus, the CSM-based method can extract better semantic relations from corpora from the viewpoint of collocation relations for information retrieval.

latency period - erythrocyte - hepatic cell
snow - school - gas
variation - death - limb
hospitalist - corneal opacities - triazolam
cross reaction - apoptoses - injuries
research - survey - altered taste - rice
environment - state interest - water - meat - diarrhea
rights - energy generating resources - cordia - education - deforestation

Fig. 5. Examples of collocations obtained from SO-data

As for the collocations obtained from SO-data, the collocation "latency period - erythrocyte - hepatic cell," the first collocation of Fig. 5, retrieves pages related to "malaria." If we input only "latency period" and "hepatic cell," Google retrieves many pages related to "hepatic trouble." Using collocations extracted by our methods, users can retrieve only the relevant and necessary pages, just like a professional who knows that during the latency period of malaria, patients have hepatic trouble. Thus, using these collocations, users can input more precise and detailed information into a search engine, and can obtain more suitable results which could not be retrieved with one keyword. Similarly, when we use "snow - school - gas," the second collocation in Fig. 5, as search terms, we obtained web pages in which "gas" is used in the sense of "fog," like "We can not leave for school because fog lay over the city on the snow day." The Japanese word "*gasu*" has two meanings, i.e. "gas" and "fog," and this collocation of words in Japanese disambiguates the meaning.

As the examples above reveal, using these collocations users can input more precise and detailed information into a search engine, and can obtain suitable results which would not be obtained using a smaller number of keywords.

In addition, we applied our method to another domain, i.e., computer science domain. We compiled experimental data from web documents within the computer science domain and extracted term collocations. There is an interesting set of collocations sharing four terms as shown below;

- file - program - environment - language - recognition - scheme
- file - program - environment - language - construction - emulation
- file - program - environment - language - image processing - download

When four common terms are input as search keys, Google retrieved 9,830,000 pages. Against this result, Google retrieved 40,500 pages with all terms in the first collocation,

11,800 pages with the second one, and 59,600 pages with the third one. There is no shared page among top 50 pages in each result. This means that each collocation directs users to different kind of web pages. In other words, the collocations extracted by CSM-based method are useful tools to direct users to more informative pages.

8 Conclusion

In this paper, we introduced a method for extracting term collocations that can direct users to informative web pages, from web documents; here, we used web documents within the medical domain as an example. We applied the Complementary Similarity Measure (CSM) which can measure a degree of inclusive relation between two vectors. In our previous research, we applied CSM to extract hierarchical structures based on hypernym-hyponym relations between two terms. In this research, we applied CSM to wider relations such as collocations of nouns (NN-data) and modifier-modifyee relations (NV-data) and showed that CSM extracts not only thesaurus-like information but also other information such as causal relations.

Thesauri are useful in order to expand queries of retrieval; however, they are not capable of obtaining specific information which is suitable to particular areas of interest. We expected other semantic relations such as causal relations are more useful for directing users to informative web pages. To verify this expectation, we deleted collocations in hierarchical relations from the collocations extracted using CSM, and executed retrieval by using the remaining collocations.

In our future work, in order to show more concretely the ability of our method for directing users to informative pages, we are developing an experimental tool by which users can actually retrieve web pages using terms extracted by our CSM-based method. We will conduct experience using the tool to get feedback from users, and improve our method to more practically available.

References

1. Hagita, N., Sawaki, M.: Robust recognition of degraded machine-printed characters using complementary similarity measure and error-correction learning. Proceedings of the SPIE – The International Society for Optical Engineering, Vol. 2442. (1995) 236–244
2. Kanzaki, K., Yamamoto, E., Ma, Q., Isahara, H.: Construction of an objective hierarchy of abstract concepts via directional similarity. Proceedings of the 20th International Conference on Computational Linguistics, Vol. 2. (2004) 1147–1153
3. Manning, D. C., Schutze, H.: Foundations of Statistical Natural Language Processing. The MIT Press (1999)
4. Nakagawa, H., Mori, T.: A simple but powerful automatic term extraction method. Proceedings of the 2nd International Workshop on Computational Terminology. (2002) 29–35
5. Yamamoto, E., Kanzaki, K., Isahara, H.: Extraction of hierarchies based on inclusion of co-occurring words with frequency information. Proceedings of the 19th International Joint Conference on Artificial Intelligence. (2005) 1166–1172
6. Yamamoto, E., Umemura, K.: A similarity measure for estimation of one–to-many relationship in corpus. Journal of Natural Language Processing, Vol.9. (2002) 45–75

Feasibility of Enriching a Chinese Synonym Dictionary with a Synchronous Chinese Corpus

Oi Yee Kwong and Benjamin K. Tsou

Language Information Sciences Research Centre
City University of Hong Kong
Tat Chee Avenue, Kowloon, Hong Kong
{rlolivia, rlbtsou}@cityu.edu.hk

Abstract. This paper reports on a first step toward the construction of a Pan-Chinese lexical resource. We investigated the plausibility of extending and enhancing an existing Chinese synonym dictionary, the *Tongyici Cilin*, with lexical items from the financial news domain obtained from a synchronous Chinese corpus, LIVAC. Results showed that 23-40% of the words from various subcorpora are unique to the individual communities, and as much as 70% of such unique items are not yet covered in *Cilin*. Our next step would be to explore automatic means for extracting related lexical items from the corpus, and to incorporate them into existing semantic classifications.

1 Introduction

Many cities have underground railway systems. Somehow one takes the *tube* in London but the *subway* in New York. In a more recent edition of the Roget's Thesaurus (Kirkpatrick, 1987), *subway*, *tube*, *underground railway* and *metro* are found in the same semicolon-separated group under head *624 Way*. Similarly if one looks up WordNet (Miller et al., 1990; http://wordnet.princeton.edu), the synset to which *subway* belongs also contains the words *metro*, *tube*, *underground*, and *subway system*; and it is further indicated that "in Paris the subway system is called the 'metro' and in London it is called the 'tube' or the 'underground'". Such variation is also found in Chinese. For instance, the subway system in Hong Kong, known as the Mass Transit Railway or MTR, is called 地鐵 in Chinese. The subway systems in Beijing and Shanghai, as well as the one in Singapore, are also known as 地鐵, but that in Taipei is known as 捷運. Such regional variation, as part of lexical knowledge, is important and useful for many natural language applications, including natural language understanding, information retrieval, and machine translation. Unfortunately, existing Chinese lexical resources often lack such comprehensiveness.

To fill this gap, Tsou and Kwong (2006) proposed a comprehensive Pan-Chinese lexical resource, based on a large and unique synchronous Chinese corpus as an authentic basis for lexical acquisition and analysis across various Chinese speech communities. For a significant world language like Chinese, a useful lexical resource should have maximum *versatility* and *portability*, such that it is not targeted at one

T. Salakoski et al. (Eds.): FinTAL 2006, LNAI 4139, pp. 322 – 332, 2006.

particular community speaking the language and thus covering only language usage observed from that particular community. Instead, it should document the core and universal substances of the language on the one hand, and also the more subtle variations found in different communities on the other. As is evident from the above example on the variation of *subway*, a lexical resource should be able to capture regional variation in order to be useful in a wide range of applications.

In this study, we make use of an existing Chinese synonym dictionary, the *Tongyici Cilin* (Mei et al., 1984) as leverage and take up a first step in this undertaking by investigating the plausibility of enriching its collection with lexical items obtained from a synchronous Chinese corpus. We focus on the financial news domain in the current study. Corpus data from four Chinese speech communities were compared with respect to their commonality and uniqueness, and also against the synonym dictionary for their coverage. Results showed that 23-40% of the words extracted from the corpus are unique to the individual communities, and as much as 70% of such unique items are not yet covered in the *Tongyici Cilin*. The results thus suggest that the synchronous corpus is a rich source for mining region-specific lexical items, and that there is plenty of room for enriching the existing synonym dictionary.

In Section 2, we will briefly review existing resources and related work. Then in Section 3, we will briefly outline the design and architecture of the Pan-Chinese lexical resource proposed in Tsou and Kwong (2006). In Section 4, we will further describe the Chinese synonym dictionary and the synchronous Chinese corpus used in this study. The comparison of their lexical items will be discussed in Section 5. Future directions will be presented in Section 6, followed by a conclusion.

2 Existing Resources and Related Work

The construction and development of large lexical resources is relying more and more on corpus-based approaches, not only as a result of the increased availability of large corpora, but also for the authoritativeness and authenticity allowed by the approach. The Collins COBUILD English Dictionary (Sinclair, 1987) is amongst the most well-known lexicographic fruit based on large corpora.

For natural language applications, much of the information in conventional dictionaries targeted at human readers must be made explicit. Lexical resources for computer use thus need considerable manipulation, customisation, and supplementation (e.g. Calzolari, 1982). WordNet (Miller et al., 1990), grouping words into synsets and linking them up with relational pointers, is probably the first broad coverage general computational lexical database. In view of the intensive time and effort required in resource building, some researchers have taken an alternative route by extracting information from existing machine-readable dictionaries and corpora semi-automatically (e.g. Vossen et al., 1989; Riloff and Shepherd, 1999; Lin et al, 2003).

Similar work in the development of thesauri and lexical databases for the Chinese language is less mature. This gap was partly due to the lack of authoritative Chinese corpora as a basis for analysis, but has been fortunately and gradually reduced with the recent availability of large Chinese corpora including the LIVAC synchronous corpus (Tsou and Lai, 2003) used in this work and further described below, the Sinica Corpus (Chen et al., 1996), the Chinese Penn Treebank (Xia et al., 2000), and the like.

An important issue which is seldom addressed in the construction of Chinese lexical databases is the problem of *versatility* and *portability*. For a language such as Chinese which is spoken in many different communities, different linguistic norms have emerged as a result of the individualistic evolution and development trends of the language within a particular community and culture. Such variations are seldom adequately reflected in existing lexical resources, as they often only draw reference from one particular source. For instance, *Tongyici Cilin* (同義詞詞林) (Mei et al., 1984) is a thesaurus containing some 70,000 Chinese lexical items in the tradition of the Roget's Thesaurus for English, that is, in a hierarchy of broad conceptual categories. It was first published in the 1980s and was based exclusively on Chinese as used in post-1949 Mainland China. Thus for the *subway* example above, the closest word group found is 火車, 列車 (train) only, let alone the *subway* itself and its regional variations.

With the recent availability of large corpora, especially synchronous ones, to construct an authoritative and timely lexical resource for Chinese is less distant than it was in the past. A large synchronous corpus provides authentic examples of the language as used in a variety of locations. It thus enables us to attempt a comprehensive and in-depth analysis of various aspects of the core common language in constructing a lexical resource; and to incorporate useful information relating to regional linguistic variations.

3 The Proposal of a Pan-Chinese Lexical Resource

The Pan-Chinese lexicon proposed in Tsou and Kwong (2006) is expected to capture not only the core senses of lexical items but also senses and uses specific to individual Chinese speech communities. The project is backed up by a very large and unique synchronous Chinese corpus, LIVAC.

The lexical database will be organised into a core database and a supplementary one. The core database will contain the core lexical information for word senses and usages which are common to most Chinese speech communities, whereas the supplementary database will contain the language uses specific to individual communities, including "marginal" and "sublanguage" uses.

A network structure will be adopted for the lexical items. The nodes could be sets of near-synonyms or single lexical items (in which case synonymy will be one type of links). The links will not only represent the paradigmatic semantic relations but also syntagmatic ones (such as selectional restrictions).

As a first step in this undertaking, we are working toward a Pan-Chinese thesaurus by acquiring near-synonyms from LIVAC, integrating them with and thus enriching existing thesauri. In the current study, we started with a Chinese synonym dictionary, the *Tongyici Cilin*, and compare its collection with data available from the LIVAC corpus to explore any room for its enrichment. In the following section, we will discuss these two resources in greater details.

4 Materials and Method

4.1 The *Tongyici Cilin*

The *Tongyici Cilin* (同義詞詞林) (Mei et al., 1984) is a Chinese synonym dictionary, or more often known as a Chinese thesaurus in the tradition of the Roget's Thesaurus for English. The Roget's Thesaurus has about 1,000 numbered semantic heads, more generally grouped under higher level semantic classes and subclasses, and more specifically differentiated into paragraphs and semicolon-separated word groups. Similarly, some 70,000 Chinese lexical items are organized into a hierarchy of broad conceptual categories in the *Tongyici Cilin*. Its classification consists of 12 top-level semantic classes, 94 sub-classes, 1,248 semantic heads and 3,925 paragraphs.

4.2 The LIVAC Synchronous Corpus

LIVAC (http://www.livac.org) stands for Linguistic Variation in Chinese Speech Communities. It is a synchronous corpus developed by the Language Information Sciences Research Centre of the City University of Hong Kong since 1995 (Tsou and Lai, 2003). The corpus contains newspaper articles collected regularly and synchronously from six Chinese speech communities, namely Hong Kong, Beijing, Taipei, Singapore, Shanghai, and Macau. Texts collected cover a variety of domains, including front page news stories, local news, international news, editorials, sports news, entertainment news, and financial news. Up to December 2005, the corpus has already accumulated about 180 million character tokens which, upon automatic word segmentation and manual verification, amount to over 900K word types.

For the present study, we make use of the subcorpora collected over the 9-year period 1995-2004 from Hong Kong (HK), Beijing (BJ), Taipei (TW), and Singapore (SG). In particular, we focus on the *finance and economic news* domain to investigate the commonality and uniqueness of the lexical items used in the various communities on the one hand, and to evaluate the adequacy of the *Tongyici Cilin* on the other. Looking at its collection of such domain-specific terms from the Pan-Chinese perspective, we intend to assess the room for its enrichment with our synchronous corpus. Table 1 shows the sizes of the subcorpora used for this study.

Table 1. Sizes of individual subcorpora in terms of character tokens and word types

Subcorpus	**Overall** (rounded to nearest 0.01M)		**Financial News** (rounded to nearest thousand)	
	Word Token	**Word Type**	**Word Token**	**Word Type**
HK	14.39M	0.22M	970K	38K
BJ	11.70M	0.19M	232K	20K
TW	12.32M	0.20M	254K	22K
SG	13.22M	0.21M	621K	28K

4.3 Procedures

Word-frequency lists were generated from the financial subcorpora from each individual community. For each resulting list, the steps below were followed to remove irrelevant items and retain only the potentially useful content words:

(a) Remove all numbers and non-Chinese words.
(b) Remove all proper names, including those annotated as personal names, geographical names, and organisation names.
(c) Remove function words[1].
(d) Remove lexical items with frequency 5 or below.

The numbers of remaining items in each subcorpus after the above steps are listed in Table 2. The lexical items retained, which are expected to contain a substantial amount of content words, are potentially useful for enriching existing lexical resources. The four lists (from the four subcorpora) were compared in terms of the items they share and those unique to individual communities. Their unique items were also compared against the *Tongyici Cilin* to investigate its adequacy and explore how it might be enriched with our synchronous corpus.

Table 2. Number of word types remaining after various data cleaning steps

Subcorpus	All	After (a)	After (b)	After (c)	After(d)
HK	37,525	27,937	20,422	17,162	5,238
BJ	20,025	17,361	14,460	12,134	2,791
TW	22,142	19,428	16,316	13,496	3,088
SG	28,193	22,829	16,863	13,822	3,836

5 Results and Discussion

5.1 Lexical Items from LIVAC

The four subcorpora of financial news texts differ considerably in their sizes. Despite this, we see from Table 2 that in general about 40-50% of all word types are numbers, non-Chinese words, and proper names. Of the remaining items, about 20-30% have frequency greater than 5. These several thousand word types are expected to be amongst the more interesting items used in the financial domain and form the "candidate sets" for further investigation.

5.2 Commonality Among Various Regions

Comparing the candidate sets from various subcorpora, which reflect the use of Chinese in various Chinese speech communities, Table 3 shows the sizes of the intersection sets among different places.

[1] A list of function words with about 5,800 types was obtained from a subset of the LIVAC corpus for filtering in the current study.

The intersection set for all four places contains slightly more than 1,000 lexical items. A quick skim through these common lexical items suggests that they contain, amongst others, the many general concepts in the financial domain (e.g. 公司 company, 市場 market, 銀行 bank, 投資 invest / investment, 業務 business, 發展 develop / development, 集團 corporation, 股份 stock shares, 股東 shareholder, 資金 capital, etc.); as well as many reportage and cognitive verbs often used in news articles (e.g. 表示 express, 認爲 reckon, 出現 appear, 反映 reflect, etc.).

Table 3. Commonality amongst various regions

Regions	Overlap	Proportion to individual lists (%)			
		HK	BJ	TW	SG
HK / BJ / TW / SG	1039	19.84	37.23	33.65	27.09
HK / BJ / TW	1126	21.50	40.34	36.46	
HK / BJ / SG	1327	25.33	47.55		34.59
HK / TW / SG	1581	30.18		51.20	41.21
BJ / TW / SG	1092		39.13	35.36	28.47
HK / BJ	1609	30.72	57.65		
HK / TW	1912	36.50		61.92	
HK / SG	2607	49.77			67.96
BJ / TW	1250		44.79	40.48	
BJ / SG	1505		53.92		39.23
TW / SG	1795			58.13	46.79

The numbers of overlaps in Table 3 also suggest that lexical items used in Mainland China (as evident from BJ data) seem to have the least in common with the rest. For instance, compared to the overlap amongst all four regions (i.e. 1,039), the overlap has increased most when BJ was not included in the comparison. This observation is further supported by the smallest overlap between BJ and TW, when we compare any two regions.

In addition, if we look at the individual regions, HK apparently shares most (about 50%) with SG, and vice versa (about 68%). At the same time, BJ also shares most with HK compared to the other two regions, and so does TW. These patterns could partly be a result of the larger size of the HK list than others, but more importantly, they tend to suggest that the lexical items used in the financial news domain in HK are more versatile and cover a wider range of topics which could be of interest to some but not all of the other regions.

5.3 Uniqueness of Various Regions

Next we compared the four lists with respect to what they have unique to themselves. Table 4 shows the numbers of unique items found in each list, together with examples from the most frequent 20 unique items in each case.

Table 4. Uniqueness of individual subcorpora in the financial news domain

Region	Unique Items and Examples		
HK	**2105 (40.19%)**		
	按揭 (mortgage)	收報 (closing price)	貨尾 (remaining stock)
	錄得 (record)	入市 (buy in)	招股 (share offer)
	樓盤 (real estate)	新盤 (new real estate)	加推 (put more to market)
	大市 (market)	銷情 (sale condition)	純利 (net profit)
	息率 (interest rate)	地產股 (real estate stock)	居屋 (Home Ownership)
	證券界 (securities)	寬頻 (broadband)	低位 (low level)
	開售 (open sale)	減價 (cut price)	
BJ	**933 (33.43%)**		
	農村 (farm village)	群眾 (the people)	水資源 (water resource)
	退耕還林 (quit farming)	優化 (improve)	質檢 (quality check)
	查處 (penalize)	運行 (operate)	品種 (breed)
	非典 (SARS)	黨 (party)	城鄉 (urban and rural)
	抽查 (sample check)	節水 (save water)	扶貧 (poverty alleviation)
	住房 (housing)	走私 (smuggling)	林業 (forestry)
	下崗 (unemployed)	專項 (project)	
TW	**891 (28.85%)**		
	金控 (financial holdings)	成長率 (growth rate)	契約 (covenant)
	計劃 (project)	升息 (rise in interest rate)	降息 (fall in interest rate)
	投資人 (investor)	買超 (over-subscribe)	執行長 (executor)
	網路 (network)	經理人 (agent)	立委 (legislator)
	營收 (revenue)	董監事 (exec)	個股 (individual stock)
	投信 (investment trust)	團隊 (team)	專案 (case)
	釋股 (stock floatation)	坪 (sq. metre)	
SG	**890 (23.20%)**		
	新元 (Sing. Dollar)	戶頭 (account)	地契 (deed)
	獻議 (proposal)	董事部 (board of directors)	私宅 (private housing)
	閉市 (close market)	共管 (joint)	海事 (marine)
	公寓 (apartment)	馬股 (Malaysian stock)	財年 (financial year)
	平方英尺 (sq. feet)	財政年 (financial year)	辦公樓 (office building)
	脫售 (sell)	文告 (message)	輪船 (ship)
	港務 (port management)	組屋 (housing)	

Again, taking the size difference among the candidate sets into account, about 40% of the lexical items found in HK data are unique to the region, which only re-echoes the versatility and wide coverage of interests in its financial domain. This is especially evident when compared to only 23% of the candidate set for SG are unique to Singapore.

Looking at the unique lexical items found in individual regions, it is not difficult to see the region-specific lexicalisation of certain concepts. For instance, in terms of housing, 居屋 (housing under the Home Ownership Scheme) is a specific kind of housing in Hong Kong, 組屋 is a specific term in Singapore (as seen in SG data), whereas housing is generally expressed as 住房 in Mainland China (as seen in BJ data). Similarly, TW uses 升息 and 降息 for the rise and fall of interest rate respectively, but these are usually expressed as 加息 and 減息 in Hong Kong.

The lists of unique items also suggest the various focus and orientation of financial news in different Chinese speech communities. For example, while Hong Kong pays much attention to the real estate market and stock market, Mainland China may be focusing more on the basic needs like water, farming, poverty alleviation, etc., and Singapore is relatively more concerned with local affairs like port management.

5.4 Comparison with *Tongyici Cilin*

As mentioned earlier, the *Tongyici Cilin* contains some 70,000 lexical items under 12 broad semantic classes, 94 subclasses, and 1,428 heads. In this section, we discuss the results obtained from comparing the unique lexical items found from individual subcorpora with the *Tongyici Cilin*, which are shown in Table 5.

Table 5. Coverage of the *Tongyici Cilin* for the unique lexical items in individual subcorpora

Region	Found in Cilin	Not Found in Cilin
HK	**560 (26.60%)** 減價、純利、居屋、戶口、拆息 憧憬、容許、倒退、通告、結餘	**1545 (73.40%)**
BJ	**369 (39.55%)** 農村、抽查、住房、運行、黨 走私、品種、林業、鄉鎮、森林	**564 (60.45%)**
TW	**265 (29.74%)** 契約、專案、不動產、改選、股利 通路、關卡、週、終場、席次	**626 (70.26%)**
SG	**333 (37.42%)** 公寓、平方英尺、港務、戶頭、共管 文告、地契、海事、輪船、開銷	**557 (62.58%)**

As mentioned in Section 2, the *Tongyici Cilin* was first published in the 1980s and was based on lexical usages mostly of post-1949 Mainland China. Hence on the one hand, its collection of words may be considerably dated and obviously will not include new concepts and neologisms arising in the last two decades. So overall speaking, for each of the unique word lists, much less that 50% are covered, particularly in view of the data sources of LIVAC, which come from newspaper materials in the 1990s.

Nevertheless, there is still an apparent gap between *Cilin*'s coverage of the unique items from various places. For BJ and SG, about 40% of the unique items are found in it; whereas for HK and TW, it is less than 30%. Again, this could be considered a result of the *Cilin*'s bias toward lexical usages in Mainland China.

In addition, while almost 40% of the unique items in BJ data are found in *Cilin*, many of these unique items covered are amongst the most frequent items. On the contrary, even though about 560 unique items in HK data are also found in *Cilin*, on the one hand only 3 out of the 20 most frequent items are amongst them, and on the other hand the semantic heads under which we find the words might not correspond exactly to the sense with which the corresponding items are used in HK context. For example, 居屋 is found under head *Bn1* together with other items like 住房, 住宅, etc., all of which only refer to the general concept of housing, instead of the housing specifically under the Home Ownership Scheme as known in Hong Kong.

Results from the above comparisons thus support that (1) different Chinese speech communities have their distinct usage of Chinese lexical items, in terms of both form and sense; (2) existing lexical resources, the *Tongyici Cilin* in particular as in our current study, should be enriched and enhanced by capturing lexical usages from a variety of Chinese speech communities, to represent the lexical items from a Pan-Chinese perspective; and (3) lexical items obtained from our synchronous Chinese corpus give a good resource to enrich the existing content of the *Tongyici Cilin*, with more contemporarily lexicalised concepts, as well as variant expressions of similar and related concepts from various Chinese speech communities.

Hence it remains for us to further investigate how the related lexical items obtained from the synchronous corpus should be grouped and incorporated into the semantic classification of existing lexical resources; and to enhance the process, further explore how they might be extracted in a large scale by automatic means. These will definitely be amongst the most important future directions as discussed in the next section.

6 Future Work

In the current study, we have investigated the plausibility of enriching the *Tongyici Cilin*, amongst many other existing Chinese lexical resources, with the lexical items obtained from financial news domain of the LIVAC synchronous corpus from a Pan-Chinese perspective. The "enrichability" is evident from the comparison between the coverage of the Chinese synonym dictionary and the lists of unique lexical items found for individual communities. Our next step would thus be to further investigate more automatic means for extracting the near-synonymous or closely related items from the various subcorpora. To this end, we would explore algorithms like those used in Lin et al. (2003). Of similar importance is the mechanism for grouping the related lexical items and incorporating them into the semantic classifications of existing lexical resources. In this regard we will proceed with further in-depth analysis of the classificatory structures of individual resources and fit in our Pan-Chinese architecture.

Apart from the *Tongyici Cilin*, there are other existing Chinese lexical resources such as *HowNet* (Dong and Dong, 2000), *SUMO* and *Chinese WordNet* (Huang et al., 2004), as well as other synonym dictionaries from which we might draw reference to build up our Pan-Chinese lexical resource.

In addition to the financial news domain, we also plan to work on the entertainment news and sports news domains for more domain-specific lexical items, with the vision to extend eventually to more general domains.

7 Conclusion

In this paper, we have taken a first step toward a Pan-Chinese lexical resource which attempts to capture both the core and region-specific usages of Chinese lexical items. We started with a Chinese synonym dictionary, the *Tongyici Cilin*, and investigated the plausibility of enriching it with lexical items from the financial news domain obtained from a synchronous Chinese corpus, LIVAC. Results are encouraging in the sense that 23-40% of the candidate words from various subcorpora are unique to the individual communities, and as much as 70% of such unique items are not yet covered in the *Tongyici Cilin*. Hence the synchronous corpus is a valuable resource for mining the region-specific expressions while existing synonym dictionaries might provide a ready-made semantic classificatory structure. Our next step would be to explore automatic means for extracting related lexical items from the corpus, and to incorporate them with existing semantic classifications.

Acknowledgements

This work is supported by Competitive Earmarked Research Grant (CERG) from the Research Grants Council of Hong Kong under grant No. CityU1317/03H.

References

Calzolari, N. (1982) Towards the organization of lexical definitions on a database structure. In E. Hajicova (Ed.), *COLING '82 Abstracts*, Charles University, Prague, pp.61-64.

Caraballo, S.A. (1999) Automatic construction of a hypernym-labeled noun hierarchy. In *Proceedings of the 37th Annual Meeting of the Association for Computational Linguistics (ACL'99)*, College Park, Maryland, pp.120-126.

Chen, K-J., Huang, C-R., Chang, L-P. and Hsu, H-L. (1996) Sinica Corpus: Design Methodology for Balanced Corpora. In *Proceedings of the 11th Pacific Asia Conference on Language, Information, and Computation (PACLIC 11)*, Seoul, Korea, pp.167-176.

Dong, Z. and Dong, Q. (2000) *HowNet*. http://www.keenage.com.

Huang, C-R., Chang, R-Y. and Lee, S-B. (2004) *Sinica BOW (Bilingual Ontological Wordnet): Integration of Bilingual WordNet and SUMO*. In *Proceedings of the 4th International Conference on Language Resources and Evaluation (LREC2004)*, Lisbon, Portugal.

Kirkpatrick, B. (1987) *Roget's Thesaurus of English Words and Phrases*. Penguin Books.

Lin, D., Zhao, S., Qin, L. and Zhou, M. (2003) Identifying Synonyms among Distributionally Similar Words. In *Proceedings of the 18th Joint International Conference on Artificial Intelligence (IJCAI-03)*, Acapulco, pp.1492-1493 .

Mei et al. 梅家駒、竺一鳴、高蘊琦、殷鴻翔 (1984) 《同義詞詞林》 (*Tongyici Cilin*). 商務印書館 (Commerical Press) / 上海辭書出版社.

Miller, G.A., Beckwith, R., Fellbaum, C., Gross, D. and Miller, K.J. (1990) Introduction to WordNet: An online lexical database. *International Journal of Lexicography, 3(4)*:235-244.

Riloff, E. and Shepherd, J. (1999) A corpus-based bootstrapping algorithm for semi-automated semantic lexicon construction. *Natural Language Engineering, 5(2)*:147-156.

Sinclair, J. (1987) *Collins COBUILD English Language Dictionary.* London, UK: HarperCollins.

Tsou, B.K. and Kwong, O.Y. (2006) Toward a Pan-Chinese Thesaurus. To appear in *Proceedings of the Fifth International Conference on Language Resources and Evaluation (LREC 2006)*, Genoa, Italy.

Tsou, B.K. and Lai, T.B.Y. 鄒嘉彥、黎邦洋 (2003) 漢語共時語料庫與信息開發. In B. Xu, M. Sun and G. Jin 徐波、孫茂松、靳光瑾 (Eds.), 《中文信息處理若干重要問題》 (*Issues in Chinese Language Processing*). 北京：科學出版社, pp.147-165.

Vossen, P., Meijs, W. and den Broeder, M. (1989) Meaning and structure in dictionary definitions. In B. Boguraev and T. Briscoe (Eds.), *Computational Lexicography for Natural Language Processing*. Essex, UK: Longman Group.

Xia, F., Palmer, M., Xue, N., Okwrowski, M.E., Kovarik, J., Huang, S., Kroch, T. and Marcus, M. (2000) Developing Guidelines and Ensuring Consistency for Chinese Text Annotation. In *Proceedings of the 2nd International Conference on Language Resources and Evaluation (LREC-2000)*, Athens, Greece.

Finding Spanish Syllabification Rules with Decision Trees

John Goddard[1] and René MacKinney-Romero[2]

[1] Departmento de Ingeniería Eléctrica, Universidad Autónoma Metropolitana
México D.F. 09950, México
jgc@xanum.uam.mx
[2] rene@xanum.uam.mx

Abstract. Syllables have been proposed as a viable alternative to phonemes for automatic speech recognition, and for use in text-to-speech systems as a way to enhance the speech quality. The question then arises of how to obtain the correct syllabification rules for a particular language. Even for a language like Spanish, which has well defined syllabification rules, linguistic knowledge is often required to discover them. It is interesting to ask whether machine learning techniques can produce effective syllabification algorithms, and our aim here is to test the usefulness of classification trees for this task. Additionally, we would like to understand the sort of problems that arise in the process, with a view to applying it to other languages.

Keywords: Automatic syllabification, decision trees, machine learning.

1 Introduction

The predominant approach to automatic speech recognition uses phonemes as the basic building blocks. This has been criticised [1], [2] given that problems, such as the pronunciation variation in spontaneous speech, coarticulation, and robust recognition in adverse conditions, have not been completely resolved. Other sub-word units, such as syllables, have been proposed as possible replacements. Syllable units, in particular, have the advantage over phones of spanning significantly longer time frames, and this could assist in overcoming these problems. Some encouraging results have been reported for English in [3].

Concatenative speech synthesis and text-to-speech systems could also benefit from syllable, or demisyllable, units. Speech quality might be enhanced with these units, and in some languages, such as those from India [4] and Spanish [5], the correct pronunciation requires a knowledge of the rules of syllabification, that is, how to divide a word into its syllable components. For example, in Spanish, a word can be pronounced correctly from its written form alone, however specific rules have to be applied in order to stress the correct syllable.

All of this raises the question of how to obtain the correct syllabification rules for a particular language. Native speakers seem to easily know these rules for their language, although some mistakes may be made. Syllabification rules have been given for Spanish [6] and Portuguese [7]. However, even in Spanish, which

T. Salakoski et al. (Eds.): FinTAL 2006, LNAI 4139, pp. 333–340, 2006.

has a well defined set of rules, there are approximately 100 such rules, and their detection is a time consuming affair. It is interesting to explore alternative approaches, and machine learning techniques offer a potentially useful option. Some related work has been carried out for other languages using genetic algorithms [8], decision trees and neural networks [9], inductive logic programming [10], and probabilistic context-free grammars [11]. In [12], an inductive logic programming technique was introduced for Spanish and some initial results obtained. In the present paper a different coding scheme to [12] is adopted for the data and a decision tree is employed, yielding encouraging results.

2 Spanish Syllable Structure

We begin by summarising a few facts about the Spanish language which will be of use in understanding the rest of the paper.

Spanish is written using the Latin alphabet, with the addition of *ñ*. The vowels *i* and *u* are termed weak vowels while the others are called strong. The letter *u* sometimes carries diaeresis, *ü*, after the letter *g*, and stressed vowels carry acute accents e.g. *á*. These accents usually indicate deviations from what would be expected if one followed the customary rules of Spanish orthography, and are essential information for text-to-speech systems. In fact, the pronunciation of any Spanish word can be perfectly predicted from its written form, even without knowing the meaning of the word. For example, the norm is to stress the last syllable of any word ending in a consonant other than *n* or *s*, in which case the penultimate syllable is stressed. If however an accented vowel appears (only one accented vowel is allowed per word), then the syllable of that vowel is stressed. As can be seen from these rules, syllables are particularly important in Spanish, and an understanding of syllabification is vital for making the correct pronunciation.

A syllable is often described as a combination or set of one or more units of sound in a language that must consist of a sonorous part, and may or may not contain less sonorous parts flanking it. This description of a syllable can be related to the syllable constituents in a binary branching model in which a syllable branches into an onset and rhyme or rime. The rhyme in turn branches into a nucleus and coda.

In the case of Spanish, the sonorous part corresponds to the nucleus and usually consists of a single vowel, although the word *y* meaning 'and' is allowed. Further, diphthongs and triphthongs also exist subject to certain rules. For example, in the case of diphthongs, the rule is: a weak vowel, without a written accent mark, will combine with a different adjacent vowel to form a single nucleus. Hence the following are the correct syllabification of words with diphthongs: *rio, ju-lio, ai-re, qui-zá, au-re-lio,* while *rí-o, ma-es-tros, le-er* and *a-é-re-a* do not contain diphthongs. Notice how an accented vowel, for example in *río*, can change the syllabification of a word.

An *h*, which is silent in Spanish, does not break a diphthong, so *ahu-ma-do* is the correct syllabification. A similar rule relates to triphthongs in which weak vowels flank the strong vowels, such as *cuau-tla, con-sen-suais.* Triphthongs are much less frequent in the language.

As these examples show, the number of syllables in a word is not always equal to the number of vowels, and the question arises as to how syllabification can be performed.

For Spanish a CV, consonant-vowel (not to be confused with the same notation for the coda), representation of a word can be used for syllabification. With this representation it is possible to develop a set of about 100 rules [6] which can be applied recursively to syllabify any Spanish word. In order to syllabify any word segment, essentially three cases are considered depending on whether the segment begins with a V, CV or CC. For example, if a segment begins with VCV, such as the first three letters of *aroma,* then it is initially syllabified as V-CV to get *a-roma.* The algorithm would then be applied to *roma,* using some of the other rules. There are also rules dealing with so-called inseparable pairs of consonants, such as *bl, dr, rr, and ll,* which are always considered as a single consonant. For example, in the case of the rule pertaining to segments of the form VCV, it would be applied to the word *arriba,* to produce *a-rriba,* whereas because *rt* is not inseparable, the word *artesano* uses a different rule, corresponding to VCCV, to initially syllabify as *ar-tesano.* This also means that the order in which the rules are applied is important for the correct syllabification.

As we can see, even for a language like Spanish with well defined syllabification rules, linguistic knowledge is required to create a rule-based syllabification algorithm. It is interesting to ask whether machine learning techniques can produce effective syllabification algorithms, and our aim here is to test the usefulness of classification trees for this task. Further, we would like to understand the sort of problems that arise in the process with a view to applying it to other languages.

3 Methods and Data

In this paper, a method to construct classification trees called CRUISE (for Classification Rule with Unbiased Interaction Selection and Estimation) was used. CRUISE was developed by [13] and is freely available from `http://www.stat.wisc.edu/~loh/`. Other tree building algorithms, such as ID3, were also tried but CRUISE was found to have several advantages, such as being a fast algorithm and building classification trees which were particularly shallow and with very few branches.

In order to build the classification trees with CRUISE, we require a collection of examples and corresponding classes which reflect the syllable structure of Spanish. Here three classes were chosen to be the onset, nucleus, and coda and represented by O, N, C. Examples were formed from a Spanish word by first converting the word to lower case and then adding a special symbol, in this case 'W', to either end to stand for the space character and so signal the beginning and end of a word. Finally a 'window' was shifted along the enlarged word, and three characters taken each time and assigned the appropriate class corresponding to the middle character. For example, the word *vieron* is syllabified as *vie-ron*. This in turn produces ONN-ONC and gives rise to the following six examples, together with their classes:

W v i O, v i e N, i e r N, e r o O, r o n N, o n W C

This meant that three attributes were used for each example, and each is referred to by their position in the example. The word *y* signifying 'and' is obviously very common and was represented by the example: W y W N.

The data used in the experiments came from three sources: a short story by Mario Benedetti, a modern Spanish spelling version of the classic work *Don Quijote de la Mancha* by Miguel de Cervantes [14], and a recent Mexican newspaper editorial. The first two are literary sources, although nearly 400 years apart in time, whilst the editorial is of a different nature, and its subject material is related to pensions in a decentralised Mexican government company. The authors have three different nationalities.

The sources were preprocessed to remove symbols such as numbers and acronyms. The first 500, 1,000, 2,000 and 4,000 words were taken from the works of Benedetti and Quijote, and 500 words from the editorial. These words were then used to create the examples as described above and were labelled as Bene500, Qui500, Pap500 etc. It was found that the 4,000 words from Benedetti and Quijote yielded 1,426 and 1,279 different words and a total of 18,629 and 17,627 examples, respectively. The 500 words of the editorial had 250 different words and produced 2,474 examples. The distribution of the examples between the O, N and C classes was roughly 39%, 47%, 13% for each set. These sets were utilised as training data to build the classification trees with CRUISE. In all the experiments conducted, the default values available in CRUISE were the ones taken to construct the classification trees.

In order to choose the test sets, it is first interesting to note that Quijote has over 370,000 words, of which nearly 22,000 are different words (c.f. [15]). Of these, over 10,000 appear just once, whilst the 1,000 most frequent words account for nearly 80% of the total number of words found in the book. Three sets, each with a 1,000 different words, were chosen from Quijote and the examples were generated from them using the method described above, and labelled Most, Rand and Least. Most is generated from the 1,000 most frequent words, Rand from a random selection of 1,000 words (from the nearly 22,000 different words), and Least from a random selection of 1,000 words which occur just once. The idea behind choosing these sets was to test the classification trees on examples which came from words which are frequently or rarely found in the language. In the end, Most had 5,618 examples, Rand had 7,833, and Least had 8,465.

4 Results

Figs 1 and 2 show the decision trees obtained from Bene4000 and Qui4000. The trees are quite shallow with a maximum depth of four levels, although constructed from over 17,000 examples. All the other trees revealed a similar behaviour. The times required to construct the trees, and test them on Least, were 44.5 and 39.7secs. For the trees constructed with Bene500, Qui500 and Pap500, approximately 4secs was needed.

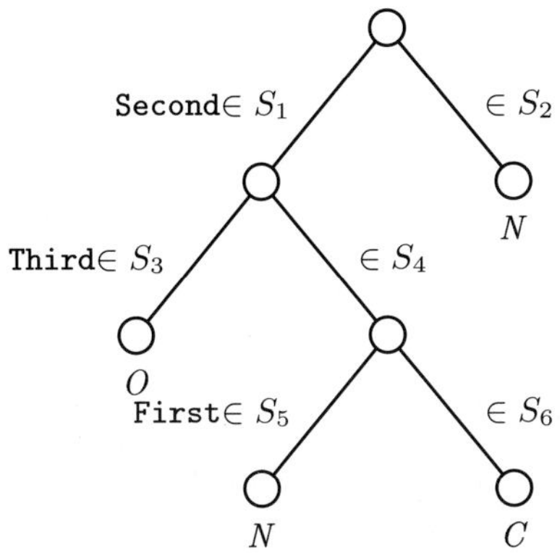

$S_1 = \{$b c d f g h j l m n p q r s t v x y z ñ$\}$
$S_2 = \{$a e i o u á é í ó ú ü$\}$ $S_3 = \{$a e h i l o r u x y á é í ñ ó ú ü$\}$
$S_4 = \{$W b c d f g j m n p q s t v z$\}$ $S_5 = \{$W$\}$
$S_6 = \{$a b c d e f g h i j l m n o p q r s t u v x y z á é í ñ ó ú ü$\}$

Fig. 1. Classification tree trained with 4000 words of Benedetti

Table 1 contains the results obtained using the decision trees built with the data set appearing in the first column. The second column gives the number of examples found in each of the data sets. The next four columns give the percentage correct results, obtained using the corresponding tree on the training set and the three test sets.

The results for all of the test sets show, as would be expected, an increasing number of correct values from those formed from the least frequent 1,000 words to the most frequent 1,000 words. All the results, with the exception of Qui500, are above 99%. An error rate of 1.2% for the case of Qui500 on Least represents 98 errors. An analysis of the errors made is given in the next section.

The results in Table 1 reveal the percentage correct on the examples in Least, Rand and Most, however we are really interested in the results pertaining to the syllabification of each word in the original word sets, each of which contained 1,000 words. Essentially each error in Table 1 corresponds to a different word, and so a total of 98 errors gives a corresponding syllabification error rate of 9.8% when calculated with respect to the 1,000 words. This is also the worst error rate found.

5 Discussion and Conclusions

In the present paper, we have investigated the use of classification trees for automatically finding Spanish syllabification rules. A coding scheme with three

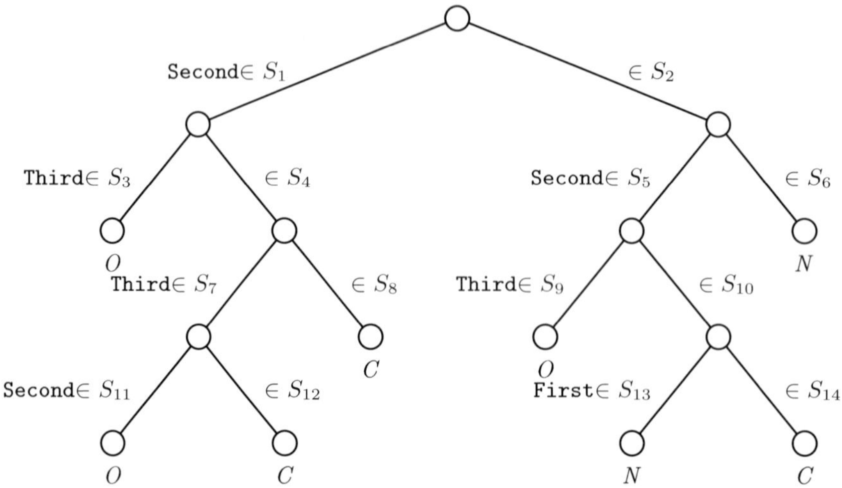

S_1 = {b c d f g h j l m n p q r s t v x z ñ}
S_2 = {a e i o u y á é í ó ú ü} S_3 = {a e i o u á é í ó ú}
S_4 = {W b c d f g h j l m n p q r s t v x y z ñ ü} S_5 = {y}
S_6 = {a b c d e f g h i j l m n o p q r s t u v x z á é í ñ ó ú ü}
S_7 = {h l r ü}
S_8 = {W a b c d e f g i j m n o p q s t u v x y z á é í ñ ó ú}
S_9 = {a b c d e f g h i j l m n o p q r s t u v x y z á é í ñ ó ú ü}
S_{10} = {W} S_{11} = {b c f g l p t}
S_{12} = {a d e h i j m n o q r s u v x y z á é í ñ ó ú ü} S_{13} = {W}
S_{14} = {a b c d e f g h i j l m n o p q r s t u v x y z á é í ñ ó ú ü}

Fig. 2. Classification tree trained with 4000 words of Quijote

Table 1. Results of the classification trees on the test sets

Data set	No. of exs	% on set	%Least	%Rand	%Most
Bene500	2,231	100	99.2	99.4	99.9
Bene1000	4,522	99.9	99.2	99.3	99.9
Bene2000	9,249	99.9	99.3	99.4	99.9
Bene4000	18,629	99.9	99.3	99.5	99.9
Qui500	2,247	99.8	98.8	98.9	99.4
Qui1000	4,440	99.7	99.3	99.5	99.7
Qui2000	8,733	99.8	99.5	99.6	99.9
Qui4000	17,627	99.8	99.4	99.5	99.7
Pap500	2,474	100	99.3	99.4	99.6

characters and three classes, corresponding to onset-nucleus-coda, has been employed and applied to different text sources to obtain training and test sets. The text sources were purposely chosen to be different in terms of their authors and content. Classification trees were constructed with the training sets using a method called CRUISE. The aim has been to see whether these techniques are effective, and what difficulties might arise in the process.

The number of characters used in the coding could be varied, especially for other languages, where contextual information contained in the language might benefit from larger windows; this is something to be explored in future work. In the present paper, however, the results in Tables 1 with three characters are already over 90%, even when as few as 500 words were used (and in that case the number of different words was about 250).

The three classes O, N, and C are a natural choice, nevertheless for Spanish, ambiguity is present in the syllabification process. For example, *rio* and *río* both produce ONN, but syllabify differently as *rio* and *rí-o.* These errors arise from the rules governing Spanish diphthongs and triphthongs, and once identified, different strategies can be employed to eliminate them, such as extending the number of classes.

If we analyse the errors made by the classification tree constructed with Qui4000, we find that there are a total of 47 errors made on Least, the worst case scenario. Of these errors, 43 correspond to splitting the inseparable pairs dr (11 errors) or rr (32 errors) and mistaking the initial letter as a coda when in fact it should be an onset. Three of the other errors occur with *alr* in *alrededores* or *alhucema,* and report an onset instead of a coda. The final error is interesting because it confuses an onset for a nucleus in *ahi,* and does not comply with the rule that an *h* should not split a diphthong.

In the case of the classification tree constructed with Bene4000, there are 59 errors on Least. Of these, 58 correspond to incorrectly changing a coda for an onset, and all occur in the context of VCC. A large number of these VCC errors take place when a pronoun appears at the end of a word, such as the errors with *arl* in *intentarla* or *osl* in *vivimosle;* however they are also found in examples such as the *alr* in the word *alrededores* or the *exh* in *exhalaciones* or *esl* in *deslumbrada.* The other error made by the tree is the same as before, confusing the diphthong in *ahi.*

The classification tree constructed with Pap500 signalled an interesting difficulty, as it was discovered that the text contained neither *ñ* nor *ü;* this accounted for over half of the errors made. Again, this is an easily identified and remedied error. The rest of the errors were similar to Bene4000 and erroneously assigned onsets instead of codas to VCC combinations. Does this suggest something about the use of pronouns found in older Spanish writing?

In any event, as we are interested in the possibility of automatically generating syllabification rules and reducing the types of errors made, it is interesting that the errors which occur for the above cases are for the most part easily explained and fall into specific categories. This provides the sort of information needed to enlarge the training examples and so reduce the type of mistakes made, albeit in an iterative fashion.

Finally, even though the texts are quite different, the syllabification performance shown is still very good on all the test sets, including the more complicated Least. These are encouraging results which we hope to pursue in future work.

References

1. Ostendorf, M.: Moving beyond the 'beads-on-a-string' model of speech. In: Proceedings of the ASRU, Keystone, Colorado (1999)
2. Greenberg, S.: Speaking in shorthand, a syllable-centric perspective for understanding pronunciation variation. Speech Communication **29** (1999) 159–176
3. Ganapathiraju, A., Hamaker, J., Ordowski, M., Doddington, G., Picone, J.: Syllable-based large vocabulary continuous speech recognition. IEEE Transactions on Speech and Audio Processing **9** (2001) 358–366
4. Rao, M.N., Thomas, S., Nagarajan, T., Murthy, H.A.: Text-to-speech synthesis using syllable-like units. In: Proceedings of National Conference on Communications, IIT, India (2005) 277–280
5. López-Gonzalo, E., Rodríguez-García, J.: Statistical methods in data-driven modeling of spanish prosody for text to speech. In: ICSLP 96. Volume 3. (1996)
6. Figueroa, K.: Síntesis de voz en español, un enfoque silábico. Tesis de Licenciatura, Asesor: Leonardo Romero (1998) Universidad Michoacana de San Nicolas de Hidalgo.
7. C.Oliveira, Mourinho, L., A.Teixeira: On european portuguese automatic syllabification. In: INTERSPEECH 2005. (2005) 2933–2936
8. Belz, A.: Computational Learning of Finite-State Models for Natural Language Processing. PhD thesis, School of Cognitive and Computing Sciences, University of Sussex, UK (2000)
9. Tian, J.: Data-driven approaches for automatic detection of syllable boundaries. In: INTERSPEECH-2004. (2004) 61–64
10. Nerbonne, J., Konstantopoulos, S.: Phonotactics in inductive logic programming. Advances in Soft Computing (2004) 493–502 Mieczyslaw A. Klopotek, Slawomir T. Wierzchon, and Krzysztof Trojanowski (eds.) Intelligent Information Processing and Web Mining.
11. Müller, K.: Probabilistic syllable modeling using unsupervised and supervised learning methods. In: AIMS 2002. Volume 8. (2002) PhD Thesis, University of Stuttgart, Institute of Natural Language Processing (IMS).
12. MacKinney-Romero, R., J. Goddard: Inferring rules for finding syllables in spanish. Lecture Notes in Computer Science **3789** (2005) 800–805 Springer-Verlag.
13. Kim, H., Loh, W.Y.: Classification trees with unbiased multiway splits. Journal of the American Statistical Association **96** (2001) 589–604
14. de Cervantes Saavedra, M.: El Ingenioso Hidalgo Don Quijote de la Mancha. F.F. Jehle (2005) Works of Miguel de Cervantes in modern-Spanish spelling, based on the 18 volume edition published by Rodolfo Schevill and Adolfo Bonilla. Edited electronically in `http://users.ipfw.edu/jehle/wcdq.htm`.
15. Goddard, J., Martínez, A.E., MacKinney, R., Martinez, F.M.: The syllable structure of don quijote. In: 10th International Conference on Speech and Computer (SPECOM'2005), Greece (2005) 251–254

Identifying Text Discourse Structure of the Narratives Describing Psychiatric Patients' Defense Mechanisms

Eunmi Ham[1] and Woojin Paik[2,*]

[1] Dept. of Nursing Science, Konkuk University,
322 Danwol-Dong, Chungju-Si, Chungcheongbuk-Do, 380-701, Korea
hem2003@kku.ac.kr

[2] Dept. of Computer Science, Konkuk University,
322 Danwol-Dong, Chungju-Si, Chungcheongbuk-Do, 380-701, Korea
wjpaik@kku.ac.kr

Abstract. Psychiatric nursing care plans include the narratives describing the defense mechanisms exhibited by the patients. These narratives form the basis for generating psychodynamic analysis, which is one of the key diagnosis outcomes about the patients. However, it is fairly difficult for the novice nurses to correctly identify the type of defense mechanism based on the observations that they made while caring for the patients. One of the main reasons for the high error rate is the lack of uniform terminology. That is, inconsistencies in the definitions and conceptualizations of defenses. Furthermore, there is lack of sufficient examples showing the wide variety of cases from which the novice nurses to learn. We developed a prototype text discourse analysis system, which assigns one or more text discourse categories to each clause in the defense mechanism narratives. The initial evaluation of the prototype system resulted in correctly identifying 85% of the defense mechanisms in the test data set. The output from the text discourse analysis system is fed into a database to augment the definition of the defense mechanisms and also to be used as a learning tool for the novice nurses.

1 Introduction

The nursing care plan includes the systematic explanation of the facts gathered from the patient assessment stage and also all intervening analysis by the nurses as well as the final diagnosis, interventions to be performed, and expected outcome of the interventions. The nurses develop a plan of care that prescribes interventions to attain outcomes. The care plan is prepared to provide continuity of care from nurse to nurse, to enhance communication, to assist with determination of agency or unit staffing needs, to document the nursing process, to serve as a teaching tool, and to coordinate provisions of care among disciplines [1].

Psychiatric nursing care plan includes the background information about the patients such as the general biographical information, the medical history, various

* Corresponding author.

T. Salakoski et al. (Eds.): FinTAL 2006, LNAI 4139, pp. 341 – 348, 2006.

health related information, physical and mental state assessment results, nursing diagnoses, suggested interventions, and expected outcomes. Much of the information is conveyed as narratives of the nurses and the direct quotes from the patients.

Defense mechanism assessment is a key part of the mental state assessment in the psychiatric nursing care plan. Defense mechanism is defined as a way of distancing oneself from a full awareness of unpleasant thoughts, feelings and desires. In psychoanalytic theory, defense mechanisms represent an unconscious mediation by the ego of id impulses which are in conflict with the wishes and needs of the ego and/or superego. By altering and distorting one's awareness of the original impulse, one makes it more tolerable [2]. There are 22 types of defense mechanisms assessed in the training and testing data for this study. Some of the defense mechanism examples are denial, projection, regression, displacement, and repression [3].

The nurses especially the novice nurses often make wrong defense mechanism assessments. One of the most serious limitations associated with defense mechanism assessment was the lack of uniform terminology or the inconsistencies in the definitions and conceptualization of the defenses [4]. However, the novice nurses still have problems in correctly identifying the defense mechanisms of the patients even with the clear definitions and explanations. We believe that the novice nurses will be able to learn to correctly assess defense mechanisms more easily if he/she can review sufficient number of actual examples. But, this is also problematic as the novice nurses have to go through many psychiatric nursing care plans to find the section describing defense mechanisms. Even after, the appropriate sections have been found, the novice nurses still have to mentally decompose the narratives, which typically consist of a definition of the assessed defense mechanism, supporting examples, and reasoning process to reach the conclusion, to fully understand why a particular defense mechanism was chosen. Thus, we developed a prototype text discourse analysis system, which automatically extracts the defense mechanism assessment narrative sections from the psychiatric nursing care plan. The system is also designed to assign one or more text discourse categories such as definition, assessment, observed, monologue by patient, question by nurse, answer by patient, and other source to each clause in the narratives. We architected the text discourse analysis system to feed its output into a database to augment the existing definitions of the various defense mechanisms and also to be used as a teaching aid for the novice nurses.

2 Text Discourse Analysis

A text discourse model specifies the necessary classes of knowledge to be identified in order to develop the skeletal conceptual structure for a class of entities. Based on a discourse linguistics observation [5], writers are often influenced by the schema of a particular text type if they produce texts of that type repeatedly. This means that the writers consider both specific content they wish to convey and usual structure for that type of text on the basis of the purpose it is intended to serve.

The existence of such predictable structures in texts is consistent with findings in cognitive psychology which suggest that human cognitive processes are facilitated by the ability to 'chunk' the vast amount of information encountered in daily life into larger units of organized data [6]. Based on schema theories, humans recode individual units of perception into increasingly larger units, which will eventually reach at the level of a schema. It has also been argued that humans possess schema for a wide range of concepts, events, and situations [7]. In discourse linguistics, this schema theory was extended to suggest that schema exist for text-types that participate regularly in the shared communication of a particular community of users.

As the text structure of a particular text type is discovered, the text's discernible and predictable superstructure is also revealed. Superstructure is defined as the text-level syntactic organization of semantic content. It can be also referred to as the global schematic structure or the recognizable template that is filled with different meaning in each particular example of that text type [8]. Some of the text types for which schemas or models have been developed with varying degree of details are: newspaper articles [8], arguments [9], editorials [10], and abstracts [11].

Our previous work focused on developing a news schema model and a legal text schema [12, 13]. For the news schema model, we started from the journalistic, hierarchical newspaper text model proposed by van Dijk [8]. By using a sample of Wall Street Journal articles from 1987 to 1999, a revised news schema was developed. The revised schema retained segmentation of the overall structure into van Dijk's higher level categories, namely, summary, story, and comment, but added several categories as warranted by the data. The categories were: circumstances, consequence, credential, definition, error, evaluation, expectation, history, lead, main event, no comment, previous event, reference, and verbal reaction. For the legal documents, we developed a legal text schema based on four basic categories [14]. The categories were: 1) summary of the facts of the case; 2) identification of the issues of law raised in arguments by counsel for each of the parties; 3) pronouncement of the legal propositions supported by the controlling authorities; and 4) declaration of a decision that resolves the issues by applying the legal propositions to the facts of the case.

3 Analysis of the Defense Mechanism Narratives

To develop a text schema for the narratives describing the defense mechanisms in the nursing care plans, we analyzed randomly selected 35 nursing care plans as a training data set.

3.2 Training Data

The generation of the nursing care plans was a part of a course assignment for the 'Psychiatric Nursing' course, which was offered at the Department of Nursing Science, Konkuk University in Chungju, Korea. The course was for Juniors who were majoring in the nursing science. Each student developed a detailed case study report of one patient while the student was working as a student intern at a psychiatric warden for two weeks. The nursing care plan was one section of the case report, which was submitted to the instructor at the end of the internship period. The case reports were from the course offered in the Spring and Fall 2005 semester. All case reports were mainly written in Korean with English translations for a number of important concepts. We also used another set of seventeen randomly selected nursing care plans as a testing data set.

The general patient information was the first section of the care plan. The second section was about the patient's current health related information. The third section was about the mental state assessment outcome. It included general appearance of the patient, attitudes & behavior, mood or affect, thoughts, perception, cognition, intellectual function, insight, expectation about the admission outcome by the patient and/or family, and patient's future plan. The third section also included narrative descriptions about the patient's defense mechanism and the psychodynamics. The fourth section included the nursing goal selected, nursing diagnoses reached, interventions to be applied, and the outcomes to be expected. It was straightforward to develop a preprocessor to extract the sub-section including the narratives describing the defense mechanism, which is a part of the third section. The preprocessor was programmed to find the text strings, which identify the heading for the defense mechanism sub-section and the heading for the next sub-section, then extract the identified sub-section for further processing.

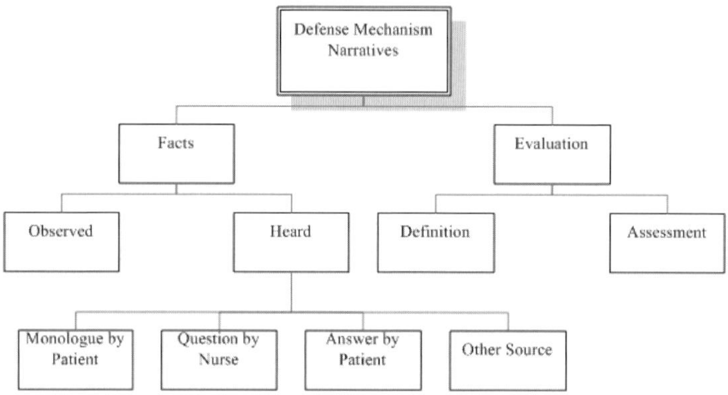

Fig. 1. Nursing Care Plan Text Schema

The nursing care plan text schema is shown in the Figure 1. It is based on the qualitative content analysis of the training data set. At the most general level, there are two major categories. They are 'Facts' and 'Evaluation'. 'Facts' refer to the factual information about the patients. 'Facts' major category is further divided into 'Observed' and 'Heard' categories according to how the information was collected. 'Observed' is for the information directly observed by the nurses without the patient usually knowing that he/she is being observed. 'Heard' is what the nurses heard about the patient. 'Heard' category is further divided into four sub-categories. Four sub-categories are: 'Monologue by Patient', 'Question by Nurse', 'Answer by Patient', and 'Other Sources'. 'Monologue by Patient' is for the information, which is based on what the patient said about him/herself without any external inquiry. 'Question by Nurse' does not convey information about the patient but it explains why certain responses are made by the patients. Nurses ask questions either to learn a particular aspect of the patient's condition or to encourage the patient to continue to talk about him/herself. 'Answer by Patient' sub-category is for the information provided by the patient in response to the nurses' questions. Finally, 'Other Sources' sub-category refers to the patient information provided by the patient's family members, friends, other nurses, or the physicians.

We decided to code each clause with one or more the discourse categories at the most specific level. There were 84 defense mechanism narratives in the 35 psychiatric nursing care plans. Thus, there are about 2.4 defense mechanism narratives per patient. However, we decided not to code eight defense mechanism narratives as the course instructor identified them to be wrongly assessed defense mechanisms. Therefore, 76 defense mechanism narratives were manually coded and used as the training data set for the text discourse analysis system. The following example is from the training data set. '<*category name*>' and '</category name>' were used to show the beginning and end of a clause, which is coded as a particular text discourse category. The following Korean example is a defense mechanism narrative about a 47-year old divorced male patient written by an internship student.

<Question by Nurse> 왜 술을 많이 마셨는지에 대해 물어보았을 때 </Question by Nurse> <Answer by Patient> 환자는 자신이 술에 손을 대게 된 계기와 폭주를 하게 된 계기가 모두 이혼한 아내 탓이라고 말하며 </Answer by Patient> <Observed> 침울한 표정을 지었다. </Observed> <Definition> 이는 자신의 불쾌한 감정, 사고 및 태도를 다른 사람의 탓으로 돌리는 </Definition> <Assessment> 투사의 방어기제로 보여진다. </Assessment>

The English translation of the first clause categorized as 'Question by Nurse' is 'when asked about why the patient had been drinking excessively'. The translation of the second clause categorized as 'Answer by Patient' is 'the patient described that he started to drink and had been drinking a lot because of his divorced wife'. The translation of the third clause categorized as 'Observed' is 'his face looked somber'. The fourth 'Definition' clause is translated as 'the preceding description indicates that the patient blames other person for his unpleasant feeling, thoughts, and attitudes'. The final clause categorized as 'Assessment' can be translated as 'the symptoms indicate the projection as the defense mechanism of the patient'.

3.2 Extracting Text Classification Features

While coding the training data, we developed both defining features and properties for each category. The defining features convey the role and purpose of that category within the defense mechanism narrative text schema. The properties provide suggestive clues for the recognition of that category. The manual coding suggested to us that we were relying on five types of linguistic information during our coding. The data, which would provide these evidence sources, were then analyzed statistically and translated into computationally recognizable text characteristics. The five sources of evidences are described in the following.

Lexical Evidences: This source of evidence is a set of one, two, three word phrases for each category. The set of lexical evidences for each category was chosen based on observed frequencies and distributions. Only the words or phrases with sufficient occurrences and statistically skewed observed frequency of occurrences in a particular category were used. Before all one and two word phrases were extracted from the text, all words were converted into their root form. Furthermore, all proper names were converted into their type. After all coded training data are processed by the lexical evidence extraction module, the frequency distribution of each piece of lexical evidence is further processed to generate the probability information. As each clause is processed, the lexical evidences for the words and phrases in the clause are combined using the Dempster-Shafer Theory of Evidence [15].

Syntactic Evidences: We utilize two types of syntactic evidences: 1) typical sentence length as measured in the average number of words per clause for each category and 2) individual part-of-speech distribution based on the output of the part-of-speech tagging. This evidence helps to recognize those categories, which tend to have a disproportionate number of their words to be of a particular part of speech.

Tense Evidences: Some categories tend to contain verbs of a particular tense more than verbs of other tenses. For example, 'Fact' clauses are almost always in the past or present perfect tense. The tense evidence is a byproduct of part-of-speech tagging.

Document Structure Evidences: We included the relative position of each clause with respect to the source narrative as a whole as another evidence source.

Order of Category Evidences: This source of evidence replies on the tendency of categories to occur in a particular, relative order. We calculated the frequency with which each category followed every other category and the frequency with which each category preceded every other category. The results are stored in two six-by-six matrices. This evidence source is not used initially. At first, the text classifier uses other evidence sources to assign one or more category tags to each clause. If there is a clause, which did not receive any category assignment by the text classifier then this order of category evidence is used to determine the most appropriate category to assign.

3.3 Text Classification

To assign a basic category label to each clause, each clause in the training data set is categorized according to the predetermined defense mechanism narrative text schema. The first text classification task involves manually coding all clauses in a set of training documents in preparation for feeding into the automatic system. Each clause is classified as "in" or "out" of the individual categories as outlined by the category definitions. The next step is to take these manually classified clauses and process them through the trainable text classification system. During this process, it builds a vector of lexical evidences, syntactic evidences, tense evidences, and document structure evidences. Multi-level Natural Language Processing outputs are the basis for these textual data feature representations.

This collection of automatically generated features is then used to determine inclusion of a clause within a particular category. The system determines the 'certainty of membership' for each of the clauses compared to each of the category. If we consider a range of one to zero where one refers to a clause that is definitely a member of a certain category, and zero means a clause is definitely a non-member of a certain category, then we can say that values of zero and one both have a 'certainty of membership' value of one. For either of these cases, we can confidently conclude that the clause either 'does' or 'does not' belong within a given category. If we look at values close to .5 on the above scale, we have a 'certainty of membership' value close to zero. For these cases, we cannot automatically determine whether or not a given clause should be assigned to a given category. These clauses are considered valuable in refining the classification system. By manually classifying these clauses, and then feeding them back into the automatic system, we train it to recognize the subtle differences that distinguish how these clauses should be classified.

4 Implementation and Evaluation

The computational modeling of instantiating a discourse-level model of the defense mechanism narratives is an ongoing effort. We developed a prototype system by manually analyzing 76 sample narratives and tested our system using 32 unseen narratives. The 32 unseen narratives are from 17 nursing care plans. Originally there were 36 unseen narratives but defense mechanisms in four narratives were wrongly assessed. Thus, only 32 narratives were used to evaluate the system. The first run and evaluation of the correctly categorizing four basic categories resulted in 85% of the clauses being correctly identified.

There is no directly comparable nursing care plan text classification system. How-ever, a news text classification system, which assigned sentences into one out of four-teen categories, performed at 72% correct rate in the fully automatic mode and 80% correct rate with various manual heuristic adjustments [12]. It should be noted that our text classifier did not utilize the second iteration of incorporating the clauses, with certainty membership value close to zero, as a part of new training data set. We believe the addition of this process will improve the correctness of our system.

5 Summary

Although we are clearly in the early stages of developing a defense mechanism narratives discourse modeling system, we find the evaluation result to be quite promising and eager to share our premature but empirical results and experiences in creating an operational text discourse analysis system with other researchers. We expect the resulting database to aid both nursing students and novice practitioners, who want to better identify defense mechanisms. They can review what others have done to learn from the examples. There are many tasks that we have yet to finish. Firstly, we need to increase the size of test data set to improve the reliability of the evaluation results. Secondly, we want to get the data from a variety of sources. Currently, all training and testing data is from the students, who were educated by the same instructor. So, we wish to confirm that our approach works by testing the system against the data obtained from the students, who attend or graduated from other institutions. Thirdly, we wish to conduct a detailed failure analysis to identify the error sources and also to come up with the remedies.

We have applied the defense mechanism narrative discourse model to the actual psychiatric nursing care plans by coding a small set of sample texts. This effort in conjunction with our previous work with the newspaper legal texts shows that we can extract a particular section of the texts by utilizing a text type specific discourse model.

References

1. Doenges, M., and Moorehead, M.F.: Application of Nursing Process and Nursing Diagnosis: An Interactive Text for Diagnostic Reasoning 4th Edition, F.A. Davis Co., Philadelphia, Pennsylvania (2003)
2. Defense Mechanisms, PlanetPsych.com: 3 April 2006 http://www.planetpsych.com/zPsychology_101/defense_mechanisms.htm
3. Bond, M., Vaillant, G.E., Vaillant, C.O.: An empirically validated hierarchy of defense mechanisms, Archives of General Psychiatry (1986)
4. Vaillant, G.E.: Ego Mechanisms of Defense: A Guide for Clinicians and Researchers, American Psychiatric Pub, Inc. (1992)
5. Jones, L.B.: Pragmatic aspects of English text structure. Summer Institute of Linguistics, Arlington, TX (1983)
6. Rumelhart, D.: Understanding and summarizing brief stories. In D. LaBerge and S.J. Samuels (Editors) Basic processes in reading: Perception and comprehension. Hillsdale, NJ: Lawrence Earlbaum Associates: 265-303. (1977)
7. Rumelhart, D.: Schemata: the building blocks of cognition. In R. Spiro, B. Bruce, & W. Brewer (Editors) Theoretical issues in reading comprehension: Perspectives from cognitive psychology, linguistics, artificial intelligence and education. Hillsdale, NJ: Lawrence Earlbaum Associates: 33-8. (1980)
8. van Dijk, T.A.: News analysis: Case studies of international and national news in the press. Hillsdale, NJ: Lawrence Earlbaum Associates. (1988)
9. Cohen, R.: Analyzing the structure of argumentative discourse. Computational Linguistics, 13. 11-24. (1987)
10. Alvarado, S.J.: Understanding editorial text: A computer model of argument comprehension. Boston, MA: Kluwer Academic Publishers. (1990)
11. Liddy, E.D.: The discourse-level structure of empirical abstracts: An exploratory study. Information Processing and Management 27.1, Tarry Town, NY, Pergamon Press: 55-81. (1991)
12. Liddy, E.D., McVearry, K.A., Paik, W., Yu, E., and McKenna, M.: Development, Implementation and Testing of a Discourse Model for Newspaper Texts. Proceedings of Human Language Technology Workshop. Plainsboro, NJ, Morgan Kaufmann Publishers: 159-164. (1993)
13. Paik, W. and Lee, J.: Extracting Legal Propositions from Appellate Decisions with Text Discourse Analysis Methods. Lecture Notes in Computer Science (LNCS) Vol. 3292, Springer-Verlag: 621-633. (2004)
14. Branting, K., Lester, J.C., and Callaway, C.B.: Automating Judicial Document Drafting: A Discourse-Based Approach. Artificial Intelligence Law 6(2-4): 111-149 (1998)
15. Pearl, J.: Probabilistic reasoning in intelligent systems: networks of plausible inference, Morgan Kaufmann Publishers, San Francisco, CA. (1988)

Implementing a Rule-Based Speech Synthesizer on a Mobile Platform

Tuomo Saarni[1], Jyri Paakkulainen[2], Tuomas Mäkilä[2], Jussi Hakokari[3], Olli Aaltonen[3], Jouni Isoaho[1], and Tapio Salakoski[1]

[1] Turku Centre for Computer Science, FI-20014, Finland
{Tuomo.Saarni, Jouni.Isoaho, Tapio.salakoski}@it.utu.fi
[2] Department of Information Technology, University of Turku, FI-20014, Finland
{Jyri.Paakkulainen, Tuomas.Makila}@it.utu.fi
[3] Phonetics Laboratory, University of Turku, FI-20014, Finland
{Jussi.Hakokari, Olli.Aaltonen}@utu.fi

Abstract. This paper describes the structure of a Finnish speech synthesis system developed at the University of Turku and evaluates the preliminary results of its implementation and performance on a platform with limited computing power. A rule-based approach was selected due to its high adaptability, low memory and computational capacity requirements. The speech synthesis system is written in Java™ MIDP 2.0 and CLDC 1.1. The synthesis is implemented on Nokia 6680 mobile device as a 65 kilobyte MIDlet. The system produces artificial speech at the sampling rate of 16 kHz. The results show that for a second of synthesized speech it takes 2.66 seconds for the system to produce it. Although the implementation was successful, improvements are needed to achieve a more acceptable level of time consumption.

1 Introduction

Speech synthesis systems have been available for decades, and several ways to produce synthesized speech have emerged. We have set out to study an older method of creating artificial speech, a rule-based speech synthesis. A rule-based speech synthesis may be considered a truly synthetic way to produce speech since it does not make use of any samples of natural, human speech as most of the other synthesis methods do. On the other hand, the rule-based speech synthesis is commonly considered to be the most challenging way to produce high-quality synthetic speech.

The development of embedded systems introduces whole new platforms with less memory capacity and computing power than in personal computers. Although technology evolves fast, we are encouraged to study possibilities in creating synthesized speech with less computational capacity than usually available. A rule-based synthesis system may be considered a small and computationally light system, and therefore suitable especially for platforms with limited capacity.

To examine the performance of the system, we have measured the time consumption of producing a second of synthesized speech signal (from hereon referred to as time cost ratio). I.e. the time consumed in creating the synthetic speech signal was

T. Salakoski et al. (Eds.): FinTAL 2006, LNAI 4139, pp. 349 – 355, 2006.

divided by the duration of the resulting signal. A real-time system would then produce more than a second of artificial speech in less than a second (the time cost ratio being less than 1). This would enable a real-time streaming of the synthesized speech simultaneously when created.

The study at hand investigates the possibility of implementing a rule-based speech synthesis on a mobile device supporting Java™ MIDP 2.0 [7] and CLDC 1.1 [1]. We are also interested of the system's time consumption on the chosen platform. The synthesis software was originally written in Java™ for personal computers; a MIDlet was the most obvious choice for implementation. The system was built at the University of Turku and was initially used to produce synthetic speech stimuli for behavioral experiments in speech sciences. Later on the system was re-evaluated by a joint project by the Phonetics Laboratory and the Department of Information Technology.

This paper first shows the overall structure of the speech synthesis program, followed by the testing procedure and the results. Finally, the results are discussed before the conclusive remarks.

2 Program Structure

This paper presents the system in two phases: the high-level synthesizer and the speech signal generator. The high-level synthesizer handles transcription, sets the segmental durations, models the fundamental frequency contour, and implements the phoneme-level rules. The signal generation phase creates the sound signal from an information matrix it receives from the high-level synthesizer. The structure is described in figure 1.

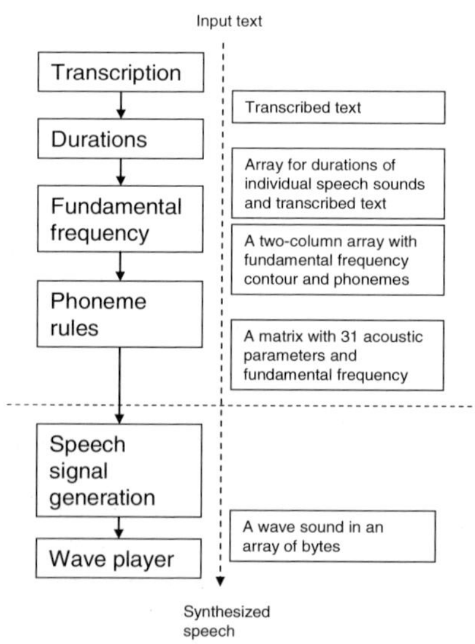

Fig. 1. The structure of the software is divided into two phases; the high-level synthesizer and the signal generation, which are separated by a horizontal dashed line. Each step in the synthesizing procedure is shown on the left and the changes in the information state is described on the right.

Implemented on a mobile device, the system does not differ much from the one on a PC. The software on the mobile device has fixed parameters that are adjustable on the PC version. Both systems operate on a time resolution of 10 milliseconds. Therefore, actual changes in the signal can only take place a hundred times per second. The synthesis software is currently used like text messaging with mobile devices. The input text is first typed and can then be synthesized.

Transcription refers to the conversion of the orthographic text to a phonetic representation. Finnish has a great advantage over many other languages from the point of view of speech synthesis. Finnish has a very high level of one-to-one correspondence between spelling and pronunciation. There are only few exceptions and most of them are possible to deal with simple rules; there is practically no need for an exception dictionary.

The durations are fixed to 70 milliseconds for short phonemes. Phonemically long phonemes are 140 ms long. A comma results in a 150 millisecond pause; a full stop introduces a 350 millisecond pause. The system has a prepausal lengthening implemented [2] [9]. Prepausal lengthening refers to the human tendency to slow down articulation right before a pause. The module now lengthens speech sounds' duration in the last word of each phrase, producing 90 ms and 180 ms long speech sounds instead of 70 ms and 140 ms. The durations are set in array which include the transcribed text and the duration of each character in transcription (including pauses).

The fundamental frequency is set to cascade model meaning that the frequency starts at 100 Hz and falls down to 70 Hz by the end of the sentence, crudely imitating a typical male speaker. Within each word of the sentence, the frequency raises 40 Hz during the first speech sound of each word. That represents the lexical stress always found on the first syllable in Finnish. If there's a comma within a sentence, this causes an additional rise of 20 Hz in the fundamental frequency.

The phoneme rules comprise of 34 acoustical parameters. Duration of each speech sound is needed to calculate its transition to the next. It has its own acoustical parameters which needs to be reached during a transitional phase between two speech sounds. The transition is currently done linearly and is usually very short, typically in the order of 30 milliseconds. The acoustical parameters are listed in Table 1. Most of the parameters are fixed in the current version so that they are shared by every speech sound.

The signal generator receives the matrix of parameters from the high-level synthesizer. The speech signal is generated by a formant synthesizer that resembles the ones described in [5] and [6]. The signal generator consists of a vocal tract model and sound sources for voicing, frication and aspiration. The vocal tract model consists of a cascade branch and a parallel branch. The cascade branch is used for generating

Table 1. Acoustical parameters used in signal signal generation with explanations

Parameter	Explanation	Parameter	Explanation
F0	Fundamental frequency	FNP	Frequency of nasal formant
AV	Amplitude of voicing	BNP	Bandwidth of nasal formant
TL	Voicing source low frequency emphasis	FNZ	Frequency of nasal antiformant
AF	Amplitude of frication	BNZ	Bandwidth of nasal antiformant
AH	Amplitude of aspiration	A1F…A6F	Amplitudes of parallel branch formants
F1…F6	Frequencies of first six formants	B1F…B6F	Bandwidths of parallel branch formants
B1…B6	Bandwidths of cascade branch formants	AB	Amplitude of bypass frication

sounds that consists of voicing and/or aspiration noise. The parallel tract is used mainly for fricative and plosive sounds. The signal generator is controlled by parameters shown in Table 1.

3 Implementation Platform

The implementation was conducted with Nokia 6680 mobile device using software version 4.04.07 (dated 22-08-05) and firmware version RM-36. The mobile device supports CLDC 1.1 (Connected Limited Device Configuration) [1] and Java™ MIDP 2.0 (Mobile Information Device Profile) [7]. The jar and heap size are only restricted by the available memory of the device [8].

The Nokia 6680 mobile device was selected as the platform due to its average MIDP 2.0 performance according to the result database of the JBenchmark J2ME benchmarking tool [4]. It should be noted that the benchmarking tool emphasizes graphical performance. Nevertheless, the results give guidelines on the overall performance of the device.

Compared to the previous versions both CLDC 1.1 and MIDP 2.0 offered several important features needed for the rule-based speech synthesis. Especially the floating-point support introduced in the CLDC 1.1 and the built-in Media API of MIDP 2.0 were valuable. However, the obvious problem in the MIDP 2.0 Media API was the lack of streaming of sounds. Speech is currently synthesized by first creating the signal in full and then playing it afterwards.

4 Testing Procedure and Time Consumption Measurements

The performance of the system was examined on the chosen platform. All non-relevant options and add-on devices were eliminated to minimize any interference. The testing was done in the following environment:

- No SIM card inserted
- No other programs installed
- No unnecessary memory usage (no calendar markings, phone numbers etc.)
- No memory card installed
- No optional devices connected
- No other programs running except the ones the device itself uses automatically when on
- The device fully charged and connected to the charger
- The device on before synthesizing a text and shut down after each synthesized passage
- Two-minute wait after the device was turned on to ensure it is fully functional
- Half-minute wait after the synthesis software was started to ensure the program has loaded
- After the text is typed, it is synthesized immediately
- The elapsed time is reported by the software itself and shown on the display

The synthesized sentences are random pickings from a Finnish periodical Suomen Kuvalehti. They represent Standard Finnish and are of varying length to provide information on the effects of varying input. Each input sentence was synthesized several times to achieve a more reliable average of the time cost ratios.

The average time consumption of the high-level synthesizer (phase 1) was 0.34 seconds per second of synthesized speech, ranging from 0.26 to 0.45. The high-level synthesis is therefore a real-time phase. The average time cost ratio of the signal generator (phase 2) was 2.32, ranging from 1.30 to 4.18. The total time cost ratio is 2.66 on the average. Consequently, the program is not a real-time system.

The results show that the time consumption increases in the signal generation phase as the input text grows longer. The same effect does not occur in the high-level synthesis. However, the time consumption of the entire synthesis consists mainly of the signal generation.

Table 2. The columns contains the input text, duration of the resulting synthetic sentence, standard deviations of time consumption of both phases (the high-level synthesis and the signal generation), the average time usage and the time cost ratios of both phases and the entire operation

Synthesized text	Dur. of the synth. speech (s)	St.dev.		Average time usage (s)			Time cost ratio		
		Phase 1	Phase 2	Phase 1	Phase 2	Total	Phase 1	Phase 2	Total
Lopulta kaipaatte tilaisuutta tunnustaa.	3.06	0.17	0.38	0.90	3.97	4.87	0.29	1.30	1.59
Muussa tapauksessa hän suunnittelee yliopistoon menemistä.	4.34	0.12	0.06	1.93	6.27	8.20	0.45	1.44	1.89
Nyt oli kiire, sillä kohta vihollinen ampuisi kaikilla pilleillä ja putkilla.	5.61	0.26	0.06	2.30	9.83	12.13	0.41	1.75	2.16
Nimityksiä perusteltiin aluksi sillä, ettei hallinnossa juuri ollut vasemmistolaisia virkamiehiä.	7.35	0.21	0.20	2.23	16.80	19.03	0.30	2.29	2.59
Sotien jälkeen suomalaisilla ei enää ole ollut mahdollisuutta käydä Valamossa, aniharvaa poikkeusta lukuunottamatta.	8.79	0.12	0.15	2.93	26.17	29.10	0.33	2.98	3.31
Nykymaailmassa ihmisviidakoita löytyy monista yhden sallitun puolueen tai sotilaiden hallitsemista yksinvaltaisista tai harvainvaltaisista maista.	10.68	0.06	0.17	2.77	44.60	47.37	0.26	4.18	4.44

The translations of the synthesized samples are as follows:

- Finally you will be longing for the chance to confess.
- He is planning on going to the university in any other case.
- We were in a hurry now, because soon the enemy would be firing with all their might.
- The nominations were first rationalized by the fact that there were really no leftist officials in the government.
- After the war the Finns had no more the opportunity to visit [the monastery island of] Valamo, with very few exceptions.
- Jungles of men are found in the modern world in countries of tyranny or oligarchy run by the military or a single allowed party.

5 Discussion and Conclusion

Our goal to implement a rule-based speech synthesis to a mobile platform was successful. The time cost ratio was close to a real-time system with the shortest input.

The real-time goal is not realized when the input grows longer. If the time cost ratio would be close to one the synthesized speech could start to play at the very moment the first waveforms are generated. Naturally, this would require streaming the audio signal and parallel synthesizing on the background. The MIDP 2.0 and CLDC 1.1 did not support streaming, which was the main reason the real-time goal was not achieved. The current version writes the sound into a buffer in 10 ms samples, which makes it easier to develop a streaming solution with the existing APIs. Unfortunately, the current buffering of samples slows down the system with higher usage of memory. The parallel synthesis on the background is also feasible with threading. On the other hand, if time consumption ratio exceeds one, it can be used to determine how many seconds must be produced before the signal can start to play (the rest of the phonemes being processed on the background). Of course, the time consumption of the wave player must be examined.

The high-level synthesizer is language-dependent, while the low-level system is not. The high-level system, on the other hand, is fully modular. Any single module that does not fit with a new language can be modified, replaced, or inactivated. Each new phoneme can be added easily, and the existing ones can be adjusted to fit the specific pronunciation of the target language.

The current version of the speech synthesis is based on a version made for non-mobile platforms. The original version was not optimized for low time consumption and therefore the solutions made affect to the mobile version. We expect a revision of the code to improve the time cost ratio significantly. Another considerable benefit would be the lowering of the sampling rate from 16 kHz to 8 kHz. This would halve the time cost ratio of the phase 2.

Java is not considered the best possible solution for real-time systems on embedded platforms [3]. We have considered the possibility to change the coding from Java™ to Symbian™, or we might use the most time critical parts in the Symbian™ code, which might solve the real-time problem completely. However, we are more interested to develop the current implementation and the solutions within.

This study did not include an examination of the memory consumption. The testing platform (Nokia 6680) has 8 MB of memory but it is expandable with a memory card. Our MIDlet takes only 65 kilobytes (the size of the jar-file) of memory and the memory usage can be considered small, though it has to be confirmed in a separate study.

We expect to achieve the real-time goal with rule-based synthesis in the near future. Another goal is to put the modular design to test by implementing a second language into the synthesizer.

Acknowledgements

This study was partially funded by the Finnish Funding Agency for Technology and Innovation (TEKES).

References

1. Connected Limited Device Configuration Specification – Version 1.1. Sun Microsystems. JSR-139. (2003)
2. Hakokari, J., Saarni, T., Salakoski, T., Isoaho, J., Aaltonen, O.: Determining Prepausal Lengthening for Finnish Rule-Based Speech Synthesis. Speech Analysis, Synthesis and Recognition, Applications of Phonetics. AGH University of Science and Technology, Kraków, Poland (2005)
3. Higuera-Toledano, M.T., Issarny, V., Banatre, M., Cabillic, G., Lesot, J.-P., Parain, F.: Java Embedded Real-Time Systems: an Overview of Existing Solutions. Object-Oriented Real-Time Distributed Computing, Third IEEE International Symposium on 15-17 March (2000) 392–399
4. JBenchmark Home Page. http://www.jbenchmark.com/, Kishonti Informatics LP. Accessed on March 31st (2006)
5. Klatt, D. H.: Software for a Cascade/Parallel Formant Synthesizer. Journal of the Acoustical Society of America 67 (1980) 971–995
6. Klatt, D. H., Klatt L. C.: Analysis, synthesis, and perception of voice quality variations among female and male talkers. Journal of the Acoustical Society of America 87 (1990) 820–857
7. Mobile Information Device Profile for Java™ 2 Micro Edition – Version 2.0. Motorola and Sun Microsystems JSR-118 (2002)
8. Nokia 6680 Developer Home Page. http://www.forum.nokia.com/devices/6680, Nokia. Accessed on March 31st (2006)
9. Vainio, M.: Artificial Neural Network Based Prosody Models for Finnish Text-to-Speech Synthesis. Academic dissertation, University of Helsinki (2001)

Improving Phrase-Based Statistical Translation Through Combination of Word Alignments

Boxing Chen and Marcello Federico

ITC-irst - Centro per la Ricerca Scientifica e Tecnologica
Via Sommarive 18, 38050 Povo (Trento), Italy
{boxing, federico}@itc.it

Abstract. This paper investigates the combination of word-alignments computed with the competitive linking algorithm and well-established IBM models. New training methods for phrase-based statistical translation are proposed, which have been evaluated on a popular traveling domain task, with English as target language, and Chinese, Japanese, Arabic and Italian as source languages. Experiments were performed with a highly competitive phrase-based translation system, which ranked at the top in the 2005 IWSLT evaluation campaign. By applying the proposed techniques, even under very different data-sparseness conditions, consistent improvements in BLEU and NIST scores were obtained on all considered language pairs.

1 Introduction

The recent years have seen a growing interest in Statistical Machine Translation (SMT). Besides its very competitive performance, a reason for its popularity is also the availability of public software to develop SMT components. A notable advance in this direction was the release of the GIZA++ tool [1], which implements the quite tricky word-alignment models introduced by IBM [2] in the early 90s, plus a few other models. Currently, most state-of-the-art SMT systems are trained on parallel texts aligned with GIZA++.

In general, phrase-based SMT [3] exploits IBM word-alignments computed in both directions, i.e. from source to target words and vice versa. Hence, a combination of the two alignments is taken, and phrase pairs are extracted from it. Up to now, this approach has proved to be successful over a range of tasks and language pairs.

Alternative word-alignment models have been recently proposed which are simpler and much faster to compute [4,5,6,7]. However, up to now, experimental comparisons between such models and the well established IBM models have only addressed the accuracy of the resulting word-alignments and not their impact on translation performance[8]. In fact, in several venues it has been argued whether alignment accuracy is indeed a good indicator of translation accuracy.

The original contribution of this work is the combined use of different word-alignment methods within a state-of-the-art phrase-based SMT system. More specifically, we focus on the comparison of translation performance of different

T. Salakoski et al. (Eds.): FinTAL 2006, LNAI 4139, pp. 356–367, 2006.

word alignments generated under a widely used IBM-model setting and with the *competitive linking algorithm* (CLA) proposed by [4]. Briefly, the CLA computes an association score between all possible word pairs within the parallel corpus, and then applies a greedy algorithm to compute the best word-alignment for each sentence pair. The algorithm works under the one-to-one assumption, i.e. each source word is aligned to one target word only, and vice versa.

Experiments were conducted on data from the BTEC corpus, which are distributed by the International Workshop on Spoken Language Translation - IWSLT [9,10]. In particular, translation into English from a variety of source languages was considered: Chinese, Arabic, Japanese, and Italian. For all language pairs, a standard training condition of 20K sentence pairs was assumed, which corresponds to the core tracks of the 2005 IWSLT Evaluation Campaign. For Italian and Chinese, training with larger amounts of data was also investigated, namely up to 60K and 160K sentence pairs, respectively.

This paper is organized as follows. Section 2 presents our phrase-based SMT framework, including IBM word-alignment settings, and the phrase-pair extraction method. Section 3 reviews the competitive linking algorithm and the adopted associative score. Section 4 and 5, respectively, present and discuss the experimental results. Section 6 is devoted to conclusions.

2 Phrase-Based SMT

In phrase-based translation, words are no longer the only units of translation, but they are complemented by strings of consecutive words, the phrases.

Our phrase-based system [11] is based on a log-linear model which extends the original IBM Model 4 [2] to phrases. The output translation for a given source sentence $\mathbf{f}$ is computed through a dynamic-programming beam-search algorithm [12] which maximizes the criterion:

$$\tilde{\mathbf{e}}^* = \arg\max_{\tilde{\mathbf{e}}} \max_{\mathbf{a}} \sum_{r=1}^{R} \lambda_r h_r(\tilde{\mathbf{e}}, \mathbf{f}, \mathbf{a}),$$

where $\tilde{\mathbf{e}}$ represents a string of phrases in the target language, $\mathbf{a}$ an alignment from the words in $\mathbf{f}$ to the phrases in $\tilde{\mathbf{e}}$, and $h_r(\tilde{\mathbf{e}}, \mathbf{f}, \mathbf{a})$ $r = 1, \ldots, R$ are *feature functions* designed to model different aspects of the translation process. In particular, feature functions are defined around the following steps of the search algorithm, which progressively add phrases $\tilde{e}$ to the target string, by covering corresponding source phrases (see Figure 1): the *permutation model*, which sets the position of the first word of the next source phrase to cover; the *fertility model*, that establishes its length; the *lexicon model* which generates target translations $\tilde{e}$; the *language model*, which measures the fluency of $\tilde{e}$ with respect to its left context. Notice that according to our model target phrases might have fertility equal to zero, hence they do not translate any source word. Moreover, uncovered source positions can be associated to a special target word (*null*), according to specific fertility and permutation models.

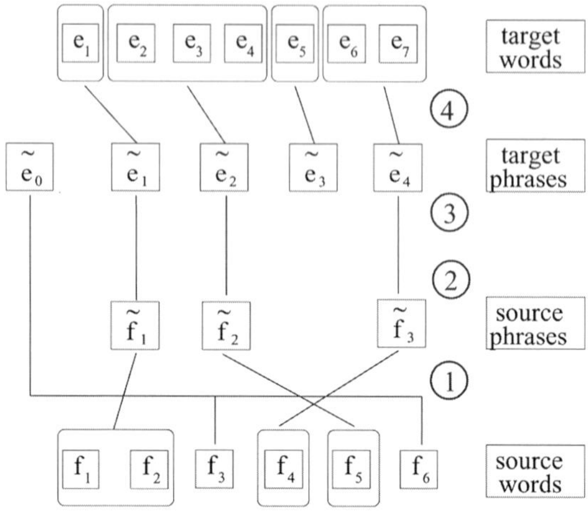

Fig. 1. Phrase-based SMT. Feature functions used in the translation process: (1) permutation model, (2) fertility model, (3) lexicon model, (4) language model.

In order to reduce the computation complexity of the search algorithm, constraints on phrase re-ordering are applied. In particular, if re-ordering is not permitted at all we have so-called monotone search, otherwise we have non-monotone search.

The resulting log-linear model has eight feature functions, whose parameters are either estimated from data or empirically fixed. In particular, fertility and lexicon models exploit relative frequencies computed on a sample of *phrase pairs* extracted from a parallel corpus. A detailed description of these features can be found in [13]. The scaling factors λ_i of the log-linear model are estimated on a development set, by applying a *minimum error training* procedure [14].

2.1 Phrase-Pair Extraction

Phrase pairs are collected from a parallel corpus containing sentence pairs $(\mathbf{f}, \mathbf{e})$ provided with some word alignment $\mathbf{c}$. For each sentence pair, all phrase-pairs are extracted corresponding to sub-intervals of the source and target positions, J and I, such that the alignment $\mathbf{c}$ links all positions of J into I and vice versa (links to the null word are disregarded). In the experiments, phrases were extracted with maximum length in the source and target set to 8.

In this work, we propose three methods to compute the alignment $\mathbf{c}$: the union of direct and inverse IBM alignments, the intersection of direct and inverse IBM alignments with expansion [15], and the competitive linking algorithm.

2.2 IBM Word-Alignment

IBM models use a many-to-one alignment scheme, i.e. each word in the source sentence is mapped to exactly one word in the target sentence. For the sake of phrase-extraction, alignments from source to target and from target to source are computed.

IBM alignments in both directions were computed through the GIZA++ toolkit [8].

3 Competitive Linking Algorithm

The competitive linking algorithm [4] works under the one-to-one assumption, i.e. each source word can be aligned to one target word only, and vice versa. An association score is computed for every possible translation pair, and a greedy algorithm is applied to select the best word-alignment. Alignment quality strongly depends on the association score. Several scores for word-pairs have been proposed in the literature, such as Mutual information, t-score, Dice coefficient, χ^2, log-likelihood ratio, etc. In this paper, we use a log-linear combination of two probabilities, as suggested in [6]: the first addresses the co-occurrence of word pairs, the other their position difference.

The first probability is defined as follows. Given two words f and e, with joint frequency n_{ef} and marginal frequencies n_f and n_e, we compute the probability that f and e co-occur just by chance with the hyper-geometric distribution

$$P_{cooc}(f,e) = \frac{\binom{n}{n_{ef}}\binom{n-n_f}{n_e-n_{ef}}}{\binom{n}{n_e}}$$

where n indicates the number of sentence pairs in the training corpus. For each word, only one occurrence per sentence is taken into account, as suggested in [4].

The probability considers the chance of observing a certain position difference between two randomly drawn positions inside two sentences of equal lengths. Hence, assuming the source and target sentences have lengths m and l, respectively, the normalized position difference between words f_j and e_i is computed by:

$$dist(j,i) = \left| j - i \cdot \frac{m}{l} \right|$$

Probabilities of observing any distance values for two randomly drawn positions were pre-computed for a fixed length $L = 50$ and tabulated as follows:

$$P_{pos}(dist) = \begin{cases} 7/L & \text{if } dist \leq 3 \\ 4/L & \text{if } 3 < dist \leq 5 \\ 1 - 11/L & \text{if } 5 < dist \end{cases}$$

The two probabilities are log-linearly combined with empirically determined weights:

$$S(f_j, e_i) = -\log P_{cooc}(f_j, e_i) + 4 \log P_{pos}(dist(j,i))$$

Notice that the negative logarithm is taken for the first score, as a small probability corresponds to a strong association score.

Table 1. Statistics of training, development and testing data used for the IWSLT 2005 supplied data condition. For Italian-English a comparable set was collected.

		IWSLT 2005				Italian-English	
		Chinese	Arabic	Japanese	English	Italian	English
Train	Sentences	20,000				20,000	
Data	Running words	173K	171K	159K	181K	149K	155K
	Vocabulary	8,536	9,251	18,150	7,348	9,611	6,885
Dev.	Sentences	500			500 × 16	100	100 × 16
Data	Running words	3,860	3,538	3,359	64,884	788	14,001
Test	Sentences	506			506 × 16	506	506 × 16
Data	Running words	3,514	3,531	3,259	65,616	3,574	65,615

Computing alignments of the training data with the CLA requires $\mathcal{O}(n\ m\ l)$ operations for the scoring function, and $\mathcal{O}(n\ m\ l\ \log m\ l)$ operations to align the corpus, where m and l indicate the lengths of the longest source and target sentences.

4 Training Modalities

Four training modalities for our phrase-based SMT system have been investigated which either change the way word-alignments are estimated or the way phrase-pairs are generated.

IBM Union

It represents the baseline modality: direct and inverse word alignments are computed by means of IBM models and successively phrase-pairs are extracted from the union of the two alignments.

IBM Intersection

Starting from the intersection alignemnt **c** of the direct and inverse IBM word alignments, additional links (i,j) are iteratively added to **c** if they satisfy the following criteria: a) links (i,j) only occur in the direct or inverse IBM alignment; b) they already have a neighbouring link in **c** or both of the words f_j and e_i are not aligned in **c**. Phrase-pairs are then extracted from the new alignment.

CLA

Word alignments are computed with the competitive linking algorithm and phrase-pairs are extracted from them.

Inter+CLA

Phrase-pairs obtained from the previous two methods (IBM Intersection and CLA) are joined.

Table 2. Examples of English sentences in the BTEC task

I'd like to take a sightseeing tour.
Do you have any of these?
Do you have travel accident insurance?
Take this baggage to the JAL counter, please.
How do you eat this?

Table 3. Statistics of extended BTEC data

Training Data	Chinese	English
Sentences	160,000	
Running words	1,106K	1,154K
Vocabulary	15,222	13,043
Training Data	Italian	English
Sentences	60,000	
Running words	463K	480K
Vocabulary	15,775	10,828

5 Experiments

5.1 Translation Tasks and Data

Experiments were carried out on the Basic Traveling Expression Corpus (BTEC) [16]. BTEC is a multilingual speech corpus that contains translation pairs taken from phrase books for tourists. We conducted experiments on four language pairs: Chinese-English, Japanese-English, Arabic-English and Italian-English. For the first three language pairs, we used data sets distributed for the IWSLT 2005 Evaluation Campaign[1], corresponding to the so-called *supplied data* evaluation condition. For Italian we used an equivalent test-suite kindly made available by the C-STAR Consortium[2], which will be distributed for IWSLT 2006. For each source sentence of the development and test sets, 16 references are available. Detailed statistics of training, development, testing data are reported in Table 1. A few examples of English sentences occurring in the test set are shown in Table 2.

To perform experiments under different data sparseness conditions, additional parallel texts available through the C-STAR Consortium were used as well. These extend the Italian-English and Chinese-English texts up to 60K and 160K sentence pairs, respectively. Statistics of the extended data are reported in Table 3. In Figure 2 vocabulary size is plotted for each language against increasing amounts of training data. Notice, that the different vocabulary-growth curves of Italian and Chinese are mainly due to different strategies used to create the Italian-English and Chinese-English corpora, rather than to intrinsic properties of the two languages.

[1] http://www.is.cs.cmu.edu/iwslt2005/

[2] httt://www.c-star.org

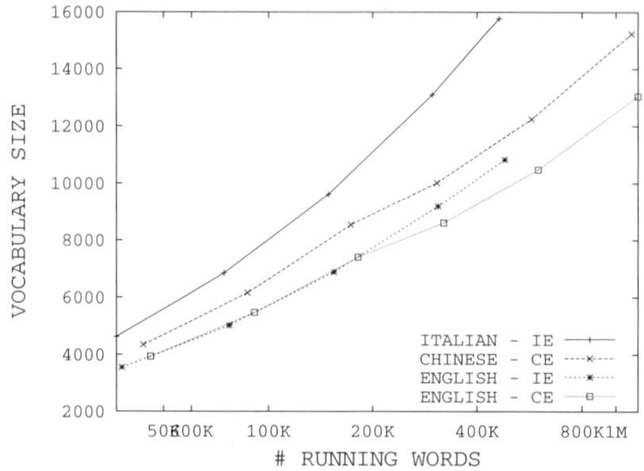

Fig. 2. Vocabulary growth in the extended BTEC data

Table 4. BLEU% scores and NIST scores under different training conditions

Language	Chinese		Japanese		Arabic		Italian	
	BLEU	NIST	BLEU	NIST	BLEU	NIST	BLEU	NIST
IBM Union	38.88	7.411	42.52	7.731	58.23	8.880	62.20	9.846
CLA	39.41	7.457	45.96	7.770	57.26	8.977	62.38	9.822
IBM Inter.	41.26	7.387	46.59	7.778	59.05	8.925	63.18	9.842
Inter+CLA	41.93	7.492	47.76	7.858	59.79	9.191	63.92	9.853

Before the experiments, some pre-processing was applied to the texts. Arabic, Chinese and Japanese characters were converted into a full ASCII encoding. Even if Chinese texts were provided with a manual segmentation at the word level, they were re-segmented with an in-house tool, trained from the original segmentation. We found that this permits the smoothing of inconsistencies in the manual segmentation. All texts were finally tokenized and put in lower case.

The search algorithm was configured similarly for all language pairs. Non-monotone search was applied for all languages, with less re-ordering allowed for Italian than for all other source languages.

Translation performance is here reported in terms of BLEU [17] score and NIST[3] score (case insensitive with punctuation).

5.2 Experimental Results

First experiments evaluated the different training modalities on all four language pairs. All experiments used the same amount of training data, i.e. 20K sentence pairs. Results are reported in Table 4.

The comparison between phrase-based training with IBM union alignments and CLA alignments shows that it is hard to say which alignment performs absolutely better. IBM union alignment works better on Arabic-English, but

[3] http://www.nist.gov/speech/tests/mt/

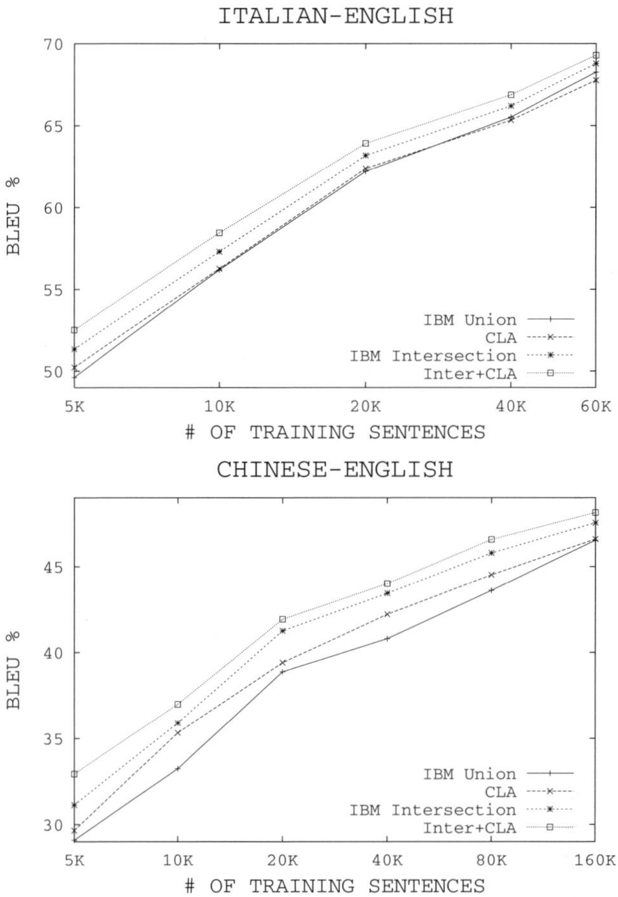

Fig. 3. Performance of training modalities against increasing amounts of training data

CLA obtains better results on the other three language-pairs. In particular, CLA alignment performs much better on Japanese-English, with a relative improvements in BLEU score around 8.1% (from 42.52 to 45.96). It is worth remarking that CLA alignments can be computed much more efficiently than IBM alignments.

IBM Intersection alignments always give better results in terms of BLEU score than union and CLA alignments. Differences in terms of NIST scores are however not so evident.

By applying the Inter+CLA training modality – i.e. concatenation of phrase-pairs from the IBM intersection alignments and CLA alignments – an improvement against IBM Intersection is observed with all four language-pairs. Relative BLEU improvements range from 1% (Italian-English) to 2% (Japanese-English). Improvements of NIST score are also consistent across all language pairs but less marked. Unfortunately, the testing samples are too small for statistically

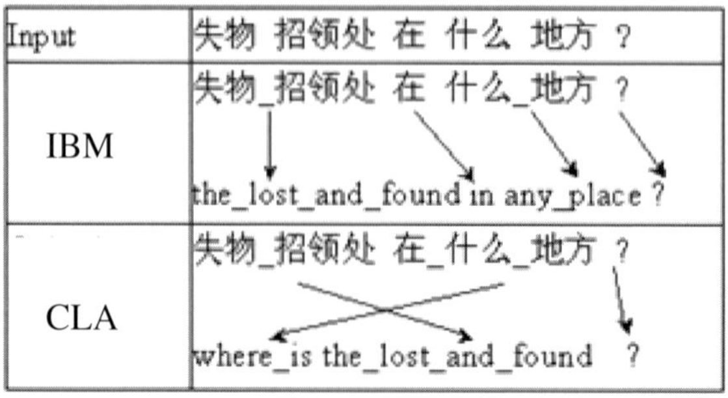

Fig. 4. MT output after training with IBM and CLA word alignments

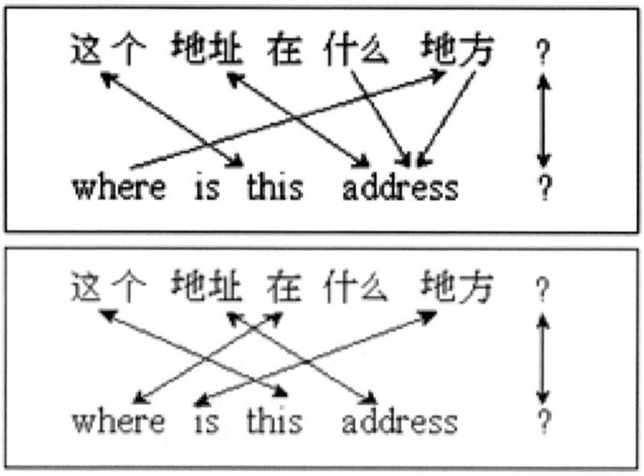

Fig. 5. Word alignments computed with IBM-models (top) and competitive linking algorithm (bottom)

assessing the reported BLEU score differences. However, a simple sign test[4] on the BLEU scores of the four tasks, with the assumption of less or equal performance, tells that improvements of the Inter+CLA method against each other method are significant at level $\alpha = 0.0625$.

A second series of experiments investigated the behavior of the training modalities against increasing amounts of data. These experiments are limited to the Chinese-English and Italian-English tasks.

Results are plotted in Figure 3. In the Chinese-English task, the superiority of the CLA over the IBM union modality consistently remains, independently from the data-sparseness condition. In the Italian-English task, IBM union modality and CLA perform very similar, CLA alignments work slightly better than IBM ones under the highest data-sparseness conditions.

Consistent conclusion can be also drawn for the combined training method Inter+CLA. For both language pairs, combined method outperform the IBM intersection modality in all considered data-sparseness conditions.

[4] http://home.clara.net/sisa/binomial.htm

6 Discussion

In order to better interpret the experimental results, a qualitative analysis of two very different word alignments can be informative, namely, CLA and IBM union alignments. A good starting point is given in Figure 4, which shows a Chinese sentence for which the system trained with CLA alignments performs better than the system training with IBM union alignments.

The problem with the IBM-model trained system is that it missed the translation of the last three Chinese words with the words *where is*. An inspection of the phrase table used by the decoder reveals that such translation is missing. By further looking into the training data we found that this translation pair could have been learned only from one sentence pair. This translation example is shown in Figure 5, together with the alignment computed with the CLA and the direct and inverse alignments computed with the IBM models. The union of the direct (arrows upward) and inverse (arrow downward) alignments is obtained by disregarding the direction of the links. Clearly, the one-to-one CLA alignment has a lower density than the IBM union alignment. According to our phrase-extraction methods, an alignment with fewer links often permits the generation of more phrase-pairs. This is indeed happens in the example shown in Figure 6, which also shows that the phrase-pair useful for the translation example in Figure 4 is indeed found in the CLA alignment.

The above example and some further manual inspections of alignments suggest the following general considerations. CLA alignments show in general lower recall and higher precision than IBM union alignments. (Formally, recall and precision of an automatic alignments should be measured by comparing all word-to-word links against some reference alignment.) From the point of view of phrase-extraction, a lower recall – i.e. number of links – can indeed result in a larger number of generated phrase pairs.

IBM Alignment		CLA Alignment	
NULL_	is	这个	this
这个	this	地址	address
这个	is this	在	where
地址	address	什么	NULL_
在	NULL_	地方	is
什么	address	?	?
地方	address	这个 地址	this address
?	?	在 什么	where
这个 地址 在 什么 地方	where is this address	什么 地方	is
这个 地址 在 什么 地方 ?	where is this address ?	在 什么 地方	where is
		这个 地址 在 什么 地方	where is this address
		这个 地址 在 什么 地方 ?	where is this address ?

Fig. 6. Phrase-pairs extracted from the IBM and CLA alignments in Figure 5, respectively. The useful translation pair for *where is* is pointed out.

CLA alignments can also induce phrase-pairs with a higher degree of non-monotonicity or, in other words, with a larger position mismatch between source and target phrases. This property could explain the better performance of CLA training in the Chinese-English task but the similar and lower performance in the Italian-English task. Translation between Italian and English seems to imply in fact much less word re-ordering than for Japanese and Chinese. Phrase-pairs extracted from CLA alignments are hence of little help. In other words, phrase-tables extracted just from CLA alignments seem less effective for language pairs with little word reordering.

Remarkably, a more consistent behavior emerges from the application of the combined training modalities. For all language pairs and data-sparseness conditions, it seems that merging information from the two types of alignments is always beneficial. More interestingly, the positive contribution is only slightly reduced when larger amounts of training data are used (see Figure 3).

7 Conclusions

We have presented novel training techniques based on the competitive linking algorithm which consistently improved performance of a phrase-based SMT system trained with conventional IBM word alignments. Extensive experiments were performed on a tourism domain including four language directions: Arabic-to-English, Chinese-to-English, Japanese-to-English, and Italian-to-English. Results showed that combining phrase-pairs extracted from IBM alignments with phrase-pairs extracted from CLA alignments gives consistent improvements in performance on all language pairs and under different data-sparseness conditions.

Acknowledgment

The authors would like to thank Laurens van der Werff and Nicola Bertoldi for useful suggestions and discussions. This work has been funded by the European Union under the integrated project TC-STAR - Technology and Corpora for Speech-to-Speech Translation - (IST-2002-FP6-506738, http://www.tc-star.org).

References

1. Och, F.J., Ney, H.: Improved statistical alignment models. In: Proceeding of the 38th Annual Meeting of the Association for Computational Linguistics, Hongkong, China (2000) 440–447
2. Brown, P.F., Della Pietra, S.A., Della Pietra, V.J., Mercer, R.L.: The mathematics of statistical machine translation: Parameter estimation. Computational Linguistics **19** (1993) 263–312
3. Koehn, P., Och, F.J., Marcu, D.: Statistical phrase-based translation. In: Proceedings of HLT/NAACL 2003, Edmonton, Canada (2003) 127–133
4. Melamed, I.D.: Models of translational equivalence among words. Computational Linguistics **26** (2000) 221–249

5. Cherry, C., Lin, D.: A probability model to improve word alignment. In: Proceedings of the 41st Meeting of the Association for Computational Linguistics (ACL), Sapporo, Japan (2003) 88–95
6. Kraif, O., Chen, B.: Combining clues for lexical level aligning using the null hypothesis approach. In: Proceedings of International Conference on Computational Linguistics (COLING), Geneva, Switzerland (2004) 1261–1264
7. Moore, R.C.: Association-based bilingual word alignment. In: Proceedings of ACL Workshop on Building and Using Parallel Texts, Ann Arbor, MI (2005) 1–8
8. Och, F.J., Ney, H.: A systematic comparison of various statistical alignment models. Computational Linguistics **29** (2003) 19–51
9. Akiba, Y., Federico, M., Kando, N., Nakaiwa, H., Paul, M., Tsujii, J.: Overview of the iwslt04 evaluation campaign. In: Proceedings of the International Workshop on Spoken Language Translation (IWSLT), Kyoto, Japan (2004) 1–12
10. Eck, M., Hori, C.: Overview of the iwslt 2005 evaluation campaign. In: Proceedings of the International Workshop on Spoken Language Translation (IWSLT), Pittsburgh, PA (2005) 11–32
11. Federico, M., Bertoldi, N.: A word-to-phrase statistical translation model. ACM Transactions on Speech and Language Processing **2** (2005) 1–24
12. Tillmann, C., Ney, H.: Word reordering and a dynamic programming beam search algorithm for statistical machine translation. Computational Linguistics **29** (2003) 97–133
13. Chen, B., Cattoni, R., Bertoldi, N., Cettolo, M., Federico, M.: The itc-irst smt system for iwslt 2005. In: Proceedings of the International Workshop on Spoken Language Translation - IWSLT, Pittsburgh, USA (2005) 98–104
14. Och, F.J.: Minimum error rate training in statistical machine translation. In: Proceedings of the 41st Meeting of the Association for Computational Linguistics (ACL), Sapporo, Japan (2003) 160–167
15. Och, F.J., Tillman, C., Ney, H.: Improved alignment models for statistical machine translation. In: Proceedings of the 1999 Joint SIGDAT Conference on Empirical Methods in Natural Language Processing and Very Large Corpora, University of Maryland, MDPA (1999) 20–28
16. Kikui, G., Sumita, E., Takezawa, T., Yamamoto, S.: Creating corpora for speech-to-speech translation. In: Proceedings of the 4th European Conference on Speech Communication and Technology. Volume 2., Madrid, Spain (1995) 1249–1252
17. Papineni, K., Roukos, S., Ward, T., Zhu, W.J.: Bleu: a method for automatic evaluation of machine translation. Research Report RC22176, IBM Research Division, Thomas J. Watson Research Center (2001)

Improving Statistical Word Alignments with Morpho-syntactic Transformations

Adrià de Gispert[1], Deepa Gupta[2], Maja Popović[3], Patrik Lambert[1], Jose B. Mariño[1], Marcello Federico[2], Hermann Ney[3], and Rafael Banchs[1]

[1] TALP Research Center, Universitat Politècnica de Catalunya, Barcelona, Spain
[2] ITC-irst, Centro per la Ricerca Scientifica e Tecnologica, Trento, Italy
[3] Lehrstuhl für Informatik 6, RWTH Aachen University, Aachen, Germany

Abstract. This paper presents a wide range of statistical word alignment experiments incorporating morphosyntactic information. By means of parallel corpus transformations according to information of POS-tagging, lemmatization or stemming, we explore which linguistic information helps improve alignment error rates. For this, evaluation against a human word alignment reference is performed, aiming at an improved machine translation training scheme which eventually leads to improved SMT performance. Experiments are carried out in a Spanish–English European Parliament Proceedings parallel corpus, both in a large and a small data track. As expected, improvements due to introducing morphosyntactic information are bigger in case of data scarcity, but significant improvement is also achieved in a large data task, meaning that certain linguistic knowledge is relevant even in situations of large data availability.

1 Introduction

Word aligned corpora are useful in a variety of fields. An obvious one is automatic extraction of bilingual lexica and terminology [1]. Word sense disambiguation is another application [2], since ambiguities are distributed differently in different languages. Word aligned corpora can also help for transferring language tools to new languages. In Yarowsky and Wicentowski [3], text analysis tools such as morphologic analyzers or part-of-speech taggers are projected to languages where such resources do not exist. Kuhn [4] presents a study of ways for exploiting statistical word alignment for grammar induction.

In statistical machine translation (SMT), word alignment is a crucial part of the training process. In approaches based on words [5], phrases [6] or n-grams [7], the basic translation units are indeed extracted from statistical word alignment [8]. Some syntax-based SMT systems [9] also rely on word alignment to estimate tree-to-string or tree-to-tree alignment models.

Och and Ney [10] have shown that translation quality depends on word alignment quality

In this paper we study ways of improving alignment quality through the incorporation of morpho-syntactic information. This type of information has already

T. Salakoski et al. (Eds.): FinTAL 2006, LNAI 4139, pp. 368–379, 2006.

been used to enhance word alignment systems: Toutanova et al. [11] augmented a HMM statistical alignment model with POS tags data; Tiedemann [12] and de Gispert [13] computed system features based on POS tags, chunk labels or lemmas. Popović and Ney [14] used hierarchical lexicon structure enriched with German base forms and POS tags for the EM training of German-English alignments.

In the experiments described here, the alignment models remain purely statistic, whereas the training corpus is transformed so as to make the statistical alignment models task easier. Results are evaluated measuring the Alignment Error Rate against a manual reference (see section 3.2).

The organization of the paper is as follows. Section 2 presents the morphosyntactic data transformations that have been considered to improve alignment, whose results are shown and discussed in section 3. Finally, section 4 concludes and gives ideas of future work.

2 Morphosyntactic Corpus Transformations

With the goal of finding out which linguistic features are relevant for improving statistical word alignment, we have followed a corpus transformation approach, ie. data has been modified using morphosyntactic information before word alignment, as shown in the flow diagram in Figure 1.

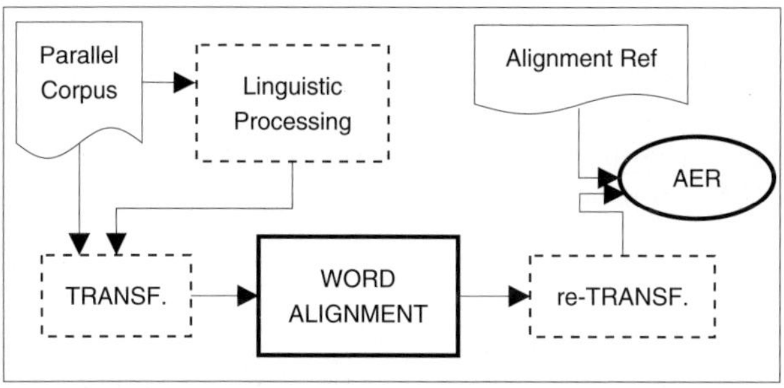

Fig. 1. Experimental configuration to evaluate impact of using morphological information on word alignment

Then, the obtained alignment of the transformed parallel corpus is mapped to the original sentence pairs in order to evaluate Alignment Error Rate against a manual reference. The same word alignment algorithm and configuration is used in all cases, therefore acting as a black-box.

In many cases, the corpus transformation can be seen as a classification from words to linguistically-enriched tokens, be it of all words or just some groups of words. However, we have also considered linguistically-motivated word order modifications, as well as combinations of both.

As most transformations are done on a word basis, aligned tokens can be directly subsituted by original text after word alignment. In case some words are grouped in a single token before aligning, all internal links are introduced when writing back original text.

Now each of the transformations carried out leading to an independent experiment, is motivated and fully described.

2.1 Word Classifications

In general, word classifications aim at reducing data sparseness, by mapping some words to a unique token according to a certain criterion. In our case, criteria are based on the linguistic information provided by state-of-the-art language tools, in the particular case of processing the Spanish and English languages.

Base forms. Also known as lemmas, base forms lack details on morphological derivation of the word (gender, number, tense, and so on) and only provide information on the head of the word. Therefore, they represent a meaning-bearing reduced version of each word, especially in the case of high morphological derivation, such as verbs, nouns or adjectives in Spanish. In English, verbs and nouns are also reduced by taking the base form, even though in lesser degree.

Stems. Same as lemmatization, stemming is another method of word transformation which truncates inflected word forms by a single stem without morphological suffixes or derivations. However, a stemmer may not necessarily produce any meaning-bearing word form, whereas a lemmatizer returns the base form, usually associated with a dictionary citation of the given word form. Table 8 gives a example of stemming and lemmatization results illustrating the differences between the two processes.

Spanish Adjective Base Forms. Spanish adjectives, in contrast to English, have gender and number inflections so that one base form can have four different full forms. For instance, the adjective "*bonito*" (beautiful/pretty) has four inflected forms ("*bonita*", "*bonitas*", "*bonito*", "*bonitos*"). Therefore, reducing the inflection from the Spanish adjectives might simplify the process of word alignment between two languages. All Spanish adjectives are replaced with its base forms whereas the English corpus remains the same.

Reduced Spanish Verbs. Spanish language has an especially rich inflectional morphology for verbs. Person and tense are expressed via suffix so that many different full forms of one verb exist, many of them without the corresponding equivalent in English. Therefore, reducing the POS information of Spanish verbs could be helpful for improving word alignments. Each verb has been reduced into its base form and reduced POS tag: parts of POS tag describing tense and/or mode which does not exist in English are removed. For example, the tag for the subjunctive mode has been removed, and the two tags representing two types of the past tense are replaced with the unique past tense tag.

Lemma plus reduced Spanish POS Morpho-attributes. As already mentioned, Spanish is morphologically richer than English. However, all inflected forms of Spanish are not relevant for translation into English. For instance, whereas Spanish adjectives may have four inflected forms, English adjectives have only one form. Therefore, it might be possible that all inflected forms of Spanish adjectives are not required for translation. Similar cases are possible to a limited extent with other words also, such as nouns, verbs, etc.

To handle this morphology-related problem of Spanish with respect to English, we can count for each Spanish part of speech (POS) tag which additional morphological attributes (morpho-attributes) do not affect the translation from Spanish to English. For this purpose, we extract bilingual lexicons from original word-based statistical word alignment for large training data from both directions (Spanish to English and English to Spanish), where each Spanish original word is replaced with its lemma plus morpho-syntactic tag. On this bilingual lexicons, entropy was calculated with respect to each morpho-attribute corresponding to each Spanish POS tag. As a result, Table 1 reports that irrelevant and relevant morpho-attributes corresponding to some Spanish POSs. Other Spanish POS (adverbs, conjunctions and interjections) have not been reported in the table as they do not convey enough morphological information. In case of some morpho-attributes for Spanish POS, the value of the entropy was not significantly reduced with respect to the value of the entropy considering only with lemma form. In this situation, we tried different combination of morpho-attributes for that POS. For instance, Table 1 reports relevant morpho-attributes for determiner are gender and number. We observed that for small data track, these morpho-attributes do not make significant effect on the translation. Therefore, in case of small data track, we have not provided this information with lemma form.

In general, Spanish words are replaced with lemma and its relevant POS tag information. The remaining ones are transformed into lemma forms in small as well as in large data (see Table 8 for example).

Table 1. Irrelevant & Relevant POS Morphological Attributes for Spanish

POS	Irrelevant POS morpho-attributes	Relevant POS morpho-attributes
Verb	type (principal, auxiliary)	mode, time, person, number, gender
Noun	type (common, proper), gender, grade	number (singular, plural, invariable)
Adjective	type, grade, gender, number, function	–
Pronoun	person, possessor, politeness	type, gender, number, case
Determiner	type (demonstrative, possessive, etc.) person, possessor	gender, number
Preposition	type, form, gender, number	–

Full Verb Forms. Undoubtedly, given a verb meaning, tense and person, each language *implements* each verbal form independently from the other language. For example, whereas the personal pronoun is compulsory in English unless the subject is present, this does not occur in Spanish, where the morphology of the verb expresses the same aspect.

Therefore, aiming at simplifying the work for the word alignment, another word classification strategy can be devised to address the rich variety of verbal forms. For this, we group all words that build up a whole verbal form (including pronouns, auxiliary verbs and head verb) into the lemma of the head verb. This is a knowledge-based detection taken using deterministic automata implementing a few simple rules. These rules require information on word forms, POS-tags and lemmas in order to map the resulting expression to the lemma of the head verb, as done in [13]. Examples of such mappings can be found in Table 2.

Table 2. Full verb forms are mapped to the lemma of the head

English		Spanish	
full form → lemma		full form → lemma	
has been found	find	introdujeran	introducir
we will find	find	han cometido	cometer
do you think	think	dijo	decir
offered	offer	está haciendo	hacer
I am doing	do	haremos	hacer

2.2 Word Order Modification

It is commonly known that non-monotonicity poses difficulties for word alignment, not to mention for statistical machine translation. The more differences in word order between two languages, the more difficult to extract a good alignment and the more challenging the translation task is. Although English and Spanish exhibit a quite remarkable monotonicity (compared to other pairs such as English and Chinese), here we study two techniques, exploring the possible gain in alignment quality of reordering one language to make word alignment more monotone.

POS-based Reordering of Spanish Nouns and Adjectives. Adjectives in Spanish are usually placed after the corresponding noun, whereas in English it is the other way round. Therefore local reordering of nouns and adjective groups might be helpful for monotonising word alignments between two languages. POS-based local reordering [15] has been used: each Spanish noun has been moved behind the correspondent adjective group. If there are two adjectives connected with a coordinate conjunction "and" or "or", the noun is moved behind the whole group of words.

Noun–Adjective swapped realignment. An alternative strategy consists of deciding which Spanish 'Noun + Adjective' structures need to be swapped according to classes extracted from an initial statistical word alignment in the original order, as introduced in [16].

Given this baseline alignment, we build up classes of nouns preceding the same adjectives and having crossed links[1]. The same classes can be extracted for the adjectives following the same nouns. From these classes, we filter out those pairs occurring less than 6 times or having a low crossed-link probability, ie. being more often monotonically linked.

Finally, we swap all remaining 'Noun + Adjective' belonging to seen pairs of classes, and realign, as we expect the increase in monotonicity to reduce the word alignment complexity and improve quality.

2.3 Combinations

Two types of combinations can be performed. On the one hand, one can combine two (or more) presented approaches to produce a new transformation. For example, any word order modification can be done together with stemming, base form substitution or full verb classification. Verb classification can also be combined with other transformation for all words outside the verb groups.

On the other hand, a new word alignment can be obtained from the combination via consensus of the different alignments generated by various transformations. Both these strategies have been tested in order to achieve the best alignment quality.

3 Experimental Framework

3.1 Corpus Description

Experiments have been carried out using the Spanish-English EPPS parallel corpus, which contains the debates proceedings of the European Parliament from 1996 to May 2005. In order to extract the linguistic information needed to perform the presented corpus modifications, we preprocessed the data as follows:

- English POS-tagging using freely-available *TnT* tagger [17].
- English lemmatization using *wnmorph*, included in the WordNet package [18].
- Spanish POS-tagging and lemmatization using *FreeLing* analysis tool [19].
- English and Spanish stemming using the Snowball stemmer[2], which is based on Porter's algorithm.

Table 3 shows the main statistics of the parallel corpus used, including number of sentences, number of words, vocabulary and average sentence length for each language. The lower part of the table shows the statistics for the 1% division used in the small data track.

[1] By crossed links, we mean that Spanish word in position n is linked to English word in position $m + 1$, and Spanish word in $n + 1$ is linked to English word in m.

[2] http://www.snowball.tartarus.org/

Table 3. Parallel corpus statistics for large and small data tracks

	sent	words	vocab.	avg len
English	1.28 M	34.9 M	106 k	27.2
Spanish		36.6 M	153 k	28.5
English 1%	13.4 k	366 k	16.3 k	27.4
Spanish 1%		385 k	22.4 k	28.8

3.2 Evaluation Measures and Manual Reference

For evaluation, an ample set of bilingual sentences was aligned manually (see table 4), following a carefully defined procedure [20] by agreement of three manual reference alignments. 66.7% of reference alignment links are Sure whereas 33.3% are Possible. This alignment test set is a subset of the training data, both in the large and the small data tracks.

Table 4. Alignment test data statistics

	sent	words	vocab.	avg len
English	400	11.7 k	2.7 k	29.1
Spanish		12.3 k	3.1 k	30.4

The alignment test data contain unambiguous links (called S or Sure) and ambiguous links (called P or Possible). If there is a P link between two words in the reference, a computed link (*i.e.* to be evaluated) between these words is acceptable, but not compulsory. On the contrary, if there would be an S link between these words in the reference, a computed link would be compulsory. In this paper, precision refers to the proportion of computed links that are present in the reference. Recall refers to the proportion of reference Sure links that were computed. The alignment error rate (AER) is given by the following formula:

$$AER = 1 - \frac{|\mathcal{A} \cap \mathcal{G}_S| + |\mathcal{A} \cap \mathcal{G}|}{|\mathcal{A}| + |\mathcal{G}_S|} \tag{1}$$

where $\mathcal{A}$ is the set of computed links, $\mathcal{G}_S$ is the set of Sure reference links and $\mathcal{G}$ is the entire set of reference links.

3.3 Baseline Statistical Word Alignment

As word alignment core algorithm, GIZA++ [21] was used. Regarding model iterations, we use the $1^4H^54^4$ configuration (meaning 4 iterations of IBM model 1, 5 iterations of HMM model and 4 iterations of IBM model 4), which provides the best AER for our task. During word alignment, we use 50 classes per language as estimated by 'mkcls', a freely-available tool along with GIZA++[3].

[3] See http://www.fjoch.com for details on both tools.

Moreover, we always work with lowercase text before aligning, as this leads to a significant AER reduction when compared with the true-case text. Note that this configuration applies for all experiments that have been done.

3.4 Alignment Results

Results with the 1% data set are shown in Table 5, where both directions and the symmetrization through union are evaluated. Each row refers to each of the corpus transformations presented.

As it can be seen, both **base forms** and **stems** produce a very significant quality improvement, especially reflected in a more than 5 point absolute precision improvement in union alignment, whereas recall is also very high in these two cases for all alignment directions. It looks like their classifications reduce sparseness and help the word alignment algorithm perform better. This improvement is best in the case of stems.

Whereas '**Spa lem+redPOS**' transformation also achieves significant improvements in recall and precision for all directions, leading to an approximate

Table 5. Word Alignment results for small-data task

	Eng→Spa			Spa→Eng			Union		
	R_S	P_P	AER	R_S	P_P	AER	R_S	P_P	AER
baseline	63.10	77.11	30.34	64.12	80.21	28.38	73.37	69.43	28.77
base forms	66.37	83.50	25.75	68.06	83.72	24.69	73.93	75.01	25.51
stems	67.02	84.30	25.01	68.61	83.80	24.32	74.66	75.65	24.82
Spa Adj base	63.96	78.29	29.33	64.17	80.31	28.31	73.59	70.19	28.25
Spa V reduced	64.25	78.39	29.13	64.09	80.16	28.44	73.17	70.05	28.51
Spa lem+redPOS	64.36	80.63	28.06	64.51	79.08	28.70	73.71	70.76	27.87
full verbs	66.50	79.72	27.13	65.44	81.30	27.10	73.96	71.36	27.45
Spa N-A reord	63.44	77.27	30.08	64.57	80.39	28.04	73.40	69.68	28.61
N-A swap realign	63.63	77.41	29.91	64.27	80.00	28.38	73.43	69.59	28.65
verbs + stems	69.58	83.17	23.89	67.33	83.96	24.85	75.47	75.17	24.69

Table 6. Word Alignment results for large-data task

	Eng→Spa			Spa→Eng			Union		
	R_S	P_P	AER	R_S	P_P	AER	R_S	P_P	AER
baseline	73.20	90.78	18.65	72.18	92.17	18.64	78.42	86.43	17.56
base forms	72.80	91.70	18.54	71.84	93.17	18.50	76.73	87.90	17.82
stems	73.56	92.40	17.79	72.72	93.78	17.68	77.81	88.94	16.74
Spa Adj base	73.01	90.78	18.77	72.40	92.47	18.39	78.30	86.70	17.50
Spa V reduced	73.07	90.69	18.77	72.07	92.22	18.70	77.97	86.43	17.80
Spa lem+redPOS	72.72	90.46	19.06	71.94	92.06	18.82	77.87	86.16	17.97
full verbs	74.27	90.77	17.85	73.03	93.31	17.56	78.60	87.37	16.97
Spa N-A reord	72.69	90.06	19.25	72.23	91.85	18.73	78.10	85.93	17.97
N-A swap realign	72.52	90.41	19.22	72.13	91.80	18.81	77.91	86.10	17.99
verbs + stems	74.74	91.83	17.14	73.23	93.84	17.23	78.36	88.82	16.42

1 point AER reduction, improvements due to '**Spa Adj base**' and '**Spa V reduced**' transformations are very slight. Yet all three cases fall short compared to stemming or lemmatizing, indicating that for data-sparse situations, classifying all words regardless of their class is a more effective strategy.

'**Full verb**' classification achieves a 1.5 AER reduction, basically thanks to an important recall increase in all alignment directions, due to the grouping effect of this classification, so that all words belonging to a verb form become linked to the same tokens. Finally, **reordering** experiments produce very slight improvements, and apparently the result is equal no matter if the reordering is *a priori* forced as in '**Spa N-A reord**' or learnt from data as in '**N-A swap realign**'.

Combining full verb classification and stemming (of the words outside verb forms) we obtain the best AER results.

Results with the full parallel corpus are shown in Table 6. Interestingly, conclusions regarding base forms and stems do not hold in this case. Whereas base forms are not useful anymore and even degrade alignment quality, stems still provide significant improvement in AER. This is expressed in a 2.5 point absolute precision increase at a cost of 0.6 recall decrease. One possible reason for this is the harder classification of stems, especially for English, where initial vocabulary of 95K words is reduced to 81K with base forms and only 69K for stems (in Spanish, from baseline 138K vocabulary we end up with 78K base forms and 79K stems). Apparently, this involves a sparsenes reduction, which makes word alignment more robust to non-literal translations. On the other hand, frequent words such as auxiliary verbs are not mapped to the same stem, thus possibly helping the aligner to discriminate compared to the case with base forms.

Partial transformations such as '**Spa lem+redPOS**', '**Spa Adj base**' and '**Spa V reduced**' do not help improve alignment quality anymore. On the other hand, '**full verb**' classification is still producing significant improvements, again reflected in the best recall figures for all alignment directions. This recall can countermeasure the recall loss when stemming and achieves the best AER (16.42) when combining these two approaches.

As about word order modification experiments, again results are not encouraging, and in this case they are even harmful for alignment quality. This holds both for deterministic Noun–Adjective reordering ('**Spa N-A reord**') and for reordering according to an initial word alignment. All combinations of order modification and stemming, base form or verb forms classification that have been tested did not yield improvements and are not reported.

These experiments provide different alignment sets which can contain complementary information, so alignment quality can be further improved if they are combined. For the large data task, the best 3, 4 and 5 best union sets were combined with a consensus criterion. For each link present in at least one of the sets, if this link is present in a majority of sets, then it is selected for the combined set. Otherwise it is absent from the combined set. For the combination of an even number of sets, the criterion can be strict (more than half of

Table 7. Combination, with a consensus criterion, of the best union alignment sets obtained in the large data task (in order: the verbs+stems, stems, full verbs, spa adj base and baseline sets)

	R_S	P_P	AER
3 best	78.50	90.04	15.79
4 best (weak)	80.29	87.35	16.10
4 best (strict)	76.51	92.59	15.87
5 best	78.37	89.70	16.07

the sets must agree) or weak (a half is enough). Results are shown in table 7. While all combinations improve the best AER presented in table 6 (that of the verbs+stems experiment), the combination of best 3 sets is particularly interesting since both recall and precision are also improved. In the 4 sets combinations, the weak criterion gives a high recall and lower precision combination, whereas the strict criterion gives a high precision but lower recall combination.

Table 8. Some English and Spanish corpus transformations as described in corresponding sections

	Asian countries have followed our example too .	Los países asiáticos han seguido también nuestro ejemplo .
2.1	Asian country have follow our example too .	El país asiático haber seguir también nuestro ejemplo .
2.1	asian countri have follow our exampl too .	los país asiátic han segu también nuestr ejempl .
2.1	Asian countries have followed our example too .	Los países asiático han seguido también nuestro ejemplo .
2.1	Asian countries have followed our example too .	Los países asiáticos haber#P seguido también nuestro ejemplo .
2.1	Asian countries have followed our example too .	el país_NP asiático haber_VIP3P0 seguir_VP00SM también nuestro ejemplo_NS .
2.1	Asian countries V[follow] our example too.	Los países asiáticos V[seguir] también nuestro ejemplo .
2.2	Asian countries have followed our example too .	Los asiáticos países han seguido también nuestro ejemplo .

4 Conclusion and Further Work

In this paper we have evaluated the impact of performing a wide range of morphology-based data transformations in automatic word alignment. Remarkably, and even though quality improvements due to morphological information are bigger in case of data scarceness, alignment error rate can be reduced by using these informations even in case large amounts of data are available.

Specifically, stemming and verb forms classification achieve significantly better recall and precision figures in all situations. In addition, consensus combination strategies of the best alignment sets produce a further improvement of both recall and precision.

As future work, we plan to evaluate the impact of these improvements in training statistical machine translation models, as well as to define alternative translation models that incorporate useful morphological information. Additionally, other language pairs should be experimented with, as long as analysis tools and human references are available.

Acknowledgements

The authors want to thank Marta R. Costa-jussà for her invaluable help. This work has been partly supported by the TC-STAR project (European Community, FP6-506738), by Generalitat de Catalunya and by the European Social Fund.

References

1. Smadja, F.A., McKeown, K.R., Hatzivassiloglou, V.: Translating collocations for bilingual lexicons: A statistical approach. Computational Linguistics **22** (1996) 1–38
2. Diab, M., Resnik, P.: An unsupervised method for word sense tagging using parallel corpora. In: Proc. of the Annual Meeting of the Association for Computational Linguistics, Philadelphia, PA (2002) 255–262
3. Yarowsky, D., Ngai, G., Wicentowski, R.: Inducing multilingual text analysis tools via robust projection across aligned corpora. In: Proc. of the 1st International Conference on Human Language Technology Research (HLT). (2001) 161–168
4. Kuhn, J.: Experiments in parallel-text based grammar induction. In: Proc. of the 42th Annual Meeting of the Association for Computational Linguistics, Barcelona, Spain (2004) 470–477
5. Brown, P., Della Pietra, S., Della Pietra, V., Mercer, R.: The mathematics of statistical machine translation: Parameter estimation. Computational Linguistics **19** (1993) 263–311
6. Zens, R., Och, F., Ney, H.: Phrase-based statistical machine translation. In Verlag, S., ed.: Proc. German Conference on Artificial Intelligence (KI). (2002)
7. Mario, J., Banchs, R., Crego, J.M., de Gispert, A., Lambert, P., Fonollosa, J., Ruiz, M.: Bilingual n-gram statistical machine translation. In: Proc. of Machine Translation Summit X, Phuket, Thailand (2005) 275–82
8. Och, F., Ney, H.: A systematic comparison of various statistical alignment models. Computational Linguistics **29** (2003) 19–51
9. Yamada, K., Knight, K.: A syntax-based statistical translation model. In: Proc. of the Annual Meeting of the Association for Computational Linguistics, Toulouse, France (2001)
10. Och, F., Ney, H.: A comparison of alignment models for statistical machine translation. In: Proc. of the 18th Int. Conf. on Computational Linguistics, Saarbrucken,Germany (2000) 1086–1090
11. Toutanova, K., Ilhan, H.T., Manning, C.D.: Extensions to hmm-based statistical word alignment models. In: Proc. of the Conference on Empirical Methods in Natural Language Processing, Philadelphia, PA (2002)

12. Tiedemann, J.: Combining clues for word alignment. In: Proc. of the 10th Conf. of the European Chapter of the ACL (EACL), Budapest, Hungary (2003)
13. de Gispert, A.: Phrase linguistic classification and generalization for improving statistical machine translation. Proc. of the ACL Student Research Workshop (2005) 67–72
14. Popović, M., Ney, H.: Improving word alignment quality using morpho-syntactic information. In: Proc. of the 20th Int. Conf. on Computational Linguistics, COLING'04, Geneva, Switzerland (2004) 310–314
15. Popović, M., Ney, H.: POS-based word reorderings for statistical machine translation. In: Proc. 5th Int. Conf. on Language Resources and Evaluation (LREC), Genoa, Italy (2006) 1278–1283
16. Costa-jussà, M., Crego, J., de Gispert, A., Lambert, P., Khalilov, M., Banchs, R., Mariño, J., Fonollosa, J.: Talp phrase-based statistical translation system for european language pairs. In: Proc. of the HLT/NAACL Workshop on Statistical Machine Translation, New York (2006)
17. Brants, T.: Tnt — a statistical part-of-speech tagger. In: Proc. of Applied Natural Language Processing (ANLP), Seattle, WA (2000)
18. Miller, G., Beckwith, R., Fellbaum, C., Gross, D., Miller, K., Tengi, R.: Five papers on wordnet. Special Issue of International Journal of Lexicography **3** (1991) 235–312
19. Carreras, X., Chao, I., Padr, L., Padr, M.: Freeling: An open-source suite of language analyzers. In: Proc. of the 4th Int. Conf. on Linguistic Resources and Evaluation (LREC), Lisbon, Portugal (2004)
20. Lambert, P., de Gispert, A., Banchs, R., Mario, J.: Guidelines for word alignment and manual alignment. Language Resources and Evaluation (2006) DOI: 10.1007/s10579-005-4822-5.
21. Och, F.: Giza++: Training of statistical translation models. http://www.fjoch.com/GIZA++.html (2000)

Improving Term Extraction with Terminological Resources

Sophie Aubin and Thierry Hamon

LIPN – UMR CNRS 7030
99 av. J.B. Clément, F-93430 Villetaneuse
Tél. : 33 1 49 40 40 82, Fax : 33 1 48 26 07 12
firstname.lastname@lipn.univ-paris13.fr,
www-lipn.univ-paris13.fr/~lastname

Abstract. Studies of different term extractors on a corpus of the biomedical domain revealed decreasing performances when applied to highly technical texts. Facing the difficulty or impossibility to customize existing tools, we developed a tunable term extractor. It exploits linguistic-based rules in combination with the reuse of existing terminologies, *i.e.* exogenous disambiguation. Experiments reported here show that the combination of the two strategies allows the extraction of a greater number of term candidates with a higher level of reliability. We further describe the extraction process involving both endogenous and exogenous disambiguation implemented in the term extractor YATEA .

1 Introduction

Identifying and extracting terms from texts is now a well-known and widely explored step in the terminology building process. Different strategies can be applied: term extraction based on lexico-syntactic markers [1], chunking based syntactic frontiers and endogenous parsing [2] , and distributional analysis [3]. Those different techniques show satisfying extraction results regarding the recall [4]. However, studying the outputs of three term extractors applied to an English biomedical corpus, we found that they are not adequate for highly technical texts [5]. The results of the extraction are generally noisy for different reasons. First, some errors result from the tagging of the corpus. The second limitation of such tools is their difficulty to distinguish terms or variants from nominal phrases that are not terms. Finally, they lack portability to new domains as it is difficult to define parsing patterns large enough with a good precision.

Extracting terms consists not only in identifying specific nominal phrases but also in providing a reliable syntactic analysis. The latter is commonly used to organise terminologies through a syntactic network and to compute hierarchical relationships using lexical inclusion. Manually written rules based on linguistic clues are insufficient for this task and must be combined with statistical methods.

Several strategies have been used and sometimes associated to finally extract the term candidates: statistical filtering [1], manual filtering through the tool

T. Salakoski et al. (Eds.): FinTAL 2006, LNAI 4139, pp. 380–387, 2006.

interface [2] or the exploitation of external resources. We propose a combination of the three methods.

The terminology extractor we implemented uses techniques comparable to state-of-the-art tools, among which chunking based on morpho-syntactic frontiers and production of the syntactic analysis of the terms extracted. We further propose new solutions for chunking and parsing by using external resources. In addition, we chose to perform positive filtering in the parsing step through the mechanism of islands of reliability (see Section 3.1). In comparison, other tools produce all parsing solutions and filter out non valid ones *a posteriori*.

We first discuss the limitations of matching existing terminologies on corpora and of automatic extraction tools. As an answer to this, we propose a combination of terminology extraction with the exploitation of testified resources. We describe the extraction process of YATEA that implements the method we propose. We finally present the results of experiments run on a biomedical corpus to characterise the effects of recycling existing terminologies in a term extractor.

2 Which Approach to Identify Terms?

Terms can be identified in corpora regarding two approaches : matching terms issued from terminological resources, or designing automatically term extraction methods.

Using terminological resources to identify terms in texts addresses the question of the usability of resources on working corpora, namely their coverage and their adequacy. This leads to evaluate how terms issued from resources, i.e. testified terms, match in the working corpus. As terminological resources are widely available in the biomedical field, many experiments have been done on recycling terminologies to identify terms in medical and biological corpora. Coverage is generally mitigated. The coverage of well-known classifications as ICD-9, ICD-10 or SNOMED III have been observed on a 14,247 word corpus of clinical texts [6]. The evaluation leads to conclude that no classification covers sufficiently the corpus, although SNOMED has the better content coverage. Similar observations have been noted regarding the evaluation of the usability of Gene Ontology for NLP [7]. 37% of the GO terms are found in a 400,000 Medline citation corpus. Results vary depending on the GO categories from 28% to 53 % in the Medline corpus. [7] consider that this low content coverage could be due to the size of the working corpus or its narrow scope. Still, content coverage is even worse on a set of 3 million randomly selected noun phrases among 14 million terms extracted from the Medline corpus [8]: most of them are not present in UMLS. In [9], we showed that, in the context of the indexation of specialized texts, even if the combination of resources is useful to identify numerous testified terms or variants, the indexation varies greatly according to the documents.

Alternatives, based on the automatic extraction of terms, have been widely proposed since the 90's. [4] give an overview of the proposed term extractors. These term identification methods generally exploit linguistic information like boundaries or, more often, patterns. Such approaches are difficult to evaluate without a golden standard and evaluations vary according to the methods. However, the recall is generally good ([2] estimates the silence to 5%), while the precision is rather low ([2] rejects 50% of the extracted term candidates, the system discussed in [10] has an error rate of 20%).

Pure term extraction methods rarely use terminological resources. Such domain information is rather exploited at the filtering step [10]. However, the usefulness of terminological resources in a term extraction process is demonstrated in FASTR [11]. Results of this term variant extraction system are rather good as term variation acquisition increases the terminological resource coverage. The limitation of this approach is the acquisition of terms unrelated to testified ones.

Regarding the works discussed above, it seems obvious that terminological resources provide precious information that must be used in a term identification task. However, exploiting terminological resources requires their availability and adequacy on the targeted corpus. On the opposite, automatic term extraction approaches suffer from a necessary human validation step. In that respect, we aim at combining both approaches by developing a term extraction method that exploits terminological resources when available.

3 Strategy of Term Extraction

The software YATEA , developed in the context of the ALVIS[1] project, aims at extracting noun phrases that look like terms from a corpus. It provides their syntactic analysis in a head-modifier format. As an input, the term extractor requires a corpus which has been segmented into words and sentences, lemmatized and tagged with part-of-speech (POS) information. The implementation of this term extractor allows to process large corpora. It is not dependent on a specific language in the sense that all linguistic features can be modified or created for a new language, sub-language or tagset. In the experiments described here, we used the GENIA tagger[2] [12] which is specifically designed for biomedical corpora and uses the Penn TreeBank tagset.

The main strategy of analysis of the term candidates is based on the exploitation of simple parsing patterns and endogenous disambiguation. Exogenous disambiguation is also made possible for the identification and the analysis of term candidates by the use of external resources, *i.e.* lists of testified terms.

This section includes the presentation of both endogenous and exogenous disambiguation strategies. We also describe the whole extraction process implemented in YATEA .

3.1 Endogenous and Exogenous Disambiguation

Endogenous disambiguation consists in the exploitation of intermediate extraction results for the parsing of a given Maximal Noun Phrase (MNP).

[1] European Project STREP IST-1-002068-STP,http://www.alvis.info/alvis/

[2] http://www-tsujii.is.s.u-tokyo.ac.jp/GENIA/tagger/

All the MNPs corresponding to parsing patterns are parsed first. In a second step, remaining unparsed MNPs are processed using the MNPs parsed during the first step as *islands of reliability*. An *island of reliability* is a subsequence (contiguous or not) of a MNP that corresponds to a shorter term candidate in either its inflected or lemmatized form. It is used as an anchor as follows: the subsequence covered by the island is reduced to the word found to be the syntactic head of the island. Parsing patterns are then applied to the simplified MNP.

This feature allows the parse of complex noun phrases using a limited number of simple parsing patterns (80 patterns containing a maximum of 3 content words were defined for the experiments described below). In addition, islands increase the degree of reliability of the parse as shown in Figure 1.

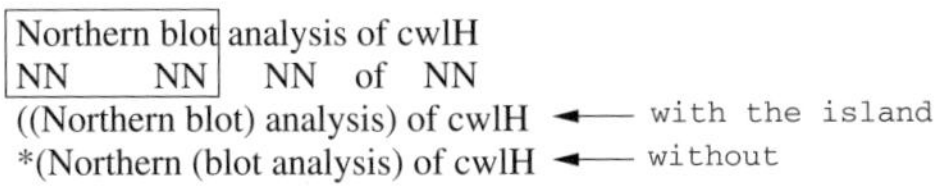

Fig. 1. Effect of an island on parsing

YATEA allows exogenous disambiguation, *i.e.* the exploitation of existing (testified) terminologies to assist the chunking, parsing and extraction steps.

During chunking, sequences of words corresponding to testified terms are identified. They cannot be further split or deleted. Their POS tags and lemmas can be corrected according to those associated to the testified term. If an MNP corresponds to a testified term for which a parse exists (provided by the user or computed using parsing patterns), it is recorded as a term candidate with the highest score of reliability. Similarly to endogenous disambiguation, subsequences of MNPs corresponding to testified terms are used as islands of reliability in order to augment the number and quality of parsed MNPs.

3.2 Term Candidate Extraction Process

A noun phrase is extracted from the corpus and considered a term candidate if at least one parse is found for it. This is performed in three main steps, (1) *chunking*, *i.e.* construction of a list of Maximal Noun Phrases from the corpus, (2) *parsing*, *i.e.* attempts to find at least one syntactic parse for each MNP and, (3) *extraction* of term candidates. The result of the term extraction process is two lists of noun phrases: one contains parsed MNPs, called *term candidates*, the other contains MNPs for which no parse was found. Both lists are proposed to the user through a validation interface (ongoing development).

1. **Chunking:** the corpus is chunked into Maximal Noun Phrases.
   The POS tags associated to the words of the corpus are used to delimit the MNPs according to the resources provided by the user: chunking frontiers and exceptions, forbidden structures and potentially, testified terms.

Chunking frontiers are tags or words that are not allowed to appear in MNPs, e.g. verbs (VBG) or prepositions (IN). *Chunking exceptions* are used to refine frontiers. For instance, *"of"* is a frontier exception to prepositions, *"many"* and *"several"* being exceptions to adjectives. *Forbidden structures* are exceptions for more complex structures and are used to prevent from extracting sequences that look like terms (syntactically valid) but are known not to be terms or parts of terms like *"of course"*. MNPs and subparts of MNPs corresponding to testified terms (when available) are protected and cannot be modified using the chunking data. For instance, the tag FW is *a priori* not allowed in MNPs. However, if an MNP is equal to or contains the testified term *"in/IN vitro/FW"*, it will be kept as such.

2. **Parsing:** for each identified MNP type, except monolexical MNPs, different parsing methods are applied in decreasing order of reliability. Once a method succeeds in parsing the MNP, the parsing process comes to an end. Still, one method can compute several parses for the same MNP, making the parsing non-deterministic if desired. We consider 3 different parsing methods:
   – TT-COVERED: the MNP inflected or lemmatized form corresponds to one or several combined testified terms (TT);
   – PATTERN-COVERED: the POS sequence of the (possibly simplified) MNP corresponds to a parsing pattern provided by user;
   – PROGRESSIVE: the MNP is progressively reduced at its left and right ends by the application of parsing patterns. Islands of reliability from term candidates or testified terms are also used to reduce the MNP sequence of the MNP to allow the application of parsing patterns.
3. **Extraction** of term candidates: MNPs that received a parse in the previous processing step are considered term candidates. Statistical measures will further be implemented to order MNPs according to their likelihood to be a term in order to facilitate their validation by the user.

4 Experiments

To characterise the effects of resources on term extraction, we compare the results provided by YATEA using or not existing terminologies on a biomedical corpus. We present and comment the effects on chunking, parsing and extraction of the term candidates.

4.1 Materials

Working corpus. We carry out an experiment on a corpus of 16,600 sentences (438,513 words) describing genomic interaction of the model organism *"Bacillus subtilis"*. The corpus was tagged and lemmatized using the GENIA tagger [12].

Terminological resources. To study the reuse of terminologies in the term extractor, we tested two types of resources: terms from two public databases and a list of terms extracted from the working corpus. We first selected and merged two specialized resources covering genomic vocabulary: Gene Ontology [13] and MeSH [14], both issued from the december 2005 release of UMLS [15]. The Gene Ontology resource[3] (henceforth GO) aims at proposing a controlled vocabulary related to the genomic description of any organism, prokaryotes as well as eukaryotes [16]. GO proposes a list of 24,803 terms. The Medical Subject Headings thesaurus[4] (henceforth MeSH) is dedicated to the indexation of the Medline database. The UMLS version of the MeSH offers 390,489 terms used in the medical domain [17].

The TAC (Terms Acquired in Corpus) resource is a list of 515 terms extracted from our working corpus using three term extractors [5]. The 515 terms occur at least 20 times in the corpus and were validated by a biologist.

4.2 Results

We present and comment the results of YATEA using no resource, the combination of GO and MeSH (GO+MeSH) and finally the TAC resource.

Chunking is affected by resources in several ways. As shown in Table 1, they allow the identification of new MNPs that were originally rejected due to their POS tag(s). In addition, the MNPs tend to be longer and monolexical terms less numerous. As MNPs are more complex, the number of types of POS sequences to be parsed is augmented. However, this increase in diversity is expected to be compensated by the parsing mechanism related to islands of reliability.

Table 1. Effects of resources on chunking

Version	MNPs		Monolexical		Words/ complex MNP	POS sequences types
	types	occ	types	occ		
no resource	45,716	84,810	6,989	30,815	3.61	2,965
GO+MeSH	46,079	85,004	6,949	30,272	3.63	3,256
TAC	46,315	84,918	6,934	29,695	3.65	3,500

Parsing MNPs is also affected by the use of resources that increase the reliability of parses since testified terms are used as islands of reliability. The contribution of each parsing method is presented in Figure 2 regarding the total types and occurrences of MNPs. Interestingly, the TT-COVERED method discharges the PROGRESSIVE method which is the least reliable. The increase in the contribution of the PATTERN-COVERED method is explained by the extraction of new short terms like species names, e.g. *"Escherichia/FW coli/FW"*, the expansion of monolexical terms like *"DNA/NNP"* to *"DNA/NNP binding/VBG"* that results from tag correction (VBG replaced by NN) and the simplification of MNPs using islands before the application of the parsing patterns.

[3] `http://www.geneontology.org/`

[4] `http://www.nlm.nih.gov/mesh`

The comparison of the diagrams on types and occurrences shows that both resources cover frequent terms. Still, GO+MeSH unsurprisingly contributes little (1777 terms out of 415,292 are used) compared to the corpus-tuned resource (TAC).

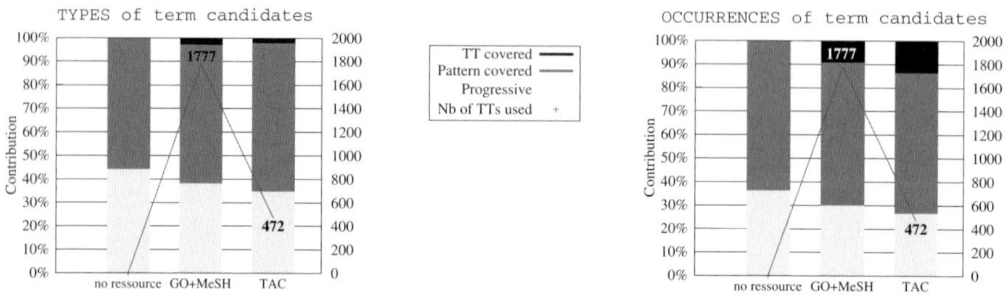

Fig. 2. Contribution of parsing methods

Extraction of term candidates is dependent on both preceding steps as an MNP found during chunking is considered a term candidate if at least one parse is found for it. Statistical filtering methods, that will be further implemented, are expected to provide qualitative information on term candidates and to allow the extraction of monolexical terms. On a quantitative point of view, using existing terminologies results in the extraction of a greater number of term candidates.

5 Conclusion and Future Works

Term extractors on the one hand and terminology matching techniques on the other hand show limitations in term acquisition and term exploitation respectively. To both reduce noisy results of the extraction and augment the coverage of existing terminologies, we proposed to combine both techniques in a term extractor. With a first experiment on a biomedical corpus, we showed that the exploitation of existing terminologies in a term extractor positively influences the identification of maximal noun phrases, their parsing and finally the extraction of lists of term candidates. The result of the extraction is a corpus-tuned list of term candidates. It is composed of a subset of the external resource(s) augmented with term candidates acquired in the corpus in conformity with the former. As future works, we intend to add statistical features to assist the endogenous and exogenous disambiguation. The handling of coordinations is also about to be integrated. Finally, a precise evaluation of the outputs of YATEA through a validation interface is planed.

References

1. Daille, B.: Conceptual structuring through term variations. In Bond, F., Kohonen, A., Carthy, D.M., Villaciencio, A., eds.: Proceedings of the ACL'2003 Workshop on Multiword Expressions: Analysis, Acquisition, and Treatment. (2003) 9–16

2. Bourigault, D.: An endogeneous corpus-based method for structural noun phrase disambiguation. In: Proceedings of the EACL'93, Utrecht, The Netherlands (1993) 81–86
3. Bourigault, D., Fabre, C.: Approche linguistique pour l'analyse syntaxique de corpus. Cahiers de Grammaire (25) (2000) 131–151
4. Cabré, M.T., Estopà, R., Vivaldi, J.: Automatic term detection: a review of current systems. In: Recent Advances in Computational Terminology. John Benjamins, Amsterdam, Philadelphia (2001)
5. Aubin, S.: Recommandations sur l'utilisation des outils terminologiques. Technical report, Projet ExtraPloDocs (2003) `http://www-lipn.univ-paris13.fr/~poibeau/Extra/D31b.pdf`.
6. Chute, C.G., Cohn, S.P., Campbell, K.E., Olivier, D.E., Campbell, J.R.: The content coverage of clinical classifications. Journal of American Medical Informatics Association **3** (1996) 224–233
7. McCray, A.T., Browne, A.C., Bodenreider, O.: The lexical properties of the gene ontology (GO). In: Proceedings of the AMIA 2002 Annual Symposium. (2002) 504–508
8. Bodenreider, O., Rindflesch, T.C., Burgun, A.: Unsupervised, corpus-based method for extending a biomedical terminology. In: Workshop on Natural Language Processing in the Biomedical Domain (ACL2002). (2002) 53–60
9. Hamon, T.: Indexer les documents spécialisés : les ressources terminologiques contrôlées sont-elles suffisantes ? In: 6ème rencontres Terminologie et Intelligence Artificielle, Rouen, France (2005) 71–82
10. Enguehard, C., Malvache, P., Trigano, P.: Indexation de textes : l'apprentissage des concepts. In: Proceedings of COLING'92, Nantes, France (1992) 1197–1202
11. Jacquemin, C., Klavans, J.L., Tzoukermann, E.: Expansion of multi-word terms for indexing and retrieval using morphology and syntax. In: Proceedings of the ACL'97/EACL'97, Barcelona, Spain (1997) 24–31
12. Tsuruoka, Y., Tateishi, Y., Kim, J.D., Ohta, T., McNaught, J., Ananiadou, S., Tsujii, J.: Developing a robust part-of-speech tagger for biomedical text. In: Proceedings of Advances in Informatics - 10th Panhellenic Conference on Informatics. LNCS 3746 (2005) 382–392
13. Consortium, T.G.O.: Gene ontology: tool for the unification of biology. Nature genetics **25** (2000) 25–29
14. MeSH: Medical subject headings. Library of Medicine, Bethesda, Maryland, WWW page `http://www.nlm.nih.gov/mesh/meshhome.html`, (1998)
15. National Library of Medicine, ed.: UMLS Knowledge Source. 13th edn. (2003)
16. Consortium, T.G.O.: Creating the Gene Ontology Resource: Design and Implementation. Genome Res. **11**(8) (2001) 1425–1433
17. Côté, R.A.: Répertoire d'anatomopathologie de la SNOMED internationale, v3.4. Université de Sherbrooke, Sherbrooke, Québec. (1996)

Improving Thai Spelling Recognition with Tone Features

Chutima Pisarn and Thanaruk Theeramunkong

Sirindhorn International Institute of Technology
131 Moo 5 Tiwanont Rd., Bangkadi, Muang, Pathumthani 12000, Thailand
{chutimap, thanaruk}@siit.tu.ac.th

Abstract. Spelling recognition has been used for several purposes, such as enhancing speech recognition systems and implementing name retrieval systems. Tone information is an important clue, in addition to phones, for recognizing speeches in tonal languages. In this paper, we present a method to improve accuracy of spelling recognition in Thai, a tonal language, by incorporating tone-related acoustic features to a well-known front-end feature named Perceptual Linear Prediction Coefficients (PLP). The proposed method makes use of three kinds of tone information: fundamental frequency (pitch), pitch delta and pitch acceleration, to enhance the original features. Compared to the baseline result gained from the original feature, our HMMs-based recognition model shows improvement of 1.73%, 2.85% and 3.16% of letter accuracy for close-type, mix-type and open-type language models, respectively.

1 Introduction

Spelling recognition is one of specific speech recognition tasks the scope of which is the domain of recognizing spelled utterances. Not only applied to assist a telephone directory system, a spelling recognition system can also be a practical way to enhance a speech recognition system. Normally, when the system cannot predict a word due to an out-of-dictionary word or signal distortion, it should request the user to spell out the word in order to recognize it. Several works on spelling recognition have widely been developed for many languages such as English [1], German [2, 3] Spanish [4] and Portuguese [5]. Most of them concentrated on how to retrieve a correct name from a telephone directory using various techniques. Unlike spelling in other languages, Thai spelling has special characteristic in the sense that one can spell Thai in several ways. In the past, there were few works on Thai spelling recognition [6].

Like Chinese, Vietnamese and some oriental language, Thai is a tonal language. For those tonal languages, tone information can be considered as a potential source in improving recognition rate. As an early stage of tonal-language speech recognition, several methods have been proposed to use tonal characteristics in speech recognition in both isolated and continuous speech of Mandarin and Cantonese [7-9]. Some works [8-11] indicated that these tonal characteristics were very helpful

T. Salakoski et al. (Eds.): FinTAL 2006, LNAI 4139, pp. 388 – 398, 2006.

in increasing speech recognition. In [8], Chen proposed a method to incorporate pitch information of only the main vowels of some syllables into feature vectors. The result showed dramatic reduction in word recognition error rate when demi-syllable pitch information was applied to the conventional method. Instead of using syllables as processing units, Chang [9] decomposed a syllable into two parts; syllable initial and syllable final as basic acoustic processing units. The basic acoustic units with a same phoneme but different tones are treated as different phonemes. The pitch information and its first-order and second-order derivatives are smoothed and then applied to feature vectors. However, this work limited the experiments to the evaluation based on individual gender. As another work, Wong [11] reported that the integration of tone-related information, such as frame energy, probability of voicing and pitch period, in addition to its derivatives to the feature vector could reduce Chinese speech syllable error rate. For Thai [12], by incorporating tone features, i.e. fundamental frequency (pitch), pitch delta and pitch acceleration, the accuracy of Thai continuous speech recognition has been improved. Unfortunately, so far there has been no work related to exploiting tone information in spelling recognition.

In this work, to improve accuracy of spelling recognition, we propose a method to incorporate tone information to the classical front-end feature vector. All experiments are performed based on three environments (i.e. close, mix, open) of bigram language model. This paper is organized as follows. In section 2, Thai phonetic characteristics, alphabet system and spelling methods are presented. Section 3 describes the pitch extraction method. The spelling recognition framework with tone incorporation is introduced in section 4. The experimental results and analysis of spelling recognition are reported in section 5. Finally, a conclusion and some future works are given in Section 6.

2 Thai Phonetic Characteristics, Alphabet System and Spelling Methods

2.1 Thai Phonetic Characteristics

Like most languages, a Thai syllable can be separated into three parts; (1) initial consonant, (2) vowel and (3) final consonant. The phonetic representation of one syllable can be expressed in the form of $/C_i\text{-}V^T\text{-}C_f/$, where C_i is an initial consonant, V is a vowel, C_f is a final consonant and T is a tone which is phonetically attached to the vowel part. Some initial consonants are cluster consonants. Each of them has a phone similar to that of a corresponding base consonant. For example, *pr* and *pl*, are similar to their corresponding base consonant *p*. In the vowel part, there are 18 vowel phones and 6 diphthongs. Following the concept in [12], there are totally 76 phonetic symbols and 5 tone symbols in Thai, as shown in Table 1.

Table 1. Phonetic symbols grouped as initial consonants, vowels, final consonants and tones

Initial Consonant *(C_i)*		Vowel *(V)*		Final Consonant *(C_f)*	Tone *(T)*
Base	Cluster	Base	Diphthong		
p,t,c,k,z,ph,	*pr,phr,pl,phl*	*a,aa,i,ii,*	*ia,iia,va,*	*p^,t^,k^,n^,*	0 Mid
th,ch,kh,b,d	*,tr,thr,kr,khr*	*v,vv,u,uu,e,e*	*vva,ua,uua*	*m^,n^,g^,j^,*	1 Low
,m,n,	*,kl,khl,kw,kh*	*e,x,xx,o,oo,*		*w^,f^,l^,s^,c*	2 Falling
ng,l,r,f,s,	*w,br,bl,dr,fr*	*@,@@,*		*h^,jf^, ts^*	3 High
h,w,j	*,fl*	*q,qq,*			4 Rising

2.2 Pronunciation of Thai Alphabet

In Thai language, there are 66 commonly used letters as shown in Table 2. These letters can be grouped into three alphabet classes by phone expression, i.e., consonant, vowel and tone. There are various styles in pronouncing Thai alphabet. An alphabet in each alphabet class may have more than one pronunciation styles. The consonantal letters can be uttered in either of the following two styles. The first style is simply pronouncing the core sound of a consonant. For example, the consonantal letter 'ก', its core sound can be represented as the phonetic sound */k-@@0/*. Normally, some consonants share a same core sound. For example, 'ค', 'ฅ', and 'ฆ' have the same phonetic sound */kh-@@0/*. In such case, the hearer may encounter with letter ambiguity. To solve this issue, the second style is generally applied by uttering a core sound of the consonant followed by the representative word of that consonant. Every consonant has its representative word. For example, the representative word of the letter 'ก' is "ไก่" (meaning: "chicken", sound: */k-a1-j^/*), and that of the letter 'ข' is "ไข่" (meaning: "egg", sound: */kh-a1-j^/*). To express the letter 'ก' using this style, the syllable */k-@@0/+/k-a1-j^/* is uttered.

Table 2. Thai alphabets: consonants, vowels and tones

Basic Classes	Alphabets in each class
Consonant (44)	ก,ข,ฃ,ค,ฅ,ฆ,ง,จ,ฉ,ช,ซ,ฌ,ญ,ฎ,ฏ,ฐ,ฑ,ฒ,ณ,ด,ต,ถ,ท,ธ,น,บ,ป,ผ,ฝ,พ,ฟ,ภ,ม,ย,ร,ล,ว,ศ,ษ,ส,ห,ฬ,อ,ฮ
First-type vowel (14)	อะ, อา, อิ, อี, อึ, อื, อุ, อู, เอ, แอ, โอ, อำ, ไอ, ใอ
Second-type vowel (4)	อั, อ็, อ์, ฤ
Tone (4)	อ่, อ้, อ๊, อ๋

Expressing letters in the vowel class is quite different from that of the consonant class. There are two types of vowels. The first-type vowels can be pronounced in two ways. One is to pronounce the word "สระ" (meaning: "vowel", sound: */s-a1//r-a1/*), followed by the core sound of the vowel. The other is to simply pronounce the core sound of the vowel. On the other hand, for the second-type vowels, they are uttered by calling their names. As the last class, tone symbols are always pronounced by calling their names. Table 3 concludes how to pronounce a letter in each alphabet class.

Table 3. Pronouncing methods for each alphabet class

Alphabet Class	Pronouncing Methods
Consonant	1. the core sound of the consonant + representative word of the consonant 2. the core sound of the consonant
First-type vowel	1. */s-a1//r-a1/* + the core sound of the vowel 2. the core sound of the vowel
Second-type vowel	1. the name of the vowel
Tone	1. the name of the tone

2.3 Thai Word Spelling Methods

Spelling a word is to utter letters in the word one by one in order. We can refer to spelling as a combination of the pronunciation of each letter in the word. In [6], Thai spelling methods were analyzed into four spelling styles. In this paper, we focus on one of the most frequently used spelling methods. In this method, for consonant letter, we pronounce only a consonant core sound. While the first-type vowel is pronounced as */s-a1//r-a1/* and then a vowel's core sound. The second-type vowel and tones are pronounced by calling their name. As mentioned above, some consonantal letters may share a same core sound. However, there will be exactly one letter, which is the most frequently used letter for each core sound, later called a representative letter. We will call the other letters with the same core sound as subordinate letters. Table 4 indicates a set of core sounds with their representative letters and subordinate letters. In order to differentiate which letter it is, a representative letter is pronounced by its core sound while a subordinate letter is pronounced by its core sound followed by its representative word.

Table 4. A set of core sounds with their representative letters and subordinate letters (consonantal letters)

Core Sound	Representative letter	Subordinate letter	Core Sound	Representative letter	Subordinate letter
/kh-@@4/	ข	ฃ	*/n-@@0/*	น	ณ
/kh-@@0/	ค	ฅ, ฆ	*/ph-@@0/*	พ	ภ
/ch-@@0/	ช	ฌ	*/j-@@0/*	ย	ญ
/d-@@0/	ด	ฎ	*/r-@@0/*	ร	ฤ
/t-@@0/	ต	ฏ	*/l-@@0/*	ล	ฬ
/th-@@4/	ถ	ฐ	*/s-@@4/*	ส	ศ, ษ
/th-@@0/	ท	ฑ, ฒ, ธ			

3 Extraction of Tone Feature

Tone (or pitch) information is considered as a potential source for improving recognition accuracy for any tonal language. Even in a non-tonal language, such tonal effect may occur when one would like to put a stress on some words or to make an interrogative utterance. The pitch information can be extracted from speech automatically and used in the recognition process. The following subsection displays the standard method to extract pitch (or tone information) and its derivatives.

3.1 Pitch Extraction

In the past, it was known that tone features could be characterized by tracing pitch or fundamental frequency (F_0) in every time unit on the voiced part of a syllable, resulting in a line shape or contour. In our work, these pitch values can be added directly to the classical feature vector in each time frame. In the past, there were two well-known pitch detection algorithms based on the time domain method called autocorrelation and the average magnitude difference function [13].

To recognize the tone of a syllable, we need normalize extracted pitch values instead of directly utilizing the extracted pitch values themselves. The aim of this task is to compensate the variety of speakers. Here, the normalized pitch value $\overline{p}_t$ can be derived by the following formula.

$$\overline{p}_t = \frac{p_t}{p_{avg}} \tag{1}$$

where p_t is the pitch value at the time frame t, and p_{avg} is the average of pitch values in the utterances. By the autocorrelation method the voice part of an utterance can be processed in order to get a pitch. However, it is impossible to get any pitch from an unvoiced part. Then the pitch is set to zero in the case of unvoiced parts. To solve the problem, we pass the normalized pitch values ($\overline{p}_t$) to a smoothing process in order to flatten pitch values for continuous speech recognition [9]. The smoothed values of a voiced part and an unvoiced part are calculated using equation (2) and (3), respectively.

Voiced :

$$f_t = \log_{10}(\overline{p}_t) + x \tag{2}$$

Unvoiced :

$$f_t = \begin{cases} f_{t-1} + \lambda(fav_{t-1} - f_{t-1}) + x, & t > 0 \\ \lambda & , \quad t = 0 \end{cases} \tag{3}$$

$$fav_t = \frac{\sum_{i=0}^{t} f_i}{t} \tag{4}$$

where fav_t is the running average of pitches in the previous frames and, x and λ are small random values determined through the experiments. In this work, they are set to 0.01 and 0.05, respectively.

3.2 Pitch Delta and Pitch Acceleration

The model can be enhanced by adding time derivatives. To grasp differences among pitch contours, the time derivatives of pitches can be used as important tone information. The pitch delta at a time frame is computed by the following formula.

$$d_t = \begin{cases} \dfrac{f_{t+\theta} - f_{t-\theta}}{2\theta}, & \theta < t < T - \theta \\ f_{t+1} - f_t \ , & t < \theta \\ f_t - f_{t-1} \ , & t \geq T - \theta \end{cases} \tag{5}$$

In the second and third equations, the end-effect problem was solved by using a simple compensation of first-order differences at the start and the end of utterances [14], where θ is the internal distance between two pitch points, f_t is a smoothed pitch value at time frame t. The same formula is applied to the delta values to obtain acceleration values.

$$a_t = \begin{cases} \dfrac{d_{t+\theta} - d_{t-\theta}}{2\theta}, & \theta < t < T - \theta \\ d_{t+1} - d_t \ , & t < \theta \\ d_t - d_{t-1} \ , & t \geq T - \theta \end{cases} \tag{6}$$

4 The Spelling Recognition Framework

In this work, HMMs are employed as the engine for recognizing continuous spelling utterances. The HMM is widely used in several works on speech recognition, especially for continuous speech since it can capture and handle a set of continuous data which are input as a sequence. Figure 1 illustrates our HMM-based automatic speech recognition (ASR) system, which consists of three major components: signal processing module, training module and recognizing module.

In the signal-processing module, speech utterances (wave signal) in the training corpus are transformed into the form of a feature vector. The feature vector used is the combination of PLP (Perceptual Linear Prediction Coefficients) and pitch information. In our work, the PLP is selected since it works well our dataset according to a number of preliminary experiments. To incorporate tone information, pitch information are extracted and integrated to the original PLP feature. Three main types of pitch information are taken into account: fundamental frequency (pitch), pitch delta and pitch acceleration. The combined feature vectors are used as input through our acoustic models. In the training module, an acoustic model and a language model are trained. For the acoustic model, the conventional phone-based HMMs are used to represent phones; i.e. one acoustic model per phone. A series of feature vectors, PLP with pitch information, are used to compute probabilities of an acoustic model. To train the language model for spelling recognition, a text corpus is used as a source for

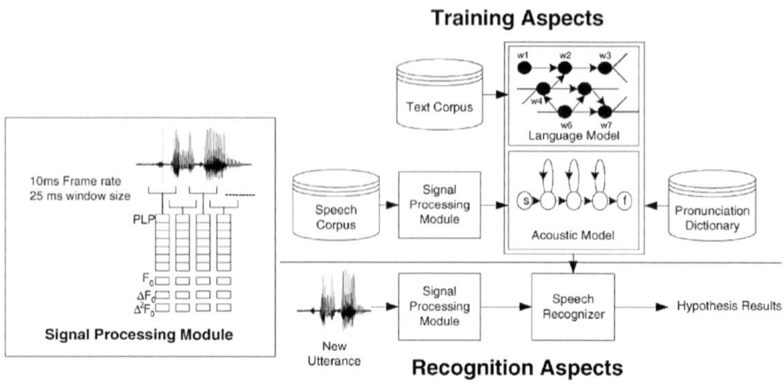

Fig. 1. The framework with a signal processing module for incorporating tone

assigning probabilities to a letter sequence. When a domain is limited to a small set of some proper names, a language model can be trained from that set and the system can yield high accuracy. As more flexible environment, a general recognizer, which accepts any spelling utterance, usually needs a larger text corpus. However, the larger the text corpus for training is, the more ambiguity the system has to cope with. In this work, we investigate both limited and flexible environments. For the recognition module, an input waveform is transformed to a set of feature vectors that are the combination of PLP and pitch information. With three main sources, i.e., acoustic model, language model and pronunciation dictionary, the system searches among all possibilities, for the letter sequence with the maximum probability and returns it as the recognition result.

5 Experimental Result and Analysis

The section describes a set of experiments and their results. The purpose is to investigate the advantage of tone exploitation.

5.1 Experimental Environment

We have constructed two speech corpora, based on two sets of spelled proper names. The spelling style is the one shown in section 2.3. The first set (A) contains 150 spelled names recorded by three males and three females while the second set (B) contains 136 spelled names recorded by three other males and three other females. There is no overlap between proper names in the sets A and B. In this work, the set A is used as the training set while the set B is for a test set. The speech signals were digitized by a 16-bit A/D converter with frequency of 16 kHz. A set of feature vectors used for forming a baseline is a 39-PLP feature vector, which consists of 12 PLP coefficients and the 0th coefficient, as well as their first and second order derivatives. Therefore, there are 39 elements in total. In our proposed system, we construct a

42-component feature vector which consists of 39-PLP feature vectors as well as three components of tone information, i.e. pitch, pitch delta and pitch acceleration. Tone information components can be acquired by the method mentioned in Section 3. The layout of feature vectors used in our approach is illustrated in Figure 2.

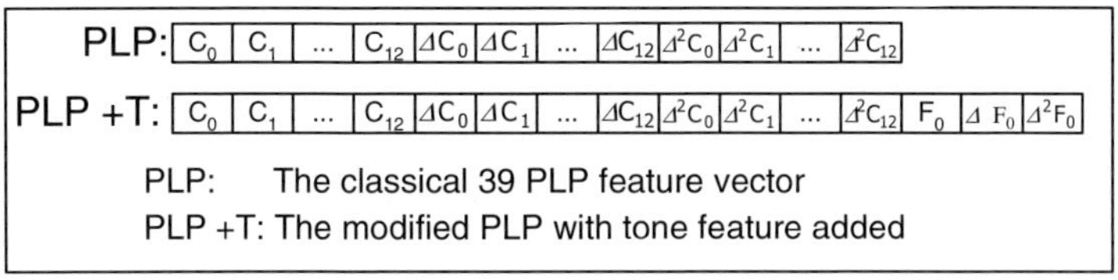

Fig. 2. Feature vector layout

The experiments are performed under three different bigram language models, LM1, LM2 and LM3. LM1 is a close-type language model constructed from the test transcription. LM3 is an open-type language model trained by another text corpus, which is not used as the test transcription. In this experiment we use 5,971 names of Thai provinces, districts and sub districts. LM2 is a mix-type language model generated from a corpus that includes both the test transcription and those 5,971 location names. In this work, Spelling recognizers are designed as phone-based HMMs. They are context-dependent in the sense that the recognition of a phone depends on its preceding and following phones. For each phone model, the topology is a 3-state left-to-right model with no skip. The number of phones is 56 as shown in Table 5. The numbers in parentheses denote the possible expansion of vowels using tones. For example "*a(0-4)*" indicates that the vowel phone '*a*' can be expanded by five different tones: 0 (mid), 1 (low), 2 (falling), 3 (high), 4 (rising).

Table 5. The list of possible acoustic models in the spelling corpora

Phonetic Types	Acoustic models (56 models)
Initial Consonant	*b,c,ch,d,f,h,j,k,kh,l,m,n,ng,r,s,t,th,tr,w,z*
Vowel	*@@(0,4),a(0-4),aa(0,1,4),e1,e(0,1),i(1,4),ii(0,4), o0,oo0, qq0,u1,u(0,2,3),uua3,v(1,3), vv0, xx0*
Final Consonant	*j^,k^,m^,n^,ng^,t^,w^*

All experiments, including automatic transcription labeling, are performed using the HTK toolkit [14]. The recognition performance is evaluated in the terms of correct rate and accuracy. Since the task concerned is spelling recognition not normal speech or word recognition, the definitions of word correct rate and word accuracy are modified to letter correct rate (LCR) and letter accuracy (LA). They are shown in equation (7) and (8) (see details in [14]). Here, H is the number of correct letters, I is the number of insertion errors, and N is the total number of letters.

$$\textit{Letter Correct Rate (LCR)} = \frac{H}{N} \tag{7}$$

$$\textit{Letter Accuracy (LA)} = \frac{H-I}{N} \tag{8}$$

5.2 Experimental Result

For comparison, we set up a baseline experiment, which employs the 39-PLP classical feature vector. By varying the grammar scale factor (GSF) [14] to adjust the appropriate weighting ratio between acoustic and language model, we can obtain the baseline result as shown in Table 6. In the table, it was observed that the best GSF for the close-type language model (LM1) is 25.0. It yields up to 80.08% LCR and 77.01% LA. In both the mix-type language model (LM2) and open-type language model (LM3), the appropriate GSF is 25.0. The best LCR and LA for LM2 are 74.18% and 60.47% while the best ones for LM3 are 73.47% and 59.48%, respectively. However, for further explanation, we will focus on the case that GSF equals to 25.0 since it gains higher accuracy in most cases. Therefore, the baseline results can be considered to 80.08% LCR and 77.01% LA for LM1 (close-type), 73.04% LCR and 68.17% LA for LM2 (mix-type), and 71.55% LCR and 66.36% LA for LM3 (open-type).

Table 6. Recognition performance for the classical PLP (the baseline)

Language model		Grammar Scale Factor (GSF) 5.0	6.25	10.0	25.0	50.0	100.0
LM1	COR	74.49	75.23	77.55	**80.08**	78.97	72.20
	ACC	55.17	58.28	65.76	77.01	**78.01**	71.01
LM2	COR	72.25	72.92	**74.18**	73.04	68.33	59.28
	ACC	51.72	54.36	60.47	**68.17**	66.02	57.08
LM3	COR	71.80	72.47	**73.47**	71.55	66.73	57.87
	ACC	51.14	53.81	59.48	**66.36**	64.02	56.11

Table 7. Recognition performance when tone information is incorporated to PLP (PLP+T)

Language model		Grammar Scale Factor (GSF) 5.0	6.25	10.0	25.0	50.0	100.0
LM1	COR	75.13	75.82	77.87	**82.28**	82.27	77.03
	ACC	64.58	66.15	70.94	78.74	**80.32**	75.43
LM2	COR	73.45	73.88	74.41	**75.11**	71.65	61.98
	ACC	62.54	63.80	66.74	**71.02**	68.95	59.61
LM3	COR	73.16	73.54	**73.92**	73.81	69.51	60.08
	ACC	62.09	63.35	66.13	**69.52**	66.56	57.54

The recognition performance in Table 7 is obtained when tone information is incorporated to the classical PLP feature vector. Independent of GSF and language models, the improvement over the baseline is observed when tone information is incorporated into the PLP feature vector. With the most suitable GSF (25.0), the system can achieve up to 82.28% LCR and 78.74% LA for LM1 (close-type), 75.11% LCR and 71.02% LA for LM2 (mix-type), and 73.81% LCR and 69.52% LA for LM3 (open-type).

6 Conclusion and Future Work

This paper presented a method to improve accuracy in Thai spelling recognition by incorporating tone information into the classical PLP feature vector. Characteristics of Thai language and its spelling method were introduced. The proposed HMM-based method recognized spelling utterances of the most popular Thai spelling method. The system was examined under three language model environments; close-type, mix-type and open-type. With the 42-component feature vector (39-PLP with three tone features), the system outperformed the baseline system (39-PLP feature vector) with improvement of 1.73%, 2.85% and 3.16% for letter accuracy in close-type, mix-type and open-type language models, respectively. As further works, we plan to explore more tone features and study spelling recognition for other types of Thai spelling methods.

References

1. Mitchell, C.D., Setlur A.R.: Improved spelling recognition using a tree-based fast lexical match. Proceedings of IEEE International Conference on Acoustics, Speech, and Signal Processing, (1999) 597-600
2. Hild, H., Waibel, A.: Recognition of spelled names over the telephone. Proceedings of the International Conference on Spoken Language Processing, ICSLP 96, Philadelphia, (1996) 346-349
3. Bauer, J.G., Junkawitsch, J.: Accurate recognition of city names with spelling as a fall back strategy. Proceedings of EUROSPEECH (1999) 263-266
4. San-Segundom, R., Colas, J., Cordoba, R., Pardo, J.M.: Spanish recognizer of continuously spelled names over the telephone, Journal of Speech Communication 38, (2002) 287-303
5. Rodrigues, F., Rodrigues R., Martins, C.: An isolated letter recognizer for proper name identification over the telephone. Proceedings of 9th Portuguese Conference on Pattern Recognition (RECPAD'97), Coimbra (1997)
6. Pisarn, C., Theeramunkong, T.: Speed compensation for improving Thai spelling recognition with a continuous speech corpus. Intelligence in Communication System, LNCS 3283, IFIP International Conference, INTELLCOMM 2004, Bangkok, Thailand, (2004) 100-111
7. Lee, T., Ching, P.C., Chan, L.W., Cheng, Y.H., Mark, B.: Tone Recognition of Isolated Cantonese Syllables, IEEE Transaction on Speech Audio Processing (1988) 988-992
8. Chen, C. Julian, Recognize Tone Languages Using Pitch Information on The Main Vowel of Each Syllable, Proceedings of IEEE International Conference on Acoustics, Speech and Signal Processing, (2001) 61-64
9. Chang, E., Zhou, J., Di, S., Huang, C., Lee, K.: Large Vocabulary Mandarin Speech Recognition with Different Approaches in Modeling Tones, Proceedings of International Conference on Spoken Language Processing 2000

10. Thubthong, N., Kijsirikul, B.,: Improving Connected Thai Digit Speech Recognition using Prosodic Information, Proceedings of The 4th National Computer Science and Engineering Conference (2000) 63-68
11. Wong, P., Siu, M., Integration of Tone Related Feature for Chinese Speech Recognition, 6th International Conference on Signal Processing, (2002) 476-479
12. Pisarn, C., Theeramunkong, T.: Incorporating tone information to improve Thai continuous speech recognition, Proc. of International Conference on Intelligent Technologies, Chiangmai, Thailand, (2003) 84-89
13. Rabiner, L.R., et. al.: A Comparative Performance Study of Several Pitch Detection Algorithms, IEEE Transaction on Acoustics, Speech, and Signal Processing, Vol. ASSP-24 No. 5, (1976)
14. Young, S., et al, The HTK Book (for HTK Version 3.1), (2000)

Incorporating External Information in Bayesian Classifiers Via Linear Feature Transformations

Tapio Pahikkala, Jorma Boberg, Aleksandr Mylläri, and Tapio Salakoski

Turku Centre for Computer Science (TUCS)
Department of Information Technology, University of Turku
Lemminkäisenkatu 14 A, FIN-20520 Turku, Finland
firstname.lastname@it.utu.fi

Abstract. Naive Bayes classifier is a frequently used method in various natural language processing tasks. Inspired by a modified version of the method called the flexible Bayes classifier, we explore the use of linear feature transformations together with the Bayesian classifiers, because it provides us an elegant way to endow the classifier with an external information that is relevant to the task. While the flexible Bayes classifier is based on the idea of using kernel density estimation to obtain the class conditional probabilities of continuously valued attributes, we use the linear transformations to smooth the feature frequency counts of discrete valued attributes. We evaluate the method on the context sensitive spelling error correction problem using the Reuters corpus. For this particular task, we define a positional feature transformation and a word feature transformation that take advantage of the positional information of the context words and the part-of-speech information of words, respectively. Our experimental results show that the performance of the Bayesian classifiers in the natural language disambiguation tasks can be improved with the proposed transformations and that the incorporation of external information via the linear feature transformations is a promising research direction.

1 Introduction

Many natural language processing applications require accurate resolution of the various kinds of ambiguity present in natural language, giving rise to a class of disambiguation problems. In this paper, we focus on lexical disambiguation problems, where disambiguation is done at the level of words. One such problem is the problem of context-sensitive spelling error correction, where the misspelling of the original word belongs to the language, such as, for example, *affect* misspelled as *effect* or vice versa. This mistake cannot be detected by standard lexicon-based checkers, since both words belongs to the English lexicon. A set of similar words that belong to the lexicon and that are often confused with the other words in the set is called a *confusion set*. For example, {*maybe*, *may be*} can be considered as a binary confusion set.

In our previous work [1,2,3], we have shown that the performance of the natural language disambiguation systems can be improved by taking advantage of

T. Salakoski et al. (Eds.): FinTAL 2006, LNAI 4139, pp. 399–410, 2006.

the positional information of the context words with position sensitive kernel functions. The methods considered in these studies were the support vector machine classifiers that have recently become the state-of-the-art machine learning algorithms. Naive Bayes classifier is another frequently used method in various natural language processing tasks that has been shown to have a high performance. John and Langley [4] introduced the flexible Bayes, a version of the naive Bayes classifier that uses kernel density estimation to estimate the class conditional probabilities of continuous attributes. We [3] used this method in context of word sense disambiguation to estimate the probabilities of word-position features. The experiment demonstrated that the performance of the Bayesian classifiers can be improved even if the attributes are ordinal (the word positions in the context of the ambiguous word in our case).

In this paper, we introduce a realization of the flexible Bayes classifier that is based on linear feature transformations, that is, we also relax the ordinality assumption of the attributes. To our knowledge, this has not been considered in the literature. Moreover, inspired by the good results obtained in the previous studies by transforming the positional information of the context words, we also define transformations for the words. We describe a method to construct the word transformations using an external source of information that is useful for the classification task in question. One such information source for the natural language disambiguation tasks is, for example, the part-of-speech information of the words (see e.g. Jurafsky and Martin [5]).

This paper is organized as follows. We start by describing the data representation and the Bayesian classifiers in Section 2. In Section 3, we consider the use of the linear feature transformations together with the Bayesian classifiers. The proposed transformations are evaluated in Section 4. We conclude the paper in Section 5 and discuss possible future directions.

2 Binary Classification with Bayesian Classifiers

We first describe the representation of the data we use in our study. Next, we give a definition of the naive Bayes classifier. Finally, we define the flexible Bayes classifier originally introduced by John and Langley [4].

2.1 Representation of the Data

In this paper, we consider the context sensitive spelling error correction as a model problem. In this kind of tasks, each data point consists of a word to be disambiguated and the context words surrounding it. We formalize the data points in the following way. Let s be a context span parameter that determines how many words to the left and to the right from the ambiguous word are included in the context, so that the size of the context window $r = 2s + 1$. If there are not enough words available in the text to the left or to the right from the ambiguous word, we use "empty" words to get a word sequence of length r. Let n be the number of words and $\mathcal{W} = \{w_1, \ldots, w_n\}$ be the set of words. Let x be a data point. We define a representation of the data point x to be a word-position matrix $A_x \in \mathcal{M}_{n \times r}(\mathbb{R})$, where $\mathcal{M}_{n \times r}(\mathbb{R})$ is the set of $n \times r$-matrices whose elements belong to $\mathbb{R}$. The word positions of a context are defined as $-s, \ldots, 0, \ldots, s$, where the word to be disambiguated is in the position zero of its context. A word-position matrix A_x generated from the context of an ambiguous word is a binary matrix in which the element $A_x(i, j)$ corresponding to the word w_i and the position $p = j - s - 1$ has the value one if the word w_i occurs in the position p of the context and zero otherwise. We also observe that there can be at most one nonzero element in each column because each position can have only one word. If the word in a certain position of a context is not in $\mathcal{W}$ or if the position in the context is empty, the corresponding column has only zeros. On the other hand, the same word can occur in several positions in the context, and therefore the rows of the matrices can have several nonzero elements.

2.2 Naive Bayes Classifier

Let F_x be the set of all features that are contained in a data point x. According to our definition of the data points as word-position matrices, the word-position features in F_x correspond to the ones in the binary valued word-position matrix constructed from the data point x. For the Naive Bayes classifier, we use the following decision function:

$$d(x) = P(+1) \prod_{f \in F_x} P(f|+1) - P(-1) \prod_{f \in F_x} P(f|-1), \tag{1}$$

where $P(f|+1)$ and $P(f|-1)$ are the probabilities that the feature f appears in a positive and in a negative example, respectively, and $P(+1)$ and $P(-1)$ are the prior probabilities of the positive and negative classes. A new data point x is given a positive (resp. negative) class label, if the value of the decision function (1) for the data point is positive (resp. negative).

The probabilities can be directly estimated from the training data using maximum likelihood estimation (MLE) as follows. Let F denote the set of all possible features the data points can contain. For each class $y \in Y$ and feature $f \in F$,

$$P(y) = \frac{\mathrm{N}(y)}{\sum_{y' \in Y} \mathrm{N}(y')},$$

$$P(f|y) = \frac{\mathrm{N}(f, y)}{\sum_{f' \in F} \mathrm{N}(f', y)},$$

where $\mathrm{N}(y)$ is the number of examples in the class $y \in Y$, and $\mathrm{N}(f, y)$ is the feature frequency count of f conditional to the class y, that is, the number of times feature f appears in the examples of the class y. The MLE estimates are typically smoothed to avoid zero probabilities in prediction; in this paper we use add-δ smoothing, where all numbers of feature occurrences are incremented by $\delta > 0$ (in our experiments, we set $\delta = 0.001$) over the counted value (see e.g. Chen and Goodman [6]).

2.3 Flexible Bayes Classifier

John and Langley [4] introduced the flexible Bayes method, a version of the naive Bayes classifier that uses kernel density estimation (we refer to Silverman [7] for more information on kernel density estimation) to estimate the class conditional probabilities of continuous attributes (this method has also been described by Hastie et al. [8]). While the word-position random variable is discrete, and hence a histogram is a natural way to estimate its density, the estimate can still be bumpy because of the lack of training data.

We now define a version of a Bayesian classifier which is similar to the flexible Bayes classifier. The class conditional probabilities of the features are estimated as follows

$$P(f|y) = \frac{\sum_{f' \in F} \mathrm{N}(f', y) g(f, f')}{\sum_{f', f'' \in F} \mathrm{N}(f', y) g(f', f'')}, \tag{2}$$

where g is a kernel function. The estimate can be considered as a convolution of the sample empirical distribution of the features with the kernel function (see e.g. Hastie et al. [8]).

In our previous study [3], our features were the word-position pairs described above and we used, among the others, a kernel function $g(f, f') : F \times F \to \mathbb{R}^+$:

$$g(f, f') = g((w, p), (v, q)) = \begin{cases} exp(-\theta(p-q))^2 & \text{when} \quad w = v \\ 0 & \text{otherwise} \end{cases}, \tag{3}$$

where $\theta \geq 0$ is a parameter, and w (resp. v) is the word and p (resp. q) is its position. We refer to this approach as the smoothed position-sensitive model. Note that if we let $\theta \to \infty$, the flexible Bayes becomes the naive Bayes classifier with the word-position features. We refer to this case as the basic position-sensitive model. If we, on the other hand, set $\theta = 0$, the different positions are identified with each other and the obtained classifier is a naive Bayes classifier constructed from the bag-of-words features.

Below, we describe how the kernel (3) can be used together with the Bayesian classifiers via linear transformations of the estimated feature frequency counts. The formalization of the approach with the linear transformations provides us a better machinery to incorporate external information into the classifier than the Gaussian kernel we use above.

3 Linear Feature Transformations

We will now describe a realization of the Bayesian classifier (2) that uses linear transformations on the word-position matrices that contain the class conditional feature frequency counts estimated from the data. Recall that we have defined our data points to be word-position matrices whose columns are the word feature vectors for different positions. Let us define for the class y a word-position matrix $A_y \in \mathcal{M}_{n \times r}(\mathbb{R})$ whose elements contain the number of occurrences of each word-position feature in class y, that is, $A_y = \sum_{x \in X_y} A_x$, where A_x is a word-position matrix corresponding to a training data point x and X_y is the set of training examples that belong to the class y. We will refer to the matrices A_y as class conditional feature frequency count matrices.

3.1 Constructing Linear Transformations for Position Vectors

We formulate the kernel function (3) as a linear transformation on the row vectors of the class conditional feature frequency count matrices. Let $P \in \mathcal{M}_{r \times r}(\mathbb{R})$ be a matrix of a transformation whose values are obtained as

$$P(i,j) = g((w,p),(w,q)), \tag{4}$$

where g is the function defined in (3), $p = i - s - 1$, and $q = j - s - 1$. The word w can be any word, because the value of the function (3) does not depend on it. We will call the matrix P a positional transformation.

We obtain the transformed feature frequency counts via the following matrix product of the original frequency counts and the positional transformation

$$\widehat{A_y} = A_y P.$$

When we normalize $\widehat{A_y}$ with the sum of the values of all its elements, we have the estimates of the class conditional probabilities of the features that can be used to construct a Bayesian classifier.

3.2 Constructing Linear Transformations for Word Vectors

Above, we defined a realization of the flexible Bayes classifier with a linear transformation of the position vectors. We can also construct linear transformations for the word vectors, that is, the column vectors of the class conditional feature frequency count matrices. Let $W \in \mathcal{M}_{n \times n}(\mathbb{R})$ be a matrix of the transformation that we call here a word transformation. The transformation is performed on the frequency count matrix A_y as

$$\widehat{A_y} = W A_y.$$

In the following, we consider a possible way to construct the word transformation.

In many natural language disambiguation tasks, the parts-of-speech (PoS) of context words are known to provide useful additional information (see e.g. Jurafsky and Martin [5]). We now use this external source of information to construct a linear feature transformation. Suppose that we know for each word all possible parts-of-speech it can have. Let us define a PoS-word matrix $V \in \mathcal{M}_{t \times n}(\mathbb{R})$ so that $V(i,j)$ is one if the jth word can have the ith PoS and zero otherwise. Let us consider an example in which the set of words consists of the words *composition*, *contribution*, *write*, and *being*, and the possible PoS are *noun* and *verb* (i.e. $n = 4$ and $t = 2$). Then

$$\begin{matrix} \mathcal{W} = \{\textit{composition, contribution, write, being}\} \\ \mathcal{P} = \{\textit{noun, verb}\} \end{matrix} \quad \text{and } V = \begin{pmatrix} 1\,1\,0\,1 \\ 0\,0\,1\,1 \end{pmatrix},$$

whete $\mathcal{P}$ denotes the set of PoS. Notice that it is possible for words to have several nonzero values in their corresponding column in W. For example, the word *being* can be a noun or a verb. From this PoS-word matrix, we construct the following word-word similarity matrix

$$W = V^{\mathrm{T}}V = \begin{pmatrix} 1\,1\,0\,1 \\ 1\,1\,0\,1 \\ 0\,0\,1\,1 \\ 1\,1\,1\,2 \end{pmatrix}, \tag{5}$$

where the rows and the columns are indexed by the four example words. The words *composition* and *contribution* are identified with each other in practice because their corresponding columns in W are equal. The word *being* is similar to all other words to some extent because it shares common PoS with them. To ensure that each word position feature is transformed to an equal amount of probability mass, we normalize the column vectors of $\widehat{W}$ with their 1-norm. By 1-norm of a vector x, we mean $\sum_i |x_i|$.

In reality there are, however, only a few PoS compared to the number of words. Therefore too many words will get identified with each other which would lead to a too powerful smoothing effect. We can control the amount of smoothing by increasing the diagonal of the transformation matrix as follows

$$\widetilde{W} = W + \mu I,$$

where $I \in \mathcal{M}_{n\times n}(\mathbb{R})$ is an identity matrix and μ is a parameter. The diagonal shift has the effect that the transformed feature frequency counts are the sum of the original frequency counts multiplied by μ and the frequency counts smoothed with the PoS information of the words.

An appropriate value of the diagonal shift parameter μ can be selected, for example, with a cross-validation. For instance, if we set $\mu = 1$, the normalized and diagonal shifted transformation matrix (5) will become

$$\widetilde{W} = \begin{pmatrix} 1.33 & 0.33 & 0 & 0.2 \\ 0.33 & 1.33 & 0 & 0.2 \\ 0 & 0 & 1.5 & 0.2 \\ 0.33 & 0.33 & 0.5 & 1.4 \end{pmatrix}. \tag{6}$$

From (6) we observe that the words *composition* and *contribution* are no longer completely identical and the similarities between the other words are also decreased compared to the values of the diagonal elements. Analogously with the above described smoothed position-sensitive model which encompasses the basic position-sensitive and bag-of-words models as extreme cases, the model based on the diagonal shifted word transformation encompasses the model based only on the word features and the model that has only the PoS information of the words. We observe that if we let $\mu \to \infty$, the information of the PoS disappears and we have just the word-position features. On the other hand, if we set $\mu = 0$, the word-position features are completely replaced with the PoS-position features.

When we select the value of the parameter μ, we choose an intermediate between these two extremes.

Note that we need the PoS-word matrix V only for the construction of the similarity matrix W of the words. If we have a source of the similarity information of the words, we can also directly construct the matrix W in a similar way that the positional transformation matrix P is obtained in (4).

3.3 Combination of Transformations

Let P be the matrix of a positional transformation and W the matrix of a word transformation. If we use both of the transformations at the same time, we obtain the transformed feature frequency counts via the following matrix product

$$\widehat{A_y} = W A_y P, \tag{7}$$

where A_y is the matrix that contains the original feature frequency counts for the class y.

3.4 Implementation Issues

Let W denote the normalized word transformation described above and $\widetilde{W}$ its diagonally shifted version. In our experiments, we defined our set of words to consist of the 10000 most common words in our data set. Therefore the transformation matrix is of dimension 10000×10000 and hence the computation of the matrix product $\widetilde{W} A_y$ for each class y may be too tedious in practice. Fortunately, because of the small number of possible PoS (in our experiments we used 10 different PoS), we are able to speed up the computation. Let V denote the PoS-word matrix from which the word transformation is constructed in the way described above. Instead of using the diagonally shifted and normalized matrix (6) directly, we perform the transformation as

$$\widetilde{W} A_y = (V^{\mathrm{T}}(V \bullet Z) + \mu I) A_y \tag{8}$$

$$= V^{\mathrm{T}}((V \bullet Z) A_y) + \mu A_y, \tag{9}$$

where $V \bullet Z$ denotes an elementwise product of the matrices V and Z of equal dimensionality and Z is a normalization matrix that ensures that the 1-norms of the column vectors of W are equal to one. The parenthesis in (9) denote the order in which the calculations are performed in the implementation. The two matrix products performed consecutively in (9) are together much faster to compute than the matrix product in the left hand side of (8).

4 Experiments

We use the task of context-sensitive spelling correction as a model problem to evaluate the performance of the proposed approach. In this task, the correct spelling of a word must be disambiguated among a set of alternative spellings based on its context, deciding, for example, between *country* and *county*. There is practical interest in improving methods at solving this task, and it is ideal as a model problem since a large dataset can be created without manual tagging. As high-quality texts such as newswire articles are widely available and unlikely to contain spelling errors, the required training and test examples can simply be extracted from such resources.

Golding and Roth [9] defined 21 sets of commonly confused words in their context-sensitive spelling correction experiments. 19 out of the 21 sets are binary (i.e. they consist only of two alternative spellings). For simplicity, we focus only on the 19 two-class problems in this paper. We create the datasets from the Reuters News corpus [10], extracting a training set of 1000 and a test set of 5000 examples for each confusion set as follows: we first search the corpus for documents containing either of the confusion set words. In each such document, every occurrence of either of the confusion set words forms a candidate example. We then form datasets of the required size by randomly selecting documents until they together contain sufficiently many examples; possible extra examples are randomly discarded from the last selected document. This sampling strategy assures that there is no overlap in documents between training and test examples. Finally, we assign one of the confusion set words the positive and the other the negative label, label each selected example, and remove from the context of each example the confusion set word.

We measure the performance of the classifier with different kernels with the area under the ROC curve (AUC) (see e.g. Fawcett [11]), and test the statistical significance of the performance difference between the various transformations and the baseline method using the Wilcoxon signed-ranks test [12].

In all the experiments, we select the value of the context span parameter s separately for each confusion set using a grid search (the grid points i.e. the possible values of s are $2^0, 2^1, \ldots, 2^6$). The grid searches are performed on the training data with a leave-one-out cross-validation (LOOCV). In some experiments, there are also other parameters to be selected, for example, the θ-parameter of the positional transformation. In those cases, we perform a two dimensional grid search over the possible values of the parameters s and θ.

First, we evaluate a naive Bayes (NB) classifier with the basic position sensitive (BP) model, that is, the NB classifier with the above described word-position features, and compare its performance to that of the NB classifier with the bag-of-words (BoW) model. The BP model clearly outperforms the BoW model on average as can be observed from Table 1. The performance gain is statistically significant ($p < 0.05$). The BoW model is better only with the data set *country-county*. In the performance comparison of our previous study [3] with the Senseval-3 data, the BoW model was better on average. Next, we test the smoothed position sensitive (SP) model, that is, the NB classifier whose class conditional probabilities are obtained from the positionally transformed feature frequency counts. The value of the θ-parameter is selected with a leave-one-out cross-validation with the training data together with the context span. Note that

Table 1. Comparison of naive Bayes classification performance with the bag-of-words (BoW) model, the basic position sensitive (BP) model, and the smoothed position sensitive (SP) model. The performances are measured with AUC. The performance difference of BP and BoW, SP and BoW, and SP and BP are denoted by Δ_1, Δ_2, and Δ_3, respectively.

	BoW	BP	Δ_1	SP	Δ_2	Δ_3
accept-except	99.17	99.76	0.59	99.80	0.63	0.04
affect-effect	97.51	98.80	1.29	98.85	1.34	0.05
among-between	88.57	90.56	1.99	90.99	2.42	0.43
amount-number	88.89	91.54	2.65	91.54	2.65	0.00
begin-being	97.77	98.61	0.84	98.60	0.82	-0.01
country-county	97.81	89.45	-8.36	97.81	0.00	8.36
fewer-less	78.67	78.79	0.11	80.79	2.11	2.00
I-me	97.17	99.27	2.11	99.27	2.10	-0.01
its-it's	94.72	96.91	2.19	96.89	2.16	-0.03
lead-led	94.60	96.90	2.30	96.92	2.32	0.02
maybe-may be	86.30	90.90	4.60	90.94	4.64	0.04
passed-past	96.12	98.71	2.59	98.75	2.62	0.03
peace-piece	97.20	97.68	0.48	97.2	0.00	-0.48
principal-principle	92.00	95.25	3.25	95.34	3.34	0.09
quiet-quite	96.07	98.68	2.60	98.68	2.60	0.00
raise-rise	90.72	97.39	6.67	97.23	6.51	-0.16
than-then	96.63	98.01	1.37	97.99	1.36	-0.01
weather-whether	97.25	98.90	1.65	98.95	1.70	0.05
your-you're	95.00	97.20	2.20	97.20	2.20	0.00
AVERAGE	93.80	95.44	1.64	95.99	2.19	0.55

this model encompasses both the BoW and the BP models as special cases because we obtain them when we set $\theta = 0$ and $\theta \to \infty$, respectively. Despite this, the classification performance with the SP model is slightly decreased compared to the performance with the BP model for some data sets (see Δ_3 in Table 1). This is possible, because the parameters selected using LOOCV with the training data are not necessarily optimal for the test data, that is, the parameter selection procedure overfits. Probably for this reason, we do not get the statistical significance for the performance difference of the BP and SP. However, the performance with SP model is always better or equal than that of the BoW model (see Δ_2 in Table 1) and the performance gain is statistically significant. The data set *country-county* favors the BoW model and this is detected by the parameter selection procedure, since it is the only one having an equal performance with the BoW and the SP models.

Next, we consider the Bayesian classifiers with the word transformations. The word transformation is constructed from the part-of-speech (PoS) information of words in the way described in Section 3. To obtain the PoS information, we used WordNet lookup, combined with the use of the WordNet *morphy* morphological analyzer for determining the PoS of inflected forms. All possibly applicable

Table 2. The naive Bayes classification performance with the basic position sensitive (BP) model compared to the performance of the Bayesian classifier with the word feature transformation (WT) (left), and to the performance of the Bayesian classifier with the combination (CB) of the word and the positional feature transformations (right). The performances are measured with AUC. The performance differences are denoted by Δ.

	BP	WT	Δ
accept-except	99.76	99.82	0.06
affect-effect	98.80	98.87	0.06
among-between	90.56	92.10	1.55
amount-number	91.54	91.37	-0.17
begin-being	98.61	98.81	0.19
country-county	89.45	91.97	2.52
fewer-less	78.79	82.66	3.87
I-me	99.27	99.34	0.07
its-it's	96.91	98.30	1.38
lead-led	96.90	97.49	0.59
maybe-may be	90.90	95.53	4.63
passed-past	98.71	98.96	0.25
peace-piece	97.68	98.63	0.95
principal-principle	95.25	96.15	0.90
quiet-quite	98.68	98.94	0.26
raise-rise	97.39	98.20	0.81
than-then	98.01	98.49	0.49
weather-whether	98.90	99.17	0.27
your-you're	97.20	98.32	1.12
AVERAGE	95.44	96.48	1.04

	BP	CB	Δ
accept-except	99.76	99.83	0.07
affect-effect	98.80	98.70	-0.10
among-between	90.56	93.91	3.36
amount-number	91.54	91.54	0.00
begin-being	98.61	98.81	0.20
country-county	89.45	97.44	7.99
fewer-less	78.79	80.26	1.47
I-me	99.27	99.27	-0.01
its-it's	96.91	98.16	1.25
lead-led	96.90	97.48	0.58
maybe-may be	90.90	95.52	4.61
passed-past	98.71	99.02	0.31
peace-piece	97.68	98.58	0.90
principal-principle	95.25	96.22	0.97
quiet-quite	98.68	98.95	0.27
raise-rise	97.39	97.99	0.61
than-then	98.01	98.48	0.47
weather-whether	98.90	99.14	0.24
your-you're	97.20	98.26	1.06
AVERAGE	95.44	96.71	1.28

parts-of-speech were assigned to words, for example, both the noun and verb PoS were assigned for the word *being*, which can be either a noun or an inflected form of the verb *be*. We used a table lookup to assign the PoS to the closed-class words, because they are not found in WordNet. Further, we included separate PoS tags for punctuation and numbers. Of the 10000 most common tokens, 8736 could be assigned at least one PoS using this procedure. The remaining 1264, consisting mostly of proper names but also containing, for example, abbreviations and multiword tokens such as *week-long*, were not assigned any PoS.

Similarly to the experiments with the positional transformations, we compare the performance of the word transformed Bayes classifier to the performance of the naive Bayes without the transformation, that is, the classifier with the BP model. Analogously to the positional transformation, we obtain the naive Bayes without transformations as a special case of the word transformed Bayes when we let $\mu \to \infty$. The results of the comparison are presented in Table 2. The performance gain between the word transformed Bayes and the Bayes without transformations is statistically significant.

Finally, we consider a Bayesian classifier together with the combination of the positional and the word transformation (see (7)). A performance comparison of the NB classifier without any transformations (i.e. with the BP model) and the word and positionally transformed Bayesian classifier is presented in Table 2. The performance gain is statistically significant. Again, due to the overfitting of the parameter selection procedure, for some data sets the classification performance with the transformation combination is slightly lower than the performance without transformations. On average, the performance with the transformation combination is better than the performance when only the positional or the word transformations is used.

5 Discussion

In this paper, we experiment with linear transformations of the feature frequency count matrices together with the Bayesian classifiers. For the particular task of natural language disambiguation that we use as a model problem, we define two types of feature transformations. The positional transformation is obtained using a Gaussian kernel on the word positions, and the word transformation is constructed from the part-of-speech information of the words. The results of the experiments show that the performance of the Bayesian classifiers in the natural language disambiguation tasks can be improved with both types of the transformations. The proposed use of linear transformations is a promising research direction in general, because it provides an elegant way to incorporate external information into the classifier.

The Gaussian kernel for the positions and the part-of-speech information of words are just examples of the information that can be incorporated into the classifiers. In the future, we plan to investigate other possibilities to construct the transformations such as variable width Gaussian kernels for the word positions. Moreover, in addition to the part-of-speech information of the words, there are many other possibilities to define the word similarities from which the word transformations can be constructed. For example, techniques based on the latent semantic analysis [13] are popularly used in several natural language processing tasks.

The proposed use of linear feature transformations is, of course, not restricted to the Bayesian classifiers. The transformations can also be used to construct kernel functions that can be applied by the kernel based learning algorithms, such as support vector machines. While the naive Bayes classifier is usually faster to train and therefore useful in situations in which small computation times are of importance, the kernel based learning algorithms are at present considered to be the state-of-the-art. Further, in our earlier experiments with the senseval-3 data [3], we found that certain disambiguation problems prefer NB while others prefer support vector machines (NB was slightly better on average). We consider the possibilities of the kernel methods in another study [14].

Acknowledgments

This work has been supported by Tekes, the Finnish National Technology Agency. We would like to thank Jouni Järvinen for his helpful comments on this manuscript.

References

1. Pahikkala, T., Ginter, F., Boberg, J., Jarvinen, J., Salakoski, T.: Contextual weighting for support vector machines in literature mining: an application to gene versus protein name disambiguation. BMC Bioinformatics **6** (2005) 157
2. Pahikkala, T., Pyysalo, S., Ginter, F., Boberg, J., Järvinen, J., Salakoski, T.: Kernels incorporating word positional information in natural language disambiguation tasks. In Russell, I., Markov, Z., eds.: Proceedings of the Eighteenth International Florida Artificial Intelligence Research Society Conference, Clearwater Beach, Florida, AAAI Press, Menlo Park, California (2005) 442–447
3. Pahikkala, T., Pyysalo, S., Boberg, J., Mylläri, A., Salakoski, T.: Improving the performance of bayesian and support vector classifiers in word sense disambiguation using positional information. In Honkela, T., Könönen, V., Pöllä, M., Simula, O., eds.: Proceedings of the International and Interdisciplinary Conference on Adaptive Knowledge Representation and Reasoning, Espoo, Finland, Helsinki University of Technology (2005) 90–97
4. John, G.H., Langley, P.: Estimating continuous distributions in bayesian classifiers. In Besnard, P., Hanks, S., eds.: Proceedings of the Eleventh Annual Conference on Uncertainty in Artificial Intelligence, San Mateo, Morgan Kaufmann Publishers (1995) 338–345
5. Jurafsky, D., Martin, J.H.: Speech and Language Processing: An Introduction to Natural Language Processing, Computational Linguistics, and Speech Recognition. Prentice Hall PTR, Upper Saddle River, New Jersey (2000)
6. Chen, S.F., Goodman, J.: An empirical study of smoothing techniques for language modeling. In Joshi, A., Palmer, M., eds.: Proceedings of the Thirty-Fourth Annual Meeting of the Association for Computational Linguistics, San Francisco, Morgan Kaufmann Publishers (1996) 310–318
7. Silverman, B.W.: Density Estimation for Statistics and Data Analysis. Chapman & Hall, London, UK (1986)
8. Hastie, T., Tibshirani, R., Friedman, J.H.: The Elements of Statistical Learning: Data Mining, Inference, and Prediction. Springer Verlag, New York (2001)
9. Golding, A.R., Roth, D.: A winnow-based approach to context-sensitive spelling correction. Machine Learning **34** (1999) 107–130
10. Rose, T.G., Stevenson, M., Whitehead, M.: The Reuters Corpus Volume 1: From yesterday's news to tomorrow's language resources. In Rodriguez, M.G., Araujo, C.P.S., eds.: Proceedings of the Third International Conference on Language Resources and Evaluation, ELRA, Paris, France (2002)
11. Fawcett, T.: Roc graphs: Notes and practical considerations for data mining researchers. Technical Report HPL-2003-4, HP Labs, Palo Alto, California (2003)
12. Wilcoxon, F.: Individual comparisons by ranking methods. Biometrics **1** (1945) 80–83
13. Deerwester, S.C., Dumais, S.T., Landauer, T.K., Furnas, G.W., Harshman, R.A.: Indexing by latent semantic analysis. Journal of the American Society of Information Science **41** (1990) 391–407
14. Pahikkala, T., Pyysalo, S., Boberg, J., Järvinen, J., Salakoski, T.: Matrix representations, linear transformations, and kernels for natural language processing (2006) Submitted.

Is a Morphologically Complex Language Really that Complex in Full-Text Retrieval?

Kimmo Kettunen and Eija Airio

University of Tampere, Department of Information Studies, Kanslerinrinne 1, FIN-33014, University of Tampere, Finland
Kimmo.kettunen@uta.fi, eija.airio@uta.fi

Abstract. In this paper we show that keyword variation of a morphologically complex language, Finnish, can be handled effectively for IR purposes by generating only the textually most frequent forms of the keyword. Theoretically Finnish nouns have about 2,000 different forms, but occurrences of most of the forms are rare. Corpus statistics showed that about 84 – 88 per cent of the occurrences of inflected noun forms are forms of only six cases out of the 14 possible. This number – maximally 2*6 – of keyword's variant forms makes it feasible to try them all in a search. IR results of the frequent keyword form variation coverage were tested with three to twelve keyword variant forms in two test collections, TUTK and CLEF 2003's Finnish material. The results show that the frequent keyword form generation method competes well with the gold standard, lemmatization, with nine and twelve variant keyword forms.

1 Introduction

Various methods for handling of the morphological variation of keywords in information retrieval (IR) have been used already for decades. Some of them are more complex than others, while some are amazingly simple but produce still quite good results in IR. So far it has been shown among other things that even a quite simple rule-based non-lexical stemmer can improve precision and recall of textual searches for languages that are morphologically quite rich, cf. [1, 2, 3]. In computational linguistics quarters it seems to have been a common belief that full coverage lemmatization is needed for languages that are morphologically complex [4], even in monolingual single term IR. This belief has been shared also by some IR researchers [5, 6.].

In the same time as simple conflation methods have been used in IR, not much attention has been given to heuristically based language aids that do not even aim to cover all the inflection of the keywords but are based, for example, on the statistically most frequent word forms of the language in question. We have earlier shown that our inflectional stem generation method and its further simulated developments compete quite well against the gold standard, FINTWOL, in a best-match IR for Finnish [7, 8]. In this paper we shall further question the need of a full coverage lemmatizer in monolingual IR of a morphologically complex language.

T. Salakoski et al. (Eds.): FinTAL 2006, LNAI 4139, pp. 411 – 422, 2006.

On a general level, our background motivations can be stated as follows:

1. The average precision and recall (P/R) of retrieval needs to be kept as high as possible without using excessively complex language technology tools; the need of lexicon-based lemmatizers in basic monolingual IR is not as high as often believed even for a morphologically complex language.
2. Performance of new methods introduced is compared to the state of art, usage of a lemmatizer, which is more challenging than use of raw words that has become all too common in IR, cf. e.g., [2, 9, 10, 11]. We have argued in [8] that the performance gained with raw words is quite meager and variable e.g. for Finnish, and thus the increases of performance given for different morphological processing methods are not as positive as they are shown to be. If comparisons are made, they should be made with respect to the state of the art or gold standard, not with respect to the worst possible result. With morphologically complex languages the best retrieval result is usually given by a lemmatizer, such as e.g. TWOL for different languages [4]. This line of argumentation is taken in the present study.

The structure of our paper is following. First we shall show the case distributions of Finnish nouns with corpus statistics. After that the discrepancy between grammatical forms and actual forms in a corpus is pinpointed. After this our research problems are stated, tested and discussed.

2 Case Distribution of Finnish Nouns

It is well known that the distributions of words and word forms are not even in texts. Some word forms occur often, some are rare. Even the distributions of different morphological categories have rates of their own, and both semantic and morphological factors play a role in distribution of word form frequencies [13, 14, 15, 16, 17, 18, 19, 20]. Karlsson [18, 19] shows with some semantically distinctive word types, how the case distributions of the words differ in Finnish. A word denoting to a place, *Helsinki*, has besides dominating nominative and genitive singular mainly occurrences of locative cases. A person's name like *Martti* occurs mostly in nominative singular. Same sort of analysis is given e.g. by Kostić et al. [20] for Serbian, although they seem to be hesitant about the semantic origins of the phenomenon. We shall not explore the semantic factors of case distribution any deeper, but analyze the distribution of cases on morphological level only.

Karlsson [21, pp. 308], citing research of Anneli Pajunen and Ulla Palomäki, presents figures about the distribution of cases for nouns in Finnish. The materials are from four different textual types of the Syntactic archives of Finnish, each comprising 5,000 word form tokens. In this data already the so called grammatical cases, nominative, genitive and partitive, cover 63.5 per cent of the overall distribution of case forms. If some marginal cases are included in this number, the resulting coverage is 67.5 per cent, over two thirds. Out of the other cases eight are so called locative cases (inner locatives: inessive, elative and illative), outer locatives (adessive, allative and ablative) and general locatives (essive and translative), and their share is 30.3 per cent, of which 17.8 per cent are inner locatives. Thus grammatical cases together with the inner locatives make 85.3 per cent of the occurrences of cases in the material.

Räsänen [22] gives a share of 78.2 % for the same six cases based on an analysis of 6 562 word form tokens in three small factual text samples.

When slightly bigger corpora are considered, almost the same distribution is found. In the whole collection of the Syntactic archives of Finnish consisting of 64,391 word form tokens of nouns, 88.2 per cent of the nouns are in the six most frequent cases [23, pp. 1180].

As e.g. Baayen [13, 14] and Biber [15, 16] emphasize, generalizations about linguistic phenomena should be based on large enough corpora. We were able to analyze or get information about two larger Finnish corpora. These were analyzed by a morphological lemmatizer, FINTWOL. We first analyzed the word form types of the inflected index of the TUTK collection [24], 719,011 word form types out of 12,109,779 word form tokens of the database, by running them through the FINTWOL program. All the noun interpretations given by FINTWOL, even ambiguous, were taken into these figures, and thus the figure is an approximation.

Our other and largest analyzed corpus was based on a 32 million word form token HUT corpus, which is one of the largest available corpora for Finnish. Out of the 32 million word form tokens about 11,3 million were analyzed by FINTWOL unambiguously as nouns [25]; these figures from data provided by [26]. In these two different and independent FINTWOL analyses case distributions for the six most frequent cases listed in Table 1 were found.

Table 1. Case distributions in the HUT and TUTK corpora

Cases	Number of noun tokens with one unambiguous TWOL analysis in the HUT corpus	Percentage	Number of noun types with all TWOL analyses in the TUTK corpus	Percentage
Nominative	3,758334	33.14	135,241	26.27
Genitive	2,900884	25.58	109,385	21.24
Partitive	1,428117	12.59	80,158	15.57
Inessive	819,333	7.23	31,007	6.02
Illative	593,513	5.23	41,778	8.11
Elative	520,101	4.59	38,392	7.45
SUM of the six cases	10,020,282/11,339,099	88.36 per cent	435 961/514,795	84. 68 per cent

After stating this, we shall shortly return to the number of forms of Finnish nouns. The usual figure given for the number of grammatical forms of Finnish nouns is about 2,000 [21: pp. 356]. This is achieved by the counting 2 (number) * 13 (cases) * 6 (possessives) * 12 (particles) = 1872. Figure 1,872 is a minimum, maximally the number is slightly over 2,000 if all the variant forms and rare cases etc. are counted for. As we can see from the figures, possessive endings and particles are mostly in charge for the huge number of grammatical word forms, because they can be combined to every inflected case form. Thus it is of interest to analyze the real occurrence of all the possessives and particles in nouns in a large enough corpus. According to the analyses [26, 29], only 3rd person possessive suffix had a share of 1,83 % when singular and plural are joined, other possessives had negligible distributions. From particles *–kin* had the biggest share, 0,25 %,. other occurrences of particles were negligible.

Relying on these analyses of four different corpora or sub-corpora, it can be argued that about 84 – 88 per cent of the case occurrences of Finnish nouns in (newspaper style) factual text are tokens of six cases only. That is about 43 % of the whole repertoire of Finnish cases. Furthermore particles and possessive endings that make the theoretical number of Finnish nouns so huge are so rare in running texts that they are not of practical importance.

3 Research Problems, Data and Methods

On the basis of these analyses we propose that reasonable or good IR performance can be achieved for Finnish by only taking maximally care of the six cases and their variation in keyword nouns. It is also possible that even with only three cases, nominative, genitive and partitive, quite realistic performance can be expected. The number of cases to be tried out in our tests will thus be three to six. This will mean three to twelve distinct forms of the search keys to be sought for in the database, as singular and plural forms of the cases are distinct. We shall call our method FCG, frequent case (form) generation. Procedures that are tested in this paper are presented and explained in Table 2.

Table 2. Frequent case form procedures to be tested.(* about, accurate number may be bigger in some cases due to variant forms in GEN PL and PTV PL; NOM = nominative, GEN = genitive, PTV = partitive; inner locatives = inessive, elative and illative, PL = plural, SG = singular)

Case forms in the procedure	Number of keyword forms in the procedure	Name of the procedure
NOM-GEN-PTV, only singular	3	FCG_3
NOM-GEN-PTV, singular and plural	6	FCG_6
NOM-GEN-PTV, singular and plural, inner locatives singular only	9*	FCG_9
NOM-GEN-PTV, singular and plural, inner locatives singular and plural	12*	FCG_12

If we contrast the numbers in column two of Table 2 to the theoretical number of Finnish noun forms, we see that in procedure FCG_12 only 0.64 % of the grammatical noun forms are counted for (12/1872). In FCG_3 only 0.16 % of the possible forms are used (3/1872). Thus the theoretical morphological complexity of Finnish in number of word forms boils down quite a bit and we still believe that reasonable or even good IR performance will be achieved with our procedures.

The emphasis of noun forms in the procedures is due to the well known fact that most of the information content of the texts is carried by nouns, and for that reason mostly nouns are important in queries [27: pp. 169]. Corpus analyses also show that about 35 – 45 per cent of the word tokens in running Finnish texts are nouns. On type level the percentage is 65 – 75 % [28, 29]. Thus the importance of other word classes than nouns in IR is small, and the variation in e.g. verbs does not affect retrieval. Besides nouns we also put adjectives in the FCG procedures in variant case forms; verbs and words of other word classes in topics (besides stop words) were taken into queries in the form they were in the topic.

Our research problem is twofold:

1. Does frequent case form generation of keywords work in IR of a morphologically complex language?
2. If it works, what is the best balance between number of generated keyword form variants and achieved mean average precision in retrieval?

We shall test our case procedures with two collections: TUTK and the Finnish CLEF 2003 material using the InQuery search engine. Both collections have almost the same number of Finnish newspaper articles: TUTK has 53,893 articles from three newspapers from years 1988 – 1992 [24], and CLEF 2003 has 55,344 articles from one newspaper from years 1994 – 1995 [3, 30]. In TUTK [24, 31] we have 30 test topics. The original four relevance levels of the collection are combined in this study: relevance level 3 of TUTK, level of most relevant documents, is called stringent, relevance levels 2 and 3 – level of most relevant and relevant documents – are joined as normal and all the three relevance levels, 1 – 3, are joined as liberal relevance; The rest of the documents, both un-judged and those judged as irrelevant, are taken as irrelevant in this study. In CLEF 2003 we have 60 test topics and binary relevance.

Queries for the test runs were formed partly manually from the topics. After automated initial inflectional stem generation and InQuery query structure generation, the needed case endings were edited to the inflectional stems of the query words, cf. [8]. Thus we simulated carefully the effects of automated rule-based frequent case form generation. Word form generators for Finnish have been implemented since the 1980's [12, 32, 33], but they were not available for this study.

As an example we can take one query from the CLEF 2003 collection. Query #144 for the FCG_3 process is as follows:

#q144 = #sum(#syn(sierra sierran sierraa) #syn(leone leonen leonea) #syn(kapina kapinan kapinaa) #syn(timantti timantin timanttia) #syn(vaikutus vaikutusta vaikutuksen) #syn(kapina kapinan kapinaa) #syn(poliittinen poliittista poliittisen) #syn(epävakaus epävakauden epävakautta) #syn(sierra sierran sierraa) #syn(leone leonen leonea) #syn(timanttiteollisuus timanttiteollisuuden timanttiteollisuutta));

The queries are of the form #SUM(#SYN() #SYN()…), and thus they are strongly structured [34]. Morphological variant forms of the keyword are treated as synonyms of the key, and InQuery treats them as instances of one key [35, 36].

Results of the FCG procedures are compared to results of FINTWOL lemmatization and Snowball stemming, which have earlier been shown to work well in Finnish best-match retrieval [3, 7, 8]. Results with plain keywords are shown for comparison as a worst case performance.

4 Results

Results with the TUTK collection are presented in Table 3. Differences in the tables are actual percentages, not relative. (* In the Plain method keywords are taken as such straight from the topics in the forms they happen to be there.)

Table 3. Results of test runs in the TUTK collection on three relevance levels

Method	Liberal relevance Mean average precision (per cent) - interpolated	Normal relevance Mean average precision (per cent) - interpolated	Stringent relevance Mean average precision (per cent) - interpolated
FINTWOL – lemmatized index, compounds split in the index	37.8	35.0	24.1
FCG_12, inflectional index	32.7 (-5.1)	30.0 (-5.0)	21.4 (-2.7)
FCG _9, inflectional index	32.4 (-5.4)	29.6 (-5.4)	21.3 (-2.8)
FCG _6, inflectional index	30.9 (-6.9)	28.0 (-7.0)	21.0 (-3.1)
Snowball, stemmed index	29.8 (-8.0)	27.7 (-7.3)	20.0 (-4.1)
FCG _3, inflectional index	26.4 (-11.4)	23.9 (-11.1)	18.9 (-5.2)
*Plain, inflectional index	19.6 (-18.2)	18.9 (-16.1)	12.4 (-11.7)

Results from the CLEF 2003 runs are in Table 4. Non-interpolated figures for FINTWOL, Snowball and Plain are from [3] and they are shown for comparison.

Results are quite similar in both collections, although FCGs perform better in the CLEF collection overall. FCG_3 performs very poorly in CLEF 2003 collection, and it outperforms plain words only slightly, while in TUTK the difference between FCG_3 and Plain keywords is clear. FCG_6 performs much better in CLEF 2003 than

Table 4. Results of test runs in CLEF 2003 collection

Method	Mean average precision (per cent) - interpolated	Mean average precision (per cent) - non-interpolated
FINTWOL		
- lemmatized index, compounds split in the index	37.6	50.5
- lemmatized index, compounds not split in the index	34.7 (-2.9)	47.0 (-3.5)
Snowball, stemmed index	35.8 (-1.8)	48.5 (-2.0)
FCG_12, inflectional index	34.0 (-3.6)	46.4 (-4.1)
FCG_9, inflectional index	33.7 (-3.9)	46.1 (-4.4)
FCG_6, inflectional index	30.1 (-7.5)	41.5 (-9.0)
FCG_3, inflectional index	24.2 (-13.4)	32.6 (-17.9)
Plain, inflectional index	22.7 (-14.9)	31.0 (-19.5)

FCG_3, but still hangs 6.5 – 9 per cent-units below Snowball and FINTWOL. In neither collection FCG_12 brings much gain to FCG_9, it is only 0.1 – 0.4 per cent-units better than FCG_9.

Our best case procedures, FCG_9 and FCG_12 perform well in both collections and they are only 3.6 – 4.4. per cent behind FINTWOL in CLEF 2003 and 2.8 - 5.4 per cent in TUTK depending on the relevance level.

We tested the statistical significance of the differences between the best methods in both collections using the Friedman test. Tested methods were FINTWOL, Snowball, FCG_12, FCG_9 and FCG_6. Although FCGs do not outperform Snowball in CLEF 2003 on any level, the differences between FCG__9, FCG__12, FCG__6 and Snowball are not statistically significant. The difference between FINTWOL using split compound index and FCG__6 was statistically significant ($p = 0.005$) in CLEF 2003. Difference between FINTWOL with compounds not split and FCG__6 was also statistically significant ($p = 0.02$). Differences between FINTWOL, FCG__9 and FCG__12 were not statistically significant in CLEF 2003.

In the TUTK collection the differences were more often statistically significant. Table 5 presents the statistical differences in the TUTK collection when the Friedman test was used. Only significant differences are listed.

Table 5. Statistically significant differences between the best methods in the TUTK collection

	Liberal relevance	Normal relevance	Stringent relevance
FINTWOL	> ALL	> ALL	> ALL but FCG_9
FCG_12	---	> Snowball p = 0.02	---
FCG_9	---	> Snowball p = 0.01	---
FCG_9	---	> FCG_6 p = 0.03	---

5 Discussion

According to the results it seems that the nine forms of FCG__9 are optimal for the search in both collections. By adding three more keyword forms to the query, only marginal gains are achieved. This is shown more clearly in Figure 1, where mean average precisions from both collections are compared to the number of variant keyword forms (for TUTK only the liberal relevance level curves are shown).

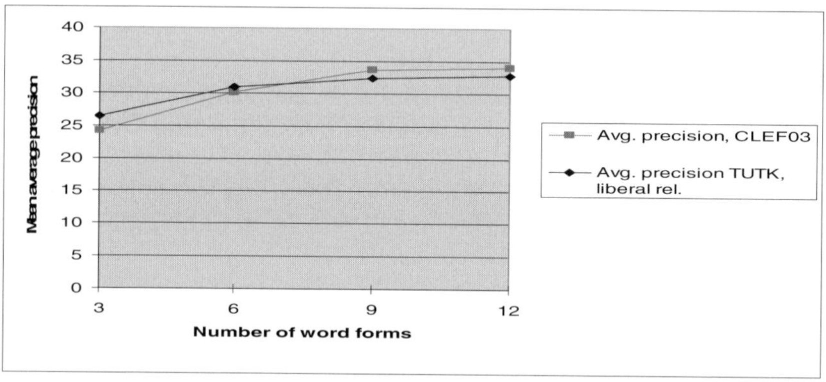

Fig. 1. Number of variant keyword forms and mean average precisions of FCG procedures

The figure shows that the mean average precisions of the queries almost stop rising in both collections after nine forms. This may be due to two reasons: either there is no large gain to be achieved with any of the added forms after nine forms, or the three additional forms in process FCG__12 are not the right ones (plural forms of inner locatives). From the results of frequency analysis it is possible that also singular forms of two outer locative cases (adessive and allative) or general locative cases (essive and translative) could be better forms to be used in addition to the nine forms. This was not tested any further. It is possible that a slight improvement of average precision over FCG__12 can be achieved by using different case forms beyond the

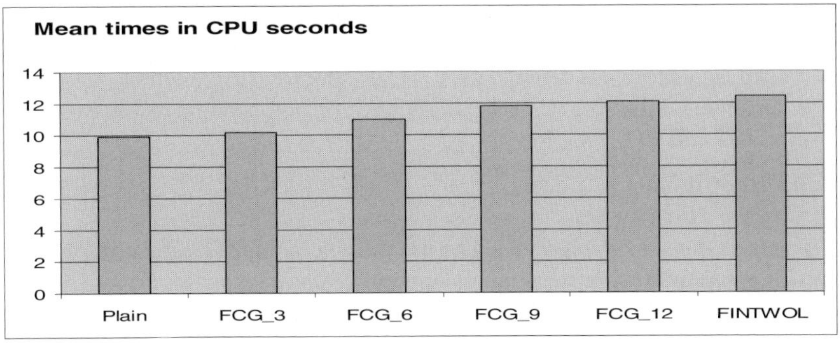

Fig. 2. Mean runtimes in CPU seconds with 60 queries of CLEF 2003

nine forms of the procedure FCG__9. In single queries this is at least certainly true, as the semantic types of the keywords may favor some other cases than those used in our FCGs.

Our experiments showed also that the use of three to twelve full form variants of each keyword is computationally tractable. Results of the CPU time tests for the whole set of 60 queries in CLEF 2003 are shown in Figure 2 (mean CPU seconds of five consecutive runs, system time + user time of Unix's *time* function added together; test system was a Sun Sparc Station with two 1,015 GHz processors and 4 GB memory under a timesharing load of a few concurrent users).

As can be seen from Figure 2, adding keyword forms to FCG procedures does not increase runtimes very much. The increase in mean CPU time is only about 20 % when maximal 12 keyword forms are used instead of three. Plain unprocessed keywords are fastest to run, and slightly surprisingly FINTWOL queries are not faster to run than FCG processes.

In earlier publications we compared other types of morphological variant handling to lemmatization. Inflectional stem generation was found to be almost as effective in average precision as lemmatization, but it resulted in slowly processed very large queries [7]. When inflectional stems were enhanced with regular expressions which restricted the choice of possibly matching words from the index, queries were faster to run and more manageable in size, but they had lower average precision [8]. When compared to these results, FCG style of keyword handling seems to be the most optimal in both average precision and runtime for inflectional indexes. The best FCG processes achieve about 86 % of the best gold standard results in TUTK and about 90 % of the best results in CLEF 2003. If best FCGs are compared to FINTWOL in CLEF 2003 with non-split compound index, FCG_12 achieves about 98 % of the mean average precision of FINTWOL and FCG_9 about 97 %. As this performance level is achieved without runtime penalties in inflected indexes, the results can be considered very good.

Thus the use of frequent case form generator as shown in this paper would be a viable alternative to be used in real query systems, such as web search engines, which do not many times have any means for handling the morphological variation of keywords in many languages. It should also be noted that the mean number of keywords given by a web-user is less than three [37]. We had long queries made out of long topics, but they ran fine. Our method has also other advantages besides a reasonable average P/R: it works with inflected form indexes and will not suffer as much from out of vocabulary words as lemmatizers; FCGs should also be simple to implement for new languages, even if they are language specific and need linguistic expertise.

6 Conclusion

The purpose of this paper was to evaluate use of only the most frequent keyword forms in a monolingual full-text retrieval of a highly inflectional language, Finnish. The forms to be used in retrieval were first analyzed from several text corpora of variable sizes. Corpus analysis showed that six cases constituted about 84 – 88 % of the token level occurrences of case forms for nouns – thus covering 84 – 88 % of the possible variation of about 2000 distinct inflectional forms of nouns. This shows that, while a language may in principle be morphologically complex, in practice it is much less so. Based on this finding, four different simulated frequent case form generation procedures (FCGs) were tested in two different full-text collections, TUTK and CLEF 2003.

The results show that frequent case form generation works in full-text retrieval in a best-match query system and competes at best well with the gold standard, lemmatization, for Finnish. Our best FCG procedures, FCG_9 and FCG_12, achieved about 86 % of the best average precisions of FINTWOL in TUTK and about 90 % in CLEF 2003. The runtimes of the FCG queries were also shown to be comparable to those of the other methods. Thus the hitherto unused method, frequent case form generation for morphologically complex languages, appears as a simple and effective alternative to more traditional methods like lemmatization or stemming in IR.

It was also shown that corpus statistics of inflectional form distributions were useful for choosing a limited set of basic case forms to cover in a language technology application of a single highly inflectional language. This finding together with general knowledge about token frequency distributions suggests that the method is suitable for other languages too, and thus our results need not be language specific only. Morphologically less complex languages may be served with simpler FCGs with quite few word forms. As the presented method is easily testable for any language of even modest morphological complexity, it can be evaluated on a language by language basis.

Acknowledgements

We wish to thank Mr. Mathias Creutz for providing the data of the HUT corpus. Kal Järvelin has commented earlier drafts of this paper insightfully. We are also grateful to the FIRE research group for helpful comments.

The InQuery search engine was provided by the Center for Intelligent Information Retrieval at the University of Massachusetts, Amherst.

FINTWOL (morphological description of Finnish). Copyright © Kimmo Koskenniemi and Lingsoft plc. 1983 – 1993.

The Snowball Finnish stemming algorithm is available at http://snowball.tartarus.org/algorithms/finnish/stemmer.html. (Accessed November 28th, 2003).

References

1. Popovič, M., Willett, P.: The Effectiveness of Stemming for Natural-Language Access to Slovene Textual Data. Journal of the American Society for Information Science 43 (1992) 384–390
2. Hollink, V., Kamps, J., Monz, C.,de Rijke, M.: Monolingual Document Retrieval for European Languages. Information Retrieval 7 (2004) 33–52
3. Airio, E.: Word Normalization and Decompounding in Mono- and Bilingual IR. Information Retrieval (2005), to appear.
4. Koskenniemi, K.: Finite State Morphology and Information Retrieval. Natural Language Engineering 2 (1996) 331 – 336
5. Galvez, C., Moya-Anegón, F., Solana, V. H.: Term Conflation Methods in Information Retrieval. Non-linguistic and Linguistic Approaches. Journal of Documentation 61 (2005) 520 – 547.
6. Jacquemin, C., Tzoukerman, E.: NLP for Term Variant Extraction: Synergy between Morphology, Lexicon, and Syntax. In Strzralkowski, T. (ed.): Natural Language Information Retrieval. Kluwer Academic Publishers, Dordrecht Boston London (1999) 25 – 74
7. Kettunen, K.: Developing an Automatic Linguistic Truncation Operator for Best-match Retrieval in Inflected Word Form Text Database Indexes. To appear in Journal of Information Science 32 (2006)
8. Kettunen, K., Kunttu, T., Järvelin, K.: To Stem or Lemmatize a Highly Inflectional Language in a Probabilistic IR Environment? Journal of Documentation 61 (2005) 476 – 496
9. Braschler, M., Ripplinger, B: How Effective is Stemming and Decompounding for German Text Retrieval? Information Retrieval 7 (2004) 291 – 316
10. Mayfield, J., McNamee, P. Single N-gram Stemming. In: Proceedings of Sigir2003, The Twenty-Sixth Annual International ACM SIGIR Conference on Research and Development in Information Retrieval (2003) 415–416
11. Tomlinson, S.: Lexical and Algorithmic Stemming Compared for 9 European Languages with Hummingbird SearchServer™ at CLEF 2003. Availabe at: http://clef.iei.pi.cnr.it/2003/WN_web/19.pdf (accessed April 28th, 2004)
12. Koskenniemi, K: A System for Generating Finnish Inflected Word Forms. In Karlsson, F. (ed.): Computational Morphosyntax. Report on research 1981 – 84. Publications of the Department of General linguistics, University of Helsinki. No. 13 (1985) 63 – 80
13. Baayen, R. H.: Statistical Models for Word Frequency Distribution. Computers and the Humanities 26 (1993) 347 – 363
14. Baayen, R. H.: Word Frequency Distributions. Kluwer Academic Publishers, Dordrecht Boston London (2001)
15. Biber, D.: Representativeness in Corpus Design. Literary and Linguistic Computing 8 (1993) 243 – 257
16. Biber, D.: Using Register-diversified Corpora for General Language Studies. Computational Linguistics 19 (1993) 219 – 241
17. Manning, C. D., Schütze, H.:. Foundations of Statistical Natural Language Processing. The MIT Press, Cambridge, Massachusetts (1999)
18. Karlsson, F.: Frequency Considerations in Morphology. Zeitsschrift für Phonetik, Sprachwissenschaft und Kommunikationsforschung 39 (1986) 19 – 28
19. Karlsson, F.: Defectivity. In: Booij G. et al. (eds.): Morphology. An International Handbook on Inflection and Word-Formation. Volume 1. Walter de Gruyter, Berlin (2000) 647 – 654

20. Kostić, A., Marković, T., Baucal, A:. Inflectional Morphology and Word Meaning: Orthogonal or Co-implicative Cognitive Domains. In: Baayen, R. H., Schreuder R. (eds.): Morphological Structure in Language Processing. Trends in Linguistics, Studies and Monographs 151. Mouton de Gruyter, Berlin (2003) 1 – 43
21. Karlsson, F.: Suomen kielen äänne- ja muotorakenne. WSOY, Helsinki (1983)
22. Räsänen, S.: Havaintoja suomen sijojen frekvensseistä. (Observations of frequencies of the Finnish cases) Sananjalka 21 (1979) 17–43
23. Hakulinen, A., Vilkuna, M., Korhonen, R., Koivisto, V., Heinonen, T.R., Alho, I. Iso suomen kielioppi.: Suomalaisen Kirjallisuuden Seura, Helsinki (2004)
24. Sormunen, E.: A Method for Measuring Wide Range Performance of Boolean Queries in Full-text Databases. Acta Universitatis Tamperensis 748, Tampere (2000)
25. Creutz, M., Linden, K.: Morpheme Segmentation Gold Standards for Finnish and English. Helsinki University of Technology. Publications in Computer and Information Science. Report A77. Espoo (2004)
26. Creutz, M.: Two E-mails, May 17, 2005
27. Baeza-Yates, R., Ribeiro-Neto B.: Modern Information Retrieval. Addison Wesley, USA 1999
28. Saukkonen, P., Haipus, M., Niemikorpi A., Sulkala, H:. Suomen kielen taajuussanasto. (A Frequency Dictionary of Finnish). WSOY, Helsinki (1979)
29. Kettunen, K.: Sijamuodot haussa - tarvitseeko kaikkea hakutermien morfologista vaihtelua kattaa? Ms. Sci. Thesis, University of Tampere, Department of Information Studies (2005)
30. Peters, C.: Introduction to the CLEF 2003 Working Notes. Available at http://www.clef-campaign.org/2003/WN_web/00.2%20-%20intro.pdf. Accessed 1st September 2005.
31. Sormunen E.: The Effectiveness of Free-text Searching in Full-text Databases Containing Newspaper Articles and Abstracts. Research Publications 790. Technical Research Centre of Finland., Espoo (In Finnish, English abstract) (1994)
32. Holman, E.: Finnmorf: A Computerized Research Tool for Students of Finnish Morphology. Computers and the Humanities 22 (1988) 165 – 172
33. Lassila, E.: Suomen kielen sanamuodot taivuttava ohjelma FORMO. In: Mäkelä, M. Linnainmaa , S., Ukkonen, E (eds.): STeP-88. Invited Papers. Contributed Papers: Applications. Helsinki: Finnish Artificial Intelligence Society (1988) 118 – 126
34. Kekäläinen, J.: The Effects of Query Complexity, Expansion and Structure on Retrieval Performance in Probabilistic Text Retrieval. Acta Universitatis Tamperensis 678 , Tampere(1999)
35. Allan, J., Callan, J., Croft, B., Ballesteros, L., Byrd, D., Swan, R., Xu, J.: INQUERY Does Battle with TREC-6. In: Voorhees, E. & Harman, D. (Eds.) Proceedings of the TREC 6 Conference. (1997). Available from http://trec.nist.gov/pubs/trec6/t6_proceedings.html. Accessed Nov 15, 2005
36. Broglio, J., Callan, J., Croft, W.B.: INQUERY System Overview. In: Proceedings of the TIPSTER text program (Phase I). San Francisco, CA: Morgan Kaufmann Publishers. (1994)
37. Jansen, B., Spink, A., Sarasevic, T.: Real Life, Real Users, and Real Needs: a Study and Analysis of User Queries on the Web. Information Processing & Management 36 (2000) 207–227

Language Independent Answer Prediction from the Web

Alejandro Figueroa and Günter Neumann*

Deutsches Forschungszentrum für Künstliche Intelligenz - DFKI,
Stuhlsatzenhausweg 3, D - 66123, Saarbrücken, Germany
alejandro@coli.uni-sb.de, neumann@dfki.de

Abstract. This work presents a strategy that aims to extract and rank predicted answers from the web based on the eigenvalues of a specially designed matrix. This matrix models the strength of the syntactic relations between words by means of the frequency of their relative positions in sentences extracted from web snippets. We assess the rank of predicted answers by extracting answer candidates for three different kinds of questions. Due to the low dependence upon a particular language, we also apply our strategy to questions from four different languages: English, German, Spanish, and Portuguese.

1 Introduction

Normally, textual Question Answering (textQA) systems receive natural language queries as input, process large unstructured document collections, and return precise answers as output. The success of current textQA technology is due to the fact that they are combining technology from different areas (e.g., information retrieval, information extraction and natural language processing) in novel ways, cf. [1]. However, scaling this new QA technology to the Web in order to improve current search engines to efficiently locating information presents extraordinary challenges, cf. [2]. Consider for example the enormous size of the Web content that is currently indexed by the best search engines (Billions of Web pages). While an indexing of TREC–like corpus (only few Gigabytes in size, mainly newspaper text sources, fixed time period) on basis of NLP–oriented preprocessing has been shown to be very fruitful for textQA technology, doing the same for the Web is out of the reach with current technology. Another important aspect of the Web is its growing multilinguality, cf. [3]. Therefore, the exploration of language independent QA core technology is requested.

There exists first web–based QA systems (webQA) that successfully demonstrate how QA technology might improve future search engines by systematically exploiting the redundancy of the Web space, e.g., [4,6,3,5]. All of these systems have a similar architecture and perform three major steps:

* The work presented here was partially supported by a research grant from the German Federal Ministry of Education, Science, Research and Technology (BMBF) to the DFKI projects Quetal (FKZ: 01 IW C02) and HyLaP (FKZ: 01 IW F02).

T. Salakoski et al. (Eds.): FinTAL 2006, LNAI 4139, pp. 423–434, 2006.

1. conversion of NL questions to search engine specific queries
2. interface to public search engines for document retrieval
3. extraction of answers from the retrieved web pages

The first step is needed in order to take advantage of a particular search engine's query syntax, and to increase the accuracy of potential relevant documents. The latter can be seen as a kind of "answer context prediction". For example a question like "Who is the president of Germany?" might be converted to search engine queries "the president of Germany is" or "Germany's president". Of course, without any corpus analysis this would just be a "blind" generate–and–test approach, so often these answering patterns are computed and weighted on basis of a statistical data analysis, cf. e.g., [6] and [7].

This sort of NL query analysis is similar to a query expansion strategy which is applied *before document retrieval*. In IR there exists also an alternative query expansion strategy, namely to perform the query expansion *after document retrieval*, which is also known as *pseudo relevance feedback* (PRF), cf. [8]. The advantage of PRF is that one can achieve a data–driven query expansion using the most relevant documents retrieved by the IR system. Applying this technology in a webQA system on basis of the retrieved documents, however might be negatively influenced by the time needed for fetching the N–best documents. Since this crawling process has to be done online, it defines a critical parameter for the latency of the subsequent webQA processes, and hence, might negatively effect the performance of the whole webQA system, cf. [6]. Fortunately, almost all modern search engines return a brief textual summary (called *snippet*) together with the URL of the candidate documents immediately as part of the query result.

In this paper, we apply the idea of PRF in the context of webQA, by performing query expansion on the set of N–best snippets retrieved using the NL query as it is, i.e., without converting it initially to possible query paraphrases. In contrast to the answer context prediction step mentioned above, we propose an *answer candidate prediction* strategy: the expanded query terms are interpreted as either direct answers to the NL user query or as terms which are semantically related to potential answer candidates. Note that answer candidates are usually not complete sentences but rather phrasal entities. Our answer predication strategy is completely data–driven. Thus it is very robust wrt. the form of the snippets and it is highly language independent. In order to evaluate our new methods we considered three specific type of questions for four languages (German, English, Spanish, Portuguese). We also designed answer extraction modules that resemble traditional systems, so to compare the extracted answers with the answers in the CLEF multilingual question/answer corpus.[1]

[1] For more information on CLEF (Cross–language Evaluation Forum) see http://www.clef-campaign.org/ .

2 System Overview

The user enters via some input device a NL query which is further passed to a search engine. The search engine returns a ranked list of document links together with a snippet for each document. The best N–snippets are passed to the answer prediction component. This component extracts from all snippets the best predicted answer strings. A predicted answer string is a substring extracted from the snippets for which a high semantic similarity to the question has been determined. Unlike PRF, the predicted answers are ranked and the M–best are submitted to the answer extraction component. It further splits the predicted answer strings into smaller units which might correspond to exact answer strings. The answer extraction component uses the NL user question in order to determine the expected answer type (EAT). For example, for a question like "Who is the president of USA?", the instance of EAT is PERSON. Since our goal is to be as language independent as possible and our focus is to evaluate the quality of the answer prediction strategy, this step resembles any traditional system based on pattern matching and lexical databases.

3 Ranking Scheme

Our system ranks two kind of strings: sentences and predicted answers. Since both are treated in the same way, we only describe the problem of ranking sentences in more detail. Formally, it can be specified as:

$$R = \{(s_1, l_1), (s_2, l_2), \ldots, (s_\sigma, l_\sigma)\}$$

where R is the rank of the set S of sentences of document D; s_s is the s–th sentence in S, $1 \leq s \leq \sigma$, where σ is the number of sentences in the document. We say that s_1 is preferred over s_2, if $l_1 > l_2$, where $l_s = rank(s_s)$, and $rank$ is a ranking rule that maps from the sentences to rank labels $rank : S \rightarrow L$.

3.1 Document Representation

In our system, a document is a multi–set of all the sentences which are extracted from all the N–best snippets returned by the search engine. We are using very simple rules for mapping a snippet to a stream of sentences, basically by using the standard punctuation signs as splitting points: colon, semicolon, coma, and dot. We will use W (the dictionary) for the set of all unique words in D, and $\omega = |W|$ the size of W. We start our description of a vector–space document representation by defining the following binary variable:

$$X_{sik} = \begin{cases} 1 \text{ if the word } w_i \text{ is in the sentence } s_s \text{ at position } k \\ 0 \text{ otherwise.} \end{cases}$$

Let $len(S_s)$ be a function which returns the number of words in a sentence S_s. Then, the frequency of the word w_i in the document is given by:

$$freq(w_i) = \sum_{s=1}^{\sigma} \sum_{k=1}^{len(s_s)} X_{sik}, \quad \forall w, \ 1 \leq i \leq \omega \tag{1}$$

Let w_j be a word in W, $1 \leq j \leq \omega$. For example, in a document D="JOHN LOVES MARY. JOHN KISSES MARY EVERY NIGHT.", we find two sentences determined by the dot. If we consider that "w_1" is "JOHN", then X_{111} will match the first occurrence of "JOHN" and X_{211} the second. X_{s1k} takes the value of one for only this two occurrences. Therefore, $freq$("JOHN") will be the sum of $X_{111} + X_{211} = 2$.

A document D is represented by the set of tuples:

$$D = \{\langle w_i, w_j, \epsilon, freq(w_i, w_j, \epsilon)\rangle, \ \forall\, i, j, \epsilon, 0 \leq \epsilon \leq \Upsilon \wedge freq(w_i, w_j, \epsilon) > 0\}$$

where $freq(w_i, w_j, \epsilon)$ is the frequency of w_i with which it appears to the left of w_j, Υ is the length of the longest sentence in the document, and ϵ is the absolute distance of their positions in the sentence:

$$freq(w_i, w_j, \epsilon) = \sum_{s=1}^{\sigma} \sum_{k=\epsilon+1}^{len(s_s)} X_{si(k-\epsilon)} X_{sjk} \tag{2}$$

For instance, $freq$("JOHN", "MARY", 1) = 2 means that the pattern JOHN * MARY was observed 2–times in document D. We also define $\Gamma(w_i, w_j, \epsilon, v) : W \times W \times N \times N \rightarrow \{0, 1\}$, as a function that returns 1 if the $freq(w_i, w_j, \epsilon)$ is equal to v, otherwise it returns zero. Using this notation, we define:

$$G(v) = \sum_{i=1}^{\omega} \sum_{j=1}^{\omega} \sum_{\epsilon=1}^{\Upsilon} \Gamma(w_i, w_j, \epsilon, v) \tag{3}$$

$G(v)$ determines the amount of pairs of words that occur v times in the document. In our example, the only tuple that occurs two times is JOHN * MARY, then $G(2) = 1$.

3.2 Ranking Sentences

We rank a sentence s_s in a document by means of a specially designed matrix M. This matrix is constructed from the tuples in D in the following way:

$$M_{ij}(s_s) = \begin{cases} freq(w_i, w_j, \epsilon) \text{ if } i < j; \\ freq(w_j, w_i, \epsilon) \text{ if } i > j; \\ 0 \qquad\qquad\quad \text{otherwise.} \end{cases}$$

w_i and w_j are two words in s_s, ϵ is the distance between w_i and w_j, ϵ=$abs(i$-$j)$, $0 \leq \epsilon \leq \alpha$, and α=$len(s_s)$. This matrix models the strength of the relation or correlation between two words w_i and w_j in a sentence s_s.

The following filtering rule (which is the same for all languages) reduces the size of the representation of D and the noise of long sequences of low correlated words:

$$\forall i, j \ M_{ij} \leq \zeta \Rightarrow M_{ij} = 0$$

where ζ is an empirical determined threshold. This rule allows us to remove some syntactic relations of a word which are probably not important. For example, the English word *of* is a *closed class word* and as such will co-occur very often with different words at different positions. However, if it is part of a phrase like *The President of Germany*, the definition above allows us to keep *of* in the noun phrase, because it typically occurs with short distance in such specific syntactic construction.

Now, we define the **rank of a sentence** s_s as follows:

$$rank(s_s) = \lambda_{max}(M(s_s))$$

where $\lambda_{max}(M(s_s))$ is the **greatest eigenvalue** of the matrix M constructed from the sentence s_s, see also [14]. This eigenvalue gives us the amount of "energy" or "syntactic bonding force" captured by the eigenvector related with λ_{max}. Note that computing the eigenvalues for a small matrix is not a demanding task, and M is a matrix of size $len(s_s)$, which in case of snippets is small. There are two more aspects of M that is worths mentioning:

1. $\forall i\, M_{ii} = 0 \Rightarrow \sum_{\forall i} M_{ii} = 0 \Rightarrow \sum_{\forall f} \lambda_f = 0$.
2. $\forall i, j\, M_{ij} = M_{ji}$, the *spectral theorem* implies that $\forall f\, \lambda_f \in \Re$, and all the eigenvectors are orthogonal.[2]

The second aspect guarantees that for each sentence S_s, we will obtain a real value for $rank(s_s)$.

3.3 Extracting Predicted Answers

The matrix M contains the frequency of each pair of words of s_s, which appears in this sentence and which has the same distance in the whole document. We interpret sequences of word pairs which frequently co–occur with same distance in M as *chains of related words*, i.e., groups of words that have an important meaning in the document. This is important if we also consider the fact that, in general, snippets are not necessary contiguous pieces of texts, and usually are not syntactically well–formed paragraphs due to some intentionally introduced breaks (e.g., denoted by some dots betweens the text fragments). We claim that these chains can be used for extracting answer prediction candidates. Algorithm 1 extracts predicted answers from a sentence s_s. It aims to replace low correlated words with a star, where a low correlated word is a word in a sentence that has a low correlation with any other word in the same sentence. Sequences of high correlated words are separated by one or more stars. Thus, low correlated words in a sentences define the points for cutting a sentence into smaller units.

[2] The *spectral theorem* claims that for a real symmetric n-by-n matrix, like M, all its eigenvalues λ_f are real, and there exist n linearly eigenvectors e_f for this matrix which are mutually orthogonal.

Algorithm 1: extractPredictedAnswers

```
input : M,s_s
begin
    predictedAnswers = s_s;
    if numberOfWords(w_i) > 3 then
        forall w_i ∈ s_s do
            flag = true;
            forall w_j ∈ s_s do
                if M_ijε > 0 then flag=false;
            end
            if flag then replace w_i with "*";
        end
        predictedAnswers = split(s_s,"*");
    end
    return predictedAnswers;
end
```

3.4 Ranking Predicted Answers

We rank every predicted answer ν extracted from a sentence s_s according to the following formula:

$$rank(\nu) = rank(s_s) * \sum_{b=2}^{\beta} P(B_b|B_{b-1})$$

where B_b are the words in ν, and β its length. This formula weights each piece of the sentence according to the probabilities of their bi–grams, which are estimated by the following formulae:

$$P(B_b|B_{b-1}) = \frac{log(freq(B_{b-1}, B_b, 1))}{log(freq(B_{b-1}))}$$

where we use the logarithm to smooth the frequencies, so to reduce the trend to favor high frequent words [9]. We consider the summation of the probabilities of bi–grams because we want to bias the ranking in such a way that longer predicted answers are preferred over shorter ones. Finally, redundant predicted answers are removed. A predicted answer ν is redundant if and only if the following conditions hold:

1. If there exists another predicted answer $\nu^{'}$, such that $rank(\nu) < rank(\nu^{'})$.
2. If ν is a substring of $\nu^{'}$.

If both conditions hold, we say that $\nu^{'}$ *contains* ν. For this comparison, we consider capitalized strings.

4 Answer Extraction

There is no standard strategy to evaluate predicted answers, but it is clear that the goal is to help the answer extraction step. Evaluating the predicted answers in a straight forward way is too ambiguous and/or unfair. For this reason, we assume that extracting answer candidates from the rank of predicted answers gives us an unbiased notion of how good is the distribution of the predicted answers which do not contain an answer candidate. During this step, no further re-ranking is performed.

In general, a *correct answer* corresponds to an instance of a concept, which is the focus or the *expected answer type* (EAT) of a question, e.g., a person name for a Who–question. This information can then be used to locate possible instances in the predicted answer.

Table 1. Some sample Wh–question keywords for the covered languages

	Keywords
Date	Wann, When, Cuándo, Qué año, Welchem Jahr, Que ano
Location	Wo, Where, Dónde, Onde
Person	Wer, Who, Quién, Quem

Usually, a sophisticated Wh–question analysis is performed in order to extract the EAT and other important control information, cf. [1]. However, since we are interested in language independent techniques and how our strategy behaves in a traditional question answering system, we are making use of a very shallow strategy for the analysis of Wh–questions, which simply searches for some Wh–keywords (see Table 1) in the question in order to determine the EAT. The predicted answers are passed on to the corresponding answer extraction module, whose main task is to remove predicted answers that has no relation with the EAT. At this step, many good predicted answers are discarded. From the remaining candidates, answer candidates are extracted applying simple specialized extraction algorithms.

Currently, we only consider Who/Where/When–questions. These are also used in TREC and CLEF QA tracks, for which annotated corpora in form of question/answer pairs exists for multiple languages. These question types are also used in other recent data–driven QA approaches for evaluation, e.g., [10] or [11].

When–Answer Extraction In general, when–questions ask for instances of the EAT DATE. First, we replace the query terms with a star and remove all characters that are not numbers afterwards. We split the remaining string into substrings by means of star sequences. If the length of a substring is greater than three and if it contains a number, is added to the set of answer candidates. The value of the rank is given by $rank(\nu)$.

Who—Answer Extraction At the beginning, characters that are not letters are removed. Then, query terms and stop-words are replaced with a star. We split the remaining string into substrings by means of star sequences. If the substring contains at least one space and its frequency is greater than two, it is added to the set of answer candidates. Here, predicted answers which contain "GEORGE BUSH" will be preferred to predicted answers which contain "BUSH", because they will have a higher correlation and therefore, a higher $rank(\nu)$.

Where–Answer Extraction is currently our most language–dependent part. This module uses geographical information about places around the world. Since we currently only make use of the English WordNet, we translate the NON–English answers (i.e., location names) using the Babelfish online MT service. The algorithm starts by removing all the characters that are not letters and we replace the query terms and stop-words with a star afterwards. We split the remaining string into substrings by means of star sequences. If the string is recognized by WordNet as a location, is added to the set of answer candidates. The value of the rank is given by $rank(\nu)$.

5 Experiments

We send a natural language Wh–question Q unmodified (i.e., without any pre–processing) to the Google search engine and extract the first 30 snippets. Each snippet is normalized by removing all HTML encoding, and by uppercasing the remaining text. We assessed the question/answering pairs from the multilingual CLEF 2004 corpus, which refers to answers from 1994/1995 newspaper articles. We consider two kinds of *correct answer*(CA):

Exact Answers(EA) are substrings that match one-to-one with the answers provided by CLEF. We should highlight that many CLEF answers are out of date and that often semantically valid alternative answers, i.e., those that are not expressed in the corpus, exist on the Web, often also decoded by using different spellings or word ordering.

Inexact Answer(IA) is an answer A that do not perfectly match with the answer A_c provided by CLEF, but for which there exists a close semantic relationship with A_c or where A corresponds to an update of A_c. For example, in case of WHERE–questions, which actually ask for a city name, we also accept the country name, and in case of WHO–questions, which requests the name of an official person, we accept the current one. Similarly, answers are also accepted, if they are just spelling variants, e.g., "George W. Bush", "G. Bush". In case of WHEN–questions, we also accept the answer "6 1945" or "1945", even though the exact answer in CLEF would be "6 August 1945".

We tested the system for 889 questions in four languages: English(EN), German(DE), Spanish(ES), and Portuguese (PT). The overall result for all languages can be inspected in Table 2. MRR stands for *Mean Reciprocal Rank*, and assigns to each question a score equal to the reciprocal of the rank of the first correct answer of the N (=3 in our case) best returned candidates. In the table, the results for the 1st, 2nd and 3rd place can be found, as well as for 0 (=NAF, which reads "no answer found, although there is one in the snippets"). Furthermore, NAG is when there was no answer in the snippets and the system returns NIL, WAG is when there was no answer in the snippets and the system gave three wrong answers. Table 2 shows the results considering the four languages altogether and Table 3 the distribution of the extracted answers considering only when there was an answer in the snippets. Table 4 displays the results for the individual languages. For the German questions we only handled WHEN and WHERE questions, because for the WHO questions our simple "Wh–keyword spotting approach" does not work out due to Wh–keyword ambiguity.

Finally, a brief note on the performance of our system. The runtime for each question averaged over all the questions of the corpus is about 2881 milliseconds.

Table 2. Results for each question type over all languages

CA	Total	MRR	NAG(%)	WAG(%)	NAF(%)	1(%)	2(%)	3(%)
WHEN	218	0.60	25.11	10.96	21.46	35.16	5.02	1.8
WHERE	232	0.57	10.77	24.14	20.68	30.60	9.91	3.87
WHO	439	0.38	11.39	27.56	32.57	18.90	6.83	2.73

Table 3. Distribution of answer candidates (all languages)

CA	NAF(%)	1(%)	2(%)	3(%)
WHEN	33.82	55.42	7.91	2.84
WHERE	31.86	47.00	15.23	5.95
WHO	53.37	30.97	11.19	4.47

Table 4. The results for the individual languages

CA(EN)	Total	MRR	NAG(%)	WAG(%)	NAF(%)	1(%)	2(%)	3(%)
when	69	0.69	15.69	15.69	17.65	45.10	3.92	1.96
where	64	0.74	7.81	12.5	15.62	53.12	10.93	0
who	148	0.50	7.43	12.83	32.43	33.78	10.14	3.38
CA(DE)	Total	MRR	NAG(%)	WAG(%)	NAF(%)	1(%)	2(%)	3(%)
Wann	58	0.45	36.20	12.07	27.59	22.03	1.17	0
Wo	58	0.46	9.37	18.75	23.43	20.31	12.5	6.25
CA(ES)	Total	MRR	NAG(%)	WAG(%)	NAF(%)	1(%)	2(%)	3(%)
Cuándo	59	0.55	16.64	11.86	23.73	32.20	10.17	11.86
Dónde	63	0.59	10.93	31.25	15.62	26.56	10.93	3.21
Quién	86	0.27	9.65	40.68	28.96	11.72	6.21	2.75
CA(PT)	Total	MRR	NAG(%)	WAG(%)	NAF(%)	1(%)	2(%)	3(%)
Quando	56	0.04	30.76	12.30	42.45	3.08	1.54	0
Onde	47	0.18	10.93	25	20.31	10.93	1.56	4.68
Quem	146	0.14	17.12	29.45	36.30	10.95	4.11	2.05

For the individual question types, we obtained: 1) When-questions: 2505, 2) Where-questions: 5591, and 3) Who: 2613 milliseconds. The extra time for the Where–questions is caused by calling Babelfish.

6 Discussion

Due to the distribution shown in Table 3, most of the extracted answers were ranked at position one, and the very few external knowledge sources and linguistic tools used for our answer extraction module, we say that our current result for the predicted answers is encouraging. If we have a closer look to the results of the different question types, then our result is competitive with current alternative data–driven approaches of QA. For example, [10] present an instance–based approach to QA in which a system (for English, only) is automatically acquired using TREC data. In particular, for 296 TEMPORAL–questions from TREC 9–12 they obtain a MRR of 0.447 using a larger corpus than we and a stricter test (checking exact answers). Their result is consistently above the sixth highest score at each TREC 9–12. That leads us to claim that our predicted answers has at least a competitive quality.

Our result also suggest, that the answer prediction strategy does not behave similar for the different question types, and for different languages. We suspect that this is due to the very shallow nature of our current answer extraction modules, and because the distribution and redundancy of web pages per languages is very different. This is an important fact, because our ranking schema assigns sequences of highly frequent word pairs a larger eigenvalue and hence a stronger weight than sequences of less frequent word pairs, cf. Sect. 3.2. This means that sequences of highly frequent words will bias in a stronger way the length of the eigenvectors in the new orthogonal spaces.

Lets consider the following ratio:

$$\bar{G}(v) = \frac{G(v)}{\sum_{v=0}^{\omega} G(v)}$$

$\bar{G}(v)$ is the probability of pairs of words with a certain distance that occur v times in a web page. The following table shows some empirical values for $\bar{G}(v)$:

Frequency	$\bar{G}(v)$
0	0.999925
1	0.000685
2	0.00005
3 and more	0.000015

Stronger relations will occur much fewer than weaker relations, and thus express more about the content of a document. It also has the advantage for representing D with a small set of pairs of words.

7 Related Work

Current webQA systems mainly use statistical methods for finding answers from the web that exploit data redundancy rather than sophisticated linguistic analyses of either questions and candidate answers, cf. also [4]. [13] present an compact overview of current state–of–the art in webQA. They also present a query reformulation process designed for the Spanish language that uses a combination of simple string rewriting, following a generate–and–test approach, i.e., no answer source feedback is used. Although they used a small non–standard question/answer corpus for evaluation (40 factoid questions), the results look promising (MRR = 0.7175). A similar strategy was earlier investigated by [6] for answer extraction from English Web snippets obtaining a MRR=0.450 for 500 TREC–9 questions. [4] describe a feedback loop approach similar to ours, in which candidate answer terms were merged back into the query used for passage retrieval. The major difference compared to our approach is that they apply the feedback strategy after answer candidates have been determined, whereas we do it before answer extraction. They seem to perform the feedback loop on retrieved passages from TREC data only, which are less noisy in general than the snippets returned by Google. Furthermore, by not considering Web snippets, they can only make use of a reduced amount of redundancy, which might explain, why their approach was of less benefit as they expected. [12] present an approach for automatic derivation of surface text patterns using Maximum Entropy Modeling. They achieve a MRR=0.2993 on 500 TREC–10 questions. [11] presents a multilingual approach to QA using supervised Machine Learning algorithms (similar in spirit to [10], cf. Sect. 6). The methods extract answers as terms biased by the question using probabilistic models constructed from question–answer pairs. The results are promising (MRR=0.36 on 2000 Japanese question–answer pairs) Although all of the mentioned approaches consider only a single language, they support our perspective that language–independent statistical methods are essential for the development of multilingual QA system.

8 Conclusion

We presented a language independent strategy for predicting and extracting answers from Web snippets. We described a strategy that uses eigenvalues determined from a specialized designed matrix, which are used for determining the implicit semantic relationship between query and answer terms from the retrieved snippets. The matrix explicitly represents word–pairs and their distance. We evaluated our approach with three different types of questions from four languages, obtaining a combined MRR=0.52 for the respective subset of the CLEF–2004 data set. Currently, we are processing only simply Wh–questions. In future work we will perform more experiments taking into account additional types of questions and languages.

References

1. Moldovan, D., Harabagui, S., Clark, C., Bowden, M., Lehmann, J., Williams, J.: Experiments and Analysis of LCC's two QA Systems over TREC 2004. TREC 2004 (2004)
2. Radev, D.: Panel on web-based question answering. AAAI Spring Symposium on New Directions in Question Answering. (2003)
3. Neumann, G., Xu, F.: Mining natural language answers from the web. Web Intelligence and Agent Systems, volume **2**. (2004) 123–135
4. Clarke, C. L. A., Cormack, G. V., Lynam, T. R.: Exploiting Redundancy in Question Answering. SIGIR. (2001) 358-365
5. Ramakrishnan, G., Paranjape, D., Chakrabarti, S., Bhattacharyya, P.: Is Question Answering an Acquired Skill?. Proceedings of the 13th international conference on World Wide Web, WWW 2004. (2004)
6. Dumais, S. T., Banko, M., Brill, E., Lin, J. J., Ng, A. Y.: Web question answering: is more always better?. SIGIR. (2002) 291-298
7. Ravichandran, D., Hovy, E. H.: Learning surface text patterns for a Question Answering System. ACL (2002) 41-47
8. Belew, R. K.:Finding out About: A Cognitive Perspective on Search Engine Technology and the WWW. Cambridge University Press. (2000)
9. Robertson, S.:Understanding Inverse Document Frequency: On theoretical arguments for IDF. Journal of Documentation, volume **60**, number **5** (2004)
10. Lita, L., Carbonell, J.: Instance-Based Question Answering: A Data-Driven Approach. EMNLP 2004 (2004)
11. Sasaki, Y., Carbonell, J.: Question Answering As Question-Biased Term Extraction: a New Approach Toward Multilingual (QA). Proceedings of ACL (2005)
12. Ravichandran, D., Ittycheriah, A., Roukos, S.: Automatic Derivation of Surface Text Patterns for a Maximum Entropy Based Question Answering System. HLT-NAACL (2003)
13. Del-Castillo-Escobedo, A., Gómez, M., Villaseñor-Pineda, L.: QA on the Web: A Preliminary Study for Spanish Language. ENC-04 (2004)
14. Deerwester, S. C., Dumais, S. T., Landauer, T. K., Furnas, G. W., Harshman, R. A.: Indexing by Latent Semantic Analysis. Journal of the American Society of Information Science, volume **41**, number **6** (1990) 391-407

Language Model Mixtures for Contextual Ad Placement in Personal Blogs

Gilad Mishne and Maarten de Rijke

ISLA, University of Amsterdam
Kruislaan 403, 1098 SJ Amsterdam, The Netherlands
{gilad, mdr}@science.uva.nl

Abstract. We introduce a method for content-based advertisement selection for personal blog pages, based on combining multiple representations of the blog. The core idea behind the method is that personal blogs represent individuals, whose interests can be modeled by the language used in the blog itself combined with the language used in related sources of information, such as comments posted to a blog post or the blogger's community. An evaluation of our ad placement method shows improvement over state-of-the-art ad placement methods which were not designed for blog pages.

1 Introduction

Blogs—frequently modified web pages in which dated entries are listed in reverse chronological order—come in a variety of genres [1]. In this paper, our focus is on personal blogs, created by individuals and serving as a vehicle for self-expression and self-empowerment; this type of blogs is by far the most common. Personal blog posts are often not topically focused—instead, they provide reports about experiences and interests of individuals, and of the objects they surround themselves with and the activities they engage in. This is one of the major differences between the text found in typical personal blog posts, and the text found in other web pages: whereas most web pages represent information, personal blogs represent individuals.

Blogs and the blogosphere form an increasingly active area of research, with interest ranging from language technology and text mining to information access, as is witnessed by e.g., the launch of a blog track at TREC 2006 [2]. Alongside the academic interest, blogs are also a rich source of information for commercial purposes. At the aggregate level, various uses have been made of blogs and their contents, e.g., predicting spikes in consumer purchase decisions using the mere volume of blog postings [3]; at the individual blog level, tools such as book recommender systems based on bloggers' writings have been proposed [4]. In this paper, we are interested in developing language technology for a different commercial aspect of blogs: advertisement placement. Specifically, we want to generate suggestions for advertisements to be displayed to readers of a blog, based on the content they are viewing. This type of ad placement is

T. Salakoski et al. (Eds.): FinTAL 2006, LNAI 4139, pp. 435–446, 2006.

Fig. 1. Contextual ads on a non-blog page

sometimes called *contextual* or *content-based*, since the displayed ads are related to the context in which they appear. For example, if the reader is viewing a blog post discussing sports, and the blogger's site uses contextual advertising, the user might see ads from advertisers such as sports memorabilia dealers or ticket sellers. Figure 1 shows an example of contextual ad placement in a non-blog page: in this example, Google's AdSense program selects ads to display in a website reviewing hotels in Turku, Finland (ads appear in the central part of the page).

Briefly, then, the task we address is this: given a personal blog post and a collection of advertisements, identify advertisements that are most relevant for the post: advertisements that are most likely to be of interest to readers of the post.

Our research is driven by two main questions. First, contextual ad placement methods have been developed for general (non-blog) web pages. How do these methods perform on personal blogs (as opposed to non-blog web pages)? We find that ad placement in personal blogs is harder than in other web pages: a state-of-the-art method developed for web pages does not achieve the same results on personal blogs. One of the truly challenging aspects of personal blogs for contextual ad placement is that personal blogs tend to be non-topical, meaning that there is no "real" topic to many of their posts—a real problem for ad placement methods that rely on identifying the general topic of a page. This observation motivates our proposal of an alternative placement algorithm, one that takes the view that a personal blog represents a person, not a topic, as its starting point. Our second research question, then, is whether this person-oriented approach yields a more effective ad placement method for personal blogs than state-of-the-art placement methods built for generic web pages.

The rest of the paper is organized as follows. In Section 2 we discuss related work. Our ad placement approach, based on person-oriented language model mixtures is presented in Section 3. Section 4 contains a description of our experimental evaluation; we conclude in Section 5.

2 Related Work

First deployed in 2003, contextual ad placement services allow websites to pay to have their advertisements displayed alongside the contents of related web pages. Programs such as Google's AdSense and Yahoo's Publisher Network are effective in generating revenue both for the advertiser and the ad-matching mediator by associating the content of a web page with the content of the displayed ads, increasing the likelihood of their usefulness. Often, the ads are non-intrusive and are clearly marked as such; on top of that, they enjoy the reputation of the ad selection platform (which is typically a well-known web search engine)—this explains much of the success of contextual ad placement [5].

As contextual ad placement has become a substantial source of revenue supporting the web today, investments in this task, and more generally, in the quality of ad placement, are increasingly important. Most of the advertisements are currently placed by search engines; advertisements that are not relevant may negatively impact the search engine's credibility and, ultimately, market share [6,7]. The more targeted the advertising, the more effective it is [8]. As a consequence, there has been a considerable amount of research on relevance in advertising for general web data (see Section 2).

As the area of content-based ad placement is relatively new, and since it involves many "trade secrets," the amount of existing published work is limited. The work most closely related to ours is that of Ribeiro-Neto et al. [9], involving an impedance coupling technique for contextual ad placement. This approach uses a variety of information sources, including the text of the advertisements, the destination web page of the ad, and the triggering words tied to a particular ad. We use the AAK_EXP method described in Ribeiro-Neto et al.'s work as state-of-the-art, for comparing with our approach. Work on ad placement prior to [9] was of a more restricted nature. E.g., [10] propose a system that is able to adapt online advertisements to a user's short-term interests; it does not directly use the content of the page viewed by the user, but relies on search keywords supplied by the user to search engines and on the URL of the page requested by the user. Finally, [11] report not on matching advertisements to web pages, but on the related task of extracting keywords from web pages for advertisement targeting. The authors use various features, ranging from *tf* and *idf* scores of potential keywords to frequency information from search engine log files.

3 Language Model-Based Blogger Profiles

Contextual placement of text advertisements boils down to matching the text of the ad to the information supplied in a web page. Typically, a textual ad is composed of a few components: the self-explanatory *title*, designed to capture the attention of the viewer, a short *description* providing additional details, a

URL, the target a surfer will be taken to if the ad is clicked, and a set of *triggering terms*. The triggering terms, which are not displayed to the surfer, are provided by the advertisers and function as terms associated with the ads, assisting the process of matching ads with context. In this paper we follow a standard approach which concatenates the text of all these different components to a single textual representation of the advertisement. The challenge we are facing is to select ads (from a collection of ads represented in this concatenated manner) that are most likely to be of interest to readers of a given blog post.

As outlined earlier, our working hypothesis is that personal blogs represent individuals. In this section we develop a framework for modeling these individuals using statistical language models, and matching these models to the advertisements. First, we provide some background about language models; we follow with an instantiation of these models for blogs.

3.1 Language Models and Model Similarity

Language models are statistical models that attempt to capture regularities of natural language phenomena [12]. Long in use by the speech recognition community, in the last decade they have been successfully adopted by researchers in other areas such as information retrieval [13] and machine translation [14].

The language models we use are probability distributions over sets of strings, where the probability assigned to a string is the likelihood of generating it by a given language. To estimate the probabilities, we use a maximum likelihood estimate generated from observed text. We use the most common type of language model: unigram models, in which the strings are single-word terms from the language's vocabulary. In practice, then, our language models consist of probabilities assigned to words according to their frequency in the text.

Since language models are probability distributions, statistical methods for comparing distributions can be used to compare them. Applying goodness-of-fit tests to two language models—one functioning as the expected distribution and the other as the observed one—indicates to what degree they differ. While a number of such tests exist, comparisons of models of the type we use is best performed by a *log likelihood* test, since the text contains a large amount of rare events [15]. This test assigns every word in the language a divergence value indicating how different its likelihood is between the two languages: words with high log likelihood values are more typical of one language than the other, and words with low values tend to be observed in both languages with similar rates.

3.2 Information Profiles

Divergence between language models provides an elegant way of building an "information profile" of a given document (or set of documents) taken from a larger collection. First, language models are estimated both for the given document and for the entire collection. Then, these two models are compared. Ordering the terms of the models according to the divergence values assigned to them functions as the profile of the document. Prominent terms in the profile—terms with higher divergence values—are more "indicative" of the content of the document, as their usage in it is higher than their usage in the rest of the documents. For example, according to this method the most indicative terms for this paper (when compared to a large collection of other scientific articles in various computer science areas) are "blog," "model," "advertisement," and "language."

3.3 Language Models of Blog Posts

Our approach to constructing profiles of blog posts is based on forming information profiles from text as just outlined. But what "text" should we use for building this profile? In the context of a specific blog post there are different sources of information about a blogger. Clearly, the blog post itself is an important source of information. Another obvious source of information is the contents of other blog posts written by the same blogger—i.e., the contents of the blog as a whole. Some properties of blogs, such as their community-oriented structure or their temporal nature, provide additional sources of knowledge. Our approach, then, attempts to distill a textual model of the blogger by combining the information present in each of these representations.

Exploiting various subsets of the information sources listed above, we build the following models for a blog post p.

Post Model. For this model we use the most straightforward content: the contents of the blog post p itself.

Blog Model. This model is built from all posts from the same blog as p which are dated earlier than p. The intuition behind this is that interests and characteristics of a blogger are likely to recur over multiple posts, so even if p itself is sparse, they can be picked up from other writings of the blogger.

Comment Model. One of the distinct properties of blogs is the ability of blog visitors to respond directly to a post by leaving a comment which is made public on the post page [16]; these are often identified as important for the blogging experience (e.g., [17]). Our comment model is constructed from all comments posted in response to p, and assumes that their content is directly related to the post.

Category Model. *Tags*—short textual labels that many bloggers use to categorize their posts [18]—are another feature often occurring in blogs. These labels range from high-level topics ("sport," "politics") to very specific ones ("Larry's birthday," "Lord of the Rings"). For this model, we used all blog posts filed under the same category as p, as the bloggers themselves decided that they are topically related.

Community Model. Given our assumption that blogs represent individuals, it is natural that the blogspace provides fertile ground for the formation and interaction of a large number of communities [19]. This model exploits this aspect of blogs by using all text of blogs which are part of the same community as the blog p is taken from. A formal definition of a blog community does not exist; in this work, we take a simple approach and mark a blog as belonging to the community of p's blog if it links at least twice to that blog.

Similar Post Model. For this model, we use the contents of the 50 blog posts which are most similar to p. To measure similarity, we used the language modeling approach described in [20]; in practice, we indexed the entire collection of blog posts and used a language modeling-based IR engine to retrieve the top 50 posts from the collection, using p itself as a query. This model attempts to overcome the vocabulary gap which exists between some of the relevant ads and the posts by adding terms from related posts, in a similar manner to that proposed in [9].

Time Model. Personal blogs function as online diaries. As such, many blog posts contain references to ongoing events at the time of publication. For example, the time-span of the blogs in our collection (see Section 4) includes New Year's Day 2006, with many references to fireworks and parties from various blogs around that day. To accommodate this, we construct a model based on all blog posts published in a 4-hour window around the publication time of p, capturing events that influence a large number of bloggers.

Each one of these models provides a weighted list of terms, where the weight assigned to a term is its divergence value when comparing the text used for the model with the entire collection of blogs.

3.4 Model Mixtures

Forming combinations of different language models is a common technique when applying these models to real-life tasks. While finding the optimal mixture is a complex task [21], there are methods of estimating good mixtures [21,22]. In our case, we are not combining pure language models, but rather lists of terms derived from language models. As with most model mixtures, we take a linear combination approach: the combined weight of a term t is $w_t = \sum_j \lambda_j \cdot w_j(t)$, where λ_j is the weight assigned to model j and $w_j(t)$ is the weight assigned to the term t by model j. To estimate the model weights λ_j, we combine static and on-line methods as detailed below.

Static weights. Clearly, the contribution of each of the models is not equal a-priori; for example, the model representing the blogger herself is arguably more important than the one representing the community. Optimal prior weights can be estimated for each model in the presence of training material; these constitute static weights, as they do not depend on a specific set of models derived from a given blog. In the absence of training material, we used a simple prior weighting scheme where all models have the same weight w, except the post model which gets a weight of $2w$ and the time model which gets $0.5w$—we mark this as λ_j^s.

On-line weights. In addition to the static model weights, we use posterior weights associated with a specific set of models; this type of weights is also called "on-line" [22] since they are calculated on the fly, once models have been induced by a given post. These weights are aimed at capturing the relative importance each model should have, compared to other models induced by the same blog post. In our setup, we associate this importance with the quality of the model—better formed models should have a higher weight. As detailed above, our models consist of lists of terms; one way to evaluate the quality of such a list is to check its coherency—the degree to which the different terms in the list are related (this idea is often used when evaluating textual clustering methods).

To measure this coherency, we need to estimate how related the different words in the list are. For this, we calculate the pointwise mutual information (PMI)—the statistical dependence—between any two terms in the list, and take the mean of these values as the coherence of the list. PMI values themselves are calculated using a method called PMI-IR which employs joint and independent counts of the two terms in a large corpus [23], which is in our case a collection of blog posts. The on-line weights obtained this way are denoted as λ_j^o.

The final weight λ_j assigned to model j is $\lambda_j = \lambda_j^s \cdot \lambda_j^o$. Note that words may appear in multiple models, boosting their final weight in the combined model.

3.5 Ad Matching

Having built a combined model for blog posts, we proceed to the final phase, where the advertisements are matched to this model.

As in [9], we take an information retrieval approach to this task. Similarity between an advertisement and a model is measured with an information retrieval ranking formula—in our case, a state-of-the-art language modeling-based one [20]. We index all ads, and "retrieve" the most similar ones using a query which contains the top terms appearing in the combined divergence model described above.

Summing up, the ad selection process for a blog post p proceeds as follows.

1. Construct the different language models relating to various aspects of p.
2. Calculate divergence values for the terms in each model, when compared to a model of a large collection of blog posts.
3. Combine the diverging terms to a single weighted list using a linear combination, with a combination of static and on-line weights.
4. Use a query consisting of the top terms in the combined model to rank all advertisements; top-ranking ads are shown to the user.

In terms of complexity, the performance of our method is similar to AAK_EXP: the most demanding phase is the retrieval of additional posts for constructing the "similar-post" model, and this is done once per blog post. The background language model is static and does not require computation per post, and inducing and comparing the rest of the models is a relatively cheap process, compared with retrieval.

3.6 A Worked Example

In Table 1 we summarize the kind of information used and generated during the ad placement process, when used with a given post from our corpus[1] (for details on the corpus, see Section 4). The blog post itself deals with birds visiting the

[1] All our data in this paper, including the examples, is in Dutch; the examples are translated into English for convenience.

Table 1. Example of model mixtures for ad-matching

Permalink	`http://alchemilla.web-log.nl/log/4549331`
Date	January 4th, 2006
Post	*Life in the Garden* Birds are flying around the tree and the garden behind our house... Hopping blackbirds, a few red-breasts, some fierce starlings and, surprisingly, a few Flemish jays. I thought Flemish jays live in the forest. I haven't heard the trouble-making magpies from the neighbors for a couple of days, they must have joined the neighbors for their winter vacation :) I see now ...
Post terms	garden, spot, starlings, blackbirds, (feeding)-balls
Blog terms	nature, bird, moon, black, hats, singing, fly, area
Comment terms	jays, hydra
Category terms	bird, moon, arise, daily
Community terms	nursery, ant, music, help, load, care
Similar-post terms	birds, garden, jays, blackbirds, Flemish, red-breasts
Time terms	(none)
Model weights	Post:0.63, Blog:0.21, Comment:0.02, Category:0.05, Similar-posts:0.09 Time:0
Combined model	birds, spot, garden, jays, blackbirds, nature ...
Selected ads	www.stepstone.nl: Interested in working in nature protection and environment? Click on StepStone. www.directplant.nl: Directplant.nl delivers direct from the nursury. This means good quality for a low price. www.ebay.nl: eBay - the worldwide marketplace for buying and selling furniture and decorations for your pets and your garden.

blogger's garden, and this is reflected in the post model. Additional models, in particular the community and category ones, expand the profile, showing that the blogger's interests (and, hence, the interests of visitors to the blog) can be generalized to nature and related areas.

4 Evaluation

In this section we describe the experiments conducted to evaluate our ad placement method and the results obtained.

4.1 Experimental Setting

Blog Corpus. We obtained a collection of 367,000 blog posts from 36,000 different blogs, all hosted by web-log.nl, the largest Dutch blogging platform. The vast majority of web-log.nl blogs are diary-like, and belong to the "personal journal" blog type [1]; their content is similar to that of LiveJournal or Xanga blogs.

Title	ArtOlive - More than 2,250 Dutch Artists
Description	The platform for promoting, lending and selling contemporary art all over the Netherlands. Click to view the current collection of more than 2,250 artists, or read about buying and renting art.
URL	`www.galerie.nl`
Trigger Words	painting, sculpture, galleries, artist, artwork, studio, artists, studios, gallery
Title	Start dating on Lexa.nl
Description	It's time for a new start. About 30,000 profiles every month. Register now for free.
URL	`www.lexa.nl`
Trigger Words	dating, meeting, dreamgirl, contacts

Fig. 2. Sample advertisements from our collection

The collection consists of all entries posted to web-log.nl blogs during the first 6 weeks of 2006, and contains 64M words and 440MB of text. In addition to the blog posts, we obtained the comments posted in response to the posts—a total of 1.5M comments, 35M words, and 320MB of text.

Ad Corpus. We acquired a set of 18,500 advertisements which are currently used for the blogs in our collection (and for other web pages: the company that operates web-log.nl, Ilse Media BV, also hosts the largest Dutch search engine and a popular portal). In total, 1,650 different web sites are advertised in the collection, and 10,400 different "triggering words" are used. Figure 2 shows examples of the advertisements in our collection.

As Dutch is a compound-rich language, we used a compound-splitting technique that has shown substantial improvements in retrieval effectiveness compared to unmodified text [24] for all components of our method employing retrieval.

4.2 Experiments

Three methods were used to match ads to blog contents. As a baseline, we indexed all ads and used the blog post as a query, ranking the ads by their retrieval score; in addition, the appearance of a trigger word in the post was required. This is similar to the AAK ("match Ads And Keywords") method described in [9], except that we use the language modeling approach to information retrieval described in [20] for ranking the ads rather than a vector space one. This most likely improves the scores of the baseline, as the language modeling retrieval method we use has shown to achieve same-or-better scores compared to top-performing retrieval algorithms, and certainly outperforms the simpler vector space model [20]. We refer to this method as AAK.

To address the first of our main research questions (How effective are state-of-the-art ad placement methods on blogs?), we implemented the impedance coupling method AAK_EXP described in [9] (the acronym stands for "match Ad And Keywords to the EXPanded page"); this represents current state-of-the-art of content-based ad matching.[2] Again, we used the language modeling

[2] The authors of [9] implement a number of methods for ad matching; AAK_EXP and AAK_EXP_H are the top-performing methods, where AAK_EXP_H shows a minor advantage over AAK_EXP but requires an additional crawling step which we did not implement.

Table 2. Ad-matching evaluation

Method	Precision@1	Precision@3
AAK [9] (baseline)	0.18	0.18
AAK_EXP [9]	0.25 (+39%)	0.24 (+33%)
LANG_MODEL_MIX	0.28 (+55%)	0.29 (+61%)

framework for the retrieval component in this method, which is likely to improve its performance.

Finally, we used the language modeling mixture method for ad placement described in Section 3. Since we did not have training material we could not tune the prior weights of the models, and used a naive weighting scheme as detailed in Section 3. Posterior weights were applied as described in Section 3, according to the coherency of the resulting models. We refer to this method as LANG_MODEL_MIX.

Assessment. For evaluation purposes we randomly selected a set of 103 blog posts as a test set. The top 3 advertisements selected by all three methods for each of these posts were assessed for relevance by two independent assessors. The assessors viewed the blog posts in their original HTML form (i.e., complete with images, links, stylesheets and other components); at the bottom of the page a number of advertisements were displayed in random order, where the method used to select an ad was not shown. The assessors were asked to mark an advertisement as "relevant" if it is likely to be of interest to readers of this blog, be they incidental visitors to the page or regular readers.

The level of agreement between the assessors was $\kappa = 0.54$. Due to this relatively low value, we decided to mark an advertisement "relevant" for a blog post only if both assessors marked it as relevant.[3]

4.3 Results

To evaluate the ad selection methods, we measured the precision levels for the top-ranked ad selected by the method, as well as the 3 top-ranked ads (a larger number of ads is likely to disturb visitors to the blog). Table 2 shows the average precision scores for all methods. All differences are strongly statistically significant using the sign test, with p values well below 0.001.

As shown in [9], the usage of the sophisticated query expansion mechanism of AAK_EXP yields a substantial improvement over the baseline. However, the improvement is somewhat lower than that gained for generic web pages: while the average improvement reported in [9] is 44%, in the case of blogs the average improvement is 36%. Usage of the LANG_MODEL_MIX method shows yet another

[3] The requirement that two independent assessors agree on an ad's relevance leads to more robust evaluation, but also reduces the scores, as fewer advertisements (on average) are marked as relevant. A different policy, marking an advertisement as relevant if *any* of the assessors decided it is relevant, boosts all scores by about 40%, but makes them less reliable.

substantial improvement, of the same order of magnitude, suggesting that this is a beneficial scheme for capturing a profile of the blog post for commercial purposes. Note that an improvement of $X\%$ in ad-matching can lead to an improvement of $X\%$ in the end result (in this case, sales from advertisements), unlike many other computational linguistic tasks where the effect of performance enhancements on the end result is not linear [11].

An in-depth analysis of the contribution of the different models to the outcome, as well as error analysis, is out of the scope of this paper, and will be made public separately.

5 Conclusions

Our aim in this work was two-fold: to determine the effectiveness of state-of-the-art ad placement methods on blogs (as opposed to general non-blog web pages), and to propose a blog-specific ad placement algorithm that builds on the intuition that a blog represents a person, not a single topic. We used manual assessments of a relatively large test set to compare our blog-specific method to a top performing state-of-the-art one—AAK_EXP. While AAK_EXP performs well, the richness of information in blogs enables us to significantly improve over it.

The success of our method is based on the use of properties which are relatively unique to blogs—the presence of a community, comments, the fact that the post itself is part of a blog, and so on. We believe that further improvements may be achieved by using non-blog specific features; among these are linguistic cues such as sentiment analysis (shown to improve other commercial-oriented tasks dealing with blogs [25]), as well as non-linguistic ones such as ad expansion, e.g., from the page pointed to by the ad [9]. Another interesting line of further work concerns the integration of additional knowledge about the blog reader, as mined from her clickstream or her own blog.

Acknowledgments. The authors wish to thank Nils Rooijmans from Ilse Media BV for providing the data used in this study, and our assessors—Leon van der Zande and Lars Wortel. This research was supported by the Netherlands Organization for Scientific Research (NWO) under project number 220-80-001.

References

1. Herring, S., Scheidt, L., Bonus, S., Wright, E.: Bridging the gap: A genre analysis of weblogs. In: HICSS. (2004)
2. TREC: Blog track (2006) URL: http://trec.nist.gov.
3. Gruhl, D., Guha, R., Kumar, R., Novak, J., Tomkins, A.: The predictive power of online chatter. In: Proceedings KDD '05. (2005)
4. Mishne, G., de Rijke, M.: Deriving wishlists from blogs: Show us your blog, and we'll tell you what books to buy. In: Proceedings WWW 2006. (2006)
5. Lingamneni, S.: Predicting the future of internet advertising (2004) http://www.stanford.edu/group/boothe/0405/PWR-Lingamneni.pdf.

6. Wang, C., Zhang, P., Choi, R., Daeredita, M.: Understanding consumers attitude toward advertising. In: Eighth Americas Conference on Information Systems. (2002) 1143–1148
7. Bhargava, H.K., Feng, J.: Paid placement strategies for internet search engines. In: Proceedings WWW 2002. (2002)
8. Novak, T.P., Hoffman, D.L.: New metrics for new media: toward the development of web measurement standards. World Wide Web J. **2** (1997) 213–246
9. Ribeiro-Neto, B., Cristo, M., Golgher, P., de Moura, E.S.: Impedance coupling in content-targeted advertising. In: Proceedings SIGIR '05. (2005)
10. Langheinrich, M., Nakamura, A., Abe, N., Kamba, T., Koseki, Y.: Unintrusive customization techniques for web advertising. Comput. Networks **31** (1999)
11. Tau-Wih, W., Goodman, J., Carvalho, V.: Finding advertising keywords on web pages. In: Proceedings WWW 2006, Edinburgh, Scotland (2006)
12. Rosenfeld, R.: Two decades of statistical language modeling: Where do we go from here? Proceedings of the IEEE **88** (2000)
13. Ponte, J., Croft, W.: A language modeling approach to information retrieval. In: Proceedings SIGIR '98. (1998)
14. Brown, R., Frederking, R.: Applying statistical english language modeling to symbolic machine translation. In: Proceedings TMI-95. (1995)
15. Dunning, T.: Accurate methods for the statistics of surprise and coincidence. Computational Linguistics **19** (1993)
16. Winer, D.: What makes a weblog a weblog? (2003) `blogs.law.harvard.edu/whatMakesAWeblogAWeblog`, accessed April 2006.
17. Gumbrecht, M.: Blogs as "protected space". In: WWW 2004 Workshop on the Weblogging Ecosystem: Aggregation, Analysis and Dynamics, 2004. (2004)
18. Golder, S., Huberman, B.: The structure of collaborative tagging systems. J. of Information Science (2006)
19. Kumar, R., Novak, J., Raghavan, P., Tomkins, A.: On the bursty evolution of blogspace. In: Proceedings WWW 2003. (2003)
20. Hiemstra, D.: Using Language Models for Information Retrieval. PhD thesis, Enschede (2001)
21. Lavrenko, V.: Optimal Mixture Models in IR. In: ECIR 2002. (2002) 193–212
22. Kalai, A., Chen, S., Blum, A., Rosenfeld, R.: On-line algorithms for combining language models. In: Proceedings ICASSP '99. (1999)
23. Turney, P.: Mining the web for synonyms: PMI-IR versus LSA on TOEFL. In: ECML 2001. (2001) 491–502
24. Hollink, V., Kamps, J., Monz, C., de Rijke, M.: Monolingual document retrieval for European languages. Information Retrieval **7** (2004)
25. Mishne, G., Glance, N.: Predicting movie sales from blogger sentiment. In: AAAI Spring Symposium on Computational Approaches to Analysing Weblogs. (2006)

Local Constraints on Arabic Word Order

Allan Ramsay[1] and Hanady Mansour[2]

[1] University of Manchester
Allan.Ramsay@manchester.ac.uk
[2] University of Alexandria
hanady_ahmed@hotmail.com

Abstract. Syntactic analysis of Arabic poses two major problems. (i) Although the canonical order of Arabic sentences is VSO, a range of other orders are possible. In order to carry out such an analysis, then, it is necessary to have a grammatical framework and an associated parsing algorithm that can cope with free word order. (ii) Although a range of non-canonical orders are possible, not all orders are possible under all circumstances.

The current paper outlines an approach to obtaining syntactic descriptions of sentences of Modern Standard Arabic, where the problems outlined above are compounded by omission of short vowels and other critical information from the written form.

1 Outline

Anyone seeking to develop a computational treatment of Arabic faces three major problems:

1. the written form of Modern Standard Arabic (MSA) omits short vowels and other material that is crucial for determining words are present, and especially for determining which forms those words have.
2. Arabic word order is comparatively free. Although the canonical order of an Arabic sentence with a simple transitive verb is VSO, most other orders can occur under appropriate circumstances.
3. Although most word orders *can* occur, non-canonical orders induce quite tight constraints on the forms of the constituents. If the subject occurs before the verb, for instance, then the agreement constraints are tighter than if it appears in its normal position.

The work reported here is part of an attempt to produce a text-to-speech (TTS) system for MSA. Clearly, the most important task for such a system is to retrieve the phonetically relevant material from the written form. We believe that determining the syntactic structure can play a major role in this task, and that if you know the syntactic structure then you can also make well informed decisions about the prosodic contour. In the current paper we discuss an approach to to coping with the the interactions between (2) and (3) above in a situation where the text that we are attempting to analyse is undiacriticised, so that we

T. Salakoski et al. (Eds.): FinTAL 2006, LNAI 4139, pp. 447–457, 2006.

are not sure which words are present and we certainly have very little idea what the form of those words is.

We will end the paper with a brief discussion of the output of the TTS system, but the emphasis is on the syntactic analysis, and especially on the use of local constraints to deal with non-canonical word orders.

2 Syntax

The main aim of the current paper is to provide a computational account of MSA syntax. Arabic poses a number of problems for such accounts:

1. Standard verbal sentences can display a variety of word orders. It is therefore essential to have a parsing algorithm that can cope with non-canonical orders, and it is also essential to be able to check that the specific constraints that non-standard orders induce.
2. Arabic allows 'nominal sentences' – sentences with just a subject NP and a predication. The order of the constituents of such a sentence is again subject to very specific constraints.
3. Arabic construct NPs, which are very similar to genetive constructions in other languages, are also subject to very tight local constraints.

None of these issues is unique to Arabic. They are, however, made particularly problematic in Arabic because their resolution often requires access to inflectional morphology (e.g. agreement and case marking) which is generally omitted from the written form.

2.1 Framework

The general framework we are using is as follows.

1. Words and phrases are combined according to modes of combination: unsaturated lexical items can combine with appropriate arguments to become saturated, and modifiers can combine with appropriate targets. The first of these modes of combination corresponds roughly to the standard categorial rules of combination, or to a combination of Schemas I-IV of [1]. The second corresponds to a combination of Schemas V and VI of [1]. (§2.1)
2. The arguments of a verb are allocated syntactic roles such as subject, first object and second object on the basis of a partial order defined on the range of possible semantic roles (θ roles). The agent of a verb, for instance, will beat the thematic object to the role of subject. This partial order is similar to [2]: we make no strong claims on behalf of the specific set of θ roles that we choose or the partial order that relates θ roles to syntactic roles, but we do believe that this general approach is sensible (see [2] for a discussion of the issues that this general notion raises).
3. The canonical order of an Arabic sentence with a transitive main verb is VSO. Numerous other orders are possible when required (e.g. for discourse

reasons), but they do induce specific local constraints. The parsing algorithm described in [3] enables us to parse languages with 'free' word order efficiently, and we will not say any more about the details of this algorithm here.

4. It is useful to maintain a distinction between the 'internal' and 'external' properties of an item. In *'He concluded the banquet by eating the owl'*, for instance, the phrase *'eating the owl'* has the internal structure of a present progressive VP, but it is being used in a context where you would normally expect an NP (see [4] for a similar approach to English gerunds).

Principles of Combination

The basic principles for combining words and phrases are shown in Fig. 1 and Fig. 2.

Fig. 1 is equivalent to the basic categorial rule `X ==> X/Y, Y` which says that a lexical item that needs a following argument can combine with something appropriate (there is an exactly parallel version for cases where the argument precedes the head).

```
{syn(B, args=R)}
 ==>{syn(B,
     subcat(args([{struct(dir(+after, -before)),
                   syn(C)} | R]))))},
 {syn(C)}
```

Fig. 1. Right-seeking categorial rule: `X/R ==> (X/R)/Y, Y`

Fig. 2 describes how a modifier can combine with an appropriate target. By allowing the rule to refer to both the target and the result we are able to cover simple adjuncts such as adjectives and PPs, where the target and the result share their main syntactic properties, and also slightly more complex cases such as determiners, where the relationship between the target (which for a determiner would be an $\overline{N}$) and the result (which in this case would be an $\overline{\overline{N}}$). Again there is an exactly parallel rule for modifiers that precede their targets.

```
{syn(B)}
==>{syn(nonfoot(minor(target({struct(dir(+after, -before)),
                              syn(C)})
                     modresult(syn(B)))))},
   {syn(C)}
```

Fig. 2. A modifier can combine with its target (right-seeking version)

From thematic roles to canonical order
The rule in Fig. 1 tells us how to combine a lexical item and its arguments. In particular, it tells us how to combine verbs and their arguments to produce sentences, so long as we know what the arguments are and where and in what order they are expected to occur. We will explain how this is treated by initially considering a straightforward transitive verb.

When we add a verb to the lexicon all we actually specify is the number and θ-roles of the arguments, so a typical entry will be as shown in Fig. 3.

```
"‘*r*f" = vtype(valency(2, [agent:living, object:nonliving]))
```

Fig. 3. Entry for a simple transitive verb

Fig. 3 says that عرف (*ʕrf*) has a sense in which requires an animate agent and and inanimate object. The notation `valency(2, [agent:living, object: nonliving])` says that this sense of the verb requires at least the first two of the items in the list. This makes no difference here, since saying that you need the first two members of a two element list is equivalent to saying that you need every member of the list, but in other cases it enables us to describe situations where a single sense of a verb can occur with varying numbers of arguments: an entry like `"open" = vtype(valency(1, [object:nonliving, agent:living, instrument:nonliving]))`, for instance, would allow us to describe [5]'s classic example of a verb which can occur with a range of different arguments:

(1) a. She opened the door with the key.
 b. She opened the door.
 c. The key opened the door.
 d. The door opened.

The order in the list of arguments in the specification reflects their obligatoriness rather than their surface order, so that the definition for *'open'* given above says that the thematic object must always be present but the other two arguments are optional. A linear order on groups of roles, of the form `[agent, ...] > [instrument, ...] > [object, recipient, ...]`, is used to decide which argument should be the surface subject (agent, then instrument, then object) and then which one should be the first object if this position is available to it (so the instrument ought to be the first object, but it cannot be because it requires a prepositional marker if it is not in subject position).

Finally, language specific rules are used to specify the surface positions of the various surface roles: for an English transitive verb, for instance, the argument list looks like [$\overrightarrow{\texttt{OBJ}}$, $\overleftarrow{\texttt{SUBJ}}$] (so an English transitive verb combines first with an NP, its object, to its right and then with an NP, its subject, to its left), whereas for Arabic it looks like [$\overrightarrow{\texttt{SUBJ}}$, $\overrightarrow{\texttt{OBJ}}$].

Marked orders
So far so good. We can use syntactic information to supplement the morphological analysis, and hence we can make decisions about fine-grained markers such as

case markers on NPs and mood and voice markers on verbs. Unfortunately, the order of the arguments of an Arabic verb is fairly unconstrained. The canonical order is VSO, but many other orders can occur.

There are two ways to cope with free word order: you can specify the variations on the canonical order which are allowed, or you can specify the variations which are not disallowed. To take the first approach, you compute the canonical order, and then generate all the allowed permutations. Having done this, you can use a standard parsing algorithm to see whether the items you are looking for are present in the specified positions. If we assume, for instance, that SOV, OSV, SVO, OVS, VSO and VOS are all acceptable orders under appropriate conditions then the parser would be required to search for six possible orders.

The alternative is to simply say that any order is potentially allowable, and to maintain a set of filters that check whether the arguments that are actually found are allowed in the positions where they turn up.

One of the advantages of this approach is that it is robust against non-standard orders. If, for instance, you simply penalise analyses that violate the constraints, rather than ruling them out entirely, then you can cover a wide range of alternative forms. Using the penalties associated with individual partial analyses to guide the search means that you will arrive at analyses that assign canonical orders before you arrive at non-standard ones, but nonetheless allows you to cope with non-standard orders when they occur. The idea of allowing arbitrary word orders subject to penalties for specific violations of the canonical order is reminiscent of the use of move-*alpha* together with a set of filters from [6], and of the treatment of constraints in optimality theory. Given that in most languages a wide range of orders *can* occur, it seems safer to allow arbitrary orders but to impose penalties on non-canonical forms than to try to enumerate the range of permissible orders in advance. You do need to adapt the underlying parsing algorithm so that it does not rely on indexing substructures on the basis of their positions, but once you can do that then this turns out to be a very robust approach.

2.2 Arabic Verbal Sentences

Canonical orders

Using these principles for determining the canonical order of the arguments in a simple Arabic sentence we can analyse a sentence like (2) as shown in Fig. 4.

(2) كتب الطالب الدرس. (*ktb āltālb āldrs.*)

If كتب (*ktb*) in (2) is a transitive verb, the principles outlined above will assign it the argument list in Fig. 4. Of course, كتب (*ktb*) could be a noun, or it could be an intransitive verb, or a passive of a transitive verb, or a ditransitive verb, or a passive of a ditransitive verb, and we have to allow for all these possibilities, though most of them will not lead to satisfactory analyses of (2). For the moment, however, we will just consider the simple transitive case.

```
{syn(args([{syn(head(cat(xbar(-v, +n))),
                      minor(specf(kspec(+specified))))},
           {syn(head(cat(xbar(-v, +n))),
                      minor(specf(kspec(+specified))))}]))}
```

Fig. 4. Arguments of a transitive verb

Clearly a word with the argument list in Fig. 4 will combine with a nominative NP immediately following it and an accusative marked one immediately after that, as required by the canonical VSO order. (2) does not, in fact, contain enough information to tell whether the following NPs have the required case-marking, but they certainly could have. We therefore assume that there is an analysis of (2) with كتب (*ktb*) as a transitive verb and the following NPs as the subject and object in their canonical positions. But since we now know the form of the verb and the case marking of the NPs we can fill in the diacritics as required.

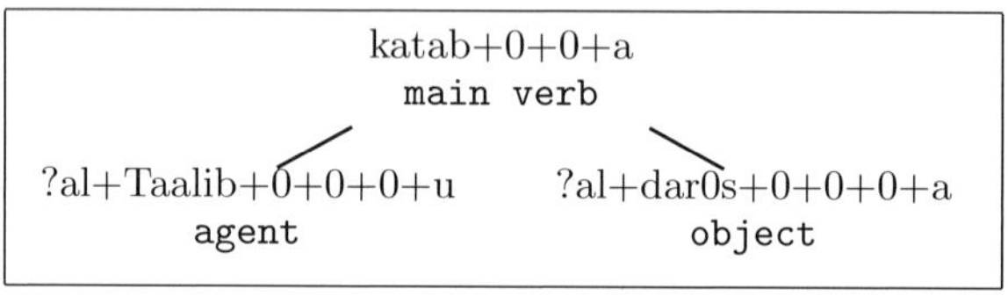

Fig. 5. Parse tree for (2)

There are, of course, a number of other possible analyses of (2), since كتب (*ktb*) has two readings as a transitive verb (كَتَبْ+٠+٠+أَ (**katab+0+0+a**) and كَتَّبْ+٠+٠+أَ (**kattab+0+0+a**)), plus a reading as a ditransitive verb كَتَّبْ+٠+٠+أَ (**kattab+0+0+a**) (which supports an analysis of (2) with a zero subject and the two explicit NPs as the direct and indirect objects) and another as the passive كُتِّبْ+٠+٠+أَ (**kuttib+0+0+a**), which again requires two NP arguments. We can rule out some of these by exploiting constraints on what kinds of things can play the various roles (e.g. the constraint that the agent of كَتَبْ+٠+٠+أَ (**katab+0+0+a**) should be animate), but ultimately obtaining the 'right' choice between the various analyses remains an open question. What we can do is to enumerate the possibilities, and to assign appropriate diacritics to each of them.

Marked orders

As noted above, Arabic allows for a number of alternative orders. In particular, SOV and OVS are both possible. However, when the subject occurs before the verb, it has to obey two constraints that are not required when it is in its canonical position immediately after the verb:

1. if an Arabic subject is not in its canonical position then it must agree with the verb in gender *and number*. Subjects in canonical position need only agree in gender.

2. only definite subjects can appear before the verb.

Consider (3):

(3) a. كاتبن بنت المدرسة. (*kātbn bnt ālmdrst.*)
b. بنت كاتبن المدرسة. (*bnt kātbn ālmdrst.*)

(3a) has two interpretations, one with بنت (*bnt*) as the subject and the other with المدرسة (*ālmdrsh*) as subject. Admittedly the second is more marked, since the subject would have to be in a non-canonical position, but it is certainly possible. For (3b), however, the reading with بنت (*bnt*) as subject is simply not possible, because indefinite subjects cannot appear before the verb.

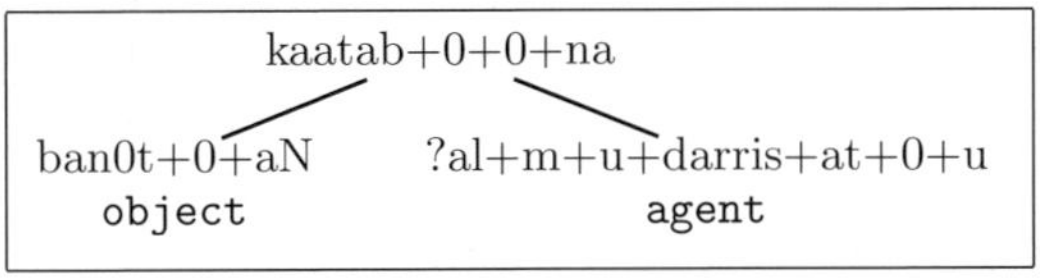

Fig. 6. Uniqueneness of (3a)

Stating the relevant constraint is fairly simple. Applying it appropriately is more difficult.

The problem here is that we do not want to generate two copies of the verb, one saying that you can have a subcat frame which specifies that the subject follows the verb and one that specifies that it precedes it but that it has to be definite, as in Fig. 7:

```
{syn(cat(xbar(+v, -n)),
     args([{struct(dir=after),
            syn(head(cat(xbar(-v, +n))),
                minor(+specified))},
           {syn(head(cat(xbar(-v, +n))),
                minor(+specified))}]))}
```

```
{syn(cat(xbar(+v, -n)),
     args([{struct(dir=before),
            syn(head(cat(xbar(-v, +n))),
                minor(+specified,
                      def(definite)))},
           {syn(head(cat(xbar(-v, +n))),
                minor(+specified))}]))}
```

Fig. 7. Alternative subcat lists for canonical and non-canonical orders

With very lexical grammars of the kind used, here the number of alternative readings of lexical items is the dominant factor in the complexity of the parsing algorithm. As such, producing multiple extremely similar analyses seems like a very bad idea. We therefore prefer to use a single interpretation of the verb with a 'just-in-time' constraint which gets applied when we have the required information, as in Fig. 8.

Fig. 8 shows a single description of the subcat list, together with a constraint that to the effect that when you know whether the subject was found before or after the verb you should check that it wasn't both before the verb and indefinite.

```
{syn(cat(xbar(+v, -n)),
     args([{struct(dir=DIR),
            syn(head(cat(xbar(-v, +n))),
                minor(+specified))},
           {syn(head(cat(xbar(-v, +n))),
                minor(+specified)
                     def(DEF))}]))}

when(known(DIR), not(DIR=before, DEF=indefinite))
```

Fig. 8. Single subcat list with just-in-time constraint

The use of delayed constraints like this allows us to generate a single highly underspecified interpretation for surface lexical forms that correspond to alternative underlying forms with quite different behaviours. The surface form أن (*ʾn*), for instance, corresponds to two underlying forms with quite different behaviours:

أن (*ʾn*) (أَنَّ (**ʾanna**)) requires a subject initial indicative clause with an accusative subject, where the clause must be a verbal clause.

أن (*ʾn*) (أَنْ (**ʾan**)) requires a verb initial subjunctive clause with a nominative subject

It can happen, then, that the surface form does not tell us which complementiser was written, nor which version of the verb. In these cases it is the embedding verb which makes the choice. We condense the two forms of أن (*ʾn*) into a single item which can manifest itself either as أَنْ (**ʾan**) or أَنَّ (**ʾanna**), and which can simultaneously provide the information required to make the verb fix its own underlying form. As soon as the embedding verb says which version of the complementiser it wants, the relevant phonetic details become clear, but until then we do not carry around multiple local analyses. The analyses of (4a) and (4b) in Fig. 9 illustrate this phenomenon: اعتقد (*āʿtqd*) requires a complement headed by أَنَّ (**ʾanna**), so the form of أن (*ʾn*) is constrained to be أَنَّ (**ʾanna**). But if the form of the complement is أنّ (**ʾanna**) then the verb must be indicative, so we can fix the right form of the mood marker. أمر (*ʾmr*) on the other hand requires the version of أن (*ʾn*) which has أَنْ (**ʾan**) as its underlying form, and this in turn requires a subjunctive form of the verb and an accusative form for its subject. We use just-in-time constraints to delay the decisions about the form of أن (*ʾn*), the mood markers and the case of the subject of the embedded clause.

(4) a. اعتقد المدرس أنّ التالبة تكتب الدرس. (*āʿtqd ālmdrs ʾn āltālbh tktb āldrs.*)
    b. أمر المدرس أن التالبة تكتب الدرس. (*ʾmr ālmdrs ʾn āltālbh tktb āldrs.*)

2.3 Nominal Sentences

Arabic, like a number of other languages, allows for sentences which consist of an NP and a predication (e.g. another NP, an adjective, a PP, or predicative VP)

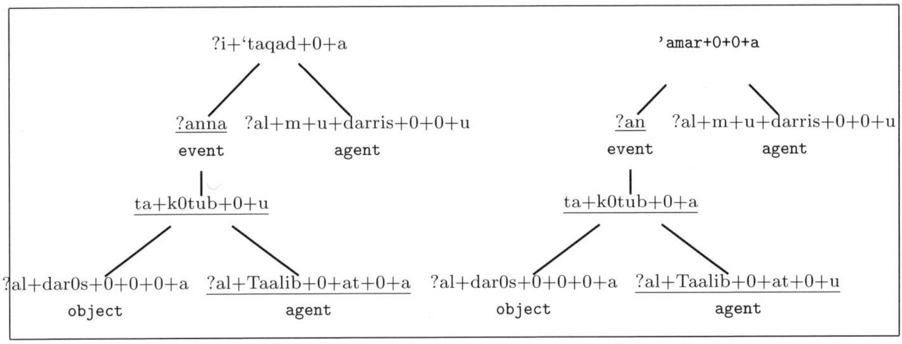

Fig. 9. (4a), (4b): Different complementisers impose different constraints

```
{syn(head(cat(xbar(+v, -n)))),
     subcat(args([{struct(dir(DIR)),
                   syn(CAT),
                   meaning(+predicative)}]))}
==>
 {syn(head(cat(xbar(-v, +n))),
      minor(specf(+specified), def(DEF)),
      subcat(args([])))}

when(known(DEF),
     if(DEF = definite)
     then DIR=after)
     else (DIR=before & CAT = pp)
```

Fig. 10. Nominal sentences

[7,8]. These ‘nominal sentences’, which also resemble English ‘small clauses’, can most easily be described by using a post-lexical rule which says that an NP can be seen as a sentence missing a predication. Fig. 10 shows the basic rule:

The first part of Fig. 10 is a post-lexical rule which says if you have an NP (a saturated `+specified` nominal) then you can see it as an unsaturated S which needs a `+predicative` item and which has the NP as its subject.

This covers the basic facts for a number of languages, including English small clauses. For Arabic, however, we have to supplement the basic rule with some rather complex ordering constraints. Roughly speaking, the situation is as follows:

- the case of the subject NP is governed by the external syntactic context.
- if the subject NP is indefinite then the order of the constituents must be reversed and the predication must in fact be a PP. This is again a constraint which can only be checked when the properties of the NP are known, and hence is included in the general rule as a just-in-time constraint.

The last part of Fig. 10 is a just-in-time rule which says that when you what the NP is you should check to see whether it is definite or not: if it is definite, then the predication should follow it, if it is indefinite then the predication should precede it, and should be a PP.

2.4 Construct NPs

Arabic allows NPs to function as possessive determiners, so that كتاب المدرسة (*ktāb ālmdrsh*) denotes 'the school's authors' [1] The basic facts here are again fairly straightforward: any genetive NP can function as the satellite in a construct NP. As in other languages, genetive marking does not always denote literal possession, and the semantic relation between the satellite and the head may be quite subtle, but the core of the structural rule is as given.

As with nominal sentences, the basic rule is embellished with a number of rather delicate caveats. The key problems relate to the case marking on the head noun. This has to be nominative marked, no matter what the function of the whole NP in the wider sentence, and the nominative marker that is assigned to it has to be the form which is appropriate for definite nouns *even if there is no definite article*. The analysis of (5) in Fig. 11 shows the assignment of the definite nominative marker to كتاب (*ktāb*) despite the lack of a definite article: كتاب (*ktāb*) is the head noun of an NP which is definite by virtue of being a construct NP, and hence the case marker has to be the definite form [9].

(5) يكتب كتاب المدرسة. (*yktb ktāb ālmdrst.*) (the school's authors write)

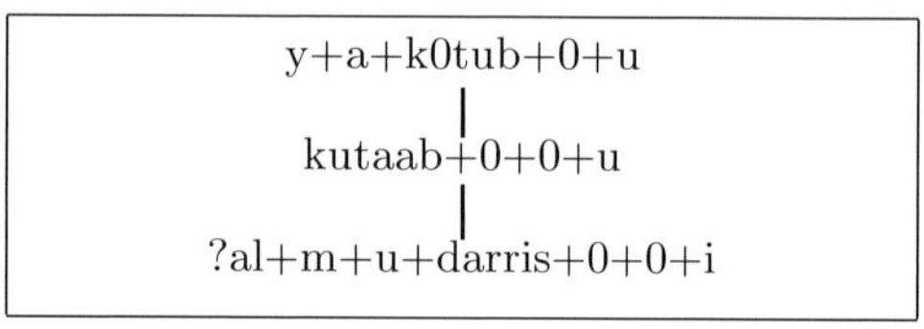

Fig. 11. Case marking in a construct NP

This example shows that we really have no chance of assigning case markers until we see the wider syntactic context. We don't know what case some noun has until we see the context, and even if we did know what the case was we wouldn't know what the marker should look like until we saw the context. Again, use of a just-in-time constraint allows us to delay the decision until we have the required information.

[1] As noted above, كتاب (*ktāb*) and المدرسة (*ālmdrsh*), like many surface forms in Arabic, have multiple interpretations. This is, after all, the reason why we have a problem in the first place. Space precludes a discussion of what we do about this widespread problem.

3 Conclusions

The work reported above is part of an attempt to produce a text-to-speech system for Modern Standard Arabic. The general problem we are faced with in this task is that syntactic analysis helps us to solve two key problems in text-to-speech for MSA, namely determining the diacritics and imposing a prosodic contour, but that until we know what the diacritics are we cannot easily determine the syntactic structure. The key to solving this chicken-and-egg problem is the use of just-in-time constraints, which are evaluated at just the point where the relevant information becomes available. Sometimes, for instance, determining what form the case marker on an NP should take requires you to know whether it is the subject or object of a verb, and also to know what complementiser, if any, the verb is governed by; but sometimes deciding whether an NP is the subject or object depends on knowing what its case marker is, and knowing what complementiser it is governed by may depend on knowing what the embedding verb is. You cannot be sure which piece of information will become available first, so the sensible thing to do is to set dynamic constraints which are activated as soon as possible.

References

1. Pollard, C.J., Sag, I.A.: An Information Based Approach to Syntax and Semantics: Vol 1 Fundamentals. CSLI lecture notes 13, Chicago University Press, Chicago (1988)
2. Dowty, D.R.: Thematic proto-roles and argument selection. Language **67** (1991) 547–619
3. Ramsay, A.M.: Direct parsing with discontinuous phrases. Natural Language Engineering **5(3)** (1999) 271–300
4. Malouf, R.: A constructional approach to English verbal gerunds. In: Proceedings of the Twenty-second Annual Meeting of the Berkeley Linguistics Society, Marseille (1996)
5. Fillmore, C.: The case for case. In Bach, E., Harms, R., eds.: Universals in Linguistic Theory, Chicago, Holt, Rinehart and Winston (1968) 1–90
6. Chomsky, N.: Lectures on Government and Binding. Foris Publications, Dordrecht (1981)
7. Fehri, A.F.: Issues in the structure of Arabic clauses and words. Kluwer Academic Publishers, Dordrecht (1993)
8. Abdul-Raof, H.: Subject, theme and agent in Modern Standard Arabic. TJ Press International, Cornwall (1998)
9. Mohammed, A.: Word order, agreement and pronominalisation in standard and Palestinian Arabic. Current Issues in Linguistic Theory (2000) 1–81

MEDITE: A Unilingual Textual Aligner

Julien Bourdaillet and Jean-Gabriel Ganascia

Université Pierre et Marie Curie - Laboratoire d'Informatique de Paris 6
8 rue du Capitaine Scott - 75015 Paris - France
julien.bourdaillet@lip6.fr, jean-gabriel.ganascia@lip6.fr

Abstract. This paper addresses a problem of natural language text alignment, from a humanities discipline called textual genetic criticism where different text versions must be compared. The paper shows that this task is hard because such versions can be very different and texts with a lot of internal repetitions present specific difficulties. MEDITE is a natural language text aligner that compares texts written in the same language. It detects modifications at character level, as opposed to related applications which either remain at word level or give poor results at character level. The detection of moved blocks in the text, induced by our formalism based on edit distance with moves, is introduced. The algorithm is closely related to sequence alignment in bioinformatics as similar building blocks are used and applied to this natural language processing task. A benchmark analysis has been carried out to compare MEDITE with other aligners and it shows that our approach is superior to existing ones especially in hard cases.

1 Introduction

MEDITE has been designed as an application to assist philologists in their practice of textual genetic criticism [1,2]. It is part of the humanities and was developped thirty years ago as an important original French school of literary study [3,4,5].

This discipline introduced a temporal dimension in literary criticism by studying not only the final version of a literary work but also writers' drafts in order to highlight the genesis of the text. It seeks to understand how a text is produced but remains close to the aesthetics of the work. Philologists suggest interpretative hypotheses when they read the final version of a text, which they corroborate (or invalidate) through the study of previous versions. This study is based on text version comparison and considers every modification between two versions. These modifications need to be character based because a writer can proceed by one- or two-character long modifications, which can seriously alter the sentence meaning, especially for a morphologically rich language such as French.

Techniques arising from genetic criticism have been applied to epistemology as in the following example. Claude Bernard was a nineteenth century physiologist who contributed to the birth of modern medicine. In order to study the evolution of his medical theories, philologists want to compare his experiment notebooks

T. Salakoski et al. (Eds.): FinTAL 2006, LNAI 4139, pp. 458–469, 2006.

and their synthesis written some years later. The notebooks relate observations in a telegraphic style while observations are written in an academic style in the synthesis (in which new ideas are also inserted). An example of comparison of these two texts using Microsoft Word is given in Figure 1 and using MEDITE in Figure 2. It can be seen that MEDITE identifies considerably more invariants (in black and white) between the two texts than Word, resulting in a better alignment (as presented in Section 4). Furthermore, the visualization interface impacts on the readability of the alignment. (This example uses French texts but MEDITE works for West-European languages.)

Comparison and visualization problems are common in existing file comparison tools. These tools are generally descendants of *diff* [6] in which two files are compared line by line and a list of inserted and deleted lines is produced. This kind of program comes from the community that created Unix where their main interest was source code comparison. For this task, line by line comparison is sufficient because program structure is very constrained and the syntax is strong. This results in well-organized texts (i.e. source code) and the assertion "one line, one instruction" is generally verified. Most of the modifications occurring between two versions are line modifications. The limits of these comparers appear with texts such as those of Claude Bernard because intra-line modifications are not well identified. For example, the modification of one character in a line will lead to a "deletion of one line, insertion of one line" analysis. This is acceptable for source code but is a bad result for natural language. The precision of detections is of crucial importance for genetic criticism and this is not addressed correctly by existing aligners.

Furthermore, Claude Bernard's texts contain a lot of repeated text blocks. In the left text of Figure 2, the word *mouvements* is repeated three times and it is repeated more times in the whole text. With simple alignment algorithms, several repetitions may not be found, resulting in missing invariant or moved blocks in the final alignment, as in Figure 1. This is due to the fact that invariants (and moves) between the two texts are blocks repeated at least twice and if some repetitions are missed then invariants will be missed. Similar problems existed in previous versions of MEDITE: when processing Claude Bernard's texts, our results were similar to those of Word. We present here a new algorithm that addresses these problems.

This task can be defined as unilingual textual alignment that compares two related texts, written in the same language, and identifies invariants and differences between them. More precisely, the term alignment refers to the identification of these invariants and their pairing. Once identified, differences can be deduced, but there is no one way of doing this. We also address the move detection task, but since moves can be seen as a deletion plus an insertion, this task involves ambiguity. Using our formalism, based on edit distance with moves, it is possible to handle moves and this is presented in Section 2.

Machine translation is based on alignment, but it is bilingual and sentence or word-based. Most of the methods rely on machine learning where a statistical model is trained from a bilingual reference corpus [7]. In our case, there exists no unilingual aligned corpus, so supervised learning is not possible. Moreover, our aim is to detect modifications between texts whereas in machine translation each word or expression in the first text must match a similar unit in the second. There are no deletions or insertions whereas they are central in our problem.

In bioinformatics, sequences of nucleic acids (DNA) or amino acids (proteins) are aligned. This is unilingual alignment because sequences are expressed in the same alphabet and the grain of the alignment is character-based.

Two alignment types exist in bioinformatics, local and global, descending from [8] and [9] respectively. Local aligners try to find regions in sequences that match exactly or with a maximum similarity. Regions of low similarity can be left unaligned because not all regions are of equal importance. On a DNA strand, coding regions (exons) will code for proteins and non-coding regions (introns) will be eliminated during the transformation process to RNA.

What global aligners try to do is to match two sequences completely. One character from one of the two sequences either matches one character of the other sequence or matches a blank character meaning it is inserted or deleted. We are not interested in finding regions of high similarity between two texts without considering low similarity regions because each character of our texts must be aligned. Our algorithm is related to bioinformatics global aligners and will be presented in Section 3 but, whereas bioinformatics aligners can hide repetitions in sequences before alignment using tools such as RepeatMasker [10], we must address this problem.

MEDITE was evaluated using a benchmark with other file comparison tools, as presented in Section 4. General conclusisons are presented in Section 5.

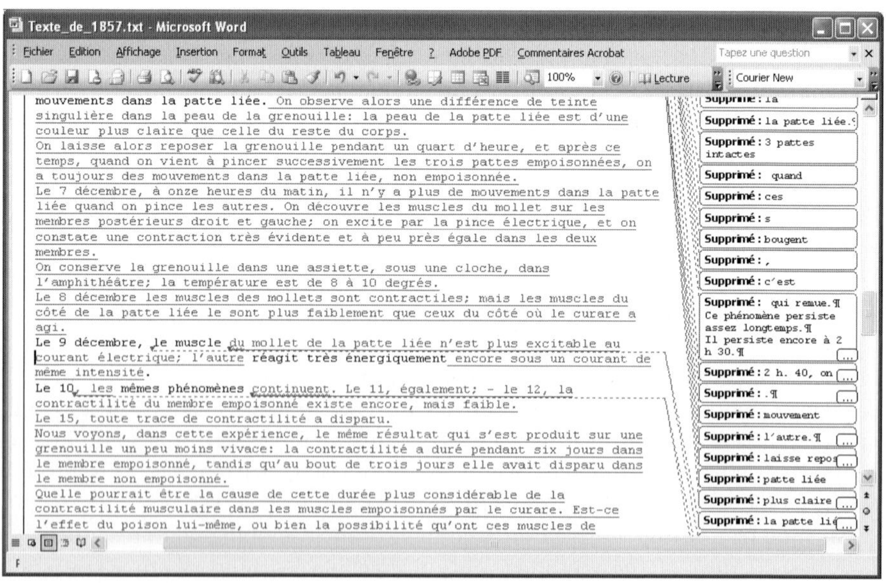

Fig. 1. The alignment of Claude Bernard's texts using Microsoft Word

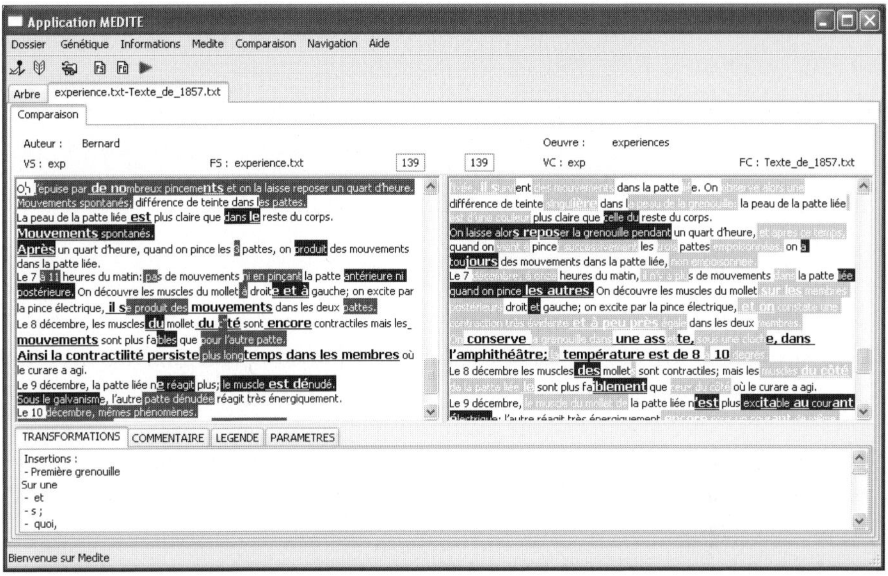

Fig. 2. The alignment of Claude Bernard's texts using MEDITE

2 Formalism

This alignment problem can be formalized as the computation of edit distance with moves [11,12] detailed below.

We have two sequences s_1 and s_2 over the common West-European Latin alphabet $\Sigma = \{a, ..., z\} \bigcup \{A, ..., Z\} \bigcup \{accentuated\ characters\} \bigcup \{separators\}$. Four operators are given: character insertion, character deletion, character substitution and block moves. A block is a 3-tuple (p, q, l) where p is the position in s_1, q the position in s_2 and l the length of the block. The goal is to find a sequence of operations of minimum cost which transforms s_1 in s_2. Characters not involved in an edit operation are called invariant characters, present in both s_1 and s_2. The decomposition of s_1 and s_2 into a list of inserted, deleted, substituted, moved and invariant blocks forms an alignment. This problem is NP-complete [13,12] and, following the formalism described in [14], it can be reduced to the block permutation problem.

The block permutation problem considers two sequences sh_1 and sh_2 over Σ such that $|sh_1| = |sh_2|$ and a predicate P that defines a bijection between every character of two strings:

$$P(S, S^{'}) = (\forall i, 1 \leq i \leq |S|, \exists! j, 1 \leq j \leq |S^{'}|, S[i] = S^{'}[j]) \wedge \\ (\forall i, 1 \leq i \leq |S^{'}|, \exists! j, 1 \leq j \leq |S|, S^{'}[i] = S[j]) \quad (1)$$

$P(sh_1, sh_2)$ defines a minimal trivial partition of the two strings in invariant or moved blocks, the 1-character long block partition. The goal is to find a maximal

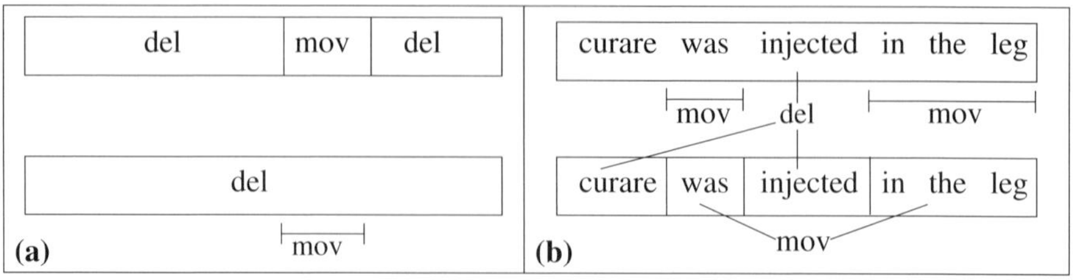

Fig. 3. (a): Decorator transformation, (b): Block split

partition under a certain measure M that is a partition maximizing invariant block size and minimizing moved block size. This enables us to define

$$M = \sum_{b_i \in \{invariants\}} |b_i| - \sum_{b_m \in \{moves\}} |b_m| \tag{2}$$

A function *part* extracts a partition from sh_1 and sh_2 such that:

$$\begin{aligned} &part\,(sh_1, sh_2) \rightarrow \{invariants\}, \{moves\} \text{ with} \\ &\qquad \forall x \in (sh_1 \cup sh_2), x \in \{invariants\} \vee x \in \{moves\} \end{aligned} \tag{3}$$

Predicate P declares that every character in sh_1 must be present in sh_2 and vice versa. The concatenation of homologies between s_1 and s_2 verify the predicate P because homologies are present in both sequences. Hence a function $hom(s_1, s_2) \rightarrow sh_1, sh_2$ transforms the problem of the computation of edit distance with moves into the block permutation problem.

The size of the set of all homologies between two related sequences s_1 and s_2 is exponential. In order to reduce this size, we consider only maximal exact matches (MEMs) that are matches which cannot be extended to the left or to the right without losing the homology property. Non maximal matches are included in MEMs and are of no interest. Furthermore, it is consistent, but not sufficient, with the necessity for homologies extracted by *hom* to be disjoint, because a block cannot be invariant and moved at the same time.

All moves can be seen as a deletion plus an insertion. When a small moved block is situated between two deleted (or inserted) blocks it may be better to consider it as part of the deleted (or inserted) blocks and to merge them. Then these moved sub-blocks can be seen as decorators of the block rather than already presented moved blocks seen as operators, as shown in Figure 3(a).

In order to capture the two different types of move, we introduce typed decorated blocks as a tuple such that:

$$\begin{aligned} block_{td} : &(type, begin, end, decorators) \text{ with } type \in \{ins, del, sub, mov, inv\}, \\ &(1 \leq begin < end \leq |s_1|) \vee (1 \leq begin < end \leq |s_2|), \\ &decorators = \{(b_d, e_d), begin \leq b_d < e_d \leq end\} \end{aligned} \tag{4}$$

As decoration makes no sense for blocks of type *mov* and *inv*, the following restriction is applied to them: $decorators = \emptyset$. An empty block named *None* is introduced for convenience. This formalism makes it possible to capture homologies considered as blocks of type *mov* as well as homologies considered as moves inside a block of another type (except *inv*).

Furthermore an alignment A becomes an increasing list of pairs of typed decorated blocks:

$$\begin{aligned} A \Leftrightarrow [(B_{s_1}, B_{s_2}) &\text{ where } B_{s_1} \text{ and } B_{s_2} \text{ are } block_{td}, \\ &1 \leq Pred(B_{s_1})[end] < B_{s_1}[begin] < B_{s_1}[end] < Succ(B_{s_1})[begin] \leq |s_1|, \\ &1 \leq Pred(B_{s_2})[end] < B_{s_2}[begin] < B_{s_2}[end] < Succ(B_{s_2})[begin] \leq |s_2|] \end{aligned} \quad (5)$$

where *Pred* and *Succ* are the predecessor and successor functions respectively. Blocks of type *sub* and *inv* are aligned pairwise whereas other blocks are aligned with *None*. We name this structure a bi-block list. Hence an alignment algorithm has to build it.

3 Algorithm

Our algorithm is an instantiation of the formalism described in Section 2. It processes text in two phases. The first phase resolves the block permutation problem and the second processes the remaining text and builds the bi-block list.

3.1 Block Permutation Problem

In bioinformatics most of the recent global aligners [15,16,17] proceed in three steps:

1. searching for anchors in sequences
2. aligning them in order to determine invariants and moves
3. processing recursively between invariants

We proceed in the same way, as shown below, and these three steps correspond to the *hom* function in Section 2.

Anchors are homologies under a certain similarity criterion. Our criterion is exact homology, where the two substrings must match exactly. Firstly, a generalized suffix tree [18] is built over the two sequences in order to extract all the homologies. A minimum size parameter is chosen by the user (by default, five characters long). This method generates overlaps between homologies. However, it is necessary to resolve them in order to obtain a proper partition of the complete sequences in disjoint blocks. We use a heuristic based on a property of natural language: if the overlap contains separators, it is better to cut it on one of them, since an inter-word cut is preferable to an intra-word cut. Most of the time this condition is verified, but if not the block is cut arbitrarily.

In the second step, blocks must be aligned to determine which are invariant and which are moved. The space of all possible alignments is browsed by an A* procedure using an alignment cost function which is a heuristic based on the measure M of Section 2. During the search, an alignment cost is decomposed into the cost of already aligned blocks plus an estimation of the cost of the remaining blocks to be aligned such that $cost = cost_{ab} + cost_{rb}$ where $cost_{ab}$ is the sum of the size of moved blocks in already aligned blocks and $cost_{rb}$ is the sum of the size of the blocks in the symmetric difference between remaining blocks to be aligned in the two sequences. Because it will not be possible to align these remaining blocks in the rest of the alignment process, they will be considered as moved in the final alignment and counted as a penalty due to M. This corresponds to the *part* function in Section 2.

Finally, these two steps are repeated recursively. The difference comes from input sequences. We loop over the alignment resulting from step two and consider the subsequences between each pair of aligned invariant blocks. Then these subsequences are used as input of the first step. The output of the recursive steps one and two is an alignment for the two subsequences. Invariants and moves identified with this alignment are included in the main invariant and moved blocks. This recursive step enables to find alignments which would otherwise have not been found.

3.2 Bi-block List Building

The first phase produces two sets of invariant and moved blocks. Text between two invariant blocks in the first sequence is a deleted block and text between two invariant blocks in the second sequence is an inserted block. By definition moved blocks overlap deleted and inserted blocks, hence all moved blocks (identified during the first phase) overlap a deleted or an inserted block and are considered as their decorators by including them in the *decorator* set of each deleted or inserted block.

Then two heuristics are used to determine substituted blocks and moved blocks considered as operators. If in the bi-block list two bi-blocks of type $(del, None)$ and $(None, ins)$ follow each other then we examine the size of blocks del and ins. If the ratio between their size reaches a certain threshold, they are considered as two substituted blocks, and are replaced in the bi-block list by one pair of type (sub, sub) with the same features. By default the ratio is set to 0.5, and the user is free to modify it. For instance, if a bi-block $((del, 'He\ saw\ me'), None)$ is immediately followed in the list by $(None, (ins, 'I\ saw\ him'))$ and their size ratio exceeds the threshold then they are replaced by $((sub, 'He\ saw\ me'), (sub, 'I\ saw\ him'))$ meaning that $'He\ saw\ me'$ has been replaced by $'I\ saw\ him'$ in the text.

In a similar way, for each block of type del and ins, we examine the ratio between the size of the block and the sum of the size of its decorators. If it is above another threshold we split the block into several blocks of type mov or the original type such that the intervals covered by these new blocks are the same as the original block. An example is presented in Figure 3(b). This ratio is also set to 0.5 by default and the user can modify it.

Finally a bi-block list that defines an alignment between the two sequences results from this phase.

4 Experiments and Evaluation

In bioinformatics, the evaluation of sequence alignment, i.e. finding an objective criterion to tell whether an alignment is good or not, is a difficult task and remains an open problem [18,19]. The first classic measure to evaluate an alignment A of two sequences sa_1 and sa_2 is the character-weight measure $M_2(sa_1, sa_2) = \Sigma_{k=1}^{|A|} S(sa_1[k], sa_2[k])$ where S is a scoring matrix between two characters of the alphabet such as Dayhoff or BLOSUM matrices. These matrices encode the probability of the substitution of one character for another. In natural language such matrices do not make sense. The second classic measure is an operator weight measure where a weight is assigned to each kind of edit operation such as $M_3(sa_1, sa_2) = \sum_{b_i \in \{invariants\}} W_i|b_i| - \sum_{b_d \in \{deletions\}} W_d|b_d| - \sum_{b_{ins} \in \{insertions\}} W_{ins}|b_{ins}| - \sum_{b_s \in \{substitutions\}} W_s|b_s| - \sum_{b_m \in \{moves\}} W_m|b_m|$.

Our measure M is similar to M_3 but it cannot be used for evaluation for three reasons. In our algorithm, M drives the alignment process, so using it to evaluate itself is of no interest. Secondly, this measure gives a blind evaluation of the alignment as it is character-based and counts each block of each type but this does not evaluate the relevance of the resulting alignment. Thirdly, there exists no processable representation of the alignments for the applications we tested in section 4.1 (except for ours), because this information is encoded only in the visualization interface.

Furthermore, there exists no annotated unilingual corpus (a corpus where texts would have been aligned correctly by human annotators) which could be considered as a reference corpus or a gold standard. Hence evaluation can not be based on measures such as precision, recall, BLEU, BLANC or ROUGE [20].

These facts led us to evaluate our system in different ways.

4.1 Benchmark

MEDITE has been compared with ten aligners, the most famous being the one present in Microsoft Word. For each application, four file comparisons were made, where three points were tested (identified with capitalized letters below).

The first comparison is between two versions of a Python language source file. In the second version, large pieces of text were inserted at the beginning and the end of the file, and a lot of lines were modified in the body of the file. These modifications occur mainly line by line, though some occur within lines. This comparison was expected to be easy and serves as a baseline. To pass the first test, inserted and deleted paragraphs must be found (A); for the second test, line by line alignment must be correct (B) and for the third test intra-line modifications must be found (C).

The second comparison is between two versions of a short story by Pascal Quignard entitled “Bernon l’Enfant”. Small modifications of some characters were introduced throughout the text. Lexical words were changed, misspellings corrected and words moved. The goal is to find such modifications. Paragraphs must be aligned (D); word modifications must be found (E) and character modifications must be found (F).

The third comparison is between a news agency dispatch and an article which is rather different but derived from it. Two paragraphs were kept with some internal modifications, and the remaining text was replaced completely by another one. The two paragraphs must be aligned (G); modifications inside these paragraphs must be found (H) and similar lexical words must be found (I).

The fourth comparison is the one described in the introduction. Texts from Claude Bernard’s experiment notebooks and their synthesis must be aligned. This task is very hard because the existing content remained the same but the form changed and new content was inserted. Paragraphs must be aligned (J); word groups must be aligned (K) and isolated words must be aligned (L).

Table 1. Benchmark Results

	A	B	C	D	E	F	G	H	I	J	K	L	Total
MEDITE	1	1	1	1	1	1	1	1	1	1	1	1	12
DiffDoc	1	1	0	1	1	0	1	1	0	1	1	0	8
Word	1	1	1	1	1	0	0	0	0	1	1	0	7
Compare It	1	1	1	1	1	1	0	0	0	0	0	0	6
Araxis Merge	1	1	1	1	0	0	0	0	0	0	0	0	4
Beyond Compare	1	1	1	1	0	0	0	0	0	0	0	0	4
Visual Comparer	1	1	0	1	0	0	0	0	0	1	0	0	4
Compare Suite	1	1	0	1	0	0	0	0	0	0	0	0	3
WinMerge	1	1	0	1	0	0	0	0	0	0	0	0	3
Active File Compare	1	1	0	0	0	0	0	0	0	0	0	0	2
Perforce P4diff	1	1	0	0	0	0	0	0	0	0	0	0	2

The results[1] of this experiment are presented in Table 1. Line by line Python code alignment (A and B) is correct for all the applications, but intra-line modifications (C) are detected only by half of them. This is a problem since intra-line modifications are necessary to detect a variable name change for instance.

Only four applications detect word changes in test E and only MEDITE and Compare It detect character changes (F). The others detect character changes as word changes, whereas often only one or two characters have been modified. By contrast MEDITE focuses on the modified characters.

For the third comparison, only DiffDoc and MEDITE align the two paragraphs (G) and find small internal modifications (H). All the other applications fail to

[1] Detailed results of each application are accessible on `http://www-poleia.lip6.fr/~bourdaillet/comparison`.

detect this. This test is useful because the longest invariant sequence is 752 characters long for two texts of 14 Ko and 18 Ko, and so represents about 5% the size of each file. As it doesn't change, we could except all software to find it but only two of them do. Because the theme of the two texts is related, common lexical words are used in the remainder of the texts but only MEDITE aligns them correctly (I).

The fourth comparison is the hardest one. Paragraphs are aligned correctly only by DiffDoc, MEDITE and Word (J). Several word groups are aligned by DiffDoc and Word but a lot are missed (K). We know they are missed because MEDITE detects them. As DiffDoc and Word miss numerous word groups, they miss isolated word changes whereas MEDITE aligns them pairwise correctly (L). The absence of these alignment anchors results in a bad alignment because a lot of information is not discovered and it impacts on the readability of the alignment. Our result can be viewed in Figure 2. The less the texts are aligned the less the visualization is good. In earlier versions of MEDITE [2] we had similar problems but the introduction of recursion in our algorithm enabled us to address them.

None of the applications except for MEDITE detects moved blocks, though we have already said that this is crucial for philology. For source code comparison, this is still the case. Detecting that a code line has been moved from one function to another is an important piece of information. It is also important for any natural language text, because it makes possible to detect rearrangements of ideas, for instance.

4.2 Visualization

As in the case of bioinformatics [21] visualization is an important criterion for the evaluation of text alignment applications. Human judges can evaluate a natural language alignment empirically but in order to do that a good visualization interface is mandatory.

Figure 2 presents MEDITE's visualization interface. Although the figure is small it can be seen that the colors identify the different types of blocks well. Deleted blocks are red (or grey in the grayscale printed proceedings), inserted blocks are green (light grey) and substituted blocks are blue (dark grey) while invariant blocks remain black and white. These colors can customized by the user. Moved blocks are underlined and have a bold font, enabling decorators to be represented.

Applications tested in section 4.1 have poor visualization in comparison to MEDITE. Not only do bad alignments result in bad visualization but in addition, graphical user interfaces (GUIs) are generally ill-suited. Another serious problem is that a lot of them present a merged text that mixes deletions and insertions: when texts are very different, the visualization is bad, as is the case with Word in Figure 1.

In MEDITE, when the user clicks on an invariant block its corresponding block is presented side-by-side on the other window. It is thus possible to browse the text in an intuitive way following the blocks the user is interested in. This differs from other applications, where scrolling bars are locked, so when big parts of text are deleted or inserted it is sometimes impossible to look at them side-by-side.

MEDITE also generates an HTML report which is a direct visualization of the bi-block list. Each block is displayed with its match and both are colored corresponding to their type. This kind of visualization can be useful especially for source code.

5 Conclusion

This paper presents a textual alignment system and addresses the problem of sequence alignment when applied to natural language. We show that it can be very difficult and that results from existing aligners are not satisfactory for texts studied by textual genetic criticism where there are a lot of repeated blocks. Our experiments show that both existing algorithms and their visualization give poor results. Only two systems, DiffDoc and Word, compete with MEDITE but nevertheless are less good.

We present a method to detect moved blocks in textual comparisons; none of the applications we tested was able to do this. In addition the way we decompose moved blocks in operators and decorators enables the user to handle them as they wish: if the user considers move detection more important, operators will be favored by shifting up the ratio and vice versa.

It is interesting to remark that this is a direct application of a current theoretical problem, edit distance with moves. This problem is harder in bioinformatics due to the huge quantity of data but it is viable in the area of file comparison.

We are also interested in medieval philology where spelling was not stable. Between two text versions, a word could be spelled in different ways because the copyist could decide arbitrarily to modify it. The challenge is to align such text versions correctly despite these difficulties.

More generally, this problem is interesting because sequence alignment is an old problem but texts resulting from genetic criticism have shown hard cases that were handled incorrectly by classic file comparison tools. In addition, and this was the original aim of this work which is now completed, natural language processing brings new facilities to researchers in textual genetic criticism via a tool such as MEDITE.

References

1. Ganascia, J.G., Fenoglio, I., Lebrave, J.L.: Manuscrits, genèse et documents numérisés. EDITE: une étude informatisée du travail de l'écrivain. Document Numérique **8** (2004) 91–110
2. Ganascia, J.G., Bourdaillet, J.: Alignements unilingues avec MEDITE. In: Huitièmes Journées Internationales d'Analyse Statistique des Données Textuelles, To appear. (2006)
3. Deppman, J., Ferrer, D., Groden, M., eds.: Genetic Criticism - Texts and Avant-textes. University of Pennsylvania Press (2004)

4. Hay, L., ed.: Essais de critique génétique. Flammarion, coll. Textes et Manuscrits (1979)
5. de Biasi, P.M.: La Génétique des Textes. Nathan Université (2000)
6. Hunt, J.W., McIlroy, M.D.: An Algorithm for Differential File Comparison. Technical Report CSTR 41, Bell Laboratories, Murray Hill, NJ (1976)
7. Manning, C.D., Schtze, H.: Foundations of Statistical Natural Language Processing. MIT Press (1999)
8. Smith, T.F., Waterman, M.S.: Identification of Common Molecular Subsequences. Journal of Molecular Biology **147** (1981) 195–197
9. Needleman, S., Wunsch, C.: A general method applicable to the search for similarities in the amino acid sequence of two proteins. Journal of Molecular Biology **48** (1970) 443–453
10. Smit, A.F.: Identification of a new, abundant superfamily of mammalian LTR-transposons. Nucleic Acids Res **21** (1993) 1863–72
11. Tichy, W.F.: The String-to-String Correction Problem with Block Moves. ACM Trans. Comput. Syst. **2** (1984) 309–321
12. Lopresti, D.P., Tomkins, A.: Block Edit Models for Approximate String Matching. Theor. Comput. Sci. **181** (1997) 159–179
13. Shapira, D., Storer, J.A.: Edit Distance with Move Operations. In Apostolico, A., Takeda, M., eds.: CPM. Volume 2373 of Lecture Notes in Computer Science., Springer (2002) 85–98
14. Kaplan, H., Shafrir, N.: The greedy algorithm for edit distance with moves. Information Processing Letters **97** (2006) 23–27
15. Delcher, A.L., Kasif, S., Fleischmann, R.D., Peterson, J., White, O., Salzberg, S.L.: Alignment of whole genomes. Nucl. Acids. Res. **27** (1999) 2369–2376
16. Bray, N., Dubchak, I., Pachter, L.: AVID: A Global Alignment Program. Genome Res. **13** (2003) 97–102
17. Darling, A.C., Mau, B., Blattner, F.R., Perna, N.T.: Mauve: Multiple Alignment of Conserved Genomic Sequence With Rearrangements. Genome Res. **14** (2004) 1394 – 1403
18. Gusfield, D.: Algorithms on Strings, Trees and Sequences: Computer Science and Computer Biology. Cambridge University Press (1997)
19. Batzoglou, S.: The many faces of sequence alignment. Briefings in Bioinformatics **6** (2005) 6–22
20. Lita, L., Rogati, M., Lavie, A.: BLANC: Learning Evaluation Metrics for MT. In: Proceedings of Human Language Technology Conference and Conference on Empirical Methods in Natural Language Processing, Vancouver, British Columbia, Canada, Association for Computational Linguistics (2005) 740–747
21. Raghava, G., Searle, S.M., Audley, P.C., Barber, J.D., Barton, G.J.: OXBench: A benchmark for evaluation of protein multiple sequence alignment accuracy. BMC Bioinformatics **4** (2003)

Maximum Likelihood Alignment of Translation Equivalents

Saba Amsalu

Universität bielefeld, Germany

Abstract. We describe a corpus-informed lexical acquisition procedure based on maximum likelihood estimate of translations. The most likely translation words in singleton parallel sentences are determined by the measure of the similarity of their distribution in the entire corpus. The results show that for the recall level obtained our procedure is quite efficient.

1 Introduction

Parallel corpora are praised for being without parallel as a source of translation data which are useful for all sorts of multilingual language engineering. However, to extract these translation data is not an easy task for many reasons. One of the challenges is that it is difficult to get a significant number of lexical entries as compared to the size of corpus used. In particular, when using statistical methods, the problem is exaggerated. Often a small set of words that occur with a higher frequency are addressed [1,4,5,7,6].

On the other hand, natural language processing operations such as machine translation, cross-language information retrieval, terminology banks and computer assisted language learning systems demand bilingual lexica of high coverage. Hence, attaining an acceptable coverage of lexicon is of paramount importance. Using a huge amount corpora have been established to cope with the problem. But again, unfortunately, for many languages large quantities of bilingual corpora are not available.

In this project we propose a method of attaining increased lexical acquisition by statistical similarity measures of maximum likelihood. We use a relatively small size of corpora to generate many translation equivalents. The algorithm is tested on Amharic-English bilingual corpora.

In Section 2, some features of aligned sentences that are relevant for text alignment are discussed. In Section 3 algorithmic analysis of the optimal alignment for parallel sentences is made. How the distribution of translation terms in parallel corpora can be indicators of similarity is also presented. Section 4 describes the evaluation of the results followed by concluding remarks and future direction in Section 5.

T. Salakoski et al. (Eds.): FinTAL 2006, LNAI 4139, pp. 470–475, 2006.

2 Characteristics of Aligned Sentences

Parallel sentences are two groups of sequences of words explaining the same message. The symbols in the words are not necessarily identical; neither are the lengths of each word or the number of words in the two sentences.

Alignment systems try to align all or some of these words in the sentences. In many statistical approaches of alignment the chances for most of the words to be aligned is very low when the dataset used is small. In fact it is not a rare case that none of the words in a sentence may be aligned. But one thing is true, these words are translations. Ideally, each word in the source language (or the meaning contained by the word) is expressed in some way in the target language. But the question of how to find these relations is not easy to answer.

For a machine the problem is as if a human translator is expected to match a pair of sentences in languages the translator does not know and with symbols not familiar. They are just sequence of symbols, but somehow they are related. For example if we have parallel sentences and each word is represented by a single symbol, say,

1 2 3 4 (sentence I)

a b c d e f g (sentence II)

We know word 1 in sentence I, is a translation to one or more of the symbols in sentence II, but don't know which one. If we have a text with several such sentences, can we use it to guess which words are the most likely correct translations?

The assumption we are basing our experiment on is that we can align words in parallel sentences extracted from a parallel corpora. I.e, based on the distributional properties of words in the entire corpus it is possible to come up with the most likely translation equivalents in sentence pairs that were extracted from the corpora itself. Subsequent sections will give detail account of the line of argument.

3 Quest for the Optimal Alignment Path

Our approach tries to align words in parallel sentences given their distribution in a larger corpora. We attempt to align words in one pair of sentences. We do not want to find the translation in some other sentences in the text but within the translation sentences. Because the translation of each of the word in the source sentence is embedded somewhere just in the target sentence. If we manage to do so, the recall for the words in the shorter sentence will simply become a hundred percent.

In an m x n matrix of words in translation sentences where m and n are the number of words in source and target sentences and m is the number of words in the shorter sentence, there are $\frac{n!}{(n-m)!}$ permutations of possible alignments. Among these alignment possibilities one of them is the optimal alignment.

Thus, each word in the source sentence must be aligned to its most likely translation in the target sentence. To get this alignment we need to have a measure of similarity of each word in the source and target text. This information is obtained in the corpora where the sentences are extracted from.

Computational linguists have devised several schemes to determine the degree of similarity of words based on their distribution in text (See [2,1,3,4]). In this paper a scoring scheme we devised in [1] is used to calculate the scores. The scoring scheme uses three parametres to describe the distributions of terms: *Global-frequency*, which is the measure of the total frequency of occurrence of a term in the corpus; *Local-frequency*, representing the frequency of occurrence of a term in a sentence; and *Placement*, indicating the sentence numbers where the term appears.

Each word is a weighted vector of its distribution; where the weight is its local frequency. For example if a term $Term_j$ is a term that exists in a corpus consisting of 5 sentences and appears three times in the text, once in sentence one and twice in sentence three, its distribution is presented as $Term_j$=(1,0,2,0,0). Now, every vector in the source language is compared to the vectors of every term in the target language. The similarity of the vectors is computed in general as the ratio of the common occurrences of the terms to the total number of appearances they make in the corpus. If $Term_j$, is an Amharic term vector, and $Term_k$ is an English term vector, then,

$$Score_{(j,k)} = \frac{2 \cdot \Sigma(Term_j \wedge Term_k)_i}{\Sigma(Term_j + Term_k)_i}$$

where $_i$ denotes the ith entry of a vector.

(See [1] for more detailed discussion of the scoring scheme).

Scores for each term in the source language with each term in the target language are stored in a repository. Note that, the bilingual corpora for calculating scores is the same corpora from which the sentences to be aligned are retrieved. These score measures are used to align words in singleton translation sentences.

Therefore we construct a matrix of scores for each translation sentence. To get a better understanding of the argument, let us take the first translation sentences of the corpus used in our experiment.

In Table 1, the scores of each word in the source language to the words in the target language is presented. This matrix is plotted in a two dimensional Cartesian plane of source words vs. scores showing the scores of the words in the source sentence with those of the target as shown in Figure 1.

To find the optimal alignment we want to find the optimal score points for each word. If the word in the target document at the optimal point of the source word is aligned with another word with even a greater score, the optimal point for the first word will be its second high point. But again the target word at this second high point also needs to be examined if it has another point where it is the optimal alignment. This process will go on until no better point is found.

Taking the first word in the chart in Figure 1, we see it is aligned with its highest score with the word *son*. We also observe that *son* does not have a score greater than this score with any other word, therefore this point is where its likely translation is found. Using the same procedure we observe that the second word in the X-axis is aligned with the highest score to the word *christ*. The third word

Table 1. Similarity Scores

	ልጅ	ክርስቶስ	ትውልድ	የዳዊት	የኢየሱስ	መጽሐፍ	የአብርሃም
a	0.056	0.004	0.016	0.012	0.008	0.004	0.004
abraham	0.022	0.138	0.148	0.100	0.154	0.364	0.545
christ	0.131	0.864	0.095	0.171	0.214	0.077	0.077
david	0.241	0.178	0.140	0.667	0.069	0.074	0.074
genealogy	0.024	0.091	0.100	0.154	0.333	0.500	0.500
jesus	0.092	0.041	0.018	0.023	0.024	0.005	0.005
of	0.154	0.021	0.015	0.026	0.009	0.004	0.007
record	0.024	0.091	0.100	0.154	0.333	0.500	0.500
son	0.776	0.101	0.029	0.171	0.033	0.017	0.017
the	0.061	0.015	0.014	0.007	0.003	0.002	0.002

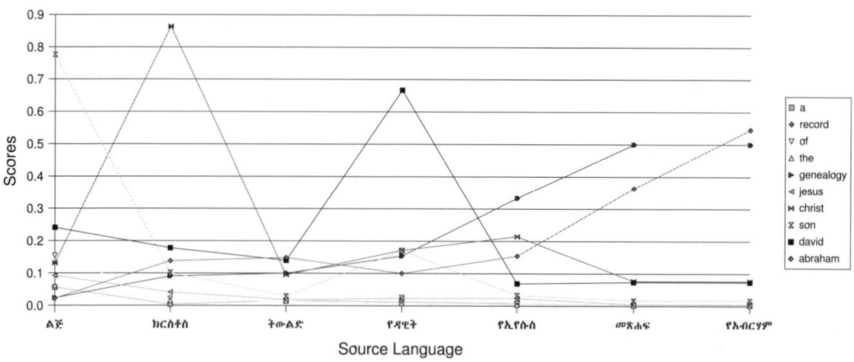

Fig. 1. Source Target Mapping

Amharic word has a best score with *abraham*, but *abraham* has even a higher score with the seventh Amharic word hence we consider the second highest point which is *david*, again *david* is aligned with a higher score with another Amharic word, so we consider the third highest score. The search goes on until we obtain a word which does not have a higher score anywhere else.

Obviously, there will be gaps for those words that do not have high points that excel over others. In most cases that happens because some words translate morphological or syntactic phenomena rather than other words. Hence, these gaps in many cases are likely to be words which are inflectional patterns for the shorter sentence. This is true assuming that we have a perfect translation i.e. there are no deletions or insertions and the translation is accurate.

4 Evaluation of the Results

The algorithm has been evaluated on a dataset of 1749 sentences taken from the bible, namely, the book of Mathew and Mark. From these sentences a repository containing the score of distribution similarity of each term in the source document to each word in the target document is generated. The total number of entries in the repository is 476,165 excluding those with zero score. The repository is used when searching for the optimal scores. We evaluate the proposed approach by first aligning the words, and then comparing the acquired lexica to manually compiled translations. Basically, two types of evaluation can be made.

1. Determine for how many of the sentences correct alignment has been obtained
2. Determine how many words are correctly aligned

Evaluation method 1 was not considered, because in many cases only some of the words in the sentences are correctly aligned. To compute the precision obtained in evaluation method 2, since the time consumption of manual evaluation of all alignments is not affordable, a sample of alignments is randomly picked and statistical measures of confidence interval were used to project for the whole set.

Out of 76 randomly selected sentences (from a total of 1749) which are constituted of 761 words, 64% of overlap with the true translations was achieved. From this we infer that at 95% confidence level the overall result has an accuracy within the confidence interval 62% - 66%. The recall values are of course 100% with respect to the language which is highly inflected.

5 Conclusion and Future Work

These results are very good to attain at such a high recall level. The fact that Amharic and English are disparate languages belonging to different language groups signifies that better results might be obtained for language pairs which are closely related. Among others the scores obtained for identically inflected language pairs are more accurate.

Two directions for gaining better results are being investigated. First, we want to increase the data size to make sure the scores used are more reliable. The second direction is in introducing filters for example by comparing the different translations in multiple sentences as a supplementary.

References

1. Saba Amsalu. Data–driven Amharic–English Bilingual Lexicon Acquisition. In Proceedings of Language Resources and Evaluation Conference (LREC2006) (2006). Genoa, Italy
2. Pascale Fung and Kenneth W. Church. Kvec: A new approach for aligning parallel texts. Proceedings of the 15th International Conference on Computational Linguistics (1994) 1096–1102. Kyoto, Japan
3. Stanley F. Chen. Aligning Sentences in Bilingual Corpora Using Lexical Information. Proceedings of ACL–93 (1993). Columbus OH
4. Magnus Sahlgren and Jussi Karlgren. Automatic Bilingual Lexicon Acquisition Using Random Indexing of Parallel Corpora. Natural Language Engineering (2005) **11** 3

5. Sur-Jin Ker, Jason J. S. Chang. Aligning more words with high precision for small bilingual corpora. Proceedings of the 16th conference on Computational linguistics (1996) 210–215. Copenhagen, Denmark
6. Martin Kay and Martin Röscheisen. Text–translation alignment. Computation Linguistics (1993) **19** 1 121–142
7. Dekai Wu and Xuanyin Xia. Large-Scale Automatic Extraction of an English-Chinese Translation Lexicon. Machine Translation (1995) 9 3–4 285–313

Measuring Intelligibility of Japanese Learner English

Emi Izumi, Kiyotaka Uchimoto, and Hitoshi Isahara

National Institute of Information and Communications Technology, Computational Linguistics Group, 3-5 Hikaridai, Seika-cho, Soraku-gun, Kyoto, 619-0289, Japan
{emi, uchimoto, isahara}@nict.go.jp

Abstract. Although pursuing accuracy is important in language learning or teaching, knowing what types of errors interfere with communication and what types do not would be more beneficial for efficiently enhancing communicative competence. Language learners could be greatly helped by a system that detected errors in learner language and automatically measured their effect on intelligibility. In this paper, we reported our attempt, based on machine learning, to measure the intelligibility of learner language. In the learning process, the system referred to the BLEU and NIST scores between the learners' original sentences and their back translation (or corrected sentences), the log-probability of the parse, sentence length, and error types (manually or automatically assigned) as a key feature. We found that the system can distinguish between intelligible sentences and others (unnatural and unintelligible) rather successfully, but still has a lot of difficulties in distinguishing the three levels of intelligibility.

1 Introduction

Non-native speakers of languages often make errors. Although pursuing accuracy is important in language learning or teaching, knowing what types of errors interfere with communication and what types do not would be more beneficial for efficiently enhancing communicative competence. Language learners could be greatly helped by a system that detected errors in learner language and automatically measured their effect on intelligibility. Automatic detection of learner errors has been attempted by Izumi, et al. (2003). In this paper, we describe a framework for measuring the intelligibility of English sentences spoken by Japanese learners. We conducted experiments with a machine learning technique that used the NICT Japanese Learner English (JLE) Corpus which is a collection of transcribed texts of English spoken by Japanese learners (Izumi et al. 2004). The remainder of this paper is organized as follows. Section 2 outlines how the intelligibility of learner language has been viewed in foreign language learning and teaching. In section 3, we review some related works on automated evaluation of languages. Section 4 explains the corpus data used in the experiment, focusing especially on data annotation of intelligibility as evaluated by humans. The relationship between intelligibility and learner errors will be analyzed in section 5. Section 6 describes the experimental procedures and the results. Finally, in section 7, we draw some general conclusions.

T. Salakoski et al. (Eds.): FinTAL 2006, LNAI 4139, pp. 476 – 487, 2006.

2 Intelligibility of Learner Language

First we would like to consider how intelligibility is positioned in foreign language learning and teaching, especially in recent language education based on the communicative approach.

Improving communicative competence is one of the major goals in a communicative approach to foreign language teaching as stated by Ellis (2003) in the following quote. "Learners need the opportunity to practice language in the same conditions that apply in real-life situations — in communication, where their primary focus is on message conveyance rather than linguistic accuracy". To successfully convey messages by producing "intelligible" utterances that can be understood by others is important. Similarly, according to Skehan (1998), meaning and task-completion are primary factors in communication task activities, and are often employed in a communicative approach.

It is true that too much concentration on accuracy sometimes prevents learners from acquiring free language production and fluency, especially in speech communication because it often introduces more time pressure than does writing. However, this does not mean that learners can hold accuracy in low account in language production because obviously if linguistic components such as grammar, lexis, or phonemes that constitute the bedrock of languages are completely inaccurate, language communication does not occur. Accuracy, especially of grammar, is often contrasted with communicability, but Canale and Swain (1980) confirm that grammatical competence is one of the important elements for building communicative competence. Since accuracy and communicability (intelligibility) are complementary, we need to know the extent to which accuracy should be taken into account in communicative foreign language production. In other words, if we could describe what kind of factors can change the level of intelligibility explicitly and could recognize the necessary degree of accuracy for making communication successful, this would effectively help improve communicative competence.

3 Related Work

Intelligibility measuring can be viewed as a similar type of task to automated essay grading. According to Williams (2001), automated essay grading has been proposed for over thirty years, and only recently have practical implementation been constructed and tested. Shermis and Burnstein (2003) also claim that most of the experiments on automatic grading have been devoted to holistic scores in the early days of this area. In much of the recent work, however, generating specific trait scores has been focused on.

A lot of efforts have been devoted to build the frameworks to score and grade essays written both in writers' native and non-native languages. Page (1994) developed the PEG (Project Essay Grade) model which mainly relies on linguistic features of the document such as the fourth root of the number of words, sentence length, and a measure of punctuation. The model showed correlations between the scores predicted by PEG and those evaluated by human raters varying between 0.389 and 0.743. Larkey (1998) reported that a text categorization technique could be implemented for automated essay grading. Bayesian independence classifiers and k-nearest-neighbor classifiers were trained to assign scores to manually-graded essays. These scores were combined with several other summary text measures using linear regressions. The proportion of essays graded the same as human graders was 0.60. Burnstein (2003) developed *E-rater* in which a hybrid approach of combining linguistic features with other document structure features was used. E-rater predicts a score using multiple linear regression techniques based on the extracted features such as essay vocabulary content, discourse structure information and syntactic information. The system can achieve a level of agreement with human raters of between 87% and 94%. Page and Petersen (1995) discussed the use of two different types of features as a way to consider the process of emulating human rater behavior. One is the characteristic dimension of interest such as fluency or grammar. The other is the observed variables with which the computer works such as part-of-speech (POS), word length, word meaning, and so on. In our experiment, we used both types of features, and as a former type of feature, we focused attention on learner errors. In the following sections, we will explain the preparatory investigation into intelligibility of learner language especially focusing on the relationship between intelligibility and error types, and then describe the actual experiment procedures.

4 Human Judgment of Intelligibility

In order to describe the level of the intelligibility of learner language explicitly, first we decided to add level-of-intelligibility information to the NICT JLE Corpus by humans.

4.1 Criterion

We asked native speakers of English to check the corpus data and measure the intelligibility of each sentence in the data. The checkers added one of the following three comments about the intelligibility of each sentence (Table 1).

Table 1. Level of Intelligibility

Comment	Level of Intelligibility
INTELLIGIBLE	There is no difficulty in understanding the meaning of the sentence.
UNNATURAL	It is possible to understand the meaning of the sentence, but the sentence is sometimes unclear or sounds unnatural.
UNINTELLIGIBLE	The sentence does not make sense at all.

Although the judgment was done sentence by sentence, the checkers had to decide the level of intelligibility depending on to what extent each sentence is "contextually" intelligible. A sentence that could be understood without problem was to be labeled INTELLIGIBLE. Even though a sentence might contain an error(s), if the meaning of the entire sentence can be understood, it was to be labeled INTELLIGIBLE. A sentence would be labeled UNNATURAL, if it made sense, but obviously did not sound like native speech or was sociolinguistically inappropriate in a specified situational context. If the checkers could not understand or even guess the meaning of a sentence at all, they judged it as UNINTELLIGIBLE. If an error(s) was found in a sentence, the checkers rewrote it. The checkers added short comments giving the reason(s) for their judgment, for instance, why it sounded unnatural, or the degree of unintelligibility.

4.2 Data: The NICT JLE Corpus

The data that was judged is a part of the NICT JLE Corpus. This corpus consists of the transcriptions of an oral proficiency test, the Standard Speaking Test (SST). The SST is a face-to-face interview between an examiner and a test-taker. This 15-minute interview test comprises five parts, commencing with an informal chat on general topics, such as the interviewee's job, hobbies, and family, for example. During the second to fourth stages of the interview, the interviewee is asked to perform three task-based activities, namely picture description, role-playing, and story telling. Two or three raters judge the proficiency level of each examinee (Levels 1 to 9. Level 9 is the most advanced.) based on an SST evaluation scheme. The entire corpus contains 1,281 interviews, which amount to 325 hours and two million words. The two checkers in our experiment were native speakers of English. They checked 49 transcribed texts from the corpus and judged the intelligibility level of each sentence. The details of the checked data are as listed in Table 2. The proficiency levels of 49 texts varied from Level 3 to Level 9, and the total number of words was 46,232, and the total number of sentences was 6,950.

Table 2. Details of Checked Data

Proficiency Level	Number of Texts	Number of Words	Number of Sentences
Level 3	7	3,294	768
Level 4	7	4,574	820
Level 5	7	6,042	992
Level 6	8	8,047	1,057
Level 7	7	6,437	1,017
Level 8	7	8,941	1,268
Level 9	6	8,897	1,028
Total	49	46,232	6,950

4.3 Results

The results of the human judgment, the numbers of INTELLIGIBLE, UNNATURAL and UNINTELLIGIBLE sentences per 100 sentences across different proficiency levels, are presented in Fig. 1.

INTELLIGIBLE sentences accounted for 67 - 70% of Level 3 and 4 data. In Level 5 and 6 data, this rose to 74 - 78%. At advanced levels (Levels 7, 8 and 9), this increased to around 80 - 90%. The number of UNNATURAL sentences did not always correlate with the proficiency level. This category accounted for 7 - 30% of all the texts. The number of UNINTELLIGIBLE sentences in Level 3 data was more remarkable (10%) than those in other proficiency levels (1 - 3%).

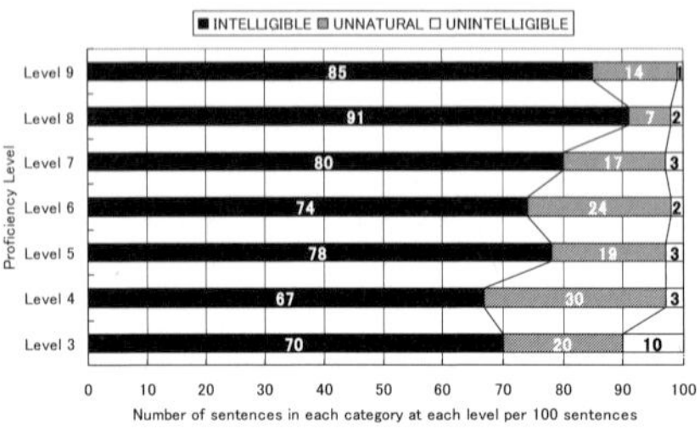

Fig. 1. Result of Human Judgment I

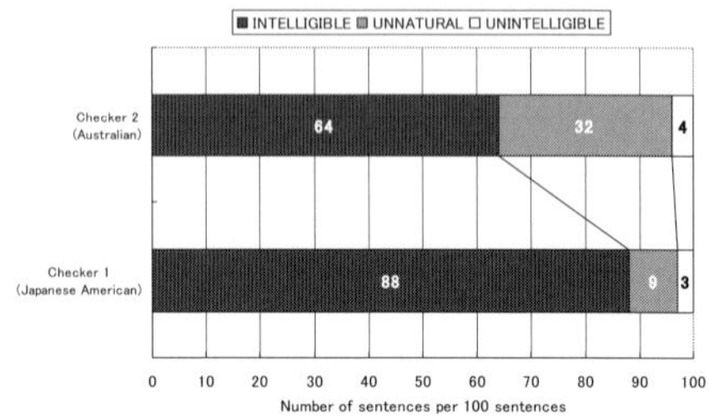

Fig. 2. Result of Human Judgment II

One of the reasons why the number of these three levels of sentence intelligibility does not completely correlate with proficiency levels might be that two people checked the data, and their judgment might have been disparate. Twenty-seven texts were checked by Checker 1, a Japanese American, and 22 texts were checked by Checker 2 from Australia. Fig. 2 shows the result of human judgment on a per-checker basis. Checker 1 judged 88% of the sentences as INTELLIGIBLE, while Checker 2 labeled 64% of the sentences as INTELLIGIBLE. The gap between the checkers' evaluations becomes bigger for UNNATURAL sentences. The sentences labeled by Checker 1 as UNNATURAL account for only 9%, while for Checker 2, this goes up to 32%. On the other hand, no big difference was found in their judgment of UNINTELLIGIBLE sentences. This accounted for 3 - 4% of the data in the evaluations of both checkers. Guessing from their background, Checker 1 might be more familiar with English spoken by Japanese people than Checker 2 because Checker 1 is Japanese American and has some knowledge of Japanese language.

5 Relationship Between Intelligibility and Error Types

Consequently, we focused attention on errors as a key feature that must have an influence on the intelligibility of a sentence. If we could find any correlation between intelligibility and errors, this will be quite beneficial not only to improve the result of automatically measuring intelligibility, but also of more explicitly describing the intelligibility in learner.

5.1 Error Tagging

To find out the relationship between intelligibility and errors, we added error tags to the data by hand. Errors were localized and categorized by referring to the corrections made by the native speakers. We used the error tags that were already implemented as part of the NICT JLE Corpus. The error tagset consists of 46 tags. Most of the tags are related to morphological, grammatical and lexical errors, which are, in most cases, local errors, but some are special tags that involve global errors such as misordering of words. The sentences judged as UNINTELLIGIBLE were not corrected by the checkers because they could not understand or even guess the meaning of a sentence intended by the speaker of these sentences. Although those sentences are unintelligible for the checkers who were native speakers of English, some of them can be understood by Japanese people because they are much more familiar with the English spoken by Japanese. In this case, a Japanese checker corrected those sentences and added error tags to them. If a sentence was unintelligible for the Japanese checker, also, an error tag was added to the sentence that means "This sentence is totally unintelligible though no error(s) can be spotted".

5.2 Correlation Between Intelligibility and Errors

We clustered the error-tagged sentences into three groups depending on their intelligibility (INTELLIGIBLE, UNNATURAL and UNINTELLIGIBLE), and then extracted the feature quantity of each type of error for each cluster. The feature quantity is the proportion of frequency of a certain type of error in a cluster out of the frequency of the same type of error in the entire data (normalized per 1,000 words). This information could help to estimate the gravity of each type of error. Fig. 4 to 9 show the feature quantity of major types of errors for three clusters. Fig. 3 shows that errors in morphological inflection of nouns, verbs and adjectives were distinctively frequent in UNNATURAL sentences. Some of them appear in INTELLIGIBLE sentences, too, but in UNINTELLIGIBLE sentences, they are not distinctively frequent at all. In this type of error, an erroneous word appears in a non-existing form and sounds quite unnatural; however, this error does not really interfere with understanding because in most cases, a listener is able to guess which word the speaker intended to produce.

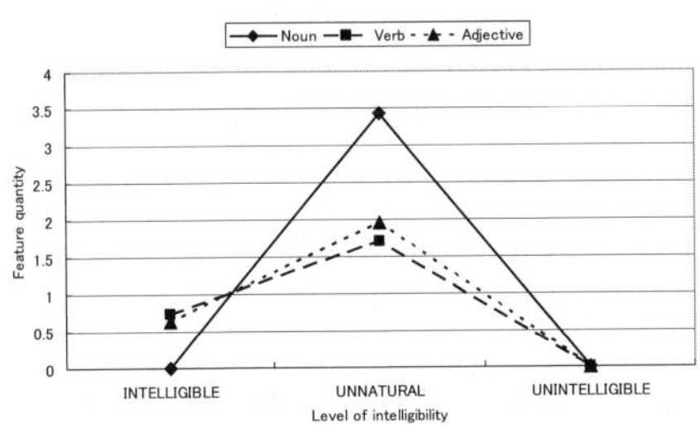

Fig. 3. Errors in Morphological Inflection

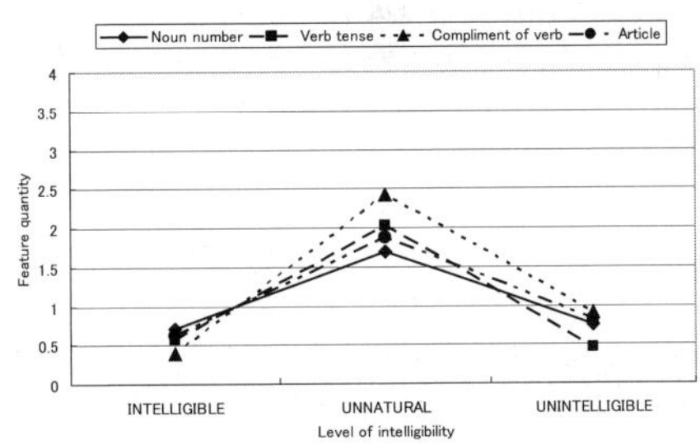

Fig. 4. Grammatical Errors

Fig. 4 reveals that major grammatical errors such as errors in noun number, verb tense, compliment of verbs and articles are also distinctively frequent in UNNATURAL sentences. Some of them appear in INTELLIGIBLE and UNINTELLIGIBLE sentences, too, so some grammatical errors appear not to interfere with understanding while others make sentences unintelligible.

On the other hand, lexical errors for content words such as nouns and adverbs are distinctively frequent in UNINTELLIGIBLE sentences (Fig. 5). Although lexical errors in verb and adjective use are still distinctively frequent in UNNATURAL sentences, the gap between this feature quantity in UNNATURAL and UNINTELLIGIBLE sentences is much smaller than in morphological and grammatical errors. Some of them appear in INTELLIGIBLE sentences, but in most cases, they were not very serious, for example lexical confusion of semantically similar vocabulary items. However, lexical errors of function words such as auxiliary verbs, normal prepositions, dependent prepositions, and conjunctions had less influence on making sentences unintelligible (Fig. 6).

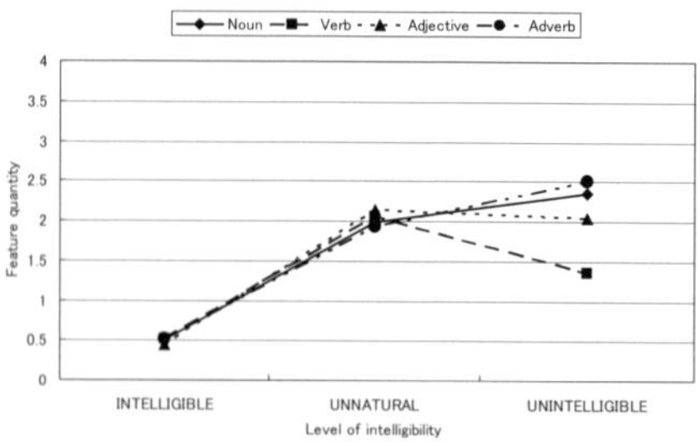

Fig. 5. Lexical Errors (Content words)

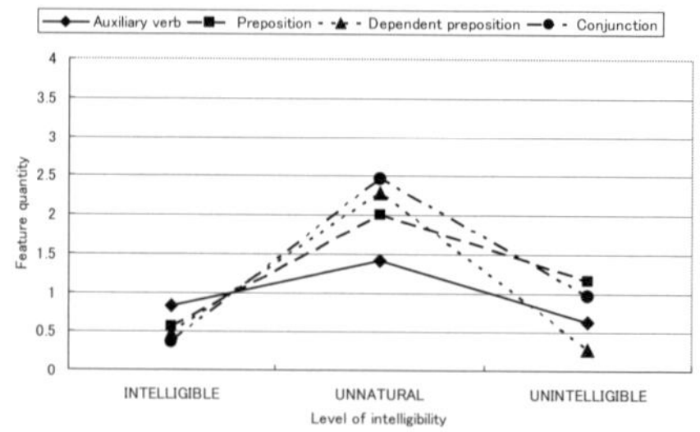

Fig. 6. Lexical Errors (Function words)

Special types of lexical errors such as Japanese English, erroneous collocational expressions, had a certain degree of influence in making sentences unintelligible, and the use of Japanese words can greatly interfere with understanding (Fig. 7).

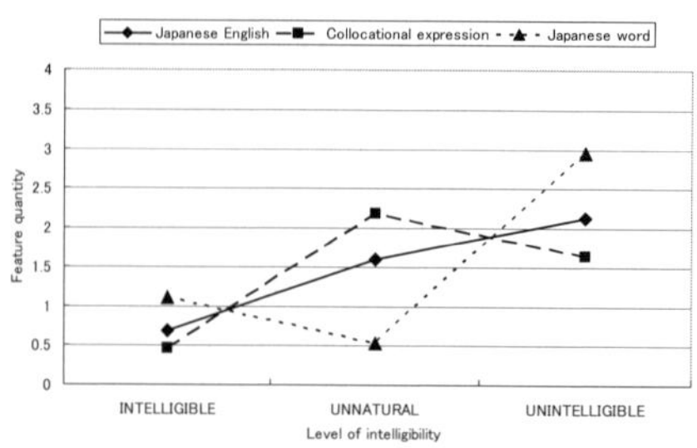

Fig. 7. Lexical Errors (Special types)

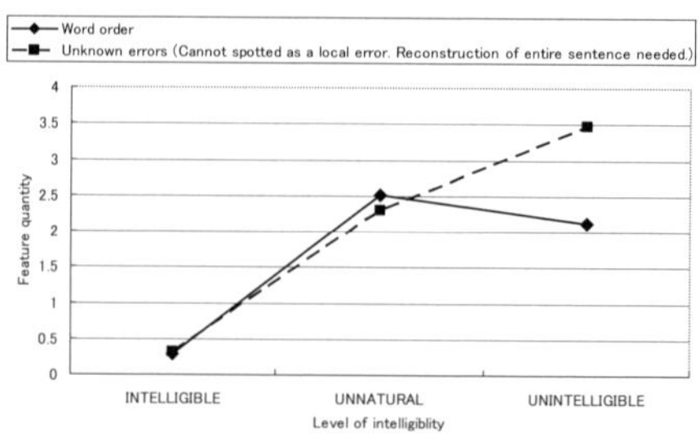

Fig. 8. Global Errors

Errors shown in Fig. 3 to 7 involve a single word or phrase, and can be localized and corrected locally. On the other hand, the errors shown in Fig. 8 are global errors that affect overall sentence structure such as misordering of words, and errors that cannot be spotted as local errors because the entire sentence must be reconstructed. In Fig. 8, one can see that global errors have a significant influence on making sentences unnatural, and even unintelligible. Furthermore, in the checkers' comments made for NINTELLIGIBLE sentences, phrases such as "no reference," "totally grammatical but doesn't make sense in this context," "does not answer the question," "contradicts the speaker's previous utterance," often appeared. These comments indicate that errors in UNINTELLIGIBLE sentences often involve more than a single sentence and involve discourse issues.

6 Automatic Measuring of Intelligibility of Learner English

In this section, we would like to describe three experiments carried out to automatically measure intelligibility based on machine learning.

6.1 Method

First we explain the method employed commonly in three experiments. The purpose of the experiments is to see to what extent learner sentences can be labeled with one of three levels of intelligibility (INTELLIGIBLE, UNNATURAL, and UNINTELLIGIBLE) correctly by using a machine learning technique. We first divided 49 texts into 42 texts for training and 7 texts for testing. For machine learning, we used the Support Vector Machine (SVM) technique that has been used to solve various classification problems (Joachims 1998). The rule for measuring intelligibility was determined through training the system on the human graded data (42 texts). The rule was then applied to a new set of data (7 texts). For training and testing, we used *Yamcha*, an SVM-based chunker developed by Kudo and Matsumoto (2001).

6.2 Experiment 1

For the first experiment, we employed error tag information added by humans and its frequency in a sentence as the features, because through the analysis in section 5, it was revealed that error type is one of the main factors that are responsible for intelligibility variation. The system also referred to the similarity between an original sentence and a corrected sentence. The similarity was obtained in a form of numerical "translation-closeness" metrics called the BLEU score (Papineni et al. 2002) and the NIST score (NIST 2002).The system also referred to other two features: log-probability of the parse of learners' original sentences and sentence length. For parsing, we used *RASP* (Briscoe and Carroll 2002). The BLEU and NIST scores were calculated using the machine translation (MT) scoring software, *mteval* (version v11a). The result of the first experiment is shown in Table 3.

Table 3. Result of Experiment 1[1]

	INTELLIGIBLE	UNNATURAL	UNINTELLIGIBLE
Recall	87.18 (660/757)	68.80(75/109)	42.85(6/14)
Precision	94.55 (660/698)	43.60(75/172)	60.00(6/10)
F-measure	90.72	53.38	50.00

The system correctly attributed 87.18% of INTELLIGIBLE sentences with a precision of 94.55%. The recall of assigning UNNATURAL sentences was 68.80% and the precision was 43.60%. 42.85% of UNINTELLIGIBLE sentences were assigned correctly, but with low precision of 60.00%.

[1] Recall stands for the percentages of sentences correctly assigned by the system out of the total number of sentences that could be assigned. Precision stands for the percentages of sentences correctly assigned by the system out of the number of sentences actually assigned by the system. F-measure is a popular combination of precision and recall into a single parameter.

6.3 Experiment 2

Although we used manually-added error tag information in experiment1, we need to automatize the processes as much as possible for putting the system into practical use. The second experiment was done based on the data without error tags. Instead of the similarity between an original sentence and a corrected sentence, the system referred to the similarity between an original sentence and its back translation. This idea was taken the method for automatically rating machine translatability of given text for a particular MT system proposed by Uchimoto et al. (2005). In this system, machine translatability is defined as a measure that indicates how well a given sentence can be translated by a particular MT system. The machine translatability of a given sentence is estimated as high when the quality of the MT result is good. The machine translatability is estimated by measuring the similarity between a source-language sentence and its back translation. A back translation is defined as a source-language sentence that is obtained by translating a sentence into a target language and then retranslating that sentence back into the source language. In our experiment, source language sentences were English sentences produced by Japanese learners. They were then translated into Japanese, and then those Japanese sentences were retranslated into English. Ideally, their similarities are rated high when the original sentence and the back translation have the same meaning. The similarity is obtained in a form of the BLEU and NIST score.

In experiment 2, back translation sentences were treated as correct sentences. In developing J-to-E or E-to-J MT systems, a lot of efforts are made to complement what the Japanese language lacks and vice versa in order to make the outputs as good and natural as possible. It is sometimes said that the method based on negative evidence like our approach may not be general because the kinds of errors found depend on the native languages of learners who generated error data. This can be considered as the limitation of this approach in terms of versatility, but, on the contrary, this can be a benefit as well because the system has the potential to become the specialized one which is more robust against errors produced by learners of a certain L1 among others. We assumed that the outputs generated by the MT system which has been developed with focusing on the differences between the specific pair of languages (Japanese and English) can help to fill the gap between the correct usages and Japanese learners' erroneous usages which are often occurred by differences between L1 and L2. If it is done successfully, we can obtain the pairs of the erroneous and corrected sentences. In other words, if the similarity between a learner's original sentence and a back translation sentence is high, this means that the original sentence has less erroneous.

In the experiment, we first obtained the back translation sentence of each sentence in the learner data by using one of the leading commercial MT systems. Second, we calculated the BLEU and the NIST scores of each sentence pair. In the learning process, the system referred to two more features: log-probability of the parse of learners' original sentences and sentence length in the same way as in the experiment 1. Table 4 shows the results of this experiment. The system correctly assigned 91.67% of INTELLIGIBLE sentences with a precision of 87.40%. The recall of assigning

UNNATURAL sentences was 20.18% and the precision was 26.82%. Only one sentence out of 14 UNINTELLIGIBLE sentences was labeled correctly with the precision of 25.00%.

Table 4. Result of Experiment 2

	INTELLIGIBLE	UNNATURAL	UNINTELLIGIBLE
Recall	91.67 (694/757)	20.18 (22/109)	7.14 (1/14)
Precision	87.40 (694/794)	26.82 (22/82)	25.00 (1/4)
F-measure	89.49	23.03	11.11

6.4 Exeperiment 3

In the third experiment, we added error tag information automatically marked up by *Eden* (*Error Detection System for English*), an automatic error detection system developed by Izumi, et al. (2004). The error types that can be detected by Eden were just 13 types[2]. The system also referred to the features used in experiment 2 (BLEU score, NIST score, log-probability of the parse of learners' original sentences and sentence length). The result of the experiment 3 is shown in Table 5. The system correctly attributed 85.20% of INTELLIGIBLE sentences with a precision of 88.11%. The recall of assigning UNNATURAL sentences was 31.19% and the precision was 24.11%. There were no INTELLIGIBLE sentences correctly assigned.

Table 5. Result of Experiment 3

	INTELLIGIBLE	UNNATURAL	UNINTELLIGIBLE
Recall	85.20 (645/757)	31.19 (34/109)	0.00 (0/14)
Precision	88.11 (645/732)	24.11 (34/141)	0.00 (0/7)
F-measure	86.63	27.20	0.00

6.5 Discussion

While we can say that the system could distinguish between INTELLIGIBLE sentences and others (UNNATURAL and UNINTELLIGIBLE) rather successfully, many difficulties still remain in distinguishing among the three types. Not surprisingly, experiment 1 where the manually-error tagged data was used marked the best overall accuracy. The best individual accuracy was found in the recall of assigning INTELLIGIBLE sentences in experiment 2 where no error tag information has been used. However, this might be just because the system heavily depended on the high proportion of INTELLIGIBLE sentences in the training data. Although the recall and precision of assigning INTELLIGIBLE sentences in experiment 3 declined compared with experiment 2, the recall of assigning UNNATURAL sentences in experiment 3 went up, which brought a balance for the overall accuracy. Therefore, although we could not find the remarkable improvement by using the result of *Eden* in experiment 3, it can be said that experiment 3 is the intermediate step to experiment 1 from experiment 2.

[2] Noun: number error, lexical error. Verb: Erroneous subject-verb agreement, tense error, compliment error, lexical error. Adjective, Adverb, Pronoun: lexical error. Preposition: lexical error (normal/dependent). Article error. Collocational error.

For future improvement, we will introduce new features for training such as learners' proficiency level information or checker's information (Which checker judged the data.). We are also planning to increase the number of error types that *Eden* can detect. Now only 13 error types are targeted in Eden, but if all error types (46 types) in our error tagset can be targeted, it will greatly help to improve accuracy. Since other features such as log-probability of the parse or sentence length provided rather superficial information about sentences, we assume that deeper information about sentence, such as errors is definitely necessary.

However, the errors that are distinctively frequent in UNINTELLGIBLE sentences are mainly lexical errors of content words and global errors including discourse errors which cannot be detected by *Eden* successfully. The reason the labeling of unintelligible sentences was so unsuccessful might be because, in most cases, they are grammatically correct as a single sentence, but do not make sense within a context. To correct these sentences, context information is needed that cannot be covered by MT and *Eden*. This means that detecting discourse errors automatically will need the context, or even cross-sentential information. This is definitely a difficult task, but we are planning to make an attempt by starting from knowing what kind of discourse errors are typically made by learners, and classifying them to build them in the error tagset.

7 Conclusion

In this paper, we reported our attempt, based on machine learning, to measure the intelligibility of learner language. Through the preparatory investigation, it has been revealed that there is a close relationship between intelligibility and error types. In the learning process, the system referred to the BLEU and NIST scores between the learners' original sentences and their back translation (or corrected sentences), the log-probability of the parse, sentence length, and error types (manually or automatically assigned) as a key feature. We found that the system can distinguish between intelligible sentences and others (unnatural and unintelligible) rather successfully, but still has a lot of difficulties in distinguishing the three levels of intelligibility. For future improvement, we will introduce new features (proficiency level and checkers' information) and focus on enhancing the quality of *Eden*. We will also work on describing learners' discourse errors and automated detection of them.

References

1. Briscoe, E., Carroll, J.: Robust Accurate Statistical Annotation of General Text. In: Proceedings of the Third International Conference on Language Resources and Evaluation. Las Palmas, Gran Canaria (2002) 1499-1504
2. Burnstein, J.: The E-rater scoring engine: Automated Essay Scoring with Natural Language Processing. In: Shermis, M. D. and Burnstein, J. (eds.): Automated Essay Scoring: A Cross-Disciplinary Perspective, Lawrence Erlbaum Associates, Inc., New Jersey (2003) 113-122
3. Canale, M., Swain, M.: Theoretical Bases of Communicative Approach to Second Language Teaching and Testing. Applied Linguistics, 1 (1980) 1-47

4. Ellis, R.: Task-based Language Learning and Teaching. Oxford University Press, Oxford (2003)
5. Izumi, E., Saiga, T., Uchimoto, K., Supnithi, T., Isahara, H.: Automatic Error Detection in the Japanese Learners' English Spoken Data. In: Companion Volume of the Proceedings of the 41st Annual Meeting of the Association of Computational Linguistics (ACL-03), Japan (2003) 145-148
6. Izumi, E., Uchimoto, K., Isahara, H.: Standard Speaking Test (SST) Speech Corpus of Japanese Learners' English and Automatic Detection of Learners' Errors. International Computer Achieves of Modern and Medieval English (ICAME) Journal, 28 (2004) 31-48
7. Joachims, T.: Text Categorization with Support Vector Machines. In: Proceedings of 10th European Conference on Machine Learning (ECML-98), Germany (1998) 137-142
8. Kudo, T., Matsumoto, Y.: Chunking with Support Vector Machines. In: Proceedings of the 2nd Meeting of the North American Chapter of the Association of Computational Linguistics, Pittsburgh (2001) 192-199
9. Larkey, L. S.: Automatic Essay Grading Using Text Categorization Techniques. In: Proceedings of the 21st Annual International Conference on Research and Development in Information Retrieval (SIGIR 98), Australia (1998) 90-95
10. NIST: Automatic Evaluation of Machine Translation Quality Using N-gram Co-Occurrence Statistics. Philadelphia (2002)
11. Page, E. B.: Computer Grading of Student Prose, Using Modern Concepts and Software. Journal of Experimental Education, 62 (1994) 127-142
12. Page, E. B., Petersen, N. S.: The Computer Moves into Essay Grading: Updating the Ancient Test. Phi Delta Kappan, 76(7) (1995) 561-565
13. Papineni, K., Roukos, S., Ward, T., Zhu, W.: BLEU: A Method for Automatic Evaluation of Machine Translation. In: Proceedings of the 40th Annual Meeting of the Association for Computational Linguistics (ACL), USA (2002) 311-318
14. Shermis, M. D., Burnstein, J. (eds.): Automated Essay Scoring: A Cross-Disciplinary Perspective. Lawrence Erlbaum Associates, Inc., New Jersey (2003) xiii-xvi
15. Skehan, P.: A Cognitive Approach to Language Learning. Oxford University Press, Oxford, (1998)
16. Uchimoto, K., Hayashida, N., Ishida, T., Isahara, H.: Automatic Rating of Machine Translatability. In: Proceedings of the MT Summit X, Thailand (2005) 235-242
17. Williams, R.: Automated Essay Grading: An Evaluation of Four Conceptual Models. In: Proceedings of the 10th Annual Teaching Learning Forum, Curtin University of Technology, Perth (2001) 7-9. http://lsn.curtin.edu.au/tlf/tlf2001/contents.html

Morphological Lexicon Extraction from Raw Text Data

Markus Forsberg, Harald Hammarström, and Aarne Ranta

Department of Computing Science
Chalmers University of Technology
Sweden
{markus, harald2, aarne}@cs.chalmers.se

Abstract. The tool *extract* enables the automatic extraction of lemma-paradigm pairs from raw text data. The tool uses search patterns that consist of regular expressions and propositional logic. These search patterns define sufficient conditions for including lemma-paradigm pairs in the lexicon, on the basis of word forms occurring in the data. This paper explains the search pattern syntax of *extract* as well as the search algorithm, and discusses the design of search patterns from the recall and precision point of view.

The *extract* tool was developed for morphologies defined in the *Functional Morphology* tool [1], but it is usable for all systems that implement a word-and-paradigm description of a morphology.

The usefulness of the tool is demonstrated by a case study on the Canadian Hansards Corpus of French. The result is evaluated in terms of precision of the extracted lemmas and statistics on coverage and rule productiveness. Competitive extraction figures show that human-written rules in a tailored tool is a time-efficient approach to the task at hand.

1 Introduction

A wide-coverage morphological lexicon is a key part of any information retrieval system, machine translation engine and of a variety of other Natural Language Processing applications. The demand is high not only for low-density languages, since existing lexica for major languages are often not publicly available. Moreover, even if they were, running text – especially newspapers and technical texts – will always contain new, not necessarily hapax, words.

Manual development of a full-scale lexicon is a time-consuming task, so it is natural to investigate how the lexicon development can be automated. The situation is usually such that access to large collections of raw language data is cheap, so cheap that it is tempting to look at ways to exploit the raw data to obtain the sought after high-quality morphological lexicon. Clearly, attempts to fully automatize the process (e.g [2,3] – most other systems for unsupervised learning of morphology cannot be used directly to build a lexicon) do not reach the kind of quality we are generally interested in. However, instead of using humans for supervised learning of lexicon extraction in some form, we believe

T. Salakoski et al. (Eds.): FinTAL 2006, LNAI 4139, pp. 488–499, 2006.

there is a more advantageous placement of the human role. With a suitable tool, humans can use their knowledge to guide a computerized extraction from raw text, with comparatively little time spent.

To be more specific, we intend to show that a profitable role for the human is to write intelligent extraction rules. The *extract* tool has been developed with this in mind. The idea behind *extract* is simple: start with a large-sized corpus and a description of the word forms in the paradigms with the varying parts, which we refer to as *technical stems*, represented with variables. In the tool's syntax, we could describe the first declension noun of Swedish with the following definition.

```
paradigm decl1 =
  x+"a"
  { x+"a"  & x+"as"  & x+"an"  & x+"ans" &
    x+"or" & x+"ors" & x+"orna & x+"ornas" } ;
```

Given that all forms in the curly brackets, called the *constraint*, are found for some prefix `x`, the tool outputs the *head* `x+"a"` tagged with the name of the paradigm. E.g., if these forms exist in the text data: `ärta`, `ärtas`, `ärtan`, `ärtans`, `ärtor`, `ärtors`, `ärtorna` and `ärtornas`, the tool will output `decl1 ärta`. Given that we have the lemma and the paradigm class label, it is a relatively simple task to generate all word forms.

The paradigm definition has a major drawback: very few lemmas appear in all word forms. It could in fact be relaxed to increase recall without sacrificing precision: to identify a Swedish word as a noun of the first declension it is often enough to find one instance of the four singular forms and one of the four plural forms. The tool offers a solution by supporting propositional logic in the constraint, further described in Sect. 2.1. Various issues of the extraction process are discussed in Sect. 3.

Another problem with the given definition is the lack of control over what the variable `x` might be. Sect. 2.2 describes how the tool improves this situation by allowing variables to be associated with regular expressions.

The stems of first declension nouns in Swedish are the same for all word forms, but this is not the case for many paradigms, e.g. German nouns with umlaut. Sect. 2.3 presents the tool's use of multiple variables as a solution to this problem.

$$
\begin{array}{rll}
\langle \mathit{Def} \rangle ::= & \texttt{paradigm} & \langle \mathit{Name} \rangle \; \langle \mathit{VarDef} \rangle = \\
 & & \langle \mathit{Head} \rangle \; \{ \; \langle \mathit{Logic} \rangle \; \} \\
 | & \texttt{regexp} & \langle \mathit{Name} \rangle = \langle \mathit{Reg} \rangle
\end{array}
$$

Fig. 1. Regexp and paradigm definitions

2 Paradigm File Format

A paradigm file consists of two kinds of definitions: `regexp` and `paradigm`. The syntax is given in Fig. 1.

A `regexp` definition associates a name (`Name`) with a regular expression (`Reg`). A `paradigm` definition consists of a name (`Name`), a set of variable-regular expression associations (`VarDef`), a set of output constituents (`Head`) and a constraint (`Logic`).

The basic unit in `Head` and `Logic` is a *pattern* that describes a word form. A pattern consists of a sequence of variables and string literals glued together with the '+' operator. An example of a pattern given previously was `x+"a"`.

Both definitions will be discussed in detail in the following sections.

2.1 Propositional Logic

Propositional logic appears in the constraint to enable a more fine-grained description of what word forms the tool should look for. The basic unit is a pattern, corresponding to a word form, which is combined with the operators `&` (*and*), `|` (*or*), and `~` (*not*).

The syntax for propositional logic is given in Fig. 2, where *Pattern* refers to one word form.

```
⟨Logic⟩ ::= ⟨Logic⟩ & ⟨Logic⟩
          | ⟨Logic⟩ | ⟨Logic⟩
          | ⟨Logic⟩
          | ~ ⟨Logic⟩
          | ⟨Pattern⟩
          | ( ⟨Logic⟩ )
```

Fig. 2. Propositional logic grammar

The addition of new operators allow the paradigm in Sect. 1 to be rewritten with disjunction to reflect that it is sufficient to find one singular and one plural word form.

```
paradigm decl1 =
      x+"a"
      { (x+"a"    | x+"as"  | x+"an"   | x+"ans") &
        (x+"or"   | x+"ors" |x+"orna   | x+"ornas") } ;
```

2.2 Regular Expressions

It was mentioned in Sect. 1 that control over the variable part of a paradigm description was desired. The solution provided by the tool is to enable the user to associate every variable with a regular expression. The association dictates which (sub-)strings a variable can match. An unannotated variable can match any string, i.e. its regular expression is Kleene star over any symbol.

As a simple example, consider German, where nouns always start with an uppercase letter. This can be expressed as follows.

```
regexp UpperWord = upper letter*;

paradigm n [x:UpperWord] = ... ;
```

The syntax of the tool's regular expressions is given in Fig. 3, with the normal connectives: union, concatenation, set minus, Kleene star, Kleene plus and optionality. *eps* refers to the empty string, *digit* to $0-9$, *letter* to an alphabetic Unicode character, *lower* and *upper* to a lowercase respectively an uppercase letter. *char* refers to any character. A regular expression can also contain a double-quoted string, which is interpreted as the concatenation of the characters in the string.

```
⟨Reg⟩ ::= ⟨Reg⟩ | ⟨Reg⟩
        | ⟨Reg⟩ – ⟨Reg⟩
        | ⟨Reg⟩ ⟨Reg⟩
        | ⟨Reg⟩ *
        | ⟨Reg⟩ +
        | ⟨Reg⟩ ?
        | eps
        | ⟨Char⟩
        | digit
        | letter
        | upper
        | lower
        | char
        | ⟨String⟩
        | ( ⟨Reg⟩ )
```

Fig. 3. Regular expression

2.3 Multiple Variables

Not all paradigm definitions are as neat as the initial example — phenomena like *umlaut* require an increased control over the variable part. The solution the tool provides is to allow multiple variables, i.e. a pattern may contain more than one variable. This is best explained with an example, where two German noun paradigms are described, both with umlaut. The change of the stem vowel is captured by introducing two variables and by letting the stem vowel be a constant string.

```
regexp Consonant = ... ;

regexp Pre = upper letter*;

regexp Aft = Consonant+ ;

paradigm n2 [F:Pre, ll:Aft] =
  F+"a"+ll
    { F+"a"+ll & F+"ä"+ll+"e" } ;

paradigm n3 [W:Pre, rt:Aft] =
   W+"o"+rt
    { W+"o"+rt & W+"ö"+rt+"er" } ;
```

The use of variables may reduce the time-performance of the tool, since every possible variable binding is considered. The use of multiple variables should be moderate, and the variables should be restricted as much as possible by their regular expression association to reduce the search space.

A variable does not need to occur in every pattern, but the tool only performs an initial match with patterns containing all variables. The reason for this is efficiency — the tool only considers one word at the time, and if the word matches one of the patterns, it searches for all other patterns with the variables instantiated by the initial match. For obvious reasons, an initial match is never performed under a negation, since this would imply that the tool searches for something it does not want to find.

It is allowed to have repeated variables, i.e. non-linear patterns, which is equivalent to *back reference* in the programming language Perl. An example where a sequence of bits is reduplicated is given. This language is known to be non-context-free [4].

```
regexp ABs = (0|1)*;

paradigm reduplication [x:ABs] =
   x+x { x+x } ;
```

2.4 Multiple Arguments

The head of a paradigm definition may have multiple arguments to support more abstract paradigms. An example is Swedish nouns, where many nouns can be correctly classified by just detecting the word forms in nominative singular and nominative plural. An example is given below, where the first and second declension is handled with the same paradigm function, where the head consists of two output forms. The constraints are omitted.

```
paradigm regNoun =
flick+"a" flick+"or"
{...} ;
```

```
paradigm regNoun =
pojk+"e" pojk+"ar"
{...} ;
```

2.5 The Algorithm

The underlying algorithm of the tool is presented in pseudo-code notation.

```
let L be the empty lexicon.
let P be the set of extraction paradigms.
let W be all word types in the corpus.
for each w : W
 for each p : P
  for each constraint C with which w matches p
   if W satisfies C with the result H,
    add H to L
   endif
  end
 end
end
```

The algorithm is initialized by reading the word types of the corpus into an array W. A word w *matches* a paradigm p, if it can match any of the patterns in the paradigm's constraint that contains all variables occurring in the constraint. The result of a successful match is an *instantiated constraint* C, i.e. a logical formula with words as atomic propositions. The corpus W *satisfies* a constraint C if the formula is true, where the truth of an atomic proposition a means that the word a occurs in W.

2.6 The Performance of the Tool

The extraction tool is implemented in Haskell. It is available as an open-source free software [1]. A typical example of using the tool, the experiment reported in Sect. 4 extracted a lexicon of 19,295 lemmas from a corpus of 66,853 word types, by using 43 paradigms. The execution time was 11min 23s on a computer with an AMD 3600+ CPU and 1 GB memory, running Kubuntu Linux 5.10. The memory consumption was 34 MB.

3 The Art of Extraction

The constraint of a paradigm describes a sub-paradigm, a subset of the word forms, considered to be evidence enough to be able to judge that the lemmas in the head are in that paradigm class. The identification of appropriate sub-paradigms requires good insights into the target language and intuitions about the distributions of the word forms. However, these insights and intuitions may be acquired while using the tool by trial and error.

Lexicon extraction is a balance between *precision*, i.e. the percentage of the extracted lemmas that are correctly classified, and *recall*, i.e. the percentage of the lemmas in the text data that are extracted. Precision, however, is by far the

[1] Extract homepage: `http://www.cs.chalmers.se/~markus/extract/`

most important, since poor recall can be compensated with more text data, but poor precision requires more human labor.

How about extracting the paradigm descriptions from a set of paradigms automatically? We use the term *minimum-size sub-paradigm* to describe the minimum-sized set of word forms needed to uniquely identify a paradigm P. More formally, a minimum-sized sub-paradigm is a minimum-size set of word forms $P' \subseteq P$ such that for any other paradigm Q, $P' \not\subseteq Q$. It turns out that the problem of finding the minimum-size sub-paradigm for a paradigm P is NP-complete[2]. Furthermore, the minimum-size sub-paradigm need not be of high practical interest since it may contain forms that are very uncommon in actual usage. Therefore there is all the more reason to let a human choose which forms to require and also weigh in which forms are likely to be common or uncommon in actual usage.

Also, some natural languages have *overshadowed paradigms*, i.e. paradigms where the form of one paradigm is a subset of another paradigm. For example, in Latin some noun paradigms are overshadowed by adjective paradigms. The distinction of Latin nouns and adjectives can be done through the use of negation where a second declension noun paradigm is defined by also stating that the feminine endings, which would indicate that it is an adjective, should not be present. This definition, however, misses e.g *filius* where the feminine parallel *filia* does exist.

```
paradigm decl2fungus =
        fung++"us"
   { fung+"us" & fung+"i" & ~(fung+"a" | fung+"ae")};
```

Negation is similar with *negation as failure* in Prolog, with the same problems associated with it. The main problem is that negation rests on the absence, not the presence, of information, which in turn means that the extraction process with negation is non-monotonic: the use of a larger corpus may lead to an extracted lexicon which is smaller. A worst-case scenario is a misspelt or foreign word that, by negation, removes large parts of the correctly classified lemmas in the extracted lexicon.

In most cases, a better alternative to negation is a more careful use of regular expressions, and in cases like Latin nouns, a rudimentary POS tagger that resolves the POS ambiguity may outperform negation.

3.1 Manual Verification

Almost all corpora have misspellings which may lead to false conclusions. Added to that are word forms that incidentally coincide. One possible solution to handle misspellings is to only consider words that occur at some frequency. However, that would remove a lot of unusual but correctly spelled words (to an extent which is unacceptable). Coincidences are in practice impossible to avoid.

[2] The minimum-size sub-paradigm problem (MSS) is equivalent to the well-known set-cover problem. Proof omitted.

Misspellings, foreign words and coincidences are the reason why manual verification of the extracted lexicon cannot be circumvented even with "perfect" paradigm definitions. However, browse-filtering a high-precision extracted lexicon requires much less time than building the same lexicon by hand. Also, nothing in principle prohibits statistical techniques to be applied in collaboration here. For instance, one can sort the extracted lemmas heuristically according to how many forms and with what frequencies they occur (cf. Sect. 5). In general, this is productive for poly-occurring lemmas but helps little for the (typically many) hapax lemmas.

4 Experiments

We will evaluate our proposed extraction technique with a study of real-world extraction on the Hansards corpus of Canadian French [5]. All words were manually annotated to enable a thorough evaluation. However, the intended practical usage of the extraction tool is to simply run the tool on the raw text data and eye-browse the output list for erroneous extractions.

The corpus consisted of approximately 15 million running tokens of 66853 types. From these 66853 types we manually removed all junk – foreign words, proper names, misspellings, numeric expressions, abbreviations as well as pronouns, prepositions, interjections and non-derived adverbs – so that a 49477 true lexical items remained. 27681 lemmas account for the 49477 forms, where verb lemmas tended to occur in more forms than noun and adjective lemmas. Of course, not all these lemmas occurred in such forms that their morphological class could be recognized by their endings alone. Many lemmas occur in only one form – usually not enough to infer its morphological class – unless, as is often the case, they contain a derivational morpheme which, together with its inflectional ending, does suffice. For example, a single occurrence of a word ending in *-e* is hardly conclusive, whereas one ending in *-tude* is almost certainly a feminine noun with a plural in *-s*. Nouns without derivational ending cannot be reliably distinguished from adjectives even when they occur in all their forms, i.e both the singular and plural. The table in Fig. 4 summarizes these data.

Tokens	15 000 000
Types	66 853
Non-junk types	49 477
Lemmas	27 681

Fig. 4. Statistics on the corpus of Canadian French Hansards used in the experiment

We now turn to the question of precision and coverage of rule-extraction of the targeted 27 681 lemmas. We quickly devised a set of 43 rules to extract French nouns (18 rules), verbs (7 rules) and adjectives (18 rules). The verb-rules aimed at *-ir* and *-er* verbs by requiring salient forms for these paradigms, whereas the noun- and adjective rules make heavy use of regularities in derivational morphology to overcome the problems of overlapping forms. Two typical example groups are given below:

```
regexp NOTi = char* (char-"i") ;

paradigm Ver [regard:NOTi]
  = regard+"er"
    {regard+"e" &
     (regard+"é"    | regard+"ée"   |
      regard+"ez"   | regard+"ont"  |
      regard+"ons"  | regard+"a"  )} ;

 paradigm Aif
  = sport+"if"
    {sport+"if"  | sport+"ifs"  |
     sport+"ive" | sport+"ives"} ;
```

The results of the extraction are shown in Fig. 5. If possible, one would like to know where one's false positives come from – sloppy rules or noisy data? At least one would like to know roughly what to expect. Since we have already annotated this corpus we can give some indicative quantitative data. To assess the impact of misspellings and foreign words – the two main sources for spurious extractions – we show the results of the same extraction performed on the corpus *with all junk removed beforehand.* As expected, false positives increase when junk is added. To be more precise, we get a lot of spurious verbs from English words and proper names in *-er* (e.g farmer, worchester) as well as many nouns, whose identification requires only one form, from misspellings (e.g qestion). Non-junk-related cases of confusion worth mentioning are nouns in *-ment* – the same ending as adverbs – and verbs which have spelling changes (manger-mangeait, appeler-appelle etc).

	Extr. All	Extr. Non-Junk
False Positives	2 031	664
Correctly Indentified	17 264	17 264
	19 295	17 928
Precision	89.5%	96.3%

Fig. 5. Extraction results on raw text vs. text with junk removed first

The rule productiveness, i.e a rule on average catches $17264/43 \approx 401$, must be considered very high. As for coverage, we can see that our rules catch the lions share of the available lemmas, 17 264 out of 27 681 (again, not all of which occur in enough forms to predict their morphological class), in the corpus. This is relevant because even if we can always find more raw text cheaply, we want our rules to make maximal use of whatever is available and more raw data is of little help unless we can actually extract a lot of its lemmas with reasonable effort. It is also relevant because a precision figure without a rule productiveness figure is meaningless. It would be easy to tailor 43 rules to perfect precision, perhaps catching one lemma per rule, so what we show is that precision and rule productiveness can be simultaneously high. In general it is of course up to the user how much of the raw-data lemmas to sacrifice for precision and rule-writing effort, which are usually more important objectives.

5 Related Work

The most important work dealing with the very same problem as addressed here, i.e extracting a morphological lexicon given a morphological description, is the study of the acquisition of French verbs and adjectives in Clément et al. [6]. Likewise, they start from an existing inflection engine and exploit the fact that a new lemma can be inferred with high probability if it occurs in raw text in predictable morphological form(s). Their algorithm ranks hypothetical lemmas based on the frequency of occurrence of its (hypothetical) forms as well as part-of-speech information signalled from surrounding closed-class words. They do not make use of human-written rules but reserve an unclear, yet crucial, role for the human to hand-validate parts of output and then let the algorithm re-iterate. Given the many differences, the results cannot be compared directly to ours but rather illustrate a complementary technique.

Tested on Russian and Croat, Oliver et al. [7,8, Ch. 3] describe a lexicon extraction strategy very similar to ours. In contrast to human-made rules, they have rules extracted from an existing (part of) a morphological lexicon and use the number of inflected forms found to heuristically choose between multiple lemma-generating rules (additionally also querying the Internet for existence of forms). The resulting rules appear not at all as sharp as hand-made rules with built-in human knowledge of the paradigms involved and their respective frequency (the latter being crucial for recall). Also, in comparison, our search engine is much more powerful and allows for greater flexibility and user convenience.

For the low-density language Assamese, Sharma et al. [3] report an experiment to induce both morphology, i.e the set of paradigms, and a morphological lexicon at the same time. Their method is based on segmentation and alignment using string counts only – involving no human annotation or intervention inside the algorithm. It is difficult to assess the strength of their acquired lexicon as it is intertwined with induction of the morphology itself. We feel that inducing morphology and extracting a morphological lexicon should be performed and evaluated separately. Many other attempts to induce morphology, usually with some human tweaking, from raw corpus data (notably Goldsmith [9]), do not aim at lexicon extraction in their current form.

There is a body of work on inducing verb subcategorization information from raw or tagged text (see [10,11,12] and references therein). However, the parallel between subcategorization frame and morphological class is only lax. The latter is a simple mapping from word forms to a paradigm membership, whereas in verb subcategorization one also has the onus discerning which parts of a sentence are relevant to a certain verb. Moreover, it is far from clear that verb subcategorization comes in well-defined paradigms – instead the goal may be to reduce the amount of parse trees in a parser that uses the extracted subcategorization constraints.

6 Conclusions and Further Work

We have shown that building a morphological lexicon requires relatively little human work. Given a morphological description, typically an inflection engine and a description of the closed word classes, such as pronouns and prepositions, and access to raw text data, a human with knowledge of the language can use a simple but versatile tool that exploits word forms alone. It remains to be seen to what extent syntactic information, e.g part-of-speech information, can further enhance the performance. A more open question is whether the suggested approach can be generalized to collect linguistic information of other kinds than morphology, such as e.g verb subcategorization frames.

References

1. Forsberg, M., Ranta, A.: Functional Morphology. Proceedings of the Ninth ACM SIGPLAN International Conference of Functional Programming, Snowbird, Utah (2004) 213–223
2. Creutz, M., Lagus, K.: Inducing the morphological lexicon of a natural language from unannotated text. In: Proceedings of the International and Interdisciplinary Conference on Adaptive Knowledge Representation and Reasoning (AKRR '05), 15-17 June, Espoo, Finland, Espoo (2005) 106–113
3. Utpal Sharma, J.K., Das, R.: Unsupervised learning of morphology for building lexicon for a highly inflectional language. In: Proceedings of the 6th Workshop of the ACL Special Interest Group in Computational Phonology (SIGPHON), Philadelphia, July 2002, Association for Computational Linguistics (2002) 1–10
4. Hopcroft, J., Ullman, J.: Introduction to Automata Theory, Languages, and Computation, Second Edition. Addison-Wesley (2001)
5. Germann, U.: Corpus of hansards of the 36th parliament of canada. Provided by the Natural Language Group of the Universtity of Southern California Information Sciences Institute. Downloadable at `http://www.isi.edu/natural-language/download/hansard/`, accessed 1 Nov 2005. (2003) 15 million words.
6. Clément, L., Sagot, B., Lang, B.: Morphology based automatic acquisition of large-coverage lexica. In: Proc. of LREC'04, Lisboa, Portugal (2004) 1841–1844
7. Oliver, A., Tadić, M.: Enlarging the croatian morphological lexicon by automatic lexical acquisition from raw corpora. In: Proc. of LREC'04, Lisboa, Portugal (2004) 1259–1262
8. Oliver, A.: Adquisició d'informació lèxica i morfosintàctica a partir de corpus sense anotar: aplicació al rus i al croat. PhD thesis, Universitat de Barcelona (2004)
9. Goldsmith, J.: Unsupervised learning of the morphology of natural language. Computational Linguistics **27**(2) (2001) 153–198

10. Kermanidis, K.L., Fakotakis, N., Kokkinakis, G.: Automatic acquisition of verb subcategorization information by exploiting minimal linguistic resources. International Journal of Corpus Linguistics **9**(1) (2004) 1–28
11. Faure, D., Nédellec, C.: Asium: Learning subcategorization frames and restrictions of selection. In Kodratoff, Y., ed.: 10th Conference on Machine Learning (ECML 98) – Workshop on Text Mining, Chemnitz, Germany, Avril 1998. Springer-Verlag, Berlin (1998)
12. Gamallo, P., Agustini, A., Lopes, G.P.: Learning subcategorisation information to model a grammar with "co-restrictions". Traitement Automatique des Langues **44**(1) (2003) 93–177

On the Use of Topic Models for Word Completion

Elisabeth Wolf[1], Shankar Vembu[1], and Tristan Miller[2,⋆]

[1] German Research Center for Artificial Intelligence
Erwin-Schroedinger-Strasse 57, 67663 Kaiserslautern, Germany
{wolf, vembu}@dfki.uni-kl.de
[2] The Socialist Party of Great Britain
52 Clapham High Street, London SW4 7UN, United Kingdom
tristan.miller@worldsocialism.org

Abstract. We investigate the use of topic models, such as probabilistic latent semantic analysis (PLSA) and latent Dirichlet allocation (LDA), for word completion tasks. The advantage of using these models for such an application is twofold. On the one hand, they allow us to exploit semantic or contextual information when predicting candidate words for completion. On the other hand, these probabilistic models have been found to outperform classical latent semantic analysis (LSA) for modeling text documents. We describe a word completion algorithm that takes into account the semantic context of the word being typed. We also present evaluation metrics to compare different models being used in our study. Our experiments validate our hypothesis of using probabilistic models for semantic analysis of text documents and their application in word completion tasks.

1 Introduction

Word completion is the task of predicting and automatically completing words that the user is in the process of typing. Such tools can prevent misspellings, help develop writing skills, and accelerate typing speed by saving keystrokes. (The last benefit is particularly important for users of keyboardless devices, such as mobile phones and PDAs, as well as for users with physical disabilities.) During typing, the user is offered a prediction list of words beginning with the letters, or word prefix, thus far typed. If the intended word is in the prediction list, the user can select it with a single keypress; otherwise, he continues typing until the word appears in the list or until he types the complete word.

The job of the word completion algorithm is to determine which words appear in the prediction list, the idea being to maximise the probability of presenting the user with the correct word. The earliest word completion algorithms [1] used simple statistical methods, such as word or word-pair frequencies, to rank words

⋆ Part of the research described in this paper was carried out while this author was at the German Research Center for Artificial Intelligence.

T. Salakoski et al. (Eds.): FinTAL 2006, LNAI 4139, pp. 500–511, 2006.

in the prediction list. The frequencies are derived from a corpus of written text, though some systems [2] dynamically update the frequency table to adapt to the user's writing style. More advanced systems [3] incorporate syntactic data, such as part-of-speech tags and grammar rules, to avoid suggesting words which are grammatically incorrect in the given context. However, even systems that combine statistical and syntactic information can suggest words that are *semantically* inappropriate. For instance, the writer of an essay on music who begins typing *Mende...* is far more likely to intend the completion to be *Mendelssohn* than *Mendel* or *Mendeleyev*, even though all three are proper nouns that may be equally statistically likely (in a unigram or a bigram model, at least).

In order to avoid suggesting semantically inappropriate words, several approaches were proposed in which semantic knowledge is incorporated into the completion task. An early attempt at incorporating semantic information was proposed by Kozima and Ito [4]. They deal with a scene-based model that uses local semantic information of each scene—i.e., a text fragment which displays a semantic unit. However, they predict words based on context-sensitive word distances, because there is no training corpus segmented into scenes to derive probabilities of the occurrence of a word given a text fragment. Other recent attempts (e.g., [5]) require language-specific tools such as WordNet [6], and many operate only on words of a particular part of speech.

All of these approaches have shown an improvement of the word completion task in predicting semantically more appropriate words. But none of these explicitly model the semantics of text documents resulting in disambiguation of polysems and synonyms, which is possible using models like latent semantic analysis (LSA) [7]. In our recent work [8], we demonstrated the advantages of exploiting the semantic context of words that have been typed for predicting a list of candidate words for completing the current word using LSA. In this paper, we investigate the application of topic models—namely, probabilistic latent semantic analysis (PLSA) [9] and latent Dirichlet allocation (LDA) [10]—to model the semantics of text documents. In recent years, these models have been gaining widespread interest as semantic models not only of text collections but also in other domains like images [11,12]. We make empirical comparisons of these models for word completion tasks with LSA as the baseline model.

The paper is organised as follows: We begin with a brief description of topic models that we intend to use in our experiments. We then present a semantic-based word completion algorithm in Section 3 and give a complexity analysis. In the following section, we describe the details of our simulator for word completion and present evaluation metrics that will be used for the comparison of the various topic models. Section 5 describes our experimental work, and is followed by conclusions and pointers to future work.

2 Topic Models

LSA has been in use for a long time for the automatic indexing and retrieval of text documents. It is based on the singular value decomposition (SVD) of the term–document matrix X giving rise to two orthogonal matrices U and V, and a diagonal matrix Σ, such that $X = U\Sigma V^T$. The elements of Σ are called singular values and the columns of U and V are called left and right singular vectors, respectively. A reduced-rank approximation of X is obtained by discarding all but the highest K singular values in Σ. The resulting matrices define the so-called *latent semantic space* in which common information retrieval operations such as comparison of two terms, two documents, or a term and a document can be performed.

PLSA is the probabilistic version of LSA and it defines a generative model for statistical modeling of discrete and count data of which text collections are an example. PLSA assumes the existence of a latent variable $z_k \in \{z_1, \ldots, z_K\}$, where K is the number of topics, for each word (or observation) in a document. The data generation process is described in three steps: a document d_i is selected with probability $p(d_i)$; a latent class variable z_k, also referred to as the topic variable, is selected with probability $p(z_k|d_i)$; a word w_j is finally generated with probability $p(w_j|z_k)$. The probability of an observation pair (d_i, w_j) is given as

$$p(d_i, w_j) = p(d_i) \sum_{k=1}^{K} p(w_j|z_k)p(z_k|d_i) \ .$$

The model parameters are estimated using the expectation-maximisation (EM) [13] algorithm. If we assume a corpus of M documents and a vocabulary of N words, the parameters of a K-topic PLSA model are K multinomial distributions of size M and N mixtures over the K hidden topics, thereby making the total number of parameters to be $KN + KM$. The linear dependence of the number of parameters on the size of the corpus results in overfitting and a tempered version of EM was proposed by Hofmann [9] to mitigate this problem. The inference step involves estimating the distribution of the topics given a new document—i.e., $p(z_k|d_{new})$—by fixing the $p(w_j|z_k)$ parameters. This step, also called *folding in* [7], projects new, unseen documents into the latent semantic space.

LDA is a three-level hierarchical Bayesian model in which each document is modeled as a mixture of an underlying set of topics, very much similar in a sense to PLSA. But the drawbacks of PLSA, such as its linear dependence on the number of documents for parameter estimation and its inability to assign probability to previously unseen documents, are mitigated in the LDA model [10]. The data generation proceeds as follows: a Dirichlet parameterised by α is sampled to yield θ; for each of the N words, a topic z_n is sampled from a multinomial parameterised by θ and a word w_n is chosen with probabibilty $p(w_n|z_n, \beta)$, which again is a multinomial conditioned on the topic z_n. The model parameters are given by α and β. The probability of a corpus D consisting of M documents having N words in each of them is given as

$$p(D|\alpha, \beta) = \prod_{m=1}^{M} \int p(\theta_m|\alpha) \left(\prod_{n=1}^{N_m} \Sigma_{z_{mn}} p(z_{mn}|\theta_m) p(w_{mn}|z_{mn}, \beta) \right) d\theta_m \ .$$

The number of parameters in a K-topic LDA model is $K + KM$—i.e., the Dirichlet parameter $\alpha \in \mathbb{R}^K$ and the K multinomial word distributions. Therefore, unlike PLSA, parameter estimation in LDA is not dependent on the number of documents N. The inferential quantity of interest is the distribution of the topics given a new document $p(\theta, z|\mathbf{w}, \alpha, \beta)$ and is estimated using approximate inference techniques for graphical models [14].

3 Semantic Word Completion

3.1 Algorithm

The first step is to build semantic models of the text corpus using LSA, PLSA and LDA. Ideally the training corpus should be large enough to contain any word the user is likely to type. Once the models are built, pairs of term or document vectors can be compared via the cosine coefficient, yielding a "semantic similarity" score in the range $[-1, 1]$. Assume the user is in the process of typing a word w with prefix pre(w). We define the *context* $C = \langle c_1, c_2, \ldots, c_{\ell-1}, c_\ell \rangle$ as the sequence of up to ℓ words immediately preceding w in the document. We refer to ℓ as the *context length*, though near the beginning of the document the actual length of the context, $|C|$, may be less than ℓ.

A *candidate word* $t \in T \subseteq V$, where V is the vocabulary of size N, is any word whose prefix is the same as that of w—i.e., $T = \{t | t \in V \wedge \text{pre}(t) = \text{pre}(w)\}$. The best candidates comprise the *prediction list* $P \subseteq T$, which the user (or system) caps at a maximum length of p. Again, it is possible that $|P| < p$ if there are fewer than p known words with the given prefix. We propose a method called *sum of similarities* (SOS) to populate P, in which we compare the candidates to each word in the context individually. The similarity score for the context is the sum of similarity scores of each word in the context and is given as

$$\text{sim}(t, C) = \sum_{i=1}^{|C|} \cos(t, c_i) .$$

We compute the similarity scores for each possible t, and populate the prediction list P with p high-scoring candidates.

3.2 Complexity Analysis

The application of topic models to word completion involves two steps: creating models (or parameter estimation) of LSA, PLSA and LDA; and simulation of word completion using the SOS algorithm. The input to our system is an $N \times M$ term–document matrix and let the desired number of topics be K. The time complexity of building an LSA model depends on the SVD of matrices. Efficient algorithms to perform SVD can be found in the literature. For example, Brand [15] introduced an algorithm that performs a reduced-rank SVD of a matrix in $\mathcal{O}(N \cdot M \cdot K)$ time, which is linear in the number of inputs and outputs. The estimation of model parameters in PLSA and LDA is performed using the EM algorithm, and therefore the time complexity is dependent on the number of operations per EM iteration and also on the number of iterations

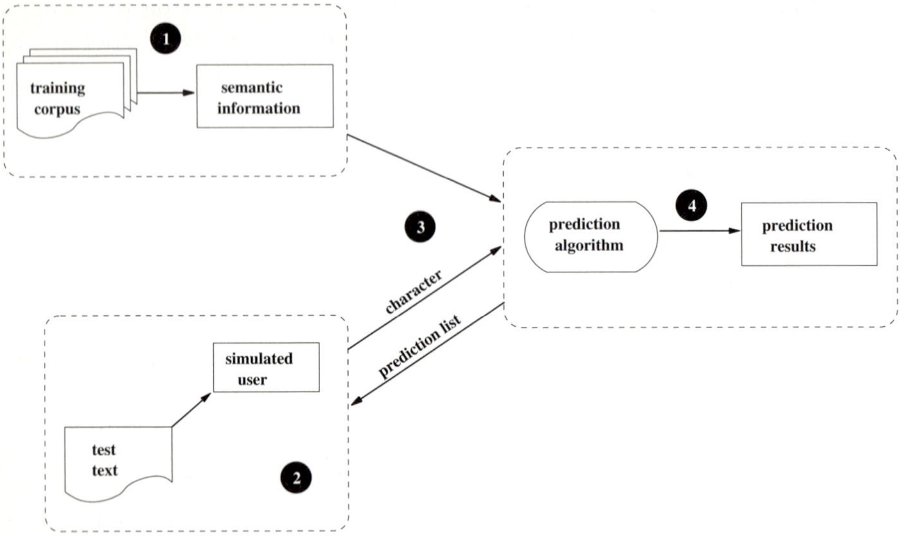

Fig. 1. Simulation architecture

that are required for convergence. Each EM iteration in PLSA requires $\mathcal{O}(R \cdot K)$ operations, where R is the number of distinct observation pairs (d_i, w_j)—i.e., $N \cdot M$ times the degree of sparseness of the term–document matrix. The number of iterations typically falls in the range 20–50 [9]. Each iteration in the varational E-step in LDA requires $\mathcal{O}((N+1) \cdot K)$ operations, with the number of iterations for a single document roughly equalling the number of words M in the document [10]. We thus observe that the time complexity of all the three models is linear in the individual inputs. In the SOS algorithm, we perform a term–term comparison i.e., a cosine operation for each word in the context, and therefore the number of comparisons is in the order of $\mathcal{O}(\ell \cdot |T|)$, where ℓ is the context length. Note that the SOS algorithm does not require the inference step of PLSA and LDA, since it performs only a term–term comparison using the K multinomial word distributions that are readily available after the parameter estimation step.

4 Test Bench

4.1 Simulation

We designed and implemented a simulator in order to evaluate the performance of our word completion algorithm. The simulator (illustrated in Figure 1) consists of three major components. The first component (❶) covers all necessary preprocessing steps and trains LSA, PLSA, LDA models in order to extract semantic information. In the second component (❷), a simulated user is integrated, who interacts (❸) with the prediction component (❹).

The simulated user types in the words of a test document by passing character after character to the prediction component, and gets p candidates presented in the prediction list in return. The population of the prediction list is dependent on the context and the semantic model being used. In order to choose a limited number of candidates for the prediction list, the prediction algorithm calculates the semantic similarity of each candidate and selects the p most appropriate words. Afterwards one of the three following cases can occur. In the explanation below, P is the prediction list and w is the typed word with prefix $\text{pre}(w)$ that has to be completed.

Case 1: $w \in P$
The word appears in the prediction list. It is selected and the system proceeds with the first character of the next word.

Case 2: $w \notin P, |\text{pre}(w)| < |w|$
The intended word does not appear in the prediction list and is not typed totally thus far. The word prefix is expanded by the next character of the current word and passed to the prediction algorithm.

Case 3: $w \notin P, |\text{pre}(w)| = |w|$
The intended word could not be completed before it was completely typed.

During the whole experimental process, detailed information is stored for further analysis. The simulation terminates after the whole test text has been processed.

4.2 Evaluation Metrics

Performance of the system is assessed with the following three metrics:

Keystroke savings, the most important metric, is the percentage of keystrokes that the user saves by using the word completion utility:

$$\text{KS} = 100 - \frac{100}{|W|} \cdot \sum_{w \in W} \frac{s_w + 1}{\text{len}(w)},$$

where $|W|$ is the number of words in the test set of documents, s_w is the number of keystrokes used to type a given word w, $+1$ is the one additional keystroke to choose the appropriate word in the prediction list, and $\text{len}(w)$ is the number of characters in w—i.e., the number of keystrokes that would have had to be typed without the word completion utility.

Hit rate refers to the percentage of keystrokes after which the intended word appears in the prediction list:

$$\text{HR} = 100 \cdot \left[\sum_{w \in W} \text{in}(w) \right] \div \sum_{w \in W} s_w,$$

where

$$\text{in}(w) = \begin{cases} 1 \text{ if } w \in P \text{ after typing } s_w \text{ characters;} \\ 0 \text{ otherwise.} \end{cases}$$

Keystrokes until prediction is the mean number of keystrokes until the intended word appears in the prediction list or is completely typed:

$$\mathrm{KUP} = \frac{1}{|W|} \cdot \sum_{w \in W} s_w \,.$$

5 Experiments and Results

5.1 Data Sets

We used Reuters-21578 [16] corpus with the ModApte splitting scheme for our experiments. The ModApte split results in a corpus of 9603 training documents and 3299 test documents. Although the original corpus has 135 topics, the ModApte split yields only 90 topics for which there is at least one training and one test document. We performed standard preprocessing techniques of stop word removal and stemming. We also removed all words that occurred in less than three documents and in more than 90% of the training documents. These operations resulted in a 5605 × 9603 term–document matrix which was used to build our models using LSA, PLSA, and LDA. Since PLSA and LDA operate on discrete or count data, we used the word counts instead of the standard tf–idf representation of documents.

5.2 Training Phase

We trained LSA, PLSA, and LDA for different values of K, the number of topics, on the training set consisting of 9603 documents. We trained the PLSA model using the tempered version of EM as described by Hofmann [9] to avoid the possibility of overfitting. The LDA model was trained using variational EM as described in Blei's paper [10]. The Dirichlet parameter α was set to an initial value of 0.5 and was allowed to be iteratively estimated along with the topic distributions. We used the same stopping criteria of 200 maximum iterations and 0.0001% change in expected log likelihood (whichever of the two occurs first) for training PLSA and LDA models. Training an LSA model simply entails performing an SVD on the term–document matrix and as such there were no free parameters to fine tune.

5.3 Simulation Results and Analysis

Simulating the word completion algorithm SOS is a computationally expensive operation, since a term–term comparison has to be made for each word in the context. We therefore could not use the entire test set of documents with all the words for our experiments. Instead, we sampled the test corpus in such a way so as to include two documents from each of the 90 topics. This resulted in 120 documents with 12 942 words that was finally used in our simulation. We note that in the Reuters corpus, a single document might be assigned to multiple topics, and therefore we have 120 instead of 180 documents.

Simulation results for $K = 25$ topics are shown in Figure 2. The figures depict the performance of LSA, PLSA, and LDA for the three metrics defined in §4.2 as a function of context length. It is evident from these graphs that the probabilistic models PLSA and LDA outperform LSA, and the best performance is achieved by LDA for all the evaluated metrics. For instance, for a context length of 14 words, LDA outperforms LSA by 8.19%, 9.94%, and 9.06% in terms of keystroke savings, hit rate, and keystrokes until prediction, respectively. An interesting observation is the dependence of these metrics on context length. In contrast to LSA, we note that PLSA and LDA show a significant increase in keystroke savings and hit rate with context length. The same holds true for keystrokes until prediction, which decreases with context length. These observations suggest that PLSA and LDA are able to model semantics or contextual information in a much better way when compared to LSA. For all three models, we observed that the performance of the system did not improve continuously for higher values of context length. For instance, we see that the keystroke savings for LSA improve until the context length is 6, but thereafter the performance goes down. The same holds true for the other metrics. For PLSA and LDA, the increase in keystroke savings was not significant for larger context lengths. This might suggest that incorporating too much semantic or contextual information for word prediction does not help; for a given application the appropriate context length could be determined by the available computational resources and with reference to these results. We also note from the complexity analysis in §3.2, that the response time of a word completion utility is linearly dependent on the context length, and therefore having large context lengths might slow down the overall response of the system.

We proceed with our analysis of results for different values of K, the number of topics. Simulation results are shown in Figure 3 for $K = 50$ and $K = 75$. We observe that there is indeed a performance gain as the number of topics increases. An interesting observation is the way PLSA behaves for higher numbers of topics. For $K = 25$, PLSA fares better than LSA at every context length and evaluation metric. But, for $K = 50$, we see that for lower values of context lengths, LSA performs better than PLSA, and this tendency becomes marked when we increase the number of topics to 75. This might be the result of overfitting due to an increase in the number of parameters. Interestingly, LDA did not suffer from any such problems and it seems to fare better with larger context lengths. For instance, with a context length of 14, LDA with $K = 75$ performs better than with $K = 25$ by 4.34%, 6.04%, and 5.63% in terms of keystroke savings, hit rate, and keystrokes until prediction, respectively. It is not computationally feasible to experiment with many values of K, and therefore we are not able to report results for a wide range of values of K. Nonetheless, as described above, we are able to draw some important conclusions regarding the behaviour of these models for different number of topics. The number of topics is indeed a bottleneck parameter, and the best value for it is dependent on the available computational resources.

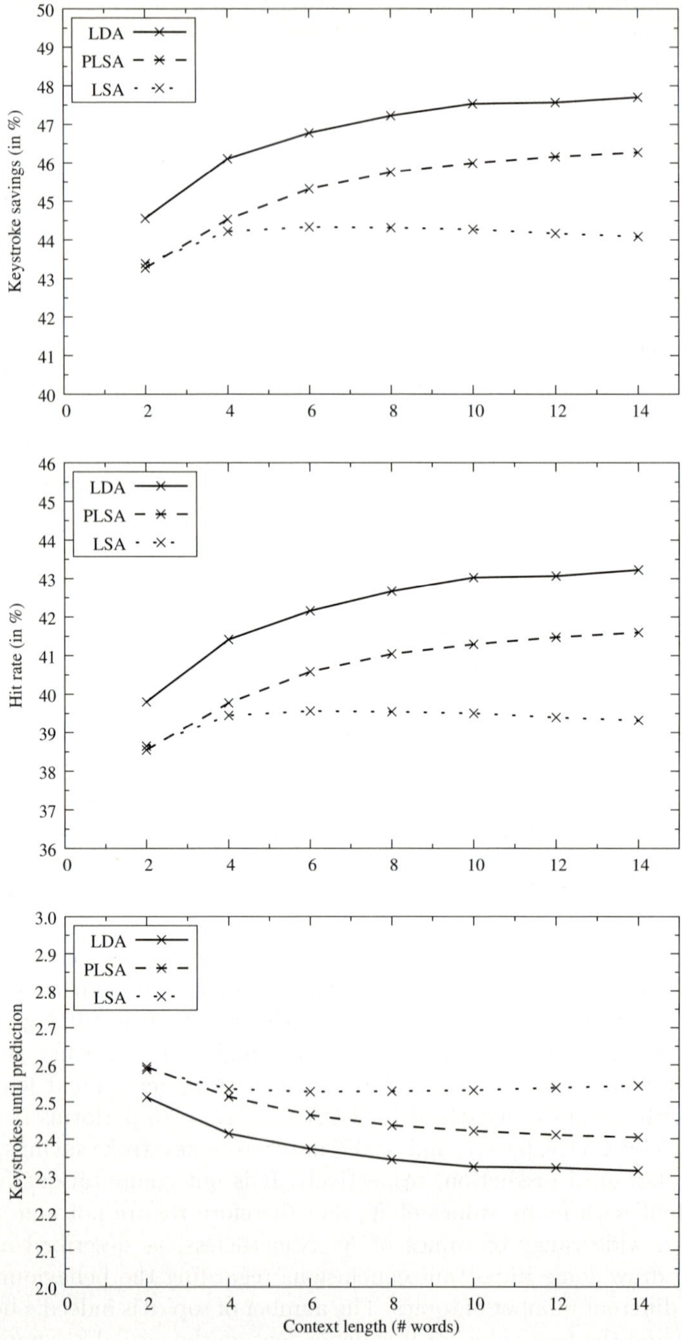

Fig. 2. Simulation results for $K = 25$ topics with keystroke savings (top), hit rate (middle), and keystrokes until prediction (bottom) as a function of context length

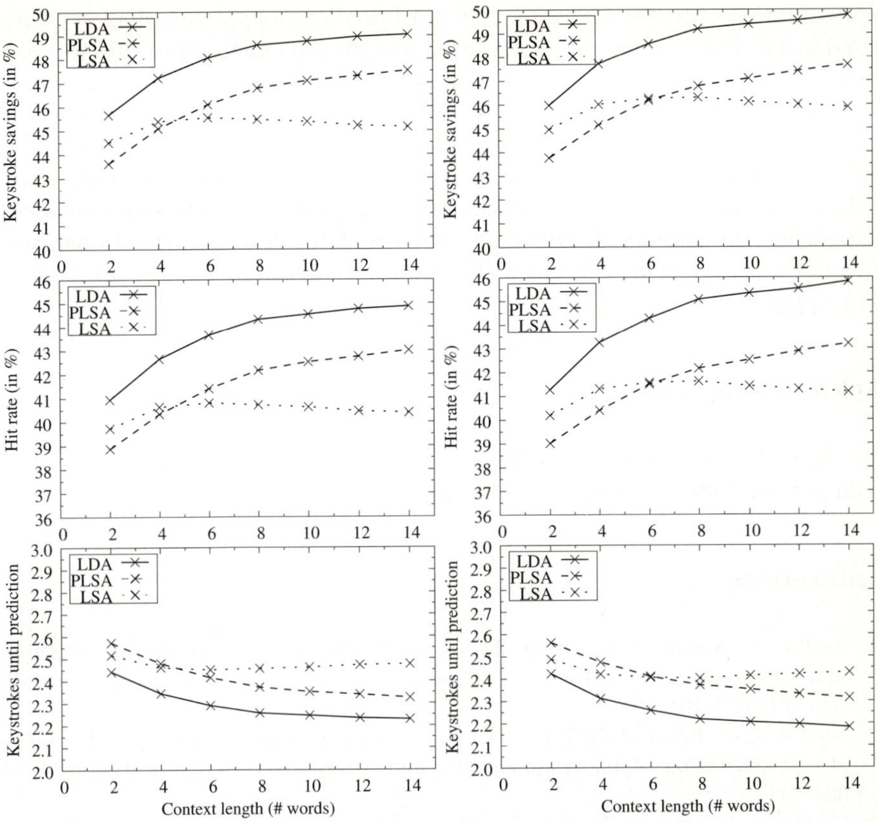

Fig. 3. Simulation results for $K = 50$ (left) and $K = 75$ (right) topics with keystroke savings (top), hit rate (middle), and keystrokes until prediction (bottom) as a function of context length

6 Conclusions

We have demonstrated the application of probabilistic models like PLSA and LDA, also called topic models, to semantic-based word completion. It has been proved elsewhere that these models are superior to their classical counterpart LSA for semantic modeling of text documents, and our experimental results corroborate their use for applications like word completion. In all our experiments, we found that LDA performed better in predicting or completing words when compared to PLSA and LSA. We also observed that there is a possibility for PLSA to overfit with increasing number of topics and that having too many words in the contextual information might not yield improved results.

We would like to point out again that we restricted ourselves to discrete inputs by simply using word counts in the term–document matrix. It would be interesting to consider extensions of these models for continuous or other non-multinomial data. This would make the models amenable to the standard tf–idf representation of text documents. Our word prediction approach suggests words based on the exclusive use of semantic knowledge. An extension to this approach would be to also integrate syntactic and statistical information to improve the efficiency of the system. Another possible extension is to make these models handle dynamic updates. This is necessary if a typed word is not part of the term–document matrix, thereby making it unpredictable. The possibility that a certain number of folding-in processes might degrade the latent semantic structure should be considered. Dynamic model updates is a non-trivial operation, though there exist some efficient SVD algorithms [17] that could be used for our LSA approach.

Acknowledgements

We thank Florent Monay (IDIAP) and David Blei (Princeton University) for making their code on PLSA and LDA available online.

References

1. Swiffin, A., Arnott, J., Pickering, J., Newell, A.: Adaptive and predictive techniques in a communication prosthesis. AAC: Augmentative and Alternative Communication **3** (1987) 181–191
2. Newell, A.F.: Effect of the PAL word prediction system on the quality and quantity of text generation. AAC: Augmentative and Alternative Communication **8** (1992) 304–311
3. Fazly, A., Hirst, G.: Testing the efficacy of part-of-speech information in word completion. In: Proceedings of the Workshop on Language Modeling for Text Entry Methods at the 10th Conference of the European Chapter of the Association for Computational Linguistics, Budapest, Hungary (2003)
4. Kozima, H., Ito, A.: A scene-based model of word prediction. In: Proceedings of the International Conference on New Methods in Language Processing (NeMLaP), Ankara, Turkey (1996) 110–120
5. Li, J., Hirst, G.: Semantic knowledge in word completion. In: Proceedings of the 7th International ACM SIGACCESS Conference on Computers and Accessibility. (2005)
6. Miller, G.A.: Wordnet: An on-line lexical database. International Journal of Lexicography **3** (1990) 235–244
7. Deerwester, S., Dumais, S.T., Furnas, G.W., Landauer, T.K., Harshman, R.: Indexing by latent semantic analysis. Journal of the American Society of Information Science **41** (1990) 391–407
8. Wolf, E.: A semantic-based word completion utility using latent semantic analysis. Diplom-Informatik thesis, Department of Technical Sciences, University of Applied Sciences, Oldenburg/Ostfriesland/Wilhelmshaven, Emden (2005)
9. Hofmann, T.: Unsupervised learning by probabilistic latent semantic analysis. Machine Learning **42** (2001) 177–196
10. Blei, D., Ng, A., Jordan, M.: Latent Dirichlet allocation. Journal of Machine Learning Research **3** (2003) 993–1022

11. Blei, D., Jordan, M.: Modeling annotated data. In: Proceedings of the 26th Annual International ACM SIGIR Conference on Research and Development in Information Retrieval, Toronto, Canada (2003)
12. Sivic, J., Russell, B., Efros, A., Zisserman, A., Freeman, W.: Discovering object categories in image collections. In: Proceedings of the 10th IEEE International Conference on Computer Vision, Beijing, China (2005)
13. Dempster, A.P., Laird, N.M., Rubin, D.B.: Maximum likelihood from incomplete data via the EM algorithm. Journal of the Royal Statistical Society, Series B **34** (1977) 1–38
14. Jordan, M.I., Ghahramani, Z., Jaakkola, T.S., Saul, L.K.: An introduction to variational methods for graphical methods. Machine Learning **37** (1999) 183–233
15. Brand, M.: Incremental singular value decomposition of uncertain data. In: Proceedings of the 7th European Conference on Computer Vision, Copenhagen, Denmark (2002)
16. Lewis, D.D.: Reuters-21578 Text Categorization Test Collection Distribution 1.0 README File v1.3. (2004)
17. Brand, M.: Fast online SVD revisions for lightweight recommender systems. In: Proceedings of the SIAM International Conference on Data Mining, San Francisco, CA, USA (2003)

Ord i Dag: Mining Norwegian Daily Newswire

Unni Cathrine Eiken[1], Anja Therese Liseth[1], Hans Friedrich Witschel[2], Matthias Richter[2], and Chris Biemann[2]

[1] University of Bergen, AKSIS
Allégaten 27, 5007 Bergen, Norway
unni@eiken.no, anjaliseth@gmail.com
[2] University of Leipzig, NLP Department
Augustusplatz 10/11, 04109 Leipzig, Germany
{witschel, mrichter, biem}@informatik.uni-leipzig.de

Abstract. We present *Ord i Dag*, a new service that displays today's most important keywords. These are extracted fully automatically from Norwegian online newspapers. Describing the complete process, we provide an entirely disclosed method for media monitoring and news summarization. For keyword extraction, a reference corpus serves as background about average language use, which is contrasted with the current day's word frequencies. Having detected the most prominent keywords of a day, we introduce several ways of grouping and displaying them in intuitive ways. A discussion about possible applications concludes.

Up to now, the service is available for Norwegian and German. As only some shallow language-specific processing is needed, it can easily be set up for other languages.

1 Introduction

Machine aided media monitoring is a service that has been offered commercially for years, typically covering thousands of channels and providing products from keyword monitoring to media resonance analysis. *Ord i Dag* (Word of the day) is a new way of monitoring news, which is interesting for academic research as well as for the layman. By using different ways of presenting today's most important keywords, we prepare a good overview of what the media considers as today's most interesting news and topics. We also present a method of monitoring these events over time.

1.1 Motivation

Media produce large and ever growing amounts of content on a regular basis. Texts account for a significant part thereof and its analysis constitutes a promising field of research. Due to the amount of data it is an obvious idea to bring into the field statistical methods which can help to single out new and interesting events and topics.

The criteria used in commercial solutions are, if at all, often not fully laid open. *Ord i dag*, as described in this work, is a fully disclosed selection and

T. Salakoski et al. (Eds.): FinTAL 2006, LNAI 4139, pp. 512 – 523, 2006.

presentation process, providing a solid data foundation for research on relations and developments.

1.2 Related Work

In recent years, topics such as summarization, clustering, filtering and tracking of news have been covered, often related to the novelty track in TREC and TDT [1]. In 1997, the Altavista search engine featured *LiveTopics* (see `http://www.samizdat.com/script/lt1.htm`), which included a graph calculated from words in current news. [2] describes *Newsblaster*, which groups stories by a Topic Detection and Tracking system and generates multi document summaries for news on a daily basis. This is comparable to approaches by *Google News* and others, but with *Newsblaster* keeping an index of past days. Another multi document summary centered approach is *NewsInEssence* [3]. Visualization interfaces for news search sites have been built and made available on the Web: *Newsmap* at `http://www.marumushi.com/ apps/newsmap/` presents the groups and stories from *Google News* in form of a treemap [4], which represents the amount of coverage of topics in differently sized labeled boxes. *In the News* at `http://news.stamen.com/` combines different data sources to display a real-time overview on news based on bar diagrams and featuring sparklines [5] for monitoring change over time. Sparklines are also used for the visual display of frequency information at the *Wörter der Woche* calculated from each issue of the German newspaper "Die Zeit" by the Berlin-Brandenburg Academy of Science. These works suggest that there is a niche for news analysis and visualization in the recently growing field of Visual Analytics [6].

1.3 Outline

In this work we cover the full process of obtaining a daily amount of 100-150 keywords that describe the most important events in the daily news. The process is split into two parts: the preparation of a reference corpus, which is outlined in section 2, and the daily processing of news data as explained in detail in section 3.

Section 4 deals with the presentation of the data: grouping related keywords for a user-friendly website layout. Visualization of daily keywords as well as time-dependent changes is exemplified. Section 5 concludes with discussing some possible extensions and applications.

All data is available in human- and machine-readable format on `http://wortschatz.uni-leipzig.de/wdtno/`.

2 Preparing the Reference Corpus

Figure 1 depicts the steps undertaken in order to prepare the reference corpus. A reference corpus is a large corpus that is used as a model for 'average' language use in the following.

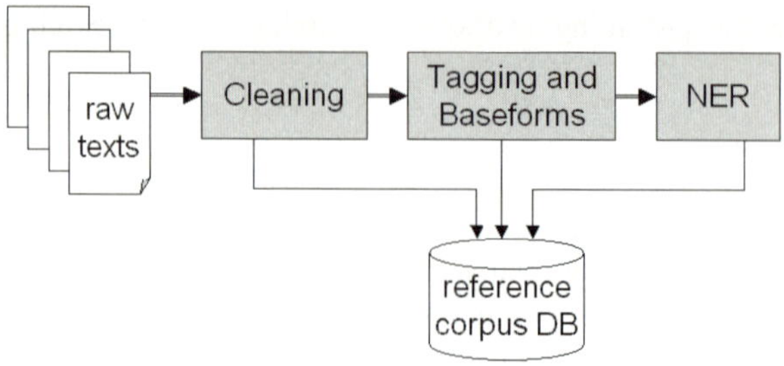

Fig. 1. Process chain for preparing the reference corpus database

2.1 Preprocessing

For the purposes of this project we make use of the Norwegian newspaper corpus Norsk aviskorpus (`http://www.avis.uib.no`, cf. [7]), which is collected by the University of Bergen and consists of approximately 440 million running words from 1.3 million texts. It is augmented every day by roughly 200,000 words from a selection of Norwegian newspapers on the internet.

When transforming the corpus into our reference corpus, some cleaning was needed, i.e. stripping of unprocessed HTML tags, broken picture headings and external links. Although the everyday routine for collecting the newspaper texts is updated constantly, a large amount of commercials, names of journalists and photographers etc. had to be removed from older material. It was also necessary to set up routines to remove such unwanted parts, should they ever re-occur in new texts.

2.2 Linguistic Processing

Tagging and base form reduction. Part-of-speech tagging and base form reduction are important steps in the linguistic pre-processing. Tagging provides information on word classes; base form reduction maps several inflected forms onto one base form. Both actions are important for linguistic filtering as elaborated in section 3.1.

For Norwegian, there exists the Oslo-Bergen-tagger, a high-quality constraint-based tagger [8] that does not only assign word class information, but also is able to annotate base forms and syntactic functions. However, this rule-based tagger is too slow for granting topicality and its output provides much more information than needed for our purpose. We therefore re-engineered the tagger in a simple way: We tagged a portion of the corpus and used the obtained triples (word, tag, base form) as training data for Compact Patricia Tree (CPT) classifiers.

Using the implementation from [9], CPT classifiers are trained to return a class, given a string. The number of classes is not restricted and the training set is perfectly reproduced. Due to the compact representation and an efficient search mechanism in the tree, CPTs can be used as lexical components for millions of words. The most important feature of CPTs, however, is their ability to generalise, i.e. to return classification guesses for unseen strings. For example, if an yet unseen word like *deministration* is classified, its class will be guessed based on training words with a longest common affix, e.g. *administration*. The same class will be assigned for similar strings. If several training words of different classes match with the same longest common affix, a class distribution is returned. CPTs can be trained on beginnings or endings of strings.

How to employ these classifiers for tagging and base form reduction is described in the following subsections.

Tagging with CPTs. As we need only rudimental word class information for filtering, we reduced the tag set of the Oslo-Bergen-tagger to the following basic categories: noun (N), verb (V), adjective (A), adverb (AV), cardinality (C), interpunctuation mark (IM) and others (S). For the most frequent 100,000 word forms of our tagged part of the corpus, we trained two CPT classifiers on these classes: one for prefixes and one for suffixes. Here, we only allowed one possible tag per string: POS-ambiguous words receive their most frequent tag, which is sufficient for our filtering task. With these top frequency words, we achieve a text coverage of about 96.3%. For these words, our classifiers yield unique classes that form the tags. For unknown words, the intersection of the two class distributions determines the tag.

This implements a unigram part-of-speech tagger that clearly does not meet the requirements of a full-fledged POS-tagger but is sufficient for the subsequent steps. A higher quality would be obtained when using e.g. a HMM tagger.

Base Form Reduction with CPTs. Unlike the low level POS-tagger, the quality of base form reduction with CPTs meets state-of-the-art requirements. Given a list of pairs (word, base form), reduction rules for the conversion from full form to base form are computed. Table 1 gives examples for the verb "stå" (to stand).

Table 1. Reduction rules for some full forms of "stå"

full form	stå	stående	står	stås	stått	sto	stod
reduction rule	0	4	1	1	2	1å	2å

The reduction rules consist of two parts: A number indicating how many characters should be cut from the suffix of the full form, and an optional string that is attached after the cut operation. We learn reduction rules as they are similar for words with the same inflection behavior.

For base form reduction, three CPTs are trained on suffixes: one for each open word class (nouns, verbs, adjectives). The tag from the unigram tagger is used for the classification.

Identification of Named Entities. The identification of named entities is a further important step in the linguistic processing of the data collection. In order to present users with an informative list of daily keywords, we need a way to recognize the multi word units that constitute named entities. We implemented a weakly supervised method described in [10] to recognize person names in the corpus. The algorithm takes very little input knowledge and performs iterative learning on unlabeled data. By drawing advantage of the fact that named entities display a high degree of regularity in their form, the algorithm bootstraps new instances of named entities based on a small set of initial names and classification rules.

The algorithm was initially supplied with a list of a few hundred common name elements, labelled as first or last names, a short list of common titles, and a set of classification rules and extraction patterns. The classification rules specify patterns that determine which tag a new name should be assigned. For example the rule TIT CAP* LN -> FN would entail that a capitalized word found between a known title and a known last name would be tagged as a first name. To ensure high classification precision, this decision is verified on other occurrences of this word.

By these means we construct a large, corpus-specific list of name parts that is used in a heavily gazetter-based Named Entity recognizer. In this NER component, the recognition of yet unseen names is carried out by the same classification rules as mentioned above (including the verification step). Using this approach, we collected a list of about 300,000 named entities from the corpus. These are used as multi word units in the following. The list includes names and titles, allowing entries such as *Jens Stoltenberg* and *statsminister Jens Stoltenberg*.

3 Processing the Daily Data

When processing daily data, the same preprocessing steps as for the reference corpus are carried out. Additionally, the reference corpus is used as a means of comparison for obtaining the words that are most prominent on that specific date. Figure 2 depicts the process chain.

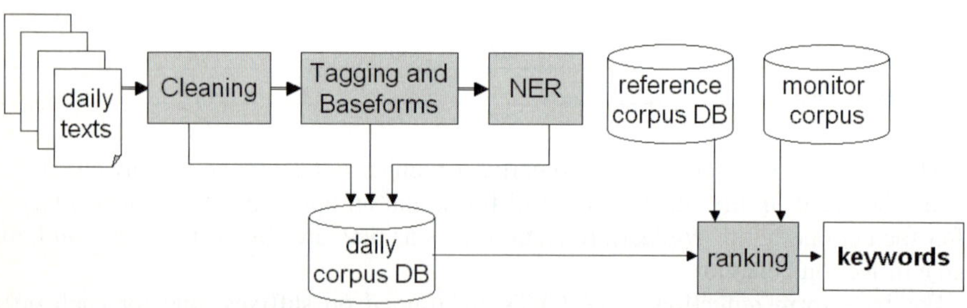

Fig. 2. Process chain for obtaining keywords from daily corpus

3.1 Extraction of Keywords

Selection Criteria. Keywords are selected following the set of assumptions proposed in [11] with an additional language specific component and a monitor corpus. Concepts can be represented best by nouns and named entities. Therefore only these word classes are considered eligible for keyword selection. There are three groups of keywords that are treated differently: words present in the reference corpus, multi words and words not present in the reference corpus.

For words seen before, a difference analysis [12] based on the Poisson measure of surprise combined with a comparison of relative frequencies is carried out. A word is considered a keyword if its Poisson significance exceeds a threshold and if it occurs with sufficient frequency. The words not covered by the reference corpus become keywords if they can pass the normal frequency threshold test.

The static reference corpus may not cover recent developments. This shortcoming is addressed by using frequency data from the recent past as a monitor corpus. An *inclusion* rule selects keywords if they occur much more often on the present day than in the preceding five week frame. An *exclusion* rule is applied to drop words if on the current day they occurred relatively less often than in the week before.

3.2 Grouping of Keywords

In order to provide a usable overview of keywords for the news topics of the day, these need to be grouped. Two alternative grouping approaches are described below.

Keyword Categorization. The reference corpus contains source URLs for each article. These can be exploited for learning a classification with only a very small amount of human interaction. The preparation process consists of the following steps:

1. Extract all possible fragments of information from the source URLs that contribute to more than 10.000 sentences. This gave 145 category candidates.
2. By eliminating in a further step senseless strings and grouping differently written variations, the number of categories for display could be reduced to only 11: "Regional" (regional), "Innenriks" (home affairs), "Utenriks" (foreign affairs), "Politikk" (politics), "Økonomi" (economy), "Kultur" (culture), "Sport" (sports), "Utdanning" (education and research), "Bil" (automobile), "Forbruker" (consumer) and "Teknologi" (technology).
3. For each pair of word and category, a dependency statistics was calculated in the form of a likelihood ratio which gives high significance to words that – in the given category – occur with higher frequency and negative values to words which appear more rarely than predicted by the entire training collection.

In the daily process, new text can be classified by assigning for each word in each sentence a category weight, which takes into account both positive and negative values for all categories and the frequency of the word in the reference corpus. An assignment of the sentence to a category is made if the sum passes a threshold, which has been set up to provide an average of 90% precision and 50 % recall in an evaluation on the training set with 10-fold cross-validation.

For texts, the sum of classifications of all sentences is calculated and the highest rated category is assigned to the text.

Clear advantages of this simplistic approach are that (except for setting up the categories) the process works fully automatically and is based on a wide coverage of vocabulary, which means that there are many features and thus enough support for reliable classification.

Candidate Clustering. Another form of organizing the *ord i dag*-keywords aims at a more granular and flexible presentation: instead of using a fixed set of categories, it might be interesting to model events using a constantly changing and more fine-grained classification that gives a quick overview of the day's events. This can be achieved by clustering the keywords and learning headlines for clusters. The headlines will be the new set of categories. As an example of why this is desirable, consider the categories and clusters presented in figure 3: The headline "Israel" in figure 3b) tells that something interesting has happened in Israel, whereas this fact is lost in figure 3a) within the general category "Utenriks" (foreign affairs).

However, a serious drawback of the cluster representation is the manual effort which it requires: headlines are assigned manually in the beginning and subsequent automatic headline assignments must be supervised.

Following is a detailed description of how we arrive at clusters and headlines:

1. *Feature Selection:* in order to describe a keyword, it is assigned a feature vector derived from its example sentences S, i.e. all of today's sentences in which it occurs. The feature vector consists of all other keywords that appear in S, weighted with their frequency.
2. *Clustering:* Now the keywords are clustered using their feature vectors via K-means with cosine as similarity measure
3. *Headline assignment:* when the process is carried out for the first time, all headlines have to be assigned manually to clusters. For each cluster which is labeled, its headline will be stored, together with a centroid of the cluster members' feature vectors.
4. *Inheriting headlines:* For the following days, the set of centroids of past clusters, together with their headlines are treated as categories and a new cluster C is classified using a Rocchio method, i.e. a centroid is computed for C and it inherits the headline from the cluster whose centroid is closest (most similar) to C's. This is only done if the similarity exceeds a threshold (currently 0.3).

Experience has shown that the system learns rather quickly, i.e. that after a few days a substantial part of the clusters receive an automatically assigned headline. The possibility to assign new headlines to newly emerging topics (i.e. to create new categories) is one of the strengths of this approach. However – since the classifier is not perfectly accurate – some "automatic" headlines need to be corrected manually. The advantage of this procedure – when compared to completely automatic headline assignment of any sort – is the fact that we can have a high level of abstraction (as can only be achieved by humans) while maintaining maximum flexibility (e.g. to invent categories when new topics emerge).

4 Presentation

4.1 Textual Web Interface

The textual web interface is split into two views: a *daily overview* and a *detailed word view* which are linked to each other via the term, respectively the date.

Overview. In the overview (figure 3a), the list of selected words is presented in alphabetical order for each of the categories, or alternatively, the cluster headlines (3b). Clicking on a word leads to its detailed view. The font size in the category view denotes the weight: the most important keywords can be spotted at a glance.

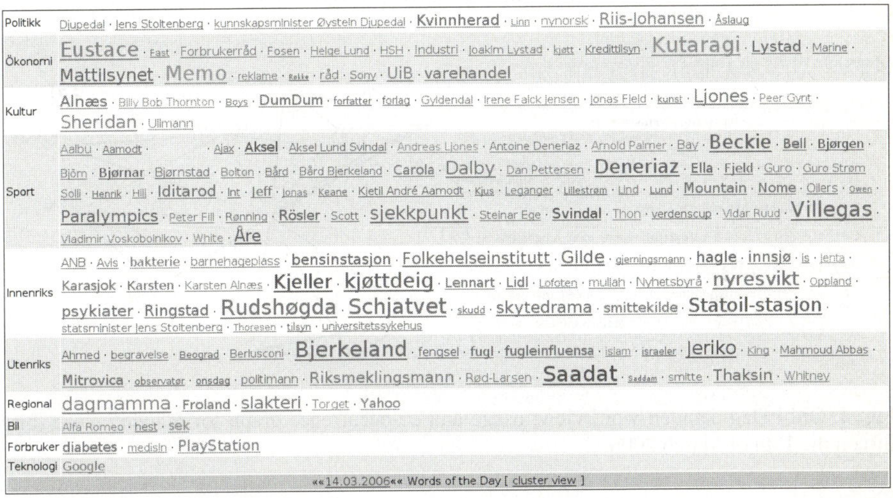

(a)

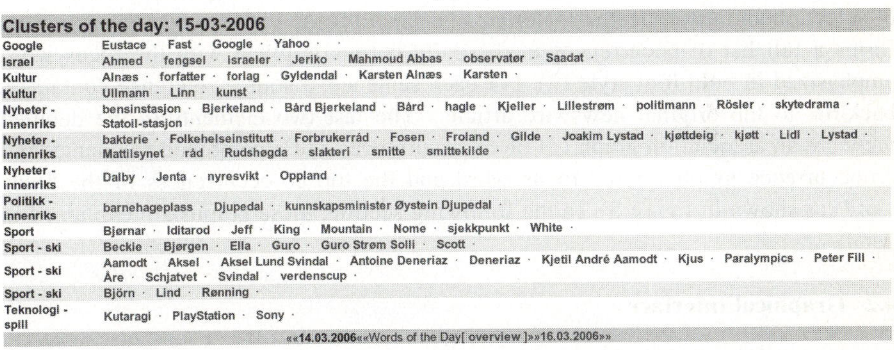

(b)

Fig. 3. Ord i dag of 15th of March, 2006 in a) category and b) cluster view

This weight is the ratio of relative frequency in the daily corpus compared to the reference corpus, called “weirdness index” in [13]. The resulting values are scaled logarithmically to font sizes of 50-200%. Furthermore, the displayed terms do not only differ in size but also in their lightness value: the light end side of the scale is used for small degrees of certainty in the classification and the dark end side for almost sure classifications.

Note that not all terms from the category view appear in the cluster view. This may be because they are contained in a cluster which has not been assigned a headline or in a cluster which is too small (≤ 2 elements) to be displayed.

Detailed word view. The detailed word view depicts information centered around one focus word. It consists of four parts as shown in figures 4 and 5.

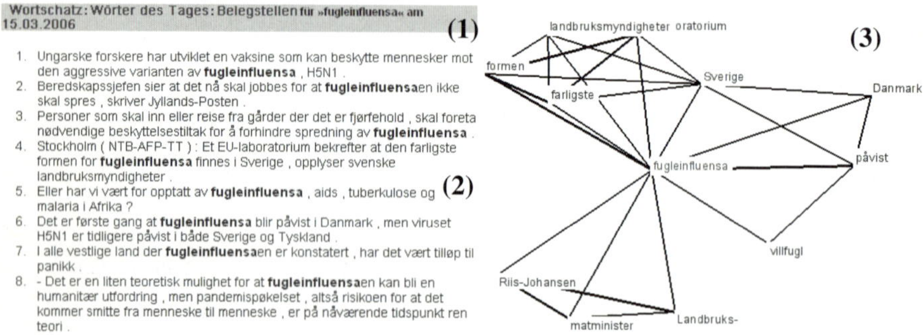

Fig. 4. Ord i Dag detailed word view: usage and co-occurrence graph for *fugleinfluensa* (bird flu) on the 15th of March 2006

First there are links back to the daily overview and pages explaining the process of selection and the collected materials (1). Then for the focus word and each of its forms a full list of occurrences in the daily corpus is given with the focus word emphasized in bold font style (2). For each sentence, a source reference contains a backlink to the original newswire article. The last two elements in the detailed view are an association graph (3) of co-occurrences and a combined frequency and co-occurrence graph for the focus word and the top co-occurrences of the focus word (as shown in figure 5). In the following section, these graphs are explained in detail.

4.2 Graphical Interface

Association Graph. For the association graph a selected fixed size set of sentence based co-occurrences is retrieved according to the co-occurrences' likelihood ratio [14]. As an additional constraint it is required for each node to have edges with at least the focus word and one more word from the set. The resulting graph is laid out fully automatically using simulated annealing as described in [15], helping the user to rapidly gain an overview of correlated terms.

4.3 Machine Readable Output

The selected terms are also made accessible in machine readable format as one RSS 2.0 (Really Simple Syndication) feed per category for use with RSS readers and for content syndication. The feeds contain a list of the words of the current day, their

Frequency / Co-occurrence Graph

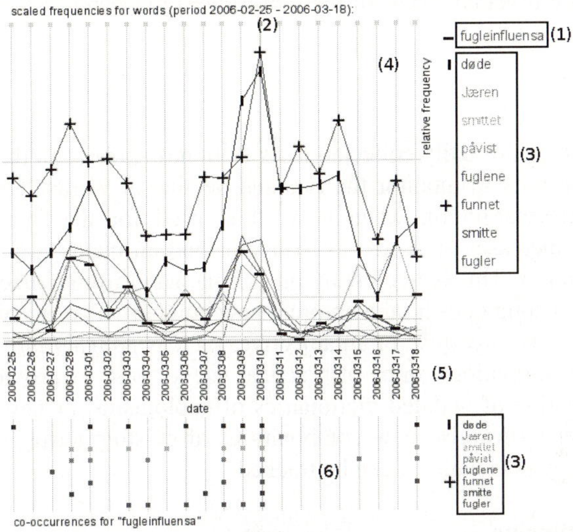

Fig. 5. Frequency / co-occurrence graph displaying the focus word *fugleinfluensa* (1) for a specific date (2) with its eight most significant co-occurrences (3). The frequency graph (4) displays the time-dependent development of those words' relative frequencies in logarithmic scale on a date line (5). The co-occurrence matrix (6) displays whether joint peaks are significant (figure edited for print, original graphs are in color).

frequency and links to the respective pages of the web interface. The RSS feeds are linked from the overview page of the *Ord i dag* in a way that they are automatically offered to an RSS autodiscovery enabled web browser such as Mozilla Firefox. As a fallback the feeds are also listed on an overview page at `http://wortschatz.uni-leipzig.de/wdtno/RSS/`.

The RSS-feeds of the German version of *Wörter des Tages*, available from `http://wortschatz.uni-leipzig.de/wort-des-tages/`, are used by the publishing house Langenscheidt to get a reasonably sized and up-to-date selection of words that are proposed to learners of English on their website.

5 Conclusion and Further Work

The implementation of *Ord i dag* shows the language independency of the framework developed by the Wortschatz project (`http://www.wortschatz.uni-leipzig.de`, [16]). Although a range of language- and data source specific amendments had to be carried out for the Norwegian version, the original framework is for the most part implemented directly with the Norwegian newspaper corpus as data source. Similar implementations could be carried out quite easily for other languages, provided the existence of sufficient corpus resources that are updated on a daily basis. But much more important than the potential of implementations for further and similar languages, the applications that now exist for Norwegian data can be used for a diversity of language related research. Some of these branches of research will be outlined in the remainder.

5.1 Neologisms

As the corpus consists of daily collected texts from newspapers on the web, it offers a convenient opportunity to monitor the rise and decline of words. The corpus can be consulted for information on when a word is used for the first time, how the frequency of use increases or decreases over time and ultimately when a word ceases being in common use. This is interesting on the one hand from a diachronic linguist's point of view; how long does it take before a new noun or name, such as *Google,* is in use as a verb, such as *to google*, or an adjective, such as *googled information*? On the other hand, this information can be of practical use as well, by providing a means of easy and fast creation of updated dictionaries of neologisms, or new words. But not only new singular terms, also new combinations of existing terms, be it multi-word units or simply new associations, can be tracked.

5.2 Trend Monitoring

A further application is trend monitoring, a task that has received increased commercial interest in recent years (see: [17], part III). By consulting the corpus we can for instance see how long a certain case is covered by the media. How long does it take before the newspapers stop writing about a particular case? Do certain cases re-appear in the media after a time? Are there foreseeable time intervals between the re-occurrences of such cases? Through analyses of co-occurrences, we can also say something about the co-dependency of the media profiling of cases; do certain cases trigger the emergence of other cases? These analyses diverge from traditional commercial media monitoring in one important aspect: rather than monitoring a set of predefined keywords, we can monitor on a more objective basis, essentially monitoring *language use* as well as *media*. The information obtainable through a media monitoring analysis of corpus data is of interest for several fields of research, ranging from linguistics, via humanities, to economic fields.

References

1. Multilingual Topic Detection and Tracking: Successful Research Enabled by Corpora and Evaluation, Wayne, C., In Proceedings of LREC (2000) 1487-1494.
2. McKeown, K. R., Barzilay, R., Evans, D., Hatzivassiloglou, V., Klavans J. L., Sable, C., Schiffman, B., and Sigelman, S.: Tracking and Summarizing News on a Daily Basis with Columbia's Newsblaster. In Proc. of the Human Language Technology Conference (2002)
3. Radev, D., Otterbacher, J., Winkel A., Blair-Goldenson, A.: NewsInEssence: Summarizing Online News Topics. Communications of the ACM. Vol. 48, No. 10, (2005) 95-98
4. Bederson, B.B., Shneiderman, B., and Wattenberg, M.: Ordered and Quantum Treemaps: Making Effective Use of 2D Space to Display Hierarchies. ACM Transactions on Graphics (TOG), 21, (4), (2002) 833-854.

5. Tufte, E.: Beautiful Evidence. To appear. Draft at: http://www.edwardtufte.com /bboard/q-and-a-fetch-msg?msg_id=0001OR&topic_id=1 (2006)
6. Thomas, J. J. and Cook, K.A. (eds.): Illuminating the Path: The Research and Development Agenda for Visual Analytics. IEEE Press (2005)
7. Hofland, K.: A Self-Expanding Corpus Based on Newspapers on the Web. Proceedings of the Second International Language Resources and Evaluation Conference. Paris: ELRA (2000)
8. Johannessen, J.-B., Hagen, K. and Nøklestad, A.: A Constraint-based tagger for Norwegian. In 17th Scandinavian Conference of Linguistics, Odense Working Papers in Language and Communication 19, University of Southern Denmark, Odense, Vol. 1, (2000) 31-47
9. Witschel, H.F. and Biemann, C.: Rigorous dimensionality reduction through linguistically motivated feature selection for text categorisation. Proceedings of NODALIDA, Joensuu, Finland (2005)
10. Quasthoff, U., Biemann, C., Wolff, C.: Named Entity Learning and Verification: Expectation Maximisation in Large Corpora, Proceedings of CoNNL-2002, Taipei, Taiwan (2002) 8-14
11. Richter, M.: Analysis and Visualization for Daily Newspaper Corpora. Proceedings of RANLP, (2005) 424-428
12. Faulstich, L., Quasthoff, U., Schmidt, F., Wolff, C.: Concept Extractor - Ein flexibler und domänen-spezifischer Web Service zur Beschlagwortung von Texten. In Proceedings of ISI 2002, Regensburg (2002)
13. Ahmad, K., Gillam, L., Tostevin, L.: Weirdness Indexing for Logical Document Extrapolation and Retrieval (WILDER). In Proceedings of TREC-8. Washington: National Institute of Standards and Technology. (2000) 717-724
14. Dunning, T.: Accurate methods for the statistics of surprise and coincidence. Computational Linguistics, 19:1. (1993)
15. Davidson, R. and Harel, D.: Drawing graphs nicely using simulated annealing. ACM Transactions on Graphics, 15(4), (1996) 301–331
16. Biemann, Chr., Bordag, S., Heyer, G., Quasthoff, U., Wolff, Chr.: Language-independent Methods for Compiling Monolingual Lexical Data, Proceedings of CicLING 2004, Seoul, Korea and Springer LNCS 2945, Springer (2004) 215-228
17. Berry, M.W.: Survey of Text Mining: Clustering, Classification and Retrieval. Springer (2003)

Paraphrase Identification on the Basis of Supervised Machine Learning Techniques

Zornitsa Kozareva and Andrés Montoyo

Departamento de Lenguajes y Sistemas Informáticos
Universidad de Alicante
{zkozareva, montoyo}@dlsi.ua.es

Abstract. This paper presents a machine learning approach for paraphrase identification which uses lexical and semantic similarity information. In the experimental studies, we examine the limitations of the designed attributes and the behavior of three machine learning classifiers. With the objective to increase the final performance of the system, we scrutinize the influence of the combination of lexical and semantic information, as well as techniques for classifier combination.

1 Introduction and Related Work

Natural language is the most powerful tool through which people establish communication and relate to each other. In our daily life we can use different words and phrases to express the same meaning. This is related to our knowledge and cultural habits, that later reflect on our written and spoken skills.

The web is the largest text repository, where millions of people share and consult information daily. In the context of Information Retrieval, given a natural language query, the search engine should identify and return documents that have similar or related meanings to the query. However, the relevant information may be present in different forms. For example a search about "operating systems" should retrieve document about "unix". In order to identify that although neither "operating" nor "systems" appear, the document is still relevant as "unix" is a type of operating system, a paraphrase identification module is needed.

Other Natural Language Processing (NLP) applications such as Information Extraction (IE) or Question Answering (QA) also have to handle lexical, semantic or syntactic variabilities. Thus, they avoid the usage of redundant information during the template filling process or find easily the correct answer which may be presented in an indirect way. Experimental studies [12] demonstrate that the identification of language variabilities is important for many NLP areas and their resolution improves the performance of the systems.

Recent paraphrase identification approaches [2] use multiple translations of a single language, where the source language guarantees the semantic equivalence in the target language. In order to extract paraphrases, [20] used named entity anchors, while [1] employed Multiple Sequence Alignment. [11] mined the web

T. Salakoski et al. (Eds.): FinTAL 2006, LNAI 4139, pp. 524–533, 2006.

to obtain verb paraphrases, while [10] constructed a broad-domain corpus of aligned paraphrase pairs through the web. [15] presented a lightweight method for unsupervised paraphrase extraction from billions of web documents.

In this paper, we focus on the paraphrase identification rather than on the paraphrase generation task. Our task consists in given two text fragments, the system has to determine weather the two texts paraphrase each other or not. For example the sentences "James sells four papers to Post International" and "Post International receives papers by James" express the same meaning therefore, they are paraphrases of each other.

Our approach is similar this of [3] who use an annotated dataset and Support Vector Machines to induce larger monolingual paraphrase corpus from a comparable corpus of news clusters found on the web. We rely on already compiled paraphrase corpus [18], so our task reduces to the identification of sentences that are paraphrases of each other, for example "the glass is half-empty" and "the glass is half-full". For this purpose, we develop a supervise machine learning approach where three classifiers are employed. The classifiers use lexical and semantic similarity information. In comparison to [6] who recognize paraphrases measuring text semantic similarity, we capture word semantic similarity.

The novelty of our approach consists in the performed experiments. First we explore the discriminating power of the individual lexical and semantic feature sets to identify paraphrases. In addition, we study the behavior of the three different machine learning classifiers with the modelled features. With the objective to improve the performance of the paraphrase identification system, we examine the impact of the combination of the lexical and semantic surface information in a big feature set and also through voting. Previous researchers did not study the effect of such combinations, therefore we believe that the direction of our approach is novel.

The paper is organized in the following way. Section 2 describes the paraphrase identification system. Section 3 outlines the paraphrasing data we worked with. The next section concerns the conducted experimental setups and finally the conclusions are exposed in Section 5.

2 The Paraphrasing System at a Glance

Most systems [9] used numerous thresholds to decide definitely whether two sentences are similar and infer the same meaning. This threshold determination process is dependent on the training data and apart may lead to incorrect paraphrase reasoning. In order to avoid the threshold settings, we use machine learning techniques. The advantages of a ML approach consists in the ability to account for a large mass of information and the possibility to incorporate different information sources such as morphologic, syntactic, semantic among others in one single execution. The major obstacle for the usage of ML techniques concerns the availability of training data. For our approach we used a standard paraphrase evaluation corpus therefore, learning from the data examples was possible.

Thus, it was reasonable to propose and possible to develop a machine learning based paraphrase identification approach. Figure 1 shows the modules of the paraphrase system.

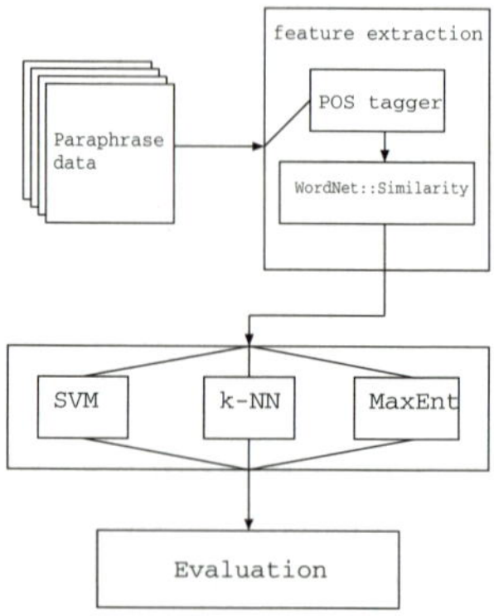

Fig. 1. Modules of the paraphrase identification system

2.1 Feature Extraction

The most important module in a machine learning system concerns the feature extraction and generation one. To perform well, every machine learning classifier needs relevant attributes calculated from the instances in the data set. For this reason, we start the description of our paraphrasing system from the feature extraction module.

As paraphrases appear on lexical, syntactic, semantic and pragmatic levels, or in a combination among them, we explore the discriminating power which can be obtained on the lexical and semantic similarity levels. All of the designed attributes capture the sentence similarity in both directions, because paraphrases are bidirectional relations [10].

The *word overlap feature set* includes well known text summarization measures. The first two attributes establish the ratio of the common consecutive *n-grams* between two texts T_1 and T_2[1], against the total number of words in T_1/T_2. For this feature, the high number of common words indicates that the two sentences are similar and we interpret it as high probability for the two sentences to paraphrase each other. However, unigrams alone fail to identify that "Mary calls the police" and "the police calls Mary" do not infer the same meaning. Therefore, to identity better the proximity of the sentences, we employ attributes sensitive to word order. Two such measures we found are the skip-gram and the longest common subsequence.

Skip-grams look for non consecutive sequences of words that may have gaps in between, compared to all combinations of words that can appear in the

[1] T_1 refers to the first sentence and T_2 refers to the second sentence.

sentences. The two measures are $skip\_gramT_1 = \frac{skip\_gram(T_1,T_2)}{C(n,skip\_gram(T_1,T_2))}$ and $skip\_gramT_2 = \frac{skip\_gram(T_1,T_2)}{C(m,skip\_gram(T_1,T_2))}$. The $skip\_gram(T_1, T_2)$ refers to the number of common skip grams (pair of words in sentence order that allow arbitrary gaps) found in T_1 and T_2 and $C(n, skip\_gram(T_1, T_2))$ is a combinatorial function, where n is the number of words in text T_1 (e.g. m corresponds to the number of words in T_2). The maximum length of the skip-gram calculation is restricted to four, because sequences higher than this do not appear very often. This measure is known in text summarization as ROUGE-S [13].

The *longest common subsequence* (LCS) determines one[2] long common subsequence of words between two sentences. Once the LCS is found, it is normalized by the number of words present in T_1/T_2. The ratio indicates how many non consecutive words appear between the two sentences in respect to all words.

So far, the presented surface features are designed to capture lexical variations. As counting n-grams is not a language dependent task, this allows their application to the recognition of paraphrases or text entailments [8] for other languages.

In order to obtain the semantic similarity attributes, first we determined the parts-of-speech tags with the TreeTagger [19] toolkit. *Word similarity features* need extrinsic knowledge which can be collected from large corpora or word repository as WordNet[3]. To establish the similarity among the nouns and verbs in the sentences, we used the WordNet::Similarity package [16] with the measure of [14].

We introduce a noun/verb semantic similarity measure obtained with the calculation of the formula $sim_{lin} = \frac{\sum_{i=1}^{n} sim(T_1,T_2)_{lin}}{n}$. This measure indicates the ratio of the noun/verb similarity with respect to the maximum noun/verb similarity for the sentences T_1 and T_2. The values of $sim(T_1, T_2)_{lin}$ are the similarity of noun/verb pairs for the text T_1 and T_2 according to the measure of [14]. For perfect similarity match, sim_{lin} has value 1 and for completely dissimilar words 0.

The *cardinal number* attribute captures that "more than 24" indicates 25 and the numbers above it, "less than 24" is 23 and the numbers below it. Writing as "twenty-five" is transformed automatically into "25", and then is lexically matched with the corresponding number. When the texts contain several cardinal numbers, this attribute matches from all possible numbers how many coincidences the two texts have.

The *proper name* attribute is 1 for perfect proper name matches such as "London" and "London", and 0 for sentences where there are no proper names at all, or when the proper names are completely distinct.

When the described features are generated for each paraphrase pair in the MSP corpus, the functioning of the feature module is terminated and the machine learning module is initiated. In the next subsection, we describe the classifiers used for the training and testing phases.

---

[2] If LCS finds two different longest common subsequence strings of the same length, only one of them is taken.

[3] wordnet.princeton.edu/

2.2 Machine Learning Module

A machine learning module can be composed of different number of classifiers. For our system, we selected three algorithms based on their processing time and generalization function.

Support Vector Machines (SVM) are known to perform well with two class problems, with high data sparcity and multiple attribute space. As parphrase recognition reduces to a two class problem, we decide that the utilization of SVM is pertinent. The software we worked with is called SVMTorch [5]. Several kernels were tested and the best performing one was the linear.

k-Nearest Neighbors (k-NN) is a lazy learner that stores every training example in the memory. This algorithm is useful when the number of training examples is not sufficient. During testing, a new case is classified by extrapolating the most similar stored examples. The similarity between a new instance X and all examples Y in the memory is computed by the distance metric $\triangle(X,Y) = \sum_{i=1}^{n} \delta(x_i, y_i)$, where $\delta(x_i, y_i) = |\frac{x_i - y_i}{max_i - min_i}|$. We used the Memory-based learning algorithm developed by [7].

Maximum Entropy (MaxEnt) estimates probabilities based on the principle of making as few assumptions as possible. The probability distribution that satisfies the above property is the one with the highest entropy. An advantage of MaxEnt framework is that even knowledge-poor features can be applied accurately. We used the MaxEnt implementation of [21].

3 Data Set and Evaluation

We evaluate the performance of our machine learning paraphrase identification system on a standard paraphrase corpus developed and provided by Microsoft[4] [18].

This corpus consists of training and testing data sets. Each line has two sentences, and the paraphrase identification task consists in determining whether these two sentences are paraphrases of each other or not. The training set consists of 4076 sentence pairs, of which 2753 are paraphrases of each other. The testing set has 1726 sentence pairs, of which 1147 are paraphrases of each other.

The evaluation measures are the traditional precision, recall and f-score. Systems are ranked and compared according to the accuracy score, which indicates the number of correct responses in respect to all test entries.

4 Experiments

Three types of experiments were conducted to answer the questions: Which machine learning algorithm is the most reliable with the presented feature sets? Does the mixture of lexical and semantic information lead to improvement? What happens through multiple classifier combination?

[4] http://research.microsoft.com/research/downloads/

4.1 Experimental Setup 1

As previously mentioned, to construct a robust multilevel paraphrase system, the resolution power of the individual machine learing classifiers should be explored. In our first experiment, we study the performance of the three machine learning algorithms with the designed *word overlap* and *word similarity* feature sets.

Initially, the three classifiers SVM, k-NN and MaxEnt were trained and tested with the *word overlap* feature set. The obtained results for the whole paraphrase identification test corpus are shown in Table 1.

Table 1. Paraphrase identification with word overlap information

System	Acc.	Prec.	Rec.	F-score
SVM	69.86	93.46	70.66	80.48
MaxEnt	68.29	69.16	59.53	63.98
k-NN	63.36	74.45	71.58	72.99
C-M	68.80	74.10	81.70	77.70
word match	66.10	72.20	79.80	75.80

Although the three classifiers use the same attributes, the yielded performances are different due to their varied machine learning philosophy. In our task, we deal with two class problem. For this experiment, the obtained results showed that the word overlap feature set indicated correctly most of the examples that do not paraphrase each other. This is related to the fact that the word overlap features penalize longer sentences as they cannot map the majority of the words.

The best generalization among all classifiers is achieved by SVM. MaxEnt and k-NN algorithms gained 68.29% and 63.36% accuracy. Comparing these results to a baseline that counts the number of common words, only k-NN could not outperform it.

In the same table, we compare the obtained results to the system of [6]. We denote their system as C-M. Although C-M measured text semantic similarity, and in our approach we compute word overlaps, the SVM run achieved better f-score and accuracy coverage. This indicates that the modelled attributes are good indicators for paraphrase identification.

A positive characteristics of the word overlap feature set is that it is simple to implement and has low computational cost. The feature set is language independent, because counting words is not a language dependent task. This property makes it easy and practical to be applied to languages with limited resources. However, a negative aspect of the lexical features is that their performance cannot be improved anymore.

For the *word similarity* feature set, the obtained results are shown in Table 2. According to the accuracy measures, three machine learning classifiers performed worse than the system of [6], but comparing the f-scores SVM performs better than C-M. One reason for the low performance is that only word to word similarity is not informative enough to identify paraphrases. In contrast to the

Table 2. Paraphrase identification with word similarity information

System	Accuracy	Prec.	Rec.	F-score
SVM	66.50	100	66.49	79.87
MaxEnt	66.49	81.15	68.20	74.11
k-NN	67.81	91.30	66.43	76.90
C-M	68.80	74.10	81.70	77.70
word match	66.10	72.20	79.80	75.80

word overlap set that determined correctly most of the non paraphrase pairs, the semantic set identified correctly the sentences that paraphrase each other. This is due to the sim_{lin} measure according to which if there is one completely similar noun/verb pair or most of the noun/verb pairs are similar, then the sentences paraphrase each other.

4.2 Experimental Setup 2

In this experimental setup, we study the combination of the lexical and semantic similarity information into a single feature set. The achieved results are shown in Table 3.

Table 3. Paraphrase identification with the combination of word overlap and similarity features

System	Accuracy	Prec.	Rec.	F-score
SVM	70.43	84.66	74.12	79.04
MaxEnt	66.44	82.13	70.50	75.87
k-NN	64.68	78.88	71.13	74.81
C-M	68.80	74.10	81.70	77.70

Compared to the previous results, in this experiment the classifiers determined correctly equally paraphrasing and non paraphrasing sentences. The best performing classifier is SVM. Only for it, the combination of word overlap and semantic features lead to increase in performace with around 1%. According to z' statistics, such improvement is insignificant. When we saw that the feature combination did not help, we performed another experiment where the generated outputs of the lexical and semantic classifiers are combined through voting.

4.3 Experimental Setup 3

For the voting scheme first the outputs of the generated lexical and semantic SVM, k-NN and MaxEnt classifiers are examined. There, test cases whose classes coincided by the two of the three classifiers, directly obtain the majority class. For the instances where the two classifiers disagree, the class of the classifier with the highest performance was adopted. The obtained results of the voting executions are shown in Table 4.

Table 4. Paraphrase identification with voting

System	Accuracy	Prec.	Rec.	F-score
SVM,k-NN,MaxEnt	76.64	94.42	68.76	79.57
C-M	68.80	74.10	81.70	77.70

According to the statistical z' test [5], the classifiers' accuracy significantly improved with voting. This improvement is due to the high complementarity of the lexical and semantic feature sets, which according to the kappa statistical measure [4] complement each other. Similar approach for complementarity examination was used by [17] who determined how to combine different word sense disambiguation systems in a beneficial way.

Through the experimental setups, we show word overlaps can identify correctly sentences that do not paraphrase each other. In addition, the combination of the lexical and semantic attributes in a single feature set did not enrich the performance. However, the combination of the lexical and semantic information through voting was beneficial. Finally, in a comparative study, we demonstrate that the proposed machine learning paraphrase identification approach can outperform more complex method like [6] which tries to measure text semantic similarity.

5 Conclusion and Future Work

We presented a machine-learning approach for the paraphrase identification task. Three machine learning algorithms were used to determine which one of them is the most appropriate for the paraphrase task. Several experiments were conducted and the obtained results were compared to a baseline and already existing systems.

The experiments revealed that simple features relying on common consecutive or insequence matches can resolve correctly 69.86% of the paraphrases. Such attributes are very useful and practical for languages with scarce resources. Unfortunately, on their own these attributes cannot be improved any more.

The combination of lexical and semantic attributes into a single feature set did not improve the accuracy of the different machine learning classifiers. Therefore, we studied a better way to combine this information. The used voting algorithm that boosted the final performance with 10%. According to z' statistics, this improvement is significant compared to the single classifier.

For all experiment, the best performance is obtained with SVM. We consider its usage for the paraphrase identification as very proper. With the analysis of the results, we saw that this is due to the ability of SVM to work with high dimensional attribute spaces.

In the future, we want to incorporate a Named Entity Recognizer which will improve the performance of the proper name attribute. As paraphrases act on different representation levels – lexical, semantic, syntactic or even a combination

[5] The tested confidence was 98%.

among them all, we believe that the incorporation of syntactic information is going to be helpful for the proposed and developed approach.

Acknowledgements

This research has been partially funded by the Spanish Government under project CICyT number TIC2003-07158-C04-01 and PROFIT number FIT-340100-2004-14 and by the Valencia Government under project numbers GV04B-276.

References

1. Regina Barzilay and Lillian Lee. Learning to paraphrase: An unsupervised approach using multiple-sequence alignment. In *HLT-NAACL 2003: Main Proceedings*, pages 16–23, 2003.
2. Regina Barzilay and Kathleen McKeown. Extracting paraphrases from a parallel corpus. In *39th Annual Meeting of the Association for Computational Linguistics*, pages 50–57, 2001.
3. Chris Brockett and William B. Dolan. Support vector machines for paraphrase identification and corpus construction. In *Second International Joint Conference on Natural Language Processing.*
4. Jacob Cohen. A coefficient of agreement for nominal scales. *Educ. Psychol. Meas*, 1960.
5. Ronan Collobert and Samy Bengio. Svmtorch: Support vector machines for large-scale regression problems. *Journal of Machine Learning Research*, 1, issn 1533-7928:143–160, 2001.
6. Courtney Corley and Rada Mihalcea. Measures of text semantic similarity. In *Proceedings of the ACL workshop on Empirical Modeling of Semantic Equivalence.*
7. Walter Daelemans, Jakub Zavrel, Ko van der Sloot, and Antal van den Bosch. Timbl: Tilburg memory-based learner. Technical Report ILK 03-10, Tilburg University, November 2003.
8. Ido Dagan and Oren Glickman. Probabilistic textual entailment: Generic applied modeling of language variability. In *PASCAL Workshop on Learning Methods for Text Understanding and Mining.*
9. Ido Dagan, Oren Glickman, and Bernardo Magnini. The pascal recognising textual entailment challenge. In *Proceedings of the PASCAL Challenges Workshop on Recognising Textual Entailment.*
10. William B. Dolan, Chris Quirk, and Chris Brockett. Unsupervised construction of large paraphrase corpora: Exploiting massively parallel news sources. In *International Conference on Computational Linguistics, COLING.*
11. Oren Glickman and Ido Dagan. Acquiring lexical paraphrases from a single corpus. In *Recent Advances in Natural Language Processing III.*
12. Zornitsa Kozareva and Andrés Montoyo. The role and resolution of textual entailment in natural language processing applications. In *11th International Conference on Applications of Natural Language to Information Systems (NLDB 2006)*, 2006.
13. Chin-Yew Lin and Eduard Hovy. Automatic evaluation of summaries using n-gram co-occurrence statistics. In *Conference of the North American Chapter of the Association for Computational Linguistics on Human Language Technology*, pages 71–78, 2003.

14. Dekang Lin. An information-theoretic definition of similarity. In *Proceddings of 15th International Conf. on Machine Learning*, pages 296–304. Morgan Kaufmann, San Francisco, CA, 1998.
15. Marius Pasca and Péter Dienes. Aligning needles in a haystack: Paraphrase acquisition across the web. In *IJCNLP*, pages 119–130, 2005.
16. Siddharth Patwardhan, Satanjeev Banerjee, and Ted Pedersen. Using measures of semantic relatedness for word sense disambiguation. In *Proceedings of the Fourth International Conference on Intelligent Text Processing and Computational Linguistics.*
17. Ted Pedersen. Assessing system agreement and instance difficulty in the lexical sample tasks of senseval-2. In *Proceedings of the 40th Annual Meeting of the Association for Computational Linguistics.*
18. Chris Quirk, Chris Brockett, and William B. Dolan. Monolingual machine translation for paraphrase generation,. In *Proceedings of the Conference on Empirical Methods in Natural Language Processing.*
19. Helmut Schmid. Probabilistic part-of-speech tagging using decision trees. In *International Conference on New Methods in Language Processing*, Manchester, UK, 1994.
20. Yusuke Shinyama, Satoshi Sekine, Kiyoshi. Sudo, and Ralf Grishman. Automatic paraphrase acquisition from news articles. 2002.
21. Armando Suárez and Manuel Palomar. A maximum entropy-based word sense disambiguation system. In *COLING*, 2002.

Passage Filtering for Open-Domain Question Answering

Elisa Noguera, Fernando Llopis, and Antonio Ferrández

Grupo de investigación en Procesamiento del Lenguaje Natural y Sistemas de Información
Departamento de Lenguajes y Sistemas Informáticos
University of Alicante, Spain
{elisa, llopis, antonio}@dlsi.ua.es

Abstract. This paper studies the problem of filtering data in Passage Retrieval applied to Question Answering. Specifically, in this paper we have proved that the Mean-Value Theorem can play an important role to improve Question Answering. We have studied the way in which this theorem can be applied in order to produce a maximum data reduction without precision loss. In the experiments, we achieve a 90% data reduction without significant data loss.

1 Introduction

Question Answering (QA) may be defined as the task that tries to locate concrete answers to questions in collections of text. This task is very useful for the users because they do not need to read all the document or fragment to obtain a specific information.

Most of QA systems (e.g. [1][2]) uses Natural Language Processing (NLP) tools that are computationally expensive, which makes difficult its application to large collections of documents. Thus, a common way to overcome this limitation is to apply Information Retrieval (IR) [3] to the whole collection and QA only to a limited set of relevant documents that IR returns. Furthermore, many QA systems use Passage Retrieval (PR) [4] because PR returns the most relevant passage of the text, instead of the whole document as IR systems do.

Although most of efforts in QA are located in the answer extraction stage, some authors [5][6][7][8] have also started to evaluate the preliminary retrieval step.

The motivation of this work is to improve PR in the context of QA. The output of the PR system is important for QA because if the answer is not in the output, then the QA system will not find the correct answer (see Fig. 1). Specifically, we propose a method which is based on the Mean-Value Theorem [9]. This method is used to obtain a threshold in order to decrease the number of passages without losing precision. Moreover, we can return a different number of passages to each kind of question.

The remainder of this paper is organized as follows: the next section explains the state-of-the-art. Section 3 describes our proposal. Section 4 presents the evaluation and the results of the experiments. Finally, section 5 gives some conclusions.

T. Salakoski et al. (Eds.): FinTAL 2006, LNAI 4139, pp. 534–540, 2006.

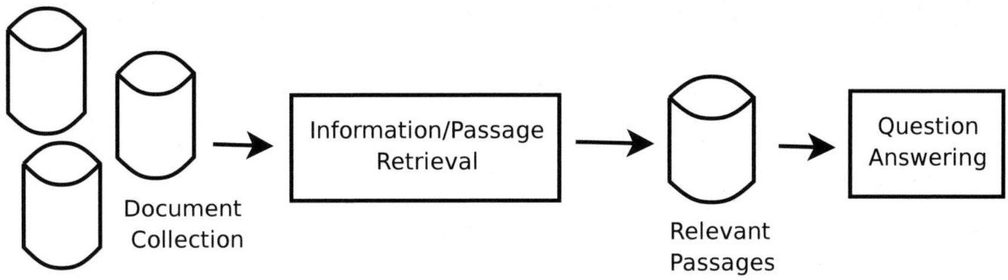

Fig. 1. Filtering process in QA

2 Background

Many QA systems [10][11] apply several methods to the output of the retrieval stage in order to filter non relevant passages.

A common approach to filtering consists on using the following two-step procedure: first we calculate a relevance score for each passage, and then we make a binary decision to accept or reject the passage based on comparison with a score threshold.

A specific method, located in the state-of-the-art which follows this approach is an algorithm used by the QALC group [12][13]. It is used to calculate the cutoff threshold associated with the weighting scheme of a given query. This algorithm detects the relative decrease of the weight of a document with respect to the preceding one (see Algorithm 1).

Algorithm 1. Method by QALC

$threshold \leftarrow numDocs$
if $\frac{w_1}{w_2} \leq 0.5$ **then**
  $threshold \leftarrow 2$
else
  for all i such that $3 \leq i \leq numDocs$ **do**
    if $\frac{w_i - w_{i-1}}{w_{i-1} - w_{i-2}} \geq 2$ and $\frac{w_i}{w_{i-1}} \leq 0.8$ **then**
      $threshold \leftarrow i$
      exit
    end if
  end for
end if

In the Figure 2 we can see an example of two queries from QA@CLEF-2003 collection. The graphic shows the relation between the weight obtained for the best 200 documents according to the questions 117 and 76:

0076 *¿En qué año se creo el Fondo Monetario Internacional?*
(What year was created the International Monetary Fund?)
0117 *¿En qué año fueron prohibidas las pruebas de armas biológicas y tóxicas?*
(What year were forbidden the tests with biological and toxin weapon?)

The threshold is 2 for the question 76 and 200 for the question 117. We can appreciate this method produces a small threshold for the question 76, because this algorithm sets the threshold when detects a relative decrease of the weight. Moreover, we can also appreciate a large threshold for the question 117, because if this method detects a slightly decreasing weight, it returns the whole of the documents.

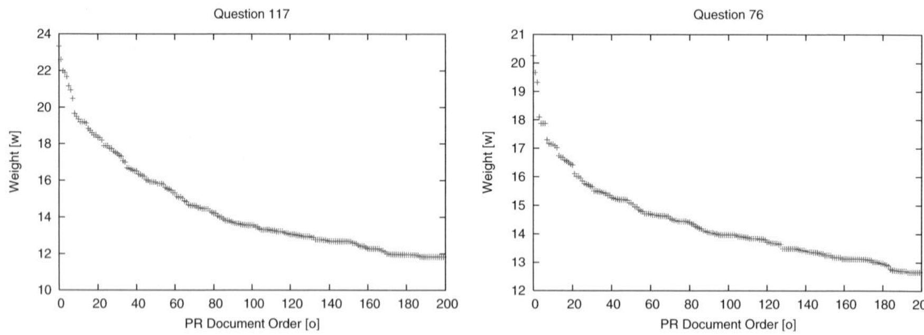

Fig. 2. Questions 117 and 76 - QA@CLEF-2003 Collection

3 Our Proposal

Our efforts have been focused to obtain a method to calculate a threshold in order to filter the passages that are not relevant.

For this reason, we have proposed a method in this work which is based on the Mean-Value Theorem (MVT) (see Theorem 1). This Theorem is one of the most important theoretical tools in Calculus, but it has not been previously used for PR and QA.

Theorem 1. *It states that if $f(x)$ is defined and continuous on the interval $[a, b]$ and differentiable on (a, b), then there is at least one number c in the interval (a, b) (that is $a < c < b$) such that:*

$$f(c)' = \frac{f(b) - f(a)}{b - a}.$$

The weights of the documents, which we have obtained with the okapy similarity measure, follow an exponential function (see Fig. 2). If we consider this relation as an interval of an exponential function then we can apply the MVT in order to calculate the point which cuts the tangent to this interval. We have considered this point as the threshold of the relevant set of documents because the weight from this point have a slight decrease. Therefore, we consider the documents from this threshold as no-relevants. For example, following this method, the threshold is 28 for the question 76 and 18 for the question 117, which are much lower than the QALC thresholds 2 and 200.

Futhermore, our proposal returns a more stable number of passages than the QALC method, because we calculate the middle point as the threshold instead of the decrease of the weight.

4 Experiments and Evaluation

We have carried out several experiments in order to evaluate and compare the previous methods. Firstly, we present the data set, resources that we have used and the evaluation metrics. Later on, we present the experiments and finally the results of our system are presented.

4.1 Evaluation Setup

Data Set. We have used the Spanish collections QA@CLEF-2003, QA@CLEF-2004 and QA@CLEF-2005 [14]. The collections of documents are the EFE1994 and EFE1995 which are made up of 454,045 documents (1086 Mb). Although the collection of queries have 600 questions, we have only evaluated the questions in which the answer is found in the collection. Therefore, the evaluation question set have 522 questions [1].

Resources. We use IR-n system [15] which is a PR system that sets, as a baseline, the passages as a fixed number of sentences. We considered 8 sentences as size passage in the experiments. It uses okapi similarity measure [16] because it is the measure that has empirically proved to obtain the best results.

Evaluation Metrics. We have used three measures to evaluate our system: Mean Reciprocal Rank (MRR) [17], Coverage (C) [18] and Redundancy (R) [18]. We consider that these measures capture aspects of IR performance specifically relevant to QA, and they are more appropriately than the traditional recall and precision measures.

MRR measure assigns to each question the inverse value of the first passage in which the answer is found or zero if the answer is not found. The final value is the average of the values for all the questions. This measure is used in QA and it gives a higher value to correct answers in earlier positions in the returned rank list. This is obtained with the formula (1).

C is the proportion of questions for which a correct answer can be found in the retrieved passages. This is obtained with (2).

R is the proportion of the retrieved passages per question which contain the correct answer. We can obtain this with (3).

$$MRR = \frac{\sum_{i=1}^{q} 1/far(i)}{q} \tag{1}$$

$$C = \frac{\sum_{i=1}^{q} a_i}{q} \tag{2}$$

$$R = \frac{\sum_{i=1}^{q} pa_i/p_i}{q} \tag{3}$$

[1] The number of questions is 180 to QA@CLEF-2003 and QA@CLEF-2004 collections and 162 to QA@CLEF-2005 collection.

Where

- $far(i)$ refers to the position of the first passage in which the correct answer is found for the query i.
- q is the number of queries.
- $1/far(i)$ will be zero if the answer is not found in any passage.
- a_i will be 1 if the answer is found for the question i in any passage and 0 in othercase.
- p_i is the number of the returned passages to the question i.
- pa_i is the number of the returned passages which contains the correct answer for the question i.

In all experiments we use the evaluation criterion which states that a passage contains the answer to a question if a substring of the passage matches a correct answer pattern for each question.

4.2 Performance Evaluation

We have evaluated our proposal (MVT method) and we have also compared it with QALC method. As the Baseline, a fixed number of passages is returned. In Table 1 we can see the evaluation of the Baseline, MVT and QALC methods. We have evaluated these methods with QA@CLEF-2003, QA@CLEF-2004, QA@CLEF-2005 collections (see 4.1). We have also done a global evaluation (Total) in order to estimate the global effectiveness of the proposals.

Table 1 shows the average of passages which are returned and the reduction of data for each method. It also shows the evaluation measures presented previously: MRR, Coverage (C) and Redundancy (R) for the different methods (see section 4.1).

MRR is almost constant for the whole of methods, because this measure gives more value to the correct answers which are in earlier positions. It is important

Table 1. Results of experiments

Collection	Method	Average Passages	Data Reduction	MRR	C	R
2003	Baseline	200	0.0%	0.649	0.98	0.22
	MVT	24	-88.0%	0.647	0.92	0.33
	QALC	105	-47.5%	0.643	0.92	0.27
2004	Baseline	200	0.0%	0.564	0.90	0.15
	MVT	20	-90.0%	0.561	0.83	0.30
	QALC	74	-63.0%	0.559	0.83	0.25
2005	Baseline	200	0.0%	0.686	0.88	0.27
	MVT	24	-88.0%	0.685	0.85	0.54
	QALC	89	-55.5%	0.684	0.85	0.39
Total	Baseline	200	0.0%	0.633	0.92	0.21
	MVT	23	-89.0%	0.631	0.86	0.39
	QALC	89	-55.3%	0.628	0.86	0.30

to note that in the MVT method, the Redundancy (R) is greater (0.39) than the others methods (Baseline (0.21) and QALC (0.30)). Obviously, the Coverage (C) decrease in MVT regarding to the Baseline, because as indicated above, MVT returns a subset of passages which are returned by the Baseline. We emphasize that MRR in MVT (0.631) is better than the QALC method (0.628) taking into account that MVT returns less passages.

5 Conclusions and Future Work

In summary, we have studied the problem of filtering data in PR applied to QA. Specifically, we have proposed a method to calculate a threshold in order to filter the passages that are not relevant. It is based on the Mean-Value theorem (MVT). Our proposal have been compared with a Baseline (a fixed number of 200 passages), and with a well-known method to filter passages (the QALC method [12][13]). The comparison experiments have been carried out on the Spanish collections QA@CLEF-2003, 2004, 2005, with a significant reduction of the number of passages (by 90%) with no apreciable reduction in the MRR. Moreover, a better Redundancy (R) is obtained by our proposal.

Finally, the future directions that we plan to undertake are to improve this model, as well as to apply some methods to detect the relevant sentences of the passages. Besides, we plan to apply some typical QA linguistic methods that can improve the results.

Acknowledgments

This research has been partially funded by the Spanish Government under project CICyT number TIC2003-07158-C04-01 and by the Valencia Government under project number GV06-161.

References

1. Roger, S., et al: AliQAn, Spanish QA System at CLEF-2005. In: Proceedings of Cross Language Evaluation Forum. (2005)
2. Narayanan, S., Harabagiu, S.: Question answering based on semantic structures. In: Proceedings of COLING 2004. (2004)
3. Baeza-Yates, R.A., Ribeiro-Neto, B.A.: Modern Information Retrieval. ACM Press / Addison-Wesley (1999)
4. Kaszkiel, M., Zobel, J., Sacks-Davis, R.: Efficient passage ranking for document databases. ACM Trans. Inf. Syst. (1999)
5. Monz, C.: From Document Retrieval to Question Answering. PhD thesis, University of Amsterdam (2003)
6. Tiedemann, J.: Improving Passage Retrieval in Question Answering Using NLP. In: Proceedings of EPIA. (2005) 634–646
7. Usunier, N., Amini, M., Gallinari, P.: Boosting Weak Ranking Functions to Enhance Passage Retrieval for Question Answering. In: Proceedings of Workshop on Information Retrieval for Question Answering (IR4QA). SIGIR 2004. (2004)

8. Gaizauskas, R., Hepple, M., , Greenwood, M.: Workshop on Information Retrieval for Question Answering (IR4QA). In: Proceedings of SIGIR 2004. (2004)
9. Tadashi, T.: A Mean Value Theorem. The american mathematical monthly **106**(7) (1999) 673
10. Fleischman, M., Hovy, E.H., Echihabi, A.: Offline Strategies for Online Question Answering: Answering Questions Before They Are Asked. In: Proceedings of ACL. (2003) 1–7
11. Kise, K., Junker, M., Dengel, A., Matsumoto, K.: Passage Retrieval Based on Density Distributions of Terms and Its Applications to Document Retrieval and Question Answering. In: Reading and Learning. (2004) 306–327
12. Ferret, O., Grau, B., Hurault-Plantet, M., Illouz, G., Jacquemin, C.: Document Selection Refinement based on linguistic features for QALC, a Question Answering System. In: Proceedings of Recent Advances on Natural Language Processing RANLP'01, Bulgaria. (2001)
13. Ferret, O., Grau, B., Illouz, G., Jacquemin, C., Masson, N.: QALC - the Question-Answering program of the Language and Cognition group at LIMSI-CNRS. In: Proceedings of TREC. (1999)
14. CLEF: Workshop of Cross-Language Evaluation Forum (CLEF) 2005. In: Workshop of Cross-Language Evaluation Forum (CLEF). Lecture notes in Computer Science, Springer-Verlag (2005)
15. Llopis, F., Noguera, E.: Combining Passages in the Monolingual Task with the IR-n System. In: Proceedings of CLEF. (2005)
16. Roberston, S., Walker, S., Beaulieu, M.: OKAPi at TREC-7. In: Proceedings of Seventh Text RETrieval Conference, volume 500-242, National Institute of Standard and Technology. Gaithersburg, USA (1998) 253–264
17. TREC: Overview of the TREC 2005 question answering track. In Voorhees, E.M., ed.: In Proceedings of TREC 2005. (2005)
18. Roberts, I., Gaizauskas, R.J.: Evaluating Passage Retrieval Approaches for Question Answering. In: Proceedings of ECIR. (2004) 72–84

Persian in MULTEXT-East Framework

Behrang QasemiZadeh[1] and Saeed Rahimi[2]

[1] Iran University of Science and Technology, Computer Department, Narmak, Tehran, Iran
QasemiZadeh@digitalclone.net
[2] Tehran University, Faculty of Literature and Humanities, Enqelab, Tehran, Iran
Saeedrahimiavval@yahoo.com

Abstract. Farsi, also known as Persian, is the official language of Iran, Tajikistan and one of the two main languages spoken in Afghanistan. It is an Indo-European agglutinating language, written in Arabic script. This paper presents the first step in creating Farsi basic language resources kit. This Step comprises the specifications for morphosyntactic encoding, which is based on the EAGLES/MULTEXT model and specific resources of MULTEXT-East. This paper introduces the language i.e. Farsi, with an emphasis on its writing system and morphological properties, and its specifications. Two other important issues introduced in this paper are; one, a novel Part of Speech (PoS) categorization and, the other, a unified orthography of Farsi in digital environment. A lexicon and an annotated corpus are under preparation.

1 Introduction

With information and communication technology (ICT) becoming more and more important, the need for language and speech technology also increases. In order for people to use their native language on the computers, a set of basic provisions (such as tools, corpora, and lexicons) is required. There have been numerous attempts to prepare basic language resources kits for the languages, especially, the languages of little or no commercial interest. With respect to Farsi, there is only little work experimented in this field. [1][2]

The MULTEXT-East project[1] was a spin-off of the EU MULTEXT[3] project. It developed standardized language resources for six languages such as Bulgarian, Czech, Estonian, Hungarian, Romanian, Slovene, as well as English, the 'hub' language of the project. The main results of the project were an annotated multilingual corpus, comprising a speech corpus, a comparable corpus and a parallel corpus, lexical resources, and tool resources for these seven languages. The most useful part of the MULTEXT-East project was the morphosyntactic resources which consist of three layers, listed in order of abstraction as follows [4]:

1. 1984 MSD: the morphosyntactically annotated 1984 corpus, where each word is assigned its context-disambiguated MSD and lemma.

[1] Multilingual Text Tools and Corpora for Eastern and Central European Languages.

T. Salakoski et al. (Eds.): FinTAL 2006, LNAI 4139, pp. 541 – 551, 2006.

2. MSD Lexicons: the morphosyntactic lexicons, which contain the full inflectional paradigms of a superset of the lemmas that appear in the 1984 corpus. Each entry gives the word-form, its lemma and MSD.
3. MSD Specs: the morphosyntactic specifications, which set out the grammar of valid morphosyntactic descriptions, MSDs. The specifications determine what, for each language, is a valid MSD and what it means, e.g., Ncms means PoS: Noun, Type: common, Gender: masculine, Number: singular.

MULTEXT-East provides a comprehensive framework for corpus development. Also, there are a lot of resources according to this framework, e.g. 1984 MSD for several languages. On the other hand, 1984 is available in Farsi and Farsi in return can be suited to this framework as we will show in the following. This can save us time, and money, moreover we can benefit from software reuse.

In this paper, we will try to propose an approach to represent an annotation of Farsi written corpora according to MULTEXT-East framework. As a result, we will have a discussion about Farsi specifications; we, then, propose our MSD Specs for Farsi. The rest of this paper is structured as follows: Section 2 introduces Farsi, its grammar, and its writing system. Section 3 explains the MSD specifications for Farsi, based on MULTEXT-East framework and the discussion in section 3. Related works are described in section 4. Finally, Conclusion and future works are discussed in section 5.

2 Farsi Language

Farsi, also known as Persian, is the official language of Iran, Tajikistan and one of the two main languages spoken in Afghanistan. Farsi is a member of the Indo-Iranian family of the Indo-European languages. Farsi has the properties of agglutinative languages. Even though Farsi is an agglutinative language, the fusional features can also be found in it. [5][6] The majority of affixes in Farsi are suffix with limited prefixes as well. There is no infix detected in Farsi.[5][6][7] Detailed morphosyntactic features of Farsi are described in section 2.1.

After the Arab's conquest in 651 A.D., the Persians adopted an extension of unified Arabic script for writing. Since Arabic is a cursive script, the number of possible shapes that letters actually can adopt exceeds the number of these letters [8]. Letters attach to each other to represent a word. Since Arabic is a Semitic language, it is obvious that how letters must be attached to each other to represent a word. In Farsi, however, due to the fact that it is an agglutinative language, there could be ambiguity in what letters should be written attached together or detached. For instance, the plural form of the word *ketäb* (book) may be written as 'کتابها' *ketäbhä* or 'کتاب ها' *ketäb hä* (books). This results in some difficulties in Farsi text analysis as cited in [9][10][11], i.e. tokenization of Farsi e-text since word boundaries are not clear. Also, the fact that short vowels are not written and capitalization is not used will result in ambiguities that impede computational analysis of the texts. In section 2.1, we will propose a standard for Farsi transcription to solve the problems mentioned above.

2.1 Farsi Transcription and Encoding in Digital Environments

Unicode standard version 4.0 reserves the range 0600 to 06FF for Arabic characters. The important design principles observed in the Unicode standard and relevant to the representation of Arabic script are characters not glyphs. As mentioned in the previous section, Arabic letters can have up to four different positional forms depending on their position relative to other letters or spaces. According to the design principle "characters, not glyphs", there is no individual code for each visual form (glyph) that an Arabic character can take in varying contexts but there exists only one code for each actual letter. The correct glyphs to be displayed for a particular sequence of Arabic characters can be determined by an algorithm. In order to display the characters properly, two special characters namely ZERO WIDTH JOINER (0x200D) and ZERO WIDTH NON JOINER (0x200C) are added to the character codes, either before or after them. The use of these special characters after a code means that a ZWJ or a ZWNJ should be added after the character if the character is not followed by a "right-join causing" character, or a "non-joining character" respectively.

The ISIRI 6219:2002 (Information Technology – Farsi Information Interchange and Display Mechanism, using Unicode) [12] has been proposed as the Farsi standard for using Unicode in digital environment. This standard indicates a subset of Arabic character set in Unicode to be used by Farsi users; but it does not specify which letters must be written in a separate or attached form. On the other hand, "Iran's Academy of Farsi Language and Literature", which is a governmental body presiding over the use of the Farsi language, has created an official orthography of the Farsi language, entitled "Dastoor-e Khatt-e Farsi" (Farsi Script Orthography) [13], for the proper representation of texts in the paper based system of writing.

Unfortunately there exists no standard for Farsi orthography in digital environent. For this reason, we have suggested an approach to represent Farsi electronic texts as we have done for 1984 corpus. According to the proposed orthography by the Academy, Farsi affixes must be written attached to their stem. In some cases when the stem ends in a letter which is a "right-join causing character", the affixe must be attached to the stem with a short space character before it. In order to fulfill this , we have used ZWNJ character as the short space. We have also used a character set based on the proposed standard in [12]. In this way, space characters represent unambiguous word boundaries and the orthography of Farsi e-texts remains consistent with the one which is proposed in [13]. Also, this transcription results in Farsi e-texts which are more consistent with the e-texts of other languages. This could be useful when developing parallel corpora of Farsi and other languages.

We should consider that the policy of text encoding, tokenization, orthography, and corpus tagging are in interaction with each other. For example, in Farsi it is possible that a bound morpheme appears detached from its stem with an intervening space; if we assume space as a delimiter in the tokenization process according to the used orthography, either we have to consider a tag for these bound morphemes during corpus tagging or, we have to consider a more complicated tokenization process as it is cited in [11] [9] (Figure1).

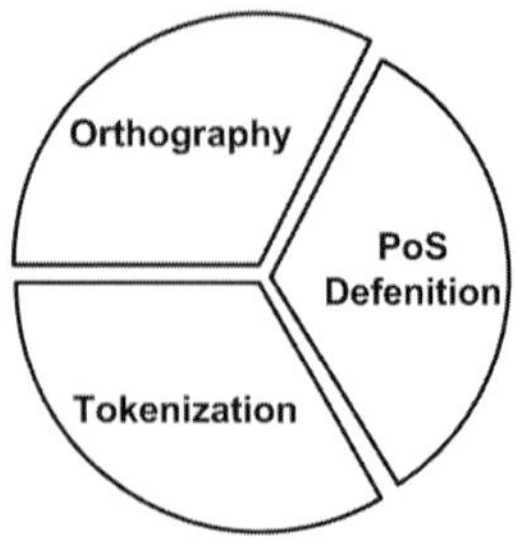

Fig. 1. Consider the whole circle as a proposed standard for corpus tagging in a specific language. Then the tokenization policy, PoS categorization, and language orthography, are fundamental elements that will directly affect the set of tags which is defined for corpus tagging.

2.2 Part of Speech in Farsi

There are seven PoS categories in traditional Farsi grammar [14]: Noun, Adjective, Verb, Adverb, Pronoun, Number, and Interjection. As cited in our previous work [10], this categorization is not adequate enough for analyzing Farsi. We can have more precise categorization considering other aspects of computational analysis of Farsi and comparing it with other languages in multilingual applications. According to our new categorization for PoSs in Farsi, there are 12 categories with their own special attributes. Our concept for this categorization is based both on the position of words in phrasal structure, and also what we have described in figure1. Nouns, Adjectives, Adverbs, Prepositions, Conjunctions, Verbs, Postpositions, Pronouns, Numbers, Determiners, and Interjections comprise our proposed categories. In the following we have discussed salient properties and morphosyntactic attributes of each of these proposed PoSs briefly.

Verbs are usually inflected with number and person. Farsi is neutral for gender. Our categorization divides verbs into 5 major types which are Main, Auxiliary, Copula, Modal, and Light. Most of these types are the same as they are in other languages. The number of Main verbs is limited in Farsi. Modal type of verbs is used to change the aspect of verbs to Subjunctive. Usually they come before Main verbs in present subjunctive form so the Main verb will have normal inflectional attributes. But if the Main verb appears in past 3rd person form, then the construction will be impersonal. Modal verbs usually are not inflected by number and person. However, there is an exception for the verb 'توانستن' (tavânestan) that can be inflected for person and number. Light verbs in Farsi are used to make a compound verb structure. Compound verb structure consists of one or more preverbal elements which could be a noun, adjective, or a prepositional phrase, followed by a Light verb. The number of Light verbs is limited. The elements of a compound verb construction can be separated by other lexical elements such as the object of the verbal construction or an adjective, adverb, etc. Therefore our suggestion is to analyze compound verb construction only at the syntactic level. We should also note that Light verbs are homographic with Main verbs. In Farsi, Past Tense verbs are made using past stem of verbs and present tense is made of present stem of verbs. Future tense is made by the help of Auxiliary verbs. In order to make progressive form in Farsi, verbs are inflected with the prefix 'می' (mī). Perfective forms of verbs are usually made using auxiliary verbs '... ام، است' (am, ast, ...). Passive form of the verbs in Farsi are made by the help of Auxiliary verbs. Passive form of the verb is made of Past Participle + Auxiliary verb 'شدن' (šodan). In some cases for courtesy, instead of the singular form of the verb, the plural one is used to refer to a singular subject. So we consider it as an attribute for Farsi Verbs. In fact, such attributes for Farsi are not found in traditional grammar books.

In Farsi, Nouns are inflected for number and Definiteness. There is no specific marker, like capitalization in English, for Farsi proper nouns. Plural form is made, similar to English, by adding Plural suffixes to the end of the nouns. Nouns may also be accompanied by the *Ezafe* Marker, a suffix that connects the elements in a phrase, and the indefinite marker. *Ezafe* Marker can appear as 'ی' (ye) when the word ends in certain characters. It can also appear as a short vowel named *Kasre* which sounds "e". In this case, according to the Farsi orthography, it can be deleted from the written text. A noun which is accompanied by *Ezafe* Marker can be considered as the genitive case of the noun.

Farsi adjectives are inflected for degree and definiteness. Adjectives, just the same as nouns, may also be accompanied by the *Ezafe* Marker and in this case we can consider it as a genitive case. Adverbs are often invariable in number. Certain adverbs may appear with the comparative suffix.

In traditional Farsi grammar, the category of determiners is not specified. Considering morphosyntactic specifications of words and the place of them in phrasal structures, we believe that determiners can be specified as a PoS in Farsi. Moreover, this consideration is more consistent with other languages. Most of the words we have considered as determiners here are categorized as adjectives in traditional grammar. There are different types of determiners namely demonstrative, indefinite, interrogative, exclamative, and article. As defined here, there is just one article in Farsi; i.e, 'یک' (yek). It is homonym with 'یک' which is a number.

Farsi has several prepositions but there is only one postposition 'را' (râ). It is an overt marker for direct object. Other categories are almost similar to traditional ones. Detailed description of Farsi grammar can be found in [16] [17] in English and [15] [18] in Farsi.

Table 1. Farsi PoSs and their proper codes according to MULTEXT-East

Part of Speech	Code	Number of Attributes
Noun	N	4
Verb	V	10
Adjective	A	4
Pronoun	P	6
Determiner	D	1
Adverb	R	2
Adposition	S	2
Conjunction	C	2
Numeral	M	1
Interjection	I	0
Abbreviation	Y	0

3 Farsi in MULTEXT-East Framework

Table 1 shows the PoSs of Farsi and the number of their attributes. Farsi MSD specification according to MULTEXT-East framework is proposed in table 2. The specification is based on the discussions in section 2. The structure of table 2 is the same as the one in [4]. Table 2 shows the attributes, their position, and the proper values of each proposed PoS. More information about the structure of the table can be found in [19]. We do not show attributes of PoSs irrelevant to Farsi due to their massive volume.

Table 2. MSD specification of Farsi(Farsi)

Nouns

P	ATT	VAL	C
1	Type	common	c
		proper	p
3	Number	singular	s
		plural	p
4	Case	genitive	g
5	Definiteness	no	n
		yes	y

Verbs

P	ATT	VAL	C
1	Type	main	m
		auxiliary	a
		modal	o
		copula	c
		light	l
2	VForm	indicative	i
		subjunctive	s
		imperative	m
		participle	p
3	Tense	present	p
		past	s
4	Person	first	1
		second	2

Table 2. (*continued*)

P	ATT	VAL	C
		third	3
5	Number	singular	s
		plural	p
8	Negative	no	n
		yes	y
10	Clitic	no	n
		yes	y
14	Aspect	progressive	p
15	Courtesy	no	n
		yes	y
16	Transitive	no	n
		yes	y
Adjectives			
P	ATT	VAL	C
1	Type	qualificative	f
2	Degree	positive	p
		comparative	c
		superlative	s
5	Case	genitive	g
6	Definiteness	no	n
		yes	y
Pronouns			
P	ATT	VAL	C
1	Type	personal	p
		demonstrative	d
		indefinite	i
		interrogative	q
		reflexive	x
		reciprocal	y
2	Person	first	1

Table 2. (*continued*)

```
                   second         2
                   third          3
- -------------- -------------- -
4 Number           singular       s
                   plural         p
- -------------- -------------- -
5 Case             genitive       g
                   accusative     a
- -------------- -------------- -
8 Clitic           no             n
                   yes            y
==================================
 Determiners
= ============== ============== =
P ATT              VAL            C
= ============== ============== =
1 Type             demonstrative  d
                   indefinite     i
                   interrogative  q
                   exclamative    e
                   article        a
- -------------- -------------- -
4 Number           singular       s
                   plural         p
==================================
 Adverbs
= ============== ============== =
P ATT              VAL            C
= ============== ============== =
2 Degree           positive       p
                   comparative    c
==================================
 Adpositions
= ============== ============== =
P ATT              VAL            C
= ============== ============== =
1 Type             preposition    p
                   postposition   t
- -------------- -------------- -
2 Formation        simple         s
                   compound       c
==================================
Conjunction
= ============== ============== =
P ATT              VAL            C
= ============== ============== =
```

Table 2. *(continued)*

P	ATT	VAL	C
1	Type	coordinating	c
		subordinating	s
2	Formation	simple	s
		compound	c
Numerals			
P	ATT	VAL	C
1	Type	cardinal	c
		ordinal	o
		fractal	f
		ordinal2	r
Interjection (No Attribute)			
Abbreviation (No Attribute)			

4 Related Works

Up until now, there are only few works done to create Farsi basic language resources kit. Keyvan et. al. introduces the work done in PersiaNet, a wordnet for Modern Farsi. [20] It has been carried out in an informal setting and is entirely on a volunteer basis. Lexical coverage is currently very sparse. The paper gives a good background about Farsi language and its writing system.

Assi and Haji [21] introduce an interactive PoS tagging system developed as a project at *the Institute for Humanities and Cultural Studies* in Tehran, Iran. It was designed as a part of the annotation procedure for a Farsi corpus called *The Farsi Linguistic Database* [22] *(FLDB)* and is the first attempt ever made to tag a Farsi corpus. The paper mainly emphasizes on the proposed system instead of the morphosyntactic specification of Farsi. The proposed tag set in [21] consists of 45 tags for lexical categories including one tag for single letters that appear in texts as lexical items, and one for unidentified word types. In the tag set, there are some tags that represent ambiguous annotations. As mentioned in [21], it was a pilot project. Studies of the tag set shows that the linguistic backgrounds are based on the traditional approaches and many morphosyntactic features of Farsi have been ignored.

A set of tools for Farsi analysis is introduced in [23]. This project focuses on English-Farsi machine translation. The tools consist of a lexicon and bilingual corpus [24], and other tools required for the analysis of Farsi. The linguistic background is based on the Machine Translation application and is different from the one proposed here.

5 Conclusion and Future Works

Unfortunately there has not been much effort made to create Farsi language resources. In summary, the significance of this paper can be fallen in two aspects: first, introducing a novel approach to represent Farsi e-text (orthography) in addition to a new PoS categorization. This could be of a great help to solve the problems which are introduced in [20][21][9][10]. Second, introducing a new tag set, according to MULTEXT-East framework, for Farsi corpus tagging.

On the one hand, MULTEXT-East introduces well-established standards with useful tools to manipulate and analyze text corpora. The MULTEXT-East resources are widely available for further researches. On the other hand, Orwell's 1984 which is tagged according to MULTEXT-East for several languages now is available in Farsi. As a result, we have fitted Farsi to this framework. We have started to tag 1984 based on the proposed tag set of Farsi to reach a multi lingual corpus consuming reasonable time and effort.

The production of the corpus and the lexicon is under preparation. Having prepared this corpus, all classical approaches to corpus based linguistics could be applied to Farsi. In this way, we can compare the results with the other efforts that have been done previously on other languages. For example, the prepared corpus can be used for training a tool for automatic PoS tagging of Farsi which uses machine learning techniques. We consider this as a future work.

In order to reach the best results, a novel PoS categorization for Farsi is introduced. One of the most important benefits of this PoS categorization is the consistency it provides for Farsi with other languages without ignoring any information of Farsi grammar. This could be of help during cross linguistic analyses. Also a unified orthography for Farsi e-text is proposed in this paper. The proposed orthography is based on the one proposed in [13] for the paper based system and computational point of view. The proposed orthography is consistent both with other languages and also Farsi grammar. Moreover it is convenient to use.

Acknowledgement

The authors would like to express their sincere gratitude to Prof. Tomaž Erjavec for many fruitful discussions. Also they would like to thank Prof. Damir Ćavar for his constructive idea.

References

1. Strik, H. Daelemans, W. Binnenpoorte, D. Sturm, J. de Vriend, F. and Cucchiarini, C.: Dutch HLT resources: From BLARK to priority lists, In Proceedings of ICSLP, Denver, USA, pp. 1549-1552, Denver, USA, (2002).
2. Krauwer, S. Maegaard, B. Choukri, K. and Damsgaard Jørgensenm, L.: Report on BLARK for Arabic, (2004).
3. Ide N. and Veronis J.: Multext: Multilingual Text Tools And Corpora. In 15th Int. Conference On Computational Linguistics, Pages 588–592, Kyoto, Japan, (1994).
4. Erjavec T., Krstev C., Petkevic V., Simov K., Tadic M., and Vitas D.: The MULTEXT-East Morphosyntactic Specifications For Slavic Languages, Proceedings Of The EACL 2003 Workshop On The Morphological Processing Of Slavic Languages, (2003).
5. Kalbasi, I.: The Derivational Structure of Word In Modern Farsi, ISBN 964-426-128-3, Tehran, (2001).

6. Samare I.: Typological Features Of Farsi, Journal Of Linguistics, Iran University Press, No. 7, pp 61-80, (1990).
7. Keshani, K.: Suffix Derivation in Contemporary Farsi, First Edition, Iran University Press, (1992).
8. Lutz, W.: Unicode and Arabic Script, Workshop "Unicode Und Mehrschriftlichkeit in Katalogen", Sbb Pk, Berlin, (2003).
9. Karine M. And Zajac R.: Processing Farsi Text: Tokenization In The Shiraz Projec,.Nmsu, Crl, Memoranda In Computer And Cognitive Scienc,(2000).
10. Qasemizadeh, B. and Rahimi, S.: Farsi Morphology, 11th Computer Society of Iran Computer Conference, IPM, Tehran, Iran, (2006).
11. Rezaie S.: Tokenizing an Arabic Script Language, Arabic Language Processing: Status And Prospects, Acl/Eacl, (2001).
12. Isiri 6219:2002: Information Technology - Farsi Information Interchange and Display Mechanism, Using Unicode, (2002).
13. Iran's Academy Of Farsi Language and Literature: Official Farsi Orthography, ISBN: 964-7531-13-3, 3rd Edition, (2005).
14. Hasan A. and Ahmadi Givi H.: Farsi Grammar, ISBN964-318-007-7, 22nd Edition, Tehran, (2002).
15. Meshkatodini M.: Introduction to Farsi Transformational Syntax, 2nd Edition, ISBN: 964-6335-80-2, Ferdowsi University Press, (2003).
16. Lazard, G.: A Grammar of Contemporary Farsi, Mazda Publishers, (1992).
17. Riazati D.: Computational Analysis of Farsi Morphology, Msc Thesis, Department Of Computer Science, RMIT, (1997).
18. Bateni, M.: Towsif-E Sakhteman-E Dastury-E Zaban-E Farsi [Description Of The Linguistic Structure Of Farsi Language], Amir Kabir Publishers, Tehran, Iran, (1995).
19. Erjavec T.: MULTEXT-East Morphosyntactic Specifications, Version 3.0. Supported By EU Projects Multext-East, Concede And TELRI, (2004).
20. Keyvan, R. Borjian, H. Kashef, M. and Fellbaum, C.: Developing Farsiet: The Farsi Wordnet, GWC 2006, Proceedings, pp. 315–318, (2005).
21. Assi, S. M. Haji Abdolhosseini, M.: Grammatical Tagging of a Farsi Corpus, International Journal of Corpus Linguistics 5:1, 69–81, (2000).
22. Assi, S. M.: Farsi Linguistic Database (FLDB), International Journal of Lexicography, Vol. 10, No. 3, Euralex Newsletter, (1997).
23. Amtrup, J. W., Mansouri Rad, H. Megerdoomian, K. and Zajac, R.: Farsi-English Machine Translation: An Overview of the Shiraz Project. NMSU, CRL, Memoranda in Computer and Cognitive Science (MCCS-00-319), (2000).
24. Megerdoomian, K. and Mansouri Rad, H.: Acquisition of Farsi Resources: Corpora and Dictionary Development in the Shiraz Project. NMSU, CRL, Memoranda in Computer and Cognitive Science (MCCS-00-323), (2000).

Prerequisites for a Comprehensive Dictionary of Serbian Compounds

Cvetana Krstev[1], Duško Vitas[2], and Agata Savary[3]

[1] Faculty of Philology, University of Belgrade, Belgrade
[2] Faculty of Mathematics, University of Belgrade, Belgrade
[3] Computer Science Laboratory, François-Rabelais University of Tours, Blois Campus

Abstract. The paper describes the steps that were undertaken in order to start the production of a comprehensive morphological dictionary of compounds for Serbian. First, the classes of multi-word expressions were determined that were to be covered by the dictionaries. In the next step the useful sources of compounds were detected. The retrieved compounds were then classified according to their inflectional properties. The recently developed special finite state transducers were constructed for each of these classes which produce all the variants and morphological forms for the compounds of the class. Finally, the software module was developed that facilitates the production of the dictionary of compound lemmas with all the necessary information in the required format.

1 Introduction

The morphological dictionary of the simple words of Serbian is being developed following the LADL methodology ([2]) during the last decade ([21]). The dictionaries have reached such a size that enables the effective processing of Serbian texts: the dictionaries of general lexica having 80,000 lemmas (yielding 1,100,000 word forms) are supplemented by special dictionaries of proper names that have 29,000 lemmas (yielding 185,000 word forms). The comprehensiveness of these dictionaries enables the text coverage that leaves from 1 to 5% of unrecognized words.

The next step in the development of the lexical resources for Serbian is to produce the dictionaries of compounds in the same format (called DELAC, cf [18]) . For Serbian, as for the other Slavic languages, this task is not easy to accomplish. The characteristics of Serbian that make it particularly demanding are:

1. *Phonologically based orthography*, the consequence of which is that a considerable number of morphophonemic processes are reproduced in written texts.
2. *Transcription* of all foreign proper names according to the Serbian orthography.
3. *The rich morphological system*, which is reflected both on the inflective and derivational level ([20]).

T. Salakoski et al. (Eds.): FinTAL 2006, LNAI 4139, pp. 552–563, 2006.

4. *Free word order* of sentence constituents, *special placement of enclitics*, and *complex agreement system* ([1]).

As a consequence, it is not recorded in the scientific literature, to our best knowledge, that a comprehensive morphological dictionary of compounds has been developed for some Slavic language.

The question often arises how many compounds exist in a language. The French DELACF dictionary of compound word forms from 2002 contains 248, 885 entries compared to the 746, 214 entries in the DELAF dictionary of simple word forms. For the languages that are starting to build such a dictionary one answer can be found in the Wordnets for particular languages. For instance, there are 12636 compound literals out of 44910 in Bulgarian Wordnet (28.14%) and respectively 4074 such literals out of 18390 existing in Serbian Wordnet (SWN) (22.15%) ([8]). It is to be supposed that in a more developed Wordnet, in which more synsets belonging deeper in the hypernym/hyponym hierarchy would be added, the contribution of the compounds would be even greater. For instance, the synset <trophy:2, prize:3> is in the eighth level node in a hypernym/hyponym branch of the Princeton Wordnet 2.0 (PWN), and its three hyponyms <bronze medal:1>, <silver medal:1>, and <gold medal:1> are all represented by compounds. The same situation exists for the corresponding synsets in the SWN.

2 Definition of Compounds

The notion of a compound is controversial among both linguists and NLP-researchers ([3], [4], [5]). In [18] compounds are defined as sequences of simple words (which are strings of alphabetic characters of a given language) that show some degree of non-compositionality from the morphological, distributional, syntactic or semantic point of view.

The limit between noun compounds and free nominal groups is not always easy to establish. For instance the noun phrase *plavo nebo* 'blue sky' is a frequent one (35 occurrences in the Corpus of Contemporary Serbian (CCS) [21]) since one often describes sky as blue; however, one can not treat it as a compound since it does not represent a new concept. The noun phrase *plava grobnica* 'blue burial chamber', however, does not represent the burial chamber that is blue but is used to refer to the burial place of those that died on the sea. The noun phrase *plavi šlemovi* 'blue helmets' referring to the UN peace forces illustrates some other compound features: *šlem* 'helmet' represents an artifact, while *plavi šlemovi* represents an organization. This example also shows that new compounds emerge in a language regularly, and it cannot be known in advance how long they will last.

The structure of a compound is stricter then that of a free noun phrase: compounds usually do not allow a change of the word order or insertions ([4] talks about the degree of "fixedness" which is the higher the more syntactic transformations are forbidden for the given phrase). In Serbian, the free noun phrase *plavi šlemovi* could be expressed equivalently as *šlemovi plavi*; the latter phrase, however, cannot be used to denote the UN peace forces. Also, the presence of the inserted adjective in *plavi zaštitni šlemovi* 'blue safety helmets' indicates that the literal meaning is used. Although this is in general true, it does not mean that there are no exceptions: for instance, *žuta tampa* 'yellow journalism' is a compound, and consequently, the occurrence *verska žuta štampa* would refer to the religious journalism of the sensationalist kind. However, the CCS records also *žuta verska štampa* which shows that in this case the adjectives can be freely distributed as in a free noun phrase.

Compounds should also be distinguished from verb phrases. For instance, *plavi dres* 'blue gym suit' is sometimes used by sport journalists to refer to the Serbian national team, regardless of the sport in question. However, it cannot be regarded as the synonym of *reprezentacija* 'national team' since these two are not interchangeable. Namely, one cannot rephrase *Jugoslovenska košarkaška reprezentacija nije otputovala na Olimpijske igre* 'Yugoslav national basketball team did not leave for the Olympic Games' by **Jugoslovenski košarkaški plavi dresovi nisu otputovali na Olimpijske igre*. The minute analysis of the usage of the expression *plavi dres* shows that it is used only in a restricted number of phrases, such as *igrati za plavi dres* 'to play for the blue gym suit', where the verb *igrati* 'to play' can be replaced only by a few other (*odigrati*, *zaigrati* 'perfective forms of to play', *voziti* 'to drive', *nositi* 'to wear', *zaslužiti* 'to deserve', etc.). The expression *plavi dres* can be replaced by *reprezentacija*, but only if the sentence is rephrased: *Poslednju utakmicu Žućko je odigrao u plavom dresu koji je nosio celu deceniju* 'Žućko has played his last game in a blue gym suit that he wore for a whole decade' can be changed to *Poslednju utakmicu Žućko je odigrao za reprezentaciju za koju je igrao celu deceniju*. This cannot be treated as a compound and it will be treated as phrase.

One of the roles compounds have in text processing is in disambiguation since in many cases compounds can be unambiguously recognized. That is, they invalidate the interpretations obtained by tagging the word forms that are their constituent parts. In Serbian, the most convincing is the case of *Crne Gore*, the genitive case form of *Crna Gora* 'Montenegro'. When dictionaries of simple word forms are applied to this sequence the following result is obtained:

```
({crne,crn.A+Col:aemp4g:aefs2g:aefw2g:aefw4g:aefp1g:aefp4g:aefp5g} +
 {crne,crneti.V547+Imperf+It+Iref+Ref+Ek:Pzp:Ays:Azs} +
 {crne,crnjeti.V747+Imperf+It+Iref+Ref+Ijk:Pzp})
({gore,gora.N:fs2q:fw2q:fw4q:fp1q:fp4q:fp5q} + {gore,gore.ADV} +
 {gore,goreti.V544+Imperf+It+Iref+Ek:Pzp:Ays:Azs} +
 {gore,gorjeti.V744+Imperf+It+Iref+Ijk:Pzp} +
 {gore,rdjav.A:bemp4g:befs2g:befw2g:befw4g:befp1g:befp4g:befp5g:bens1g...} +
 {gore,zao.A:bemp4g:befs2g:befw2g:befw4g:befp1g:befp4g:befp5g:bens1g...})
```

The word form *crne* obtains 11 grammatical interpretations for 3 different lemmas, while *gore* obtains 31 grammatical interpretations for 6 different lemmas. These are all the cases of a "false ambiguity" ([12]) since a human reader does not see them as such; if written in this way, with both simple word forms with initial capitals, it represents the Republic Montenegro, and it can be unambiguously tagged: Crne Gore,Crna Gora.AN+C+Nprop+Top+Dr:fs2q

3 Collecting

The compounds that will be covered by our Serbian DELAC can be grouped in various Parts-of-Speech. In Serbian the compounds that do not inflect are compound prepositions (*bez obzira na* 'regardless of'), conjunctions (*kao da* 'as if'), interjections (*blago tebi* 'lucky you'), and adverbs (*od srca* literally 'from heart' meaning 'willingly', *iz dana u dan* 'day in day out'). The compound numerals occur often in texts (*dvadeset i pet miliona* 'twenty five millions'), but as they are built in regular way from a small number of constituents, they are usually not part of a dictionary but are recognized using other tools, such as FSTs. The same is valid for many adverbial phrases, as *januara prošle godine* 'in January last year' and they are treated in the similar way. The compounds that inflect can be categorized as adjectives (*kulturno-umetnički* 'cultural and artistic') and nouns (*general pukovnik* 'general colonel', *ministar spoljnih poslova* 'minister of the foreign affairs').

There exist many approaches dedicated to manual, semi-automatic or automatic extraction of compounds of various types such as frozen expressions, complex terms (see [6] for a comparative study of some of them), multi-word named entities (e.g. [13]), etc. We know of no such method for Serbian. Some extraction systems, based mainly on statistical estimation of token co-occurrences, are meant to be language-independent. One such system has been used for term extraction from Serbian texts in restricted domains but the results were not very promising ([14]).

As stated the section 1 Wordnet can be regarded as a valuable source of potential compounds. However, not all literals in Wordnet that contain non-alphabetic characters are compounds, since quite a number of them are just descriptions of some concepts. For instance, in PWN the synset <group action:1> is defined as an 'action taken by a group of people'. The corresponding synset in SWN is <grupna akcija:X> and although the English literal may be regarded as a compound, the Serbian one can hardly be.

Another source of compounds is the list of unknown words produced during the lexical analysis since the constituents of various compounds can be found in it. For example, in *akten-tašna* 'briefcase' and *saher-torta* 'Sacher cake' *akten* and *saher* are not simple word forms in Serbian so they would be listed among unrecognized words. Quite a number of simple word forms found in this list belong to the compound proper names, like *Šri Lanka* 'Sri Lanka', *Skotland Jard* 'Scotland Yard', and *Ajfelova kula* 'Eiffel Tower'.

Specific patterns can be used in order to try to discover the compounds, as suggested in [15]. Useful patterns can be constructed by using the syntactic and semantic markers that are added to the entries in the dictionary of simple lemmas. For instance, all the adjectives that represent colors are marked in the Serbian dictionary of lemmas by the marker +Col, and thus the pattern <A+Col>

`<N>`[1] used on various texts can reveal quite a number of compounds. Among the retrieved compounds there are common names, such as *bela kafa* 'coffee with milk', *crno tržište* 'black market', *siva ekonomija* 'gray economy', but also quite a number of proper names: *Crno more* 'Black Sea', *Crveni krst* 'Red Cross', *Žuta reka* 'Yellow river'. Some, but not many, additional compounds are retrieved by the pattern `<A+Col> <A>* <N>`, for instance *siva moždana masa* 'cerebral cortical gray matter'.

Beside the color maker `+Col`, other markers that can be used in the same pattern are those indicating relational adjectives such as `+Zool`, `+Mat`, and `+NProp+Top`, referring to animals, substances and geographical proper names, respectively. They allow to retrieve compounds such as *labudji pev* 'swan song', *staklena bašta* (literally 'glass garden', meaning 'greenhouse'), *šećerna bolest* (literally 'sugar disease', meaning 'diabetes mellitus'), *Saudijska Arabija* 'Saudi Arabia', *Jadransko more* 'Adriatic Sea', *Versajski mir* 'the Peace Treaty of Versailles', *užička pršuta*, a type of prosciuto from Užice (town in Serbia), etc. A certain number of compounds is also retrieved with the marker `+Ord` that denotes ordinal numbers, e.g. *treći svet* 'third world', *na prvi pogled* 'at the first sight'.

Some more complex patterns were used to retrieve compound nouns. A grammar in a form of finite state graphs has been developed that recognizes functions, professions and titles of people. It is particularly successful when applied to newspaper texts in order to retrieve personal names followed or preceded by such designations ([10]). Some compounds retrieved are *narodni heroj* 'national hero', *književni kritičar* 'literary critic', *vršilac dužnosti* 'acting officer', *kandidat za predsednika* 'candidate for the president', etc.

4 Inflection

Morphological dictionaries of simple word forms of the DELAF type are produced automatically from the dictionaries of lemmas (of DELAS type). Namely, an inflectional class code is attached to every lemma which determines the FST that produces all the members of the lemma's paradigm with appropriate values of grammatical categories. The programming environments such as Intex[2], Unitex[3] and NooJ[4] incorporate these transducers and enable the automatic production of the DELAF. All three systems enable work with compounds but do not offer means for automatic production of a DELACF. In NooJ a step has been done towards it by introducing some new operators that can be used for inflection, for instance, "go to the end of the previous word", but serious linguistic problems have not been tackled (see [19]). Another, lexicographically based, approach relying on a systematic compound per compound description ([11]) is too specific to be efficiently applied to Serbian. In other corpus-oriented contexts the

[1] This is the over-simplified version of the pattern used; the actual pattern is more complex since it takes care about the agreement.

[2] http://msh.univ-fcomte.fr/intex/

[3] http://www-igm.univ-mlv.fr/~unitex/

[4] http://www.nooj4nlp.net

inflectional morphology of compounds is dealt with via automatic stemming or lemmatizing of their component words, or via combinations of all their inflected forms. As discussed in [16], these methods suffer from excessive generalizations or from overlooking of exceptions.

The Xerox finite-state lexicon compiler, *lexc* ([7]), based on the two-level morphology, allows the representation of inflectional and derivational morphology in terms of morpho-phonological phenomena. In particular, via a cascaded composition of lexical transducers, it enables the description of inflected forms of compounds. An example for French shows that a number of mechanisms, including unification, allows the *lexc* rules to combine different inflected forms of single constituents in order to obtain the inflected forms of the whole compound, as is the case in our formalism described below. The *lexc* rules probably allow to cover most of the compound inflection paradigms within the same framework as the simple words' morphology. However, if the description of the simple words has been done by a different formalism, its integration to *lexc* for compounds' inflection seems difficult. Moreover, it remains to be examined how some morpho-syntactic variants of compounds, which require constituent insertion, deletion, or order change, may be modeled by *lexc* rules.

The problem of the inflection of compounds is regarded as serious for English and French. However, in [17] the most complex example for English is *student union* that has three possible single forms: *student union*, *students union*, and *students' union*, and three possible plural forms: *student unions*, *students unions*, and *students' unions*. For Serbian, and other Slavic languages, the problem is more complex. For instance, in Serbian, nouns are characterized by four categories: gender, number, case, and animateness, and they inflect in two of them, number and case. There are seven cases and three numbers: singular, plural, and paukal that is used only with the small numbers two, three, and four, and only in genitive and accusative case. A compound noun, like a simple noun, has thus, in most cases, 16 different possible realizations, and in order to produce them different agreement conditions have to be taken into consideration for all of its *characteristic constituents* (CC), that is, the headword and all the constituents that agree with it. For instance, if the headword is a noun, and the other CC is an adjective, than the adjective has to agree with the noun in gender, which can change in a noun paradigm but not freely, in number and case for which the noun inflects, and in certain cases with the animateness which is fixed for a noun. In addition, the adjectives inflect in degree (positive, comparative, and superlative), and definiteness (definite and indefinite), independently from the noun.

In [16] a method is suggested that enables an effective inflection of compounds that satisfies both the condition of *correctness* and *exhaustivity*, that is, nothing that does not belong to the compound's paradigm is produced, and everything that belongs to it is. The method is based on a "two-level" approach[5] that separates the inflectional characteristics of compounds from the inflectional characteristics of its constituents. Namely, two compounds as a whole can behave in

[5] Not to be confused with Koskenniemi's two-level morphology.

the same way, although their characteristic constituents inflect in different ways, for instance, *Ujedinjene nacije* 'United Nations' and *Crno more* 'Black Sea'. As compounds they have the same structure, that is, the structure of an adjective followed by a noun, adjective and noun agree in gender, number, and case, and noun in either compound does not inflect in number. The constituent adjectives and nouns in the given examples inflect in a different way, as suggested by their different inflectional codes listed in the Serbian DELAS:

```
(ujedinjen,A1 nacija,N600) and (crn,A10 more,N300)
```

Moreover, the constituent noun is in the first compound always in plural, and consequently the compound has only plural number, while in the second compound the constituent noun is only in singular and as a result the compound is also always in singular. However, according to this method, these two compounds would belong to the same class, regardless of the different characteristics of their constituents.

In order to describe the inflectional characteristics of compounds, two formalisms are defined: *inheritance* and *unification.* The compound can inherit some category values from some of its constituents through the inheritance mechanism, for instance in the example of *Ujedinjene nacije* the value of the category number is inherited from the headword *nacije*, and it is plural. Some categories are neither fixed nor inherited but can take all the values allowed for them. These values, however, have to be in accord for the CC, which is established by the unification mechanism. For instance, for the same example, the different forms of the CC for the category case, when category number, gender and animateness are inherited, are as follows:

```
ujedinjene:1    nacije:1      ujedinjene:5    nacije:5
ujedinjenih:2   nacija:2      ujedinjenim:6   nacijama:6
ujedinjenim:3   nacijama:3    ujedinjenim:7   nacijama:7
ujedinjene:4    nacije:4
```

The word forms in these two columns cannot combine freely, only those that have the same value of the case category can combine. The unification mechanism is, thus, similar to the natural join operation in relational algebra.

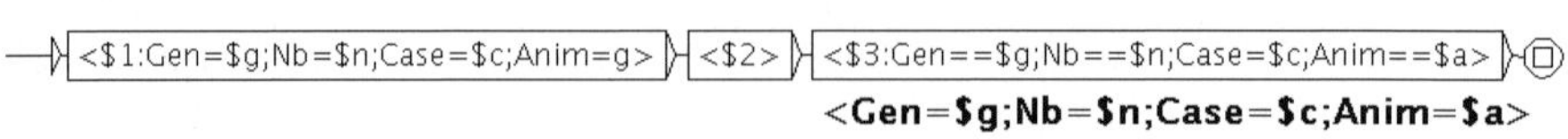

Fig. 1. The inflectional FST for the compounds of the type *Ujedinjene nacije*

These two mechanisms are supported by a new type of a graph[6], which generates all the inflected forms of a compound. Such a graph for compounds *Ujedinjene nacije* and *Crno More* is presented on Figure 1. All the compound constituents are represented in the FST by ordinal numbers, non-alphabetic

[6] These FSTs rely on Unitex inflectional FSTs.

characters being constituents on their own. The headword is the third constituent ($3) since the values of the categories gender (Gen), number (Nb), and animateness (Anim) are inherited from it (which is signaled by the double equal sign). The first ($1) and third constituent both inflect in case (signaled by the single equal sign for Case), but they have to agree (signaled by the use of the same variable $c for the category Case). The use of the same variable $c for Case in the first and the third constituent actually extends the only path in the graph in Figure 1 into seven paths with seven different output values – if two different variables were used that path would be extended into 49 paths. To continue the analogy with the relational algebra, that would correspond to the Cartesian product. Two DELAC entries for the given example illustrate the usage of the inflectional graph (named NC_A3XN2) from the Figure 1 and the "two-level" approach:

```
Ujedinjene(Ujedinjen.A1:aefp1g) nacije(nacija.N600:fp1q),NC_A3XN2
Crno(crn.A10:aens1g) more(more.N300:ns1q),NC_A3XN2
```

In order to use this method, the compounds have to be analyzed and classified according to their different characteristics:

1. *The number of constituents.* This is usually not difficult to establish, but this point is connected to the establishment of the lemma. Consider the adjective *vojno-tehnički* 'military and technical' that can also be written *vojnotehnički*; however, the latter cannot be chosen for lemma since it is not possible to unambiguously distinguish the constituents in it. For the constituents that do not inflect in the compound the corresponding DELAF entry need not be given. As a result, one compound inflectional class can contain syntactically different compounds. For instance, *Ministarstvo za informacije* 'Ministry for Information' and *Ministarstvo spoljašnjih poslova* 'Ministry of Foreign Affairs' would be in one inflectional class although the first one has the structure `<N> <PREP> <N>` and the second `<N> <A:2> <N:2>`, because in both cases the last two constituents do not inflect.
2. The identification of the constituents that can be omitted, e.g. *profesor engleskog jezika* 'professor of English language' is often used in a shorter form *professor engleskog* (the third constituent is optional).
3. The identification of optional replacements, e.g. *žiro račun* 'giro account' can also be written with the hyphen *žiro-račun.*
4. The identification of the allowed word reordering, e.g. *Božji sud* and *sud Božji* 'ordeal'.
5. The identification of characteristic constituents and their agreement conditions. Although this seems straightforward, it is by no means so. Consider the example of a compound adjective *gladan kao vuk* 'hungry as a wolf'. The characteristic constituent is the adjective *gladan* that inflects in gender, number, case, but can inflect neither in degree (**gladniji kao vuk* is not syntactically correct) nor animateness. The problem is whether *vuk* inflects as well, and, if it does, how it agrees with the noun to which the adjective is applied. The following examples from the CCS illustrate the problem:

(a) *Posle takvih vežbi Grmalj je bio <gladan kao vuk>.* 'After these exercises Grmalj was hungry as a wolf'.
(b) *Kad dodju sa treninga, <gladni kao vukovi> i otvore frižidera,...* 'When they come back from training, hungry as wolfs and open the refrigerator...'
(c) *Ako ste <gladni kao vuk>, možete pojesti i porciju barenog žutog pirinča...* 'If you are hungry as a wolf you can eat a portion of boiled yellow rice...'
(d) *Posle pušenja kanabisa osoba je pospana, nervozna, <gladna kao vuk>.* 'After smoking cannabis, one is sleepy, nervous, hungry as a wolf.'

The examples (a) and (b) show that *vuk* inflects in number and agrees with the noun or pronoun the adjective is applied to. The example (c) shows that the adjective can be in plural and *vuk* in singular if the plural form is used as a form of a polite address. The example (d) shows that the adjective can be in a feminine form although *vuk* is in masculine (**gladna kao vučica*, 'hungry as a female volf' is not used). After this considerations, the inflectional graph for this type of compound adjectives is given on Figure 2.

6. The identification of the categories for which the constituents inflect and those for which the values are inherited. For instance, in *Crno more* the noun *more* does not inflect in number (**Crna mora*), in *redovni profesor* 'full-time professor' the adjective *redovan* does not inflect in degree (**redovniji profesor*) and only its definite forms are used (**redovan profesor*).
7. The identification of the output values of grammatical categories. For many types of compounds this is straightforward, for instance for the compounds with the structure <A> <N>, the compound will inherit its gender and animateness from the noun, it will inflect in number (or inhert the number) and in case. The following examples show that some compounds are more complex:

(a) *Komanda Unprofora za bivšu <Bosnu i Hercegovinu> nije prihvatila...* 'The command of Unprofor for the former Bosnia and Herzegovina has not accepted...'
(b) *<Bosna i Hercegovina> su na 70-tom mestu....* 'Bosnia and Herzegovina are on the 70th place...'.
(c) *<Kosovo i Metohija> je postalo leglo organizovanog kriminala...* 'Kosovo and Metohija has become the nest of the organized crime...'.
(d) *<Kosovo i Metohija> su bili, sada su i ostaće multietnička sredina.* 'Kosovo and Metohija were, are now and will remain a multiethnic'.

The examples (a) and (b) show that the gender of *Bosna i Hercegovina* 'Bosnia and Herzegovina' is feminine because both *Bosna* and *Hercegovina* have feminine gender. Its number, however, can be both singular (a) and plural (b). Even more complex is the case of *Kosovo i Metohija* 'Kosovo and Metohija'. If used as singular its gender is neuter since *Kosovo*, the first constituent is neuter (c), but if used as plural its gender is masculine (d), although neither *Kosovo* nor *Metohija* are.

The application of this method to the Serbian compounds has shown that the "two-level" principle cannot be applied to all cases. Namely, in Serbian there

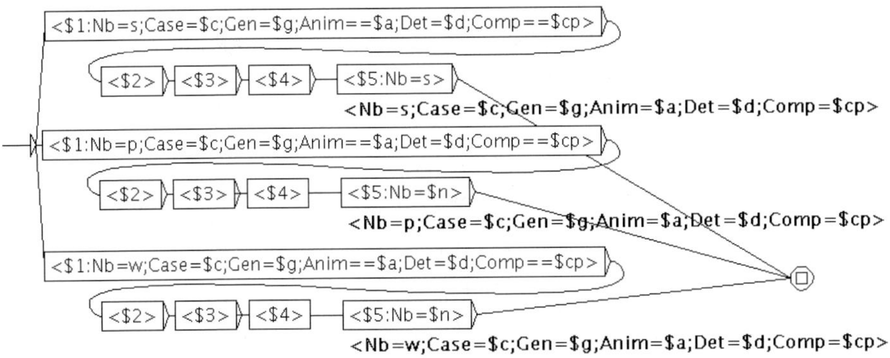

Fig. 2. The inflectional FST (called NC_A3XN2) for the compound adjective of the type *gladan kao vuk*

are come classes of nouns that change their gender with the number: *papa.ms* 'pope' vs. *pape.fp*, *sudija.ms* 'judge' vs. *sudije.fp*. In this case, gender is not an independent category as it is usually treated, so it can be neither inherited nor can it inflect freely. As a consequence, when a noun of this type is a constituent of a compound a different FST for the compound inflection has to be constructed. In addition, there are both nouns and adjectives that do not inflect at all, and ask for a special treatment as well.

Although the principle of exhaustivity can always be satisfied, the principle of correctness is sometimes disrupted. Namely, in Serbian the adjectives for some cases and numbers have shorter and longer forms that are not treated as special categories in the traditional grammars, and thus we have not specifically marked them in the Serbian DELAS. In compounds, as well as in nominal phrases, these different forms cannot combine. However, since we have not marked them appropriately some erroneous compound forms are generated, as for *okružni javni tužilac* 'district attorney':

```
okružnoga javnoga tužioca,okružni javni tužilac.NC+Comp:ms2v
*okružnoga javnog tužioca,okružni javni tužilac.NC+Comp:ms2v
*okružnog javnoga tužioca,okružni javni tužilac.NC+Comp:ms2v
okružnog javnog tužioca,okružni javni tužilac.NC+Comp:ms2v
```

The application of the compound inflection FSTs has thus detected a serious flow in the dictionaries that we have to correct in order to achieve a full correctness. On the other hand, creating an extensive DELAC/DELACF sample for an inflectionally reach language such as Serbian allowed for the new compound inflection formalism and software to undergo their first large-scale test of adequateness and correctness.

5 Production

The final step in the production of the dictionary of compounds is the preparation of the list of entries in the desired format. Due to the "two-level" approach the preparation of one entry in DELAC is much more complex then the preparation of one entry in DELAS. Namely, besides the correct inflectional code of a compound, one has to add, for each constituent that inflects, the full DELAF entry of the form that appears in a compound lemma, that is: (a) simple word lemma; (b) inflectional code; (c) grammatical categories. In order to facilitate this work a module has been developed within the software named WS4LR — workstation for the lexical resources ([9]). First of all, this module enables the existing entries to be copied, and in that way for the compounds that share the same structure the compound inflectional code is copied. For each word form that inflects, the Unitex routines are invoked that retrieve from the appropriate DELAF dictionaries all the necessary information. Often, more then one DELAF entry satisfies the query, and in that case the user has to choose the correct one. The only case when the user actually has to fill in all the fields is when the word form does not appear in the dictionary of simple words. The only data that has to be entered for all the new entries are the semantic markers since, in general, they cannot be inherited from the constituent lemmas.

6 Conclusion and Perspectives

The dictionary of compounds for Serbian has at this moment around one thousand lemmas. Much more of them have been collected but have not yet been classified and processed accordingly. However, now that all the prerequisites have been achieved it is expected that this dictionary will grow quickly. The description of compounds is not finished. Some lemma variations can be described by the mechanism shown in section 4, for instance for the lemma *ministar za saobraćaj* 'minister for traffic' the syntactically variant form *ministar sobraćaja* can be generated. However, for *kandidat za predsednika* 'candidate for the president' the variant form *predsednički kandidat* cannot be produced since its constituent is the relational adjective *predsednički* derived from *predsednik* and it is not part of the noun paradigm. Similarly, from many compound geographic names simple derivational forms are obtained, e.g. *Novi Sad*, town in Serbia, and *novosadski* 'related to Novi Sad', *Novosadjanin* 'the inhabitant of Novi Sad', and presently they have to be treated separately.

A reliable quantitative and qualitative evaluation of the proposed methodology will only be possible when the dictionary reaches a large-coverage size. However, having linguistically studied various, even rare, compound inflection paradigms for Serbian, Polish, English and French, allows us to believe that a very high percentage of existing compounds may be correctly described by our formalism. Naturally, this human-controlled process will be labor intensive but will also allow a very reliable and easily maintainable lexicographic data.

References

1. Corbett, G. G.: Number. Cambridge University Press (2000)
2. Courtois, B., Silberztein, M., eds.: Dictionnaires électroniques du français. Langue Française, 87. Larousse (1990)

3. Downing, P.: On the Creation and Use of English Compound Nouns. In Language, 153(4), Linguistic Society of America (1977)
4. Gross, G. Définition des noms composés dans un lexique-grammaire. In Langue Française, 87, Larousse, Paris (1990)
5. Habert, B., Jacquemin, Ch.: Noms composés, termes, dénominations complexes : problématiques linguistiques et traitements automatiques. In TAL, 2 (1993)
6. Jacquemin, Ch.: Spotting and Discovering Terms through Natural Language Processing. MIT Press (2001)
7. Karttunen, L.: Finite-State Lexicon Compiler. Technical Report. ISTL-NLTT2993-04-02. Xerox Palo Alto Research Center. Xerox Corporation (1993)
8. Koeva, S, Krstev, C., Obradović, I., Vitas,D.: Resources for Processing Bulgarian and Serbian — a brief overview of Completeness, Compatibility and Similarities. In S. Piperidis and E. Paskaleva, eds.: Workshop on Language and Speech Infrastructure for Information Access in the Balkanic Countries, 25 September 2005, Borovets, Bulgaria. (2005) 31–38
9. Krstev, C. Stanković, R., Vitas, D., Obradović, I.: WS4LR: A Workstation for Lexical Resources. In: Proc. of LREC'06, Genoa, ELRA (2006).
10. Krstev, C., Vitas, D., Gucul, S.: Recognition of Personal Names in Serbian Texts. In G. Angelova, ed.: Proc. of the International Conference Recent Advances in Natural Language Processing, 21-23 September 2005, Borovets, Bulgaria. (2005) 288–292
11. Kyriacopoulou, T., Mrabti, S., Yannacopoulou, A.: Le dictionnaire électronique des noms composés en grec moderne. In Lingvisticae Investigationes, 25(1), John Benjamins B.V. (2002) 7–28
12. Laporte, E.: Reduction of lexical ambiguity. Lingvisticae Investigationes, 24(1), John Benjamins B.V. (2001) 67–103
13. Mikheev, A., Grover, C., Moens, M: Description of the LTG System Used for MUC-7. In Proceedings of the 7th Message Understanding Conference (MUC-7).
14. Monachini, M., Soria, C.: Building Multilingual Terminological Lexicon for Less Widely Available Languages. In Proc. of LTC'05, Poznań, Poland (2005) 129–133
15. Ranchhod, E.M.: Using Corpora to Increase Portuguese MWE Dictionaries. Tagging MWE in a Portuguese Corpus. Proc. of the Corpus Linguistics Conference Series 1(1) (2005) [to appear].
16. Savary, A.: A formalism for the computational morphology of multi-word units. Archives of Control Sciences, 15(LI) (2005) 437–449
17. Savary, A.: Multiflex — User's Manual and Technical Documentation, version 1.0. Technical Report 285, LI-University of Tours, Tours (2005)
18. Silberztein, M.: Le dictionnaire électronique des mots composés. Langue Française, 87 (1990) 71–83
19. Silberztein, M.: NooJ Manual. Université de Franche-Comté (2005) http://perso.wanadoo.fr/rosavram/NooJ
20. Vitas, D., Krstev, C.: Derivational Morphology in an E-Dictionary of Serbian. In Z. Vetulani, ed.: Proc. of LTC'05, Poznań, Poland (2005) 139–143
21. Vitas, D., Pavlović-Lažetić, G., Krstev, C., Popović, Lj., Obradović, I.: Processing Serbian Written Texts: An Overview of Resources and Basic Tools. In S. Piperidis and V. Karkaletisis, eds.: Workshop on Balkan Language Resources and Tools, 21 November 2003, Thessaloniki, Greece. (2003) 97–104

Regular Approximation of Link Grammar

Filip Ginter, Sampo Pyysalo, Jorma Boberg, and Tapio Salakoski

Turku Centre for Computer Science (TUCS)
and Department of IT, University of Turku
Lemminkäisenkatu 14 A
20520 Turku, Finland
first.last@it.utu.fi

Abstract. We present a regular approximation of Link Grammar, a dependency-type formalism with context-free expressive power, as a first step toward a finite-state joint inference system. The approximation is implemented by limiting the maximum nesting depth of links, and otherwise retains the features of the original formalism. We present a string encoding of Link Grammar parses and describe finite-state machines implementing the grammar rules as well as the planarity, connectivity, ordering and exclusion axioms constraining grammatical Link Grammar parses. The regular approximation is then defined as the intersection of these machines. Finally, we implement two approaches to finite-state parsing using the approximation and discuss their feasibility. We find that parsing in the intersection grammars framework using the approximation is feasible, although inefficient, and we discuss several approaches to improve the efficiency.

1 Introduction

Finite-state techniques provide simple and efficient models in natural language processing. They have been successfully applied to many basic problems such as tokenization, phonological and morphological analysis, parsing, and language modeling [1]. With the well-studied mathematical apparatus for combining and transforming finite-state machines, including the standard algorithms for intersection, composition, determinization and minimization, it is possible to build large efficient systems by combining many simple, small machines. Moreover, weighted formulations of finite-state machines allow for probabilistic models.

In natural language parsing, context-free parsing algorithms currently form the basis for almost all full parsing approaches producing either a hierarchical phrase structure or a full dependency structure, while finite-state techniques are most commonly applied in shallow parsing which produces no, or very limited, hierarchical structure [2]. There is, however, a growing interest in the application of finite-state techniques to full parsing. Although finite-state models are weaker in terms of expressive power, they are applicable in practical cases, for example as approximations of context-free grammars. Such an approximation recognizes a regular subset or superset of the original context-free language. Approximation approaches have primarily been developed in the context of phrase

T. Salakoski et al. (Eds.): FinTAL 2006, LNAI 4139, pp. 564–575, 2006.

structure grammars (see Nederhof [3] for a detailed discussion). For instance, Grimley Evans [4] obtains a finite-state approximation in an intersection framework, where finite-state representation of the dotted rules in phrase structure parsing is intersected with regular languages expressing constraints on their usage. The result is a finite-state automaton that recognizes the language as sequence of terminals, but does not encode the parse trees. Further, Johnson [5] implements the approximation through left-corner grammar transforms, allowing unlimited left and right recursion without increasing stack depth. By contrast with these phrase-structure based approaches, we focus on dependency grammars. We also have the additional requirement of obtaining a representation of the full dependency analysis.

Several approaches have been introduced for finite-state dependency parsing. Oflazer [6] has developed a robust finite-state full dependency parser as a transducer that is iteratively applied to the input string, each time producing one level of analysis. Elworthy [7] presents a parser with dependency output based on deterministic finite-state transducers. In the framework of finite-state intersection grammars [8], parsing is treated as an intersection problem. For each sentence, a finite-state automaton (FSA) is built that generates the sentence together with all syntactic hypotheses allowed by the grammar for the individual words. This FSA is then intersected with automata that implement the grammatical constraints. The result of the intersection is an FSA that describes all grammatical analyses of the sentence. Yli-Jyrä has recently advanced the finite-state intersection grammars to allow full tree structures and resolve all structural ambiguities. This paper is mainly related to Yli-Jyrä [9], where a finite-state approximation of Hays and Gaifman dependency grammars [10,11] is introduced.

In this paper, we present a finite-state approximation of Link Grammar (LG) [12], a dependency-type formalism with context-free expressive power. LG and its parser[1] represent one of the major computational dependency grammar implementations with a wide coverage of general English. Recently, there has been an increased interest in applications of LG in NLP tasks such as information extraction.

One of the key motivations for introducing a finite-state approximation of link grammar is to facilitate the integration of the parser into a finite-state system which identifies the globally optimal solution through joint inference across all different levels of linguistic analysis in Information Extraction [13]. In such an integrated model, each level of analysis produces a set of alternate hypotheses encoded as a finite-state automaton, and the intersection of these automata then encodes the set of all possible analyses structurally compatible with all levels in the system. Subsequently, the globally optimal solution can be identified by a search through this unified automaton, taking into account the local preferences of the individual levels of analysis [14]. The finite-state approximation of LG presented in this paper is a first step toward a finite-state joint inference system.

For the purpose of integration into a unified model, each component must be developed in the context of the whole system. Most importantly, each of the

[1] Available at `http://link.cs.cmu.edu`

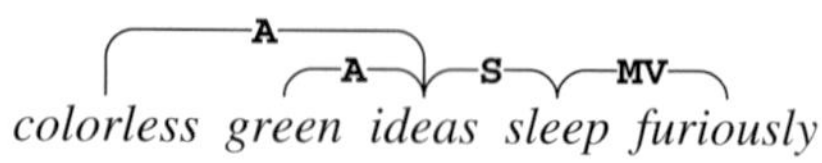

Fig. 1. Example LG linkage

components must share a representation that allows intersection, in this case, that of finite-state machines. Thus, the representation constrains the implementation, and, at least initially, takes priority over considerations of the efficiency and expressive power of the parser.

Additionally, a finite-state formulation of LG could, for example, in combination with FSA weighting and unsupervised FSA weight estimation algorithms, provide means for developing a statistical model of LG in terms of weighted finite-state machines.

2 Link Grammar

The LG formalism is closely related to dependency grammars. An LG parse of a sentence, termed a *linkage*, consists of a set of undirected, typed *links* connecting pairs of words of the sentence (see Figure 1). The links connecting each word to others must fulfill the *linking requirements* given to the word in the grammar: for example, verbs could require a `S` link to the left to connect to their subject.

LG is highly lexical: the grammar rules are only expressed through the linking requirements assigned to individual words. LG differs from traditional dependency grammars in that linkages are unrooted and links do not explicitly identify which word is the governor and which the dependent.

Linkages must further fulfill a set of axioms (termed *meta-rules* by Sleator and Temperley) which, together with the linking requirements of the words, specify the set of grammatical sentences and their analyses. The following sections describe the specification of the linking requirements and the linkage axioms.

2.1 Linking Requirements

The linking requirements of each word in the grammar are specified by a formula of *connectors*, each of which has a *type* and a *direction*. The type of a connector is specified by a string of characters, and the direction is either `-` for left or `+` for right. LG linking requirement formulas are built of connectors joined by the *and* and *or* operators (written `&` and `or`). Parentheses are used to specify precedence in formulas. Connectors or larger parts of linking requirement formulas can be made optional by enclosing them in curly brackets (e.g. `{MV+}`), and connectors can be allowed to repeat one or more times by prepending the `@` character. In parsing, links must be formed by connecting left and right connectors of matching types so that all non-optional connectors participate in a link.

As an example, consider the following grammar:

```
colorless red green: A+
ideas theories proofs: {@A-} & (O- or S+)
```

```
sleep dream rest: S- & {O+} & {MV+}
furiously symbolically: MV-
```

The language specified by this grammar requires that the adjectives take an `A` connector to the right, the nouns take any number of `A` connectors to the left and either an `O` connector further to the left or an `S` connector to the right, the verbs take an `S` connector to the left and optionally `O` and `MV` connectors to the right, and the adverbs require an `MV` connector to the left. This language thus includes linkages such as that shown in Figure 1.

2.2 Connector Matching

LG connector type strings can consist of any sequence of capital letters, followed by a *subscript* containing any sequence of lowercase letters and a wild-card character. When comparing connectors, shorter subscripts are (conceptually) padded with wild-cards. Two connectors are defined to match if they are equal when wild-cards are considered equal to any lowercase character.

2.3 Linkage Axioms

The following four axioms constrain the set of grammatical LG linkages. The *planarity axiom* states that the links of a linkage must not cross when drawn above the sentence. This axiom is closely related to projectivity constraints of dependency grammars. The *connectivity axiom* requires that, when considered as an undirected graph with the words as nodes and the links as edges, the linkage must be connected. The *ordering axiom* specifies that when traversing the connectors of the linking requirement formula of a word from left to right, the words which the connectors link to proceed from near to far. The *exclusion axiom* states that any two words are directly connected by at most one link.

3 The Approximation

We now present the components of the regular LG approximation. Note that we approximate the LG grammar, and grammar-external LG features implemented in the parser code, such as the special treatment of coordination, the post-processing mechanism and the robust parsing algorithm [15], are not considered.

3.1 String Encoding

We define a string encoding of linkages as follows. The words of the sentence are preceded by a word boundary marker $\#$. Each word is followed by a $\Downarrow$ character separating it from the links *closing* at the word, i.e. links connecting to the word from the left. These are in turn separated by a $\Uparrow$ character from the links *opening* at the word. Opening links are represented by an opening angle bracket character ($<$) followed by the connector type string, and closing links are represented by the type string followed by a closing angle bracket ($>$). Finally, the sentence is terminated by a $\#$ character. An example is given in Figure 2.

#green⇓⇑<A#ideas⇓A>⇑<S#sleep⇓S>⇑ #

Fig. 2. Example linkage with string encoding

3.2 Lexicon Language

The linking requirement formulas of words can be expressed in equivalent *disjunctive forms*. For example, the formula `{@A-} & (O- or S+)` has the disjunctive form `({@A-} & S+) or ({@A-} & O-)`. In the LG terminology, the elementary conjunctions in the disjunctive form are referred to as *disjuncts*. Each disjunct represents a particular way of satisfying the linking requirements of the word. We define disjuncts in terms of regular expressions that describe their string representation: for example, the conjunction operator & corresponds to concatenation, the optionality operator {} corresponds to disjunction with an empty string, and optional repetition {@} corresponds to the Kleene star operator. The order of concatenation respects the interpretation of the formula according to the ordering axiom as well as the grouping by connector direction according to the string encoding whereby left connectors are separated from right connectors by the ⇑ symbol.

The regular expression for the whole formula is then a disjunction of the regular expressions of its disjuncts, prefixed with the symbol ⇓. For the disjunctive form above, the corresponding expression is ⇓(((A>)*⇑<S)|((A>)*O>⇑)).

Let R_f be the regular expression corresponding to the linking requirement formula f. A grammar entry for a word w with requirement formula f is then represented by the regular expression R_w

$$R_w = \#wR_f$$

For example, for the word *ideas* with a grammar entry `ideas: {@A-} & (O- or S+)`, the language R_{ideas} contains the following strings:

#ideas⇓O>⇑	#ideas⇓⇑<S
#ideas⇓A>O>⇑	#ideas⇓A>⇑<S
#ideas⇓A>A>O>⇑	#ideas⇓A>A>⇑<S
...	...

Let further L be the *lexicon language* defined by the regular expression

$$L = (R_{w_1}|\dots|R_{w_n}) + \#$$

where $w_1 \dots w_n$ are the words defined in the grammar. The lexicon language L thus consists of sequences of words with linking requirements, terminated with the boundary symbol #. L contains strings such as

#green⇓⇑<A#ideas⇓A>⇑<S#sleep⇓S>⇑ #
#sleep⇓S>⇑ #ideas⇓A>⇑<S#green⇓⇑<A#
#sleep⇓S>⇑<MV#furiously⇓MV>⇑ #

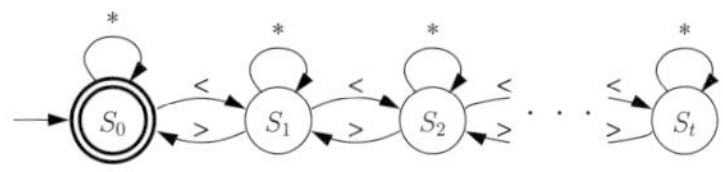

Fig. 3. Untyped balanced bracketing FSA B_t. The states S_0–S_t serve as a memory of the number of currently open brackets.

#green⇓⇑<A#ideas⇓A>O>⇑ #

...

Note that of the strings above, only the first string encodes a valid LG linkage.

3.3 Planarity and the Nature of the Approximation

Let us define a *typed balanced bracketing* in the context of the strings encoding LG linkages as a bracketing where brackets do not cross and the connector types associated with the corresponding opening and closing brackets match.

By definition, an LG linkage is planar[2] if and only if its links when drawn above the sentence do not cross. As crossing links directly translate to crossing typed brackets and vice versa, it is easy to see that the string representation contains a typed balanced bracketing if and only if the linkage it encodes does not contain crossing links. Thus, an LG linkage is planar if and only if its encoding string contains a typed balanced bracketing. Enforcing the planarity axiom is thus equivalent to enforcing a typed balanced bracketing in the string representation.

Let us consider the untyped bracketing case, disregarding the connector type matching. It is a well-known fact that a balanced bracketing with unrestricted depth is not a regular language. A balanced bracketing with a finite fixed maximum depth $t \in \mathbb{N}$, however, is a regular language and can be defined by the simple $t+1$-state FSA B_t illustrated in Figure 3. Following Yli-Jyrä [9], we limit the maximum depth of the bracketing, thus approximating LG. The maximum bracketing depth t is a parameter of the approximation.

In order to enforce the planarity axiom, it is necessary to enforce the LG connector type matching in addition to the untyped balanced bracketing. Let Δ be the alphabet of all connector types used in right connectors in a particular LG grammar. Similarly, ∇ is the alphabet of left connector types[3]. Let further $M(c) \subseteq \nabla$ be the set of all connector types in ∇ matching a connector type $c \in \Delta$. For each bracketing depth d, we define an FSA $P_{d,t}$ (Figure 4) which accepts a string only if for each link opened with a connector type $c \in \Delta$ at the depth d, the link is closed with a connector type $c' \in M(c)$. This approach implements the connector type matching algorithm by simple enumeration, since in any given grammar, the number of unique connector types is finite. The intersection FSA

[2] More correctly, the term *semi-planar* is often used.

[3] Roughly, Δ corresponds to the alphabets B_L and B_l in [9] and ∇ corresponds to B_R and B_r.

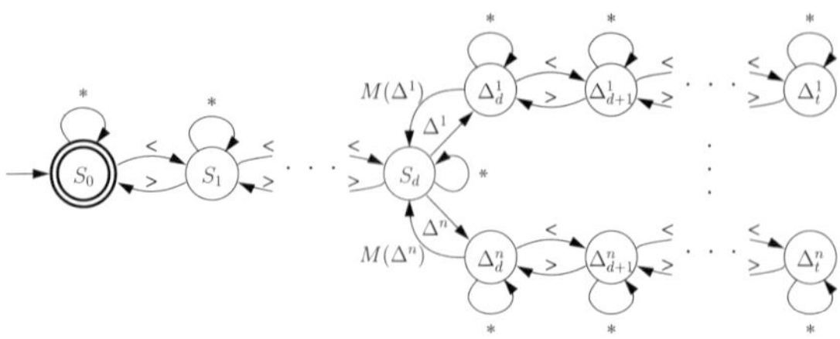

Fig. 4. Planarity FSA $P_{d,t}$. The states S_0–S_d maintain a balanced bracketing up to the depth d. From the state S_d, there is an outgoing edge and a new state Δ^i_d for every connector type $\Delta^1 \ldots \Delta^n \in \Delta$. For every such state Δ^i_d, there is a sequence of states $\Delta^i_d \ldots \Delta^i_t$ that maintain a balanced bracketing up to the total depth t. Further, there is an edge from Δ^i_d to S_d for each connector type in $M(\Delta^i)$. Consequently, the states $\Delta^1_d \ldots \Delta^n_d$ serve as a memory of which right connector type was used to open the link at depth d. A transition back to the state S_d is only possible through a matching left connector type.

$$P_t = \bigcap_{d=1}^{t} P_{d,t}$$

then accepts a language where all connector types associated with corresponding open/close bracket pairs match. Any string from $L \cap P_t$ thus encodes a planar LG linkage graph.

3.4 Exclusion

The exclusion FSA $E_{d,t}$ accepts only strings such that if the bracketing depths d and $d+1$ are opened by the same word, then they are closed by two different words, thus enforcing the exclusion axiom at the two adjacent bracketing depths. It is easy to see that the intersection FSA

$$E_t = \bigcap_{d=1}^{t-1} E_{d,t}$$

then accepts only strings where no two words are connected by more than one link. The FSA $E_{d,t}$ is detailed in Figure 5.

3.5 Connectivity

Words in a linkage that do not connect to any other words to the left (resp. right) are called *left-bare words* (resp. *right-bare words*). Further, an *island* in a linkage is a connected component of the linkage graph. The connectivity axiom requires that a linkage only has one connected component. Trivially, any island starts with a left-bare word and ends with a right-bare word. By the projectivity axiom, any island consists of a balanced bracketing. The depth d at the boundary symbol preceding the first word of an island is therefore equal to the depth at the

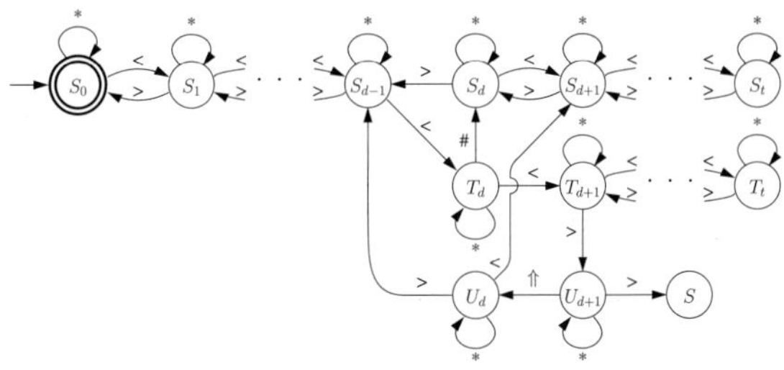

Fig. 5. Exclusion FSA $E_{d,t}$. The states S_0–S_t maintain balanced bracketing up to the depth t. If a link is opened at the depth $d-1$, thus opening the depth d, the FSA reaches the state T_d. If another link is opened by the same word, the state T_{d+1} is reached, otherwise the FSA continues in S_d. When the depth $d+1$ is closed the FSA reaches the state U_{d+1}. If the depth d is closed by the same word, the sink state S is reached and the string is rejected. Otherwise the states S_{d-1} or S_{d+1} are reached through U_d.

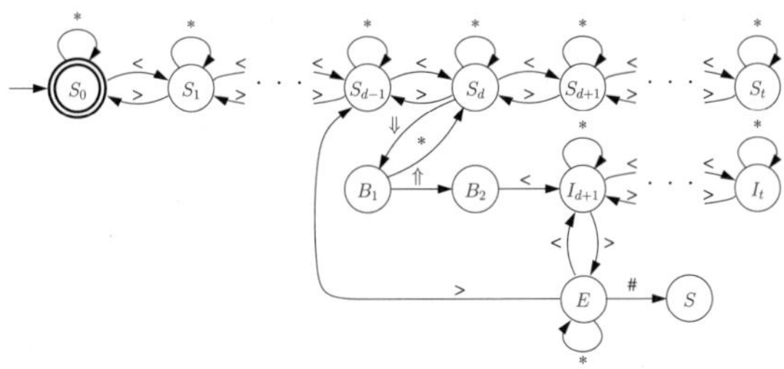

Fig. 6. Connectivity FSA $C_{d,t}$. The states S_0–S_d maintain balanced bracketing up to the depth d. If the current word is a left-bare word at depth d, the FSA reaches state B_2, otherwise it returns to state S_d. States I_{d+1}–I_t maintain a balanced bracketing from the left-bare word onward and the state E is reached upon closing the depth d. If, at this point, also the depth $d-1$ is closed, it means that the left-bare word did not open an island since the current depth is smaller than d. The FSA then returns to state S_{d-1}. If, on the other hand, the FSA proceeds from the state E to S, it has reached a right-bare word and the depth within the island was never been smaller than d. Therefore, an island was found and since S is a sink state, the string is rejected.

boundary symbol following the last word of the island. Moreover, at any point within the island, the depth is $\geq d$. These properties are used in the construction of an FSA $C_{d,t}$ that only accepts strings that do not have islands opened at the depth d. The FSA $C_{0,t}$ must, however, accept the single island comprising the whole linkage. The intersection FSA

$$C_t = \bigcap_{d=0}^{t-1} C_{d,t}$$

then accepts strings encoding connected linkages. The FSA $C_{d,t}$ is detailed in Figure 6. Note that the FSA $C_{0,t}$ cannot be constructed as in the figure. Its construction is, however, trivial.

3.6 Approximation Language

The approximation language $\mathcal{L}_t$ is defined as an intersection of the lexicon language L with the languages P_t, E_t, and C_t which implement the LG axioms of planarity, exclusion, and connectivity. The LG axiom of ordering is implicit in L.

$$\mathcal{L}_t = L \cap P_t \cap E_t \cap C_t$$

The definition of $\mathcal{L}_t$ concludes the construction of the regular LG approximation.

4 Parsing with the Finite-State LG Approximation

We now introduce two ways to implement a parser based on the finite-state approximation of LG.

4.1 LG as a Monolithic Transducer

Let us consider $\mathcal{L}_t$ as an identity finite-state transducer (FST) with edge input:output symbol pairs $z : z$. Let us define a FST $\mathcal{T}_t$ based on $\mathcal{L}_t$ such that every edge symbol pair $z : z$ in $\mathcal{L}_t$ where $z \in \Delta \cup \nabla \cup \{\Uparrow, \Downarrow, <, >\}$ is replaced with $\epsilon : z$, where ϵ is the empty transition symbol. The FST $\mathcal{T}_t$ thus generates the parse encoding on the output string via ϵ-transitions on the input string.

4.2 LG as a Finite-State Intersection Grammar

We now cast LG finite-state parsing as an intersection problem within the framework of finite-state intersection grammars [8].

For a sentence $s = w_1 w_2 \ldots w_n$ we define the language R_s as the regular expression

$$R_s = R_{w_1} R_{w_2} \ldots R_{w_n} \#$$

that is, the concatenation of the regular languages representing the grammar entries for the individual words as defined in Section 3.2. The sentence s is then parsed by computing the intersection

$$R_s \cap P_t \cap E_t \cap C_t$$

The resulting language encodes all parses of s with bracketing depth $\leq t$.

Note that for a sentence s with n words, the planarity and exclusion axioms imply that the maximum possible bracketing depth is $n - 1$. A *perfect approximation*, where the set of parses in the regular language R_s is exactly the set of all parses possible for the sentence in the context-free language, can therefore theoretically be achieved by setting $t = n - 1$.

5 Practical Considerations

We have created proof-of-concept implementations of the two finite-state LG parsers. We have implemented the automata with the FSA utilities [16] and, for efficiency reasons, executed the automata and operations such as intersections and minimizations in the AT&T FSM utilities [17].

The efficiency of the intersection algorithm critically depends on the size of the intersected FSAs. When sequentially intersecting several FSAs, the size of the intermediate automata has a strong influence on the efficiency of the computation. For illustration, we list the sizes (as the number of states/transitions) of several determinized and minimized automata constructed based on a broad-coverage English LG grammar[4] with 47K words: $P_{1,6}$ (1.1K/465K), C_6 (159/40K), E_6 (157/52K), $C_6 \cap E_6$ (1.2K/337K), L (45K/110K).

Given the size of the automata, it is not surprising that building the monolithic FST has proven impractical. Even for a very simple grammar[5] and $t = 3$ the FSA $\mathcal{L}_t$ has over 20M states. The explicit computation of the monolithic parser for a broad-coverage grammar is thus infeasible.

Parsing within the framework of finite-state intersection grammars is more practical. For illustration, when considering a complex sentence with 41 words and depth up to 6, R_s has 2.2K states and 4K transitions. The parsing of this complex sentence, however, takes on the order of minutes, while the LG parser takes on the order of seconds. Hence, unlike the monolithic approach, LG parsing as a finite-state intersection grammar is feasible, but inefficient due to the computation of intermediate results, where, although the result FSA has 130K states, the largest intermediate result has 1M states.

The problem of the large size of intermediate results is inherent to the finite-state intersection grammars. Several approaches to alleviate the problem are discussed, for example, by Tapanainen in [1]. For instance, the size of intermediate results strongly depends on the order in which the FSAs are intersected and optimizing the order can result in improved efficiency. We first compute $R_s \cap E_t \cap C_t$ and then intersect sequentially with $P_{d,t}$ for the individual depths d. We observed that intersecting the FSAs $P_{d,t}$ in the inverse order, starting with $P_{t,t}$, leads to several times faster intersection (largest intermediate result has 1M states) than intersecting $P_{1,t}$ first and $P_{t,t}$ last (largest intermediate result has 2.5M states). Other approaches discussed by Tapanainen include using a parallel intersection algorithm, or alternatively avoiding the explicit computation of the intersection by using a depth-first search through the FSA R_s, backtracking any time an axiom FSA rejects the string.

The efficiency of the original LG parser depends critically on *pruning*, where, prior to execution of the main parsing algorithm, the set of disjuncts assigned to each word is pruned so that, for example, if a disjunct contains a right connector and no disjunct of any following word contains a matching left connector, the disjunct cannot be satisfied and can thus be discarded [12]. The decrease in

---

[4] `4.0.dict` in the LG distribution

[5] `tiny.dict` in the LG distribution

the number of disjuncts and hence the decrease in the size of the search space is very substantial, often several orders of magnitude. As the number of disjuncts directly relates to the number of paths through the machine, pruning, once implemented, should result in a substantial decrease in parsing time also for the finite-state approximation of LG. Additionally, Yli-Jyrä [9] proposed several techniques which, through extension of the internal alphabets, achieve local testability of some of the linking axioms — with a corresponding positive effect on the size of intermediate results. Adapting Yli-Jyrä's techniques to the current implementation is thus another potential direction of research.

The explosion in the number of states can also potentially be avoided by the use of *extended* finite-state approaches, where the finite-state formalism is augmented in order to allow for more compact machines. Commonly, for every extended FSM there exists an equivalent, but considerably larger, pure FSM. However, some extended FSM techniques result in non-regular languages. An example of a practical application of an extended finite-state approach to parsing is that of Oflazer [6]. Additionally, *lazy evaluation*, supported for example by the AT&T FSM library, avoids explicitly expanding the machines in terms of atomic states and transitions and could result in a further decrease in parsing time.

Optimizing the computation of the intersection through the techniques discussed above or, alternatively, avoiding its explicit computation with an extended finite-state approach can be expected to increase the practicability and efficiency of finite-state LG parsing.

6 Conclusions

In this study, we have introduced a finite-state approximation of Link Grammar. The regular language approximating a given LG grammar was constructed by intersecting finite-state machines implementing the LG grammar and the LG axioms that constrain the set of grammatical parses. The approximation language is a subset of the corresponding context-free LG language with a limited maximum nesting depth of links.

Further, as a preliminary study of the practical applicability of the presented approximation, we have implemented finite-state LG parsers in terms of a monolithic transducer and in the framework of finite-state intersection grammars.

We have shown that a finite-state approximation of LG can be constructed and that finite-state parsing based on the approximation is feasible. Whether efficiency comparable to that of the original LG parser can be achieved using intersection optimization techniques or extended finite-state approaches remains a question for future research.

Acknowledgments

This work has been supported by Tekes, the Finnish Funding Agency for Technology and Innovation. We would like to thank the anonymous reviewers for their detailed and enlightening comments.

References

1. Roche, E., Schabes, Y., eds.: Finite-State Language Processing. MIT Press (1997)
2. Carroll, J.: Parsing. In Mitkov, R., ed.: The Oxford Handbook of Computational Linguistics. Oxford University Press (2003) 233–248
3. Nederhof, M.J.: Practical experiments with regular approximation of context-free languages. Computational Linguistics **26**(1) (2000) 17–44
4. Grimley Evans, E.: Approximating context-free grammars with a finite-state calculus. In: Proceedings of ACL/EACL '97, Association for Computational Linguistics (1997) 452–459
5. Johnson, M.: Finite-state approximation of constraint-based grammars using left-corner grammar transforms. In: Proceedings of ACL/COLING '98, Association for Computational Linguistics (1998) 619–623
6. Oflazer, K.: Dependency parsing with an extended finite-state approach. Computational Linguistics **29**(4) (2003) 515–544
7. Elworthy, D.: A finite state parser with dependency structure output. In: Proceedings of the Sixth International Workshop on Parsing Technologies IWPT 2000, Trento, Italy. (2000)
8. Koskenniemi, K.: Finite-state parsing and disambiguation. In Karlgren, H., ed.: Proceedings of the 13th International Conference on Computational Linguistics COLING 90, Helsinki, Finland, ACL (1990) 229–232
9. Yli-Jyrä, A.M.: Approximating dependency grammars through intersection of star-free regular languages. International Journal of Foundations of Computer Science **16**(3) (2005) 565–579
10. Hays, D.G.: Dependency theory: A formalism and some observations. Language **40** (1964) 511–525
11. Gaifman, H.: Dependency systems and phrase-structure systems. Information and Control **8** (1965) 304–337
12. Sleator, D.D., Temperley, D.: Parsing English with a Link Grammar. In: Proceedings of the Third International Workshop on Parsing Technologies IWPT 93, Tilburg, Netherlands. (1993)
13. Miller, S., Fox, H., Ramshaw, L., Weischedel, R.: A novel use of statistical parsing to extract information from text. In: Proceedings of NAACL '00, Morgan Kaufmann (2000) 226–233
14. Ginter, F., Mylläri, A., Salakoski, T.: A probabilistic search for the best solution among partially completed candidates. In: Proceedings of the HLT/NAACL'06 Workshop on Computationally Hard Problems and Joint Inference in Speech and Language Processing, Association for Computational Linguistics (2006) 33–40
15. Grinberg, D., Lafferty, J., Sleator, D.D.: A robust parsing algorithm for link grammars. In: Proceedings of the Fourth International Workshop on Parsing Technologies IWPT 95, Prague, Czech Republic. (1995)
16. van Noord, G.: FSA utilities: A toolbox to manipulate finite-state automata. In Wood, D., Darrell, R., Yu, S., eds.: Automata Implementation. Volume 1260 of Lecture Notes in Computer Science (LNCS)., Springer, Heidelberg (1997) 87–108
17. Mohri, M., Pereira, F.C.N., Riley, M.: A rational design for a weighted finite-state transducer library. In Wood, D., Yu, S., eds.: Proceedings of the Second International Workshop on Implementing Automata WIA 97, London, Canada. Volume 1436 of Lecture Notes in Computer Science (LNCS)., Springer, Heidelberg (1998) 144–158

Segmental Duration in Utterance-Initial Environment: Evidence from Finnish Speech Corpora

Tuomo Saarni[1], Jussi Hakokari[2], Jouni Isoaho[1], Olli Aaltonen[2], and Tapio Salakoski[1]

[1] Turku Centre for Computer Science, Finland
{tuomo.saarni, jouni.isoaho, tapio.salakoski}@it.utu.fi
[2] Phonetics Laboratory, University of Turku, Finland
{jussi.hakokari, olli.aaltonen}@utu.fi

Abstract. This study examines segmental durations produced by Finnish speakers in utterance-initial environments. We have established a method to statistically examine segmental duration on the phone level in speech corpora. The two corpora represented in this study consist mainly of television news broadcasts and short texts read aloud by professional speakers. Previous studies conducted have been contradictory; there are reports of initial shortening in certain languages and lengthening in others. Our results are conclusive in neither way, but suggest a qualitatively differentiated behavior. We have observed lengthening of all utterance-initial vowels, diphthongs included, and shortening of phonologically long plosive (stop) consonants. No other speech sounds are significantly affected. These findings hold in both corpora, in despite of different speakers and annotators.

1 Introduction

Final, prepausal, and pre-boundary lengthening have been reported in a great number of languages, leading us to believe it is in fact, depending on the point of view, either a phonetic or a linguistic universal. Final lengthening refers to the human tendency to slow down articulatory movements in the ends of utterances or syntactic units, effectively increasing the duration of individual speech sounds. There is debate over what are the origin and the possible function of the phenomenon. We do know lengthening is a powerful boundary signal, especially since lengthening alone at a boundary can produce a sensation of the speaker temporarily pausing [3]. White [12] calls such modulations of speech in both initial and final environments domain-edge processes.

There are reports of domain-edge processes at the other end of the utterance, as well. Unlike final lengthening, on which the studies mostly agree, domain-initial processes have produced conflicting results. Some languages are mentioned to display shortening of initial speech sounds in the literature, while perhaps the majority is reputed to lengthen utterance-initial speech sounds. Kaiki et al. [8] report having found shortening in Japanese, although Campbell [1] has criticized their corpus of imbalance. Nagano-Madsen [10] reports initial shortening in Eskimo. Hansson [6] makes a very strong case for initial shortening in Southern Swedish. Initial lengthening has been

T. Salakoski et al. (Eds.): FinTAL 2006, LNAI 4139, pp. 576 – 584, 2006.

reported, among others, in Korean [2], Standard Chinese [13], and English [12]. The locus and extent of lengthening or shortening varies from language and method to another. White [12], for instance, has found certain speech sounds to occur shorter while the others are lengthened. Furthermore, initial lengthening is sometimes credited as a consequence of initial strengthening, a phenomenon causing stronger contact between the tongue and the palate in domain-initial consonant articulations. The study at hand will only address segmental duration in Finnish. We will move phoneme by phoneme from phrase-initial towards medial positions and observe how long different kinds of phonemes are realized.

2 Methods and Materials

Many studies into domain-edge processes and segmental duration have relied on behavioral experimental designs, such as reading aloud nonsense words embedded into carefully designed sentence structures. Our methodology is different; we wish to observe segmental duration statistically in vivo; in ordinary, unrestricted speech flow. Furthermore, while the studies generally operate on word or syllable level, we have chosen a phone-level approach. The method appears novel in speech timing research. We designed search scripts to read the annotation files which contained the speech sounds' identities along with their position and duration information. The output of the scripts was manually inspected to verify the resulting data.

2.1 Speech Corpora

We studied the effect of utterance-initial position on segmental durations using two corpora. Both are in Standard Finnish, the literary language of both spoken and print media. The first one is a single-speaker corpus consisting of 964 utterances, read aloud by a 39-year-old male. The corpus is described in more detail in Vainio [11]. The other one is a multi-speaker corpus featuring 9 men and 4 women, all professional speakers. It originates with the Finnish Broadcasting Company and consists of news reading, interviews, and oral presentations. There are 802 utterances altogether. Both corpora were annotated manually by trained phoneticians, although the annotation strategies were slightly different due to independent annotators.

2.2 Procedure

Segmental duration was examined by two criteria: position by position and by the phoneme category. We mapped all vowels, consonants, etc. into a chart by their position in their respective utterances. The phoneme categories were vowels, non-plosive consonants, and voiceless plosives. Their phonologically contrasting short and long counterparts were further separated. The annotation of the multi-speaker corpus also recognized diphthongs, which were marked as two consecutive short vowels in the single-speaker corpus. Therefore short vowels are not entirely comparable between the two corpora, as the single-speaker material contains short vowels that are in fact diphthongs cut in two halves. To clarify the method established, let us consider the following example from the single-speaker corpus:

/suʊi mene:/ (transl. 'the summer passes')

In the short non-plosive consonant chart (below in the results section), the first value (position 1) is the mean duration of all short non-plosive consonants that are the very first phone in an utterance (/s̲uʊi/). The phonemically long vowel /e:/ in /mene:/ is therefore in the eight position of the long vowel chart. /ʊ/ in /suʊi/ is in the third position of the short non-plosive consonant chart. By organizing the phones separately by the category, we are not tied to higher-level units such as syllable or word duration, as the previous studies have. We can get accurate information on as how long different kinds of phones are realized in the utterance-initial position, and how their duration evolves as we move further towards the end. For reference, the mean duration of all phones of a category (regardless of their position) is represented as horizontal lines in the charts.

Our studies have revealed a significant prepausal lengthening effect in both the single-speaker [5] and the multi-speaker corpora (unpublished). The lengthening takes place as early as the 10th last phone in the utterance. To study duration in initial position, it was necessary to eliminate any prepausal lengthening from the speech material. It was done by removing the last ten phones from each utterance in the corpora, effectively excluding all utterances with 10 or less phones in them. For instance, we have found very short utterances entirely affected by lengthening, and they will not give accurate information on specifically utterance-initial phenomena. The procedure left 934 utterances of the original 964 (all remaining ones 10 phones shorter than before) for the single-speaker corpus, and 679 of the 802 utterances for the multi-speaker one. Utterance is used in a purely acoustic sense here; any single, continuous chunk of speech, limited by silence (pauses) at both ends, qualified as an utterance. While those pauses usually co-occur with syntactic boundaries, the annotation was not syntactically motivated.

Table 1. The sample sizes and mean durations in milliseconds of the phoneme categories in both corpora (having removed the 10 last phones of each utterance)

	Single-speaker corpus		Multi-speaker corpus	
	Sample size	Mean duration	Sample size	Mean duration
Diphthongs			817	117,4
Long vowels	1456	121,6	649	105,9
Short vowels	15014	65,1	5484	58,6
Long non-plosive consonants	934	91,9	456	85,2
Short non-plosive consonants	11157	60,3	5359	60,7
Long plosives	667	142,4	284	130,0
Short plosives	5043	85,3	2452	74,4

3 Results

The data is shown in the following charts. The positions are on the horizontal axis and the mean durations (absolute values) on the vertical axis. The bold line represents the mean duration of the given phoneme category in, and only in its respective position. The dotted lines represent the confidence limit (level of confidence $p \leq 0.05$). The straight grey line is the mean duration of all phones of the given category, regardless of their position. We considered statistically significant a case in which the entire confidence limit is situated above or below the mean.

The phonologically long sounds, presented as the upper line in the graphs below, have more variation because they are relatively infrequent in Finnish, even when compared to other quantity languages [4]. In our data, the phonologically long speech sounds make up less than 10 % of all sounds [table 1]. The variation occasionally

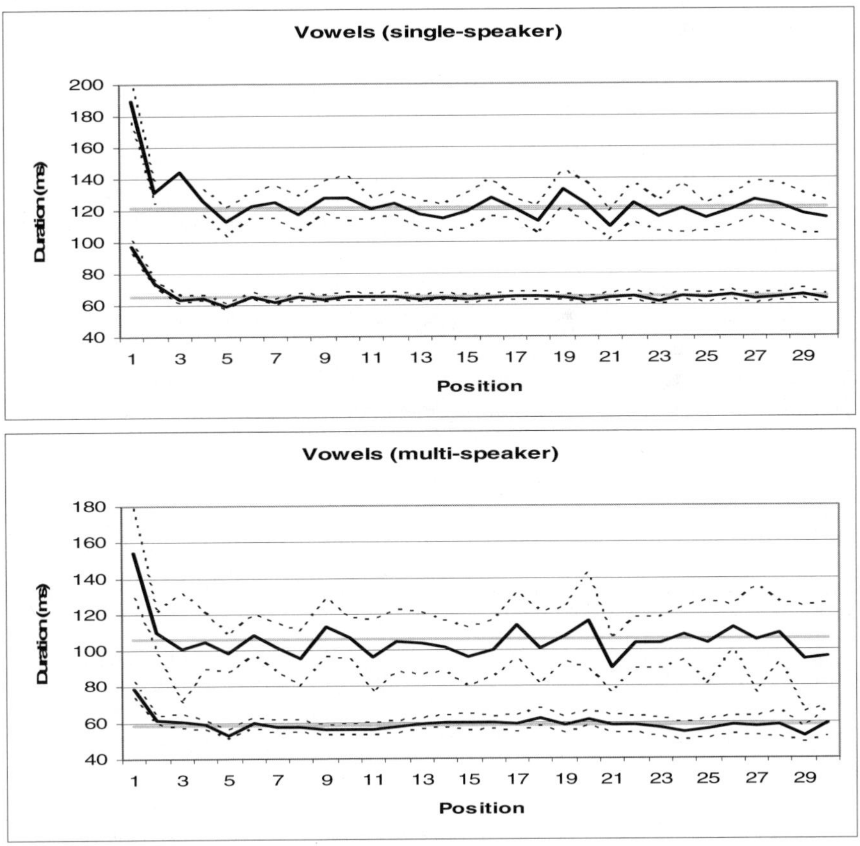

Fig. 1. Short and long vowels. The upper solid lines represent phonologically long sounds.

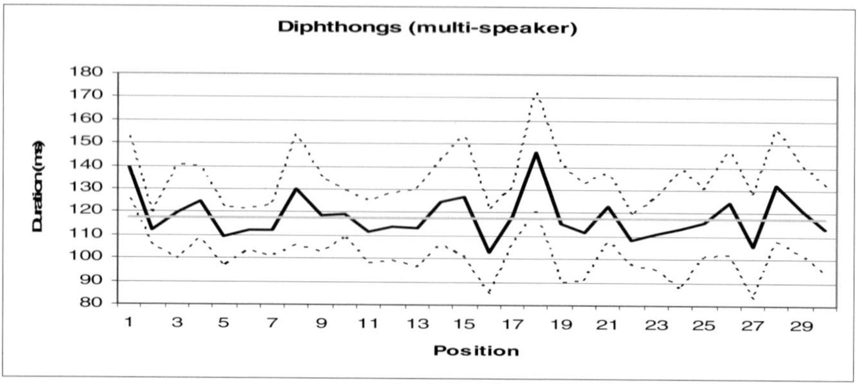

Fig. 2. Diphthongs (not available in the single-speaker corpus)

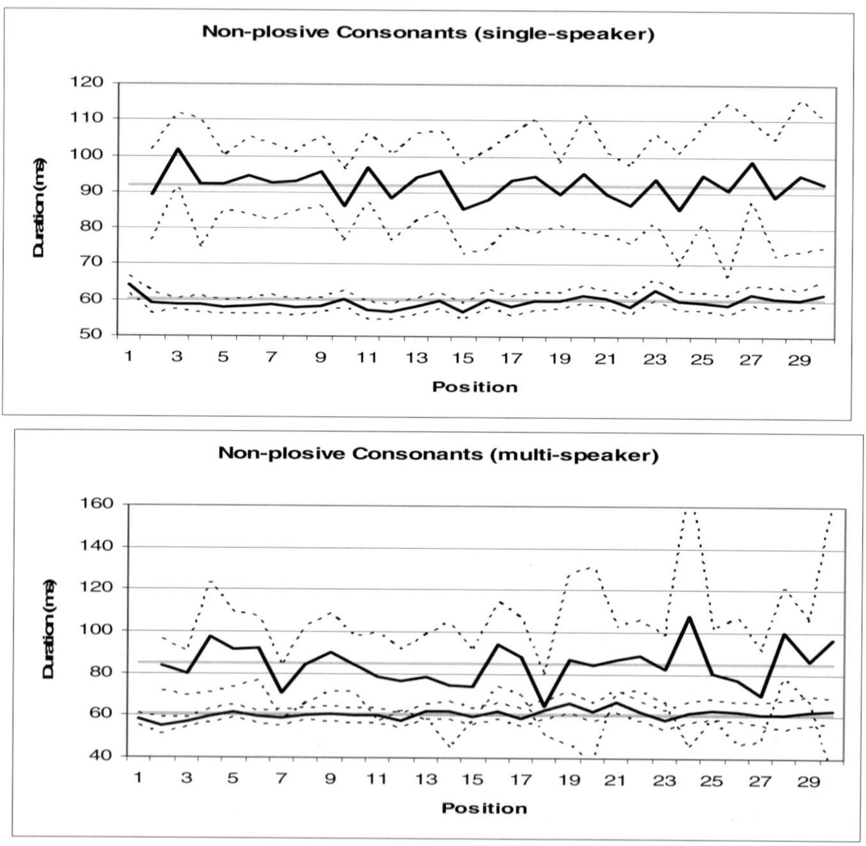

Fig. 3. Non-plosive consonants. The upper solid lines represent phonologically long sounds.

introduces statistically significant points in seemingly haphazard positions, and we will only discuss issues we feel may carry weight. Generally, the figures are more reliable towards the initial position, since the sample size decreases towards the end of the scale. Every utterance in the study is at least one phone long, of course, and therefore contributes to the first position.

Figure 1 shows that vowels, both short and long, are lengthened in the first position in both materials. There is a trace amount of lengthening in the second position, as well. The third position appears longer with long vowels in the single-speaker data, but that is insignificant as there is only one sample of the position (hence the missing level of confidence). The difference between the two materials is most likely due to individual variation.

According to figure 2, diphthongs in the multi-speaker corpus behave in the same fashion as the rest of the vowels. The lengthening is clear in the first position. The diphthongs were annotated only in the multi-speaker corpus, hence the lacking single-speaker figure. A statistically significant lengthening effect also appears in position 18, which we suspect is merely an artifact.

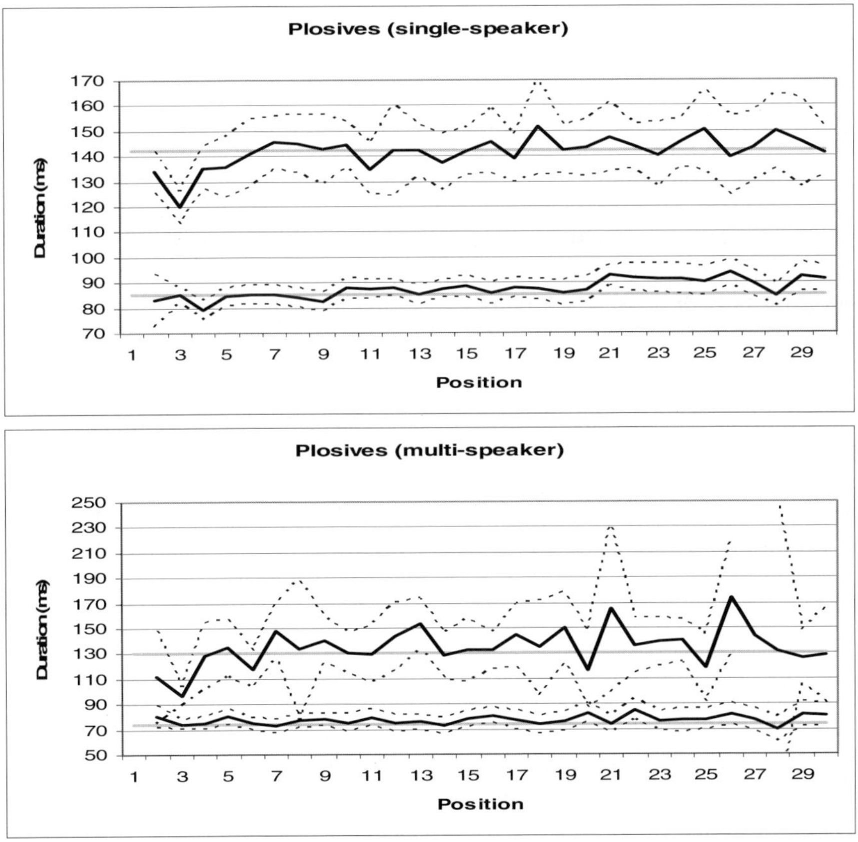

Fig. 4. Plosive consonants. The upper solid lines represent phonologically long sounds.

Figure 3 suggests the short non-plosive consonants are slightly longer in the 1st position in the single-speaker corpus, but not in the multi-speaker corpus. Instead, the short ones are slightly shorter until the 2nd position. We are uncertain whether those minimal deviations are meaningful. The long consonants did not deviate from the average duration significantly. Long consonants, plosives included, have no value in the 1st position; they are invariably geminates occurring in medial positions.

Figure 4 indicates the phonologically long plosives (geminates) were shorter in initial environment. The shortening was strongest in the 3rd position in both materials. The second position is similarly shorter than the mean in both, but lacks statistical significance in the multi-speaker data. The 3rd position corresponds to the boundary between first and the second syllable. The short plosives were not affected significantly.

There are no initial long consonants, and the short plosives were excluded since the majority of them have no reliably discernible duration. We can usually only spot the explosion phase, while the actual onset of articulation remains invisible and inaudible. The 27th position in the multi-speaker data has only one sample and therefore no confidence limit.

4 Discussion

The Finnish language is characterized by a very small phoneme inventory, restrictive phonotactics, and a fixed first-syllable lexical stress. However, a pervasive quantity system (almost doubling the inventory) and long, multi-syllabic words compensate in preventing homophony. The phonological structure makes Finnish different from many other European languages, and has in fact led some to question whether domain-edge processes, such as final lengthening, can be observed in the language. Our work [5] with both corpora clearly indicates Finnish is not exempt. Final lengthening has also been confirmed in Hungarian [7] and Estonian [9], both genetically related quantity languages previously thought not to display lengthening on similar grounds as Finnish.

The stressed syllable (always the first one in Finnish) is generally thought to prescribe longer duration. The lengthening of the vowels in the first position cannot be explained away as a simple stress issue, however. Namely, the second position of a vowel, showing little if any lengthening, corresponds to a consonant-initial first syllable, such as /su.ʊi/ ('summer'). That points toward a boundary process. The applicable structures are either a single-vowel syllable, such as /e.si.ne/ ('an object') or vowel-initial closed syllable /is.ku/ ('an impact'). Furthermore, the lengthening applies to long vowels as well as diphthongs, such as /ei.len/ ('yesterday') and /uː.ti.nen/ ('a piece of news'). We would also expect lengthening of consonants until the 3rd position if we were dealing with lengthening of the stressed syllable. There is nothing of such nature in our data.

Phonologically long plosive consonants are affected in reverse fashion. While they cannot exist word-initially, they occur significantly until the second and the third position. The phonologically long consonants are all voiceless and geminate

(/pː tː kː/); they do not occur within syllables but at syllable boundaries. Expected cases of shortening thus include structures such as /kuk.ka/ ('a flower'), /ilk.ka/, (a given name), /uːt.ta/ ('something new'), and /ap.pi/ ('a father-in-law'). We have not conducted behavioral listening tests, but the acoustic results suggest the shortening does not obscure the phonemic contrast between short and long plosives in these positions. The ratio is narrowed from ~1:1.7 to ~1:1.4 in the single-speaker data, and from ~1:1.7 to ~1:1.3 in the multi-speaker data.

A future investigation would benefit from at least three expansions. The inclusion of a spontaneous or conversational speech corpus is needed to determine whether the effects are style-specific. Examining not categories (vowels, plosives, etc.), but phonemes separately, would be useful, since any lengthening or shortening may have to do with specific articulatory dynamics of certain speech sounds. A simple division into categories may be too crude. Nevertheless, increasing sample sizes would yield more reliable and more easily interpreted results.

It is notable that the two corpora used in this study are very different. The first one has only one speaker reading aloud short passages of text, while the other is a mixture of speakers in various environments with considerably varying speaking rates. The annotation is also conducted independently by different annotators. Still the somewhat unexpected results are congruent between the corpora.

5 Conclusion

Various studies suggest speakers tend to articulate either faster or slower when they begin to speak or carry on speaking having paused. The phenomenon, although not studied to a great extent, has become known as initial lengthening or shortening. We have studied the effect of utterance-initial environment on segmental duration in Finnish. We have established a method of studying segmental duration on the level of individual phones instead of syllables or words. While it does forfeit the advantage of other domains, especially the syllabic structure, it allows us to examine the speakers' behavior in greater detail.

In the light of our current data, initial environment does affect segmental duration in Finnish, but it cannot be described as either initial lengthening or initial shortening. Vowels and phonologically long plosive consonants were significantly affected, but in the opposite manner. Utterance-initial vowels (as opposed to all first-syllable vowels) were lengthened, while long plosives were shortened up until the third syllable. The rest were affected minimally if at all. If the initial environment does shorten certain speech sounds while lengthening the others, the conflicting results from the other languages may be based on biased material and call for a re-evaluation of the methods used. Or, we should accept the asymmetry and recognize that the initial processes are not so uniformly represented in natural languages as final lengthening. Our materials and method showed a combination of the lengthening and shortening, necessitating further studies before we can establish on what principles utterance-initial duration operates in Finnish.

Acknowledgements

This study was funded by the Finnish Funding Agency for Technology and Innovation (TEKES). Our studies in segmental duration are aimed at developing duration modeling for speech synthesis. We would like to thank Professor Martti Vainio (University of Helsinki) for providing us with the single-speaker corpus.

References

1. Campbell, N.: Segmental Elasticity and Timing in Japanese Speech. In Speech Perception, Production, and Linguistic Structure. Y. Tohkura, E.Vatikiotis-Bateson, andY. Sagisaka, Eds. IOS Press (1992) 403-418
2. Chung, H., Gim, G., Huckvale, M.: Consonantal and Prosodic Influences on Korean Vowel Duration. Proceedings of Eurospeech, Vol.2. Budapest, Hungary (1999) 707-710
3. Duez, D.: Acoustic Correlates of Subjective Pauses. Journal of Psycholinguistic Research, Vol. 22(1). (1993) 21-39
4. Greenberg, J.: Language Universals: with Special Reference to Feature Hierarchies. Mouton (1966)
5. Hakokari, J., Saarni, T., Salakoski, T., Isoaho, J., Aaltonen, O.: Determining Prepausal Lengthening for Finnish Rule-Based Speech Synthesis. Proceedings of Speech Analysis, Synthesis and Recognition: Applications of Phonetics (SASR 2005). Krakow, Poland (2005)
6. Hansson, P.: Prosodic Phrasing in Spontaneous Swedish. Academic Dissertation. Travaux de l'institut de linguistique de Lund 43. Lund: Lund University (2003)
7. Hockey, B.A., Fagyal, Zs.: Phonemic Length and Pre-Boundary Lengthening: an Experimental Investigation on the Use of Durational Cues in Hungarian. Proceedings of the XIVth International Congress of Phonetics Sciences, San Francisco (1999) 313-316.
8. Kaiki, N., Takeda, K., Sakisaga, Y.: Statistical Analysis for Segmental Duration Rules in Japanese Speech Synthesis. In proceedings of the 1990 International Conference on Spoken Language Processing. Kobe, Japan (1990) 17-20
9. Krull, D.: Prepausal Lengthening in Estonian: Evidence from Conversational Speech. In Lehiste, I., Ross, J. (eds.), Estonian Prosody: Papers from a Symposium, Proceedings of the International Symposium on Estonian Prosody, Tallinn, Estonia. Tallinn: Institute of Estonian Language (1997) 136-148
10. Nagano-Madsen, Y.: Temporal Characteristics in Eskimo and Yoruba: a Typological Consideration. In Papers from the Sixth Swedish Phonetics Conference. Göteborg (1992)
11. Vainio, M.: Artificial Neural Network Based Prosody Models for Finnish Text-to-Speech Synthesis. Academic dissertation, University of Helsinki. (2001)
12. White, L.S.: English Speech Timing: a Domain and Locus Approach. University of Edinburgh PhD dissertation (2002)
13. Zu, Y., Chen, X.: Segmental Durations of a Labelled Speech Database and its Relation to Prosodic Boundaries. In Proceedings of the 1st International Symposium on Chinese Spoken Language Processing (ISCSLP 1998) (1998)

Selection Strategies for Multi-label Text Categorization

Arturo Montejo-Ráez and Luis Alfonso Ureña-López

Department of Computer Science
University of Jaén, Spain
amontejo@ujaen.es, laurena@ujaen.es

Abstract. In multi-label text categorization, determining the final set of classes that will label a given document is not trivial. It implies first to determine whether a class is suitable of being attached to the text and, secondly, the number of them that we have to consider. Different strategies for determining the size of the final set of assigned labels are studied here. We analyze several classification algorithms along with two main strategies for selection: by a fixed number of top ranked labels, or using per-class thresholds. Our experiments show the effects of each approach and the issues to consider when using them.

1 Introduction

Multi-label text categorization allows a classification were plain text documents are indexed with terms (also referred to as *key-words* or *descriptors*) selected from a controlled vocabulary. A given document can be associated to a variable number of classes at the same time, so we have to decide not only if a class is close enough to the document, but also about the number of them to be selected. Usually, supervised algorithms are trained in order to produce standalone classifiers [15].

Methods proposed for solving this classification case (multiple labels for a single document) are not common, despite the fact that multi-label classifiers can be constructed from binary classifiers (like in the case of the Adaptive Selection of Base Classifiers [11]) or generated using algorithms that rank all classes according to a coherent value (as in the case of the AdaBoost algorithm [14]). Binary classifiers decide between two possible choices: YES/NO answers or two disjoint classes. This is the most common behaviour of well known classifiers, like Support Vector Machines [4], PLAUM [17], Bayesian Logistic Regression [3], while linear classifiers produce values that can be viewed as distances to the class, like for Rocchio, Widrow Hoff and many others [8].

Whatever algorithm we may choose, at the end we need "hard" classification (*yes/no* answers) and if our classifier outputs a value of matching between a document and a class, we can decide whether to assign the document to the category by applying a threshold to the value returned by the classifier. In approaches like the *S-Cut* or the *P-Cut* ([18]) the threshold is a fixed value used

T. Salakoski et al. (Eds.): FinTAL 2006, LNAI 4139, pp. 585–592, 2006.

as decision boundary. Another approach is to apply the limit not on the *classification status value* (that is the reason to also call the previous cut-based approaches *CSV thresholding*), but rather on the number of classes to be assigned to a document. In this case, a fixed number of classes will be attached to each document ([10,18,1]). In this paper we compare two of these strategies for selection of candidate classes: *global ranking* and *local S-cut.*

2 Thresholding Strategies

As pointed out previously, we can reduce any multi-label or multi-class classification to binary problems, where a document is classified as either relevant or not relevant with respect to a predefined topic or class. There are two main straightforward approaches to combine binary decisions to produce a multi-label one:

- *By CSV thresholding.* Each binary classifier will produce a *classification status value*. The final set of automatically assigned classes are those with a CSV over a predefined threshold, i.e. for each classifier, we know if the class will be assigned to the document or not. This approach has the benefit of considering each classifier independent from the rest, therefore we can decide whether to return a label or not as soon as each classifier finishes its computation, which allowes distributed computing. The number of resulting classes for a document is only tuned by adjusting the threshold, but might certainly produce a different number of classes for each document, desirable in many cases. This threshold can be *global* or *local*, i.e. we may have a unique threshold over all the classifiers or a different one per class. A global threshold makes sense only when CSVs are comparable, and that is something that is not always so easy to assert: margin based values are not good indicators of the proximity of a document to a class and, moreover, we may have a different classification algorithm per class. All these problems are not present when using local thresholds.
- *By Ranking.* If we rank all the resulting CSVs and then select only the top N classifiers we can control precisely the number of classes assigned to a document, but we have to wait for all the classifiers to finish to compute the final assignment. Again, comparable CSVs are needed, so the same imposed restrictions found in global thresholding are present here.

The result of binary classifiers will be a sequence of values (margin distances, similarity measures, probabilities, etc.), one per class, that will help us in determining the n most related classes, i.e. the classes that will be the final output of the multi-label classifier for every given document to be categorized. The expected result from a binary classifier is just a *yes* or *no* answer, and to select the final choice the resulting measure of the algorithm must be *thresholded*, that is, compared to a threshold to establish the discrete goodness of the class for the document: if the value is under the threshold, the class is discarded. This threshold is usually called *cut*. The most well known cuts defined in the literature are those ones determined empirically, that is, over evaluation samples to adjust it to the one we hope will provide best performance (Yiming Yang has a nice review of them [20]):

- **R-cut.** This is, simply, directly applied when selecting a set of categories. The t top ranked classes are selected as positive classes, the rest is considered negative (not assigned). This is what we also refer to as *global ranking.*
- **P-cut.** Here, the focus is on documents, rather than on categories. The documents are ranked for a given category, and the k_j top-ranking documents are assigned to the class:

$$k_j = P(c_j) \times x \times m \tag{1}$$

  where
  k_j is the number of documents assigned to category c_j,
  $P(c_j)$ is the prior probability (over the training set) for a document to be member of class c_j,
  m is the total number of classes in the collection, and
  x is a real value that must be tuned to get best global performance (its range is $[0, n]$, being n is the total number of documents in the training set)
- **S-cut.** This threshold is fixed per category, setting the cut that produces the best performance over an evaluation set (i.e. we take the threshold that shows the best value of a predefined evaluation measure, F1 in our case). The difference with respect to the former two is that it is optimized in a per class basis. It does not guarantee that the global optimum for the training set will be reached.

Yang observed that *S-cut* tends to over-fit while *P-cut* performed well on rare categories. Nevertheless, *P-cut* is not applicable in our experiments, since we want to consider each document as an isolated classification problem. Therefore, the *S-cut* strategy is the local threshold to be applied in our experiments and the *R-cut* the global approach to be compared.

3 Experiments and Results

3.1 HEP Corpus and Data Preparation

The HEP corpus[1] is a collection of papers related to *High Energy Physics*, and manually indexed with DESY labels. These documents have been compiled by Montejo-Ráez and Jens Vigen from the CERN Document Server[2] and have motivated intensive study of text categorization systems in recent years [2,10,9,11].

[1] The collection is freely available for academic purposes from `http://sinai.ujaen.es/wiki/index.php/HepCorpus`

[2] `http://cds.cern.ch`

For performing these experiments we have used the TECAT[3] implementation of the adaptive selection algorithm. The corpus used was the *hep-ex* partition of abstracts documents. The keywords have been processed to only consider first-level ones (known in DESY thesaurus as *primary* keywords). Reactions and energy related keywords have been omitted. Abstracts have been processed as follows:

- Punctuation was removed
- Every character was lower-cased
- Stop words were removed
- The Porter stemming algorithm [12] was applied
- Resulting stems were weighted according to the TF.IDF scheme [13]

For the evaluation of experiments, *ten-fold cross validation* [5] was used in order to produce stable results that do not depend on the partitioning of the collection into training, evaluation and test sets. Extensive experiments have shown that this is the best choice to get an accurate estimate. The measures computed are *precision* and *recall*. The F_1 measure (introduced by Rijsbergen [16]) is used as an overall indicator based on the two former ones. Final values are computed using macro-averaging on a per-document basis, rather than the usual micro-averaging over classes. The reason is that if we average by class, rare classes will influence the result as much as the most frequent ones, which will not provide a good estimate on the performance of the multi-label classifier over documents. Since the goal of this study is to focus on automated classification of individual documents, we considered to be far more useful to concentrate on these measurements for our evaluation of the system. More details about these concepts can be found in [15,6,19].

For the rank strategy the number of top classes selected was modified to produce 5 different runs over each base algorithm: {5, 10, 15, 20, 50} were set as the number of classes for each document. Since we wanted to compare it also against the Boolean strategy where all positive class are returned, i.e. thresholds are set to zero, we have in total 12 runs of the multi-label classifier over the corpus. Again, 10-fold cross validation computation was applied.

3.2 Results

We can briefly summarize the results obtained listed in table 1 by graphically presenting them as in figures 1 (for PLAUM algorithm) and 2 (for Rocchio algorithm). As we can see at first sight, the behavior strongly depends on the algorithm used.

These two algorithms differ totally in the approach used: PLAUM is a margin-based one (similar to SVM), and Rocchio is a well known linear classifier. It is clear that, for them both, ranking strategy is in general a bad idea, since precision and recall only converge when the number of classes is 10, due to the fact that precisely the average number of classes per document in the corpus is close to 11.

[3] Available at `http://sinai.ujaen.es/wiki/index.php/TeCat`

Table 1. Performance measures registered for PLAUM and Rocchio algorithms using ranking strategy

n-top ranked	Precision	Recall	F1	Algorithm
all positive	0.472300	0.543758	**0.461417**	Rocchio
S-cut	0.469709	0.541668	0.459714	Rocchio
5	0.255107	0.130831	0.166047	Rocchio
10	0.219876	0.221002	0.212103	Rocchio
15	0.196147	0.290238	0.226044	Rocchio
20	0.175423	0.342289	0.224755	Rocchio
50	0.107944	0.510858	0.174812	Rocchio
all positive	0.697099	0.421487	0.499468	PLAUM
S-cut	0.510057	0.573596	**0.520278**	PLAUM
5	0.703932	0.356124	0.457544	PLAUM
10	0.539713	0.526894	0.516098	PLAUM
15	0.415165	0.597558	0.475219	PLAUM
20	0.332678	0.633238	0.424067	PLAUM
50	0.150648	0.709563	0.244088	PLAUM

When individual thresholds per class are considered (like zero for the *all-positive* results, or the computed S-cut), the behaviour of the multi-label classifier is more robust, showing high values of performance.

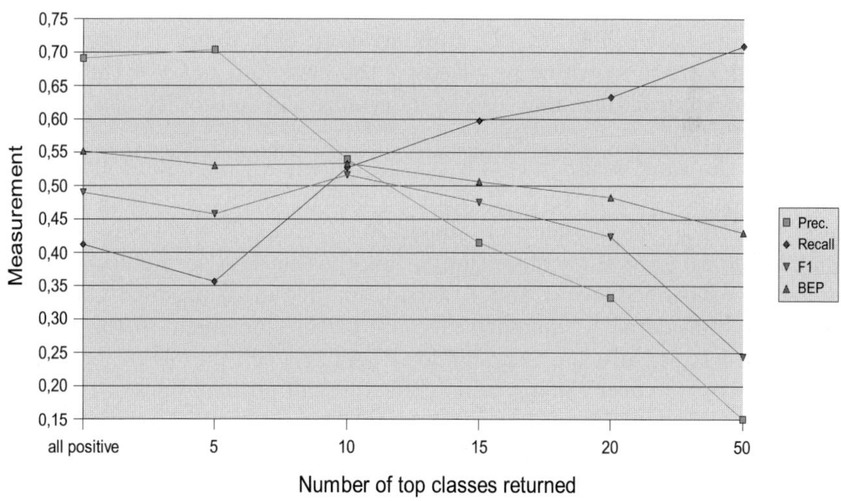

Fig. 1. Rank strategy results for **PLAUM** algorithm

3.3 Conclusions and Open Issues

The main conclusion is straightforward: the rank strategy is not a good solution for merging classifiers predictions into final set of labels as far as it has been

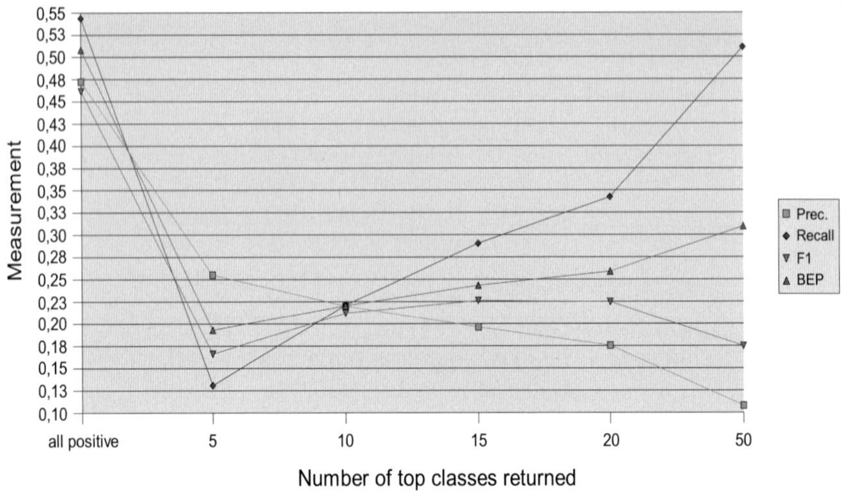

Fig. 2. Rank strategy results for **Rocchio** algorithm

reported by experimental results on this set of data. Although we can control whether precision should be penalized in favor of a higher recall, specifying a fixed set of final classes is not a recommended option. This is due to the fact that we may select classes that were refused by the associated binary classifier, and symmetrically, some classes that were found positive by the originator classifier my be discarded. That is, the rank strategy is a "blind" strategy, since it only consider the CSV value returned by the classifier, but not the internal threshold that the classifier may use to determine the suitability of a class for the document.

Moreover, the rank strategy is only applicable when CSV values are comparable, and that is a very difficult question to answer: even when using the same learning algorithm, the classifier obtained after training it for a class may not be comparable with the same algorithm for another class. Also, some algorithms like margin based ones (SVM and PLAUM, for instance) produce CSVs that could not be considered as distance measure of the document to the class. A maximum on F1 measure is observable for PLAUM when taking 10 top classes. This higher F1 value over the one registered when all positive ones are returned is consequence of the behavior of the PLAUM algorithm, which reports usually higher values of precision than for recall. By taking top 10 classes always (even when some of them may be negative) we are penalizing precision in favor of the recall index, so we register that overall increment in F1 measure.

Anyhow, the decision of when to use zero as threshold or the computation of another value like the S-cut threshold depends on the measure were emphasis has to be placed, that is, S-cut threshold shows a high benefit for recall, but decreases precision (although the overall F1 gets better). Thus, if we may prefer a classifier with high values of precision, then a threshold zero should be taken, or S-Cut could be calculated focusing on improving precision.

All these results are in direct relation with Lewis study on autonomous text classification systems when using binary classifiers [7]. Here, *Probability Ranking Principle for Binary Classifier* does not hold because we are *not* using probabilities, that why our paradigm seems to obey the *Probability Thresholding Principlefor Binary Classification*, because, in this way, we can make an individual decision (therefore, without needing to have comparable CSVs).

This study leaves some aspects opened for further research. We plan to experiment with a global ranking strategy with variable size in the set of final documents, for example, determining a global cut (we could also use S-cut algorithm). Anyhow, it is clear that the problem of this size only appears in multi-label classification tasks, and that it needs more research in order to reach solid strategies. This work identifies that all componentes involved (characteristics of the labels, base algorithm used, importance of precision over recall, etc.) must be considered in the process of determining the final solution to this problem. Also, in order to validate previous conclusions, additional corpora should be considered.

Acknowledgements

This work has been partially supported by the Spanish Government under project R2D2-RIM (TIC2003-07158-C04-04).

References

1. Bruno Pouliquen, Ralf Steinberger, and Camelia Ignat. Automatic Annotation of Multilingual Text Collections with a Conceptual Thesaurus. In A. Todirascu, editor, *Proceedings of the workshop 'Ontologies and Information Extraction' at the EuroLan Summer School 'The Semantic Web and Language Technology'(EUROLAN'2003)*, page 8 pages, Bucharest (Romania), 2003.
2. D. Dallman and J. Y. L. Meur. Automatic keywording of High Energy Physics. In *4th International Conference on Grey Literature : New Frontiers in Grey Literature Washington, DC, USA*, Oct 1999.
3. A. Genkin, D. D. Lewis, and D. Madigan. Large-scale bayesian logistic regression for text categorization. Technical report, Center for Discrete Mathematics and Theoretical Computer Science, 2004.
4. T. Joachims. Text categorization with support vector machines: learning with many relevant features. In C. Nédellec and C. Rouveirol, editors, *Proceedings of ECML-98, 10th European Conference on Machine Learning*, number 1398, pages 137–142, Chemnitz, DE, 1998. Springer Verlag, Heidelberg, DE.
5. R. Kohavi. A study of cross-validation and bootstrap for accuracy estimation and model selection. In *Proc. of the Fourteenth International Joint Conference on Artificial Intelligence*, pages 1137–1145. Morgan Kaufmann, San Mateo, CA, 1995.
6. D. D. Lewis. Evaluating Text Categorization. In *Proceedings of Speech and Natural Language Workshop*, pages 312–318. Morgan Kaufmann, 1991.
7. D. D. Lewis. Evaluating and Optimizing Autonomous Text Classification Systems. In E. A. Fox, P. Ingwersen, and R. Fidel, editors, *Proceedings of the 18th Annual International ACM SIGIR Conference on Research and Development in Information Retrieval*, pages 246–254, Seattle, Washington, 1995. ACM Press.

8. D. D. Lewis, R. E. Schapire, J. P. Callan, and R. Papka. Training algorithms for linear text classifiers. In H.-P. Frei, D. Harman, P. Schäuble, and R. Wilkinson, editors, *Proceedings of SIGIR-96, 19th ACM International Conference on Research and Development in Information Retrieval*, pages 298–306, Zürich, CH, 1996. ACM Press, New York, US.
9. A. Montejo-Ráez. Towards conceptual indexing using automatic assignment of descriptors. Workshop in Personalization Techniques in Electronic Publishing on the Web: Trends and Perspectives, Málaga, Spain, May 2002.
10. A. Montejo-Ráez and D. Dallman. Experiences in automatic keywording of particle physics literature. *High Energy Physics Libraries Webzine*, (issue 5), November 2001. URL: http://library.cern.ch/HEPLW/5/papers/3/.
11. A. Montejo-Ráez, R. Steinberger, and L. A. Ureña-López. Adaptive selection of base classifiers in one-against-all learning for large multi-labeled collections. (3230):1–12, 2004.
12. M. F. Porter. *An algorithm for suffix stripping*, pages 313–316. Morgan Kaufmann Publishers Inc., 1997.
13. G. Salton, A. Wong, and C. S. Yang. A Vector Space Model for Automatic Indexing. Technical Report TR74-218, Cornell University, Computer Science Department, July 1974.
14. R. E. Schapire and Y. Singer. BoosTexter: A boosting-based system for text categorization. *Machine Learning*, 39(2/3):135–168, 2000.
15. F. Sebastiani. Machine learning in automated text categorization. *ACM Comput. Surv.*, 34(1):1–47, 2002.
16. C. J. van Rijsbergen. *Information Retrieval.* London: Butterworths, 1975. http://www.dcs.gla.ac.uk/Keith/Preface.html.
17. L. Y., Z. H., H. R., S.-T. J., and K. J. The perceptron algorithm with uneven margins. In *Proceedings of the International Conference of Machine Learning (ICML'2002)*, 2002.
18. Y. Yang. A study on thresholding strategies for text categorization. In W. B. Croft, D. J. Harper, D. H. Kraft, and J. Zobel, editors, *Proceedings of SIGIR-01, 24th ACM International Conference on Research and Development in Information Retrieval*, pages 137–145, New Orleans, US, 2001. ACM Press, New York, US. Describes RCut, Scut, etc.
19. Y. Yang and X. Liu. A re-examination of text categorization methods. In M. A. Hearst, F. Gey, and R. Tong, editors, *Proceedings of SIGIR-99, 22nd ACM International Conference on Research and Development in Information Retrieval*, pages 42–49, Berkeley, US, 1999. ACM Press, New York, US.
20. Y. Yang and J. O. Pedersen. A comparative study on feature selection in text categorization. In *Proceedings of the Fourteenth International Conference on Machine Learning*, pages 412–420. Morgan Kaufmann Publishers Inc., 1997.

Some Problems of Prepositional Phrases in Machine Translation

Xiaohong Wu, Sylviane Cardey, and Peter Greenfield

Centre de Recherche en Linguistique et traitement automatique des langues Lucien Tesnière
Faculté des Lettres, Université de Franche-Comté, Besançon, France
wuxiaohongfr@yahoo.com.cn,
sylviane.cardey@univ-fcomte.fr,
peter.greenfield@univ-fcomte.fr

Abstract. Prepositions as functional words play an important role in the construction of phrases and sentences. They connect typically a noun or a pronoun to another word and show their relationships in a sentence. They are a kind of "small" word and can not stand alone in the sentences. However, they often pose great problems in the identification of their relationships to other constituents. Prepositional phrase (PP) attachment is especially problematic in machine translation. Besides, as prepositions by themselves are semantically very ambiguous, the translation of these words poses challenge to machine translation (MT) too. This paper discusses how some of the PP attachments and other problems concerned with PPs are resolved in an experimental English-Chinese MT system by applying controlled language technique that we have developed in the context of safety-critical applications. Examples are extracted from a small parallel bilingual corpus focused on medical protocols in English and Chinese, where the usages, in particular some of the syntactic structures, vary a lot in many aspects. It is suggested that such ambiguities can be resolved by means of lexical information, such as subcategorizations, selection constraints and other additional information.

Keywords: prepositional phrase attachment (PP attachment), machine translation (MT), controlled language technique, disambiguation, equivalent, grammatical functions, translation information.

1 Introduction

Prepositional phrase attachment is one of the major sources of ambiguity in English. It poses a great challenge to Machine Translation (MT), especially to systems that translate English to other languages that are less ambiguous in this aspect. The identification of non-predicative PP attachment (noun phrase (NP) attachment or verb phrase (VP) attachment) is one of the major problems to have to be solved at the very beginning of the linguistic analysis since ambiguities might occur if the PP attachment is not well recognized. However, this is not easy. The English PP attachment is problematic not only for MT but for human beings as well. We cite one of the well-known examples to illustrate this problem:

T. Salakoski et al. (Eds.): FinTAL 2006, LNAI 4139, pp. 593 – 603, 2006.

1) *John saw the man with a telescope.*

With such a sentence, two different images might come into our mind:

1 a) John, with his telescope, saw the man; and
b) John saw a man who had a telescope.

How can we disambiguate such kinds of attachment without any indications? Furthermore, how can we make things easier for the machine to perform better facing such a dilemma?

However, this kind of PP attachment ambiguity might not exhibit the same characteristics in another language or it is not or less ambiguous in another language, for example, Chinese. The different interpretations of the above sentence will not show any ambiguity in Chinese as they will be expressed by different syntactic positions. For example, for the first interpretation, the Chinese equivalent is:

1 a) 约翰用望远镜看见了一个人。
(linear sequence of the Chinese literal translation into English: John, with telescope, see, LE(Asp)[1], a GE (CLS)[2] person)

The second interpretation is shown below:

1 b) 约翰看见了一个拿着[3]望远镜的人。
(John, see, LE, a GE, hold telescope, DE (Str)[4], person)

As is shown in the above sentences, in Chinese the positions of PPs in the sentence are different according to which constituent a PP modifies. Generally speaking, in Chinese the adverbial constituents are often placed between the subject and the verb when they modify the verb. So if the prepositional phrase modifies the verb, it will be placed between the subject and the verb (sometimes it can be put at the beginning of the sentence, if it is the focus (or theme) of the discourse, or at the end of the sentence, as additional information; see below). Otherwise the PP will precede directly the noun phrase it modifies (as in 1 b). So the first English interpretation can also be expressed in Chinese as:

1 c) 用望远镜，约翰看见了一个人。(with telescope, John, see, LE, a GE person; *theme*)
1 c) 约翰看见了一个人，用望远镜。(John, see, LE, a GE person, with telescope, *additional information*)

However, never (for 1 b):

---

[1] LE: aspectual word indicating the action of past (also called particle).
[2] CLS: classifier.
[3] Note: the Chinese equivalent for 'with' can have several alternatives, e.g. '有', '带着', etc. We choose '拿着' as correspondence. All of these words refer to 'possession' with minor semantic differences.
[4] DE: structural word indicating the relation between a noun and its pre-posed modifier (also called particle).

1 d) *[5]拿着望远镜，约翰看见了一个（的）人。(holding telescope, John, see, LE a GE, (DE), person)

Or:

1 d) *约翰看见了一个（的）人，拿着望远镜。(John, see, LE, a GE, (DE), person, holding telescope)

If we put the "拿着望远镜" of the second interpretation in front of or at the end of the sentence and separate it with the noun ("人) (as shown in 1 d's), then the meaning of the whole sentence changes. In this case it has almost the same meaning with the first interpretation instead of the intended second one (the Chinese 1d's indicate that John saw the man but not necessarily with the help of the telescope; it states only the fact that John has a telescope in his hand). In fact the second interpretation for (1 d) becomes ambiguous as we are no longer sure who is "*holding the telescope*". Therefore, in Chinese the position of the PP in the sentence plays an extremely important role in transferring the intended meanings of such kind of constituents. As they are assigned in different positions, they do not show the same ambiguity as that seen in the English sentence. Let us take one more example to demonstrate this:

2 a) 我在花园里看见了一个女孩。(I, in the garden, see, LE, a GE (CLS) girl)

I saw a girl in the garden (I saw her when I was in the garden).

b) 我看见一个女孩在花园里。 (I, see LE, a GE girl, in the garden)
I saw a girl in the garden (I saw a girl who was in the garden).

The deep syntactic structure of the example (1 b and 2 b) is similar to that of the English syntactic structure shown below:

3) *We elected him president.*

The subjects of the above sentences are "I" and "we" respectively, and the objects "a girl" and "him" are also the logical subject of "in the garden" and "president". Usually the constituents which are semantically related are placed together in the sentence and by doing so, the Chinese language successfully avoids a lot of these ambiguities and also other kinds of ambiguities.

2 Finding the Problems

We are working on an experimental English-Chinese MT system applied in the safety critical domain of medicine by introducing controlled language techniques [1] and [2]. For this purpose, we construct a small parallel bilingual corpus for the purpose of extracting a domain-specific lexicon and designing a controlled language rule set. Our texts are selected from two sub-domains, of which one is on

---

[5] *: here the asterisk does not mean that the sentences are ungrammatical, but means that they are confusing and do not convey the intended interpretation.

echinoccocosis, a kind of transmissible disease shared by animals and humans (clinical practice); and the other is on molecular cloning (laboratory practice). To narrow down the linguistic difficulties, we focus on the linguistic analysis of protocols of these two sub-domains so that we do not need to face all kinds of linguistic phenomena. We first choose the types of protocols to work with and then we carefully study the general structure of the protocols from which we construct a small lexicon of more than two thousand domain-specific words. We also build a unification-based grammar for this small system. In respect of the problem of PP attachment we first do a statistical study to the frequency of occurrence of each preposition in the sentences in order to identify and compare its usages, for example how a preposition is used in the sentence in both languages and how many kinds of semantic meanings it may convey. This work is very important as it provides important raw data for further decision making on the constraints of the PP attachments. Our findings show that these protocols show a high degree of homogeneity in both textual structure and sentence typology. The lexical usages also show a high conformity throughout the sample examples. One of the most important features is that both the sentential structures and lexical usage are very repetitive. This characteristic makes it easier to identify the possible problems that we have to deal with. We finally classify the prepositions or prepositional phrases into limited types and list the ambiguous structures separately so that a better solution can be found to tackle these problems by comparing them in both languages.

As we have mentioned in the first section, Chinese PP structures show less or sometimes no ambiguity than that of the English PPs in some cases. However, we find other problems in the Chinese equivalents for English prepositions which are caused by the complex nature of the Chinese preposition itself. Most Chinese prepositions come from verbs (classical Chinese) and they exhibit many of the characteristics of verbs. In some cases it is hard to tell the real grammatical status of a Chinese equivalent for a particular English preposition. This fact can be reflected from some of the arguments once held by different linguists. Whilst most linguists agree that the Chinese language has prepositions, there were others who argued that the Chinese language did not possess prepositions (the same disagreement on whether Chinese language really has ‘parts of speech’, [3]). This suggests that some of the Chinese prepositions can be used both as a verb or a preposition. This is not at all the case of English prepositions. The Chinese prepositions which can also function as verbs are sometimes called ‘coverbs’ (literally: sub-verbs) which can stand alone as main verbs. For example, in the above example, the Chinese equivalent for (1 b), for the English prepositional phrase ‘with a telescope’, is “<u>拿着</u>望远镜”. The word “拿着” can be used as a verb, for example,

4) 他手里<u>拿着</u>一本书。(he, hand, in, take a BEN (ClS[6]) book)
He takes a book in his hand.

In this sentence the word “<u>拿着</u>” is typically a verb functioning as the predicate of the sentence. Syntactically, we will not see any differences from this “<u>拿着</u>一本书”

---

[6] ClS: classifier.

and the above "拿着望远镜". They both share the same syntactic structure and both can be considered as the 'verb + object' formation. However, they do not share the same grammatical functions in the above sentences. In (1 b) the "拿着望远镜" functions as a pre-posed modifier of the noun '人' (person); but in (4), the "拿着一本书" functions as the predicate of the sentence. The problem here is what should the true grammatical category of the "拿着" in Chinese be, a verb or a preposition, or both? Furthermore, if we call a word which exhibits these properties a 'coverb', what is the true grammatical status of a 'coverb' and how do we differentiate it for MT?

Further examination of the above sentences (1 a) and (1 b) shows that the same preposition does not have the same lexical equivalents in the target language (TL) and different words might share the same Chinese characters in the TL. This phenomenon, being another feature of prepositions (prepositions are polysemous by nature), produces an extra difficulty for MT. For example, in the example (1 a), the first interpretation of the preposition "*with*" takes "用" as its equivalent in the TL; but the second interpretation for the same preposition "*with*" has "拿着" as its equivalent. Furthermore, in example (4), the same word "拿着" becomes a verb and has a verb as its correspondence in English. Multiple parts-of-speech and polysemy intersect with the same lexical item.

Three major kinds of problems are thus shown here (there are still other problems, e.g. the English PP takes a bare NP correspondence in Chinese, etc. but they will not be discussed here): first, how to disambiguate the English PP attachments when ambiguity occurs; second, how to define the grammatical functions of some of the Chinese prepositions if they share the status of both a preposition and a verb; and third, how the different kinds of translation information can be linked to the same preposition or even the same translation information to different words without causing any problems?

3 Solutions

3.1 English PP Attachment Disambiguation

Ambiguities concerned with PP attachments often occur when a structure contains a verb plus an NP object and then is followed by a prepositional phrase as is already shown in the above examples. Many methods have been proposed for the disambiguation of such kinds of English PP attachments; see for example in [4], [5]. In our corpus we have observed other phrases including NPs such as "*Preparation of Plasmid DNA by Alkaline Lysis with SDS*" where the head noun is derived from a verb and thus still keeps some of the features of a verb, for example having objects and/or PP adjuncts. To minimize the possible ambiguities, in our work the ambiguities of PP attachments are resolved mainly in the following carefully controlled ways:

- **The preposition is first constrained semantically by limiting the types of NP complement it can take**
- **Some complicated PP structures are proscribed**
- **If the preposition is used in a fixed collocation, it is treated with the word with which it is connected**

We now describe these three ways that we have devised for the resolution of PP attachment ambiguities and other problems.

The preposition is first constrained semantically by limiting the types of NP complement it can take

Working in a relatively narrow domain, we profit from the fact that both syntactic structures and lexical items are used narrowly. We observe that some prepositions are much less ambiguous than when they are used in general texts where they might be used much more broadly. Our first solution to tackle the PP attachment problem is to restrict the selection of NP complement. In this way, some of the PP attachment problems can be semantically excluded. In other words, from the semantic content that a preposition carries we can easily exclude them being a NP/VP attachment, for example,

5) *Preparation of Plasmid DNA by Alkaline Lysis with SDS*

In this complicated noun phrase, the prepositional phrases "*by Alkaline Lysis*", and "*with SDS*" might be wrongly attached to the immediate preceding nouns, in particular the second PP. In our work, the preposition 'by' is restricted to no more than two usages and both take a NP complement in which the head noun is related to a kind of 'action', thereby, a phrase starting with "by" can only be an adjunct of either the verb of the sentence or the head noun of a nominal phrase (usually a noun derived from a verb, or a noun which implies 'action'). Furthermore, in this phrase the head noun "*Lysis*" does imply an action, so the first "*by*" PP is the adjunct of the '*preparation*' rather than "*Plasmid DNA*". For the second phrase "*with SDS*", first, similar processing is applied. The preposition '*with*' is restricted to have a NP complement indicating an instrument, a material, or a method. In other words, it is also assigned an adjunct role. Besides, with the subcategorization information, we can deduce that the derived noun "*preparation*" can have another complement with a prepositional head "*with*" as its verb framework shows: "prepare something with something else". Thus the second PP is excluded from being wrongly attached to the preceding NP "*Alkaline Lysis*".

Some complicated structures of a PP are proscribed

In our work, the PPs are framed to function more as adjuncts of the head word, with the PP headed by "of" as an exception. The "of" structure in our work modifies always its preceding noun, for example,

6) *PAIR for the treatment of hydatid cysts of liver*

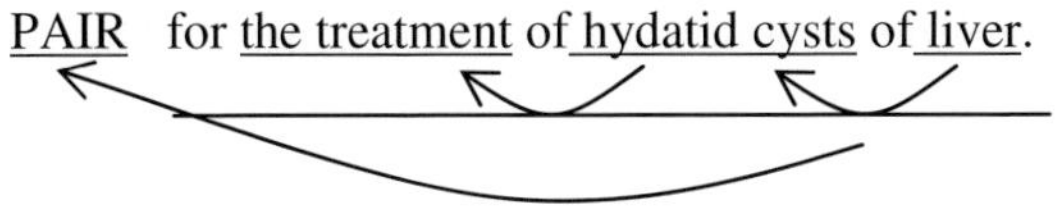

Take again example 5), unlike the preceding example 6):

Preparation of Plasmid DNA by Alkaline Lysis with SDS

in which both 'by' and 'with' phrases are related to the head noun of 'preparation' with only the 'of' phrase connected with its preceding noun which is also 'preparation' but implies a different semantic content.

Traditionally, a preposition is defined as a word that governs and normally precedes a noun or pronoun to express the latter's relation to another word in a sentence. Again, traditionally, it is considered that a preposition takes an NP as its complement. However, some researchers argue that much evidence can be found where a PP can take as a complement other phrases rather than only NP. See in the example cited from [6]

7 a) *The magician emerged from behind the curtain (PP).*
b) *I didn't know about it until recently (AdvP).*
c) *We can't agree on whether we should call in the police. (Interrogative clause)*
d) *They took me for dead (AdjP).*

Besides, some researchers declare that a preposition can accept some adverbs (for example, very much, just right) as modifiers. Examples can be seen below [6]:

8 a) *She seems very much in control of things*
b) *It happened just inside the penalty area.*

And even with NP modifiers:

9) *She died two years after their divorce.*

In our work, the above examples (7) and (8) are not allowed and (9) is treated differently. The '*two years*' are treated as a bare NP instead of as a PP modifier.

If the preposition is used in a fixed collocation, it is treated with the word with which it is connected

This is concerned again with the subcategorization framework which is quite powerful for the disambiguation of PP attachments. The grammatical complements and syntactic functions of a preposition should be judged by its specific usage, together with some necessary semantic analysis. Prepositions are mostly used to indicate the relationships of direction, location, manner, purpose, cause, time and so on. These kinds of semantic information can differentiate many of the grammatical functions of PPs for disambiguation, for instance, whether a prepositional phrase functions as an adverbial adjunct or as an attributive can only be detected through grammatical and semantic analysis. In addition, some words, in particular verbs, idiosyncratically select prepositional phrases as their complements. This is very useful in detecting the ambiguities in Verb + NP + PP structures, for example:

10) *Obtain informal oral informed-consent from the patient.*
11) *Puncture the cyst with the needle under US guidance.*
12) *Pour 1.5 mL of the culture into a microfuge tube.*

The same method can be applied to derived nominal phrases, such as:

13) *Preparation of Plasmid DNA by Alkaline Lysis with SDS*
14) *Plasmid DNA is isolated from small-scale (1-2 mL) bacterial cultures by treatment with alkali and SDS.*

In example (14), the final PP "with alkali and SDS" might be wrongly considered as the adjunct of the main verb "isolate" if this information is missing. This kind of information is defined in our lexicon as one of the properties of the lexical item, for example,

15) Perform V, (↑PRED) = 'perform 1 < (↑SUBJ) (↑OBJ)>'
V, (↑PRED) = 'perform 2 < (↑SUBJ) (↑OBJ) (↑OBL 'with')>'

This formula means that the verb "perform" can be used in two ways, either having a subject and an object as its arguments, or having a subject, an object and another object with a prepositional head "with" as its arguments.

3.2 The Grammatical Functions of Chinese PPs

In Chinese the major grammatical function of the preposition is that of acting as an adverbial adjunct [7]. However, we can find many PP-like structures which superficially take up the positions of other grammatical constituents, for example, the subject, the predicate, the attributive etc., and almost all of them correspond to an English prepositional phrase. Compare the following pairs of sentences:

16 a) 桌子上有一本书。(table, on, have, a, BEN(Cls), book) (There is a book on the table. *subject*)
b) 她把书放在桌子上。(she, BA[7], book, put, table, on) (She put the book on the table. *adjunct*)

17 a) 这栋大楼面朝北。(this building, face, to, north) (This building faces to the north/north. *predicate*)
b) 我们朝北走。(we, to north, walk) (We walk toward north. *adjunct*)

18 a) 他在教室里。(he, in, classroom) (He is in the classroom. *predicate*)
b) 他坐在教室里。(he, sit, in, classroom) (He sits in the classroom; *adjunct*)

---

[7] BA: refers to a special structure called 'BA construction' in Chinese. The BA is considered as a preposition with which the object of the verb is put before the verb. It is thus also referred to as marker of the patient.

19 a) 我看到了在他房间里的那个人。(I, see, LE, in, his room, DE, that person; I saw the person in his room; *attributive*)

b) 我在他房间里看见了她。(I, in his room, see, LE, she; I saw her in his room; *adjunct*)

All the constituents underlined in the Chinese sentences (group a) superficially share the same syntactic structures with the sentences in (group b). Furthermore, we can see that though in the Chinese sentences these structures take up the positions of different grammatical functions, their correspondences in English are all prepositional phrases. This suggests that English PPs have to be represented by Chinese words of different grammatical categories (verbs or prepositions) in different positions of the sentence. This can become a big problem if their grammatical status is not well represented.

In our work, the grammatical functions of the preposition we have observed are mostly concerned with the prepositional phrases being post-posed modifiers of a noun in English (corresponding to Chinese pre-posed attributives), for example:

20) *Lumbar puncture needles for percutaneous puncture*
用于经皮穿刺*的*腰穿针 (a PP correspondence in Chinese)

21) *Safety and reliability of PAIR*
PAIR*的安*全性和可靠性 (a noun correspondence in Chinese)

When these English PPs are transferred into Chinese equivalents, one important feature is that between these phrases and the head noun, a structural particle 'DE *的*' should be added. Another feature is that almost all of the post-posed SL PP modifiers of a noun have to be moved to the front of the head noun in Chinese (but the linear sequence might differ according to the semantic contents and the modification relationships). It is also the same case for English relative clauses. When English relative clauses are translated into Chinese, they are either translated as pre-posed attributives of nouns or they are translated into different sentences in Chinese (if the relative clause is too long or structurally complicated). For example:

22) *Portable ultrasound equipment that has a 3.5 – 5 MHz probe*
带有一根3.5－5 MHz探头的便携式B超设备

In addition, the English preposition which can function both as a preposition and as a verb in a Chinese sentence is 'with' signifying "contain", "possess" or "have" etc. in our corpus, for example:

23) *Portable ultrasound equipment with a 3.5 – 5 MHz probe*
带有一个3.5－5 MHz 探头的便携式超声设备

In this phrase, the correspondence of the preposition 'with' is '带有' which can be used as a verb in Chinese, for instance:

24) 这张桌子带有两个抽屉。(this table, take, two drawer) (This table has two drawers.)

To avoid possible confusion in both languages, what we suggest is to change the 'with' structure of this kind in the source language to a relative clause:

Portable ultrasound equipment <u>that has</u> a 3.5 – 5 MHz probe

3.3 Translation Information

As we have mentioned in the above sections, the preposition is by nature polysemous. Furthermore, very often there is no one-to-one correspondence for a particular preposition in two languages. We take a few simple examples to illustrate this problem. The nearest Chinese equivalent of the English preposition "*in*" (indicating location) in many cases is "在 … （里）", as in "*in the house*" (在房子里); "*in the school*" (在学校里); "*in China*" (在中国); however, "*in bed*" does not correspond to "*[8]在床里", as "*in bed*" can have two possible interpretations: one refers to "*somebody lies in bed*", and the other might imply "somebody *is asleep*". The best Chinese correspondences should be "在床上" (*on bed*) and "在睡觉" (*is sleeping*) respectively. Another similar example is the English expression "*in the sun*" as in "*We lie in the sun"*. If we translate this sentence literally into Chinese as "*我们躺<u>在</u>太阳<u>里</u>", it will sound not only ridiculous, but also impossible. Nobody could lie within the territory of the burning star. The best translation in Chinese should be "我们躺<u>在</u>太阳<u>底下</u>" (Literally: *We lie <u>under</u> the sun*).

This reveals the problems of many-to-one or one-to-many correspondences in the target language (TL). In our case, we constrain the possible semantic meanings of a preposition to limited kinds in order to avoid this problem. This means that controlled translation information is assigned to every individual preposition in the source language (SL) if it has a correspondence in the target language. For instance, the preposition "by" is limited to have an NP complement expressing an action (suggested structure: *by doing something*), and we assign a fixed equivalent in Chinese as "通过". So whenever "by" is used, it has to satisfy this criterion and it will always be translated into "通过" in Chinese, for example:

25) *Remove the medium <u>by aspiration</u>.*
<u>通过抽吸</u>除去培养基。

26) *Resuspend the bacterial pellet in 100µl of ice-cold Alkaline-lysis-solution-I <u>by vigorous vortexing</u>.*
<u>通过剧烈振荡</u>，将细菌重新悬浮在100 µl冰冷的碱裂解液I中。

Similar processing is applied to the other prepositions too. For example, the preposition "at" can be used in two ways in our domain, one is to have an NP complement expressing temperature and the other is speed. We see this in the following examples:

27) *Centrifuge the bacterial lysate in a microfuge for 5 minutes <u>at maximum speed</u> <u>at 4°C</u>.*
<u>于4°C以最大转速</u>在一微量离心机中离心细菌裂解物5分钟。

---

[8] *: here * means ungrammatical.

28) *Leave the mixture for 2 minutes at room temperature.*
于室温下放置混合物2分钟。

In these two examples, we assign two different Chinese equivalents (one-to-many correspondence) to the English preposition "at", of which one is for the temperature "于 … (下)", and the other is for the speed "以".

Besides the above mentioned problems we still find some other complex and tricky problems related to the prepositions and which can not be easily resolved with the above mentioned methods. More sophisticated ways have to be designed to solve such problems.

4 Conclusions

This paper has discussed some of the problems concerned with the prepositions and prepositional phrases which are observed in a small corpus of medical protocols. The problems detected are also based on the comparison of the usages in both the source language – English and the target language – Chinese. Some methods are suggested on how they can be initially tackled for better MT performance in order that the English PPs can be correctly translated into the target language. Though the complexity of PPs is tricky and hard to solve with the limited methods that we have described, however, with the help of the controlled language technique that we have developed in the context of safety-critical applications, the problems can be greatly reduced and further smoothed away little by little.

References

1. Wu, X.: Controlled Language – A Useful Technique to Facilitate Machine Translation of Technical Documents. In: Lingvisticæ Investigationes 28:1, John Benjamins Publishing Company, ISSN 0378-4169 / E-ISSN 1569-9927 (2005) 123-131
2. Cardey, S.,Greenfield, P.,Wu, X.: Designing a Controlled Language for the Machine Translation of Medical Protocols: the Case of English to Chinese. In: Proceedings of the AMTA 2004, LNAI 3265, Springer-Verlag, ISBN 3-540-23300-8 (2004) 37-47
3. Guo, R, 郭锐: "现代汉语词类研究 (The Study of the Parts-of-Speech of Modern Chinese Language)", 商务印书馆 ISBN 7-100-03621-6/H-920 (2002)
4. Saint-Dizier, P.: PrepNet: a Framework for Describing Prepositions: Preliminary Investigation Results. In: IWCS06, Tilburg, NL, 7 janvier 9 janvier 2005. Harry Bunt (Eds.), Univ. of Tilburg (2005) 145-157
5. Volk, M.: Exploiting the WWW as a corpus to resolve PP attachment ambiguities. In: Proceedings of Corpus Linguistics 2001, Lancaster: March 2001 (2001)
6. Huddleston, R., Pullum, G.K.: The Cambridge Grammar of the English Language. Cambridge University Press. ISBN 0 521 43146 8 (2002)
7. Zhou, J., Pu, K.: 周靖, 濮侃: "现代汉语 (Modern Chinese)", 华东师范大学出版社, ISBN 7135 104 (1985)

Speech Confusion Index (Ø): A Recognition Rate Indicator for Dysarthric Speakers

Prakasith Kayasith[1, 2], Thanaruk Theeramunkong[1], and Nuttakorn Thubthong[3]

[1] School of Information and Computer Technology, Sirindhorn International Institute of Technology (SIIT), Thammasat University, Klong Luang, Pathumthani 12121, Thailand
p.kayasith@nectec.or.th, thanaruk@siit.tu.ac.th
[2] Assistive Technology Center, National Electronics and Computer Technology Center (NECTEC), Thailand Science Park, Klong Luang, Pathumthani 12120, Thailand
[3] Acoustics and Speech Research Laboratory (ASRL), Department of Physics, Faculty of Science, Chulalongkorn University, Bangkok 10330, Thailand

Abstract. This paper presents an automated method to help us assess speech quality of a dysarthric speaker, instead of traditional manual methods that are laborious and subjective. The assessment result can also be a good indicator for predicting the accuracy of speech recognition that the speaker can benefit from the current speech technology. The so-called *speech confusion index (Ø)* is proposed to measure the severity of speech disorder. Based on the dynamic time wrapping (DTW) technique with adaptive slope constraint and accumulate mismatch score, Ø is developed as a measure of difference between two speech signals. Compared to the manual methods, i.e. articulatory and intelligibility tests, the proposed indicator was shown to be more predictive on recognition rate obtained from HMM and ANN. The evaluation was done in terms of three measures, *root-mean-square difference*, *correlation coefficient* and *rank-order inconsistency*. The experimental results on the control set showed that Ø achieved better prediction than both articulatory and intelligibility tests with the average improvement of 9.56% and 7.86%, respectively.

1 Introduction

Dysarthria is a term given to a group of speech disorder in which the transmission of messages controlled by the motor movements for speech is interrupted. Our research assumption is that for a certain dysarthric speaker, if his/her familiar communication partner can recognize (or learn to recognize) his/her speech, some modern speech processing techniques (i.e., speech recognition) should be able to learn to recognize those patterns as well. Several previous studies [1- 4] showed some advantages of incorporating a speech recognition system into assistive devices for dysarthric speakers. Due to the fact that there is high variety in dysarthric speech, it is impossible to build a general recognition system that can handle well on all types of dysarthric speech. A system needs to be tailored (or trained) in order to match with

T. Salakoski et al. (Eds.): FinTAL 2006, LNAI 4139, pp. 604 – 615, 2006.

individual condition. However, training a system is a time-consuming task. Towards this problem, it is necessary to develop a method to preliminarily indicate whether an individual dysarthria could benefit from such technologies or not.

Nowadays, there are two common tests for speech assessments based on speech-perceptual analysis. The articulatory test has been widely used as a clinical tool relied on perceptions of clinicians (speech therapist or pathologist). The main objective of the assessment is to specify a level of severity and to diagnose errors of dysarthric speech. Since the results of the test mainly depend on the clinicians' knowledge and experience about the disorder assessed, the test is very subjective. Therefore, it is necessary to consider the standardization and the reliability of this method, especially when it is performed by clinicians who may have different common knowledge and training [5].

The intelligibility test, the other standard assessment, is performed by a group of normal non-hearing impaired listeners rather than some speech specialists or trained listeners. The main objective of the test is to measure the level of understanding between a speaker and a listener. Therefore the absolute correctness (or clearness) of a speech done by the speaker is not important as long as the message (or information) of the speaker can be understood by the listener. The results of the test come from the average value of all assessments done by the listeners.

Although both articulatory and intelligibility tests are commonly used in many aspects, they are labor-intensive and subjective to human perception. This paper presents an automatic method where an assessment indicator called *speech confusion index (Ø)*, is developed to predict a possibly outcome performance of those alternative speech technologies without those laborious pre-processing processes. The performance of the indicator is compared with two standard assessments based on three measures, i.e., *root-mean-square difference* (Δ_{rms}), *correlation coefficient* (R^2), and *rank-order inconsistency* (*ROI*).

In the rest of this paper, conceptual idea and mathematical terms of those key steps are presented in section 2. The experimental details including characteristics of subjects, speech corpuses, and evaluation methods are shown in section 3. Section 4 and section 5 describe discussion and conclusion, respectively.

2 Speech Confusion Index (Ø)

To simplify the process of speech assessment, it is necessary to invent an automated process that gives us some outputs to indicate the quality of a speech. For this purpose, *speech confusion index* (Ø) is proposed to measure a distinctive property of one's speech by means of grouping. Basically, the Ø of a speaker is defined as the probability in which an utterance (e.g. word pronunciation) done by the speaker may be placed in probably one or more wrong sound-groups produced by that speaker. In one of our previous works [8], a severity of dysarthria was measured by a ratio of similarity to dissimilarity of speech signal. In this paper presents an alternative way by applying a grouping method to severity evaluation. The value of Ø represents a chance that an input speech could be mis-grouped. If Ø is high (high confusion), the severity is high and the recognition rate is expected to be low (and vise versa). To obtain the index Ø, it is necessary to perform the following four major steps, i.e., feature extraction, feature comparison, group representative selection, and confusion index calculation.

In feature extraction, a signal is divided into a sequence of smaller frames (typically 25 ms width). Let X be a speech signal that is divided into a sequence of frames. Each frame is encoded into a standard feature vector. While the definition of features is arbitrary in general, this work applied the standard Mel-Frequency Cepstral Coefficient (MFCC) since it is widely used in speech recognition. In the feature comparison process, we need to cope with the problem of time variation of speech samples. For this purpose, a modified technique of dynamic time wrapping (DTW) [6-7] with adaptive slope constraint and accumulated mismatch score is applied to measure difference between speech signals. To cope with the representative selection and the confusion index calculation, the method starts with choosing a representative for each group, and then calculates a group boundary for each word's group. The representative template for each word w (T^w) is chosen by selecting a sample from m utterances of the same word w (each speaker would be asked to speak the same word m times). The selection criterion is to choose the utterance with the minimum sum of distances away from the others, as shown in equation (1). The difference between the ith and j^{th} samples (X_i^w and X_j^w) of a word w, denoted by $DTW[X_i^w, X_j^w]$, is calculated by the DTW technique with Euclidean's distance for frame comparison. A group boundary (b_w), for the word w, is defined as an average distance of all utterances within that word, as shown in equation (2).

$$T^w = \arg\min_{X_i^w}\Big(\sum_{j=1}^{m} DTW[X_i^w, X_j^w]\Big) \tag{1}$$

$$b_w = \frac{1}{{}^mC_2}\sum_{i=1}^{m}\sum_{j=i+1}^{m} DTW[X_i^w, X_j^w] \tag{2}$$

Next, for every template, the distance between templates is calculated and filled into a distance matrix (D), where $D_{ij} = DTW[T^i, T^j] = D_{ji}$. The grouping criterion is defined by a threshold function (δ):

$$\delta(a,b) = \begin{cases} 1 & \text{if } a \le b \\ 0 & \text{otherwise} \end{cases} \tag{3}.$$

Taking into account of n groups, the *confusion index* (Ø) is defined as a ratio of mis-grouped probability in which a template could be placed in any wrong groups (probably more than one group), as shown in equation (4).

$$\varnothing = \frac{1}{n^2}\sum_{i=1}^{n}\sum_{j=1}^{n}\delta(D_{ij}, b_j) \tag{4}$$

Clearly, the value of Ø varies between 0 and 1, representing the probability of mis-grouping (or overlapping) of a signal in the data set. It equals 0 when speech signals of different words are highly distinctive and then there is no confusion among words.

On the other hand, the Ø reaches its maximum value of 1 when the confusion among words becomes the highest. In other words, all data are overlapped to each others. Its inverted value (1–Ø), therefore, represents non-overlapping probability of words uttered by a speaker. The hypothesis of this work bases on the assumption that a speaker who has a low (high) value of Ø should have a high (low) value of speech recognition rate.

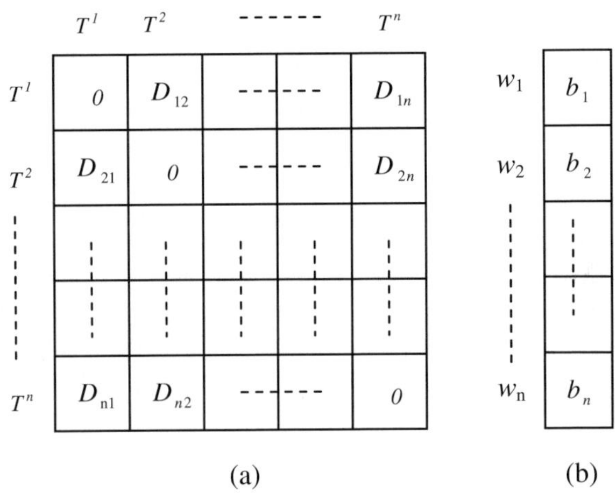

Fig. 2.1. (a) Distance matrix (D) and (b) a group boundary for each group

3 The Experiments

3.1 The Subjects

To evaluate our method, a speech corpus of sixteen speakers had been constructed from eight CP-Dysarthric children, (7 – 14 years old), and eight normal speakers including four adults (23 – 36 years old) and four children (7 – 12 years old). The corpus was created with the balance set of males and females. All CP-Dysarthric children were recruited from the Srisungwan compulsive school, a school for children with disabilities. The selection criteria are to select cerebral palsied children who had dysarthric speech, hearing acuity within normal range, and had no mental retardation problem (IQ more than 70 or above). The details of the dysarthric speakers and the evaluations of severity by an articulatory test (**Arti**) and intelligibility test (**Intel**) are presented in Table 3.1 and Table 3.2.

All dysarthric speakers have been evaluated by two standard methods. The first assessment (an articulatory test) had been done by two experts. The test consists of 68 target words from the control set, which included all basic Thai phonemes. A severity measurement criterion is considered from "Percentage of Correct Phoneme (PCP)" which is a modification of "Percentage of Consonant Correct (PCC)" presented in [9-10]. The PCP was calculated in the following manner.

$$PCP = \frac{Number\ of\ correctly\ pronounced\ phonemes}{Total\ number\ of\ tested\ phonemes} \times 100.$$

Table 3.1. Cerebral palsy children's demographic and characteristics

Code	Age	Sex	Cerebral Palsy	Dysarthria
DF01	11	F	Athetoid	Hypokinetic
DF02	12	F	Flaccid	Flaccid
DF03	7	F	Spactic Diplegia	Spastic
DF04	12	F	Athetoid	Hypokinetic
DM01	12	M	Spastic Diplegia	Spastic
DM02	13	M	Athetoid	Hypokinetic
DM03	10	M	Athetoid	Hypokinetic
DM04	14	M	Athetoid	Hypokinetic

The second assessment (an intelligibility test) had been done by twelve non-hearing impaired listeners. The test consists of three sessions; *word transcription, multiple choices, and rating scale* [11]. The average of those three sessions from all listeners is calculated to evaluate the intelligibility level of each speaker.

Table 3.2. Cerebral palsy children's evaluation by the standard articulatory test and intelligibility test

Code	Severity Level (Articulatory Test)	Arti Score	Severity Level (Intelligibility Test)	Intel Score
DF01	Moderate	0.63	Moderate	0.53
DF02	Severe	0.49	Severe	0.39
DF03	Moderate	0.66	Moderate	0.77
DF04	Severe	0.51	Severe	0.48
DM01	Severe	0.56	Severe	0.41
DM02	Moderate	0.69	Moderate	0.63
DM03	Moderate	0.69	Moderate	0.77
DM04	Moderate	0.63	Moderate	0.68

3.2 Speech Corpus

The proposed method is evaluated using two speech corpora, named the control set and the unknown set. The *control set* was designed especially for Thai phonemes error analysis. There are totally 70 Thai phonemes, however, only 68 phonemes were selected to construct 68 target words using the criteria that every word was a single syllable word and was able to be represented by a picture in order to get speech data of natural conversation, i.e. not a reading speech. Two diphthongs [ɯa, ua] were excluded because they were scarce and could not be used for constructing any target word represented by a picture.

The *unknown set* was designed as a set of words that are frequently used for controlling assistive devices and/or emergency call. It is comprised of 96 words usually used for an environmental control unit, power wheelchair, emergency case, and to control household electronic devices. Some examples are, "left", "right", "forward", "backward", "turn", "stop", "lock", and "unlock" which are commonly used for a voice-command power wheelchair.

Using our developed speech recording program, both speech corpus were recorded under a semi-controlled environmental conditions, i.e. in a quiet room with the door closed but no additional sound proof materials. A dynamic headset microphone (Shure model SM2) was used at a position approximately 1.5 cm. from the right side of the speaker's mouth. The subjects were instructed to utter each word in isolation with their habitual tone accent and volume. During the recording process, the speech stimuli (the target picture) were presented to the subjects on a computer screen. In the case of unknown pictures for CP-children, the target words will be told and those pictures will be repeated after a pre-setup order. The speech sample was recorded through a Sound Blaster Extigy card connected to IBM ThinkPad model T42 by USB port, with a 16-bit A/D converter at a sampling rate of 16 kHz.

3.3 Evaluation Methods

The results of Ø were compared with the evaluation results obtained from the articulatory assessment and intelligibility test, as well as recognition rates of two well-known speech recognition (SRR) models; HMM and ANN. From the research assumption, Ø could be used as a powerful indicator for predicting recognition rate. To this end, the result of Ø and that of recognition systems from the control set are used to generate a prediction function. By the function, the predicted speech recognition rate of each speaker is calculated and compared with HMM recognition rate of the unknown set. All results were evaluated using the average of *root-mean-square difference* (Δ_{rms}) and the *Pearson's correlation coefficient* (R^2). As for a reliability evaluation, a *margin of distance* (an acceptable distance-bound) is calculated. The margin is set to an average root-mean-square difference between two reference recognition systems (HMM and ANN). If the difference of our prediction rate and the reference rate is less than a margin of error, then the prediction method is acceptable.

Besides Δ_{rms} and R^2, the third evaluation criterion is *rank-order inconsistency* (*ROI*). In this criterion, first the results of prediction are sorted by the accuracy rate. The reference orders are arranged by the results from speech recognition systems. The mismatched rank is counted and accumulated. The counting method is based on two techniques called *pairwise comparison* and *rank-order comparison*. Given ranking results of the two methods of interest, we find the inconsistency (or mismatch) of decisions made by those methods on the question of which speaker gains better performance than the others. For an individual case, if two methods give different outcomes, it will be counted as an inconsistent decision. To this end, the number of rank mismatches between the results of a test method (*test*) and that of the reference method (*ref*) is defined as equation (5).

$$\#Mismatch_{(test,ref)} = \sum_{i=1}^{n}\sum_{j=i+1}^{n}\left|\delta(S_i^{ref}, S_j^{ref}) - \delta(S_i^{test}, S_j^{test})\right| \qquad (5)$$

where n is the number of speakers and δ is the threshold function shown in equation (3). In (5) S_i^{ref} represents the score of the ith speaker on the reference (*ref*) system, while S_i^{test} is the score of the same speaker on the test (*test*) system. The score mentioned here can be speech recognition rate, the value of Ø, Arti, or Intel.

The ROI is calculated by dividing the number of rank mismatches by the total number of comparison, i.e. $^{n}C_2$.The rank-order inconsistency ranges between 0 and 1. Same as the previous criteria, an acceptable bound of inconsistency is also calculated by comparing the results of HMM to ANN or vise versa.

4 Results and Discussion

4.1 Evaluation by Root-Mean-Square Difference and Correlation Coefficient

Table 4.1.1 shows the results (on the control set) of Ø and 1- Ø values in the case of normal speakers (the code's names starting with **A** and **N**) and dysarthric speakers (the code's names starting with **D**), respectively. According to Table 4.1.1, the average of Ø for normal speakers is 0.04 (σ = 0.03) while that of dysarthric speakers is 0.51 (σ = 0.18). For each individual speaker, a smaller value of Ø represents less confusion between different words.

Table 4.1.1. Experiment results with normal speeches and dysarthric speeches (on the control set)

Code	SRR (HMM)	SRR (ANN)	Ø	1-Ø
AF01	0.99	0.93	0.04	0.96
AF02	0.99	0.97	0.02	0.98
AM01	0.98	0.95	0.02	0.98
AM02	0.98	0.97	0.07	0.93
NF01	0.98	0.95	0.01	0.99
NF02	0.92	0.84	0.03	0.97
NM01	0.95	0.84	0.10	0.90
NM02	0.94	0.91	0.03	0.97
	Average		**0.04**	**0.96**
	Standard division		**0.03**	**0.03**

Code	SRR (HMM)	SRR (ANN)	Ø	1-Ø
DF01	0.38	0.38	0.75	0.25
DF02	0.49	0.54	0.49	0.51
DF03	0.77	0.65	0.42	0.58
DF04	0.51	0.47	0.63	0.37
DM01	0.55	0.53	0.51	0.49
DM02	0.49	0.37	0.70	0.30
DM03	0.72	0.60	0.40	0.60
DM04	0.75	0.77	0.20	0.80
	Average		**0.51**	**0.49**
	Standard division		**0.18**	**0.18**

Figure 4.1.1 shows a graphical comparison relation between Ø and speech recognition rates gained from HMM and ANN (SRR_{HMM} and SRR_{ANN}). As expected, a speaker with a low confusion value gains high recognition rate. A higher Ø shows more confusion (high possibility of mis-grouping) among different words for a speaker. The value of 1-Ø, in contrary, represents a probability of correct grouping and then is naturally proportional to the recognition rate. Intuitively, we can expect a high correlation between the values of 1-Ø and the recognition rates. To confirm this, the correlation between them is investigated. Figure 4.1.2 and Figure 4.1.3 show the correlation between 1-Ø and speech recognition rates (SRRs) for both recognition models, HMM and ANN respectively.

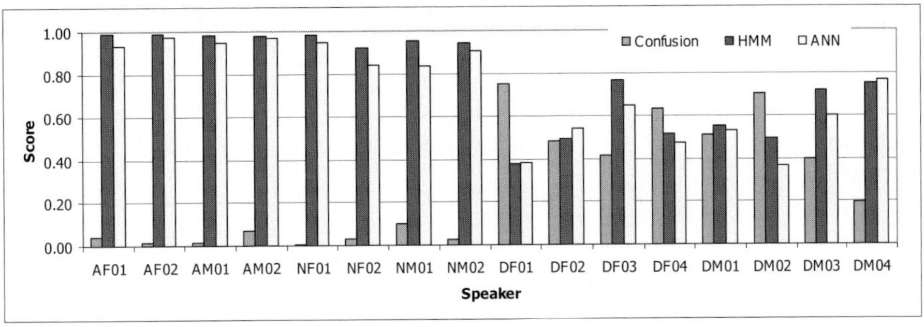

Fig. 4.1.1. Comparing of speech confusion index (Ø), speech recognition rates gained from HMM and ANN

Plotting a graph of 1-Ø and SRR showed in Table 4.1.1, we can generate the *prediction function* of 1-Ø and $SRR_Ø$. As the result, the calculated *correlation coefficient* (R^2) is nearly 0.94 for HMM and 0.97 for ANN. That is the correlation between Ø and the recognition rate of ANN is higher than a correlation between Ø and the recognition rate of HMM. The result suggests that Ø matches better to the performance obtained from the ANN model than to that gained from HMM.

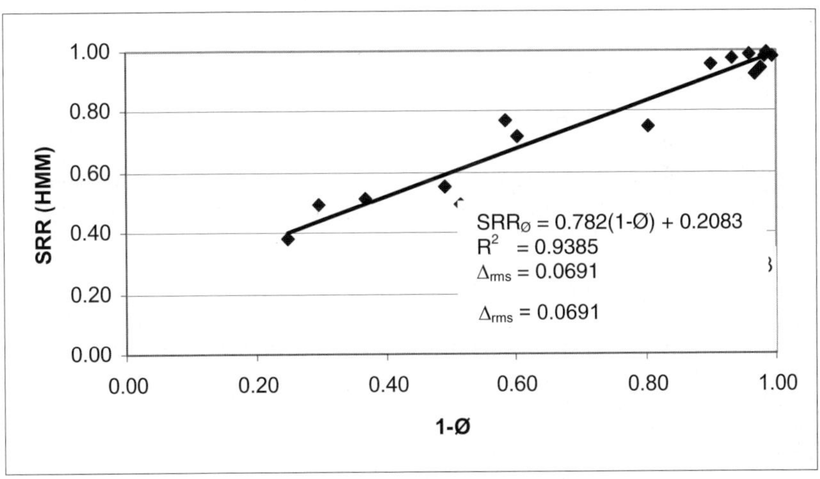

Fig. 4.1.2. Correlation between 1-Ø and HMM recognition rate (all speakers and the control data set)

From the prediction functions calculated by Ø (shown in Figure 4.1.2 and 4.1.3), the predicted recognition rates ($SRR_Ø$) based on each dysarthric speaker were calculated and shown in Table 4.1.2 and Table 4.1.3, respectively. At the end of both tables are *root-mean-square differences* (Δ_{rms}) calculated from a reference recognition method and each speech evaluations (Ø, speech articulatory test, and speech intelligibility test, denoted by $\Delta_Ø$, Δ_{Arti}, and Δ_{Intel}, respectively).

According to the experiments on the control data set, our proposed method (Ø) shows the lowest prediction errors of 6.91% and 2.45% for HMM and ANN, respectively, when compared to the others (articulatory test and intelligibility test). Moreover, from the calculation of difference between HMM and ANN, the acceptable bound for the error is 7.79%. That means the results from the proposed method are acceptable.

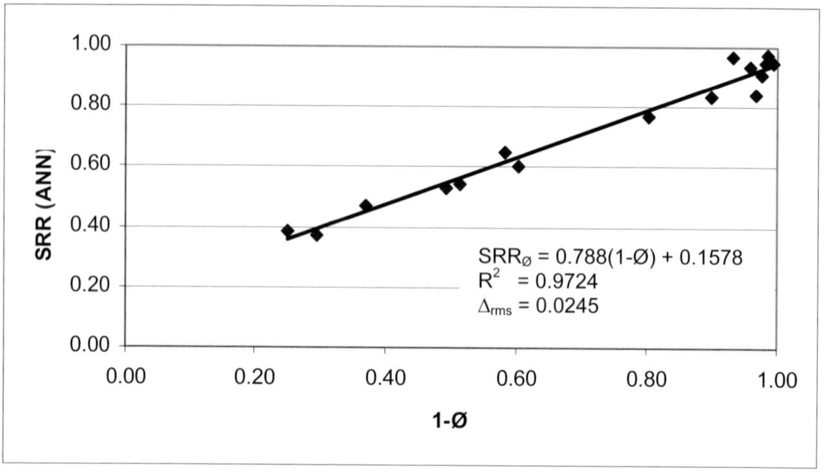

Fig. 4.1.3. Correlation between 1-Ø and ANN's recognition rate (all speakers and the control data set)

Table 4.1.2. Recognition rates and root-mean-square difference of speech recognition rates from HMM (SRR_{HMM}) compared to recognition rates calculated from Ø ($SRR_{Ø}$), articulatory test (Arti), and intelligibility test (Intel)

Code	SRR_{HMM}	$SRR_{Ø}$	Arti	Intel	$\Delta_{Ø}$	Δ_{Arti}	Δ_{Intel}
DF01	0.38	0.40	0.63	0.53	0.0006	0.0641	0.0240
DF02	0.49	0.61	0.49	0.39	0.0139	0.0001	0.0112
DF03	0.77	0.66	0.66	0.77	0.0105	0.0111	0.0000
DF04	0.51	0.50	0.51	0.48	0.0003	0.0000	0.0015
DM01	0.55	0.59	0.56	0.41	0.0017	0.0000	0.0207
DM02	0.49	0.44	0.69	0.63	0.0028	0.0395	0.0184
DM03	0.72	0.68	0.69	0.77	0.0016	0.0008	0.0025
DM04	0.75	0.84	0.63	0.68	0.0069	0.0144	0.0053
Accepted distance = 0.0779				**Mean**	**0.0048**	**0.0162**	**0.0105**
				Δ_{rms}	**0.0691**	**0.1274**	**0.1023**

The experiment on the unknown data set (Table 4.1.4) showed a comparable result with all standard methods. The lowest prediction error came from intelligibility test followed by our method and the articulatory test with the errors of 9.7%, 11.33%, and 12.21%, consecutively. In this case, the accepted distance bound is 12.15%. The acceptable error in this case comes from an error when using the HMM result on the control set to predict the result on the unknown set. The acceptable bound for this case is 6.73%. The results from all methods are out of bound. This result is not surprising since there are differences of word (or sound) distribution among both data sets.

Table 4.1.3. Recognition rates and root-mean-square difference of speech recognition rates from ANN (SRR_{ANN}) compared to recognition rates calculated from Ø ($SRR_{Ø}$), articulatory test (Arti), and intelligibility test (Intel)

Code	SRR_{ANN}	$SRR_{Ø}$	Arti	Intel	$\Delta_{Ø}$	Δ_{Arti}	Δ_{Intel}
DF01	0.38	0.35	0.63	0.53	0.0008	0.0621	0.0228
DF02	0.54	0.56	0.49	0.39	0.0004	0.0033	0.0242
DF03	0.65	0.62	0.66	0.77	0.0009	0.0002	0.0162
DF04	0.47	0.45	0.51	0.48	0.0006	0.0018	0.0000
DM01	0.53	0.55	0.56	0.41	0.0002	0.0007	0.0153
DM02	0.37	0.39	0.69	0.63	0.0005	0.1044	0.0677
DM03	0.60	0.63	0.69	0.77	0.0009	0.0079	0.0281
DM04	0.77	0.79	0.63	0.68	0.0005	0.0179	0.0076
Accepted distance = 0.0779				**Mean**	**0.0006**	**0.0248**	**0.0227**
				Δ_{rms}	**0.0245**	**0.1574**	**0.1508**

Table 4.1.4. Results of predicted speech recognition rate ($SRR_{Ø}$) and HMM's results for the *unknown data set*

Code	SRR_{HMM}	$SRR_{Ø}$	Arti	Intel	$\Delta_{Ø}$	Δ_{Arti}	Δ_{Intel}
DF01	0.41	0.40	0.63	0.53	0.0001	0.0474	0.0143
DF02	0.39	0.61	0.49	0.39	0.0488	0.0092	0.0000
DF03	0.78	0.66	0.66	0.77	0.0141	0.0148	0.0001
DF04	0.58	0.50	0.51	0.48	0.0064	0.0039	0.0104
DM01	0.58	0.59	0.56	0.41	0.0002	0.0004	0.0291
DM02	0.61	0.44	0.69	0.63	0.0300	0.0062	0.0002
DM03	0.74	0.68	0.69	0.77	0.0032	0.0020	0.0012
DM04	0.82	0.84	0.63	0.68	0.0002	0.0355	0.0201
Accepted distance = 0.0673				**Mean**	**0.0129**	**0.0149**	**0.0094**
				Δ_{rms}	**0.1134**	**0.1221**	**0.0971**

4.2 Evaluation by Rank-Order Inconsistency

This evaluation focuses on the correctness of ranking order when compared to the reference systems. In Table 4.2.1, on the control set, the Ø method is the best method with the lowest inconsistency scores for both reference systems (HMM and ANN) followed by an intelligibility test and then an articulatory test. The accepted inconsistency score is calculated by comparing the result HMM to that of ANN which is 14.29%. Therefore, the results from Ø method are a little bit off bound for the HMM but acceptable for the ANN system.

Table 4.2.1. Speech recognition rate ranking and inconsistency scores of three methods (Ø, Articulatory test, and Intelligibility test) on the *control data set*, when the HMM system (left) and the ANN system (right) were used as the references

HMM Reference	$ROI_Ø$	ROI_{Arti}	ROI_{Intel}	ANN Reference	$ROI_Ø$	ROI_{Arti}	ROI_{Intel}
DF01	DF01	DF02	DF02	**DM02**	DF01	DF02	DF02
DF02	DM02	DF04	DM01	**DF01**	DM02	DF04	DM01
DM02	DF04	DM01	DF04	**DF04**	DF04	DM01	DF04
DF04	DM01	DF01	DF01	**DM01**	DM01	DF01	DF01
DM01	DF02	DM04	DM02	**DF02**	DF02	DM04	DM02
DM03	DF03	DF03	DM04	**DM03**	DF03	DF03	DM04
DM04	DM03	DM03	DM03	**DF03**	DM03	DM03	DM03
DF03	DM04	DM02	DF03	**DM04**	DM04	DM02	DF03
Score	**0.18**	**0.36**	**0.25**	**Score**	**0.07**	**0.54**	**0.43**

Accepted Inconsistency Score = 0.14

Table 4.2.2 shows the results on the unknown set. An intelligibility test has the lowest inconsistency score (i.e. 18%) in this case. The next best ones are the Ø index and an articulatory test with the inconsistency score of 25% and 29%, respectively. Only the result from the intelligibility test is acceptable.

Table 4.2.2. Speech recognition rate ranking and inconsistency scores of three methods (Ø, Articulatory test, and Intelligibility test) on the *unknown data set*, when the HMM system was used as the reference

HMM Reference	$ROI_Ø$	ROI_{Arti}	ROI_{Intel}
DF02	DF01	DF02	DF02
DF01	DM02	DF04	DM01
DF04	DF04	DM01	DF04
DM01	DM01	DF01	DF01
DM02	DF02	DM04	DM02
DM03	DF03	DF03	DM04
DF03	DM03	DM03	DM03
DM04	DM04	DM02	DF03
Inconsistency Score	**0.25**	**0.29**	**0.18**

Accepted Inconsistency Score = 0.18

5 Conclusion and Future Work

In this work, we present an automated method for speech assessment before building a speech recognition system. The so-called *speech confusion index* (Ø) is proposed to measure the severity of speech disorder. Besides, it can be used to predict the recognition rate obtained from two well-known speech recognition systems, i.e., HMM and ANN. Comparing to two standard speech assessments, Ø achieves better prediction ability and need no laborious task. The prediction can be served as a decision index whether this dysarthric speaker could be benefit from such technology or not. All results from the experiment are comparable to the standard methods, and quite promising to be an assessment for modern speech assessment. However, the prediction on the unknown set still needs more consideration.

As our future works, the research will scope on exploring more parameters such as the overlap factor, the consistency of energy, and time, to improve the accuracy of prediction for the unknown set. Another issue is how to figure out the relation of word or *phoneme density distribution* of an unknown set. If the density distribution can be added into the prediction function then the function can be used in general case for any unknown set.

Acknowledgement

The research is a part of the project granted by the Royal Golden Jubilee Ph.D. Program, Thailand Research Fund and the National Electronics and Computer Technology Center (NECTEC), National Science and Technology Development Agency (NSTDA), Thailand.

References

1. Deller, J., Hsu, D., Ferrier, L.: On the use of hidden Markov Modeling for Recognition of Dysarthric Speech. *Computer Methods and Programs in Biomedicine* **35** (1991) 125 -139
2. Kotler, A., and Thomas-Stonel, N.: Effects of speech training on the accuracy of speech recognition for an individual with speech impairment. *Journal of Augmentative and Alternative Communication* **12** (1997) 71- 80
3. Rosen, K., and Yampolsky, S.: Automatic Speech Recognition and a Review of Its Functioning with Dysarthric Speech. *Journal of Augmentative and Alternative Communication* **16** (2000) 46 - 60
4. Thubthong, N. and Kayasith, P.: Incorporated Tone model speech recognition for Thai dysarthria. *In Proc. of 11th International Society for Augmentive and Alternate Communication.* Natal Brazil (2004)
5. Kent, R.D.: Hearing and believing: Some limits to auditory-perceptual assessment of speech and voice disorders. *Journal of Speech and Hearing Disorders* **7** (1996) 7-23
6. Corman, T.H., Leiserson, C.E., Rivet, R.L.: *Introduction to Algorithms*. MIT Press (1990)
7. Itakura, F.: Minimum Prediction Residual Principle Applied to Speech Recognition. *IEEE Transaction on acoustics, speech, and signal processing*, ASSP-23, 1 (1975) 67-72.
8. Kayasith, P., Thubthong, N., Theeramunkong, T.: Consistency Score: Dysarthric Speech Indicator for Modren Speech Technologies. *In Proc. of 12th International Society for Augmentive and Alternate Communication (ISAA -2006)*. Dusseldorf German.
9. Shriberg, L., Kwiatkowski, J.: Phonological disorders III: A procedure for assessing severity of involvement. *Journal of Speech and Hearing Disorders*, **47**(3), (1982) 256–70.
10. Shriberg, L., Austin, D., Lewis, B.A., McSweeny, J.L., Wilson, D.L.: The percentage of consonants correct (PCC) metric. Extensions and reliability data. *Journal of Speech, Language, and Hearing Research,* 40, (1997) 708–22.
11. Kayasith, P., Thubthong, N.: Computerized Intelligibility Test for Thai Speech Disorder. *US - Thailand Symposium on Biomedical Engineering* , Bangkok Thailand. (2005)

Statistical Machine Translation of German Compound Words

Maja Popović, Daniel Stein, and Hermann Ney

Lehrstuhl für Informatik VI - Computer Science Department
RWTH Aachen University
Ahornstrasse 55
52056 Aachen, Germany
{popovic, stein, ney}@informatik.rwth-aachen.de

Abstract. German compound words pose special problems to statistical machine translation systems: the occurence of each of the components in the training data is not sufficient for successful translation. Even if the compound itself has been seen during training, the system may not be capable of translating it properly into two or more words. If German is the target language, the system might generate only separated components or may not be capable of choosing the correct compound. In this work, we investigate and compare different strategies for the treatment of German compound words in statistical machine translation systems. For translation from German, we compare linguistic-based and corpus-based compound splitting. For translation into German, we investigate splitting and rejoining German compounds, as well as joining English potential components. Additionaly, we investigate word alignments enhanced with knowledge about the splitting points of German compounds. The translation quality is consistently improved by all methods for both translation directions.

1 Introduction

The goal of statistical machine translation is to translate an input word sequence in the source language into a target language word sequence. Given the source language sequence, we should choose the target language sequence which maximises the posterior probability. The translation system used in this work models this posterior probability directly as a log-linear combination of seven different models. The most important ones are phrase-based models in both directions. Additionaly, phrase level IBM1 models in both directions, a language model of the target language, as well as phrase penalty and word penalty are used. For detailed description of the system see [7,8].

In order to improve the translation process, it is possible to perform preprocessing steps based on morphological and/or syntactic knowlegde in both the source and/or target language sequence. If necessary, after the translation the inverse transformations are applied to the generated target sequence.

In this work, we investigate and compare strategies for treatment of German compound words. For translation from German, we compare linguistic-based

T. Salakoski et al. (Eds.): FinTAL 2006, LNAI 4139, pp. 616–624, 2006.

and corpus-based approaches for splitting compounds in the source language. For translation into German, we explore two possibilities for improving the translation quality: splitting and rejoining German compounds and joining English words. Additionaly, we investigate how much the translation quality can be improved by incorporating knowledge about compound splitting points into the word alignments. This method is applied for both translation directions.

Related Work

Several publications adress the problem of German compound words in statistical machine translation.

In [3], a morpho-syntactic analyser is used to split German compounds and improve the quality of the generated English output.

Corpus-based splitting for the same translation direction has been proposed in [1]. They compare several corpus-based methods and report that the one based on word frequencies yields the best translation improvements.

In this work, we compare these two methods on the European Parliament corpus. We propose several methods for treating German compounds when German is the target language. This problem has not be investigated yet to the best of our knowledge.

Some publications have proposed the use of morpho-syntactic knowledge for improving statistical alignment quality, for example [5,6]. However, introducing knowledge about compound words has not been investigated so far.

In our work, we investigate the effects of introducing information about German compound words into the word alignments.

2 Treatment of German Compound Words

Compounding of words is common in many languages (German, Dutch, Finnish, etc.). Compound words are created by joining an arbitrary number of existing words together, and this can lead to a large increase of the vocabulary size, and thus also to sparse data problems. Therefore the problem of compound words poses challenges for many NLP applications. In this work, we investigate and compare different methods for treating German compound words in order to improve the quality of statistical machine translation both from German and into German.

2.1 Translation from German into English

For translation from German into English, the lingustic-based method proposed in [3] and the corpus-based method proposed in [1] are used in order to compare two approaches. For the linguistic-based splitting we used the Constraint Grammar Parser for German (GERCG) as described in [3]. For the corpus-based splitting we used the frequency-based method described in [1]:

- each capitalised word which consists of two or more words occuring in the training vocabulary is considered as a compound word

- for each compound word:
  - the frequency of the compound itself $N(w)$ and the frequencies of its components $N(w_1), ..., N(w_K)$ are collected
  - the geometric mean of the component frequencies is calculated $GM(f_1, ..., f_K) = (\prod_{k=1}^{K} N(f_k))^{\frac{1}{K}}$
  - compound word is split if $GM(f_1, ..., f_K) > N(f)$

The main difference between the two approaches is that the linguistic-based one leads to a larger number of split compounds because it does not depend on component frequencies, so even those compounds whose components have not been seen in the training will be split.

Examples of the splittings can be seen in Table 1. The first compound word "Arbeitnehmer" consists of two components, "Arbeit" and "Nehmer". Since the word "Nehmer" has not been seen in the training corpus, the geometric mean of component frequencies is equal to zero and therefore the word is not been split by the corpus-based method. The second compound word consists of three components, and each of them has been seen in the training corpus. However, the geometric mean of component frequencies is 17.9 whereas the frequency of the word itself is 51 which means that the word remains unsplit by the corpus-based method. Those values for the compound word "Treibhauseffekt" are also the reason for splitting the third word "Treibhauseffektgase" into two components instead of four.

Table 1. Examples of splitting German words

original word	splitted word	
	linguistic-based	corpus-based
Arbeitnehmer	Arbeit Nehmer	Arbeitnehmer
Treibhauseffekt	Treib Haus Effekt	Treibhauseffekt
Treibhauseffektgase	Treib Haus Effekt Gase	Treibhauseffekt Gase

2.2 Translation from English into German

For translation from English into German we propose three methods:

- splitting and merging German compounds
- POS-based joining of English words
- alignment-based joining of English words

Splitting and Merging German Compounds: German compound words in the training corpus are split using the corpus-based frequency method because it allows a straightforward and simple approach for merging components after the translation process. After training, translation is performed from English into the modified German language. The generated output is then postprocessed, i.e. the components are merged using the following method:

- a list of compounds and a list of components are extracted from the original German training corpus
- if the word in the generated output is in the component list
  - check if this word merged with the next word is in the compound list
  - if yes, merge two words

Joining English Words: Another possible approach for treatment of the compound words in the target language is joining the corresponding words in the source language. Such transformation increases the English vocabulary size, but the word structure in the transformed English corpus becomes more similar to the German one.

- POS-based joining:
  English words which correspond to one German compound are usually two or more consecutive nouns. Therefore each sequence of English nouns is merged into one word.
- alignment-based joining:
  Distinct English words which are aligned to one German word are considered as potential components. All successive components are merged into one word.

Table 2. Examples of joining English words

original words	joined words	
	POS-based	alignment-based
energy certificate	energy_certificate	energy certificate
order of business	order of business	order_of business

As in the case of the German compound word splitting, the linguistic-based approach for joining English words (POS-based) leads to a larger number of English "compounds". An example can be seen in Table 2. The example shows two merged English nouns which have not been joined by alignment-based approach because in the baseline alignment they are not aligned to the same German word. The example also shows an aligment-based joining of a noun and a following preposition.

2.3 Improved Word Alignments

Knowlegde about splitting points of German compound words can also be used to enhance the word alignments. The alignments are trained using the modified German corpus with compound words split using the corpus-based frequency method described in Section 2.1. After the alignments are created, positions of the component words belonging to the same compound word are merged and the training of translation models is done on the original German corpus. The advantage of this approach is that it can be applied to both translation directions without preprocessing of the input test text or postprocessing of the generated output.

3 Experiments

The experiments are performed on the European Parliament corpus described in [2]. It contains German and English parliamentary speeches. The corpus statistics can be seen in Table 3. The original corpus consists of about 700k sentences and 15M running words. In order to investigate effects of sparse training data, we have randomly extracted a small subset containing about 7k sentences and 144k running words (about 1% of the original corpus).

Table 3. Corpus statistics

		German	English
Train:	Sentences	751088	
	Running Words+Punctuation	15257678	16052330
	Vocabulary	205374	74708
	Singletons [%]	49.8	38.3
Dev:	Sentences	2000	
	Running Words+Punctuation	55147	58655
	Distinct Words	9213	6547
	OOVs [%]	0.8	0.2
Test:	Sentences	2000	
	Running Words+Punctuation	54260	57951
	Distinct Words	9048	6496
	OOVs [%]	0.7	0.2

As already pointed out, transformations were applied as a preprocessing step, then training and search were performed using the transformed data. In the case of improved alignments, the preprocessed corpus is used only for the alignment training, whereas the translation training is performed on the original corpus. The translation system we used is the phrase-based system described in [8]. Modifications of the training and search procedure were not necessary. In the case of the target language transformation, the inverse transformation step described in Section 2.2 was necessary after the translation.

The evaluation metrics used in our experiments are WER (Word Error Rate), PER (Position-independent word Error Rate) and BLEU (BiLingual Evaluation Understudy) [4].

4 Translation Results

4.1 Translation from German into English

Table 4 presents the results for translation from German into English. It can be seen that the treatment of German compound words leads to small but consistent improvements of all error measures for both sizes of the training corpus. The improvements obtained by the linguistic-based approach of compound splitting are similar to those of the corpus-based approach as well as to those obtained by improved word alignments.

Table 4. Translation results for German→English

German→English		dev			test		
		WER	PER	BLEU	WER	PER	BLEU
700k	baseline	63.4	48.6	20.5	63.6	48.6	20.9
	linguistic split	63.2	47.9	21.4	63.2	47.3	22.0
	corpus-based split	62.9	47.6	21.5	63.2	47.5	21.9
	improved alignment	63.1	48.4	21.1	63.3	48.3	21.5
7k	baseline	71.4	55.2	14.1	71.2	54.8	14.6
	linguistic split	71.5	54.5	15.0	71.1	53.7	15.6
	corpus-based split	71.3	54.5	15.0	71.0	53.7	15.4
	improved alignment	71.1	54.2	15.2	70.8	54.0	15.5

More details considering translation with the full corpus and corpus-based compound splitting are shown in Table 5.

Table 5. Detailed translation results for German→English

German→English			dev			test		
			WER	PER	BLEU	WER	PER	BLEU
700k	transformed	baseline	63.8	47.7	20.3	63.8	47.9	21.3
		split	63.2	46.5	21.4	63.4	46.6	22.5
	rest	baseline	63.0	49.3	21.0	63.4	49.2	20.8
		split	62.6	48.8	21.0	63.0	48.5	21.4

Table 6. Translation examples for German→English without and with compound splitting

original German sentence:	...die artgerechte und umweltfreundliche **Produktionsmethode**...
transformed German sentence:	...die artgerechte und umweltfreundliche **Produktion Methode**...
generated English sentence:	
without splitting:	...the animal and environmentally friendly **production**...
with splitting:	...the animal and environmentally friendly **production methods**...
reference English sentence:	...the animal and environmentally friendly **production methods**...

Development and test corpus were divided into two parts: one containing sentences with split compound words (which is about 45%)[1] and other which remained the same. Then these two sets were evaluated separately for each translation system. Results show that the compound splitting improves translation quality for both sets, slightly more for the transformed set. This means that the new system allows better learning of models so that the translation quality has been improved both directly as well as indirectly.

From the translation example in Table 6 it can be seen that the system trained on the transformed corpus is better able to produce the correct English output.

4.2 Translation from English into German

The results for this translation direction are reported in Table 7.

Table 7. Translation results for English→German

English→German		dev			test		
		WER	PER	BLEU	WER	PER	BLEU
700k	baseline	68.6	56.4	19.8	68.5	56.2	19.8
	split+merge	68.4	55.9	20.4	68.3	55.5	20.4
	join-eng POS	68.5	56.1	20.1	68.2	55.5	20.6
	join-eng aligned	68.5	56.3	20.0	68.2	55.5	20.3
	improved alignment	68.2	55.9	20.2	67.7	55.2	20.6
7k	baseline	76.9	61.6	15.0	76.6	61.4	15.4
	split+merge	76.0	61.3	15.8	75.9	61.2	16.2
	join-eng POS	76.7	61.6	15.4	76.4	61.3	15.8
	join-eng aligned	76.8	61.8	15.2	76.4	61.4	15.8
	improved alignment	76.4	61.0	16.1	76.3	61.0	16.3

It can be seen that the treatment of German compounds is also helpful for this translation direction, namely when the German language is the target language.

For the full training corpus all four methods yield similar results, the splitting and merging method and the enhanced alignment yield slightly larger improvements. For the small training corpus, both methods for joining English words result to similar small improvements whereas the splitting and merging method and enhanced alignment have more impact.

Details for the translation with the full corpus and splitting-merging method can be seen in Table 8. Like for the other translation direction, the improvements are present for both evaluation sets, i.e. the translation quality has been improved both directly and indirectly.

The translation example in Table 9 shows the advantage of the new system. Without compound treatment the system translated two English words belonging to one German compound into two German words. The output of the new system where German compounds have been split and merged is correct.

[1] It should be noted that only about 2.5% of running words are affected by compound splitting, therefore significant changes in error measures cannot be expected.

Table 8. Detailed translation results for English→German

English→German			dev			test		
			WER	PER	BLEU	WER	PER	BLEU
700k	transformed	baseline	69.7	56.8	18.9	69.4	56.3	19.9
		split	69.2	56.0	19.9	69.3	55.5	20.5
	rest	baseline	67.5	56.4	20.4	67.4	56.4	19.6
		split	67.4	55.8	21.0	67.1	55.4	20.3

Table 9. Translation examples for English→German without and with compound splitting and merging

English sentence:	...the animal and environmentally friendly production methods...
generated German sentence:	
without splitting and merging:	...die artgerechte und umweltverträgliche **Produktion Methoden**...
with splitting and merging:	...die artgerechte und umweltfreundliche **Produktionsmethode**...
reference German sentence:	...die artgerechte und umweltfreundliche **Produktionsmethode**...

5 Conclusions

In this work we introduced several methods for dealing with German compound words in order to improve the translation quality of the German output. For translation from German into English we compared two approaches proposed in a previous work. We also proposed incorporating knowledge about German compound words into the word alignments and tested it for both translation directions.

Our experimental results show that both linguistic-based and corpus-based compound splitting, as well as enhanced word alignment, yield similar improvements for translation from German into English.

It has been shown that these treatments of compound words also improve the quality of translation into German. For translation with a large tranining corpus, all proposed methods lead to similar improvements. For the small training corpus, splitting and merging German compounds and enhanced word alignment are slightly superior in comparison to the two other methods for joining English words.

In future work we plan to investigate possible treatments of compound words for other languages and language pairs (e.g. German-Spanish, Finnish, etc.). We also plan to investigate other methods for merging components in the generated output.

Acknowledgement

This work was partly supported by the TC-STAR project by the European Community (FP6-506738).

References

1. Koehn, P., Knight, K.: Empirical Methods for Compound Splitting. Proc. 10th Conf. of the European Chapter of the Association for Computational Linguistics (EACL). Budapest, Hungary (2003) 347–354
2. Koehn, P., Montz, C.: Shared task: statistical machine translation between European languages. Proc. ACL Workshop on Building and Using Parallel Texts. Ann Arbor, Michigan (2005) 119–124
3. Niessen, S., Ney, H.: Improving SMT quality with morpho-syntactic analysis. Proc. 18th Int. Conf. on Computational Linguistics (COLING). Saarbrücken, Germany (2000) 1081–1085
4. Papineni, K., Roukos, S., Ward, T., Zhu, W. J.: BLEU: a method for automatic evaluation of machine translation. Proc. 40th Annual Meeting of the Assoc. for Computational Linguistics (ACL). Philadelphia, PA (2002) 311–318
5. Popović, M., Ney, H.: Improving Word Alignment Quality using Morpho-syntactic Information. Proc. 20th Int. Conf. on Computational Linguistics (COLING). Geneva, Switzerland (2004) 310–314
6. Toutanova, K., Tolga Ilhan, H., Manning, C.: Extensions to HMM-based statistical word alignment models. Proc. Conf. on Empirical Methods for Natural Language Processing (EMNLP). Philadelphia, PA (2002) 87–94
7. Vilar, D., Matusov, E., Hasan, S., Zens, R., Ney, H.: Statistical Machine Translation of European Parliamentary Speeches. Proc. MT Summit X. Phuket, Thailand (2005) 259–266
8. Zens, R., Bender, O., Hasan, S., Khadivi, S., Matusov, E., Xu, J., Zhang, Y., Ney, H.: The RWTH Phrase-based Statistical Machine Translation System. Proc. Int. Workshop on Spoken Language Translation (IWSLT) Pittsburgh, PA (2005) 155–162

Summarizing Documents in Context: Modeling the User's Information Need

Yllias Chali

Department of Computer Science, University of Lethbridge
4401 University Drive, Lethbridge, Alberta, Canada, T1K 3M4
chali@cs.uleth.ca

Abstract. Popularity of the Internet has contributed towards the explosive growth of the information available to users for day to day usage, and people are faced with information overload problems because of the spread of the information across various kinds of sources - documents, web pages, mails, faxes, manuals, reports, books, etc. In this paper, we present a text summarization system that models the real-world application in which the user would be interested in learning about a sequence of events. Also, we focus on some evaluation procedures.

1 Introduction

Popularity of the Internet, the articles, the reports, the books, have contributed towards the explosive growth of the information available to users for day to day usage. Search engines provide a means to access huge volumes of online information by retrieving the documents considered relevant to the user's query. Even with search engines, the user has to go through the entire document content to judge its relevance. This contributes towards a well recognized information overload problem.

Similar information overload problems are also faced by corporate networks and people in general, which have information spread across various kinds of sources - documents, web pages, mails, faxes, manuals, reports, books, etc. It has become a necessity to have tools that can digest the information present across various sources and provide the user with condensed form of the most relevant information. Summarization is one such technology that can satisfy these needs.

Summaries are frequently used in our daily life to serve variety of purposes. Headlines of news articles, market reports, movie previews, abstracts of journal articles, TV listings, are some of the commonly used forms of summaries. Oracle's Text uses the summarization technology to mine textual databases. InXight summarizer [1] provides summaries for the documents retrieved by the information retrieval engine. Microsoft's Word provides the AutoSummarize option to highlight the main concepts of the given document. BT's ProSum, IBM's Intelligent Miner [2] are some of the other tools providing summaries to speed the process of information access.

Several advanced tools have been developed in recent times using summarization techniques to meet certain requirements. Newsblaster [1], and NewsInEssence [2]

[1] http://www.inxight.com/products/sdks/sum/
[2] http://www-306.ibm.com/software/data/iminer/

T. Salakoski et al. (Eds.): FinTAL 2006, LNAI 4139, pp. 625–631, 2006.

allow the users to be updated about the interesting events happening around the world, without the need to spend time searching for the related news articles. They group the articles from various news sources into event related clusters, and generate a summary for each cluster. Meeting summarizer [3] combines the speech recognition and summarization techniques to browse the contents of the meeting. Persival [4], and Healthdoc [5], aid physicians by providing a "recommended treatment", for particular patient's symptoms, from the vast online medical literature. Broadcast news navigator [6] is capable of understanding the news broadcast and present the user with the condensed version of the news. IBM's Re-Mail [7] and [8] can summarize the threads of e-mail messages based on simple sentence extraction techniques.

We are proposing in this paper a summarization tool that models the real-world application in which the user would be interested in learning about a sequence of events. Since the level of interest is a factor in summarization [9], we have to consider the user's interest explicitly.

The system that we are proposing performs as follows. *Given a topic, a user's demands (i.e., a series of questions related to the same topic, as in question answering systems), and a collection of documents judged relevant, create a fluent summary (<= 250 words) responding to the information request in a manner specific to the user's questions.* We are interested to experiment with the usage of information retrieval techniques to consider only a subset of the document collection and with information extraction techniques for summary generation. Also, we are interested in the evaluation task.

For instance, considering the recent Pakistan earthquake. One could be concerned to know *where exactly did the earthquake hit*? *What was the scale of the earthquake*? *How many people died so far*? *What are the damages*? *What are the needs for help*? and so on. Another user could be interested in a different topic such as the *folic acid* and she wants to know *what is the folic acid*? *What are its benefits*? *How many folic acid should an expectant mother get daily*?, etc. We are interested in generating summaries that discover and gather useful information from a collection of documents according to the user's demands.

This paper is organized as follows. In the following section, we give a brief overview of our system. We then discuss about the measures and approaches used in the evaluation task.

2 System Overview

The system is outlined in Figure 1. In the following, we give brief overview of each module in the system.

2.1 Pre-processing

In this module, we extract the text from the source document collection and tokenize the text using OAK system[3]. Tokenized text is then segmented into smaller portions using

[3] http://nlp.cs.nyu.edu/oak/

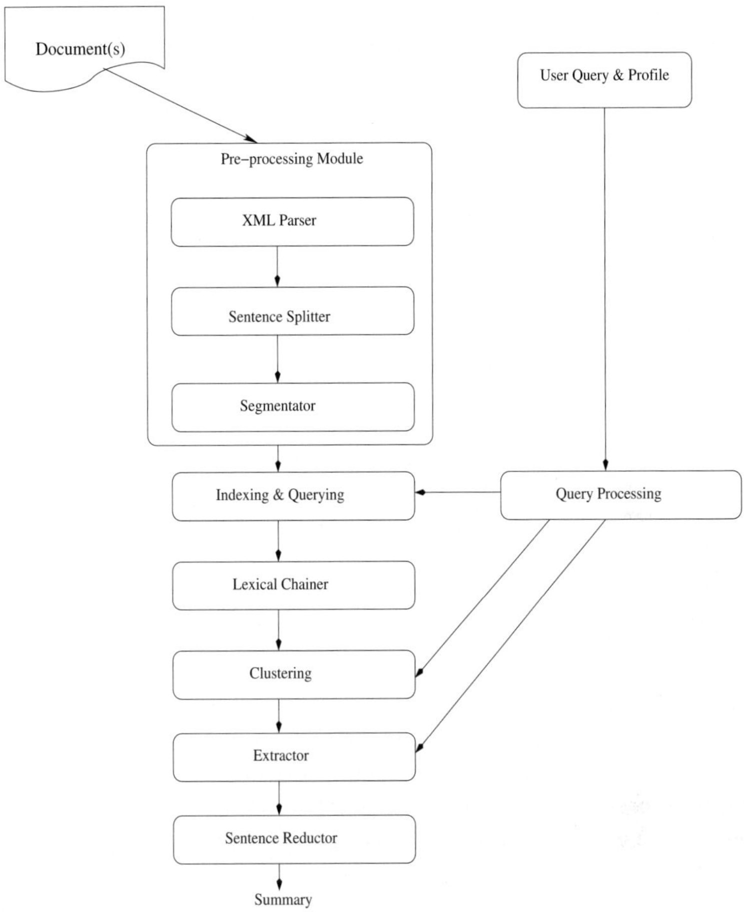

Fig. 1. System Overview

C99 segmentator [10]. Segments are obtained by dividing the document at the point of maximum shift in topic boundaries identified using the maximization algorithm [11]. We then index the segments using Lucene Indexer[4] for the purpose of searching.

2.2 Query Processing

Given a query of the form:

<Topic>
<title>
Development of Magnetic Levitation (MAGLEV) Rail Systems
</title>

[4] http://lucene.apache.org/

<narr>
In what countries are MAGLEV rail systems being proposed?
Are the proposals for short or long haul?
Is government financing required for construction?
</narr>
</Topic>

We identify the noun phrases (NPs) from the title and the narrative portion of the topic. For the above example, the query terms extracted are:

maglev rail systems short or long haul countries government financing proposals magnetic levitation (maglev) rail systems construction development

Now, we query the indexed document collection, with the above extracted query terms and retain the top 50 segments. This would allow us to filter the portions of the document, which are not relevant to the topic. On the other hand, there is a possibility that we lose some segments which are relevant but which do not have an occurrence of the query term.

2.3 Clustering

Extracted segments are grouped into clusters, based on their topical similarity as explained in [12]. We first compute the lexical chains for each segment and then compute the similarity between the segments based on the lexical chain overlap. Segments are then retained in the cluster, in which they contribute the most. Lexical chains are lists of related words spanning the entire segment. They are computed using a machine readable dictionary such as Wordnet (http://wordnet.princeton.edu), and used as indicators of the segment topic [13].

2.4 Extraction

Once the clusters are generated, we rank the clusters based on the *tf.idf*() values [14] of the query terms. Given query terms Q(1..n), score of a cluster C_j can be computed as:

$$score(C_j) = \sum_{i=1}^{n} tf(Q_{ij}).idf(Q_i) \qquad (1)$$

where

$tf(Q_{ij})$ - is the frequency of the query term Q_i in C_j.
$idf(Q_i)$ - is the *idf* value of the term Q_i.

We then calculate the score of segments and sentences within the cluster(s) in the similar way. Summary is then generated by extracting the top-ranked n sentence(s) from each cluster, i.e., first ranked sentences from all clusters, followed by second ranked ones and so on, until the length of the summary required is reached.

3 Evaluation

Evaluating content selection in summarization has proven to be a difficult problem, and summarization evaluation has been always a challenge to researchers in the document summarization field. Usually, human involvement is necessary to evaluate the quality of summaries, the fact that no single best model summary exists, and the lack of reliable automatic evaluation of text summaries. The National Institute for Standards and Technology (NIST) provides in the context of Document Understanding Conference (DUC) an evaluation series for text summarization.

We evaluated our system generated summaries using the Document Understanding Conference (DUC) 2005 datasets, provided by NIST, and ROUGE evaluation package [15]. ROUGE, Recall-Oriented Understudy of Gisting Evaluation, is a collection of measures to automatically evaluate the quality of summaries, based on *n-gram* overlap (n = 1, 2, 3, 4) and word sequence similarity between the peer and model summaries. In our evaluation, we used ROUGE-2 and ROUGE-SU4 measures. Lin [15] found that ROUGE measures correlate well with the human evaluation.

In 2005, NIST provided a collection of 30 clusters of documents relevant to the topic, and defined the task as to create from the documents a brief (<= 250 words), well-organized, fluent summary which answers the need for information expressed in the topic, at the level of user's demands specified in the narrations. Apart from the test data, NIST also provides four human generated 'model' summaries for each of the clusters.

We compared the summaries of our system against the model summaries using ROUGE with the parameters set in the same way as in DUC 2005 evaluation. Table 1 shows the evaluation results of our system in comparison with the average of human summarizers. Our system is among the top ranked systems with respect to ROUGE-2, and ROUGE-SU4 measures.

Table 1. ROUGE Evaluation

System	ROUGE-SU4	ROUGE-2
Baseline	0.09	0.04
Our System	0.11	0.06
Avg. Human	0.16	0.10

Even though ROUGE provides an automatic method to evaluate the systems, in comparison with the human summaries, a study [16] showed that ROUGE measures cannot be used as an absolute measure of the system's performance. They proposed a method to evaluate summaries based on the content overlap among a pool of human summaries rather than one model summary.

In the Document Understanding Conference [17], that we participated using this system, NIST judges carried out the manual evaluation of the summaries to measure the responsiveness (relative) and linguistic quality. Responsiveness can be defined as the measure of the extent to which the summary is able to satisfy the information need of the user. Each summary is assigned a value between 1 and 5, where 5 being the best. NIST also evaluated the linguistic quality of the summaries. Each judge was asked to determine the readability, grammatical correctness etc. of the summaries. The following linguistic qualities were evaluated independent of the model summaries.

- Grammaticality
- Non-redundancy
- Referential clarity
- Focus
- Structure and coherence.

Each summary is judged for each of the above linguistic quality and is given a value from 1 to 5, where 5 is the best. Table 2 shows the responsiveness and linguistic quality of our system.

Table 2. Responsiveness and Linguistic Quality Measures

System	Responsiveness	Avg. Quality
Baseline	1.98	4.41
Our System	2.06	3.18
Avg. Human	4.67	4.86

4 Discussion and Conclusion

In this paper, we gave a brief description of our summarization system, in context of modeling real-world scenarios of information need. The system creates from a cluster of documents a brief summary which answers the need for information expressed in the topic, at the level of details specified by the user's demands. We also briefed the various evaluation measures. It would be interesting to see if we could project the system's performance based on the topics used in the evaluation.

In our system, we assumed that the query terms are independent of each other and hence converted them to their baseform before querying. This approach would not work for complex queries, which require more deeper analysis to obtain the user's need.

Acknowledgments

We would like to thank Ali Karim, a co-op student for his work in the development of the system. This work was supported by the Natural Science and Engineering Research Council (NSERC) research grant and the University of Lethbridge research support.

References

1. McKeown, K., Barzilay, R., Chen, J., Elson, D., Evans, D., Klavans, J., Nenkova, A., Schiffman, B., Sigelman, S.: Columbia's newsblaster: New features and future directions (demo). In: Proceedings of NAACL-HLT'03, Edmonton, Canada (2003)
2. Radev, D.R., Blair-Goldensohn, S., Zhang, Z., Sundara Raghavan, R.: Newsinessence: A system for domain-independent, real-time news clustering and multi-document summarization. In: Demo Presentation, Human Language Technology Conference, San Diego, CA (2001)
3. Waibel, A., Bett, M., Finke, M., Stiefelhagen, R.: Meeting browser:tracking and summarization meetings. In: Proceedings of the 1998 DARPA Broadcast News Workshop, Lansdowne, Virginia (1998)
4. McKeown, K.R., Jordan, D.A., Hatzivassiloglou, V.: Generating patient-specific summaries of online literature. In: AAAI 98 Spring Symposium on Intelligent Text Summarization, Stanford University (1998) 34-43
5. Hirst, G., DiMarco, C., Hovy, E., Parsons, K.: Authoring and generating health-education documents that are tailored to the needs of the individual patient. In: Proceedings of the Sixth International Conference on User Modeling, Sardinia Italy (1997) 107-118
6. Maybury, M., Merlino, A.: Multimedia summaries of broadcast news. In Maybury, M., ed.: Multimedia Information Retrieval. (1997)
7. Rohall, S.L., Gruen, D., Moody, P., Wattenberg, M., Stern, M., Kerr, B., Stachel, B., Dave, K., Armes, R., Wilcox, E.: Remail: a reinvented email prototype. In: Extended abstracts of the 2004 conference on Human factors and computing systems, ACM Press (2004) 791–792
8. Rambow, O., Shrestha, L., Chen, J., Lauridsen, C.: Summarizing email threads. In: Proceedings of HLT-NAACL 2004: Short Papers, Boston, MA (2004)
9. Sparck-Jones, K.: Automatic summarizing: Factors and directions. In Mani, Maybury, eds.: Advances in Automatic Text Summarization. MIT press. (1999)
10. Choi, F.Y.Y.: Advances in domain independent linear text segmentation. In: Proceedings of the 1st North American Chapter of the Association for Computational Linguistics, Seattle, Washington (2000) 26 - 33
11. Reynar, J.: Topic Segmentation: Algorithms and applications. PhD thesis, Computer and Information Science, University of Pennsylvania (1998)
12. Chali, Y., Noureddine, S.: Document clustering with grouping and chaining algorthms. In Dale, R. et al., eds.: Proceedings of International Joint Conference on Natural Language Processing. LNAI 3651. (2005) 280–291
13. Chali, Y.: Topic detection of unrestricted texts: Approaches and evaluations. Journal of Applied Artificial Intelligence **19**(2) (2005) 119–136
14. Salton, G., Buckley, C.: Term weighting approaches in automatic text retrieval. Technical report, Ithaca, NY, USA (1987)
15. Lin, C.Y.: ROUGE: A package for automatic evaluation of summaries. In: Proceedings of the Workshop on Text Summarization Branches Out, Barcelona, Spain (2004) 74 - 81
16. Nenkova, A., Passonneau, R.: Evaluating content selection in summarization: the Pyramid method. In: Proceedings of the Human Language Technology Research Conference/North American Chapter of the Association of COmputation Linguistics, Boston, MA (2004) 145-152
17. DUC, ed.: Document Understanding Conference, NIST (2005)

Supervised TextRank*

Fermín Cruz, José A. Troyano, and Fernando Enríquez

Department of Languages and Computer Systems
University of Seville
Av. Reina Mercedes s/n 41012, Sevilla Spain
troyano@lsi.us.es

Abstract. In this paper we investigate how to adapt the TextRank method to make it work in a supervised way. TextRank is a graph based method that applies the ideas of the ranking algorithm used in Google (PageRank) to Natural Language Processing (NLP) tasks. This approach has given very good results in many NLP tasks like text summarization, keyword extraction or word sense disambiguation. In all these tasks TextRank operates in an unsupervised way, without using any training corpus. Our main contribution is the definition of a method that allows to apply TextRank to a graph that includes information generated from a training tagged corpus. We have tested our method with the Part of Speech (POS) tagging task, comparing the results with those obtained with tools specialized in this task. The performance of our system is quite near to these tools, improving the results of two of them when the corpus tagset is big and therefore the tagging task more complicated.

1 Introduction

Graphs are a very natural representation for many NLP problems. In fact, we have a graph just splitting a text into words and linking them by means of some syntactic or semantic relationship. However, this obvious relationship between texts and graphs is not always present in the models employed to implement NLP applications. For example, generative approaches based on grammars tend to use trees as representation model as a natural consequence of derivation trees.

In the other hand, statistical methods (based on corpus) rely on a great variety of representations but only a few make use of the relationship between graphs and language. Techniques like Maximun Entropy Modelling, Decision Trees, Memory Based Learning or Transformation Based Learning are quite far of including graph representations in their models. Examples of graph based techniques are Markov Models and Neural Networks, though in this cases graphs are not used to represent texts and they just give a way of connecting various elements to build a model.

Recently, there have appeared research works that begin to make use of graphs as the central representation for their models. There are even workshops

* Partially funded by Spanish Ministry of Science and Technology (TIN2004-07246-C03-03).

T. Salakoski et al. (Eds.): FinTAL 2006, LNAI 4139, pp. 632–639, 2006.

(like [9]) whose main subject is the use of general graph methods and algorithms for text processing tasks.

TextRank [6] is one of these approaches. This algorithm is based on the same idea used originally by Google [4] to calculate the relevance of each web page in Internet. It has been successfully applied to several NLP tasks. Despite of being an unsupervised method it reaches similar results in these tasks than systems that make use of additional information through annotated training corpora.

In this paper we investigate how to use TextRank in a supervised way. To do that, we have collected information from a tagged training corpus and we have included this information into a graph that is subsequently processed by the TextRank algorithm. Our intuition says that if TextRank has behaved so good working without training material, it would work better if we include in the graph information extracted from thousands of examples of a task. The key is to find the graph representation for a given problem that best exploits the power of TextRank.

We have defined a general method for constructing a graph from a tagged training corpus. This method is independent of the corpus tagset, so it can be applied to any task that attachs tags to words. We have chosen the POS tagging task for our experiments because it is easy to find resources to train the models and because there are many specialized tagger generators to compare with. We are aware that POS tagging is a well studied problem and that it is quite difficult to improve the results reached by well tested techniques like Markov Models [2] or Transformation Based Learning [3]. However, our aim is to learn from these initial experiments in order to apply these ideas to more complex tasks in the future.

The organization of the paper is as follows. In section two we present the original version of TextRank, in the third section we show how to build a graph from a training tagged corpus, fourth section includes the experimental design and the results. Finally, in section five we draw the final conclusions and point out some future work.

2 TextRank Algorithm

The main idea of TextRank is to apply a graph based ranking algorithm to NLP tasks. It uses the well known PageRank algorithm [4], one of the keys that converted Google in one of the most used browsers in Internet. PageRank provides a web page ranking that relies on the knowledge stored in web page links. It is used to calculate a relevance indicator for each page in Internet that allows Google to decide which pages would be more interesting given a user query. This idea has been successfully used in other domains, like social nets analysis or citation analysis.

Formalization of PageRank is quite easy, let $G = (V, E)$ be a graph where V is a set of vertices and E is a a set of directed edges between two vertices. Two functions are defined for a given vertex V_i:

– $In(V_i)$ calculates the set of vertices that point to V_i.
– $Out(V_i)$ calculates the set of vertices that V_i points to.

The score of a vertex V_i is computed by the following formula from In and Out operations:

$$PR(V_i) = (1 - d) + d \sum_{j \in In(V_i)} \frac{1}{|Out(V_j)|} PR(V_j)$$

where d is a dumping factor that is used to include in the model the probability of a random jump from a vertex to any other, not necessarily linked to the first one. The formula models the behavior of an Internet user that chooses randomly a link with probability d and visit a completely new page with probability $1 - d$. In the original definition of PageRank a value of 0.85 is recommended for this factor d, we have also used this value in our experiments.

An iterative algorithm is used to compute the PageRank value of each vertex of the graph. This algorithm initially assigns arbitrary values to each node and then applies iteratively the formula until convergence. This convergence is achieved when the difference of the PageRank values in two consecutive iterations is less than a predefined threshold for all the vertices in the graph. Once the iteration has finished, the value calculated for each vertex represents the importance that the algorithm has associated it.

This formula can be easily extended to admit weighted graphs. In this case the score is computed using the following formula, where p_{ji} is the weight of the edge that goes from vertex V_i to V_j:

$$WPR(V_i) = (1 - d) + d \sum_{j \in In(V_i)} \frac{p_{ji}}{\sum_{k \in Out(V_j)} p_{jk}} WPR(V_j)$$

TextRank applies the ideas of PageRank to NLP tasks. To do that it is necessary to find a way of representing the task by means of a graph. Then, PageRank can be run and the resulting scores of each nodes can be used to make decisions about the textual entities that they represent. The authors of TextRank have successfully applied it to several NLP tasks, including Keyword Extraction and Text Summarization [6] or Word Sense Disambiguation [7]. In each task the method for building the graph is different. For example, in Keyword Extraction vertices denote words, and edges represent that two words appear close in a phrase.

3 Building the Graph from an Annotated Corpus

Until now, applications developed using TextRank have followed a non supervised approach. That is, the graph is built directly from the test corpus avoiding the use of any annotated training corpus. Despite of it, TextRank achieves results comparable to supervised learning systems that use annotated corpus in the three tasks mentioned earlier. Perhaps, the reason for such an unexpected fact (the same results are achieved using less information) may be found in the nature of the selected tasks, that fit very well to graph models.

So, how good a task fits to graph models seems to be a critical factor for using TextRank to solve it. In fact, we have not found any application to other classic tasks of NLP such as POS tagging, syntactic analysis or information extraction. The goal of this work is indeed to explore other application targets for this algorithm while trying to adapt its use to a supervised framework that takes advantage of the information available in a training annotated corpus.

The first thing we have to do is to decide a graph representation of our problem from all the possible ones, in order to apply a ranking algorithm as TextRank. We have chosen a representation as general as possible, so it could be used to any tagging task. Vertices of our graphs are composed by two information units, a word w and a tag t ($V = (w, t)$). For an ambiguous word (several tags can be associated to it), as many vertices as possible tags to the word are created. The main idea of our approach is building a graph for each sentence to be tagged, applying TextRank to each of them and assigning to each word the tag from its best ranked vertex. If a word appears more that once in a sentence, independent vertices are created for each of them, this way it is possible to assign different tags to each instance of the repeated word.

Edges in our graphs represent word cooccurrence, so between two vertexes $V_i = (w_i, t_i)$ and $V_j = (w_j, t_j)$ there is an edge if the word w_j appears in the sentence just after the word w_i.

Finally, information extracted from the training corpus appears in the graph as the weights of the edges. We have tested a few metrics to this purpose and the best results have been achieved using a combination between emission probabilities $P(w|t)$ and transition probabilities $P(t|t')$, the same ones used by the bigrams based Hidden Markov Models. These probabilities are estimated counting words and tags in the corpus:

$$P(w|t) = \frac{C(w,t)}{C(t)} \qquad\qquad P(t|t') = \frac{C(t',t)}{C(t')}$$

where $C(t)$ is the count of the tag t in the training corpus, $C(w|t)$ is the count of the word w tagged with tag t and $C(t', t)$ is the count of the tag t' appearing just before the tag t.

In the Hidden Markov Models, these probabilities are used to compute the best tagged sentence maximizing this probability:

$$P(t_{1,n}|w_{1,n}) = \prod_{i=1}^{n} P(w_i|t_i)P(t_i|t_{i-1})$$

We use the probability $P(w_i|t_i)P(t_i|t_{i-1})$ to weigh the edge going from vertex $V_{i-1} = (w_{i-1}, t_{i-1})$ to vertex $V_i = (w_i, t_i)$, and then we let TextRank to compute the importance of each node. Unlike Markov Models which consider all possible solution paths of the graph as competitors, searching for the one maximizing the earlier expression, our TextRank based approach is more collaborative, because probabilities from different edges are combined in order to compute a score for each vertex.

Many of the classic improvements of Markov Models, like trigrams and unigrams computing, unknown words estimations, or interpolation, may be easily added to our system, just redefining the expression that weights the edges.

4 Experimental Design and Results

In this section we present the results we have obtained by applying different variants of the supervised TextRank with two corpus annotated with POS tags. There are many resources for this task and there are also many approaches which we can compare the results to. This task, like many others in PLN, consists of deciding which tags must be associated to a word. The set of labels is usually medium size (between 50 and 100), there are words that can only be tagged with one tag and others for which there are several possibilities. The hardest problem in this task is raised by the unknown words, that are those that previously have not been observed in the training corpus.

We have compared our results with the ones obtained with the most used tools for the POS tagging. Both corpus used are written in English, one is the Susanne corpus and the other one is made up of the four first sections of the Penn TreeBank corpus, in table 1 there can be seen the sizes of the train and test partitions for both corpus.

Table 1. Sizes of the corpus

	Words (train)	Words (test)	Tags
Susanne Corpus	141140	15482	131
Penn Corpus	198550	46461	35

The most significant difference between both corpus is the number of tags. The Penn corpus has a quite small set of tags of only 35 tags, whereas the Susanne corpus triples that number with 131. In practice this can be translated in the fact that tagging using the Susanne corpus is a much more difficult task than with the Penn corpus, as it is verified in the results.

4.1 Other Systems

In order to compare the results obtained with our supervised version of TextRank we have trained both corpus with tools specialized in the task of POS tagging. Concretely we have used the following systems:

- **TnT** [2], is one of the most widely used, based in Markov Models, is very fast and usually obtains very good results.
- **TreeTagger** [10], is based in decision trees, it generates a database register for each word that is later used to obtain the decision tree.
- **MBT** [5], carries out the training by means of example based learning, an efficient implementation of the nearest neighbour technique.

- **fnTBL** [8], is an efficient implementation of the Brill method based in the generation of transformation rules guided by error discovery.
- **MaxEnt** [1], uses maximum entropy modelling to integrate, using restrictions, the problem knowledge provided by the training corpus.

Furthermore, we have a simple tagger that we have used as the baseline in our experiments. This simple tagger associates to each word the most repeated tag in the training corpus for it.

4.2 TextRank Variants

Besides the supervised method for TextRank presented in section 3 of this article, we have included in our group of experiments two variants of the original idea.

The first variant, namely inverse TextRank, consists in calculating the transition probabilities in reverse way. Therefore, $P(t|t')$ shows the probability of tag t' being found after the tag t, and it is estimated with the following formula from the examples of the training corpus:

$$P(t|t') = \frac{C(t,t')}{C(t')}$$

In this model, the edges of the graph represent the coocurrence relations of the viewed words from right to left.

The second variant consists of the combination of the results of TextRank and inverse TextRank. In order to do this we have applied the technique of stacking, that consists of using the results of a first stage of learning to train a second level classifier. In our case, for each word of the training corpus we have created a register that contains the three tags better located according to TextRank and inverse TextRank for this word, as well as the scores obtained by each proposal. The register is completed with the real tag that is extracted directly from the training corpus. With all the registers obtained from the training corpus, we trained a decision tree that determines the tag to assign to a word based on the proposals of TextRank and inverse TextRank.

4.3 Results

Before running these experiments we knew that it was going to be difficult to obtain better results than the tools with which we would compare ourselves. The reason: these tools are very specialized in the task of the POS tagging and include special heuristics to solve this problem in the best possible way.

The table 2 shows the results of all the systems described in this article. With respect to the baseline, TextRank fully surpasses the established ones for both corpus. Considering the comparative with the other tools, our method beats TreeTagger and MBT with the Susanne corpus, and remains quite close to the rest of taggers for this corpus. In the case of the Penn corpus we did not beat any of these tools, although our results are near to MBT and TreeTagger.

Table 2. Results of the experiments

	Susanne Corpus	Penn Corpus
Baseline	79.15%	80.01%
TnT	93.61%	95.48%
TreeTagger	91.27%	94.28%
fnTBL	93.01%	95.04%
MBT	91.16%	94.40%
MaxEnt	93.09%	95.47%
TextRank	90.32%	92.14%
Inverse TextRank	89.84%	91.70%
Combined TextRank	91.51%	93.28%

Although we have obtained worse results than most of the tools, it is necessary to emphasize that our method is still in a very preliminary phase. For example, no special heuristic for the unknown words is included. It is to expect that the results will improve when this type of information is included in the construction of the graph, as most of the tools which we have compared it with includes this information. It is also necessary to emphasize that the method has behaved better with the most difficult corpus (Susanne with 131 tags as opposed to the 35 tags of the Penn corpus), which makes us think that it can work better in another type of harder tasks.

As an interpretation of these results we can conclude that the supervised TextRank method can be an alternative to other learning methods used in NLP tasks, although it is still necessary to make a deeper study to know how far it can improve and in what tasks it can give better results.

5 Conclusions and Future Work

We have studied how to adapt the unsupervised algorithm TextRank to make it work in a supervised way. We have defined a method to build a graph from a phrase that integrates information extracted from a tagged training corpus. We apply TextRank to this graph and use the ranking of each node to assign the most plausible tag to each word of the phrase. The method is based on word coocurrence and emission and transition probabilities similar to those used in Markov Models.

We have developed an experimental study using two corpus (Susanne and Penn TreeBank) tagged with POS information, and we have compared our results with those obtained by specialized tools for this kind of task. Results show that our method produces a satisfactory tagging, improving the results of two of them when we train with the Susanne corpus (this corpus sets out a more difficult problem than Penn corpus because its tagset is bigger).

Our future work will concern three main lines: 1) to study different ways of building graphs that include more information extracted from the corpus, 2) to define heuristics to manage special cases like unknown words, and 3) to apply our method to other NLP tasks like Information Extraction or Shallow Parsing to check out how it behaves with more complex tasks than POS tagging.

References

[1] Baldridge, J., Morton, T., Bierner, G.: Maxent, Mature Java package for training and using maximum entropy models. An *OpenNLP* project. (2005)

[2] Brants, T.: TnT. A statistical part-of-speech tagger. In *Proceedings of the 6th Applied NLP Conference (ANLP00).* USA (2000)

[3] Brill, E.: Transformation-based error-driven learning and natural language processing: A case study in part of speech tagging. In *Computational Linguistics* 21(4), (1995)

[4] Brin, S., Page, L.: The anatomy of a large-scale hypertextual Web search engine. In *Computer Networks and ISDN Systems.* (1998)

[5] Daelemans, W., Zavrel, J., van der Sloot, K., van den Bosch, A.: TiMBL Memory Based Learner, version 5.1, Reference Guide. ILK Research Group Technical Report Series no. 04-02. The Netherlands (2004)

[6] Mihalcea, R., Tarau, P.: TextRank. Bringing Order into Texts. In *Proceedings of the Conference on Empirical Methods in Natural Language Processing.* Barcelona, Spain (2004)

[7] Mihalcea, R., Tarau, P. Figa, E.: PageRank on Semantic Networks, with application to Word Sense Disambiguation. In *Proceedings of The 20st International Conference on Computational Linguistics* . Switzerland, Geneva (2004)

[8] Ngai, G., Florian, R.: Transformation-based learning in the fast lane. In *Proceedings of North Americal ACL 2001*, (2001)

[9] Radev, D., Mihalcea, R. (organizers): Graph-based Algorithms for Natural Language Processing. Workshop at *HLT/NAACL.* New York, USA (2006)

[10] Schmid, H.: Probabilistic Part-of-Speech Tagging Using Decision Trees. In *International Conference on New Methods in Language Processing.* Manchester, UK (1994)

Tagging a Morphologically Complex Language Using Heuristics*

Hrafn Loftsson

University of Sheffield, Department of Computer Science,
Regent Court, 211 Portobello Street,
Sheffield S1 4DP, United Kingdom
h.loftsson@dcs.shef.ac.uk

Abstract. We describe and evaluate heuristics, a collection of algorithmic procedures, which have been developed as a part of a linguistic rule-based tagger, *IceTagger*, for POS tagging Icelandic text. The purpose of the heuristics is to mark grammatical functions and prepositional phrases, and use this information to force feature agreement where appropriate. The heuristics are run after the application of local rules, i.e. rules which perform initial disambiguation based on a local context. Evaluation shows that the accuracy of two of the heuristics, which guess subjects and objects of verbs, is relatively high when compared to the results of parsing-based systems. Similar heuristics could be used for POS tagging texts in other morphologically complex languages.

1 Introduction

Part-of-speech (POS) tagging is the process of classifying word tokens according to their POS. Each word is assigned a string label, a tag, denoting information about the word class and morphological features. The tag is selected from a set of allowable tags, referred to as a tagset. Tagging text is needed for several natural language processing tasks, e.g. grammar correction, syntactic parsing, information extraction, question-answering and corpus annotation.

Tagging methods fall into two categories: data-driven methods (DDMs), (e.g. [1–3]) and linguistic rule-based methods (LRBMs) (e.g. [4, 5]). In the former approach, a pre-tagged training corpus is used to obtain, automatically, information later to be used during disambiguation. In contrast, most LRBMs use hand-crafted rules for disambiguation, as opposed to information automatically deduced from corpora.

Due to the scarcity of tagged corpora for other languages than English, German and French, the usage of DDMs may not always be a viable option. Additionally, in the case where a tagged corpus does indeed exist, data sparseness

* The author would like to thank Professor Yorick Wilks for valuable comments and suggestions in the preparation of this paper. Additionally, the Institute of Lexicography at the University of Iceland receives gratitude, for kindly providing access to the *IFD* corpus used in this research.

T. Salakoski et al. (Eds.): FinTAL 2006, LNAI 4139, pp. 640–651, 2006.

problems can occur when the size of the corpus is small, in relation to the size of the tagset [6].

In our previous work, we showed that developing a LRBM for a morphologically complex language, like Icelandic, can be a feasible option [5]. We showed that our tagger, *IceTagger*, based on this method, achieves 91.47% average tagging accuracy, when tested (using a tagset of about 660 tags) against the Icelandic Frequency Dictionary (*IFD*) corpus, a balanced corpus consisting of 590k tokens [7]. This is substantially higher than the 90.36% accuracy, achieved by the best performing DDM, using the same corpus and tagset [8] (our tagger makes about 11% less errors than the best DDM).

In this paper, we describe the heuristics used by *IceTagger*. The purpose of the heuristics is to tag grammatical functions and prepositional phrases, and use these tags to force feature agreement where appropriate. The heuristics are used by the tagger after the application of local rules, i.e. rules which perform initial disambiguation based on local context. The development of these heuristics is the main reason for a relatively short development time of the tagging system (consisting of a tokeniser, a sentence segmentiser, an unknown word guesser and a disambiguator), i.e. only 7 man-months.

This paper is organised as follows. In Sect. 2, we briefly describe the Icelandic language and its tagset. Section 3 describes different tagging methods and previous work. The tagger is described in Sect. 4, and Sect. 5 covers the heuristics in detail. In Sect. 6, we present an evaluation of the heuristics, and Sect. 7 discusses the errors and refinements. We conclude, in Sect. 8, with a summary.

2 The Icelandic Language and Its Tagset

The Icelandic language is one of the Nordic languages which comprise the North-Germanic branch of the Germanic language tree. From a syntactic point of view, Icelandic has a subject-verb-object (SVO) word order, which is, nevertheless, relatively free. The Icelandic language is a morphologically rich language, mainly due to inflectional complexity. A thorough description of the language can, for example, be found in [9].

Due to the morphological richness of the Icelandic language, the main tagset (about 660 tags), constructed in the compilation of the *IFD* corpus, is large and makes fine distinctions. We can illustrate the preciseness of the tags by the following. Each character in the tag has a particular function. The first character denotes the word class. For each word class there is a predefined number of additional characters (at most six) which describe morphological features, like gender, number and case for nouns; degree and declension for adjectives; voice, mood and tense for verbs, etc. Table 1 shows the semantics of the noun and the adjective tags.

To illustrate, consider the sentence "*fallegu hestarnir hoppuðu*" (beautiful horses jumped). The corresponding tag for "*fallegu*" is "*lkfnvf*" denoting adjective, masculine, plural, nominative, weak declension, positive; the tag for "*hestarnir*" is "*nkfng*" denoting noun, masculine, plural, nominative with suffixed

Table 1. The semantics of the noun and the adjective tags

Char #	Category/ Feature	Symbol – semantics
1	Word class	**n**–noun, **l**–adjective
2	Gender	**k**–masculine, **v**–feminine, **h**–neuter, **x**–unspecified
3	Number	**e**–singular, **f**–plural,
4	Case	**n**–nominative, **o**–accusative, **þ**–dative, **e**–genitive
5	Article	**g**–with suffixed article
5	Declension	**s**–strong, **v**–weak
6	Proper noun	**m**–person, **ö**–place, **s**–other proper name
6	Comparison	**f**–positive, **m**–comparative, **e**–superlative

definite article, and the tag for "*hoppuðu*" is "*sfg3fþ*" denoting verb, indicative mood, active voice, 3rd person, plural and past tense. Note the agreement in gender, number and case between the adjective and the noun, and the agreement in person and number between the adjective/noun and the verb.

3 Tagging Methods and Previous Work

Various DDMs have been developed in the last ten to fifteen years. Well known methods include probabilistic trigram methods [3], maximum entropy methods [2] and the transformation-based learning approach [1]. The main advantage of the DDMs is that they are both language and tagset independent, and no (or limited) human effort is needed for rule writing. On the other hand, the disadvantage is that a pre-tagged corpus is essential for training, and a limited window size is used for disambiguation (e.g. three words in the case of a trigram tagger).

Most LRBMs use hand-crafted rules for disambiguation and are developed for tagging a specific language using a particular tagset. The advantage of LRBMs is that they do not rely on the existence of a pre-tagged corpus, and rules can be written to refer to words and tags in the entire sentence. Developing a LRBM, able to compete with data-driven taggers, has, however, been considered a difficult and time-consuming task [4, 10, 11] (a different opinion has been expressed in [5, 12]).

One of the better known LRBMs is the *Constraint Grammar* (CG) framework [13], in which both POS and grammatical functions are tagged. The English CG project *EngCG-2*, developed over several years, consists of 3,600 rules [14]. Another example of a CG project is a tagger for Norwegian which took seven man-years to develop [15]. The time effort needed in these two CG systems, for developing rules for POS tagging alone, is not available, but is probably measured in man-years. A disadvantage of the Constraint Grammar Framework is *that constraints cannot be generalised, but have to be stated in a case by case fashion* [16]. This is probably the reason for the large number of rules usually developed under this framework.

The error rate of the EngCG-2 system has been reported as an order-of-magnitude lower than the error rate of a statistical tagger [14]. It is important to note, however, that the EngCG-2 system does not perform full disambiguation and the results are, thus, only presented for the same amount of remaining ambiguity. Additionally, as previously stated, the EngCG-2 has been developed over several years.

Obtaining high tagging accuracy on Icelandic text is hard, due to the morphological complexity of the language and the large tagset used. Baseline accuracy on Icelandic text is only about 76% [5].

The first tagging results for Icelandic text were presented in [8], using the *IFD* corpus and the three data-driven taggers: *TnT* [3], *fnTBL* [17] and MXPOST [2]. The highest average accuracy, 90.36%, was obtained by the TnT tagger. By combining taggers using a simple voting scheme, i.e. selecting the tag chosen by two or more of the taggers and selecting TnT's tag in the case where all the three taggers disagreed, the total accuracy increased to 91.54%.

We have, previously, developed a linguistic rule-based tagger, *IceTagger*, and an unknown word guesser, *IceMorphy*, with the purpose of, first, achieving higher tagging accuracy than previously published, and, secondly, for improving the tagging accuracy using simple voting [5]. The average tagging accuracy of *IceTagger* is 91.47%. The error rate is about 11% lower compared to using the TnT tagger. Moreover, by combining *IceTagger* with versions of *fnTBL* and *TnT*, which use features of *IceMorphy*, the tagging accuracy increased to 92.94%.

4 The Linguistic Rule-Based Tagger

Our linguistic rule-based tagger, *IceTagger*, consists of two phases: introduction of ambiguity and disambiguation. In the former phase, the set of possible tags for each word, both known words (for which tags are sorted by descending frequency) and unknown words, is introduced. This is achieved with the help of a lexicon, automatically derived from the *IFD* corpus, and *IceMorphy*, whose function is to guess the possible tags for words not known to the lexicon. For a thorough description of *IceTagger* and *IceMorphy* the reader is referred to [5].

The main characteristic in the disambiguation part of *IceTagger* is the usage of only about 200 local rules along with heuristics that perform further disambiguation based on feature agreement. The purpose of a local rule is to eliminate inappropriate tags from words based on a window of 5 words; two words to the left and right of the focus word. A typical local rule uses the word class feature of surrounding tags to eliminate a particular tag of the focus word (in fact, a rule can refer to all the individual features of a tag), e.g. to eliminate a preposition tag if the following word does only have verb tags.

Henceforth, we will use the following main illustrative sentence: "*gamli maðurinn borðar kalda súpu með mjög góðri lyst*" (*old man eats cold soup with very good appetite*[1]). After introduction of ambiguity and the application of local

[1] When translating examples to English we use word-by-word translation.

disambiguation rules by *IceTagger*, the words of this sentence have the following tags ("_" is used as a separator between tags for a given word):

Sentence 1. gamli/**lkenvf** maðurinn/**nkeng** borðar/**sfg3en_sfg2en** kalda/**lhenvf_lkfosf_lveosf_lkeþvf_lheþvf_lheovf_lheevf** súpu/**nveo_nveþ_nvee** með/**aþ_aa** mjög/**aa** góðri/**lveþsf** lyst/**nveþ_nveo_nven**[2]

5 The Heuristics

Once local disambiguation has been carried out, each sentence is sent to a global heuristic module. The heuristics are used to tag grammatical functions and prepositional phrases (PPs), and force feature agreement where appropriate. We call these heuristics global because, when disambiguating a particular word, a heuristic can refer to another word which is not necessarily in the nearest neighbourhood. Each heuristic is general, in the sense that it can be applied to a sequence of words of different word classes, as opposed to the local rules which are written on a case by case basis.

Before the heuristics are applied, each sentence is partitioned into clauses using tokens like comma, semicolon and coordinating/relative conjunctions as separators (care is taken not to break enumerations up into individual parts). The heuristics then repeatedly scan each clause and perform the following: 1) mark PPs, 2) mark verbs, 3) mark subjects, 4) force subject-verb agreement, 5) mark objects, 6) force subject-object agreement, 7) force verb-object agreement, 8) force nominal agreement and 9) force PP agreement.

We will now consider each heuristic above in turn, as well as briefly describing other miscellaneous heuristics. For space reasons, we will describe the main functionality without going into too much detail or describing exceptions. Recall that, before the heuristics are run, local rules have been applied and the list of tags for each known word is sorted by descending frequency.

5.1 Marking Prepositional Phrases

The first heuristic searches for words, in the current clause, having a prepositional tag as their first (i.e. most frequent) remaining tag. Each such word is assumed to be a preposition and, thus, all non-prepositional POS tags for the word are removed. Additionally, the word is marked with a syntactic *PP* tag. Nominals following the assumed preposition are marked with a *PP* tag as well, if there is a case feature agreement match between the nominals and the preposition.

In Sentence 1, each word (with the exception of the adverb) in the PP "*með mjög góðri lyst*" is marked with a *PP* tag, resulting in the following POS and syntactic tags:

Sentence 2. með/**aþ** PP mjög/**aa** góðri/**lveþsf** PP lyst/**nveþ_nveo_nven** PP

[2] **sfg3en/sfg2en**: verb, indicative, active, $3^{rd}/2^{nd}$ pers., sing., present tense., **aþ**: preposition governing dat., **aa**: adverb. See Table 1 for the semantics of the noun and the adjective tags.

5.2 Marking Verbs

When marking verbs in the current clause, words are searched which have a verb tag as their first remaining tag. Each such word is assumed to be a verb and, hence, all non-verb POS tags, for the word, are removed. Each verb found is marked with a functional verb tag *VERB*.

In Sentence 1, "*borðar*" is marked with the tag *VERB*.

5.3 Marking Subjects of Verbs

The third heuristic marks the one closest subject of a given verb, i.e. in most cases the head noun of a subject noun phrase (NP). Since Icelandic word order is relatively free, both "*Jón gaf eina bók*" (*John gave one book*) and "*eina bók gaf Jón*" (*one book gave John*) are possible. The heuristic thus assumes that subjects can be found either preceding or following the verb.

For each verb v, already marked with a *VERB* tag, the tokens are first scanned starting from the left of v (since SVO order is more likely than OVS order). If the immediate token to the left of v is a relative conjunction or a comma, then it is assumed that the subject can be found in the previous clause (see below). Otherwise, if the current token is a nominal (not marked with a *PP* tag) and it agrees with v in person and number, it is marked with a functional tag *SUBJ* – if not, the scanning continues.

If no subject candidate is found to the left of v, a search continues using the next two tokens to the right of v (it is thus assumed that subjects appearing further away to the right are unlikely), using the same feature agreement criterion as before.

If at this point a subject candidate has still not been found, a search is performed in the previous clause, and the first nominal found is then marked with a *SUBJ* tag (if it is not already marked as an object of a verb in the previous clause).

In Sentence 1, "*maðurinn*" is marked as a subject because it agrees with the verb "*borðar*" in person and number (notice that the modifier "*gamli*" is not marked – the heuristic described in section 5.8 will force an agreement between modifiers and heads of NPs), i.e.:

Sentence 3. gamli/**lkenvf** maðurinn/**nkeng** SUBJ borðar/**sfg3en_sfg2en** VERB

5.4 Forcing Subject-Verb Agreement

Once verbs and subjects of verbs have been identified, feature agreement is forced between the respective words.

In Sentence 3, this means removing the second person tag from the verb "*borðar*" because the subject "*maðurinn*" is third person. Moreover, if the subject is in the nominative case (which is generally the case except for subjects of special verbs that demand oblique case subjects) all non-nominative cases are removed from the subject.

5.5 Marking Objects of Verbs

This heuristic marks direct objects and verb complements. Both types receive the same functional tag *OBJ*. For each verb already marked with a *VERB* tag, a search is performed for objects following the verb or, if the search is unsuccessful, for objects preceding the verb.

Objects can be nominals (direct objects or complements) or past participle verbs (only complements). When searching for nominals, words which have already been marked with *PP* or *SUBJ* tags are ignored. Only the last word in a sequence of nominals is marked. Effectively, in most cases, this means that only the head of a NP is marked as an object. For the purpose of enforcing feature agreement between adjacent nominals, marking the head is sufficient, because, as previously stated, internal NP agreement is forced by the heuristic described in section 5.8.

In Sentence 1, the noun of the NP "*kalda súpu*" is marked as an object and the whole sentence now has the following tags:

Sentence 4. gamli/**lkenvf** maðurinn/**nkeng** SUBJ borðar/**sfg3en** VERB
kalda/**lhenvf_lkfosf_lveosf_lkeþvf_lheþvf_lheovf_lheevf**
súpu/**nveo_nveþ_nvee** OBJ
með/**aþ_aa** PP mjög/**aa** góðri/**lveþsf** PP lyst/**nveþ_nveo_nven** PP

5.6 Forcing Subject-Object Agreement

In Icelandic, feature agreement is needed between a subject and a verb complement. For example, in sentences like "*Jón er fallegur*" and "*María er falleg*" (*John/Mary is beautiful*), the complement adjusts itself to the subject. This heuristic forces such an agreement.

5.7 Forcing Verb-Object Agreement

Icelandic verbs govern the case of their direct objects which is, generally, either accusative or dative. A verb complement is, however, always in the nominative case. The correct case of a direct object must be "learnt" for each verb, because no general rule applies. For example, "*Jón gaf bókina*" (accusative object; *John gave book*) is correct but not "*Jón henti bókina*" but rather "*Jón henti bókinni*" (dative object; *John threw book*).

A lookup table, automatically derived from the *IFD* corpus, is used for determining the correct case for direct objects (this table thus provides partial verb subcategorisation information). A lookup is performed for a given verb lexeme and the correct case is returned. Tags of the associated object that do not include the correct case are then removed. If the lookup is unsuccessful, and the marked object is not a complement, then only the nominative case tags are removed from the object (in this case, as discussed in Section 5.10, the most frequent tag of the object is used).

In Sentence 4, the verb "*borðar*" demands an accusative object, and, as a result, all non-accusative case tags are removed from the object "*súpu*". After this removal, the sentence part "*borðar kalda súpu*", thus, contains the following tags:

Sentence 5. borðar/**sfg3en** VERB
kalda/**lhenvf_lkfosf_lveosf_lkeþvf_lheþvf_lheovf_lheevf**
súpu/**nveo** OBJ

5.8 Forcing Agreement Between Nominals

Agreement in gender, number and case between a noun and its modifiers is a characteristic of Icelandic NPs. This heuristic forces such an agreement in the following manner. Starting at the end of a clause, it searches for a nominal *n*, i.e. a head of a NP. If a head is found, the heuristic searches for modifiers to the left of *n* (care must be taken not to step inside a PP phrase if *n* itself is not part of that PP phrase). Agreement is forced between the head and its modifiers by removing inappropriate tags from either word.

In Sentence 5, the heuristic removes the six tags **lhenvf_lkfosf_lkeþvf_-lheþvf_lheovf_lheevf** from the adjective "*kalda*", in order to force gender, number and case agreement with the tags of the following noun "*súpu*". Additionally, this heuristic removes the tags **nveo_nven** from the noun "*lyst*" (see Sentence 2) because of the feature agreement with the preceding adjective "*góðri*". Notice that an agreement already holds in the first NP, "*gamli maðurinn*" (see Sentence 3). After these tag eliminations, the final disambiguated sentence looks like:

Sentence 6. gamli/**lkenvf** maðurinn/**nkeng** SUBJ borðar/**sfg3en** VERB
kalda/**lveosf** súpu/**nveo** OBJ
með/**aþ** PP mjög/**aa** góðri/**lveþsf** PP lyst/**nveþ** PP

5.9 Forcing Prepositional Phrase Agreement

The last main heuristic forces feature agreement in prepositional phrases. Two things need to be accounted for. First, when a preposition has two possible case tags, i.e. accusative and dative tags (which is common for prepositions like "*á, eftir, fyrir, í, með*" (*on, after, for, in, with*)), the heuristic removes one of the case tags based on the case of a following word in the PP.

If a following word does not unambiguously select the correct tag for the preposition then a search is performed for a preceding verb. A verb-preposition pair does, usually, unambiguously determine the correct case of the preposition. For example, in the sentence "*Jón settist á plötu*" (*John sat-down on brick*) the verb-preposition pair "*settist á*" determines an accusative case for the preposition "*á*". In contrast, in the sentence "*Jón lá á plötu*" (*John lay on brick*) the pair "*lá á*" determines a dative case for the preposition "*á*". In this case, a lookup table, automatically derived from the *IFD* corpus, is used for determining the correct case of the preposition. A lookup is performed for a given verb-preposition lexeme, the correct case returned and the conflicting tag of the preposition is removed. If the lookup is unsuccessful the most frequent tag of the preposition is used.

Secondly, once the correct preposition case tag is determined, a case agreement between the preposition and the rest of the words in the PP is forced. This is straight-forward, since the correct case is now known and the words to search for have already been marked by the heuristic described in section 5.1.

This heuristic does not have any effect on our example sentence because the sentence is, at this point, already fully disambiguated.

5.10 Other Miscellaneous Heuristics

In addition to the above main heuristics, specific heuristics are used to choose between supine and past participle verb forms, infinitive or active verb forms, and ensuring agreement between reflexive pronouns and their antecedents. Finally, for words that have still not yet been fully disambiguated, the default heuristic is simply to choose the most frequent tag.

6 Evaluation

In this section, we evaluate the heuristics *per se*, i.e. the accuracy of the syntactic and functional (SynFunc) tagging, which the heuristics base their disambiguation process on.

We built a *gold standard* by randomly selecting 150 sentences from the *IFD* corpus and hand-tagged these sentences with SynFun tags, i.e. *PP* tags and *SUBJ*, *VERB* and *OBJ* tags. The sentences contain a total of 2,868 tokens, i.e. 19.1 tokens per sentence, on the average. During hand-tagging, 1,691 (59%) tokens received a SynFun tag.

We then ran *IceTagger* on the 150 sentences and computed precision and recall[3] for the SynFun tags generated by the tagger. The POS tagging accuracy of *IceTagger* for these sentences was 92.29%, and the ratio of unknown words was 8.26%.

Table 2 shows how the 1,691 tokens divide between the four SynFun tags. Not surprisingly, the number of *PP* tags is highest because each word in a PP (with the exception of an adverb) is tagged. Furthermore, *VERB* tags outnumber *SUBJ* and *OBJ* tags because a verb(s) occurs in almost every sentence. More *SUBJ* tags than *OBJ* tags are found which can be explained by the fact that not all verbs are transitive, but a subject is, generally, needed.

Table 3 shows precision (p), recall (r) and F-measure, $F_{\beta=1}$ (2*p*r/(p+r)), for the different tag types, guessed by the heuristics. The table shows much higher F-measure for *VERB* and *PP* tags compared to *SUBJ* and *OBJ* tags. This is to be expected because guessing the former is much easier than guessing the latter. As explained in section 5.2, a token receives a *VERB* functional tag if the first POS tag, in its (locally disambiguated) tag list, is a verb tag.

[3] *Precision* = # of correct generated tags / # of generated tags. *Recall* = # of correct generated tags / # of tags in the *gold standard*.

Table 2. Partition of SynFun tag types

Tag type	Gold standard		Generated by *IceTagger*	
SUBJ	265	(15.7%)	254	(15.4%)
VERB	425	(25.1%)	423	(25.6%)
OBJ	216	(12.8%)	219	(13.3%)
PP	785	(46.4%)	754	(45.7%)
Total	1,691	(100.0%)	1,650	(100.0%)

Table 3. Precision, recall and F-measure for SynFun tag types

Tag type	Precision	Recall	F-measure	F-measure no unknown words
SUBJ	85.43%	81.89%	83.62%	85.11%
VERB	94.56%	94.12%	94.34%	94.95%
OBJ	72.60%	73.61%	73.10%	74.59%
PP	97.61%	93.76%	95.65%	95.73%

Similarly, a preposition candidate is easy to guess and the accompanying PP words are just those nominals having the same case as the preposition. Guessing the functional *SUBJ* and *OBJ* tags is, however, more difficult because the correct guess is not only dependent on the word class, but also on word order and verb subcategorisation information.

Recall that 8.26% of the tokens, behind the figures in columns 2-4 in Table 3, were unknown to the tagger. As expected, the accuracy improves when including the unknown words in the lexicon as can be seen in column 5.

7 Discussion

There are various different causes for errors in the *SUBJ* and *OBJ* tagging. One source of error is the lack of verb subcategorisation information in *IceTagger*. For example, in the sentence "*þarna svelgdist ykkur á bjórnum*" (*there quaff you on beer*) the verb "*svelgdist*" demands a dative subject (but not the usual nominative subject) and, hence, the pronoun "*ykkur*" should be tagged with a *SUBJ* tag, but not an *OBJ* tag.

Table 3 shows substantially higher F-measure for *SUBJ* vs. *OBJ*. We have noticed that PPs are responsible for many of the *OBJ* errors (and, indeed, some of the *SUBJ* errors as well). In the sentence "*hann heyrði með öðru eyranu hljóðin*" (*he heard with one ear sounds*), the noun "*hljóðin*" is a direct object of the verb "*heyrði*", but the PP "*með öðru eyranu*" lies between the verb and the object. The heuristic described in section 5.5 does not handle such intervening PPs. Furthermore, in some cases, *IceTagger* tags OBJs as VERBs, due to lack of an appropriate local disambiguation rule.

Our error analysis implies that the accuracy of *SUBJ / OBJ* tagging may be improved by the following. First, by adding more thorough verb subcategorisation information to *IceTagger*. Secondly, by "stepping over" intervening PPs, between the verb and the corresponding *SUBJ* or/and *OBJ*, when searching for subjects and objects. Lastly, by writing more local rules, thus eliminating more inappropriate tags before the heuristics are applied. Improving the accuracy of *SUBJ / OBJ* tagging will most probably increase the POS tagging accuracy of *IceTagger*.

It would be interesting to compare the figures for the functional *SUBJ* and *OBJ* tags with corresponding evaluation figures produced by a parser for Icelandic text. Unfortunately, no such figures are available. Several results on tagging grammatical functions have, however, been published for related languages. A recent study on grammatical function assignment for German (using memory-based learning from a corpus annotated with grammatical functions tags), showed $F_{\beta=1}$ as 87.23%, 78.60% and 75.32%, for subjects, accusative objects and verb complements, respectively [18] (recall that our figures for *OBJ* tags include both direct objects and verb complements). In another German study (using finite-state cascades to annotate grammatical functions on top of a shallow constituent structure), the corresponding $F_{\beta=1}$ were 90.77%, 81.86% and 79.61%, respectively [19].

Since both these methods are based on parsing, higher scores are to be expected in comparison to our (non-parsing) heuristics. Nevertheless, this comparison shows that the accuracy of our heuristics for tagging subjects and objects of verbs is relatively high. Moreover, improving the accuracy of these heuristics is possible, as discussed above.

8 Conclusion

We have described heuristics used by *IceTagger*, a linguistic rule-based tagger for tagging Icelandic text. The purpose of the heuristics is to tag grammatical functions and prepositional phrases, and use these tags to force feature agreement where appropriate.

Our linguistic rule-based framework, consisting of relatively few local rules for initial disambiguation and heuristics for further disambiguation, could be applicable to other morphologically complex languages. The development of a tagging framework like ours is a feasible option when the usage of a data-driven method is difficult, due to lack of pre-tagged corpora or due to data sparseness.

Our error analysis demonstrates that the accuracy of the heuristics can still be improved which, in turn, will most probably increase the overall tagging accuracy of *IceTagger*.

References

1. Brill, E.: Transformation-Based Error-Driven Learning and Natural Language Processing: A Case Study in Part of Speech Tagging. Computational Linguistics **21** (1995) 543–565

2. Ratnaparkhi, A.: A Maximum Entropy Part-of-Speech Tagger. In: Proceedings of the Empirical Methods in Natural Language Processing Conference, Philadelphia, PA, USA (1996)
3. Brants, T.: TnT: A statistical part-of-speech tagger. In: Proceedings of the 6th Conference on Applied natural language processing, Seattle, WA, USA (2000)
4. Voutilainen, A.: A syntax-based part-of-speech analyzer. In: Proceedings of the 7th Conference on European Chapter of the ACL, Dublin, Ireland (1995)
5. Loftsson, H.: Tagging Icelandic text: A linguistic rule-based approach. Technical Report CS-06-04, Department of Computer Science, University of Sheffield (2006)
6. Schmid, H.: Improvements in Part-of-Speech Tagging with an Application to German. In: European Chapter of the ACL SIGDAT workshop, Dublin, Ireland (1995)
7. Pind, J., Magnússon, F., Briem, S.: The Icelandic Frequency Dictionary. The Institute of Lexicography at the University of Iceland, Reykjavik, Iceland (1991)
8. Helgadóttir, S.: Testing Data-Driven Learning Algorithms for PoS Tagging of Icelandic. In Holmboe, H., ed.: Nordisk Sprogteknologi 2004. Museum Tusculanums Forlag (2004)
9. Þráinsson, H.: Icelandic. In König, E., Auwera, J., eds.: The Germanic Languages. Routledge, London (1994)
10. Brill, E.: A Simple Rule-Based Part of Speech Tagger. In: Proceedings of the 3rd Conference on Applied natural language processing, Trento, Italy (1992)
11. Samuelsson, C.: Morphological tagging based entirely on Bayesian inference. In Eklund, R., ed.: 9th Scandinavian Conference on Computational Linguistics, Stockholm, Sweden (1994)
12. Chanod, J.P., Tapanainen, P.: Tagging French – comparing a statistical and a constraint-based method. In: Proceedings of the 7th Conference on European Chapter of the ACL Conference, Dublin, Ireland (1995)
13. Karlsson, F.: Constraint Grammar as a Framework for Parsing Running Text. In Karlgren, H., ed.: Papers presented to the 13th International Conference on Computational Linguistics, Helsinki, Finland (1990)
14. Samuelsson, C., Voutilainen, A.: Comparing a Linguistic and a Stochastic tagger. In: Proceedings of the 8th Conference on European Chapter of the ACL, Madrid, Spain (1997)
15. Hagen, K., Johannessen, J., Nøklestad, A.: A Constraint-Based Tagger for Norwegian. In Lindberg, C.E., Lund, S.N., eds.: 17th Scandinavian Conference on Computational Linguistics. Odense Working Papers in Language and Communication. Volume 19. Odense, Denmark (2000) 31–48
16. Hinrichs, E., Trushkina, J.: Getting a Grip on Morphological Disambiguation. In: Proceedings of KONVENS 2002, 6. Konferenz zur Verarbeitung natürlicher Sprache, Saarbrücken, Germany (2002)
17. Ngai, G., Florian, R.: Transformation-Based Learning in the Fast Lane. In: Proceedings of the 2nd Conference of the North American Chapter of the ACL, Pittsburgh, PA, USA (2001)
18. Kouchnir, B.: Knowledge-Poor Grammatical Function Assignment for German. Manuscript. Seminar für Sprachwissenschaft (2004)
19. Müller, F.H.: Annotating Grammatical Functions in German Using Finite-State Cascades. In: 20th International Conference on Computational Linguistics, Geneva, Switzerland (2004)

Terminology Structuring Through the Derivational Morphology

Natalia Grabar[1] and Thierry Hamon[2]

[1] Université Paris Descartes, Faculté de Médecine; Inserm, UMR_S 729; SPIM, 75006 Paris, France
natalia.grabar@spim.jussieu.fr
[2] LIPN – UMR CNRS 7030, Université Paris-Nord, Avenue J.B. Clément, 93430 Villetaneuse, France
thierry.hamon@lipn.univ-paris13.fr

Abstract. In this work, we address the deciphering of semantic relations between terms in order to build structured terminologies. We study particularly the contribution of morphological clues. Among linguistic operations proposed by the morphology, we analyze affixation and suppletion. We show interpretative schemata emerging from morphologically formed lexemes and corresponding terminological relations. Morphology appears to be a useful tool for the deciphering of semantic relations between terms.

1 Introduction

Terminological resources allow to encode knowledge of a given technical or scientific area. The content of such resources is known to depend on the application needs [1], furthermore collected terms can be organized in a more or less sophisticated way: a simple list of terms, term records in term banks, structured terminology, etc. In this work, we focus on the building of structured terminologies from textual corpora. We rely particularly on the deciphering of semantic relationships between terms based on their morphological structure. We address here mainly affixation clues and show how they can be used for terminology structuring. Using morphological operations for such a task is suggested by the fact that these operations are one of the basics for the formation of vocabulary.

We start with the presentation of types of semantic relationships between terms in structured terminologies (sec. 2), and approaches currently used for the deciphering of such relationships (sec. 3). We then present the material we need for the deciphering of semantic relations through morphological operations (sec. 4), and we describe and analyze clues provided by morphology as well as types of relationships which can be induced with these clues (sec. 5). We apply this method on terms from two areas: medicine and cogeneration[1] [2]. We finally conclude and draw some perspectives (sec. 6).

[1] Cogeneration is a technology used for the generation of electricity. It allows to combine the generation of electricity and of heat (hot water, steam, ...)

T. Salakoski et al. (Eds.): FinTAL 2006, LNAI 4139, pp. 652–663, 2006.

2 Semantic Relationships in Structured Terminologies

The structuring of terms can be obtained using different types of semantic relationships. According to the nature of related terms, we distinguish three types of relationships [3]: taxonomic, lexical and transversal.

Taxonomic relationships organize terms within a tree. Two kinds of taxonomic relations can be distinguished: hierarchical and partitive. *Hierarchical* (`is-a`, *subsumption*, *hyperonymy* or *hyponymy*) relationships link a generic term to its specific terms. These relationships are most present in structured terminological resources and traditionally forms their backbone. Examples above are from medical terminology SNOMED [4]:

pneumonie (*pneumonia*)	`is-a`	*bronchopneumonie* (*bronchopneumonia*)
pneumopathie inflammatoire (*pneumonitis*)	`is-a`	*bronchopneumonie* (*bronchopneumonia*)
bronchopneumonie (*bronchopneumonia*)	`is-a`	*maladie de l'appareil respiratoire* (*diseases of the respiratory system*)

Partitive (*meronymy*, *mereology*, `part-whole` or `part-of`) relationships are often used to describe artefacts and living organisms through the enumeration of their constituant parts. When they are assimilated to hierarchical relationships, they can ensure the hierarchical structuring of terms as well:

poumon (*lung*) `part-of` *appareil respiratoire* (*respiratory system*)

Lexical relationships are established between terms which are subsumed by the same hyperonym. These relationships correspond to two types: synonymy and antonymy. They are less frequently identified in terminologies than taxonomic relationships. *Equivalence* relationships (*synonymy*) link terms which refer to the same entity. For instance, the terms *pneumonie* (*pneumonia*) and *pneumopathie inflammatoire* (*pneumonitis*) are synonymous within the medical terminology SNOMED. Synonymy can also relate variants of a given term. *Opposite* (*adverse* or *antonymy*) relationship relies on co-hyponyms which are not synonyms [5]. This relationship exists for instance between cogeneration terms *électricité nucléaire* (*nuclear power*) and *électricité non nucléaire* (*not nuclear power*) [2].

Transversal relationships relate terms which are located in different branches of hierarchical tree. When these relationships are under-specified they are addressed as `see-also` relationships. They can also be used to finely depict the domain knowledge. In postcoordinated terminologies these relationships ensure defining complex terms on the basis of their known semantic primitives and composition rules [6,7]. For instance, the diagnosys *pneumonie* (*pneumonia*) can be defined as a morphological affection *inflammation* (*inflammation*) which is located in a body part *poumon* (*lung*):

pneumonie (*pneumonia*) → `is-a` → *inflammation* (*inflammation*)
↘ `located-in` → *poumon* (*lung*)

3 Approaches for Mining Relationships Between Terms

Two types of approaches for the deciphering of semantic relationships between terms are usually distinguished: external approaches based on the analysis of contexts in which terms occur, and internal approaches based on the analysis of the internal structure of terms. Both are related to given types of relationships and are necessarily overseen by human expertise. Automatic tools based on these approaches are often designed for the detection of taxonomic relatioships, whereas synonymy pays less attention. As for transversal relationships, they are neglected but can take advantage of the acquisition of taxonomic and synonymous relationships, being sometimes their side effect.

External approaches rely on text corpora. On one hand, they aim at the detection of expressions and phrases sensitive to contain given type of relationships between two terms, i.e. markers and lexico-syntactic patterns [8,9,10,11,12]. On the other hand, they aim at the detection of common contexts or cooccurrences of terms and then group them into homogeneous classes [13,14,15]. They can provide with various semantic relationships.

Among internal approaches for terms structuring, we distinguish lexical inclusion analysis for the deciphering of taxonomic relationships [16,17,18], transformation rules for detection of synonyms and morpho-syntactic variants of terms [19,20], and analysis of morphological structure of words. As we are particularly interested in this last work, we present it in more detail.

Lexical functions [21], can thus be used for the encoding of semantic relationships between terms [22] or even for their automated detection [23,24]:

$\mathbf{Real}_1(\textit{logiciel}) = \textit{excuter, faire tourner}$
$\quad(\mathbf{Real}_1(\textit{program}) = \textit{to run})$
$\mathbf{S}_0(\textit{programmer}) = \textit{programmation}$
$\quad(\mathbf{S}_0(\textit{to program}) = \textit{programming})$

In these examples, lexical functions indicate the nature of semantic relationships between lexemes ($\mathbf{Real}_1$ for `realizes`, $\mathbf{S}_0$ for `subject`) and can lead to semantic and terminological relationships between them. Furthermore, the work described in [25] presents denominal adjectives as clues for the detection of semantic relations between terms. The aim of our work is to propose a more complete investigation of morphological clues for terminology structuring. We rely on the analysis of these clues which are suggested by derivational morphology, and specifically by affixation and suppletion.

4 Material

The main condition needed for the deciphering of semantic relationships between terms through the morphology is the understanding of morphological operations as well as their impact on the semantics of formed lexemes. This can be performed when studying linguistic morphological description of languages. Indeed, derivational morphology proposes a set of linguistic operations which allow the creation of "new" lexemes (nouns, adjectives, verbs, etc.). We adopt here the approach of morphological analysis of lexemes as proposed in [26], which is particularly suitable for natural language processing, as it allows to explain the construction of the meaning of lexemes. In this approach, the meaning is conveyed by morphological operations and operators (affixes, bases, compounds), and the meaning of complex lexemes is constructed at the same time as their form. Derivational morphology proposes the following main types of operations:

- *Affixation* (*derivation*), which combines bases (*artery*, *stenosis*) and affixes (suffixes, such as *-al*, *-ic*, prefixes or infixes):
  {*artère*, *artér*iel} ({*artery*, *arter*ial})
  {*sténose*, *sténot*ique} ({*stenosis*, *stenot*ic})
- *Conversion* describes formations where morphologically related lexemes have the same form but different syntactic categories:
  {*muqueuse*/A, *muqueuse*/N} ({*mucous*/A, *mucous membrane*/N})
  {*wound*/N, *wound*/V}
- *Compounding* combines at least two bases and forms compound lexemes:
  artery and *scopy* gives *arterio*scopy

Suppletion, which is not a morphological operation, allows relating and substituting bases which have the same meaning but are provided by different languages, often Greek and Latin. Suppletion can appear both in affixation and compounding operations. For instance, *estomac* (*stomach*) (latin word) can be substituted with *gastr-* (greek word) and *foie* (*liver*) with *hepat-* (greek word):

{*estomac*, *gastr*ique} ({*stomach*, *gastr*ic})
{*foie*, *hépat*ique} ({*liver*, *hepat*ic})

Affixation is a basic morphological operation widely used in many languages. But both compounding and suppletion, being related to the use of greek and latin words, are often reserved for some specialized languages, like medecine, agronomics or biology. We assume that all morphological operations can potentially lead to the deciphering of semantic relations between terms and are then useful for terminology structuring.

Morphological parsing and the analysis of lexemes can be reached with a list of morphological operators [27], morphological lexicon [28,29,30,31] or automated tools [32]. In this work, we mainly use a morphological lexicon built in a previous work [33] and some affixes which convey suitable semantic relations for terminology structuring. Both are related to suppletion and affixation operations. We use a medical dictionary [34] as reference knowledge for the validation of the morphologically built meaning of medical lexemes and terms.

5 Morphologically-Induced Terminology Structuring

5.1 Suppletion

Suppletion provides with relations of equivalence and pseudo-synonymy between two bases from different languages: *estomac* (*stomach*) and *gastr-*, *foie* (*liver*) and *hepat-* in previous examples. By extension, affixed and compound lexemes in which suppletive bases are the only difference can be considered as equivalent or (quasi-)synonymous [35]. The semantic proximity between lexemes coined with suppletive bases is reinforced if involved morphological operations are equivalent. The following first example corresponds to the coining of verbs from two noun bases with the same meaning *pierre* (*stone*), the second example corresponds to the coining of adjectives from two bases which mean *estomac* (*stomach*):

1. *pért-* and *lith-* ⟶ *pétr*ifier and *lith*ifier
2. *estomac* and *gastr-* ⟶ *stomac*al (*stomach*al) and *gastr*ique (*gastr*ic)

Both examples allow the construction of lexemes with very close meanings.

5.2 Affixation

Affixation refers to the creation of lexemes by adding affixes to bases. The meaning of affixed lexemes is the result of influence of the meaning conveyed by affix on its base. We present here prefixation and suffixation operations and their possible semantic involvement in the terminology structuring.

Prefixation

Construction of opposite meaning. The opposite meaning can be constructed with negation prefixes *dé-*, *ir-*, *anti-*, *non-*, *in-*, or with privative prefixes *a-*, *dys-* [36]. The usefulness of some of such prefixes for terminology structuring has already been noticed in [23]. In the present work, we used a set of 52 word pairs linked together with such morphological operations (*i.e.*, {*accessible*, *inaccessible*}, {*fonction*, *dysfonction*}), and this allowed us relating 40 pairs of medical terms, among which 30 pairs comprise complex terms. All the induced pairs have been validated as correct:

- {*activateur du plasminogène*, *inactivateur du plasminogène*} ({*plasminogen activator*, *plasminogen inactivator*})
- {*kératose*, *dyskératose*} ({*keratosis*, *dyskeratosis*})
- {*continence fécale*, *incontinence fécale*} ({*fecal continence*, *fecal incontinence*})
- {*cycle mensuel normal*, *cycle mensuel anormal*} ({*normal menstrual cycle*, *abnormal menstrual cycle*})

Construction of meaning for spatial localization. Transversal relations for relative spatial localization can be detected through prefixes like *sur-*, *sous-*, *contre-*, *péri-* [36]. We used 99 word pairs linked with 12 such prefixes, and related 40 term pairs, among which 21 pairs with complex terms. All the induced pairs have been considered as correct:

- {*abcès rénal*, *abcès périrénal*} ({*renal abscess*, *perirenal abscess*})
- {*hyperplasie kystique*, *hyperplasie intrakystique*} ({*cystic hyperplasia*, *intracystic hyperplasia*})
- {*cervicite chronique*, *endocervicite chronique*} ({*chronic cervicitis*, *chronic endocervicitis*})
- {*région auriculaire*, *région sous-auriculaire*} ({*auricular region*, *infraauricular region*})

Other prefixes can lead to other meanings possibly useful for terminology structuring: temporal localization (*pré-*, *post-*), comparison (*super-*), etc.

Suffixation

*Construction of agent and action nouns.*When constructing agent and action nouns, morphological rules apply suffixes to verbal bases V. Agent nouns are mainly formed with the suffix *-eur* (*-or*, *-er*), and receive the general semantic instruction *The agent that V*. Action nouns are formed with suffixes *-age*, *-ade*, *-erie*, *-ment*, *-tion* or *-ure* (*-age*, *-ing*, *-ment*, *-tion*), and receive the general semantic instruction *Action of V* or *Result of V*. These rules allow the detection of transversal relations among terms, called respectively `actor-of`, `action-of` and`result-of` [23]. The suffix *-eur* (*-or*, *-er*) is ambiguous and can match with substrings which are not affixes, like in the following examples:

vapeurs de métal (*metal fumes*)
tumeur à cellules géantes (*giant cell tumor*)

Despite this the suffix *-eur* allows the deciphering of semantic relations between terms with a good precision. Here are few examples from medicine (ME) and electricity (EL) areas:

ME - *activateur du plasmogène* (*plasminogen activator*)
- *buveur modéré de boisson alcoolisée* (*alcoholic beverage moderate drinker*)
- *gros fumeur de cigarettes (plus de 20 cigarettes par jour)* (*heavy smoker (over 20 per day)*)
- *marqueur lymphocytaire* (*lymphocyte marker*)
- *dialyseur péritonéal* (*peritoneal dialyzer*)

EL - *producteur d'électricité* (*electricty producer*)
- *capteur solaire* (*solar panel*)
- *consommateur éligible* (*eligible consumer*, *eligible customer*)
- *disjoncteur de couplage* (*circuit breaker*)
- *cogénérateur* (*cogenerator*)
- *constructeur de turbine* (*turbine manufacturer*)
- *compresseur gaz* (*gas compressor*)

As for suffixes that label process or its result they allow the detection of terms which introduce `action-of` and `result-of` relations:

ME - *blessure par balle* (*gunshot wound*)
- *brûlure avec carbonisation* (*burn injury with charring*)
- *blocage congénital* (*congenital obstruction*, *congenital blocking*)
- *tamponade* (*compression*, *compressed structure*, *tamponade*)
- *tatouage* (*tattoo*)
- *ablation* (*excision*, *ablation*, *abscission*, *extirpation*)
- *absorption intestinale anormale* (*abnormal intestinal absorption*)

EL - *alimentation électrique* (*electricity supply, electricity supplying*)
- *production éolienne* (*production of aeolian energy*)
- *raccordement au réseau* (*connection to the mains*)
- *aspiration* (*sucking, suction*)
- *refoulement* (*delivery*)
- *protection électrique* (*electric protection, electric depositing*)

Construction of nouns with partitive meaning. The morphological rule for the construction of nouns with collective meaning operates suffixes: *-ade*, *-age*, -*ail(le)* and *-ure* [37], which sometimes correspond to *-ing* in English. Constructed nouns mean that they contain one or more occurrences of base noun. It possibly introduces the `part-of` relations [37,23]. These suffixes are ambiguous and require human validation of induced relations.

ME *ossature* (*skeletal system, skeleton*)
palmature congénitale (*congenital webbing, congenital membrane*)
vergeture (*linear atrophy, stretch marks*)
vomissure gastrique (*gastric vomitus*)
arcade sus-pyramidale du rein (*arcuate artery of kidney*)
cordage tendineux (*chordae tendineae*)

EL *sciure* (*sawdust*)
outillage (*tools, equipment*)
câblage électrique (*electric cabling*)

Construction of relational meaning: denominal adjectives. The rule, which coins denominal or relational adjectives, applies a set of suffixes to noun bases. Among these suffixes we have *-aire*, *-el*, *-al*, *-ique*, *-eux*, *-ien*, *-in*, *-ois* and *-é* (e.g. -*al*, *-ant*, *-ary*, *-ic*, *-ous*, *-ive* and *-'s*). Constructed adjectives receive the general semantic instruction *Relative to N* and allow then the indentification of semantic relations among base nouns and their derived adjectives:

{*aorte/Nom, aortique/Adj*} ({*aorta/Noun, aortic/Adj*})
{*germe/Nom, germinal/Adj*} ({*germ/Noun, germinal/Adj*})

But, when occurring in noun phrases, relational adjectives establish semantic relations among base nouns as well (*aorte* (*aorta*), *germe* (*germ*)) and their head nouns (*sténose* (*stenosis*), *cellule* (*cell*)) [38]:

sténose aortique (*aortic stenosis*)
cellule germinale (*germinal cell*)

These indications can be used for the deciphering of semantic relations between terms t_1 and t_2, especially when t_2 contains adjective formed with such suffixes on the basis of the head noun of the term t_1. [38] distinguishes two types of relations among relational adjective and its head noun. These relations are close to the `part-of` relation, namely belonging and possession:

– The belonging relation is constructed, in French, with suffixes *-é*, *-aire*, *-eux*, *-in* and *-ique*. The head noun corresponds to the whole entity, while the base noun of the adjective to its part:
  nerf denté (*dentate nerve*, *toothed nerve*): which means that the
  Nerve is tooth-shaped or *Nerve has teeth.*
– The possession relation is constructed, in French, with suffixes *-al*, *-aire*, *-el*, *-ien*, *-in*, *-ique* and *-ois*. The head noun corresponds to the part of an entity and the base noun of the adjective to whole entity:
  nerf dental (*dental nerve*): which means that the
  Nerve is located in the tooth.

In other words, in a noun phrase with relation of belonging base noun belongs to head noun, and in a noun phrase with possession base noun possesses head noun.

We applied these clues to medical and cogeneration terms and noticed that these semantic relations are particularly reliable when linking simple noun terms t_1 (*abdomen*) with noun phrase terms t_2 (*abdominal abscess*). When occuring in more complex terms, this operation has to be supported by strong syntactic analysis and then by manual validation. In table 1 we present few examples with medical terms. The first column contains simple term t_1 (base noun). The second column contains complex term t_2 (with the relational adjective). In the last column we indicate type of relations: p for possession and b for belonging.

Table 1. Examples of belonging/possession relations in medical terms

term t_1 (base noun)	term t_2 (with affixed adjective)	rel.
abdomen (*abdomen*)	⇒ *abcès abdominal* (*abdominal abscess*)	p
amygdale (*tonsil*)	⇒ *noyau amygdalien* (*amygdaloid nucleus*)	p
anévrisme (*aneurysm*)	⇒ *hématome anévrismal* (*aneurysmal hematoma*)	p
artère (*artery*)	⇒ *cône artériel* (*conus arteriosus*)	p
achromie (*achromasia*)	⇒ *mélanome achromique* (*amelanotic melanoma*)	b
actinomycose (*actinomycosis*)	⇒ *infection actinomycosique* (*actinomycotic infection*)	b
athérome (atheroma)	⇒ *embolie athéromateuse* (*atheromatous embolus*)	b

Furthermore, in specialized languages, such global semantic instructions (belonging and possession) can lead to more specific meaning. For instance, in examples of possession, when (1) the base noun of the adjective means a part of body or a tissue (*abdomen*, *amygdale*, etc.) and (2) when the head noun of the adjective means an illness or injury (*abcès*, *fibrosarcome*, etc.), the resulting relation corresponds typically to localisation:
  abcès abdominal (*abdominal abscess*) `located-in` *abdomen* (*abdomen*),
  noyau amygdalien (*amygdaloid nucleus*) `located-in` *amygdale* (*tonsil*)
But possession couples can also induce other types of semantic relations:
  cône artériel (*conus arteriosus*) `conducts-to` *artère* (*artery*)
  hématome anévrismal (*aneurysmal hematoma*) `produced-by` *anévrisme* (*aneurysm*)
When terms comprise more that one relational adjective, which builds both possession and belonging relations, interpretation schemas get more complex:

- *ganglion lymphatique abdominal* (*abdominal lymph node*):
ganglion (*node*) `contains` *lymphe* (*lymph*) `located-in` *abdomen*
- *vésicule cutanée acantholytique* (*acantholytic blister*):
(*vésicule* `located-in` *peau*) (*blister*) `caused-by` *acantholyse* (*acantholysis*)

Such analysis of medical terms can be qualified through the semantic axes of their primitives, for instance those from SNOMED, as it has been done with compound terms [39]. Term *ganglion lymphatique abdominal* (*abdominal lymph node*) can thus be described as the combination of axes M (morphology or illness) and T (topology or body parts): *ganglion* (*node*) from axis M, *lymphe* (*lymph*) from axis T, and *abdomen abdomen* from axis T.

Below, we give a few similar examples from the cogeneration area (possession `p` and belonging `b` relations):

term t_1 (base noun)		term t_2 (with affixed adjective)	rel.
atmosphère (*atmosphere*)	⇒	*polluant atmosphérique* (*atmospheric contaminants*)	`p`
industrie (*industry*)	⇒	*déchet industriel* (*industrial waste*)	`p`
troposphère (*troposphere*)	⇒	*ozone troposphérique* (*tropospheric ozone*)	`p`
gaz (*gas*)	⇒	*acide gazeux* (*acid gas*)	`b`
métallurgie (*metallurgy*)	⇒	*industrie métallurgique* (*metallurgical industry*)	`b`
carbone (*carbon*)	⇒	*gaz carbonique* (*carbonic gas*)	`b`
soufre (*sulfur*)	⇒	*rejet soufré* (*sulfur rejection*)	`b`

These examples can be analyzed in the same way and lead to specific terminological relations. For instance, with possession, when the head noun means chemical substance (*polluant*, *ozone*), the resulting relation is localisation:

polluant atmosphérique (*atmospheric contaminants*) `located-in` *atmosphère*
ozone troposphérique (*tropospheric ozone*) `located-in` *troposphère*

In all studied examples, affixation can lead to the detection of different semantic relations between terms: meronymy, antonymy and many transversal relations. It is obvious that the precision and completeness of used morphological resources define the quality and completeness of generated semantic relations between terms.

6 Conclusion and Perspectives

In this work we studied the contribution of morphological clues for the deciphering of semantic relations between terms in order to build structured terminologies. We particularly addressed clues given by affixation and suppletion. Morphology then appears to be useful for the deciphering of a large variety of semantic relations (synonymy, antonymie, taxonomy or transversal relations). We assume that the morphology allows complimenting results obtained with other methods for terminology structuring. This method has been applied to medical and cogeneration terms.

However such approach requires suitable morphological resources or a morphological analyser, and it especially requires the understanding of the meanings conveyed by morphological units and rules. This approach must be supported by linguistic research in the area of morphology. Furthermore, it is obvious that the precision and completeness of used morphological knowledge define the quality and completeness of generated semantic relations between terms.

We demonstrated that morphological operations, which allow the inducing of general semantic meanings of constructed lexemes, can indicate more specialized meanings specific to given scientific and technical areas. For instance, relational adjectives formed on the base of nouns receive the general meaning *Relative to N*, but can lead to possession and belonging relations, and further more to specific relations such as `located-in`, `caused-by`, etc. These final relations are suitable for the organization of knowledge from different areas. They allow particularly to describe complex terms through their atomic primitives.

In the medical area, numerous affixations are applied to nouns referring to body parts. When these affixed formations are parts of complex terms, they allow anchoring diseases, injuries, medical procedures, etc. in a given body part (*affection musculaire* (*disorder of muscle*), *anévrisme cardiaque* (*aneurysm of heart*), *angiome capillaire* (*capillary hemangioma*)). As the topography, or body part localizations, corresponds to widely used entities in medicine, it should be studied in a more detailed way.

One of the issues that were not addressed in this work is related to the polysemy and homonymy of affixes. For instance, the French language has two suffixes *-aire*: the first is applied to noun bases and used for the formation of relational adjectives {*cellule, cellulaire*}, the second is applied to verb bases and used for the formation of agent nouns {*contest(er), contestataire*}. It is obvious that the homonymy, as well as the polysemy, of affixes raise an ambiguity in the resulting semantic relations between terms. In order to manage this ambiguity, linguistic features of studied operations and their affixes must be taken into account at different levels (syntactic, phonological, morphological and semantic) which should bring the first disambiguation of clues for terminology structuring.

In a further work, we plan to extend this study on compounding, which is widely used in sublanguages like medicine, biology, etc. The analysis of compound lexemes leads to a large set of semantic relations between terms, and is also useful for terminology structuring. In a further work, we also plan to apply morphological clues to terms from other areas.

References

1. Bourigault, D., Slodzian, M.: Pour une terminologie textuelle. In: Terminologie et Intelligence Artificielle (TIA), Nantes (1999)
2. Grabar, N., Jeannin, B.: Contribution de différents outils la construction d'une terminologie pour la recherche d'information. In Gréboval, C., ed.: Ingénierie des connaissances (IC), Rouen (2002) Poster.
3. Grabar, N., Hamon, T.: Les relations dans les terminologies structurées : de la théorie la pratique. Revue d'Intelligence Artificielle (RIA) **18**(1) (2004)

4. Côté, R.A.: Répertoire d'anatomopathologie de la SNOMED internationale, v3.4. Université de Sherbrooke, Sherbrooke, Québec. (1996)
5. Amsili, P.: L'antonymie en terminologie : quelques remarques. In: Terminologie et Intelligence Artificielle (TIA), Strasbourg (2003) 31–40
6. Spackman, K., Campbell, K.: Compositional concept representation using SNOMED: Towards further convergence of clinical terminologies. In: Journal of American Medical Informatics Association (JAMIA). (1998) 740–744
7. Zweigenbaum, P.: Encoder l'information médicale : des terminologies aux systèmes de représentation des connaissances. Information de Santé Innovation Stratégie (ISIS) **2**(3) (1999) 27–47
8. Hearst, M.A.: Automatic acquisition of hyponyms from large text corpora. In: Proceedings of the Fourteenth International Conference on Computational Linguistics, Nantes, France (1992) Disponible `http://sern.ucalgary.ca/KSI/KAW/KAW99/papers/Gery1/index.html`. Visité le 26/08/99.
9. Séguéla, P., Aussenac-Gilles, N.: Extraction de relations sémantiques entre termes et enrichissement de modèles du domaine. In: Actes d'Ingénierie des Connaissances (IC), Palaiseau, France (1999) 79–88
10. Morin, E.: Acquisition de patrons lexico-syntaxiques caractéristiques d'une relation sémantique. Traitement Automatique des Langues (TAL) **40**(1) (1999) 143–166
11. Garcia, D.: Structuration du lexique de la causalité et réalisation d'un système d'aide au repérage de l'action dans les textes. In: Terminologie et Intelligence Artificielle (TIA), Toulouse (1997) 7–26
12. Pearson, J.: Terms in Context. Volume 1 of Studies in Corpus Linguistics. John Benjamins, Amsterdam/Philadelphia (1998)
13. Grefenstette, G.: Explorations in automatic thesaurus discovery. Kluwer Academic Publishers (1994)
14. Nazarenko, A., Zweigenbaum, P., Habert, B., Bouaud, J.: Corpus-based extension of a terminological semantic lexicon. In: Recent Advances in Computational Terminology. John Benjamins (2001) 327–351
15. Assadi, H.: Construction d'ontologies partir de textes techniques – Application aux systèmes documentaires. Thèse de doctorat en informatique, Université de Paris 6, Paris, France (1998)
16. Bourigault, D.: Analyse syntaxique locale pour le repérage de termes complexes dans un texte. Traitement Automatique des Langues (TAL) (1993) 105–117
17. Bodenreider, O., Burgun, A., Rindflesch, T.C.: Lexically-suggested hyponymic relations among medical terms and their representation in the UMLS. In URI INIST CNRS, ed.: Terminologie et Intelligence artificielle (TIA), Nancy (2001) 11–21
18. Grabar, N., Zweigenbaum, P.: Lexically-based terminology structuring: Some inherent limits. In Chien, L.F., Daille, B., Kageura, K., Nakagawa, H., eds.: Proceedings of Second International Workshop on Computational Terminology (COMPUTERM 2002), Taipei, Taiwan, ACLCLP (2002) 36–42
19. Jacquemin, C.: A symbolic and surgical acquisition of terms through variation. In Wermter, S., Riloff, E., Scheler, G., eds.: Connectionist, Statistical and Symbolic Approaches to Learning for Natural Language Processing, Springer (1996) 425–438
20. Hamon, T., Nazarenko, A., Gros, C.: A step towards the detection of semantic variants of terms in technical documents. In: International Conference on Computational Linguistics (COLING-ACL'98), Université de Montréal, Montréal, Quebec, Canada (1998) 498–504

21. Melčuk, I.: Dictionnaire explicatif et combinatoire du français contemporain. Recherches lexico-s'emantiques. Presses Universitaires de Montréal, Montréal (1984-1999)
22. L'Homme, M.C.: Fonctions lexicales pour repr'esenter les relations s'emantiques entre termes. Traitement automatique de la langue (TAL) **43**(1) (2002) 19–41
23. Daille, B.: Conceptual structuring through term variations. In: Proceedings of the ACL Workshop on Multiword Expressions : Analysis, Acquisition and Treatment. (2003) 9–16
24. Claveau, V., L'Homme, M.C.: Discovering specific semantic relationships between nouns and verbs in a specialized French corpora. In: Computerm. (2004)
25. L'Homme, M.C.: Adjectifs dérivés sémantiques (ADS) dans la structuration des terminologies. In: Journées d'étude Terminologie, Ontologie et représentation des connaissances, Lyon (2004)
26. Corbin, D.: Morphologie dérivationnelle et structuration du lexique. Volume 1. Presse universitaire de Lille, Lille (1987)
27. Creutz, M.: Unsupervised segmentation of words using prior distributions of morph length and frequency. In: Proc of ACL-03, Sapporo, Japan (2003) 280–287
28. Burnage, G.: CELEX - A Guide for Users. Centre for Lexical Information, University of Nijmegen (1990)
29. Dal, G., Namer, F., Hathout, N.: Construire un lexique dérivationnel : théorie et réalisations. In Amsili, P., ed.: Traitement Automatique des Langues Naturelles (TALN), Cargèse (1999) 115–124
30. Hathout, N., Namer, F., Dal, G.: An experimental constructional database: the MorTAL project. In Boucher, P., ed.: Morphology book. Cascadilla Press, Cambridge, MA (2001)
31. NLM: UMLS Knowledge Sources Manual. National Library of Medicine, Bethesda, Maryland. (2005) www.nlm.nih.gov/research/umls/.
32. Namer, F.: Acquisition automatique de sens partir d'opérations morphologiques en français : étude de cas. In: Traitement Automatique de la Langue Naturelle (TALN), Nancy (2002) 235–244
33. Grabar, N., Zweigenbaum, P.: A general method for sifting linguistic knowledge from structured terminologies. JAMIASUP (2000) 310–314
34. Manuila, L., Manuila, A., Lewalle, P., Nicoulin, M.: Dictionnaire médical. Masson, Paris (2001) 9e édition.
35. Namer, F., Zweigenbaum, P.: Acquiring meaning for French medical terminology: contribution of morphosemantics. In: Annual Symposium of the American Medical Informatics Association (AMIA), San-Francisco (2004)
36. Amiot, D.: Préfixes ou prépositions ? Les cas de *sur-*, *sans* , *contre-* et les autres. Lexique **16** (2001)
37. Aliquot-Suengas, S.: Référence collective/Sens collectif. La notion du collectif travers les noms suffixés du lexique français. Thèse de doctorat en linguistique, Université de Lille III, Lille, France (1996)
38. Mélis-Puchulu, A.: Les adjectifs dénominaux : les adjectifs de 'relation'. Lexique **10** (1991) 33–60
39. Pacak, M.G., Norton, L.M., Dunham, G.S.: Morphosemantic analysis of -itis forms in medical language. Methods in Medical Informatics (MIM) **19**(2) (1980) 99–105

Text Segmentation Criteria for Statistical Machine Translation

Mauro Cettolo and Marcello Federico

ITC-irst, Istituto per la Ricerca Scientifica e Tecnologica
via Sommarive, 18
38050 Povo di Trento, Italy
{cettolo, federico}@itc.it
http://hermes.itc.it

Abstract. For several reasons machine translation systems are today unsuited to process long texts in one shot. In particular, in statistical machine translation, heuristic search algorithms are employed whose level of approximation depends on the length of the input. Moreover, processing time can be a bottleneck with long sentences, whereas multiple text chunks can be quickly processed in parallel. Hence, in real working conditions the problem arises of how to optimally split the input text. In this work, we investigate several text segmentation criteria and verify their impact on translation performance by means of a statistical phrase-based translation system. Experiments are reported on a popular as well as difficult task, namely the translation of news agencies from Chinese-English as proposed by the NIST MT evaluation workshops. Results reveal that best performance can be achieved by taking into account both linguistic and input length constraints.

1 Introduction

Current machine translation (MT) systems are in general unable to process long texts in a single step. Long documents are typically split into smaller and more manageable chunks, here simply called segments. For the sake of our exposition, a segment is here a generic sequence of words, not necessarily corresponding to a linguistic unit.

At first sight, text segmentation based on linguistic criteria should be the best choice; however, any segmentation method should also take into account the way a specific system works.

Statistical MT (SMT), for instance, typically relies on a beam search algorithm to control the growth of the solution space, and on statistical models or feature functions to compute scores of translation hypotheses. Moreover, several SMT systems use multi-stage decoding strategies. That is, the search algorithm first generates a list of N-best translation candidates, then these translations are re-scored and re-ranked by means of additional and richer feature functions. In this framework, the length of the input string plays indeed a relevant role.

T. Salakoski et al. (Eds.): FinTAL 2006, LNAI 4139, pp. 664–673, 2006.

The longer the input string, the more drastic will be the cut of hypotheses by the beam. Moreover, at a fixed length N of the N-best list, the longer the input string the less the list will represent the solution space. From the point of view of efficiency, shorter segments can in generally lead to faster and less memory consuming translation and better exploitation of multi-processing resources.

The above issues would suggest to opt for short input strings; however, statistical models applied in SMT can deliver better translation quality if sufficient context is available for all words in the input. Hence, requirements by the statistical models act in opposition to those of the search algorithm.

In this work, we investigate different text segmentation criteria and look at their impact on translation performance by using a state-of-the-art phrase-based SMT system. The investigated methods address real working conditions, such as the translation of documents or spoken language, where the text to be translated is produced by a speech recognizer. In this case, linguistically motivated segments are difficult to obtain, given the difficulty to reliably detect sentence boundaries from linguistic and acoustic cues.

The basic goal of this work is to understand if better performance can be gained by combining linguistically motivated criteria with length-based methods that take into account the peculiarities of the used SMT system.

The paper is organized as follows. In Section 2, several aspects of the statistical SMT system developed at ITC-irst are introduced, namely: the statistical model, the system architecture, some details on the decoding algorithm and rescoring module, and finally its domain. In Section 3, the segmentation types to be compared are presented and their pros and cons are commented. Finally, Section 4 shows and discusses results. A section with conclusions ends the paper.

2 Phrase-Based Translation System

Given a string $\mathbf{f}$ in the source language, the goal of statistical machine translation is to select the string $\mathbf{e}$ in the target language which maximizes the posterior distribution $\Pr(\mathbf{e} \mid \mathbf{f})$. In phrase-based translation, words are no longer the only units of translation, but they are complemented by strings of consecutive words, the phrases. By assuming a log-linear model [1,2] and by introducing the concept of word alignment[3], the optimal translation can be searched for with the criterion:

$$\tilde{\mathbf{e}}^* = \arg\max_{\tilde{\mathbf{e}}} \max_{\mathbf{a}} \sum_{r=1}^{R} \lambda_r h_r(\tilde{\mathbf{e}},\ f, \mathbf{a}),$$

where $\tilde{\mathbf{e}}$ represents a string of phrases in the target language, $\mathbf{a}$ an alignment from the words in $\mathbf{f}$ to the phrases in $\tilde{\mathbf{e}}$, and $h_r(\tilde{\mathbf{e}}, \mathbf{f}, \mathbf{a})$ $r = 1, \ldots, R$ are *feature functions*, designed to model different aspects of the translation process.

The assumed translation process extends step by step the target string by covering new source positions until all of them are covered. For each added target phrase, a source phrase within the source string is chosen, and the corresponding score is computed on the basis of its position and phrase-to-phrase translation probabilities. The fluency of the added target phrase with respect to its left context is evaluated by a 4-gram language model. Some exceptions are also managed: target phrases might be added which do not translate any source word, and some of the source words can be left untranslated, that is they are translated with a special empty word.

Model Training

The resulting log-linear model embeds feature functions whose parameters are either estimated from data or empirically fixed. The scaling factors λ of the log-linear model are instead estimated on a development set, by applying a *minimum error training* procedure [4,5].

The language model feature function is estimated on unsegmented monolingual texts.

The phrase-to-phrase probability feature is estimated from phrase-pair statistics extracted from word-aligned parallel texts. Alignments are computed with the GIZA++ software tool [6] which implements statistical models developed by [3,6]. Phrase pairs are extracted from the segment pairs by means of the algorithm described in [7].

For the sake of this work, it is worth explaining how phrase-pair statistics are extracted. Since long parallel texts represent a problem in training word-alignment models, they are split into smaller parallel segments by means of a binary and recursive procedure. The method relies on a likelihood measure which evaluates the correspondence of a segment pair in the source and target language, respectively. Text break candidates are chosen both according to strong punctuation and segment length. For our training, the final length of parallel segments is at most 30 words.

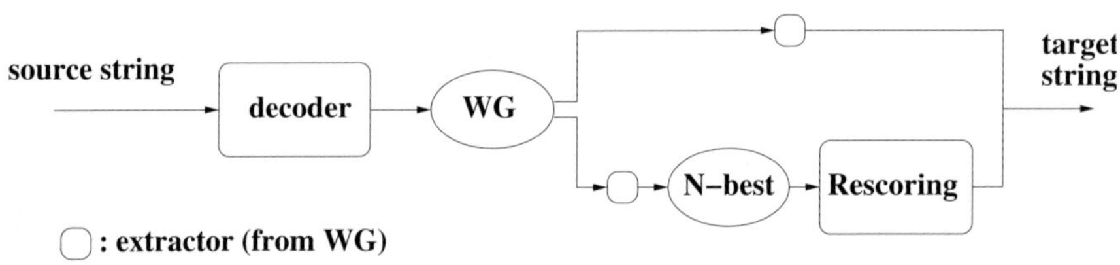

Fig. 1. Architecture of the ITC-irst SMT system. The decoder produces a word-graph (WG) of translation hypotheses. In single-stage translation the most probable string is output. In two-stage decoding, N-best translations are extracted, re-scored, and re-ranked by applying additional feature functions.

Decoding Strategy

Figure 1 illustrates how the translation of an input string is performed by the ITC-irst SMT system [7]. In the first stage, a beam search algorithm (decoder) computes a word graph of translation hypotheses. Hence, either the best translation hypothesis is directly extracted from the word graph and output, or an

N-best list of translations is computed by means of an exact algorithm [8]. The N-best translations are then re-ranked by applying additional features and the top ranking translation is finally output. Additional feature functions include: IBM models 1 and 3, a broad 5-gram LM and task-specific 3-gram LMs.

The decoder [9] exploits dynamic programming, i.e. the optimal solution is computed by expanding and recombining previously computed partial theories. Theory expansion basically follows the translation process explained above.

To cope with the large number of generated theories, a beam is used to prune out partial theories that are less promising and constraints are set to possible word re-ordering.

Pruning is applied on all theories covering the same set of source positions, and on all theories with the same output length.

Word re-ordering constraints are applied during translation each time a new source position is covered, by limiting the number of vacant positions on the left and the distance from the left most vacant position. In the following experiments, both parameters were set to 3, which results in a good compromise between quality and speed.

Table 1. Statistics (number of words) of training and test data. The size of the English side of the test set refers only to the gold reference.

	parallel resources		monolingual resources
	Chinese	English	English
training	82M	88M	464M
test	26K	29K	–

Translation Task

The task considered in this paper is the translation of news agency texts from Chinese to English as proposed in the NIST MT Evaluation Workshops.[1] The ITC-irst system was trained according to the so-called large data condition. Table 1 gives figures about training and test corpora, which also include punctuation marks in both languages. As testing data we used the NIST 2003 evaluation set.

Translation performance are reported in terms of BLEU [10] and NIST [11] scores, that were computed with the case-insensitive modality and by exploiting four reference translations.

Since segment boundaries of the reference translations are those prepared by the Linguistic Data Consortium (LDC), the problem arises of how to score translations computed with different segmentations of the input. A reasonable solution is provided by a publicly available tool developed by RWTH [12], which automatically aligns, with possible errors, the translation hypotheses to the multiple reference translations.

[1] `www.nist.gov/speech/tests/mt/`.

3 Segmentation Criteria

The segmentation criteria we investigated are the following.

Linguistic-Based Criteria

- *ldc*: original segmentation provided by LDC. Most segments end with a strong punctuation mark, but not all of them. Possibly, sentences separated by strong punctuation marks are joined into a single segment: this happens when sentences are semantically tied.
- *strongPnct*: segmentation obtained by splitting the input text stream on strong punctuation (".", "!" and "?"). Possibly, segments can be either very short or very long. Segments do not contain semantic breaks, but it happens that contiguous sentences are split even if they are semantically related.

Length-Based Segmentation

- *fixedLEN*: segmentation obtained by cutting the text into segments of fixed length LEN, whatever are the tokens around each break. Breaks are not linguistically motivated, moreover feature functions of the SMT system are not expected to model well words on the segment boundaries. On the other side, since decoder computes hypotheses of about the same length for each input segment, all N-best lists should have similar content variability, allowing an easier qualitative evaluation of the re-ranking module.

Combined Criteria

- *pnct&lenLEN*: this is a linguistically refined version of the *fixedLEN* segmentation. It is obtained by first looking for strong punctuation and then for weak punctuation (",", ";", ":" and "-") within a window (of size LEN) centered at distance LEN from the beginning of the segment. If no punctuation mark is found, the segment size is set to LEN. Differently from *strongPnct* segmentation, segments can neither be very short nor very long (according to the LEN value). Most breaks are linguistically motivated and the average segment length can be tuned by means of the LEN value.
- *pnct&maxLEN*: segmentation obtained by further splitting segments of *strongPnct* segmentation which are longer than LEN. They are split on weak punctuation, if present, or anyway at length LEN. The rationale behind this type of segmentation is the elimination of long segments from *strongPnct* which cause long decoding time and low variability inside the N-best lists.

4 Results

Table 2 collects results of all experiments. Each line refers to a complete translation run of the test set segmented according to one of the segmentations described above; for those depending on the parameter LEN, the most significant

LEN values have been tested. For each translation run, the following numbers are supplied:

- total number of segments and their minimum, average and maximum length;
- BLEU and NIST scores of the first best output by the decoder;
- total number of theories generated during decoding; this value is approximately a linear function of the decoding time, but it is preferable to that as it is independent from the hardware;
- BLEU and NIST values of the highest scored translation hypothesis after the re-ranking of the 5000-best lists provided by the decoder;
- performance gain due to the re-scoring stage.

In the following subsections, results are commented.

Table 2. Performance measured with different types of source text segmentation

SegType	#Seg	SegLength min	avg	max	Decoder bleu/nist	GenTh ($\times 10^9$)	Rescoring bleu/nist	Rescoring Δ bleu/nist
linguistic-based criteria								
ldc	919	4	27.8	93	29.22/8.841	1.23	30.96/9.060	+1.74/+.219
strongPnct	825	3	31.0	103	28.79/8.764	1.25	30.52/9.006	+1.73/+.242
length-based segmentation								
fixed10	2558	10	10.0	11	24.36/8.207	0.39	24.85/7.979	+0.49/ −.228
fixed20	1279	20	20.0	21	26.55/8.498	0.85	28.33/8.609	+1.78/+.111
fixed31	825	31	31.0	32	27.30/8.588	1.24	28.95/8.782	+1.65/+.194
fixed40	639	40	40.0	41	27.80/8.658	1.36	29.10/8.833	+1.30/+.175
fixed50	511	50	50.0	51	28.05/8.705	1.41	29.29/8.888	+1.24/+.183
fixed60	426	60	60.0	61	27.80/8.666	1.44	29.01/8.867	+1.21/+.201
fixed70	365	70	70.0	71	28.08/8.690	1.47	29.43/8.889	+1.35/+.199
combined criteria								
pnct&len20	1265	11	20.2	29	28.31/8.720	0.91	30.00/8.850	+1.69/+.130
pnct&len30	840	16	30.5	44	28.73/8.777	1.23	30.75/9.046	+2.02/+.269
pnct&len50	510	27	50.2	74	29.04/8.807	1.43	30.45/9.023	+1.41/+.216
pnct&len70	367	38	69.7	103	28.90/8.794	1.49	29.89/8.985	+0.99/+.191
pnct&max40	1082	2	23.6	41	28.72/8.793	1.11	30.56/9.011	+1.84/+.218
pnct&max50	948	2	27.0	51	28.89/8.793	1.18	30.74/9.031	+1.85/+.238
pnct&max60	875	2	29.2	61	28.98/8.809	1.23	30.63/9.029	+1.65/+.220

4.1 Linguistic-Based Segmentation

The *ldc* segmentation has segments whose length is very variable (4 to 93 words) and about 28 on average. Performance of both decoder and re-scoring stages are good, yielding to the best global BLEU and NIST scores. Probably, this is because breaks were selected by humans on a linguistic basis; anyway, one must also consider that the system was trained and tuned on data provided by LDC, which processed in a coherent way also the evaluation set.

The quality of the decoder output generated on strong punctuation (*strongPnct*) is lower than that generated from *ldc*. This reveals the importance of keeping in the same segment sentences which are semantically related even if they are separated by a strong punctuation mark. Length of segments of *strongPnct* is quite similar to that of *ldc*; this is why the gains of the second stage are comparable.

4.2 Length-Based Segmentation

Fixed length segmentations were tested for lengths ranging from 10 to 70 words. As expected, the trend shows that the longer the segments, the higher are the translation quality and computational cost by the decoder.

The decoder improves its performance up to 50-word segments; long segments mean few segment boundaries, that is little processing with poor translation context. With segments longer than 50 words, a performance saturation is observed. Anyway, the quality of the decoder output is definitely worse than the translations generated from linguistic-based segmentations. Hence, the decoder models seem to suffer from random breaks.

Concerning the re-scoring stage, the longer the segments the lower is the gain, since the variability of the 5000-best lists reduces. One exception is the low performance increment observed with very short segments (10 words). This is probably due to the large number of segment boundaries where words are difficult to translate due to the lack of context. For segments of length comparable to that of *ldc* and *strongPnct* segmentations, the re-scoring gain is similar. This tells that for the sake of re-scoring, the length of segments is at least as important as having linguistically motivated breaks.

4.3 Linguistic- and Length-Based Segmentation

The *pnct&lenLEN* segmentations produce segments whose length is less variable than linguistic-based segmentations.

The decoder guarantees good quality, thanks to the non-randomness of sentence breaks. Translation quality tends to increase by increasing the length of segments, as for fixed length segmentation. Hence, for the sake of the decoder it seems to be preferable to reduce as much as possible the number of breaks.

The re-scoring module works well. In particular, when segments include on average around 30 words, BLUE and NIST scores increase, respectively, by 2.02% and 0.269, which are the highest advances observed in our experiments. This outcome together with the good re-scoring performance for *fixed20* and *fixed30* segmentations show that the re-scoring stage improves if segments are: (i) not too short in order to have an high number of plausible translations; (ii) not too long so that N-best lists include many different translations; (iii) linguistically motivated; and (iv) coherent with training and system tuning conditions.

The behavior of *pnct&maxLEN* segmentations is clear. The decoder performs well, favored also by the match with training and tuning conditions. Rescoring is good since breaks are linguistically motivated, but not so much as for

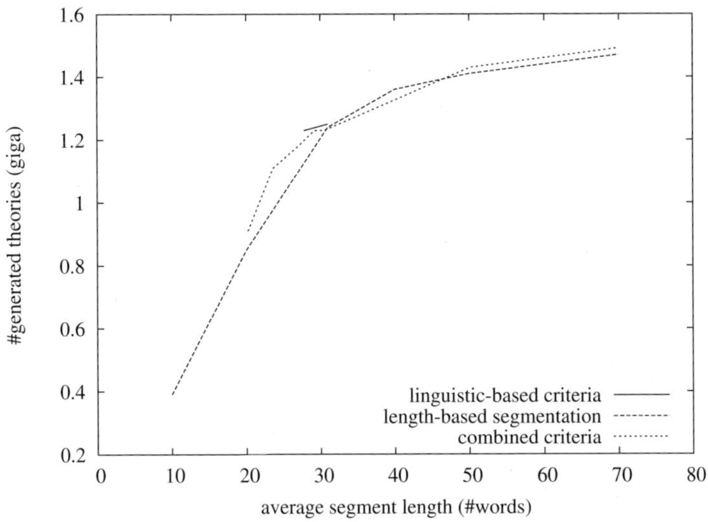

Fig. 2. Generated theories (decoding time) as a function of the average segment length for the segmentation criteria under investigation

pnct&lenLEN segmentations, due to the presence of very short segments (up to 2 words). The split of *strongPnct* long segments results to be useful both for decoder and re-scoring stage.

4.4 Decoding Time vs. Segment Length

Figure 2 plots the number of generated theories, which is proportional to decoding time, versus the average segment length for each segmentation criteria analyzed in this work. It is evident that the decoder searches portions of the search space whose size depends only on the average number of words to be translated, and not on the segmentation criterion. Moreover, the impact of the beam approximation is plain: in spite of the exponential growth of possible translations with the input length, the corresponding number of actually generated theories tends to saturate, proving that the cut of theories by the beam search is larger for longer inputs. Hence, it could happen that for very long inputs the decoder performance degrades. However, this phenomenon was not observed with the here considered segment lengths.

5 Conclusions

Current MT systems are unable to process huge blocks of text in one shot. Input text stream must be split in manageable segments. Hence, the problem arises of how to automatically segment the input text. Linguistic-based criteria are expected to work well in theory, but in practice segments should also suit the features of the used MT system. In statistical MT it is known that segment length affects the behavior of the search algorithms and its embedded statistical models.

In this work, we dealt with the problem of source text segmentation with respect to a state-of-the-art phrase-based SMT system, based on a two stage decoding strategy.

The quality of translations was measured when these were originated from different input segmentation types: linguistic-based, length-based, and a combination of the two.

Results reveal that it is important to break the source text stream by fulfilling linguistic constraints, but performance of a real SMT system can be improved by providing segments of adequate length. From the decoder perspective, long segments favor translation quality. From the re-scoring point of view, the length of segment should balance content variability inside the N-best list and the matching of conditions used to train the system.

Acknowledgments

This work has been funded by the European Union under the integrated project TC-STAR - Technology and Corpora for Speech to Speech Translation - (IST-2002-FP6-506738, http://www.tc-star.org).

References

1. A. Berger, S. A. Della Pietra, and V. J. Della Pietra. A Maximum Entropy Approach to Natural Language Processing. *Computational Linguistics*, 22(1):39–71, 1996.
2. F. J. Och and H. Ney. Discriminative training and maximum entropy models for stati stical machine translation. In *Proceedings of the 40th Annual Meeting of the Association for Computational Linguistics*, PA, Philadelphia, USA, 2002.
3. P. F. Brown, S. A. Della Pietra, V. J. Della Pietra, and R. L. Mercer. The Mathematics of Statistical Machine Translation: Parameter Estimation. *Computational Linguistics*, 19(2):263–312, 1993.
4. Franz Joseph Och. Minimum error rate training in statistical machine translation. In *Proceedings of the 41st Meeting of the Association for Computational Linguistics (ACL)*, pages 160–167, Sapporo, Japan, 2003.
5. M. Cettolo and M. Federico. Minimum Error Training of Log-Linear Translation Models. In *Proceedings of the International Workshop on Spoken Language Translation (IWSLT)*, pages 103–106, Kyoto, Japan, September 2004. http://www.slt.atr.jp/IWSLT2004/archives/000619.html.
6. F. J. Och and H. Ney. Improved Statistical Alignment Models. In *Proceedings of the 38th Annual Meeting of the Association for Computational Linguistics*, Hong Kong, China, 2000.
7. B. Chen, R. Cattoni, N. Bertoldi, M. Cettolo, and M. Federico. The ITC-irst SMT System for IWSLT-2005. In *Proceedings of IWSLT*, 2005. http://www.is.cs.cmu.edu/iwslt2005/proceedings.html.
8. B.H. Tran, F. Seide, and V. Steinbiss. A Word Graph based N-Best Search in Continuous Speech Recognition. In *Proceedings of ICLSP*, 1996.

9. Marcello Federico and Nicola Bertoldi. A word-to-phrase statistical translation model. *ACM Transaction on Speech Language Processing*, 2(2):1–24, 2005.
10. K. Papineni, S. Roukos, T. Ward, and W.-J. Zhu. Bleu: a Method for Automatic Evaluation of Machine Translation. Research Report RC22176, IBM Research Division, Thomas J. Watson Research Center, 2001.
11. G. Doddington. Automatic Evaluation of Machine Translation Quality using N-gram Co-occurrence Statistics. In *Proceedings of the ARPA Workshop on Human Language Technology*, 2002.
12. E. Matusov, G. Leusch, O. Bender, and H. Ney. Evaluating Machine Translation Output with Automatic Sentence Segmentation. In *Proceedings of IWSLT*, 2005. http://www.is.cs.cmu.edu/iwslt2005/proceedings.html.

The Classificatim Sense-Mining System

Sylviane Cardey, Peter Greenfield, Mounira Bioud, Aleksandra Dziadkiewicz, Kyoko Kuroda, Izabel Marcelino, Ciprian Melian, Helena Morgadinho, Guillaume Robardet, and Séverine Vienney

Centre de recherche en linguistique et traitement automatique des langues Lucien Tesnière, Faculté des lettres, Université de Franche-Comté, 30 rue Mégevand, F-25030 Besançon, France
ctesniere@univ-fcomte.fr
http://tesniere.univ-fcomte.fr

Abstract. In this paper, we present the theory from which a methodology has been developed to create Classificatim, a system for sense mining. The system is rule-based and has been conceived with micro-systems in interrelation. Classificatim is composed of 3 systems, Labelgram - a disambiguating parts of speech tagger, Semegram - a sense tagger and a kernel - Classificatim ('verbatim classifier'). The corpus provided by an agro-food industry enterprise has been used to test the system. We explain how the different micro-systems function, what is peculiar to each of them and in what manner our research is original.

Keywords: ambiguity, neologism, POS-tagger, rule-based, sense-mining, sense tagger.

1 Introduction

Data mining is a major application for natural language processing and computational linguistics. In this paper we present the SyGuLAC theory from which a methodology used to create the system Classificatim has been developed. Classificatim is a 'verbatim' classifier. Each component of the system is then described, these being: Labelgram - a parts of speech disambiguating tagger, and Semegram - a sense tagger. We then discuss the tests to which our system has been submitted and the results obtained.

2 SyGuLAC

The theory called SyGuLAC (Systemic Grammar using a Linguistically motivated Algebra and Calculus) has been developed by Sylviane Cardey and Peter Greenfield [1, 2] in Centre Tesnière in the University of Franche-Comté, France. This systemic grammar which is in reality a micro systemic or μ systemic grammar (for a definition of μ system see [3]) proposes that to be processed safely languages have to be decomposed into systems which can be analysed by a human being and by machine because they are small enough but also complete so as to be able to work as a unified system. As well as this, the systems so delimited can interact with other such systems, and this interaction is a property of language. Nothing is independent; lexis, morphology and syntax are linked.

T. Salakoski et al. (Eds.): FinTAL 2006, LNAI 4139, pp. 674–683, 2006.

2.1 μ Systems

We give below examples which show how what have originally been proposed as different layers of language analysis are in fact interrelated. We then discuss this and

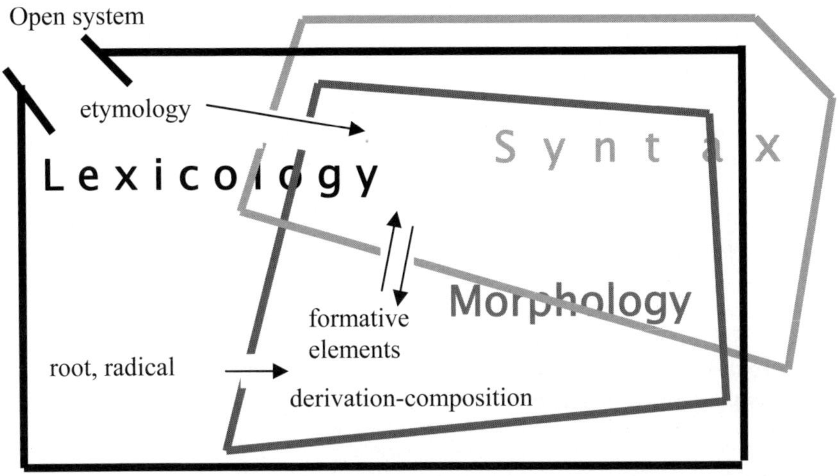

Fig. 1. The morphological system of the French Language

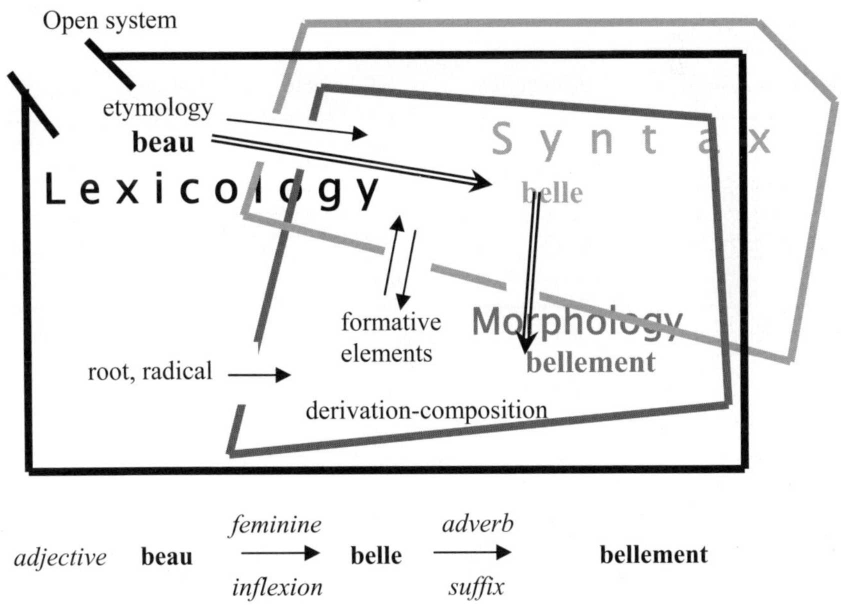

Fig. 2. French Morphological Systems for beau → bellement

propose that it is better to organise or decompose-recompose languages in systems according to needs. The schema in Fig. 1 shows what morphology is in at least some Indo-European languages.

We can see here how morphology in fact is also part of syntax and lexis. Let us take an example showing how the morphological system of the French Language functions.

If we take the adjective in its canonical base form (masculine singular) *beau*, an intermediary system (inflexional system) is needed dealing with inflexion (feminine) *belle* to be able finally to form the adverb *bellement* by means of the system of (adverbial) suffixes (derivation system) – see Fig. 2.

When we want to analyse languages, instead of talking about lexicology, syntax, and morphology, we should use 'lexico-morpho-syntax'.

3 The Labelgram System

For our system Classificatim we first need a reliable morpho-syntactic analyser. From the theory SyGuLAC, a system called Labelgram [4], a desambiguating parts of speech tagger, has been devised.

Consider the French sentence:

la méchante rigole car le petit est malade
(the nasty woman laughs because the little boy is ill)

where, out of context, all the units are ambiguous. Labelgram tags sentences even containing successive ambiguities, as shown for the French tagger in Fig. 3.

Labelgram					
Word form	**Tagger ref.**	**Categories**	**Disambig n°**	**Disambig ref.**	**Category**
la	2.12/	[Art.,Noun,Pro. pers.]	5	45/	Art.
méchante	41.2/	[Noun,Adj.]	28	339/	Noun
rigole	360.4/	[Noun,Verb conj.]	8	79/	Verb conj.
car	144/	[Noun,Conj.]	10	144/	Conj.
le	Pre_dict	[Art.,Pro. pers.]	5	45/	Art.
petit	279.1/	[Noun,Adj.]	28	339/	Noun
est	Pre_dict	[Noun,Verb conj.]	8	74/	Verb conj.
malade	13.1/	[Noun,Adj.]	28	346a/	Adj.

source relations target source relations **target**

super-system 1 super-system 2

super-super-system

Fig. 3. Example of tagging by Labelgram

The Labelgram system gives the trace of the disambiguation. The two principal µ systems constituting Labelgram, the raw tagger and the disambiguator are formed of µ systems which are numbered (this can be seen in Fig. 3). If one takes the word *car* (meaning *because* or *bus*) the raw tagger µ system gives a tag with two possible parts of speech out of context due to the rule number 144 and the disambiguator μ system disambiguates in context by means of its μ system 10 and sub-μ system 144.

Labelgram can also tag and disambiguate sentences containing many neologisms. Let us take as example a sentence from Jabberwocky from Lewis Carroll [5] containing words invented by Lewis Carroll but morphologically adequate in respect of English language morphology:

*'Twas **brillig**, and the **slithy toves***
*Did **gyre** and **gimble** in the **wabe**;*

where the results are shown in Fig. 4.

Lexical unit	Out-of-context Categories	In-context Category
It	{PROpers}	PROpers
was	{V}	V
brillig	{ADJ}	ADJ
,	{PUNCT}	PUNCT
and	{CONJ}	CONJ
the	{ADV, DET}	DET
slithy	{ADJ}	ADJ
toves	{Nplu, V3sing}	Nplu
Did	{Aux}	Aux
gyre	{V}	V
and	{CONJ}	CONJ
gimble	{V}	V
in	{ADV, ADJ, PREP}	PREP
the	{ADV, DET}	DET
wabe	{N}	N
;	{PUNCT}	PUNCT

Fig. 4. Results of the disambiguated tagging of the first two lines of Lewis Carroll's Jabberwocky, with *'Twas* being expanded to *It was*

We know how important it is to be able to tag and disambiguate properly to ensure good results at the end. Labelgram is the first step for our Classificatim system, this latter system being the main purpose of the paper.

4 Classificatim

Classificatim is a system which processes verbatims.

What is a verbatim? A verbatim is the transcription word by word of speech. In our context due to our corpus, verbatims refer also to other items (designated this way by the industry with which we have collaborated). Verbatims are messages (contacts) from consumers; they could be:

- emails
- letters
- verbatims (transcription of telephone calls from consumers)
- etc.

The problem to be solved is that millions of messages are received every day by industries or organisations in general, and each of the messages should be analysed and classified to be then routed to the right departments who will have to deal with the information transmitted by means of these verbatims. Our corpus came from an international agro-food industry enterprise which wanted to analyse and classify the verbatims coming from their consumers. The research has been done on 7 languages. The corpus is made up of verbatims from different countries' consumers with different backgrounds and from varied socio-cultural levels. We also have to deal with a mixture of everyday common language and specialised languages and this for a specific use by industry, and also with different varieties of the same language. For example for Spanish we have Iberian and Latin American varieties, for English we have British, American and South African, and for Portuguese we have Lusitanian and Brazilian varieties. All sorts of ambiguities have to be solved. The system has to take as input a list of verbatims in French, for example (from Belgium, France, and others), and produce as output the same list of verbatims as input but in addition with their associated meanings.

5 Semegram

The first thing was to define what sort of information will be relevant for the industry.

Each type of information has been ranked in what we call a 'seme' or 'sub-seme'. These semes or concepts could be imprecise or indeed be very refined. Here is a well known example taken from outside the domain studied:

> If you ask for a seat, it could be answered what sort of seat do you want?
> With a back and legs (a chair)
> With a back, legs and arms (an armchair)
> Without a back, with legs (a stool)
> Without legs and without back (a cushion)

Semegram is organised as a µ system composed of rules, grouped in sets and subsets which are linked to a same seme. Semegram includes the set of semes and different sets of rules and sub-rules dealing with morphology, lexis, syntax and semantic fields. One rule represents one meaning, that is one seme, but one seme can be represented by different rules. We call such rules synonymous rules. A rule can analyse many verbatims. To enable this, we have what we call canonical formulae for representing our rules and these have an abstract representation but whose application is extensive, and being maximal thus represent in reality a great number of subformulae.

Generality is an important factor in the system. Due to Labelgram and Semegram having been designed in intension and not in extension, the tag *verb* for example represents all the verbs in the language and *Be* represents all the conjugated forms of the English verb *to be*. We also have sets of semantic categories which are rather like classifiers in Chinese.

Our seme classification has up to 5 levels. These semes could be expressed differently by consumers according to lexis and syntax. This classification has been done by hand for the 7 languages. We have to remark that the verbatims were not always well structured and that some contained mistakes. Labelgram which is used first to tag the verbatims can tag words even if they contain mistakes and as we have already said, it can tag and disambiguate neologisms.

6 Comparison Between Different Data Mining Methodologies and Classificatim

We would like to show some of the problems encountered in information retrieval or data mining. Let us take two methodologies which are currently practised and also Classificatim:

- Keyword methodology
- Statistical methodology
- Linguistic methodology (data + sense mining): Classificatim

The examples we give are drawn from another domain than that of agro-food.

6.1 Keyword Methodology

The keyword methodology is based on the notion of important words and non-important words. The problem is, what is an important word? The main question is in fact, what is a word?

Let us consider the following sentence:

He is a has been, he has been working on the same methodology far too long.

Here we have *has been* twice, the first occurrence refers to a person, and the second is a verb.

Concerning important words, let us take another example:

the product ought to be <u>perfect</u>

perfect here does not indicate a compliment, instead it implies the understatement:

...but it is not.

The consumer is really saying:

the product ought to be perfect ***but it is not***

If one tries to detect what the consumer feels using the keyword methodology with important words (*<u>perfect</u>*), the interpretation will be that the consumer is confident but the implied rest of the sentence says that you are probably going to loose the consumer. The interpretation is wrong if you use the said important words.

Let us take the following examples:

For some months this product is no longer as it was before

Here who can tell what are the important words or keywords?

The product inspires me with confidence and I would never have thought that I could find a product that smells.

If we take the important words here we have *confidence*, but in reality the information given by the consumer is not really this.

6.2 Statistical Methodology

We are going to see that the statistical methodology could be of limited use. Being based on counting keyword occurrences, doing calculations of words out of context can effectively lead to false interpretations. As well as this, the same problem as with the keyword methodology appears, that is: what are important words? For example:

The product would be very good without perfume.

Here we have the word sequence *very good*. However, what the consumer is saying is nearly the contrary.

6.3 Linguistics Methodology

In comparison with both the keyword and the statistical methodologies, our methodology can:

- interpret a text even if it does not contain any keywords
- analyse the full verbatim

Our methodology uses μ systemic methodology, mixing lexis, morphology and syntax and has already been applied on many languages: English, French, German, Italian, Japanese, Portuguese and Spanish.

Some languages (e.g. Japanese) are agglutinative languages. This means that in say Japanese, units are the concatenation of 'non-empty' words and 'empty' words. This causes a real problem with keyword methodologies that keep only 'important' non-empty words, as would be so in Japanese for example with auxiliary verbs and non-autonomous verbs, which change the verb meaning especially at the level of voice, aspect, tense and mood. This is demonstrated with the following attested examples of the verb 'Oshieru' (= inform, tell) followed by a set of non and semi-content words:

- 'Oshie'+te-hoshii = I wish that you inform me;
- 'Oshie'+te-kudasai = Please inform me;
- 'Oshie'+rareta = I was informed;
- 'Oshie'+te-ageru = I will inform (you, him...);
- 'Oshie'+te-morae-masen-de-shita = I did not get any information,
- 'Oshie'+te-morae-masen-ka = Could you kindly inform me, etc.

To conclude this section, we can say that in safety critical domains, methodologies have to be trusted. Languages are not made of words independent of each other;

meaning can be conveyed by all sorts of structures. A preposition can play the role of a verb in Chinese for example. The order of the words could also change the meaning.

7 The Classificatim System

The Classificatim system can be represented as shown in Fig. 5.

Classificatim

Rules for raw tagging + disambiguation ↓ | Seme rules + semes ↓

verbatims → **Labelgram** → *tagged verbatims* → **Semegram** → *classified verbatims*

Fig. 5. Representation of the Classificatim system

The kernel of the Classificatim system is composed of the following:

- Labelgram: morpho-syntactic analyser that tags and disambiguates verbatims for parts of speech.
- Semegram: semantico-morpho-syntactic analyser that identifies the semes in a given consumer verbatim using pre-established rules and semes.

The important features of our methodology are

- Easy updating – our methodology is fully traceable; unlike statistical methods we can pinpoint problems and omissions.
- Our methodology allows disregarding certain spelling mistakes.
  For example in the verbatim:

  Power would not thicken up after adding water as instructed.

  Power is correctly recognise as *powder* even with the spelling mistake.

- Our methodology allows the recognition of meanings with other representations than keywords (e.g. syntax as in the previous examples).
- As the work has been prepared manually, words and structures not present in the actual verbatims studied (corpora) have been formulated, this due to the linguists' intuition (competence).

8 Testing and the Classification Rate

In terms of the classification rate, our methodology gives better results than the other methodologies mentioned above; these giving between 40% and 60% of good results against 84% for our own.

The test procedure which also enables calculating the classification rate is illustrated by the schema in Fig. 6.

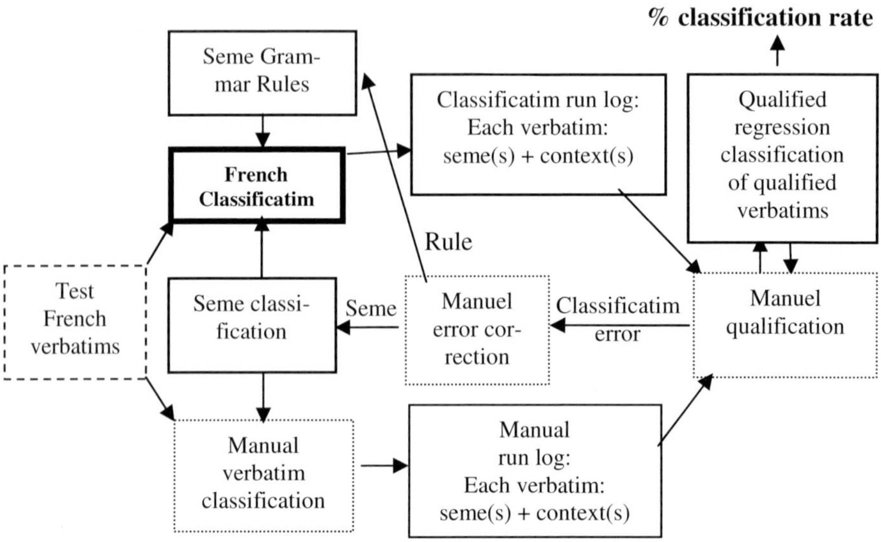

Fig. 6. Testing of the Classificatim system enabling calculating the classification rate

Seme recognition		**Nature of rule**		**Demonstrates**	**Action**
Correctly recognised		Corpus attested rule		Specific analysis	None – success
		Linguist's competence rule	Attested seme in other rule(s) in same language	Generality	Add attestation to rule
			Seme not attested in same language, but attested in other language(s)	Cross language generality	Add attestation to rule
Error	Not recognised	Lack of cover: seme and/or rule missing		Location of error	Insert seme and/or rule, do regression test
	Incorrectly recognised	Rule error		Location of error	Correction of rule, do regression test

Fig. 7. Manual qualification procedure for a given seme in the Classificatim system

Tests have been carried out on approximately 250,000 verbatims. The success rate with raw text (emails, verbatims and letters) and with neither any preparation of the text nor 'training' of the system is 84%, and after normalisation of the text the success rate is 99%. Languages respect some norms; if not, it would be impossible to learn a language.

The manual qualification procedure for a given seme recognised in a given verbatim by the Classificatim system is illustrated in the schema shown in Fig.7.

9 Conclusion

To conclude, we can say that other methodologies (Boolean, retrieval (extended or not), vector space model, fuzzy set model, network model) that use key words (lexis and not all of it) create stop lists to filter (eliminate) what are called empty words so as to keep what are called important words (not empty words). Our methodology uses lexis, morphology, syntax and semantics represented by rules and sets in interrelated μ systems. Furthermore our methodolgy solves ambiguities.

In our methodology, on completion of the analysis we have a grammar of synonymous formulae (rules) which allows the finding of one or many senses in a given text knowing that different texts can have the same meaning and that all sorts of ambiguities have to be solved.

References

1. Cardey, S., Greenfield P.: Systemic Linguistics with Applications. In: Proceedings of the 9th International Symposium on Social Communication. Actas II. Santiago de Cuba, January 24-28, (2005) 649-653
2. Cardey, S., Greenfield P.: A Core Model of Systemic Linguistic Analysis. In: Proceedings of the International Conference RANLP-2005 Recent Advances in Natural Language Processing, Borovets, Bulgaria, 21-23 September (2005) 134-138
3. Gentilhomme, Y.: Essai d'approche micro-systémique, Peter Lang (1985)
4. Cardey, S., Greenfield, P.: Disambiguating and Tagging Using Systemic Grammar. In: Proceedings of the 8th International Symposium on Social Communication, Santiago de Cuba, January 20-24, (2003) 559-564
5. Carroll, L.: Through the Looking Glass (1872). In: Alice's Adventures in Wonderland and Through the Looking Glass, Puffin Books, Penguin Books Ltd (1974)

The Role of Verb Sense Disambiguation in Semantic Role Labeling

Paloma Moreda and Manuel Palomar

Natural Language Processing Research Group
University of Alicante. Alicante, Spain
{moreda, mpalomar}@dlsi.ua.es

Abstract. In this paper an exhaustive evaluation of the behavior of the most relevant features used in Semantic Role Disambiguation tasks when the senses of the verbs are considered and when they are not, is presented. This evaluation analyzes the influence of Verb Sense Disambiguation in the task. In order to do this, a whole system of Semantic Role Labeling is used and it is compared with similar methods. Our main results show how using the senses of the verbs improves the results for verb-specific roles, such as A2 or A3, and while not using them improves the results for adjuncts, such as modal or negative.

1 Introduction

A semantic role is the relationship between a syntactic constituent (verb's argument) and a predicate. It identifies the role of a verbal argument in the event expressed by the verb: an agent, a patient, an instrument, etc. and also adjuncts such as locative, temporal, manner, cause, etc. So, the semantic role is the role given by the predicate to its arguments. For instance, in the following sentence

(E0) The executives gave the chefs a standing ovation

The executives has the agent role, *the chefs* the recipient role and *a standing ovation* the theme role.

Recognizing and labeling semantic arguments is a key task for answering "Who", "When", or "Where" questions. For instance, the following questions could be answered with the sentence (E0).

(E1) Who gave the chefs a standing ovation?
(E2) What did the executives give the chefs?

The agent role answers the question (E1) and the theme role answers the question (E2).

The Semantic Role Labeling (SRL) task consists of analyzing and recognizing the arguments of the verbs and determining the role that play for a sentence. In particular, for each verb all the constituents in the sentence which fill a semantic role of the verb have to be extracted. The problem of the SRL is not trivial. Several approaches using machine learning strategies, have been proposed to

T. Salakoski et al. (Eds.): FinTAL 2006, LNAI 4139, pp. 684–695, 2006.

identify semantic roles or to build semantic classifiers. The task has usually been approached as a two phase procedure consisting of recognition and labeling arguments [3] and [12].

Regarding the information used, some systems have use a full syntactic parse ([18], [16]) but other systems only use shallow syntactic information at the level of phrase chunk ([9], [19]).

Regarding the learning component the main systems are based on pure probabilistic models, such as [6] and [7], or on different kind of machine learning approaches, such as Maximum Entropy [10], Memory-based Learning [20], Support Vector Machines [17] and more.

In any case, it is necessary to involve additional semantic information in this kind of systems in order to obtain high precision SRL systems. Among the different kind of semantic information which would improve the SRL task it is found Word Sense Disambiguation (WSD). In this paper the influence of Verb Sense Disambiguation in the SRL task is evaluated. Taking into account the sense of the verb, an exhaustive study of different kind of features is presented.

The remaining paper is organized as follows: First, our SRL system is presented in section 2. Next, the influence of WSD technique in the SRL task is measured in section 3. So, an exhaustive evaluation is shown in subsection 3.2 and how the verb sense disambiguation technique is able to improve or not the SRL task is shown 3.3. Besides, our system is compared with similar systems in section 3.4. Finally, section 4 concludes.

2 The SemRol Method

The SRL task has usually been approached as a two phase procedure consisting of recognition and labeling arguments. From our point of view to carry out the SRL task a previous phase of the recognition and labeling arguments phases is needed. In this previous phase the sense of the verb in the sentence must be disambiguated. Next, during the recognition phase, the argument boundaries of the disambiguated verb must be identified. Finally, during the labeling phase, the roles that fill these arguments must be disambiguated. These three modules are explain as follows.

2.1 Phases of SemRol

First, the sense of the verb has to be obtained, because semantic roles are related with the specific sense of the verb. Therefore, polysemous verbs could assign a different set of semantic roles to their arguments depending on the sense. The two following sentences use of the verb *give*.

(E1) John gives out lots of candy on Halloween to the kids on his block
(E2) The radiator gives off a lot of heat

Depending on the sense of the verb a different set of roles must be considered. For instance, Figure 1 shows three senses of the verb *give* (give#1, give#4, and give#6)) and the set of roles of each sense. So, sentence (E0) matches with the sense give#1. Therefore, the roles *giver*, *thing given* and *entity given to* are considered. Nevertheless, sentence (E1) matches with sense give#6 and sentence (E2) matches with sense give#4. Then, the sets of roles are (*distributor*, *thing distributed*, *distributed*) and (*emitter*, *thing emitted*), respectively. In sentence (E1), *John* has the distributor role, *lots of candy* the thing distributed role, *the kids on his block* the distributed role and *on Halloween* the temporal role. In sentence (E2), *the radiator* has the emitter role and *a lot of heat* the thing emitted role. These examples show the relevance of WSD in the process of the assignment of semantic roles.

Give#1	Give#4	Give#6
role A0 *giver* role A1 *thing given* role A2 *entity given*	role A0 *emitter* role A1 *thing emitted*	role A0 *distributor* role A1 *thing distributed* role A2 *distributed*

Fig. 1. Some senses and roles of the frame *give* in PropBank [15]

In the second phase, the argument boundaries are determined. For instance, in the sentence (E0), the argument boundaries recognized are the following:

[The executives] gave [the chefs] [a standing ovation]

Once these two phases are applied, the assignment of semantic roles can be carried out.

So, our SRL method, named SemRol, presented in this paper consists of three phases:

1. Verb Sense Disambiguation phase (VSD)
2. Argument Boundaries Disambiguation phase (ABD)
3. Semantic Role Disambiguation phase (SRD)

Concerning the information used by this learning component, the SemRol method uses features about words, lemmas, PoS tags and shallow parsing informatio at the level of phrase chunk.

2.2 The Learning Component

All the three previous phases are corpus-based approaches. In this paper two different classifiers have been used: the TiMBL program, a Memory-based Learning algorithm[5], and a conditional Maximum Entropy probability model[21].

TiMBL [5] is a program implementing several memory-based learning algorithms. All implemented algorithms have in common that they store some representation of the training set explicitly in memory. During testing, new cases are classified by extrapolation from the most similar stored cases.

A classifier obtained by means of an ME technique consists of a set of parameters or coefficients which are estimated using an optimization procedure. Each coefficient is associated with one feature observed in the training data. The main purpose is to obtain the probability distribution that maximizes the entropy, that is, maximum ignorance is assumed and nothing apart from the training data is considered.

In order to do so, different kind of features using words, lemmas part-of-speech tags, named entities and shallow parsing have been defined for each phase. Follows, a summary of most relevant of them used in SRD phase is presented.

- Features of the SRD phase
  - Features based on arguments
    - **Predicate position (F6)**. The position of the argument regarding the verb, before (-1) or after (+1) the predicate.
    - **Clause position (F7)**. It indicates if the argument is inside (-1), outside (+1) or in the same (0) clause which contains the predicate.
    - **Distance in words (F8), phrases (F9) and arguments (F10)**. Distance from the argument to the predicate as a number of words, phrases or arguments. The possible values are 0, 1 or 2, when the number of words is 0, or is between 1 or 2, or is more than 2, respectively.
    - **Distance in number of words (F11), phrases (F12), and arguments (F13)**. Number of words, phrases or arguments between the argument and the predicate.
    - **Number of words (F128)**. Number of words in the argument.
  - Features based on Words
    - **First and Last word (F129)**. The first and the last word in the argument.
    - **Lemma[1] of the First and Last word (F133)**. Lemma of the first and the last word in the argument.
  - Features based on Named Entities (NE)
    - **Kind/List of Named Entities (F14), (F16)**. Different kinds/list of NE in the argument.
  - Features based on phrases
    - **List of Phrases (F17), (F18)**. List of phrases in the argument including or not the position in the phrase.
    - **Prepositions (F19), (F51)**. If the argument begins with a preposition, the preposition and the part-of-speech tag of the preposition, respectively.
    - **Headwords (F20)**. Headwords of the phrases included in the argument. Heads in syntactic phrases refer to words with part-of-speech related to noun, in a noun phrase; or related to verb, in a verb phrase.
    - **Lemma of the headwords (F109)**. The lemmas of the headwords of the phrases included in the argument.
  - Features based on Part-of-Speech tag
    - **Content-words (F30)**. Words in the argument with part-of-speech related to noun, adjective, adverb or verb.

[1] In all features that make use of lemma, we don't really refer to the lemma of the word. It is just the middle of the letters of the words for words with long bigger than four, and the word for words with long equal to or smaller than four.

  * **PoS/Lemma of Content-words (F112),(F107)**. Part-of-speech/ lemma of content-words in the argument.
  * **Words (F111)**. Part-of-speech of the words in the argument.
  * **Headwords (F22)**. Part-of-speech of headwords of the phrases included in the argument.
  * **Nouns (F27), Adjectives (F28) or Adverbs (F29)**. Nouns, adjectives or adverbs in the argument.
  * **PoS of Last and First word (F137)**. Part-of-speech of the first and the last word in the argument.
- Features based on sentence
  * **Voice (F2)**. Voice of the sentence. The possible values are P or A, depending on if the voice is passive or active, respectively.
  * **Verb (F113)**. The predicate of the argument.
  * **Sense (F114)**. The sense of the predicate of the argument.
  * **Verb disambiguated (F115)**. The predicate and its sense.
  * **Words around (F139)**. The previous and the next word of the argument.
  * **PoS around (F141)**. The Part-of-Speech tag of the previous and the next word of the argument.
  * **Lemma around (F147)**. The lemma of the previous and the next word of the argument.
  * **Phrases around (F149)**. The kind of the previous and the next phrase of the argument.
- Features combined
  * **Lemma and PoS (F124), (F126), (F131), (F145)**. Lemma and Part-of-Speech tag of content-words, of the headwords of the phrases, of the first and the last word and of the previous and the next word of the argument.
  * **Word and PoS (F120), (F121), (F122), (F123), (F135), (143)**. Words and Part-of-Speech tag of the first and the last word, of the previous and next word, of the headwords of the phrases and of the nouns, adjectives, adverbs and content-words of the argument.

3 Evaluation

The goal of this evaluation is to measure the role of Verb Sense Disambiguation in Semantic Role Labeling. In order to do so, it is necessary to determine the behavior of the features used in the classification process when the senses of the verbs are considered and when they are not. Additionally, how the tuning process of these features is affected by the VSD is studied.

When the senses of the verbs are considered the classification is done by each sense of verb. So, the classes considered are the roles for each sense of each verb. In this case, information about features is extracted for each argument, for every sense of each verb. Instead of this, when the senses of the verbs are not considered, the classes considered are the general set of roles. Then information about features is extracted just for each argument. So, let's remember the verb *give* and its three senses, #1,#4, and #6, shown in Figure 1. If the senses are considered, we will have three different classifiers: the #1 classifier with three classes, the roles A0, A1 and A2; the #4 classifier with two classes, the roles A0 and A1; and the #6 classifier with three classes, the roles A0, A1 and A2. If the senses are not considered, we will have just a classifier with three classes, the roles A0, A1 and A2.

The features have been evaluated about precision, recall and F1 measure. Precision (p) is the proportion of roles predicted by the system which are correct. Recall (r) is the proportion of correct roles which are predicted by the system. F1 measure computes the harmonic mean the precision and recall. It is formulated as $F_{\beta=1}=(2pr)/(p+r)$.

3.1 Experimental Data

In order to build this three-phase learning system, training and development data set are used. It is used the PropBank corpus [15], which is the Wall Street Journal part of the Penn Treebank corpus [13] enriched with predicate-arguments structures.

PropBank annotates the Penn Treebank with argument structures related to verbs. The set of tags considered is the following:

- Tags for Arguments (A0-A5, AA): Arguments defining verb-specific roles. Their semantics depend on the sense of the verb usage in a sentence. In general, A0 stands for the agent and A1 corresponds to the patient or theme of the proposition. However, no consistent generalization can be made across different verbs or different senses of the same verb. AA refers to volitional motion.
- Tags for Adjuncts (AM-): General arguments that any verb may take optionally. There are 12 types of adjuncts:
  - AM-LOC: location
  - AM-EXT: extent
  - AM-DIS: discourse marker
  - AM-ADV: general-porpouse
  - AM-NEG: negation marker
  - AM-MOD: modal verb
  - AM-CAU: cause
  - AM-TMP: temporal
  - AM-PRD: purpose
  - AM-MNR: manner
  - AM-DIR: direction
  - AM-PNC
- Tags of References (R-): Arguments representing arguments realized in other parts of the sentence. The role of a reference is the same as the role of the referenced argument. The label is an R-tag preceded to the label of the referent, e.g. R-A1.

The data set consists of 39832 sentences, with 239858 arguments and 3101 distinct verbs. Apart from the correct output, this data set contain the output of several annotation processors: PoS tags [8], chunks and clauses [2] and named entities [4].

3.2 Behavior of Combined Features

In any corpus-based approach a tuning process is needed in order to obtain a set of features that maximizes the results.

In order to do this, we have used a k-fold cross validation evaluation method, with $K=3$. In this kind of methods the data set is divided into k subsets, and the holdout method[2] is repeated k times. Each time, one of the k subsets is used as the test set and the other k-1 subsets are put together to form a training set. Then the average error across all k trials is computed. The advantage of this method is that it matters less how the data gets divided. Every data point will be in a test set exactly once, and will be in a training set k-1 times.

Taking into account the proposal of Langley [11], the feature selection process of our semantic role annotation tool has been defined as follows [14]:

- The **starting point** of the search will be the empty set. It is determined by the algorithm used in the organization of the search.
- The **organization of the search**. In order to obtain one of the best sets of features the Forward Selection (FS) algorithm will be applied. This algorithm starts with the empty set and greedily adds features, one at a time, until all features are added. First, the feature which results in the best fit is selected. Next, this feature is used to test all combinations with the remaining features in order to find the best pair of features. In all further steps, additional features are added until either all features are used up, or some stopping criterion is reached. Once a feature is added FS cannot remove it later.
- The **strategy used to evaluate** will be a wrapper method. In this case two different approaches will be used, the TiMBL program and a Maximum Entropy classifier.
- The **criterion for halting search**. In order to further reduce the number of possible subsets, the search will stop if the results are not improved.

Results about this tuning procedure are shown in Tables 1 and 2. These results show how additional attributes interfere with other more useful attributes. For example, in Table 1 the precision using a random selected set of twenty five features is 64.90%. This precision is exceeded by sets of two features (69.83%) and more. So, the highest precision is obtained with a set of twelve features (76.91%). The last row of this table shows the results obtained by the ten features with the best individual results (72.48%).

Table 1 results refer to the tuning procedure when the senses of the verbs are considered. To measure the influence of these senses a different tuning procedure has been done without considering the senses of the verbs. These results are shown in Table 2. In this case, the best results are obtained when a set of ten features is used (80.84% of precision). Sets of eleven or twelve features obtain lower results (80.75% and 80.63%, respectively).

Tables 1 and 2 show how the tuning process is affected by the VSD module. If the sense of the verb is used or not, the set of features to be considered is

[2] The holdout method is the simplest kind of cross validation. The data set is separated into two sets, called the training set and the testing set.

Table 1. Behavior of features applied in a combined form when the senses of the verbs are used (vs). TiMBL algorithm is used.

Features	P	R	$F_{\beta=1}$
F137	61.69	60.98	61.33
F6,F137	69.83	68.99	69.41
F6,F19,F137	72.31	71.43	71.87
F6,F19,F137,F145	74.19	73.15	73.67
F6,19,F129,F137,F145	75.99	74.52	75.05
F6,F7,F19,F129,F137,F145	76.15	75.05	75.60
F2,F6,F7,F19,F129,F137,F145	76.33	75.22	75.77
F2,F6,F7,F19,F29,F129,F137,F145	76.47	75.36	75.91
F2,F6,7,F19,F29,F109,F129,F137,F145	76.50	75.47	76.02
F2,F6,F7,F19,F29,F109,F129,F137,F145,F149	76.71	75.58	76.14
F2,F6,F7,F19,F29,F51,F109,F129,F137,F145,F149	76.82	75.78	76.24
F2,F6,F7,F19,F29,F51,F109,F129,F133,F137,F145,F149	**76.91**	**75.78**	**76.34**
F2,F6,F7,F19,F27,F29,F51,F109,F129,F133,F137,F145,F149	76.91	75.78	76.34
F2,F6,F7,F19,F27,F29,F51,F109,F115,F129,F133,F137,F145,F149	76.91	75.78	76.34
Set of twenty five	64.90	61.30	63.05
F6,F17,F18,F111,F112,F137,F141,F145,F147,F149	72.48	71.45	71.96

Table 2. Behavior of features applied in a combined form when the senses of the verbs are not used (u). TiMBL algorithm is used.

Features	P	R	$F_{\beta=1}$
F135	63.22	63.92	63.57
F135,F143	70.25	70.95	70.59
F115,F135,F143	73.66	74.15	73.91
F19,F115,F135,F143	76.55	77.06	76.81
F6,F19,F115,F135,F143	78.87	79.38	79.12
F6,F7,F19,F115,F135,F143	80.00	80.52	80.26
F2,F6,F7,F19,F115,F135,F143	80.38	80.89	80.63
F2,F6,F7,F19,F29,F115,F135,F143	80.48	81.03	80.76
F2,F6,F7,F19,F29,F113,F115,F135,F143	80.56	81.09	80.82
F2,F6,F7,F8,F19,F29,F113,F115,F135,F143	**80.84**	**81.34**	**81.09**
F2,F6,F7,F8,F19,F29,F113,F115,F135,F137,F143	80.75	81.26	81.01
F2,F6,F7,F8,F19,F29,F113,F115,F135,F137,F143,F147	80.63	81.14	80.89

Table 3. Detail of features when the senses of the verbs are used (vs) and not (u). TiMBL algorithm is used.

Features vs	Features u
F2 - Voice	F2 - Voice
F6 - Position of the argument	F6 - Position of the argument
F7 - Position in the clause	F7 - Position in the clause
F19 - Initial preposition	F8 - Distance in words to the verb
F29 - Adverbs	F19 - Initial preposition
F51 - PoS of initial preposition	F29 - Adverbs
F109 - Lemma of headwords	F113 - Verb
F129 - First and last word of the argument	F115 - Sense of verb
F133 - Lemmas of the first and last word of the argument	F135 - Lemmas of the first and last word of the argument and their PoS
F137 - PoS of the first and last word of the argument	F143 - previous and next word of the argument and their PoS
F145 - Lemma of the previous and next word of the argument	
F149 - Kind of previous and next phase	

Table 4. Behavior of features applied in a combined form when the senses of the verbs are used (vs) and the ME algorithm is applied

Features	P	R	$F_{\beta=1}$
F137	61.91	62.44	62.17
F137,F149	68.38	38.85	68.61
F133,F137,F149	71.24	71.81	71.53
F18,F133,F137,F149	**71.33**	**71.92**	**71.62**
F8,F133,F137,F145,F149	72.06	71.15	71.60

different. Indeed, the number of features needed when the senses are considered is bigger than they are not. However the kind of information used is very similar in both approaches although in a different format. See Table 3.

Other similar tuning process has been carried out using the ME classifier. Table 4 shows the result of this process. In this case, the best results have been obtained using a set of four features (71,62% de F1). Sets of five features has better precision but worse recall. So, the F1 measure goes down (71,60%). This tuning process has considered the sense of the verbs. An additional tuning should be done without the sense of the verbs. However, taking into account the results about TiMBL, the results do not justify the computational cost of this process.

3.3 Behavior of Roles

Table 5 shows detailed results of the different kinds of roles and our two different machine learning approaches, with and without senses.

When specific roles are considered the results with senses are higher (A1, A2, A3, A4, AA). When adjuncts, or general arguments, are considered the results without senses are higher (see for example modal, negative, location or temporal roles).

These results confirm our initial approach shown in section 2. It is because roles such as A2, A3 or A4 are specific to the sense of a verb. However, the adjunct information, such as modal or negative, is independent of the sense.

Table 5. Behavior of roles when the senses of the verbs are used (vs) and not (u). Results about $F_{\beta=1}$ measure.

Roles	TiMBL (vs)	TiMBL (u)	ME (vs)	ME (u)	Roles	TiMBL (vs)	TiMBL (u)	ME (vs)	ME (u)
A0	83.95	84.93	72.76	76.57	AM-MOD	89.79	96.57	80.30	98.59
A1	84.49	83.99	73.39	70.27	AM-NEG	76.06	96.62	65.55	88.22
A2	81.97	73.46	66.92	34.48	AM-PNC	43.17	39.46	25.60	29.75
A3	74.01	58.82	56.87	24.37	AM-PRD	100.00	57.14	50.00	0.00
A4	76.80	64.00	60.47	57.36	AM-TMP	48.96	77.52	35.16	61.63
A5	50.00	50.00	0.00	0.00	R-A0	76.29	85.91	60.87	82.65
AA	100.00	0.00	0.00	0.00	R-A1	58.06	68.71	51.81	44.30
AM-ADV	36.82	55.24	26.49	46.44	R-A2	47.06	50.00	47.06	0.00
AM-CAU	16.00	25.40	6.15	3.64	R-A3	0.00	0.00	0.00	0.00
AM-DIR	64.79	50.00	51.92	40.00	R-AM-CAU	0.00	40.00	0.00	0.00
AM-DIS	57.22	85.99	43.28	81.53	R-AM-EXT	0.00	0.00	0.00	0.00
AM-EXT	50.00	52.00	59.26	34.48	R-AM-LOC	46.15	81.82	0.00	87.50
AM-LOC	41.36	64.62	32.00	46.28	R-AM-MNR	50.00	90.91	0.00	0.00
AM-MNR	39.79	54.15	23.26	31.13	R-AM-TMP	72.73	96.67	46.15	91.67

Moreover, this table shows how the results are independent of the machine learning algorithm used. The behavior of the specific roles and adjuncts is equivalent for the two approaches, TiMBL and ME classifiers. In both, the average of A2, A3, A4 and A5 roles[3] is upper when the senses are considered (70.70 for TiMBL and 46,07 for ME) when they are not (55.33 for TiMBL and 41.48 for ME). On the other hand, the average of adjuncts is upper when the senses are not taken into account (62.89 for TiMBL and 46.81 for ME) when they are (61.57 for TiMBL and 29.05 for ME).

3.4 Comparison with Other Methods

Our method has been compared with methods of CoNLL2004 shared task[4]

The results obtained in the CoNLL 2004 shared task[5] are shown in Table 6. As this table shows, the results obtained using the SemRol method, when the TiMBL classifier is used, are higher than the best results obtained in the CoNLL competition.

To obtain these results the corpus used for training and testing have been the corpus used in the competition (WSJ sections: 15-18 training, 21 test).

Table 6. Comparison of SemRol with other SRL methods

Features	P	R	$F_{\beta=1}$
SemRol u	**77.75**	**78.23**	**77.99**
hacioglu	78.61	72.47	75.42
punyakanok	77.82	70.04	73.72
carreras	79.22	67.41	72.84
park	73.64	70.05	71.80
lim	75.43	67.76	71.39
SemRol vs	**72.97**	**69.318**	**71.10**
higgins	70.72	63.40	66.86
vandenbosch	75.48	61.23	67.61
kouchnir	66.52	58.43	62.21
baldewein	75.13	48.70	59.09
williams	70.62	42.25	52.87

4 Conclusion and Work in Progress

In this paper the role of Verb Sense Disambiguation in Semantic Role Labeling has been evaluated. In order to do this, our SRL method, named , has been used. This method introduces a new phase in the SRL task because depending on the sense of the verb a different set of roles must be considered. Our method first disambiguates the sense of the verb in the sentence. Next, during the recognition phase, the argument boundaries of the disambiguated verb are identified. Finally, during the labeling phase, the roles that fill these arguments are determined.

[3] A0 and A1 roles have not been considered because they are common to almost all the verbs.

[4] Our results are not compared with CoNLL 2005 shared task because we do not use a full syntactic parser.

[5] http://www.lsi.upc.edu/ srlconll/st04/slides/intor.psf slide 33

Using SemRol the behavior of the most relevant features for the SRD phase has been analyzed when the senses of the verbs are used and when they are not. As a result we have establish a set of good features for the classification using senses, and a set of good features for the classification without them. Furthermore, the results show how specific roles are better disambiguated when the senses of the verbs are considered.

Beside of this, the results obtained are independent of the algorithm used in the classification process. Equivalents results have been shown using two different classification approaches, TiMBL, a Memory-based Learning algorithm, and a conditional Maximum Entropy probability model.

Finally, the SemRol method has been compared with other SRL methods that make use of the same kind of learning information. The results obtained using the SemRol method when the senses of the verbs are not considered (77.75% of precision, 78.23% of recall and 77.99% of $F_{\beta=1}$) are higher than the best results obtained in the CoNLL 2004 shared task competition.

Actually, we are applying the semantic role information to improve QA systems. Depending on the kind of question or the class of verb, the answer is a specific or a generic role. So, the verb sense disambiguation approach must be used or not.

Acknowledgement

This paper has been supported by the Spanish Government under project "R2D2: Recuperación de Respuestas de Documentos Digitalizados" (TIC2003-07158-C04-01).

References

1. *Ninth Conference on Natural Language Learning (CoNLL-2005)*, Ann Arbor, Michigan, USA, Junio 2005.
2. X. Carreras and L. Màrquez. Phrase recognition by filtering and ranking with perceptrons. In *Proceedings of Recent Advances in Natural Language Processing (RANLP)*, Borovets, Bulgaria, Septiembre 2003.
3. X. Carreras and L. Màrquez. Introduction to the CoNLL-2005 Shared Task: Semantic Role Labeling. In *Proceedings of the Ninth Conference on Natural Language Learning (CoNLL-2005)* [1].
4. H.L. Chieu and H.T. Ng. Named Entity Recognition With a Maximum Entropy Approach. In *Proceedings of the Seventh Conference on Natural Language Learning (CoNLL)*, Edmonton, Alberta, Canada, Mayo-Junio 2003.
5. W. Daelemans, J. Zavrel, K. van der Sloot, and A. van den Bosch. TiMBL: Tilburg Memory Based Learner, version 5.0, Reference Guide. ILK Research Group Technical Report Series 03-10, Tilburg, 2003. 56 pages.
6. D. Gildea and D. Jurafsky. Automatic labeling of semantic roles. *Computational Linguistics*, 28(3):245–288, 2002.
7. D. Gildea and M. Palmer. The necessity of parsing for predicate argument recognition. In *Proceedings of the 40th Annual Meeting of the Association for Computational Linguistic (ACL)*, Philadelphia, Julio 2002.

8. J. Giménez and L. Màrquez. Fast and Accurate Part-of-Speech Tagging: The SVM Approach Revisited. In *Proceedings of Recent Advances in Natural Language Processing (RANLP)*, Borovets, Bulgaria, Septiembre 2003.
9. K. Hacioglu, S. Pradhan, W. Ward, J.H. Martin, and D. Jurafsky. Semantic Role Labeling by Tagging Syntactic Chunks. In *Proceedings of the Eighth Conference on Natural Language Learning (CoNLL-2004)*, Boston, MA, USA, Mayo 2004.
10. A. Haghighi, K. Toutanova, and C. Manning. A Joint Model for Semantic Role Labeling. In *Proceedings of the Ninth Conference on Natural Language Learning (CoNLL-2005)* [1].
11. P. Langley. Selection of Relevant Features in Machine Learning. In AAAI Press, editor, *Proceedings of the AAAI Fall Symposium on Relevance (AAAI)*, New Orleans, LA, 1994.
12. K. Litkowski. Senseval-3 task: Automatic Labeling of Semantic Roles. In *Proceedings of the Third International Workshop on the Evaluation of Systems for the Semantic Analysis of Text*, Barcela, Spain, July 2004. ACL-SIGLEX.
13. M.P. Marcus, B. Santorini, and M.A. Marcinkiewicz. Building a Large Annotated Corpus of English: the Penn Treebank. *Computational Linguistics*, 19(2):313–330, 1993.
14. P. Moreda and M. Palomar. Selecting Features for Semantic Roles in QA Systems. In *Proceedings of Recent Advances in Natural Language Processing (RANLP)*, Borovets, Bulgaria, Septiembre 2005.
15. M. Palmer, D. Gildea, and P. Kingsbury. The Proposition Bank: An Annotated Corpus of Semantic Roles. *Computational Linguistics*, 31(1):71–106, 2005.
16. S. Pradhan, K. Hacioglu, V. Krugler, W. Ward, J. Martin, and D. Jurafsky. Support Vector Learning for Semantic Argument Classification. *Machine Learning*, page To appear, 2005.
17. S. Pradhan, K. Hacioglu, W. Ward, J.H. Martin, and D.Jurafsky. Semantic role chunking combining complementary syntactic views. In *Proceedings of the Ninth Conference on Natural Language Learning (CoNLL-2005)* [1].
18. V. Punyakanok, D. Roth, W. Yih, and D. Zimak. Generalized inference with multiple semantic role labeling systems. In *Proceedings of the Ninth Conference on Natural Language Learning (CoNLL-2005)* [1].
19. V. Punyakanok, D. Roth, W. Yih, D. Zimak, and Y. Tu. Semantic Role Labeling Via Generalized Inference Over Classifiers. In *Proceedings of the 20th International Conference on Computational Linguistics (COLING)*, Switzerland, Agosto 2004.
20. E.F.Tjong Kim Sang, S.Canisius, and A. van den Bosch adn T. Bogers. Applying spelling error correction techniques for improving semantic role labeling. In *Proceedings of the Ninth Conference on Natural Language Learning (CoNLL-2005)* [1].
21. A. Suárez and M. Palomar. A Maximum Entropy-based Word Sense Disambiguation System. In *Proceedings of the 19th International Conference on Computational Linguistics (COLING)*, pages 960–966, Taipei, Taiwan, Agosto 2002.

The Vowel Game: Continuous Real-Time Visualization for Pronunciation Learning with Vowel Charts

Annu Paganus[1], Vesa-Petteri Mikkonen[2], Tomi Mäntylä[1], Sami Nuuttila[1], Jouni Isoaho[1], Olli Aaltonen[2], and Tapio Salakoski[1]

[1] University of Turku, Department of Information Technology, FI-20014 Turku Finland
{Annu.Paganus, Tomi.Heikkimikael.Mantyla, Sami.Nuuttila, Jouni.Isoaho, Tapio.Salakoski}@utu.fi
[2] University of Turku, Department of Phonetics, FI-20014 Turku Finland
{Petteri.Mikkonen, Olli.Aaltonen}@utu.fi

Abstract. Learning to pronounce new speech sounds is difficult. Visual feedback helps in identifying the errors and indicating the achieved progress. The Vowel Game uses a visualization method that symbolizes the vocal tract. This instructs the user on how to adjust e.g. the tongue position during pronunciation. It gives information about the correctness and goodness of the uttered vowel. Preliminary evaluation suggests that continuous real-time feedback can be obtained, but the effect on learning remains to be tested.

1 Introduction

Visual feedback has been proven to be beneficial in language learning applications. When using Sona-Speech 3600-ESL [2] from KAY Elemetrics the user pronounces a vowel according to an example sound. Then the application draws a dot in real-time into a vowel chart where correct places of the vowels are presented with IPA-symbols. The application also opens a new window where it presents the "closest vowel" to the user's production. There is also authentic video material of native speakers pronouncing the sample vowels. Baldi [12] is an animated 3D talking head that have been used, for example, for training the perception and production of speech for people with hearing loss. The head provides the learner with examples and feedback (smiling etc.) on whether or not one is making the right interpretation of words the head says. In their investigation Massaro and Light [12] have used also the voice recognition system in the CSLU toolkit to evaluate the validity of the learner's ability to produce certain words. In the Video Voice system [6] the learner gets information about how near his/her pronunciation is to the right phoneme. Those phonemes are shown at the coordinate system in which the axes are F1 and F2 values. Dowd, Smith and Wolfe [5] have visualized vowels with separate oval areas for each vowel. They don't use formants but resonances of the vocal tract using an acoustic impedance spectrometer. Their paper describes this technique as more precise than using formants. They have got encouraging results in learning: results with visual feedback and training were 25 percent units better than with only auditory feedback. The Optical

T. Salakoski et al. (Eds.): FinTAL 2006, LNAI 4139, pp. 696 – 703, 2006.

Logo Therapy (OLT) [7] provides same kind of real-time feedback. It shows e.g. phonemes /s/, /z/, /sh/, /i/ and /u/ in the same picture. There is undefined space between the presented phonemes which they consider to be a problem. The tool tells when the learner has said the right phoneme but doesn't give information about how to improve.

In this paper we introduce the Vowel Game, a pronunciation learning tool based on formants. The phonetic background underlying the game is based on the Turku Vowel Test, which is a research project build up to study the perception of vowels by speakers of different languages [15]. It is a perception test where the listener is asked to judge first what category the stimulus belongs to and second how good of an example of the given category the stimulus is. Application then produces a vowel chart according to listener's choices. While the study had been going on for several years, an idea emerged of how the produced vowel charts could be used in pronunciation training. If we can produce a vowel plotter that shows the exact relevant acoustic values of the utterance, we could use it as an instructional tool on a vowel chart of any given language.

The phonetic background underlying the game is discussed first in section 2. Third section describes the workings of the game. The learning with the system and real-time issues are discussed in section 4. Finally the paper is concluded with a discussion on future work.

2 Phonetic Background

A vowel chart is a simple tool for visualizing speech. Place in the chart is determined by first and second formant frequency. Formants are energy peaks at a certain frequency resulted from vocal tract resonances. A vowel chart is a diagram where the first formant is presented as values of hertz or mels growing from top to bottom. The second formant is presented similarly from right to left. Vowel chart can be viewed as a simplification of a person's individual vocal tract. Width of the vowel chart corresponds to the length of the vocal tract, and height of the vowel chart corresponds to vocal tract height. Figure 1 shows two correspondences.

The perception of speech sounds is categorical. Liberman et al. [11] found out that people tend to have little difficulties in discriminating sounds near phoneme boundaries, even though the acoustic qualities of phonemes are continuous. In cooing a prelingual infant produces all vowels of the vowel space. She can also discriminate sounds nonexistent in her native language. The infant listens and mimics adult speech. That makes her brains to start constructing permanent memory traces about the nature of her native speech sounds. At the age of six months, all humans have usually learned the phonetic categories and prototypes of their native language, making it extremely difficult to distinguish foreign speech sounds. The prototype is the best example of a phoneme category. This best example acts like a magnet drawing the other phonemes of the category towards it perceptually. This results in better discrimination and identification of phonemes. It also creates structure inside categories, making it possible to rate goodness within a category [10].

Fig. 1. Vowel chart and vocal tract correspondences of phonemes /i/ and /o/. Notice how the tongue positions correspond to the phoneme locations on the chart.

Learning foreign speech sounds can be extremely difficult. The native system causes interferences and can block the acquisition of foreign speech sounds [8]. Learning native vowel categories can be viewed as dividing the vowel space, which includes all the possible vowels, to a certain set of vowel categories, with a prototype at the center, surrounded by the less typical examples. All sounds may belong to a completely different category in another language. Figure 2 shows a Finnish and a Finland Swedish vowel chart. Notice how the Finland Swedish vowel /ʉ/ occupies space from both Finnish /y/ and /u/.

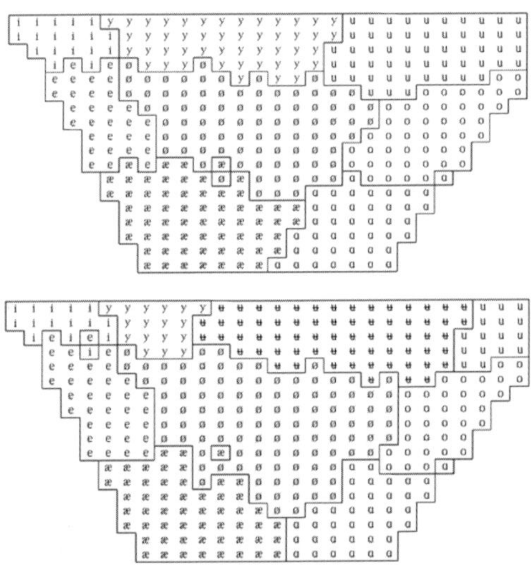

Fig. 2. Category charts of Finnish (the upper diagram) and Finland Swedish (the lower diagram). [15].

A prototype chart demonstrates the structures inside categories. An example of a Finnish prototype chart is presented in Figure 3. The chart is based on perceived goodness at a scale of 1 to 7. Goodness is demonstrated by grey scale colors. Lighter grey areas represent the more prototypical vowels.

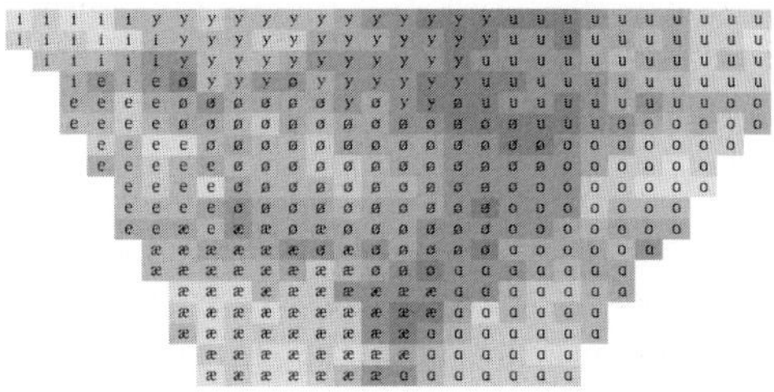

Fig. 3. Prototype chart of the eight Finnish vowels. Lighter areas represent the more prototypical vowels, whereas darker areas are rarely used in Finnish. [15].

3 The Vowel Game

The Vowel Game is an application that uses vowel charts in order to let the user train to pronounce vowels. The software is built with Java^{TM} using version 1.5.0.

3.1 The Idea of the Vowel Game

When the application is started, the user sees the Finnish vowel chart and the target phonemes circled at the chart as illustrated in Figure 4. The idea of the game is to learn to pronounce all the target vowels. The *Play* button starts the game. The user is expected to pronounce a vowel, which is continuously traced on the chart. When the

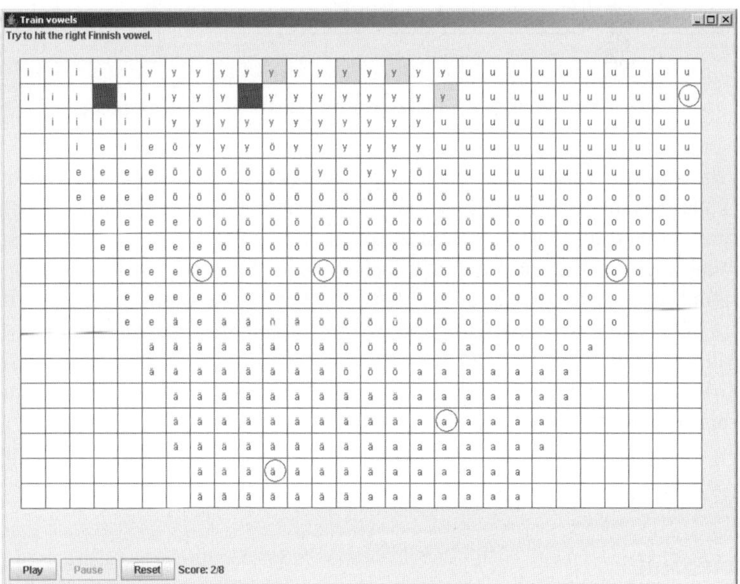

Fig. 4. A snap shot of the Vowel Game while user is saying vowel /y/ and has been hit the target vowels /i/ and /y/

user's utterance is located on the chart, it is shown by switching the vowel yellow. Last five locations are shown at a time. When a target vowel has been hit it turns red. The *Pause* button pauses the speech data recording.

Figure 4 illustrates how the game looks like when the user is uttering the vowel /y/ and has already hit the vowels /i/ and /y/. Notice that the IPA-symbols are not used in the game, instead the written characters of standard Finnish of the corresponding phonemes are used.

We are currently working to offer auditory feedback with formant speech synthesis. When it is ready the user can get a sample from each vowel by clicking on the chart.

3.2 Implementation Aspects

Figure 5 shows the steps that are taken while the formant locations are determined. The sampling frequency we use is 8 kHz. This enables us to review formants at frequencies below 4 kHz according to Nyquist theorem [4]. The voice signal is windowed using a Hann window (aka Hanning) of length 256 samples. One window takes then 32 ms which should include at least one glottal pulse. The signal is then pre-emphasized by a whitening filter that increases the spectral slope by 6 dB per each octave. The pre-emphasis stage thus increases the relative energy of the high-frequency spectrum [4] so that the higher frequencies with naturally lower relative energy get the same weight as the lower ones.

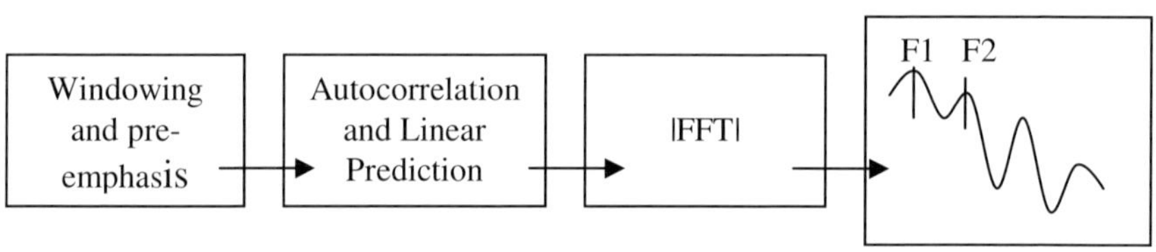

Fig. 5. Steps taken while the formant locations are determined

Next, the autocorrelation coefficients are calculated for the 10th order Linear Prediction (LP) analysis that is used. The actual LP coefficients are then found by using a decomposition method to solve the normal equations [4]. Finally, the impulse response of the resulting analysis filter is Fourier transformed to find the spectral envelope of the speech signal. In this the Fast Fourier Transform (FFT) algorithm is used. Formants F1 and F2 are then found by locating the first two maxima in the spectral envelope.

Generally it is difficult to determine the formants precisely, rapidly and automatically [5]. In the current state of development of the Vowel Game the values are extracted rapidly and automatically but not always precisely. Problems occur when F1 and F2 are merged to one peak. That happens e.g. sometimes when the user utters the Finnish vowel /u/.

4 Discussion

Visual feedback has positive influences in learning foreign languages [5], and overcoming problems with speech production [6, 7]. The challenge in providing visual feedback is to make it easy to understand [6]. The Vowel Game shows how close the pronunciation is to the prototype, as the Sona-Speech [2] does, and also, if it falls within the correct category. This is a guide to shift the pronunciation, for example, towards a familiar phoneme in the same direction as the target prototype. Unlike in OLT [7] there is no undefined area between the prototypes, so the presentation is continuous.

We believe it would serve a purpose to have the feedback in real-time instead of after each attempt. The speaker shouldn't have to wait to see, how close the attempt came, before trying again. Another important factor is continuity of the training session. Real-time and continuous feedback can be used to search the correct pronunciation, or play around and see how the outcome is affected.

Systems delivering non-judgmental, immediate feedback during the pronunciation, such as our application and many parts of the SPECO system at KTH [17], are also seen beneficial by Zhang [18]. There was also a weakness noted in the Baldi system, where it occasionally gave false negative feedback [12], which can be seen as an argument on behalf of using directing, non-judgmental feedback.

The probable future of the system is to be a part of a toolbox of several applications. This game is for a teacher to apply, when the student's mastery of the language is at a point, where focusing on the correct pronunciation is useful.

The Vowel Game helps visual learners, as they can see what the vowel "looks like". For kinesthetic learners, real-time feedback would seem to us as equally helpful, as the learner given the visual guidance can feel the vowel around the mouth, and work with their own vocal tract and see what is happening. For people with hearing loss, visual feedback has also been found successful [12]. People with no hearing at all might find our application helpful e.g. on a mobile device as a tool for pronunciation confirmation when they talk. A third group of people who should be interested in the game are language professionals. They could use the application to train the awareness of their own vocal tract and the nature of speech production.

Providing the system for a PDA-platform poses a real challenge. We use Java to achieve code mobility at the cost of efficiency. It remains to be seen how well we can comply with the real-time requirements in the PDA environments.

A research by Alais and Carlile [1] supports, that the human perception system is capable of adapting to a time difference of at least 68 ms, which is consistent with other researches mentioning the requirement of maximum video delay of 16-42 ms [14] and even 150 ms [16]. The risk in failing to achieve real-time is that the effects of notable delay "include overcompensation, lack of trust in the feedback and confusion and disorientation" [3].

Cost efficiency is one practical aspect. As noted by Zhang [18], feedback of this kind has been impractically expensive in the past. Today, a typical PC with enough processing power is affordable. Where a small elementary school can not afford a real language studio, a desktop computer might be a low cost equivalent.

Because the vowel chart is a simplification of the vocal tract, and there are as many vocal tract sizes and shapes as there are speakers, our tool needs to be calibrated. This can be done, for example, by the use of the so called "point vowels", /i/, /a/ and /u/. Because these vowels are the articulatory and acoustic extremes of the vowel space [9], we can ask the user to articulate them and then set the vowel chart size accordingly. There are also more sophisticated methods for calculating vocal tract length and shape. These methods use formant data and pitch period estimations [13].

Another problem for accurate analysis of formants comes from differences in fundamental frequency. Because there is acoustic energy present only at the multiples of the fundamental frequency, there is more "empty space" between the multiples when the fundamental frequency is higher. This kind of "empty space" can in some cases be at a crucial point in the spectra. There are also ways to normalize the effect of fundamental frequency, in which we will look into in the future.

Preliminary tests suggest that the game is currently more suitable for men than for women. Women's F1 values are sometimes higher than the values in the used chart, which is natural because the used vowel chart is based on synthesized male voice samples. However, once the calibration is finalized the problem should be solved.

The vowel chart is a simplification also in that there are other ways to inflict formants than tongue position. One of these ways is lip rounding. In the two dimensional model it is impossible to analyze or visualize whether a certain change in the second formant frequency is a cause of lip rounding or movement of the tongue. An application of the third formant could prove to be beneficial in determining lip rounding, but would also cause the system to become seriously more complex. At the current time we feel that the information provided by the two formants gives us satisfactory outcome and the application of higher formants seems unnecessary.

5 Conclusion and Future Work

In this paper we introduced the Vowel Game - a tool to help people to learn to pronounce vowels. The study shows that real-time continuous visual feedback about correctness and goodness of the pronunciation is viable through formant charts. The game will be a part of a larger system including consonants and prosody training. Future work will also include e.g. fundamental frequency normalization and research on the applicability of the third formant. Also the effect on learning has to be studied.

References

1. Alais, D., Carlile, S.: Synchronizing to real events: Subjective audiovisual alignment scales with perceived auditory depth and speed of sound. Proc Natl Acad Sci USA. 2005 Feb 8; 102(6), (2005) 2244-7
2. Carey, M.: CALL visual feedback for pronunciation of vowels: KAY Sona Speech. CALICO Journal 21, (3) (2004)
3. Day, P.N. Holt, P.O'B. Russell, G.T.: Modelling the Effects of Delayed Visual Feedback in Real-Time Operator Control Loops: A Cognitive Perspective. Proceedings of XVII European Annual Conference on Human Decision Making and Manual Control, Loughborough October, Group D Publications Ltd (1999) 70-79
4. Deller, J.R., Proakis, J.G., Hansen, J.H.L.: Discrete-Time Processing of Speech Signals. Macmillan, New York (1993)
5. Dowd, A., Smith, J.R., Wolfe, J.: Learning to pronounce vowel sounds in a foreign language using acoustic measurements of the vocal tract as feedback in real time. Language and Speech, 41 (1998) 1-20

6. Fitzgerald M., Gruenwald A., Stoker R.: Software review – Video Voice Speech Training System, Volta Review, vol. 89 (1989) 171-173
7. Hatzis, A.: Optical Logo-Therapy (OLT): Computer-Based Audio-Visual Feedback Using Interactive Visual Displays for Speech Training. PhD thesis, Department of Computer Science, University of Sheffield (1999)
8. Iverson P, Kuhl P.K, Akahane-Yamada R, Diesch E, Tohkura Y, Kettermann A, Siebert C.: A perceptual interference account of acquisition difficulties for non-native phonemes. Cognition 87 (2003) B47-B57
9. Jakobson, R., Fant, G., Halle, M.: Preliminaries to speech analysis: The distinctive features and their correlates. Cambridge, Massachusetts. MIT Press. (1969)
10. Kuhl P.K.: Human adults and human infants show a "perceptual magnet effect" for the prototypes of speech categories, monkeys do not. Perception and Psychophysics 50(2) (1991) 93-107
11. Liberman. A.M., Harris, K.S. Hoffman, H.S., Griffith, B.C.: The discrimination of speech sounds within and across phoneme boundaries. Journal of Experimental Psychology, 54, (1957) 358-368
12. Massaro, D.W., Light, J.: Using Visible Speech to Train Perception and Production of Speech for Individuals With Hearing Loss, Journal of Speech, Language and Hearing Research, Vol. 47, April (2004) 304-320
13. Paige A., Zue V.: Calculation of Vocal Tract Length, IEEE Transactions on Audio and Electroacoustics 18, no. 3 (1970) 268-70
14. Regan, M. Pose, R.: Priority rendering with a virtual reality address recalculation pipeline. In Proceedings of the 21st Annual Conference on Computer Graphics and interactive Techniques SIGGRAPH '94. ACM Press, New York, NY (1994)
15. The Turku Vowel Test. Dept. of Phonetics, University of Turku. http://fon.utu.fi/ 3.4.2006
16. Vaghi, I., Greenhalgh, C., Benford, S.: Coping with inconsistency due to network delays in collaborative virtual environments. In Proceedings of the ACM Symposium on Virtual Reality Software and Technology (London, United Kingdom, December 20 - 22, 1999). VRST '99. ACM Press, New York, NY (1999) 42-49
17. Vicsi, K. Roach, P. Öster, A-M. Kacic, Z. Csatári, F. Sfakianaki, A., Veronik, R.: A multilingual, Multimodal, Speech Training System SPECO, Proceedings of Eurospeech 2001 (2001) 2807-2810
18. Zhang, F.: Using interactive feedback tool to enhance pronunciation in language learning. S. Mishra & R.C. Sharma (Eds.) Interactive Multimedia in Education and Training, Idea Group Publishing (2004) 377-399

Towards a Framework for Evaluating Syntactic Parsers

Tuomo Kakkonen and Erkki Sutinen

University of Joensuu, Finland
{tuomo.kakkonen, erkki.sutinen}@cs.joensuu.fi

Abstract. Despite its great importance to developing parsing systems, the task of evaluating the performance of a syntactic parser of natural language is poorly defined. This paper provides a survey of parser evaluation methods and outlines a framework for experimental parser evaluation. Clearly, there is a lack of a comprehensive evaluation framework and a generic evaluation tool for parsers in the research community. Several evaluation methods exist and some practical evaluations have been carried out, but they usually concentrate on a single level of parsers' performance. The proposed framework focuses on intrinsic evaluation, providing useful information for parser developers. We provide a fuller picture of parser's performance compared to using the standard precision and recall measures. In addition, we consider ways of using the framework for comparative evaluations. The main motivation for this work is to serve as a requirements analysis for a parser evaluation tool to be implemented.

1 Introduction

A parser is a crucial component in any NLP system because it performs the structural analysis utilized by the other components, such as semantic interpreters and document classifiers. The output of a parser is a structural description of an analyzed language fragment. A natural language parser should be able to perform the tasks of segmentation and syntactic analysis [1]. Segmentation or tokenization refers to the process of identifying text units (*i.e.* sentences and words). In syntactic analysis, the syntactic segments (noun and verb phrases*etc.*) of each sentence are recognized and tagged. Many parsers also perform morphological analysis, assigning morphosyntactic labels (*e.g. part-of-speech*, (POS) tags) to each word.

Natural language parser evaluation has three distinct foci: developers need means to track the development of the system they are working on, users are interested in comparisons between different parsers, and managers need information as a basis for their decisions on resource allocation. For providing information for each groups' needs, several types of evaluation need to be carried out [2]: *Intrinsic evaluation* focuses on the performance of a parser in the context of the framework that it is developed in. Intrinsic evaluation provides developers

T. Salakoski et al. (Eds.): FinTAL 2006, LNAI 4139, pp. 704–715, 2006.

with means to identify improvements that are needed for the parser. As changes to grammar and the processing component of a parser have effects on the performance of the system, monitoring system evolution is important. In *extrinsic evaluation* the performance of a parser is measured as an embedded component of an *natural language processing* (NLP) application. *Comparative evaluation* aims to directly compare parsers based on different linguistic formalisms.

Empirical evaluation has become increasingly important in developing NLP systems. Evaluation tools are needed to allow developers and users to assess NLP systems. Although parsers are used as components of larger NLP applications, evaluation cannot be solely based on the comparison of their performance as a part of whole systems. Methods for direct evaluation of parsers are needed. Natural language parsers are evaluated by comparing their output to comparison materials, *gold standard*, usually taken from a manually constructed treebank - a syntactically annotated corpus. In addition to the gold standard, a metric is needed for performing the evaluation.

The diversity in the detail and the method of presentation of the output forms a major obstacle to directly comparing parsers' performance. Therefore, a transformation method between the outputs must be available or the comparison must be based on a general enough format to allow inter-system evaluation. The levels of detail in the output of parsers vary. An annotation scheme defines the format of the parser's output. Full parsers aim to produce a full, detailed parse whereas partial / shallow parsers focus on efficiency and reliability, thus producing a less detailed analysis. In terms of practical NLP applications, the preferred type of parser output depends on the application. For some purposes shallow parsing may be sufficient, whereas for other purposes, more detailed information on sentence structure is needed. Also, the representation format of the output varies. *Dependency* (D) and *phrase structure* (PS) (or constituent) structures are the two main ways to represent parses. The status of these two types of representations is a controversial one. Constituent structure has been favored by the transformational syntax community since Chomsky [3]. On the other hand, many researchers consider D structure as the fundamental representation. Some theories (such as *LFG*) see both of the structures as primitive.

There is clearly a need for framework for evaluating parsers and comparing the characteristics of parsing systems. Such a framework could be used by both practitioners of NLP to compare the strengths and weaknesses of diverse parsers and by parser developers to guide their work by pinpointing problems and providing analytical information on the parser's performance. In addition, there are no comprehensive evaluation tools currently available. Thus, an evaluation tool enabling practical evaluations to be carried out in the framework is needed.

The paper is organized in the following way. Previous work in evaluation methods and resources in discussed in Sections 2 and 3. Section 4 describes the evaluation framework. Section 5 concludes with outlining open problems and directions for future research.

2 Linguistic Resources for Parser Evaluation

Most of the work in parser evaluation has so far been concentrated on measuring the correctness of the structures assigned by parsers. Evaluating a parser's output consists of making judgments about the grammaticality or "the correctness" of structural descriptions assigned by the system. Parser evaluation is generally done by comparing system output to human-constructed, correct parses. The *gold standard* is usually a treebank or a test suite. Treebanks consist of a set of sentences which have been manually assigned parse trees with syntactic and morphosyntactic annotation. The aim of a test suite is to provide a means for testing of a wide range of linguistic phenomena by classifying each sentence (or test item) into a certain category, such as negation, agreement *etc.* Special type of resources are used for evaluating the parsers' ability to handle ill-formed input.

2.1 Resources for Accuracy and Coverage Evaluation

Evaluation resources, *i.e.* treebanks and test suites, exist for several languages (overviews of existing treebanks can be found in *e.g.* [4]). Nevertheless, the large diversity of annotation conventions employed limit their applicability for evaluation purposes. There are several possible solutions to the problem: either (a) mapping algorithms between the annotation schemes must be constructed, (b) evaluation resources must be represented in theory-independent format, or (c) resources must be annotated in parallel.

An alternative for mapping the parser output to the format used in the gold standard is to construct an evaluation resource with a type of annotation that is abstract enough to be compared to diverse kinds of annotations. There are XML-based exchange formats, such as *TigerXML* [5] and *XCES* [6], which can be applied to exchange between annotation schemes. A specific annotation scheme should be convertible to the theory-independent abstraction and vice versa. Only a set of tools that is able to understand the exchange format is needed to manipulate and search any of the resources.

Another possibility for facilitating the use of a treebank for comparative evaluation is to construct a multi-treebank consisting of sentences annotated according to several schemes. An example of such a treebank is the *AMALGAM MultiTreebank*, a multi-parsed corpus of English that has annotations according to nine different schemes [7].

A test suite is a type of linguistic resource especially tailored for evaluation purposes. Test suite -based evaluation is generally used by the system developers to evaluate the development of the parser and to pinpoint the strengths and weaknesses of the system in a controlled manner. Such an evaluation offers a way to evaluate the coverage of the grammar and check its consistency. In test suites, such as the *TSNLP* [1], sentences are divided into test items and grouped into test groups, allowing controlled experiments on a pre-defined set of phenomena to be carried out. Some test suites include negative, ill-formed test items.

2.2 Resources for Evaluating Robustness

A special type of evaluation resource, a corpus of ungrammatical English sentences have been reported by Foster [8]. The error types in the corpus include incorrect word forms, extraneous words, omitted words, and composite errors. For each sentence, the corpus has parallel correct and ungrammatical versions, both expressing the same meaning. Comparing the parsers' output on well-formed and ill-formed inputs is used for evaluating the robustness of a parser when faced with ill-formed input sentences. Bigert *et al.* [9] create ill-formed sentences for robustness evaluation by introducing spelling errors to input sentences by an automatic tool. The tool simulates naturally occurring typing errors. The automatic induction of errors enables controlled testing of degradation, the effect of increased error rate to the output of a parser.

3 Methods for Comparative Evaluation

The most widely used method in comparative parser evaluation is *PARSEVAL* [10]. The scheme uses PS bracketings to compare the output of a parser and a treebank. The *Penn Treebank* [11] is most commonly utilized in PARSEVAL evaluations. Three metrics are used for measuring the quality of the parser output: precision, recall and the number of crossing brackets. An advantage of the PARSEVAL method is that a treebank with only quite a low level of annotation detail is needed. The method also provides a means to compare parsers that use different output schemes. Several objections to PARSEVAL have been presented, though. Lin [12] argues that the crossing brackets measure counts a single bracketing error more than once in some cases. Srinivas *et al.* [13] point out that the precision measure penalizes parsers that generate detailed analyses when compared to a treebank with a low level of detail. They also argue that PARSEVAL is not suitable for evaluating partial parsers. One problem with the metrics is that they cannot be used for error analysis on the level of syntactic phenomena because of the lack of detail [2]. Carroll *et al.* [14] conclude that PARSEVAL evaluation "is...objective, but the results are not reliable."

A wide range of evaluation methods and metrics have been proposed to overcome the shortcomings of PARSEVAL and other evaluation methods based on phrase boundaries. Work has been done in an attempt to construct mapping methods between syntactic annotations. Lin [12] has proposed a method based on mapping the parser output to D structures. Precision and recall based on D relations are applied as the measure of the similarity between the parser output and the treebank. Algorithms for transformations between D and PS have been introduced *e.g.* in [15].

Also Carroll *et al.* [14,16], Srinivas *et al.* [13,2], [17], and Clark and Hockenmaier [18] have proposed evaluation methods based on D structures. The *Relation Model* by Srinivas *et al.* aims to combine PS and D representations by adding D relations between phrasal constituent chunks. The *Grammatical Relations* (GR) scheme by Carroll *et al.* uses an annotation scheme with grammatical relations between heads and dependents. These relations are used for calculating precision, recall and F-measure based on comparison between corpus and parser output. The evaluation methods mentioned above have all been applied for parsers of English. Some effort has been made to apply them to other languages ([17,19]).

There are several problems in direct comparative evaluation of parsers' accuracy. First, only the dimensions common to all parsers can be evaluated. *E.g.* diverse POS tagsets, syntactic labels and the varying detail of parsers' output cannot be taken into consideration in direct comparison. Many parsers fail to agree even on such low-level tasks as segmentation or basic word classes, let alone the syntactic description.

Second, an evaluation metrics for comparative evaluation should provide a comparable basis for comparison across systems. The PARSEVAL measure, for example, penalizes more rich output. An advantage of D-based evaluation is that since semantic dependencies are embedded in the syntactic ones, the results of D-based evaluation are much more meaningful that those of phrase-boundary based methods. The problem with Lin's approach is similar to the main problem of PARSEVAL: a lot of syntactic information is lost in the transformation [20]. The GR scheme is similar to Lin's proposal. The main difference is that the GR scheme defines a specific inventory of grammatical relations. In addition, the relations are organized into a hierarchy, enabling parsers with shallow output to be compared against a GR-style treebank. The main disadvantage of the GR scheme is that it requires a specially-built test set to be constructed.

Each approach to parsing has its distinct strengths and weaknesses and a single scalar value cannot fully reflect the quality of a parse [21]. Thus, in addition to measures such as precision and recall of tag assignment accuracy, methods enabling more fine-grained analysis are needed. For example, in D-based evaluation, the performance of a parser can be measured with respect to specific types of D relations [12]. Both the GR and Lin's models compare favorably against PARSEVAL in their ability to provide detailed information on accuracy of parsing. For example in the GR scheme, precision and recall scores can be provided for relation groups or single relations.

Third, the comparison material must be compatible with the outputs of the parsers. All the three methods discussed above, mapping, parallel treebanks and abstract annotation formats, have some problems. The problem with the general models of linguistic categories is that they lead to the loss of theory-specific information. There are several problems in the mapping approach [22,23]: First, the tag sets may not be identical: the number of tags may be different and the mapping is necessarily not one-to-one. Second, not all the syntactic structures of the treebanks might be uniquely mapped. Third, some constructs in one scheme may not be representable by the other scheme. Devising mappings between annotation schemes is extremely complicated. For example, the Penn Treebank [11] contains more than 10,000 distinct context-free productions, the majority occurring only once [24]. In addition, the categories should be interrelated in several steps, making use of information on multiple levels of linguistic description.

It is well-known that PS trees can be converted into D trees. A D parse that specifies word-order can be converted into an equivalent constituency parse provided that the D parse does not have nonterminals with labels or features, and that each phrase it contains has a head [25]. Converting back to D structure will cause loss of information if the head of the constituencies are not known. The problem is that most of the PS treebanks do not provide information to unambiguously identify the heads. Furthermore, the notion of head might not be compatible in the source and target annotations.

There are two main problems related to the multi-treebank approach: First, as constructing even a treebank with a single annotation is an expensive process, the costs of building a multi-treebank are manifold. Given the high costs of building such a treebank, it is not a realistic option for most languages and parsers, at least until more automated methods of treebank creation are available. In addition, a major problem with the multi-treebank approach lies in guaranteeing the consistency of different annotations. As pointed out by Atwell [20], given the size and complexity of treebank annotation schemes, it is too much to ask for a single annotator to master several of them. Thus, creating a multi-treebank calls for cooperation from several research teams, adding a source for inconsistencies.

4 FEPa – A Framework for Evaluating Parsers

In the preceding sections, methods and resources for evaluations were discussed. Most of the existing methods concentrate on a single aspect of performance (*e.g.* accuracy, robustness). Consequently, there is a need for a full-scale framework that incorporates several aspects of quality of output as well as the "engineering" aspects of parsers. The framework outlined in this Section focuses on intrinsic evaluation, providing useful information for parser developers. The aim is to provide a fuller picture of parser's performance than simply using the standard precision and recall measures. The goal of FEPa (Framework for Evaluating Parsers) is to provide a framework for practical evaluations of parsers' performance and provide a set of measures for evaluating parsers within their own framework. Thus, FEPa supports intrinsic evaluation. Due to the preliminary state of the research, some details of the framework need further revision. We believe that these modifications are best done based on practical evaluation experiments with the framework.

Based on the analysis of the problems in comparative parser evaluation discussed in Section 3, we concluded (following Santos [26]) that the problem of harmonizing parsers' outputs for comparative evaluation is totally unrealistic. Black [27] sums up that it may never be possible to compare all parsers of a given language in a uniform way. He suggests that, instead of comparing parsers across frameworks using coarse-grained scores based on dubious technical compromises, evaluation could be carried out with highly accurate methods *within* the framework of the parser to be evaluated. We take this approach.

Although our framework does not provide direct measures of relative performance of parsing systems, it offers a common ground for measuring and representing the performance of parsers according to several dimensions, thus providing a way to compare their strengths and weaknesses. The framework is well suited for progress evaluation between different versions of a system. Furthermore, for parsers for which there are more direct ways of comparing the relative performances (*i.e.* are using the same or highly similar output format or have a parallel treebank available), such measures can be incorporated to evaluation to provide more direct measures of parsers' relative performance.

An evaluation framework has to address the following four questions:

1. Purpose: What is the purpose of the evaluation?
2. Criteria: What is being measured?
3. Metrics: How is the performance of a system measured and reported?
4. Materials: What kinds of resources are used for evaluation?

Two *purposes* for evaluating parsers can be distinguished: First, providing information for developers of the systems to guide their work. The system developers with information needs can be divided into two groups: grammar writers and parsing algorithm developers. Second, to provide NLP practitioners and system developers alike information on the relative performances of parsing systems. Our proposal aims to offer a comprehensive framework for the first purpose, and also offers a means to perform evaluations of the latter type.

In FEPa, the *criteria* of evaluation are preciseness, coverage, robustness, efficiency, and subtlety of a parser. The two first criteria are most well-suited for grammar developers, while robustness and efficiency measures are needed mostly by the developers of parsing algorithms. The last criteria is useful for inter-system comparisons and for NLP system developers looking for a suitable parser for their needs. The evaluation process for each of the criteria consists of selecting the resources for evaluation, parsing the selected texts with the parser being evaluated and performing the calculations needed to measure the performance of a parser. Distinct methods and metrics are needed for each criteria.

4.1 Criteria and Metrics

Preciseness. We use the term *preciseness* to refer to the correctness of analyses assigned by a parser. We avoid using terms accuracy and precision because of their technical use in evaluation context. The preciseness of a parser is most commonly measured by means of precision, recall and F-measure of the parses covered correctly. The correctness of a parse is defined by comparing it to a manually annotated parse from a treebank or a test suite. The method used should measure the parser's accuracy in assigning syntactic tags. In addition, for the parser that performs morphological analysis, the accuracy of morphological tagging should me measured. Since the tags cannot be assigned correctly if segmentation has failed, obviously, the accuracy of word and sentence segmentation will also be assessed indirectly. Furthermore, it is possible to provide detailed information on accuracy of a parser in assigning certain POS or syntactic tags. In addition, when using a test suite as an evaluation resource, detailed analysis of parser's accuracy on analyzing specific types types of linguistic phenomena can be provided. It is interesting to note that many current evaluation metrics lack a sentence-level measure of accuracy. What normally makes parsing hard is that many consecutive decisions has to be made correctly in order to succeed [28]. Thus, the overall success rate is the nth power of the individual decision success rate. As for example the PARSEVAL precision, recall, and crossing brackets measure success at the level of individual decisions, and actually are quite easy measures to do well on. In addition to PS nonterminal/D link -level analysis we see it reasonable to report the percentage of sentences that were parsed correctly.

Coverage. The notion of coverage has two meanings [29]: *Grammatical coverage* is the parser's ability to handle different linguistic phenomena. *Parsing coverage* is a measure of how many sentences of naturally occurring, free-text can a parser produce a parse. We divide parsing coverage further into *domain coverages* on different text types, such as prose, newspaper, law, financial *etc.* Parsing coverage can be measured as the percentage of input sentences that a parser is able to assign a parse to. A more strict measure of parsing coverage is the percentage of sentences covered correctly. However, the advantage of the former definition is that no annotated text is needed for performing the evaluation and the results are directly comparable across parsers. A test suite is needed for measuring the grammatical coverage of a parser. One can simply list or report the percentage of linguistic phenomena that the parser is able to treat correctly. Both coverage measures are comparable over parsing systems.

Robustness. *Robustness* of a parser refers to its ability to produce an error-free or a just slightly altered output when faced with noisy input [8]. A total failure to produce an output might be only accepted in case of sufficiently distorted input. Parsers are often applied to texts that contain errors. For example, a parser processing user inputs may encounter misspelled words, wrong usage of cases, missing or extra words, or dialect variations. The method proposed by Bigert *et al.* [9] is well-suited for robustness evaluation. First, an error-free text is parsed with the parser to be evaluated. Second, ill-formed input texts are parsed and compared to the parses obtained in the previous stage. The ill-formed input consists in the case of Bigert *et al.* of texts with automatically induced errors. Ill-formed input can also be taken from a corpus of ill-formed sentences or consist of negative test items from a test suite. The *degradation* of a parser's output when faced with ill-formed input can be measured by comparing the parser's accuracy on error-free texts obtained in the accuracy evaluation phase to its accuracy on ill-formed inputs. The experiments can be repeated for several levels of distortion (*e.g.* 1%, 2% and 5% of the input words).

Some parsers are, by design, grammar-checking, and returning "failure to parse" for an ungrammatical sentence is for these a "correct" result. The evaluation approach discussed above is not applicable to such systems. In such cases, one might either leave robustness of the parser undefined or measure the proportion of ill-formed sentences that the parser accepts.

Efficiency. *Efficiency* is the most easily measurable and comparable of the five criteria. In practical terms, the efficiency of a parser can be measured by observing the time and space it takes for a parser to analyze a sentence. The efficiency measures can be broken down according to the sentence length to provide more insight in the time and space-complexity of the parser. Furthermore, parser's efficiency in parsing ill-formed input can provide insight of the way that the robustness mechanisms of the parser are implemented. When the same input texts are used for a set of parsers, their performance can be directly compared. The subtlety of the parsers output can be applied as a factor of the measure to be fair in comparison across systems that use different levels of richness in their outputs.

Subtlety. By *subtlety* of parser's output we refer to the level of detail in its output. We avoid using the term delicacy coined by Atwell [20] because it may imply "fragility" and be intuitively taken to be a negative property for a parser. The detail in the parsers' outputs may vary *e.g.* in the number of tags in the morphological and syntactic tagsets. Furthermore, some parsers leave part of the ambiguities unresolved in the output. The subtlety of a parsing scheme can be defined automatically by observing the complexity of the tagset and the number of remaining ambiguities in the parser's output.

As discussed earlier, varying levels of detail in parser output is needed for different NLP tasks. Thus, information on the subtlety of the output is needed by NLP developers looking for a suitable parser for their application. In addition, it is obvious that more detailed the analysis, more decisions have to be done while parsing, making it more difficult and time-consuming to assign a correct analysis.

4.2 Evaluation Materials

As for the resource for the evaluation, it can be debated if the resource should be tailored towards linguistically interesting sentences, which often are rare in running text or more commonly occurring "normal" cases. The division roughly corresponds to the distinction between treebank and test-suite based evaluation. Test suite based evaluation provides better directions for improving the system, whereas treebank based evaluation measures the performance of a parser on unrestricted texts [29]. A disadvantage of test suite -based evaluation is the lack of variation in the lexical items. In addition, test items usually contain a single grammatical phenomenon, thus leaving interactions between phenomenon untested. Prasad & Sarkar [29] report low overlap between the error types found by using treebank and test suite-based evaluation methods. As Balkan *et al.* [30] have pointed out, treebanks and test suites have different roles in evaluation, and are thus complementary rather than competing techniques.

Optimally, an evaluation should be performed by using both, a treebank and a test suite. For measuring efficiency, preciseness, and subtlety both types of resources are equally useful. The same holds for robustness evaluation provided that the applied resource includes ill-formed examples. Test suite -based evaluation is more suitable for measuring grammatical coverage, whereas evaluation based on a treebank or unannotated texts accounts better for parsing coverage. If evaluation is carried out on a treebank text, an error analysis can be performed for the rejected parses in order to pinpoint problems. In test suite evaluation, more detailed information on the level of morphological and syntactic phenomena can be produced.

4.3 Comparative Evaluation in FEPa

For providing comparative evaluations between parsing systems within the framework, we apply an approach where the overall score of a parser uses information on the level of detail in parser's output. In addition, in order to take into account the possible overacceptance of the grammar, we need to include the level of ambiguity in the parser's output. Thus, the overall score for an annotation of a layer for a parser can be defined according to Equation (1).

$$score_l = preciseness_l * subtlety_{sl} / ambiguity_l \qquad (1)$$

where $preciseness_l$ is the preciseness of an annotation layer l, say POS tagging, measured on framework-specific evaluation resource using F-measure. $Subtlety_{sl}$ is the subtlety factor of the parsing scheme s for the layer l. This factor is difficult to measure and without doubt open to dispute. However, if one wants to compare diverse parsing systems, one has to take into account the difference in the "difficulty" of the structure assigned by a parser. Atwell [7] is a rare example of an attempt to compare annotation schemes. A way to measure the subtlety of a parser's output is to automatically observe the complexity (*e.g.* the number of tags) of the tagset. For example, the subtlety of the syntactic description of a D-based parser could be defined based on the number of D link types in its tagset. The factor $ambiguity_l$ is used for accounting for remaining ambiguity in the output. If the parser returns, say 1.05 POS tags per word, it should be penalized when comparing against a parser that produces only a single tag per word. Determining the level of ambiguity for a syntactic analysis is a more complicated issue; in order to distinguish between overacceptance and real, inherent ambiguity, the treebank used for evaluation should include several parses for sentences that cannot be disambiguated based purely on syntactic information.

5 Conclusion

In this paper, the existing methods and resources for evaluation of syntactic parsers were discussed. In addition, we outlined a framework for carrying out empirical evaluations and discussed how such evaluation could be performed. The task of the model is to provide a basis for characterizing how well and efficiently a parser can analyze syntax. Furthermore, we discussed how the framework could be utilized to compare the performance of different parsing systems, without the need for using "compromising" direct comparison metrics.

The future research activities include the following:

1. Implementation of a tool for performing evaluations in the proposed framework. Such a system must be able to make use of several existing linguistic resources and provide the user with detailed information on all the five aspects of the evaluation framework.
2. Experimentation with the framework and the tool in practical parser evaluation.
3. Revising the framework.
4. Incorporating to the framework methods for providing more capability for inter-system comparisons.

References

1. Balkan, L., Meijer, S., Arnold, D., Dauphin, E., Estival, D., Falkedal, K., Lehmann, S., Reginier-Prost, S.: Test Suite Design Guidelines and Methodology. Report to LRE 62-089 (D-WP2.1) (1994)
2. Bangalore, S., Sarkar, A., Doran, C., Hockey, B.: Grammar & Parser Evaluation in the XTAG Project. In: Proceedings of the 1st International Conference on Language Resources and Evaluation (LREC), Granada, Spain (1998)
3. Chomsky, N.: Aspects of the Theory of Syntax, Cambridge, Massachusetts, USA (1965)
4. Kakkonen, T.: Dependency Treebanks: Methods, Annotation Schemes and Tools. In: Proceedings of the 15th Nordic Conference of Computational Linguistics, Joensuu, Finland (2005)
5. Mengel, A., Lezius, W.: An XML-based Representation Format for Syntactically Annotated Corpora. In: Proceedings of the 2nd LREC, Athens, Greece (2000)
6. Ide, N., Romary, L.: A Common Frameworks for Syntactic Annotation. In: Proceedings of the Association for Computational Linguistic, 39th Annual Meeting and 10th Conference of the European Chapter, Toulouse, France (2001)
7. Atwell, E., Demetriou, G., Hughes, J., Schiffrin, A., Souter, C., Wilcock, S.: A Comparative Evaluation of Modern English Corpus Grammatical Annotation Schemes. ICAME Journal **24** (2000) 7–23
8. Foster, J.: Parsing Ungrammatical Input: An Evaluation Procedure. In: Proceedings of the 4th LREC, Lisbon, Portugal (2004)
9. (Bigert, J., Sj J.)
10. E. Black et al.: A Procedure for Quantitatively Comparing the Syntactic Coverage of English Grammars. In: Proceedings of the 4th DARPA Speech and Natural Language Workshop, Pacific Grove, California, USA (1991)
11. Marcus, M.P., Santorini, B., Marcinkiewicz, M.A.: Building a Large Annotated Corpus of English: The Penn Treebank. Computational Linguistics **19** (1993) 313–330
12. Lin, D.: Dependency-Based Evaluation of MINIPAR. In: Proceedings of the 1st LREC, Granada, Spain (1998)
13. Bangalore, S., Doran, C., Hockey, B., Joshi, A.K.: An Approach to Robust Partial Parsing and Evaluation Metrics. In: Proceedings of the Workshop on Robust Parsing at European Summer School in Logic, Language and Information, Prague, Czech Republic (1996)

14. Carroll, J., Briscoe, T., Sanfilippo, A.: Parser Evaluation: A Survey and a New Proposal. In: Proceedings of the 1st LREC, Granada, Spain (1998)
15. Xia, F., Palmer, M.: Converting Dependency Structures to Phrase Structures. In: Proceedings of the 1st Human Language Technology Conference, San Diego, California, USA (2001)
16. Carroll, J., Minnen, G., Briscoe, T.: Corpus Annotation for Parser Evaluation. In: Proceedings of the EACL-99 Post-Conference Workshop on Linguistically Interpreted Corpora, Bergen, Norway (1999)
17. Kübler, S., Telljohann, H.: Towards a Dependency-Oriented Evaluation for Partial Parsing. In: Proceedings of the Beyond PARSEVAL Workshop at the 3rd LREC, Las Palmas, Gran Canaria, Spain (2002)
18. Clark, S., Hockenmaier, J.: Evaluating a Wide-Coverage CCG Parser. In: Proceedings of the Beyond PARSEVAL Workshop at the 3rd LREC, Las Palmas, Gran Canaria, Spain (2002)
19. Suzuki, H.: Phrase-Based Dependency Evaluation of a Japanese Parser. In: Proceedings of the 5th LREC, Lisbon, Portugal (2004)
20. Atwell, E.: Comparative Evaluation of Grammatical Annotation Models. Rodopi, Amsterdam, The Netherlands (1996)
21. Magerman, D.: Natural Language Parsing as Statistical Pattern Recognition. Ph.D. Thesis, Stanford University, California, USA (1994)
22. Sasaki, F., Witt, A., Metzing, D.: Declarations of Relations, Differences and Transformations between Theory-specific Treebanks: A New Methodology. In: Proceedings of the 2nd Workshop on Treebanks and Linguistic Theories, Växjö, Sweden (2003)
23. Wang, J.N., Chang, J.S., Su, K.Y.: An Automatic Treebank Conversion Algorithm for Corpus Sharing. In: Proceedings of the 32nd Annual Meeting of the Association for Computational Linguistics, Las Cruces, New Mexico, USA (1994)
24. Charniak, E.: Tree-bank Grammars. Technical Report CS-96-02, Brown University, Providence, Rhode Island, USA (1996)
25. Covington, M.A.: A Dependency Parser for Variable-Word-Order Languages. Research Report AI-1990-01, Artificial Intelligence Center, The University of Georgia, Athens, Georgia, USA. (1990)
26. Santos, D.: Timber! Issues in Treebank Building and Use. In: Proceedings of the 6th International Workshop on Computational Processing of the Portuguese Language, Faro, Portugal (2003)
27. Black, E.: Evaluation of Broad-Coverage Natural-Language Parsers. Cambridge University Press, Cambridge, UK (1998)
28. Manning, C.D., Carpenter, C.: Probabilistic Parsing Using Left Corner Language Models. In: Proceedings of the 5th International Workshop on Parsing Technologies, Boston, Massachusetts, USA (1995)
29. Prasad, R., Sarkar, A.: Comparing Test-suite Based Evaluation and Corpus-based Evaluation of a Wide Coverage Grammar for English. In: Proceedings of the Using Evaluation within HLT Programs: Results and Trends Workshop at the 2nd LREC, Athens, Greece (2000)
30. Balkan, L., Arnold, D., Fouvry, F.: Test Suites for Evaluation in Natural Language Engineering. In: Proceedings of the 2nd Language Engineering Convention, London, UK (1995)

Towards the Improvement of Statistical Translation Models Using Linguistic Features*

Alicia Pérez[1], Inés Torres[1], and Francisco Casacuberta[2]

[1] Departamento de Electricidad y Electrónica.
Facultad de Ciencia y Tecnología.
Universidad del País Vasco
manes@we.lc.ehu.es

[2] Departamento de Sistemas Informáticos y Computación
Institut Tecnològic d'Informàtica
Universidad Politécnica de Valencia
fcn@dsic.upv.es

Abstract. Statistical translation models can be inferred from bilingual samples whenever enough training data are available. However, bilingual corpora are usually too scarce resources so as to get reliable statistical models, particularly, when we are dealing with very inflected languages, or with agglutinative languages, where many words appear just once. Such events often distort the statistics. In order to cope with this problem, we have turned to morphological knowledge. Instead of dealing directly with running words, we also take advantage of lemmas, thus, producing the translation in two stages. In the first stage we transform the source sentence into a lemmatized target sentence, and in the second stage we convert the lemmatized target sentence into the target full forms.

1 Introduction

Current trends in machine translation suggest cooperation between classical knowledge-based methods and modern statistical methods. Some efforts have already been made to look for a clear technique that joins linguistic and statistical knowledge sources. With the CLSP workshop, which took place in 2003 at The Johns Hopkins University, [1] being an outstanding example. However, there is currently no commonly accepted and standarized technique for dealing with this problem. Thus, our aim is to contribute to the improvement of statistical translation models on the basis of specific linguistic information.

Another goal of this study is to deal with a highly practical application of Spanish-to-Basque. Basque is a minority language, with around 600,000 speakers, but enjoys official status along with Spanish in the Basque Country. Even though they coexist in the same area, these languages are very different both in syntax and semantics. Translation is not therefore a straightforward task. Statistical

* This work has been partially supported by the Industry Department of the Basque Government and by the University of the Basque Country under grants INTEK CN02AD02 and 9/UPV 00224.310-15900/2004 respectively.

T. Salakoski et al. (Eds.): FinTAL 2006, LNAI 4139, pp. 716–725, 2006.

machine translation seems to be a good choice in this framework, since it is cheap and very fast but we must deal with the problem of the scarcity of training data. It has to be taken into account that the available resources are quite limited.

The remainder of this paper is organised as follows: in Section 2 we introduce statistical translation models and explain how they are learned from samples; the way in which statistical models can take advantage of the linguistic features is described in Section 3; Section 4 is focused on the features of the task under study; Section 5, shows the results obtained both with traditional one-stage device and the proposed two-stage transducer; finally, in Section 6, the conclussions and the future direction of this work are discussed.

2 Finite-State Transducers

Stochastic finite-state transducers (SFST) constitute an interesting class of statistical translation models that have proved to be highly suitable for text-input and speech-input translation in specific tasks [2,3]. In this section we describe the transducers of this kind, and how they are trained.

Definition 1. *An **stochastic finite-state transducer** (SFST) is a tuple* $\mathcal{T} = \langle \Sigma, \Delta, Q, q_0, R, F, P \rangle$, *where:*

Σ *is a finite set of input symbols (source words);*
Δ *is a finite set of output symbols (target words);*
Q *is a finite set of states;*
$q_0 \in Q$ *is the initial state;*
$R \subseteq Q \times \Sigma \times \Delta^* \times Q$ *is a set of transitions such as* $(q, s, \tilde{t}, q')$, *which is a transition from the state* q *to the state* q', *with the source word* s *and producing the substring* $\tilde{t}$;
$P : R \rightarrow [0, 1]$ *transition probability;*
$F : Q \rightarrow [0, 1]$ *final state probability;*

The probability distributions satisfy the stochastic constraint:

$$\forall q \in Q \quad F(q) + \sum_{\forall s, \tilde{t}, q'} P(q, s, \tilde{t}, q') = 1 \tag{1}$$

■

A *translation form*, $d(\mathbf{s}, \mathbf{t})$, is a sequence of transitions in the SFST compatible with both the input string $\mathbf{s} \in \Sigma^*$ (source sentence) and the output string $\mathbf{t} \in \Delta^*$ (target sentence).

$$d(\mathbf{s}, \mathbf{t}) : (q_0, s_1, \tilde{t}_1, q1)(q_1, s_2, \tilde{t}_2, q2) \ldots (q_{J-1}, s_J, \tilde{t}_J, q_J)$$

where the input string ($\mathbf{s}$) is a sequence of input symbols, $\mathbf{s} = s_1 s_2 \ldots s_J$ and the output string ($\mathbf{t}$) is a sequence of output substrings $\mathbf{t} = \tilde{t}_1 \tilde{t}_2 \ldots \tilde{t}_J$. The probability supplied by the SFST to the translation form is thus:

$$P_{\mathcal{T}}(d(\mathbf{s}, \mathbf{t})) = F(q_J) \prod_{j=1}^{J} P(q_{j-1}, s_j, \tilde{t}_j, q_j) \tag{2}$$

Therefore, the probability of the pair $(\mathbf{s}, \mathbf{t})$, is the sum of all the possible ways compatible with that pair.

$$P_{\mathcal{T}}(\mathbf{s}, \mathbf{t}) = \sum_{\forall d(\mathbf{s},\mathbf{t})} P_{\mathcal{T}}(d(\mathbf{s}, \mathbf{t})) \tag{3}$$

SFSTs operate as follows: the expected translation is the string which maximizes the joint probability described by eq. (4):

$$\widehat{t} = \arg\max_{\mathbf{t}} P_{\mathcal{T}}(\mathbf{s}, \mathbf{t}) = \arg\max_{\mathbf{t}} \sum_{\forall d(\mathbf{s},\mathbf{t})} P_{\mathcal{T}}(d(\mathbf{s}, \mathbf{t})) \tag{4}$$

Resolving eq. (4) has proved to be a hard computational problem [4], but it can be efficiently computed by the *maximum approximation*, which replaces the sum by the maximum ($P_{\mathcal{T}}(\mathbf{s}, \mathbf{t}) \approx \max_{d(\mathbf{s},\mathbf{t})} P_{\mathcal{T}}(d(\mathbf{s}, \mathbf{t}))$). Under this maximum approximation, the *Viterbi algorithm* can be used to find the best sequence of states through the SFST given the input string [3]. The translation is the concatenation of the output strings through the optimal path.

2.1 Learning Finite-State Transducers: GIATI

Given a *bitext*, i.e. a set of training pairs consisting of sentences in the source and target languages, the structural and probabilistic components of the SFST can be automatically learned by resorting to a grammatical inference technique such as GIATI (*Grammar Inference and Alignments for Transducers Inference*). This method provides hybrid translation models since it combines the two main trends in statistical machine translation: statistical alignment models [5] and finite state automaton models [3].

The transducer learning method can be summarized in three steps: 1) building extended strings; 2) inferring a finite-state automaton and 3) transforming the automaton into a transducer. These setps are presented in the following subsections.

Building Extended Strings

Using a *labeling function* ($\mathcal{L}$) based on statistical word-alignments [5], each translation pair is transformed into a single string from an *extended vocabulary* ($\Gamma^* \subseteq \Sigma \times \Delta^*$). This transformation associates each source word with those target words aligned with it, in a monotone fashion. Each *extended word* consists of a word from the source language plus zero or more words from the target language.

Inferring a Regular Grammar k-TSS

Once we have the corpus of extended strings, we can infer a regular grammar (finite-state automaton) from it. In this study we introduce the use of a *k-Testable in the Strict Sense* (*k-TSS*) language model instead of n-gram models, since k-TSS models keep the syntactic constraints of the language as shown in previous works [6,7].

A k-TSS language model is said to be a syntactic extension of an n-gram model, and it works like k n-gram models ($1 \leq n \leq k$) integrated taking into account structural information.

Given an alphabet Σ, the k-TSS language, L_{kTSS}, is a subset of Σ^* which contains all the strings with a prefix from a set I_k, with a suffix from a set F_k and without any substring from the set T_k, where $I_k, F_k \subseteq \bigcup_{i=1}^{k-1} \Sigma^i$ and $T_k \subseteq \Sigma^k$.

$$L_{kTSS}(\Sigma, I_k, F_k, T_k) \equiv (I_k\Sigma^* \bigcap \Sigma^* F_k) - \Sigma^* T_k \Sigma^* \tag{5}$$

The k-TSS grammar is a subset of the regular grammars and thus it can be represented as a stochastic finite state automaton (SFSA). Here we include the definitio of a k-TSS SFSA in terms of commonly accepted standard definition for an automaton.

Definition 2. *The* ***k-Testable in the Strict Sense Stochastic Finite State Automaton*** *(k-TSS SFSA) is a six-tuple $\mathcal{A} = \langle \Sigma, Q, q_0, F, \delta, F, P \rangle$, where:*

Σ is the vocabulary;
Q is a finite set of states that satisfy:

$$Q = \bigcup_{n=0}^{k-1} Q^n \quad \textit{where} \quad Q^n \subseteq \Sigma^n \tag{6}$$

$q_0 \in Q$ is the initial state;
$\delta \subseteq Q \times \Sigma \times Q$ is a subset of transitions, $\{(q, w, q')\}$, from the state q to q', with the input word w. The set of transitions satisfies

$$\delta = \bigcup_{n=0}^{k-1} \delta_n \tag{7}$$

where

$$\delta_n \subseteq \begin{cases} Q^n \times \Sigma \times Q^{n+1} & n \in [0, k-2] \\ Q^{k-1} \times \Sigma \times Q^{k-1} & n = k-1 \end{cases} \tag{8}$$

$F : Q \rightarrow [0, 1]$ final state probability distribution;
$P : \delta \rightarrow [0, 1]$ transition probability distribution;

Probability distributions, F and P, satisfy the stochastic constraint of eq. (9):

$$\forall q \in Q \qquad F(q) + \sum_{\substack{w \in \Sigma \\ q' \in Q}} P(q, w, q') = 1 \tag{9}$$

■

Both the structure and the probability distribution of the k-TSS SFSA are easy to learn from samples and can be carried out using efficient algorithms based on a maximum likelihood approach [8].

Although sparseness of data often leads to the assignment of null probabilities, the use of k-TSS grammar based models makes it possible to perform smoothing in a natural way. In fact, several syntactic smoothing techniques have been proposed and tested in previous papers [9]. At this point, let us note that smoothing is carried out on the extended symbols and not only on the input strings, even though the automaton goes from one node to other one merely by taking into account the input word. Finding a suitable smoothing for this kind of transducer is still an open problem.

Transforming the Automaton into a Transducer
The extended symbols associated with the finite-state transitions in the k-TSS automaton ($\mathcal{A}$) are transformed into input/output symbols by the inverse labeling function ($\mathcal{L}^{-1}$). In this way a transducer ($\mathcal{T}$) is obtained.

The automaton, which accepts extended strings, is deterministic (except for the back-off transitions introduced for smoothing). Nevertheless, once it is transformed into a transducer becomes non-deterministic.

3 On the Use of Linguistics Within Statistics

The probability distributions of the SFST are directly inferred from samples, i.e. from the bilingual corpus under consideration, on the basis of the maximum likelihood criterion.

Statistical models require no further information other than the sentences of the corpus. But, it is necessary the corpus to cover as many real events as possible. When referring to events, we do not mean all possible sentences of the application, but all possible word combinations. Moreover, those word combinations should appear among the sentence-samples in a well balanced way, just as they would appear in a realistic situation.

Anyway, the smoothed k-TSS grammar under use guarantees that the SFST can cope with any input string, even those which contain unknown input words ($w \notin \Sigma$). However, bilingual corpora are usually too scarce so as to obtein reliable statistical models, particularly when dealing with highly inflected languages, or with agglutinative languages. In these cases, there are many running words that appear just once in the whole training corpus. Such isolated events, the so called *singletons*, often distort the statistics.

In this study we propose the use of lemmas, instead of full forms, in order to deal with this problem. A *lemma* is defined as "the head of an annotation or gloss". The vocabulary size in terms of lemmas is smaller than in terms of running words, since many words share the same lemma. Hence, with the same number of sentences, more events are covered in terms of lemmas than in terms of running words.

In [10], *two-stage* translation was proposed, consisting of two translators in a serial architecture. The first allows translation from the source language into a pseudo-target language, while the second allows translation from that intermediate language into the real target language. In that work, the performance of the two-stage device was slightly worse than the performance of the direct device. The lack of improvement in those results could be attributed to the training corpus considered, which was small, and also to the fact that the intermediate language was not simple enough.

In this study we try a *two-stage* system, where the intermediate language is the lemmatized-target language. Specifically, in stage one, we take natural Spanish as the input language, and translated it into lemmatized-Basque. Then, in stage two, the lemmatized-Basque is translated into natural-Basque.

The first stage is the most critical one, since both the appropriate target lemmas and their order must be choosen. The second stage just has to choose the right full-form for each lemma.

4 Task and Corpus

The METEUS corpus [11] consists of bilingual sentences of weather forecast reports picked from among those published on the Internet by the Basque Institute of Meteorology. The main features of METEUS are shown in Table 1.

Table 1. Main features of the METEUS corpus

		words		lemmas	
		Spanish	**Basque**	**Spanish**	**Basque**
Training	number of sentences	14,615			
	different sentences	7,226	7,523	7,190	7,324
	running words	191,156	187,462	191,156	187,462
	vocabulary	720	1,147	462	578
	mean length	13.0	12.8	13.0	12.8
Test	sentences	1500			
	running words	18,978	18,711	18,978	18,711
	PP (3-grams)	3.6	4.3	3.6	4.0

Note that the Basque language vocabulary in terms of running words, is 1.6 times greater than the Spanish. However, the vocabulary size for the two languages is simmilar in terms of lemmas. This is quite usual due to the language agglutination of Basque (see Section 4.1). Perplexity (PP), nevertheles, remains almost equal after the lemmatization process.

In Spanish, there are 178 words (of 720) which are seen only once among the 14,615 sentences. In Basque there are 294 (of 1,147). So the 25% of the words are singletons. These figures highlight the sparseness of data in the METEUS corpus.

4.1 Spanish and Basque: Main Differences

The main differences between the two languages can be summarized as follows:

Origin: Spanish is an Iberian Romance language, while Basque is pre-Indoeuropean, and it's origin is unknown.

Speakers: Spanish is spoken by around 420,000,000 people (including non-native speakers), whereas Basque is a minority language, spoken by around 600,000 people.

Syntax: in Spanish, the order of the phrases within a sentence is *Subject plus Verb plus Objects*, while in Basque is much more free, although usually it is *Subject plus Objects plus Verb*. Basque (like Japanese), unlike Spanish (or English), suffers from left recursion.

Morphology: unlike Spanish, Basque is head-final, that is, it has a strong tendency to place the heads of phrases at the end of the phrase. In contrast to sentences, where phrases can be arranged in many different ways, noun phrases have a very strict word order in Basque. Another difference with Spanish is that Basque is an extremely agglutinative language, in both noun and verbs.

5 Experimental Results

The SFST was learned from the training set described in Table 1. Then, the sentences from the test set were translated by that SFST. The translation given by the system was compared with the reference sentence. Two evaluation measures were taken into account:

WER: *Word Error Rate* is the relative number of error edit operations between the reference sentence and the system's output (the lower the better).

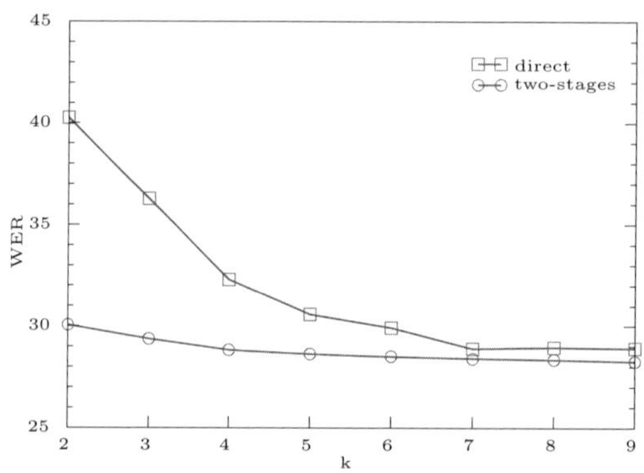

(a) WER for several k-TSS models.

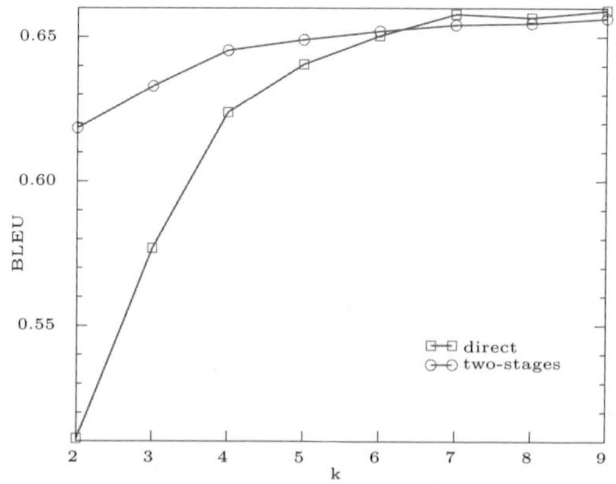

(b) BLEU for several k-TSS models.

Fig. 1. Comparison of the performance of the direct and two-stage systems for Spanish into Basque translation. WER, the lower the better; BLEU, the lower the worst.

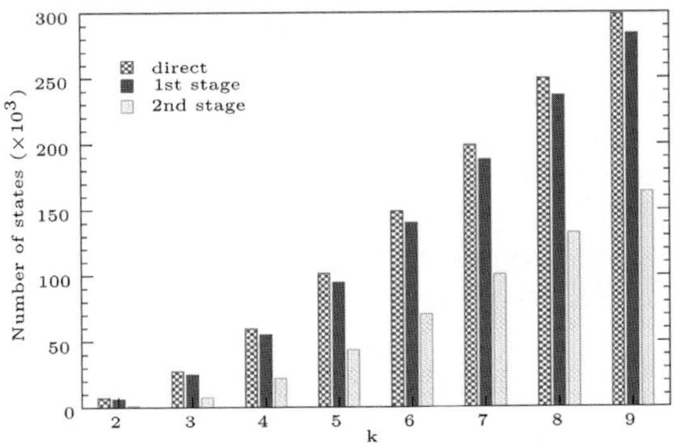

(a) Number of states.

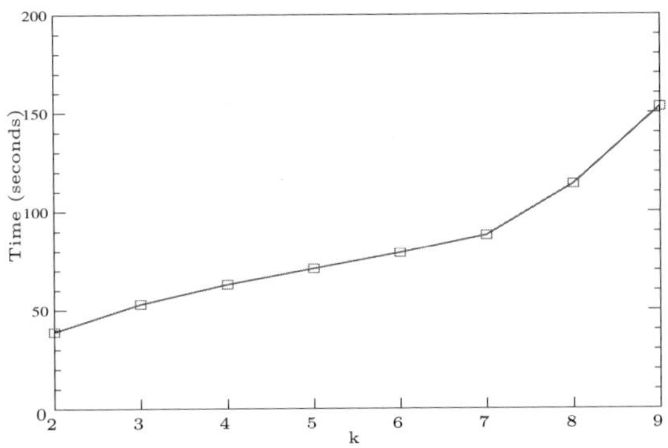

(b) Search time.

Fig. 2. Spatial and temporal costs. Figure 2(a) The size, in terms of number of states, of k-TSS models for several values of k; the first column refers to the direct model, and the second and third to the two-stage model. Figure 2(b) The translation time for 1,500 test sentences.

BLEU: *BiLingual Evaluation Understudy* is based on the n-grams of the hypothesized translation that occur in the reference translations. The BLEU metric ranges from 0.0 (worst score) to 1.0 (best score) [12].

The WER is in Figure 1(a) and BLEU in Figure 1(b), both for several values of k in the k-TSS model. The error rate decreases as k increases, for both the direct-architecture and for two-stages architecture. However, two-stages architecture provides much better performance. The error rates always remain below the error rates provided by the direct systems. This improvement is specially noticeable for lower values of k.

Figure 2(a) shows the size of the k-TSS-like transducers in terms of the number of states: first column for the direct model, second and third columns for two-stage model (second column for the Spanish into lemmatized-Basque transducer, and third column for lemmatized-Basque into natural-Basque transducer).

The time needed to translate the 1,500 test sentences is shown in Figure 2(b). Since there is no appreciable difference between the direct and two-stage systems, we show a single drawing rather than both.

The higher the value of k the better performance, as shown in Figure 1. Nevertheless, the number of states of the model increases as k does, and searching through the transducer thus takes more time (see Figure 2).

The results in Figure 1 point out that the *two-stages* architecture works better than the direct one. For low values of k, in particular, the improvement is quite considerable.

6 Concluding Remarks

Stochastic finite state transducers can be learned from bilingual samples. In order to estimate reliable probability distributions, we reduce the number of symbols to estimate the translation models. Thus, a *two-stage* translation is studied. The goal is to translate from the source language, Spanish, into the target language, Basque, through an easier intermediate language, that is, lemmatized-Basque. This architecture performs better than the direct one with respect to word error rates, less memory is needed and almost the same speed is obtained.

Acknowledgements

We would like to thank *Ametzagaiña group* (`http://www.ametza.com`), and Josu Landa, in particular, for providing us with the bilingual corpus split into morpho-syntactic tags, which made possible this work.

References

1. Och, F.J., Gildea, D., Khudanpur, S., Sarkar, A., Yamada, K., Fraser, A., Kumar, S., Shen, L., Smith, D., Eng, K., Jain, V., Jin, Z., Radev, D.: Final report of johns hopkins 2003 summer workshop on syntax for statistical machine translation. Technical report, Johns Hopkins University (2004)
2. Casacuberta, F., Ney, H., Och, F.J., Vidal, E., Vilar, J.M., Barrachina, S., García-Varea, I., Llorens, D., Martínez, C., Molau, S., Nevado, F., Pastor, M., Picó, D., Sanchis, A., Tillmann, C.: Some approaches to statistical and finite-state speech-to-speech translation. Computer Speech and Language **18** (2004) 25–47
3. Casacuberta, F., Vidal, E.: Machine translation with inferred stochastic finite-state transducers. Computational Linguistics **30** (2004) 205–225
4. Casacuberta, F., de la Higuera, C.: Computational complexity of problems on probabilistic grammars and transducers. In Oliveira, A.L., ed.: ICGI. Volume 1891 of Lecture Notes in Computer Science. Springer-Verlag (2000) 15–24
5. Brown, P.F., Della Pietra, S.A., Della Pietra, V.J., Mercer, R.L.: The mathematics of statistical machine translation: Parameter estimation. Computational Linguistics **19** (1993) 263–311
6. Torres, I., Varona, A.: k-tss language models in a speech recognition systems. Computer Speech and Language **15** (2001) 127–149

7. Pérez, A., Casacuberta, F., Torres, M., Guijarrubia, V.: Finite-state transducers based on k-tss grammars for speech translation. In: Proceedings of Finite-State Methods and Natural Language Processing (FSMNLP 2005), Helsinki, Finland (2005) 270–272
8. García, P., Vidal, E.: Inference of k-testable languages in the strict sense and application to syntactic pattern recognition. IEEE Transactions on Pattern Analysis and Machine Intelligence **12** (1990) 920–925
9. Varona, A., Torres, I.: Back-off smoothing evaluation over syntactic language models. In: Proc. of European Conference on Speech Technology. Volume 3. (2001) 2135–2138
10. Nießen, S.: Improving statistical machine translation using morpho-syntactic information. PhD thesis, Computer Science Department, RWTH Aachen University (2002) Advisors: Dr. Ing. Hermann Ney and Dr. Enrique Vidal.
11. Pérez, A., Torres, I., Casacuberta, F., Guijarrubia, V.: A Spanish-Basque weather forecast corpus for probabilistic speech translation. In: Proceedings of the 5th SALTMIL Workshop on Minority Languages, Genoa, Italy (2006)
12. Papineni, K., Roukos, S., Ward, T., Zhu, W.J.: BLEU: a method for automatic evaluation of machine translation. In: Proceedings of the 40th Annual Meeting of the Association Computational Linguistics (ACL), Philadelphia (2002) 311–318

Treating Unknown Light Verb Construction in Korean-to-English Patent MT

Munpyo Hong, Chang-Hyun Kim, and Sang-Kyu Park

ETRI, NLP Team
161 Gajeong-dong, Yuseong-gu
305-350 Daejeon, Korea
{munpyo, chkim, parksk}@etri.re.kr

Abstract. This paper addresses the problem of the unknown light verb construction in Korean in the context of Korean-to-English patent machine translation. The light verb construction in Korean is composed of a light verb 'ha' and a predicative noun. The predicative nouns are generally sino-Korean words or loan words mostly from English in deverbal form. Previous researches on the light verb construction were mostly focused on the linguistic explanation about the thematic role assignment and the argument realization. In this paper, we will present a method for treating the LVC words that are not in the dictionary of Korean-to-English patent MT system. We introduce 4 types of unknown LVCs and present a method for generating the target word automatically. The evaluation of the automatically translated unknown words by professional translators showed 70.06% accuracy.

1 Introduction

In this paper, we provide a method for treating the so-called light verb construction (LVC henceforth) in Korean in the context of Korean-to-English patent machine translation. The LVC in Korean is composed of a light verb 'ha' and a predicative noun. Generally, it is assumed that the semantically vacuous light verb does not assign any thematic role to the arguments. The thematic role is assigned by the predicative noun, which has its own argument structure. The predicative noun in the LVC is mostly sino-Korean words. However, as the language use is very much influenced by western culture and technology, new loan words are emerging very frequently. These words are mostly loaned from English and combine with the light verb 'ha' to form an LVC. This linguistic phenomenon is very often encountered in technical documents as well as patent documents, because there are many brand new ideas and technologies introduced in such text types. Previous researches on the LVC were mainly focused on the linguistic explanations about the thematic role assignment and the argument realizations in the formal linguistic frameworks such as HPSG, TAG, LFG and GB.

From the viewpoint of MT, the LVC poses a new question regarding the target word generation for unknown words. As the word formation rule for the LVC is highly productive in Korean, it is almost impossible to contain all the words in the

T. Salakoski et al. (Eds.): FinTAL 2006, LNAI 4139, pp. 726 – 737, 2006.

dictionary. However, a robust MT system should be able to deal with such unknown words properly.

In this paper we will present a method for treating the unknown LVC words for Korean-to-English patent MT. Automatic target word generation of unknown LVC words is very much dependent on the semantic analysis of LVC. We classify the unknown LVC words into four types according to the semantic relations among the nouns participating in the LVC. To classify the types, our method employed the lexical co-occurrence pattern, an adverbial noun list, and a verb dictionary.

In the following section we will introduce the LVC in Korean with examples. In 2.2, the Korean-to-English patent MT system will be presented briefly. In section 3, we will discuss previous researches on the LVC. In section 4, we present our method for generating target words for unknown LVC words based on the type classification. Section 5 will show the evaluation result of the proposed method. Finally, in section 6, we will sum up the discussion and present the future research direction.

2 Background

2.1 Light Verb Construction in Korean

Light verb construction is an often-encountered linguistic form in Korean consisting of a light verb 'ha' and a predicative noun. The predicative nouns are generally sino-Korean words or loan words mostly from English in deverbal form. (1)

(1) a.	Peter-ka	Enehak-ul	kongpwu-lul	ha-n-ta
	Peter-NOM	Linguistics-ACC	study-ACC	LV-PRES-DECL
	'Peter studies Linguistics'			
b.	Peter-ka	Jane-ul	pickup-ul	hay-ss-ta
	Peter-NOM	Jane-ACC	pickup-ACC	LV-PAST-DECL
	Peter picked up Jane'			

In LVC, it is the predicative noun that assigns thematic roles to the arguments, not the light verb, as the following example indicates:

(2) a.	Peter-ka	Enehak-ul	kongpwu-lul	ha-n-ta	
	Peter-NOM	Linguistics-ACC	study-ACC	LV-PRES-DECL	
	'Peter studies Linguistics'				
b.	Peter-ka	Jane-eykey	inhyeng-ul	senmwul-ul	hay-ss-ta
	Peter-NOM	Jane-DAT	doll-ACC	present-ACC	LV-PAST-DECL
	'Peter presented Jane a doll'				

The light verb 'ha' does not assign any thematic roles to the arguments, otherwise the arguments in (2.a) and (2.b) should share the same roles. The predicative nouns are activity-denoting nouns that are mostly either sino-Korean words or English loan words. The activity-denoting predicative noun can be modified like any other nouns, as in (3).

(3) a.	Peter-ka	elyewu-n	kyelceng-ul	hay-ss-ta
	Peter-NOM	difficult-mod	decision-ACC	LV-PAST-DECL
	'Peter made a difficult decision'			
b.	Peter-ka	himtu-n	arubaitu-lul	hay-ss-ta
	Peter-NOM	strenuous-mod	part-time job-ACC	LV-PAST-DECL
	'Peter did a strenuous part-time job'			

One of the linguistic properties of LVC is that the LVC can also be used as an incorporated form, as in (4).

(4) a.	Peter-ka	Enehak-ul	kongpwu-ha-n-ta
	Peter-NOM	linguistics-ACC	study-LV-PRES-DECL
	'Peter studies linguistics'		
b.	Peter-ka	Jane-ul	pickup-hay-ss-ta
	Peter-NOM	Jane-ACC	pickup-LV- PAST-DECL
	'Peter picked up Jane'		

We assume in this work that the meaning of the both forms (kongpwu-lul hata, kongpwu-hata) is identical.

(5) a.	File-ul	DB server-ey	kakong-cecang-ha-sio
	File-ACC	DB server-DAT	manage and save-LV-IMPER
	'Manage and save the file in the DB server'		
b.	Sayongca-ka	pwuphwum-ul	kasang-selkye-hay-ss-ta
	User-NOM	part-ACC	virtually design-LV-PAST-DECL
	'The user designed the part virtually'		

In (5), the predicative nouns are compound nouns, 'kakong-cecang (manage and save)' and 'kasang-selkye (virtually design)'. As the word formation rule for LVC in this form is very productive, there is a high possibility that some unknown words in this form may appear in a text, especially in technical texts. Such unknown words can cause serious problems in MT, because the mistranslation or non-translation of the predicates may affect the overall translation quality seriously.

2.2 Korean-English Patent MT

ETRI (Electronics and Telecommunication Research Institute)[1] developed a Korean-English MT system for patent documents under the auspices of Ministry of

---

[1] www.etri.re.kr

Information and Communication from 2004 to 2005. The MT system was customized for patent documents based on a general domain Korean-English MT system. The customization process includes the construction of terminology DB and the modification of engine modules after linguistic studies of patent documents. (cf. [4]) The Korean-to-English patent MT system was installed at KIPO (Korean Intellectual Property Office) and is currently being used by foreign patent examiners. The MT system translates Korean patent documents to English in real time.

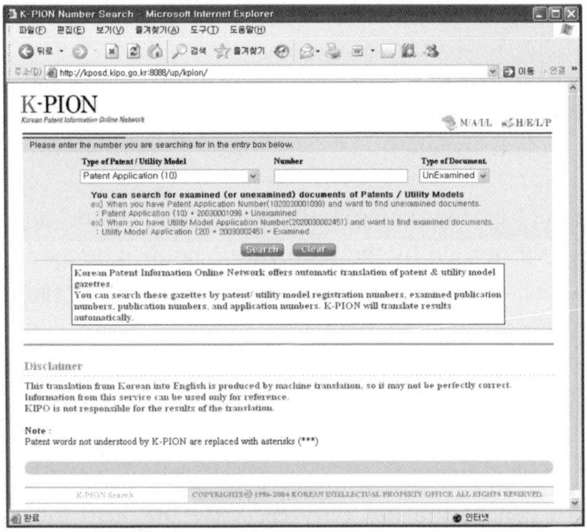

Fig. 1. Korean-English Patent MT Service K-PION

The MT system can be classified as a pattern-based MT system. After the syntactic analysis, the dependency structure of Korean input sentence is generated. For the transfer, patterns are employed, as in (6). In case there is no matching pattern for the input, the default translation of the input word based on the dictionary information is triggered. As to the unknown LVC words, as there is no pattern, the automatically generated target word functions as a predicate in the target sentence.

(6)

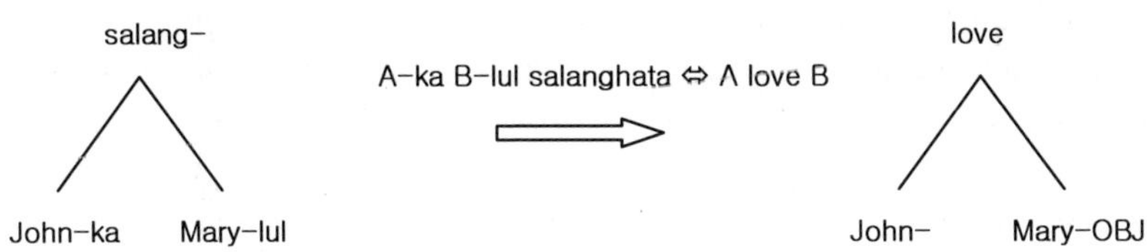

3 Previous Researches

The LVC has been a hot research topic among Korean theoretical- as well as computational linguists. The major linguistic issues concerning the LVC can be summarized as follows:

i) if the thematic roles are assigned by the predicative noun in LVC, why are they not inside the NP headed by the predicative noun, but inside the VP?

ii) how can be the varying grammaticality regarding the word order of the arguments of the LVC explained?

(1) a.	Peter-ka	enehak-ul	kongpwu-lul	ha-n-ta
	Peter-NOM	linguistics-ACC	study-ACC	LV-PRES-DECL
	'Peter studies linguistics'			
b.	Peter-ka	Jane-ul	pickup-ul	hay-ss-ta
	Peter-NOM	Jane-ACC	pickup-ACC	LV-PRES-DECL
	'Peter picked up Jane'			

As we can see in (1.a), for example, the arguments, 'Peter' and 'linguistics' are not realized inside the NP headed by the predicative noun 'kongpwu (study)'. Otherwise, they would have been marked by the possessive 'uy'. The case marker 'ka' and 'ul' indicates that they are assigned by the verb.

In order to explain the discrepancy between the case marking and the thematic role assignment, many ideas have been proposed. [1] proposed the idea of 'Argument Transfer'. The core of the idea is that the predicative noun in the LVC can transfer some of its arguments to the argument structure of the light verb. Through this, the light verb can assign not only the case but also the thematic roles to its arguments.

The varying grammaticality of the word order was explained by introducing the concept of argument hierarchy according to the prominence among the arguments. [2] proposed an XTAG based method to solve the linguistic puzzles of LVC. [5] proposed an HPSG based explanation for the LVC. Their approach is based on the multiple classification of category types with systematic inheritance mechanism. [7] dealt with the Japanese LVC in the framework of HPSG.

From the viewpoint of MT, there has not been much work on Korean LVC. [3] presented a unification-based approach for LVC in Korean to German MT. His work is focused on the analysis of Korean LVC in the unification-based CAT2 formalism. [6] treated the LVC in Korean to Chinese MT. They issued the transfer problem of LVC, in case the predicative noun is modified. However, the transfer problem of unknown LVC was not dealt with.

[9] treated the compound noun analysis problem using word co-occurrence relation. Their approach is quite similar to ours in using the lexical co-occurrence relation. However, their research is limited to the problem of Korean analysis.

[8] employed the lexical conceptual structure to analyze the semantic structure of deverbal compound noun. However, to build the lexical conceptual structure for every noun in patent domain in order to apply the method does not seem to be feasible for the present purpose.

4 Unknown LVC

4.1 The Types of Unknown LVC

However big a dictionary size may be, a dictionary cannot contain all the possible words that may appear in a patent document. If the unknown word is a predicate, the translation of the sentence may be damaged seriously compared with other word categories.

In order to deal with the unknown LVC in a patent text, we propose an automatic target word generation algorithm based on 4 unknown LVC types. The unknown light verb is relatively easy to detect. Among the unknown words, the words with the light verb 'ha' in its base form (e.g. 'salang-hata') or separately (e.g. 'salang-ul hata'), are detected as an LVC. The unknown LVC words can be classified into four types as follows:

~ **Type1: SUBJ/OBJ + Predicate Noun + Light Verb**
e.g) kakyek (OBJ)-selceng (PN)-hata (LV) : 'set price'

~ **Type2: ADV + Predicate Noun + Light Verb**
e.g) yekswun (ADV)-silhayng (PN)-hata (LV): 'execute reversely'

~ **Type3: Predicate Noun + Predicate Noun + Light Verb**
e.g) phanpyel (PN)-cecang (PN)-hata (LV): 'distinguish and store'

~ **Type4: More than 2 nouns + Light Verb**
e.g) tunglok (PN)-sakcey (PN)-chwullyek (PN)-hata (LV): 'register, de lete and print'

Type 1 shows the LVC in which an argument of the predicative noun is incorporated into the predicative noun to form a compound noun. The status of such words can be argued in favor of orthographic errors. However, type 1 construction appears so often in a patent document that there must be an apparatus to deal with the case properly. Type 2 shows that the first component ('yekswun') functions semantically as an adverb, although its POS is a noun. In such cases, the Korean noun is translated into an adverb. In type 3, the first noun in the nominal compound is also a predicative noun. The English translation of each component is often coordinated with 'and'. Finally, type 4 shows the case where the compound noun is composed of more than 2 components. The inner structure of such words can be type 1, 2, and 3 recursively.

The empirical study of 1,000 randomly extracted unknown LVC shows that type 1 and 3 are two major types of unknown LVCs.[2]

Table 1. Number of LVC types among 1,000 unknown LVCs

Type	Type 1	Type 2	Type 3	Type 4	Etc.
Number	261	202	290	171	76

[2] 76 LVCs could not be classified into any of 4 types.

4.2 Type 1 LVC

After the detection of unknown LVCs, automatic type classification is followed. The input for the type classification is the following form:

$$PN(NOUN_1 - NOUN_2\text{-} \ldots NOUN_n)\text{–}LV$$

To deal with the type 1 LVC, we extracted the lexical co-occurrence patterns from patent corpus. The size of the patent corpus is about 500 million eojeols.[3,4] The lexical co-occurrence patterns are extracted by running Korean morphological analyzer and tagger and applying heuristic rules on patent corpus. The patterns take the form of '<noun, case marker, predicate>'. To minimize the errors, the heuristic rules are limited to the most reliable ones. The basic heuristic rules to extract the lexical co-occurrence patterns are the following two. To every extracted pattern was the frequency 1 added.

In a setting in which nominal arguments (N_1, N_2, … N_k) are located between two predicates P(n) and P(n-1)

… P(n-1) N_1 N_2 … N_k P(n)[5]

Extract

(N_1,P(n)), (N_2,P(n)), … , (N_k, P(n))

For example, in the following sentence

(7)	pap-ul	mek-ko	cip-ey	ka-n-ta
	meal-AKK	eat-CONJ	house-DIR	go-PRES-DECL
	'After ϕ having a meal, ϕ go home'			

the following lexical co-occurrence pattern is extracted:

<cip, ey, kata>

In case a noun is modified, <the modified noun, nominative case marker, modifier> is extracted. For example,

(8)	yeyppu-un	kkoch-ul	sa-ss-ta
	beautiful-mod	flower-ACC	buy-PAST-DECL
	'ϕ bought a beautiful flower'		

<kkoch, ka, yeypputa> is extracted.

Above heuristic rules are most reliable ones so that the frequency 1 can be assigned to the extracted patterns. However, in doing this, we can encounter the data sparseness problem. As a smoothing technique for the problem, the following rules are added:

[3] 'Eojeol' is a spacing unit in Korean sentence.
[4] It corresponds to the size of all the patent documents applied in last five years in Korea.
[5] This algorithm is based on the fact that Korean is a head-final language.

```
If (a verb Vt is not the last predicate in a sentence
and is transitive)
        If (there is an object in the preceding two
words except an adverb)
        then  Extract the object, and
              Extract also the words between Vt and
              the object
        Elseif (the preceding word bears an adverbial
               case),
        then extract it
if (the verb Vi is not the last predicate in a sentence
and is intransitive, and the preceding word except an ad-
verb does not bear an adverbial case),
          then extract it
if (the adjective Ai is not the last predicate in a sen-
tence)
            if (it is a pronominal, and the preceding
word bears an adverbial case)
            then extract it
            elseif (if the ending is not 'key', and if
                   the preceding word bears an adver-
                   bial case)
             then extract it
```

The data extracted by applying the algorithm is used only when it is over than the threshold value. In case the extracted noun bears a nominative or accusative case, the threshold value is defined by using <noun, case marker, predicate> or <noun sense, case marker, predicate>. If the case is adverbial, <case marker, predicate> is employed to set the threshold. It is due to the fact that nouns with adverbial case marker are relatively fewer than other cases. Furthermore, the adverbial case marker has a meaning by itself in compare to other case markers. Having applied this method, we could get about 15 million patterns with frequency information from the corpus of 500 million eojeols.

Now, let's come back to the algorithm for the automatic target word generation of the type 1 LVC. If the noun 1 and noun 2 which comprise the predicative noun in the LVC can be found in the lexical co-occurrence pattern data constructed in the above-described manner, the case relation between them is consulted. Consequently, the automatic generation of target word takes place. Take an example of 'kakyek-selceng-hata (to set price)'. The first noun in the compound, 'kakyek (price)', and the second one, 'selceng (set)' are found in the lexical co-occurrence pattern data. The pair appears 170 times in 'obj-pred' relation. Thus, we assume that the semantic relation between 'kakyek (price)' and 'selceng (set)' is that of predicate and object. From this, we generate the target word 'to set the price' using the dictionary information of each word.

4.3 Type 2 LVC

In type 2 LVC, the first noun in the compound predicative noun functions as an adverb semantically. Thus, they are mostly translated to an adverb. In some cases, the translation to an adverb makes the translation unnatural. However, the information of the input sentence can be delivered without much loss. The nouns that appear in the type 2 construction are limited.

We built manually a list of nouns that can function as an adverb in type 2 LVC. The list contains 362 nouns. Each noun is connected to its English translation. Thus the first noun in the compound predicative noun is in the list, the translation of the unknown LVC is triggered by the translation in the list. Take an example of 'yekswun (reverse)-silhayng (execute)-hata (execute reversely)'. The first noun 'yekswun' is included in the list, then the translation of the unknown LVC is simply the translation of the second noun with the first noun, i.e. an adverb.

Table 2. The sample list of adverbial nouns with the translation

Noun	Translation
cungphok	with amplification
cwunghwa	with neutralization
...	...

Even if a noun is not in the list, if it appears in the lexical co-occurrence pattern in the adverbial case-predicate relation often, it is regarded as a noun that must be translated as an adverb. As the translation of such nouns is not in the list, the translation is performed simply by attaching 'with' to the translation of the noun.

4.4 Type 3 LVC

In type 3 LVC, we have two predicative nouns in the compound. The resource used to classify type 3 is a verb dictionary. We have currently a verb dictionary containing about 85,000 verbs. Thus, if both the noun 1 and noun 2 are found in the verb dictionary, the translation of the unknown LVC is simply the translation of noun 1 and noun 2 conjoined with 'and'. For example, in case of 'phanpyel (distinguish)-cecang (save)-hata (distinguish and save)', both 'phanpyel-hata' and 'cecang-hata' exist in the verb dictionary. Thus, the translation of the unknown LVC is simply the conjunction of the two.

4.5 Type 4 LVC

We have dealt with the case in which there are two noun components in the compound. However, there are many cases (171 out of 1,000) in which there are more than 2 components in the compound. In this case, we process from left to right. For example, in the case of 'tunglok (register)-sakcey (delete)-chwullyek (print)-hata (register, delete and print)', the semantic relation of the first two words, i.e. 'tunglok' and 'sakcey' is calculated. In fact, both words are not in the lexical co-occurrence pattern, and 'tunglok' is not the noun which triggers the adverbial translation. Finally, 'tunglok-hata' and 'sakcey-hata' are both contained in the verb dictionary. As a next step of the automatic target word generation of the unknown LVC, the second word 'sakcey' and 'chwullyek' are considered. These two words are not in the lexical co-occurrence pattern either, and 'sakcey' is not the noun which triggers the adverbial translation. Finally, 'sakcey-hata' and 'chwullyek-hata' are contained in the verb dictionary. Therefore the final translation of the unknown LVC is 'to register, delete and print'.

5 Evaluation

The evaluation of the proposed method was conducted in the following manner: Firstly, we extracted randomly 1,012 unknown LVC words from patent corpus. All the extracted words have the form "compound noun + ha". Secondly, human evaluators classified the unknown LVCs into the four categories introduced in section 4. Thirdly, human evaluators evaluated the automatically generated words. In doing this, if the automatic classification is correct, and the automatically generated word is acceptable, even if it is not perfect, the evaluators took them for correct. The human evaluators were professional translators specializing in patent translation with at least 5 years experience. The following table shows the experiment result:

Table 3. Evaluation result of the method

	Type 1	Type 2	Type 3	Type 4	Total
Evaluator	286	154	352	220	1012
Our Method	220	66	308	114	709
Precision	**76.92%**	**42.86%**	**87.5%**	**52.27%**	**70.06%**

The overall precision of the proposed method was 70.06%. Type 3 algorithm was most reliable, showing 87.5%. In 44 errors, the verbs were not contained in the dictionary.

Type 1 rule was also relatively reliable. It showed 76.92% precision. Most of the errors were due to the data sparseness problem of the patent corpus, e.g. 'kamsan (reduced production) – phyosi (display)'-hata'. The object-predicate relation 'kamsan-phyosi (reducted production – display)' was not found in the patent corpus.

In case of the type 2 and type 4, the result was rather disappointing. As to type 4, most of the errors were caused by the erroneous analysis of the compound noun structure. In the proposed algorithm, we simply analyze the relation between the first noun and the second noun, then the relation between the second noun and the third noun, etc. However, as there are cases in which, for example, the third noun relates to the inner compound semantically, our method failed to deal with such cases.

(9) a. kaip (subscription)-sincheng (application)-ywuto (promote)-hata : "to promote subscription"

b. ((kaip-sincheng) ywuto)

Our method produced for the above example a wrong translation "to induce apply subscription". As our method did not consider the left-branching or right-branching structure of the compound nouns, it showed the low accuracy rate for type 4.

The type 2 showed the lowest precision. In many cases, a noun that must be translated adverbially was not in the list, or not in the lexical co-occurrence pattern, either. In some other cases, the nouns that were in the adverbial noun list could not be translated as an adverb depending on the context.

6 Conclusion

In this paper we presented a method for treating unknown LVC words in Korean patent documents. LVC is an often encountered linguistic form in Korean which is composed of a predicative noun and a light verb. Because the word formation rule for the LVC is very productive in Korean, there is a high possibility in patent documents that unknown LVC words appear. In order to deal with the problem, we proposed 4 types of unknown LVC words. For each type, we presented a method for automatic generation of target words. Our method employs a lexical co-occurrence pattern DB, an adverbial noun list, and a verb dictionary. The proposed method showed 70.06% accuracy. The method can be integrated to an MT engine as a robust processing mechanism. Although the proposed method was successfully applied to the Korean-to-English patent MT system, there is still much room for improvement. The left-branching and the right-branching of the inner structure of compound nouns must be taken into account in order to deal with type 4 LVC better. As we currently assume the flat structure of the compound only, translation errors can occur. The adverbial translation of the nouns in type 2 is the next topic to tackle in depth.

Acknowledgement

This work was funded by the Ministry of Information and Communication of Korean government.

References

1. Grimshaw, J., Mester, A.: Light verbs and theta-marking, *Linguistic Inquiry* 19 (1988), 205-232
2. Han, C., Rambow, O.: The Sino-Korean Light Verb Construction and Lexical Argument Structure, in Proceedings of TAG+5 (2000)
3. Hong, M.: Linguistische Probleme in der Maschinellen Uebersetzung, Ph.D. Diss., Universitaet des Saarlandes (2001)
4. Hong, M., Kim, Y., Kim, C., Yang, S., Seo, Y., Ryu, C., Park, S.: Customizing a Korean-English MT System for Patent Translation, in Proceedings of the tenth MT Summit (2005)

5. Kim, J., Yang, J., Choi, I.: Capturing and Parsing the Mixed Properties of Light Verb Constructions in a Typed Feature Structure Grammar, in Proceedings of PACLIC18 (2004)
6. Seo, Y., Huang, Y., Hong, M., Choi, S.: Treating 'hata'-construction in Korean-Chinese MT, in Proceedings of IASTED (2003)
7. Shimada, A., Kordoni, V.: Japanese "Verbal Noun and *suru*" Constructions, in Proceedings of the Workshop on Multi-Verb constructions, Trondheim Summer School (2003)
8. Takeuchi, K., Kageura, K., Koyama, T.: Deverbal Compound Noun Analysis Based on Lexical Conceptual Structure, in Proceedings of 41st ACL (2003)
9. Yoon, J., Song, M.: Yet Another Compound Noun Analysis Using Word Co-occurrence Relation, in Proceedings of NLPRS'97 (1997)

Trees as Contexts in Formal Language Generation*

Adrian-Horia Dediu[1,2] and Gabriela Martín[1]

[1] Research Group on Mathematical Linguistics, Rovira i Virgili University
Pl. Imperial Tàrraco 1, 43005 Tarragona, Spain
adrian.dediu@urv.cat, gabrielasusana.martin@estudiants.urv.cat
[2] Faculty of Engineering in Foreign Languages
University "Politehnica" of Bucharest, Romania

Abstract. Initially designed to generate languages without rewriting of some nonterminals, contextual grammars are used in formal language theories as well as models for several particular aspects of natural languages. However, despite their power, contextual grammars do not provide a structural description of the generated languages. We present several modalities to add structures to classical contextual grammars. We are studying the relations of these structured contextual languages comparing with other structured languages. Several examples show the potential of the newly introduced grammars.

Keywords: Contextual grammars, tree languages, bracketed languages, structured contextual grammars.

1 Introduction

Contextual grammars were introduced by Solomon Marcus in 1969; he defined the class known as *external* contextual grammars in which the contexts are added at the extremities of the strings. In the *internal* contextual grammars, introduced by Paun and Nguyen in 1980, the contexts are adjoined using selectors, which are considered as substrings of the words in the generated languages. Initially designed to generate languages without nonterminal rewriting, only by adjoining contexts using a selection procedure, contextual grammars were discovered to have some limitations. Yet, as the term contextual seems to be very appropriate to model linguistic aspects, soon a large variety of such grammars appeared. We mention here only several types, like the *internal* case, *total contextual*, *grammars with choices* respectively, etc. For more information regarding particular types of contextual grammars, the reader may consult [1].

Despite the large variety of contextual grammars, it is difficult to put together strings and structures, a very important intrinsic quality of natural languages.

* This work was possible for the first author thanks to the grant 2002CAJAL-BURV4, and for the second author thanks to the grant 1323U07 E30 N-2003BRDI/12-03 both provided by the University Rovira i Virgili.

T. Salakoski et al. (Eds.): FinTAL 2006, LNAI 4139, pp. 738–747, 2006.

There were several proposals to introduce bracketed contextual grammars [2,3,4] in order to enhance the words in the generated languages with a tree structure, or to add a dependency relation to contexts, axioms and to generated words.

Analyzing possible structures that might be attached to one string, we can enumerate the syntactic structure, semantic structure, rhetoric structure, etc. Several of these structures are hierarchical and might be represented as trees, others like the one for *anaphora solving* might be represented as dependencies.

In section 5 we show how to attach a tree structure (in the Gcseg and Steinby sense) to the words and contexts in a contextual grammar, taking advantage of the simple shape and good computational behavior of this objects. In sections 6 and 7 we study the relation of the obtained classes of languages comparing with other two existent structured languages. We prove that the conjecture proposed in [3] is true, showing that the yield of *fully bracketed contextual languages* is CF. Several examples show the potential of the newly introduced grammars.

2 Preliminaries

In this section, we recall all the notions and notations as needed in this paper.

We denote by $\mathbb{N}$ the set of natural numbers. For $n \in \mathbb{N}$, $[n]$ represents the finite set $\{1, \ldots, n\}$, with $[0] = \emptyset$.

For a given finite set A, $|A|$ denotes the number of elements in A. We use the notation $\mathcal{P}(A)$ for the powerset of A, i.e. the set of all subsets of A. A function $w : [n] \to A$ is called a *string* over A, also denoted by $w = a_1 \ldots a_n$ for $i \in [n]$. The set A is also called an *alphabet* and strings over A are *words*. For a given string $w = a_1 \ldots a_n$, $|w| = n$ is the length of the string and $w(i) = a_i$ denotes the i-th symbol of the string. We denote by λ the empty string with $|\lambda| = 0$. The set of all strings over A is denoted by A^*.

For a given function $f : A \to B$, we may define the canonical extension to strings as the function $f^* : A^* \to B^*$ defined as $f^*(\lambda) = \lambda$, and $f^*(aw) = f(a)f^*(w)$ for $a \in A$ and $w \in A^*$. By convention if $A = \emptyset$, then $\emptyset^* = \{\lambda\}$ and the canonical extension to strings is also defined.

A *language* over an alphabet A is a subset of A^*. A language $L \subseteq A^*$ has *bounded length increase* (BLI) property if there is a constant ℓ such that for each $x \in L$ having $|x| > \ell$ there exists a word $y \in L$ such that $|y| < |x|$ but $|y| + \ell \geq |x|$.

We can find information regarding *Chomsky grammars, productions, derivations, generated languages* in [5]. We just recall that we denote by *RE (Recursively Enumerable)*, *CS*, *CF*, *LIN* and *REG* the families of languages generated by arbitrary (type 0), context-sensitive (also by length-increasing), context-free, linear and regular (also by left-linear and right-linear) grammars respectively. We denote by *FIN* the family of finite languages.

Context-free grammars (CFGs) are a well known class of grammars extensively used for programming languages and they can also describe almost all structures of natural languages. Yet for several exceptions like multiple agreement languages $\{a_1^n a_2^n \ldots a_k^n | n \geq 1, k \geq 3\}$, copy languages $\{ww | w \in \{a, b\}^*\}$

and cross agreement $\{a^n b^m c^n d^m | n, m \geq 1\}$, the context-free grammars are not the most appropriate investigation instrument for natural languages analysis. That is why we present several notions about *tree adjoining grammars.* We can find the basic information about this kind of grammars, *elementary trees* (initial and auxiliary trees), *lexicalized TAGs*, *adjoining* and *substitution* operations, constraints on adjunction such that *Selective Adjunction*, *Null Adjunction*, *Obligatory adjunction*, *TAG derivation trees*, *string language* and *tree language* definitions in [6].

3 Contextual Grammars

We give the definition of total contextual grammars according to [1].

Definition 1 (Total Contextual Grammars). *A (string)* total contextual grammar *is a construct* $TCG = (\Sigma, A, C, \varphi)$*, where* Σ *is an alphabet,* A *is a finite subset of* Σ^**,* C *is a finite subset of* $\Sigma^* \times \Sigma^*$ *and* $\varphi : \Sigma^* \times \Sigma^* \times \Sigma^* \to \mathcal{P}(C)$*. The elements of* A *are called* axioms*, the elements of* C *are called* contexts*, and* φ *is a* choice function.

A derivation relation $\underset{TC}{\Rightarrow}$ *is defined as* $x \underset{TC}{\Rightarrow} y$ *if and only if* $x = x_1x_2x_3$, $y = x_1ux_2vx_3$*, for* $x_1, x_2, x_3 \in \Sigma^*$*, and* $(u, v) \in C$*, s.t.* $(u, v) \in \varphi(x_1, x_2, x_3)$*. The reflexive transitive closure of the relation* $\underset{TC}{\Rightarrow}$ *is denoted by* $\underset{TC}{\overset{*}{\Rightarrow}}$*.*

The generated language is $L(TCG) = \{w \in \Sigma^* \mid a \underset{TC}{\overset{*}{\Rightarrow}} w, \text{ for } a \in A\}$*.*

Introducing several restrictions for function φ, we get particular types of contextual grammars such as:

1. *external contextual grammars with choice (ECC)*, $\varphi(x_1, x_2, x_3) = \emptyset$ whenever $x_1 \neq \lambda$ or $x_3 \neq \lambda$, we add contexts only outside of the derived strings
2. *internal contextual grammars with choice (ICC)*, $\varphi(x_1, x_2, x_3) = \psi(x_2)$, the selection depends only by x_2
3. *without choice (EC, IC)*, the values of φ are either C or $\emptyset$.

If # is a symbol not contained in Σ then if the set $S_{(u,v)} = \{x_1\#x_2\#x_3 | (u, v) \in \varphi(x_1, x_2, x_3)\}$ is a language in a given family F, then we say that G is a contextual grammar *with* F *– choice.* F is one of FIN, REG, CF, CS, RE.

When we think of the selection function as an if instruction (*if* exists x_2 *then* "add" a context) we may give the modular presentation of internal contextual grammars in the form $G = (\Sigma, A, \{(S_i, C_i) | i \in [n]\})$ where S_i is a subset of Σ^* and C_i is a finite subset of $\Sigma^* \times \Sigma^*$. We call $\{S_i | i \in [n]\}$ the *selector set.* Again, we can have the same discussion regarding the language of selectors.

Example 1. $G = (\Sigma = \{John,\ really,\ loves,\ Mary\}$,
$A = \{John\ loves\ Mary\}$, $C = \{(really, \lambda)\}$, $\varphi(x_1,\ loves,\ x_3) = C$, for all x_1, $x_3 \in \Sigma^*)$.

$L(G) = \{John\ loves\ Mary,\ John\ really\ loves\ Mary,\ John\ really\ really\ loves\ Mary, \dots\}$.

Let us consider several computational properties of contextual languages. As we defined the BLI property for languages, we can define external and internal bounded step properties.

A language $L \subseteq \Sigma^*$ has *external bounded step* (EBS) property if there is a constant ℓ such that for each $x \in L$ having $|x| > \ell$ there exists a word $y \in L$, $x = uyv$ such that $|x| \leq |y| + \ell$.

A language $L \subseteq \Sigma^*$ has *internal bounded step* (IBS) property if there is a constant ℓ such that for each $x \in L$ having $|x| > \ell$ there exists a word $y \in L$, $x = x_1ux_2vx_3$, $y = x_1ux_2vx_3$ such that $|x| \leq |y| + \ell$.

If a language has EBS or IBS property, then it has also BLI.

Lemma 1 (Properties of Contextual Languages)

- *A language belongs to the ECC family if and only if it has the EBS property.*
- *A language is in the TC family if and only if it has the IBS property.*

Proof. Let us chose $\ell = max\{|x| \mid (x \in A) \text{ or } (x = uv, (u, v) \in C)\}$. According to the definition of the derivation relation it is easy to see that contextual languages have the mentioned properties. Conversely, we construct grammars having axioms and the pair of contexts as the words in the language shorter than ℓ. The selection function is constructed accordingly.

Corollary 1. *All contextual languages have BLI property.*

4 Tree Languages and Contexts

We give here basic definitions from tree language theory, for a complete exposition of this topic we refer the reader to the book [7]. A *ranked alphabet* Σ is a finite set of symbols such that each one has been assigned a nonnegative integer called the *arity* of the symbol. For any $m \geq 0$, Σ_m is the set of all $m-$ary symbols in Σ.

The set T_Σ of $\Sigma-$*terms* is the smallest set T such that:

1. $\Sigma_0 \subseteq T$, and
2. $\sigma(t_1, ...t_m) \in T$ whenever $m \geq 0$, $t_1, ..., t_m \in T$ and $\sigma \in \Sigma_m$.

It is required that $\Sigma_0 \neq \emptyset$, this way T_Σ is always nonempty. Terms are regarded as formal representations of labelled, left to right oriented trees and we call them $\Sigma-$ *trees*. Subsets of T_Σ are called $\Sigma -$ *tree languages* or just *tree languages*.

A $\Sigma -$ *recognizer* $\mathbf{A} = (\mathcal{A}, A')$ consists of a $\Sigma-$algebra $\mathcal{A} = (A, \Sigma)$, and a set of *final states* $A' \subseteq A$. The elements of A are called the *states* of $\mathbf{A}$. The $\Sigma-$recognizer is finite if A is finite. The $\Sigma-$tree language *recognized* by $\mathbf{A}$ is

$$T(\mathbf{A}) = \{t \in T_\Sigma : t^{\mathcal{A}} \in A'\}$$

Where $t^{\mathcal{A}}$ is the value of the term t in the algebra $\mathcal{A}$. A $\Sigma-$ tree language is called *recognizable* or *regular* if it is recognized by a $\Sigma-$tree recognizer. The set of all recognizable Σ-tree languages is denoted also by Rec_Σ.

A $\Sigma(A)$- rewriting system is a set of rules of the form $l \rightarrow r$ with $l, r \in T_{\Sigma(A)}$, $\Sigma(A)_k = \Sigma_k$ for $k > 0$ and $\Sigma(A)_0 = \Sigma_0 \cup A$

It is well known [7] that a *non deterministic bottom up* $\Sigma-$ *recognizer* (ndB) recognizes exactly the same class of languages. We recall that a *non deterministic bottom up* $\Sigma-$*recognizer* (ndB) is an object $\mathbf{A} = (A, F, R)$ where A is a finite set of states, $F \subseteq A$, and R is a $\Sigma(A)$- rewriting system such that each rule is of the form:

1. $c \rightarrow a$, where $c \in \Sigma_0$ and $a \in A$
2. $f(a_1, ...a_n) \rightarrow a$, where $f \in \Sigma_n$, $a_1, ...a_n, a \in A$

Let $\overset{*}{\Rightarrow}_R$ be the reflexive, transitive closure of the rewrite $\Rightarrow_R$ relation thus defined. The Σ- tree language defined by $\mathbf{A}$ is $T(\mathbf{A}) = \{t \in T_\Sigma : t \overset{*}{\Rightarrow}_R a,\ a \in F\}$. More information about tree automata one can find in [8].

Example 2. Let Σ defined by $\Sigma_2 = \{f\}$ and $\Sigma_0 = \{c, d\}$ the ndB $\mathbf{A} = (\{a, b\}, \{a\}, R)$ with $R = \{c \rightarrow a, d \rightarrow b, f(a, a) \rightarrow a, f(a, a) \rightarrow b, f(b, b) \rightarrow a\}$ accepts the tree $t = f(d, f(c, c))$ by the computation $f(d, f(c, c)) \Rightarrow_R^3 f(b, f(a, a)) \Rightarrow_R f(b, b) \Rightarrow_R a$.

Next, we recall the well known notion of *yield* of a tree as well as an extension of it that is needed for the purpose of comparing our approach to the bracketed one proposed in [3].

For a tree $t \in T_\Sigma$ we define the *yield* of the tree as follows
$yd(t) = c$ if $t = c \in \Sigma_0$.
$yd(t) = yd(t_1)...yd(t_n)$ if $t = \sigma(t_1, ...t_n)$, $\sigma \in \Sigma_n$
The *extended yield* of a tree is defined as follows
$Ey(t) = c$, for each $t = c \in \Sigma_0$.
$Ey(t) = [Ey(t_1)...Ey(t_n)]$. if $t = \sigma(t_1, ...t_n)$, $\sigma \in \Sigma_n$
If $L \subseteq T_\Sigma$, the yield of the language is $yd(L) = \{yd(w) : w \in L\}$ while the extended yield of the language is $Ey(L) = \{Ey(w) : w \in L\}$.

Example 3. If $\Sigma = \Sigma_0 \cup \Sigma_1 \cup \Sigma_2$, $\Sigma_0 = \{a, b\}$, $\Sigma_1 = \{g\}$, $\Sigma_2 = \{f\}$, then $yd(f(a, f(a, g(b)))) = aab$, $Ey(f(a, f(a, g(b)))) = [a[a[b]]]$.

Let ξ be a symbol which does not appear in Σ. Let $\Sigma' = \Sigma \cup \{\xi\}$, where it is understood that ξ is a new symbol in Σ_0. A $\Sigma-$*context* is a $\Sigma'-$ tree in which the symbol ξ appears exactly once. The set of contexts is denoted also by C_Σ. If $p \in C_\Sigma$ and $t \in T_\Sigma$, $p(t)$ denotes the tree obtained by replacing ξ in p by t, this is if $p = \xi$, then $p(t) = t$, otherwise $p = \sigma(t_1, ...\xi, ...t_n)$ for some $\sigma \in \Sigma_n$ and then $p(t) = \sigma(t_1, ...t, ...t_n)$. One can find information about tree contexts and even multidimensional tree contexts in [8].

If we consider the *length* of a tree as being the length of its term expression then we can define the BLI, EBS, IBS properties for tree languages.

5 Contextual Tree Grammars

In this section we introduce the new concept of contextual tree grammars and their generated tree language. Besides a ranked alphabet and a leaf alphabet a contextual tree grammar consists of two finite sets of trees, a set of axioms and a set of contexts, as well as an operator that specifies how each context can be used to derive trees from trees.

Definition 2 (Contextual Tree Grammar). *For a given ranked alphabet Σ, a* contextual tree grammar *(CTG) is an object* $(A, \{(S_i, C_i) : i = 1, ...m\})$ *(axioms, (selectors, contexts)) such that* $A, S_i \subseteq T_\Sigma$, $C_i \subseteq C_\Sigma$ *for every* $i = 1, ...m$. *We refer to the pairs* (S_i, C_i) *as* productions, *and denote* $P = \{(S_i, C_i) : i = 1, ...m\}$.

If $t_1, t_2 \in T_\Sigma$ *we define the derivation relation in this grammar as follows:* $t_1 \Rightarrow t_2$ *if for some* $i, j = 1, ...m$ *there are* $r \in S_i$, $r' \in C_i$, $p \in C_\Sigma$ *such that* $t_1 = p(r)$ *and* $t_2 = p(r'(r))$.

We denote as $\stackrel{*}{\Rightarrow}$ *the reflexive transitive closure of* $\Rightarrow$, *and if* $t_1 \stackrel{*}{\Rightarrow} t_2$.

The language generated by a CTG grammar G is $L(G) = \{t \in T_\Sigma : a \stackrel{*}{\Rightarrow} t,\ a \in A\}$.

If in a grammar G as above all selectors $S_1, ...S_n$ are languages in a given family F, then we say that G is a contextual tree grammar *with* $F - choice$. The class of all this languages is called $\mathbf{CTL}(F)$.

Example 4. $\Sigma_0 = \{R, really, loves, S\}$, $\Sigma_1 = \{V\}$, $\Sigma_2 = \{A\}$, $\Sigma_3 = \{F\}$,
$A = \{F(R, V(loves), S)\}$
$P = \{(V(loves), A(really, \xi))\}$
$L = \{F(R, V(loves), S),$
$F(R, A(really, V(loves)), S)$
$F(R, A(really, A(really, V(loves))), S)$
$.......\}$
$Ey(L) = \{\ [R[loves]S],$
$[R, [really[loves]]S]$
$[R[really[really[loves]]]S]$
$.......\}$
$yd(L) = \{R\ (really)^n\ loves\ S : n \geq 0\}$

Example 5. Let Σ be the alphabet formed by
$\Sigma_2 = \{S, VP\}$,
$\Sigma_1 = \{NP\}$,
$\Sigma_0 = \{N, V, adv\}$
$G = (\{S(NP(N), VP(adv, V))\},$
$\{(VP(adv, V), VP(adv, \xi))\})$.

We can easily recognize that G generates sentences (S) with their syntactic structures (NP, VP) consisting in a noun (N) and a verb (V) preceded by one or more adverbs (adv).

As the set of contexts and the set of axioms is finite it is easy to see that:

Proposition 1. *CTL has BLI.*

Observe that $\mathbf{CTL}(FIN) \subseteq \mathbf{Rec}_\Sigma$; it is easy to construct a non deterministic bottom up recognizer for this class of languages.

Example 6. Consider the ranked alphabet $\Sigma = \Sigma_0 \cup \Sigma_1 \cup \Sigma_2$, $\Sigma_0 = \{a, b\}$, $\Sigma_1 = \{g\}$, $\Sigma_2 = \{f\}$, and the contextual tree grammar

$$G = (\{g(f(a, g(b)))\}, \{(g(b), f(a, \xi))\}).$$

If we call $p = f(a, \xi)$, the generated language is $L(G) = \{g(p^k(g(b))) : k \geq 1\}$. The following ndB recognizes the same language $\mathbf{A} = (\{a', b', c, d\}, \{d\}, R)$ with $R = \{a \to a',\ b \to b',\ g(b') \to c,\ f(a', c) \to c,\ g(c) \to d\}$. For example: $g(f(a, f(a, g(b)))) \Rightarrow_R^3 g(f(a', f(a', g(b')))) \Rightarrow_R g(f(a', f(a', c))) \Rightarrow_R g(f(a', c))$ $\Rightarrow_R g(c) \Rightarrow_R d$.

From this it is clear that this objects are natural parsers of this class of languages.

6 Relation with the Bracketed Contextual Grammars

In this section we consider the relation between the proposed structure for contextual grammars and that given by Paun-Vide in [3]. They define the Dyck covered languages ($DC(V)$) over $(V \cup B)^*$ where V is an alphabet and $B = \{[,]\}$ as the languages $L \subseteq (V \cup B)^*$ such that for each $x \in L$, x can be reduced to λ ($x \stackrel{*}{\Rightarrow} \lambda$) by means of rules of the form $[w] \to \lambda$ only, where $w \in V^*$. The *projection* pr_V is the canonical extension to strings of a function $f_V : (V \cup B) \to V$ defined as $f_V(a) = a$ if $a \in V$ and $f_V(a) = \lambda$ if $a \in B$.

Paun-Vide restrict their attention to a subset of the class of Dyck covered languages in order to be able to associate a tree structure to the resulting strings. In this paper we look at the term structure of strings, therefore we consider the *minimally Dyck covered language* over V ($MDC(V)$) as the least set such that:

1. $[u] \in MDC(V)$ if $u \in V^*$
2. $[u_1...u_n] \in MDC(V)$ if $u_i \in MDC(V) \cup V^*$ for every $i \in \{1, ...n\}$.

We observe that $MDC(V) \subseteq DC(V)$ and it fails to contain words of the form uv with $u, v \in MDC(V)$ but it does contain $[uv]$.

The strings in V^* that occur inside an element of $MDC(V)$ are taken maximal; i.e. for any $[u_1...u_n] \in MDC(V)$ if $u_i \in V^*$, $2 \leq i \leq n-1$ then u_{i+1} starts with a '[', and u_{i-1} ends with a ']', if $u_1 \in V^*$, the first condition holds and if $u_n \in V^*$, the second condition holds. The following lemmas have elementary proofs.

Lemma 2. *For every $u \in MDC(V)$ there exist a unique sequence $u_1, ...u_n \in MDC(V) \cup V^*$ such that $u = [u_1...u_n]$.*

Lemma 3. *For every $u \in MDC(V)$ there exists a ranked alphabet Σ and a $t \in T_\Sigma$ such that $Ey(t) = u$.*

We use this $MCD(V)$ set to define the *fully bracketed contextual grammar* in a more general way than it is done in the Paun-Vide paper:

Definition 3. *A* fully bracketed contextual grammar *(FBCG) is a construct* $G = (V, A, (S_1, C_1), ...(S_n, C_n))$ $n \geq 1$

where V *is an alphabet,* A *is a finite subset of* $MDC(V)$, $S_i \subseteq MDC(V) \cup V$ *and* $C_1, ...C_n$ *are finite subsets of* $(MDC(V) \cup V^*) \times (MDC(V) \cup V^*) - (\lambda, \lambda)$.

For $x, y \in MDC(V)$ *we define*

$x \Rightarrow_G y$ *if and only if* $x = x_1 x_2 x_3$, $y = x_1[u x_2 v] x_3$

where $x_2 \in S_i$, $x_1, x_3 \in (V \cup B)^*$, $(u, v) \in C_i$ *for some* $i \in \{1, ...n\}$.

The language generated by this G *denoted* $L(G)$ *is* $L(G) = \{w \in V^* : a \overset{*}{\Rightarrow}_G w$ *for some* $a \in A\}$.

The string language *generated by this* G *denoted* $StrL(G)$ *is* $StrL(G) = \{pr_V(w) \in V^* : a \overset{*}{\Rightarrow}_G w$ *for some* $a \in A\}$.

If all selectors $S_1, ...S_n$ are languages in a given family F, then we say that G is a fully bracketed contextual grammar *with* $F -$ *choice*.

We denote the class of such languages **FBCL**(F) and **StrFBCL**(F) From the previous lemma we have that:

Lemma 4. *If* $x = x_1 x_2 x_3 \in MDC(V)$, $u, v \in MDC(V) \cup V^*$ *then there exist a CTG over a ranked alphabet* Σ, $r, t \in T_\Sigma$ *such that* $t \Rightarrow r$ *with* $x = Ey(t)$, $x_1[u x_2 v] x_3 = Ey(r)$.

Proposition 2

1. **FBCL**$(FIN) \subseteq Ey($**CTL**$(FIN))$
2. **StrFBCL**$(FIN) \subseteq yd($**CTL**$(FIN))$

Proof. Is straightforward from the previous lemma.

In the paper [3] the authors conjecture that the **StrFBCL**(FIN) are included in the class of Context Free languages. Now we see from the last proposition and the well known fact that the yield of a recognizable language is context free, that this conjecture is true:

Theorem 1. StrFBCL$(FIN) \subseteq CFL$

7 Relation with Tree Adjoining Grammars

Tree-Adjoining Grammars, or TAGs for short, were introduced by Joshi, Levy and Takahashi in 1975. TAGs represent an important class of grammars, originally motivated by some linguistic considerations, which later have yielded some important mathematical and computational results. We can find an overview of TAGs in [6]. Yet TAGs have several limitations, $a^n b^n c^n d^n e^n$ is not a TAG language. There are known extensions of TAGs that could solve this problem [9], yet other structures than trees are hard to imagine in the TAGs context.

The reader may be noted that the derivation procedure in a CTG grammar is very similar to the adjoining operation in a TAG, in fact we have

Lemma 5. *Let* $G_1 = (T, N, I, A, S)$ *a pure* TAG *(without local constraints) and without substitution (no non-terminals marked for substitution), then there exists a CTG grammar* $G_2 = (A, (S_i, C_i)_{i \in I})$ *such that* $L(G_1) = L(G_2)$.

Proof. It is enough to take the terminals of G_1 as Σ_0, the non terminals as symbols in Σ_n with $n \geq 1$ (regarding at the branching at each node in the elementary trees), and the rules as $(r, r') \in T_\Sigma \times C_\Sigma$ such that r is a subtree of an elementary tree, r' is an auxiliary tree in which the foot node has been changed by ξ, $root(r') = root(r)$.

Note that the CTG's are stronger than this restricted type of TAG, for in the former the labels of the root and the foot node need not to be the same.

This pure TAG without substitution were the first model of TAG's introduced by Joshi, Levy and Takahashi (1975).

Now, regarding at the substitution operation, it is not possible to emulate it in a contextual tree grammar as we defined it from the beginning. Nevertheless, the needed modification is very simple. Let us allow rules in the extended set $T_\Sigma \times (T_\Sigma \cup C_\Sigma)$ (instead of just $T_\Sigma \times C_\Sigma$), this is, for each tree $t = p(r)$ with $p \in C_\Sigma$ and $r \in T_\Sigma$ if (r, r') is a rule and $r' \in T_\Sigma$, $t \Rightarrow p(r')$. Let $G_1 = (T, N, I, A, S)$ be a pure TAG. Perform the following replacements, if α is an elementary tree with a node A marked for substitution then replace it with a new symbol $\sigma_A (\notin T \cup N)$. This set of new symbols will be called Σ'_0. Take Σ' such that $\Sigma_0 = T \cup \Sigma'_0$ and $\Sigma'_k = \{A \in N : A \text{ is an inner node, and the number of branches at the node labelled by } A \text{ is } k\}$ for every $k \geq 1$. Add the rules prescribed by the lemma for the auxiliary trees and for each initial tree β with $root(\beta) = A$ add the rule (σ_A, β). The axioms are taken as the S rooted initial trees. If we name the resulting grammar G_2 and $\Sigma = \Sigma' - \Sigma'_0$ then $L(G_1) = L(G_2) \cap T_\Sigma$. This is to say $L(G_1) = \{t \in T_\Sigma : a \overset{*}{\Rightarrow} t\}$.

Example 7. Consider the TAG grammar:
Axioms (only one): $S(NP_\downarrow, (VP(V(likes), NP_\downarrow))$
Elementary trees:

$VP(VP^*, ADV(passionately))$
$NP(Harry)$
$NP(peanuts)$

We now define the ranked alphabet Σ like $\Sigma_0 = \{Harry,\ peanuts,\ like,\ passionately,\ \sigma_{NP}\}$, $\Sigma_1 = \{NP, ADV, V\}$, $\Sigma_2 = \{VP, S\}$. The rules are:

$\{(VP(V(likes), \sigma_{NP}), VP(\xi, ADV(passionately))),$
$(\sigma_{NP}, NP(Harry)),$
$(\sigma_{NP}, NP(peanuts))\}$

and the axiom:

$S(\sigma_{NP}, (VP(V(likes), \sigma_{NP}))$

8 Concluding Remarks

We introduced a new type of structured grammar, that gives a natural structure to the strings generated by the Solomon's contextual grammars strategy.

This is a contribution to filling a gap in the theory of contextual grammars, which has been (with a few exceptions) mainly concerned with the weak generative capacity. The new model has simple computational features to be exploit (in generating and parsing issues) and allows the derivation of structured strings adding contexts with its own structure, thought as encoding the dependencies between a word an its arguments, relating in this regard with others formalisms as Tree Adjoining Grammars. Our model for structuring a contextual grammars is compared as well with other attempts given for this aim, like Bracketed Contextual Grammars. The relation of the formalism with other interesting structures like Sleator's linkages, Kappes's Multiple Contextual Grammars and Marcus's Structured Strings remains to be studied. As possible applications of it we mention the annotation of documents with multiple structures (including syntactic, semantic, dependencies) using appropriate XML tags.

Acknowledgement

We would like to thank the anonymous referees for their helpful comments and observations.

References

1. Păun, G.: Marcus Contextual Grammars. Kluwer Academic Publishers, Norwell, MA, USA (1997)
2. Kudlek, M., Martín-Vide, C., Mateescu, A., Mitrana, V.: Contexts and the concept of mild context-sensitivity. Linguistics and Philosophy (26) (2002) 703–725
3. Marcus, S., Păun, G., Martín-Vide, C.: Contextual grammars as generative models of natural languages. Comput. Linguist. **24**(2) (1998) 245–274
4. Kappes, M.: Combining contextual grammars and tree adjoining grammars. Grammars A Journal of Mathematical Research on Formal and Natural Languages **3**(2-3) (2000) 175–187
5. Aho, A.V., Ullman, J.D.: The Theory of Parsing, Translation, and Compiling. Volume I: Parsing of Series in Automatic Computation. Prentice Hall, Englewood Cliffs, New Jersey (1972)
6. Joshi, A., Schabes, Y.: Tree-adjoining grammars. In Rozenberg, G., Salomaa, A., eds.: Handbook of Formal Languages, vol3. Springer Verlag (1997) 69–120
7. Gécseg, F., Steinby, M.: Tree automata. Akadémiai Kiadó (Publishing House of the Hungarian Academy of Sciences), Budapest (1984)
8. Comon, H., Dauchet, M., Gilleron, R., Jacquemard, F., Lugiez, D., Tison, S., Tommasi, M.: Tree automata techniques and applications. Available on: `http://www.grappa.univ-lille3.fr/tata` (1997) release October, 1rst 2002.
9. Hotz, G., Pitsch, G.: On using semi-dyck sets to analyse coupled-context-free languages. Fundam. Inform. **29**(1-2) (1997) 1–26

Two String-Based Finite-State Models of the Semantics of Calendar Expressions

Jyrki Niemi[1], Lauri Carlson[2], and Kimmo Koskenniemi[1]

[1] University of Helsinki, Department of General Linguistics,
{jyrki.niemi, kimmo.koskenniemi}@helsinki.fi
[2] University of Helsinki, Department of Translation Studies
lauri.carlson@helsinki.fi

Abstract. This paper presents two string-based finite-state approaches to modelling the semantics of natural-language calendar expressions: extended regular expressions (XREs) over a timeline string of unique symbols, and a string of hierarchical periods of time constructed by finite-state transducers (FSTs). The approaches cover expressions ranging from plain dates and times of the day to more complex ones, such as *the second Tuesday following Easter*. The paper outlines the representations of sample calendar expressions in the two models, presents a possible application in temporal reasoning, and informally compares the models.

1 Introduction

Temporal information and calendar expressions are essential in various applications, for example, in event calendars, appointment scheduling and timetables. Calendar expressions range from simple dates and times of the day to more complex ones, such as *the second Tuesday following Easter*. The information should often be both processed by software and presented in a human-readable form.

A calendar expression denotes a period of time that does not depend on the time of use of the expression, such as *1 September 2005*. However, the denotation may be vague or underspecified without context, such as *September* or *in the morning*, or ambiguous, such as *a week*, which may denote either a calendar period or a duration. We model the disambiguated meanings of natural-language expressions, trying to retain underspecification wherever possible. The approaches presented here can also model disconnected periods (non-convex intervals) of time, such as *two Sundays*, which denotes a period consisting of two Sundays without the intervening days.

In [1], we proposed extended regular expressions (called calendar XREs) for modelling the semantics of natural-language calendar expressions, following Carlson [2]. While the well-known semantics of regular expressions could in principle be used in reasoning with temporal information represented as calendar XREs, such reasoning remains in general intractable. Thus, in [3], we presented a temporal model and a representation of calendar expressions that makes reasoning tractable in more cases. The model is based on a string of hierarchical periods,

T. Salakoski et al. (Eds.): FinTAL 2006, LNAI 4139, pp. 748–755, 2006.

expanded to finer granularities by finite-state transducers (FSTs) as needed. In this paper, we informally compare the two approaches.

In [1], we modelled time as a long string of consecutive basic periods of time, such as minutes, each represented by a unique symbol. Hours, days and other basic calendar periods were then represented as sets of substrings of this timeline string. These sets were further combined with XRE operations to represent more complex calendar expressions. In the FST-based model of [3], the timeline consists of start and end markers for calendar periods. There are only a fixed number of symbols. It is also easy to adjust the granularity of the timeline, either globally or locally. The denotation of a calendar expression is represented by marking the corresponding periods of time on a timeline.

In our view, finite-state methods suit well to representing and processing temporal information, as they lend themselves naturally to processing cycles and repetition. Finite-state methods have a sound theoretical basis, and they are easier to control than ad hoc methods. On the other hand, numerical calculations related to temporal information require more powerful methods.

In general, more information and details of the unique-symbol model and calendar XREs can be found in [1] and [4], and of the FST-based model, in [3].

2 Regular Expression Operations and Notations

The usual (extended) regular expression operations are concatenation ($A\ .\ B$), union ($A \cup B$), Kleene star (A^*), intersection ($A \cap B$), difference ($A \setminus B$) and complement ($\neg A$). In addition, calendar XREs use operations defined using regular relations (FSTs), for example, non-empty substrings ($\mathbf{in}_+ A$), non-empty subwords (possibly disconnected substrings) ($\mathbf{in}_+^* A$) and (typed) suffix ($A \backslash\backslash B$). Concatenation power (A^n) is a notational shorthand. Simple parametrized macros simplify calendar XREs containing repeating subexpressions and make them structurally closer to natural language. The main FST operation is composition ($A \circ B$). $L(R)$ denotes the regular language specified by the XRE R.

3 Two String-Based Models of Time

3.1 Timeline as a String of Unique Symbols

Since regular expressions can specify strings only over a finite alphabet, we choose a finite subsequence of an infinite timeline partitioned into basic periods, such as minutes or seconds. Each basic period t_i has a unique corresponding symbol a_i in the alphabet $\Sigma = \bigcup_{i=1}^{n} \{a_i\}$. The string $T = a_1 a_2 \ldots a_n$ corresponds to the finite timeline. A single calendar XRE defines a regular language over Σ, corresponding to a set of possibly disconnected periods of time.

The language of an XRE may contain strings x that are not subwords of the timeline string: $x \notin L(\mathbf{in}_+^* T)$. Such a string contains a symbol a_i followed by an a_j with $i \geq j$. However, as a period of time may not be followed by the same or a preceding period, we limit the languages of calendar XREs to representing meaningful periods by intersecting them with $L(\mathbf{in}^*_+ T)$. The calendar XRE for an inconsistent expression, such as *30 February*, denotes the empty set.

This model allows a fairly clean and compositional representation of the semantics of calendar expressions using XRE operations. However, the alphabet Σ may need to be huge. Computing $L(\mathbf{in}^*_+ T)$ is intractable even for a string of a few thousand symbols. The model also requires using the base granularity even if the expression referred to only longer periods of time.

3.2 Timeline as a String of Hierarchical Period Markers

In this model, a string corresponding to a finite timeline is constructed by a cascade of compositions of FSTs. The FSTs mark periods of time and expand appropriately marked parts of the timeline to a finer granularity. Granularities need not be strictly nested, allowing the representation of weeks. A calendar expression is represented by marking on a timeline the denoted periods of time.

Each calendar period on a timeline is delimited by granularity-specific begin and end markers: for example, [y marks the beginning of a year and d] marks the end of a day. A begin marker is followed by a symbol indicating a specific period, such as y2006 for the year 2006 and Jan for January. A day is marked for both the day of the month and the day of the week. The period symbol may in turn be followed by a sequence of markers for a finer granularity. Between the begin marker and the period symbol can be inserted various kinds of marker symbols, for example, to mark the period relevant or to be expanded.

To be able to expand the months of a year and the days of a month independently of the neighbouring periods, each year contains information about its leap-year status and the day of the week of its first day, and each month, the number of its days and the day of the week of its first day. For example, a timeline denoting the year 2006 would be [y y2006 nly Sun y], where nly indicates that the year is not a leap year, and Sun that its first day is a Sunday.

The level of detail in a calendar expression timeline can vary: for example, if hours are not referred to in the expression, they need not be introduced into the timeline. Moreover, if the expression refers to days only within May, explicitly or implicitly, only that month is expanded to the level of days.

4 Calendar Expressions and Their Representations

In this section, we present a few central constructs appearing in natural-language calendar expressions and their representations in the two models. We describe the FSTs (or rather regular relation expressions) at the level of macros. An example of the implementation of an FST macro can be found in [3].

4.1 Basic Calendar Expressions

Unqualified natural-language calendar expressions, such as *May*, typically refer to the nearest past or future period relevant in the context. In this work, however, we interpret them as underspecified, for example, referring to any May.

In the unique-symbol model, we regarded the basic expressions as predefined constants specifying sets of substrings of the timeline string T. They included expressions corresponding to the generic periods of the Gregorian calendar, such as day, month and year, and specific ones, such as each month. We also assumed appropriately defined sets for seasons and holidays, such as Christmas Day.

In the FST-based model, basic calendar expressions are not used to as parts of FSTs. Their representation is needed only when they alone constitute a complete calendar expression. Their denotation is marked directly in the relevant periods of an appropriately expanded timeline. For example, unless otherwise constrained, the expression *Monday* or *Mondays* would require expanding all years and all months to the level of days, in order to mark each Monday.

4.2 Lists, Refinement and Intervals

Lists, refinement and intervals are three basic constructs combining calendar expressions to more complex ones. Lists are conjunctions or disjunctions, such as *Mondays and Wednesdays.* Refinement combines multiple subexpressions, each of which refines or restricts the period of time denoted, as in *Christmas Eve falling on a Friday* and *23 August 2006.* An interval *Monday to Friday* begins from a Monday and almost always ends in the closest following Friday.

In the unique-symbol model, lists were in general represented disjunctively using union. Refinement was implemented with intersection and a substring operation, and intervals with the help of a not-containing construct. The calendar expression *Mon–Fri in January to April and Sat–Wed in June to August 2006* illustrates all the three constructs. It is represented by the calendar XRE

$$((\mathit{interval}(\mathit{Mon},\ \mathit{Fri}) \cap \mathbf{in}_{+}\mathit{interval}(\mathit{Jan},\ \mathit{Apr})) \\ \cup (\mathit{interval}(\mathit{Sat},\ \mathit{Wed}) \cap \mathbf{in}_{+}\mathit{interval}(\mathit{Jun},\ \mathit{Aug}))) \cap \mathbf{in}_{+}\mathit{y2006}.$$

The macro $\mathit{interval}(A,\ B)$ corresponds to $A\ .\ \neg\,(\Sigma^*\ .\ B\ .\ \Sigma^*)\ .\ B$, meaning "$A$, followed by any connected period not containing B, followed by B". The substring operation $\mathbf{in}_{+}$ is applied to longer periods before intersection with shorter ones.

In the FST-based approach, FSTs are used to mark the denotation of a calendar expression in several phases with intermediate markings. We first generate a string containing the year: *make_year*(y2006) produces [y y2006 nly Sun y]. To expand the year to the level of months, we first mark it with E by composing the previous expression with *mark*(E, y2006), resulting in [y E y2006 nly Sun y]. We then add months within each marked year using *add_months*: [y E y2006 nly Sun [m Jan 31 Sun m] [m Feb 28 Wed m] ... [m Dec 31 Fri m] y].

Next we mark January as the beginning of an interval (IB) and April as the end (IE), mark for expansion the periods within an interval, and expand the marked months to contain days. We then mark the day intervals Monday to Friday as above. As there are no finer granularities in the expression, we then mark them as relevant (R) instead of for further expansion. The second conjunct in the list of month intervals is processed similarly. However, before that, we mark the months of the first conjunct (January to April) as inactive (I), to avoid marking Saturdays and Sundays in them.

The final timeline for the expression *Mon–Fri in January to April and Sat–Wed in June to August 2006* is then as follows:

[y E y2006 nly Sun
  [m I Jan 31 Sun [d 1st Sun d] [d R 2nd Mon d]
  ... [d R 6th Fri d] [d 7th Sat d] ... [d R 31st Tue ... d] m]
... [m I Apr 30 Sat ... m] [m May 31 Mon m]
  [m E Jun 30 Thu [d 1st Thu d] ... [d 30th Fri d] m]
... [m E Aug 31 Tue [d R 1st Tue d] ... [d 31st Thu d] m]
... [m Dec 31 Fri m] y]

The whole FST cascade producing the above is:

make_year(y2006) ∘ *mark*(E, y2006) ∘ *add_months* ∘ *mark*(IB, Jan)
∘ *mark*(IE, Apr) ∘ *mark_interval*(E) ∘ *add_days* ∘ *mark*(IB, Mon)
∘ *mark*(IE, Fri) ∘ *mark_interval*(R) ∘ *change_marks*([m, E, I)
∘ *mark*(IB, Jun) ∘ *mark*(IE, Aug) ∘ *mark_interval*(E) ∘ *add_days*
∘ *mark*(IB, Sat) ∘ *mark*(IE, Wed) ∘ *mark_interval*(R)

The periods marked as relevant in the final timeline are the denotation of the calendar expression. Some periods of time of the final timeline may be irrelevant to the denotation. The details within such periods can be collapsed (that is, finer-granularity periods deleted) without affecting the denotation.

4.3 Exception and Anchored Expressions

The expression *8 am, except Mondays 9 am* is an exception expression consisting of a default time (here *8 am*), an exception scope (*Mondays*) and an optional exception time (*9 am*). In the unique-symbol model, this is expressed with union, difference and intersection: $(\mathsf{h08} \setminus \mathbf{in}_+ \mathit{Mon}) \cup (\mathsf{h09} \cap \mathbf{in}_+ \mathit{Mon})$. If the exception time is omitted, the difference alone suffices. In the FST-based model, the denotation is computed by first marking the default time with marker m_1, next marking the exception scope with m_2, then removing markers m_1 contained in periods marked with m_2, and finally marking with m_1 the exception time within m_2. The periods marked with m_1 provide the denotation.

An anchored expression denotes a time relative to an anchor time. For example, *the second Tuesday following Easter* refers to a time relative to Easter: the last day in a string of days beginning from Easter, containing exactly two Tuesdays and ending in a Tuesday. This can be expressed as the calendar XRE $\mathit{Easter}\,.\,(\neg\,(\Sigma^*\,.\,\mathit{Tue}\,.\,\Sigma^*)\,.\,\mathit{Tue})^2 \,\backslash\backslash\, \mathit{Tue}$. In the FST-based model, one FST marks Easter with an anchor marker, and another one marks the second Tuesday following the marked day as the denotation. We assume an FST that knows the time of Easter, possibly by having the dates enumerated. The second following Tuesday can easily be expressed in a way similar to the above calendar XRE.

A general complication with anchored expressions is to know which periods of time should be expanded. For example, if Easter falls at the end of March, the second Tuesday following it is in April, which should also be expanded. As the calculating ability of FSTs is very limited, we assume that a compiler compiling calendar expressions to FSTs decides the periods to be expanded in such cases.

5 Temporal Reasoning with Calendar Expressions

We have mainly considered a form of temporal reasoning that finds the common periods of time denoted by two calendar expressions. For example, a query to an event database could find out at what time certain museums are open on Mondays in December, or which museums are open on Mondays in December. The former query should find for each target calendar expression in the database the set of periods of time denoted by both the query and the target, and the latter, whether the query and the target denote some common periods or not. Both the query and target expressions would be similar calendar expressions.

In the unique-symbol model of time, both types of queries require computing the intersection of the calendar XREs. In principle, it would be straightforward to construct finite-state automata from the XREs, intersect them, and either enumerate the strings or check for the emptiness of each intersection. In practice, however, constructing the automata is often intractable. Moreover, the enumerated language may be very large and incomprehensible to a human.

Similar reasoning in the FST-based model using FST compositions should in general be significantly more efficient. The common periods of two calendar expressions can be computed by considering for the second expression only the periods of time marked relevant in the first expression. While not necessarily efficient enough for on-line processing, it might be of use in an application in which some information is generated periodically from a database, such as a Web page showing events of the week. It would also be easier to convert the reasoning result to a human-readable form. As mentioned in [1], calendar XREs could also be used as a language-independent representation of calendar expressions in a natural-language generation system.

6 Comparing the Models and Representations

In our view, both XREs and FSTs would be fairly well suited to modelling the semantics of calendar expressions. Compared to the unique-symbol model and calendar XREs, the hierarchical FST-based model is more procedural and less compositional. It uses FSTs applied (composed) in a certain order. While the reduced compositionality is a drawback, the FST-based model is much more efficient in practice, a step towards tractable reasoning.

The structure of a calendar XRE is usually fairly close to the corresponding natural-language calendar expression, largely thanks to the use of macros. In contrast, the corresponding composition of FSTs is structurally very different. We therefore envisage an intermediate representation, structurally close to natural-language calendar expressions and compilable to the FST representation. The representation might be XREs or the term-based one proposed in [3].

The FST-based model does not need the intersection with the set of subwords of the timeline string. Not having to compute this set makes significantly longer timelines practical. The alphabet is also much smaller and of a fixed size.

In the FST-based model, all the periods of time denoted by a calendar expression are typically represented by a single string, while in the unique-symbol model the elements of a set denoted separate periods of time. An advantage of the former is a more compact representation. However, the set-based approach made it fairly straightforward to represent disconnected periods of time, such as *two Sundays a month*, by juxtaposing symbols denoting non-adjacent periods of time, while a similar distinction cannot be made within a single string. Neither can overlapping or disjunctive periods of time be represented in a single string.

We now think that the need for such a distinction is specific to a purpose: while disjunctions of (possibly disconnected) periods of time are indeed useful in queries, an information source, such as an event database, would probably not in general need them. For example, *Monday and Wednesday or Tuesday and Thursday* would hardly make sense as the opening days of a museum. In contrast, a customer might well want to organize a visit to a museum either on Monday and Wednesday or on Tuesday and Thursday. Combining such an expression with a single-string target expression in an event database would yield a set of denotations, each in its own string, represented by an automaton with several paths. The models thus seem equally powerful in this respect.

We have not yet tested in the FST-based model all the calendar expression constructs whose calendar XREs were presented in [1], but we strongly expect that they all can be represented in it as well, as both representations are based on regular language and regular relation operations over a timeline string.

7 Related Work

Temporal expressions have been widely researched, including modelling and reasoning with calendar expressions. Our main inspiration has been Carlson's [2] event calculus, which includes modelling calendar expressions as XREs.

The Verbmobil project [5] had its own formalism to represent and reason with temporal expressions in appointment negotiation dialogues [6]. Its coverage of calendar expressions was similar to ours. The calendar logic of Ohlbach and Gabbay [7] can represent calendar expressions of various kinds. However, calendar logic expressions are not structurally as close to natural-language expressions as calendar XREs. Han and Lavie [8] use their own formalism to reason using temporal constraint propagation. They cover more types of expressions than we do, including underspecified and quantified ones, such as *every week in May*.

Karttunen et al. [9] express the syntax of dates as regular expressions to check their validity. Fernando (for example, [10]) uses regular expressions to represent events with optional temporal information, such as *(for) an hour*.

8 Further Work

We intend to research further various options for a tractable, practical reasoning method for calendar expressions. One option would be to process calendar XREs syntactically using term rewriting. We could also combine several approaches.

Finite-state methods cannot naturally represent fuzzy expressions, such as *about 8 o'clock*, internally anaphoric expressions, such as *9 to 17, an hour later in winter*, or fractional expressions, such as *the second quarter of the year*. A major goal would be to extend the representation to cover these expression types.

It might also be worthwhile to explore options of representing events combined with calendar expressions, or at least to examine calendar expressions in their context. Such approaches might sometimes help to resolve the meaning of a single fuzzy or underspecified calendar expression.

Lastly, we need to evaluate the coverage and performance of our models and representations more thoroughly, and compare them to other temporal models.

Acknowledgements

This paper represents independent work by the junior author based on the suggestions of the senior authors.

We are grateful for the anonymous reviewers for their valuable comments. We are also grateful to Nathan Vaillette (personal communication) for his suggestion to represent basic calendar periods as finite-state transducers.

References

1. Niemi, J., Carlson, L.: Modelling the semantics of calendar expressions as extended regular expressions. In Yli-Jyrä, A., Karttunen, L., Karhumäki, J., eds.: Proceedings of the FSMNLP 2005. Number 4002 in Lecture Notes in Artificial Intelligence, Springer (2006) 179–190
2. Carlson, L.: Tense, mood, aspect, diathesis: Their logic and typology. Unpublished manuscript (2003)
3. Niemi, J., Koskenniemi, K., Carlson, L.: Finite-state transducers and a variable-granularity timeline in modelling the semantics of calendar expressions. In: ECAI'06 Workshop on Spatial and Temporal Reasoning. (2006) In press.
4. Niemi, J.: Kalenteriajanilmausten semantiikka ja generointi: semantiikan mallintaminen laajennettuina säännöllisinä lausekkeina ja lausekkeiden luonnolliskielisten vastineiden XSLT-pohjainen generointi [The semantics and generation of calendar expressions: Modelling the semantics as extended regular expressions and generating the corresponding natural-language expressions using XSLT]. Master's thesis, University of Helsinki, Department of General Linguistics, Helsinki (2004)
5. Wahlster, W., ed.: Verbmobil: Foundations of Speech-to-Speech Translation. Artificial Intelligence. Springer, Berlin (2000)
6. Endriss, U.: Semantik zeitlicher Ausdrücke in Terminvereinbarungsdialogen. Verbmobil Report 227, Technische Universität Berlin, Fachbereich Informatik, Berlin (1998)
7. Ohlbach, H.J., Gabbay, D.: Calendar logic. Journal of Applied Non-classical Logics **8** (1998) 291–324
8. Han, B., Lavie, A.: A framework for resolution of time in natural language. ACM Transactions on Asian Language Information Processing (TALIP) **3** (2004) 11–32
9. Karttunen, L., Chanod, J.P., Grefenstette, G., Schiller, A.: Regular expressions for language engineering. Natural Language Engineering **2** (1996) 305–328
10. Fernando, T.: A finite-state approach to events in natural language semantics. Journal of Logic and Computation **14** (2004) 79–92

Using Alignment Templates to Infer Shallow-Transfer Machine Translation Rules

Felipe Sánchez-Martínez* and Hermann Ney

Lehrstuhl für Informatik VI – Computer Science Department
RWTH Aachen University, D-52056 Aachen, Germany
fsanchez@dlsi.ua.es, ney@informatik.rwth-aachen.de

Abstract. When building rule-based machine translation systems, a considerable human effort is needed to code the transfer rules that are able to translate source-language sentences into grammatically correct target-language sentences. In this paper we describe how to adapt the alignment templates used in statistical machine translation to the rule-based machine translation framework. The alignment templates are converted into structural transfer rules that are used by a shallow-transfer machine translation engine to produce grammatically correct translations. As the experimental results show there is a considerable improvement in the translation quality as compared to word-for-word translation (when no transfer rules are used), and the translation quality is close to that achieved when hand-coded transfer rules are used. The method presented is entirely unsupervised, and needs only a parallel corpus, two morphological analysers, and two part-of-speech taggers, such as those used by the machine translation system in which the inferred transfer rules are integrated.

1 Introduction

When building rule-based machine translation (MT) systems, a considerable human effort is needed to code transfer rules. Transfer rules are needed when translating source language (SL) into target language (TL) to perform some syntactic and lexical changes. In this paper we explore the use of alignment templates (ATs) [1,2,3], already used in the statistical machine translation framework, as structural transfer rules within a shallow-transfer MT system. An alignment template (AT) can be defined as a generalization performed over aligned phrase pairs (or *translation units*) using word classes instead of the words themselves. Our approach uses some linguistic information to automatically learn from a parallel corpus a set of ATs that are then used as transfer rules. The method is entirely unsupervised and only needs a parallel corpus, two morphological analysers, and two part-of-speech taggers, more likely the two morphological analysers, and the two part-of-speech taggers used by the MT system in which the learned rules are then integrated.

* Permanent address: Transducens Group, Departament de Llenguatges i Sistemes Informàtics, Universitat d'Alacant, E-03071, Alacant, Spain.

T. Salakoski et al. (Eds.): FinTAL 2006, LNAI 4139, pp. 756–767, 2006.

To adapt the ATs to a shallow-transfer MT system the part-of-speech, or lexical category, of each word is used as the word class when extracting the ATs (see section 2). Moreover, the method needs to be provided with some linguistic information, such as the set of *closed lexical categories*[1] on both languages. After extracting the ATs two different criteria have been tested to choose the AT to apply when more than one can be applied. Those criteria are: (1) to choose always the longest AT that can be applied, and (2) to choose always the most frequent AT that can be applied. Nevertheless, before applying either criterion, infrequent ATs are discarded (see section 3.3). The method we present has been tested using an existing shallow-transfer MT system, and the experimental results show that the use of ATs within a shallow-transfer MT system drastically improves the translation quality as compared to word-for-word translation, i. e. when no transfer rules are used.

There have been other attempts to learn automatically or semi-automatically those structural transformations needed to produce correct translations into the TL. Those approaches can be classified according to the translation framework to which the learned rules are applied. On the one hand, some approaches learn transfer rules to be used in rule-based MT [4,5]. In [4,5] transfer rules for MT involving "minor" languages (e. g. Quechua) are learned with very limited resources. To this end, a small parallel corpus (of a few thousand sentences) is built with the help of a small set of bilingual speakers of the two languages. The parallel corpus is obtained by translating a controlled corpus from a "major" language (English or Spanish) to a "minor" language by means of an elicitation tool. This tool is also used to graphically annotate the word alignments between the two sentences. Finally, some hierarchical syntactic rules, that can be seen as a context-free transfer grammar, are inferred from the aligned parallel corpus.

On the other hand, in the example-based machine translation (EBMT) framework some research works deal with the problem of inferring some kind of translations rules called *translation templates* [6,7,8]. A translation template can be defined as a bilingual pair of sentences in which corresponding units (words or phrases) are coupled and replaced by variables. In [9] there is an interesting review of the different research works dealing with translation templates. In [7] the author uses a parallel corpus and some linguistic knowledge in the form of equivalence classes (both syntactic and semantic) to perform a generalization over the bilingual examples collected. The method works by replacing each word by its corresponding equivalence class and then using a set of grammar rules to replace patterns of words and tokens by more general tokens. In [8] the authors formulate the acquisition of translation templates as a machine learning problem. In that work the translation templates are learned from the differences and similarities observed in a set of different translation examples, using no morphological information at all. In [6] a bilingual dictionary and a syntactic parser are used to determine the correspondences between translation units while learning the

[1] Closed lexical categories are those categories that cannot easily grow by adding new words to the dictionaries (articles, pronouns, conjunctions, etc.).

translation templates. In any case, the translation templates used in EBMT differ from the approach presented in this paper, firstly because our approach is largely based on part-of-speech information and the inferred translation rules are flatter, less structured and non-hierarchical (because of this, they are suitable for shallow-transfer MT translation); and secondly, because the way in which the transformations to apply are chosen differs from those used in the EBMT framework.

The rest of the paper is organized as follows: the next section overviews the alignment templates approach; section 3 explains how to adapt the ATs in order to use them as transfer rules within a shallow-transfer MT system. Section 4 overviews the shallow-transfer MT system used to evaluate the presented approach, and describes the experiments conducted and the results achieved. Finally, in section 5 we draw some conclusions and outline future work.

2 The Alignment Templates Approach

Alignment templates (ATs) [1,2,3] were introduced in the statistical machine translation framework as a feature function to be used in the log-linear maximum entropy model [10]. An AT represents a generalization performed over aligned phrase pairs[2] using word classes. The ATs are learned following a three-stage procedure: First, word alignments are computed, then aligned phrase pairs are extracted; and finally, a generalization over the extracted aligned phrase pairs is performed using word classes instead of the words themselves. In [2] the word classes used to perform such generalization were automatically obtained using the method described in [11]. However, using non-automatic classes such as part-of-speech or semantic categories is feasible as suggested in [2]. The use of word classes allows for generalization, considering word reordering, preposition changes and other dissimilarities between SL and TL.

Formally, an AT is a tuple $z = (S_n, T_m, A)$ that describes the alignment A between a source sequence S_n of n SL word classes and a target sequence T_m of m TL word classes.

3 Alignment Templates for Shallow-Transfer Machine Translation

For a correct extraction, filtering, and application of the alignment templates (ATs) as transfer rules some linguistic knowledge needs to be used. This section explains how an indirect rule-based MT systems works and introduces the

[2] Linguists would not agree with our use of the word *"phrase"*. In this paper phrase means any sequence of consecutive words, not necessarily whole syntactic constituents.

Fig. 1. Main structure of an (indirect) rule-based transfer MT system. Source language (SL) text is analyzed and converted into an intermediate representation (SLIR), then transformations are applied giving as a result a target language intermediate representation (TLIR), finally the TLIR is used to generate the output translation into the target language (TL).

linguistic knowledge used. Then it explains in detail how to extract, filter and apply the ATs.

3.1 Indirect Rule-Based Machine Translation

Shallow-transfer MT is an special case of the (indirect) rule-based transfer MT framework. Shallow transfer rules simply detect patterns of lexical forms and perform some lexical and syntactic changes. Figure 1 summarizes how an indirect rule-based MT system works. First, the SL text is analyzed and converted into a source-language intermediate representation (SLIR); then, transformations are applied, transforming the SLIR into a target language intermediate representation (TLIR); finally, the TLIR is used to generate the output translation.

Usually the transformations to apply consist in using a bilingual dictionary to translate each word (lexical transfer) and applying some rules to ensure the grammatical correctness of the translation output (structural transfer). The work reported in this paper focused on automatically learning the structural transfer rules needed to produce correct translations; to this end, the ATs approach already introduced in section 2 is used.

In order to apply the ATs within a shallow-transfer MT system the parallel corpus must be preprocessed. The SL part must be in the format in which the input will be presented to the transfer module, that is the SLIR; analogously, the TL part must be in the format in which the transfer module will produce the output, that is, the TLIR. Notice that for the SL this preprocessing is exactly the same done by the MT system when translating an input text, and that the preprocessing of the TL part is equivalent to that for the SL.

Indirect rule-based MT systems, such as the shallow-transfer MT system used in the experiments (see section 4.1), are usually based on morphological and bilingual dictionaries. In shallow-transfer MT systems the source language intermediate representation (SLIR) and the target language intermediate representation (TLIR) are usually based on lexical forms containing the lemma, the part-of-speech, and the inflection information for each word. For example, an intermediate representation for the English sentence *The green houses* would be *the*-`(art)` *green*-`(adj)` *house*-`(noun,plural)`.

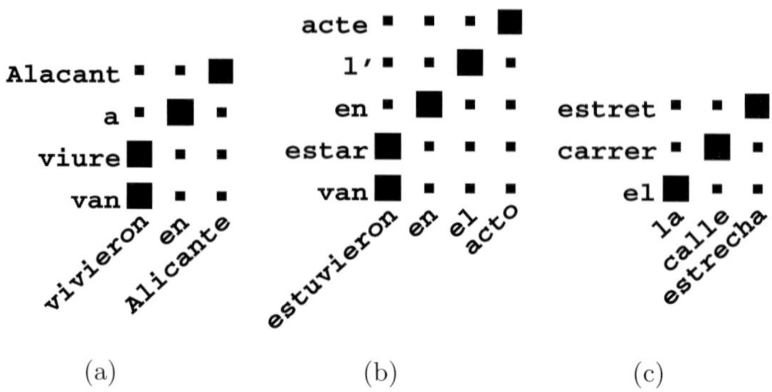

Fig. 2. Examples of the kind of alignments that can be found in a Spanish–Catalan parallel corpus

3.2 Extraction and Filtering of the Alignment Templates

As the transformations to apply are mainly based on the part-of-speech of SL and TL words, the method to adapt the ATs to a shallow-transfer MT system needs to be provided with the following linguistic information:

- The set of *closed lexical categories* in both source and target languages. Closed lexical categories are those categories that cannot easily grow by adding new words to the dictionaries: articles, auxiliary verbs, pronouns, etc. From now on we will refer as *closed words* to those words whose part-of-speech is in the set of closed lexical categories. Analogously, we will refer as *open words* to those words whose part-of-speech is not in the set of closed lexical categories.
- The set of *dominant categories* in the target language. A dominant category is a lexical category which usually propagates its inflection information (such as gender or number) to neighboring lexical categories. Usually the only dominant category is the noun, which propagates its gender and number to articles and adjectives. From now on we will refer as *dominant words* to those words whose part-of-speech is in the set of dominant categories.

To extract the ATs, the part-of-speech (including all the inflection information such as gender, number or verb tense) is used to assign a word class to each open word. For closed words, the lemma is also used to define the word class, therefore each closed word is in its own single class. For example, the English nouns *book* and *house* would be in the same word class, but the prepositions *to* and *for* would be in different classes even if they have the same part-of-speech. In this way the method is allowed to learn some changes such as preposition changes or auxiliary verbs usages in the target language.

Figure 2 shows examples of the kind of alignments that can be found in a Spanish–Catalan parallel corpus. In figure 3 the ATs extracted from the alignments found in figure 2 are shown. To extract these ATs the part-of-speech of each word has been used as word class; remember however, that closed words

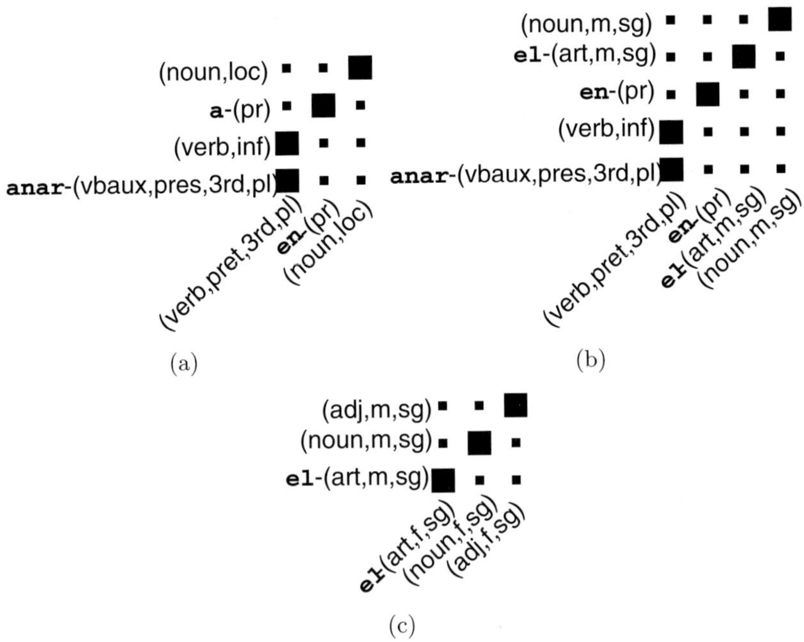

Fig. 3. Alignment templates (ATs) obtained from the alignments found in figure 2. These ATs have been extracted using the part-of-speech as word classes, but putting each closed word in its own single word class (see section 3.2) .

have their own single class (in the example reported, the prepositions *en* and *a*, the article *el*, and the Catalan verb *anar* that works as an auxiliary verb). As can be seen the ATs represent a generalization of the transformations to apply when translating from Spanish to Catalan and vice versa. The AT 3(c) generalizes the rule to apply in order to propagate the gender from the noun (a dominant category) to the article and the adjective. The AT 3(a) generalizes, on the one hand, the use of the auxiliary Catalan verb *anar* to express the past (preterite) tense and, on the other hand, the preposition change when it refers to a place name, such as the name of a city or a country. The AT 3(b) also generalizes the use of the auxiliary Catalan verb *anar*, but it does not specify any preposition change because the noun does not refer to a location name.

Finally it must be noticed that those ATs that have a different number of *open* lexical categories on both sides (source and target) of the AT cannot be applied. This is because it makes no sense to delete or introduce an open word (i. e. a noun or an adjective) when translating from SL into TL.

3.3 Application of the Alignment Templates

When translating an input SL text into the TL, the ATs are applied from left to right. Once an AT has been applied, the search for a new AT to apply starts from the next SL word that was not covered by the previous applied AT. If there is not any AT to apply the word from which the search was started is translated in isolation (by looking it up in the bilingual dictionary) and a new search is started from the next SL word.

In our approach we have used two different criteria to select the AT to apply. The first criterion uses the number of times each AT has been seen in the training corpus to select the most frequent AT that matches a SL text segment; the second one chooses the longest AT.[3] In both cases, the transfer module is provided with a frequency threshold that is used to discard infrequent ATs according to their counts.

Matching of alignment templates. To apply an AT its SL part must match exactly the SL text segment being translated, and it must be *applicable.* An AT is *applicable* if the TL inflection information provided by the bilingual dictionary for the dominant words being translated (see section 3.2) is not modified by the TL part of the AT. The last must hold because it usually makes no sense to change the TL gender or number provided by the bilingual dictionary for a dominant category (a noun for example).

Application of alignment templates. The application of an AT is done by translating each open word by looking it up in a bilingual dictionary, and replacing the part-of-speech information provided by the bilingual dictionary by the part-of-speech information provided by the TL part of the AT. The alignment information is used to put each word in their correct place in the TL. Closed words are not translated, they are taken from the TL part of the AT; in this way the method can perform transformations such as preposition or verb tense changes when translating.

The next example illustrates how an AT is applied. Suppose that we are translating to Catalan the Spanish text segment *permanecieron en Alemania*[4] with the following source language intermediate representation (SLIR): *permanecer*-`(verb,pret,3rd,pl)` *en*-`(pr)` *Alemania*-`(noun,loc)`. The AT shown in figure 3(a) matches the given Spanish text segment and is applicable. To apply this AT, first all open words are translated into TL (Catalan) by looking them up in a bilingual dictionary: *permanecer*-`(verb,pret,3rd,pl)` is translated as *romandre*-`(verb,pret,3rd,pl)` and *Alemania*-`(noun,loc)` is translated as *Alemanya*-`(noun,loc)`. After that, the output of the transfer module is constructed taking into account the inflection information provided by the TL part of the AT for the open words and copying closed words to the output as they appear in the TL part of the AT. The alignment information is used to put each word in the correct place in the TL. For the running example we have, after applying the AT, the following target language intermediate representation (TLIR): *anar*-`(vbaux,pres,3rd,pl)` *romandre*-`(verb,inf)` *a*-`(pr)` *Alemanya*-`(noun,loc)`, which the generation module transforms into the Catalan phrase *van romandre a Alemanya.*

[3] Note that in this case the ATs can be applied in a left-to-right longest-match (LRLM) way, as in OpenTrad Apertium (`http://apertium.sourceforge.net` [12,13]).

[4] Translated into English as *They remained in Germany.*

4 Experiments

In this section we overview the shallow-transfer MT system used to test the approach presented in this paper, then we describe the experiments conducted and the results achieved. The performance of the presented approach is compared to that of a word-for-word MT system and that of a MT system using hand-coded transfer rules.

4.1 Shallow-Transfer Machine Translation Engine

For the experiments we used the Spanish–Catalan MT system interNOSTRUM [14],[5] which basically follows a (shallow) transfer architecture with the following pipelined modules:

- A *morphological analyzer* that divides the text in surface forms and delivers, for each surface form, one or more lexical forms consisting of *lemma*, *lexical category* and morphological inflection information.
- A *part-of-speech tagger* (categorial disambiguator) that chooses, using a first-order hidden Markov model, one of the lexical forms corresponding to each ambiguous surface form.
- A *lexical transfer* module that reads each SL lexical form and delivers the corresponding TL lexical form.
- A *structural transfer* module that (parallel to the lexical transfer) detects patterns of lexical forms, like "article–noun–adjective", which need to be processed for word reordering, agreement, etc. This is the module we are trying to automatically learn from bilingual corpora.
- A *morphological generator* delivers a TL surface form for each TL lexical form, by suitably inflecting it; in addition, it performs some inter-word orthographical operations such as contractions and apostrophations.

4.2 Results

We have done the experiments using the MT system presented above when translating in both directions, from Spanish to Catalan and from Catalan to Spanish. To train the word alignments and to extract the alignment templates (ATs) we have used a Spanish–Catalan parallel corpus from *El Periódico de Catalunya*, a daily newspaper published both in Catalan and Spanish.

Before training the word alignments, the parallel corpus was preprocessed so as to have it in the intermediate representations used by the shallow-transfer MT system. The preprocessing consisted on analyzing both sides of the parallel corpus by means of the morphological analysers and part-of-speech taggers used by the MT system when translating.

[5] A complete rewriting of this MT engine [12,13] (together with data for several language pairs) was released in July 2005 under an open source license (`http://apertium.sourceforge.net`).

Table 1. Data about the training corpus used to compute the word alignments, the part of the corpus used to extract the alignment templates, and the disjoint corpora used for evaluation (test)

Language	Sentences	Running words	Vocabulary size
Spanish (training)	400 000	7 480 909	157 841
Catalan (training)	400 000	7 285 133	155 446
Spanish (AT extraction)	15 000	288 084	31 409
Catalan (AT extraction)	15 000	296 409	30 228
Spanish (test)	1 498	32 092	7 473
Catalan (test)	1 498	31 468	7 088

Once the parallel corpus was preprocessed, the word alignments were trained using the open-source GIZA++ toolkit.[6] The training of the word alignments consisted in training the IBM model 1 [15] for 4 iterations, the hidden Markov model (HMM) alignment model [16] for 5 iterations, and the IBM model 4 [15] for 8 iterations. After training the word alignment a symmetrization that applies an heuristic postprocessing is performed to combine the alignments on both translation directions; in this way, a source word is allowed to be aligned with more than one target word. For a deeper description of the symmetrization method see [17].

After training the word alignments the alignment templates (ATs) were extracted using a small part of the training corpus because this is a very resource-consuming task. Therefore, it must be said that the experiments did not exploit the full strength of the statistical approach; much better results must be expected for the alignment templates approach when the full training corpus is used to extract the ATs.

Once the ATs are extracted, they are filtered according to the guidelines explained in section 3.2 to discard those ATs that cannot be applied. Table 1 summarizes basic data about the training corpus, the part of the training corpus used to extract the ATs, and the disjoint corpora used for evaluation.

In the experiments we have tested two different criteria to select the AT to apply when processing the SL text from left to right (see section 3.3). Remember that the first criterion chooses the most frequent AT that can be applied, and in case of equal frequency the AT that covers the longest SL word sequence, i. e. the longest AT. The second criterion chooses the AT that covers the longest SL word sequence, and in case of equal length, the most frequent AT.

Table 2 shows the results achieved when using the ATs automatically extracted from bilingual corpora. For comparison purposes the results of a word-for-word translation (that is, when no structural transformations are applied and all words are translated in isolation by looking them up in a bilingual dictionary), and the results achieved when using hand-coded transfer rules are reported; in both cases the same MT system was used. The errors reported in table 2 were cal-

[6] http://www.fjoch.com/GIZA++.html

Table 2. Results for the two translation directions and the different MT setups used in the experiment. The error measures reported are, from left to right, word error rate, position independent error rate, the NIST score, and the BLEU score. The results reported are for word-for-word translation (baseline), hand-coded transfer rules, and the two different approaches tested to choose the automatically-extracted ATs to apply.

Translation direction	MT setup	WER	PER	NIST	BLEU
Spanish→Catalan	word-for-word	29.41	26.99	10.07	53.07
	longest AT	24.63	22.86	10.75	59.41
	most frequent AT	24.50	22.70	10.77	59.75
	hand-coded rules	22.94	21.05	10.88	62.50
Catalan→Spanish	word-for-word	30.01	27.46	9.76	52.59
	longest AT	25.32	23.25	10.51	57.69
	most frequent AT	25.90	23.78	10.44	56.66
	hand-coded rules	23.77	22.19	10.53	60.23

culated on a test corpus extracted from the newspaper *El Periódico de Catalunya* with only one reference translation (see table 1).

As can be seen in table 2 the room for improvement between word-for-word and hand-coded rules is about 9.4 BLEU points for the Spanish→Catalan translation, and about 7.6 BLEU points for the Catalan→Spanish translation. As can be seen the improvement in the translation quality is around 6 BLEU points in the Spanish→Catalan translation, and about 4.5 BLEU points in the Catalan→Spanish. Moreover, both selecting criteria give comparable results, but slightly better (around 1 BLEU point) when the translation is from Catalan into Spanish and the longest AT is selected for application.

5 Discussion

In this paper the introduction of statistically-inferred alignment templates (ATs) as transfer rules within a shallow-transfer MT system has been tested. To this end, some linguistic information has been used in order to learn the transformations to apply when translating SL into TL. In any case, the linguistic information used can be easily provided to the alignment templates extraction algorithm, and is a commonly used information in indirect rule-based transfer MT systems, which rely on monolingual and bilingual dictionaries.

The approach presented has been tested using an existing shallow-transfer MT system. The performance of the system when using the automatically extracted ATs has been compared to that of word-for-word translation (when no structural transformations are applied) and that of hand-coded rules application using the same MT engine. In both translation directions there is a significant improvement in the translation qualities compared to word-for-word translation. Furthermore, the translation quality is very close to that achieved when using hand-coded transfer rules. Moreover, it must be noticed that the relative improvement in both translation directions, if the best translation quality that can be achieved is assumed to be that of hand-coded rules, is about 70% for the Spanish→Catalan translation, and around 60% for the Catalan→Spanish translation.

Two different selection criteria has been tested to choose the AT to apply (longest or most frequent) when more than one can be applied to the same SL text segment. The performance for both selecting criteria is more or less the same when translating Spanish into Catalan. However, when translating Catalan into Spanish, choosing the longest AT gives better results (around 1 BLEU point) than choosing the most frequent AT. As future work we plan to study the reason why choosing the longest AT gives better results and why the improvement in the translation quality is lower in the Catalan→Spanish translation.

Finally we plan to merge both selecting criteria into a single one by means of a log-linear combination, despite the fact that due to the comparable translation results for both criteria we do not expect a great improvement.

Acknowledgements

Work funded by the Spanish Comisión Interministerial de Ciencia y Tecnología through project TIC2003-08681-C02-01 and by the Spanish Ministerio de Educación y Ciencia and the European Social Fund through grant BES-2004-4711. We thank Mikel L. Forcada (Universitat d'Alacant) and Richard Zens (RWTH Aachen University) for useful comments on this work.

References

1. Och, F.J.: Statistical Machine Translation: From Single-Word Models to Alignment Templates. PhD thesis, RWTH Aachen University, Aachen, Germany (2002)
2. Och, F.J., Ney, H.: The alignment template approach to statistical machine translation. Computational Linguistics **30**(4) (2004) 417–449
3. Bender, O., Zens, R., Matusov, E., Ney, H.: Alignment templates: the RWTH SMT system. In: Proceedings of the International Workshop on Spoken Language Translation (IWSLT), Kyoto, Japan (2004) 79–84
4. Probst, K., Levin, L., Peterson, E., Lavie, A., Carbonell, J.: MT for minority languages using elicitation-based learning of syntactic transfer rules. Machine Translation **17**(4) (2002) 245–270
5. Lavie, A., Probst, K., Peterson, E., Vogel, S., Levin, L., Font-Llitjós, A., Carbonell, J.: A trainable transfer-based machine translation approach for languages with limited resources. In: Proceedings of Workshop of the European Association for Machine Translation (EAMT-2004), Valletta, Malta (2004)
6. Kaji, H., Kida, Y., Morimoto, Y.: Learning translation templates from bilingual text. In: Proceedings of the 14th Conference on Computational Linguistics, Morristown, NJ, USA, Association for Computational Linguistics (1992) 672–678
7. Brown, R.D.: Adding linguistic knowledge to a lexical example-based translation system. In: Proceedings of the Eighth International Conference on Theoretical and Methodological Issues in Machine Translation (TMI-99), Chester, England (1999) 22–32
8. Cicekli, I., Güvenir, H.A.: Learning translation templates from bilingual translation examples. Applied Intelligence **15**(1) (2001) 57–76

9. Liu, Y., Zong, C.: The technical analysis on translation templates. In: Proceedings of the IEEE International Conference on Systems, Man & Cybernetics (SMC), The Hague, Netherlands, IEEE (2004) 4799–4803
10. Och, F.J., Ney, H.: Discriminative training and maxium entropy models for statistical machine translation. In: Proceedings of the 40th Annual Meeting of the Association for Computational Lingustics (ACL), Philadelphia, PA (2002) 295–302
11. Och, F.J.: An efficient method for determining bilingual word classes. In: EACL'99: Ninth Conference of the European Chapter of the Association for Computational Lingustics, Bergen, Norway (1999) 71–76
12. Corbí-Bellot, A.M., Forcada, M.L., Ortiz-Rojas, S., Pérez-Ortiz, J.A., Ramírez-Sánchez, G., Sánchez-Martínez, F., Alegria, I., Mayor, A., Sarasola, K.: An open-source shallow-transfer machine translation engine for the Romance languages of Spain. In: Proceedings of the 10th European Associtation for Machine Translation Conference, Budapest, Hungary (2005) 79–86
13. Armentano-Oller, C., Carrasco, R.C., Corb-Bellot, A.M., Forcada, M.L., Ginestí-Rosell, M., Ortiz-Rojas, S., Pérez-Ortiz, J.A., Ramírez-Sánchez, G., Sánchez-Martínez, F., Scalco, M.A.: Open-source Portuguese-Spanish machine translation. In: Computational Processing of the Portuguese Language, Proceedings of the 7th International Workshop on Computational Processing of Written and Spoken Portuguese, PROPOR 2006. Volume 3960 of Lecture Notes in Computer Science. Springer-Verlag (2006) 50–59
14. Canals-Marote, R., Esteve-Guillén, A., Garrido-Alenda, A., Guardiola-Savall, M., Iturraspe-Bellver, A., Montserrat-Buendia, S., Ortiz-Rojas, S., Pastor-Pina, H., Perez-Antón, P., Forcada, M.: The Spanish-Catalan machine translation system interNOSTRUM. In: Proceedings of MT Summit VIII: Machine Translation in the Information Age, Santiago de Compostela, Spain (2001) 73–76
15. Brown, P.F., Pietra, S.A.D., Pietra, V.J.D., Mercer, R.L.: The mathematics of statistical machine translation: Parameter estimation. Computational Linguistics **19**(2) (1993) 263–311
16. Vogel, S., Ney, H., Tillmann, C.: HMM-based word alignment in statistical translation. In: COLING '96: The 16th International Conference on Computational Linguistics, Copenhagen (1996) 836–841
17. Och, F.J., Ney, H.: A systematic comparison of various statistical alignment models. Computational Linguistics **29**(1) (2003) 19–51

Author Index

Lecture Notes in Artificial Intelligence (LNAI)

Vol. 4139: T. Salakoski, F. Ginter, S. Pyysalo, T. Pahikkala (Eds.), Advances in Natural Language Processing. XIV, 771 pages. 2006.

Vol. 4114: D.-S. Huang, K. Li, G.W. Irwin (Eds.), Computational Intelligence, Part II. XXVII, 1337 pages. 2006.

Vol. 4108: J.M. Borwein, W.M. Farmer (Eds.), Mathematical Knowledge Management. VIII, 295 pages. 2006.

Vol. 4106: T.R. Roth-Berghofer, M.H. Göker, H. A. Güvenir (Eds.), Advances in Case-Based Reasoning. XIV, 566 pages. 2006.

Vol. 4099: Q. Yang, G. Webb (Eds.), PRICAI 2006: Trends in Artificial Intelligence. XXVIII, 1263 pages. 2006.

Vol. 4093: X. Li, O.R. Zaiane, Z. Li (Eds.), Advanced Data Mining and Applications. XXI, 1110 pages. 2006.

Vol. 4092: J. Lang, F. Lin, J. Wang (Eds.), Knowledge Science, Engineering and Management. XV, 664 pages. 2006.

Vol. 4088: Z.-Z. Shi, R. Sadananda (Eds.), Agent Computing and Multi-Agent Systems. XVII, 827 pages. 2006.

Vol. 4068: H. Schärfe, P. Hitzler, P. Øhrstrøm (Eds.), Conceptual Structures: Inspiration and Application. XI, 455 pages. 2006.

Vol. 4065: P. Perner (Ed.), Advances in Data Mining. XI, 592 pages. 2006.

Vol. 4062: G. Wang, J.F. Peters, A. Skowron, Y. Yao (Eds.), Rough Sets and Knowledge Technology. XX, 810 pages. 2006.

Vol. 4049: S. Parsons, N. Maudet, P. Moraitis, I. Rahwan (Eds.), Argumentation in Multi-Agent Systems. XIV, 313 pages. 2006.

Vol. 4048: L. Goble, J.-J.C.. Meyer (Eds.), Deontic Logic and Artificial Normative Systems. X, 273 pages. 2006.

Vol. 4045: D. Barker-Plummer, R. Cox, N. Swoboda (Eds.), Diagrammatic Representation and Inference. XII, 301 pages. 2006.

Vol. 4031: M. Ali, R. Dapoigny (Eds.), Advances in Applied Artificial Intelligence. XXIII, 1353 pages. 2006.

Vol. 4029: L. Rutkowski, R. Tadeusiewicz, L.A. Zadeh, J.M. Zurada (Eds.), Artificial Intelligence and Soft Computing – ICAISC 2006. XXI, 1235 pages. 2006.

Vol. 4027: H.L. Larsen, G. Pasi, D. Ortiz-Arroyo, T. Andreasen, H. Christiansen (Eds.), Flexible Query Answering Systems. XVIII, 714 pages. 2006.

Vol. 4021: E. André, L. Dybkjær, W. Minker, H. Neumann, M. Weber (Eds.), Perception and Interactive Technologies. XI, 217 pages. 2006.

Vol. 4020: A. Bredenfeld, A. Jacoff, I. Noda, Y. Takahashi (Eds.), RoboCup 2005: Robot Soccer World Cup IX. XVII, 727 pages. 2006.

Vol. 4013: L. Lamontagne, M. Marchand (Eds.), Advances in Artificial Intelligence. XIII, 564 pages. 2006.

Vol. 4012: T. Washio, A. Sakurai, K. Nakajima, H. Takeda, S. Tojo, M. Yokoo (Eds.), New Frontiers in Artificial Intelligence. XIII, 484 pages. 2006.

Vol. 4008: J.C. Augusto, C.D. Nugent (Eds.), Designing Smart Homes. XI, 183 pages. 2006.

Vol. 4005: G. Lugosi, H.U. Simon (Eds.), Learning Theory. XI, 656 pages. 2006.

Vol. 3978: B. Hnich, M. Carlsson, F. Fages, F. Rossi (Eds.), Recent Advances in Constraints. VIII, 179 pages. 2006.

Vol. 3963: O. Dikenelli, M.-P. Gleizes, A. Ricci (Eds.), Engineering Societies in the Agents World VI. XII, 303 pages. 2006.

Vol. 3960: R. Vieira, P. Quaresma, M.d.G.V. Nunes, N.J. Mamede, C. Oliveira, M.C. Dias (Eds.), Computational Processing of the Portuguese Language. XII, 274 pages. 2006.

Vol. 3955: G. Antoniou, G. Potamias, C. Spyropoulos, D. Plexousakis (Eds.), Advances in Artificial Intelligence. XVII, 611 pages. 2006.

Vol. 3949: F. A. Savacı (Ed.), Artificial Intelligence and Neural Networks. IX, 227 pages. 2006.

Vol. 3946: T.R. Roth-Berghofer, S. Schulz, D.B. Leake (Eds.), Modeling and Retrieval of Context. XI, 149 pages. 2006.

Vol. 3944: J. Quiñonero-Candela, I. Dagan, B. Magnini, F. d'Alché-Buc (Eds.), Machine Learning Challenges. XIII, 462 pages. 2006.

Vol. 3930: D.S. Yeung, Z.-Q. Liu, X.-Z. Wang, H. Yan (Eds.), Advances in Machine Learning and Cybernetics. XXI, 1110 pages. 2006.

Vol. 3918: W.K. Ng, M. Kitsuregawa, J. Li, K. Chang (Eds.), Advances in Knowledge Discovery and Data Mining. XXIV, 879 pages. 2006.

Vol. 3913: O. Boissier, J. Padget, V. Dignum, G. Lindemann, E. Matson, S. Ossowski, J.S. Sichman, J. Vázquez-Salceda (Eds.), Coordination, Organizations, Institutions, and Norms in Multi-Agent Systems. XII, 259 pages. 2006.

Vol. 3910: S.A. Brueckner, G.D.M. Serugendo, D. Hales, F. Zambonelli (Eds.), Engineering Self-Organising Systems. XII, 245 pages. 2006.

Vol. 3904: M. Baldoni, U. Endriss, A. Omicini, P. Torroni (Eds.), Declarative Agent Languages and Technologies III. XII, 245 pages. 2006.

Vol. 3900: F. Toni, P. Torroni (Eds.), Computational Logic in Multi-Agent Systems. XVII, 427 pages. 2006.

Vol. 3899: S. Frintrop, VOCUS: A Visual Attention System for Object Detection and Goal-Directed Search. XIV, 216 pages. 2006.

Vol. 3898: K. Tuyls, P.J. 't Hoen, K. Verbeeck, S. Sen (Eds.), Learning and Adaption in Multi-Agent Systems. X, 217 pages. 2006.

Vol. 3891: J.S. Sichman, L. Antunes (Eds.), Multi-Agent-Based Simulation VI. X, 191 pages. 2006.

Vol. 3890: S.G. Thompson, R. Ghanea-Hercock (Eds.), Defence Applications of Multi-Agent Systems. XII, 141 pages. 2006.

Vol. 3885: V. Torra, Y. Narukawa, A. Valls, J. Domingo-Ferrer (Eds.), Modeling Decisions for Artificial Intelligence. XII, 374 pages. 2006.

Vol. 3881: S. Gibet, N. Courty, J.-F. Kamp (Eds.), Gesture in Human-Computer Interaction and Simulation. XIII, 344 pages. 2006.

Vol. 3874: R. Missaoui, J. Schmidt (Eds.), Formal Concept Analysis. X, 309 pages. 2006.

Vol. 3873: L. Maicher, J. Park (Eds.), Charting the Topic Maps Research and Applications Landscape. VIII, 281 pages. 2006.

Vol. 3863: M. Kohlhase (Ed.), Mathematical Knowledge Management. XI, 405 pages. 2006.

Vol. 3862: R.H. Bordini, M. Dastani, J. Dix, A.E.F. Seghrouchni (Eds.), Programming Multi-Agent Systems. XIV, 267 pages. 2006.

Vol. 3849: I. Bloch, A. Petrosino, A.G.B. Tettamanzi (Eds.), Fuzzy Logic and Applications. XIV, 438 pages. 2006.

Vol. 3848: J.-F. Boulicaut, L. De Raedt, H. Mannila (Eds.), Constraint-Based Mining and Inductive Databases. X, 401 pages. 2006.

Vol. 3847: K.P. Jantke, A. Lunzer, N. Spyratos, Y. Tanaka (Eds.), Federation over the Web. X, 215 pages. 2006.

Vol. 3835: G. Sutcliffe, A. Voronkov (Eds.), Logic for Programming, Artificial Intelligence, and Reasoning. XIV, 744 pages. 2005.

Vol. 3830: D. Weyns, H. V.D. Parunak, F. Michel (Eds.), Environments for Multi-Agent Systems II. VIII, 291 pages. 2006.

Vol. 3817: M. Faundez-Zanuy, L. Janer, A. Esposito, A. Satue-Villar, J. Roure, V. Espinosa-Duro (Eds.), Nonlinear Analyses and Algorithms for Speech Processing. XII, 380 pages. 2006.

Vol. 3814: M. Maybury, O. Stock, W. Wahlster (Eds.), Intelligent Technologies for Interactive Entertainment. XV, 342 pages. 2005.

Vol. 3809: S. Zhang, R. Jarvis (Eds.), AI 2005: Advances in Artificial Intelligence. XXVII, 1344 pages. 2005.

Vol. 3808: C. Bento, A. Cardoso, G. Dias (Eds.), Progress in Artificial Intelligence. XVIII, 704 pages. 2005.

Vol. 3802: Y. Hao, J. Liu, Y.-P. Wang, Y.-m. Cheung, H. Yin, L. Jiao, J. Ma, Y.-C. Jiao (Eds.), Computational Intelligence and Security, Part II. XLII, 1166 pages. 2005.

Vol. 3[illegible], J. Liu, Y.-P. Wang, Y.-m. Cheung, H. Yin, L. Jiao, J. Ma, Y.-C. Jiao (Eds.), Computational Intelligence and Security, Part I. XLI, 1122 pages. 2005.

Vol. 3789: A. Gelbukh, Á. de Albornoz, H. Terashima-Marín (Eds.), MICAI 2005: Advances in Artificial Intelligence. XXVI, 1198 pages. 2005.

Vol. 3782: K.-D. Althoff, A. Dengel, R. Bergmann, M. Nick, T.R. Roth-Berghofer (Eds.), Professional Knowledge Management. XXIII, 739 pages. 2005.

Vol. 3763: H. Hong, D. Wang (Eds.), Automated Deduction in Geometry. X, 213 pages. 2006.

Vol. 3755: G.J. Williams, S.J. Simoff (Eds.), Data Mining. XI, 331 pages. 2006.

Vol. 3735: A. Hoffmann, H. Motoda, T. Scheffer (Eds.), Discovery Science. XVI, 400 pages. 2005.

Vol. 3734: S. Jain, H.U. Simon, E. Tomita (Eds.), Algorithmic Learning Theory. XII, 490 pages. 2005.

Vol. 3721: A.M. Jorge, L. Torgo, P.B. Brazdil, R. Camacho, J. Gama (Eds.), Knowledge Discovery in Databases: PKDD 2005. XXIII, 719 pages. 2005.

Vol. 3720: J. Gama, R. Camacho, P.B. Brazdil, A.M. Jorge, L. Torgo (Eds.), Machine Learning: ECML 2005. XXIII, 769 pages. 2005.

Vol. 3717: B. Gramlich (Ed.), Frontiers of Combining Systems. X, 321 pages. 2005.

Vol. 3702: B. Beckert (Ed.), Automated Reasoning with Analytic Tableaux and Related Methods. XIII, 343 pages. 2005.

Vol. 3698: U. Furbach (Ed.), KI 2005: Advances in Artificial Intelligence. XIII, 409 pages. 2005.

Vol. 3690: M. Pěchouček, P. Petta, L.Z. Varga (Eds.), Multi-Agent Systems and Applications IV. XVII, 667 pages. 2005.

Vol. 3684: R. Khosla, R.J. Howlett, L.C. Jain (Eds.), Knowledge-Based Intelligent Information and Engineering Systems, Part IV. LXXIX, 933 pages. 2005.

Vol. 3683: R. Khosla, R.J. Howlett, L.C. Jain (Eds.), Knowledge-Based Intelligent Information and Engineering Systems, Part III. LXXX, 1397 pages. 2005.

Vol. 3682: R. Khosla, R.J. Howlett, L.C. Jain (Eds.), Knowledge-Based Intelligent Information and Engineering Systems, Part II. LXXIX, 1371 pages. 2005.

Vol. 3681: R. Khosla, R.J. Howlett, L.C. Jain (Eds.), Knowledge-Based Intelligent Information and Engineering Systems, Part I. LXXX, 1319 pages. 2005.

Vol. 3673: S. Bandini, S. Manzoni (Eds.), AI*IA 2005: Advances in Artificial Intelligence. XIV, 614 pages. 2005.

Vol. 3662: C. Baral, G. Greco, N. Leone, G. Terracina (Eds.), Logic Programming and Nonmonotonic Reasoning. XIII, 454 pages. 2005.

Vol. 3661: T. Panayiotopoulos, J. Gratch, R. Aylett, D. Ballin, P. Olivier, T. Rist (Eds.), Intelligent Virtual Agents. XIII, 506 pages. 2005.

Vol. 3658: V. Matoušek, P. Mautner, T. Pavelka (Eds.), Text, Speech and Dialogue. XV, 460 pages. 2005.